MW00953111

# Baseball Prospectus Futures Guide 2014

### THE WORLD'S FINEST ANALYSIS OF BASEBALL'S FINEST MINOR-LEAGUERS
Featuring a cavalcade of hundreds of tomorrow's major league stars

*Jason Parks*

*Mark Anderson, Nick Faleris, Chris Mellen*

*Ben Carsley, Patrick Ebert, Mike Gianella, Todd Gold, Craig Goldstein, Jordan Gorosh, Max Jensen,
Chris King, Rob McQuown, Jeff Moore, Ryan Parker, Ethan Purser, David Rawnsley, Chris Rodriguez,
Mauricio Rubio, Bret Sayre, Steffan Segui, Ronit Shah, Paul Sporer, CJ Wittmann*

*Geoff Young, Editor*

*Dave Pease, Publisher*

*Foreword by Allan Simpson*

.

# Table of Contents

# Foreword

*by Allan Simpson*

In mainstream baseball circles, 1981 is remembered as the year when the game was brought to its knees by its first prolonged work stoppage. For 50 long, arduous days at the height of that season, baseball went dark in major-league stadiums around the United States and Canada.

But out of the rubble of that strike-stained 1981 season came a series of developments that conspired to change the traditional way that baseball would be viewed and followed in the years to come. No longer was Major League Baseball the only game in town that mattered.

With nowhere else to turn to satisfy their appetite for baseball, disgruntled fans and media alike shifted the bulk of their focus 33 years ago to the minor leagues, which were unaffected by the strike. Not only was rare national attention showered on the minors, but it coincidentally came at a time when a groundswell surge of renewed interest was already beginning to take shape in the minor leagues, which had fallen on relatively hard times over the previous quarter century.

Moreover, the baseball draft, which had been cloaked in anonymity since its creation in 1965, witnessed a sudden and dramatic switch in demographics in 1981, with more-recognizable college talent populating the early part of the process for the first time. That only helped to fuel a quiet surge of national interest in college baseball and played right into the hands of ESPN, then a fledgling network that was looking for meaningful TV programming and had cast its lot with the College World Series.

And there to chronicle all the developments in a changing baseball landscape that marked the 1981 season was a brand new all-baseball publication by the name of *Baseball America*—an oxymoron if there ever was one, as the bi-weekly newspaper was born in obscurity in Canada, or more specifically, a garage in White Rock, B.C.

From the start, my emphasis was establishing a culture aimed at promoting prospects—both minor-league prospects as they endured their journey to the big leagues, and college and high-school prospects as they prepared for the draft (the bridge that connects amateur and professional baseball). Who knew, with a little publicity, long-ignored areas of the game like college baseball and the draft, in addition to the minor leagues, might begin to develop more of a national following—all to the benefit and long-term growth of Major League Baseball.

I also had the belief that lists and rankings were a popular way to generate interest in a topic, so it was only natural that rankings of the top 10 prospects in each major-league organization were a *Baseball America* staple from the outset.

Obviously, the lists and rankings we created needed to be as accurate as possible for them to be taken seriously by fans and industry insiders alike, but nothing is for certain when it comes to ranking baseball prospects. Just like with the baseball draft, where only 69 percent of first-round picks have ever played in the big leagues, the practice of evaluating prospects is not an exact science.

But our prospect lists, along with relevant and often-privileged scouting information on the players, were always assembled by going to the best sources available, namely to scouting and player-development experts in the game. We tapped into those people as a matter of routine in formulating our lists, and they unquestionably remain the best judges of projecting the future value of unpolished baseball nuggets.

The practice of ranking and analyzing prospects became so popular through the years that it has almost become an industry unto itself. No longer do players ascend through the minor leagues in near anonymity, and Baseball Prospectus has embraced this popularity by authoring its second version of its popular *Futures Guide*.

BP's *Futures Guide* offers a unique perspective on prospects that cannot be found elsewhere and, most importantly, the BP staff has gathered its information the tried-and-true way by tapping extensively into the right sources to get the best information available. The publication has quickly become one of the best and most insightful of its kind, and is already a definitive source on prospect coverage.

So while we might still lament the labor unrest that ripped apart the 1981 major-league season, we can at least be thankful for some of the fallout that occurred that year and ultimately led to a whole new way to look at baseball, with this book as a prime exhibit. ■

# Preface

*by Geoff Young*

---

Who do you take: Chris James or Barry Bonds? The answer is obvious three decades later, but at the time, I chose Chris James.

My information was bad. Or rather, it failed to tell the whole story. I had numbers, but lacked context and understanding of how they were achieved. Those would have been useful.

Lucky for me, this was a Rotisserie League minor-league draft. Aside from the shame of my having made a mistake and now admitting this to you, no real harm was done.

Big money wasn't at stake, as it was when the Pirates took Bonds sixth overall in the 1985 draft. Careers and businesses didn't depend on the success of my decision. Heck, I got a fun anecdote out of it.

The White Sox, picking one slot ahead of Pittsburgh in '85, were less fortunate. They took catcher Kurt Brown, who spent seven seasons in their organization and hit .243/.306/.325 with 23 home runs in 586 minor-league games. He made it to Triple-A before retiring at age 24.

They had better information than I had when I chose James, and it still didn't help. Such is the nature of studying young men, evaluating their physical tools, and attempting to imagine what baseball skills those might yield several years later.

There are no guarantees, but with a reliable guide that pushes beyond the numbers and explains why a young player is likely or not to succeed at higher levels, you at least give yourself a fighting chance. This book is that guide.

It starts with the Baseball Prospectus Top 101, a high-level view of baseball's brightest as judged by BP's prospect expert Jason Parks. Past lists have included Clayton Kershaw, Andrew McCutchen, Evan Longoria, Joey Votto, David Price—look, this could take a while; the point is, you'll want to pay attention because tomorrow's stars are hiding in here.

Next, Parks gives detailed reports on his top 10 prospects from each of the 30 teams. Using information culled from his and his staff's eyewitness accounts, as well as from industry sources, Parks identifies the strengths, weaknesses, and expected roles of 360 young players. With snapshots of six more names to know for every team, the total number of prospects to dream on approaches 500. That's a lot of dreams.

You'll also find even more detailed reports on 44 of those players as viewed in person by the BP prospect team throughout the 2013 season. If you want to know what Javier Baez looked like at the plate in August, drool at descriptions of Joey Gallo's power, or comfort yourself with tales of Noah Syndergaard's fastball ("with natural cut at 99-100 mph"), we've got that.

Then come the organizational rankings, which show how teams stack up against one another in terms of players on the rise, depth, and so forth. This is followed by Perfect Game's top 100 draft prospects list, which will come in handy as you track your team's adventures in the First-Year Player Draft. Perfect Game also takes an in-depth look at how several current top prospects were viewed when they were amateurs.

From here we steer toward the fantasy side and take a quick break from lists with Paul Sporer's "Making Sense of Pitching Prospects," which introduces strategies for mitigating risk when targeting young arms. They are an inherently volatile group, but if you bear a few key points in mind (I won't reveal Sporer's secrets here; you'll have to read the chapter), you just might beat the odds.

Ben Carsley follows with a discussion on finding post-hype prospect sleepers. Whether they need to make adjustments, jump an organizational hurdle or three, or just stay healthy, some guys don't "click" right away. Many fantasy owners gave up on Brandon Belt and Domonic Brown before they finally blossomed. You don't want to do that. Nor do you want to miss on the next one, whoever that might be. Carsley has ideas and even names names, but you'll have to—well, you know the drill.

Having stretched out and examined some broader concepts, we then return to the lists you crave. Bret Sayre gives his top 101 fantasy prospects, which is like Parks' list, only different. Sayre's, as you might expect, focuses on the value each prospect is likely to contribute to fantasy players. For example, Austin Hedges is a terrific major-league prospect, but his ability to handle a pitching staff and throw behind runners is useless in all but the strangest of fantasy formats.

Next up, Craig Goldstein's "The Ones Who Could Jump" provides insights into 24 players who could take a big step forward in 2014. Twenty-four players! That's one for every hour in the day. When will you sleep?

Assuming you do find time to catch a few winks and maybe grab a snack, you'll want to hurry back for Mike Gianella's 50 prospects most likely to pay immediate dividends in 2014. It's great to know who the best and brightest are, but maybe you aren't ready to do a full rebuild. If your roster just needs a few minor tweaks, this is the list for you.

Sometimes more drastic actions are required. "The Top 50 2013 Signees for Dynasty Drafts" can help. Everyone knows about Kris Bryant and Masahiro Tanaka, but what about Hunter Harvey, Hunter Renfroe, Hunter Dozier, and Hunter Green? Furthermore, what's up with everyone being named "Hunter"?

Finally, we close with "The Top 40 Fantasy Prospects Outside of Major League Baseball," which examines the next wave of talent to come from, well, wherever. Some of these guys are in high school, some are in college. Others are in Japan or Cuba. Increasingly, baseball is being played all over the planet (maybe elsewhere, too, but that's a topic for another day), and if you're in one of those leagues where anything goes, you'll want to know these names before they sell out and go mainstream.

But the end isn't really the end. Rather, it's a launching point for further discovery. The learning process never ceases, and we'll bet that you find yourself referring to this book again and again.

Whether you work for a major-league organization, play fantasy, or just love baseball, the Futures Guide will help you navigate the vast rivers of information available today. It will enhance your understanding of and appreciation for the up-and-coming stars of this great game.

We may never see another Barry Bonds, but if we do, thanks to the folks who study prospects and tell us about them, we'll be better equipped to distinguish him from the next Chris James or Kurt Brown. The baseball world will be a better place for this. ∎

# Prospect Preamble

*by Jason Parks*

Scouting is the clever combination of art and science—a tug-of-war between the tangible realities of the present and the abstract projections of the future—mixed with a dash of subjective bias, timing, and luck, served on the geometry of our favorite pastime. In a reductive sense, scouting is searching, a professional act of surveying the physical qualities of a specific action and extrapolating the trends to an assumed level of quality. While this is accurate on a base level, the complexities of the evaluation process are where the real beauty is found. In my eight years on the backfields of baseball, learning the ropes from the industry I'm now tasked with covering, I've learned that scouting is not so much about the search [itself] as it's about the emotional and intellectual sacrifices required in that search, a forced acceptance that binary conclusions can limit the size of the lens we use and that the necessity of observational fluidity is paramount to any long-term evaluation process.

I joined Baseball Prospectus as a contributor in 2010, and began writing a bi-weekly column called "Prospects Will Break Your Heart" before the 2011 season. When then-minor-league guru Kevin Goldstein received the call to the majors in the summer of 2012, I officially took over the helm as the national prospect writer for the site, a move I was initially hesitant to embrace. That initial reluctance was rooted in vision and process and possibilities, as I wanted to borrow some of the characteristics of a major-league scouting department, creating a network of evaluators in different parts of the country, putting their eyes on the prospects they were writing about, throwing all the information into one internal repository to feed and support our content when applicable for the foreseeable future. Easier said than done on all fronts, but with the unwavering support of Baseball Prospectus President Joe Hamrahi, and the other powers that be, we moved ahead with our plan to put as many eyes on as many physical prizes as possible, negotiating the logistics as we went along. We expected some bumps in the road, but if we stumbled too violently, the goodwill associated with Goldstein's established work and subsequent industry hire would eventually subside, and the minor-league content on the site would suffer as a result—perhaps even finding a fate worse than failure itself: becoming common, nondescript, and insignificant.

In our first year, we started with a small staff of hungry writers and would-be scouts, producing eyewitness reports from early spring until late summer, starting on the backfields and continuing until our coverage included players at the major-league level at the end of the season. Our range wasn't as large as our conceptual vision, but the firsthand reporting helped keep our content pertinent, and more importantly, free from the stain often associated with secondhand scouting accounts. It's vital to our product to be authentic in our approach, and that means putting in the wrench work at the fields where the action actually takes place. While it's beneficial to have industry sources—and I call upon them with regularity to help augment, support, or refute our opinions—if you don't have the proper context established through firsthand scouting, you are simply a mouthpiece for somebody else's thoughts, which creates a product that lacks any personal accountability. It's far too common on the Internet to chase the satisfaction of being "right" with the same fervor as eluding the responsibility of being "wrong." We wanted to be held to a higher standard. We wanted to be held by the industry standard.

Along the way, the spotlight fell on several deserving members of the prospect staff, and the baseball industry saw the quality of their work and acquired their services, leaving us full of pride but low on personnel. I spent the offseason restocking the Baseball Prospectus system with more evaluators, more than doubling the personnel from the previous campaign, and streamlining our approach so we could maximize our collective efforts in 2014. Never have I felt more confident about the site or the content being delivered, and the following collection of work is just one of the sleeves on which we wear that confidence. On the following pages, you will read the Baseball Prospectus 101—with scouting capsules on every prospect on the list; top-10 lists for every team in the game—compiled using our prospect-based Socratic method of debate and discussion, augmented by the opinions of some of the brightest minds in the baseball industry; mini-eyewitness reports on several key prospects on the 101, written by some of the up-and-coming talent ready to become household names on the site in 2014; and much more. This is the Baseball Prospectus Futures Guide. This is just the beginning of the vision. ∎

# Top 101 Prospects

*by Jason Parks, with contributions by Nick Faleris, Chris Mellen, Mark Anderson, and Jeff Moore*

## 1. Byron Buxton, OF, Minnesota Twins

*2013 Ranking: 8*

The premier talent in the minor leagues, Buxton has the type of impact tools to develop into a franchise player at the major-league level. With elite speed, well-above-average potential with the glove in center, a plus arm, a plus-plus potential hit tool complemented by an advanced approach, and power potential that he is only scratching the surface of, Buxton has the highest tool-based ceiling of any player in the minors. If everything comes together, he could change the Twins' fortunes.

## 2. Xander Bogaerts, SS, Boston Red Sox

*2013 Ranking: 12*

The 21-year-old shortstop showed the world his mettle in October, flashing the type of big-game coolness that helped define him as a prospect in the minors. Now a prospect in name and eligibility only, Bogaerts is perhaps the safest bet on the 101 to develop into a frontline player, a shortstop with a middle-of-the-order bat and the type of feel for the game to take him above his tool-based ceiling. If everything clicks, he's a perennial all-star and one of the most valuable players in the game.

## 3. Oscar Taveras, OF, St. Louis Cardinals

*2013 Ranking: 2*

In what was supposed to be his spotlight season in the upper minors and his major-league arrival, Taveras suffered through an ankle injury that limited his effectiveness in the field and eventually put him on the shelf. When healthy, Taveras has one of the most dangerous bats in the minors, a swing with the controlled violence of a Vlad Guerrero or Gary Sheffield, the type of hit/power combination that could lead to future batting titles and Most Valuable Player consideration. Assuming the lingering ankle injury is a thing of the past, Taveras won't be long for the minors, and is likely to blossom into an impact bat at the major-league level right out of the gate.

## 4. Javier Baez, SS, Chicago Cubs

*2013 Ranking: 20*

Often labeled a boom-or-bust prospect, 2013 saw Baez boom, hitting his way to Double-A with the type of game power his elite bat speed always suggested was possible. Unlike most top-tier prospects, Baez still comes with considerable risk, mostly because of his ultra-aggressive approach on both sides of the ball. At the plate, Baez is very fastball happy and can be susceptible to off-speed offerings. In the field, he can play too fast and rush his actions despite easy plus hands and arm. The ultimate profile is an all-star, a borderline-elite player who can stick at shortstop and hit in the middle of a lineup.

## 5. Carlos Correa, SS, Houston Astros

*2013 Ranking: 26*

With some of the best instincts of any prospect, and a unique blend of high-ceiling tools and feel for the game, Correa could be sitting atop this list next year. He has above-average actions in the field, a very big arm, a very advanced approach at the plate and highly projectable pop in the stick. The former first overall pick in the draft looks like a future cornerstone.

## 6. Francisco Lindor, SS, Cleveland Indians

*2013 Ranking: 10*

With a plus-plus glove at a premium position, Lindor could justify his lofty prospect status with his defensive profile alone. But the 20-year-old can swing the bat as well, working himself into favorable hitting conditions with a discerning eye while using a contact-heavy swing to spray hits to all fields. With only 21 Double-A games under his belt, it might seem premature to project Lindor for major-league service in 2014, but the precocious talent has the tools and the makeup to hold his own at the highest level if given a chance to break camp with the major-league team.

## 7. Addison Russell, SS, Oakland Athletics

*2013 Ranking: 22*

Russell is the rare middle infielder who projects to hit for both average and power at the plate. Despite concerns in his amateur days about his long-term defensive home, the 20-year-old has removed doubts as a professional by showing well-above-average actions and enough range to stick at the position for a long time. Despite his age and limited professional experience, Russell could reach the major leagues at some point in the 2014 season, a highly aggressive yet completely justifiable projection.

## 8. Taijuan Walker, RHP, Seattle Mariners

*2013 Ranking: 9*

Across three levels (including a three-game spot in the majors), Walker flashed his top-of-the-rotation potential, highlighted by an electric plus-plus fastball, criminally dangerous low-90s cutter and low-70s curve with big depth. Once the command refines and the changeup continues in the maturation process, Walker is going to be one of the better young arms in the game, a long and lively pitcher with knockout stuff and feel for his craft. Dangerous combination.

## 9. Archie Bradley, RHP, Arizona Diamondbacks

*2013 Ranking: 31*

Bradley has all the characteristics of a true power pitcher, with workhorse size, a high-impact arsenal that includes a heavy plus-plus fastball and a violent power curve, and the type of approach and work ethic that scouts champion at every available opportunity. With 21 Double-A starts already under his belt, the 21-year-old righty is primed for a rotation spot in 2014, and it shouldn't take long for him to establish himself as one of the premier young starters in the National League.

### 10. Kevin Gausman, RHP, Baltimore Orioles

*2013 Ranking: 13*

A dominating run in the minors was overshadowed by mixed results in his sporadic major-league spots, as Gausman's command wasn't sharp and his fastball found too many barrels. The former fourth overall pick in the 2012 draft, the idiosyncratic righty can work comfortably in the mid-90s, ratcheting up for more when necessary, and backing up the heater with two distinct change pieces, including one with fall-off-the-table action that is effective against both righties and lefties and can be deployed in any sequence. The refinement of the breaking ball and the transition from good control to good command could be the difference between a solid-average major leaguer and a frontline starter and perennial all-star.

### 11. Noah Syndergaard, RHP, New York Mets

*2013 Ranking: 28*

Not much separates Syndergaard from the top arms in the minors, as the 21-year-old righty shares all the characteristics of a prototypical power arm like Archie Bradley, complete with size, strength, fluidity, and athleticism in the delivery, a heavy plus-plus fastball, a breaking ball that has well-above-average potential and an overall feel for pitching. Syndergaard's underdeveloped changeup is still a work in progress, but when all the parts come together, the Mets might be able to boast the best young rotation trio in baseball.

### 12. Yordano Ventura, RHP, Kansas City Royals

*2013 Ranking: 62*

My early pick to be this year's AL Rookie of the Year, Ventura is a perfect fit for the reliever box, but with a starter's arsenal and the ability to hold velocity deep into games the slight righty is going to defy the stereotype and emerge as a frontline starter. Durability will be an early concern, as will fastball command and utility of the secondary arsenal, but the near-elite fastball gives the 23-year-old more wiggle room than the average pitcher, and any step forward with the curveball and changeup could finally give the Royals a homegrown arm worthy of the hype.

### 13. Lucas Giolito, RHP, Washington Nationals

*2013 Ranking: 70*

You can make a case that Giolito has the highest ceiling of any arm in the minors, a distinction he can wear despite a limited professional record and a Tommy John surgery already on his resume. With exceptional size and a frontline arsenal—which includes a fastball and curveball with elite potential and a highly projectable changeup that is still in its infancy—Giolito is ready to explode in 2014. Barring any setback, the 19-year-old could challenge the likes of Buxton and Correa for prospect supremacy in 2015.

### 14. Miguel Sano, 3B, Minnesota Twins

*2013 Ranking: 21*

Sano is a physical beast with 80-grade raw power and the type of athleticism you would expect from an NFL tight end. The swing-and-miss in his game was exploited at Double-A, as he was more prone to expand his zone and chase spin down and away. But the game power still found a way to play—despite the poor contact—and his defensive chops at third, long a subject of scouting debate, improved to the point where some scouts suggest he could end up above average at the position. There is still risk involved with his profile, but the payoff is enormous, a legit middle-of-the order bat capable of hitting 35-plus bombs from the left side of the infield.

### 15. Dylan Bundy, RHP, Baltimore Orioles

*2013 Ranking: 4*

2013 was a lost year for Bundy, as he hit the shelf after Tommy John surgery and didn't resume a throwing program until December. When fully healthy, Bundy is one of the top young arms in baseball, a power pitcher with a power arsenal, complete with a near-elite fastball that he can manipulate, a big up-and-down curveball with depth and a highly projectable changeup. The arsenal—in combination with his advanced pitchability, hyper-competitiveness, and legendary work ethic—will eventually make Bundy a frontline arm in the Orioles' rotation and half of one of the best one-two rotation punches in baseball, along with Gausman.

### 16. Jonathan Gray, RHP, Colorado Rockies

*2013 Ranking: N/A*

Selected third overall in the 2013 draft, Gray exploded into a legit 1:1 candidate while at Oklahoma, and he didn't lose a step in his transition to professional ball, shoving it in his brief nine-start run in the minors. With excellent size, strength, dominating fastball/slider combination, and developing changeup, Gray fits the mold of a future no. 1 starter. Although some scouts have concerns about the stiff front leg in his delivery and his command profile, most industry sources seem to agree that Gray will develop into a high-end starter, the only debate being whether he blossoms into a legit ace or falls a bit short.

### 17. Kris Bryant, 3B, Chicago Cubs

*2013 Ranking: N/A*

The best college bat available in the 2013 draft, Bryant didn't mess around in his professional debut, hitting his way to the Florida State League and then putting on a show in the Arizona Fall League, where the now-22-year-old slugged .727 in 20 games. You can debate his defensive profile at third and the projected utility of his hit tool—both of which could limit his ultimate value—but what isn't up for discussion is his plus-plus power potential, which could easily make him a middle-of-the-order threat for the Cubs as early as 2015.

### 18. Austin Hedges, C, San Diego Padres

*2013 Ranking: 19*

When it comes to catching prospects, you won't find a young player with a more complete defensive package than Hedges, a future Gold Glove-level backstop with an easy plus arm, plus-plus glove, excellent balance and footwork, and the necessary intangibles to develop into a general on the field. The bat is probably more down-the-lineup than one with impact potential, but the swing is simple and easy, so he should be able to make solid contact; the bat speed and strength are present, so some gap and even over-the-fence power could add to the offensive profile. If Hedges can muster a .260 average with some pop, he's a first-division talent. If the bat plays above projection, Hedges could be a perennial All-Star and one of the best all-around catchers in the game. Don't discount the value of an elite defensive catcher, even if the bat fails to impress.

### 19. Jameson Taillon, RHP, Pittsburgh Pirates

*2013 Ranking: 11*

Taillon reached Triple-A Indianapolis last summer as a 21-year-old, holding his own over six starts. The arsenal is loud, headlined by a plus to plus-plus fastball that can climb to triple digits and a low-80s power curve that plays both in the zone and as a bury pitch. The changeup remains his third-best offering, but it took a step forward in 2013, earning more consistent 5 grades (on the 2-to-8 scouting scale) from evaluators. He'll also mix in an average slider from time to time, which serves to keep barrels off his fastball. A half grade improvement in command could mean a big jump in production, and he figures to arrive in Pittsburgh for good in 2014.

### 20. George Springer, OF, Houston Astros

*2013 Ranking: 55*

After starting the 2013 season with a strong return trip to the Texas League, Springer exploded after moving up a level to Triple-A, hitting for average and power and stealing bases at a healthy clip while playing above-average defense at an up-the-middle position. The former 11th overall pick positioned himself as the Astros' center fielder of the future, although some are still pessimistic about his hit tool—specifically, the swing-and-miss tendencies and struggles against quality off-speed offerings. In all likelihood, the 24-year-old will struggle to hit for a high average against major-league pitching, but he will show plus power and speed, to go along with plus defensive chops in center, and that profile should make him a first-division player.

### 21. Mark Appel, RHP, Houston Astros

*2013 Ranking: N/A*

Appel stepped into the Houston organization as its top pitching prospect, bringing mid-90s heat to go with a changeup and breaker that can both register as plus offerings. The stuff has a tendency to play down at times due to a lack of deception and consistent execution, and while Appel earns praise for his even demeanor on the mound, critics counter that he is too passive and too often struggles to assert himself. Overall, the former Stanford ace looks the part of a high-floor starter with a chance to grow into a legit front-end arm if it all comes together.

### 22. Robert Stephenson, RHP, Cincinnati Reds

*2013 Ranking: 78*

The former first-round pick took a big developmental step forward in 2013, pitching his way to Double-A and missing a lot of barrels along the way. The 21-year-old righty has one of the best fastballs in the minors, a lively mid-to-upper-90s pitch that he complements with a hard curveball that is already a plus offering. The changeup and command need refinement, but with an athletic delivery and good overall feel for pitching, Stephenson should eventually put the pieces together and develop into an impact arm at the top of the Reds' rotation.

### 23. Jackie Bradley Jr., CF, Boston Red Sox

*2013 Ranking: 27*

Despite a rocky major-league debut, few question Bradley's future as a fixture in Fenway's spacious center field. The defense grades to plus off the strength of his reads and routes, solid speed, and a strong and accurate arm that will play to the deep reaches of Fenway's gaps. He is a disciplined hitter who should fit well at the top of the order with a gap-to-gap approach, top-shelf bat speed, and enough pop to keep pitchers honest. With an advanced game and the departure of Jacoby Ellsbury, Bradley should have the inside track on the Opening Day job in Boston and figures to hold it for the foreseeable future.

### 24. Gregory Polanco, CF, Pittsburgh Pirates

*2013 Ranking: 44*

Polanco is a potential five-tool talent with a chance to show impact in each aspect of his game. The bat comes with torque and leverage, regularly producing hard contact, particularly from the middle out, where he can get fully extended. There are some holes on the inner half due to swing length and load. The power could play anywhere from average to plus, and a not-unlikely trajectory could be a slow build in pop through his 20s as the body matures, with the speed running counter and ticking down from plus to average. He has the physical tools to project to center, though Andrew McCutchen's presence makes a corner spot the more likely point of entry.

### 25. Albert Almora, CF, Chicago Cubs

*2013 Ranking: 18*

Despite average straight-line speed, Almora profiles easily as a top-tier defensive center fielder due to an almost prescient first step and instinctive routes to the ball. In the box he shows an advanced understanding of the strike zone and impressive bat-to-ball ability, with a chance for a plus hit tool and average-or-better power. Almora saw an uptick in his physicality in 2013, but he also drew some criticism, rightly or wrongly, for missing too many games for "ticky tack" injuries. His feel for the game is elite and should help him to move quickly through the system, with a 2015 debut not unreasonable.

### 26. Eddie Butler, RHP, Colorado Rockies

*2013 Ranking: N/A*

Butler carved through three levels in his first taste of full-season ball, arguably improving his stock more than any other prospect in the process. The former supplemental first-rounder showcases three potential plus-or-better offerings, highlighted by a lively 93 to 97 mph fastball thrown with four- and two-seam variations. The changeup carries deception and mirrors Butler's heavy two-seam action, while the slider flashes plus with mid-to-upper-80s velocity. A long arm action and some crossfire can leave his offerings visible and imprecise, though most believe in the package enough to project him as a potential front-end starter.

### 27. Marcus Stroman, RHP, Toronto Blue Jays

*2013 Ranking: N/A*

The diminutive former Duke Blue Devil and USA Baseball standout showcases a dynamic arsenal and, with a plus-plus fastball and slider, one of the most explosive one-two combos in the minors. The heater is a low- to mid-90s offering with late giddy-up, while the slider comes with sharp wipeout action. He shows excellent feel for the slide piece, with an additional ability to tighten it up to cutter depth with upper-80s to low-90s velocity. He'll also flash a plus changeup with abrupt late fade and good trajectory deception. While pitch plane will be a concern against more advanced bats, Stroman's polish, command, and multiple-look finishes on his offerings give him the weapons necessary to remain a starter, and one with true impact potential.

### 28. Chris Owings, SS, Arizona Diamondbacks

*2013 Ranking: 81*

No one tool screams "impact," but the sum of Owings' parts might be a first-division regular with a long and productive career. He lacks premium range or arm strength, but will get the job done at the six spot due to solid hands, good footwork, and a quick and clean release. The bat-to-ball ability took a step forward last summer, resulting in regular loud contact as he showed the potential for fringe-average over-the-fence power. He's an instinctive baserunner with the wherewithal to swipe a bag or grab an extra base when the opportunity arises. After crushing the PCL in 2013, Owings should compete for a spot on the 25-man this spring.

### 29. Raul Mondesi, SS, Kansas City Royals

*2013 Ranking: 58*

One of the youngest players to land on the Top 101, Mondesi played most of the year as a 17-year-old in the Sally, showcasing a skill set that belied his age and carried the potential to impact the game in all facets, albeit through unrefined means. The glove, arm, and athleticism give him the chance to profile as a plus defender once he's able to slow the game down, and his natural contact ability from both boxes could push the hit tool to plus provided the approach tightens with reps. Given the likelihood the Royals continue to challenge Mondesi via aggressive promotion, it might take some time for the numbers to catch up with the scouting. But the end result should be well worth the wait.

### 30. Andrew Heaney, LHP, Miami Marlins

*2013 Ranking: N/A*

Heaney enjoyed a breakout year in his first full professional season, breezing through 12 Florida State League starts before finishing strong at Double-A Jacksonville. The hard-throwing lefty utilizes a loose and easy arm to produce his plus fastball, which he can dial up to 97 mph when he needs it. His best secondary is a true plus slider with hard, late bite and good depth, and he can also drop an average change piece with slot and plane deception. With three future average-to-plus weapons with which to attack advanced bats, and solid command of each, Heaney projects as a mid-rotation arm capable of no. 2 production with continued refinement.

### 31. Aaron Sanchez, RHP, Toronto Blue Jays

*2013 Ranking: 32*

Four seasons into his pro career, the story of Sanchez remains one of immense upside and inconsistent performance. The long and projectable former supplemental first-rounder boasts a loose and whippy arm capable of regularly producing heavy mid-90s heat and a low-80s power breaker. Sanchez can also turn over a plus changeup with disappearing action and arm-speed deception. He has yet to develop the ability to repeat his mechanics and frequently loses his release point, limiting his command and execution. The ceiling remains that of a front-end starter, but it's a high-risk profile that is perhaps more likely to settle in as a solid, if erratic, no. 3 or 4.

### 32. Alex Meyer, RHP, Minnesota Twins

*2013 Ranking: 88*

Evaluators continue to bifurcate along starter/reliever lines when projecting Meyer, though the former Kentucky Wildcat should have an impact regardless of ultimate role. The long and lanky righty utilizes a mid- to upper-90s plus-plus fastball, with premium extension helping the pitch play up even further. While inconsistent at times, the slider gives Meyer a second plus to plus-plus offering, and even the changeup drew the occasional 6 grade from evaluators in the Arizona Fall League this year. While his long limbs help create angles and extension, Meyer regularly struggles to keep them in sync, leading to mechanical inconsistencies and imprecise execution. There's mid-rotation or front-end upside here, with a late-inning safety net.

### 33. Kolten Wong, 2B, St. Louis Cardinals

*2013 Ranking: 90*

Wong is a baseball player in every sense of the phrase, a gamer who makes plays on all sides of the ball despite a cache of tools more solid than special. The baseball instincts allow everything to play up, which remains true despite the World Series mental lapse that had some questioning his readiness for the big stage. Wong is going to put his bat to the ball with consistency, and he's going to show above-average chops at the keystone, but it remains to be seen whether he'll develop into a true up-the-lineup type or settles into a down-the-lineup role on a veteran-laden World Series contender.

### 34. Kyle Zimmer, RHP, Kansas City Royals

*2013 Ranking: 41*

The former San Francisco Don boasts a clean delivery and a potential front-end four-pitch arsenal. The fastball is a plus offering that sits comfortably between 92 and 96 mph with arm-side life, and Zimmer shows the ability to work the quadrants with it. He can bring two distinct breakers in his curve and slider, and he can manipulate the shape and speed of the former, drawing consistent plus to plus-plus grades. The changeup is inconsistent but projects to average, and he has been known to mix in a cutter as an "off-speed" offering if needed. Zimmer could be major-league ready this year, and profiles as a solid no. 3 with no. 2 upside.

### 35. Julio Urias, LHP, Los Angeles Dodgers

*2013 Ranking: N/A*

At age 16, Urias averaged more than a strikeout per inning in the Midwest League while showing poise and feel for a three-pitch arsenal, the likes of which you simply don't see from arms at his developmental stage. The three-way fastball (two-seam, four-seam, cut) clocks anywhere from 91 to 96 mph and works well to the bottom "U" of the zone. He can manipulate the speed and depth of his curve, which already grades as plus, and the changeup will flash as well. There's limited projection in the body, and we have yet to see if the stuff will play deeper into games, but these are small issues at this point.

### 36. Clint Frazier, CF, Cleveland Indians

*2013 Ranking: N/A*

Frazier's swing can be best described as beautifully violent, with quick-twitch actions and strong hands and wrists delivering the barrel with enough force to bring his back foot off the ground at contact. The bat speed is special, producing easy plus power with a chance for plus hit if he can rein in the approach a bit and limit the empty swings. A recent convert to the outfield, Frazier has the raw tools to grow into an average defender in center, and should benefit greatly from reps and pro instruction. The upside is that of a top 10 prospect in the game if everything clicks.

### 37. Nick Castellanos, 3B, Detroit Tigers

*2013 Ranking: 37*

With the departure of Prince Fielder and Miguel Cabrera's shift across the diamond, the door has opened for Castellanos to return to third base, where his defensive profile fits best. The carrying tools, however, reside in the bat, as Castellanos boasts an impressive ability to barrel up balls on the regular. There's little question he has the feel for the craft to hit for average, and the leverage in the swing combined with a projectable and ever-strengthening frame indicate the potential for plus over-the-fence pop as well. He'll compete for a starting job this spring and could produce from day one.

### 38. Kyle Crick, RHP, San Francisco Giants

*2013 Ranking: 65*

Crick's fastball is a plus-plus weapon capable of reaching the upper 90s and sitting 93 to 96 deep into starts. He rolls out three secondaries, with his change and curve both showing above-average potential and the slider projecting just behind. Mechanical quirks, including a short stride and late hand break, have thus far prevented Crick from throwing with precision in the zone, and at times he's clunky enough to visibly lose balance through his finish. Believers point to his age and argue that he'll refine and stick as a potential front-end arm, while more conservative evaluators see a shift to the 'pen, where he could excel as a shutdown closer.

### 39. Rougned Odor, 2B, Texas Rangers

*2013 Ranking: N/A*

An intense competitor on both sides of the ball, Odor looks the part of a first-division regular. He squares up velocity with ease and is at his best when he focuses on simply making obnoxiously hard contact with a compact barrel delivery. He can get loose and uphill when trying to lift and drive, which advanced arms will exploit if given the chance. Defensively he's prone to errors of aggression, but the overall production should be a net positive. He could debut in 2014 with a chance to quickly grow into a plus-plus bat capable of wearing out the gaps and notching 14 to 18 home runs a year in hitter-friendly Arlington.

### 40. Lucas Sims, RHP, Atlanta Braves

*2013 Ranking: N/A*

Full-season ball didn't slow Sims down, thanks to his 91 to 95 mph fastball and hammer curveball, a pitch that some project to be a plus-plus offering. For those scoring at home, that's two plus pitches at 19 years old, just a year and a half removed from high school. Last year was a breakout season for Sims, and if the changeup takes a step forward the athletic righty could be on the fast track to the majors, where his three-pitch mix and plus command profile could make him a no. 2 or 3 starter.

### 41. Jorge Alfaro, C, Texas Rangers

*2013 Ranking: 76*

As far as tool-based ceilings are concerned, there aren't many prospects who can stand with Alfaro, a true five-tool talent at a premium position. On the merits of his projection alone, he could be a top 10 prospect in baseball, but questions about his approach and the utility of his hit tool keep the risk high and the assessments optimistic but prudent. He could blossom into an all-star if everything clicks, but Double-A will present a good test for the young Colombian backstop.

### 42. Tyler Glasnow, RHP, Pittsburgh Pirates

*2013 Ranking: N/A*

The paragon of the Pirates' "draft projectable high school pitchers" strategy, Glasnow blossomed in his first full season of pro ball. At 6-foot-7, there's still some projection remaining. Glasnow sat in the mid-90s with his fastball, but he'll have to command it better against better competition. His curveball flashes plus potential and he could have an average changeup, but that has a long way to go. Glasnow's fastball will get him to the majors, especially in a Pirates system that stresses pounding the zone with fastballs, but his off-speed pitches will determine his future role.

### 43. Mike Foltynewicz, RHP, Houston Astros

*2013 Ranking: N/A*

Foltynewicz walks too many batters and lacks a plus secondary offering, but 100-mph fastballs are rare enough that his make him stand out. The past two years have seen the big right-hander take significant steps forward, but if he wants to remain a starter, he'll have to take another step with either his curveball or his changeup. If either can become an average pitch, it might be enough for him to remain a starter. If not, his fastball alone should make him a solid late-inning reliever.

### 44. Corey Seager, SS, Los Angeles Dodgers

*2013 Ranking: N/A*

Seager battered the Midwest League over 74 games before running out of steam upon promotion to High-A Rancho Cucamonga. He has an advanced approach at the plate and does a good job of matching swing plane to pitch plane, allowing him to make hard contact across the quadrants and work pole to pole. With a projectable body already maturing, it's only a matter of time before the raw power starts to emerge with regularity. A return to the homer-friendly California League in 2014 could help jump-start a big offensive breakout for Seager, making the likely shift from short to third a non-issue.

### 45. Jorge Soler, RF, Chicago Cubs

*2013 Ranking: 36*

Injury limited Soler to just 55 High-A games in 2013, but even in small doses it was easy to see the huge offensive upside in his game. A physically imposing presence, Soler relies on a strong core and good barrel acceleration to create heavy backspin and carry, aided by natural loft in his swing. He will be tested by advanced arms capable of effectively working east and west, but most evaluators see enough discipline in the approach to believe Soler will be able to find his pitches and punish them. The result could be 30-plus home runs to go with average defense and a plus to plus-plus arm in right.

### 46. Miguel Almonte, RHP, Kansas City Royals

*2013 Ranking: N/A*

Behind an advanced changeup and lively plus fastball, Almonte has been able to carve up low-level bats, but the immature breaking ball could stall his progress as he climbs the professional ladder. He shows both a curveball and a slider, but neither offering has stepped up to the standard set by the rest of the arsenal, and sources are mixed as to which pitch projects higher. Almonte is going to shove in the friendly confines of the Carolina League, with the real test looming in Double-A, where his command and breaking ball will need to be sharper to find the same level of success.

### 47. Matt Wisler, RHP, San Diego Padres

*2013 Ranking: N/A*

Sitting comfortably between 92 and 94 mph, Wisler pounds the strike zone with a deceptive and repeatable delivery, and complements the fastball with what will one day be a plus slider. It's a profile that allowed him to find success at an advanced level at a young age. He profiles as a mid-rotation starter who could continue to move quickly and eventually thrive by generating weak contact in Petco Park. If the crossfire delivery limits his command or the growth of his secondary arsenal, Wisler could still find success as a max-effort reliever in the 'pen.

### 48. Travis d'Arnaud, C, New York Mets

*2013 Ranking: 15*

Most prospects would lose serious points in rankings such as these for being 25, but d'Arnaud is a catcher who can hit, so he gets extra chances. Had he been healthy, d'Arnaud would have left his prospect status behind long ago. Unfortunately, his list of injuries looks like the Declaration of Independence. He's a solid hitter with good power and solid receiving skills. That's a heck of a catcher, if he can stay on the field.

### 49. Billy Hamilton, CF, Cincinnati Reds

*2013 Ranking: 14*

Will he hit? The speed is game-changing, as Hamilton proved in September that even the best catchers in the world will have a hard time throwing him out. He's still learning center field but has the speed to make up for mistakes and will be better than average on defense for the next decade with the potential for more. But will he hit? It's the only question that matters for Hamilton, as his legs will always make things interesting if he can make enough contact for them to matter.

### 50. Joc Pederson, OF, Los Angeles Dodgers

*2013 Ranking: N/A*

Pederson broke out with a strong .278/.381/.497 line at Double-A in 2013 and his prospect stock rose with each passing day. With a broad skill set, Pederson can do a little of everything. He projects as an average hitter, though he is currently anemic against same-side arms, and he should have at least average power. His average speed plays well on the bases and in the field, and there are scouts who believe he can handle center field long term. The overall profile lacks impact, but Pederson does have the potential to be a solid major leaguer.

### 51. Garin Cecchini, 3B, Boston Red Sox

*2013 Ranking: N/A*

The third baseman from Louisiana made stops at two levels in 2013 and continued to show solid hitting chops. Cecchini unfolds from a balanced left-handed stroke that's driven by quick-firing hands and a strong base. While the bat speed isn't elite, the 23-year-old shows the ability to adjust his swing to the path of the ball and possesses a sharply tuned hitting eye. Questions surround Cecchini's ability to stick at the hot corner, with a move to a corner outfield spot the likely destination. It's the profile of a major leaguer, not an upper-echelon player, but one who can be an average to slightly above-average regular on a contending team.

### 52. Maikel Franco, 3B, Philadelphia Phillies

*2013 Ranking: N/A*

Franco is a naturally gifted hitter who does a lot of things wrong, which is a scary combination for scouts who never know how it will translate against better competition. What we do know is that he put up consecutive .900-plus OPS's in the Florida State League and the Eastern League, both tough hitting environments. His plate discipline is all over the map and he's no lock to stick at third base, but there's enough talent there to carve out a career, with the potential for an impact player with just a little refinement.

### 53. A.J. Cole, RHP, Washington Nationals

*2013 Ranking: N/A*

Cole has a big-league, mid-90s fastball coming from a prototypical starter's body, a profile that is both highly projectable and risky because of the present utility of the secondary arsenal. The knock on Cole has been his organizational travels, as he is an oft-traded player who carries the stigma of being disposable despite his enticing profile. But after a very strong Double-A debut in 2013, Cole is starting to look the part of a future no. 3 starter, a reality that could come to fruition by 2014.

### 54. Kohl Stewart, RHP, Minnesota Twins

*2013 Ranking: N/A*

A strong, athletic build, a plus fastball, and a plus slider already give Stewart more to work with than most pitching prospects, and there's the potential for another plus pitch (curveball) in his repertoire, giving him the type of profile that can stand atop a rotation. If he dominates the low minors the way he's expected to do this season, he should quickly put himself among the top tier of pitching prospects in the minors, perhaps emerging as a top 10 prospect in the game.

### 55. Max Fried, LHP, San Diego Padres

*2013 Ranking: 61*

Fried has the potential for as much success as any left-hander on this list, but he also has a considerable distance between his current and future abilities. His low-90s fastball has good life (especially the two-seamer that features late action), and both his curveball and changeup feature plus potential. He needs to finish his pitches and refine his command, but the arsenal is there for future success. The package has yet to come together, and if he takes the mound in the hitter-friendly California League, the stat sheet might not be kind to the young southpaw.

### 56. Josmil Pinto, C, Minnesota Twins

*2013 Ranking: N/A*

After a slow marinade that began all the way back in 2006, Pinto took strong steps forward last year and broke out in a major way. The defensive package is highlighted by solid receiving skills behind the plate, coupled with a quick release. The offense is headed up by a no-nonsense swing and some over-the-fence pop. The 25-year-old's overall game isn't flashy, but it can be steady and dependable in a lineup. The time is now for Pinto to put his claim on the Twins' catching spot, with the outcome potentially adding up to a solid-average big leaguer at a premium spot.

### 57. Jonathan Singleton, 1B, Houston Astros

*2013 Ranking: 25*

The big slugger from California lost some of his shine with a drug-of-abuse suspension and a subsequent return in less-than-ideal shape, but the potential for big power at first base remains. The left-handed hitter generates both impressive bat speed and the type of torque to launch high arcing drives deep into the seats. Singleton's defense at first will be adequate at best, but if the hit tool plays at the highest level it will more than carry the overall profile. It comes down to the 22-year-old's desire to maximize his talent into a first-division role, or else drift toward second-division status.

### 58. Hunter Harvey, RHP, Baltimore Orioles

*2013 Ranking: N/A*

The Orioles found a big-time arm late in the first round last summer, and Harvey showed his potential immediately. His curveball proved to be far too advanced for Gulf Coast and New York-Penn League hitters, as he struck out 11.7 batters per nine innings between the two. His fastball is no slouch, sitting from 91 to 94 mph, giving him the potential for two plus pitches. Harvey is another arm who could make a big move up prospect lists after a full-season debut this year.

### 59. Reese McGuire, C, Pittsburgh Pirates

*2013 Ranking: N/A*

As Austin Hedges and Jorge Alfaro make their way to the majors in the next few years, McGuire has the skill set to develop into the top all-around catching prospect in the game: plus potential glove with a bat that is stronger than you might think. If it weren't for his having only 50 professional games—none in full-season ball—under his belt, he'd be even higher on this list. He comes in where he does because of the inherent risk of developing high school catchers, but once he proves himself in full-season ball, he'll jump.

### 60. Eddie Rosario, 2B, Minnesota Twins

*2013 Ranking: N/A*

Rosario's excellent hitting ability gives him a legitimate major-league future, but how the rest of his game plays will determine his impact. Rosario has good power to the gaps, projecting for plenty of doubles and possibly 15 home runs per season. His defense gives scouts pause as he looks uncomfortable at second base and seems a more natural fit for the outfield, where his speed and arm can have more of an impact. If he can find a way to stay on the dirt as a fringe-average defender, Rosario's bat could carry him to an everyday profile.

### 61. Eduardo Rodriguez, LHP, Baltimore Orioles

*2013 Ranking: N/A*

This left-hander out of Venezuela has both the size and diversity of arsenal that you look for in a starting pitcher. Featuring a low-90s fastball that touches 95, a biting slider with tilt and a changeup that can fade quickly off the table, Rodriguez uses multiple options to get the upper hand on opponents. While his stuff is more solid-average to plus and he lacks a true wipeout secondary pitch, the 21-year-old shows solid pitchability and a knowledge of how to execute his craft. It's a profile that points toward eating innings at the back of a rotation, with third starter upside.

### 62. Braden Shipley, RHP, Arizona Diamondbacks

*2013 Ranking: N/A*

The Diamondbacks drafted the athletic right-hander 15th overall in June, and Shipley used his mid-90s fastball and plus changeup to strike out more than a batter per inning between the Northwest and Midwest Leagues. His curveball gives him the potential for another plus pitch and the chance to move quickly through the Diamondbacks' system. His changeup could be a savior as he battles the tough hitting environments of the California League next season.

### 63. Phillip Ervin, OF, Cincinnati Reds

*2013 Ranking: N/A*

The 2013 first-round pick out of Samford University blends high contact ability with the potential for up-the-middle defense. Ervin utilizes a short, compact swing that enables the right-handed hitter to rifle the barrel through the zone. The outfielder profiles as a gap-to-gap hitter who can flash consistent extra-base ability. Opinions are mixed on whether the 21-year-old has enough glove to stick in center. There's enough arm for right field, but the pressure on the bat might be too much in a corner. Expect Ervin to hit his way to Double-A quickly, where he'll get his first true test as a professional and bring the projection into clearer focus.

### 64. Matt Barnes, RHP, Boston Red Sox

*2013 Ranking: 38*

A casting call for a big-league pitcher would end up with Barnes at the top of the list. The right-hander possesses the size, stuff, and mound presence to play the part of no. 3 starter. Barnes' bread and butter is a fastball that approaches the mid-90s, with the ability to routinely rack up quality strikes within the zone. The inconsistency of the 24-year-old's secondary stuff causes some hesitation, as both the curveball and changeup need to be firing on all cylinders to churn through unforgiving lineups. Barnes is tasked with pushing his arsenal to the next level in the finishing stages of his minor-league development, and with proving he's ready for the chance to cement his spot in Boston's rotation.

### 65. D.J. Peterson, 3B, Seattle Mariners

*2013 Ranking: N/A*

The Mariners' top pick in June, Peterson came off the board in the first round almost entirely because of the potential value in his bat. With a ceiling that includes plus hitting ability and plus power, Peterson has the potential to be an impact middle-of-the-order bat. Defensively, he has plenty of work to do at third base, and most scouts believe he is destined to move across the infield, a move that will put plenty of pressure on him to maximize his offensive talents.

### 66. Stephen Piscotty, OF, St. Louis Cardinals

*2013 Ranking: N/A*

The Stanford product has entered the upper minors after making short work of the lower levels. His calling card continues to be an above-average hit tool accentuated by loose hands that enable the right-handed hitter to explode to the point of contact and control the head of the bat. The results are plenty of hard line drives to all fields and a projection of a high-average hitter in The Show. Drafted as a third baseman in 2012, Piscotty has moved out to the outfield, where his plus-plus arm plays up in right. While the home-run power is likely to be modest, the 22-year-old has the chance to develop into a solid-average major league player.

### 67. Erik Johnson, RHP, Chicago White Sox

*2013 Ranking: N/A*

Built to log innings, Johnson's future rests in the middle or back of a big-league rotation, where his broad arsenal should allow him to work through lineups multiple times. Johnson's best pitch is a slider that grades plus, and he supports that swing-and-miss offering with a 90- to 93-mph fastball, average curveball, and fringy changeup. With improved command in 2013, Johnson stepped forward as a viable rotation candidate for the White Sox this season, and he could peak as high as a no. 3 starter once he settles in.

### 68. James Paxton, LHP, Seattle Mariners

*2013 Ranking: 92*

Paxton has been a known commodity for a while now, and at 25 he's one of the oldest prospects on this list. He was underwhelming in Triple-A in 2013 but put together four solid starts in the majors toward the end of the season. His mid-90s fastball gives him a solid ceiling, but his inability to repeat his mechanics will likely keep him a no. 3 or 4 starter or reliever. He's ready for the majors and will get a chance to start in 2014, although with the Mariners going for it this season he won't have much slack on the leash.

### 69. Henry Owens, LHP, Boston Red Sox

*2013 Ranking: N/A*

Standing 6-foot-6 and on the lanky side, Owens brings a lot of arms, legs, and body for opposing hitters to deal with. The 2011 first-round pick isn't just deception, however. The left-handed starter easily delivers a low-90s fastball that will touch up to 94 and get late swings. Owens' best pitch is a bat-missing changeup, which profiles as a true plus weapon. The curveball lags behind, but will show flashes of being a big-league offering when the lefty stays on top of it. The package has third-starter upside, and with more near-term polish on pitchability he can begin to challenge for a look in Boston's rotation.

### 70. Chi Chi Gonzalez, RHP, Texas Rangers

*2013 Ranking: N/A*

The Rangers grabbed Alex "Chi Chi" Gonzalez 23rd overall in June, and he looked like a steal after finishing the year with five impressive outings in the Carolina League. His best pitch is a naturally cutting low-to-mid-90s fastball, which is essentially a 93 mph cutter generating weak contact. He also has a slider that grades out with plus potential. At 6-foot-3, he's got a solid build to be a mid-rotation starter, but he'll have to refine something off-speed to really bring out his potential. His unique repertoire could allow him to move quickly through the Rangers system this season.

### 71. Wilmer Flores, 2B/3B, New York Mets

*2013 Ranking: N/A*

A controversial prospect in scouting circles, Flores' supporters believe he has a chance to be an average hitter with at least average power while playing a position of at least some defensive value. His detractors see an average offensive talent destined to continue sliding down the defensive spectrum until he ultimately lands at first base. The reality likely lies somewhere in between, with Flores settling in as a .270 hitter with 17 to 20

home runs at an unknown defensive home, which should be enough for a lengthy major-league career.

### 72. Luis Sardinas, SS, Texas Rangers

*2013 Ranking: 86*

Sardinas has a plus hit tool and a plus glove up the middle, which alone make him a solid prospect. The fact that he should be able to stay at shortstop bumps it up a notch, and his well-above-average speed puts another feather in his cap. Sardinas has well-below-average power, but his game is built on speed and defense, and if he can stay healthy and focused, he has a first-division ceiling with an 1980s throwback profile.

### 73. Blake Swihart, C, Boston Red Sox

*2013 Ranking: N/A*

A glance at the statistical output won't tip off anything out of the ordinary, but it's the scouting and long-term vision that make Swihart an attractive prospect. The 22-year-old switch-hitter has the type of hit tool to maintain high rates of contact and lace line drives to all fields. The bat can produce high averages with extra-base pop at full utility. Behind the dish, Swihart's athleticism plays up nicely, with a plus arm, quick reflexes, and fast feet. If things come together he's a first-division player, but there's still a large enough gap between the present and the vision to keep him lower... for now.

### 74. Colin Moran, 3B, Miami Marlins

*2013 Ranking: N/A*

Moran came out of the University of North Carolina as one the most polished hitters in the 2013 draft, and was popped sixth overall by the Marlins. His best tool is his ability to barrel up the ball, but the power potential is the subject of debate, which could limit his ultimate value if the game power doesn't arrive. His hit tool alone is enough to make Moran a solid regular, and if he can stick at third (another scouting debate) and the power steps up, he could develop into a first-division player and occasional all-star. For a polished college bat, the risk is higher than you would expect.

### 75. Jose Berrios, RHP, Minnesota Twins

*2013 Ranking: N/A*

The 2012 first-round pick hit the ground running in full-season ball and continued to sharpen an already mature arsenal. Berrios works his lively fastball at 92 to 96 mph, while flashing the ability to dot both sides of the plate. The 20-year-old leans on a hard curveball to miss bats later in counts and also shows the makings of a changeup that can grow into a plus pitch at his disposal. The downside is his size, which draws concerns about future durability, but the Puerto Rico native pitches with both the fortitude and approach of a future major leaguer. The clues point toward a potential mid-rotation arm and a prospect who can rise into the next tier of this list in short order.

### 76. Alberto Tirado, RHP, Toronto Blue Jays

*2013 Ranking: N/A*

Though he's yet to reach full-season ball, this is a name to keep an eye on. Tirado flashes a maturing arsenal consisting of a 91- to 95-mph fastball, disappearing changeup, and late-breaking slider. The right-hander also oozes the easiness you love to see. While the command is presently below average due to inconsistent mechanics, Tirado displays an aptitude for his craft and has a body that can develop further to bring more balance to his delivery. With the potential for three plus pitches and large developmental gains, this is a prospect who can explode and push frontline-starter upside.

### 77. Josh Bell, OF, Pittsburgh Pirates

*2013 Ranking: N/A*

A solid athlete with a frame designed to pack on muscle, this switch-hitting outfielder possesses big raw power fueled by a loose, easy swing from both sides of the plate. After a knee injury derailed his first professional season, Bell showed that he was healthy in 2013 and made progress polishing his overall tools. The 21-year-old still has questions to answer about his hit tool and pitch recognition, but the ingredients are there for a power-hitting corner outfielder who can rise quickly into the next tier of prospects.

### 78. Sean Manaea, LHP, Kansas City Royals

*2013 Ranking: N/A*

Manaea emerged as a candidate to go first overall in the 2013 draft after dominating the prestigious Cape Cod League, but saw a regression in stuff and control over the course of an injury-plagued junior year. Despite the disappointing spring, Kansas City saw enough upside to invest the draft's fifth highest signing bonus in the southpaw after selecting him in the supplemental first round. At his best, Manaea spits 93 to 96 mph gas from a low slot and tough angle, showing a sharp slider and improving split-change. There's projection in the body, and if Manaea can remain healthy and return to Cape form, he represents a potential mid-rotation starter with a chance to vault into the top tier of prospect arms with further development.

### 79. Michael Choice, OF, Texas Rangers

*2013 Ranking: 82*

A new addition to the Rangers' outfield mix, Choice has the potential to help in left field over the long term. He is an average runner who plays solid defense, but his arm is below average and does not support a long-term future in center or right field. Choice's calling card is his plus-plus raw power, though it plays down a grade because of considerable swing-and-miss issues. Choice has a solid approach and will take some walks, which combined with 25 home runs a year will help buoy what projects to be a .250-ish batting average.

### 80. Nick Kingham, RHP, Pittsburgh Pirates

*2013 Ranking: N/A*

Standing 6-foot-5 and 220 pounds, Kingham's physicality stands out the second he steps on the field. He backs up his physical presence with an impressive array of pitches that includes a fastball that can reach 95 to 96 mph and a curveball and changeup that are both promising. With his height and long arms, Kingham's fastball appears harder than radar guns suggest, and his ability to locate the pitch helps it play up even more. Despite his impressive raw stuff, Kingham can struggle to miss bats and profiles as a mid-rotation workhorse rather than a front-of-the-rotation arm.

### 81. C.J. Edwards, RHP, Chicago Cubs

*2013 Ranking: N/A*

Edwards has gone from relative obscurity to "on the radar" thanks to the strength of his fastball and the promise of his secondary stuff. A loose thrower with an easy delivery and fast arm, the right-hander currently sits in the low-90s and can touch 94. Edwards also shows feel for both a mid-70s curveball and changeup, though the latter is still a fairly raw offering. The 22-year-old is presently very slender and lean, which highlights the need for added strength so he can maintain his stuff into outings and over the grind of the season. The package points toward a future reliever, but large physical gains can keep the arm on a starter's track.

### 82. Jonathan Schoop, 2B, Baltimore Orioles

*2013 Ranking: 80*

Schoop might be the Orioles' long-term answer at second base, but he desperately needs additional seasoning in Triple-A before being called on to fill a full-time major-league role. Impressive physically and athletically, Schoop has a host of tools that could make him a quality everyday player. He is a potentially average defender with a plus arm at second base. At his best he makes easy contact with at least average power, but his offensive game remains inconsistent because of a raw approach and a lack of experience against upper-level arms.

### 83. Arismendy Alcantara, 2B, Chicago Cubs

*2013 Ranking: N/A*

Alcantara had a bit of a coming-out party at the 2013 Futures Game and cemented his breakout status with a very strong season at Double-A as a 21-year-old. Every part of Alcantara's game stepped forward in 2013. His defense at second base now projects to be above average, and his arm is still a plus tool. His feel for the game on offense took a big step forward, allowing him to work deeper counts and drive the ball more consistently. All told, Alcantara has potential as an everyday second baseman.

### 84. Zach Lee, RHP, Los Angeles Dodgers

*2013 Ranking: 87*

Given a massive signing bonus out of a Texas high school in 2010, expectations for Lee were immediately extreme. A gifted athlete, Lee repeats his delivery well and pounds the zone with an average fastball that plays up because of plus sink. His slider and changeup are both average offerings and his curveball can be effective when set up properly. Once projected as a front-of-the-rotation arm, Lee looks the part of a durable third or fourth starter who could help the Dodgers as early as the second half of this year.

### 85. Gary Sanchez, C, New York Yankees

*2013 Ranking: 47*

Possessing big raw power and a swing with excellent extension, Sanchez can drive baseballs with authority to all fields. The 21-year-old catcher typically punishes mistakes. Behind the dish Sanchez shows a plus-plus arm and fluidity with his catch-and-release mechanics, but the receiving skills need refinement to stick long-term. If everything comes together, Sanchez can be a first-division catcher with 25-homer power and an arm to control the run game. But with his level of engagement drifting for stretches and questions about whether there's enough desire to maximize his talent, he might ultimately end up an average regular at first base at his peak.

### 86. Brian Goodwin, OF, Washington Nationals

*2013 Ranking: 74*

Even after posting a pedestrian .252/.355/.407 line in Double-A, Goodwin still has an all-star ceiling thanks to an impressive set of tools. He has the speed to play center field if he can continue to refine his reads and routes, something he made progress with in 2013. The ball jumps off his bat when he makes contact, and if he can develop enough consistency with his swing to hit .270 to .280, then he could contribute 25 to 30 doubles and 15-plus home runs to the lineup. Goodwin still carries considerable risk despite reaching Double-A, but the payoff could be an outstanding everyday player.

### 87. Christian Bethancourt, C, Atlanta Braves

*2013 Ranking: 93*

When going through the checklist of desirable defensive attributes in a catcher, this prospect's scores are at the top. The glove is firm when receiving offerings. The footwork is crisp and there's athleticism for his size. To top it all off, the arm grades as an 8 with a hair-trigger release, leaving Bethancourt more than capable of controlling the running game. The defense screams elite, but the potential offensive contributions may very well end up weak thanks to an uneven approach. This is a big leaguer, but a career as a regular will come down to whether Bethancourt can avoid being an automatic out at the bottom of the lineup.

### 88. Nick Williams, OF, Texas Rangers

*2013 Ranking: N/A*

There's a distinct sound heard off the bat from players with legit major-league hitting talent. The "crack" always turns heads in its direction. Williams turned those heads not only with explosive sounds but with his innate barrel-to-ball ability and easy, controlled swing. The hit tool has the potential to round to plus-plus, with natural raw power that can crest toward 20 home runs at peak. Williams still has a ways to go developing the other aspects of his game, including outfield defense that needs work to reach average, but the bat is good enough to potentially carry him as a regular, with All-Star upside if the baseball skills click.

### 89. Austin Meadows, OF, Pittsburgh Pirates

*2013 Ranking: N/A*

Sweet left-handed stroke? Check. Frame to hang dreams on? Check. Easy raw power? Check. Pittsburgh selected Meadows ninth overall in 2013 with aspirations of slow-cooking this raw talent into an outfield fixture at PNC Park for years to come. The hit tool and approach are advanced for his age, though Meadows is going to be challenged to make adjustments during his early career. With the potential for continued physical development, the 19-year-old likely slots into a corner spot down the road. The potential is there for a middle-of-the-order threat, and one who can rise quickly up both the ranks of the minors and prospect lists.

### 90. Enny Romero, LHP, Tampa Bay Rays

*2013 Ranking: N/A*

Romero has two paths to an impact role in the big leagues: With improved command, he could profile as a third or fourth starter; without improved command he could profile as a high-powered late-inning reliever. In either scenario he attacks hitters with two plus-plus pitches, a fastball that can reach 96 mph and a hard curveball. Romero lacks feel for his changeup and he is generally considered more of a thrower than pitcher, but his overall ceiling remains tantalizing.

### 91. Pierce Johnson, RHP, Chicago Cubs

*2013 Ranking: N/A*

Johnson pushed his way to High-A in his first full season of pro ball, posting impressive numbers in the second half with Daytona.

At his best he attacks hitters with a low-to-mid-90s fastball, a hard curveball that can be a true swing-and-miss pitch, and a changeup that is making rapid strides. Johnson still has to prove that his thin frame can handle the rigors of starting every five days over a long season, but if he can demonstrate his durability, he could develop into a quality no. 3 starter in short order.

### 92. Jake Odorizzi, RHP, Tampa Bay Rays

*2013 Ranking: 83*

Part of the package that sent James Shields to the Royals, Odorizzi is on the verge of securing a spot in the Rays' rotation. No part of Odorizzi's game truly stands out, but he makes up for that with three pitches that each grade at least average: a fastball that sits in the low-90s, a solid slider, and an above-average changeup. While he lacks the profile to miss bats at the major-league level, he carries minimal risk and should become a no. 4 starter very soon.

### 93. Matt Davidson, 3B, Chicago White Sox

*2013 Ranking: 89*

A classic right-handed power hitter, Davidson's long arms are both his strength and vulnerability. The third baseman generates plenty of extension through the hitting zone and is capable of lifting balls out of the park to all fields. The home-run power can play into the mid-20s. Davidson also shows a developed idea of his strike zone and a willingness to work himself into favorable counts. The big concern surrounds his ability to consistently hit for average. The 23-year-old's propensity to overextend leaves him prone to stuff above the belt and on the inner third. Davidson has the ingredients to round into a regular at the hot corner for a handful of seasons, but if the hit tool is exposed over the long haul the profile becomes a likely up-and-down player.

### 94. Jesse Biddle, LHP, Philadelphia Phillies

*2013 Ranking: 67*

Biddle made the leap to Double-A in 2013 and more than held his own despite an increased walk rate against more advanced hitters. With a low-90s fastball, plus curveball, and developing changeup, Biddle can miss bats and work through lineups with ease. As his command develops— which it should with his clean delivery—Biddle should develop into a workhorse fourth starter, possibly earning a taste of the big leagues in 2014 and getting a full shot in 2015.

### 95. Joey Gallo, 3B, Texas Rangers

*2013 Ranking: N/A*

Gallo's raw power is the stuff of legend, and is the most impressive in the minors. He can drive any pitch out of any park, to any field, and that effort does not require square contact. Gallo has work to do at the plate, however, as his hit tool projects well below average, and might never reach the heights necessary for his raw power to play. He has improved enough to now project as a solid third baseman with a 70-grade arm. Gallo's future depends entirely on his ability to make contact,, and if he improves enough he could be a monster talent.

### 96. Hunter Dozier, SS, Kansas City Royals

*2013 Ranking: N/A*

Dozier was the eighth overall selection in the 2013 draft, signing for below slot and allowing the Royals to push the savings to supplemental first rounder Sean Manaea. The former Stephen F. Austin State standout is a fundamental player with power serving as his carrying tool. Well put together and boasting a leveraged swing with natural lift, he could grow into a threat to hit 25 home runs annually and should provide good defensive value once he completes the likely transition from short to the hot corner. The ceiling is limited, but the overall profile could provide lots of surplus value for the Royals in the form of a solid everyday contributor who does everything pretty well.

## 97. Raimel Tapia, OF, Colorado Rockies

*2013 Ranking: N/A*

A potential breakout prospect for 2014, Tapia has the type of raw tools that cause prospects to explode onto the national scene. A gifted hitter, he has the potential to develop into an easy plus at the plate, and possibly better, at his peak. He backs up his hitting ability with impressive raw power that could max out in the 20-25 home-run range. Defensively, he fits well in right field as an above-average defender with at least a plus arm. Tapia turns 20 before spring training, and he could be in line for a monster full-season debut.

## 98. Alexander Reyes, RHP, St. Louis Cardinals

*2013 Ranking: N/A*

Reyes arrived on the scene in 2013 and showed well in the Appalachian League after an unusual path to professional baseball. An excellent prep pitcher, Reyes moved to the Dominican Republic to avoid the draft and signed in December 2012 for nearly $1 million. Armed with a 93-95 mph fastball that peaks around 97-98 and a curveball that earns plus grades, Reyes has the raw stuff to dominate the lower levels as he continues to develop his changeup and command. It remains early in the developmental process but Reyes has high-end potential that could make him a no. 2 or 3 starter.

## 99. Jorge Bonifacio, OF, Kansas City Royals

*2013 Ranking: N/A*

The Royals' major-league roster is slowly heading in the right direction, and Bonifacio could be part of the future of that roster if he continues to develop the way he did in 2013. A classic right fielder with a big arm and solid defensive skills, Bonifacio has the raw power at the plate to fulfill the other side of the profile as well. A natural hitter, Bonifacio could hit .280 at the highest level, and his power could play in the 20-home-run range if he can begin applying more power in game action.

## 100. David Dahl, OF, Colorado Rockies

*2013 Ranking: 40*

A year after Dahl went 10th overall, injuries turned 2013 into a lost season. When healthy, he displays the type of natural hitting ability rarely found in prospects. He demonstrates a quality approach in his at-bats and uses the whole field well, and his above-average raw power should arrive in games as he matures. Dahl's supporters stand behind his ability to play center field and believe he can be an above-average defender down the line. While his first full season was a lost one, Dahl still maintains considerable potential as a middle-of-the-order hitter at a premium position.

## 101. Lewis Thorpe, LHP, Minnesota Twins

*2013 Ranking: N/A*

Signed out of Australia in 2012, Thorpe's professional debut was nothing short of a rousing success. Not only did he perform exceptionally well, but his stuff took a substantial step forward as well. Armed with an arsenal that could include a plus-plus fastball, plus curveball, and plus changeup at his peak, Thorpe also shows an excellent feel for his craft and a promising command profile. He must still adjust to his remaining physical development and the demands of a heavier workload, but Thorpe's future is as promising as any arm in the Twins system. ■

# Team Top 10 Prospects 2014

**W**elcome to the team top 10s. Before immersing yourself in what follows, you'll need to know a few things:

## Terminology

**20/80:** Scouting scale; often used as the 2/8 scale; used to denote physical tool grades both in the present and the future. The scale can also indicate a future player role, i.e., future major league grade (overall) at tool maturity. This is the break-down:

- 20=Very poor
- 30=Well below-average
- 40=Below-average
- 50=Average; major-league regular
- 60=Above-average (plus); first-division
- 70=Well above-average (plus-plus); all-star
- 80=Elite; bacon

**Big Raw:** Power (or the power tool) is often just referred to as "raw."

**Bore:** A pitch that shows intense arm-side movement into the hitter standing in the arm-side box (RHP/RH; LHP/LH).

**First-division:** A player that could start for a playoff-caliber team.

**Hittability:** Put simply, the overall command and feel for the act of hitting. It's a broad term, but it's usually used to describe hitters who put the barrel of the bat on the baseball, command of the bat, the ability to make contact all over the zone against all types of offerings, etc.

**Life:** action/movement on a particular pitch; usually used to described the late movement on a fastball.

**Makeup:** For me, makeup is about work ethic and the desire to improve and maximize the potential suggested by the raw physical tools. Makeup is not about being a jerk or being like-able or being a sweetheart to fans in the stands. Makeup is a major component in a player's ability to respond and adjust to failure and setbacks on the field.

**OFP (Overall Future Potential):** The measure of all tool futures based on the projected growth and maturity of those tools. The individual grades are calculated and assigned proper weight, and the result of that division is the player's OFP, or projected ceiling.

**Pitchability:** Put simply, the overall command and feel for the act of pitching. It's a broad term, but it's usually used to describe pitchers with instincts for their craft, sequencing ability, understanding of how to get hitters out, how to pitch east, west, north, and south, etc.

**Run:** Another way of describing the speed tool; also used to described a pitch that will show movement to the arm-side of the pitcher, hence running away from a hitter in the opposite box.

**Secs:** Secondary pitches.

**#Want:** The manifestation of human desire and physical yield; when the yearning for perfection becomes visible to the naked eye.

## Toolbar

We've also included a graphical display of each player's future projected (i.e., not present) physical tools.
For hitters, it looks like this:

| MLB ETA | Hit | Power | Run | Glove | Arm | | OFP | Realistic |
|---------|-----|-------|-----|-------|-----|---|-----|-----------|
| 2014 | – | 55 | 50 | 65 | 80 | | 60<br>1ST DIV PLAYER | 45<br>BACKUP C/<AVG REG |

These are the traditional five tools used to evaluate hitters. OFP is explained above, while "realistic" represents a less optimistic overall view of the future. Both come with number grades as well as descriptions to give you some idea of the type of player we're envisioning.
For pitchers, it looks like this:

| MLB ETA | CT | FB | CH | CB | SL | | OFP | Realistic |
|---------|----|----|----|----|----|---|-----|-----------|
| 2016 | – | 65 | 60 | 60 | – | | 65<br>NO.2 STARTER | 55<br>NO.3 STARTER |

CT = cutter, FB = fastball, CH = changeup, CB = curve ball, SL = slider.

## Order of Team Top 10s

Teams are listed alphabetically by city. Following is the list of teams and their corresponding page numbers.

Now you know how this chapter works. Read and enjoy.

## 1. Archie Bradley   RHP

**Born:** 8/10/92   **Age:** 21   **Bats:** R   **Throws:** R   **Height:** 6' 4"   **Weight:** 225

| MLB ETA | | CT | FB | CH | CB | SL | | OFP | Realistic |
|---------|--|----|----|----|----|----|--|-----|-----------|
| 2014 | | – | 70 | 65 | 70 | – | | 70 NO.1 STARTER | 65 NO.2 STARTER |

| YEAR | TEAM | LVL | AGE | W | L | SV | G | GS | IP | H | HR | BB | SO | BB9 | SO9 | GB% | BABIP | WHIP | ERA | FIP | FRA | WARP |
|------|------|-----|-----|---|---|----|----|----|----|----|----|----|----|----|-----|-----|-------|------|-----|-----|-----|------|
| 2013 | VIS | A+ | 20 | 2 | 0 | 0 | 5 | 5 | 28.7 | 22 | 1 | 10 | 43 | 3.1 | 13.5 | 44% | .362 | 1.12 | 1.26 | 2.48 | 2.41 | 1.2 |
| 2013 | MOB | AA | 20 | 12 | 5 | 0 | 21 | 21 | 123.3 | 93 | 5 | 59 | 119 | 4.3 | 8.7 | 47% | .276 | 1.23 | 1.97 | 3.04 | 3.70 | 1.4 |
| 2014 | ARI | MLB | 21 | 7 | 8 | 0 | 23 | 23 | 123.3 | 109 | 12 | 66 | 114 | 4.8 | 8.3 | 48% | .307 | 1.42 | 4.31 | 4.42 | 4.69 | 0.4 |
| 2015 | ARI | MLB | 22 | 9 | 10 | 0 | 31 | 31 | 200.7 | 173 | 22 | 94 | 168 | 4.2 | 7.5 | 47% | .287 | 1.33 | 4.06 | 4.32 | 4.42 | 1.0 |

Breakout: 0%   Improve: 0%   Collapse: 0%   Attrition: 0%   MLB: 0%      *Comparables: Chris Tillman, Carlos Martinez, Trevor Cahill*

**Drafted/Acquired:** 1st round, 2011 draft, Broken Arrow HS (Broken Arrow, OK)

**Previous Ranking:** #2 (Org), #31 (Top 101)

**What Happened in 2013:** The former seventh overall pick in 2011 took a big developmental step forward in his second full season, pitching his way to Double-A and showing more refinement without sacrificing the intensity of his raw stuff.

**Strengths:** Big, strong frame; fantastic arm speed/strength; fastball is plus-plus monster; routinely works 93-97; touches higher; late arm-side burst; misses bats and barrels; hard knuckle curveball is second plus-plus offering; big velocity and vertical depth; big-time hammer; changeup can show plus; action with improving deception from fastball; aggressive competitor with 80-grade work ethic.

**Weaknesses:** Athletic but can lose his delivery; struggles to stay over the ball and finish his pitches; deception with the high leg and arm swing, but can struggle with balance and pace on the secondary offerings; command is below average at present; could limit full utility of arsenal; can start curveball too high in the zone; changeup needs more developmental time.

**Risk Factor/Injury History:** Moderate risk; 21 Double-A starts on resume.

**Bret Sayre's Fantasy Take:** Bradley has the makings of a special fantasy pitcher, with his workhorse build and three future plus pitches. There will be lots of strikeouts—potential for 220 in a season—and he should contribute a lot in ERA and wins as well. The only question mark is whether he'll walk too many batters to be an impact WHIP guy. If he hovers above the 1.20 range, it will be tough for him to be an elite fantasy option, as the lowest WHIP recorded by a top-10 starter in 2013 was Jordan Zimmermann's 1.09 mark.

**The Year Ahead:** Bradley is a true frontline power arm, with size, strength, and a highly intense arsenal that already features two well-above-average offerings. The delivery can lack consistency and he struggles to finish his pitches, which can leave the ball up and arm side and cause his power curve to play too high in the zone. If the command continues to refine, a number one starter is a possible outcome; a true top-of-the-rotation starter capable of a heavy innings workload and gaudy strikeout totals. Even without sharp command, Bradley will find success in a major-league rotation, especially if the changeup lives up to its projection. Bradley is going to be one of the best young arms in baseball very soon.

> #9
> BP Top
> 101
> Prospects

## 2. Chris Owings   SS

**Born:** 8/12/91   **Age:** 22   **Bats:** R   **Throws:** R   **Height:** 5' 10"   **Weight:** 180

| MLB ETA | Hit | Power | Run | Glove | Arm | | OFP | Realistic |
|---------|-----|-------|-----|-------|-----|--|-----|-----------|
| Debuted in 2013 | 65 | 50 | 50 | 50 | 60 | | 60 1ST DIV PLAYER | 50 ML REGULAR |

| YEAR | TEAM | LVL | AGE | PA | R | 2B | 3B | HR | RBI | BB | SO | SB | CS | AVG/OBP/SLG | TAv | BABIP | BRR | FRAA | WARP |
|------|------|-----|-----|----|---|----|----|----|-----|----|----|----|----|-------------|-----|-------|-----|------|------|
| 2013 | RNO | AAA | 21 | 575 | 104 | 31 | 8 | 12 | 81 | 22 | 99 | 20 | 7 | .330/.359/.482 | .272 | .386 | 6.3 | SS(111): 8.7, 2B(11): -0.8 | 4.2 |
| 2013 | ARI | MLB | 21 | 61 | 5 | 5 | 0 | 0 | 5 | 6 | 10 | 2 | 0 | .291/.361/.382 | .254 | .356 | -0.9 | SS(13): -0.6, 2B(3): 0.2 | 0.0 |
| 2014 | ARI | MLB | 22 | 250 | 27 | 11 | 2 | 5 | 22 | 6 | 59 | 4 | 2 | .248/.266/.368 | .229 | .300 | 0.2 | SS 3, 2B -0 | 0.6 |
| 2015 | ARI | MLB | 23 | 452 | 47 | 20 | 4 | 9 | 48 | 16 | 97 | 7 | 3 | .260/.291/.393 | .250 | .312 | 0.3 | SS 6 | 2.2 |

Breakout: 0%   Improve: 0%   Collapse: 0%   Attrition: 0%   MLB: 0%      *Comparables: Junior Lake, Chris Nelson, Alcides Escobar*

**Drafted/Acquired:** 1st round, 2009 draft, Gilbert HS (Gilbert, SC)

**Previous Ranking:** #3 (Org), #81 (Top 101)

**What Happened in 2013:** Owings exceeded expectations with a very strong campaign in the upper minors and 20-game splash in the majors, where his tools played up to the level of competition.

**Strengths:** Plus athlete with excellent hand-eye coordination; sound swing with good bat speed and barrel control; very good fastball hitter that can sting velocity; hands work well at the plate and in the field; solid glove-

> #28
> BP Top
> 101
> Prospects

work and actions; arm plays plus, and capable of left-side throws; instincts and quick reactions help range play up; makes things happen on a field.

**Weaknesses:** Approach at the plate can get too fastball happy and aggressive; can struggle against quality off-speed/spin; lacks plus range at short; solid defender but lacks special defensive attributes; power might play below average at major-league level.

**Risk Factor/Injury History:** Low risk; achieved major-league level

**Bret Sayre's Fantasy Take:** It's taken the fantasy community a while to warm up to Owings as a legitimate potential starting shortstop in all leagues, but we're finally here. His 2013 season saw two nice progressions that we look for in fantasy—an increase in contact rate and more aggressiveness on the basepaths. Playing in a park that will draw out some extra juice from his bat, Owings has the potential to hit .290 with 15 homers and 15 steals. Oh, and he's ready now.

**The Year Ahead:** Owings is a highly skilled baseball player despite not owning highly acclaimed or projectable raw tools. The ability to strike a baseball will make him a solid-average major leaguer, regardless of his defensive home, but the infield skill set is good enough to stick at shortstop if the opportunity presents itself. Owings can bring all five tools into game action, and could develop into a well-rounded first-division player if the approach doesn't limit the utility of the hit tool and he plays up (or beyond) his on-paper tool grades. The ability to make adjustments at the plate will be paramount to his success, especially when the book is written and circulated around the league. I think Owings continues to refine and takes another step forward in 2014, developing into the type of player that we will look back on and wonder why he wasn't rated higher when he was a prospect.

## 3. Braden Shipley   RHP

**Born:** 2/22/92   **Age:** 22   **Bats:** R   **Throws:** R   **Height:** 6'3"   **Weight:** 190

| MLB ETA | | CT | FB | CH | CB | SL | | OFP | Realistic |
|---------|--|----|----|----|----|----|--|-----|-----------|
| Late 2015 | | – | 70 | 65 | 70 | – | | 65<br>NO.2 STARTER | 60<br>NO.3 STARTER |

| YEAR | TEAM | LVL | AGE | W | L | SV | G | GS | IP | H | HR | BB | SO | BB9 | SO9 | GB% | BABIP | WHIP | ERA | FIP | FRA | WARP |
|------|------|-----|-----|---|---|----|----|----|-----|-----|----|----|-----|-----|-----|-----|-------|------|-----|-----|-----|------|
| 2013 | SBN | A | 21 | 0 | 1 | 0 | 4 | 4 | 20.7 | 14 | 2 | 8 | 16 | 3.5 | 7.0 | 46% | .218 | 1.06 | 2.61 | 4.35 | 4.92 | 0.1 |
| 2013 | YAK | A- | 21 | 0 | 2 | 0 | 8 | 8 | 19.0 | 30 | 1 | 6 | 24 | 2.8 | 11.4 | 44% | .475 | 1.89 | 7.58 | 2.58 | 3.65 | 0.5 |
| 2014 | ARI | MLB | 22 | 2 | 3 | 0 | 9 | 9 | 34.7 | 38 | 5 | 18 | 22 | 4.7 | 5.7 | 43% | .319 | 1.60 | 5.54 | 5.57 | 6.02 | -0.3 |
| 2015 | ARI | MLB | 23 | 5 | 9 | 0 | 29 | 29 | 177.0 | 190 | 23 | 84 | 130 | 4.3 | 6.6 | 43% | .324 | 1.55 | 5.30 | 4.81 | 5.76 | -1.7 |

Breakout: 0%    Improve: 0%    Collapse: 0%    Attrition: 0%    MLB: 0%        *Comparables: Drake Britton, J.C. Ramirez, Zach Phillips*

**Drafted/Acquired:** 1st round, 2013 draft, University of Nevada-Reno (Reno, NV)

**Previous Ranking:** NR

**What Happened in 2013:** Selected 15th overall in the draft, Shipley could end up looking like a steal, as the well-above-average fastball and changeup arrived as advertised, and the curveball showed up better than expected.

**Strengths:** Athletic; excellent size and present strength; delivery works; good arm action; fastball is lively in the 93-98 range; very comfortable in the mid-90s with arm-side giddy-up; changeup plays very well off fastball; good arm speed and heavy vertical action; curveball is a hammer, with velocity in the low-80s and two-plane break; good command projections; attacks hitters.

**Weaknesses:** Command is fringe at present; doesn't always finish his pitches; tendency to miss arm side; excellent changeup but loses action when he leaves it up; can play too firm in the upper-80s; curveball can get wild out of his hand; easy plus projection but not a plus pitch at present.

**Risk Factor/Injury History:** Moderate risk; limited professional experience.

**Bret Sayre's Fantasy Take:** Another good-sized right-hander with three potential plus pitches, Shipley can miss bats with the best of the arms in his 2013 draft class. He should be considered toward the end of the first round in dynasty drafts this year, and could be a big riser during 2014 with strong potential in all four categories.

**The Year Ahead:** Shipley has the size, strength, and arsenal to stand in the shadow of Archie Bradley without losing his light. Delivery is athletic with good command projection, the arm is fresh, the action is fluid and fast, and he could end up with two well-above-average pitches and a third plus offering at maturity. It's a number two profile with some risk, but a full season of development will push him up prospect lists and into the national spotlight, where graduations from Bradley and Owings should make Shipley the top prospect in the Diamondbacks system.

**#62**
BP Top 101 Prospects

## 4. Jose Martinez   RHP

**Born:** 4/14/94   **Age:** 20   **Bats:** R   **Throws:** R   **Height:** 6'1"   **Weight:** 160

| MLB ETA | | CT | FB | CH | CB | SL | | OFP | Realistic |
|---------|--|----|----|----|----|----|--|-----|-----------|
| 2017 | | – | 75 | 55 | 70 | – | | 65<br>NO.2 STARTER | 60<br>LATE-INN RP (CLOSER) |

| YEAR | TEAM | LVL | AGE | W | L | SV | G | GS | IP | H | HR | BB | SO | BB9 | SO9 | GB% | BABIP | WHIP | ERA | FIP | FRA | WARP |
|------|------|-----|-----|---|---|----|----|----|-----|-----|----|----|-----|-----|-----|-----|-------|------|-----|-----|-----|------|
| 2013 | YAK | A- | 19 | 2 | 3 | 0 | 10 | 10 | 38.0 | 20 | 3 | 25 | 30 | 5.9 | 7.1 | 52% | .179 | 1.18 | 4.03 | 5.37 | 7.05 | -0.4 |
| 2014 | ARI | MLB | 20 | 1 | 1 | 0 | 8 | 3 | 37.7 | 41 | 5 | 23 | 24 | 5.5 | 5.7 | 52% | .316 | 1.69 | 5.84 | 5.79 | 6.35 | -0.5 |
| 2015 | ARI | MLB | 21 | 2 | 2 | 0 | 17 | 6 | 92.0 | 96 | 12 | 47 | 66 | 4.6 | 6.5 | 52% | .315 | 1.55 | 5.34 | 5.03 | 5.81 | -0.9 |

Breakout: 0%    Improve: 0%    Collapse: 0%    Attrition: 0%    MLB: 0%        *Comparables: Kevin Siegrist, Rafael Dolis, Yordano Ventura*

**Drafted/Acquired:** International free agent, 2011, Dominican Republic

**Previous Ranking:** NR

**What Happened in 2013:** In a return trip to the Northwest League, Martinez flashed his ridiculous fastball and curveball combination, but struggled with his delivery and control, walking 25 hitters in only 38 innings.

**Strengths:** Elite arm strength; elite arm speed; whippy fastball from 3/4 slot that will work 92-97; has touched elite velocity in bursts; creates good angle; projects to settle in as true plus-plus weapon in the 96+ range; curveball is second plus-plus potential offering; slider-like but with more snap; true wipeout pitch with more command and consistency; some feel for turning over a changeup.

**Weaknesses:** Slight frame; needs to add strength; well-below-average command at present; more thrower than pitcher; flies open in the delivery and gets very arm heavy; changeup is often overthrown and deliberate in the release; projectable but below average at present.

**Risk Factor/Injury History:** High risk; yet to pitch at full-season level.

**Bret Sayre's Fantasy Take:** Targeting short-season arms can be a tricky proposition, but the group of those arms who have more upside than Martinez can be counted on one hand. The role and future are all to be determined, but as I keep saying in this series, when you dig into the guppy pool for these teenage pitchers, always bet on velocity and stuff—and Martinez has that in spades.

**The Year Ahead:** When it comes to ceiling, Martinez can stand tall with the big boys in the system, but the risk associated with the profile is much higher. The 20-year-old has some of the best arm speed in the minors, a lighting-fast release that makes an already sexy fastball play even sexier because of its combination of velocity and late action. The build, the arm speed, and the potent fastball/curveball combo remind some scouts of Yordano Ventura, but the overall pitchability is below average and drags the utility of the arsenal down. With improved command, Martinez could emerge as a premier prospect in baseball, but that's a much easier statement to make on paper than it is to execute on a mound. Martinez will move to the full-season level in 2014, and I wouldn't be surprised if the strikeout totals start turning heads even if the strike throwing remains a work in progress.

---

## 5. Aaron Blair RHP

**Born:** 5/26/92    **Age:** 22    **Bats:** R    **Throws:** R    **Height:** 6'5"    **Weight:** 230

| MLB ETA | CT | FB | CH | CB | SL | OFP | Realistic |
|---|---|---|---|---|---|---|---|
| Late 2015 | — | 60 | 60 | 50 | 50 | 60 NO.3 STARTER | 50 NO.4 STARTER |

| YEAR | TEAM | LVL | AGE | W | L | SV | G | GS | IP | H | HR | BB | SO | BB9 | SO9 | GB% | BABIP | WHIP | ERA | FIP | FRA | WARP |
|---|---|---|---|---|---|---|---|---|---|---|---|---|---|---|---|---|---|---|---|---|---|---|
| 2013 | YAK | A- | 21 | 1 | 1 | 0 | 8 | 8 | 31.0 | 25 | 2 | 13 | 28 | 3.8 | 8.1 | 42% | .280 | 1.23 | 2.90 | 3.80 | 4.68 | 0.2 |
| 2013 | SBN | A | 21 | 0 | 2 | 0 | 3 | 3 | 17.7 | 19 | 0 | 4 | 13 | 2.0 | 6.6 | 45% | .328 | 1.30 | 3.57 | 2.72 | 3.25 | 0.4 |
| 2014 | ARI | MLB | 22 | 2 | 3 | 0 | 7 | 7 | 34.3 | 39 | 4 | 17 | 20 | 4.5 | 5.2 | 42% | .319 | 1.62 | 5.65 | 5.24 | 6.14 | -0.4 |
| 2015 | ARI | MLB | 23 | 7 | 10 | 0 | 29 | 29 | 183.7 | 192 | 24 | 75 | 140 | 3.7 | 6.9 | 42% | .320 | 1.46 | 4.94 | 4.56 | 5.37 | -1.0 |

Breakout: 0%    Improve: 0%    Collapse: 0%    Attrition: 0%    MLB: 0%      *Comparables: Chad Bettis, Michael Belfiore, Brett Marshall*

**Drafted/Acquired:** 1st round, 2013 draft, Marshall University (Huntington, WV)

**Previous Ranking:** NR

**What Happened in 2013:** Popped 36th overall in the 2013 draft, Blair is a safe yet unspectacular starter who wasted little time showing off his mature arsenal in 11 starts after signing.

**Strengths:** Big, strong body; shows athleticism in the delivery; repeatable mechanics; arm works well; fastball is solid-average to plus; works low-90s and can bump higher; good arm-side boring action; changeup is above-average pitch and should play as plus; good fastball disguise and off-the-barrel action; can locate both a slider and a curveball; solid command profile and workload projection.

**Weaknesses:** Physically mature; limited arsenal projection; fastball velocity can play average in the 90-91 range; breaking balls play as fringe-average offerings at present; both pitches lack intensity and bat-missing bite; what you see is probably what you will get; needs to work down and sequence to find success.

**Risk Factor/Injury History:** Moderate risk; limited professional experience

**Bret Sayre's Fantasy Take:** Blair gets a little lost with other arms from the 2013 draft class, but he should be able to be somewhat solid in all four categories. His ERA may struggle because he likes to elevate, leaving him susceptible to the long ball, and the strikeouts won't make a huge difference (think 150-160 in a full season). He's a better target the deeper your league is.

**The Year Ahead:** Blair should be an innings-chewer in a major-league rotation, a big-bodied and durable starter with a four-pitch mix, including a zone-pounding low-90s fastball and a quality changeup. He can reach his ultimate projection with improved command and refined breaking ball utility, but there isn't a big gap between his ceiling and his floor. Blair should move quickly in the Arizona system, with a chance to reach Double-A at some point in 2014, and with good results, could pitch his way to the majors by the end of the 2015 season.

## 6. Stryker Trahan    C

**Born:** 4/25/94    **Age:** 20    **Bats:** L    **Throws:** R    **Height:** 6' 1"    **Weight:** 215

| MLB ETA | Hit | Power | Run | Glove | Arm | OFP | Realistic |
|---|---|---|---|---|---|---|---|
| 2017 | – | 60 | 50 | 50 | 70 | 60<br>1ST DIV PLAYER | 50<br>2ND DIV PLAYER |

| YEAR | TEAM | LVL | AGE | PA | R | 2B | 3B | HR | RBI | BB | SO | SB | CS | AVG/OBP/SLG | TAv | BABIP | BRR | FRAA | WARP |
|---|---|---|---|---|---|---|---|---|---|---|---|---|---|---|---|---|---|---|---|
| 2013 | MSO | Rk | 19 | 262 | 44 | 15 | 2 | 10 | 33 | 24 | 57 | 1 | 0 | .254/.328/.462 | .270 | .296 | 2.7 | C(44): -1.1 | 1.5 |
| 2014 | ARI | MLB | 20 | 250 | 20 | 8 | 1 | 5 | 24 | 18 | 79 | 1 | 0 | .186/.245/.294 | .198 | .250 | -0.3 | C -0 | -0.6 |
| 2015 | ARI | MLB | 21 | 250 | 27 | 9 | 1 | 7 | 27 | 19 | 71 | 0 | 0 | .205/.267/.346 | .225 | .257 | -0.5 | C 0 | -0.7 |

Breakout: 0%    Improve: 0%    Collapse: 0%    Attrition: 0%    MLB: 0%        *Comparables: Max Stassi, Wilin Rosario, Travis d'Arnaud*

**Drafted/Acquired:** 1st round, 2012 draft, Acadiana HS (Lafayette, LA)

**Previous Ranking:** #6 (Org)

**What Happened in 2013:** Trahan moved up a level to the Pioneer League in 2013, and while his power still oozes projection, the hit tool and defensive profile continue to leave scouts on the fence about his future.

**Strengths:** Football body; plus strength and good athleticism; power swing from the left-side; generates loft and leverage; plus power potential; raw arm is plus-plus; utility should play over plus; runs well for position.

**Weaknesses:** Lost some fluidity in actions because of body bulk; below-average receiver at present; can get casual with footwork and framing; hit tool likely to play below average; struggles with pitch recognition and bat control; will likely struggle against sequence and spin.

**Risk Factor/Injury History:** High risk; dual-threat development; yet to play at full-season level.

**Bret Sayre's Fantasy Take:** This past season does little to mute the type of offensive upside that Trahan has behind the plate, if he does indeed stay there. However, therein lies the problem. As an outfielder, he'd be far less interesting for fantasy (as a potential .275+ hitter capable of hitting 20 homers), but he certainly clears the bar for ownership among fantasy catching prospects.

**The Year Ahead:** Trahan's career path is still undetermined, as sources are mixed on his long-term defensive home, and having seen Trahan in person and behind the plate, I'm still on the fence as well about his ability to make it work. He has all the necessary physical gifts, but the receiving has a long way to go, and some believe that his bat would be better served if the focus shifted from a dual-threat development to a more narrow approach. This will play out over the next few years, but in addition to the glove, the bat will need to take big steps forward in the coming years if it's going to play, even more so if Trahan moves to a corner outfield spot. Full-season ball is going to be a huge challenge for the 20-year-old, and I can see the swing-and-miss getting exploited by better stuff and the stock dropping throughout the season.

## 7. Jake Barrett    RHP

**Born:** 7/22/91    **Age:** 22    **Bats:** R    **Throws:** R    **Height:** 6' 3"    **Weight:** 230

| MLB ETA | CT | FB | CH | CB | SL | OFP | Realistic |
|---|---|---|---|---|---|---|---|
| 2014 | – | 65 | – | – | 60 | 55<br>LATE INN RP (CLOSER) | 50<br>LATE INN RP (SETUP) |

| YEAR | TEAM | LVL | AGE | W | L | SV | G | GS | IP | H | HR | BB | SO | BB9 | SO9 | GB% | BABIP | WHIP | ERA | FIP | FRA | WARP |
|---|---|---|---|---|---|---|---|---|---|---|---|---|---|---|---|---|---|---|---|---|---|---|
| 2013 | VIS | A+ | 21 | 2 | 1 | 15 | 28 | 0 | 27.3 | 21 | 2 | 9 | 37 | 3.0 | 12.2 | 49% | .284 | 1.10 | 1.98 | 3.33 | 3.66 | 0.7 |
| 2013 | MOB | AA | 21 | 1 | 1 | 14 | 24 | 0 | 24.7 | 18 | 2 | 3 | 22 | 1.1 | 8.0 | 46% | .232 | 0.85 | 0.36 | 2.55 | 3.64 | 0.3 |
| 2014 | ARI | MLB | 22 | 2 | 1 | 2 | 42 | 0 | 41.3 | 40 | 5 | 16 | 35 | 3.5 | 7.6 | 47% | .311 | 1.35 | 4.27 | 4.46 | 4.64 | 0.0 |
| 2015 | ARI | MLB | 23 | 3 | 1 | 2 | 54 | 0 | 53.7 | 48 | 5 | 16 | 52 | 2.7 | 8.7 | 47% | .308 | 1.20 | 3.50 | 3.32 | 3.81 | 0.7 |

Breakout: 0%    Improve: 0%    Collapse: 0%    Attrition: 0%    MLB: 0%        *Comparables: Joe Ortiz, Daniel Stange, Rich Thompson*

**Drafted/Acquired:** Arizona State University (Tempe, AZ)

**Previous Ranking:** On The Rise

**What Happened in 2013:** In his first full season of action, the former third-round pick pitched his way to Double-A, allowing only 7 earned runs in 52 innings of relief work.

**Strengths:** Excellent size/present strength; excellent fastball; routinely works 95+; good life; slider is second plus offering; mid-80s velocity and sharp two-plane movement; can drop tumbling changeup; delivery works well and has some pitchability despite short-burst profile.

**Weaknesses:** Fastball command is fringe; can overthrow the slider and lose the depth; more deliberate when showing the changeup.

**Risk Factor/Injury History:** Low risk; Double-A/AFL experience; stuff to play at present.

**Bret Sayre's Fantasy Take:** The relief profile is not a sexy one for fantasy purposes, and the fact that Addison Reed just arrived in the desert likely means that Barrett will be looking up in the depth chart at him even if he does develop into a shutdown reliever quickly. Saves are saves, and relievers who don't get them can only do so much for you.

**The Year Ahead:** As much I dislike ranking relievers on prospect lists—I realize their value to a major-league team but they are also more ubiquitous in nature—Barrett's proximity to the majors and likelihood of sustainable success at the back of a major-league bullpen warrants the inclusion. With two highly potent offerings in the fastball and slider, and good overall feel for strike throwing, the 22-year-old righty is able to miss a lot of bats by attacking the zone. It shouldn't take long for Barrett to develop into a frontline setup option, and if the command refines, he has the stuff and the approach to close games at the major-league level.

## 8.   Sergio Alcantara   SS

**Born:** 7/10/96   **Age:** 17   **Bats:** B   **Throws:** R   **Height:** 5' 10"   **Weight:** 150

| MLB ETA | Hit | Power | Run | Glove | Arm | OFP | Realistic |
|---|---|---|---|---|---|---|---|
| 2018 | 60 | – | – | 65 | 70 | 60<br>1ST DIV PLAYER | 45<br>UTILITY |

| YEAR | TEAM | LVL | AGE | PA | R | 2B | 3B | HR | RBI | BB | SO | SB | CS | AVG/OBP/SLG | TAv | BABIP | BRR | FRAA | WARP |
|---|---|---|---|---|---|---|---|---|---|---|---|---|---|---|---|---|---|---|---|
| 2013 | DIA | Rk | 16 | 218 | 31 | 5 | 4 | 0 | 16 | 44 | 36 | 3 | 2 | .243/.398/.320 | .299 | .304 | -1.4 | SS(47): 0.3 | 1.7 |
| 2014 | ARI | MLB | 17 | 250 | 22 | 8 | 1 | 2 | 15 | 22 | 69 | 0 | 0 | .188/.262/.253 | .196 | .260 | -0.3 | SS -0 | -0.6 |
| 2015 | ARI | MLB | 18 | 250 | 23 | 6 | 1 | 2 | 17 | 22 | 62 | 0 | 0 | .195/.269/.256 | .202 | .255 | -0.3 | SS 0 | -1.9 |

Breakout: 0%   Improve: 0%   Collapse: 0%   Attrition: 0%   MLB: 0%   *Comparables: Ruben Tejada, Jonathan Schoop, Freddy Galvis*

**Drafted/Acquired:** International Free Agent, 2012, Dominican Republic

**Previous Ranking:** NR

**What Happened in 2013:** After receiving a high six-figure bonus in the 2012 J2 window, Alcantara skipped over a Dominican complex assignment in 2013 and jumped straight to stateside ball, where he was the youngest player in the Arizona league.

**Strengths:** Special instincts; impressive glovework at shortstop; easy and fluid actions; soft hands; glove could grade over plus; arm is well above average; a true weapon; instincts and a quick first step allow for range; good bat-to-ball-skills; mature approach tracks the ball very well; uses the middle of the diamond.

**Weaknesses:** Fringe run at present; lacks much projection with that tool; limited size and strength; bat could be empty (hit tool only); well-below-average power potential.

**Risk Factor/Injury History:** Extreme risk; complex-league resume; 17 years old

**Bret Sayre's Fantasy Take: :** The defense moves him onto this list from a real-life perspective, but Alcantara isn't worth paying attention to for fantasy yet. We'll check back in on him in another year.

**The Year Ahead:** Alcantara has the type of skill set to develop into a premier prospect, with instincts and feel for the game that you can't teach, an impact arm, and slick actions in the field. The bat could be light, but the 17-year-old already shows an advanced approach and ability to track and react to pitches, so there's a chance he can offer more than just slappy contact. The lack of speed could also be an issue, but the instincts and first step help in the field, and with improved strength and conditioning, the speed might be able to play to average. Keep an eye on this kid.

## 9.   Justin Williams   LF

**Born:** 8/20/95   **Age:** 18   **Bats:** L   **Throws:** R   **Height:** 6' 2"   **Weight:** 215

| MLB ETA | Hit | Power | Run | Glove | Arm | OFP | Realistic |
|---|---|---|---|---|---|---|---|
| 2017 | 50 | 70 | – | 50 | 50 | 60<br>1ST DIV PLAYER | 45<br>PLATOON/<AVG ML |

| YEAR | TEAM | LVL | AGE | PA | R | 2B | 3B | HR | RBI | BB | SO | SB | CS | AVG/OBP/SLG | TAv | BABIP | BRR | FRAA | WARP |
|---|---|---|---|---|---|---|---|---|---|---|---|---|---|---|---|---|---|---|---|
| 2013 | SBN | A | 17 | 11 | 3 | 0 | 0 | 0 | 0 | 2 | 2 | 0 | 0 | .111/.273/.111 | .171 | .143 | 0.0 | LF(2): 0.6 | 0.0 |
| 2013 | DIA | Rk | 17 | 161 | 17 | 12 | 0 | 1 | 32 | 8 | 35 | 0 | 1 | .345/.398/.446 | .313 | .446 | 0.7 | LF(31): -2.6 | 1.0 |
| 2013 | MSO | Rk | 17 | 52 | 12 | 6 | 0 | 0 | 5 | 1 | 7 | 0 | 0 | .412/.423/.529 | .328 | .477 | 0.8 | LF(10): -2.6 | 0.3 |
| 2014 | ARI | MLB | 18 | 250 | 16 | 9 | 0 | 2 | 19 | 10 | 73 | 0 | 0 | .199/.235/.265 | .185 | .270 | -0.4 | LF -1 | -1.5 |
| 2015 | ARI | MLB | 19 | 250 | 22 | 9 | 1 | 3 | 21 | 9 | 70 | 0 | 0 | .209/.243/.297 | .200 | .276 | -0.5 | LF -1 | -2.5 |

Breakout: 0%   Improve: 0%   Collapse: 0%   Attrition: 0%   MLB: 0%   *Comparables: Caleb Gindl, Joe Benson, Che-Hsuan Lin*

**Drafted/Acquired:** 2nd round, 2013 draft, Terrebonne High School (Houma, LA)

**Previous Ranking:** NR

**What Happened in 2013:** Despite being a young high school draftee at age 17, Williams ripped the ball after signing, showing a good feel for loud contact against older competition.

**Strengths:** Physical and strong; monster power potential in the bat; rotational swing and quick hands produce easy plus bat speed; loose and easy; good feel for contact; shows some bat control

**Weaknesses:** Body could become high-maintenance; room to add bad weight; speed is fringe; overall athletic profile isn't great; will expand and chase at the plate; can get overly aggressive; questions about projection/ utility of hit tool against better arms; throwing mechanics need work in the outfield; fringe-average at present; read/routes are very raw.

**Risk Factor/Injury History:** High risk; limited professional experience.

**Bret Sayre's Fantasy Take:** The power is very tempting with Williams, as it could be of the 30-homer variety if it plays up to his potential. Of course, we're a long way from that, so for now he's an interesting flier for fantasy and someone to look at as you draw toward the end of your dynasty drafts.

**The Year Ahead:** Williams has some of the best raw power on the scene, but concerns about his approach and hit tool stemming from his amateur days give pause when it comes to projecting his game power. He can get aggressive at the plate, and has a tendency to expand and chase secondary stuff, which could get exploited in a full season at the full-season level. If the hit tool and approach prove to be better than advertised, the raw left-handed power could really make Williams a standout prospect, regardless of the limitations on defense. As a recent convert to the outfield, his defense is understandably raw and unrefined, but he should develop into a passable corner glove, with several sources calling left field his future home.

## 10.  Jacob Lamb  3B

**Born:** 10/9/90    **Age:** 23    **Bats:** L    **Throws:** R    **Height:** 6'2"    **Weight:** 200

| MLB ETA | Hit | Power | Run | Glove | Arm | | OFP | Realistic |
|---|---|---|---|---|---|---|---|---|
| **2015** | **55** | **55** | – | **50** | **60** | | **50** ML REGULAR | **45** <AVG REGULAR |

| YEAR | TEAM | LVL | AGE | PA | R | 2B | 3B | HR | RBI | BB | SO | SB | CS | AVG/OBP/SLG | TAv | BABIP | BRR | FRAA | WARP |
|---|---|---|---|---|---|---|---|---|---|---|---|---|---|---|---|---|---|---|---|
| 2013 | VIS | A+ | 22 | 283 | 44 | 20 | 0 | 13 | 47 | 48 | 70 | 0 | 0 | .303/.424/.558 | .331 | .380 | -0.1 | 3B(55): -2.3 | 2.8 |
| 2013 | DIA | Rk | 22 | 21 | 4 | 2 | 0 | 0 | 5 | 2 | 5 | 0 | 0 | .294/.381/.412 | .288 | .385 | 0.3 | 3B(4): 0.1 | 0.2 |
| 2014 | ARI | MLB | 23 | 250 | 25 | 10 | 0 | 7 | 28 | 24 | 68 | 0 | 0 | .226/.301/.369 | .246 | .290 | -0.4 | 3B -2 | 0.1 |
| 2015 | ARI | MLB | 24 | 250 | 29 | 11 | 0 | 7 | 27 | 25 | 67 | 0 | 0 | .221/.297/.370 | .245 | .278 | -0.6 | 3B -1 | 0.4 |

Breakout: 1%    Improve: 12%    Collapse: 2%    Attrition: 11%    MLB: 27%    *Comparables: Josh Bell, Mike Olt, Mat Gamel*

**Drafted/Acquired:** 6th round, 2012 draft, University of Washington (Seattle, WA)

**Previous Ranking:** NR

**What Happened in 2013:** In his full-season debut, Lamb jumped to the California League and continued his professional trend of hitting for average and power, despite losing time to a broken bone in his hand.

**Strengths:** Well-rounded player; good athlete with present strength; shows the ability to drive the baseball to all fields; works at-bats and puts himself in favorable hitting conditions; shows above-average power potential; good hands in the field; solid-average glove; strong arm; can make plays.

**Weaknesses:** Swing features some swing-and-miss in the zone; struggles to cover the outer third; footwork at third can get casual; lacks big range; questions about game power against better pitching.

**Risk Factor/Injury History:** Moderate risk; yet to play at Double-A level

**Bret Sayre's Fantasy Take:** With Lamb's future fantasy value, it's all about the power. He's shown it in high-offensive environments thus far, but if he's a 12-15 homer guy in the end versus 20+, it's essentially the difference between being replacement level (or below) and a bona fide fantasy starter. He's another guy, like Blair, who is a better target in deep leagues.

**The Year Ahead:** Lamb is a prospect that seems to get more love from the statistical community than the scouts, as the 23-year-old has put up impressive offensive numbers at every stop—including a very high on-base percentage in High-A—but his swing might not have the characteristics to make him a big threat against better pitching; with some swing-and-miss on offerings in the zone, and reports about exploitable holes in the swing [itself], more advanced arms could expose Lamb at the plate. He does show some bat speed and barreling ability, especially against weaker stuff, but several sources called him a bad-ball hitter that is likely to struggle against quality velocity and secondary arsenals, and despite projecting to the major-league level, the bat might not play enough to make him a regular. Double-A will be a big test for the bat.

### Prospects on the Rise

**1. SS Jose Munoz:** An "On the Rise" prospect on last year's rankings, Munoz's bat made a case for his inclusion on the top ten this year, but the strong draft crop of 2013 left him waiting in the wings. The offensive profile is projectable, with a strong swing and power to dream on, but he is likely to outgrow shortstop and will be a better fit for the hot corner, where his actions and arm will be weapons. I think he's ready to take another step forward in 2014 and finally etch his name onto a top-10 list.

**2. RHP Brad Keller:** Even with workhorse size and strength, Keller fell to the eighth round in the 2013 draft, but wasted little time making his name known, pounding the zone with a low-90s fastball and throwing two secondary offerings for strikes, and pitching his way to the Pioneer League. The 18-year-old lacks frontline stuff or projections, but a solid-average mix or a strong, physical body could give the D-Backs an innings-chewer type.

**3. 3B Brandon Drury:** Acquired from the Braves in the Justin Upton trade, Drury really stepped forward on both sides of the ball in 2013, showing a well-rounded stick at the plate and better chops in the field. There are still questions about the power utility and if it will play enough for Drury to profile as a major-league regular, but if he makes the same developmental progress in 2014 as he did in 2013, the 21-year-old will jump into the top 10 in this system.

## Factors on the Farm

### Prospects likely to contribute at the major-league level in 2014

**1. LHP Andrew Chafin:** The former first-round pick was slotted seventh on last season's top 10, but fell after an uneven run in Double-A, where the lefty limited damage but failed to miss many bats. The profile might be a better fit in relief, where the solid-average to plus fastball could play up and the slider could miss more bats and not just barrels. In the rotation, he can bring a solid three-pitch mix and some pitchability, but the command profile would need to be sharp to find a sustainable home at the back of a major-league rotation.

**2. RHP Matt Stites:** Short in size but not lacking in stuff, Stites is well on his way to developing into a late-innings options for the Diamondbacks. The 23-year-old can miss bats with a plus-plus fastball that works in the 95+ range, backed up with an above-average mid-80s slider. The delivery has effort and the command comes and goes, but the combination of stuff, approach, and control should make him a setup option at some point in 2014.

**3. RHP Willy Paredes:** Relatively unknown reliever signed by the Diamondbacks in 2011, the 25-year-old Dominican arm features a grotesquely heavy mid-90s sinker that can touch higher in bursts that he can ride all the way to a late-innings opportunity at the major-league level in 2014. He can miss bats. Keep him on your radar.

## FROM THE FIELD

### Braden Shipley

**Player:** Braden Shipley

**Team:** Arizona Diamondbacks

**Filed by:** Ryan Parker

**Date(s) Seen:** July 2, 2013

**Physical:** Very athletic frame, long-limbed but not lanky

**Mechanics/Delivery:** High-energy mechanics, slight hip twist, quick arm, high 3/4 arm slot, repeats well.

**Fastball:** 60 grade; 92-95, throws both four- and two-seam. Improving command; four-seam can flatten out at times.

**Curveball:** 50 grade; 80-82, inconsistent; when thrown right it has 60 movement, showing late downward break; lacks command; will throw to righties and lefties.

**Changeup:** 70 grade; 86-88, best changeup I've personally seen in the minors; movement is average but has incredible deception; occasionally will be too firm with pitch.

**Makeup:** 60 grade; very hard worker; takes instruction well and picks up teammates rather than belittle them.

**OFP:** 60; no. 2 or high 3 starter

**Realistic Role:** 55; no. 3 starter or Ryan Madson type reliever

**Risk:** Moderate; never dealt with high workload; command is currently shaky at best; still should make it to MLB.

## 1. Lucas Sims   RHP

**Born:** 5/10/94   **Age:** 20   **Bats:** R   **Throws:** R   **Height:** 6'2"   **Weight:** 195

| MLB ETA | CT | FB | CH | CB | SL | OFP | Realistic |
|---------|----|----|----|----|----|-----|-----------|
| **2016** | --- | **65** | **60** | **60** | --- | **65**<br>NO.2 STARTER | **55**<br>NO.3 STARTER |

| YEAR | TEAM | LVL | AGE | W | L | SV | G | GS | IP | H | HR | BB | SO | BB9 | SO9 | GB% | BABIP | WHIP | ERA | FIP | FRA | WARP |
|------|------|-----|-----|---|---|----|----|----|----|----|----|----|----|-----|-----|-----|-------|------|-----|-----|-----|------|
| 2013 | ROM | A | 19 | 12 | 4 | 0 | 28 | 18 | 116.7 | 83 | 3 | 46 | 134 | 3.5 | 10.3 | 44% | .284 | 1.11 | 2.62 | 3.09 | 3.47 | 2.0 |
| 2014 | ATL | MLB | 20 | 4 | 6 | 0 | 22 | 16 | 86.7 | 81 | 9 | 44 | 78 | 4.6 | 8.1 | 42% | .313 | 1.43 | 4.53 | 4.52 | 4.92 | 0.0 |
| 2015 | ATL | MLB | 21 | 7 | 8 | 0 | 35 | 24 | 170.7 | 156 | 20 | 73 | 165 | 3.8 | 8.7 | 42% | .313 | 1.34 | 4.30 | 4.09 | 4.68 | 0.2 |

Breakout: 0%    Improve: 0%    Collapse: 0%    Attrition: 0%    MLB: 0%         *Comparables: Julio Teheran, Trevor Cahill, Chris Tillman*

**Drafted/Acquired:** 1st round, 2012 draft, Brookwood HS (Snellville, GA)

**Previous Ranking:** #3 (Org)

**What Happened in 2013:** In his full-season debut, Sims established himself as one of the better young arms in the minors, missing plenty of bats and barrels, allowing 83 hits in 116 innings while striking out 134.

**Strengths:** Very athletic; smooth/easy mechanics; repeats well; fastball works 90-95; touches 96; pitch shows late wiggle; curveball plays above average at present; true hammer in the upper-70s; bat-missing pitch with big vertical depth; 82- to 86-mph changeup with late sink; pitchability and good command projection; competitor.

**Weaknesses:** Needs to add strength/stamina; fastball command needs refinement; curveball can get slurvy when he doesn't stay over it; changeup can get a little firm in the 86 range and lose action.

**Risk Factor/Injury History:** Moderate risk; limited professional experience; yet to achieve Double-A level.

**Bret Sayre's Fantasy Take:** As the lone representative of the Braves on the Fantasy 101, Sims has impressive stuff across the board, which at peak could lead to strong numbers across the board—including 180+ strikeouts. The questions with Sims from a fantasy standpoint are more about his ability to provide the quantity required of a frontline fantasy starter than the quality portion of the equation.

**The Year Ahead:** Sims draws scouting comps to a young Matt Cain, an athletic strike-thrower who can take the ball every fifth day and beat you with his entire arsenal. He still has some rough edges, but this is a safer prospect than the resume suggests. Sims can work the fastball in the low- to mid-90s, back it up with a very impressive upper-70s curve with depth, and show feel for a future above-average changeup. Add to the profile an athletic and clean delivery and good pitchability, and you have the making of a very solid major-league starter, with a ceiling of a number two but a high floor in the middle of a rotation. He's likely to shove it at the High-A level, and could emerge as a top-20 prospect in the game by the end of the season. Underrated prospect.

**#40**
BP Top
101
Prospects

## 2. Christian Bethancourt   C

**Born:** 9/2/91   **Age:** 22   **Bats:** R   **Throws:** R   **Height:** 6'2"   **Weight:** 215

| MLB ETA | Hit | Power | Run | Glove | Arm | OFP | Realistic |
|---------|-----|-------|-----|-------|-----|-----|-----------|
| **2014** | --- | **55** | **50** | **65** | **80** | **60**<br>1ST DIV PLAYER | **45**<br>BACKUP C/<AVG REG |

| YEAR | TEAM | LVL | AGE | PA | R | 2B | 3B | HR | RBI | BB | SO | SB | CS | AVG/OBP/SLG | TAv | BABIP | BRR | FRAA | WARP |
|------|------|-----|-----|----|---|----|----|----|-----|----|----|----|----|-------------|-----|-------|-----|------|------|
| 2013 | MIS | AA | 21 | 388 | 42 | 21 | 0 | 12 | 45 | 16 | 57 | 11 | 7 | .277/.305/.436 | .273 | .294 | -0.4 | C(85): 0.8 | 2.4 |
| 2013 | ATL | MLB | 21 | 1 | 0 | 0 | 0 | 0 | 0 | 0 | 1 | 0 | 0 | .000/.000/.000 | .053 | -- | 0.0 | | 0.0 |
| 2014 | ATL | MLB | 22 | 250 | 27 | 10 | 1 | 5 | 22 | 4 | 52 | 4 | 2 | .242/.254/.352 | .222 | .280 | -0.2 | C 1 | 0.2 |
| 2015 | ATL | MLB | 23 | 297 | 30 | 13 | 0 | 7 | 31 | 10 | 55 | 4 | 2 | .241/.267/.365 | .230 | .270 | -0.5 | C 1 | 0.1 |

Breakout: 0%    Improve: 0%    Collapse: 0%    Attrition: 0%    MLB: 0%         *Comparables: Tony Cruz, Angel Salome, Tim Federowicz*

**Drafted/Acquired:** International Free Agent, 2008, Panama

**Previous Ranking:** #5 (Org), #93 (Top 101)

**What Happened in 2013:** The Panamanian catcher returned to the Double-A level, where his arm continued to show elite promise and his bat took a much needed step forward.

**Strengths:** Athletic, with good size and strength; elite arm strength; capable of unbelievable pop times in the sub-1.7 range; quick release and accurate; glovework has improved; more focus behind the plate; plus glove; well-above-average defensive potential; has good raw power; runs well for the position; better bat-to-ball in 2013; shows bat speed.

**Weaknesses:** Can get too casual behind the plate with his footwork; blocking needs work; needs work with game management/game calling; aggressive approach; looks to swing and can get beat by stuff and sequence; hit tool likely to play below average; game power likely to play fringe-average at best; can play with low energy.

**#87**
BP Top
101
Prospects

**Risk Factor/Injury History:** Moderate risk; achieved Double-A level; big questions about bat.

**Bret Sayre's Fantasy Take:** While his defense will likely keep Bethancourt in the lineup barring being an absolute zero at the plate, we can't say the same about his fantasy value. Even if things break right for Bethancourt in his development at the plate, he's still unlikely to be a good option as a starter in a one-catcher league.

**The Year Ahead:** If you like elite arm strength and a true weapon in the catch/throw game, Bethancourt is worth the price of admission. The problem with the profile is the stick, as he isn't a natural hitter and is highly unlikely to develop into a true dual-threat player at the highest level. Against better arms, the 22-year-old Panamanian struggles to stay on quality stuff inside, and when worked away with spin, is prone to off-balance cuts that produce weak contact. At the end of the day, I think Bethancourt's bat will play below average but find a home at the back of a lineup, a .250 type with the power to hit 10-15 bombs coupled with plus defense and the potential for elite catch/throw impact. Even without much help from the bat, Bethancourt could carve out a very long career as a backup catcher, but he's still young enough and offers enough projection with the stick that he could develop into more.

## 3. Mauricio Cabrera RHP

**Born:** 9/22/93 **Age:** 20 **Bats:** R **Throws:** R **Height:** 6' 2" **Weight:** 180

| MLB ETA | CT | FB | CH | CB | SL | OFP | Realistic |
|---|---|---|---|---|---|---|---|
| 2016 | – | 80 | 60 | 50 | – | 65<br>NO.2 STARTER | 50<br>LATE-INN RP (SETUP) |

| YEAR | TEAM | LVL | AGE | W | L | SV | G | GS | IP | H | HR | BB | SO | BB9 | SO9 | GB% | BABIP | WHIP | ERA | FIP | FRA | WARP |
|---|---|---|---|---|---|---|---|---|---|---|---|---|---|---|---|---|---|---|---|---|---|---|
| 2013 | ROM | A | 19 | 3 | 8 | 0 | 24 | 24 | 131.3 | 118 | 3 | 71 | 107 | 4.9 | 7.3 | 51% | .298 | 1.44 | 4.18 | 3.91 | 5.01 | 0.2 |
| 2014 | ATL | MLB | 20 | 4 | 9 | 0 | 20 | 20 | 101.0 | 109 | 12 | 60 | 60 | 5.3 | 5.3 | 47% | .314 | 1.68 | 5.75 | 5.59 | 6.25 | -1.5 |
| 2015 | ATL | MLB | 21 | 8 | 10 | 0 | 28 | 28 | 168.3 | 157 | 18 | 87 | 119 | 4.7 | 6.4 | 46% | .291 | 1.45 | 4.59 | 4.69 | 4.99 | -0.5 |

Breakout: 0%    Improve: 0%    Collapse: 0%    Attrition: 0%    MLB: 0%    *Comparables: Jeurys Familia, Brett Marshall, Jonathan Pettibone*

**Drafted/Acquired:** International free agent, 2010, Dominican Republic

**Previous Ranking:** #4 (Org)

**The Tools:** 8 potential FB; 6 potential CH; 5 potential CB

**What Happened in 2013:** In his full-season debut, the then-19-year-old Dominican made 24 starts and logged over 130 innings, although the scouting reports are still ahead of the on-the-field production.

**Strengths:** Elite arm strength; electric; fastball can work comfortably in the mid- to upper-90s; touches over 100; potential to be 80-grade pitch; changeup will flash plus potential; works as average offering with some deception off the fastball and late action; curveball can flash average potential.

**Weaknesses:** Delivery can get messy; comes across his body and struggles with release point consistency; command is well below average at present; can get deliberate on secondaries; curveball plays below average at present; lacks big upside; pitch can get soft and loose; not sure the pitch will play to major-league standards.

**Risk Factor/Injury History:** High risk; yet to pitch in upper minors; possible bullpen profile; shaky command.

**Bret Sayre's Fantasy Take:** It's very easy to fall in love with the fastball, but without more refinement and command of his secondary stuff, Cabrera's strikeout numbers will not be proportional with his velocity. In fact, he may be more valuable from a fantasy standpoint as an intimidating reliever in deeper leagues.

**The Year Ahead:** Based on the power of one singular pitch, Cabrera has one of the highest projections in the Braves organization, but the pitchability and secondary stuff are still underdeveloped at present and could limit the ultimate upside. Cabrera has monster arm strength and can routinely push his fastball near triple digits, and when he can turn it over and maintain the arm speed, the changeup shows plus potential and plays effectively off the big heater. Once he refines his command and improves his overall feel, Cabrera could really explode as a prospect, but that below-average curveball worries some scouts and might point toward a bullpen future.

## 4. J.R. Graham RHP

**Born:** 1/14/90 **Age:** 24 **Bats:** R **Throws:** R **Height:** 5' 10" **Weight:** 195

| MLB ETA | CT | FB | CH | CB | SL | OFP | Realistic |
|---|---|---|---|---|---|---|---|
| 2014 | – | 70 | 50 | – | 60 | 60<br>NO.3 STARTER | 50<br>LATE-INN RP (SETUP) |

| YEAR | TEAM | LVL | AGE | W | L | SV | G | GS | IP | H | HR | BB | SO | BB9 | SO9 | GB% | BABIP | WHIP | ERA | FIP | FRA | WARP |
|---|---|---|---|---|---|---|---|---|---|---|---|---|---|---|---|---|---|---|---|---|---|---|
| 2013 | MIS | AA | 23 | 1 | 3 | 0 | 8 | 8 | 35.7 | 39 | 0 | 10 | 28 | 2.5 | 7.1 | 68% | .348 | 1.37 | 4.04 | 2.18 | 3.14 | 0.7 |
| 2014 | ATL | MLB | 24 | 2 | 3 | 0 | 9 | 9 | 47.0 | 48 | 5 | 17 | 32 | 3.3 | 6.1 | 54% | .312 | 1.38 | 4.43 | 4.44 | 4.81 | 0.0 |
| 2015 | ATL | MLB | 25 | 10 | 10 | 0 | 32 | 32 | 205.7 | 194 | 22 | 65 | 161 | 2.8 | 7.0 | 54% | .304 | 1.26 | 3.82 | 3.90 | 4.15 | 1.4 |

Breakout: 0%    Improve: 0%    Collapse: 0%    Attrition: 0%    MLB: 0%    *Comparables: David Phelps, Dillon Gee, Jeff Manship*

**Drafted/Acquired:** 4th round, 2011 draft, Santa Clara University (Santa Clara, CA)

**Previous Ranking:** #2 (Org), #63 (Top 101)

**What Happened in 2013:** In his return trip to Double-A, Graham was looking the part before a shoulder injury shut him down and sent his prospect status into a tailspin.

**Strengths:** Short but incredibly strong; balanced on the mound; holds his stuff deep into games; clean arm action; multiple fastball looks; pushes four-seamer easy into mid-90s; two-seamer shows very heavy life in the 93-94 range; plus-plus offering; slider is plus offering; thrown in the upper-80s and touching 90; late sharp dart to the glove side; changeup is solid-average in the 86-89 range; good late life; strong feel for command; highly competitive and aggressive approach.

**Weaknesses:** Lacks height and has to work down to create angle; struggles when he works up in the zone; loses movement and is hittable; slider can lack big depth; more cutter-like in the upper-80s without big tilt; changeup can get too firm in the 88-90 range; sinks but not as effective as two-seamer.

**Risk Factor/Injury History:** Moderate risk; Double-A experience; shoulder injury on resume (2013).

**Bret Sayre's Fantasy Take:** There are a few philosophies that I stand behind in making decisions for fantasy purposes, and one of them is never put much faith in a pitcher with a shoulder injury. Of course, the long-term ramifications of Graham's injury are to be determined, but tread carefully, as he's a likely 'pen candidate in the long run anyway.

**The Year Ahead:** Everybody is worried about the shoulder, and with good reason. But a healthy Graham (and reports suggest he is fully recovered from the shoulder injury of 2013) is an impact arm that several sources think can be an effective mid-rotation starter despite limited height. What the 24-year-old lacks in height he makes up for with strength and intensity, as Graham will batter you with heavy fastballs in the lower zone and then elevate his hard cut-slider and dare you to match the barrel to it. Assuming health, he's a no-doubt late-innings arm as a floor, as he can sit in the mid-90s and touch 97+ in bursts with the knockout slider that can be quite effective missing bats and barrels in the upper-80s. But he can hold his stuff deep into games and has the command and pitchability to start, so if he can stay on the mound, his prospect stock should return to previous levels. But the shoulder injury that spoiled his 2013 season will continue to be talked about until he proves [on the mound] that it is no longer worth talking about.

---

# 5.   Jose Peraza   SS

**Born:** 4/30/94   **Age:** 20   **Bats:** R   **Throws:** R   **Height:** 6' 0"   **Weight:** 165

| MLB ETA | Hit | Power | Run | Glove | Arm | | OFP | Realistic |
|---|---|---|---|---|---|---|---|---|
| **Late 2015** | **55** | – | **65** | **60** | **60** | | **60**<br>1ST DIV PLAYER | **45**<br>UT/<AVG REGULAR |

| YEAR | TEAM | LVL | AGE | PA | R | 2B | 3B | HR | RBI | BB | SO | SB | CS | AVG/OBP/SLG | TAv | BABIP | BRR | FRAA | WARP |
|---|---|---|---|---|---|---|---|---|---|---|---|---|---|---|---|---|---|---|---|
| 2013 | ROM | A | 19 | 504 | 72 | 18 | 8 | 1 | 47 | 34 | 64 | 64 | 15 | .288/.341/.371 | .275 | .328 | 7.0 | SS(104): 20.4 | 5.6 |
| 2014 | ATL | MLB | 20 | 250 | 29 | 8 | 2 | 2 | 14 | 9 | 52 | 16 | 4 | .229/.259/.297 | .208 | .280 | 1.9 | SS 8, 2B -0 | 0.7 |
| 2015 | ATL | MLB | 21 | 250 | 24 | 7 | 2 | 3 | 21 | 10 | 47 | 16 | 4 | .246/.279/.333 | .229 | .287 | 2.2 | SS 8 | 1.0 |

Breakout: 0%    Improve: 0%    Collapse: 0%    Attrition: 0%    MLB: 0%    *Comparables: Carlos Triunfel, Tyler Pastornicky, Elvis Andrus*

**Drafted/Acquired:** International free agent, 2010, Venezuela

**Previous Ranking:** #7 (Org)

**What Happened in 2013:** In his full-season debut, the slick Venezuelan shortstop continued to show good life at the plate, making a lot of contact and hitting for average while showing off his near plus-plus speed on base.

**Strengths:** Well-above-average athlete; plus to plus-plus run; quick feet; highly coordinated in the field; slick actions; excellent backhand pickup; plus arm; plus defensive profile at short; good bat-to-ball ability; can square up velocity; makeup for accelerated developmental path.

**Weaknesses:** Needs to add strength; swing for contact but it can play light; well-below-average power potential; swings at pitches he shouldn't; will expand and chase spin.

**Risk Factor/Injury History:** High risk; Low-A resume; questions about the offensive profile.

**Bret Sayre's Fantasy Take:** There's some fantasy upside here, as anyone (especially a middle infielder) who steals 64 bases in a minor-league season is worth taking note of. Unfortunately, there's little else to his game that will add fantasy value, and the presence of defensive wizard Andrelton Simmons will push Peraza to second base (at best) barring a trade.

**The Year Ahead:** Peraza is a very strong defender at a premium position with high-end speed and contact ability, but he plays in the wrong organization and won't have a future on the left side of the Braves major-league infield. I bring up the major leagues because Peraza has the potential to move through the minors very quickly, despite his age and limited upside with the stick. This kid is very advanced and can bring a lot to the table, and if he can maintain his contact ability as he climbs, you could see 20-year-old playing his way to the highest level by late 2015, which seems like an extreme developmental plan but one that his overall skill set suggests is very possible. The profile is probably more utility than first division, as the offensive tools are more contact and speed with limited pop or power, but the glove is legit and Peraza would bring a lot to a 25-man roster, even if the bat plays a bit light.

## 6. Tommy La Stella  2B

**Born:** 1/31/89  **Age:** 25  **Bats:** L  **Throws:** R  **Height:** 5'11"  **Weight:** 185

| MLB ETA | Hit | Power | Run | Glove | Arm | OFP | Realistic |
|---|---|---|---|---|---|---|---|
| 2014 | 65 | – | – | 50 | – | 55 >AVG REGULAR | 50 2ND DIV PLAYER |

| YEAR | TEAM | LVL | AGE | PA | R | 2B | 3B | HR | RBI | BB | SO | SB | CS | AVG/OBP/SLG | TAv | BABIP | BRR | FRAA | WARP |
|---|---|---|---|---|---|---|---|---|---|---|---|---|---|---|---|---|---|---|---|
| 2013 | MIS | AA | 24 | 324 | 32 | 21 | 2 | 4 | 41 | 37 | 34 | 7 | 1 | .343/.422/.473 | .339 | .380 | -1.8 | 2B(73): -3.2 | 3.1 |
| 2013 | LYN | A+ | 24 | 29 | 7 | 1 | 0 | 1 | 4 | 8 | 1 | 1 | 1 | .550/.690/.750 | .488 | .556 | 0.9 | 2B(3): 0.1 | 0.9 |
| 2014 | ATL | MLB | 25 | 250 | 26 | 12 | 1 | 5 | 27 | 21 | 39 | 3 | 1 | .272/.339/.399 | .273 | .310 | 0.0 | 2B -3 | 0.8 |
| 2015 | ATL | MLB | 26 | 519 | 62 | 23 | 3 | 12 | 57 | 42 | 78 | 2 | 1 | .266/.332/.407 | .270 | .292 | -0.6 | 2B -7 | 1.0 |

Breakout: 1%    Improve: 7%    Collapse: 16%    Attrition: 33%    MLB: 48%    *Comparables: Jarrett Hoffpauir, Eric Sogard, Scott Sizemore*

**Drafted/Acquired:** 8th round, 2011 draft, Coastal Carolina University (Conway, SC)

**Previous Ranking:** #9 (Org)

**What Happened in 2013:** The former eighth-round pick showed a good bat in 2012, but he really exploded in 2013, hitting over .340 at the Double-A level and carrying that success over to the Arizona Fall League, where he had 18 hits in 18 games.

**Strengths:** Excellent bat-to-ball skills; strong/quick hands; knack for putting the barrel on the ball; knows his pitch; game doesn't feature a lot of swing-and-miss; hit tool could play plus or better; fundamentally sound on defense; glove is average; high-energy player.

**Weaknesses:** Lacks big athleticism; run is below average; arm is fringe-average at best; lacks first-step quickness or range; relies on fundamentals and positioning in the field; power is well below average; works gaps but lacks over-the-fence pop; has to hit to have any value.

**Risk Factor/Injury History:** Moderate risk; Double-A experience; mature hit tool.

**Bret Sayre's Fantasy Take:** The best player on this list in terms of "now" value, La Stella is in competition for the second-base job out of spring training. He doesn't have much to offer besides a strong hit tool, but at a weak position, someone who can hit .280-.290 with minimal (but nonzero) production all around doesn't sound like such a bad proposition in deeper leagues.

**The Year Ahead:** La Stella is the type of player that evaluators will discount, and despite his strong Double-A performance in 2013, I'm still not sold in the profile. The 25-year-old can swing the bat and knows what he can drive and what he can't, but he lacks power and speed, and his defensive profile is fringe-average at best, mostly on the strength of his fundamental glove and overall feel for the game. The hit tool has to really shine against even better arms for La Stella to emerge as a major-league regular, but as one source aptly stated, "give me a guy with a plus hit tool and baseball instincts over a guy with elite tools and no clue how to use them." La Stella is one of those players evaluators often miss on because the body doesn't look the part, the tools are fringy at best, and the overall profile doesn't exactly make you weak in the knees when writing the report. But La Stella can hit the baseball, and at the end of the day, that's the one tool that can not only make you a major leaguer but keep you around at that level for a long time.

## 7. Wes Parsons  RHP

**Born:** 9/6/92  **Age:** 21  **Bats:** R  **Throws:** R  **Height:** 6'5"  **Weight:** 190

| MLB ETA | CT | FB | CH | CB | SL | OFP | Realistic |
|---|---|---|---|---|---|---|---|
| 2016 | – | 60 | 55 | – | 60 | 50 NO.4 STARTER | 50 NO.5 SP/LONG RP |

| YEAR | TEAM | LVL | AGE | W | L | SV | G | GS | IP | H | HR | BB | SO | BB9 | SO9 | GB% | BABIP | WHIP | ERA | FIP | FRA | WARP |
|---|---|---|---|---|---|---|---|---|---|---|---|---|---|---|---|---|---|---|---|---|---|---|
| 2013 | ROM | A | 20 | 7 | 7 | 0 | 19 | 19 | 109.7 | 91 | 5 | 21 | 101 | 1.7 | 8.3 | 52% | .280 | 1.02 | 2.63 | 3.05 | 4.06 | 1.3 |
| 2014 | ATL | MLB | 21 | 4 | 5 | 0 | 13 | 13 | 75.3 | 78 | 9 | 29 | 53 | 3.5 | 6.3 | 47% | .313 | 1.42 | 4.76 | 4.70 | 5.18 | -0.4 |
| 2015 | ATL | MLB | 22 | 9 | 10 | 0 | 27 | 27 | 165.7 | 160 | 17 | 60 | 131 | 3.3 | 7.1 | 47% | .310 | 1.33 | 4.19 | 3.99 | 4.56 | 0.4 |

Breakout: 0%    Improve: 0%    Collapse: 0%    Attrition: 0%    MLB: 0%    *Comparables: Patrick Corbin, Will Smith, Carter Capps*

**Drafted/Acquired:** Nondrafted free agent, 2012, Jackson State Community College (Jackson, Tennessee)

**Previous Ranking:** NR

**The Tools:** 6 potential FB; 6 potential SL; 5+ potential CH

**What Happened in 2013:** In his first professional season, the virtually unknown and undrafted prospect had a nearly 5:1 strikeout rate at the full-season level.

**Strengths:** Excellent size and physical projection; easy arm action; fastball works 90-95; shows good sink; good command; slider shows plus potential; sharp tilt and effective to both left- and right-handed hitters; changeup shows solid-average potential; plus pitchability; intelligent with strong makeup.

**Weaknesses:** Fastball can play more pedestrian in the lower-90s; pitch can flatten out when he elevates; slider can get slurvy and loose; emerging weapon but needs refinement; changeup can play a little soft; limited professional sample.

**Risk Factor/Injury History:** Moderate risk; limited professional experience; good overall feel for the pitching.

**Bret Sayre's Fantasy Take:** There's not a whole lot of ceiling here, but if you're looking for a name that could be of use in deeper leagues and is (in all likelihood) unowned, Parsons is a good player to grab or keep an eye on. He won't be a big strikeout guy, but the ratios could be strong.

**The Year Ahead:** Parsons is a pop-out prospect but a legit one nonetheless. He has size, mound smarts, and solid-average to plus stuff, and the bow on the package is above-average pitchability. It will be interesting to see if the stuff ticks up as the body continues to mature, but even without much additional projection, the present profile is very promising, with a low-90s fastball that can touch 95, a slider that can show a sharp two-plane break and a changeup he can turn over and play off his fastball. The 21-year-old righty is a strong bet to continue the trend at the High-A level, and if he does start to tick up a bit, we might have something even more substantial emerge on the prospect landscape.

---

## 8.   Victor Caratini    3B

**Born:** 8/17/93    **Age:** 20    **Bats:** B    **Throws:** R    **Height:** 6' 0"    **Weight:** 192

| MLB ETA | Hit | Power | Run | Glove | Arm | OFP | Realistic |
|---|---|---|---|---|---|---|---|
| **2017** | **60** | – | – | – | **60** | **60** 1ST DIV CATCHER | **50** 2ND DIV PLAYER |

| YEAR | TEAM | LVL | AGE | PA | R | 2B | 3B | HR | RBI | BB | SO | SB | CS | AVG/OBP/SLG | TAv | BABIP | BRR | FRAA | WARP |
|---|---|---|---|---|---|---|---|---|---|---|---|---|---|---|---|---|---|---|---|
| 2013 | DNV | Rk | 19 | 246 | 29 | 23 | 1 | 1 | 25 | 39 | 49 | 0 | 2 | .290/.415/.430 | .311 | .375 | -0.6 | 3B(47): 2.1, SS(1): -0.2 | 2.2 |
| 2014 | ATL | MLB | 20 | 250 | 17 | 8 | 0 | 2 | 19 | 19 | 76 | 0 | 0 | .185/.251/.249 | .192 | .260 | -0.5 | 3B 1, SS -0 | -1.1 |
| 2015 | ATL | MLB | 21 | 250 | 24 | 9 | 1 | 3 | 19 | 23 | 72 | 0 | 0 | .194/.271/.276 | .208 | .267 | -0.6 | 3B 1, SS 0 | -1.7 |

Breakout: 0%    Improve: 0%    Collapse: 0%    Attrition: 0%    MLB: 0%          *Comparables: Alex Liddi, Will Middlebrooks, Josh Bell*

**Drafted/Acquired:** 2nd round, 2013 draft, Miami Dade South CC (Miami, FL)

**Previous Ranking:** NR

**What Happened in 2013:** Drafted in the second round, Caratini showed off the strong bat in his short-season debut, and a possible move behind the plate has the trajectory of his prospect status on the way up.

**Strengths:** Very strong and physical at present; built like a square block; natural hitter; short/sweet swing that is line-drive oriented; good eye at the plate; works counts and knows his pitch; arm is plus.

**Weaknesses:** Body lacks projection; limited room for additional weight/muscle; well-below-average power potential; swing isn't built for the long ball; glove and range would play below average at third; touch profile in the infield.

**Risk Factor/Injury History:** High risk; rookie-level experience.

**Bret Sayre's Fantasy Take:** If Caratini stays on the dirt, he could be a very low level fantasy play in the long term, but his upside jumps if he does make the transition behind the plate. The potential is there for a .275 average and 15-18 homers if he can stick and develop, but like any transition project, this is going to take a long time.

**The Year Ahead:** This is a tale of two players, a possible first-division catcher with a very strong hit tool or a third baseman with a fringe-average (at best) defensive profile and little to no power in the offensive game. Caratini is maxed out physically, a compact and strong player that looks built for the backstop. With a short swing and an advanced approach, there is a good chance that he hits all the way up the ladder, but when it comes to prospect status, the 20-year-old needs to make a successful conversion behind the plate to really blossom on the national level. It's not going to be an overnight event, but all sources seem to agree that the additional developmental patience required will be worth it at the end of the day.

---

## 9.   Jason Hursh    RHP

**Born:** 10/2/91    **Age:** 22    **Bats:** R    **Throws:** R    **Height:** 6' 3"    **Weight:** 190

| MLB ETA | CT | FB | CH | CB | SL | OFP | Realistic |
|---|---|---|---|---|---|---|---|
| **Late 2015** | – | **70** | **50** | – | **50** | **60** NO.3 STARTER | **50** LATE-INN RP (SETUP) |

| YEAR | TEAM | LVL | AGE | W | L | SV | G | GS | IP | H | HR | BB | SO | BB9 | SO9 | GB% | BABIP | WHIP | ERA | FIP | FRA | WARP |
|---|---|---|---|---|---|---|---|---|---|---|---|---|---|---|---|---|---|---|---|---|---|---|
| 2013 | ROM | A | 21 | 1 | 1 | 0 | 9 | 9 | 27.0 | 20 | 1 | 10 | 15 | 3.3 | 5.0 | 63% | .235 | 1.11 | 0.67 | 4.07 | 5.04 | 0.3 |
| 2014 | ATL | MLB | 22 | 2 | 3 | 0 | 9 | 9 | 34.3 | 39 | 5 | 17 | 18 | 4.5 | 4.7 | 49% | .315 | 1.63 | 5.66 | 5.75 | 6.16 | -0.4 |
| 2015 | ATL | MLB | 23 | 5 | 9 | 0 | 29 | 29 | 180.3 | 196 | 23 | 76 | 106 | 3.8 | 5.3 | 49% | .313 | 1.51 | 5.11 | 4.91 | 5.55 | -1.6 |

Breakout: 0%    Improve: 0%    Collapse: 0%    Attrition: 0%    MLB: 0%          *Comparables: Robert Carson, Kyle Waldrop, Daniel Webb*

**Drafted/Acquired:** 1st round, 2013 draft, Oklahoma University (Stillwater, OK)

**Previous Ranking:** NR

**What Happened in 2013:** Hursh was drafted in the first round but several sources questioned his first-round bona fides, especially with a Tommy John surgery in his immediate rear-view.

**Strengths:** Good size/strength; shows pitchability; works off of his heavy mid-90s fastball that shows excellent life; slider shows some promise off the fastball and projects to be solid-average; shows a playable changeup; arm is considered fresh with some remaining projection.

**Weaknesses:** Mechanics can get out of whack; command is fringe-average; fastball is strong pitch but secondary arsenal is fringe; slider lacks big intensity; changeup is below average at present.

**Risk Factor/Injury History:** Moderate risk; limited professional experience; Tommy John on resume (2012).

**Bret Sayre's Fantasy Take:** A low-end pick in dynasty league drafts this offseason, Hursh brings a lot of the risk inherent in young pitchers, but without a huge amount of upside. The fastball is great, but if he's a starter, major-league hitters aren't going to oblige and give him the punchouts that his fantasy owners desire.

**The Year Ahead:** Hursh gets some prospect love because of his draft status and easy plus fastball, but the overall profile is a bit lacking, with an average-at-best slider, a below-average changeup, and iffy command. The 22-year-old isn't far removed from Tommy John surgery, so you can expect some rust on the overall profile. But the projections on the secondary stuff don't offer much to dream on, and the command needs to be sharp to ride the back of the fastball to rotation glory. 2014 will tell us a lot about the direction Hursh will take, with some sources seeing a setup reliever at the end of the day, which is a respectable outcome but not ideal from a first-round pick.

## 10. Victor Reyes OF

**Born:** 10/05/94 **Age:** 19 **Bats:** L **Throws:** R **Height:** 6'3" **Weight:** 170

| MLB ETA | Hit | Power | Run | Glove | Arm | OFP | Realistic |
|---|---|---|---|---|---|---|---|
| 2017 | 65 | 60 | – | 50 | 55 | 60 1ST DIV PLAYER | 45 <AVG REGULAR/PLTN |

| YEAR | TEAM | LVL | AGE | PA | R | 2B | 3B | HR | RBI | BB | SO | SB | CS | AVG/OBP/SLG | TAv | BABIP | BRR | FRAA | WARP |
|---|---|---|---|---|---|---|---|---|---|---|---|---|---|---|---|---|---|---|
| 2013 | BRA | Rk | 18 | 129 | 22 | 8 | 1 | 0 | 21 | 12 | 20 | 5 | 1 | .357/.414/.446 | .326 | .421 | 4.5 | LF(25): 2.5, RF(1): -0.1 | 2.3 |
| 2013 | DNV | Rk | 18 | 84 | 12 | 3 | 0 | 0 | 4 | 3 | 9 | 0 | 0 | .321/.345/.358 | .297 | .361 | -0.1 | LF(15): -1.4 | 0.3 |
| 2014 | ATL | MLB | 19 | 250 | 18 | 8 | 0 | 2 | 18 | 14 | 75 | 2 | 1 | .199/.244/.257 | .192 | .280 | -0.3 | LF 0, RF -0 | -1.0 |
| 2015 | ATL | MLB | 20 | 250 | 18 | 8 | 0 | 2 | 18 | 14 | 75 | 2 | 1 | .199/.244/.257 | .192 | .280 | -0.3 | LF 0, RF -0 | -1.0 |

Breakout: 0%    Improve: 0%    Collapse: 0%    Attrition: 0%    MLB: 0%    *Comparables: Caleb Gindl, Andrew McCutchen, Che-Hsuan Lin*

**Drafted/Acquired:** International free agent, 2011, Venezuela

**Previous Ranking:** NR

**The Tools:** 6+ potential hit; 6 potential power; 5+ arm; 5 potential glove

**What Happened in 2013:** In his stateside debut, the high-ceiling talent really impressed with the stick, showing a sweet left-handed stroke and excellent bat-to-ball ability.

**Strengths:** Highly projectable; frame to add strength/muscle; sweet stroke from the left side; shows plus bat speed and very good bat control; really jumps on fastballs and will look for his pitch; hit tool could play to plus; power could play to plus at maturity; shows impressive present pop to opposite field; arm for a corner; good athlete with good feel.

**Weaknesses:** Needs to continue to add strength; lets the ball travel and goes to the opposite field, but has yet to learn how to really turn on the baseball; will struggle against quality arm-side stuff; still underdeveloped in the field; reads/routes aren't crisp; long way to go.

**Risk Factor/Injury History:** High risk; yet to play at full-season level.

**Bret Sayre's Fantasy Take:** Reyes has strong bat-to-ball skills, which could lead to a batting average around .290 down the road. Of course, he's going to have to develop some secondary fantasy skills to go with it, or else he's not that interesting to us and won't warrant the playing time for it to matter. If the power comes, he's one to watch.

**The Year Ahead:** Reyes has the highest tool-based ceiling of any position player on the Braves farm, which is impressive, but he's also 19 years old without full-season experience, so the risk is very high. Every source gushed about Reyes' swing; the bat speed in combination with control really stands out and gets you excited about the future, especially when the Venezuelan learns how to tap into his power. He has a highly projectable body and could add a great deal of additional muscle and strength, and once he starts to put it all together, look out. It might not look super pretty in the short term, as he's still unrefined and raw, but the natural bat-to-ball ability will keep his head above water against more advanced arms; when the light goes on and the pop starts to play, Reyes could develop into a top-101 prospect.

## Prospects on the Rise

**1. SS Johan Camargo:** A Panamanian shortstop with a strong stick, Camargo projects to hit for average and some power (10+ bombs) , with a strong approach at the plate and a strong arm in the field. The 20-year-old lacks speed and is unlikely to stick at shortstop as he climbs, but the bat could play legit, and he has the chops to develop into a quality defender on the right side of the infield.

**2. RHP Alec Grosser:** An 11th-round pick in the 2013 draft, Grosser was strong in his professional debut, touching the mid-90s from a lower slot with good feel for a breaking ball. With a lean and athletic body, scouts see some additional projection, and the 19-year-old righty could be in for a step forward in 2014. Sleeper.

**3. LHP Luis Barrios:** The Braves are one of the best in the business when it comes to recognizing and acquiring Latin American talent, so when they popped the hyped Colombian lefty, my interest in the prospect soared. Barrios is a projectable southpaw with good feel for pitching, already working the fastball in the upper-80s and touching the 90s, and as he adds strength and takes to pro instruction, he should step forward as a prospect in the Braves organization. The resume will likely feature a few seasons of complex-league action, but the scouting reports could push his stock after his debut summer.

## Factors on the Farm
### Prospects likely to contribute at the ML level in 2014

**1. RHP Shae Simmons:** A 22nd-round selection in the 2012 draft, diminutive righty Shae Simmons will likely pitch his way to the major league level in 2014. On the back of an explosive 93- to 97-mph fastball, plus slider, and playable splitter, the 23-year-old arm misses a disgusting number of bats and barrels, and despite his 5'9" size, projects to be an impact arm at the back of a major-league bullpen.

**2. RHP David Hale:** It's not the sexiest profile, but former third-round pick David Hale can pitch, with good athleticism (former two-way player at Princeton), strike-throwing ability, and a solid-average arsenal. The 26-year-old's ultimate role might come as a swingman or emergency starter, although he has the arsenal to stick around in a rotation if the command is sharp, with a low-90s fastball, quality slider, and good changeup.

**3. RHP Gus Schlosser:** A 17th-round pick in the 2011 draft, Schlosser has found some success as a starter in the minors, but his major-league profile is more of a situational reliever. From a sidearm slot, the 25-year-old righty brings a low-90s fastball to the table, a pitch he can manipulate for heavy sink or even cut it into the hands of lefties. He backs it up with an average secondary arsenal but he shows pitchability and average command, so he can keep hitters off-balance and prove to be quite effective against right-handed bats.

## 1. Kevin Gausman   RHP

**Born:** 1/6/91   **Age:** 23   **Bats:** R   **Throws:** R   **Height:** 6' 3"   **Weight:** 190

| MLB ETA | CT | FB | CH | CB | SL | OFP | Realistic |
|---|---|---|---|---|---|---|---|
| Debuted in 2013 | – | 70 | 70 | – | 60 | 70<br>NO.2 STARTER | 65<br>NO.2-3 STARTER |

| YEAR | TEAM | LVL | AGE | W | L | SV | G | GS | IP | H | HR | BB | SO | BB9 | SO9 | GB% | BABIP | WHIP | ERA | FIP | FRA | WARP |
|---|---|---|---|---|---|---|---|---|---|---|---|---|---|---|---|---|---|---|---|---|---|---|
| 2013 | BAL | MLB | 22 | 3 | 5 | 0 | 20 | 5 | 47.7 | 51 | 8 | 13 | 49 | 2.5 | 9.3 | 45% | .328 | 1.34 | 5.66 | 4.02 | 4.68 | 0.4 |
| 2013 | NOR | AAA | 22 | 1 | 2 | 0 | 8 | 7 | 35.7 | 36 | 1 | 9 | 33 | 2.3 | 8.3 | 48% | .354 | 1.26 | 4.04 | 2.56 | 3.81 | 0.7 |
| 2013 | BOW | AA | 22 | 2 | 4 | 0 | 8 | 8 | 46.3 | 44 | 3 | 5 | 49 | 1.0 | 9.5 | 54% | .313 | 1.06 | 3.11 | 2.57 | 2.73 | 1.5 |
| 2014 | BAL | MLB | 23 | 6 | 5 | 0 | 26 | 16 | 92.7 | 92 | 12 | 23 | 85 | 2.2 | 8.3 | 46% | .303 | 1.24 | 3.82 | 4.06 | 4.15 | 1.1 |
| 2015 | BAL | MLB | 24 | 10 | 10 | 0 | 31 | 31 | 199.3 | 195 | 27 | 41 | 174 | 1.9 | 7.9 | 46% | .294 | 1.19 | 3.68 | 3.88 | 4.00 | 2.4 |

**Breakout:** 26%   **Improve:** 63%   **Collapse:** 10%   **Attrition:** 25%   **MLB:** 85%   *Comparables: Brian Matusz, Derek Holland, Michael Pineda*

**Drafted/Acquired:** 1st round, 2012 draft, Louisiana State University (Baton Rouge, LA)

**Previous Ranking:** #2 (Org), #13 (Top 101)

**What Happened in 2013:** Gausman was on the professional roller coaster in 2013, making stops in Double-A, Triple-A, and several trips to the majors.

**Strengths:** Elite arm strength; good delivery; repeats well; fastball works 95-98; touches 100; good arm-side life; good command; total package pitch; multiple changeup looks; plus-plus offering in the 84-86 range with splitter movement; knockout pitch to both left-handers and right-handers; slider shows above-average potential; good overall feel for strike throwing.

**Weaknesses:** Fastball can be visible; some cross fire in delivery; struggles with hard contact when he elevates; slider comes and goes; shows sharp tilt and good depth but can flatten out and become a hard slurve; pitchability still needs work.

**Risk Factor/Injury History:** Low risk; ready for major leagues

**Bret Sayre's Fantasy Take:** Projection be damned, Gausman is staring down a rotation spot to start the 2014 season. And don't let those 2013 MLB raw stats fool you, he had a 3.99 FIP (and 3.04 xFIP, if you're into that sort of thing). He'll always be at a slight disadvantage pitching in Baltimore, but this is a pitcher who can make very strong contributions in all four categories regardless—and, at his ceiling, projects to be a guy you can get away with as your fantasy ace if you have a strong staff.

**The Year Ahead:** Gausman is a beast, with a near elite fastball, a plus-plus changeup, and the makings of a plus slider. If the command stays sharp and the slider takes a step forward (in confidence and consistency), Gausman has all the necessary ingredients to be a frontline starter. The stuff can be a little visible, and he's hittable when he throws too many strikes and not enough good strikes (control vs. command), but the floor is obnoxiously high, and the ceiling suggests he could be one of the better arms in baseball very soon.

> **#10**
> BP Top 101 Prospects

## 2. Dylan Bundy   RHP

**Born:** 11/15/92   **Age:** 21   **Bats:** B   **Throws:** R   **Height:** 6' 1"   **Weight:** 195

| MLB ETA | CT | FB | CH | CB | SL | OFP | Realistic |
|---|---|---|---|---|---|---|---|
| Debuted in 2012 | 80 | 70 | 70 | 60 | – | 75<br>NO.1 STARTER | 60<br>NO.3 STARTER |

| YEAR | TEAM | LVL | AGE | W | L | SV | G | GS | IP | H | HR | BB | SO | BB9 | SO9 | GB% | BABIP | WHIP | ERA | FIP | FRA | WARP |
|---|---|---|---|---|---|---|---|---|---|---|---|---|---|---|---|---|---|---|---|---|---|---|
| 2014 | BAL | MLB | 21 | 2 | 2 | 0 | 8 | 8 | 35.0 | 33 | 4 | 15 | 32 | 3.9 | 8.2 | 42% | .292 | 1.36 | 4.11 | 4.42 | 4.47 | 0.3 |
| 2015 | BAL | MLB | 22 | 8 | 11 | 0 | 29 | 29 | 180.3 | 193 | 30 | 67 | 141 | 3.3 | 7.0 | 42% | .298 | 1.44 | 4.96 | 4.96 | 5.39 | -0.7 |

**Breakout:** 0%   **Improve:** 0%   **Collapse:** 0%   **Attrition:** 0%   **MLB:** 0%   *Comparables: Drew Hutchison, Shelby Miller, Chris Tillman*

**Drafted/Acquired:** 1st round, 2011 draft, Owasso HS (Owasso, OK)

**Previous Ranking:** #1 (Org), #4 (Top 101)

**What Happened in 2013:** Thomas Edward John Jr.

**Strengths:** Elite combination of stuff and pitchability; plus-plus arm strength; excellent arm action; excellent delivery; from high 3/4 slot, creates good plane; fastball is near elite pitch; works 94-98; explosive life; very easy; curveball has intense late bite/tight rotation; 12/6 shape; plus pitch; changeup comes from fastball arm; good deception; future plus pitch; best secondary pitch not used in minors; 8 potential cutter; devastating pitch; velo/late glove-side cut; feel for pitching; dangerous power arm.

**Weaknesses:** Good control, but command within the zone is still loose; needs to finish delivery and work down; curveball thrown for strikes, but often high in the zone; changeup is more deception than action; can get too firm.

> **#15**
> BP Top 101 Prospects

**Risk Factor/Injury History:** Moderate risk; Tommy John on resume

**Bret Sayre's Fantasy Take:** Among all prospects, it seems that Bundy has been on the move most in dynasty leagues this offseason—and it comes down to two things: owners trying to cash out ahead of the risk and owners buying into the remaining ace upside. That second group sounds good to me. Tommy John recovery is no cakewalk, but his kind of fantasy upside doesn't grow on trees. In fact, it's second to only one pitcher in the minors right now. Trade him away at your own risk.

**The Year Ahead:** Bundy is a workout freak with work ethic and makeup for days, so there is a very good chance that he not only comes back at full strength, but a better version of himself. Bundy could be a number one starter, with a plus-plus fastball, an elite cutter that some think could possess religious properties, a very good curve and change, and the pitchability to bring everything together. He's going to shove.

## 3. Hunter Harvey RHP

**Born:** 12/9/94   **Age:** 19   **Bats:** R   **Throws:** R   **Height:** 6' 3"   **Weight:** 175

| MLB ETA | CT | FB | CH | CB | SL | OFP | Realistic |
|---|---|---|---|---|---|---|---|
| Late 2016 | – | 65 | 60 | 70 | – | 70<br>NO.2 STARTER | 55<br>NO.3-4 STARTER |

| YEAR | TEAM | LVL | AGE | W | L | SV | G | GS | IP | H | HR | BB | SO | BB9 | SO9 | GB% | BABIP | WHIP | ERA | FIP | FRA | WARP |
|---|---|---|---|---|---|---|---|---|---|---|---|---|---|---|---|---|---|---|---|---|---|---|
| 2013 | ABE | A- | 18 | 0 | 0 | 1 | 3 | 3 | 12.0 | 11 | 0 | 4 | 15 | 3.0 | 11.2 | 68% | .355 | 1.25 | 2.25 | 1.60 | 2.71 | 0.3 |
| 2013 | ORI | Rk | 18 | 0 | 0 | 0 | 5 | 5 | 13.3 | 10 | 0 | 2 | 18 | 1.4 | 12.1 | 47% | .333 | 0.90 | 1.35 | 1.21 | 2.81 | 0.4 |
| 2014 | BAL | MLB | 19 | 2 | 3 | 0 | 8 | 8 | 32.0 | 36 | 5 | 19 | 21 | 5.3 | 5.9 | 46% | .306 | 1.74 | 5.92 | 6.06 | 6.43 | -0.4 |
| 2015 | BAL | MLB | 20 | 5 | 9 | 0 | 28 | 28 | 172.0 | 187 | 25 | 83 | 128 | 4.3 | 6.7 | 46% | .303 | 1.57 | 5.26 | 5.11 | 5.71 | -1.2 |

Breakout: 0%    Improve: 0%    Collapse: 0%    Attrition: 0%    MLB: 0%        *Comparables: Jonathan Pettibone, Julio Teheran, Tyler Chatwood*

**Drafted/Acquired:** 1st round, 2013 draft, Bandys HS (Catawba, NC)

**Previous Ranking:** NR

**What Happened in 2013:** Harvey only made eight starts at short-season levels after signing, but it was enough to send scouts away salivating at his upside.

**Strengths:** Good present size; physical projection; athletic; easy release; fastball works 91-95; late life; some natural cut; could end up a plus-plus pitch with improved command and velocity spike; curveball is legit power breaker in the upper-70s/low-80s; tight rotation and hard vertical action; could be monster offering; changeup flashes above-average potential, with arm-side fade.

**Weaknesses:** Command is below average at present; some arm slot inconsistency; more thrower than pitcher; more deliberate on changeup; slows arm/loses deception.

**Risk Factor/Injury History:** High risk

**Bret Sayre's Fantasy Take:** The overwhelming odds are that the person who takes Harvey in your dynasty draft this offseason is a BP reader. However, I still would not take him in that first or second tier of players available this offseason (after the top seven it's a free-for-all). But if you can snag him with a pick outside the top 10, he could be a huge boon, as he has the potential to be a high-strikeout pitcher with strong ratios.

**The Year Ahead:** Harvey's ceiling is just a tick below Gausman and Bundy, thanks to his athletic delivery and easy release and impact potential arsenal. He comes at a much higher risk and the ceiling could lower as the developmental process exposes some of the realities of his skill set, but right now, Harvey looks the part of a future frontline prospect. Despite below-average command at present, Harvey has the stuff to move quickly through the lower minors, and could find himself in Double-A by 2015. He won't be a "sleeper" for much longer. He'll be a featured player in most national top 50 lists.

**#58**

BP Top 101 Prospects

## 4. Eduardo Rodriguez LHP

**Born:** 4/7/93   **Age:** 21   **Bats:** L   **Throws:** L   **Height:** 6' 2"   **Weight:** 200

| MLB ETA | CT | FB | CH | CB | SL | OFP | Realistic |
|---|---|---|---|---|---|---|---|
| 2014 | – | 60 | 55 | – | 60 | 60<br>NO.3 STARTER | 50<br>NO.4 STARTER |

| YEAR | TEAM | LVL | AGE | W | L | SV | G | GS | IP | H | HR | BB | SO | BB9 | SO9 | GB% | BABIP | WHIP | ERA | FIP | FRA | WARP |
|---|---|---|---|---|---|---|---|---|---|---|---|---|---|---|---|---|---|---|---|---|---|---|
| 2013 | BOW | AA | 20 | 4 | 3 | 0 | 11 | 11 | 59.7 | 53 | 5 | 24 | 59 | 3.6 | 8.9 | 42% | .296 | 1.29 | 4.22 | 3.74 | 3.77 | 1.3 |
| 2013 | FRD | A+ | 20 | 6 | 4 | 0 | 14 | 14 | 85.3 | 78 | 4 | 25 | 66 | 2.6 | 7.0 | 48% | .292 | 1.21 | 2.85 | 3.36 | 4.18 | 1.6 |
| 2014 | BAL | MLB | 21 | 6 | 6 | 0 | 22 | 18 | 112.3 | 123 | 15 | 46 | 68 | 3.7 | 5.4 | 46% | .296 | 1.51 | 5.08 | 5.29 | 5.52 | -0.5 |
| 2015 | BAL | MLB | 22 | 2 | 1 | 1 | 49 | 0 | 51.7 | 51 | 7 | 17 | 39 | 3.0 | 6.8 | 46% | .281 | 1.32 | 4.26 | 4.52 | 4.63 | 0.2 |

Breakout: 0%    Improve: 0%    Collapse: 0%    Attrition: 0%    MLB: 0%        *Comparables: Ian Krol, Patrick Corbin, Michael Bowden*

**Drafted/Acquired:** International free agent, 2010, Venezuela

**Previous Ranking:** #4 (Org)

**What Happened in 2013:** The then-20-year-old pitched his way to Double-A, and even made five starts in the prospect-heavy Arizona Fall League, setting himself up for a major-league opportunity at some point in 2014.

**Strengths:** Sturdy build; good delivery; repeatable; creates good angle; fastball is plus offering; works 90-94; can touch higher; can move the ball around; changeup flashes above-average; works 82-84 with arm-side run and

**#61**

BP Top 101 Prospects

some sink; slider is sharp two-plane breaker in the 81-84 range; could end up a bat-missing plus pitch; good pitchability.

**Weaknesses:** Fastball can lack movement; more control than command; can slip to the side on the slider and lose bite/depth; tendency to cast changeup; throw it too hard; lacks true knockout secondary pitch.

**Risk Factor/Injury History:** Moderate risk; limited Double-A experience

**Bret Sayre's Fantasy Take:** It's easy to overlook Rodriguez with the other arms ahead of him in this system, but just because he doesn't have that lofty upside doesn't mean he's worth shrugging off. With strong across-the-board potential, he can put up the type of numbers that Chris Tillman did in 2013—and Tillman was nearly a top-30 starter.

**The Year Ahead:** While scouts seem to agree that Rodriguez is a future major-league starter, the ultimate projections vary from source to source, as some don't see the high-impact upside that the production/stuff might suggest. The stuff is solid-average to plus, but he lacks true wipeout stuff, and without sharp command, it's hard to see Rodriguez developing into a frontline arm. But a number three or four starter under team control is a very valuable commodity, and it shouldn't take Rodriguez long to make that projection a reality.

---

## 5.  Jonathan Schoop   2B

**Born:** 10/16/91   **Age:** 22   **Bats:** R   **Throws:** R   **Height:** 6' 2"   **Weight:** 210

| MLB ETA | Hit | Power | Run | Glove | Arm | | OFP | Realistic |
|---|---|---|---|---|---|---|---|---|
| Debuted in 2013 | 50 | 50 | – | 50 | 60 | | 55<br>>AVG ML REGULAR | 50<br>2ND DIV PLAYER |

| YEAR | TEAM | LVL | AGE | PA | R | 2B | 3B | HR | RBI | BB | SO | SB | CS | AVG/OBP/SLG | TAv | BABIP | BRR | FRAA | WARP |
|---|---|---|---|---|---|---|---|---|---|---|---|---|---|---|---|---|---|---|---|
| 2013 | ABE | A- | 21 | 15 | 3 | 1 | 0 | 2 | 9 | 1 | 1 | 0 | 1 | .571/.600/1.071 | .595 | .545 | -0.1 | 2B(2): -0.2 | 0.5 |
| 2013 | NOR | AAA | 21 | 289 | 30 | 11 | 0 | 9 | 34 | 13 | 55 | 1 | 2 | .256/.301/.396 | .247 | .290 | 0.1 | 2B(48): -0.1, SS(20): 2.8 | 0.7 |
| 2013 | ORI | Rk | 21 | 32 | 9 | 2 | 0 | 3 | 9 | 6 | 6 | 0 | 0 | .360/.469/.800 | .432 | .353 | 0.3 | 2B(5): 0.5 | 0.7 |
| 2013 | BAL | MLB | 21 | 15 | 5 | 0 | 0 | 1 | 1 | 1 | 2 | 0 | 0 | .286/.333/.500 | .257 | .273 | 0.0 | 2B(4): -0.4 | 0.0 |
| 2014 | BAL | MLB | 22 | 250 | 28 | 10 | 1 | 7 | 26 | 13 | 52 | 1 | 1 | .237/.285/.377 | .243 | .270 | -0.5 | 2B -1, SS 0 | 0.4 |
| 2015 | BAL | MLB | 23 | 401 | 47 | 18 | 1 | 13 | 48 | 22 | 81 | 1 | 0 | .247/.296/.406 | .255 | .279 | -0.9 | 2B -1, SS 0 | 1.3 |

Breakout: 0%    Improve: 0%    Collapse: 0%    Attrition: 0%    MLB: 0%    *Comparables: Adrian Cardenas, Travis Denker, Kolten Wong*

**Drafted/Acquired:** International free agent, 2008, Curacao

**Previous Ranking:** #3 (Org), #80 (Top 101)

**The Tools:** 6 arm; 5 glove; 5 potential hit/power

**What Happened in 2013:** Up and down year for Schoop, who struggled in Triple-A, sat on the shelf for a few months with a back injury, and oddly enough found himself called up to the major-league level for a five-game taste.

**Strengths:** Wiry strength; good athlete; good hands; shows bat speed at the plate; good bat control; strong wrists and barreling ability; shows power potential; average glove; strong arm; baseball skills; versatile skill set on defense.

**Weaknesses:** Struggles against quality arm-side stuff; can get tied up inside and above the hands; swing has some length; looks to extend early; approach can get aggressive/will lose counts; footwork can get a little sloppy in the field; stiff lower half.

**Risk Factor/Injury History:** Low risk; achieved major-league level

**Bret Sayre's Fantasy Take:** Judging Schoop by his minor-league stats is not a great approach, as he was pushed pretty aggressively during his minor-league career. Assuming he stays middle infield eligible, he projects to be a consistently above-replacement player, who retains more value in deeper leagues. Schoop may top out as a Neil Walker-type second baseman with decent average, near 20-homer pop and a couple of steals sprinkled in.

**The Year Ahead:** Schoop could use a full season in the upper minors to refine his approach and adjust to quality secondary stuff. Because of the back injury, Schoop missed valuable developmental time and never found his footing at the plate; in fact, the 22-year-old infielder hasn't found any consistency at the plate since the 2011 season, when he was at the A-ball level. It's easy to see the potential in Schoop, from the body to the athleticism to the easy swing and power potential at the plate. But the pieces have yet to come together against quality competition, and my scout sources are very mixed when it comes to his ultimate role.

#82
BP Top
101
Prospects

## 6.  Mike Wright  RHP

**Born:** 1/3/90   **Age:** 24   **Bats:** R   **Throws:** R   **Height:** 6' 6"   **Weight:** 215

| MLB ETA | CT | FB | CH | CB | SL | OFP | Realistic |
|---|---|---|---|---|---|---|---|
| 2014 | – | 55 | 50 | – | 55 | 50<br>NO.3-4 STARTER | 50<br>NO.4-5 STARTER |

| YEAR | TEAM | LVL | AGE | W | L | SV | G | GS | IP | H | HR | BB | SO | BB9 | SO9 | GB% | BABIP | WHIP | ERA | FIP | FRA | WARP |
|---|---|---|---|---|---|---|---|---|---|---|---|---|---|---|---|---|---|---|---|---|---|---|
| 2013 | NOR | AAA | 23 | 0 | 0 | 0 | 1 | 1 | 6.7 | 6 | 0 | 0 | 2 | 0.0 | 2.7 | 33% | .250 | 0.90 | 0.00 | 2.60 | 3.48 | 0.1 |
| 2013 | BOW | AA | 23 | 11 | 3 | 0 | 26 | 26 | 143.7 | 152 | 9 | 39 | 136 | 2.4 | 8.5 | 44% | .332 | 1.33 | 3.26 | 3.27 | 3.44 | 3.6 |
| 2014 | BAL | MLB | 24 | 7 | 8 | 0 | 23 | 23 | 121.3 | 137 | 17 | 36 | 84 | 2.7 | 6.2 | 45% | .307 | 1.43 | 4.82 | 4.86 | 5.24 | -0.1 |
| 2015 | BAL | MLB | 25 | 8 | 9 | 0 | 27 | 27 | 162.0 | 176 | 20 | 46 | 124 | 2.6 | 6.9 | 45% | .311 | 1.37 | 4.33 | 4.22 | 4.71 | 0.6 |

**Breakout:** 20%   **Improve:** 32%   **Collapse:** 7%   **Attrition:** 28%   **MLB:** 44%   *Comparables: Tommy Milone, Brandon Workman, Kyle Gibson*

**Drafted/Acquired:** 3rd round, 2011 draft, East Carolina University

**Previous Ranking:** #5 (Org)

**What Happened in 2013:** Strong season for the then-23-year-old righty, making 27 starts (26 at the Double-A level), and logging a workhorse-like 150 innings.

**Strengths:** Tall, with a strong, durable body; good delivery; arm is clean and quick; fastball works low- 90s with good weight; good angle to the plate; hard slider in the mid-80s; good tilt; can miss bats; changeup plays well off fastball with some fade; shows slow curve in lower-70s; feel for strike throwing.

**Weaknesses:** Throws too many strikes; finds barrels; stuff is more solid-average than plus; lacks electric secondary arsenal; could struggle to miss bats against better competition.

**Risk Factor/Injury History:** Low risk; mature arsenal; 27 starts in upper minors

**Bret Sayre's Fantasy Take:** Here's where I'd put the line of demarcation on this list, as I'd rather take a chance with a high upside, unproven arm in short-season ball over a guy like Wright. In deep leagues, he's worth a look (as he may have some value this season), but as a guy who doesn't keep the ball on the ground very well in a park that binges on homers, expectations should be kept in check.

**The Year Ahead:** Wright has the frame, delivery, and arsenal to pound the zone as a league-average workhorse type, a number four or five starter. He lacks impact stuff, although the fastball can work in the low-90s and touch higher, and the slider will flash the potential to miss barrels. While it's most certainly not a sexy profile, a league-average starter capable of logging innings has a lot of value, and without much risk involved, Wright could step into the back of a major-league rotation at some point in 2014.

## 7.  Tim Berry  LHP

**Born:** 3/18/91   **Age:** 23   **Bats:** L   **Throws:** L   **Height:** 6' 3"   **Weight:** 180

| MLB ETA | CT | FB | CH | CB | SL | OFP | Realistic |
|---|---|---|---|---|---|---|---|
| Late 2014 | – | 60 | 60 | 55 | – | 55<br>NO.3 STARTER | 50<br>NO.5 SP/LONG RP |

| YEAR | TEAM | LVL | AGE | W | L | SV | G | GS | IP | H | HR | BB | SO | BB9 | SO9 | GB% | BABIP | WHIP | ERA | FIP | FRA | WARP |
|---|---|---|---|---|---|---|---|---|---|---|---|---|---|---|---|---|---|---|---|---|---|---|
| 2013 | FRD | A+ | 22 | 11 | 7 | 0 | 27 | 27 | 152.0 | 156 | 13 | 40 | 119 | 2.4 | 7.0 | 47% | .310 | 1.29 | 3.85 | 3.84 | 4.61 | 2.1 |
| 2014 | BAL | MLB | 23 | 6 | 9 | 0 | 23 | 23 | 118.3 | 141 | 18 | 54 | 69 | 4.1 | 5.2 | 44% | .308 | 1.65 | 5.85 | 5.76 | 6.36 | -1.5 |
| 2015 | BAL | MLB | 24 | 2 | 1 | 0 | 36 | 0 | 38.0 | 44 | 6 | 14 | 24 | 3.3 | 5.7 | 44% | .306 | 1.54 | 5.48 | 5.21 | 5.96 | -0.4 |

**Breakout:** 0%   **Improve:** 0%   **Collapse:** 0%   **Attrition:** 0%   **MLB:** 0%   *Comparables: Stolmy Pimentel, Nick Tepesch, Yoervis Medina*

**Drafted/Acquired:** 50th round, 2009 draft, San Marcos HS (San Marcos, CA)

**Previous Ranking:** NR

**What Happened in 2013:** A solid but not spectacular Carolina League campaign culminated in a very strong Arizona Fall League performance, where Berry was able to miss some bats and hold the prospect-heavy lineups to a .212 average.

**Strengths:** Projectable body; loose arm; smooth and easy; fastball is solid-average at present; routinely works low-90s with fastball; some arm-side movement; good feel for curveball; flashes above-average with big depth; changeup is another average offering with above-average potential; good arm-speed deception and some fade; can throw strikes.

**Weaknesses:** Lacks overpowering stuff; fastball can be hittable and he doesn't always hold velocity well; curveball can get big and visible, especially when the fastball doesn't set up the swing; finds too much of the plate; command needs grade improvement.

**Risk Factor/Injury History:** Moderate; yet to pitch at Double-A level; Tommy John surgery on resume.

**Bret Sayre's Fantasy Take:** There is fantasy potential here, but he'll need to improve upon his relatively low strikeout rates in order to be much more than a waiver-wire type guy in shallower leagues. And for that to happen, his secondary pitches are going to have to progress to bat-missers at the major-league level.

**The Year Ahead:** Berry is a lefty with solid-average stuff, and if you project the body a little bit more (added strength), you can see a tick more on the gun. He has some pitchability, and with improved command, Berry has mid-rotation potential. The stuff is unlikely to blow anybody away as a starter, but lefties with a three-pitch mix of average or better stuff and some feel for craft find a way to stick around for a long time. Berry will face a strong test in Double-A, but if he adds strength and continues to refine, he should set himself up for a major-league job in 2015.

## 8. Zachary Davies RHP

**Born:** 2/7/93    **Age:** 21    **Bats:** R    **Throws:** R    **Height:** 6' 0"    **Weight:** 150

| MLB ETA | CT | FB | CH | CB | SL | OFP | Realistic |
|---------|----|----|----|----|----|-----|-----------|
| 2015 | – | 50 | 55 | 50 | 50 | 50<br>NO.4 STARTER | 50<br>NO.5 STARTER |

| YEAR | TEAM | LVL | AGE | W | L | SV | G | GS | IP | H | HR | BB | SO | BB9 | SO9 | GB% | BABIP | WHIP | ERA | FIP | FRA | WARP |
|------|------|-----|-----|---|---|----|---|----|----|----|----|----|----|-----|-----|-----|-------|------|-----|-----|-----|------|
| 2013 | FRD | A+ | 20 | 7 | 9 | 0 | 26 | 26 | 148.7 | 145 | 10 | 38 | 132 | 2.3 | 8.0 | 52% | .310 | 1.23 | 3.69 | 3.28 | 4.12 | 2.9 |
| 2014 | BAL | MLB | 21 | 7 | 8 | 0 | 21 | 21 | 114.7 | 130 | 17 | 48 | 72 | 3.8 | 5.6 | 49% | .300 | 1.54 | 5.21 | 5.45 | 5.66 | -0.7 |
| 2015 | BAL | MLB | 22 | 7 | 8 | 0 | 22 | 22 | 128.7 | 134 | 18 | 49 | 99 | 3.4 | 6.9 | 49% | .298 | 1.42 | 4.55 | 4.65 | 4.94 | 0.2 |

Breakout: 0%    Improve: 0%    Collapse: 0%    Attrition: 0%    MLB: 0%    *Comparables: Will Smith, Casey Kelly, Michael Bowden*

**Drafted/Acquired:** 26th round, 2011 draft, Mesquite HS (Gilbert, AZ)

**Previous Ranking:** On The Rise

**What Happened in 2013:** After making 17 starts in his debut season, Davies took a step forward in the Carolina League, making 26 starts and logging 148 innings, despite concerns about his limited size.

**Strengths:** Athletic; smooth delivery; nice arm action; fastball is average, but works all zones and has some sink; changeup is solid-average offering with more in the tank; plays well off fastball; good deception and fading action; shows two breaking balls; can throw strikes; plus pitchability.

**Weaknesses:** Limited size; has to work down in the zone to create angle; fastball is pedestrian and relies on location more than velocity; has to hit his spots to be effective; breaking balls are average at best; lack plus projections.

**Risk Factor/Injury History:** Moderate risk; yet to achieve Double-A; small margin for error with stuff.

**Bret Sayre's Fantasy Take:** Probably not a whole lot. This isn't the type of player you want to own on your minor-league roster, as he likely tops out as a replacement-level guy unless you're playing in an AL-only format.

**The Year Ahead:** Davies is a small right-hander with small stuff, but a strong competitor with excellent feel for pitching and the ability to change speeds and hit his spots with a deep arsenal. The ceiling is limited, and I don't see a lot of projection in the arsenal, but with plus command potential the 21-year-old Davies has a chance to make it all work. The big test comes in Double-A, where big boy hitters are going to feast on upper-80s fastballs, especially if they arrive on a flat plane served on a platter. Davies will need to continue to refine his already strong command, and mix his offerings to keep hitters off-balance and off his average-at-best fastball.

## 9. Chance Sisco C

**Born:** 2/24/95    **Age:** 19    **Bats:** L    **Throws:** R    **Height:** 6' 2"    **Weight:** 193

| MLB ETA | Hit | Power | Run | Glove | Arm | OFP | Realistic |
|---------|-----|-------|-----|-------|-----|-----|-----------|
| 2018 | 50 | 50 | – | 55 | 50 | 60<br>1ST DIV PLAYER | 45<br>BACKUP C/<AVG REG |

| YEAR | TEAM | LVL | AGE | PA | R | 2B | 3B | HR | RBI | BB | SO | SB | CS | AVG/OBP/SLG | TAv | BABIP | BRR | FRAA | WARP |
|------|------|-----|-----|----|---|----|----|----|-----|----|----|----|----|-------------|-----|-------|-----|------|------|
| 2013 | ABE | A- | 18 | 6 | 1 | 0 | 0 | 0 | 0 | 1 | 2 | 0 | 0 | .200/.333/.200 | .244 | .333 | 0.0 | C(1): -0.0 | -0.1 |
| 2013 | ORI | Rk | 18 | 118 | 15 | 4 | 1 | 1 | 11 | 17 | 21 | 1 | 1 | .371/.475/.464 | .351 | .461 | 0.1 | C(19): 0.5 | 1.5 |
| 2014 | BAL | MLB | 19 | 250 | 19 | 8 | 0 | 3 | 21 | 16 | 75 | 0 | 0 | .193/.247/.273 | .194 | .260 | -0.4 | C 0 | -0.8 |
| 2015 | BAL | MLB | 20 | 250 | 26 | 8 | 1 | 5 | 23 | 16 | 69 | 0 | 0 | .229/.281/.329 | .225 | .300 | -0.5 | C 0 | -0.7 |

Breakout: 0%    Improve: 0%    Collapse: 0%    Attrition: 0%    MLB: 0%    *Comparables: Cedric Hunter, Christian Bethancourt, Marcell Ozuna*

**Drafted/Acquired:** 2nd round, 2013 draft, Santiago HS (Corona, CA)

**Previous Ranking:** NR

**What Happened in 2013:** A second-round pick in the 2013 draft, Sisco is a dual-threat catcher that could be a household name at this time next season.

**Strengths:** Good body to work with; athletic; arm is strong (solid-average); strong feel for baseball; new to catching but shows highly projectable skills; good hands; projectable bat; shows bat speed and good extension; can drive the baseball; power potential down the line with added strength; gamer.

**Weaknesses:** Still new to catching; receiving needs work; arm isn't big weapon; quick swing but questions about power upside; might be more average across the board than impact.

**Risk Factor/Injury History:** Extreme risk; limited professional experience; dual-threat development.

**Bret Sayre's Fantasy Take:** It's a tough bar to clear to be a catching prospect with potential mixed league fantasy relevance, but Cisco has the tools to stay above that fray. The second-rounder is a sneaky endgame pick in deep league dynasty drafts, and even more so in OBP/points leagues, due to potentially strong plate discipline numbers.

**The Year Ahead:** Sisco has a very long way to go, much like fellow high school draftee Josh Hart, but his overall feel for the game and impressive developmental steps forward in a very short amount of time are highly encouraging. The defensive profile isn't of the high-impact variety, with a solid-average arm and decent quickness, and the bat doesn't project to middle-of-the-order production, but a solid-average all-around catcher can represent a lot of value. It might take several years, but Sisco has a chance to develop into a very legit prospect, despite not possessing a cache of plus tools.

## 10. Josh Hart OF

**Born:** 10/2/94 **Age:** 19 **Bats:** L **Throws:** L **Height:** 6'1" **Weight:** 180

| MLB ETA | Hit | Power | Run | Glove | Arm | OFP | Realistic |
|---------|-----|-------|-----|-------|-----|-----|-----------|
| 2018 | 55 | — | 60 | 60 | — | 55 ML REGULAR | 45 BENCH/<AVG REG |

| YEAR | TEAM | LVL | AGE | PA | R | 2B | 3B | HR | RBI | BB | SO | SB | CS | AVG/OBP/SLG | TAv | BABIP | BRR | FRAA | WARP |
|------|------|-----|-----|----|----|----|----|----|-----|----|----|----|----|-------------|-----|-------|-----|------|------|
| 2013 | ABE | A- | 18 | 11 | 0 | 0 | 0 | 0 | 0 | 1 | 4 | 0 | 0 | .100/.182/.100 | .124 | .167 | 0.0 | CF(3): -0.2 | -0.2 |
| 2013 | ORI | Rk | 18 | 139 | 14 | 5 | 2 | 0 | 9 | 13 | 23 | 11 | 3 | .228/.312/.301 | .227 | .280 | 0.5 | CF(33): 5.1 | 0.5 |
| 2014 | BAL | MLB | 19 | 250 | 25 | 8 | 0 | 3 | 15 | 12 | 74 | 8 | 3 | .184/.226/.255 | .179 | .250 | 0.7 | CF 5 | -0.8 |
| 2015 | BAL | MLB | 20 | 250 | 21 | 9 | 1 | 2 | 18 | 14 | 70 | 7 | 2 | .188/.240/.264 | .192 | .253 | 0.4 | CF 4 | -2.2 |

Breakout: 0%   Improve: 0%   Collapse: 0%   Attrition: 0%   MLB: 0%          *Comparables: Che-Hsuan Lin, Andrew McCutchen, Joe Benson*

**Drafted/Acquired:** 1st round, 2013 draft, Parkview HS (Lilburn, GA)

**Previous Ranking:** NR

**What Happened in 2013:** Taken 37th overall in the 2013 draft, Hart is a prototypical center fielder/leadoff type, with more athleticism than baseball skills at present.

**Strengths:** Plus athlete; good body; easy plus run; very good range potential in center; glove could get to plus; swing built for steady contact; quick to the ball; good control; body to add more strength and pop to the offensive profile.

**Weaknesses:** Raw baseball skills; big upside but long developmental path; reads/routes need work in center; arm is fringy; bat is more weak contact than line drive; slappy at times; power could play well below average.

**Risk Factor/Injury History:** High risk; limited professional record; wide gap between present/future grades.

**Bret Sayre's Fantasy Take:** Now this is a more interesting fantasy stash. Hart's speed makes all the difference here, as he was one of the most interesting players in the 2013 draft class from a stolen-base perspective. He won't contribute much else outside of steals and average, but if he can rob 30-40 bases, he doesn't have to.

**The Year Ahead:** Hart is a long-term project, but the ceiling is an above-average player at a premium position, with plus speed that could affect the game on all sides. The swing and setup need work, from the trigger, to the balance, to the bat speed. He has the potential to develop into a high-contact hitter, one that can bring his best attribute (speed) into the equation. With a refined approach, he could develop into a leadoff threat down the line, but he could spend several years in the lower minors, struggling at the plate, before he is ready to take a big step forward.

## Prospects on the Rise

**1. 3B Hector Veloz:** I was able to watch the 19-year-old several times in 2013, and it was ugly more than it was awesome. But he has something in that swing, and if you had the opportunity to watch him rip it in batting practice, you might fall for his charms as well. I'll be honest: I'm not sure he can hit. But with good present strength and impressive bat speed, it will be interesting to see if it comes together with another pass at the short-season level. Right-handed power can take a long time to develop, so extra patience will be necessary with this player.

**2. LHP Daniel Ayers:** Big over-slot signing in the 2013 draft, Ayers is a (relatively) mature lefty with a good fastball, good curveball, and the feel for an average potential changeup. It's not a flashy profile—more of the solid-average variety—but lefties with solid-average stuff can go a very long way, and Ayers should jump into the top 10 next season with a strong full-season debut.

### FROM THE FIELD

**Eduardo Rodriguez**

**Player:** Eduardo Rodriguez
**Team:** Baltimore Orioles
**Filed by:** Tucker Blair
**Date(s) Seen:** July 3, July 23, and August 26, 2013
**Physical:** Athletic and sturdy frame, mild room for growth left.
**Mechanics/Delivery:** Smooth arm action, good extension. Quick arm. Falls off mound to third base side at times.
**Fastball:** 60 grade; 91-94 mph with mild, late movement with some run and sink. Becomes flat if he overthrows it.
**Slider:** 60 grade; 82-86 mph with depth and some late break. Good spin. Overthrows at times, losing depth, and becomes very hittable.
**Changeup:** 55 grade; 81-86 mph with plus fade, pulls the string well. Inconsistent at times, loses grip and command of it.
**Makeup:** 60 grade; Hardworking, determined on the mound. Good head on his shoulders. Very social and fun.
**OFP:** 6; no. 2 starter
**Realistic Role:** 5; no. 5 starter
**Risk:** Moderate; good feel for pitching, solid-average arsenal with potential plus fastball. Needs more time at Double-A for secondary pitches.

---

**Player:** Eduardo Rodriguez
**Team:** Baltimore Orioles
**Filed by:** CJ Wittmann
**Date(s) Seen:** Multiple times
**Physical:** Compact build, muscular for 6'2"; good base in legs; not a high-maintenance body.
**Mechanics/Delivery:** Easy, repeatable delivery from traditional 3/4 arm slot; shorter arm action; long stride to home; very effective fast worker; advanced pitchability; great feel.
**Fastball:** 60 grade; 90-94 mph; downhill plane; showed ability to cut it; most with arm-side run; above-average command profile.
**Slider:** 55 grade; 80-83 mph; short, tight breaker; sharp bite with some tilt; spots well to arm side.
**Changeup:** 55 grade; 80-84 mph; sinking action; can get firm at times.
**Makeup:** 60 grade; very rich demeanor and confidence; very good pitcher's mentality
**OFP:** 60; no. 3 starter
**Realistic Role:** 50; no. 4/5 starter
**Risk:** Low; advanced pitchability for limited professional profile.

**3. LHP Stephen Tarpley:** A third-round pick in the 2013 draft, several sources pushed for Tarpley in the top 10, mostly on the back of his strong lefty fastball, plus potential slider, and solid curveball. He has some rough edges, particularly in the delivery—high leg, loses balance, struggles to finish—but lefties with good stuff find homes on prospect lists, and a strong season in 2014 will push the 20-year-old up the rankings.

## Factors on the Farm

### Prospects likely to contribute at the major-league level in 2014

**1. 1B Christian Walker:** It's a tough profile because of the defensive limitations, but Walker is a stick, and he showed off that natural bat-to-ball ability in 2013 by hitting his way to Double-A in his first full season. Will he hit for big power? Probably not. But he can put a charge into the ball, and if injuries or opportunities arise at the major-league level Walker is the type of player capable of stepping up and holding his own at the plate.

**2. LHP Jason Gurka:** Diminutive lefty with a 90-91 mph fastball and a good curve, Gurka might not have a high-leverage bullpen role in his future, but if he can spot his heavy fastball down in the zone and miss bats with his two-plane breaker, he has a chance to contribute to the major-league bullpen in some capacity in 2014.

**3. LHP Michael Belfiore:** A former supplemental first-round pick of the D-Backs in 2009, Belfiore finally got a taste of the major-league level in 2013, and looks to carve out a larger role in 2014. Armed with a lively low-90s fastball and quality slider, Belfiore might lack the upside of a late-innings arm, but could find a home as a situational reliever.

## FROM THE FIELD

### Hunter Harvey

**Player:** Hunter Harvey

**Team:** Baltimore Orioles

**Filed by:** Chris Mellen

**Date(s) Seen:** August 26, 2013

**Mechanics/Delivery:** 3/4 arm slot; uses size to throw downhill; can land toward first base and crossfire; loose delivery; will jerk head—eyes drift off target and arm slot wavers

**Fastball:** 65 grade; velocity: 91-94, top 95; command: below-average; movement: cut and late finish in lower velocity band; ride when elevated; lot of life; will work down in the zone.

**Curveball:** 70 grade; velocity 78-81; command: average; movement: overhand break with power; strong wrist rotation; shows advanced feel for age; bite and depth.

**Changeup:** 60 grade; velocity 83-85; command: below-average; movement: arm-side fade; shows feel and arm speed; will telegraph at times; needs to improve throwing for a strike to get enough chases.

**Other:** Presently a thrower with fastball; even-keeled on mound; comes after hitters; confident in ability; advanced for age; will be pushed by better hitters to refine fastball command.

**Makeup:** 55 grade

**OFP:** 70; no. 2 starter

**Realistic Role:** 55; no. 3/4 starter

**Risk:** High; in the infancies of career; age and position present high volatility.

# BOSTON RED SOX

## 1.  Xander Bogaerts    SS

**Born:** 10/1/92    **Age:** 21    **Bats:** R    **Throws:** R    **Height:** 6'3"    **Weight:** 185

| MLB ETA | Hit | Power | Run | Glove | Arm | OFP | Realistic |
|---|---|---|---|---|---|---|---|
| Debuted in 2013 | 65 | 65 | -- | 50 | 60 | 70<br>ALL-STAR | 60<br>1ST DIV PLAYER |

| YEAR | TEAM | LVL | AGE | PA | R | 2B | 3B | HR | RBI | BB | SO | SB | CS | AVG/OBP/SLG | TAv | BABIP | BRR | FRAA | WARP |
|---|---|---|---|---|---|---|---|---|---|---|---|---|---|---|---|---|---|---|---|
| 2013 | PME | AA | 20 | 259 | 40 | 12 | 6 | 6 | 35 | 35 | 51 | 5 | 1 | .311/.407/.502 | .324 | .378 | 1.9 | SS(47): -3.1 | 2.4 |
| 2013 | PAW | AAA | 20 | 256 | 32 | 11 | 0 | 9 | 32 | 28 | 44 | 2 | 2 | .284/.369/.453 | .285 | .320 | 1.5 | SS(49): -5.9, 3B(10): -0.7 | 1.2 |
| 2013 | BOS | MLB | 20 | 50 | 7 | 2 | 0 | 1 | 5 | 5 | 13 | 1 | 0 | .250/.320/.364 | .300 | .323 | 1.1 | 3B(9): -0.4, SS(8): 0.9 | 0.5 |
| 2014 | BOS | MLB | 21 | 250 | 27 | 12 | 1 | 8 | 31 | 19 | 60 | 1 | 1 | .259/.319/.427 | .271 | .320 | -0.3 | SS -1, 3B -0 | 1.1 |
| 2015 | BOS | MLB | 22 | 633 | 77 | 29 | 4 | 19 | 75 | 56 | 147 | 1 | 1 | .253/.321/.416 | .273 | .306 | -1.1 | SS -4 | 2.8 |

Breakout: 5%    Improve: 21%    Collapse: 2%    Attrition: 13%    MLB: 32%          *Comparables: Reid Brignac, Joel Guzman, Christian Yelich*

**Drafted/Acquired:** International free agent, 2009, Aruba

**Previous Ranking:** #1 (Org), #12 (Top 101)

**What Happened in 2013:** Bogaerts crushed in two upper-level stops before arriving at the major-league level, where the now-21-year-old made his presence felt in the regular season before blossoming under the bright lights of the postseason.

**Strengths:** Great hands and coordination; easy, fluid swing; shows bat speed and bat control; projects to hit for both a high average and game power; advanced approach; instincts enhance profile at short; arm is plus.

**Weaknesses:** Defensive profile at short is average; actions can get stiff; range isn't ideal because of fringe run, but plays up because of instincts and good first step; over-the-fence pop still immature.

**Risk Factor/Injury History:** Low risk; achieved major-league level

**Bret Sayre's Fantasy Take:** Bogaerts is ready, willing, and able to be one of the next great middle infielders in the fantasy realm. Even without the ability to add much value on the bases (he's 17-for-33 on the basepaths in his minor-league career), he can provide Troy Tulowitzki-type value everywhere else. A potential .300 hitter with 25+ homers and potentially huge RBI totals is a special player, and makes Bogaerts the top fantasy prospect in baseball.

**The Year Ahead:** Bogaerts has the type of profile to develop into a star, a middle of-the-diamond defender with a high-upside bat capable of producing a high average and game power. The makeup is insane, and any setback or failure on the field won't derail or dissuade his progression toward his ultimate goal. Adjustments will be necessary after the book on Bogaerts is passed around, but his feel for the game and speed of adaptation will allow him to thrive at the highest level despite his inexperience and age.

**#2**

BP Top
101
Prospects

---

## 2.  Jackie Bradley Jr.    CF

**Born:** 4/19/90    **Age:** 24    **Bats:** L    **Throws:** R    **Height:** 5'10"    **Weight:** 195

| MLB ETA | Hit | Power | Run | Glove | Arm | OFP | Realistic |
|---|---|---|---|---|---|---|---|
| Debuted in 2013 | 55 | -- | -- | 65 | 60 | 60<br>1ST DIV PLAYER | 50<br>ML REGULAR |

| YEAR | TEAM | LVL | AGE | PA | R | 2B | 3B | HR | RBI | BB | SO | SB | CS | AVG/OBP/SLG | TAv | BABIP | BRR | FRAA | WARP |
|---|---|---|---|---|---|---|---|---|---|---|---|---|---|---|---|---|---|---|---|
| 2013 | PAW | AAA | 23 | 374 | 57 | 26 | 3 | 10 | 35 | 41 | 75 | 7 | 7 | .275/.374/.469 | .302 | .331 | 0.1 | CF(58): 3.0, RF(7): 0.4 | 3.3 |
| 2013 | BOS | MLB | 23 | 107 | 18 | 5 | 0 | 3 | 10 | 10 | 31 | 2 | 0 | .189/.280/.337 | .236 | .246 | -2.2 | CF(19): 0.5, LF(14): -0.1 | -0.3 |
| 2014 | BOS | MLB | 24 | 250 | 32 | 14 | 1 | 5 | 24 | 26 | 55 | 5 | 3 | .254/.343/.399 | .273 | .310 | -0.2 | CF 1, LF 0 | 1.2 |
| 2015 | BOS | MLB | 25 | 640 | 79 | 33 | 3 | 14 | 70 | 67 | 145 | 11 | 5 | .259/.348/.407 | .280 | .322 | -0.8 | CF 4 | 3.4 |

Breakout: 2%    Improve: 22%    Collapse: 15%    Attrition: 23%    MLB: 61%          *Comparables: Ryan Kalish, Desmond Jennings, Carlos Quentin*

**Drafted/Acquired:** 1st round, 2011 draft, University of South Carolina, (Columbia, SC)

**Previous Ranking:** #2 (Org), #27 (Top 101)

**What Happened in 2013:** After a strong spring, Bradley unexpectedly made the Red Sox out of camp, but struggled with the stick against major-league arms and failed to establish himself as a permanent fixture on the 25-man roster.

**Strengths:** Plus-plus instincts in the field; plus arm, with carry and accuracy; glove is a 7; range plays up because of good reads/routes; quick path to the ball; easy swing that produces hard contact; advanced approach; tracks well; big makeup.

**Weaknesses:** Lacks an impact bat; hit tool more solid-average than plus; struggles against good arm-side stuff; power will play well below average; speed is average at best.

**#23**

BP Top
101
Prospects

**Risk Factor/Injury History:** Low risk; achieved major-league level

**Bret Sayre's Fantasy Take:** Bradley is a cookie-cutter example of someone who is far more interesting in real life than fantasy. At his best, he could be a top-of-the-order hitter who gets on base at a very good clip and scores a bunch of runs without providing much value in the other three categories. From a fantasy viewpoint, that sounds an awful lot like Denard Span. He gets a bump up in on-base percentage leagues.

**The Year Ahead:** Bradley isn't a flashy player, and he's not going to show pole-to-pole range, flash game-changing speed on base, or force pitchers to work around him at the plate. But he's going to get the job done at a premium position, and with an advanced approach and a good swing, he's going to prove to be a tough out, even if he's a down-the-lineup bat. This is an instinctual player of the highest order, and once he finds his rhythm at the plate, you can chisel his name on the lineup card for the next decade.

## 3. Garin Cecchini 3B

**Born:** 4/20/91 **Age:** 23 **Bats:** L **Throws:** R **Height:** 6' 2" **Weight:** 200

| MLB ETA | Hit | Power | Run | Glove | Arm | OFP | Realistic |
|---|---|---|---|---|---|---|---|
| Late 2014 | 65 | 50 | – | 50 | 60 | 60 1ST DIV PLAYER | 50 ML REGULAR |

| YEAR | TEAM | LVL | AGE | PA | R | 2B | 3B | HR | RBI | BB | SO | SB | CS | AVG/OBP/SLG | TAv | BABIP | BRR | FRAA | WARP |
|---|---|---|---|---|---|---|---|---|---|---|---|---|---|---|---|---|---|---|---|
| 2013 | PME | AA | 22 | 295 | 36 | 14 | 3 | 2 | 28 | 51 | 52 | 8 | 2 | .296/.420/.404 | .312 | .367 | 0.6 | 3B(44): 3.4 | 3.2 |
| 2013 | SLM | A+ | 22 | 262 | 44 | 19 | 4 | 5 | 33 | 43 | 34 | 15 | 7 | .350/.469/.547 | .349 | .400 | 2.2 | 3B(59): -8.2 | 2.9 |
| 2014 | BOS | MLB | 23 | 250 | 27 | 12 | 1 | 2 | 22 | 27 | 55 | 10 | 2 | .252/.338/.352 | .255 | .320 | 0.9 | 3B -2 | 0.4 |
| 2015 | BOS | MLB | 24 | 250 | 28 | 13 | 1 | 3 | 23 | 26 | 55 | 8 | 2 | .255/.339/.371 | .264 | .323 | 0.6 | 3B -2 | 1.7 |

Breakout: 3%   Improve: 15%   Collapse: 2%   Attrition: 15%   MLB: 28%   *Comparables: Logan Forsythe, James Darnell, Taylor Green*

**Drafted/Acquired:** 4th round, 2010 draft, Alfred M. Barbe HS (Lake Charles, LA)

**Previous Ranking:** #6 (Org)

**What Happened in 2013:** After a strong full-season debut in 2012, Cecchini took a big step forward in 2013, crushing the Carolina League before earning a promotion to Double-A, where the bat continued to impress.

**Strengths:** Excellent hand-eye coordination; natural bat-to-ball skills; hit tool could end up well above average; line-drive stroke; advanced approach; arm is plus; glove could play to average; good makeup/instincts.

**Weaknesses:** Game power yet to arrive; struggles to create backspin on the ball; can struggle against quality secondary stuff; fringe run; lacks above-average defensive profile at third.

**Risk Factor/Injury History:** Low risk; 66 games at Double-A level; mature offensive skill set.

**Bret Sayre's Fantasy Take:** Thankfully, Cecchini's 2013 was more representative of his potential for fantasy than his career up to that point. His 63 stolen bases in only 150 games during his first two seasons were a hint of something that was never to come, but the average/on-base skill driven value his most recent stat line hinted at is a more realistic outcome. Cecchini is not an impact fantasy player, and that will be only further cemented if he has to move to the outfield.

**The Year Ahead:** Polarizing prospect in scouting circles, as some see an impact bat at third base—a future .300 hitter with 20+ home run pop—while others see a solid-average type—good average and on-base skills, but limited game power and a better fit for an outfield corner. A disappointing season from the incumbent Middlebrooks opens the door for Cecchini to force the issue with a strong spring and early run through Triple-A. But there are still questions about the 23-year-old's profile, and until the game power starts to show its face, the questions about the offensive upside will persist.

**#51** BP Top 101 Prospects

## 4. Matt Barnes RHP

**Born:** 6/17/90 **Age:** 24 **Bats:** R **Throws:** R **Height:** 6' 4" **Weight:** 205

| MLB ETA | CT | FB | CH | CB | SL | OFP | Realistic |
|---|---|---|---|---|---|---|---|
| 2014 | – | 70 | 50 | 55 | – | 60 NO.3 STARTER | 50 LATE-INN RP (SETUP) |

| YEAR | TEAM | LVL | AGE | W | L | SV | G | GS | IP | H | HR | BB | SO | BB9 | SO9 | GB% | BABIP | WHIP | ERA | FIP | FRA | WARP |
|---|---|---|---|---|---|---|---|---|---|---|---|---|---|---|---|---|---|---|---|---|---|---|
| 2013 | PAW | AAA | 23 | 1 | 0 | 0 | 1 | 1 | 5.3 | 3 | 0 | 2 | 7 | 3.4 | 11.8 | 45% | .273 | 0.94 | 0.00 | 1.70 | 2.03 | 0.2 |
| 2013 | PME | AA | 23 | 5 | 10 | 0 | 24 | 24 | 108.0 | 112 | 11 | 46 | 135 | 3.8 | 11.2 | 46% | .356 | 1.46 | 4.33 | 3.54 | 3.51 | 2.9 |
| 2014 | BOS | MLB | 24 | 6 | 7 | 0 | 21 | 21 | 98.0 | 99 | 11 | 40 | 97 | 3.7 | 8.9 | 46% | .318 | 1.42 | 4.39 | 4.20 | 4.77 | 0.6 |
| 2015 | BOS | MLB | 25 | 8 | 9 | 0 | 29 | 29 | 178.7 | 170 | 20 | 62 | 194 | 3.1 | 9.8 | 46% | .314 | 1.30 | 3.84 | 3.62 | 4.17 | 1.9 |

Breakout: 24%   Improve: 43%   Collapse: 7%   Attrition: 33%   MLB: 56%   *Comparables: James Paxton, Scott Barnes, J.J. Hoover*

**Drafted/Acquired:** 1st round, 2011 draft, University of Connecticut (Storrs, CT)

**Previous Ranking:** #3 (Org), #38 (Top 101)

**What Happened in 2013:** In his Double-A debut, Barnes was solid but not special, showing off the big boy fastball and missing barrels, but failing to take the secondary stuff to the next developmental level.

**Strengths:** Excellent size; power arm strength; fastball is meaty offering; routinely works 93-96; touches higher when needed; arm-side life; curveball flashes knockout potential; mid- to upper-70s with two-plane break and occasional late snap; shows some feel for fading changeup; projects as average offering.

**#64** BP Top 101 Prospects

**Weaknesses:** Below-average command; delivery can get out of whack; struggles to stay over and finish his pitches; fastball can flatten out; curveball can break too early and get big and visible; changeup lacks plus projection and isn't a weapon.

**Risk Factor/Injury History:** Moderate risk; 24 starts at Double-A level

**Bret Sayre's Fantasy Take:** The shine has certainly come off of Barnes' star, but he still remains a very solid investment—especially in deeper leagues. The strikeouts (and wins, in turn) should be there, but pitching in the AL East could make his ratios less than stellar.

**The Year Ahead:** Barnes has more potential than he often shows; the young righty can get by with his superior fastball against inferior bats, but the secondary stuff only teases and rarely tantalizes. If he can bring it together—which several sources think will happen in 2014—Barnes has middle-of-the-rotation potential, with a plus-plus fastball that he can use to set up hitters for the plus curveball. The command needs work, and the curveball needs to find more consistency, but the ingredients are there for major-league success.

## 5. Henry Owens  LHP

**Born:** 7/21/92  **Age:** 21  **Bats:** L  **Throws:** L  **Height:** 6'6"  **Weight:** 205

| MLB ETA | CT | FB | CH | CB | SL | OFP | Realistic |
|---|---|---|---|---|---|---|---|
| Late 2014 | – | 60 | 55 | 55 | – | 55 NO.3 STARTER | 50 NO.4 STARTER |

| YEAR | TEAM | LVL | AGE | W | L | SV | G | GS | IP | H | HR | BB | SO | BB9 | SO9 | GB% | BABIP | WHIP | ERA | FIP | FRA | WARP |
|---|---|---|---|---|---|---|---|---|---|---|---|---|---|---|---|---|---|---|---|---|---|---|
| 2013 | SLM | A+ | 20 | 8 | 5 | 0 | 20 | 20 | 104.7 | 66 | 6 | 53 | 123 | 4.6 | 10.6 | 45% | .249 | 1.14 | 2.92 | 3.46 | 4.28 | 2.1 |
| 2013 | PME | AA | 20 | 3 | 1 | 0 | 6 | 6 | 30.3 | 18 | 3 | 15 | 46 | 4.5 | 13.6 | 29% | .254 | 1.09 | 1.78 | 3.26 | 3.67 | 0.7 |
| 2014 | BOS | MLB | 21 | 6 | 7 | 0 | 21 | 21 | 104.3 | 98 | 12 | 56 | 113 | 4.8 | 9.8 | 40% | .308 | 1.47 | 4.38 | 4.47 | 4.76 | 0.6 |
| 2015 | BOS | MLB | 22 | 8 | 8 | 0 | 26 | 26 | 153.7 | 134 | 17 | 77 | 165 | 4.5 | 9.7 | 40% | .289 | 1.37 | 3.87 | 4.09 | 4.21 | 1.6 |

Breakout: 0%  Improve: 0%  Collapse: 0%  Attrition: 0%  MLB: 0%  *Comparables: Joel Zumaya, Jake McGee, Trevor Bauer*

**#69** BP Top 101 Prospects

**Drafted/Acquired:** 1st round, 2011 draft, Edison HS (Huntington Beach, CA)

**Previous Ranking:** #7 (Org)

**What Happened in 2013:** In his 20 starts in High-A, Owens started to live up to his first-round talent and the prospect world took note, but it wasn't until his impressive six-start run in Double-A that the status really exploded.

**Strengths:** Long, lanky body; projectable; easy delivery; fastball is solid-average and can show more; works 89-92; touches 94+; good late life (arm-side); changeup is best secondary offering; good arm-speed deception and action; curveball with plus shape; can flash above-average potential; good feel for pitching.

**Weaknesses:** Fastball can play down; pedestrian at times; needs to add strength to frame; command is below average; curveball can get too big and lack bite; changeup can get soft.

**Risk Factor/Injury History:** Moderate risk; limited experience in upper-minors.

**Bret Sayre's Fantasy Take:** For my money, Owens is the arm you want in dynasty formats over the similarly ranked Barnes and Webster—though it's admittedly close all around. His 11.4 career K/9 rate certainly shows his ability to miss bats, but he gives some of that potential value back in WHIP by walking too many batters—not too dissimilar from C.J. Wilson (if it all works).

**The Year Ahead:** Owens is going to pitch in the major leagues for a long time, but I don't see a high-impact starter; rather, I see a back-end type capable of logging innings and keeping hitters off-balance with a solid three-pitch mix. But the curveball that misses bats in the minors will struggle to do the same against major-league hitters, especially if the fastball command continues to play below average and doesn't get the bats moving. But with added strength, more consistent fastball velocity, and more refined command, Owens could find his way to the middle of a major-league rotation.

## 6. Blake Swihart  C

**Born:** 4/3/92  **Age:** 22  **Bats:** B  **Throws:** R  **Height:** 6'1"  **Weight:** 175

| MLB ETA | Hit | Power | Run | Glove | Arm | OFP | Realistic |
|---|---|---|---|---|---|---|---|
| Late 2015 | 55 | 50 | – | 55 | 60 | 60 1ST DIV PLAYER | 50 ML REGULAR |

| YEAR | TEAM | LVL | AGE | PA | R | 2B | 3B | HR | RBI | BB | SO | SB | CS | AVG/OBP/SLG | TAv | BABIP | BRR | FRAA | WARP |
|---|---|---|---|---|---|---|---|---|---|---|---|---|---|---|---|---|---|---|---|
| 2013 | SLM | A+ | 21 | 422 | 45 | 29 | 7 | 2 | 42 | 41 | 63 | 7 | 8 | .298/.366/.428 | .271 | .350 | -6.9 | C(101): 2.6 | 2.4 |
| 2014 | BOS | MLB | 22 | 250 | 20 | 12 | 2 | 2 | 22 | 13 | 58 | 2 | 1 | .232/.272/.328 | .219 | .290 | -0.3 | C 0 | 0.1 |
| 2015 | BOS | MLB | 23 | 250 | 24 | 12 | 2 | 3 | 22 | 15 | 59 | 1 | 0 | .234/.280/.337 | .226 | .296 | -0.4 | C 0 | -0.4 |

Breakout: 0%  Improve: 0%  Collapse: 0%  Attrition: 0%  MLB: 0%  *Comparables: Josmil Pinto, J.R. Murphy, Rob Brantly*

**#73** BP Top 101 Prospects

**Drafted/Acquired:** 1st round, 2011 draft, V Sue Cleveland HS (Rio Rancho, NM)

**Previous Ranking:** #5 (Org)

**What Happened in 2013:** In his Carolina League debut, the switch-hitting catcher showed off his stick and his arm, slugging 112 hits in 103 games and throwing out 42 percent of would-be basestealers.

**Strengths:** Elite makeup; plus athlete; shows consistent swing mechanics from both sides of the plate; bat speed and barrel control; hit tool has above-average potential; mature approach; good gap pop; very good footwork behind the plate; plus arm; quick release for good pops; projects as plus defender.

**Weaknesses:** Will chase fastballs up; game power likely to play below plus; low-rider behind the plate (backside close to the ground) can shrink target size; still refining as a receiver.

**Risk Factor/Injury History:** Moderate risk; dual-threat development; yet to play at Double-A level

**Bret Sayre's Fantasy Take:** Another catching prospect worth waiting for, Swihart has the potential to hit .280 with 15+ homers. He also has the athleticism to steal 5-10 bases, which is just gravy from a catcher. He'll never be the number one fantasy option at the position, but has the ability to be a starter in even the shallowest of formats.

**The Year Ahead:** Swihart has the type of makeup, work ethic, and physical skills to develop to his potential, regardless of the complexities of his dual-threat profile. The bat is solid, with a good approach, good hand-eye coordination and strength, and the defensive skill set should be plus, with a strong arm, quick feet, and a high baseball IQ. Double-A will present a challenge for the 22-year-old, especially at the plate, where better arms can exploit his tastes for shoulder-level heat and force him to chase spin down and away. If he adjusts and the bat takes a step forward, his stock could really explode, as legit two-way catchers are the rarest breed found in baseball.

## 7. Allen Webster   RHP

**Born:** 2/10/90   **Age:** 24   **Bats:** R   **Throws:** R   **Height:** 6' 2"   **Weight:** 190

| MLB ETA | CT | FB | CH | CB | SL | OFP | Realistic |
|---|---|---|---|---|---|---|---|
| Debuted in 2013 | -- | 70 | 60 | -- | 55 | 60 NO.3 STARTER | 50 LATE-INN RP (SETUP) |

| YEAR | TEAM | LVL | AGE | W | L | SV | G | GS | IP | H | HR | BB | SO | BB9 | SO9 | GB% | BABIP | WHIP | ERA | FIP | FRA | WARP |
|---|---|---|---|---|---|---|---|---|---|---|---|---|---|---|---|---|---|---|---|---|---|---|
| 2013 | BOS | MLB | 23 | 1 | 2 | 0 | 8 | 7 | 30.3 | 37 | 7 | 18 | 23 | 5.3 | 6.8 | 44% | .316 | 1.81 | 8.60 | 6.54 | 7.21 | -0.5 |
| 2013 | PAW | AAA | 23 | 8 | 4 | 0 | 21 | 21 | 105.0 | 71 | 9 | 43 | 116 | 3.7 | 9.9 | 51% | .246 | 1.09 | 3.60 | 3.80 | 4.21 | 1.3 |
| 2014 | BOS | MLB | 24 | 6 | 8 | 0 | 21 | 21 | 109.7 | 118 | 12 | 51 | 87 | 4.2 | 7.1 | 50% | .311 | 1.54 | 5.06 | 4.92 | 5.50 | -0.3 |
| 2015 | BOS | MLB | 25 | 6 | 5 | 0 | 65 | 11 | 120.3 | 121 | 12 | 46 | 101 | 3.4 | 7.6 | 49% | .303 | 1.38 | 4.35 | 4.17 | 4.73 | 0.4 |

Breakout: 20%   Improve: 41%   Collapse: 14%   Attrition: 31%   MLB: 59%     *Comparables: Wily Peralta, Casey Crosby, Felix Doubront*

**Drafted/Acquired:** 18th round, 2008 draft, McMichael HS (Mayodan, NC)

**Previous Ranking:** #4 (Org), #69 (Top 101)

**What Happened in 2013:** While he proved to be quite hard to hit in his Triple-A debut, Webster found plenty of hard contact in his seven major-league starts, as the 23-year-old allowed seven home runs in only 30 innings of work.

**Strengths:** Good body; good arm strength; fastball is plus-plus offering; routinely works 94-96; touches higher; good vertical life; changeup is plus; mid-80s with arm-speed deception and sink; slider flashes wipeout potential at times; sharp in the 84-86 range; shows an upper-70s curveball; competitive/aggressive approach.

**Weaknesses:** Below-average command; struggles to repeat delivery/release points; tendency to work up and flatten out; slider can get slurvy and lose bite; arsenal can get too firm; curveball more for show and sneak.

**Risk Factor/Injury History:** Low risk; achieved major-league level

**Bret Sayre's Fantasy Take:** Webster would be a more attractive proposition if he had a better chance of avoiding a career in the bullpen. He has the stuff to get above-average strikeouts in a starting role, but as his major-league numbers showed, Webster has a lot of work to do in order to not drown you with his ratios. He has the highest fantasy upside of the big three arms in this system, but also carries the most risk.

**The Year Ahead:** Webster has all the components of a very good starting pitcher, but when he fails to locate his fastball, he struggles to get back into counts and loses the effectiveness of his bat-missing secondary stuff, which is often best deployed out of the zone. Sources are mixed on his future role, but the louder chorus is coming from the reliever camp, where the arsenal depth and intensity could make him a very good late-innings arm, even if the command remains fringy.

## 8. Mookie Betts   2B

**Born:** 10/7/92   **Age:** 21   **Bats:** R   **Throws:** R   **Height:** 5' 9"   **Weight:** 156

| MLB ETA | Hit | Power | Run | Glove | Arm | OFP | Realistic |
|---|---|---|---|---|---|---|---|
| 2015 | 60 | -- | 60 | 60 | 55 | 55 >AVG REGULAR | 50 FRINGE-AVG ML REG |

| YEAR | TEAM | LVL | AGE | PA | R | 2B | 3B | HR | RBI | BB | SO | SB | CS | AVG/OBP/SLG | TAv | BABIP | BRR | FRAA | WARP |
|---|---|---|---|---|---|---|---|---|---|---|---|---|---|---|---|---|---|---|---|
| 2013 | SLM | A+ | 20 | 211 | 30 | 12 | 3 | 7 | 39 | 23 | 17 | 20 | 2 | .341/.414/.551 | .331 | .346 | 3.0 | 2B(50): 7.1 | 3.5 |
| 2013 | GRN | A | 20 | 340 | 63 | 24 | 1 | 8 | 26 | 58 | 40 | 18 | 2 | .296/.418/.477 | .329 | .322 | 4.7 | 2B(76): -4.0 | 3.4 |
| 2014 | BOS | MLB | 21 | 250 | 28 | 12 | 1 | 5 | 25 | 24 | 42 | 9 | 2 | .257/.328/.381 | .260 | .290 | 0.9 | 2B 2, SS 0 | 1.2 |
| 2015 | BOS | MLB | 22 | 250 | 30 | 12 | 1 | 5 | 27 | 23 | 37 | 7 | 1 | .274/.342/.413 | .277 | .302 | 0.6 | 2B 2, SS 0 | 3.1 |

Breakout: 0%   Improve: 0%   Collapse: 0%   Attrition: 0%   MLB: 0%     *Comparables: Kolten Wong, Jonathan Schoop, Alexi Amarista*

**Drafted/Acquired:** 5th round, 2011 draft, John Overton HS (Brentwood, TN)

**Previous Ranking:** NR

**What Happened in 2013:** In his full-season debut, Betts destroyed A-ball pitching across two levels and finished the year in the prospect-heavy Arizona Fall League, where he continued to show off his hit tool and mature approach.

**Strengths:** Plus athlete; plus instincts; excellent hand-eye coordination; well-above-average pitch-recognition skills; shows bat control and ability to use all fields; plus potential hit; easy plus runner; plus-plus range at 2B; glove projects to plus; arm is strong enough to make all the throws.

**Weaknesses:** Limited size; power likely to play well below average; questions about timing/balance in swing against better stuff (getting front foot down); good actions and hands on defense, but still finding familiarity with position.

**Risk Factor/Injury History:** Moderate risk; yet to play at Double-A level

**Bret Sayre's Fantasy Take:** The stat line is sexy, and his fantasy potential is only a slightly lesser version of said sexiness. The average/speed combination is attractive at such a shallow position and when you add potential 10-homer pop, there's Jean Segura-lite potential here.

**The Year Ahead:** Sources are mixed on Betts, despite his impressive run through the A-ball levels and a strong showing in the Arizona Fall League; some see an impact player on all sides of the ball, with a plus hit, plus approach, plus run, and plus defensive chops at second base, while others see more of a utility profile, a catalytic player that doesn't have enough offensive punch to profile as a regular. Double-A will be a huge test for the catalytic player, a level that often exposes players for what they really are (or what they are likely to become).

---

## 9. Christian Vazquez C

**Born:** 8/21/90  **Age:** 23  **Bats:** R  **Throws:** R  **Height:** 5'9"  **Weight:** 195

| MLB ETA | Hit | Power | Run | Glove | Arm | OFP | Realistic |
|---|---|---|---|---|---|---|---|
| 2015 | 50 | – | – | 65 | 70 | 60<br>1ST DIV PLAYER | 50<br>ML REGULAR |

| YEAR | TEAM | LVL | AGE | PA | R | 2B | 3B | HR | RBI | BB | SO | SB | CS | AVG/OBP/SLG | TAv | BABIP | BRR | FRAA | WARP |
|---|---|---|---|---|---|---|---|---|---|---|---|---|---|---|---|---|---|---|---|
| 2013 | PAW | AAA | 22 | 4 | 0 | 0 | 0 | 0 | 0 | 1 | 0 | 0 | 0 | .000/.250/.000 | .153 | .000 | 0.0 | C(1): -0.0 | 0.0 |
| 2013 | PME | AA | 22 | 399 | 48 | 19 | 1 | 5 | 48 | 47 | 44 | 7 | 5 | .289/.376/.395 | .285 | .316 | 1.2 | C(93): 0.7 | 3.7 |
| 2014 | BOS | MLB | 23 | 250 | 23 | 11 | 0 | 4 | 25 | 21 | 51 | 1 | 1 | .236/.303/.346 | .238 | .280 | -0.5 | C 1 | 0.7 |
| 2015 | BOS | MLB | 24 | 250 | 29 | 11 | 1 | 5 | 26 | 21 | 44 | 1 | 0 | .255/.322/.386 | .259 | .291 | -0.5 | C 1 | 1.8 |

Breakout: 2%   Improve: 13%   Collapse: 0%   Attrition: 10%   MLB: 23%          *Comparables: Russell Martin, Jason Castro, Bryan Anderson*

**Drafted/Acquired:** 9th round, 2008 draft, Puerto Rico Baseball Academy (Gurabo, PR)

**Previous Ranking:** NR

**What Happened in 2013:** In his second pass in Double-A, Vazquez's bat started to show signs of life, a promising progression to go along with his already highly impressive defensive profile.

**Strengths:** Plus-plus arm strength; quick release and accurate; good footwork and movements behind the plate; good receiver; well-above-average defensive potential; has some pop in the stick; tracks well with good approach.

**Weaknesses:** Can get too aggressive with the arm; hit tool could play below average; struggles against velocity and quality secondary stuff; some pop but doesn't project for much over the fence power.

**Risk Factor/Injury History:** Low risk; high-end defensive skill set; Double-A experience.

**Bret Sayre's Fantasy Take:** I saw Vazquez throw out both of the runners who tried to steal against him when I saw him in Trenton last April. That's about as positive of a comment as I can make in regards to his fantasy value in this space. He doesn't have the bat to warrant a roster spot in dynasty leagues.

**The Year Ahead:** The defensive profile is better than people realize, with a plus-plus arm, a quick release, good receiving skills, and improving footwork and blocking ability. That's Vazquez's meal ticket and, regardless of the bat, what will eventually give him a career at the major-league level. But if the bat shows some life and he can prove to be a tougher out than his projections suggest—even in a down-the-lineup capacity—the overall profile could make him a first-division player because of the impact potential of his defense.

---

## 10. Trey Ball LHP

**Born:** 6/27/94  **Age:** 20  **Bats:** L  **Throws:** L  **Height:** 6'6"  **Weight:** 185

| MLB ETA | CT | FB | CH | CB | SL | OFP | Realistic |
|---|---|---|---|---|---|---|---|
| 2017 | – | 65 | 65 | 55 | – | 65<br>NO.2 STARTER | 50<br>NO.4 STARTER |

| YEAR | TEAM | LVL | AGE | W | L | SV | G | GS | IP | H | HR | BB | SO | BB9 | SO9 | GB% | BABIP | WHIP | ERA | FIP | FRA | WARP |
|---|---|---|---|---|---|---|---|---|---|---|---|---|---|---|---|---|---|---|---|---|---|---|
| 2013 | RSX | Rk | 19 | 0 | 1 | 0 | 5 | 5 | 7.0 | 10 | 1 | 6 | 5 | 7.7 | 6.4 | 28% | .375 | 2.29 | 6.43 | 6.46 | 7.91 | -0.1 |
| 2014 | BOS | MLB | 20 | 1 | 3 | 0 | 7 | 7 | 30.0 | 40 | 4 | 21 | 12 | 6.3 | 3.6 | 43% | .321 | 2.04 | 7.40 | 6.73 | 8.04 | -0.8 |
| 2015 | BOS | MLB | 21 | 2 | 6 | 0 | 22 | 22 | 130.7 | 155 | 19 | 81 | 73 | 5.6 | 5.0 | 43% | .307 | 1.81 | 6.43 | 6.00 | 6.99 | -2.3 |

Breakout: 0%   Improve: 0%   Collapse: 0%   Attrition: 0%   MLB: 0%          *Comparables: Matt Magill, Jeanmar Gomez, Alberto Cabrera*

**Drafted/Acquired:** 1st round, 2013 draft, New Castle Chrysler HS (New Castle, IN)

**Previous Ranking:** NR

**What Happened in 2013:** Ball was selected seventh overall in the 2013 draft, a two-way talent that brings more upside on the mound thanks to his high-end projection.

**Strengths:** Highly projectable body; very long and lean; plus athlete; delivery is smooth and easy; arm action is very impressive; fastball has late jump in the upper-80s/low-90s; projects to easy plus; changeup receives high marks for deception and action; could be difference maker pitch; curveball already shows average and projects to be an above-average offering.

**Weaknesses:** Long developmental road ahead; needs to add strength/muscle to frame; adjust to pitching full time; improve fastball and fastball command; curveball is still underdeveloped.

**Risk Factor/Injury History:** High risk; limited professional experience.

**Bret Sayre's Fantasy Take:** Unlikely to crack the top 15 in my 2013 dynasty league rankings despite being a top-10 pick, Ball is a high-upside starter with a long, long ways to go. It's too early to know what he'll become from a fantasy standpoint, but if he does become a lefty with a plus fastball and plus change, the strikeouts will come.

**The Year Ahead:** Ball has the type of physical projection to dream on, with a plus potential arsenal from an ultra-athletic and easy delivery and release. In his first full season, you will see a heavy dose of fastball action to build up arm strength and establish command, so the results might not match the hype, at least initially. But once the full arsenal comes together, which already includes a very good changeup, Ball will start to miss more bats and start to blossom as a pitching prospect.

## Prospects on the Rise

**1. CF Manuel Margot:** You can make a case that the 19-year-old Dominican already belongs in the top 10 in this system, with an above-average defensive profile in center field and impact speed. The bat still has question marks and Margot lacks high-end offensive upside, but the overall profile could be a first-division player, and with a strong full-season debut in 2014, he could find himself in the top 10 without much debate.

**2. IF Rafael Devers:** One of the sweetest swings I've ever seen from a 16-year-old, Devers was highly impressive when I saw him in a Dominican showcase last January, with the type of bat speed that you just can't teach. It's not hyperbole to compare the swing to that of Robinson Cano, although the overall athleticism and defensive projection leaves a lot to be desired. But this kid can absolutely hit the baseball, and if he shows that offensive prowess at the complex level in 2014, he should climb prospect lists and start to emerge as a national name.

**3. 2B Wendell Rijo:** Rijo suffered a substantial knee injury before signing in the J2 window in 2012, which impacted his debut season, although the then-17-year-old still showed off his natural bat-to-ball ability at the complex level. The swing and setup are a bit unorthodox, but the toolsy Dominican makes it work, and if he continues to hit in the New York-Penn League, the now-healthy second baseman could really step forward as a prospect. I really like this kid.

## Factors on the Farm

### Prospects likely to contribute at the major-league level in 2014

**1. RHP Anthony Ranaudo:** An injury-plagued 2012 depressed Ranaudo's once-lofty standing in the prospect world, but the former first-round pick got back on the right track in 2013, pitching his way to Triple-A and logging a career-high 140 innings. The ceiling isn't as high as his hype, as the fastball can get flat and pedestrian and the secondary arsenal inconsistent, but the large 24-year-old righty still

---

## FROM THE FIELD

### Matt Barnes

**Player:** Matt Barnes

**Team:** Boston Red Sox

**Filed by:** Chris Mellen

**Date(s) Seen:** April 19, 2013

**Mechanics/Delivery:** 3/4 arm slot; easy and controlled delivery; creates leverage/steep plane via leg drive and follow-through in line with home plate; at times loses balance on landing, causing feet to drift and weight to veer toward first base

**Fastball:** 70 grade; velocity: 91-95, top 96; command: solid-average; movement: arm-side run in lower tier of zone; late downward finish in lower tier when thrown glove side; flat when elevated above the middle of thighs; can miss target and back into plate on the glove side

**Curveball:** 55 grade; velocity: 75-78; command: fringe-average; movement: 11-5 break; flashes deep, overhand break, but inconsistent; loose and slurvy in upper range of velocity; tends to wrap wrist rather than pull downward.

**Changeup:** 50 grade; velocity: 83-85; command: average; movement: arm-side fade with drop; occasional cut to glove side; more of a contact inducing pitch; will hold onto too long.

**Other:** Level demeanor and body language on the mound; was not rattled; did not have best fastball velocity, but blended elements of power and finesse when situation called for it; showed understanding of how to execute craft.

**Makeup:** 55 grade

**OFP:** 60; no. 3 starter

**Realistic Role:** 50; no. 4 starter or late-innings reliever

**Risk:** Low; one step from The Show; will pitch in majors; comes down to adjustments.

---

## FROM THE FIELD

### Xander Bogaerts

**Player:** Xander Bogaerts

**Team:** Boston Red Sox

**Filed by:** Chris Mellen

**Date(s) Seen:** April 4-5, April 19, July 28, and August 14-15, 2013

**Physical:** Ideal frame; room to continue filling out and add more muscle; developing core and lower body; built for the rigors of a long season.

**Hit:** 60 grade; explosive hands; elite bat speed; easy swing, with upward plane through hitting zone; loose hands; capable of adjusting swing; will fish and get out on front foot.

**Power:** 65 grade; easy power; ball jumps off bat with carry; doesn't seem to sell out to drive the ball; 30- to 35-home-run potential.

**Glove:** 55 grade; improving actions in the field; at times stiff when reaching down and moving to his left; solid instincts; decreasing foot speed into mid-to-late twenties will limit range; capable of becoming above average at hot corner.

**Arm:** 60 grade; quick release; throws can die from deep in the hole; solid-average accuracy; smart thrower; knows competition and when he needs more.

**Speed:** 45 grade; 4.37 down the line on best clocking opportunity; smart baserunner; stolen bases not a big part of game, but can swipe one from time to time.

**Makeup:** 70 grade; high baseball IQ; consistently shows ability to adjust and soak in instruction.

**OFP:** 70; perennial all-star

**Realistic Role:** 65; first-division player/occasional all-star

**Risk:** Low; achieved major leagues.

holds a back-end rotation projection and should contribute in some form to the major-league team in 2014.

**2. RHP Brandon Workman:** A former second-round pick in 2010, Workman's progress has been slow and steady, and the former Longhorns starter finally reached the major-league level in 2013 and pitched in the World Series. The future role is still a subject of debate, with some seeing a capable starter while others prefer the 25-year-old as a seventh-inning reliever, a bridge arm with the potential to give you more than just a short-burst appearance.

**3. OF Alex Hassan:** He lacks impact potential or roster sex appeal, but Hassan could offer some value to a 25-man, thanks to his mature approach at the plate and strong arm in the outfield. You can suggest he makes pitchers work, which is a nice way of saying he doesn't project to hit much against major-league pitching. But if the bat can play to average—to go along with the on-base skills—the 25-year-old could get a major-league look if injuries open the door for opportunity.

## FROM THE FIELD

### Garin Cecchini

**Player:** Garin Cecchini

**Team:** Boston Red Sox

**Filed by:** Chris Mellen

**Date(s) Seen:** June 4-6 and August 19, 2013

**Physical:** Baseball frame; can add a bit more weight; athletic; shows no affects from prior ACL injury; body to handle daily rigors of a regular.

**Hit:** 55 grade; adjusts well to path of the ball; controlled swing; average bat speed; brings a plan to the plate; will be tested against quality stuff when seen on a consistent basis—lunges at spin; hands stay inside of ball.

**Power:** 50 grade; strong base; has strength to tap into; swing not overly leveraged; needs improvement generating lift to produce more loft to drives; creates too much topspin presently; capable of growing into mid-teens or so home-run outputs.

**Glove:** 45 grade; average reads at the crack of the bat; slow lateral movements; robotic at times; fronts balls well; will make routine plays; needs more confidence; not a sure bet to stick at third.

**Arm:** 55 grade; possesses arm strength, but doesn't play up as much on field; tends to aim ball across diamond to first base; choppy footwork tends to affect throws; can play in a corner outfield spot.

**Speed:** 40 grade; Timed at 4.36-4.42 down the line digging for hits; on the slower side out of the box; smart baserunner; reads pitcher well to get good jumps.

**Makeup:** 55 grade

**OFP:** 55; solid-average regular

**Realistic Role:** 50; major-league regular

**Risk:** Low; will reach highest level; comes down to how bat will adjust to elite competition on daily basis.

---

**Player:** Garin Cecchini

**Team:** Boston Red Sox

**Filed by:** CJ Wittmann

**Date(s) Seen:** Multiple times

**Physical:** Physical, muscular frame; sturdy base.

**Hit:** 60 grade; good approach to hitting; recognizes off-speed early; good hand-eye coordination; line-drive-oriented swing; can spray the ball all over; strong, quick wrists.

**Power:** 40 grade; line-dive/contact-oriented swing; linear swing path creating minimum loft; has natural strength to still put balls over the fence.

**Glove:** 50 grade; can make plays to left and right; not silky smooth but gets job done; good instincts when reacting; not mechanically sound but could play to average.

**Arm:** 60 grade; strong arm; kept accuracy when throwing on the run.

**Speed:** 40 grade; fringe runner; 4.2ish range to first base from left side.

**Makeup:** 60 grade; from scout: "Cecchini is a hard worker who loves the game. He's the first one at the facility and last to leave."

**OFP:** 55; major-league regular

**Realistic Role:** 50; major-league regular

**Risk:** Low; Double-A experience.

## FROM THE FIELD

### Henry Owens

**Player:** Henry Owens

**Team:** Boston Red Sox

**Filed by:** Chris Mellen

**Date(s) Seen:** June 5, 2013

**Mechanics/Delivery:** 3/4 arm slot; easy, low energy expending delivery; even-paced; long-levered; frame to generate downward leverage; inconsistent using body to his advantage

**Fastball:** 60 grade; velocity: 89-93, top 93; command: below-average; movement: arm-side run in lower tier of velocity band; downward finish and arm-side run when between knees/thighs; flat when at belt or above.

**Curveball:** 55 grade; velocity: 71-75; command: average; movement; big, slow bend, with deep break; slower break allows hitters to wait back on the ball.

**Changeup:** 60 grade; velocity: 77-81; command: fringe-average; movement: arm-side fade when thrown arm side; drop and arm-side fade when thrown to the glove side; will need to improve command and ability to throw for strikes against more advanced hitters.

**Other:** Relaxed on mound; kept an even pace; 1.37-1.47 out of the stretch to home; deceptive release point out of delivery; held stuff for five innings; went deep in a lot of counts; tended to waver between overthrowing fastball and releasing early.

**Makeup:** 50 grade

**OFP:** 60; no. 3 starter

**Realistic Role:** 50; no. 4 starter

**Risk:** Moderate; reached upper levels; advanced bats can stall development.

---

**Player:** Henry Owens

**Team:** Boston Red Sox

**Filed by:** CJ Wittmann

**Date(s) Seen:** April 29, 2013

**Physical:** Tall, lanky frame; should add weight; needs to thicken lower half.

**Mechanics/Delivery:** Very easy, repeatable delivery; comes from high 3/4 arm slot, creating good downhill plane on all pitches; hides ball well; good pitchability.

**Fastball:** 55 grade; 90-94 mph; throws downhill; arm-side life; spotted well to all four quadrants.

**Curveball:** 55 grade; 72-75 mph; good shape; tight spin; diagonal diving action type; can get slurvy.

**Changeup:** 70 grade; 77-81 mph; great arm speed, plays off fastball well; good fade and tumbling action; best secondary offering; can get too soft and lose effectiveness; "Cole Hamels like pitch"—from scout.

**OFP:** 55; no. 3 starter

**Realistic Role:** 50; no. 4 starter

**Risk:** Moderate; only a few starts above High-A.

## FROM THE FIELD

# Blake Swihart

**Player:** Blake Swihart

**Team:** Boston Red Sox

**Filed by:** Chris Mellen

**Date(s) Seen:** June 4-6, 2013

**Physical:** Lean body; room to fill out in both upper and lower body; athletic build.

**Hit:** 55 grade; quick hands; loose swing; improving creating lift; ability to drive balls hard into both gaps with backspin; some present hook in swing, resulting in too much top hand and topspin.

**Power:** 50 grade; below-average present strength; line-drive hitter; can occasionally muscle up; power zone against offerings middle-to-slightly away; projects as pull-side power—not likely to hit many out the other way.

**Glove:** 55 grade; Receives ball with palm square to pitch; firm with glove hand; keeps target on plate; moves better to left than right; ball control when blocking needs work.

**Arm:** 60 grade; quick release; fluidly comes out of crouch; loose throwing mechanics; needs improvement getting throws down into runner on second base.

**Speed:** 45 grade; 4.32 down the line on best clocking opportunity; shows speed making the turn at first base and running from first to third; intelligent runner on bases; will slow due to wear and tear.

**Makeup:** 65 grade; driven to succeed and get better.

**OFP:** 60; first-division regular

**Realistic Role:** 50; major-league regular

**Risk:** Moderate; dual development of offense and defense may take its toll.

---

### Blake Swihart

**Player:** Blake Swihart

**Team:** Boston Red Sox

**Filed by:** CJ Wittmann

**Date(s) Seen:** April 29-30, 2013

**Physical:** Good build; muscular frame but not as thick as some catchers; could add weight but not a necessity.

**Hit:** 50 grade; aggressive but smart hitting style; good bat speed and approach; similar swing from both sides; line-drive-oriented swing; will use all parts of the field; has good pitch recognition and lets ball travel deep into hitting zone;

**Power:** 40 grade; swing does not have natural leverage; has strength to still show good gap pop present.

**Glove:** 60 grade; limited experience for catching; receiving skills improving; shows strong wrist and improving frame work; can get small behind plate at times; smooth transfers from glove to hand without distraction behind plate.

**Arm:** 60 grade; strong, aggressive arm; not afraid to back pick; good footwork and quick release; pop time in 1.9 range consistently.

**Speed:** 50 grade; very athletic but not extremely fast; 4.2 range to first base from right side.

**Makeup:** 80 grade; literally have never heard a bad thing.

**OFP:** 60; first-division player

**Realistic Role:** 50; major-league regular

**Risk:** Moderate; no experience above High-A.

## 1. Javier Baez  SS

**Born:** 12/1/92   **Age:** 21   **Bats:** R   **Throws:** R   **Height:** 6'0"   **Weight:** 195

| MLB ETA | Hit | Power | Run | Glove | Arm | OFP | Realistic |
|---|---|---|---|---|---|---|---|
| 2014 | 65 | 80 | – | 60 | 70 | 75 PERENNIAL ALL-STAR | 65 1ST DIV/ALL-STAR |

| YEAR | TEAM | LVL | AGE | PA | R | 2B | 3B | HR | RBI | BB | SO | SB | CS | AVG/OBP/SLG | TAv | BABIP | BRR | FRAA | WARP |
|---|---|---|---|---|---|---|---|---|---|---|---|---|---|---|---|---|---|---|---|
| 2013 | TEN | AA | 20 | 240 | 39 | 15 | 0 | 20 | 54 | 19 | 69 | 8 | 2 | .294/.346/.638 | .343 | .333 | 1.0 | SS(50): 1.5 | 3.4 |
| 2013 | DAY | A+ | 20 | 337 | 59 | 19 | 4 | 17 | 57 | 21 | 78 | 12 | 2 | .274/.338/.535 | .299 | .310 | 2.2 | SS(73): 2.9 | 3.3 |
| 2014 | CHN | MLB | 21 | 250 | 34 | 11 | 1 | 14 | 38 | 9 | 74 | 7 | 2 | .244/.281/.475 | .268 | .290 | 0.9 | SS 2 | 1.6 |
| 2015 | CHN | MLB | 22 | 585 | 77 | 23 | 3 | 32 | 89 | 25 | 172 | 13 | 3 | .234/.277/.461 | .266 | .278 | 1.4 | 3B 0 | 1.2 |

**Breakout:** 6%    **Improve:** 24%    **Collapse:** 2%    **Attrition:** 8%    **MLB:** 34%    *Comparables: Jay Bruce, Reid Brignac, Travis Snider*

**Drafted/Acquired:** 1st round, 2011 draft, Arlington Country Day School (Jacksonville FL)

**Previous Ranking:** #2 (Org), #20 (Top 101)

**What Happened in 2013:** You can't ask for more from a prospect than Baez offered at the plate in 2013, launching 75 extra-base hits in 130 games across two levels and pushing himself into the top tier of all prospects in baseball.

**Strengths:** Elite bat speed; elite hands; plus hand-eye coordination; can make hard contact to all fields; natural ability to barrel the ball; raw power is elite; game power could play to elite; arm is plus-plus; actions are easy plus in the field; baseball instincts; superstar profile.

**Weaknesses:** Can get impatient at the plate and attempt to hit bad balls out of the park; can get tied up by off-speed offerings; early weight shift/fastball cheat; will expand and chase; struggles against quality arm-side stuff; big swing-and-miss; loves to swing it; slick actions in the field but can get overly passive and let the ball play him; can make ill-advised throws; needs to learn when to eat it.

**Risk Factor/Injury History:** Moderate risk; Double-A experience; sizeable gap between present/future.

**Bret Sayre's Fantasy Take:** The upside that Baez holds from a fantasy perspective is likely second to only Byron Buxton—and the likely gets added in there because Baez may actually have more, given his potential eligibility. The tools are crazy and even though he doesn't have the strongest run tool, he's still 46-for-55 in stolen bases during his 215 minor-league games. Even if you can't put him at shortstop (which is far from a definitive outcome), you'd take 30 homers, 15+ steals and a .280 average from just about anywhere on the diamond. He's a no-doubt top-five fantasy prospect in baseball.

**The Year Ahead:** Baez might lack Buxton's overall athleticism or Bogaerts' polish, but the 21-year-old Puerto Rican might have the highest offensive ceiling of any player in the minors, a potential middle-of-the-order force capable of hitting for average and obnoxious game power. While he's no longer a true boom-or-bust prospect, Baez carries more risk than the average high-end prospect with Double-A experience because of the extreme projections on his tools and the balls-to-the-wall approach he often brings to all sides of the game. As Baez matures and adds more patience at the plate and more confidence in the field, he should develop into one of the game's elite players, a left-side infielder (short or third) with an offensive attack that some scouts project to achieve Miguel Cabrera-level heights, an extreme comparison but one that his elite bat speed and power potential could make a reality if everything clicks. He needs to shorten up against arm-side pitching and stay in his approach, and he needs to slow the game down in the field and let his hands and arm help the cause rather than hurt it, but he should continue to crush in the upper minors and force a major-league decision at some point in 2014. The Cubs could have a generational talent in Baez.

#4

BP Top 101 Prospects

## 2. Kris Bryant  3B

**Born:** 1/4/92   **Age:** 22   **Bats:** R   **Throws:** R   **Height:** 6'5"   **Weight:** 215

| MLB ETA | Hit | Power | Run | Glove | Arm | OFP | Realistic |
|---|---|---|---|---|---|---|---|
| Late 2014 | 55 | 75 | – | 50 | 65 | 70 ALL-STAR | 60 1ST DIV PLAYER |

| YEAR | TEAM | LVL | AGE | PA | R | 2B | 3B | HR | RBI | BB | SO | SB | CS | AVG/OBP/SLG | TAv | BABIP | BRR | FRAA | WARP |
|---|---|---|---|---|---|---|---|---|---|---|---|---|---|---|---|---|---|---|---|
| 2013 | BOI | A- | 21 | 77 | 13 | 8 | 1 | 4 | 16 | 8 | 17 | 0 | 0 | .354/.416/.692 | .372 | .404 | -0.2 | 3B(16): 1.5 | 1.1 |
| 2013 | CUB | Rk | 21 | 7 | 0 | 1 | 0 | 0 | 2 | 0 | 1 | 0 | 0 | .167/.143/.333 | .213 | .167 | 0.0 | 3B(2): -0.2 | -0.1 |
| 2013 | DAY | A+ | 21 | 62 | 9 | 5 | 1 | 5 | 14 | 3 | 17 | 1 | 0 | .333/.387/.719 | .362 | .400 | -0.6 | 3B(13): 1.4 | 1.0 |
| 2014 | CHN | MLB | 22 | 250 | 26 | 10 | 1 | 10 | 32 | 13 | 71 | 1 | 0 | .228/.274/.404 | .243 | .280 | -0.3 | 3B 5 | 0.7 |
| 2015 | CHN | MLB | 23 | 250 | 30 | 11 | 1 | 10 | 32 | 13 | 72 | 1 | 0 | .231/.278/.412 | .248 | .287 | -0.5 | 3B 6 | 1.4 |

**Breakout:** 0%    **Improve:** 0%    **Collapse:** 0%    **Attrition:** 0%    **MLB:** 0%    *Comparables: Alex Liddi, Matt Davidson, Josh Bell*

**Drafted/Acquired:** 1st round, 2013 draft, University of San Diego (San Diego, CA)

**Previous Ranking:** NR

**What Happened in 2013:** The best bat in the 2013 draft, Bryant slipped to the Cubs with the second overall pick in the draft, and he wasted little time proving his offensive profile was well above average.

**Strengths:** Excellent size and present strength; good athlete; elite raw power; game power could play plus-plus or better; highly leveraged swing built for over-the-fence production; some bat-to-ball ability and hit tool utility; plus arm; glove should play to average; fringe run but good athlete and coordinated for size.

**Weaknesses:** Hit tool could limit full utility of power tool; can get tied up inside by quality stuff; bat path/plane limits time in the zone; sources suggest more swing-and-miss to come against better arms; lower half actions can get stiff at third; lacks first-step quickness/ideal range.

**Risk Factor/Injury History:** Low risk; limited professional experience; mature bat.

**Bret Sayre's Fantasy Take:** Power, power, and more power. With home runs down across the league, prospects who can hit 30+ at their peak become very valuable commodities. Bryant has that potential, has a good chance at third base eligibility, and could see the majors in relatively short order. There are fewer major-league third basemen I'd prefer to Bryant than I can count on two hands, and he's my clear number one in dynasty drafts this year.

**The Year Ahead:** Bryant is ready to start his first full season at the Double-A level, and with any luck, he will be forcing the issue at the major-league level at some point in 2014. The power is enormous and is going to play at the highest level, although he might end up hitting for a lower average and swinging and missing more than some are projecting. While the 22-year-old can play passable defense at the hot corner, his athleticism and arm are a better fit for right field, a position most sources seem to agree is Bryant's long-term home. Regardless of where he plays, the bat could make him an all-star, a true 35+ home-run force in the middle of a lineup.

**#17**
BP Top 101 Prospects

## 3.    Albert Almora    CF

**Born:** 4/16/94    **Age:** 20    **Bats:** R    **Throws:** R    **Height:** 6' 2"    **Weight:** 180

| MLB ETA | Hit | Power | Run | Glove | Arm | | OFP | Realistic |
|---|---|---|---|---|---|---|---|---|
| 2015 | 65 | 60 | --- | 65 | 55 | | 65 1ST DIV/ALL STAR | 55 >AVG PLAYER |

| YEAR | TEAM | LVL | AGE | PA | R | 2B | 3B | HR | RBI | BB | SO | SB | CS | AVG/OBP/SLG | TAv | BABIP | BRR | FRAA | WARP |
|---|---|---|---|---|---|---|---|---|---|---|---|---|---|---|---|---|---|---|---|
| 2013 | KNC | A | 19 | 272 | 39 | 17 | 4 | 3 | 23 | 17 | 30 | 4 | 4 | .329/.376/.466 | .286 | .362 | -0.7 | CF(59): 9.2 | 2.7 |
| 2014 | CHN | MLB | 20 | 250 | 24 | 12 | 1 | 3 | 20 | 8 | 51 | 2 | 1 | .238/.266/.340 | .220 | .280 | -0.3 | CF 6 | 0.4 |
| 2015 | CHN | MLB | 21 | 250 | 24 | 11 | 2 | 3 | 23 | 10 | 45 | 0 | 0 | .246/.281/.350 | .231 | .287 | -0.4 | CF 6 | 0.4 |

Breakout: 0%     Improve: 0%     Collapse: 0%     Attrition: 0%     MLB: 0%          *Comparables: Cedric Hunter, Abraham Almonte, Fernando Martinez*

**Drafted/Acquired:** 1st round, 2012 draft, Mater Academy Charter School (Hialeah, FL)

**Previous Ranking:** #1 (Org), #18 (Top 101)

**What Happened in 2013:** Assorted injuries limited his full-season debut to 61 games, but the former sixth overall selection in the 2012 draft returned to play in the Arizona Fall League, where he managed to hit over .300 despite being the second youngest player in the league.

**Strengths:** High level baseball skills and instincts; natural bat-to-ball ability; can make hard contact to all fields; hit tool projects to be plus (or better); tracks well and shows advanced approach; has above-average raw power; swing more gap-to-gap at present but over-the-fence power could show up as he matures; glove in center is easy plus; quick reactions and proper reads help range; arm is solid-average to plus; cocky/confident player.

**Weaknesses:** Concerns about durability; game power is several grades away from projection; speed is fringe-average at present; range dependent on crisp reads/routes; body development could drag speed below average and limit major-league quality range.

**Risk Factor/Injury History:** Moderate risk; yet to achieve Double-A level

**Bret Sayre's Fantasy Take:** The big separator as to whether Almora will be a very good fantasy outfielder or just a guy whose real life value doesn't line up with his fantasy value will depend on his power. He could be a near .300 hitter, but with middling stolen base potential, he'll have to hit 20 homers to reach the type of fantasy heights that being ranked third on a very strong Cubs list would indicate.

**The Year Ahead:** Almora is a highly skilled all-around player, with an impact hit tool and the ability to play above-average defense in center. While he lacks graphic tools or middle-of-the-lineup power, the 20-year-old has that rare ability to make the game look easy, both in the field and at the plate. The speed is the only tool that projects to play below average at the major-league level, and even with his advanced feel for the game and instincts, his range in center will be limited by the lack of wheels; despite his quick reactions and almost preternatural feel for tracking balls, his foot speed can't recover from mistakes like most athletes at the position. Almora is going to hit at every stop, and if he can avoid the injury bug in 2014, he should be able to move quickly, reaching the Double-A level and positioning himself for a major-league opportunity in 2015.

**#25**
BP Top 101 Prospects

## 4.   Jorge Soler   RF

**Born:** 2/25/92   **Age:** 22   **Bats:** R   **Throws:** R   **Height:** 6' 4"   **Weight:** 215

| MLB ETA | Hit | Power | Run | Glove | Arm | OFP | Realistic |
|---|---|---|---|---|---|---|---|
| 2015 | 55 | 70 | – | 50 | 70 | 60<br>1ST DIV PLAYER | 50<br>ML REGULAR |

| YEAR | TEAM | LVL | AGE | PA | R | 2B | 3B | HR | RBI | BB | SO | SB | CS | AVG/OBP/SLG | TAv | BABIP | BRR | FRAA | WARP |
|---|---|---|---|---|---|---|---|---|---|---|---|---|---|---|---|---|---|---|---|
| 2013 | DAY | A+ | 21 | 237 | 38 | 13 | 1 | 8 | 35 | 21 | 38 | 5 | 1 | .281/.343/.467 | .283 | .304 | 1.8 | RF(55): -0.9 | 1.1 |
| 2014 | CHN | MLB | 22 | 250 | 27 | 11 | 1 | 7 | 29 | 14 | 52 | 4 | 1 | .240/.286/.385 | .242 | .280 | 0.3 | RF -1 | 0.0 |
| 2015 | CHN | MLB | 23 | 250 | 29 | 11 | 1 | 8 | 29 | 16 | 53 | 2 | 0 | .241/.294/.396 | .251 | .278 | -0.1 | RF -1 | 0.8 |

**Breakout:** 3%   **Improve:** 18%   **Collapse:** 2%   **Attrition:** 22%   **MLB:** 32%   *Comparables: Domonic Brown, Shane Peterson, Carlos Gonzalez*

**Drafted/Acquired:** International free agent, 2012, Cuba

**Previous Ranking:** #3 (Org), #36 (Top 101)

**What Happened in 2013:** After only 20 games at the full-season level in 2012, Soler was set to explode on the prospect world in 2013, but suspensions and a leg injury limited his playing time and offered more questions than answers.

**#45**

BP Top
101
Prospects

**Strengths:** Elite raw power; extreme strength and leverage in swing; game power could play to plus-plus; shows some hit tool quality; could play above average; arm is well above average; glove plays; runs well; looks the part.

**Weaknesses:** Struggles with adjustments at the plate; questionable pitch recognition; hit tool is likely to limit full power potential; struggles against good arm-side stuff; arm is well above average but doesn't always play as a weapon; focus has been questioned.

**Risk Factor/Injury History:** Moderate risk; yet to achieve Double-A level; questions about hit tool.

**Bret Sayre's Fantasy Take:** It only seems like the Cubs grow power prospects on trees. Soler carries more risk than any of the names ahead of him, but has the 30-homer ability to be a number two outfielder. With strong contact abilities for a potential slugger, Soler should be able to hit in the .270-.280 range—which, along with around 10 steals, makes him very appealing in dynasty leagues.

**The Year Ahead:** Soler has a prototypical right field profile, with the high-powered arm and the enormous raw power, the kind you can't truly appreciate unless you get to see him rip balls over mountains in batting practice. But the 22-year-old Cuban struggles making in-bat adjustments, and as a result, pitchers with a good plan of attack can eat his lunch. With his type of power, he can punish mistakes and make you pay for improper placement of a fastball, but his recognition skills and aggressive style open him up to sequence and spin, and the inability to make quick adjustments to his approach could spoil his ultimate potential at the plate. If he can stay on the field, Soler should rake in the minors and push himself to the majors by 2015. But the higher-level arms are going to present a problem for him, so he will need to improve his focus and plan of attack at the plate in order to maximize his talent.

## 5.   C.J. Edwards   RHP

**Born:** 9/3/91   **Age:** 22   **Bats:** R   **Throws:** R   **Height:** 6' 2"   **Weight:** 155

| MLB ETA | CT | FB | CH | CB | SL | OFP | Realistic |
|---|---|---|---|---|---|---|---|
| 2015 | – | 70 | 60 | 60 | – | 60<br>NO.3 STARTER | 50<br>LATE-INN RP (SETUP) |

| YEAR | TEAM | LVL | AGE | W | L | SV | G | GS | IP | H | HR | BB | SO | BB9 | SO9 | GB% | BABIP | WHIP | ERA | FIP | FRA | WARP |
|---|---|---|---|---|---|---|---|---|---|---|---|---|---|---|---|---|---|---|---|---|---|---|
| 2013 | HIC | A | 21 | 8 | 2 | 0 | 18 | 18 | 93.3 | 62 | 0 | 34 | 122 | 3.3 | 11.8 | 54% | .268 | 1.03 | 1.83 | 2.06 | 2.57 | 2.9 |
| 2013 | DAY | A+ | 21 | 0 | 0 | 0 | 6 | 6 | 23.0 | 14 | 1 | 7 | 33 | 2.7 | 12.9 | 43% | .260 | 0.91 | 1.96 | 1.85 | 2.37 | 0.7 |
| 2014 | CHN | MLB | 22 | 5 | 5 | 0 | 18 | 16 | 88.0 | 75 | 9 | 40 | 88 | 4.1 | 9.0 | 47% | .309 | 1.32 | 3.93 | 4.05 | 4.27 | 0.7 |
| 2015 | CHN | MLB | 23 | 9 | 8 | 0 | 32 | 28 | 200.0 | 155 | 17 | 84 | 219 | 3.8 | 9.9 | 47% | .299 | 1.20 | 3.29 | 3.31 | 3.57 | 3.2 |

**Breakout:** 0%   **Improve:** 0%   **Collapse:** 0%   **Attrition:** 0%   **MLB:** 0%   *Comparables: Christian Friedrich, Danny Duffy, Fautino De Los Santo*

**Drafted/Acquired:** 48th round, 2011 draft, Mid-Carolina HS (Prosperity, SC)

**Previous Ranking:** NR

**What Happened in 2013:** In his full-season debut, the former 48th-round pick exploded on the prospect world, finishing the season by missing 33 bats in only 23 Florida State League innings.

**#81**

BP Top
101
Prospects

**Strengths:** Loose, easy delivery; near elite release; ball just explodes out of his hand; fastball very comfortable in the 92-95 range; can work higher; very good angle and arm-side life; easy release helps secondary arsenal play up; changeup projects as plus offering; very good deception and fade; curveball is bat-missing weapon at present; above-average shape and depth; pitchability; good makeup.

**Weaknesses:** Long and slender frame; very narrow at the waist; body doesn't project to hold much strength or additional mass; fastball command is fringe; curveball can get too big and easy to track.

**Risk Factor/Injury History:** Moderate risk; yet to achieve Double-A level; questions about body/durability

**Bret Sayre's Fantasy Take:** The stats are ridiculous, but unfortunately paint an unrealistic picture of Edwards in fantasy. He certainly has the potential raw stuff to strike out nearly a batter an inning at the major-league level, but it's still more likely to be coming from the bullpen than the rotation. However, in the bullpen, he could be a dominant reliever with the potential for huge strikeout and save totals. That helps elevate his floor a bit.

**The Year Ahead:** Edwards is a very legit prospect whose statistical output creates a slightly more promising profile than the scouting reports. On paper, Edwards looks like a frontline arm, and at times, he can flash that sort of future on the mound. But when/if you watch Edwards in person, you can see that his advanced arsenal is simply too good for the level of competition he is facing, and the same curveball that is making A-Ball hitters look foolish is unlikely to encourage the same result from major-league quality bats. This isn't to take anything away from Edwards, who has one of the easiest releases in the minors, which along with the crisp velocity makes his fastball a potential well-above-average offering. The keys for Edwards will be the body and the fastball command, each of which could limit his overall effectiveness in a rotation. While he's certainly bigger than the listed weight of 155 pounds, the frame itself is very narrow and it raises concerns about potential workload and durability; frontline arms project to log 200+ innings season after season. The fastball command might end up being an even bigger hurdle, as the ability to spot the fastball will help the already solid secondary stuff play against more advanced bats, the kind that can track a big curveball out of the hand. The end result could be a mid-rotation arm, or perhaps a late-innings reliever if the durability concerns prove to be true. Regardless, Edwards is going to be a major-league quality arm with impact potential, which is a win for everybody involved in the procurement and developmental process.

## 6. Arismendy Alcantara    SS

**Born:** 10/29/91   **Age:** 22   **Bats:** B   **Throws:** R   **Height:** 5' 10"   **Weight:** 160

| MLB ETA | Hit | Power | Run | Glove | Arm | OFP | Realistic |
|---|---|---|---|---|---|---|---|
| 2014 | 55 | 55 | 65 | 55 | 60 | 60 1ST DIV PLAYER | 50 ML REGULAR |

| YEAR | TEAM | LVL | AGE | PA | R | 2B | 3B | HR | RBI | BB | SO | SB | CS | AVG/OBP/SLG | TAv | BABIP | BRR | FRAA | WARP |
|---|---|---|---|---|---|---|---|---|---|---|---|---|---|---|---|---|---|---|---|
| 2013 | TEN | AA | 21 | 571 | 69 | 36 | 4 | 15 | 69 | 62 | 125 | 31 | 6 | .271/.352/.451 | .287 | .332 | 5.2 | SS(66): 4.1, 2B(64): -0.1 | 4.2 |
| 2014 | CHN | MLB | 22 | 250 | 30 | 11 | 1 | 5 | 22 | 13 | 63 | 8 | 2 | .242/.282/.371 | .236 | .300 | 0.9 | SS 0, 2B -1 | 0.4 |
| 2015 | CHN | MLB | 23 | 359 | 39 | 17 | 3 | 9 | 40 | 20 | 91 | 11 | 3 | .247/.294/.396 | .251 | .308 | 1.1 | SS 1 | 1.3 |

Breakout: 0%   Improve: 0%   Collapse: 0%   Attrition: 0%   MLB: 0%       *Comparables: Jordany Valdespin, Henry Rodriguez, Scooter Gennett*

**Drafted/Acquired:** International free agent, 2008, Dominican Republic

**Previous Ranking:** NR

**What Happened in 2013:** Slow and steady up the ladder, Alcantara arrived at the Double-A level as a 21-year-old and set career highs in games played, home runs, and stolen bases.

**Strengths:** Plus athlete with good present strength; excellent hands; creates plus bat speed and above-average power; short, clean path to the ball; makes hard contact; easy plus run; multidimensional offensive threat; plus arm; above-average glove at second; five-tool talent.

**Weaknesses:** Swing from the right side lacks the same punch; contact is softer; some swing-and-miss in his game; right-side defensive profile (glove); hit tool might only play as average.

**Risk Factor/Injury History:** Moderate risk; Double-A experience; needs refinement at the plate/in the field.

**Bret Sayre's Fantasy Take:** A five-tool middle infielder with 30-steal potential? Sign me up, please. The best part about Alcantara for fantasy is that even if the power potential doesn't come through and he's more of a 10-homer guy, he's still a potential top-10 shortstop or second baseman. That puts his realistic floor around Jose Altuve type value. It also puts his ceiling closer to Jason Kipnis. There's risk, but lots of fantasy potential here.

**The Year Ahead:** Alcantara would receive more attention in a weaker system, as the 22-year-old infielder has impact tools and could develop into a first-division talent at the major-league level. From the left side, Alcantara is an offensive threat, with bat speed and game power, but he struggles from his weaker right side, as the plane is flatter and the contact not nearly as hard. The speed is a weapon on base and in the field, and with more refinement should give him another above-average tool. A heavy dose of Triple-A secondary stuff will help the five-tool talent refine at the plate, and with any luck, Alcantara could get a major-league taste in 2014. While I'm not a big fan of comps, especially if they are forced, the industry-suggested Jose Reyes-lite fits Alcantara very well.

**#83**
BP Top 101 Prospects

## 7. Pierce Johnson    RHP

**Born:** 5/10/91   **Age:** 23   **Bats:** R   **Throws:** R   **Height:** 6' 3"   **Weight:** 170

| MLB ETA | CT | FB | CH | CB | SL | OFP | Realistic |
|---|---|---|---|---|---|---|---|
| 2015 | – | 60 | 55 | 60 | – | 60 NO.3 STARTER | 50 NO.4 STARTER |

| YEAR | TEAM | LVL | AGE | W | L | SV | G | GS | IP | H | HR | BB | SO | BB9 | SO9 | GB% | BABIP | WHIP | ERA | FIP | FRA | WARP |
|---|---|---|---|---|---|---|---|---|---|---|---|---|---|---|---|---|---|---|---|---|---|---|
| 2013 | KNC | A | 22 | 5 | 5 | 0 | 13 | 13 | 69.7 | 68 | 4 | 22 | 74 | 2.8 | 9.6 | 52% | .335 | 1.29 | 3.10 | 3.12 | 3.52 | 1.8 |
| 2013 | DAY | A+ | 22 | 6 | 1 | 0 | 10 | 8 | 48.7 | 41 | 1 | 21 | 50 | 3.9 | 9.2 | 43% | .333 | 1.27 | 2.22 | 2.99 | 4.23 | 0.6 |
| 2014 | CHN | MLB | 23 | 4 | 6 | 0 | 18 | 18 | 85.0 | 84 | 10 | 38 | 72 | 4.0 | 7.6 | 46% | .323 | 1.44 | 4.64 | 4.59 | 5.04 | 0.0 |
| 2015 | CHN | MLB | 24 | 8 | 10 | 0 | 29 | 29 | 179.7 | 177 | 19 | 74 | 156 | 3.7 | 7.8 | 46% | .327 | 1.40 | 4.42 | 4.07 | 4.81 | 0.2 |

Breakout: 0%   Improve: 0%   Collapse: 0%   Attrition: 0%   MLB: 0%       *Comparables: Matt Magill, Garrett Richards, Cesar Carrillo*

**Drafted/Acquired:** 1st round, 2012 draft, Missouri State University (Springfield, MO)

**Previous Ranking:** #7 (Org)

**What Happened in 2013:** In his full-season debut, Johnson seemed to improve with each start, pitching his way to High-A and emerging as a top-101 talent in the minors.

**Strengths:** Prototypical starter's body; long, lean, and athletic; very good arm strength; fastball is plus; low-90s velocity that routinely pops the mid-90s on the gun; breaking is easy plus and could end up even better if the command improves; low-80s hammer curve with serious snap; some feel for an average changeup that has some projection.

**Weaknesses:** Below-average command at present; can lose some zip on the fastball and work 90-mph range; changeup is clear third offering; can get deliberate in the arm; overthrows the pitch.

**Risk Factor/Injury History:** Moderate risk; yet to achieve Double-A level

**Bret Sayre's Fantasy Take:** Johnson doesn't have the gaudy numbers that Edwards has, but he has a safer future as a starting pitcher. If he continues to make strides with the change, he can settle into a 3.50 ERA or better, with enough strikeouts for even the shallowest of fantasy leagues (think 165-175 at peak).

**The Year Ahead:** Several sources prefer Johnson to Edwards in the Cubs system because of his body and breaking ball, which is one of the better offerings in the entire organization. To really step forward, the 23-year-old righty will need to refine his command, spotting his fastball early and knocking the pins down with the aforementioned curve. The ceiling isn't frontline, but much like Edwards, the developmental path and projection should provide impact, most likely in the middle of a major-league rotation. Johnson will move up to the Double-A level in 2013, and if the command and changeup continue to improve, he could position himself as a legit major-league rotation option in 2015. I really like this arm.

## 8.  Dan Vogelbach   1B

**Born:** 12/17/92  **Age:** 21  **Bats:** L  **Throws:** R  **Height:** 6'0"  **Weight:** 250

| MLB ETA | Hit | Power | Run | Glove | Arm | OFP | Realistic |
|---------|-----|-------|-----|-------|-----|-----|-----------|
| 2015 | 65 | 70 | – | – | – | 60 <br> 1ST DIV PLAYER | 50 <br> ML REGULAR |

| YEAR | TEAM | LVL | AGE | PA | R | 2B | 3B | HR | RBI | BB | SO | SB | CS | AVG/OBP/SLG | TAv | BABIP | BRR | FRAA | WARP |
|------|------|-----|-----|-----|-----|-----|-----|-----|-----|-----|-----|-----|-----|--------------|------|-------|------|------|------|
| 2013 | KNC | A | 20 | 502 | 55 | 21 | 0 | 17 | 71 | 57 | 76 | 4 | 4 | .284/.364/.450 | .288 | .305 | -5.6 | 1B(85): -0.7 | 1.4 |
| 2013 | DAY | A+ | 20 | 66 | 13 | 2 | 0 | 2 | 5 | 16 | 13 | 1 | 0 | .280/.455/.440 | .322 | .343 | 0.7 | 1B(7): -0.2 | 0.6 |
| 2014 | CHN | MLB | 21 | 250 | 26 | 10 | 0 | 9 | 31 | 21 | 60 | 0 | 0 | .230/.297/.390 | .249 | .270 | -0.5 | 1B -1 | -0.1 |
| 2015 | CHN | MLB | 22 | 250 | 32 | 11 | 0 | 9 | 32 | 24 | 53 | 0 | 0 | .252/.323/.427 | .274 | .287 | -0.7 | 1B -1 | 2.0 |

Breakout: 0%    Improve: 0%    Collapse: 0%    Attrition: 0%    MLB: 0%          *Comparables: Anthony Rizzo, Freddie Freeman, Chris Marrero*

**Drafted/Acquired:** 2nd round, 2011 draft, Bishop Verot HS (Fort Myers, FL)

**Previous Ranking:** #5 (Org)

**What Happened in 2013:** After spending the 2012 season at two short-season stops, Vogelbach moved to the full-season levels in 2013, hitting 17 bombs in the Midwest League before finishing the year in High-A.

**Strengths:** Big boy strength; big boy raw power; doesn't sell out swing for game power; generates impressive bat speed with quick, strong stroke that is short to the ball/long through it; projects to hit for both average and power; makes pitchers work and doesn't give away outs.

**Weaknesses:** Bat-only profile; body is fat; doesn't project for much defensively, even at first base; can struggle against arm-side stuff; can be his own worst enemy and hold onto on-the-field setbacks.

**Risk Factor/Injury History:** Moderate risk; yet to achieve Double-A level; bat only profile.

**Bret Sayre's Fantasy Take:** Some men were put on this planet to hit, and Vogelbach is one of those men. For fantasy purposes, we don't care that he doesn't field his position well (or potentially at all)—we only care that he hits and hits for power. Even if he is a full-time DH in short order, the upside is there for him to be a near-.300 hitter with 30+ homers annually. He's even a slightly stronger option in OBP and points leagues, where his career 139:110 strikeout-to-walk rate can shine.

**The Year Ahead:** Vogelbach is a natural hitter with near elite raw power, and because of his approach and swing, should bring a healthy chunk of the raw into game action. The downside is that Vogelbach is a big-bodied player who is already viewed as a future designated hitter, so his future home will most likely be with an American League team. I don't care that Vogelbach is fat or that he is a natural DH; I care if he can crush a baseball, and Vogelbach can absolutely crush baseballs. Talent is talent, regardless of what it looks like in a uniform, and if he continues to rake—like almost every source thinks he will—the Cubs are going to have a valuable commodity to trade when things start to get serious at the major-league level in 2015. This kid can hit and teams will covet his bat.

## 9.   Christian Villanueva   3B

**Born:** 6/19/91   **Age:** 23   **Bats:** R   **Throws:** R   **Height:** 5' 11"   **Weight:** 160

| MLB ETA | Hit | Power | Run | Glove | Arm | OFP | Realistic |
|---|---|---|---|---|---|---|---|
| 2014 | 55 | 55 | – | 70 | 60 | 55 <br> >AVG PLAYER | 50 <br> ML REGULAR |

| YEAR | TEAM | LVL | AGE | PA | R | 2B | 3B | HR | RBI | BB | SO | SB | CS | AVG/OBP/SLG | TAv | BABIP | BRR | FRAA | WARP |
|---|---|---|---|---|---|---|---|---|---|---|---|---|---|---|---|---|---|---|---|
| 2013 | TEN | AA | 22 | 542 | 60 | 41 | 2 | 19 | 72 | 34 | 117 | 5 | 7 | .261/.317/.469 | .275 | .303 | 1.8 | 3B(124): -1.1 | 2.3 |
| 2014 | CHN | MLB | 23 | 250 | 26 | 13 | 0 | 7 | 29 | 10 | 62 | 4 | 2 | .233/.275/.388 | .239 | .280 | -0.3 | 3B 1, 2B 0 | 0.2 |
| 2015 | CHN | MLB | 24 | 250 | 28 | 14 | 0 | 8 | 29 | 10 | 59 | 3 | 2 | .238/.281/.396 | .245 | .282 | -0.5 | 3B 1 | 0.4 |

Breakout: 1%   Improve: 16%   Collapse: 3%   Attrition: 10%   MLB: 25%        *Comparables: Cody Asche, Brandon Laird, Jedd Gyorko*

**Drafted/Acquired:** International free agent, Mexico, 2008 (Rangers)

**Previous Ranking:** #9 (Org)

**What Happened in 2013:** I'm not sure people realize that Villanueva had 62 extra-base hits in 133 games, while showing well-above-average defense at the hot corner.

**Strengths:** Broad-shouldered with good present strength; hands are exceptional in the field; fluid actions; excellent backhand pickup; easy plus arm; can make every play in, side, or back; fast hands at the plate; shows bat speed and some power potential; very heady player with plus makeup.

**Weaknesses:** Can get pull happy at the plate; can struggle against quality off-speed; bat profiles as average at highest level; below-average run; will have to watch the body as he ages.

**Risk Factor/Injury History:** Low risk; Double-A experience; mature skill set/plus makeup.

**Bret Sayre's Fantasy Take:** Villanueva isn't the most attractive fantasy option, but it's not really his fault. Right now the market is flooded with potential 20-homer bats at the hot corner with middling hit tools. Add in his competition for playing time as the minor-league bats rise to the surface and there's just not much need to own Villanueva in anything but deep leagues.

**The Year Ahead:** Villanueva gets overlooked in a system with Baez, Bryant, and Olt, but the glove at third is the best in the entire org—and one of the best hot corner profiles in the minors—and the bat is capable of hard contact and some over-the-fence power. While he's unlikely to hit for a high batting average, especially against quality arm-side stuff, Villanueva has fast hands and a quick bat, and he should be able to find average utility with the hit tool, which will allow his above-average raw power to play in game action. His bat isn't going to set the world ablaze and single-handedly change the fortunes of the franchise, but he could emerge as the best overall candidate to be the Cubs third baseman of the future, with the type of makeup and work ethic to get the most of his physical gifts and the best glove in the organization. Don't forget about Villanueva.

## 10.   Jeimer Candelario   3B

**Born:** 11/24/93   **Age:** 20   **Bats:** B   **Throws:** R   **Height:** 6' 1"   **Weight:** 180

| MLB ETA | Hit | Power | Run | Glove | Arm | OFP | Realistic |
|---|---|---|---|---|---|---|---|
| 2016 | 55 | 60 | – | 50 | 60 | 60 <br> 1ST DIV PLAYER | 50 <br> ML REGULAR |

| YEAR | TEAM | LVL | AGE | PA | R | 2B | 3B | HR | RBI | BB | SO | SB | CS | AVG/OBP/SLG | TAv | BABIP | BRR | FRAA | WARP |
|---|---|---|---|---|---|---|---|---|---|---|---|---|---|---|---|---|---|---|---|
| 2013 | KNC | A | 19 | 572 | 71 | 35 | 1 | 11 | 57 | 68 | 88 | 1 | 0 | .256/.346/.396 | .257 | .290 | -0.6 | 3B(121): -4.8 | 1.2 |
| 2014 | CHN | MLB | 20 | 250 | 21 | 11 | 0 | 5 | 24 | 18 | 60 | 0 | 0 | .213/.272/.322 | .218 | .260 | -0.5 | 3B -2, 1B 0 | -0.6 |
| 2015 | CHN | MLB | 21 | 250 | 28 | 13 | 0 | 6 | 27 | 17 | 53 | 1 | 0 | .237/.291/.373 | .245 | .279 | -0.7 | 3B -2, 1B 0 | 0.3 |

Breakout: 0%   Improve: 0%   Collapse: 0%   Attrition: 0%   MLB: 0%        *Comparables: Matt Dominguez, Mike Moustakas, Matt Davidson*

**Drafted/Acquired:** International free agent, 2010, Dominican Republic

**Previous Ranking:** On The Rise

**What Happened in 2013:** After a strong season in Boise in 2012, Candelario took on a full-season assignment with Kane County, playing in 130 games, racking up 128 hits and 68 walks while showing improvements in the field.

**Strengths:** Good present strength; fluid swing from both sides of the plate; shows excellent bat speed and quick path to the ball; very mature approach; tracks the ball well; has a plan at the plate; power could play above average; arm is strong; work ethic to refine with the glove.

**Weaknesses:** Body could escape him; below-average run; range will be suspect at third; glove is below average at present; power stroke is more hard contact and gap-based at present; hit tool could work against power against better pitching.

**Risk Factor/Injury History:** High risk; Low-A resume; bat-first profile.

**Bret Sayre's Fantasy Take:** It may have been a relatively underwhelming full-season debut from Candelario, but the offensive potential remains. A .275 hitter with 20 homers at the hot corner might not sound like something worth breaking the bank for, but it's essentially what Kyle Seager did this year and he just missed the top-10 third basemen. And there's upside on top of that.

**The Year Ahead:** Candy Candelario gets a lot of love from scouts, as the 20-year-old has serious pop in the bat and could develop into another impact player in a system full of impact players. The defensive profile needs a lot of refinement, and the body could make the task more difficult if he loses sight of it as he continues to mature. But with good pitch-recognition skills and a discernible plan of attack at the plate, Candelario can take advantage of opportunities and bring his physical tools into game action. Look for Candelario to continue his surge up prospect lists with a strong 2014 season, where his over-the-fence power will start to play a bigger role in his hype.

## Prospects on the Rise

**1. RHP Paul Blackburn:** A supplemental first-round pick in 2012, the athletic righty moved up to short-season Boise in 2013, making 12 starts with uneven results; the fastball has the potential to develop into a true plus-plus offering, but the command was well below average at times and the secondary arsenal was inconsistent. But several sources really liked what they saw from the 20-year-old, and a step forward in fastball command could allow the plus potential curve to miss more bats. The ceiling could go as high as a number two or three starter, and at this time next season, we should be talking about Blackburn as a no-brainer top-10 prospect in the system. Based on ceiling, he has a legit case for inclusion on this year's list.

**2. C Mark Malave:** Since signing out of Venezuela in 2011, Malave has logged time at every infield position but had yet to find a home. As we approach the 2014 season, the athletic and physically projectable 19-year-old will transition to catcher, where his raw defensive tools have a chance to make him a very interesting prospect going forward. The bat has a chance to play, as he shows bat speed and some power projection to go along with a good approach. It's going to take time, and extra patience will be required because of the dual-threat development, but Malave has a chance to be more than just a name on a short-season roster.

**3. LHP Rob Zastryzny:** A second-round pick in the 2013 draft, Zastryzny has a chance to move quickly through the minors and quickly up the rankings queue in 2014. After a long amateur workload, the 21-year-old lefty's stuff was a little soft in his professional debut, but a fresh arm should offer up a commandable fastball in the 90-91 range—spiking in the mid-90s on occasion—with a good changeup and slider combination. The profile is more a number three or four starter, but Zastryzny has the pitchability and arsenal depth to reach his potential.

## FROM THE FIELD

### Javier Baez

**Player:** Javier Baez

**Team:** Chicago Cubs

**Filed by:** Steffan Segui

**Date(s) Seen:** August 13-17 and August 29-September 2, 2013

**Physical:** Small, muscular frame. Still has some room to fill out. Should remain lean and athletic.

**Hit:** 60 grade. Gary Sheffield-esque in his approach and swing. Outer worldly hands with incredible bat speed. Has considerable bat wrap but starts early. Stands close to plate giving him issues in but has substantial plate coverage. Shaky plate discipline especially down. Will chase, especially changeups.

**Power:** 80 grade. Ball jumps off his bat to all fields. Still immature and max efforts every time but almost unrivaled power potential. Stays through the ball as well as anyone I have seen.

**Glove:** 60 grade. Only thing holding him back at shortstop is top range and footwork. Arm can make up for some of the footwork issues but range will likely push him to third base before long. Will be plus at third base.

**Arm:** 70 grade. Shows off arm every throw. Often throws from bad positions but remains fairly accurate. Trusts too much.

**Speed:** 50 grade. Uses average speed and plus instincts to be a base stealer. 10-15 steals a year. Experience will help improve footwork on defense.

**Makeup:** 50 grade. Comes from rough area in Jacksonville. Loud on the field, quiet off it.

**OFP:** 70; perennial all-star/MVP-type talent

**Realistic Role:** 65; well above average

**Risk:** Low; proved he could hit well in best pitching league in minors. No makeup concerns. No major injuries.

## FROM THE FIELD

### C.J. Edwards

**Player:** C.J. Edwards

**Team:** Chicago Cubs

**Filed by:** Chris Mellen

**Date(s) Seen:** June 9, 2013

**Mechanics/Delivery:** 3/4 arm slot; long body; long arms; easy delivery; loose thrower; fast arm.

**Fastball:** 65 grade; velocity: 89-93, top 94; command: fringe-average; movement: arm-side run in lower tier of zone; ride when elevated; potential to sit closer to current peak with added strength; velocity dropped after first inning.

**Curve:** 55 grade; velocity: 72-77; command: fringe-average; movement: overhand break; flashes deep teeth; good shape to offering in upper tier of velocity band; keeps wrist above the ball; inconsistent with grip.

**Changeup:** 50 grade; velocity: 80-85; command: below-average; movement: arm-side fade; slows arm down frequently; feels pitch in hand; flashes bat-missing action; presently raw with offering.

**Other:** Pounds strike zone with fastball; came out amped up and lost some juice by third inning; needs to control pace better; level mentality on the hill; body needs to mature to stick as a starter.

**Makeup:** 50 grade

**OFP:** 60; no. 3 starter

**Realistic Role:** 50; 7th-inning reliever

**Risk:** Moderate; yet to reach upper minors; unsure how body is going to handle rigors of professional season year in and year out.

---

**Player:** C.J. Edwards

**Team:** Chicago Cubs

**Filed by:** CJ Wittmann

**Date(s) Seen:** May 19, 2013

**Physical:** String-bean skinny; narrow frame from shoulders to waist; will be difficult to add weight and strength; skinny legs.

**Mechanics/Delivery:** Very fast arm with repeatable delivery; ball jumps out of hand; natural arm strength; lacks finish on some off-speed; tends to land on stiff front leg at times; creates good plane from 3/4 arm slot; long stride to home; very good pitchability.

**Fastball:** 60 grade; 91-95 mph; ball jumps out of hand; arm-side life with good plane; inconsistent command at present.

**Curveball:** 60 grade; 73-79 mph; 12-6 shape; great depth and bite; will add/subtract to give different looks; hammer.

**Changeup:** 55 grade; 81-86 mph; can cut it; has great deception and some with good fading action; will add/subtract.

**Makeup:** 60 grade; very nice kid who has an idea of what he needs to improve on.

**OFP:** 60; no. 3 starter

**Realistic Role:** 55; late-innings reliever

**Risk:** High; inconsistent command profile with limited experience at High-A level.

## Factors on the Farm
### Prospects likely to contribute at the major-league level in 2014

**1. 3B Mike Olt:** There is no way to sugarcoat Mike Olt's 2013 campaign. Regardless of the eye issue or the trade or anything else that might have played a role, the reality is that Olt's performance at the plate was very poor and his stock plummeted as a result. But we are a fickle and judgmental bunch, and a strong bounce-back season and Olt will once again be a darling with a bright future, Captain America. The problems at the plate are multi-faceted, with an unorthodox swing that was exposed by plus velocity or questionable balance in the setup and a trigger that was exploited by outside spin. But renewed comfort and confidence in the box could help his cause, as the 25-year-old didn't suddenly lose all the physical attributes that once made him a top prospect. Upper level pitching won't make this recovery easy, but Olt should rebound from the disappointment and emerge as a stronger player as a result. It's a crowded field and opportunities will be limited, so this tale of redemption will need a positive development out of camp.

**2. RHP Arodys Vizcaino:** Vizcaino is a prospect that has been kissed a lot; first by the Yankees, then the Braves, then Cubs, and then by Tommy John in 2012, the effects of which continue to keep the 23-year-old on the shelf. When health finally allows him to pitch in game action for the Cubs, the likely destination will be in the bullpen, where the plus-plus fastball and hard curve should allow him to excel in a late-innings role.

**3. RHP Neil Ramirez:** Acquired from the Rangers in the [now] one-sided Matt Garza exchange, Ramirez is a power arm with some injury red flags that could either stay healthy and consistent in a major-league rotation, or up the intensity of his arsenal in short bursts out of the bullpen. The latter is the more likely scenario, as Ramirez has an inconsistent mechanical profile that limits his command and causes his secondary arsenal to play down. In bursts, Ramirez's fastball has been clocked in the upper-90s, a pitch he can back up with multiple breaking ball looks and a surprisingly decent changeup with sharp action.

## 1. Erik Johnson   RHP

**Born:** 12/30/89   **Age:** 24   **Bats:** R   **Throws:** R   **Height:** 6' 3"   **Weight:** 235

| MLB ETA | CT | FB | CH | CB | SL | OFP | Realistic |
|---|---|---|---|---|---|---|---|
| Debuted in 2013 | – | 60 | 60 | 50 | 60 | 60 NO.3 STARTER | 55 NO.4 STARTER |

| YEAR | TEAM | LVL | AGE | W | L | SV | G | GS | IP | H | HR | BB | SO | BB9 | SO9 | GB% | BABIP | WHIP | ERA | FIP | FRA | WARP |
|---|---|---|---|---|---|---|---|---|---|---|---|---|---|---|---|---|---|---|---|---|---|---|
| 2013 | CHR | AAA | 23 | 4 | 1 | 0 | 10 | 10 | 57.3 | 43 | 1 | 19 | 57 | 3.0 | 8.9 | 48% | .295 | 1.08 | 1.57 | 2.59 | 3.38 | 0.9 |
| 2013 | CHA | MLB | 23 | 3 | 2 | 0 | 5 | 5 | 27.7 | 32 | 5 | 11 | 18 | 3.6 | 5.9 | 48% | .290 | 1.55 | 3.25 | 5.42 | 4.87 | 0.1 |
| 2013 | BIR | AA | 23 | 8 | 2 | 0 | 14 | 14 | 84.7 | 57 | 6 | 21 | 74 | 2.2 | 7.9 | 50% | .228 | 0.92 | 2.23 | 2.90 | 4.40 | 0.7 |
| 2014 | CHA | MLB | 24 | 7 | 8 | 0 | 22 | 22 | 122.7 | 120 | 14 | 45 | 97 | 3.3 | 7.1 | 46% | .288 | 1.34 | 4.06 | 4.49 | 4.41 | 0.9 |
| 2015 | CHA | MLB | 25 | 10 | 10 | 0 | 29 | 29 | 183.3 | 178 | 22 | 55 | 155 | 2.7 | 7.6 | 46% | .292 | 1.28 | 3.87 | 4.04 | 4.21 | 1.7 |

Breakout: 24%   Improve: 52%   Collapse: 12%   Attrition: 27%   MLB: 73%   *Comparables: Alex Cobb, Wade Davis, Jason Windsor*

**Drafted/Acquired:** 2nd round, 2011 draft, University of California, Berkeley (Berkeley, CA)

**Previous Ranking:** #4 (Org)

**What Happened in 2013:** Johnson continued to take developmental steps forward in 2013, pitching his way across three levels, including five starts in the majors.

**Strengths:** Big, strong body; delivery has refined and works well; fastball works 91-93; can touch higher; thrown with good angle; can work it east/west; slider is a good, hard breaking ball in the mid- to upper-80s; above-average offering; curveball good sight line/change of pace offering in the low-70s; changeup is average pitch; good strike-thrower.

**Weaknesses:** Lacks high-end stuff; relies on location and changing speeds; doesn't project to be a big bat-misser; more pitch to contact; changeup is fourth offering; not a big weapon.

**Risk Factor/Injury History:** Low risk; achieved major-league level

**Bret Sayre's Fantasy Take:** Johnson's time is now, but as far as top prospects across organizations go, he's one of the weakest from a fantasy perspective. In a more neutral park, his profile would be more attractive, but I wouldn't expect him to be better than a SP4 while pitching half his games at U.S. Cellular. Think an ERA around 4.00 and a league-average strikeout rate.

**The Year Ahead:** After a taste of major-league action, Johnson is ready for a rotation spot in 2014. He has good but not great stuff, and with an improved delivery, the command has taken a good step forward and he can execute a four-pitch mix. The slider might become his out-pitch weapon, but the rest of his stuff is average to solid-average, so he will need to hit his spots and keep hitters off-balance to find sustainable success. He should find his footing as a middle-of-the-rotation innings horse, with solid but not special outcomes.

**#67**
BP Top 101 Prospects

## 2. Matt Davidson   3B

**Born:** 3/26/91   **Age:** 23   **Bats:** R   **Throws:** R   **Height:** 6' 1"   **Weight:** 225

| MLB ETA | Hit | Power | Run | Glove | Arm | OFP | Realistic |
|---|---|---|---|---|---|---|---|
| Debuted in 2013 | – | 60 | – | – | 55 | 50 ML REGULAR | 50 2ND DIV PLAYER |

| YEAR | TEAM | LVL | AGE | PA | R | 2B | 3B | HR | RBI | BB | SO | SB | CS | AVG/OBP/SLG | TAv | BABIP | BRR | FRAA | WARP |
|---|---|---|---|---|---|---|---|---|---|---|---|---|---|---|---|---|---|---|---|
| 2013 | RNO | AAA | 22 | 500 | 55 | 32 | 3 | 17 | 74 | 46 | 134 | 1 | 0 | .280/.350/.481 | 0.264 | 0.359 | -2.6 | 3B(108): -0.7 | 1.5 |
| 2013 | ARI | MLB | 22 | 87 | 8 | 6 | 0 | 3 | 12 | 10 | 24 | 0 | 1 | .237/.333/.434 | 0.258 | 0.306 | -0.8 | 3B(20): -2.0 | -0.2 |
| 2014 | CHA | MLB | 23 | 250 | 26 | 11 | 0 | 9 | 31 | 19 | 69 | 0 | 0 | .231/.297/.396 | 0.252 | 0.29 | -0.6 | 3B -2, 1B 0 | 0.1 |
| 2015 | CHA | MLB | 24 | 388 | 47 | 18 | 0 | 14 | 47 | 31 | 109 | 0 | 0 | .227/.297/.394 | 0.252 | 0.286 | -1.1 | 3B -3 | 0.6 |

Breakout: 1%   Improve: 16%   Collapse: 3%   Attrition: 11%   MLB: 41%   *Comparables: Josh Bell, Alex Liddi, Alex Gordon*

**Drafted/Acquired:** 1st round, 2009 draft, Yucaipa High School (Yucaipa, CA)

**Previous Ranking:** #4 (Org; D-Backs)

**What Happened in 2013:** The 23-year-old hit his way to the majors, and an offseason trade to the White Sox will give him the opportunity to step into a major-league lineup and prove he belongs.

**Strengths:** Plus power potential; can drive the ball out to all fields; leveraged swing with power characteristics (loft/back spin); brings a plan to the plate; glove is playable; arm is solid-average to plus; can make the throws; shows athleticism coming in on balls.

**Weaknesses:** Good approach but has swing-and-miss; bat doesn't stay in the zone long; exaggerated plane built for bombs; hit tool might play fringe-average; lacks a plus glove at third; below-average run; bat has to play to have value.

**#93**
BP Top 101 Prospects

**Risk Factor/Injury History:** Low risk; already achieved major-league level.

**Bret Sayre's Fantasy Take:** The trade that sent Davidson to the White Sox helped his fantasy value most by ridding him of his roadblocks to playing time. In U.S. Celluar, Davidson should be able to hit 25 homers, although he's unlikely to help in batting average (in fact, you should probably expect him to hurt you there). However, with third base very shallow these days, he's a strong value—especially in deeper and OBP leagues.

**The Year Ahead:** Davidson can show legit power, and if he can continue to work counts and put himself in friendly hitting positions, he could tap into that raw power and end up a 20+ home-run type at the major-league level. He will likely sacrifice average to find that game power, and despite being able to stick at third, he's not a flashy defender with much upside in the field, putting more pressure on the power to carry the load.

---

## 3.  Tim Anderson  SS

**Born:** 6/23/93  **Age:** 21  **Bats:** R  **Throws:** R  **Height:** 6' 1"  **Weight:** 180

| MLB ETA | Hit | Power | Run | Glove | Arm | OFP | Realistic |
|---|---|---|---|---|---|---|---|
| 2016 | 60 | 70 | 70 | – | 55 | 65<br>1ST DIV/ALL-STAR | 45<br><AVG ML PLAYER |

| YEAR | TEAM | LVL | AGE | PA | R | 2B | 3B | HR | RBI | BB | SO | SB | CS | AVG/OBP/SLG | TAv | BABIP | BRR | FRAA | WARP |
|---|---|---|---|---|---|---|---|---|---|---|---|---|---|---|---|---|---|---|---|
| 2013 | KAN | A | 20 | 301 | 45 | 10 | 5 | 1 | 21 | 23 | 78 | 24 | 4 | .277/.348/.363 | .272 | .384 | 6.3 | SS(63): 2.8 | 2.6 |
| 2014 | CHA | MLB | 21 | 250 | 27 | 8 | 1 | 2 | 16 | 14 | 73 | 10 | 2 | .209/.260/.283 | .203 | .290 | 1.2 | SS 2 | -0.1 |
| 2015 | CHA | MLB | 22 | 250 | 24 | 7 | 1 | 3 | 21 | 15 | 71 | 8 | 2 | .216/.272/.298 | .214 | .292 | 0.9 | SS 2 | -0.7 |

Breakout: 0%    Improve: 0%    Collapse: 0%    Attrition: 0%    MLB: 0%    *Comparables: Marcus Semien, Trevor Plouffe, Tim Beckham*

**Drafted/Acquired:** 1st round, 2013 draft, East Central Community College (Decatur, MS)

**Previous Ranking:** NR

**What Happened in 2013:** Anderson was pushed straight to the full-season level after signing, and the then-20-year-old more than held his own in a 68-game sample

**Strengths:** Impact athlete; plus-plus run; really good-looking swing; shows bat speed and power potential; raw is easy 6; arm is a 5 (maybe a little more).

**Weaknesses:** Glove needs refinement at short; arm isn't a weapon on left side; whispers of a future move to the outfield (outside organization sources); hit/power have a long way to go.

**Risk Factor/Injury History:** High risk; limited professional resume

**Bret Sayre's Fantasy Take:** If I'm targeting a single player from this organization in a dynasty format, it's Anderson. He comes with equal (if not better) upside than Hawkins, mostly due to potential eligibility, and it comes with a far better baseline of performance. Sure, there may be plenty of reasons he doesn't get there, but this could be an Ian Desmond type of package if the dream lives.

**The Year Ahead:** Anderson can show all five tools, including plus-plus run, plus raw power, and a swing that looks conducive to consistent hard contact. The glove is still unrefined at short, but several sources think he has a chance to make it work in the infield, while others see a better fit in center field, where the fast-twitch athleticism could make him a plus (or better) defender. He was pushed to start his career, but with a lot of development left in his future, the White Sox don't need to throw Anderson into the deep end quite yet. Regardless of where he starts or where he finishes, the continued development of his bat and his glove are paramount to his statistical output in his first full season.

---

## 4.  Courtney Hawkins  CF

**Born:** 11/12/93  **Age:** 20  **Bats:** R  **Throws:** R  **Height:** 6' 3"  **Weight:** 220

| MLB ETA | Hit | Power | Run | Glove | Arm | OFP | Realistic |
|---|---|---|---|---|---|---|---|
| 2016 | – | 70 | – | – | 60 | 60<br>1ST DIV PLAYER | 40<br><AVG ML PLAYER |

| YEAR | TEAM | LVL | AGE | PA | R | 2B | 3B | HR | RBI | BB | SO | SB | CS | AVG/OBP/SLG | TAv | BABIP | BRR | FRAA | WARP |
|---|---|---|---|---|---|---|---|---|---|---|---|---|---|---|---|---|---|---|---|
| 2013 | WNS | A+ | 19 | 425 | 48 | 16 | 3 | 19 | 62 | 29 | 160 | 10 | 5 | .178/.249/.384 | .216 | .236 | 1.7 | CF(100): 2.3 | -0.7 |
| 2014 | CHA | MLB | 20 | 250 | 26 | 7 | 1 | 9 | 29 | 10 | 95 | 4 | 2 | .187/.227/.344 | .208 | .260 | 0.1 | CF 0, LF 0 | -0.5 |
| 2015 | CHA | MLB | 21 | 250 | 28 | 8 | 1 | 10 | 31 | 13 | 94 | 3 | 1 | .197/.243/.372 | .225 | .270 | -0.2 | CF 0, LF 0 | -0.6 |

Breakout: 0%    Improve: 0%    Collapse: 0%    Attrition: 0%    MLB: 0%    *Comparables: Marcell Ozuna, Greg Halman, Travis Snider*

**Drafted/Acquired:** 1st round, 2012 draft, Mary Carroll HS (Corpus Christi, TX)

**Previous Ranking:** #1 (Org)

**What Happened in 2013:** Hawkins spent the entire season in the Carolina League, a small eight-team league where advance scouting can play a larger role in the exploitation of young hitters.

**Strengths:** Plus athlete; plus-plus raw power; shows impressive bat speed; good run for size; arm is plus; makeup is praised.

**Weaknesses:** Big swing-and-miss; shows bat speed but the swing [itself] can get very long; struggles with pitch recognition; chewed up by arm-side stuff; approach is ultra-aggressive; lacks up-the-middle defensive profile.

**Risk Factor/Injury History:** High risk; wide gap between present/future

**Bret Sayre's Fantasy Take:** Oh, the power. And oh, the strikeouts. A better fit for shallower dynasty leagues, Hawkins possesses great ultimate fantasy upside (think a notch shy of Nelson Cruz), but the risk of getting next to nothing out of him is very real.

**The Year Ahead:** Hawkins had a disappointing season, and after a certain point, it just started to get worse when he lost all forms of comfort and confidence at the plate. You can argue that his assignment was too aggressive or that the league was quick to adjust and exploit because of the small roster of teams, but he just never settled into a groove and it never clicked. On a positive note, Hawkins did rip 38 extra-base hits (including 19 bombs) as a 19-year-old in a pitcher-friendly league, so the season wasn't a complete bust. The pitch recognition and long swing are legit issues, but the power potential, makeup, and youth are all on Hawkins' side. His stock has slipped, but he's not off the radar and it's way too early to write him off.

---

## 5.  Chris Beck  RHP

**Born:** 9/4/90  **Age:** 23  **Bats:** R  **Throws:** R  **Height:** 6'3"  **Weight:** 210

| MLB ETA | CT | FB | CH | CB | SL | OFP | Realistic |
|---|---|---|---|---|---|---|---|
| Late 2014 | – | 60 | 50 | 50 | 50 | 50<br>NO.3-4 STARTER | 50<br>NO.5 STARTER |

| YEAR | TEAM | LVL | AGE | W | L | SV | G | GS | IP | H | HR | BB | SO | BB9 | SO9 | GB% | BABIP | WHIP | ERA | FIP | FRA | WARP |
|---|---|---|---|---|---|---|---|---|---|---|---|---|---|---|---|---|---|---|---|---|---|---|
| 2013 | WNS | A+ | 22 | 11 | 8 | 0 | 21 | 21 | 118.7 | 117 | 11 | 42 | 57 | 3.2 | 4.3 | 59% | .275 | 1.34 | 3.11 | 4.76 | 5.73 | 0.6 |
| 2013 | BIR | AA | 22 | 2 | 2 | 0 | 5 | 5 | 28.0 | 26 | 0 | 3 | 22 | 1.0 | 7.1 | 45% | .313 | 1.04 | 2.89 | 1.88 | 2.97 | 0.6 |
| 2014 | CHA | MLB | 23 | 5 | 8 | 0 | 19 | 19 | 100.7 | 121 | 15 | 43 | 44 | 3.8 | 3.9 | 51% | .299 | 1.63 | 5.58 | 5.92 | 6.07 | -1.0 |
| 2015 | CHA | MLB | 24 | 2 | 1 | 0 | 36 | 0 | 37.7 | 45 | 6 | 14 | 21 | 3.3 | 5.0 | 51% | .308 | 1.57 | 5.37 | 5.31 | 5.84 | -0.4 |

Breakout: 0%    Improve: 0%    Collapse: 0%    Attrition: 0%    MLB: 0%        *Comparables: Brandon Cumpton, Luke French, Ivan Nova*

**Drafted/Acquired:** 2nd round, 2012 draft, Georgia Southern University (Statesboro, GA)

**Previous Ranking:** #8 (Org)

**What Happened in 2013:** Making his full-season debut in the Carolina League, Beck put his four-pitch mix to work, eventually finding his way to Double-A, where everything started to come into focus for the former second-round pick.

**Strengths:** Big, strong durable frame; shows utility of a four-pitch mix; fastball is solid-average to plus; works in the low-90s with good sink; can ramp up to higher velo when he needs it; short cut-slider is solid-average; can show plus; late horizontal action and effective off fastball; can turn over a good changeup with some fade; will throw a curveball into the mix; can throw strikes and work deep into games.

**Weaknesses:** Lacks knockout stuff; more of pitch to weak contact approach; conditioning has been an issue in the past; delivery can be nonathletic; secondary stuff might be a tad weak at the major-league level.

**Risk Factor/Injury History:** Moderate risk; mature arsenal, with some mechanical inconsistencies in the delivery and small margin of error.

**Bret Sayre's Fantasy Take:** Beck also has a strong ability to keep the ball on the ground, but it won't help him be fantasy relevant in anything but deeper leagues. That said, he's an interesting name to file away in AL-only leagues for the second half of the season (should injuries strike).

**The Year Ahead:** Beck is likely to return to Double-A, where he will hope to build on a promising 2013 season and possibly pitch his way to the majors. The delivery improved last season, and with the delivery came better command and a more consistent secondary arsenal. He has a good fastball that he can manipulate to force poor contact, and his secondary arsenal is average with a chance to play a little higher. He's not a high-ceiling arm, but one that can log innings and limit damage, and if everything continues on course, he should arrive in Chicago at some point in 2014, most likely settling in to the back of the rotation.

---

## 6.  Tyler Danish  RHP

**Born:** 9/12/94  **Age:** 19  **Bats:** R  **Throws:** R  **Height:** 6'2"  **Weight:** 190

| MLB ETA | CT | FB | CH | CB | SL | OFP | Realistic |
|---|---|---|---|---|---|---|---|
| Late 2016 | – | 60 | 55 | – | 65 | 50<br>NO.3 STARTER | 50<br>LATE-INN RP (SETUP) |

| YEAR | TEAM | LVL | AGE | W | L | SV | G | GS | IP | H | HR | BB | SO | BB9 | SO9 | GB% | BABIP | WHIP | ERA | FIP | FRA | WARP |
|---|---|---|---|---|---|---|---|---|---|---|---|---|---|---|---|---|---|---|---|---|---|---|
| 2013 | KAN | A | 18 | 0 | 0 | 0 | 2 | 0 | 4.0 | 2 | 0 | 0 | 6 | 0.0 | 13.5 | 62% | .250 | 0.50 | 0.00 | 0.48 | 1.82 | 0.1 |
| 2013 | BRI | Rk | 18 | 1 | 0 | 0 | 13 | 1 | 26.0 | 15 | 1 | 5 | 22 | 1.7 | 7.6 | 74% | .209 | 0.77 | 1.38 | 2.82 | 4.40 | 0.3 |
| 2014 | CHA | MLB | 19 | 1 | 0 | 1 | 16 | 0 | 31.7 | 38 | 5 | 19 | 17 | 5.4 | 4.8 | 50% | .306 | 1.81 | 6.29 | 6.35 | 6.83 | -0.5 |
| 2015 | CHA | MLB | 20 | 1 | 0 | 1 | 17 | 0 | 34.7 | 37 | 4 | 17 | 20 | 4.4 | 5.2 | 50% | .288 | 1.56 | 5.10 | 5.15 | 5.54 | -0.2 |

Breakout: 0%    Improve: 0%    Collapse: 0%    Attrition: 0%    MLB: 0%        *Comparables: Joe Ortiz, Brett Oberholtzer, Eduardo Sanchez*

**Drafted/Acquired:** 2nd round, 2013 draft, Durant HS (Plant City, FL)

**Previous Ranking:** NR

**What Happened in 2013:** After not allowing an earned run during his senior season of high school, Danish only allowed four in his professional debut, which spanned two stops and 30 innings.

**Strengths:** Big competitor; arm works very well from lower slot; creates angle; fastball works 89-91 with big life;

slider is a plus potential offering; very difficult on right-handers; sharp tilt; changeup could be third plus offering with more refinement; shows good sink and deception; plus pitchability; rubber arm.

**Weaknesses:** Unconventional delivery with lower three-quarter slot; some question how that plays in rotation long-term or against lefties; fastball lacks plus velo; relies on movement and location; slider can saucer across the zone; changeup not there yet.

**Risk Factor/Injury History:** High risk; limited professional resume

**Bret Sayre's Fantasy Take:** While it's not an inevitability at this point, Danish should be valued as a reliever in fantasy leagues. If he does make it through the gantlet as a starter, his ability to keep the ball on the ground will mix very well with U.S. Cellular—which punishes fly-ball pitchers. Regardless, it's still not a sexy profile.

**The Year Ahead:** Danish is the type of arm that I normally discount or place in the reliever box ahead of developmental reality, but with Danish I've been convinced to support the unconventional candidate. In big spots, Danish pitches his best games, and attacks hitters like his stuff has top of the rotation grades when it doesn't. He relies on deception and movement, and when he can hit his spots, hitters don't have much of a chance. He might look like a future righty specialist, and perhaps that is his realistic role. But discount this kid at your own peril, because he wants the ball all the time and loves to take on the opposition. I absolutely love that type of a competitor. If you ever get a chance, ask an amateur scout about Danish's cojones. He wears them outside of his uniform when games matter the most.

## 7.  Marcus Semien  SS

**Born:** 9/17/90   **Age:** 23   **Bats:** R   **Throws:** R   **Height:** 6' 1"   **Weight:** 190

| MLB ETA | Hit | Power | Run | Glove | Arm | OFP | Realistic |
|---|---|---|---|---|---|---|---|
| Debuted in 2013 | – | – | 50 | 50 | 50 | 50<br>2ND DIV PLAYER | 45<br>UTILITY/PLATOON |

| YEAR | TEAM | LVL | AGE | PA | R | 2B | 3B | HR | RBI | BB | SO | SB | CS | AVG/OBP/SLG | TAv | BABIP | BRR | FRAA | WARP |
|---|---|---|---|---|---|---|---|---|---|---|---|---|---|---|---|---|---|---|---|
| 2013 | BIR | AA | 22 | 484 | 90 | 21 | 5 | 15 | 49 | 84 | 66 | 20 | 5 | .290/.420/.483 | .329 | .317 | 2.9 | SS(47): 3.3, 2B(41): -2.7 | 5.9 |
| 2013 | CHR | AAA | 22 | 142 | 20 | 11 | 1 | 4 | 17 | 14 | 24 | 4 | 0 | .264/.338/.464 | .275 | .293 | -0.9 | SS(25): -3.9, 3B(6): 0.8 | 0.5 |
| 2013 | CHA | MLB | 22 | 71 | 7 | 4 | 0 | 2 | 7 | 1 | 22 | 2 | 2 | .261/.268/.406 | .266 | .348 | -0.6 | 3B(17): 0.1, SS(3): 0.5 | 0.3 |
| 2014 | CHA | MLB | 23 | 250 | 32 | 11 | 1 | 7 | 25 | 24 | 55 | 5 | 2 | .244/.321/.394 | .263 | .290 | 0.1 | SS -1, 2B -0 | 1.0 |
| 2015 | CHA | MLB | 24 | 551 | 65 | 25 | 2 | 13 | 59 | 52 | 125 | 7 | 2 | .246/.322/.386 | .262 | .299 | -0.4 | SS -3 | 1.3 |

Breakout: 3%   Improve: 22%   Collapse: 3%   Attrition: 16%   MLB: 43%   *Comparables: Brad Miller, Josh Rodriguez, James Darnell*

**Drafted/Acquired:** 6th round, 2011 draft, University of California, Berkeley (Berkeley, CA)

**Previous Ranking:** NR

**What Happened in 2013:** Semien took a magic ride in 2013, crushing the Southern League before promotions to both Triple-A and then the majors, where the now-23-year-old infielder put his name into the mix for a major-league job in 2014.

**Strengths:** Shows good all-around baseball skills; has bat-to-ball ability; has pop in the bat; can put the ball in the gaps; crushes left-handed pitching; runs well; arm is average but can make throws from left side; glove plays around average; has fundamental ability on all sides of the ball.

**Weaknesses:** Lacks a plus tool; can make contact but hit tool likely to play fringe-average or below; can sting a baseball but not a big over-the-fence threat; struggles against arm-side pitching; arm isn't a weapon on the left side.

**Risk Factor/Injury History:** Low risk; achieved major-league level

**Bret Sayre's Fantasy Take:** If he can take advantage of his home park, Semien could turn his fringy power into a couple of 15-homer seasons—as many before him have. That combined with the potential for 15 steals leaves him on the fantasy map, just not by any means a star attraction.

**The Year Ahead:** Semien is ready for a full season of major-league exposure, and with versatility and the ability to hit left-handed pitching, he will likely find a way to carve out a role on the 25, either as a starter at third, or maybe at second, or as a quality utility option. He lacks impact tools and is unlikely to exceed expectations and develop into a first-division type, but he will provide a valuable service for a major-league team, and given the skill set, has a chance to stick around for a long time.

## 8.  Carlos Sanchez  2B

**Born:** 6/29/92   **Age:** 22   **Bats:** B   **Throws:** R   **Height:** 5' 11"   **Weight:** 195

| MLB ETA | Hit | Power | Run | Glove | Arm | OFP | Realistic |
|---|---|---|---|---|---|---|---|
| 2014 | 60 | – | – | 65 | – | 50<br>AVG ML PLAYER | 45<br>UTILITY |

| YEAR | TEAM | LVL | AGE | PA | R | 2B | 3B | HR | RBI | BB | SO | SB | CS | AVG/OBP/SLG | TAv | BABIP | BRR | FRAA | WARP |
|---|---|---|---|---|---|---|---|---|---|---|---|---|---|---|---|---|---|---|---|
| 2013 | CHR | AAA | 21 | 479 | 50 | 20 | 2 | 0 | 28 | 29 | 76 | 16 | 7 | .241/.293/.296 | .220 | .290 | -1.9 | 2B(61): -2.2, SS(52): 0.4 | -1.2 |
| 2014 | CHA | MLB | 22 | 250 | 26 | 9 | 1 | 2 | 17 | 12 | 48 | 6 | 4 | .249/.290/.319 | .228 | .300 | -0.2 | 2B -1, SS -1 | 0.0 |
| 2015 | CHA | MLB | 23 | 250 | 24 | 8 | 2 | 2 | 20 | 13 | 50 | 5 | 3 | .244/.290/.320 | .229 | .294 | -0.1 | 2B -1, SS 0 | -0.3 |

Breakout: 0%   Improve: 0%   Collapse: 0%   Attrition: 0%   MLB: 0%   *Comparables: Adrian Cardenas, DJ LeMahieu, Logan Watkins*

**Drafted/Acquired:** International free agent, 2009, Venezuela

**Previous Ranking:** #3 (Org)

**The Tools:** 6+ glove; 6 potential hit

**What Happened in 2013:** Sanchez had a down year, but he was a 21-year-old playing at the Triple-A level, not exactly a prospect behind the developmental curve.

**Strengths:** Advanced for his age; good with the bat; shows bat speed and control; from both sides; can use all fields and work against all types of stuff; it's the hands; glove is easy plus; easy actions; makeup to fail; gamer.

**Weaknesses:** Well-below-average power; arm can make throws but isn't a weapon from left side of the infield; glove-first player with some contact ability but limited high-end impact potential.

**Risk Factor/Injury History:** Low risk; development is near major-league ready

**Bret Sayre's Fantasy Take:** Even at second base, a player that has minimal power and is not a good bet to steal 20 bases just doesn't have the type of foundation to be a reasonable fantasy option—even if his hit tool is all it could be.

**The Year Ahead:** After a very long 2012 campaign that stretched year round without much of a break, Sanchez wasn't as sharp in 2013, and fatigue (along with an assignment to an advanced level) was certainly a factor in his disappointing season. But the 22-year-old is far from a finished product, and with versatility on defense, instincts for the game, and a contact bat from both sides of the plate, Sanchez is going to eventually bring something to the 25-man roster. The floor is utility, but the bat offers a little more than that, possibly even a major-league regular if everything comes together.

---

# 9. Micah Johnson 2B

**Born:** 12/18/90   **Age:** 23   **Bats:** L   **Throws:** R   **Height:** 5'11"   **Weight:** 190

| MLB ETA | Hit | Power | Run | Glove | Arm | | OFP | Realistic |
|---|---|---|---|---|---|---|---|---|
| 2015 | 50 | – | 70 | – | – | | 50 <br> 2ND DIV PLAYER | 45 <br> UTILITY/<AVG ML |

| YEAR | TEAM | LVL | AGE | PA | R | 2B | 3B | HR | RBI | BB | SO | SB | CS | AVG/OBP/SLG | TAv | BABIP | BRR | FRAA | WARP |
|---|---|---|---|---|---|---|---|---|---|---|---|---|---|---|---|---|---|---|---|
| 2013 | BIR | AA | 22 | 22 | 2 | 0 | 0 | 0 | 1 | 0 | 4 | 1 | 0 | .238/.227/.238 | .175 | .278 | 0.3 | 2B(5): 0.1 | -0.1 |
| 2013 | WNS | A+ | 22 | 228 | 28 | 7 | 4 | 1 | 15 | 10 | 27 | 22 | 7 | .275/.309/.360 | .234 | .310 | -1.0 | 2B(47): 6.6 | 0.4 |
| 2013 | KAN | A | 22 | 351 | 76 | 17 | 11 | 6 | 42 | 40 | 67 | 61 | 19 | .342/.422/.530 | .357 | .422 | 5.5 | 2B(72): 8.2 | 6.0 |
| 2014 | CHA | MLB | 23 | 250 | 33 | 8 | 2 | 3 | 17 | 15 | 58 | 18 | 6 | .234/.282/.331 | .226 | .290 | 1.7 | 2B 5 | 0.7 |
| 2015 | CHA | MLB | 24 | 250 | 24 | 7 | 2 | 3 | 21 | 15 | 55 | 15 | 5 | .224/.271/.313 | .217 | .274 | 1.7 | 2B 6 | -0.3 |

Breakout: 0%    Improve: 0%    Collapse: 0%    Attrition: 0%    MLB: 0%      *Comparables: Josh Barfield, Eric Young, Luke Hughes*

**Drafted/Acquired:** 9th round, 2012 draft, Indiana University-Bloomington (Bloomington, IN)

**Previous Ranking:** NR

**What Happened in 2013:** Johnson set the Sally League on fire to start the season, but some of the weaknesses in his game were exposed as he was promoted up the professional ladder.

**Strengths:** Plus-plus run; high-end athlete; has a good swing; can put the barrel on the ball; shows an approach at the plate; becomes a weapon when he reaches base.

**Weaknesses:** Real questions about defensive profile at second; glove is below average; arm is strong enough but not a real weapon; bat lacks plus potential; well-below-average power; plus-plus athlete but doesn't show a lot of baseball instincts.

**Risk Factor/Injury History:** Moderate risk; yet to pass extended Double-A test; elbow surgery on resume (amateur).

**Bret Sayre's Fantasy Take:** If a player steals 80 bases, I will pay attention. That's a simple fact. Jose Altuve led all second basemen with 35 steals this past season, so if Johnson could hit enough to steal 40 bases, he's almost certainly going to be a top-10 fantasy option—anything else would be gravy.

**The Year Ahead:** After his explosive Low-A production, the questions started to roll in about Johnson, and some of the stat-based projections started to paint him as a future impact first-division type in the making. The reality is that Johnson is a very fast individual that can swing a decent bat and can bring his legs into the offensive equation, and that will eventually take him to the major-league level and possibly keep him there in a starting capacity. But the defensive profile is more athletic than skilled, and the offensive skill set—while potentially catalytic—lacks a plus punch. He's going to struggle to hit against better pitching, and without another step forward with the stick, it's hard to see a major-league regular emerging from that profile.

# 10. Trayce Thompson   OF

**Born:** 3/15/91   **Age:** 23   **Bats:** R   **Throws:** R   **Height:** 6'3"   **Weight:** 215

| MLB ETA | Hit | Power | Run | Glove | Arm | OFP | Realistic |
|---|---|---|---|---|---|---|---|
| **2015** | – | **65** | – | **55** | **60** | **50**<br>AVG ML PLAYER | **45**<br>BENCH OF |

| YEAR | TEAM | LVL | AGE | PA | R | 2B | 3B | HR | RBI | BB | SO | SB | CS | AVG/OBP/SLG | TAv | BABIP | BRR | FRAA | WARP |
|---|---|---|---|---|---|---|---|---|---|---|---|---|---|---|---|---|---|---|---|
| 2013 | BIR | AA | 22 | 590 | 78 | 23 | 5 | 15 | 73 | 60 | 139 | 25 | 8 | .229/.321/.383 | .274 | .280 | 3.8 | CF(67): -10.1, RF(62): 2.0 | 2.0 |
| 2014 | CHA | MLB | 23 | 250 | 28 | 9 | 1 | 9 | 29 | 18 | 78 | 5 | 1 | .209/.274/.369 | .236 | .270 | 0.4 | CF -1, RF 0 | 0.0 |
| 2015 | CHA | MLB | 24 | 250 | 27 | 9 | 1 | 7 | 27 | 17 | 79 | 4 | 1 | .216/.277/.360 | .233 | .289 | 0.2 | CF -2, RF 0 | -0.3 |

Breakout: 0%   Improve: 0%   Collapse: 0%   Attrition: 0%   MLB: 0%   *Comparables: Kirk Nieuwenhuis, Corey Brown, Michael Choice*

**Drafted/Acquired:** 2nd round, 2009 draft, Santa Margarita Catholic HS (Rancho Santa Margarita, CA)

**Previous Ranking:** #2 (Org)

**What Happened in 2013:** Thompson played a full season in the Southern League, and after a productive and promising May and June, the then-22-year-old outfielder came crashing back down to earth, finishing the season with an anemic .229.

**Strengths:** Plus athlete, with excellent size and strength; runs well; raw power is easy plus; can launch balls for distance; arm is strong and a weapon in center; glove is at least solid-average.

**Weaknesses:** Hit tool is well below average; swing is long and difficult to control; limited time in the zone; plus power unlikely to play; reads/routes in center aren't always crisp; more tools than usable skills.

**Risk Factor/Injury History:** Moderate risk; still lacks refinement at the plate; failed Double-A test.

**Bret Sayre's Fantasy Take:** The career minor-league home run and stolen base numbers hint at a good amount of fantasy upside with Thompson, but his deficiencies are so large at the plate that he's better off left as someone else's dream (and likely waste of a roster spot).

**The Year Ahead:** Thompson is a frustrating prospect because he has the raw physical qualities of an impact level player but lacks the feel and utility to bring it to the field. The hit tool isn't very good, and unless he completely restructures the swing or taps into certain neurological reactions at an advanced stage of development, it's unlikely that he will ever hit. This limits his future role, but doesn't crush his potential to reach and contribute at the major-league level. He has defensive chops and the big raw power, so it's easy to see a bench bat if the hit tool can offer a little cooperation. If everything comes together, he's a major-league regular, but that dream drifts further away from reality with each passing season.

## Notable Omission—Jose Abreu

It's hard for me to justify ranking a prospect who will bypass the traditional developmental process and start his professional career on the 25-man roster. Were Abreu eligible (by the aforementioned standard), he would rank number one on this list based on his huge raw power. The value is tied to his bat, and sources are mixed on power utility he will be able to bring into game action against major-league pitching; the power is very strength based and some question the bat speed and ability to keep his hands inside the ball when worked inside. I was able to talk to one Latin American scout who absolutely loved what Abreu brings to the table, both in terms of hit and power, suggesting a .275+ hitter with 30+ home run potential. That's a monster player, regardless of the defensive limitations.

## Prospects on the Rise

**1. OF Micker Zapata:** In January, I wrote that Micker Zapata was one of my favorite prospects at the MLB Dominican Showcase, mostly because of his swing and strong arm. He's a very long ways off, but the power potential makes him a prospect that could jump into the top 10 in this system with a strong stateside showing in 2014.

**2. OF Jacob May:** A third-round pick in 2013, May was a strong candidate for inclusion in the top 10, as scouts seem to really like this kid. Perhaps the bloodlines play a role in the affection (May is the grandson of Lee May and son of Lee May Jr.), but his up-the-middle profile with a strong bat drives the positive reports.

**3. LHP Chris Freudenberg:** An eighth-round pick in 2013, Freudenberg is an under-the-radar player who just might surprise people in 2014. Injuries and inconsistencies limited his rise as an amateur, and his debut in the Appalachian League was rather insignificant, but the 6'3" lefty showed off his impressive stuff during instructs, including a plus curveball and a low-90s fastball.

## FROM THE FIELD

### Erik Johnson

**Player:** Erik Johnson

**Team:** Chicago White Sox

**Filed by:** Steffan Segui

**Date(s) Seen:** April 17 and May 3, 2013

**Physical:** Big fluffy build. Weight could be issue going forward. Looks similar to Josh Beckett with more rotational mechanics.

**Mechanics/Delivery:** Quick pace. A lot of moving parts for a big guy. Throws across body and gets on side of the ball occasionally. Delivers over high front side. Good deception. Mechanics get better as game progresses. Not as repeatable from windup.

**Fastball:** 60 grade. Good life, especially coming back over corner to right-handed hitters. Often misses arm-side away vs. left-handed hitters and it flattens out. Maintains velocity.

**Slider/Cutter:** 70 grade. Throws both very effectively. Very tight spin. Slider disappears back foot to left-handed hitters and can throw for strikes. Cutter misses right-handed hitters' barrels. Out pitch.

**Curveball:** 50 grade. Compliment. Change-of-pace pitch with alright depth when he stays on top of it.

**Changeup:** 55 grade. Increased use in 2013. Better feel with good fade.

**Makeup:** 60 grade. Moved very fast, not making more than 14 starts at any level. Made it to MLB two years after being drafted. Went to Cal.

**OFP:** 60; no. 2 starter

**Realistic Role:** 55; no. 3/4 starter

**Risk:** Very low. Five MLB starts with success. Mechanical issues much improved from 2012.

## Factors on the Farm
### Prospects likely to contribute at the major-league level in 2014

**1. RHP Daniel Webb:** Webb was my final cut from the top-10 list, and that has more to do with my preference for ceiling rather than safety. Webb is a very good relief prospect, with a lively mid-90s fastball and slider, and as his major-league sample showed, he can miss bats with both offerings. I think he ends up a seventh-inning type right now, and if the breaking ball tightens up he could pitch in higher leverage situations.

**2. RHP Chris Bassitt:** A tall pitcher with good sinker and multiple breaking ball looks, Bassitt could eventually find a home in either the back of the rotation or the bullpen. The command is below average, but he can miss barrels, and when he does find them, hitters struggle to square him up.

**3. LHP Scott Snodgress:** From the left side, Snodgress shows a plus fastball and tumbling curve, but he struggles to control his body in the delivery, and the command is well below average as a result. The fastball is strong enough for the bullpen if he fails to develop into a quality starter, but even then he will need to find more consistency in his release points and refine his command and secondary stuff before that is a realistic option. But being 6'6'' and left-handed buys you a lot of development patience, and it's too early to write Snodgress off either way.

# CINCINNATI REDS

## 1. Robert Stephenson   RHP

**Born:** 2/24/93   **Age:** 21   **Bats:** R   **Throws:** R   **Height:** 6'3"   **Weight:** 195

| MLB ETA | CT | FB | CH | CB | SL | OFP | Realistic |
|---|---|---|---|---|---|---|---|
| 2014 | – | 75 | 60 | 70 | -- | 70<br>NO.2 STARTER | 60<br>NO.3 STARTER |

| YEAR | TEAM | LVL | AGE | W | L | SV | G | GS | IP | H | HR | BB | SO | BB9 | SO9 | GB% | BABIP | WHIP | ERA | FIP | FRA | WARP |
|---|---|---|---|---|---|---|---|---|---|---|---|---|---|---|---|---|---|---|---|---|---|---|
| 2013 | BAK | A+ | 20 | 2 | 2 | 0 | 4 | 4 | 20.7 | 19 | 3 | 2 | 22 | 0.9 | 9.6 | 39% | .286 | 1.02 | 3.05 | 3.82 | 3.97 | 0.5 |
| 2013 | DYT | A | 20 | 5 | 3 | 0 | 14 | 14 | 77.0 | 56 | 5 | 20 | 96 | 2.3 | 11.2 | 51% | .279 | 0.99 | 2.57 | 2.59 | 4.12 | 1.4 |
| 2013 | PEN | AA | 20 | 0 | 2 | 0 | 4 | 4 | 16.7 | 17 | 2 | 13 | 18 | 7.0 | 9.7 | 34% | .357 | 1.80 | 4.86 | 4.65 | 4.20 | 0.1 |
| 2014 | CIN | MLB | 21 | 5 | 6 | 0 | 18 | 18 | 89.3 | 84 | 12 | 39 | 83 | 3.9 | 8.4 | 44% | .311 | 1.38 | 4.51 | 4.57 | 4.90 | 0.1 |
| 2015 | CIN | MLB | 22 | 9 | 10 | 0 | 31 | 31 | 200.7 | 179 | 26 | 80 | 183 | 3.6 | 8.2 | 44% | .297 | 1.29 | 4.10 | 4.23 | 4.45 | 0.8 |

**Breakout:** 0%   **Improve:** 0%   **Collapse:** 0%   **Attrition:** 0%   **MLB:** 0%     *Comparables: Randall Delgado, Danny Duffy, Jarrod Parker*

**Drafted/Acquired:** 1st round, 2011 draft, Alhambra HS (Martinez, CA)

**Previous Ranking:** #2 (Org), #78 (Top 101)

**What Happened in 2013:** The then-20-year-old pitched across three professional levels, finishing the year in Double-A, missing more than a bat an inning and holding hitters near the Mendoza line.

**Strengths:** Easy plus athlete; fluid delivery; creates sharp angle to the plate and excellent extension; fastball is plus-plus offering; routinely works in the mid-90s; touches upper-90s in most outings; curveball flashes well-above-average potential; thrown with velocity and hard vertical snap; true wipeout offering; shows feel for a changeup; good control for power arm; ultra-competitive.

**Weaknesses:** Can lose plane because of the delivery; pitches can flatten out; tendency to work up in the zone; changeup is fringe at present; flashes plus but overthrows the pitch; too firm in the upper-80s with a more deliberate release; more control than command at present.

**Risk Factor/Injury History:** Moderate risk; limited Double-A experience.

**Bret Sayre's Fantasy Take:** There's no doubt that the fantasy upside is huge for this fireballer. Stephenson has the raw stuff to strike out a batter per inning and log a lot of them—the question is where his ratios will fall. His realistic ceiling, especially pitching at Great American Ball Park, is that he's around a 3.40 ERA and 1.20 WHIP, which gives him top-20 starter potential.

**The Year Ahead:** Stephenson is one of the most electric arms in the minors, a true frontline type with two 70 (or better) pitches and the makings of a quality changeup. He's still turning his control into command, but for a power arm, he shows advanced pitchability and feel for sequencing and location. This could be a special arm, one that reaches heights above his paper projection, especially if the changeup matures into a plus pitch and the fastball command refines. Stephenson will continue to miss bats at the Double-A level in 2014, and could reach the majors over the summer if he continues to take steps forward.

> **#22**
> BP Top 101 Prospects

## 2. Billy Hamilton   CF

**Born:** 9/9/90   **Age:** 23   **Bats:** B   **Throws:** R   **Height:** 6'0"   **Weight:** 160

| MLB ETA | Hit | Power | Run | Glove | Arm | OFP | Realistic |
|---|---|---|---|---|---|---|---|
| Debuted in 2013 | 55 | – | 80 | 65 | 50 | 60<br>1ST DIV PLAYER | 50<br>ML REGULAR |

| YEAR | TEAM | LVL | AGE | PA | R | 2B | 3B | HR | RBI | BB | SO | SB | CS | AVG/OBP/SLG | TAv | BABIP | BRR | FRAA | WARP |
|---|---|---|---|---|---|---|---|---|---|---|---|---|---|---|---|---|---|---|---|
| 2013 | LOU | AAA | 22 | 547 | 75 | 18 | 4 | 6 | 41 | 38 | 102 | 75 | 15 | .256/.308/.343 | .232 | .310 | 10.7 | CF(118): 18.7, SS(1): 0.0 | 3.0 |
| 2013 | CIN | MLB | 22 | 22 | 9 | 2 | 0 | 0 | 1 | 2 | 4 | 13 | 1 | .368/.429/.474 | .358 | .467 | 1.1 | CF(7): 0.5 | 0.5 |
| 2014 | CIN | MLB | 23 | 250 | 39 | 8 | 2 | 3 | 14 | 18 | 59 | 36 | 8 | .245/.300/.333 | .236 | .310 | 4.7 | SS 2, CF 4 | 1.4 |
| 2015 | CIN | MLB | 24 | 388 | 41 | 13 | 4 | 5 | 36 | 28 | 84 | 59 | 12 | .256/.312/.364 | .249 | .314 | 8.8 | CF 11 | 3.2 |

**Breakout:** 3%   **Improve:** 10%   **Collapse:** 4%   **Attrition:** 8%   **MLB:** 23%     *Comparables: Ezequiel Carrera, Peter Bourjos, Gorkys Hernandez*

**Drafted/Acquired:** 2nd round, 2009 draft, Taylorsville HS (Taylorsville, MS)

**Previous Ranking:** #1 (Org), #14 (Top 101)

**What Happened in 2013:** Hamilton continued to ride to glory on the back of his legendary game speed, but the bat played soft in a lengthy Triple-A look.

**Strengths:** Fast-twitch athlete; elite speed; elite stolen base potential; catalytic wheels help hit tool play up; can put bat to ball; has more strength than assumed; can drive the ball; showed easy plus potential after transition to center; arm plays well; range is well above average.

**Weaknesses:** Aggressive approach at the plate; struggles against quality spin; struggles to put together quality at-bats; can get power hungry and try to lift balls he shouldn't lift; game contact can play soft; would put a

> **#49**
> BP Top 101 Prospects

– 69 –

below-average future on hit tool without his speed; reads/routes need refinement; power will play well below average.

**Risk Factor/Injury History:** Low risk; achieved major-league level

**Bret Sayre's Fantasy Take:** The minor-league season wasn't full of success for Hamilton, but his time in the majors in September (with 13 steals in 13 games) hints at his future value. Hamilton has the potential for more impact in steals than any other player in baseball at any other category—prospect or otherwise. Still a top-10 fantasy prospect in baseball, he projects as around a .270 hitter with 80-100 steals, if he just takes that last step forward in the hit tool.

**The Year Ahead:** Hamilton is the fastest player I've ever seen on a baseball field, but his baseball skills can still play raw, especially at the plate; he shows bat speed and some pop, but takes himself out of counts early and doesn't drive the ball with consistency. If Hamilton can refine his approach, his speed would make him a destructive force at the front of lineup, an 80-100 stolen base threat, and a premium defender in center because of his pole-to-pole range. But Hamilton's bat is likely a better fit for down-the-lineup, and despite the elite run, the 23-year-old might fail to live up to the lofty ceiling created by his lofty speed. Regardless, Hamilton should be considered a favorite for the NL Rookie of the Year because of his prowess on the bases, despite a bat that might underachieve.

## 3. Phillip Ervin OF

**Born:** 7/17/92    **Age:** 21    **Bats:** R    **Throws:** R    **Height:** 5'11"    **Weight:** 190

| MLB ETA | Hit | Power | Run | Glove | Arm | OFP | Realistic |
|---|---|---|---|---|---|---|---|
| 2016 | 60 | 60 | 65 | 50 | 65 | 60 <br> 1ST DIV PLAYER | 50 <br> ML REGULAR |

| YEAR | TEAM | LVL | AGE | PA | R | 2B | 3B | HR | RBI | BB | SO | SB | CS | AVG/OBP/SLG | TAv | BABIP | BRR | FRAA | WARP |
|---|---|---|---|---|---|---|---|---|---|---|---|---|---|---|---|---|---|---|---|
| 2013 | BIL | Rk | 20 | 149 | 27 | 9 | 1 | 8 | 29 | 17 | 24 | 12 | 0 | .326/.416/.597 | .363 | .351 | 0.7 | RF(18): -0.7, CF(9): 0.4 | 2.0 |
| 2013 | DYT | A | 20 | 51 | 7 | 2 | 0 | 1 | 6 | 8 | 10 | 2 | 1 | .349/.451/.465 | .354 | .438 | -1.4 | CF(8): -0.1, RF(4): -0.3 | 0.5 |
| 2014 | CIN | MLB | 21 | 250 | 26 | 8 | 0 | 6 | 26 | 17 | 71 | 6 | 1 | .213/.272/.337 | .225 | .270 | 0.5 | RF -2, CF -0 | -0.5 |
| 2015 | CIN | MLB | 22 | 250 | 28 | 8 | 1 | 7 | 27 | 20 | 69 | 3 | 0 | .212/.281/.349 | .234 | .265 | 0.0 | RF -2, CF 0 | -0.4 |

Breakout: 0%    Improve: 0%    Collapse: 0%    Attrition: 0%    MLB: 0%    *Comparables: Moises Sierra, Ryan Kalish, Caleb Gindl*

**Drafted/Acquired:** 1st round, 2013 draft, Samford University (Birmingham, AL)

**Previous Ranking:** NR

**What Happened in 2013:** Selected 27th overall in the 2013 draft, Ervin exploded at the plate in his professional debut, hitting 21 extra-base hits in 46 games while walking 25 times.

**Strengths:** Easy plus athlete; good present strength; hands work very well on both sides of the ball; generates above-average bat speed; short/easy path to the ball; feel for hard contact; both hit and power could play above average; puts together good at-bats; when healthy, can show well-above-average straight-line speed; can play center field at present; five-tool talent; loud impact potential.

**Weaknesses:** Has struggled with assorted injuries; lacks much size or physical remaining projection; stocky body could push him to right field; can get fastball aggressive and look to pull everything; reads/routes need work up the middle.

**Risk Factor/Injury History:** Moderate risk; limited professional experience/yet to play in upper minors; assorted injuries on resume.

**Bret Sayre's Fantasy Take:** There's a lot to really like about Ervin's overall package from a fantasy standpoint. For his debut, he was one of the top performers in the Pioneer League—and while it's an offensive league, the stat line looked eerily similar to David Dahl's from 2012. And while he doesn't have Dahl's upside for fantasy, the potential is there for a 20/15 player, who could be even more valuable in OBP leagues.

**The Year Ahead:** Even with the impressive statistical debut, people are still underrating Ervin, a legit five-tool player with a lot of impact potential with the bat. He tracks the ball well and puts himself in good hitting conditions, and when he tees it up, his short-to-the-ball stroke and above-average strength allow him to make hard contact. It's not a stretch to see a .275+ hitter with 25 bombs, a first-division type even if he can't stay in center field. Minor injuries have derailed his rise since his amateur days, and could limit his upside if he can't stay on the field and get his repetitions at the plate and on defense. But assuming health, Ervin is going to continue to hit the baseball, and should be in the discussion for the midseason top 50 this summer.

**#63**

BP Top 101 Prospects

## 4. Yorman Rodriguez  RF

**Born:** 8/15/92  **Age:** 21  **Bats:** R  **Throws:** R  **Height:** 6' 3"  **Weight:** 195

| MLB ETA | Hit | Power | Run | Glove | Arm | OFP | Realistic |
|---------|-----|-------|-----|-------|-----|-----|-----------|
| 2015 | — | 65 | 60 | 55 | 70 | 60<br>1ST DIV PLAYER | 45<br><AVG REG/BENCH OF |

| YEAR | TEAM | LVL | AGE | PA | R | 2B | 3B | HR | RBI | BB | SO | SB | CS | AVG/OBP/SLG | TAv | BABIP | BRR | FRAA | WARP |
|------|------|-----|-----|-----|----|----|----|----|-----|----|----|----|----|-------------|-----|-------|-----|------|------|
| 2013 | BAK | A+ | 20 | 278 | 41 | 20 | 4 | 9 | 35 | 22 | 77 | 6 | 3 | .251/.319/.470 | .265 | .327 | 0.9 | CF(55): -10.5, RF(1): -0.0 | 0.0 |
| 2013 | PEN | AA | 20 | 289 | 30 | 15 | 2 | 4 | 31 | 25 | 76 | 4 | 0 | .267/.329/.385 | .261 | .359 | -0.3 | RF(66): -4.1 | 0.5 |
| 2014 | CIN | MLB | 21 | 250 | 22 | 10 | 1 | 5 | 24 | 11 | 80 | 4 | 2 | .214/.251/.331 | .213 | .300 | 0.1 | RF -3, CF -2 | -1.2 |
| 2015 | CIN | MLB | 22 | 250 | 23 | 10 | 1 | 4 | 22 | 13 | 82 | 3 | 1 | .205/.250/.313 | .209 | .291 | -0.2 | RF -3, CF -3 | -2.4 |

**Breakout:** 0%  **Improve:** 0%  **Collapse:** 0%  **Attrition:** 0%  **MLB:** 0%  *Comparables: Marcell Ozuna, Moises Sierra, Avisail Garcia*

**Drafted/Acquired:** International free agent, 2008, Venezuela

**Previous Ranking:** NR

**What Happened in 2013:** Rodriguez has the highest tool-based ceiling of any player in the system, and after a shaky 2012 campaign, the 21-year-old hit his way to Double-A and showed off his loud tools in the prospect-heavy Arizona Fall League.

**Strengths:** Excellent size and athleticism; still room for physical growth/strength; arm is plus-plus; strong and accurate; plus run; glove is solid-average or better in right field; power potential is plus; better hitter than stats have shown.

**Weaknesses:** Still raw around the edges; glove better for right field; plus runner but long strider that is more underway speed than quickness; will expand and chase spin on the outer half; hit tool likely to play average or lower; lots of swing-and-miss; over-the-fence power yet to really emerge; still carries boom/bust label.

**Risk Factor/Injury History:** High risk; achieved Double-A level as 21-year-old; hit tool questions; needs refinement

**Bret Sayre's Fantasy Take:** If it seems like Rodriguez has been around forever, that's because he has. The power and speed tools are great and exciting, but counting on him to develop anything beyond a below-average hit tool at this point is a fool's errand. Even with that said, if he's a .240 hitter with 20+ homers and 15-20 steals, that's still a plenty valuable player. Unfortunately, his floor is well below that.

**The Year Ahead:** Rodriguez has been on the prospect landscape since 2008, and with each year, he adds a little more refinement to the profile and brings more baseball skills to the field. But despite all the professional experience (over 1,500 at-bats, not counting fall/winter leagues), the 21-year-old Venezuelan is still a prospect enigma, a high-reward talent that maintains his high risk even with Double-A and AFL on his resume. His hit tool isn't great, and he's unlikely to hit for much batting average against upper-minors arms, which could end up limiting the full potential of his raw power. More than one source compared Yorman to Alex Rios, a lengthy and athletic power/speed outfielder who isn't afraid to swing the bat. That's quite the lofty outcome, but entirely possible if Rodriguez can continue to refine on all sides of the ball, especially at the plate, where his big power just needs a little help from his approach and his hit tool to find its way into game action.

## 5. Jesse Winker  LF

**Born:** 8/17/93  **Age:** 20  **Bats:** L  **Throws:** L  **Height:** 6' 2"  **Weight:** 210

| MLB ETA | Hit | Power | Run | Glove | Arm | OFP | Realistic |
|---------|-----|-------|-----|-------|-----|-----|-----------|
| 2016 | 55 | 55 | — | 55 | — | 55<br>>AVG REGULAR | 50<br>ML REGULAR |

| YEAR | TEAM | LVL | AGE | PA | R | 2B | 3B | HR | RBI | BB | SO | SB | CS | AVG/OBP/SLG | TAv | BABIP | BRR | FRAA | WARP |
|------|------|-----|-----|-----|----|----|----|----|-----|----|----|----|----|-------------|-----|-------|-----|------|------|
| 2013 | DYT | A | 19 | 486 | 73 | 18 | 5 | 16 | 76 | 63 | 75 | 6 | 1 | .281/.379/.463 | .290 | .308 | -1.6 | LF(100): -6.1, RF(1): -0.0 | 2.1 |
| 2014 | CIN | MLB | 20 | 250 | 25 | 8 | 1 | 7 | 28 | 22 | 60 | 0 | 0 | .224/.293/.361 | .239 | .270 | -0.4 | LF -2, RF -1 | -0.3 |
| 2015 | CIN | MLB | 21 | 250 | 30 | 10 | 1 | 8 | 30 | 24 | 60 | 0 | 0 | .225/.303/.390 | .255 | .266 | -0.5 | LF -2, RF -1 | 0.9 |

**Breakout:** 0%  **Improve:** 0%  **Collapse:** 0%  **Attrition:** 0%  **MLB:** 0%  *Comparables: Christian Yelich, Andrew Lambo, Matt Dominguez*

**Drafted/Acquired:** 1st round, 2012 draft, Olympia HS (Olympia, FL)

**Previous Ranking:** #7 (Org)

**What Happened in 2013:** The former supplemental first-round pick became a prospect darling in his full-season debut, showing a mature bat and a mature approach for his age/level.

**Strengths:** Good present strength; plus hittability; easy stroke; quick to the ball and good extension; projects for above-average hit and power; advanced approach at the plate; puts himself in good hitting conditions; good feel for the game.

**Weaknesses:** Average at best athlete; limited defensively; arm is fringe; run is below average; left field profile; offensive tools have to play to potential for impact; bat speed isn't crazy.

**Risk Factor/Injury History:** Moderate risk; Low-A resume; lacks high-impact tools; good present skills

**Bret Sayre's Fantasy Take:** From a fantasy perspective, Winker is essentially what Phillip Ervin could look like in a year with less speed—a little more advanced, a little less projection. The ballpark will help Winker's average power play up, but .270 with 20 homers is probably where he'll max out, unless he takes an unexpected step forward.

**The Year Ahead:** Winker gets a lot of national love, and for some, his ability to get on-base [read: walk] elevates his status beyond the realities of the scouting report. The 20-year-old is a legit prospect with baseball skills that translate to the field, but he lacks huge upside because the offensive tools are simply good but not great, and the limitations on defense put all the pressure on his bat to carry the value. He has natural bat-to-ball ability and a precocious approach, so he's likely to find success at the plate at the minor-league level, but several sources doubt the future impact of the tools at the highest level, seeing more of an average regular at his peak than a first-division talent.

## 6. Jon Moscot   RHP

**Born:** 8/15/91   **Age:** 22   **Bats:** R   **Throws:** R   **Height:** 6'4"   **Weight:** 205

| MLB ETA | CT | FB | CH | CB | SL | OFP | Realistic |
|---|---|---|---|---|---|---|---|
| 2015 | --- | 60 | 60 | – | 55 | 55 NO.3 STARTER | 50 NO.4 STARTER |

| YEAR | TEAM | LVL | AGE | W | L | SV | G | GS | IP | H | HR | BB | SO | BB9 | SO9 | GB% | BABIP | WHIP | ERA | FIP | FRA | WARP |
|---|---|---|---|---|---|---|---|---|---|---|---|---|---|---|---|---|---|---|---|---|---|---|
| 2013 | PEN | AA | 21 | 2 | 1 | 0 | 6 | 6 | 31.0 | 34 | 3 | 12 | 28 | 3.5 | 8.1 | 32% | .337 | 1.48 | 3.19 | 3.82 | 4.28 | 0.6 |
| 2013 | BAK | A+ | 21 | 2 | 14 | 0 | 22 | 22 | 115.7 | 109 | 17 | 36 | 112 | 2.8 | 8.7 | 47% | .287 | 1.25 | 4.59 | 4.83 | 5.33 | 1.2 |
| 2014 | CIN | MLB | 22 | 6 | 8 | 0 | 24 | 24 | 109.7 | 111 | 16 | 44 | 86 | 3.6 | 7.1 | 45% | .310 | 1.41 | 4.75 | 4.96 | 5.16 | -0.2 |
| 2015 | CIN | MLB | 23 | 8 | 10 | 0 | 30 | 30 | 191.0 | 191 | 26 | 69 | 157 | 3.3 | 7.4 | 45% | .314 | 1.36 | 4.42 | 4.36 | 4.80 | 0.0 |

Breakout: 0%     Improve: 0%     Collapse: 0%     Attrition: 0%     MLB: 0%     *Comparables: Alex Wood, Jarrod Parker, Anthony Swarzak*

**Drafted/Acquired:** 4th round, 2012 draft, Pepperdine University (Malibu, CA)

**Previous Ranking:** NR

**What Happened in 2013:** Moscot was hit and hit hard in Bakersfield, giving up 17 bombs in 22 starts, and finished the level with a 2-14 record, an unfortunate statistical tattoo that soured some on the promising arm.

**Strengths:** Excellent size; sharp angles; pounds lower zone with low-90s fastball; aggressive; shows quality changeup; solid-average with a chance for a little more; good arm speed and some sink; slider plays average; project to solid-average; shows pitchability and workhorse potential.

**Weaknesses:** More control than command; tendency for arm to fall behind and struggle to finish his pitches; will elevate and find barrels; fastball shows plus velocity but can play pedestrian; lacks a knockout breaking ball; modest ceiling.

**Risk Factor/Injury History:** Moderate risk; limited exposure to Double-A; breaking ball needs grade improvement.

**Bret Sayre's Fantasy Take:** The concern with right-handed starting pitchers who need to hit their projections to have an average breaking ball is that even if they get to the rotation, the strikeout numbers are likely to be on the low side. Moscot is no exception, and a realistic outcome for him might be right around Mike Leake's 2013 season.

**The Year Ahead:** Moscot took his lumps in his first full season, but has the combination of size and pitchability to find success in a major-league rotation. He's aggressive with the fastball, and when he can work down in the zone it's a very effective offering because of the low-90s velocity and plane. The changeup has a chance to play above average, but the command is fringe and the slider can play a little soft, so the ultimate upside will require refinement on those fronts. Moscot should return to Double-A in 2014, and if he takes any step forward, he could find himself fighting for a rotation spot in 2015. Nothing fancy, but a mid-rotation arm is entirely possible, especially if he can tease the stuff up a bit without sacrificing the strike-throwing ability.

## 7. Ben Lively   RHP

**Born:** 3/5/92   **Age:** 22   **Bats:** R   **Throws:** R   **Height:** 6'4"   **Weight:** 190

| MLB ETA | CT | FB | CH | CB | SL | OFP | Realistic |
|---|---|---|---|---|---|---|---|
| 2016 | – | 60 | 55 | 50 | 60 | 55 NO.3 STARTER | 50 LATE INN RP (SETUP) |

| YEAR | TEAM | LVL | AGE | W | L | SV | G | GS | IP | H | HR | BB | SO | BB9 | SO9 | GB% | BABIP | WHIP | ERA | FIP | FRA | WARP |
|---|---|---|---|---|---|---|---|---|---|---|---|---|---|---|---|---|---|---|---|---|---|---|
| 2013 | DYT | A | 21 | 0 | 1 | 0 | 1 | 1 | 4.0 | 2 | 0 | 1 | 7 | 2.2 | 15.8 | 62% | .250 | 0.75 | 2.25 | 0.59 | 1.92 | 0.2 |
| 2013 | BIL | Rk | 21 | 0 | 3 | 0 | 12 | 12 | 37.0 | 21 | 0 | 12 | 49 | 2.9 | 11.9 | 48% | .250 | 0.89 | 0.73 | 2.49 | 2.89 | 1.4 |
| 2014 | CIN | MLB | 22 | 2 | 3 | 0 | 9 | 9 | 34.7 | 35 | 5 | 19 | 30 | 4.9 | 7.8 | 45% | .319 | 1.55 | 5.15 | 5.27 | 5.60 | -0.2 |
| 2015 | CIN | MLB | 23 | 5 | 9 | 0 | 28 | 28 | 172.7 | 170 | 22 | 106 | 155 | 5.5 | 8.1 | 45% | .320 | 1.60 | 5.37 | 4.97 | 5.84 | -1.8 |

Breakout: 0%     Improve: 0%     Collapse: 0%     Attrition: 0%     MLB: 0%     *Comparables: Tony Cingrani, Alex Colome, Duane Below*

**Drafted/Acquired:** 4th round, 2013 draft, University of Central Florida (Orlando, FL)

**Previous Ranking:** NR

**What Happened in 2013:** A fourth-round pick in 2013, Lively looked sharp in his debut, making 13 starts across two levels and missing 56 bats in 41 innings.

**Strengths:** Excellent size; above-average arm strength; aggressive with fastball; works in plus velocity range; touches mid-90s in bursts; slider can play sharp, with velocity and some tilt; has pitchability and can show playable curveball and change.

**Weaknesses:** Concerns about command profile/projection because of delivery; effort and length of action; secondary arsenal is inconsistent; slider flashes but can get slurvy; changeup overthrown and too firm.

**Risk Factor/Injury History:** Moderate risk; limited professional record; potential to move fast.

**Bret Sayre's Fantasy Take:** Lively has the slider that projects to miss bats, and that will go a long way toward helping him achieve fantasy-relevant strikeout levels in the majors. The rest of the arsenal will determine whether he ends up being ownable in shallow leagues. He could be a nice deep-league add now, someone to deal if he puts up strong full-season numbers, and someone to consider at the end of dynasty drafts.

**The Year Ahead:** Sources seemed mixed on Lively, with some seeing a future mid-rotation starter with at least two above-average offerings and the pitchability to pound the zone, while others aren't fans of the delivery or the arm action and see more of a max-effort two-pitch type in the back of a bullpen. Lively has a live arm and excellent size, so he should be given all opportunities to start, and if the delivery concerns prove false, he could really move up the lists next season with a strong showing in full-season ball.

## 8. Michael Lorenzen RHP

**Born:** 1/4/92 **Age:** 22 **Bats:** R **Throws:** R **Height:** 6'3" **Weight:** 195

| MLB ETA | CT | FB | CH | CB | SL | OFP | Realistic |
|---|---|---|---|---|---|---|---|
| 2015 | – | 70 | – | – | 60 | 60<br>NO.2-3 STARTER | 50<br>LATE-INN RP (SETUP) |

| YEAR | TEAM | LVL | AGE | W | L | SV | G | GS | IP | H | HR | BB | SO | BB9 | SO9 | GB% | BABIP | WHIP | ERA | FIP | FRA | WARP |
|---|---|---|---|---|---|---|---|---|---|---|---|---|---|---|---|---|---|---|---|---|---|---|
| 2013 | CIN | Rk | 21 | 0 | 0 | 0 | 1 | 1 | 1.0 | 1 | 0 | 0 | 1 | 0.0 | 9.0 | 100% | .250 | 1.00 | 0.00 | 2.00 | 3.17 | 0.0 |
| 2013 | DYT | A | 21 | 1 | 0 | 2 | 9 | 0 | 8.3 | 7 | 0 | 2 | 7 | 2.2 | 7.6 | 57% | .304 | 1.08 | 0.00 | 2.38 | 3.24 | 0.2 |
| 2013 | BAK | A+ | 21 | 0 | 1 | 2 | 5 | 0 | 5.7 | 6 | 1 | 5 | 6 | 7.9 | 9.5 | 50% | .333 | 1.94 | 6.35 | 8.18 | 9.47 | -0.2 |
| 2013 | PEN | AA | 21 | 0 | 0 | 0 | 7 | 0 | 6.0 | 6 | 1 | 6 | 5 | 9.0 | 7.5 | 47% | .312 | 2.00 | 4.50 | 6.41 | 7.97 | -0.3 |
| 2014 | CIN | MLB | 22 | 2 | 1 | 1 | 37 | 0 | 35.0 | 36 | 5 | 17 | 25 | 4.4 | 6.4 | 46% | .313 | 1.53 | 5.23 | 5.37 | 5.68 | -0.4 |
| 2015 | CIN | MLB | 23 | 3 | 1 | 2 | 53 | 0 | 50.7 | 49 | 6 | 22 | 40 | 3.9 | 7.1 | 46% | .310 | 1.42 | 4.57 | 4.42 | 4.97 | 0.0 |

Breakout: 0%    Improve: 0%    Collapse: 0%    Attrition: 0%    MLB: 0%    *Comparables: Jose Ortega, Rich Thompson, Emiliano Fruto*

**Drafted/Acquired:** 1st round, 2013 draft, California State University Fullerton (Fullerton, CA)

**Previous Ranking:** NR

**What Happened in 2013:** Strange year for a strange player, a dual-threat player in college that was popped in the first round and ended up pitching at four professional levels and the Arizona Fall League.

**Strengths:** Well-above-average athlete; fast-twitch; long and lean; arm strength is huge; fastball can work mid-upper-90s at times; some arm-side life; shows long slider that can flash plus; developmental versatility.

**Weaknesses:** Has yet to focus on pitching; raw on the mound; fastball command is below average; slider is more of a slurve; changeup is well below average at present; not many sources think starting is a real outcome; more unknowns than knowns.

**Risk Factor/Injury History:** Moderate risk; limited focus on pitching

**Bret Sayre's Fantasy Take:** A true flier, there's so much risk with his transition to starter and if he ends up in the bullpen (as is most likely) he's going to have to close to matter in fantasy leagues. He's worth keeping an eye on, but not someone who should take up one of your roster spots right now.

**The Year Ahead:** In his amateur days, Michael Lorenzen received a lot of prospect love, both as a center fielder and as a late-innings arm, and one team told me they considered drafting him and putting him straight in the major-league bullpen because of the power of his fastball. The Reds intend to try Lorenzen as a starter, a developmental track that will likely fail because of his inexperience on the mound, but an angle worth exploring because of the high upside of the outcome. It will be interesting to see how the 22-year-old will respond to a full focus on pitching, which will make him one of the more interesting prospect projects in the minor leagues in 2014. The likely outcome is a major-league reliever, but the unknowns in his profile leave open the magic of a grand what-if, and that alone should intrigue all prospect hounds in the coming years. I have no idea how this will turn out.

## 9. Ismael Guillon LHP

**Born:** 2/13/92 **Age:** 22 **Bats:** L **Throws:** L **Height:** 6'2" **Weight:** 210

| MLB ETA | CT | FB | CH | CB | SL | OFP | Realistic |
|---|---|---|---|---|---|---|---|
| 2016 | ---- | 60 | 70 | 55 | ---- | 65<br>NO.2 STARTER | 45<br>MIDDLE RELIEF |

| YEAR | TEAM | LVL | AGE | W | L | SV | G | GS | IP | H | HR | BB | SO | BB9 | SO9 | GB% | BABIP | WHIP | ERA | FIP | FRA | WARP |
|---|---|---|---|---|---|---|---|---|---|---|---|---|---|---|---|---|---|---|---|---|---|---|
| 2013 | DYT | A | 21 | 7 | 8 | 0 | 27 | 26 | 121.3 | 95 | 14 | 95 | 134 | 7.0 | 9.9 | 29% | .275 | 1.57 | 4.75 | 5.00 | 5.47 | 1.0 |
| 2014 | CIN | MLB | 22 | 4 | 7 | 0 | 21 | 16 | 97.0 | 97 | 14 | 68 | 82 | 6.3 | 7.6 | 35% | .313 | 1.70 | 5.77 | 5.71 | 6.27 | -1.3 |
| 2015 | CIN | MLB | 23 | 4 | 6 | 0 | 22 | 16 | 122.7 | 105 | 17 | 85 | 112 | 6.2 | 8.2 | 35% | .286 | 1.55 | 4.95 | 5.24 | 5.38 | -0.7 |

Breakout: 0%    Improve: 0%    Collapse: 0%    Attrition: 0%    MLB: 0%    *Comparables: Jose Cisnero, Alex Colome, Javy Guerra*

**Drafted/Acquired:** International free agent, 2008, Venezuela

**Previous Ranking:** #6 org

**What Happened in 2013:** In his return to the Midwest League, Guillon had a nightmare first half, walking more than a batter an inning before rebounding (relatively) in the second half.

**Strengths:** Strong, physical frame; big arm strength; fastball can show plus velocity; will work anywhere from 90 to 95; can touch higher; good arm-side movement; changeup is money pitch; deceptive with big, late action; could be a well-above-average pitch; shows a curveball with some snap.

**Weaknesses:** Messy mechanics; loses delivery and release point; fastball is rarely consistent; will show pedestrian velo and then pop 97 on the next pitch; command is poor; curveball is inconsistent; below-average at present.

**Risk Factor/Injury History:** High risk; well-below-average command; Tommy John on resume.

**Bret Sayre's Fantasy Take:** Guillon has a lot of scary things from a fantasy perspective in his profile—serious control issues, an injury history, stalled developmental progress—but he also has more upside than any arm not named Robert Stephenson on this list. Expect nothing, but in a deep league, his ceiling makes him worth a flier.

**The Year Ahead:** I love this pitcher, even though the command profile would scare Max Schreck. If you want to focus on the positives in Guillon's game, you can see a plus fastball and a plus-plus changeup backed up by a playable curveball, all from the left-side. The negatives are obvious and likely to limit the Venezuelan's upside, but any step forward on the command front could allow the plus raw stuff to play and elevate his status as a result. I like to think of Guillon as the Venezuelan C.J. Wilson, a pitcher that will always struggle with the free pass but has the stuff to overcome that obstacle. I might be too high on this arm, but it's hard to turn away from a changeup that has this much potential. He's a number two/three starter if everything clicks, but that seems like an unrealistic outcome given the delivery and pitchability profile. I'll keep dreaming.

---

## 10.  Jose Ortiz  C

**Born:** 6/11/94  **Age:** 20  **Bats:** R  **Throws:** R  **Height:** 5'11"  **Weight:** 205

| MLB ETA | Hit | Power | Run | Glove | Arm | OFP | Realistic |
|---|---|---|---|---|---|---|---|
| 2017 | – | 60 | – | 55 | 65 | 55 >AVG ML PLAYER | 45 BACKUP C/<AVG ML |

| YEAR | TEAM | LVL | AGE | PA | R | 2B | 3B | HR | RBI | BB | SO | SB | CS | AVG/OBP/SLG | TAv | BABIP | BRR | FRAA | WARP |
|---|---|---|---|---|---|---|---|---|---|---|---|---|---|---|---|---|---|---|---|
| 2013 | BIL | Rk | 19 | 186 | 21 | 14 | 0 | 8 | 32 | 14 | 42 | 1 | 0 | .262/.321/.494 | .287 | .297 | -2.0 | C(41): -0.7 | 1.0 |
| 2014 | CIN | MLB | 20 | 250 | 20 | 8 | 0 | 6 | 24 | 12 | 81 | 1 | 0 | .187/.229/.294 | .192 | .250 | -0.3 | C -0 | -0.7 |
| 2015 | CIN | MLB | 21 | 250 | 28 | 9 | 0 | 9 | 29 | 13 | 69 | 1 | 0 | .215/.261/.370 | .229 | .260 | -0.6 | C 0 | -0.4 |

Breakout: 0%   Improve: 0%   Collapse: 0%   Attrition: 0%   MLB: 0%   *Comparables: Wilin Rosario, Kyle Skipworth, Max Stassi*

**Drafted/Acquired:** 17th round, 2012 draft, Juana Colon High School (Comerio, PR)

**Previous Ranking:** NR

**What Happened in 2013:** Ortiz moved up a level to short-season Billings with solid results given his age and the developmental demands on his position, hitting 22 extra-base hits while taking steps forward behind the plate.

**Strengths:** Strong, sturdy build; looks the part of a backstop; arm is very strong; can pop sub-1.9; shows some feel for glovework; projects to be above average defensively; aggressive stroke at the plate; can drive the ball; shows power potential; has game intelligence.

**Weaknesses:** Still learning the finer points of catching; footwork needs refinement; approach at the plate needs work; needs to improve at-bats; generally raw on all sides of the ball; well-below-average run; hit tool doesn't project for much impact.

**Risk Factor/Injury History:** High risk; dual-threat development; raw at present.

**Bret Sayre's Fantasy Take:** We've talked a lot about the bar of relevance for fantasy catchers a lot throughout the top-10 lists. Ortiz may be a long way from the majors, but his power potential puts him above that line. With a chance to be a catcher who can hit more than 20 homers, he's a worthy deep-league flier—especially if you play in a two-catcher format.

**The Year Ahead:** Ortiz shows potential at the plate and behind it, with an easy plus arm, a body built for backstop, and a clean, powerful stroke at the plate that is capable of driving the baseball. He needs to refine on all fronts, and it's going to be a long developmental journey, but legit catchers with pop in the bat are extremely valuable commodities and players worth keeping close tabs on. This could be the year he takes a very big step forward, or it could be 2015, but regardless of the results, any developmental progress is a positive at this point in the process.

### Prospects on the Rise

**1. OF Reydel Medina:** A Cuban outfielder with well-above-average bat speed, Medina is ready to make his professional debut in 2014, and several sources think he could explode up prospect lists. The pitch

---

### FROM THE FIELD

**Billy Hamilton**

**Player:** Billy Hamilton

**Team:** Cincinnati Reds

**Filed by:** Jeff Moore

**Date(s) Seen:** September 20-22, 2013

**Physical:** Slender and scrawny. Built for speed, not power. Realistic questions about how his body holds up to the grind of a 162-game season.

**Hit:** 50 grade, would be lower if not for his speed. Struggles with advanced pitching, but understands his game well and embraces it.

**Power:** 20 grade; Makes no attempt to drive the ball, nor should he. Any extra-base power comes as a result of his speed.

**Glove:** 50 grade in center field, but could improve with more experience. Makes up for poor routes and jumps with plus-plus speed. Has only been playing outfield for one season so could improve over time.

**Arm:** 50 grade; Has enough arm for center field.

**Speed:** 80 grade; would be higher if possible. Fastest man in baseball. Good baserunner as well, with aggressive instincts. Has refined base-stealing ability over minor-league career and doesn't just rely on speed. Steals third base at will.

**Makeup:** 60 grade; No off-field discretions. From small town so could have issues with big-league spotlight but has handled increased fame and attention well.

**OFP:** 60; first-division player

**Realistic Role:** 50; second-division player

**Risk:** Low; will be in majors in 2014.

recognition needs work, and it will be interesting to see how the bat plays against quality arms, as spin could give him fits. But the raw strength, bat speed, and power potential could make the 20-year-old a household name with a strong debut season.

**2. RHP Nick Travieso:** We ranked the former first-round pick fifth in the system last season, but the arsenal showed up flatter than expected in 2013, and unfortunately, the body showed up rounder. The fastball/slider combo could once again push him up the list, but it will take a return to his amateur velocity and a more refined physical form before I jump back on the bandwagon. Too promising to completely ignore, though.

**3. RHP Jackson Stephens:** An 18th-round pick in the 2012 draft, Stephens took a step forward in his full-season debut, working mostly in a tandem situation, but showing off his easy plus fastball in the shorter stints. He has the body and the delivery to start, and should take another step forward in 2014, especially if the secondary stuff can play sharper without losing his feel for the zone.

## Factors on the Farm
### Prospects likely to contribute at the major-league level in 2014

**1. LHP David Holmberg:** A solid but far from spectacular arm, acquired from the D-Backs in the three-way trade that sent Ryan Hanigan to the Rays. The 22-year-old southpaw has a solid-average arsenal that can play down because of command woes, which will limit his potential in a major-league rotation without refinement. You can make a case that he belongs in the top 10 because of the safety of his floor, but I prefer ceiling to safety, so Holmberg just missed the cut.

**2. C Tucker Barnhart:** A 10th-round pick in 2009, Barnhart has slowly developed into a legit major-league-caliber player, a quality backstop who can swing the stick a little bit. While he's likely a backup at the major-league level, his glove and catch/throw skills would be good enough to make him a full-time regular if the bat had more to offer.

**3. RHP Chad Rogers:** A starter since getting drafted in the 28th round in 2010, Rogers really took a step forward in the bullpen in the Arizona Fall League, showing a good low-90s fastball and sharp cutter. His future looks brighter out of the 'pen than in a rotation, as the diminutive Texan can push his arsenal up a notch in short bursts and eventually carve out a role in middle relief at the major-league level.

---

## FROM THE FIELD

### Robert Stephenson

**Player:** Robert Stephenson
**Team:** Cincinnati Reds
**Filed by:** Jordan Gorosh
**Date(s) Seen:** Opening Day 2013
**Physical:** Athletic, pitcher's body; still has some room to grow
**Mechanics/Delivery:** simple; repeatable; some drop and drive; loose arm; preposterous arm speed; downward plane.
**Fastball:** 80 grade; explodes like a cannon; 95-98 T 100 with elite life; challenges hitters; attacks.
**Curveball:** 60 grade; 10-4 break; generates plus spin; looks like fastball out of hand; swing-and-miss pitch; consistency issues at present.
**Changeup:** 60 grade; still developing; needs to trust grip; pitch will play due to sheer arm speed.
**Control:** 60 grade; zone-pounder; attacks hitters at present; doesn't issue free passes; throws strikes when he needs to.
**Command:** 5+; attacks all quadrants with fastball; repeatable delivery allows him to be consistent with arm slot; will pitch inside or outside.
**Makeup:** high pitching IQ; bulldog on the mound; competitive; wants the ball.
**OFP:** 7; no. 2 starter; near top-of-the-rotation arm; should have no trouble throwing 200-plus innings
**Realistic Role:** 6; no. 3 starter; can eat innings and have ERA in the mid-3s
**Risk:** Moderate; only 20 years old; hasn't had upper minors success.

---

**Player:** Robert Stephenson
**Team:** Cincinnati Reds
**Filed by:** Ronit Shah
**Date(s) Seen:** July 19 and 29, 2013
**Physical:** Good athletic, live body with room to add strength.
**Delivery/Mechanics:** There is effort in the delivery and how player generates his power; head bobble and neck snap, but he is able to repeat the delivery and show control; electric arm speed.
**Fastball:** 70 grade; velocity sits in the mid-90s; tops out at upper-90s; movement is there in the mid-90s but flattens as it climbs the ladder; opposing hitters forced to cheat on the pitch.
**Curveball:** 70 grade; present plus curveball with 11-5 break; comes in at lower-70s; projects to be a plus-plus hammer once player is able to add strength and add more finish on the offering. Throws it for chase pitches and quality strikes.
**Changeup:** 60 grade; developing offering that comes in the upper-80s; may be thrown too firm at times; needs to create larger velocity separation when compared to fastball; present feel and movement at time of observation were impressive; projects to be a plus offering.
**Other:** Fastball command needs improvement; not afraid to throw inside; attacks hitters and doesn't get behind; showed fatigue in second observed start; needs to be challenged.
**Makeup:** 60 grade; poised and confident on the mound; mentality of an attacker who wants to dominate opposing hitters.
**OFP:** 80; no. 1 starter
**Realistic Role:** 70; no. 2 starter
**Risk:** Moderate; limited exposure in Double-A.
**in field.**

# CLEVELAND INDIANS

## 1. Francisco Lindor   SS

**Born:** 11/14/93   **Age:** 20   **Bats:** B   **Throws:** R   **Height:** 5' 11"   **Weight:** 175

| MLB ETA | | Hit | Power | Run | Glove | Arm | | OFP | Realistic |
|---|---|---|---|---|---|---|---|---|---|
| 2014 | | 65 | -- | -- | 70 | 60 | | 70<br>ALL-STAR | 60<br>1ST DIV PLAYER |

| YEAR | TEAM | LVL | AGE | PA | R | 2B | 3B | HR | RBI | BB | SO | SB | CS | AVG/OBP/SLG | TAv | BABIP | BRR | FRAA | WARP |
|---|---|---|---|---|---|---|---|---|---|---|---|---|---|---|---|---|---|---|---|
| 2013 | CAR | A+ | 19 | 373 | 51 | 19 | 6 | 1 | 27 | 35 | 39 | 20 | 5 | .306/.373/.410 | .274 | .341 | -2.3 | SS(82): 2.6 | 2.5 |
| 2013 | AKR | AA | 19 | 91 | 14 | 3 | 1 | 1 | 7 | 14 | 7 | 5 | 2 | .289/.407/.395 | .305 | .309 | -0.8 | SS(21): -2.0 | 0.5 |
| 2014 | CLE | MLB | 20 | 250 | 27 | 10 | 1 | 2 | 17 | 19 | 47 | 7 | 3 | .236/.298/.316 | .231 | .280 | 0.3 | SS 0 | 0.4 |
| 2015 | CLE | MLB | 21 | 440 | 47 | 16 | 3 | 5 | 39 | 34 | 72 | 10 | 3 | .255/.318/.347 | .249 | .293 | 0.3 | SS 0 | 1.2 |

Breakout: 0%     Improve: 0%     Collapse: 0%     Attrition: 0%     MLB: 0%     *Comparables: Ruben Tejada, Ehire Adrianza, Starlin Castro*

**Drafted/Acquired:** 1st round, 2011 draft, Montverde HS (Montverde, FL)

**Previous Ranking:** #1 (Org), #10 (Top 101)

**What Happened in 2013:** As a 19-year-old, Lindor made his way to the Double-A level, showing skills on all sides of the ball and securing his status as one of the top prospects in baseball.

**Strengths:** Incredible instincts for the game; near elite potential with the glove; silky actions; excellent backhand pickup; range plays up; arm is plus; total package at shortstop; balanced at the plate; clean path into the ball; consistent contact from both sides of the plate; advanced approach; tracks and reacts very well; good baserunner despite average speed; makeup is plus.

**Weaknesses:** Hit tool might lack impact; could play below projection and play to (only) solid-average; contact can be soft and slappy; well-below-average power; not a burner; doesn't play for your team.

**Risk Factor/Injury History:** Moderate risk; limited Double-A experience.

**Bret Sayre's Fantasy Take:** One of the ultimate fantasy vs. reality prospects, Lindor does not have nearly the shine in our world as he does for the Indians—unless your league counts defensive statistics. A potential .300 hitter at the major-league level, he just doesn't project to have the power or speed at this point to have top-five shortstop upside in standard leagues. He gets a tick up in points leagues due to his approach at the plate.

**The Year Ahead:** Lindor is likely to reach the major-league level as a 20-year-old, as his glove is a game changer and his overall approach will make him a tough out even if the bat falls short of high-end projection. What makes Lindor special is the ease with which he plays baseball, as he shows an intrinsic feel for all aspects of the game, which could allow his already highly projected tools to play beyond their assumed limitations. He's going to be a fixture at the major-league level for the next 15 years.

#6

BP Top
101
Prospects

## 2. Clint Frazier   OF

**Born:** 9/6/94   **Age:** 19   **Bats:** R   **Throws:** R   **Height:** 6' 1"   **Weight:** 190

| MLB ETA | | Hit | Power | Run | Glove | Arm | | OFP | Realistic |
|---|---|---|---|---|---|---|---|---|---|
| Late 2016 | | 60 | 65 | 60 | 50 | 55 | | 70<br>ALL-STAR | 60<br>1ST DIV PLAYER |

| YEAR | TEAM | LVL | AGE | PA | R | 2B | 3B | HR | RBI | BB | SO | SB | CS | AVG/OBP/SLG | TAv | BABIP | BRR | FRAA | WARP |
|---|---|---|---|---|---|---|---|---|---|---|---|---|---|---|---|---|---|---|---|
| 2013 | CLE | Rk | 18 | 196 | 32 | 11 | 5 | 5 | 28 | 17 | 61 | 3 | 2 | .297/.362/.506 | .309 | .418 | 0.0 | CF(35): -1.0 | 1.5 |
| 2014 | CLE | MLB | 19 | 250 | 18 | 8 | 1 | 4 | 22 | 12 | 87 | 0 | 0 | .184/.224/.273 | .185 | .270 | -0.4 | CF -1 | -1.4 |
| 2015 | CLE | MLB | 20 | 250 | 23 | 10 | 1 | 4 | 21 | 13 | 83 | 0 | 0 | .197/.245/.296 | .200 | .283 | -0.4 | CF -1 | -2.4 |

Breakout: 0%     Improve: 0%     Collapse: 0%     Attrition: 0%     MLB: 0%     *Comparables: Joe Benson, Che-Hsuan Lin, Aaron Hicks*

**Drafted/Acquired:** 1st round, 2013 draft, Loganville HS (Loganville, GA)

**Previous Ranking:** NR

**What Happened in 2013:** The fifth pick in the draft, Frazier showed all five tools in his 44-game complex-level debut.

**Strengths:** Fast-twitch athlete; good present strength; bat speed is near elite; impressive hands/wrists; easy plus power potential; solid-average arm; solid-average to plus run; glove could play to average; plays with intensity.

**Weaknesses:** Glove in center is current underdeveloped/below average; sources mixed on ability to stick up the middle; aggressive at the plate; tendency to expand the zone; lots of swing-and-miss; risk in the hit tool.

**Risk Factor/Injury History:** High risk; complex-level resume; ultimate ceiling depends on ability to stay up the middle.

**Bret Sayre's Fantasy Take:** The top fantasy prospect in this system (with a bullet), Frazier has all the tools you'd want to see from a future franchise player. He can hit, hit for power, steal bases—and once the season starts, any chance to pay a reasonable price for him may be gone. Behind only Kris Bryant, Frazier is the second best fantasy prospect from the 2013 draft.

#36

BP Top
101
Prospects

**The Year Ahead:** Frazier might not look the part of a future all-star (aesthetically), but he certainly fits the bill physically, with legit five-tool potential and the makeup to make it work. If you believe in the up-the-middle projection, you believe Frazier is a future all-star, an impact player on all sides of the ball. Even if you aren't sold on his future in center, the end result could be a .285+ hitter with 25+ bombs in a corner, more than enough to earn a first-division label. Frazier's likely to jump straight to the full-season level in 2014, and he could emerge as a top-10 prospect in the game by the end of the year.

## 3. Tyler Naquin    CF

**Born:** 4/24/91    **Age:** 23    **Bats:** L    **Throws:** R    **Height:** 6' 2"    **Weight:** 175

| MLB ETA | Hit | Power | Run | Glove | Arm | | OFP | Realistic |
|---|---|---|---|---|---|---|---|---|
| 2015 | 55 | — | 50 | 55 | 70 | | 50<br>ML REGULAR | 45<br><AVG REG/4TH OF |

| YEAR | TEAM | LVL | AGE | PA | R | 2B | 3B | HR | RBI | BB | SO | SB | CS | AVG/OBP/SLG | TAv | BABIP | BRR | FRAA | WARP |
|---|---|---|---|---|---|---|---|---|---|---|---|---|---|---|---|---|---|---|---|
| 2013 | CAR | A+ | 22 | 498 | 69 | 27 | 6 | 9 | 42 | 41 | 112 | 14 | 7 | .277/.345/.424 | .264 | .351 | 0.9 | CF(102): 1.6 | 2.8 |
| 2013 | AKR | AA | 22 | 85 | 9 | 3 | 0 | 1 | 6 | 5 | 22 | 1 | 3 | .225/.271/.300 | .237 | .298 | -1.0 | CF(18): -1.0 | -0.1 |
| 2014 | CLE | MLB | 23 | 250 | 26 | 10 | 1 | 4 | 19 | 13 | 70 | 3 | 2 | .224/.270/.322 | .221 | .300 | -0.3 | CF 0 | -0.3 |
| 2015 | CLE | MLB | 24 | 250 | 25 | 10 | 1 | 4 | 22 | 15 | 68 | 2 | 1 | .225/.277/.330 | .227 | .299 | -0.4 | CF 0 | -0.5 |

Breakout: 0%    Improve: 0%    Collapse: 0%    Attrition: 0%    MLB: 0%          *Comparables: Gorkys Hernandez, Peter Bourjos, Alex Presley*

**Drafted/Acquired:** 1st round, 2012 draft, Texas A&M University (College Station, TX)

**Previous Ranking:** #8 (Org)

**What Happened in 2013:** I wasn't a believer in Naquin coming into the season, but the then-22-year-old outfielder took big steps forward throughout the season, culminating in an eye-opening run in the Arizona Fall League.

**Strengths:** The glove has really improved; plays solid-average; arm is true weapon; plus-plus arm strength; good athlete; runs well; swing has improved; shows good bat speed and line-drive ability.

**Weaknesses:** Some still question ability to hit quality pitching; some swing-and-miss in the zone; will chase off-speed; power is below-average; could end up with a tweener profile.

**Risk Factor/Injury History:** Moderate risk; limited exposure to Double-A

**Bret Sayre's Fantasy Take:** A more interesting prospect for deeper leagues, Naquin may not be able to provide the type of punch that those in 10- and 12-team leagues are looking for in an outfielder—and that's not just a power thing. He does not project to have impact in any individual fantasy category, but double-digit steals and homers with a reasonable batting average can help in the right format. He could do Michael Brantley things in fantasy.

**The Year Ahead:** I was wrong about Naquin in 2013, as he took steps forward in the field and at the plate, turning some of his biggest doubters into skeptical believers. While it's not a given that he develops to his potential, he looks like a no-doubt major leaguer with a carrying weapon in the arm and enough athleticism to handle center field. The bat might be unremarkable, but he has shown the ability to make adjustments and improve his swing, so I wouldn't be as quick as I once was to discount his potential.

## 4. Cody Anderson    RHP

**Born:** 9/14/90    **Age:** 23    **Bats:** R    **Throws:** R    **Height:** 6' 4"    **Weight:** 220

| MLB ETA | CT | FB | CH | CB | SL | | OFP | Realistic |
|---|---|---|---|---|---|---|---|---|
| 2015 | — | 65 | — | — | 60 | | 55<br>NO.3 STARTER | 50<br>NO.4 STARTER |

| YEAR | TEAM | LVL | AGE | W | L | SV | G | GS | IP | H | HR | BB | SO | BB9 | SO9 | GB% | BABIP | WHIP | ERA | FIP | FRA | WARP |
|---|---|---|---|---|---|---|---|---|---|---|---|---|---|---|---|---|---|---|---|---|---|---|
| 2013 | CAR | A+ | 22 | 9 | 4 | 0 | 23 | 23 | 123.3 | 105 | 6 | 31 | 112 | 2.3 | 8.2 | 40% | .296 | 1.10 | 2.34 | 3.04 | 3.55 | 3.0 |
| 2013 | AKR | AA | 22 | 0 | 0 | 0 | 3 | 3 | 12.7 | 16 | 2 | 9 | 10 | 6.4 | 7.1 | 24% | .359 | 1.97 | 5.68 | 5.93 | 5.67 | 0.0 |
| 2014 | CLE | MLB | 23 | 6 | 7 | 0 | 21 | 21 | 100.7 | 113 | 13 | 43 | 67 | 3.8 | 6.0 | 40% | .306 | 1.55 | 5.02 | 5.14 | 5.46 | -0.4 |
| 2015 | CLE | MLB | 24 | 7 | 9 | 0 | 26 | 26 | 157.7 | 180 | 19 | 63 | 109 | 3.6 | 6.2 | 40% | .315 | 1.54 | 4.93 | 4.60 | 5.36 | -0.7 |

Breakout: 0%    Improve: 0%    Collapse: 0%    Attrition: 0%    MLB: 0%          *Comparables: Justin Grimm, Brandon Workman, Erik Johnson*

**Drafted/Acquired:** 14th round, 2011 draft, Feather River College (Quincy, CA)

**Previous Ranking:** NR

**What Happened in 2013:** A 14th-round pick in the 2011 draft, Anderson had successfully stayed under the prospect radar until he took a big step forward in the Carolina League, missing bats with a much-improved secondary arsenal.

**Strengths:** Big, strong frame; good arm action; fastball works 91-95; good sink; can work higher in bursts; slider is a future plus pitch; sharp with good tilt; shows average curveball that he can get over; feel for strike throwing; workhorse potential.

**Weaknesses:** More control than command; struggles to finish his delivery and will work up/find contact; curveball is inconsistent; rotation gets loose and movement slurvy; shows changeup but it's currently below average; deliberate.

**Risk Factor/Injury History:** Moderate risk; limited exposure to high minors.

**Bret Sayre's Fantasy Take:** He's a name for fantasy more because of proximity than upside, as Anderson likely does not have the strikeout potential you'd ideally want in a starter. That said, he has the profile to put up a solid WHIP with potentially strong control and fly-ball tendencies—but hopefully those tendencies don't get him into too much trouble.

**The Year Ahead:** It's not sexy but the profile points to a workhorse starter at the highest level, and if you can get that out of a 14th-round pick, you take it all day long. He can pitch off his fastball, although his command needs to improve and he needs to keep the ball down because his stuff isn't all that lively up in the zone and it finds barrels. The slider could be a plus breaking ball, and he shows the curveball enough for it to change sight lines and timing. But the secondary stuff isn't knockout, so the ceiling is limited to mid-rotation. He needs another year in Double-A before he's ready for the majors, but he has a chance to be a solid-average pitcher as soon as 2015.

---

## 5.   Francisco Mejia   C

**Born:** 10/27/95   **Age:** 18   **Bats:** B   **Throws:** R   **Height:** 5' 10"   **Weight:** 175

| MLB ETA | Hit | Power | Run | Glove | Arm | OFP | Realistic |
|---------|-----|-------|-----|-------|-----|-----|-----------|
| 2018 | 65 | 60 | – | 55 | 75 | 65<br>1ST DIV/ALL-STAR | 50<br>ML REGULAR |

| YEAR | TEAM | LVL | AGE | PA | R | 2B | 3B | HR | RBI | BB | SO | SB | CS | AVG/OBP/SLG | TAv | BABIP | BRR | FRAA | WARP |
|------|------|-----|-----|----|----|----|----|----|-----|----|----|----|----|-------------|-----|-------|-----|------|------|
| 2013 | CLE | Rk | 17 | 113 | 16 | 9 | 1 | 4 | 24 | 5 | 18 | 3 | 1 | .305/.348/.524 | .314 | .337 | 1.3 | C(25): -0.0, LF(1): 0.3 | 1.3 |
| 2014 | CLE | MLB | 18 | 250 | 19 | 8 | 0 | 4 | 22 | 9 | 73 | 2 | 1 | .197/.229/.291 | .192 | .260 | -0.2 | C 0, LF 0 | -0.7 |
| 2015 | CLE | MLB | 19 | 250 | 25 | 9 | 0 | 5 | 25 | 9 | 66 | 1 | 0 | .232/.262/.344 | .221 | .294 | -0.5 | C 0, LF 0 | -0.8 |

Breakout: 0%    Improve: 0%    Collapse: 0%    Attrition: 0%    MLB: 0%    *Comparables: Christian Bethancourt, Josh Vitters, Marcell Ozuna*

**Drafted/Acquired:** International free agent, 2012, Dominican Republic

**Previous Ranking:** NR

**What Happened in 2013:** Mejia made his professional debut, flashing plus bat speed and plus-plus arm strength in the Arizona League.

**Strengths:** Balanced setup and easy swing; shows plus bat speed from both sides of the plate; natural hitting ability; plus power potential; arm strength is near elite; glove could get to solid-average eventually; good makeup reports.

**Weaknesses:** Still very raw and unrefined; makes good contact but approach is aggressive; footwork behind the plate needs work; receiving skills are underdeveloped; impact arm but utility isn't there yet.

**Risk Factor/Injury History:** Extreme risk; dual-threat profile; complex-level resume

**Bret Sayre's Fantasy Take:** If you like to bet on raw tools, Mejia is certainly someone to target. In fact, outside of Jorge Alfaro, there may not be a catcher in the minor leagues with more fantasy upside than him. With that said, he is forever away both in terms of ETA and development, so let's all just take a deep breath here. Or at least try to.

**The Year Ahead:** This kid has monster potential, with the type of bat speed you can't teach and a rocket arm from a premium defensive position. He will play the entire 2014 season as an 18-year-old, so there is no reason to rush him; I expect him to start in extended spring training before moving on to the New York-Penn League. Outside of Lindor and Frazier, Mejia has the highest ceiling on the farm, and even though he comes with tremendous risk, the payoff could be enormous.

---

## 6.   Jose Ramirez   2B

**Born:** 9/17/92   **Age:** 21   **Bats:** B   **Throws:** R   **Height:** 5' 9"   **Weight:** 165

| MLB ETA | Hit | Power | Run | Glove | Arm | OFP | Realistic |
|---------|-----|-------|-----|-------|-----|-----|-----------|
| Debuted in 2013 | 55 | – | 65 | 55 | – | 50<br>ML REGULAR | 45<br><AVG ML/UTILITY |

| YEAR | TEAM | LVL | AGE | PA | R | 2B | 3B | HR | RBI | BB | SO | SB | CS | AVG/OBP/SLG | TAv | BABIP | BRR | FRAA | WARP |
|------|------|-----|-----|----|----|----|----|----|-----|----|----|----|----|-------------|-----|-------|-----|------|------|
| 2013 | AKR | AA | 20 | 533 | 78 | 16 | 6 | 3 | 38 | 39 | 41 | 38 | 16 | .272/.325/.349 | .261 | .290 | 3.0 | 2B(53): -0.6, SS(50): 3.0 | 3.0 |
| 2013 | CLE | MLB | 20 | 14 | 5 | 0 | 1 | 0 | 0 | 2 | 2 | 0 | 1 | .333/.429/.500 | .338 | .400 | 0.5 | 2B(5): 0.3, 3B(2): 0.1 | 0.3 |
| 2014 | CLE | MLB | 21 | 250 | 29 | 9 | 2 | 2 | 18 | 12 | 34 | 10 | 4 | .258/.293/.340 | .234 | .290 | 0.5 | 2B 1, SS 1 | 0.6 |
| 2015 | CLE | MLB | 22 | 250 | 26 | 9 | 2 | 3 | 23 | 13 | 28 | 11 | 5 | .279/.318/.370 | .252 | .298 | 0.5 | 2B 1, SS 1 | 1.6 |

Breakout: 0%    Improve: 0%    Collapse: 0%    Attrition: 0%    MLB: 0%    *Comparables: Alexi Amarista, Johnny Giavotella, Jose Altuve*

**Drafted/Acquired:** International free agent, 2009, Dominican Republic

**Previous Ranking:** #10 (Org)

**What Happened in 2013:** As a 20-year-old, Ramirez started the season in Double-A and unexpectedly found himself in the major leagues at the end of the season, where the diminutive infielder hit over .300 in a 15-game sample.

**Strengths:** Good bat-to-ball skills; limited size but good pop in the bat; line-drive swing; shows bat speed (especially from right side) and balance; easy plus run; very good glove at second; has some defensive versatility; good overall fundamentals.

**Weaknesses:** Hit tool could be above average but power will play well below average; down-the-lineup bat at best; arm is fringe; not a good fit for the left side of the infield; left-handed bat isn't as strong; bat speed not as good.

**Risk Factor/Injury History:** Low risk; achieved major-league level

**Bret Sayre's Fantasy Take:** Ramirez has the now skills to contribute to a fantasy roster given playing time. Unfortunately for him, that playing time is going to be tough to come by as long as he's behind one of the best second basemen in the game. With 30+ steal potential and a career 7.9 percent strikeout rate in the minors, Ramirez can contribute in both roto and points leagues.

**The Year Ahead:** Ramirez was rushed to the majors in 2013, and could use another pass through the high minors before he's ready for a full-time position at the highest level. He can make contact at the plate, and that brings his legs into the equation, giving him a chance to hit for average. Power will not be a part of his game, but he can still drive mistakes, especially from the right side of the plate. The glove is very good, but the arm will limit his effectiveness off second, so if he is to develop into a starter, it will have to come at the keystone. But the floor is a good utility player, and there is minimal risk in that outcome.

# 7. Ronny Rodriguez  SS

**Born:** 4/17/92   **Age:** 22   **Bats:** R   **Throws:** R   **Height:** 6' 0"   **Weight:** 170

| MLB ETA | Hit | Power | Run | Glove | Arm | OFP | Realistic |
|---|---|---|---|---|---|---|---|
| 2015 | 50 | 60 | – | 50 | 65 | 60<br>1ST DIV PLAYER | 45<br><AVG ML/UTILITY |

| YEAR | TEAM | LVL | AGE | PA | R | 2B | 3B | HR | RBI | BB | SO | SB | CS | AVG/OBP/SLG | TAv | BABIP | BRR | FRAA | WARP |
|---|---|---|---|---|---|---|---|---|---|---|---|---|---|---|---|---|---|---|---|
| 2013 | AKR | AA | 21 | 498 | 62 | 25 | 6 | 5 | 52 | 16 | 76 | 12 | 3 | .265/.291/.376 | .244 | .304 | 2.9 | SS(71): -3.8, 2B(44): -0.3 | 0.6 |
| 2014 | CLE | MLB | 22 | 250 | 22 | 11 | 1 | 5 | 26 | 4 | 57 | 3 | 2 | .229/.242/.353 | .217 | .270 | 0.0 | SS -1, 2B 1 | -0.1 |
| 2015 | CLE | MLB | 23 | 250 | 25 | 9 | 2 | 6 | 26 | 7 | 49 | 3 | 2 | .243/.268/.374 | .231 | .276 | 0.0 | SS -1, 2B 1 | 0.0 |

Breakout: 0%   Improve: 0%   Collapse: 0%   Attrition: 0%   MLB: 0%   *Comparables: Alcides Escobar, Eduardo Escobar, Hector Gomez*

**Drafted/Acquired:** International free agent, 2010, Dominican Republic

**Previous Ranking:** #3 (Org)

**What Happened in 2013:** After a solid but not spectacular High-A season in 2012, Rodriguez moved up a level and fell a bit short of solid, as the toolsy infielder offered some flash but very little consistency.

**Strengths:** Exciting tools; fast hands on both sides of the ball; big bat speed; power potential is there; arm is very strong; weapon from second; good actions.

**Weaknesses:** Very aggressive at the plate; fooled by off-speed stuff; tries to yank outside offerings to the pull side; doesn't work counts; good athlete but not a plus runner; smooth actions but will make fundamental errors; range is better to glove side, but not ideal for shortstop; power has yet to show up in games.

**Risk Factor/Injury History:** High risk; despite Double-A experience, wide gap between present/future grades.

**Bret Sayre's Fantasy Take:** If you're in an OBP league, you can probably start moving onto the next player already. Rodriguez has the tools to hit .270 with 20 homers at a middle infield position, but with Kipnis/Lindor taking those positions long term, his future may be at third—where those numbers would be less impactful. With his performance and eligibility risk, Rodriguez is a good flier, but just a flier.

**The Year Ahead:** Rodriguez has impact potential based on his raw tools, but he has yet to put the package together on the field. He shows impressive bat speed and big-play ability at second, but frustrates scouts with his inconsistency and tool utility. He could use a return trip to Double-A, where he could work to refine his approach and bring his plus tools into game action. If he clicks, he's a legit major leaguer with above-average potential, but he's still a high-risk, boom/bust type despite his age and level.

# 8. Dorssys Paulino  SS

**Born:** 11/21/94   **Age:** 19   **Bats:** R   **Throws:** R   **Height:** 6' 0"   **Weight:** 175

| MLB ETA | Hit | Power | Run | Glove | Arm | OFP | Realistic |
|---|---|---|---|---|---|---|---|
| Late 2016 | 50 | 60 | – | – | 55 | 60<br>1ST DIV PLAYER | 45<br><AVG ML PLAYER |

| YEAR | TEAM | LVL | AGE | PA | R | 2B | 3B | HR | RBI | BB | SO | SB | CS | AVG/OBP/SLG | TAv | BABIP | BRR | FRAA | WARP |
|---|---|---|---|---|---|---|---|---|---|---|---|---|---|---|---|---|---|---|---|
| 2013 | LKC | A | 18 | 523 | 56 | 28 | 3 | 5 | 46 | 30 | 91 | 12 | 7 | .246/.297/.349 | .229 | .294 | 0.0 | SS(116): -10.3 | -0.8 |
| 2014 | CLE | MLB | 19 | 250 | 23 | 11 | 1 | 3 | 17 | 8 | 63 | 3 | 1 | .215/.241/.297 | .199 | .270 | -0.2 | SS -4 | -1.0 |
| 2015 | CLE | MLB | 20 | 250 | 22 | 10 | 1 | 3 | 21 | 7 | 58 | 1 | 0 | .231/.255/.322 | .213 | .285 | -0.4 | SS -4 | -1.7 |

Breakout: 0%   Improve: 0%   Collapse: 0%   Attrition: 0%   MLB: 0%   *Comparables: Jonathan Schoop, Chris Owings, Wilfredo Tovar*

**Drafted/Acquired:** International free agent, 2011, Dominican Republic

**Previous Ranking:** #2 (Org), #96 (Top 101)

**What Happened in 2013:** In his full-season debut, the then-18-year-old struggled against much older competition in a tough hitter's league, but he did manage to produce 36 extra-base hits in 120 games for Lake County.

**Strengths:** Legit projections on the bat, both hit and power; good hands; generates above-average bat speed; swing has natural lift; line drives will eventually turn into over-the-fence power; arm is strong; has good straight-line speed

**Weaknesses:** Glove is below average; lacks the quickness or instincts for shortstop; profiles better at third or second; approach is aggressive; struggles against spin/off-speed; some makeup concerns.

**Risk Factor/Injury History:** High risk; long developmental road; limited professional experience.

**Bret Sayre's Fantasy Take:** Like Rodriguez before him, the combination of performance and eligibility risk weighs heavily on Paulino's value—but for fantasy purposes, I'd take him fifth in this system (over Naquin and Anderson) even after losing some prospect luster. He's not worth dropping for that next big thing yet.

**The Year Ahead:** I'm not quick to write off Paulino as a prospect just because he struggled (on all sides of the ball) in his full-season debut. The scouting reports did sour a bit on the player, as the reality of the defensive skill set became clearer and the pressure on the bat increased as a result. Despite the defensive profile, I think Paulino is going to hit, eventually bringing above-average power to the table. He'll probably struggle for a while, as the approach is aggressive and better arms can exploit his taste for fastballs, but the bat will find a way to play and the value will come from that. His prospect status will ebb and flow as a result, but he's super young and has very good bat speed, so that buys him a lot of developmental leeway.

## 9. Joe Wendle 2B

**Born:** 4/26/90 **Age:** 24 **Bats:** L **Throws:** R **Height:** 5' 11" **Weight:** 190

| MLB ETA | Hit | Power | Run | Glove | Arm | | OFP | Realistic |
|---|---|---|---|---|---|---|---|---|
| 2015 | 60 | – | – | – | – | | 50 ML REGULAR | 45 <AVG ML PLAYER |

| YEAR | TEAM | LVL | AGE | PA | R | 2B | 3B | HR | RBI | BB | SO | SB | CS | AVG/OBP/SLG | TAv | BABIP | BRR | FRAA | WARP |
|---|---|---|---|---|---|---|---|---|---|---|---|---|---|---|---|---|---|---|---|
| 2013 | CAR | A+ | 23 | 474 | 73 | 32 | 5 | 16 | 64 | 44 | 79 | 10 | 2 | .295/.372/.513 | .298 | .327 | 3.3 | 2B(101): 6.7 | 4.1 |
| 2014 | CLE | MLB | 24 | 250 | 25 | 11 | 1 | 7 | 29 | 14 | 55 | 1 | 0 | .243/.292/.387 | .249 | .290 | -0.2 | 2B 2, 3B 0 | 0.8 |
| 2015 | CLE | MLB | 25 | 250 | 29 | 10 | 1 | 7 | 28 | 17 | 52 | 0 | 0 | .242/.298/.389 | .251 | .279 | -0.4 | 2B 2, 3B 1 | 1.4 |

Breakout: 3%    Improve: 24%    Collapse: 6%    Attrition: 16%    MLB: 37%    *Comparables: Jason Kipnis, David Adams, Ryan Adams*

**Drafted/Acquired:** 6th round, 2012 draft, West Chester University of Pennsylvania (West Chester, PA)

**Previous Ranking:** NR

**What Happened in 2013:** A sixth-round pick in the 2012 draft, Wendle isn't exactly a toolshed, but he showed off his ability to square up a baseball in the Carolina League and continued that trend in the Arizona Fall League.

**Strengths:** Natural bat-to-ball ability; smooth, easy stroke from the left side; no frills; regular hard contact; good approach; works himself into favorable counts; okay pop; baseball skills.

**Weaknesses:** Lacks impact tools; hit tool only carrying attribute; below-average glove; arm isn't a weapon; below-average run; pop but not over-the-fence power projection; very limited profile.

**Risk Factor/Injury History:** Moderate risk; hit is only carrying tool

**Fantasy Future:** Wendle put himself on the map with a very strong season, but it's not wise to read too much into it from a fantasy perspective right now. The power and speed just don't project particularly well, and middle infield is the biggest source of organizational depth for the Indians.

**The Year Ahead:** Wendle isn't a sexy prospect, and you can argue that he was old for High-A and was expected to produce good numbers at the plate. This ranking has nothing to do with his numbers; rather, this ranking has everything to do with the scouting, more specifically, his hit tool, which several sources said has a chance to really play at the highest level. He's always going to be limited in the field, and without much power, he's unlikely to be an impact stick, but the kid can hit a baseball, and with a fundamental approach to the game has a chance to maximize his limited skill set and bring the bat-to-ball ability to the highest level. He will move up to Double-A in 2014, and I absolutely expect him to keep hitting. Again, this is not a sexy prospect and he's easy to discount, but guys who can hit find a way to carve out major-league careers, and it wouldn't shock me to see Wendle holding his own against major-league pitching in the next few seasons.

## 10. Dace Kime RHP

**Born:** 3/6/92 **Age:** 22 **Bats:** R **Throws:** R **Height:** 6' 4" **Weight:** 200

| MLB ETA | CT | FB | CH | CB | SL | | OFP | Realistic |
|---|---|---|---|---|---|---|---|---|
| 2016 | 55 | 55 | 55 | – | – | | 50 NO.4 STARTER | 50 NO.5 SP/LONG RP |

| YEAR | TEAM | LVL | AGE | W | L | SV | G | GS | IP | H | HR | BB | SO | BB9 | SO9 | GB% | BABIP | WHIP | ERA | FIP | FRA | WARP |
|---|---|---|---|---|---|---|---|---|---|---|---|---|---|---|---|---|---|---|---|---|---|---|
| 2013 | MHV | A- | 21 | 0 | 2 | 0 | 9 | 9 | 24.7 | 19 | 0 | 16 | 26 | 5.8 | 9.5 | 52% | .317 | 1.42 | 2.92 | 2.93 | 4.25 | 0.2 |
| 2014 | CLE | MLB | 22 | 2 | 3 | 0 | 8 | 8 | 31.7 | 37 | 4 | 19 | 19 | 5.4 | 5.4 | 45% | .313 | 1.80 | 6.14 | 5.80 | 6.68 | -0.5 |
| 2015 | CLE | MLB | 23 | 4 | 8 | 0 | 28 | 28 | 168.0 | 191 | 23 | 79 | 113 | 4.2 | 6.1 | 45% | .309 | 1.61 | 5.39 | 5.13 | 5.86 | -1.6 |

Breakout: 0%    Improve: 0%    Collapse: 0%    Attrition: 0%    MLB: 0%    *Comparables: Nick Maronde, Bryan Morris, Blake Wood*

**Drafted/Acquired:** 3rd round, 2013 draft, University of Louisville (Louisville, KY)

**Previous Ranking:** NR

**What Happened in 2013:** More of a bullpen arm in college, Kime is viewed by the Indians as a long-term starter, as he has all the necessary ingredients to make it work in that role.

**Strengths:** Big, strong frame; good arm strength; good arm action; fastball works low-90s (90-92); can go get more when he needs it; good plane; cutter is above-average; late and sharp; can turn over a changeup that shows above-average potential.

**Weaknesses:** Below-average command at present; fastball can look pedestrian; too true and visible when elevated; cutter is more of an escape pitch than a bat-misser; lacks a true plus offering; tendency to cast changeup.

**Risk Factor/Injury History:** Moderate risk; limited professional experience

**Bret Sayre's Fantasy Take:** There's plenty of value to having pitchers like Kime in your organization, but when it comes to fantasy, you're better off targeting players with more upside. A lot would have to go right for him to be fantasy viable in anything other than very deep leagues.

**The Year Ahead:** Kime's command is going to improve, as the arm action and delivery are good and he controls his body well. The stuff isn't especially nasty, but he could end up with three solid-average pitches and the physicality to log innings in a rotation. If the stuff ticks up as he adjusts to the role, he might have more in the tank than just a back-end starter, which is why his status is higher than most arms with his profile. When you get a guy with good size, a good delivery and good arm action, never discount the stuff even if it only looks to be average. He is a good candidate to step forward in 2014 when he makes his full-season debut.

## Prospects on the Rise

**1. OF Anthony Santander:** The young outfielder was featured as an On the Rise player on last season's list, and a tepid full-season debut didn't elevate his status like I expected. But I really like this kid and I think he's going to hit. It's a corner profile, but Santander has a feel for the game and a really good-looking swing from the left side, so I'm staying on this bandwagon and encouraging others to do so as well.

**2. SS Erik Gonzalez:** It's a glove-first profile, but his ability to play a legit shortstop gives him value. He's unlikely to emerge as a top-10 prospect (in any system), but if the bat can take a step forward, Gonzalez could have a major-league future, most likely as a utility option. Again, not the sexiest prospect on the planet, but don't discount the ability to play the shortstop position at the highest level. These guys find a way to stick around and play roles on 25-man rosters.

**3. 1B/DH Nellie Rodriguez:** A 15th-round pick in 2012, Rodriguez has big raw power from the right side, and has a chance to make it play as he climbs the professional ladder. It's a tough profile, as he's already marooned at first base, but the bat has a chance to carry the value, and a strong full-season debut could propel him up prospects lists in 2014.

### FROM THE FIELD

## Francisco Lindor

**Player:** Francisco Lindor

**Team:** Cleveland Indians

**Filed by:** CJ Wittmann

**Date(s) Seen:** Multiple times

**Physical:** Small, short frame; not skinny but could add some weight for durability purposes;

**Hit:** 60 grade; balanced, quiet load and stride from both sides of the plate; natural bat-to-ball skills; good bat speed from both sides; short, compact swing making loud contact often; quick, strong wrists; uses all parts of the field; advanced approach and has very good pitch recognition skills.

**Power:** 40 grade; ability to turn on a mistake; natural leverage in swing; below average.

**Glove:** 70 grade; extreme instincts for the game; not a burner but first-step quickness makes range plus; smooth actions when fielding and transferring to hand.

**Arm:** 60 grade; strong, accurate throws from all places.

**Speed:** 55 grade; quick, agile movements; not a burner; 4.17 to first base from left side.

**Makeup:** 70 grade; first one in, first one out type attitude; strong work ethic and passion for game from scouts.

**OFP:** 70; all-star

**Realistic Role:** 60; first-division player

**Risk:** Moderate; limited professional profile in upper minors.

### FROM THE FIELD

## Clint Frazier

**Player:** Clint Frazier

**Team:** Cleveland Indians

**Filed by:** Ethan Purser

**Date(s) Seen:** March 12, 2013

**Physical:** Compact and explosive athlete. Medium frame. Full-on man strength in forearms and upper body. Lower half shows room for continued muscle development. Close to being physically maxed.

**Hit:** 60 grade; tip-and-rip hitter with insanely quick hands/wrists. Compact swing with top-shelf bat speed. Bat plane will occasionally become too steep, leading to nonoptimal contact point with the ball. Will flash the necessary ingredients for good lower-half leverage; great hip action. Aggressive approach; will expand the zone. Can ID soft stuff but has appetite for contact.

**Power:** 70 grade; graphic raw power. Pulverizes baseballs. Already shows massive in-game pop. Swing displays the type of bat speed and lift necessary to send balls over the fence with regularity. Doesn't have to sell out; power is currently driven by insane bat speed and wrist strength. Can sting balls without squaring them up.

**Glove:** 50 grade; new to center field. Shows good agility, but reads and routes are still raw. Could play center at maturity but will more than likely move to a corner down the line as he gains additional mass.

**Arm:** 60 grade; high front side; deep arm plunge. Throws exhibit plenty of exit velocity and good overall carry. Would play well in right field.

**Speed:** 55 grade; current plus runner; will likely slow down a tick as the body continues to add bulk. Should still exhibit above-average speed due to impressive athleticism.

**Makeup:** Plays the game with intensity. Ability to take games into his own hands; elite competitor. Displays the confidence necessary to succeed at the highest level.

**OFP:** 7; all-star player

**Realistic Role:** 6; first-division player

**Risk:** High. Hit tool requires projection. Swing-and-miss needs to be tamed.

## Factors on the Farm
**Prospects likely to contribute at the major-league level in 2014**

**1. 1B Jesus Aguilar:** Aguilar has a case to be a top-10 prospect in the system, as the power has the potential to play at plus at the highest level. Sources aren't sold that his hit tool is strong enough, and as a first-base-only type, he has to hit to have any value in the majors. But if you believe in the power he's a top-10 prospect and potential second-division type. If you have doubts, you probably see a platoon bat at best. Regardless, he's going to taste the major leagues in 2014.

**2. RHP C.C. Lee:** It's not an impact arm, and a prolonged look vs. lefties could expose him as a situational type, but with a low-90s sinker and slider combo from a low 3/4 slot, Lee has the stuff to play a role in a major-league bullpen.

**3. RHP Shawn Armstrong:** Live-armed righty with late-innings stuff but below-average command, Armstrong has a chance to not only reach the majors in 2014 but stick around at that level. When he can stay in his delivery, the former 18th-round pick can work in the mid-90s and touch higher, showing a hard cutter and low-80s breaking ball. The delivery isn't conducive for command, but any step forward in that regard could turn the 23-year-old righty into a power arm in a late-innings capacity.

## 1. Jonathan Gray RHP

**Born:** 11/5/91 **Age:** 22 **Bats:** R **Throws:** R **Height:** 6' 4" **Weight:** 255

| MLB ETA | | CT | FB | CH | CB | SL | | OFP | | Realistic |
|---------|---|----|----|----|----|----|---|-----|---|-----------|
| Late 2014 | | — | 80 | 65 | — | 70 | | 75 NO.1 STARTER | | 70 NO.2 STARTER |

| YEAR | TEAM | LVL | AGE | W | L | SV | G | GS | IP | H | HR | BB | SO | BB9 | SO9 | GB% | BABIP | WHIP | ERA | FIP | FRA | WARP |
|------|------|-----|-----|---|---|----|---|----|----|---|----|----|----|-----|-----|-----|-------|------|-----|-----|-----|------|
| 2013 | GJR | Rk | 21 | 0 | 0 | 0 | 4 | 4 | 13.3 | 15 | 0 | 2 | 15 | 1.4 | 10.1 | 38% | .385 | 1.27 | 4.05 | 2.51 | 3.14 | 0.6 |
| 2013 | MOD | A+ | 21 | 4 | 0 | 0 | 5 | 5 | 24.0 | 10 | 0 | 6 | 36 | 2.2 | 13.5 | 50% | .227 | 0.67 | 0.75 | 1.52 | 2.42 | 0.9 |
| 2014 | COL | MLB | 22 | 2 | 2 | 0 | 8 | 8 | 36.3 | 35 | 4 | 16 | 35 | 4.0 | 8.7 | 44% | .327 | 1.40 | 4.36 | 4.16 | 4.74 | 0.3 |
| 2015 | COL | MLB | 23 | 8 | 9 | 0 | 32 | 32 | 203.3 | 179 | 18 | 81 | 211 | 3.6 | 9.3 | 44% | .322 | 1.28 | 3.90 | 3.43 | 4.23 | 2.5 |

**Breakout:** 0%   **Improve:** 0%   **Collapse:** 0%   **Attrition:** 0%   **MLB:** 0%   *Comparables: Christian Friedrich, Danny Duffy, Tommy Hanson*

**Drafted/Acquired:** 1st round, 2013 draft, University of Oklahoma (Norman, OK)

**Previous Ranking:** NR

**What Happened in 2013:** A 1:1 candidate coming into the draft, Gray slid to the Rockies with the number three pick despite possessing the best stuff in the draft.

**Strengths:** Big, strong frame; physical on the mound; elite arm strength; fastball routinely works in the plus-plus range and can touch triple digits; shows good command of the offering; works to all quadrants; slider is wipeout pitch; fastball disguise with sharp, late tilt; changeup another plus offering; arm-speed consistency with some late fade; frontline characteristics.

**Weaknesses:** Stiff front leg landing in delivery; can cause inconsistency in his release points and tendency to yank off target; changeup yet to be featured player in the arsenal; limited professional experience (not many weaknesses).

**Risk Factor/Injury History:** Moderate risk; yet to pitch in upper minors; limited professional experience.

**Bret Sayre's Fantasy Take:** If you were going to build a pitcher designed to succeed in Coors Field, Gray may be the prototype. He's unlikely to have extreme ground-ball rates, but with a big fastball and a slider/change combination, he should be able to pitch at altitude while maintaining a strong stat line. Said stat line should include a lot of strikeouts and modest ratios if he can fulfill his potential. Don't let Coors scare you, Gray is worthy of a top-five selection in dynasty drafts this year.

**The Year Ahead:** Gray is a top 20 prospect in baseball, and that is probably going to look foolishly conservative by midseason, as Gray has the size, stuff, and pitchability to develop into a legit frontline starter at the major-league level. The fastball is elite, the slider is plus-plus and scary as all hell to both lefties and righties, and the changeup —the pitch I suggested could be a 6+ offering—might end up exceeding those lofty projections and developing into his separator pitch at the highest level. If the command stays strong and the stuff stays sharp, it won't take long for Gray to emerge as one of the best young arms in baseball.

**#16**

BP Top 101 Prospects

## 2. Eddie Butler RHP

**Born:** 3/13/91 **Age:** 23 **Bats:** B **Throws:** R **Height:** 6' 2" **Weight:** 180

| MLB ETA | | CT | FB | CH | CB | SL | | OFP | | Realistic |
|---------|---|----|----|----|----|----|---|-----|---|-----------|
| 2014 | | — | 75 | 70 | — | 65 | | 70 NO.2 STARTER | | 60 NO.3 STARTER |

| YEAR | TEAM | LVL | AGE | W | L | SV | G | GS | IP | H | HR | BB | SO | BB9 | SO9 | GB% | BABIP | WHIP | ERA | FIP | FRA | WARP |
|------|------|-----|-----|---|---|----|---|----|----|---|----|----|----|-----|-----|-----|-------|------|-----|-----|-----|------|
| 2013 | ASH | A | 22 | 5 | 1 | 0 | 9 | 9 | 54.3 | 25 | 2 | 25 | 51 | 4.1 | 8.4 | 76% | .172 | 0.92 | 1.66 | 3.63 | 5.30 | 0.3 |
| 2013 | TUL | AA | 22 | 1 | 0 | 0 | 6 | 6 | 27.7 | 13 | 0 | 6 | 25 | 2.0 | 8.1 | 58% | .188 | 0.69 | 0.65 | 2.11 | 2.44 | 0.9 |
| 2013 | MOD | A+ | 22 | 3 | 4 | 0 | 13 | 13 | 67.7 | 58 | 7 | 21 | 67 | 2.8 | 8.9 | 49% | .280 | 1.17 | 2.39 | 4.16 | 4.67 | 0.9 |
| 2014 | COL | MLB | 23 | 7 | 7 | 0 | 21 | 21 | 110.3 | 112 | 13 | 49 | 75 | 4.0 | 6.1 | 55% | .307 | 1.46 | 4.79 | 4.88 | 5.21 | 0.2 |
| 2015 | COL | MLB | 24 | 10 | 10 | 0 | 32 | 32 | 203.7 | 187 | 23 | 73 | 143 | 3.2 | 6.3 | 55% | .284 | 1.27 | 4.06 | 4.26 | 4.42 | 2.1 |

**Breakout:** 0%   **Improve:** 0%   **Collapse:** 0%   **Attrition:** 0%   **MLB:** 0%   *Comparables: Justin Grimm, Erik Johnson, Travis Wood*

**Drafted/Acquired:** 1st round, 2012, Radford University (Radford, VA)

**Previous Ranking:** On The Rise

**What Happened in 2013:** From "On the Rise" prospect coming into the season, to number two talent in a solid system and one of the premier arms in the minors.

**Strengths:** Athletic; long arms; good body with more room to add strength; repeatable delivery; fastball is power offering; works 93-98; huge life to the arm side; holds velocity; two-seamer with heavy life; bat-smasher; changeup is money pitch; plus-plus potential with mid- to upper-80s velo, good deception, and heavy two-seamer action; slider is third plus potential offering; hard and cutter-like in mid- to upper-80s; longer in the 83-85 range with more tilt; shows low-80s curveball with some bite.

**#26**

BP Top 101 Prospects

**Weaknesses:** Repeats but delivery can show effort; cross fire; can lose deception by getting long in the back (showing too much of the ball); command is loose and could cause arsenal to play down.

**Risk Factor/Injury History:** Moderate risk; limited experience at Double-A level (6 starts)

**Bret Sayre's Fantasy Take:** Butler has been able to get the ground-ball rates that Gray likely will not, but the 2013 breakout prospect remains second in line for fantasy value in the organization. Another slider/change pitcher who can succeed despite Coors, Butler may not quite be a strikeout-per-inning type of arm—though he can make inroads in all four categories. He likely does not have top-20 fantasy starter upside, but a 3.50 ERA and 180 strikeouts would be nothing sneeze at.

**The Year Ahead:** Butler has a very deep arsenal of nasty, grimy stuff, highlighted by his multiple fastball looks and power changeup with heavy action. The delivery doesn't always look the part and he lacks deception in the release, but he holds velocity deep into games and repeats, so he finds a way to make it play. Most sources see a long-term starter, despite the delivery concerns, as the stuff is very sharp and the movement he achieves with each offering is well above average and helps quell some of the concerns about early pickup out of the hand. Butler should have every chance to earn a rotation spot out of camp, and even if he starts in the high-minors, the 23-year-old should be pitching in the major-league rotation by summer.

## 3.  Raimel Tapia    RF

**Born:** 2/4/94    **Age:** 20    **Bats:** L    **Throws:** L    **Height:** 6' 2"    **Weight:** 160

| MLB ETA | Hit | Power | Run | Glove | Arm | OFP | Realistic |
|---------|-----|-------|-----|-------|-----|-----|-----------|
| 2017 | 70 | 60 | 60 | 55 | 60 | 70<br>ALL-STAR | 60<br>1ST DIV PLAYER |

| YEAR | TEAM | LVL | AGE | PA | R | 2B | 3B | HR | RBI | BB | SO | SB | CS | AVG/OBP/SLG | TAv | BABIP | BRR | FRAA | WARP |
|------|------|-----|-----|-----|-----|-----|-----|-----|-----|-----|-----|-----|-----|-------------|-----|-------|-----|------|------|
| 2013 | GJR | Rk | 19 | 286 | 53 | 20 | 6 | 7 | 47 | 15 | 31 | 10 | 9 | .357/.399/.562 | .336 | .381 | 1.6 | CF(49): 1.9, RF(11): -0.0 | 3.4 |
| 2014 | COL | MLB | 20 | 250 | 24 | 9 | 1 | 2 | 17 | 10 | 62 | 4 | 3 | .215/.249/.291 | .190 | .280 | -0.4 | CF 0, RF 1 | -1.1 |
| 2015 | COL | MLB | 21 | 250 | 24 | 8 | 2 | 3 | 21 | 12 | 55 | 2 | 2 | .233/.275/.320 | .220 | .285 | -0.4 | CF 0, RF 1 | -1.0 |

Breakout: 0%    Improve: 0%    Collapse: 0%    Attrition: 0%    MLB: 0%        *Comparables: Rafael Ortega, Eury Perez, Xavier Avery*

**#97**
BP Top
101
Prospects

**Drafted/Acquired:** International free agent, 2010, Dominican Republic

**Previous Ranking:** NR

**What Happened in 2013:** The stats paint a glowing picture of Tapia from his stateside debut in the Pioneer League, but the scouting is what pushed the young Dominican up the Rockies list and onto the Baseball Prospectus 101.

**Strengths:** Five-tool potential; natural bat-to-ball ability; plus bat speed and bat control; could be special tool; shows ability to drive the ball; above-average power potential; easy plus run; strong arm; high energy/plus makeup.

**Weaknesses:** Tools still raw and unrefined; needs to add strength; needs to improve reads/routes in center; unorthodox setup and swing; aggressive approach; can play at one speed.

**Risk Factor/Injury History:** High risk; yet to play at full-season level; big gap between present/future grades.

**Bret Sayre's Fantasy Take:** Tapia is a player who will be available alongside the 2013 signees in your offseason draft, outside of the deepest of leagues—and he's well worth considering for a reasonably high pick. It's easy to look at the tool grades above and drool considering the Coors factor, but don't get too carried away yet. That said, a strong debut in the Midwest League and he could be a top-10 fantasy prospect in 2015—and be subjected to way too many Carlos Gonzalez comps.

**The Year Ahead:** It's early in the developmental process and I don't want to live in the projection at the expense of the present, but Tapia has all the ingredients to blossom into one of the premier prospects in the game. Despite an aggressive (and often violent) swing that looks for contact regardless of where the ball is thrown, Tapia has the natural ability to barrel up velocity and spin alike, and with well-above-average underway speed, a plus arm, and feel for the game, he should be able to develop into a very good center fielder. That's one hell of profile. Full-season ball will be a good test for the 20-year-old, but I expect the results to match the tools, and it won't be long until Tapia is a national name in the prospect world.

## 4.  David Dahl    CF

**Born:** 4/1/94    **Age:** 20    **Bats:** L    **Throws:** R    **Height:** 6' 2"    **Weight:** 185

| MLB ETA | Hit | Power | Run | Glove | Arm | OFP | Realistic |
|---------|-----|-------|-----|-------|-----|-----|-----------|
| 2016 | 70 | 50 | 60 | 60 | 65 | 70<br>ALL-STAR | 60<br>1ST DIV PLAYER |

| YEAR | TEAM | LVL | AGE | PA | R | 2B | 3B | HR | RBI | BB | SO | SB | CS | AVG/OBP/SLG | TAv | BABIP | BRR | FRAA | WARP |
|------|------|-----|-----|-----|-----|-----|-----|-----|-----|-----|-----|-----|-----|-------------|-----|-------|-----|------|------|
| 2013 | ASH | A | 19 | 42 | 9 | 4 | 1 | 0 | 7 | 2 | 8 | 2 | 0 | .275/.310/.425 | .259 | .344 | -0.1 | CF(8): -1.1 | 0.0 |
| 2014 | COL | MLB | 20 | 250 | 24 | 10 | 2 | 4 | 19 | 10 | 62 | 3 | 2 | .224/.254/.323 | .201 | .280 | 0.0 | CF -5, LF 0 | -1.3 |
| 2015 | COL | MLB | 21 | 250 | 24 | 9 | 2 | 3 | 22 | 14 | 53 | 1 | 1 | .228/.272/.330 | .221 | .276 | -0.1 | CF -5, LF 0 | -1.5 |

Breakout: 0%    Improve: 0%    Collapse: 0%    Attrition: 0%    MLB: 0%        *Comparables: Xavier Avery, Abraham Almonte, Eury Perez*

**Drafted/Acquired:** 1st round, 2012 draft, Oak Mountain HS (Birmingham, AL)

**Previous Ranking:** #2 (Org), #40 (Top 101)

**What Happened in 2013:** A hamstring injury derailed his much-anticipated full-season debut and an early-season disciplinary issue received more media attention and significance than necessary.

**Strengths:** Athletic and strong; natural hitter; easy, line-drive stroke; plus bat speed and bat control; plus run; strong arm; glove with above-average projection; could be legit five-tool player; strong work ethic and high baseball IQ.

**Weaknesses:** Reads/routes need refinement in the field; swing is more short to the ball and linear than leveraged for over-the-fence; power might not develop into plus tool; can get fastball happy and aggressive.

**Risk Factor/Injury History:** High risk; limited professional experience; season-ending injury in 2013 (right hamstring).

**Bret Sayre's Fantasy Take:** The same fantasy upside that surrounded him after his Pioneer League MVP season is still there. However, with some of the shine off, he may be undervalued at the moment. It's hard to wrangle a hitting prospect in the Colorado system away from his owner, but Dahl is worth inquiring about before the 2014 season starts. He could be a .300 hitting top-of-the-order player with 15 homers and 30 steals if it breaks right.

**The Year Ahead:** 2013 was a wash for Dahl, but now fully healthy and ready for action, the five-tool talent should waste little time establishing (anew) his standing as a top tier prospect. With Dahl's advanced and projectable hit tool, Low-A pitchers won't have much success against him, and if the game power can continue to grow, the offensive profile—in combination with his projectable defensive chops in the outfield—could push his developmental ascent into high gear. After a lost year and only 10 games above the short-season level, it's aggressive to assume Dahl could reach Double-A in 2014. But several sources think he has the bat to move quickly once he regains his footing and suggested it was possible if everything clicks.

#100
BP Top 101 Prospects

## 5.  Ryan McMahon   3B

**Born:** 12/14/94   **Age:** 19   **Bats:** L   **Throws:** R   **Height:** 6'2"   **Weight:** 185

| MLB ETA | Hit | Power | Run | Glove | Arm | OFP | Realistic |
|---|---|---|---|---|---|---|---|
| 2017 | 60 | 65 | – | 55 | 50 | 60<br>1ST DIV PLAYER | 50<br>ML REGULAR |

| YEAR | TEAM | LVL | AGE | PA | R | 2B | 3B | HR | RBI | BB | SO | SB | CS | AVG/OBP/SLG | TAv | BABIP | BRR | FRAA | WARP |
|---|---|---|---|---|---|---|---|---|---|---|---|---|---|---|---|---|---|---|---|
| 2013 | GJR | Rk | 18 | 251 | 42 | 18 | 3 | 11 | 52 | 28 | 59 | 4 | 6 | .321/.402/.583 | .323 | .396 | -0.9 | 3B(54): 2.5 | 2.4 |
| 2014 | COL | MLB | 19 | 250 | 21 | 9 | 1 | 5 | 25 | 15 | 79 | 1 | 1 | .203/.252/.316 | .199 | .270 | -0.5 | 3B 1 | -0.9 |
| 2015 | COL | MLB | 20 | 250 | 28 | 10 | 0 | 8 | 29 | 16 | 75 | 0 | 0 | .220/.272/.373 | .234 | .283 | -0.6 | 3B 1 | 0.0 |

Breakout: 0%   Improve: 0%   Collapse: 0%   Attrition: 0%   MLB: 0%     *Comparables: Alex Liddi, Josh Vitters, Matt Dominguez*

**Drafted/Acquired:** 2nd round, 2013 draft, Mater Dei HS (Santa Ana, CA)

**Previous Ranking:** NR

**What Happened in 2013:** The 42nd overall pick in the 2013 draft showed off his impressive offensive tool collection in the Pioneer League, hitting for average and power against both lefties and righties alike.

**Strengths:** Projectable body; athletic with good present strength; loose and fluid swing; plus bat speed; controls it well and makes hard contact; power has plus projection; generates backspin and lift in the swing; arm is solid-average; glove projects to be at least average; strong competitive background and makeup.

**Weaknesses:** Can get aggressive in his approach; fastball setup and will struggle with good sequence; arm isn't a big weapon at third; glove/footwork still unrefined; actions can get stiff; fringe-average likely to play below average at physical maturity.

**Risk Factor/Injury History:** High risk; limited professional experience.

**Bret Sayre's Fantasy Take:** A surprise name in the back end of the top 20 players available in first-year dynasty drafts, McMahon showed off his .280, 25-homer potential immediately last summer. With the help of Coors Field, he could put up stats similar to Josh Donaldson from 2013—value everywhere except on the basepaths, where he's unlikely to be much of a contributor.

**The Year Ahead:** For a multisport athlete in high school (quarterback at Mater Dei High), a chiseled focus on baseball could push McMahon into the national spotlight in 2014, as the 19-year-old already has the requisite tools and intangibles to take a big step forward, and now he will have the dedication to one sport. The ceiling could be even higher than projected if the hit and power tools expand and start to flash ceilings greater than plus, but there are still many unknowns about the profile, such as how the approach will play against better arms and how the glove will develop at third. Scouts seem to love this kid, with many suggesting he was a clear first-round talent that was a gift to the Rockies in the second round. McMahon is likely to continue hitting at the full-season level, and the Rockies will soon be able to boast one of the most talented positional prospect trios in the game in Tapia, Dahl, and McMahon.

## 6. Rosell Herrera    SS

**Born:** 10/16/92   **Age:** 21   **Bats:** B   **Throws:** R   **Height:** 6' 3"   **Weight:** 180

| MLB ETA | Hit | Power | Run | Glove | Arm | OFP | Realistic |
|---------|-----|-------|-----|-------|-----|-----|-----------|
| 2016 | 50 | 50 | 50 | – | 50 | 50 AVG ML REGULAR | 50 SUPER UTILITY |

| YEAR | TEAM | LVL | AGE | PA | R | 2B | 3B | HR | RBI | BB | SO | SB | CS | AVG/OBP/SLG | TAv | BABIP | BRR | FRAA | WARP |
|------|------|-----|-----|----|----|----|----|----|-----|----|----|----|----|-------------|-----|-------|-----|------|------|
| 2013 | ASH | A | 20 | 546 | 83 | 33 | 0 | 16 | 76 | 61 | 96 | 21 | 8 | .343/.419/.515 | .316 | .401 | -0.8 | SS(93): -4.1 | 4.9 |
| 2014 | COL | MLB | 21 | 250 | 23 | 9 | 1 | 4 | 24 | 17 | 59 | 3 | 1 | .238/.289/.340 | .222 | .300 | -0.2 | SS -0, 3B -0 | -0.1 |
| 2015 | COL | MLB | 22 | 250 | 29 | 9 | 1 | 6 | 26 | 20 | 53 | 1 | 1 | .257/.316/.377 | .254 | .306 | -0.4 | SS 0, 3B 0 | 1.3 |

Breakout: 0%   Improve: 0%   Collapse: 0%   Attrition: 0%   MLB: 0%        *Comparables: Asdrubal Cabrera, Tim Beckham, Trevor Plouffe*

**Drafted/Acquired:** International free agent, 2009, Dominican Republic

**Previous Ranking:** NR

**What Happened in 2013:** In a return trip to the Sally League, Herrera took a step forward at the plate; of course, hitting an incredible .384 at home on the season certainly helped his cause.

**Strengths:** Good size/athleticism; frame to add more strength; okay swing; can make good contact and will use all fields; shows present pop and some power projection; more lift and leverage from left side; arm is solid-average; can show good actions in the field; projects to have good defensive versatility; took a step forward after disappointing 2012 season.

**Weaknesses:** Lacks a plus tool; swing is timing heavy and can get out of whack, especially against quality stuff; tendency to cheat on fastballs; swing from the right side is more linear and contact driven; plays soft; good actions in the field but footwork and execution can get sloppy; range is limited; run is average and projects to be fringe or lower.

**Risk Factor/Injury History:** High risk; yet to play in upper minors; lacks impact tools.

**Bret Sayre's Fantasy Take:** There's no question that Asheville is a great place to hit if you're a left-handed bat, and Herrera took full advantage of that in 2013 by hitting .384/.455/.635 in those friendly confines. The power is noticeable, as he slugged just .411 on the road. After all, a stadium that is 320 feet to right-center and 297 feet to dead right will enhance the power numbers of many. This is more Josh Rutledge than Troy Tulowitzki, but he can hit 20 homers at Coors.

**The Year Ahead:** If you scout Herrera by the numbers, you see a shortstop that hit .343 in a full-season league as a 20-year-old, a noble accomplishment regardless of the scouting particulars involved. But closer investigation of the player reveals some flaws in the profile, at least when it comes to projecting the player at the highest level. Herrera's swing improved a great deal in 2013, as his timing and balance were better, and the contact was louder and more consistent. But scouts seem down on his chances to find similar success against better arms, and on the other side of the ball, Herrera's future home doesn't project to be at shortstop, so the overall profile isn't as glamorous as the numbers might suggest. On a more positive note, Herrera has the type of skill set to develop into a superutility type, a player capable of playing passable defense at several positions in the infield and outfield, with enough stick to make it interesting at the plate.

## 7. Chad Bettis    RHP

**Born:** 4/26/89   **Age:** 25   **Bats:** R   **Throws:** R   **Height:** 6' 1"   **Weight:** 200

| MLB ETA | CT | FB | CH | CB | SL | OFP | Realistic |
|---------|----|----|----|----|----|-----|-----------|
| Debuted in 2013 | 50 | 70 | 60 | 50 | – | 50 NO.4 STARTER | 50 LATE INN RP (SETUP) |

| YEAR | TEAM | LVL | AGE | W | L | SV | G | GS | IP | H | HR | BB | SO | BB9 | SO9 | GB% | BABIP | WHIP | ERA | FIP | FRA | WARP |
|------|------|-----|-----|---|---|----|---|----|----|---|----|----|----|-----|-----|-----|-------|------|-----|-----|-----|------|
| 2013 | COL | MLB | 24 | 1 | 3 | 0 | 16 | 8 | 44.7 | 55 | 6 | 20 | 30 | 4.0 | 6.0 | 49% | .327 | 1.68 | 5.64 | 4.90 | 5.04 | 0.4 |
| 2013 | TUL | AA | 24 | 3 | 4 | 0 | 12 | 12 | 63.0 | 60 | 9 | 13 | 68 | 1.9 | 9.7 | 50% | .307 | 1.16 | 3.71 | 3.52 | 4.26 | 0.7 |
| 2014 | COL | MLB | 25 | 5 | 5 | 0 | 13 | 13 | 76.0 | 79 | 9 | 27 | 60 | 3.2 | 7.1 | 46% | .320 | 1.39 | 4.69 | 4.37 | 5.10 | 0.2 |
| 2015 | COL | MLB | 26 | 9 | 11 | 0 | 31 | 31 | 196.7 | 200 | 24 | 60 | 166 | 2.7 | 7.6 | 47% | .321 | 1.32 | 4.38 | 3.95 | 4.76 | 1.3 |

Breakout: 20%   Improve: 44%   Collapse: 14%   Attrition: 35%   MLB: 76%        *Comparables: Wade LeBlanc, Christian Friedrich, Juan Nicasio*

**Drafted/Acquired:** 2nd round, 2010 draft, Texas Tech University (Lubbock, TX)

**Previous Ranking:** #5 (Org)

**What Happened in 2013:** A shoulder injury spoiled his 2012 season, but Bettis returned to the mound in 2013 (despite missing yet another chuck of time to injury), and managed to log 12 starts in Double-A before getting the call to the majors, where the then-24-year-old righty struggled to find his stuff or his command.

**Strengths:** When healthy, plus-plus arm strength; fastball easily works in the plus velocity range; could return to pre-shoulder range in the mid-90s; good natural weight to the pitch; changeup has swing/miss action and good deception from fastball; shows major-league average cutter and okay curveball; highly competitive on the mound; attacks hitters.

**Weaknesses:** Effort in the delivery; below-average command and doesn't project well because of the rushed mechanics and follow-through; hard slider took step back after injury; tendency to flatten out without much tilt; curveball can play as sight line/change-of-pace, but not an impact pitch; overall profile better suited for the bullpen.

**Risk Factor/Injury History:** Low risk; achieved major-league level; injury history on resume (shoulder/oblique).

**Bret Sayre's Fantasy Take:** For better or worse, Bettis is the type of pitcher who becomes far less interesting for fantasy because of Coors Field. With a curveball as his only usable breaking pitch, he is going to have a tough time warranting ownership in anything outside of deep leagues. In fact, he'd probably have more future fantasy value if he were moved to the bullpen.

**The Year Ahead:** Bettis is a former power arm who suffered a season-ending shoulder injury in 2012 and struggled to regain full form in his return to the mound in 2013. If the velocity comes all the way back—most likely in shorter bursts—Bettis can find a home in the back of major-league bullpen, using his deep secondary arsenal—including a much-improved changeup—to miss bats and force weak contact on the ground. If the slider can return to its preinjury glory, Bettis could really develop into a weapon.

---

## 8.   Tom Murphy   C

**Born:** 4/3/91   **Age:** 23   **Bats:** R   **Throws:** R   **Height:** 6' 1"   **Weight:** 220

| MLB ETA | Hit | Power | Run | Glove | Arm | OFP | Realistic |
|---|---|---|---|---|---|---|---|
| 2015 | – | 55 | – | 55 | 60 | 60<br>1ST DIV PLAYER | 50<br>2ND DIV PLAYER |

| YEAR | TEAM | LVL | AGE | PA | R | 2B | 3B | HR | RBI | BB | SO | SB | CS | AVG/OBP/SLG | TAv | BABIP | BRR | FRAA | WARP |
|---|---|---|---|---|---|---|---|---|---|---|---|---|---|---|---|---|---|---|---|
| 2013 | TUL | AA | 22 | 74 | 9 | 5 | 0 | 3 | 9 | 4 | 16 | 0 | 0 | .290/.338/.493 | .294 | .340 | -1.9 | C(14): -0.1 | 0.4 |
| 2013 | ASH | A | 22 | 341 | 55 | 26 | 2 | 19 | 74 | 37 | 87 | 4 | 5 | .288/.385/.590 | .324 | .346 | -3.2 | C(69): -0.7 | 3.5 |
| 2014 | COL | MLB | 23 | 250 | 27 | 11 | 1 | 9 | 32 | 16 | 70 | 1 | 1 | .238/.295/.417 | .248 | .300 | -0.4 | C -0 | 0.7 |
| 2015 | COL | MLB | 24 | 250 | 30 | 11 | 1 | 8 | 30 | 18 | 65 | 0 | 0 | .236/.302/.404 | .259 | .291 | -0.6 | C 0 | 1.5 |

Breakout: 4%   Improve: 14%   Collapse: 3%   Attrition: 15%   MLB: 32%        *Comparables: Devin Mesoraco, Travis d'Arnaud, Yasmani Grandal*

**Drafted/Acquired:** 3rd round, 2012 draft, University of Buffalo, State University of New York (Buffalo, NY)

**Previous Ranking:** NR

**What Happened in 2013:** In his full-season debut, the former third-round pick hit his way to the Double-A level, showing more promise and production with the bat than expected.

**Strengths:** Strong frame; good receiver; strong wrists; good footwork and coordination; excellent on balls in the dirt; good catch-and-throw skills; plus arm; intangibles for position; quick to the ball with an easy, uncomplicated trigger/swing; legit above-average power potential in the stick.

**Weaknesses:** Questions about hit tool utility, despite easy mechanics and smooth trigger; bat speed is only okay; power is more strength derived; will struggle against quality stuff; can beat him with velocity; below-average run; arm is strong but won't impact game on its own.

**Risk Factor/Injury History:** Moderate risk; limited experience at Double-A; hit tool could bring game power down.

**Bret Sayre's Fantasy Take:** Murphy falls above the line of upside demarcation when it comes to owning catching prospects. In fact, he's one of the top five prospects at the position for fantasy purposes. If he sticks behind the plate, a .260 hitting catcher with 20 homers is not something to shake your head at these days.

**The Year Ahead:** Quality backstops are hard to find, and the ones that are found tend to stick around at the highest level for a long time. Murphy has a good swing and very good strength, so he's going to run into game power, especially against weaker arms. The better the stuff, the more exposed his bat will be, but he should hit enough to keep his solid-average to plus defensive profile on the field, which could make him a first-division player if everything clicks, and a long-time major leaguer even if it doesn't.

---

## 9.   Kyle Parker   RF

**Born:** 9/30/89   **Age:** 24   **Bats:** R   **Throws:** R   **Height:** 6' 0"   **Weight:** 200

| MLB ETA | Hit | Power | Run | Glove | Arm | OFP | Realistic |
|---|---|---|---|---|---|---|---|
| Late 2014 | – | 60 | – | – | 55 | 50<br>2ND DIV PLAYER | 45<br><AVG ML PLAYER |

| YEAR | TEAM | LVL | AGE | PA | R | 2B | 3B | HR | RBI | BB | SO | SB | CS | AVG/OBP/SLG | TAv | BABIP | BRR | FRAA | WARP |
|---|---|---|---|---|---|---|---|---|---|---|---|---|---|---|---|---|---|---|---|
| 2013 | TUL | AA | 23 | 528 | 70 | 23 | 3 | 23 | 74 | 40 | 99 | 6 | 6 | .288/.345/.492 | .300 | .318 | -2.0 | LF(77): -7.0, RF(20): -0.8 | 2.0 |
| 2014 | COL | MLB | 24 | 250 | 28 | 10 | 1 | 9 | 33 | 19 | 60 | 1 | 1 | .256/.317/.429 | .262 | .300 | -0.3 | RF -1, LF -2 | 0.2 |
| 2015 | COL | MLB | 25 | 250 | 32 | 10 | 1 | 9 | 33 | 22 | 62 | 0 | 0 | .266/.329/.445 | .282 | .324 | -0.5 | RF -1, LF -2 | 2.5 |

Breakout: 0%   Improve: 41%   Collapse: 5%   Attrition: 7%   MLB: 52%        *Comparables: Eric Thames, Khris Davis, Todd Frazier*

**Drafted/Acquired:** 1st round, 2010 draft, Clemson University (Clemson, SC)

**Previous Ranking:** #8 (Org)

**What Happened in 2013:** Parker had a strong season—all things considered—showing actualized power in Double-A without selling out for it, a trend he continued in the Arizona Fall League.

**Strengths:** Strong, physical player; shows good bat speed; gets good extension and can create backspin; power could play has potential to play to plus; arm is strong.

**Weaknesses:** Lacks defensive value; below-average run; hit tool could limit game power against better pitching; could play below average; has swing-and-miss in the zone; tendency to pull off the bat and yank.

**Risk Factor/Injury History:** Moderate risk; Double-A/Arizona Fall League experience; questionable hit tool and defensive value.

**Bret Sayre's Fantasy Take:** There may not be a player with a bigger gap between fantasy value and real life value than Parker's. His minimal defensive value and home park are big helps there, and could help push him close to 30 homers at elevation, if the hit tool can play at even a fringe-average level.

**The Year Ahead:** I've never been very high on Parker, mostly because of questions about the swing and defensive profile, but reports about the bat were much better in 2013 even if the defensive limitations remain. It's not an impact profile unless the power plays to (or beyond) potential, and that still seems unlikely to me against major-league-caliber pitching. But if he can keep progressing at the plate—putting himself in favorable hitting conditions, forcing pitchers to work, keeping short to the ball and long through it, etc.—Parker could emerge as a solid major-league regular.

## 10. Trevor Story SS

**Born:** 11/15/92 **Age:** 21 **Bats:** R **Throws:** R **Height:** 6' 1" **Weight:** 175

| MLB ETA | Hit | Power | Run | Glove | Arm | OFP | Realistic |
|---------|-----|-------|-----|-------|-----|-----|-----------|
| 2016 | – | 50 | 50 | 50 | 60 | 60<br>1ST DIV PLAYER | 45<br>UTILITY |

| YEAR | TEAM | LVL | AGE | PA | R | 2B | 3B | HR | RBI | BB | SO | SB | CS | AVG/OBP/SLG | TAv | BABIP | BRR | FRAA | WARP |
|------|------|-----|-----|----|---|----|----|----|-----|----|----|----|----|-------------|-----|-------|-----|------|------|
| 2013 | MOD | A+ | 20 | 554 | 71 | 34 | 5 | 12 | 65 | 45 | 183 | 23 | 1 | .233/.305/.394 | .270 | .343 | 1.8 | SS(125): -4.7, 3B(4): -0.1 | 3.0 |
| 2014 | COL | MLB | 21 | 250 | 28 | 11 | 1 | 6 | 22 | 17 | 78 | 5 | 1 | .218/.273/.350 | .219 | .300 | 0.5 | SS -0, 3B 0 | 0.0 |
| 2015 | COL | MLB | 22 | 250 | 28 | 12 | 1 | 7 | 28 | 20 | 75 | 3 | 0 | .229/.295/.388 | .249 | .305 | 0.1 | SS 0, 3B 0 | 1.2 |

Breakout: 0%    Improve: 0%    Collapse: 0%    Attrition: 0%    MLB: 0%    *Comparables: Nick Franklin, Jonathan Villar, Joel Guzman*

**Drafted/Acquired:** 1st round, 2011 draft, Irving HS (Irving, TX)

**Previous Ranking:** #1 (Org), #34 (Top 101)

**What Happened in 2013:** The former top prospect in the Rockies organization and number 34 in the minors fell into a prospect pit of despair, struggling so mightily with the stick that his stock plummeted and even his most ardent supporters (me) were forced to accept a new reality.

**Strengths:** Good athlete with baseball skills and instincts; gets high marks for makeup; hands are still very good; swing improved in second half; showed improved bat speed and control; has legit pop in the stick; power could play to average; arm is plus; makes plays at shortstop; good actions; good footwork around the bag.

**Weaknesses:** Swing was a mess in 2013; poor balance; inconsistent and erratic mechanics; poor timing and hitchy trigger; struggled with pitch recognition and reaction; killed by sharp breaking balls; makes plays at shortstop but lacks glove; is more average than plus.

**Risk Factor/Injury History:** High risk; hit tool is well below average; yet to play at Double-A level.

**Bret Sayre's Fantasy Take:** Despite the setback, Story is still worth owning in fantasy based on the potential that remains (even if the risk has only increased). With a reasonable eye at the plate and the batting average risk, Story is more valuable in OBP leagues—though he's unlikely to be a huge help in that category. There's still 15/15 upside here.

**The Year Ahead:** Story could put himself back on the prospect roller coaster in 2014 with a strong season, but his shortcomings in High-A could be magnified by the superior arms in Double-A, particularly, his aggressive, fastball-timed approach. If he can stay consistent in his setup and swing, and stay on the ball with a more nuanced approach, he has the bat speed and strength to make things happen at the plate, and that along with his average defensive profile at shortstop could once again push his stock back up on the tracks and on its way.

## Prospects on the Rise

**1. RHP Raul Fernandez:** Remove a few ERA-inflating outings from the seasonal resume and Fernandez would look like a different arm, as the 23-year-old has a bat-missing power arsenal with good control. It's most likely a setup future and therefore not the sexiest prospect profile, but with a lively mid- to upper-90s fastball and splitter-like changeup, Fernandez could be ready for a fast ride in 2014. Don't sleep on the name.

**2. OF Terry McClure:** McClure was a part of the strong Georgia prep class of 2013, and lucky for the Rockies, fell all the way to the eighth round despite the lofty tool-based ceiling. With plus athleticism and the potential for all five tools, McClure has the physical characteristics to take a big step forward and climb into the Rockies top 10 next season, especially if the bat catches up to the promise he already shows on defense.

**3. RF Jordan Patterson:** A fourth-round selection in 2013 from the University of South Alabama, Patterson has the type of size, strength, and feel for hitting to step out of the shadows in 2014 as a legit offensive prospect. The arm is very strong, and despite his size, he is a good athlete and should be able to find a home in right field. But the bat will determine his fate, and if he crushes at the full-season level like several scouts envision, his name will be in the mix for top-10 consideration come next offseason.

## Factors on the Farm
### Prospects likely to contribute at the major-league level in 2014

**1. LHP Tyler Anderson:** Injuries and inconsistencies have kept Anderson from developing into the fast-to-the-majors starter the Rockies envisioned when they selected the southpaw 20th overall in the 2011 draft, ahead of arms like Alex Meyer, Taylor Guerrieri, and Robert Stephenson. With only a limited High-A resume to boast, it's time for Anderson to step forward in 2014, to use his mature approach of a solid-average arsenal to launch himself ahead in the queue of arms lining up to compete for innings at the major-league level. If he can stay healthy and log innings, a hot start in Double-A could expedite his arrival and punch his ticket to Colorado by season's end.

**2. LHP Tyler Matzek:** Matzek finally fell out of the Rockies top 10 after years of tantalizing and teasing observers with his plus stuff but minus control. The shortcomings of the past remained present in his 26-game run through Double-A, as the now-23-year-old arm struggled with mechanical consistency and arsenal execution. With command pulling down his once-vibrant rotation projection, a likely home will come in the bullpen, where shorter stints could enhance his stuff and hopefully allow the former first-round pick to regain his ability to repeat his mechanics and get the ball over the plate.

**3. OF Tim Wheeler:** Another prospect list recidivist, Wheeler's disappointing 2013 campaign depressed his stock and major-league projection, as the 25-year-old outfielder was removed from the 40-man roster and exposed to waivers. But he still offers some defensive versatility in the outfield and can swing it enough to keep pitchers honest, so he could find himself in the discussion for a possible bench role if the opportunity presents itself.

## FROM THE FIELD

### Eddie Butler

**Player:** Eddie Butler

**Team:** Colorado Rockies

**Filed by:** Chris Rodriguez

**Date(s) Seen:** July 17, 2013

**Physical:** Wiry but athletic; workload will be questioned because of his lack of size; don't see it to be an issue at the moment.

**Mechanics/Delivery:** Repeats well; ball comes out of his hand free and easy; delivery can get a little loose; which can negatively affect his command; shows too much ball in the back of his delivery.

**Fastball:** 70 grade; monster pitch; sat 92-94; hard two-seam bore to the arm side; tough to square; pounded down in the zone with it early and often; four-seam was 95-96; liked to elevate for some swings and misses; held velocity throughout.

**Slider:** 60 grade; quick and darting; thrown 84-86 mph; very confident in pitch; thrown in any count to both left-handers and right-handers; showed good command; deadly against right-handed hitters; threw more of a cutter at 88 mph; also very effective.

**Curveball:** 60 grade; good bite; plenty of depth; thrown around 82 mph; didn't throw many, but the few he did through were promising.

**Changeup:** 70 grade; best secondary pitch; thrown 87-88 mph; disappearing sinking action; huge vertical drop and movement to the arm side; confident throwing to both left-handers and right-handers.

**Other:** Command was solid; pounded that fastball on the outer half for first-pitch strikes; mixed in the slider and change beautifully; did not rack up the strikeouts (only two) but got a bunch of weak contact and ugly swings.

**Makeup:** 60 grade; poised; pumped up the fastball to 96 to get out of a bases-loaded jam; big competitor.

**OFP:** 70; no. 2 starter

**Realistic Role:** 60; no. 3 starter

**Risk:** Low; reached Double-A; advanced arsenal and solid command should play well at the highest level.

## 1. Nick Castellanos   3B/LF

**Born:** 3/4/92   **Age:** 22   **Bats:** R   **Throws:** R   **Height:** 6' 4"   **Weight:** 210

| MLB ETA | Hit | Power | Run | Glove | Arm | OFP | Realistic |
|---|---|---|---|---|---|---|---|
| Debuted in 2013 | 65 | 60 | — | — | 60 | 60<br>1ST DIV PLAYER | 50<br>ML REGULAR |

| YEAR | TEAM | LVL | AGE | PA | R | 2B | 3B | HR | RBI | BB | SO | SB | CS | AVG/OBP/SLG | TAv | BABIP | BRR | FRAA | WARP |
|---|---|---|---|---|---|---|---|---|---|---|---|---|---|---|---|---|---|---|---|
| 2013 | TOL | AAA | 21 | 595 | 81 | 37 | 1 | 18 | 76 | 54 | 100 | 4 | 1 | .276/.343/.450 | .282 | .307 | -0.6 | LF(130): 2.6 | 3.1 |
| 2013 | DET | MLB | 21 | 18 | 1 | 0 | 0 | 0 | 0 | 0 | 1 | 0 | 0 | .278/.278/.278 | .206 | .294 | -0.1 | LF(9): -0.3 | -0.1 |
| 2014 | DET | MLB | 22 | 250 | 24 | 12 | 1 | 5 | 27 | 13 | 57 | 1 | 0 | .263/.302/.390 | .250 | .320 | -0.4 | LF 0, 3B -2 | 0.1 |
| 2015 | DET | MLB | 23 | 364 | 40 | 18 | 2 | 8 | 39 | 21 | 85 | 1 | 0 | .254/.299/.391 | .254 | .313 | -0.7 | 3B -6 | 0.4 |

Breakout: 0%   Improve: 0%   Collapse: 0%   Attrition: 0%   MLB: 0%   *Comparables: Joel Guzman, Andrew Lambo, Carlos Gonzalez*

**Drafted/Acquired:** 1st round, 2010 draft, Archbishop McCarthy HS (Southwest Ranches, FL)

**Previous Ranking:** #1 (Org), #37 (Top 101)

**What Happened in 2013:** As a 21-year-old, Castellanos played a full season of Triple-A baseball, working to refine his plus bat against more advanced pitching.

**Strengths:** Excellent hands at the plate; creates plus bat speed; has some leverage and lift; projects to hit for both average and power; strong arm; good athlete for size; aptitude for the game; some defensive versatility.

**Weaknesses:** Trigger can be a bit slow; swing can get long; struggles against quality arm-side velocity; some question the offensive projection (more solid-average than impact); glove unlikely to play solid-average at third; below-average profile in outfield corner.

**Risk Factor/Injury History:** Low risk; ready for major-league challenge

**Bret Sayre's Fantasy Take:** With a move back to the hot corner potentially on the horizon, Castellanos' fantasy value takes a nice tick up as the eligibility is much sexier there. Even if he does switch back to third, there's always the chance that his defensive performance there warrants a return to the outfield. Regardless, if he hits to his full potential he could be a near-.300 hitter with 20+ homers and a lot of RBIs (as he's more likely to be in a run-producing slot in the lineup).

**The Year Ahead:** Of all the prospects in the minors, Castellanos might receive the most mixed reviews, as he's either a top-20 talent with future 6/6 hit/power at the major-league level, or he's just an average player, a top-50 prospect that has some ability with the bat but not nearly the impact talent some project. I've seen it and I like it, but I tend to fall in the middle of the two camps; I think Castellanos is going to hit for a high average but I'm not sold the power shows up in the 25+ home-run range without selling out the contact to achieve it. While I don't see a future 6/6 type, I do think he develops into a solid-average major-league player, and if he can stick around at third, there is a lot of value to be found in that profile.

## 2. Jonathon Crawford   RHP

**Born:** 11/1/91   **Age:** 22   **Bats:** R   **Throws:** R   **Height:** 6' 2"   **Weight:** 205

| MLB ETA | CT | FB | CH | CB | SL | OFP | Realistic |
|---|---|---|---|---|---|---|---|
| 2015 | — | 70 | — | — | 65 | 60<br>NO.3 STARTER | 50<br>LATE INN RP (SETUP) |

| YEAR | TEAM | LVL | AGE | W | L | SV | G | GS | IP | H | HR | BB | SO | BB9 | SO9 | GB% | BABIP | WHIP | ERA | FIP | FRA | WARP |
|---|---|---|---|---|---|---|---|---|---|---|---|---|---|---|---|---|---|---|---|---|---|---|
| 2013 | ONE | A- | 21 | 0 | 2 | 0 | 8 | 8 | 19.0 | 15 | 0 | 9 | 21 | 4.3 | 9.9 | 60% | .288 | 1.26 | 1.89 | 2.46 | 3.22 | 0.4 |
| 2014 | DET | MLB | 22 | 1 | 3 | 0 | 8 | 8 | 31.3 | 39 | 4 | 18 | 18 | 5.2 | 5.2 | 47% | .317 | 1.81 | 6.29 | 5.79 | 6.83 | -0.4 |
| 2015 | DET | MLB | 23 | 4 | 8 | 0 | 28 | 28 | 169.0 | 194 | 23 | 75 | 110 | 4.0 | 5.9 | 47% | .309 | 1.59 | 5.36 | 5.08 | 5.83 | -1.2 |

Breakout: 0%   Improve: 0%   Collapse: 0%   Attrition: 0%   MLB: 0%   *Comparables: Nick Maronde, Adam Warren, Ricky Romero*

**Drafted/Acquired:** 1st round, 2013 draft, University of Florida (Gainesville, FL)

**Previous Ranking:** NR

**What Happened in 2013:** Taken 20th overall in the 2013 draft. Crawford only dipped his toes into professional waters after signing, but should jump on an accelerated plan and move quickly up the minor-league ranks in 2014.

**Strengths:** Big arm strength; fastball is lively in the low-90s; touches mid-90s; strong offering; slider is second plus potential pitch; hard breaker with good tilt and bat-missing ability; mature build; ready to advance quickly.

**Weaknesses:** Command profile is fringe; can lose his delivery; struggles to finish and will elevate offerings; changeup is below average; power arsenal with limited nuance.

**Risk Factor/Injury History:** Moderate risk; short-season resume; should move fast going forward.

**Bret Sayre's Fantasy Take:** Crawford is a big arm, and carries the most upside in the system when it comes to potential starting pitchers. He has two weapons that may allow him to maintain very strong strikeout rates, but there might not be a ton of impact in the other three categories. If he's a reliever, it's a poor value proposition, but there's endgame potential.

**The Year Ahead:** Crawford has the arm strength and hard breaking ball to pitch in the majors, but the long-term outcome will depend on his ability to find consistency in his delivery, which will aid in his ability to throw strikes and to execute his changeup. If he can refine, this is future mid-rotation starter with good bat-missing potential. If he fails to reach that ceiling, he can still carve out a valuable career as a late-innings reliever, one who could probably work the fastball in the mid-90s (touching higher) to go along with the sharp slider.

## 3. Robbie Ray   LHP

**Born:** 10/1/91   **Age:** 22   **Bats:** L   **Throws:** L   **Height:** 6' 2"   **Weight:** 170

| MLB ETA | CT | FB | CH | CB | SL | OFP | Realistic |
|---|---|---|---|---|---|---|---|
| Late 2014 | — | 60 | 50 | 50 | — | 55<br>NO.3-4 STARTER | 50<br>NO.5 STARTER |

| YEAR | TEAM | LVL | AGE | W | L | SV | G | GS | IP | H | HR | BB | SO | BB9 | SO9 | GB% | BABIP | WHIP | ERA | FIP | FRA | WARP |
|---|---|---|---|---|---|---|---|---|---|---|---|---|---|---|---|---|---|---|---|---|---|---|
| 2013 | HAR | AA | 21 | 5 | 2 | 0 | 11 | 11 | 58.0 | 56 | 4 | 21 | 60 | 3.3 | 9.3 | 45% | .317 | 1.33 | 3.72 | 3.55 | 3.59 | 1.1 |
| 2013 | POT | A+ | 21 | 6 | 3 | 0 | 16 | 16 | 84.0 | 60 | 9 | 41 | 100 | 4.4 | 10.7 | 45% | .273 | 1.20 | 3.11 | 3.97 | 4.77 | 1.2 |
| 2014 | DET | MLB | 22 | 5 | 9 | 0 | 22 | 22 | 107.0 | 118 | 14 | 55 | 84 | 4.6 | 7.1 | 40% | .309 | 1.61 | 5.44 | 5.30 | 5.91 | -0.7 |
| 2015 | DET | MLB | 23 | 8 | 10 | 0 | 29 | 29 | 178.3 | 188 | 24 | 77 | 148 | 3.9 | 7.5 | 41% | .305 | 1.49 | 4.81 | 4.70 | 5.23 | -0.2 |

Breakout: 0%    Improve: 0%    Collapse: 0%    Attrition: 0%    MLB: 0%    *Comparables: Jeurys Familia, Alex Wood, Jarrod Parker*

**Drafted/Acquired:** 12th round, 2010 draft (Nationals), Brentwood High School (Brentwood, TN)

**Previous Ranking:** NR

**What Happened in 2013:** Ray has been a solid prospect since he was drafted, but he started to smooth out some of the rough edges in 2013, before a trade sent him to Detroit in early December.

**Strengths:** Good size/athleticism; simple delivery; fastball works in the low-90s; can bump 95; some lefty run; has some sneaky qualities and can miss bats; changeup is average with some fading action; curveball can flash average with big tumble from a high release; some strike-throwing ability.

**Weaknesses:** Delivery is simple but can show some effort; arm action can get short and rigid; fastball command is fringe-average; changeup can get deliberate and lacks disguise from the release; curveball is very slurvy and easy to track with long, slow break.

**Risk Factor/Injury History:** Moderate risk; some Double-A experience.

**Bret Sayre's Fantasy Take:** The left-hander will naturally have his fantasy value deflated because the general public's perception of the Doug Fister trade was that Washington got a steal. However, if you look past that, you see a starter who is capable of all the potential numbers people are projecting Drew Smyly for—and while that's not a star, it's worthy of investment.

**The Year Ahead:** Ray is an athletic lefty that can pump the fastball in the 92-95 range on a consistent basis, but lacks the secondary arsenal or command profile to project high in a major-league rotation. He's a solid arm and should eventually find a home in the back of a major-league rotation, but unless the secondary stuff improves or the command because extra sharp, his ceiling is limited and he will likely struggle to find sustainable results against big-league bats.

## 4. James McCann   C

**Born:** 6/13/90   **Age:** 24   **Bats:** R   **Throws:** R   **Height:** 6' 2"   **Weight:** 210

| MLB ETA | Hit | Power | Run | Glove | Arm | OFP | Realistic |
|---|---|---|---|---|---|---|---|
| Late 2014 | 50 | — | — | 55 | 60 | 50<br>ML REGULAR | 45<br>BACKUP C/<AVG REG |

| YEAR | TEAM | LVL | AGE | PA | R | 2B | 3B | HR | RBI | BB | SO | SB | CS | AVG/OBP/SLG | TAv | BABIP | BRR | FRAA | WARP |
|---|---|---|---|---|---|---|---|---|---|---|---|---|---|---|---|---|---|---|---|
| 2013 | ERI | AA | 23 | 486 | 50 | 30 | 1 | 8 | 54 | 30 | 85 | 3 | 3 | .277/.328/.404 | .266 | .321 | -0.5 | C(100): -0.3 | 2.0 |
| 2014 | DET | MLB | 24 | 250 | 19 | 12 | 0 | 3 | 23 | 8 | 55 | 1 | 0 | .231/.261/.322 | .213 | .280 | -0.5 | C -0 | -0.1 |
| 2015 | DET | MLB | 25 | 250 | 24 | 12 | 0 | 4 | 22 | 11 | 58 | 0 | 0 | .223/.265/.323 | .218 | .276 | -0.7 | C 0 | -0.4 |

Breakout: 0%    Improve: 0%    Collapse: 0%    Attrition: 0%    MLB: 0%    *Comparables: Brett Hayes, Manny Pina, John Hester*

**Drafted/Acquired:** 2nd round, 2011 draft, University of Arkansas (Fayetteville, AR)

**Previous Ranking:** NR

**What Happened in 2013:** After a disappointing run in his first pass in Double-A, McCann rebounded in 2013, showing good gap pop to go along with his solid defensive skills behind the plate.

**Strengths:** Athletic and strong; good receiver; frames well; good game caller; arm is solid-average; quick release and accurate; necessary intangibles for position; bat could get to average; shows gap power.

**Weaknesses:** Glove-first profile; weak contact against arm-side pitching; hit most likely to play below average; power will play below average; athletic but below-average run.

**Risk Factor/Injury History:** Moderate risk; solid in Double-A debut; bat needs grade improvement.

**Bret Sayre's Fantasy Take:** Unless you're in a deep league or one that plays two catchers, McCann is not a name worth worrying about at this point. His real-life value is much higher than his fantasy value. He profiles similarly with the bat to former Tigers' farmhand Rob Brantly.

**The Year Ahead:** Dual-threat catchers don't grow on trees, and given his progress with the stick in 2013, it's not a stretch to see McCann developing his way into that category. It's always going to be a glove-first profile—with solid-average attributes that play up in combination—but the bat has a chance to play up to average and show respectable gap pop, so its not an empty out. If that's a .260 hitter with some extra-base potential coming from a 5+ glove at a premium spot, that's a valuable player.

## 5.  Jake Thompson   RHP

**Born:** 1/31/94  **Age:** 20  **Bats:** R  **Throws:** R  **Height:** 6' 4"  **Weight:** 235

| MLB ETA | CT | FB | CH | CB | SL | OFP | Realistic |
|---|---|---|---|---|---|---|---|
| 2016 | – | 60 | 50 | 50 | 65 | 55 NO.3 STARTER | 50 NO.5 SP/LATE INN RP |

| YEAR | TEAM | LVL | AGE | W | L | SV | G | GS | IP | H | HR | BB | SO | BB9 | SO9 | GB% | BABIP | WHIP | ERA | FIP | FRA | WARP |
|---|---|---|---|---|---|---|---|---|---|---|---|---|---|---|---|---|---|---|---|---|---|---|
| 2013 | WMI | A | 19 | 3 | 3 | 0 | 17 | 16 | 83.3 | 79 | 4 | 32 | 91 | 3.5 | 9.8 | 45% | .325 | 1.33 | 3.13 | 3.33 | 3.91 | 1.6 |
| 2014 | DET | MLB | 20 | 3 | 5 | 0 | 13 | 13 | 60.0 | 67 | 8 | 32 | 45 | 4.8 | 6.8 | 45% | .313 | 1.64 | 5.47 | 5.42 | 5.95 | -0.4 |
| 2015 | DET | MLB | 21 | 7 | 10 | 0 | 27 | 27 | 164.7 | 177 | 22 | 82 | 131 | 4.5 | 7.2 | 45% | .306 | 1.58 | 5.24 | 4.98 | 5.70 | -0.9 |

Breakout: 0%    Improve: 0%    Collapse: 0%    Attrition: 0%    MLB: 0%    *Comparables: Jenrry Mejia, Jarrod Parker, David Holmberg*

**Drafted/Acquired:** 2nd round, 2012 draft, Rockwall-Heath HS (Heath, TX)

**Previous Ranking:** #5 (Org)

**What Happened in 2013:** The then-19-year-old made his full-season debut, making 16 starts in the Midwest League, missing 91 bats in 83 innings.

**Strengths:** Big, physical frame; delivery and arm work well; fastball works 89-92; touches higher; some late arm-side wiggle; slider is money pitch; already above average, thrown with velocity and tilt; shows some feel for promising changeup.

**Weaknesses:** More control than command at this point; fastball command is below average; will pitch off his slider; show a curveball but it's below average (present); changeup is below average (present); physically mature without much projection remaining.

**Risk Factor/Injury History:** High risk; limited professional experience

**Bret Sayre's Fantasy Take:** Of all the pitchers on this list, Thompson likely has the best chance to stay in the rotation long term, but his upside is not something to get extremely excited about. He projects as more of a back-end starter who could be solid all around, but lacks a ton of fantasy potential.

**The Year Ahead:** Thompson looks the part of a workhorse type, complete with a big, sturdy frame and at least two pitches that project to plus (slider is close to that point already). He needs to refine his fastball command and take a grade step with the changeup and curveball, but you have to like the profile. It might be more slow and steady than accelerated and sexy, but if he eventually finds his way to a major-league rotation and settles in as a solid-average number three or four starter, the luster and shine of his prospect status won't matter.

## 6.  Corey Knebel   RHP

**Born:** 11/26/91  **Age:** 22  **Bats:** R  **Throws:** R  **Height:** 6' 3"  **Weight:** 195

| MLB ETA | CT | FB | CH | CB | SL | OFP | Realistic |
|---|---|---|---|---|---|---|---|
| Late 2014 | – | 70 | – | 70 | – | 55 LATE INN RP (CLOSER) | 50 LATE INN RP (SETUP) |

| YEAR | TEAM | LVL | AGE | W | L | SV | G | GS | IP | H | HR | BB | SO | BB9 | SO9 | GB% | BABIP | WHIP | ERA | FIP | FRA | WARP |
|---|---|---|---|---|---|---|---|---|---|---|---|---|---|---|---|---|---|---|---|---|---|---|
| 2013 | WMI | A | 21 | 2 | 1 | 15 | 31 | 0 | 31.0 | 14 | 0 | 10 | 41 | 2.9 | 11.9 | 56% | .212 | 0.77 | 0.87 | 1.66 | 2.69 | 0.8 |
| 2014 | DET | MLB | 22 | 2 | 1 | 1 | 34 | 0 | 33.7 | 34 | 4 | 16 | 31 | 4.3 | 8.3 | 47% | .310 | 1.49 | 4.57 | 4.62 | 4.96 | 0.0 |
| 2015 | DET | MLB | 23 | 3 | 1 | 2 | 50 | 0 | 50.3 | 45 | 5 | 20 | 47 | 3.6 | 8.4 | 47% | .283 | 1.30 | 3.61 | 3.90 | 3.93 | 0.6 |

Breakout: 0%    Improve: 0%    Collapse: 0%    Attrition: 0%    MLB: 0%    *Comparables: Drew Storen, Eduardo Sanchez, Steven Geltz*

**Drafted/Acquired:** 1st round, 2013 draft, University of Texas at Austin (Austin, TX)

**Previous Ranking:** NR

**What Happened in 2013:** Knebel wasted little time after signing, shoving in the Midwest League before making a nine-game cameo in the Arizona Fall League.

**Strengths:** Big fastball; delivered on steep plane; velocity works easy in the 93-97 range; power pitch; hard curve can be true hammer; thrown in the low-80s with big snap and depth; can turn over a decent cambio; late-innings approach/mentality.

**Weaknesses:** Makeup concerns; emotions can get the better of him; fastball lacks big movement; can flatten out when he works up; more control than command.

**Risk Factor/Injury History:** Low risk; mature arsenal

**Bret Sayre's Fantasy Take:** The leader in the clubhouse for Tigers' closer of the future, Knebel could be an impact reliever at the major-league level and soon. The slider should keep him racking up strikeouts, but with his value being so role dependent (and the Tigers' willingness to reach outside the organization to fill the closer role), he shouldn't be high up on your dynasty draft boards.

**The Year Ahead:** Knebel is a natural late-innings arm, with a power arsenal and aggressive approach to execution. The makeup should be a legit concern, as immaturity has been a red flag since his college days. But the stuff is there to develop into a major-league caliber closer, and if he can channel his emotions without losing the intensity he brings to the table, he could move fast and contribute to the major-league team in 2014.

## 7.   Endrys Briceno   RHP

**Born:** 2/7/92   **Age:** 22   **Bats:** R   **Throws:** R   **Height:** 6'5"   **Weight:** 171

| MLB ETA | CT | FB | CH | CB | SL | OFP | Realistic |
|---|---|---|---|---|---|---|---|
| 2016 | – | 70 | 65 | 50 | – | 55 NO.2-3 STARTER | 50 NO.4 STARTER |

| YEAR | TEAM | LVL | AGE | W | L | SV | G | GS | IP | H | HR | BB | SO | BB9 | SO9 | GB% | BABIP | WHIP | ERA | FIP | FRA | WARP |
|---|---|---|---|---|---|---|---|---|---|---|---|---|---|---|---|---|---|---|---|---|---|---|
| 2013 | WMI | A | 21 | 7 | 9 | 0 | 25 | 25 | 116.7 | 124 | 5 | 51 | 65 | 3.9 | 5.0 | 53% | .305 | 1.50 | 4.47 | 4.25 | 5.65 | -0.1 |
| 2014 | DET | MLB | 22 | 3 | 7 | 0 | 19 | 14 | 82.7 | 112 | 12 | 48 | 26 | 5.2 | 2.8 | 46% | .318 | 1.93 | 7.10 | 6.68 | 7.72 | -1.9 |
| 2015 | DET | MLB | 23 | 4 | 6 | 0 | 21 | 16 | 111.7 | 134 | 13 | 54 | 59 | 4.4 | 4.8 | 46% | .315 | 1.68 | 5.75 | 5.23 | 6.25 | -1.3 |

Breakout: 0%   Improve: 0%   Collapse: 0%   Attrition: 0%   MLB: 0%          *Comparables: Charlie Haeger, Jordan Smith, Jared Hughes*

**Drafted/Acquired:** International free agent, 2009, Venezuela

**Previous Ranking:** On The Rise

**What Happened in 2013:** Briceno made his full-season debut, finding mixed results, but he did make 25 starts and logged an impressive 116 innings, quite the progression from last season's body of work.

**Strengths:** Highly projectable body; easy delivery and release; fastball will work 90-95; touches higher; projects to be a 7 pitch; turns over an impressive changeup; good arm speed and late action; plus potential pitch; athletic and clean delivery suggests average or better command at maturity.

**Weaknesses:** Fastball velocity ebbs and flows; will work 90-92 then work 94-95; general inconsistencies in delivery; breaking ball is below average; slurvy offering that lacks bite; pitchability needs work; command below average at present.

**Risk Factor/Injury History:** High risk; big gap between present/future

**Bret Sayre's Fantasy Take:** If drafting for ceiling is what you're into, Briceno should probably be the second pitcher in this system off the board. He's too raw to have a feel for what he'll be at peak, but the stuff is worth taking a chance toward the end of your farm system.

**The Year Ahead:** The system lacks many high-ceiling prospects, but Briceno has the size and the stuff to emerge as a top talent. He has a good delivery, but is still learning how to control his body and repeat his mechanics. The fastball is a potential monster offering, and the changeup is ahead of the developmental curve and shows the making of an impact pitch. The breaking ball needs a lot of work, and it could take a few years for him to really take off. But once his stuff stabilizes and he starts to miss more bats, Briceno is a likely candidate to take a major step forward in the prospect world.

## 8.   Drew VerHagen   RHP

**Born:** 10/22/90   **Age:** 23   **Bats:** R   **Throws:** R   **Height:** 6'6"   **Weight:** 230

| MLB ETA | CT | FB | CH | CB | SL | OFP | Realistic |
|---|---|---|---|---|---|---|---|
| Late 2014 | – | 60 | 55 | 50 | – | 50 NO.4 STARTER | 50 LATE INN RP (SETUP) |

| YEAR | TEAM | LVL | AGE | W | L | SV | G | GS | IP | H | HR | BB | SO | BB9 | SO9 | GB% | BABIP | WHIP | ERA | FIP | FRA | WARP |
|---|---|---|---|---|---|---|---|---|---|---|---|---|---|---|---|---|---|---|---|---|---|---|
| 2013 | LAK | A+ | 22 | 5 | 3 | 0 | 12 | 11 | 67.3 | 49 | 1 | 27 | 35 | 3.6 | 4.7 | 58% | .231 | 1.13 | 2.81 | 3.82 | 5.24 | -0.1 |
| 2013 | ERI | AA | 22 | 2 | 5 | 0 | 12 | 12 | 60.0 | 53 | 3 | 17 | 40 | 2.5 | 6.0 | 60% | .272 | 1.17 | 3.00 | 3.69 | 4.54 | 0.5 |
| 2014 | DET | MLB | 23 | 4 | 6 | 0 | 19 | 16 | 86.7 | 98 | 10 | 38 | 42 | 3.9 | 4.4 | 55% | .297 | 1.57 | 5.20 | 5.43 | 5.66 | -0.4 |
| 2015 | DET | MLB | 24 | 7 | 9 | 0 | 30 | 25 | 168.3 | 172 | 18 | 67 | 104 | 3.6 | 5.6 | 55% | .286 | 1.42 | 4.51 | 4.67 | 4.91 | 0.4 |

Breakout: 0%   Improve: 0%   Collapse: 0%   Attrition: 0%   MLB: 0%          *Comparables: Anthony Ortega, Kevin Mulvey, Ivan Nova*

**Drafted/Acquired:** 4th round, 2012 draft, Vanderbilt University (Nashville, TN)

**Previous Ranking:** NR

**What Happened in 2013:** A fourth-round pick out of Vandy in 2012, VerHagen advanced to the Double-A level in 2013, setting himself up for a potential call-up at some point in the coming season.

**Strengths:** Huge size; athletic; fastball is heavy and can work in the 91-95 range and touch higher; hard to lift when he works low in the zone; strike-thrower; curve and change could be average to solid-average.

**Weaknesses:** Fastball-dominant arsenal; secondary arsenal is fringe-average; lacks plus projections; command needs refinement; can lose his delivery/struggle to stay over the ball.

**Risk Factor/Injury History:** Moderate risk; mature build; limited projection

**Bret Sayre's Fantasy Take:** The upside is just not there for VerHagen to be owned outside of very deep dynasty leagues. Even if he makes it to Detroit as a starter, his quality of raw stuff isn't going to lead to a ton of missed bats (as it hasn't thus far in the minors), though his ground-ball tendencies will help insulate his ratios a bit.

**The Year Ahead:** VerHagen is a big-bodied sinkerballer who knows how to pound the zone and force ground-ball outs. He's not sexy but if the secondary stuff can improve a bit, he should end up a solid back-of-the-rotation starter. If the curve and changeup remain fringe offerings, a bullpen future is still likely given the power of the fastball and the ability to throw strikes. He should start back in Double-A, and with any luck, VerHagen could taste the majors at some point this season.

---

## 9.  Steven Moya  RF

**Born:** 9/8/91  **Age:** 22  **Bats:** L  **Throws:** R  **Height:** 6'6"  **Weight:** 230

| MLB ETA | Hit | Power | Run | Glove | Arm | OFP | Realistic |
|---|---|---|---|---|---|---|---|
| Late 2016 | – | 80 | – | – | – | 60<br>1ST DIV PLAYER | 45<br>PLATOON /<AVG REG |

| YEAR | TEAM | LVL | AGE | PA | R | 2B | 3B | HR | RBI | BB | SO | SB | CS | AVG/OBP/SLG | TAv | BABIP | BRR | FRAA | WARP |
|---|---|---|---|---|---|---|---|---|---|---|---|---|---|---|---|---|---|---|---|
| 2013 | LAK | A+ | 21 | 388 | 52 | 19 | 5 | 12 | 55 | 18 | 106 | 6 | 0 | .255/.296/.433 | .254 | .327 | 1.3 | RF(78): -4.0 | -0.1 |
| 2014 | DET | MLB | 22 | 250 | 22 | 9 | 1 | 8 | 28 | 5 | 88 | 1 | 0 | .210/.227/.350 | .208 | .290 | -0.1 | RF -1 | -1.0 |
| 2015 | DET | MLB | 23 | 250 | 26 | 10 | 2 | 8 | 29 | 8 | 87 | 0 | 0 | .220/.247/.378 | .229 | .305 | -0.3 | RF -2 | -0.8 |

Breakout: 0%   Improve: 0%   Collapse: 0%   Attrition: 0%   MLB: 0%      *Comparables: Carlos Peguero, Jeremy Moore, Cole Garner*

**Drafted/Acquired:** International free agent, 2008, Dominican Republic

**Previous Ranking:** #9 (Org)

**What Happened in 2013:** After 566 at-bats at the Low-A level over the last two seasons, Moya finally made his way to the Florida State League, where his batting practice displays still received more acclaim than his on-the-field performance.

**Strengths:** Abnormally large human; raw power is off the charts; good athlete for his enormous size; raw arm strength for corner spot; glove should be average.

**Weaknesses:** Swing is long and leveraged; issues with pitch recognition; chewed up by arm-side stuff; hit tool will play well below average; game power will play under raw; glove is average at best; needs power to play.

**Risk Factor/Injury History:** High risk; big developmental gains needed to play

**Bret Sayre's Fantasy Take:** Moya is a fantasy of sorts, as he still has a long way to turn his One True Tool into fantasy relevance. If you're in a league where a two true outcome player (he doesn't walk) has value, Moya may be worth a flier, but he's most likely not worth the roster spot.

**The Year Ahead:** Moya has some of the best raw power in the minors, with batting practice heroics that force observers to worship the long ball like it was a sun god. The biggest problem with Moya's profile is that his future is tied to his ability to bring that raw power into game action, and the reality is that his hit tool is going to limit that utility. The swing isn't especially quick, as he relies more on his superhuman strength than pure bat speed, and he has holes that better pitching will exploit with greater efficiency. He's still very young, and it might take three more years in the minors to refine his swing and approach, but if he can find a way to get the power to play, it's an impact bat in the middle of a lineup. Hard to see that actually happening, though.

---

## 10.  Eugenio Suarez  SS

**Born:** 7/18/91  **Age:** 22  **Bats:** R  **Throws:** R  **Height:** 5'11"  **Weight:** 180

| MLB ETA | Hit | Power | Run | Glove | Arm | OFP | Realistic |
|---|---|---|---|---|---|---|---|
| Late 2014 | 50 | – | – | 55 | 55 | 50<br>ML REGULAR | 45<br>UTILITY |

| YEAR | TEAM | LVL | AGE | PA | R | 2B | 3B | HR | RBI | BB | SO | SB | CS | AVG/OBP/SLG | TAv | BABIP | BRR | FRAA | WARP |
|---|---|---|---|---|---|---|---|---|---|---|---|---|---|---|---|---|---|---|---|
| 2013 | LAK | A+ | 21 | 122 | 17 | 6 | 2 | 1 | 12 | 14 | 25 | 2 | 3 | .311/.410/.437 | .305 | .397 | -0.3 | SS(24): 1.1, 2B(1): 0.1 | 1.4 |
| 2013 | ERI | AA | 21 | 496 | 53 | 24 | 4 | 9 | 45 | 46 | 98 | 9 | 11 | .253/.332/.387 | .268 | .307 | 4.3 | SS(111): 4.3 | 3.2 |
| 2014 | DET | MLB | 22 | 250 | 27 | 11 | 1 | 4 | 20 | 17 | 62 | 4 | 3 | .235/.296/.341 | .235 | .300 | -0.4 | SS 0, 2B 0 | 0.5 |
| 2015 | DET | MLB | 23 | 250 | 27 | 10 | 2 | 4 | 24 | 19 | 57 | 3 | 2 | .249/.317/.361 | .254 | .313 | -0.5 | SS 1, 2B 0 | 1.6 |

Breakout: 0%   Improve: 0%   Collapse: 0%   Attrition: 0%   MLB: 0%      *Comparables: Marcus Semien, Tim Beckham, Nick Franklin*

**Drafted/Acquired:** International Free Agent, 2008, Venezuela

**Previous Ranking:** #7 (Org)

**What Happened in 2013:** The then-21-year-old proved to be a tough out over two levels, while showing above-average defense at shortstop.

**Strengths:** Left-side defensive skills; good actions; good backhand pickup; arm is strong enough to make the throws; shows instincts for the position; can put the bat on the ball at the plate; good hands; quick to the ball; hit tool could play to solid-average.

**Weaknesses:** Lacks impact tools; defensive profile is solid-average but will make fundamental errors; arm isn't a weapon; well-below-average power; hit tool might play below average; not a burner; limited upside.

**Risk Factor/Injury History:** Moderate risk; Double-A experience; quality glove

**Bret Sayre's Fantasy Take:** Another low-upside fantasy option in the Tigers system. Suarez might have the potential to be a valuable member of the Detroit organization, but if he's on your fantasy roster, you may have to rethink your strategy for acquiring minor leaguers.

**The Year Ahead:** It was a toss-up between Suarez and Hernan Perez for this spot, as both look like future utility options at the highest level. Suarez gets the nod on this list because of the better left-side profile, even though Perez has the superior stick. It's close, but I think Suarez takes a step forward in 2014 and shows more life at the plate than he did in his first run through Double-A.

## Prospects on the Rise

**1. INF Javier Betancourt:** The Tigers have been aggressive with the 18-year-old Betancourt, offering him the chance to make his stateside debut in 2013. He rewarded that aggressiveness with a .333/.379/.441 performance while playing shortstop, third base and second base. The nephew of former major leaguer Edgardo Alfonzo, Betancourt's tools won't blow you away but he has a great feel for the game and just enough tools to profile as a potential everyday player, most likely at second base, where his modest range and average arm will play best.

**2. INF Steven Fuentes:** Betancourt's teammate each of the last two seasons, Fuentes has the raw tools Betancourt lacks. Fuentes is compact with exceptional athleticism, plus speed, a plus arm, and good feel for the barrel. He has the ingredients to remain at shortstop but could move to third base if he doesn't settle into the defensive profile. The developmental arc may be bumpier for Fuentes because he is so raw, but he has some of the most impactful tools in the system.

**3. RHP Joe Jimenez:** A nondrafted free agent out of Puerto Rico, Jimenez was widely considered the top pitcher on the island heading into the 2013 draft. He fell out of the draft after not budging from his lofty bonus demands, and the Tigers used a close relationship with the player to sign him away from a college commitment. A physically mature 6-foot-3 and 200 pounds, Jimenez offers a low-90s sinking fastball, quality slider, and some feel for a changeup, allowing him to profile as a mid-rotation inning eater.

## Factors on the Farm

### Prospects likely to contribute at the major-league level in 2014

**1. LHP Kyle Lobstein:** After coming over from the Rays in the Rule 5 draft, Lobstein logged 28 starts between Double-A and Triple-A in 2013, and was added to the Tigers 40-man roster in November. Though the overall profile lacks flash, Lobstein has the durability and breadth of arsenal to serve as a fifth starter, or he could fill in as a second lefty out of the bullpen. In either capacity, he will be in line for a major-league look at some point in 2014.

**2. RHP Justin Miller:** The Tigers moved quickly to sign the former Rangers farmhand as a minor-league free agent following the 2013 season. After evaluating his progress as he recovers from surgery, they added Miller to the 40-man roster, and he will be a candidate to contribute out of the bullpen this season. At his best Miller can show an easy plus fastball with a good slider, giving him two distinct offerings that could work against major-league hitters.

**3. RHP Melvin Mercedes:** Another product of the Tigers' Latin American pipeline, Mercedes has already survived Tommy John surgery and put together an impressive 2013 season that included a 1.19 ERA across High-A and Double-A. Mercedes' fastball can work in the 93-95 mph range and has touched 98 mph at times. On top of his impressive velocity, Mercedes has a heavy fastball that is extremely difficult to lift, and when combined with his slider he can induce plenty of weak contact. Mercedes may only pitch in the middle innings in 2014, but he has the potential to develop into a quality setup arm.

---

## FROM THE FIELD

### Nick Castellanos

**Player:** Nick Castellanos

**Team:** Detroit Tigers

**Filed by:** Jordan Gorosh

**Date(s) Seen:** Multiple times

**Physical:** Large, physical, still not in "man" body. Bit of room to grow.

**Hit:** 65 grade; superb barrel control; excellent hand-eye; lets ball travel deep in hitting zone; trusts hands implicitly; right center field is comfort zone.

**Approach:** must look for better pitches to drive; low heartbeat hitter; can get a bit overaggressive because of his outstanding coordination.

**Power:** 60 grade; 35 doubles, 55 extra-base hits possible; over-the-fence power still developing; needs to pull ball more with authority.

**Glove:** 40 grade; good athlete for size; side-to-side movement below average; limited range; average hands.

**Arm:** 50; major-league-average arm; good carry on throws from third base; can make all necessary throws.

**Speed:** 40 grade; not a part of his game; may even slow down a tick more; below-average runner.

**Makeup:** hard worker; looking to improve; always honing his skills; good work ethic.

**OFP:** 6+; if everything clicks, all-star ceiling at third, position that is down in recent years

**Realistic Role:** 5+; first-division player

**Risk:** Low; has hit at every minor league level, ready to go in MLB.

## 1. Carlos Correa   SS

**Born:** 9/22/94   **Age:** 19   **Bats:** R   **Throws:** R   **Height:** 6' 4"   **Weight:** 205

| MLB ETA | Hit | Power | Run | Glove | Arm | OFP | Realistic |
|---|---|---|---|---|---|---|---|
| Late 2014 | 60 | 65 | -- | 60 | 70 | 70 ALL-STAR | 60 1ST DIV PLAYER |

| YEAR | TEAM | LVL | AGE | PA | R | 2B | 3B | HR | RBI | BB | SO | SB | CS | AVG/OBP/SLG | TAv | BABIP | BRR | FRAA | WARP |
|---|---|---|---|---|---|---|---|---|---|---|---|---|---|---|---|---|---|---|---|
| 2013 | QUD | A | 18 | 519 | 73 | 33 | 3 | 9 | 86 | 58 | 83 | 10 | 10 | .320/.405/.467 | .314 | .375 | -2.3 | SS(115): -6.8 | 4.7 |
| 2014 | HOU | MLB | 19 | 250 | 27 | 11 | 1 | 5 | 22 | 17 | 60 | 2 | 1 | .242/.300/.355 | .242 | .300 | -0.5 | SS -3 | 0.3 |
| 2015 | HOU | MLB | 20 | 250 | 30 | 13 | 1 | 5 | 27 | 19 | 51 | 0 | 0 | .275/.336/.413 | .275 | .329 | -0.6 | SS -3 | 2.5 |

**Breakout:** 0%   **Improve:** 0%   **Collapse:** 0%   **Attrition:** 0%   **MLB:** 0%   *Comparables: Manny Machado, Jurickson Profar, Jason Heyward*

**Drafted/Acquired:** 1st round, 2012 draft, Puerto Rican Baseball Academy (Gurabo, PR)

**Previous Ranking:** #2 (Org), #26 (Top 101)

**What Happened in 2013:** Correa emerged as a potential superstar, showing four tools with impact potential, all from a premium position on the diamond.

**Strengths:** 80-grade makeup; high-end tool projections with present skills; advanced approach to the game; can make quick adjustments; plus potential hit; power could be bigger than projected; above-average glove; well-above-average arm; actions and instincts can keep him at shortstop.

**Weaknesses:** Body could outgrow shortstop; run is average at best; range at shortstop dependent on instincts/first step; swing can get long at times; can swing through velocity in the zone; power potential is a big debate (could be 5, could be 7).

**Risk Factor/Injury History:** Moderate risk; can make a case for low risk based on makeup and present skills; very high floor.

**Bret Sayre's Fantasy Take:** One of the top fantasy prospects in the game, Correa is a potential perennial first-round talent, especially if he does stick at shortstop long term. Think Troy Tulowitzki without the constant injury risk, from a statistical perspective. Even if he does move to the hot corner, he can still be a top performer from that position as well.

**The Year Ahead:** After a year of steady development at one level, Correa looks ready to take another big step forward in 2014, with a very good chance of playing in Double-A early and perhaps even reaching the majors by the end of the season. It's aggressive and perhaps unnecessary, but Correa is already the best shortstop in the organization, and despite being 19 years old, he could hold his own at the higher levels because of the elite makeup.

**#5**
BP Top 101 Prospects

## 2. George Springer   CF

**Born:** 9/19/89   **Age:** 24   **Bats:** R   **Throws:** R   **Height:** 6' 3"   **Weight:** 200

| MLB ETA | Hit | Power | Run | Glove | Arm | OFP | Realistic |
|---|---|---|---|---|---|---|---|
| 2014 | -- | 60 | 60 | 60 | 60 | 60 1ST DIV PLAYER | 55 >AVG PLAYER |

| YEAR | TEAM | LVL | AGE | PA | R | 2B | 3B | HR | RBI | BB | SO | SB | CS | AVG/OBP/SLG | TAv | BABIP | BRR | FRAA | WARP |
|---|---|---|---|---|---|---|---|---|---|---|---|---|---|---|---|---|---|---|---|
| 2013 | OKL | AAA | 23 | 267 | 50 | 7 | 4 | 18 | 53 | 41 | 65 | 22 | 3 | .311/.425/.626 | .373 | .362 | 1.6 | CF(47): -0.7, RF(11): -0.4 | 4.1 |
| 2013 | CCH | AA | 23 | 323 | 56 | 20 | 0 | 19 | 55 | 42 | 96 | 23 | 5 | .297/.399/.579 | .350 | .390 | 4.9 | CF(70): -2.8, LF(3): -0.0 | 4.4 |
| 2014 | HOU | MLB | 24 | 250 | 36 | 8 | 2 | 11 | 35 | 26 | 78 | 12 | 2 | .248/.332/.457 | .290 | .320 | 1.5 | CF -1, RF -0 | 1.5 |
| 2015 | HOU | MLB | 25 | 609 | 82 | 21 | 4 | 25 | 82 | 63 | 189 | 26 | 5 | .244/.329/.440 | .285 | .323 | 3.3 | RF -6, CF -1 | 2.6 |

**Breakout:** 3%   **Improve:** 26%   **Collapse:** 15%   **Attrition:** 16%   **MLB:** 55%   *Comparables: Joe Benson, Mike Olt, Brett Jackson*

**Drafted/Acquired:** 1st round, 2011 draft, University of Connecticut (Storrs, CT)

**Previous Ranking:** #3 (Org), #55 (Top 101)

**What Happened in 2013:** Springer exploded in 2013, ripping 37 bombs over two stops in the high minors, and positioning himself as the Astros' center fielder of the future.

**Strengths:** Lively power; should achieve at least solid-average to plus game power; multidimensional player; brings plus run to offense/defense; glove in center should end up a 6; arm is a weapon.

**Weaknesses:** Swing-and-miss concerns; approach can get loose; two-strike approach can lack adjustment; tendency to miss in the zone; hit tool might play below-average; could limit some of the power potential.

**Risk Factor/Injury History:** Low risk; ready for major leagues

**Bret Sayre's Fantasy Take:** Potential fantasy stud, even if he ends up as a .250 hitter. Springer is one of the few prospects in baseball with 30/30 upside, although he's more likely to reach the plateau on the steals side. There's certainly concern in points league with the strikeout rate, but don't make too much of an adjustment for it.

**#20**
BP Top 101 Prospects

**The Year Ahead:** Springer is ready for Houston, but some sources aren't sold that his hit tool/approach will be conducive to sustainable success at the highest level, at least not right away. Springer is a more electric version of Chris Young, with similar issues with the hit tool that could limit the overall utility of the power. The defensive profile and speed will give his bat a very long leash, but if he doesn't learn to make adjustments at the plate, especially when he's down in the count, major-league arms will exploit him at will and it could lead to a very high strikeout total.

---

## 3. Mark Appel RHP

**Born:** 7/15/91 **Age:** 22 **Bats:** R **Throws:** R **Height:** 6' 5" **Weight:** 190

| MLB ETA | CT | FB | CH | CB | SL | OFP | Realistic |
|---|---|---|---|---|---|---|---|
| 2014 | -- | 70 | 60 | -- | 60 | 65<br>NO.2 STARTER | 60<br>NO.2-3 STARTER |

| YEAR | TEAM | LVL | AGE | W | L | SV | G | GS | IP | H | HR | BB | SO | BB9 | SO9 | GB% | BABIP | WHIP | ERA | FIP | FRA | WARP |
|---|---|---|---|---|---|---|---|---|---|---|---|---|---|---|---|---|---|---|---|---|---|---|
| 2013 | TCV | A- | 21 | 0 | 0 | 0 | 2 | 2 | 5.0 | 6 | 0 | 0 | 6 | 0.0 | 10.8 | 71% | .429 | 1.20 | 3.60 | 0.70 | 2.67 | 0.2 |
| 2013 | QUD | A | 21 | 3 | 1 | 0 | 8 | 8 | 33.0 | 30 | 2 | 9 | 27 | 2.5 | 7.4 | 54% | .277 | 1.18 | 3.82 | 3.40 | 4.58 | 0.4 |
| 2014 | HOU | MLB | 22 | 1 | 3 | 0 | 8 | 8 | 32.0 | 38 | 5 | 16 | 18 | 4.5 | 5.1 | 47% | .308 | 1.70 | 5.89 | 5.96 | 6.40 | -0.4 |
| 2015 | HOU | MLB | 23 | 8 | 11 | 0 | 28 | 28 | 172.0 | 190 | 24 | 79 | 115 | 4.1 | 6.0 | 47% | .302 | 1.57 | 5.21 | 5.12 | 5.67 | -1.1 |

Breakout: 0%    Improve: 0%    Collapse: 0%    Attrition: 0%    MLB: 0%        *Comparables: Alex Cobb, Brett Marshall, J.C. Ramirez*

**Drafted/Acquired:** 1st round, 2013 draft, Stanford University (Palo Alto, CA)

**Previous Ranking:** NR

**What Happened in 2013:** After being selected 1:1 in the amateur draft, Appel made 10 starts over two levels, finishing the season with an impressive run in the Midwest League.

**Strengths:** Clean delivery; fastball works 92-96; can touch higher; thrown with good angle; can offer two-seamer look with good arm-side movement; slider is a weapon pitch; can flash plus-plus potential in the mid-80s; good tilt and dive; bat-misser when it's on; changeup works solid-average to plus; low-80s with tumble; good command projection.

**Weaknesses:** Fastball can lack deception; seems to find barrels; both slider and changeup flash plus (or better) but can play lower; struggles to bring every pitch to the table in the same game; aggressiveness in the zone needs work; can pitch with passivity (a few sources questioned his fortitude on the mound).

**Risk Factor/Injury History:** Low risk; very high floor

**Bret Sayre's Fantasy Take:** While he may not be someone you want anchoring your pitching staff, Appel is as certain of a bet as there is from the 2013 draft class to return usable fantasy value. He's likely to offer solid production across the board, with more of a focus on ratios than strikeouts.

**The Year Ahead:** Appel is basically major-league ready, but I assume he starts in Double-A before finding his way to Houston by the summer. As far as pitching prospects go, Appel is probably the safest bet in the minors to develop into a quality mid-rotation arm, with the ceiling offering a little more to dream on. That's a very safe and comforting reality. However, the knock on Appel (from some) is that the ceiling in question isn't that of a true number one starter, a projection usually associated with a player drafted first overall.

**#21**
BP Top
101
Prospects

---

## 4. Mike Foltynewicz RHP

**Born:** 10/7/91 **Age:** 22 **Bats:** R **Throws:** R **Height:** 6' 4" **Weight:** 200

| MLB ETA | CT | FB | CH | CB | SL | OFP | Realistic |
|---|---|---|---|---|---|---|---|
| 2014 | -- | 80 | -- | 55 | -- | 60<br>NO.2-3 STARTER | 55<br>LATE INN RP (CLOSER) |

| YEAR | TEAM | LVL | AGE | W | L | SV | G | GS | IP | H | HR | BB | SO | BB9 | SO9 | GB% | BABIP | WHIP | ERA | FIP | FRA | WARP |
|---|---|---|---|---|---|---|---|---|---|---|---|---|---|---|---|---|---|---|---|---|---|---|
| 2013 | CCH | AA | 21 | 5 | 3 | 3 | 23 | 16 | 103.3 | 75 | 8 | 52 | 95 | 4.5 | 8.3 | 55% | .254 | 1.23 | 2.87 | 3.88 | 4.71 | 1.0 |
| 2013 | LNC | A+ | 21 | 1 | 0 | 0 | 7 | 5 | 26.0 | 31 | 4 | 14 | 29 | 4.8 | 10.0 | 46% | .360 | 1.73 | 3.81 | 5.16 | 4.63 | 0.9 |
| 2014 | HOU | MLB | 22 | 4 | 10 | 0 | 21 | 21 | 105.7 | 118 | 14 | 60 | 67 | 5.1 | 5.7 | 46% | .302 | 1.69 | 5.67 | 5.72 | 6.16 | -1.1 |
| 2015 | HOU | MLB | 23 | 8 | 11 | 0 | 28 | 28 | 174.3 | 180 | 23 | 90 | 131 | 4.6 | 6.8 | 47% | .295 | 1.55 | 5.05 | 5.06 | 5.49 | -0.8 |

Breakout: 0%    Improve: 0%    Collapse: 0%    Attrition: 0%    MLB: 0%        *Comparables: Brett Marshall, Brian Flynn, J.C. Ramirez*

**Drafted/Acquired:** 1st round, 2010 draft, Minooka HS (Minooka, IL)

**Previous Ranking:** #10 (Org)

**What Happened in 2013:** After a slow and low developmental start to his career, which included 53 starts at the Low-A level, Foltynewicz's elite velocity finally pushed him up the ladder, as he finished the season at Double-A and put himself in contention for a major-league role at some point in 2014.

**Strengths:** Huge fastball; works in the upper-90s and can touch over 100; big, strong, durable frame; could horse innings; shows multiple breaking ball looks; both can flash; intimidation factor.

**Weaknesses:** Command is below average; fastball can work up and lose effectiveness; lacks a true wipeout breaking ball; changeup is below average; gets too firm and lacks movement.

**Risk Factor/Injury History:** Moderate risk; he can throw 102 mph, but can be one-dimensional.

**#43**
BP Top
101
Prospects

**Bret Sayre's Fantasy Take:** The chasm of starting pitching at the major-league level for Houston works in his favor, as Foltynewicz should be given every opportunity to prove himself as a starter. If he makes it, it's a high-strike-out profile with some give back in WHIP. If he doesn't, there's still plenty of opportunity for him to redeem himself by racking up saves.

**The Year Ahead:** Foltynewicz has the body and the fastball to project high up in a major-league rotation, but the secondary arsenal will flash only above-average potential, and the command profile is below average with only an average projection. If everything clicks, he's a rotation beast who can log innings and pitch off an elite fastball, but the likely role will come in relief, where the shortcomings in the arsenal can be somewhat muted.

## 5.  Jonathan Singleton   1B

**Born:** 9/18/91  **Age:** 22  **Bats:** L  **Throws:** L  **Height:** 6' 2"  **Weight:** 235

| MLB ETA | Hit | Power | Run | Glove | Arm | OFP | Realistic |
|---------|-----|-------|-----|-------|-----|-----|-----------|
| 2014 | 50 | 70 | – | – | – | 60<br>1ST DIV PLAYER | 50<br>2ND DIV PLAYER |

| YEAR | TEAM | LVL | AGE | PA | R | 2B | 3B | HR | RBI | BB | SO | SB | CS | AVG/OBP/SLG | TAv | BABIP | BRR | FRAA | WARP |
|------|------|-----|-----|----|---|----|----|----|-----|----|----|----|----|-------------|-----|-------|-----|------|------|
| 2013 | OKL | AAA | 21 | 294 | 31 | 13 | 0 | 6 | 31 | 46 | 89 | 1 | 0 | .220/.340/.347 | .247 | .314 | -1.4 | 1B(68): -5.0 | -1.1 |
| 2013 | CCH | AA | 21 | 48 | 5 | 2 | 1 | 2 | 8 | 9 | 16 | 0 | 0 | .263/.396/.526 | .351 | .381 | -0.7 | 1B(10): -0.5 | 0.4 |
| 2013 | QUD | A | 21 | 25 | 6 | 2 | 0 | 3 | 5 | 4 | 5 | 0 | 0 | .286/.400/.810 | .420 | .231 | 0.5 | 1B(5): 0.3 | 0.6 |
| 2014 | HOU | MLB | 22 | 250 | 27 | 9 | 1 | 7 | 28 | 32 | 74 | 1 | 0 | .228/.328/.376 | .261 | .310 | -0.3 | 1B 1, LF -0 | 0.3 |
| 2015 | HOU | MLB | 23 | 283 | 35 | 12 | 1 | 8 | 31 | 40 | 84 | 0 | 0 | .227/.336/.384 | .267 | .311 | -0.5 | 1B 0 | 1.3 |

Breakout: 3%    Improve: 21%    Collapse: 0%    Attrition: 10%    MLB: 32%          *Comparables: Kyle Blanks, Anthony Rizzo, Chris Parmelee*

**Drafted/Acquired:** 8th round, 2009 draft, Millikan HS (Long Beach, CA)

**Previous Ranking:** #1 (Org), #25 (Top 101)

**What Happened in 2013:** Singleton was popped for a drug of abuse, and when he arrived back on the field after 50 games off, his body wore the effects of the layoff, as the young first baseman could best be defined as "thick."

**Strengths:** Big raw power; 7 raw; game power should play to plus; generates excellent bat speed; hands are impressive; big torque in the swing, but shows bat control; has a plan at the plate; knows balls/strikes.

**Weaknesses:** Hit tool receives mixed reviews; struggles against arm-side pitching; power utility will be limited by contact ability; body got sloppy in layoff; speaks to iffy makeup; limited to first base defensively; below-average arm; doesn't move well.

**Risk Factor/Injury History:** Moderate risk; drug suspension; makeup concerns

**Bret Sayre's Fantasy Take:** Despite the step back in 2013, Singleton still maintains the same fantasy upside he did prior to the suspension—it's the risk that has changed. But with power down across the game—only seven first basemen hit 25 homers in 2013—he certainly is still worth investing in. Singleton should have no issue working himself into a run-producing spot in the Astros' lineup.

**The Year Ahead:** Singleton was knocking on the door of the majors before he was suspended for marijuana and ate himself into a new physique. If he wants it, the opportunity is waiting for him at the highest level, but the 22-year-old has to dedicate himself to the cause. The power potential is there for a middle-of-the-order presence, but the likely role is a second-division player who flashes his potential but never quite lives up to the hype.

**#57**
BP Top 101 Prospects

## 6.  Vincent Velasquez   RHP

**Born:** 6/7/92  **Age:** 22  **Bats:** B  **Throws:** R  **Height:** 6' 3"  **Weight:** 203

| MLB ETA | CT | FB | CH | CB | SL | OFP | Realistic |
|---------|----|----|----|----|----|-----|-----------|
| 2015 | – | 65 | 65 | 50 | – | 60<br>NO.2-3 STARTER | 50<br>NO.4 STARTER |

| YEAR | TEAM | LVL | AGE | W | L | SV | G | GS | IP | H | HR | BB | SO | BB9 | SO9 | GB% | BABIP | WHIP | ERA | FIP | FRA | WARP |
|------|------|-----|-----|---|---|----|---|----|----|---|----|----|----|-----|-----|-----|-------|------|-----|-----|-----|------|
| 2013 | QUD | A | 21 | 9 | 4 | 3 | 25 | 16 | 110.0 | 90 | 7 | 33 | 123 | 2.7 | 10.1 | 52% | .292 | 1.12 | 3.19 | 4.24 | 4.24 | 1.8 |
| 2013 | LNC | A+ | 21 | 0 | 2 | 0 | 3 | 3 | 14.7 | 14 | 2 | 8 | 19 | 4.9 | 11.7 | 33% | .353 | 1.50 | 6.14 | 5.00 | 5.75 | 0.1 |
| 2014 | HOU | MLB | 22 | 3 | 7 | 0 | 20 | 15 | 87.7 | 93 | 12 | 45 | 72 | 4.6 | 7.4 | 44% | .306 | 1.57 | 5.17 | 5.24 | 5.62 | -0.4 |
| 2015 | HOU | MLB | 23 | 7 | 8 | 0 | 31 | 23 | 158.7 | 161 | 22 | 71 | 127 | 4.0 | 7.2 | 44% | .293 | 1.46 | 4.85 | 4.86 | 5.27 | -0.4 |

Breakout: 0%    Improve: 0%    Collapse: 0%    Attrition: 0%    MLB: 0%          *Comparables: Dan Straily, Simon Castro, Sean Nolin*

**Drafted/Acquired:** 2nd round, 2010 draft, Garey HS (Garey, CA)

**Previous Ranking:** On The Rise

**What Happened in 2013:** Making his full-season debut, Velasquez erased all doubts about his post-Tommy John arm, pitching his way to the California League on the back of the potent fastball/changeup combo.

**Strengths:** Really crisp fastball; easy plus velocity in the 92-95 range; routinely works higher; holds velocity; clean arm action; changeup is a plus pitch at present; some sources project it higher; excellent arm-speed deception; major-league-quality pitch; good overall feel for craft; good command profile.

**Weaknesses:** Breaking ball not very impressive; several reports had it below average at present and didn't project it over fringe-average; success in lower minors on the back of fastball location and velocity in combination with big boy changeup; needs full-grade breaking ball improvement.

**Risk Factor/Injury History:** Moderate; Tommy John surgery in September 2010

**Bret Sayre's Fantasy Take:** High probability of sticking in a starting role, but whether he's a back-end fantasy starter or a number two or three type almost all depends on where the curveball ends up. Most likely to be strong in WHIP and good everywhere else, but not elite. Lower fantasy upside than Appel/Foltynewicz, but strong profile, especially in deeper leagues.

**The Year Ahead:** The development of the breaking ball is key for Velasquez's long-term success, although his fastball/changeup combo is strong enough to carry him to the majors, even with a fringe curveball. Depending on the source, projections on the present offering range from below average to average, with one source suggesting it could develop into a plus pitch next season. If that's the case, Velasquez's placement on this list could look foolish at this time next year.

---

## 7.  Lance McCullers   RHP

**Born:** 10/2/93   **Age:** 20   **Bats:** L   **Throws:** R   **Height:** 6' 2"   **Weight:** 205

| MLB ETA | | CT | FB | CH | CB | SL | | OFP | Realistic |
|---|---|---|---|---|---|---|---|---|---|
| 2015 | | – | 70 | – | 70 | – | | 60<br>NO.2-3 STARTER | 55<br>LATE INN RP (SETUP) |

| YEAR | TEAM | LVL | AGE | W | L | SV | G | GS | IP | H | HR | BB | SO | BB9 | SO9 | GB% | BABIP | WHIP | ERA | FIP | FRA | WARP |
|---|---|---|---|---|---|---|---|---|---|---|---|---|---|---|---|---|---|---|---|---|---|---|
| 2013 | QUD | A | 19 | 6 | 5 | 0 | 25 | 19 | 104.7 | 92 | 3 | 49 | 117 | 4.2 | 10.1 | 57% | .327 | 1.35 | 3.18 | 3.05 | 3.99 | 1.9 |
| 2014 | HOU | MLB | 20 | 3 | 6 | 0 | 18 | 14 | 72.0 | 77 | 9 | 43 | 59 | 5.4 | 7.4 | 50% | .311 | 1.67 | 5.38 | 5.38 | 5.85 | -0.4 |
| 2015 | HOU | MLB | 21 | 5 | 8 | 0 | 30 | 22 | 154.3 | 156 | 20 | 86 | 130 | 5.0 | 7.6 | 50% | .298 | 1.57 | 5.03 | 4.99 | 5.47 | -0.7 |

Breakout: 0%    Improve: 0%    Collapse: 0%    Attrition: 0%    MLB: 0%          *Comparables: Jenrry Mejia, Trevor Cahill, Chris Tillman*

**Drafted/Acquired:** 1st round, 2012 draft, Jesuit High School (Tampa, FL)

**Previous Ranking:** #9 (Org)

**What Happened in 2013:** The former supplemental first-round pick made his full-season debut, logging 19 starts and missing more than a bat an inning.

**Strengths:** Plus-plus arm strength; easy cheese; works comfortably in the low- to mid-90s; can go get more; power breaking ball is close to a plus pitch at present; projects higher; big-league-quality bat-misser; competitor on the mound; attacks hitters.

**Weaknesses:** Delivery isn't super easy or clean; tendency to lose some of the stuff later in games; changeup is below average; several sources don't think it plays above fringe-average at maturity; command is spotty; lacks plus projection.

**Risk Factor/Injury History:** Moderate; has the fastball/curveball to reach realistic role

**Bret Sayre's Fantasy Take:** If McCullers does make it as a starter, the strikeouts will leave fantasy owners happy (as he could get up to one per inning), but his ratios could be a drag on his value. If not, he should be in the mix for saves down the road.

**The Year Ahead:** After a strong full-season campaign last year, McCullers could reach Double-A at some point in 2014, perhaps faster than expected given some of the developmental hurdles associated with the California League. The fastball/curve combo is intense, but the rotation package won't come together without improved command of the arsenal and a better changeup. The cambio can take time and he's still early in the process, so there is no need to move him into the 'pen right now. But his delivery is what scouts point to when it comes to the bullpen projection, not the inability to develop a playable changeup.

---

## 8.  Domingo Santana   RF

**Born:** 8/5/92   **Age:** 21   **Bats:** R   **Throws:** R   **Height:** 6' 5"   **Weight:** 230

| MLB ETA | | Hit | Power | Run | Glove | Arm | | OFP | Realistic |
|---|---|---|---|---|---|---|---|---|---|
| Late 2014 | | – | 65 | – | – | 65 | | 60<br>1ST DIV PLAYER | 50<br>2ND DIV PLAYER |

| YEAR | TEAM | LVL | AGE | PA | R | 2B | 3B | HR | RBI | BB | SO | SB | CS | AVG/OBP/SLG | TAv | BABIP | BRR | FRAA | WARP |
|---|---|---|---|---|---|---|---|---|---|---|---|---|---|---|---|---|---|---|---|
| 2013 | CCH | AA | 20 | 476 | 72 | 23 | 2 | 25 | 64 | 46 | 139 | 12 | 5 | .252/.345/.498 | .296 | .316 | 0.2 | RF(100): -3.9, CF(8): 0.0 | 2.9 |
| 2014 | HOU | MLB | 21 | 250 | 28 | 10 | 1 | 9 | 31 | 17 | 84 | 2 | 1 | .228/.295/.400 | .256 | .320 | -0.1 | RF -2, CF -0 | 0.1 |
| 2015 | HOU | MLB | 22 | 316 | 39 | 12 | 2 | 11 | 39 | 25 | 100 | 2 | 1 | .233/.305/.408 | .264 | .314 | -0.3 | RF -3, CF 0 | 0.3 |

Breakout: 3%    Improve: 17%    Collapse: 1%    Attrition: 7%    MLB: 24%          *Comparables: Jay Bruce, Travis Snider, Colby Rasmus*

**Drafted/Acquired:** International free agent, 2009, Dominican Republic

**Previous Ranking:** #7 (Org)

**What Happened in 2013:** A 20-year-old for most of the season, Santana held his own at the Double-A level, hitting 50 extra-base hits in 112 games, including 25 bombs.

**Strengths:** Big boy raw power; can launch tape-measure shots; leveraged swing that can produce very loud contact, especially when he can get extended on balls out over the plate; can handle right field; easy plus arm; good athlete for his size.

**Weaknesses:** Hit tool is below average; lacks much projection; tremendous strength, but swing can get heavy and pitchers can work him inside; lots of swing-and-miss; hit tool could limit power output.

**Overall Future Potential:** 6; first-division player

**Realistic Role:** Low 5; second-division player

**Risk Factor/Injury History:** Moderate risk; power is legit

**Bret Sayre's Fantasy Take:** A 30-homer hitter these days is an endangered species of sorts, regardless of batting average risk or positional eligibility. Due to the issues with his hit tool, he's most valuable in OBP leagues and carries some strikeout drag in points formats.

**The Year Ahead:** Santana has a lot of supporters in the scouting community, and those who really believe in him see a Nelson Cruz type; big raw, suspect hit tool, awkward at times in his routes but a good athlete for the size, with a very good arm. Santana has a tendency to expand his zone and help pitchers out in counts, so he will need to continue to refine and learn to stay back on off-speed offerings if he wants to let the full potential of his power out. He could reach the majors in 2014, although a healthy dose of Triple-A off-speed stuff could benefit the 21-year-old's development at the plate.

---

## 9. Rio Ruiz  3B

**Born:** 5/22/94  **Age:** 20  **Bats:** L  **Throws:** R  **Height:** 6'2"  **Weight:** 215

| MLB ETA | Hit | Power | Run | Glove | Arm | OFP | Realistic |
|---|---|---|---|---|---|---|---|
| Late 2015 | 60 | 60 | – | – | 60 | 60<br>1ST DIVISION 3B | 50<br>2ND DIVISION 1B |

| YEAR | TEAM | LVL | AGE | PA | R | 2B | 3B | HR | RBI | BB | SO | SB | CS | AVG/OBP/SLG | TAv | BABIP | BRR | FRAA | WARP |
|---|---|---|---|---|---|---|---|---|---|---|---|---|---|---|---|---|---|---|---|
| 2013 | QUD | A | 19 | 472 | 46 | 33 | 1 | 12 | 63 | 50 | 92 | 12 | 3 | .260/.335/.430 | .275 | .303 | -3.6 | 3B(111): -8.0 | 1.3 |
| 2014 | HOU | MLB | 20 | 250 | 23 | 10 | 1 | 5 | 25 | 18 | 66 | 2 | 1 | .211/.269/.330 | .221 | .270 | -0.1 | 3B -4 | -0.8 |
| 2015 | HOU | MLB | 21 | 250 | 28 | 13 | 0 | 7 | 28 | 16 | 58 | 0 | 0 | .238/.288/.389 | .247 | .284 | -0.6 | 3B -4 | 0.3 |

Breakout: 0%   Improve: 0%   Collapse: 0%   Attrition: 0%   MLB: 0%   *Comparables: Matt Dominguez, Mike Moustakas, Matt Davidson*

**Drafted/Acquired:** 4th round, 2012 draft, Bishop Amat Memorial HS (La Puente, CA)

**Previous Ranking:** #8 (Org)

**What Happened in 2013:** It was a tale of two seasons, as Ruiz struggled mightily in the first half before finding his stroke in the second, slugging a robust .520 with 34 extra-base hits.

**Strengths:** Sweet stroke from the left side; clean and quick to the ball; generates good bat speed; shows plus power potential; good approach at the plate; will work counts; shows recognition skills; strong arm at third.

**Weaknesses:** Glove at third is below average; might not get to average; lacks range; below-average run; mixed reviews on the hit tool; several sources really like it; others not sold it's a plus tool (more average at best).

**Risk Factor/Injury History:** High risk; injury history: blood clots

**Bret Sayre's Fantasy Take:** In shallower dynasty leagues, Ruiz is exactly the kind of player you want to take a chance on toward the end of your minor-league roster. The upside is there for a long-term solution at a corner in any league, but if he doesn't work out from either a health or developmental standpoint, there's always another train coming.

**The Year Ahead:** The second half of Ruiz's season showed his offensive potential, and a move to the friendly confines of the California League could help inflate his numbers and elevate his prospect stock. The glove needs work, and some aren't sold he sticks at the position long term. But if the bat is legit—meaning he shows the ability to hit for both average and power—his defensive home won't be a big issue.

---

## 10. Michael Feliz  RHP

**Born:** 9/28/93  **Age:** 20  **Bats:** R  **Throws:** R  **Height:** 6'4"  **Weight:** 210

| MLB ETA | CT | FB | CH | CB | SL | OFP | Realistic |
|---|---|---|---|---|---|---|---|
| 2016 | ---- | 70 | – | – | 60 | 60<br>NO.2-3 STARTER | 50<br>LATE INN RP (SETUP) |

| YEAR | TEAM | LVL | AGE | W | L | SV | G | GS | IP | H | HR | BB | SO | BB9 | SO9 | GB% | BABIP | WHIP | ERA | FIP | FRA | WARP |
|---|---|---|---|---|---|---|---|---|---|---|---|---|---|---|---|---|---|---|---|---|---|---|
| 2013 | TCV | A- | 19 | 4 | 2 | 1 | 14 | 10 | 69.0 | 53 | 2 | 13 | 78 | 1.7 | 10.2 | 53% | .288 | 0.96 | 1.96 | 1.91 | 2.96 | 1.7 |
| 2014 | HOU | MLB | 20 | 1 | 4 | 0 | 11 | 7 | 49.3 | 58 | 7 | 31 | 31 | 5.7 | 5.7 | 48% | .311 | 1.79 | 6.19 | 6.07 | 6.73 | -0.8 |
| 2015 | HOU | MLB | 21 | 5 | 6 | 0 | 25 | 16 | 131.7 | 141 | 18 | 65 | 95 | 4.4 | 6.5 | 47% | .297 | 1.56 | 5.25 | 5.11 | 5.70 | -0.9 |

Breakout: 0%   Improve: 0%   Collapse: 0%   Attrition: 0%   MLB: 0%   *Comparables: J.C. Ramirez, Alex Sanabia, Carlos Carrasco*

**Drafted/Acquired:** International free agent, 2010, Dominican Republic

**Previous Ranking:** NR

**What Happened in 2013:** Feliz shoved in the New York-Penn League, using his lively mid-90s fastball to miss 78 bats in 69 short-season innings.

**Strengths:** Plus-plus arm strength; fastball works in the 94-96 range, touching 98 with big wiggle; slider shows plus potential; big, strong frame; has some feel for craft; strike-thrower.

**Weaknesses:** Control ahead of command; changeup is below average at present; sources not high on changeup projection; slider flashes but can get loose and slurvy.

**Risk Factor/Injury History:** High risk; great stuff but short-season resume

**Bret Sayre's Fantasy Take:** Pitching prospects who haven't yet reached full-season ball are always a risky proposition, but when you bet, bet on velocity. Right now, Feliz doesn't project as a huge strikeout guy if he sticks in the rotation, but there's plenty of time for that to change as he develops.

**The Year Ahead:** Feliz is the type of arm who will need to prove he is a starter all the way up the chain, mostly because of the fastball-first arsenal that features an okay slider and an immature changeup. Feliz shows a lot of feel for pitching, and the delivery is pretty easy given the fact that his fastball can touch 98 mph, so it's not a given that he ends up in the bullpen. But it's also easy to dream of that explosive fastball in short bursts, and if you add an improved slider to the mix, that's an impact arm at the major-league level.

## Notable Omission

**Delino DeShields Jr.:** DeShields will likely be a featured prospect on most Astros-specific lists, and I've even seen his name kicked around as a top-100 prospect in the minors. The reports I've received throughout the season haven't painted the best picture of the player, a direct contrast to the positive statistical output that will no doubt influence his placement on most lists. The biggest complaint from scouts has to do with makeup, or more specifically, visible effort and maturity displayed on the field. DeShields might be a plus-plus runner, but his low-energy approach to the game can rub some the wrong way, and almost every single source I spoke to suggested he would fall short of his ceiling.

## Prospects on the Rise

**1. OF Teoscar Hernandez:** On the list for the second straight season, the young outfielder had a strong case for inclusion in the top 10, but fell short because of the strength of the system. With a good glove at a premium spot on the diamond (center), a good feel for hitting, and an infectious approach to the game, Hernandez will likely emerge as a name prospect in 2014.

**2. LHP Reymin Guduan:** I'm a sucker for southpaw velocity, and Guduan stands in elite company when it comes to arm strength from the left side. A relatively unknown prospect-—he has only 2 1/3 innings above the complex level—the 21-year-old Dominican can pump upper-90s heat like it's a common outcome. Relief prospects don't offer much, especially when they will be 22 coming into the season with a very limited professional record at the full-season level. But 6'4'' lefties who can touch 100 mph on the radar gun are always worth keeping a very close eye on.

**3. RHP Andrew Thurman:** The 40th overall pick in the 2013 draft, UC Irvine's Friday starter is a solid and safe prospect, one who will likely progress quickly in the system and land in the top 10 next season. The projection isn't going to change the fortunes of the franchise, but with a solid-average fastball, two passable breaking balls, a good changeup, and sharp command, Thurman could eventually settle in as a number four starter at the major-league level.

## Factors on the Farm

### Prospects likely to contribute in the majors in 2014

**1. RHP Nick Tropeano:** With a solid fastball/changeup combo, the former fifth-round pick can miss bats and force weak contact. He's a back-end type at the highest level, but he has the delivery, the body, and the arsenal to contribute to a major-league rotation in 2014.

**2. C Max Stassi:** Stassi's bat really took off in the Texas League, producing 38 extra-base hits in 76 games. The league and home environment certainly played a role in the offensive explosion, but don't overlook the fact that Stassi was finally healthy, as nagging injuries have slowed the former fourth-round pick's rise to the majors. With good receiving skills and some punch in his stick, Stassi could eventually carve out a career as a major-league regular.

**3. OF Leo Heras:** The Astros jumped into the Mexican League market this summer and snatched one of the league's best hitters, a 5'9'' outfielder from the Diablos Rojos of Mexico City. The 23-year-old isn't a physical specimen, but with a good approach, bat speed and a balanced stroke from the left side, Heras has the skill set to hit at the highest level. He should get a look at some point in 2014.

## 1. Yordano Ventura   RHP

**Born:** 6/3/91   **Age:** 23   **Bats:** R   **Throws:** R   **Height:** 5'11"   **Weight:** 180

| MLB ETA | CT | FB | CH | CB | SL | OFP | Realistic |
|---|---|---|---|---|---|---|---|
| Debuted in 2013 | — | 80 | 65 | 65 | — | 70<br>NO.2 STARTER | 65<br>NO.3 STARTER |

| YEAR | TEAM | LVL | AGE | W | L | SV | G | GS | IP | H | HR | BB | SO | BB9 | SO9 | GB% | BABIP | WHIP | ERA | FIP | FRA | WARP |
|---|---|---|---|---|---|---|---|---|---|---|---|---|---|---|---|---|---|---|---|---|---|---|
| 2013 | OMA | AAA | 22 | 5 | 4 | 0 | 15 | 14 | 77.0 | 80 | 4 | 33 | 81 | 3.9 | 9.5 | 42% | .357 | 1.47 | 3.74 | 3.54 | 3.53 | 1.7 |
| 2013 | NWA | AA | 22 | 3 | 2 | 0 | 11 | 11 | 57.7 | 39 | 3 | 20 | 74 | 3.1 | 11.5 | 43% | .279 | 1.02 | 2.34 | 2.41 | 2.91 | 1.6 |
| 2013 | KCA | MLB | 22 | 0 | 1 | 0 | 3 | 3 | 15.3 | 13 | 3 | 6 | 11 | 3.5 | 6.5 | 51% | .227 | 1.24 | 3.52 | 5.36 | 5.17 | 0.0 |
| 2014 | KCA | MLB | 23 | 7 | 7 | 0 | 25 | 22 | 117.3 | 120 | 13 | 50 | 104 | 3.8 | 8.0 | 43% | .311 | 1.45 | 4.52 | 4.49 | 4.91 | 0.4 |
| 2015 | KCA | MLB | 24 | 8 | 8 | 0 | 26 | 26 | 152.0 | 148 | 15 | 60 | 147 | 3.6 | 8.7 | 44% | .310 | 1.37 | 4.06 | 3.83 | 4.41 | 1.2 |

Breakout: 26%   Improve: 33%   Collapse: 8%   Attrition: 29%   MLB: 48%   *Comparables: Jake Odorizzi, Carlos Carrasco, Christian Friedrich*

**Drafted/Acquired:** International free agent, 2008, Dominican Republic

**Previous Ranking:** #5 (Org), #62 (Top 101)

**What Happened in 2013:** Ventura logged a career high in innings pitched—spanning three levels—and concluded his impressive run with three starts in the majors.

**Strengths:** Elite arm speed; fastball sits mid- to upper-90s; can hit triple digits deep into games; can manipulate the movement; gets cutting action at lower velo; curveball is plus pitch; hard breaker with tight rotation and excellent depth; changeup could end up another well-above-average pitch; offers deception from fastball and good action.

**Weaknesses:** Slight build; concerns about workload ability; tendency to lose command by overthrowing; change-up can get too firm; requires more refinement than other offerings; curveball plays down when fastball command is loose.

**Risk Factor/Injury History:** Low risk; achieved major-league level; ready for extended look.

**Bret Sayre's Fantasy Take:** We already got a sneak peak at his heat in September, but with the inside track to a rotation spot on Opening Day, Ventura is ready to make a fantasy impact. The immediate future may not feature the type of strikeout numbers you'd expect long term, but he is still the type of pitcher to take a shot with at the back end of your rotation in 2014. Beyond that, he has the potential to be a full four-category contributor if he can handle the workload.

**The Year Ahead:** Ventura has been throwing gas since he could walk, but the progression of his secondary arsenal has turned him from a future relief prospect to a frontline arm that can pitch atop a major-league rotation. The body is slight and short, and normally I'd be quick to put him into a late-innings box. But Ventura can hold velocity like a workhorse, gaining strength as he goes along, not losing it. I do have some concerns about long-term workload and what 200 innings might do to the stuff, but it's hard to ignore the electricity in his arm and the potential that creates. I wouldn't be shocked if Ventura takes another step forward in 2014, and pitches his way into Rookie of the Year discussions.

**#12**
BP Top 101 Prospects

## 2. Raul Mondesi   SS

**Born:** 7/27/95   **Age:** 18   **Bats:** B   **Throws:** R   **Height:** 6'1"   **Weight:** 165

| MLB ETA | Hit | Power | Run | Glove | Arm | OFP | Realistic |
|---|---|---|---|---|---|---|---|
| 2016 | 60 | — | 60 | 60 | 60 | 65<br>1ST DIV/ALL-STAR | 50<br>ML REGULAR |

| YEAR | TEAM | LVL | AGE | PA | R | 2B | 3B | HR | RBI | BB | SO | SB | CS | AVG/OBP/SLG | TAv | BABIP | BRR | FRAA | WARP |
|---|---|---|---|---|---|---|---|---|---|---|---|---|---|---|---|---|---|---|---|
| 2013 | LEX | A | 17 | 536 | 61 | 13 | 7 | 7 | 47 | 34 | 118 | 24 | 10 | .261/.311/.361 | .257 | .331 | 1.1 | SS(108): 2.3 | 2.0 |
| 2014 | KCA | MLB | 18 | 250 | 24 | 7 | 2 | 2 | 16 | 9 | 65 | 5 | 2 | .223/.250/.293 | .197 | .290 | 0.4 | SS 1 | -0.4 |
| 2015 | KCA | MLB | 19 | 250 | 23 | 7 | 2 | 3 | 21 | 8 | 61 | 3 | 1 | .244/.267/.327 | .216 | .304 | 0.2 | SS 1 | -0.8 |

Breakout: 0%   Improve: 0%   Collapse: 0%   Attrition: 0%   MLB: 0%   *Comparables: Elvis Andrus, Chris Owings, Jonathan Schoop*

**Drafted/Acquired:** International free agent, 2011, Dominican Republic

**Previous Ranking:** #4 (Org), #58 (Top 101)

**What Happened in 2013:** I took a calculated risk by ranking Mondesi third in the system last season and 58th overall, as he was still an unknown commodity to most fans and prognosticators alike. He rewarded our belief in his ability by jumping to a full-season league and holding his own despite being 17 years old for a healthy chunk of the season.

**Strengths:** Advanced talent; shows high-impact skills on all sides of the ball; slick actions on defense; plus glove

**#29**
BP Top 101 Prospects

potential with more repetition; plus arm, capable of all the throws; instincts could push tools up; plus run; good bat-to-ball ability from both sides of the plate; could develop average power down the line.

**Weaknesses:** Needs to learn to slow the game down; can play fast, rush his actions and throws in the field; overly aggressive at the plate; susceptible to secondary stuff; power potential is questionable.

**Risk Factor/Injury History:** High risk; 18 years old; yet to play in high minors

**Bret Sayre's Fantasy Take:** The fantasy upside of Mondesi is overshadowed by the real-life impact he can have on the Royals. If he doesn't develop even average power, we're talking more about a 10-homer, 20-steal threat with the ability to post a helpful batting average. That's not a fantasy stud, but at shortstop, it's still a back of the top-10 guy.

**The Year Ahead:** Mondesi is a special talent, a gifted defender at a premium position, with speed and a quick stroke to the ball from both sides of the plate. He is unrefined and eager in his game, but he has a chance to develop into an impact talent at the highest level. The developmental process will present setbacks and failures along the way, and 2014 might look similar to 2013 on the stat sheet, but Mondesi's ceiling is worth the patience.

## 3. Kyle Zimmer    RHP

**Born:** 9/13/91    **Age:** 22    **Bats:** R    **Throws:** R    **Height:** 6'3"    **Weight:** 215

| MLB ETA | CT | FB | CH | CB | SL | OFP | Realistic |
|---|---|---|---|---|---|---|---|
| Late 2014 | – | 70 | 50 | 70 | 60 | 60<br>NO.2-3 STARTER | 55<br>NO.3 STARTER |

| YEAR | TEAM | LVL | AGE | W | L | SV | G | GS | IP | H | HR | BB | SO | BB9 | SO9 | GB% | BABIP | WHIP | ERA | FIP | FRA | WARP |
|---|---|---|---|---|---|---|---|---|---|---|---|---|---|---|---|---|---|---|---|---|---|---|
| 2013 | NWA | AA | 21 | 2 | 1 | 0 | 4 | 4 | 18.7 | 11 | 2 | 5 | 27 | 2.4 | 13.0 | 56% | .231 | 0.86 | 1.93 | 2.68 | 3.21 | 0.5 |
| 2013 | WIL | A+ | 21 | 4 | 8 | 0 | 18 | 18 | 89.7 | 80 | 9 | 31 | 113 | 3.1 | 11.3 | 55% | .318 | 1.24 | 4.82 | 3.27 | 4.37 | 1.3 |
| 2014 | KCA | MLB | 22 | 5 | 5 | 0 | 16 | 16 | 79.3 | 81 | 9 | 31 | 73 | 3.5 | 8.3 | 52% | .312 | 1.42 | 4.44 | 4.34 | 4.83 | 0.4 |
| 2015 | KCA | MLB | 23 | 10 | 10 | 0 | 30 | 30 | 191.0 | 190 | 19 | 62 | 179 | 2.9 | 8.4 | 52% | .311 | 1.32 | 3.91 | 3.69 | 4.25 | 1.8 |

Breakout: 0%    Improve: 0%    Collapse: 0%    Attrition: 0%    MLB: 0%    *Comparables: Danny Duffy, Jake McGee, Tommy Hanson*

**Drafted/Acquired:** 1st round, 2012 draft, University of San Francisco (San Francisco, CA)

**Previous Ranking:** #2 (Org), #41 (Top 101)

**What Happened in 2013:** In his first full season of professional ball, Zimmer made 22 starts across two levels before getting shut down in August with tightness in his right shoulder.

**Strengths:** Clean delivery; easy and repeatable; excellent arm strength; fastball can work 92-97; touching as high as 99 in short bursts; some arm-side life; curveball is big boy pitch; multiple looks; can throw the pitch for strikes with heavy vertical action or show more two-plane break and drop it out of the zone; slider at 85-88 with short break and late tilt; future plus offering; can turn over changeup with some sink and fade; very good command profile.

**Weaknesses:** Delivery offers little deception; hitters seem to pick up the ball early; changeup is fringe-average (present); below-average command of the offering; can cut off his extension and cut the ball back into left-handers.

**Risk Factor/Injury History:** Moderate risk; minor injury concerns (tightness in right shoulder); limited Double-A exposure.

**Bret Sayre's Fantasy Take:** With Zimmer, it's all about the strikeouts. His potential plus-plus curve, when combined with the rest of his arsenal, can lead to very strong strikeout totals. He's one of fewer than 10 starting pitchers in the minors who projects as a potential impact player in strikeouts (think 200+ if he is who we think he is). Kauffman Stadium is also a nice match for him, as he could be prone to the long ball.

**The Year Ahead:** Zimmer is a polished arm with high-end stuff and in a lighter system would be the marquee name on the farm. The fastball is an easy plus offering, working low-to-mid-90s as a starter and touching higher when he needs to go get it. The curveball is one of the better hammers in the minors, a plus pitch that some already have plus-plus grades on. He can drop it for strikes or for chase, and with a slider also in the arsenal, Zimmer has a potent assortment of secondary stuff to miss barrels and force weak contact. He's going to reach the major-league level in 2014, and should develop into rotation horse as a floor and an impact number two starter if everything falls into place.

> **#34**
> BP Top 101 Prospects

## 4. Miguel Almonte    RHP

**Born:** 4/4/93    **Age:** 21    **Bats:** R    **Throws:** R    **Height:** 6'2"    **Weight:** 180

| MLB ETA | CT | FB | CH | CB | SL | OFP | Realistic |
|---|---|---|---|---|---|---|---|
| Late 2015 | – | 65 | 70 | 50 | – | 60<br>NO.3 STARTER | 50<br>NO.4-5 STARTER |

| YEAR | TEAM | LVL | AGE | W | L | SV | G | GS | IP | H | HR | BB | SO | BB9 | SO9 | GB% | BABIP | WHIP | ERA | FIP | FRA | WARP |
|---|---|---|---|---|---|---|---|---|---|---|---|---|---|---|---|---|---|---|---|---|---|---|
| 2013 | LEX | A | 20 | 6 | 9 | 0 | 25 | 25 | 130.7 | 115 | 6 | 36 | 132 | 2.5 | 9.1 | 47% | .297 | 1.16 | 3.10 | 3.04 | 3.98 | 1.1 |
| 2014 | KCA | MLB | 21 | 3 | 4 | 0 | 19 | 11 | 90.7 | 106 | 11 | 41 | 52 | 4.1 | 5.2 | 47% | .310 | 1.62 | 5.44 | 5.35 | 5.91 | -0.7 |
| 2015 | KCA | MLB | 22 | 5 | 5 | 0 | 24 | 14 | 128.7 | 138 | 13 | 57 | 101 | 4.0 | 7.1 | 47% | .313 | 1.51 | 4.75 | 4.35 | 5.16 | -0.1 |

Breakout: 0%    Improve: 0%    Collapse: 0%    Attrition: 0%    MLB: 0%    *Comparables: Zach McAllister, Brett Oberholtzer, Jake Odorizzi*

**Drafted/Acquired:** International free agent, 2010, Dominican Republic

**Previous Ranking:** #9 (Org)

**What Happened in 2013:** In his full-season debut, Almonte took another step forward on the field, missing a bat an inning thanks to his potent fastball/changeup combo.

**Strengths:** Loose, easy arm; great action; delivery is repeatable; fastball works 92-96; can touch higher; good arm-side movement; changeup is money pitch; excellent deception in the arm and plus-plus action; effective against both left-handers and right-handers; shows multiple breaking balls; curve can flash above-average; strike-throwing ability.

**Weaknesses:** More control than command; can live loose in the zone; tendency to come across his body in the delivery and struggles to hit arm-side spots; both breaking balls are inconsistent; curveball has best chance to play to average.

**Risk Factor/Injury History:** High risk; yet to pitch in upper minors

**Bret Sayre's Fantasy Take:** Another pitcher who could put up strong strikeout numbers, Almonte also could be a very strong contributor in WHIP. From June 1 to the end of the season, he had 90 strikeouts versus just 16 walks in 86 1/3 innings—and limiting walks like that will also net him more wins, as he'll be able to pitch deeper into games at the major-league level.

**The Year Ahead:** Almonte is going to move onto the pitcher-friendly confines of High-A Wilmington, and he's probably going to shove it with excellent results. His fastball is a plus offering, his changeup is well above average, and his ability to throw strikes should allow him to produce statistical results that will elevate his prospect status. The real test will come in Double-A, and I wouldn't be shocked if he gets promoted to that level at some point during the summer. His breaking ball (whichever one steps forward) needs improvement, and the control needs to continue developing into command, but this is a very legit arm with a high ceiling.

> **#46**
> BP Top 101 Prospects

## 5. Sean Manaea  LHP
**Born:** 2/1/91  **Age:** 23  **Bats:** L  **Throws:** L  **Height:** 6' 5"  **Weight:** 235

| MLB ETA | CT | FB | CH | CB | SL | OFP | Realistic |
|---|---|---|---|---|---|---|---|
| 2015 | --- | 70 | 65 | --- | 60 | 65 NO.2 STARTER | 60 NO.3 STARTER |

| YEAR | TEAM | LVL | AGE | W | L | SV | G | GS | IP | H | HR | BB | SO | BB9 | SO9 | GB% | BABIP | WHIP | ERA | FIP | FRA | WARP |
|---|---|---|---|---|---|---|---|---|---|---|---|---|---|---|---|---|---|---|---|---|---|---|
| | | | | | | | | No Professional Experience | | | | | | | | | | | | | |

**Drafted/Acquired:** 1st round, 2013 draft, Indiana State University (Terre Haute, IN)
**Previous Ranking:** NR

**What Happened in 2013:** Manaea was a legit 1:1 candidate coming into the spring, but injures (hip/shoulder) and inconsistency allowed him to the fall to the 34th pick, where the Royals popped and signed him for $3.55 million.

**Strengths:** Big, athletic body; impressive arm strength; from 3/4 slot, fastball can work 92-96; touch 97; good movement; arm-side run and some sink; slider can flash well-above-average potential; low-80s with sharp tilt; changeup could be high-impact pitch; excellent deception and late action; good command profile.

**Weaknesses:** Inconsistent fastball velocity reports this spring; abnormal for him but worth noting; slider can get slurvy and lose effectiveness; changeup is promising offering but hasn't been a heavily featured player in arsenal; can get a little deliberate in the delivery.

**Risk Factor/Injury History:** High risk; no professional record; injury concerns

**Bret Sayre's Fantasy Take:** Manaea's fantasy upside is intense and higher than any of the other arms on this list—even Kyle Zimmer. The raw tools are there for him to be a full four-category contributor and top-20 fantasy starter. He's a great chance to take in dynasty drafts if you're looking for a potentially fast riser in value—just don't ignore the risks.

**The Year Ahead:** If healthy, Manaea is a monster, a left-handed power arm with easy plus velocity, good movement, sharp slider, and the foundation of a very good changeup. Add athleticism and pitchability into the mix, and you can see why several teams had Manaea ranked as the top arm in the 2013 class. He will need to prove he is both healthy and effective, but it's not going to take the 23-year-old long to shoot up prospect lists and emerge as one of the top arms in the minors.

> **#78**
> BP Top 101 Prospects

## 6. Hunter Dozier  SS
**Born:** 8/22/91  **Age:** 22  **Bats:** R  **Throws:** R  **Height:** 6' 4"  **Weight:** 220

| MLB ETA | Hit | Power | Run | Glove | Arm | OFP | Realistic |
|---|---|---|---|---|---|---|---|
| 2016 | --- | 60 | 50 | 50 | 60 | 60 1ST DIV PLAYER | 50 ML REGULAR |

| YEAR | TEAM | LVL | AGE | PA | R | 2B | 3B | HR | RBI | BB | SO | SB | CS | AVG/OBP/SLG | TAv | BABIP | BRR | FRAA | WARP |
|---|---|---|---|---|---|---|---|---|---|---|---|---|---|---|---|---|---|---|---|
| 2013 | LEX | A | 21 | 59 | 6 | 6 | 0 | 0 | 9 | 3 | 5 | 0 | 0 | .327/.373/.436 | .322 | .360 | -0.5 | 3B(13): 0.1 | 0.6 |
| 2013 | IDA | Rk | 21 | 258 | 43 | 24 | 0 | 7 | 43 | 35 | 32 | 3 | 1 | .303/.403/.509 | .314 | .326 | 3.1 | 3B(37): -0.7, SS(9): -0.1 | 2.6 |
| 2014 | KCA | MLB | 22 | 250 | 19 | 10 | 0 | 3 | 21 | 15 | 55 | 0 | 0 | .215/.265/.296 | .208 | .270 | -0.4 | 3B -1, SS -0 | -0.8 |
| 2015 | KCA | MLB | 23 | 250 | 26 | 11 | 0 | 5 | 24 | 16 | 51 | 0 | 0 | .232/.284/.347 | .233 | .274 | -0.6 | 3B -1, SS 0 | -0.3 |

Breakout: 0%    Improve: 0%    Collapse: 0%    Attrition: 0%    MLB: 0%        *Comparables: Jedd Gyorko, Jesus Guzman, Chase Headley*

**Drafted/Acquired:** 1st round, 2013 draft, Stephen F. Austin State University (Nacogdoches, TX)

**Previous Ranking:** NR

**What Happened in 2013:** A first-round talent but a surprise pick at number eight overall, Dozier has been saddled with the burden of enhanced expectations as a result.

**Strengths:** Baseball skills; good overall approach to the game; has a plan at the plate and understands the strike zone; has good leverage in the swing and projects to hit for solid-average to plus power; arm is strong; can make routine plays up the middle; athletic with solid run.

**Weaknesses:** Lacks impact tools; swing can get hitchy and long; velocity concerns; lacks ideal range for shortstop; third base is likely long-term defensive home; more polish than projection.

**Risk Factor/Injury History:** Moderate risk; limited professional experience; shows baseball skills.

**Bret Sayre's Fantasy Take:** The talk of Dozier being a reach in the June draft could help you nab him later than he should go in your dynasty league drafts this year. The college standout brings a strong overall fantasy profile to the table, but more in the Kyle Seager vein than someone who will be a top-five option at the position. Dozier also could be an even stronger value in points leagues, where his potentially strong strikeout and walk rates can shine.

**The Year Ahead:** Dozier is a baseball player, with game skills and good instincts. The problem with the skill set is impact, which is an expectation built in to his lofty draft status. While Dozier is unlikely to develop into a star or a high-impact player, he has the tools to become a solid major-league regular, one with a good approach, good pop from the right side, and the defensive chops to play a solid third base. That's not a Longoria-esque profile, and perhaps you want a little more out of a top-10 selection, but it's hard to find fault in the outcome if the Royals are able to develop a major-league player out of the deal, especially given the financial flexibility his signing offered, which allowed the team to sign Sean Manaea.

> **#96**
> BP Top
> 101
> Prospects

---

## 7. Jorge Bonifacio    RF

**Born:** 6/4/93    **Age:** 21    **Bats:** R    **Throws:** R    **Height:** 6' 1"    **Weight:** 195

| MLB ETA | Hit | Power | Run | Glove | Arm | | OFP | Realistic |
|---|---|---|---|---|---|---|---|---|
| **Late 2014** | **50** | **60** | – | – | **70** | | **60**<br>1ST DIV PLAYER | **50**<br>2ND DIV PLAYER |

| YEAR | TEAM | LVL | AGE | PA | R | 2B | 3B | HR | RBI | BB | SO | SB | CS | AVG/OBP/SLG | TAv | BABIP | BRR | FRAA | WARP |
|---|---|---|---|---|---|---|---|---|---|---|---|---|---|---|---|---|---|---|---|
| 2013 | NWA | AA | 20 | 105 | 15 | 7 | 0 | 2 | 19 | 11 | 23 | 2 | 1 | .301/.371/.441 | .302 | .377 | 0.8 | RF(23): -1.8 | 0.8 |
| 2013 | WIL | A+ | 20 | 234 | 32 | 11 | 3 | 2 | 29 | 23 | 40 | 0 | 2 | .296/.368/.408 | .289 | .353 | -1.7 | RF(50): 0.9 | 1.1 |
| 2013 | ROY | Rk | 20 | 35 | 4 | 3 | 2 | 0 | 6 | 4 | 6 | 1 | 0 | .300/.400/.533 | .311 | .375 | -0.1 | RF(8): -0.9 | 0.1 |
| 2014 | KCA | MLB | 21 | 250 | 21 | 10 | 1 | 4 | 24 | 12 | 60 | 1 | 1 | .241/.279/.347 | .229 | .300 | -0.3 | RF -2, CF -0 | -0.6 |
| 2015 | KCA | MLB | 22 | 250 | 25 | 10 | 2 | 4 | 23 | 15 | 59 | 1 | 1 | .241/.289/.348 | .236 | .303 | -0.4 | RF -3, CF 0 | -0.4 |

Breakout: 0%    Improve: 0%    Collapse: 0%    Attrition: 0%    MLB: 0%    *Comparables: Moises Sierra, Josh Reddick, Oswaldo Arcia*

**Drafted/Acquired:** International free agent, 2009, Dominican Republic

**Previous Ranking:** #7 (Org)

**What Happened in 2013:** Bonifacio hit his way to Double-A, after a hamate injury threatened to derail his breakout campaign.

**Strengths:** Big raw strength; all-fields power potential; brings a plan to the plate; not just a power hacker; arm in right field is very strong; receives some plus-plus grades; runs well for size (average); hit tool should allow power to play.

**Weaknesses:** Big power has yet to show up in game action; hamate injury didn't help; swing is compact; more linear than loft necessary for over-the-fence power; body is high maintenance; questions about hit tool against higher level pitching.

**Risk Factor/Injury History:** Moderate risk; limited Double-A experience

**Bret Sayre's Fantasy Take:** The fact that Bonifacio could be the type of hitter to smack 25 bombs in a season might still be hidden on his stat page, as he's never hit more than 10 in his minor-league career. This year may be no different, as hamate bone fractures can sap power for an extended period of time. If he starts off slow in 2014, there might never be a better time to acquire him in a trade.

**The Year Ahead:** Bonifacio can hit, but it remains to be seen what type of hitter he will develop into. Sources disagree on offensive outcome, as some see the power coming but at the expense of contact—a potential .260 type with 20+ bombs—while others see a more complete hitter, one where the power flows from the hit tool without compromising contact. It's a right-field profile and a solid-average one, with the arm being a weapon, but the ceiling is dependent on the power showing up, and that is still debatable heading into the 2014 season. This year should tell us a lot about the player Bonifacio will develop into, either pushing him up this list or leaving us with more questions than answers.

> **#99**
> BP Top
> 101
> Prospects

## 8. Bubba Starling   CF

**Born:** 8/3/92   **Age:** 21   **Bats:** R   **Throws:** R   **Height:** 6'4"   **Weight:** 180

| MLB ETA | Hit | Power | Run | Glove | Arm | OFP | Realistic |
|---------|-----|-------|-----|-------|-----|-----|-----------|
| 2016 | — | 60 | 70 | 60 | 70 | 65<br>1ST DIV/ALL-STAR | 45<br><AVG ML/BENCH OF |

| YEAR | TEAM | LVL | AGE | PA | R | 2B | 3B | HR | RBI | BB | SO | SB | CS | AVG/OBP/SLG | TAv | BABIP | BRR | FRAA | WARP |
|------|------|-----|-----|-----|----|----|----|----|-----|----|-----|----|----|-------------|------|-------|-----|------|------|
| 2013 | LEX | A | 20 | 498 | 51 | 21 | 4 | 13 | 63 | 53 | 128 | 22 | 3 | .241/.329/.398 | .287 | .309 | 1.0 | CF(117): 2.2 | 3.3 |
| 2014 | KCA | MLB | 21 | 250 | 25 | 8 | 1 | 6 | 25 | 17 | 74 | 5 | 1 | .214/.270/.336 | .222 | .280 | 0.5 | CF 2 | 0.0 |
| 2015 | KCA | MLB | 22 | 250 | 28 | 9 | 2 | 6 | 26 | 20 | 72 | 2 | 0 | .228/.291/.364 | .240 | .301 | 0.1 | CF 1 | 0.5 |

Breakout: 0%   Improve: 0%   Collapse: 0%   Attrition: 0%   MLB: 0%   *Comparables: Brett Jackson, Austin Jackson, Michael Saunders*

**Drafted/Acquired:** 1st round, 2011 draft, Gardner-Edgerton HS (Gardner, KS)

**Previous Ranking:** #3 (Org), #49 (Top 101)

**What Happened in 2013:** A disappointing first half of the season gave way to a promising second half, as Starling started to show some of the impact flash that made him a high first-round pick back in 2011.

**Strengths:** Plus-plus athlete; potential for loud tools; 7 run; 6 glove in center; arm is a weapon (7); power potential is easy plus; true impact ceiling.

**Weaknesses:** Inconsistency at the plate; needs to find rhythm in his swing; approach needs a lot of work; pitch-recognition and reaction issues; hit tool is well below average; could damage power potential; long way to go.

**Risk Factor/Injury History:** High risk; long developmental process

**Bret Sayre's Fantasy Take:** There are still plenty of reasons why Starling is worth owning in fantasy leagues, but the 25-homer, 25-steal upside is his meal ticket. Even with all his warts, Starling still possesses the highest fantasy ceiling of any prospect in this farm system.

**The Year Ahead:** Starling has the tools to develop into an all-star, a plus defender at a premium position, with big power potential and well-above-average speed. That's a monster player. But the overall bat-to-ball ability is suspect, and the culprit might be his pitch-recognition skills, which could end up limiting his overall potential at the plate. Even if he's a .260 hitter (~5 hit), his overall attributes would make him a very valuable major leaguer. But several sources are in agreement with me that his hit tool is likely to play well below average and will limit his power from impacting games. Any developmental step forward for Starling is a step toward stardom, and I will gladly admit I was wrong about his evaluation if he starts to show signs of a more projectable hit tool.

## 9. Jason Adam   RHP

**Born:** 8/4/91   **Age:** 22   **Bats:** R   **Throws:** R   **Height:** 6'4"   **Weight:** 219

| MLB ETA | CT | FB | CH | CB | SL | OFP | Realistic |
|---------|----|----|----|----|----|-----|-----------|
| Late 2014 | — | 60 | 50 | 55 | — | 50<br>NO.4 STARTER | 50<br>NO.5 SP/LONG RP |

| YEAR | TEAM | LVL | AGE | W | L | SV | G | GS | IP | H | HR | BB | SO | BB9 | SO9 | GB% | BABIP | WHIP | ERA | FIP | FRA | WARP |
|------|------|-----|-----|---|----|----|----|----|-------|-----|----|----|-----|-----|-----|-----|-------|------|------|------|------|------|
| 2013 | NWA | AA | 21 | 8 | 11 | 0 | 26 | 26 | 144.0 | 153 | 12 | 54 | 126 | 3.4 | 7.9 | 42% | .328 | 1.44 | 5.19 | 3.83 | 4.72 | 1.1 |
| 2014 | KCA | MLB | 22 | 7 | 9 | 0 | 22 | 22 | 120.7 | 144 | 17 | 48 | 68 | 3.6 | 5.1 | 43% | .308 | 1.59 | 5.60 | 5.54 | 6.09 | -1.2 |
| 2015 | KCA | MLB | 23 | 9 | 10 | 0 | 27 | 27 | 162.7 | 176 | 20 | 52 | 118 | 2.9 | 6.5 | 43% | .304 | 1.40 | 4.61 | 4.43 | 5.01 | 0.2 |

Breakout: 0%   Improve: 0%   Collapse: 0%   Attrition: 0%   MLB: 0%   *Comparables: Vance Worley, Jeanmar Gomez, Collin Balester*

**Drafted/Acquired:** 5th round, 2010 draft, Blue Valley Northwest HS (Overland Park, KS)

**Previous Ranking:** #10 (Org)

**What Happened in 2013:** Slow and steady, Adam moved up to the Double-A level, made 26 starts, logged 144 innings, took developmental steps forward that didn't show up on the stat sheet.

**Strengths:** Big, durable frame; arm works well; gets great extension; fastball can work 90-95; good sink; pitches off the fastball; curveball flashes plus; upper-70s with tight rotation and depth; changeup will play above average at times; good sink; pitchability.

**Weaknesses:** Delivery can get segmented; slows down the body; offerings can be easy to pick up; fastball floats between average and plus; secondary arsenal lacks a plus pitch; still refining command.

**Risk Factor/Injury History:** Moderate risk; mature arm; 26 starts at Double-A level

**Bret Sayre's Fantasy Take:** Adam's fantasy relevance relies more on floor than ceiling, as he does not project to have a strong impact on any of the pitching categories. In deeper leagues, Adam is a nice value because he's likely to have a major-league future as a starter, and he can miss enough bats to matter.

**The Year Ahead:** Adam has the stuff and the body to develop into a major-league-average workhorse, the type of pitcher that can give you 200 innings of solid but not spectacular performance. He will most likely end up with three 55 pitches (20/80), and a good feel for strike throwing, giving him the tools to find success but a small margin for error at the highest level. His delivery still needs work and the secondary arsenal needs more consistency, but after another season in the upper minors, Adam will be ready to compete for a rotation spot in 2015.

## 10. Orlando Calixte SS

**Born:** 2/3/92  **Age:** 22  **Bats:** R  **Throws:** R  **Height:** 5'11"  **Weight:** 160

| MLB ETA | Hit | Power | Run | Glove | Arm | | OFP | Realistic |
|---|---|---|---|---|---|---|---|---|
| **2015** | — | **60** | — | **50** | **60** | | **50**<br>ML REGULAR | **45**<br>UTILITY PLAYER |

| YEAR | TEAM | LVL | AGE | PA | R | 2B | 3B | HR | RBI | BB | SO | SB | CS | AVG/OBP/SLG | TAv | BABIP | BRR | FRAA | WARP |
|---|---|---|---|---|---|---|---|---|---|---|---|---|---|---|---|---|---|---|---|
| 2013 | NWA | AA | 21 | 536 | 59 | 25 | 4 | 8 | 36 | 42 | 131 | 14 | 11 | .250/.312/.368 | .243 | .325 | 1.0 | SS(101): -5.6, 3B(11): -0.7 | 0.5 |
| 2014 | KCA | MLB | 22 | 250 | 25 | 9 | 1 | 4 | 19 | 12 | 65 | 4 | 3 | .221/.259/.320 | .212 | .280 | -0.2 | SS -1, 3B -0 | -0.3 |
| 2015 | KCA | MLB | 23 | 250 | 26 | 10 | 2 | 4 | 23 | 16 | 59 | 4 | 3 | .244/.296/.351 | .240 | .307 | -0.3 | SS 0, 3B 0 | 0.5 |

Breakout: 0%   Improve: 0%   Collapse: 0%   Attrition: 0%   MLB: 0%   *Comparables: Danny Worth, Brock Holt, Todd Frazier*

**Drafted/Acquired:** International free agent, 2010, Dominican Republic

**Previous Ranking:** NR

**What Happened in 2013:** Calixte was pushed to the Double-A level, and he struggled against quality pitching, but the tools are still present to develop into a solid-average major-league regular.

**Strengths:** Plus raw power; has some bat-to-ball ability; arm is plus; glove is at least average at shortstop; range is average.

**Weaknesses:** Plate discipline needs work; can get overly aggressive; hit tool profiles as below average; defensive profile might be a better fit for third base; game power might play below projection.

**Risk Factor/Injury History:** Moderate risk; struggled in first pass at Double-A.

**The Year Ahead:** Calixte was a bit over his head in Double-A, but his struggles could be a developmental positive, and he has shown the ability to make adjustments in the past. His defensive profile at shortstop is average and could play, but he will need to find more consistency and learn to slow the game down. The power potential is legit, but the hit tool might limit the utility, and the overall approach needs work if he wants to put himself in favorable hitting conditions and add an on-base dimension to his offensive game. He is likely to repeat Double-A, and hopefully take a step forward at the plate and in the field.

### Prospects on the Rise

**1. RHP Christian Binford:** A tall right-hander with a projectable fastball, Binford was impressive in his full-season debut. The secondary stuff is inconsistent, and the fastball velocity would dip under plus, but when it clicked, the fastball was angular and firm in the low-90s and the secondary arsenal flashed above-average potential. He should take a step forward in 2014, joining Almonte in the Wilmington rotation.

**2. OF Daniel Rockett:** A ninth-round pick in 2013, Rockett has the bat to move quickly and the defensive versatility to offer value at all three spots. As an older prospect, he will be pushed aggressively and will have to perform to move up the ranks, but several sources were high on his bat and put better grades on his glove in center than some of his amateur reports suggested.

**3. OF Elier Hernandez:** Strong case for inclusion in the top 10, Hernandez has both tools and instincts for the game, a promising combination to find in a young player. It's a corner-outfield profile but plenty of raw power to dream and a good overall feel for hitting. He could be in the top five in this system at this time next season.

### Factors on the Farm

**Prospects likely to contribute at the major-league level in 2014**

**1. LHP Chris Dwyer:** The stuff is solid-average but it plays down because of an inconsistent delivery and poor command. Dwyer has a chance to right the ship and contribute to the major-league team in 2014.

**2. IF Christian Colon:** Ignore the obvious narrative about Colon— that the fourth overall pick in the draft would end up a fringy

### FROM THE FIELD

**Miguel Almonte**

**Player:** Miguel Almonte

**Team:** Kansas City Royals

**Filed by:** CJ Wittmann

**Date(s) Seen:** May 1, 2013

**Physical:** Starter's build; strong lower half; room to add strength for more durability.

**Mechanics/Delivery:** very smooth, easy delivery; easy, fast arm; very repeatable from 3/4 arm slot; has great deception in delivery, hides ball well.

**Fastball:** 65 grade; 94-96 mph; good running arm-side life; more control than command at present.

**Slider:** 50 grade; 79-82 mph; sharp late break; flashed minimum tilt.

**Changeup:** 70 grade; 80-84 mph; great fading action; drop; great arm action; plays extremely well off fastball.

**Curveball:** 40 grade; 73-76 mph; slurvy type shape; breaks and can see it early; inconsistent.

**Makeup:** 50 grade; visibly frustrated at times on the mound; a bit immature presently

**OFP:** 60; no. 3 starter

**Realistic Role:** 50; no. 4 starter

**Risk:** High; limited professional profile.

### FROM THE FIELD

**Kyle Zimmer**

**Player:** Kyle Zimmer

**Team:** Kansas City Royals

**Filed by:** CJ Wittmann

**Date(s) Seen:** Multiple times

**Physical:** Strong, physical build; thick lower half with deceptive athleticism; build of an innings-eating horse.

**Mechanics/Delivery:** Smooth, traditional 3/4 arm slot delivery; strong leg drive and momentum toward plate, stays balanced throughout and keeps arm online; very repeatable and clean delivery creating minimal deception.

**Fastball:** 60 grade; 94-99 mph; premium velocity but minimal movement; lacks extreme plane from a 6'3" pitching frame; above-average command profile.

**Curveball:** 70 grade; 79-84 mph; 12-6 shape; late downward hard break; hard snap and bite; depth; ability to throw for a strike (early in count) and strikeout (burial) pitch.

**Changeup:** 50 grade; 83-88 mph; good sink; can get firm at times.

**Slider:** 55 grade; late sharp break with tilt; needs to stay on top.

**Makeup:** 60 grade; very cool demeanor on mound; strong work ethic; almost "too cool" according to a scout.

**OFP:** 65; no. 2 starter.

**Realistic Role:** 60; no. 3 starter.

**Risk:** Moderate; limited experience at Double-A.

utility option—and focus on what he might end up bringing to the table at the highest level. It's not an impact profile, but with good baseball skills and enough stick to force a pitcher to work, Colon has a chance to develop into a productive player for the Royals, most likely in a utility role, but there is always a chance he rises to the challenge and becomes a viable option at second base.

**3. LHP Donnie Joseph:** The 26-year-old lefty can miss bats, and that alone is reason to be optimistic about his contribution to the 25-man roster in 2014. On the back of his potent fastball/slider combo, Joseph missed 84 bats in only 55 innings at the Triple-A level in 2013, and with improved command, he could make an already good bullpen even better.

---

## FROM THE FIELD

### Jorge Bonifacio

**Player:** Jorge Bonifacio

**Team:** Kansas City Royals

**Filed by:** CJ Wittmann

**Date(s) Seen:** Multiple times

**Physical:** Big frame with room to add weight; smaller lower half; big broad shoulders; immature young looking body; body could be high-maintenance upkeep going forward.

**Hit:** 50 grade; strong wrists with good bat speed and barrel control; advanced approach and plate discipline; quick hands leading to a short stroke; can get pull-happy at times; questions about hitting quality off-speed; could eventually sacrifice power for more average.

**Power:** 60 grade; good raw strength; good leverage in swing but not great; hit tool will allow plus raw to play above average; with added strength could allow game power to play above.

**Glove:** 50 grade; tracked ball well in outfield (down line and in alley); routes could use refinement; corner outfielder only.

**Arm:** 70 grade; right-field profile arm; gets behind ball and uses necessary footwork to use all of body to make throws; throws were on target.

**Speed:** 50 grade; sneaky athletic; quick and lengthy strides; 4.23 from right side to first base.

**Makeup:** 60 grade; shows willingness to work at craft in pregame (drills, working with coaches, etc.).

**OFP:** 60; first-division regular

**Realistic Role:** 50; major-league regular

**Risk:** High; injuries on resume/limited experience in upper minors.

---

## FROM THE FIELD

### Raul A. Mondesi

**Player:** Raul A. Mondesi

**Team:** Kansas City Royals

**Filed by:** CJ Wittmann

**Date(s) Seen:** Multiple times

**Physical:** Broad-shouldered frame; slender build with plenty of room to add weight; very athletic; long way from maturity.

**Hit:** 60 grade; quiet load from both sides of the plate with plus bat speed; natural bat-to-ball skills, making hard contact often; tracks pitches deep into hitting zone with very good pitch recognition; good plate discipline but will expand zone at times; present trouble with quality spin down in the zone.

**Power:** 50 grade; present gap-to-gap pop;

**Glove:** 65 grade; plus instincts with a very quick first step; extreme range; silky, smooth actions when fielding; lightening quick transfers to arm.

**Arm:** 65 grade; strong, accurate throws; fast arm; capable of making all types of throws.

**Speed:** 60 grade; 4.0 range from left side to first base; long, graceful strides.

**Makeup:** 60 grade; very good teammate and influence to others on the field

**OFP:** 65; all-star

**Realistic Role:** 55; major-league regular

**Risk:** High; 18-year-old with one year of full-season ball.

## 1. Taylor Lindsey 2B

**Born:** 12/2/91 **Age:** 22 **Bats:** L **Throws:** R **Height:** 6'0" **Weight:** 195

| MLB ETA | Hit | Power | Run | Glove | Arm | OFP | Realistic |
|---|---|---|---|---|---|---|---|
| Late 2014 | 60 | •••• | ••••• | ••••• | ••••• | 55 >AVG PLAYER | 50 2ND DIV PLAYER |

| YEAR | TEAM | LVL | AGE | PA | R | 2B | 3B | HR | RBI | BB | SO | SB | CS | AVG/OBP/SLG | TAv | BABIP | BRR | FRAA | WARP |
|---|---|---|---|---|---|---|---|---|---|---|---|---|---|---|---|---|---|---|---|
| 2013 | ARK | AA | 21 | 567 | 68 | 22 | 6 | 17 | 56 | 48 | 91 | 4 | 4 | .274/.339/.441 | .288 | .303 | 0.0 | 2B(134): -6.2 | 2.3 |
| 2014 | ANA | MLB | 22 | 250 | 26 | 10 | 1 | 4 | 22 | 12 | 47 | 1 | 1 | .245/.282/.356 | .237 | .280 | -0.3 | 2B -0 | 0.2 |
| 2015 | ANA | MLB | 23 | 367 | 40 | 16 | 3 | 8 | 39 | 21 | 64 | 1 | 0 | .255/.300/.388 | .251 | .289 | -0.6 | 2B 0 | 0.8 |

Breakout: 0%    Improve: 0%    Collapse: 0%    Attrition: 0%    MLB: 0%        *Comparables: Henry Rodriguez, Adrian Cardenas, Luis Valbuena*

**Drafted/Acquired:** 1st round, 2010 draft, Desert Mountain HS (Scottsdale, AZ)

**Previous Ranking:** #5 (Org)

**What Happened in 2013:** Lindsey took a step forward to the Texas League and took a step forward with the stick, impressing scouts with his ability to square the baseball to all fields.

**Strengths:** The hit tool could be plus; shows above-average bat speed; quick hands; can square velocity; can track off-speed; good gap pop; has athleticism to play a passable second base.

**Weaknesses:** Wide-base setup and leg movement can effect timing and balance; power potential is fringe-average at best; below-average run; below-average range; hands in the field are fringy; arm is average but not a weapon; has to hit.

**Risk Factor/Injury History:** Moderate risk; already achieved Double-A level

**Bret Sayre's Fantasy Take:** A much more interesting prospect in deeper leagues, Lindsey is one of the least exciting number one prospects for fantasy that this series will feature. The batting average could be helpful, but the production everywhere else is likely to be middling at best. His best-case scenario is somewhere around Martin Prado for fantasy, which, while underrated, is not a star.

**The Year Ahead:** Lindsey is the top prospect in the Angels system, but I doubt he would sit atop the list for any other team in baseball. He has a really nice hit tool, and if you are one of those people who really, really believes in it—meaning you think he can develop into a .285+ hitter at the major-league level—perhaps you can look beyond his other "average-at-best" attributes to see a first-division talent. I like the player and I think he will hit for a good average with some doubles power, but I don't see a lot of over-the-fence power coming, and the overall profile is a bit one dimensional.

## 2. Kaleb Cowart 3B

**Born:** 6/2/92 **Age:** 22 **Bats:** B **Throws:** R **Height:** 6'3" **Weight:** 195

| MLB ETA | Hit | Power | Run | Glove | Arm | OFP | Realistic |
|---|---|---|---|---|---|---|---|
| 2015 | — | 60 | — | 55 | 70 | 55 >AVG PLAYER | 50 2ND DIV PLAYER |

| YEAR | TEAM | LVL | AGE | PA | R | 2B | 3B | HR | RBI | BB | SO | SB | CS | AVG/OBP/SLG | TAv | BABIP | BRR | FRAA | WARP |
|---|---|---|---|---|---|---|---|---|---|---|---|---|---|---|---|---|---|---|---|
| 2013 | ARK | AA | 21 | 546 | 48 | 20 | 1 | 6 | 42 | 38 | 124 | 14 | 5 | .221/.279/.301 | .216 | .280 | 3.1 | 3B(131): -10.8 | -1.5 |
| 2014 | ANA | MLB | 22 | 250 | 21 | 9 | 1 | 3 | 21 | 16 | 65 | 3 | 1 | .214/.266/.302 | .216 | .280 | -0.1 | 3B -2, 1B 0 | -0.7 |
| 2015 | ANA | MLB | 23 | 250 | 26 | 10 | 1 | 6 | 25 | 17 | 65 | 2 | 1 | .223/.278/.351 | .234 | .281 | -0.3 | 3B -1, 1B 0 | -0.2 |

Breakout: 0%    Improve: 0%    Collapse: 0%    Attrition: 0%    MLB: 0%        *Comparables: Jesus Guzman, Ian Stewart, Brent Morel*

**Drafted/Acquired:** 1st round, 2010 draft, Cook HS (Adel, GA)

**Previous Ranking:** #1 (Org), #42 (Top 101)

**What Happened in 2013:** An aggressive assignment to Double-A was met with disappointing results, as Cowart never found any comfort at the plate, especially from the left side, as he hit an anemic .202 against right-handed pitching.

**Strengths:** Good athlete; good defensive profile at third; arm is plus-plus; glove is above average; in the past, has shown bat speed and control from both sides of the plate; better contact from the right side; bigger power potential from the left side.

**Weaknesses:** Was a mess at the plate in 2013; timing was off; unbalanced; hands/front foot not in sync; bat speed was noticeably slower; lost his approach; was overmatched and visibly frustrated at times.

**Risk Factor/Injury History:** Moderate risk; unsuccessful in first pass at Double-A; skills to reach major-league level.

**Bret Sayre's Fantasy Take:** The power is still there for Cowart to be a potential 25-homer guy at the hot corner, and if that can even come with a .250 average, it's a skill set that will make him sought after in all leagues. But another year like 2013 and he'll be on the fast track to fantasy irrelevance.

**The Year Ahead:** Cowart needs to hit the reset button and start anew in Double-A. He never looked comfortable at the plate, and his struggles would compound when he started pressing. The defensive profile at third is nice, and if the bat can get back on track, this is a prospect worthy of top-50 consideration.

## 3. C.J. Cron 1B

**Born:** 1/5/90 **Age:** 24 **Bats:** R **Throws:** R **Height:** 6' 4" **Weight:** 235

| MLB ETA | Hit | Power | Run | Glove | Arm | OFP | Realistic |
|---|---|---|---|---|---|---|---|
| Late 2014 | – | 80 | – | – | – | 50 ML REGULAR | 45 PLATOON BAT |

| YEAR | TEAM | LVL | AGE | PA | R | 2B | 3B | HR | RBI | BB | SO | SB | CS | AVG/OBP/SLG | TAv | BABIP | BRR | FRAA | WARP |
|---|---|---|---|---|---|---|---|---|---|---|---|---|---|---|---|---|---|---|---|
| 2013 | ARK | AA | 23 | 565 | 56 | 36 | 1 | 14 | 83 | 23 | 83 | 8 | 4 | .274/.319/.428 | .278 | .298 | -1.5 | 1B(124): 2.2 | 1.6 |
| 2014 | ANA | MLB | 24 | 250 | 24 | 12 | 0 | 7 | 29 | 6 | 47 | 1 | 1 | .248/.275/.393 | .246 | .280 | -0.4 | 1B 0 | -0.1 |
| 2015 | ANA | MLB | 25 | 250 | 30 | 13 | 0 | 9 | 32 | 8 | 45 | 1 | 0 | .257/.291/.430 | .262 | .281 | -0.6 | 1B 0 | 0.6 |

Breakout: 2%   Improve: 6%   Collapse: 6%   Attrition: 17%   MLB: 17%   *Comparables: Mark Trumbo, Wes Bankston, Joey Terdoslavich*

**Drafted/Acquired:** 1st round, 2011 draft, University of Utah (Salt Lake City, UT)

**Previous Ranking:** #3 (Org)

**What Happened in 2013:** Cron arrived at the Double-A level and slugged 51 extra-base hits, but his streaky nature and one-dimensional skill set limit his value and leave his long-term projection up for debate.

**Strengths:** Monster raw; capable of tape-measure shots; game power could play to plus; crushes left-handed pitching; body has improved year-to-year; better movement at first.

**Weaknesses:** Struggles against arm-side pitching; hit tool is below average and unlikely to play to average; power is only carrying tool; well-below-average run; fringe defender at first.

**Overall Future Potential:** 5; major-league regular

**Bret Sayre's Fantasy Take:** The big man has both his eligibility and his potential hit tool working against him from a fantasy perspective, but the power will be worth all of the headaches if he can become a 25+ homer guy. His value in the near term also takes a hit, as being a 1B/DH prospect in an organization long on age and short on defensive flexibility clouds his path.

**The Year Ahead:** Cron is a powerful human with plus right-handed power potential, but the overall profile is tough to sell. He's unlikely to hit for a high average, and major-league-quality pitching will be able to exploit his weaknesses at the plate, which include putting poor swings on spin on the outer half. But he has the potential to hit 25 bombs, and you can overlook a lot of skill-set deficiencies for 25 bombs. He should start in Triple-A and produce, but the real test will come at the highest level, where the power isn't as easy to bring into games as it at the minor-league level. He will be tested.

## 4. R.J. Alvarez RHP

**Born:** 6/8/91 **Age:** 23 **Bats:** R **Throws:** R **Height:** 6' 1" **Weight:** 180

| MLB ETA | CT | FB | CH | CB | SL | OFP | Realistic |
|---|---|---|---|---|---|---|---|
| Late 2014 | – | 70 | – | – | 60 | 60 LATE INN RP (SETUP) | 50 MIDDLE RELIEF |

| YEAR | TEAM | LVL | AGE | W | L | SV | G | GS | IP | H | HR | BB | SO | BB9 | SO9 | GB% | BABIP | WHIP | ERA | FIP | FRA | WARP |
|---|---|---|---|---|---|---|---|---|---|---|---|---|---|---|---|---|---|---|---|---|---|---|
| 2013 | SBR | A+ | 22 | 4 | 2 | 4 | 37 | 2 | 48.7 | 34 | 2 | 27 | 79 | 5.0 | 14.6 | 38% | .327 | 1.25 | 2.96 | 2.85 | 2.56 | 1.6 |
| 2014 | ANA | MLB | 23 | 2 | 1 | 1 | 32 | 0 | 38.3 | 34 | 4 | 20 | 44 | 4.7 | 10.3 | 42% | .309 | 1.41 | 3.97 | 4.15 | 4.32 | 0.2 |
| 2015 | ANA | MLB | 24 | 2 | 1 | 0 | 46 | 0 | 49.0 | 44 | 6 | 27 | 56 | 5.0 | 10.3 | 42% | .300 | 1.43 | 4.21 | 4.24 | 4.58 | 0.2 |

Breakout: 0%   Improve: 0%   Collapse: 0%   Attrition: 0%   MLB: 0%   *Comparables: Steven Geltz, Donnie Joseph, Heath Hembree*

**Drafted/Acquired:** 3rd round, 2012 draft, Florida Atlantic University (Boca Raton, FL)

**Previous Ranking:** #6 (Org)

**What Happened in 2013:** Alvarez was pure filth in the California League, missing 79 bats in only ~48 innings, holding opposing hitters to a .191 average.

**Strengths:** Big arm strength; fastball is impact weapon; works mid-90s and higher with ease; good vertical life; shows quality slider in the mid-80s; attacks hitters; late-innings mentality.

**Weaknesses:** Delivery has effort; arm-slot inconsistency (now throwing from low 3/4); slider can flatten out; shows both a curveball and changeup that don't grade to average; command is below average at present.

**Risk Factor/Injury History:** Low risk; has the fastball to pitch at highest level

**Bret Sayre's Fantasy Take:** As a pure relief prospect, Alvarez has very limited value. He could be a big strikeout guy (think 80+ in a good season), but using minor-league roster spots on players who are so role dependent for value isn't the best use of resources.

**The Year Ahead:** Alvarez is on the fast track to the majors, and could show up as soon as 2014. The fastball is a weapon, working in the 95-97 range with life. The slider flashes plus, and it should get there, giving him two impact pitches to work with in short bursts. The command isn't sharp, but with a little more refinement he could develop into a late-innings arm, one capable of an eventual setup role.

## 5. Mark Sappington  RHP

**Born:** 11/17/90  **Age:** 23  **Bats:** R  **Throws:** R  **Height:** 6' 5"  **Weight:** 210

| MLB ETA | CT | FB | CH | CB | SL | OFP | Realistic |
|---|---|---|---|---|---|---|---|
| 2015 | – | 60 | – | – | 60 | 55<br>NO.3-4 STARTER | 50<br>MID/LONG RELIEF |

| YEAR | TEAM | LVL | AGE | W | L | SV | G | GS | IP | H | HR | BB | SO | BB9 | SO9 | GB% | BABIP | WHIP | ERA | FIP | FRA | WARP |
|---|---|---|---|---|---|---|---|---|---|---|---|---|---|---|---|---|---|---|---|---|---|---|
| 2013 | ARK | AA | 22 | 1 | 1 | 0 | 5 | 5 | 25.7 | 23 | 1 | 20 | 26 | 7.0 | 9.1 | 52% | .306 | 1.68 | 3.86 | 4.11 | 4.30 | 0.2 |
| 2013 | SBR | A+ | 22 | 11 | 4 | 0 | 22 | 22 | 130.7 | 103 | 10 | 62 | 110 | 4.3 | 7.6 | 47% | .262 | 1.26 | 3.38 | 4.62 | 4.97 | 0.9 |
| 2014 | ANA | MLB | 23 | 6 | 8 | 0 | 22 | 22 | 107.0 | 114 | 13 | 64 | 72 | 5.4 | 6.1 | 48% | .298 | 1.66 | 5.27 | 5.59 | 5.73 | -0.7 |
| 2015 | ANA | MLB | 24 | 7 | 8 | 0 | 25 | 25 | 147.7 | 146 | 16 | 76 | 107 | 4.6 | 6.5 | 48% | .287 | 1.50 | 4.56 | 4.79 | 4.96 | 0.0 |

Breakout: 0%    Improve: 0%    Collapse: 0%    Attrition: 0%    MLB: 0%        *Comparables: Alex Colome, Kyle Weiland, Rafael Dolis*

**Drafted/Acquired:** 5th round, 2012 draft, Rockhurst University (Kansas City, MO)

**Previous Ranking:** #7 (Org)

**What Happened in 2013:** Across two stops and 27 starts, Sappington showed off the impressive arm strength, routinely working the fastball into the mid-90s and backing it up with a very good slider.

**Strengths:** Big arm; excellent size/strength; fastball can start slow (90-93) but builds as he goes along, often sitting in the 95-96 range by midgame; pitch has some vertical action; slider is preferred breaking ball; can flash plus in the mid-80s with good tilt; intense competitor; high energy; works fast.

**Weaknesses:** Command is well below average; slows body down on secondary offerings; will show a curveball and a changeup, neither of which projects to be an average pitch.

**Risk Factor/Injury History:** Moderate risk; fastball to play but command needs improvement.

**Bret Sayre's Fantasy Take:** The stuff is there for Sappington to do some damage in strikeouts, but he'll give back all of that value (and more) if he doesn't start finding the plate more consistently. With that said, the ballpark and lack of pitching depth in Los Angeles will help his cause—it's just not a profile to get all that excited about right now.

**The Year Ahead:** Sappington should continue to be developed as a starter, as he will offer more value as a number four in a rotation than as a middle or long reliever. But the delivery isn't sexy smooth, and the command profile and secondary execution are inconsistent, so he might not be able to avoid his long-term fate in the bullpen. But with a very good fastball and a very competitive streak, Sappington might exceed his projection in this role and develop into an arm with late-innings impact potential.

## 6. Alex Yarbrough  2B

**Born:** 8/3/91  **Age:** 22  **Bats:** B  **Throws:** R  **Height:** 5' 11"  **Weight:** 180

| MLB ETA | Hit | Power | Run | Glove | Arm | OFP | Realistic |
|---|---|---|---|---|---|---|---|
| Late 2015 | 60 | – | 50 | – | – | 50<br>AVG ML PLAYER | 45<br><AVG ML PLAYER |

| YEAR | TEAM | LVL | AGE | PA | R | 2B | 3B | HR | RBI | BB | SO | SB | CS | AVG/OBP/SLG | TAv | BABIP | BRR | FRAA | WARP |
|---|---|---|---|---|---|---|---|---|---|---|---|---|---|---|---|---|---|---|---|
| 2013 | SBR | A+ | 21 | 615 | 77 | 32 | 10 | 11 | 80 | 27 | 106 | 14 | 4 | .313/.341/.459 | .302 | .364 | 0.5 | 2B(126): -19.9 | 2.4 |
| 2014 | ANA | MLB | 22 | 250 | 19 | 10 | 2 | 2 | 22 | 6 | 50 | 3 | 1 | .245/.263/.331 | .223 | .300 | 0.2 | 2B -6 | -0.7 |
| 2015 | ANA | MLB | 23 | 250 | 24 | 10 | 2 | 3 | 22 | 8 | 47 | 1 | 0 | .256/.280/.348 | .235 | .305 | -0.1 | 2B -6 | -0.5 |

Breakout: 0%    Improve: 0%    Collapse: 0%    Attrition: 0%    MLB: 0%        *Comparables: Scooter Gennett, Henry Rodriguez, Tony Abreu*

**Drafted/Acquired:** 4th round, 2012 draft, University of Mississippi (Oxford, MS)

**Previous Ranking:** On The Rise

**What Happened in 2013:** I know it's the California League, but Yarbrough had a really good season at the plate, hitting 32 doubles, 10 triples, 11 home runs, while also swiping 14 bases.

**Strengths:** Lacks loud tools, but shows baseball skills; fast hands at the plate; can square velocity; can use the entire field; good gap pop; hit tool could reach plus; balanced from both sides of the plate; runs well; instincts for the game.

**Weaknesses:** Aggressive approach; can get beat by off-speed; power is below average; makes plays, but defensive profile is fringe-average; hit tool is only weapon.

**Risk Factor/Injury History:** Moderate risk; shows baseball skills; ready for Double-A test.

**Bret Sayre's Fantasy Take:** Playing a full season in the California League can pump up a prospect's trade value in dynasty league formats, and Yarbrough's solid statistical year overstates his fantasy case. Best left for only the deepest of formats, as an okay average and a few steals just isn't an exciting package, even at second base.

**The Year Ahead:** Yarbrough has a difficult profile, as he's a hit-tool second baseman who lacks above-average weapons on either side of the ball. He can play the game, and his bat might be better than people realize; he can square velocity from both sides of the plate and use the entire field, so the bat has a chance to play. The over-the-fence power is unremarkable, but he can put a change into the ball, so you can't just sleep on him. Thanks to his instincts, Yarbrough's overall game is better than what the individual tool grades might suggest, and I wouldn't be shocked if he developed into a decent little player at the highest level.

## 7.  Jose Rondon   SS

**Born:** 3/3/94  **Age:** 20  **Bats:** R  **Throws:** R  **Height:** 6' 1"  **Weight:** 160

| MLB ETA | Hit | Power | Run | Glove | Arm | OFP | Realistic |
|---|---|---|---|---|---|---|---|
| 2017 | 55 | – | 50 | 50 | 50 | 50 AVG PLAYER | 45 UTILITY PLAYER |

| YEAR | TEAM | LVL | AGE | PA | R | 2B | 3B | HR | RBI | BB | SO | SB | CS | AVG/OBP/SLG | TAv | BABIP | BRR | FRAA | WARP |
|---|---|---|---|---|---|---|---|---|---|---|---|---|---|---|---|---|---|---|---|
| 2013 | ORM | Rk | 19 | 316 | 45 | 22 | 2 | 1 | 50 | 30 | 31 | 13 | 8 | .293/.359/.399 | .273 | .319 | -1.6 | SS(66): -1.4 | 1.5 |
| 2014 | ANA | MLB | 20 | 250 | 21 | 9 | 0 | 1 | 14 | 11 | 60 | 3 | 2 | .194/.229/.246 | .181 | .250 | -0.3 | SS 1, 3B 0 | -0.9 |
| 2015 | ANA | MLB | 21 | 250 | 20 | 6 | 1 | 1 | 16 | 11 | 51 | 1 | 1 | .204/.239/.251 | .186 | .251 | -0.4 | SS 0 | -2.9 |

Breakout: 0%    Improve: 0%    Collapse: 0%    Attrition: 0%    MLB: 0%    *Comparables: Juan Diaz, Didi Gregorius, Osvaldo Martinez*

**Drafted/Acquired:** International free agent, 2011, Venezuela

**Previous Ranking:** #9 (Org)

**What Happened in 2013:** The then-19-year-old Venezuelan returned to short-season ball, putting up impressive numbers at the plate and showing scouts his well-rounded defense up the middle.

**Strengths:** Advanced player; clean actions in the field; smooth; arm is solid-average; can make the throws; has instincts for the game; quick hands at the plate; can drive the ball; has some pop; good approach; not a burner but can run.

**Weaknesses:** Lacks high-end tools; arm isn't a weapon; more polish than projection; range could be an issue at short; could grow out of the position.

**Risk Factor/Injury History:** High risk; yet to achieve full-season level

**Bret Sayre's Fantasy Take:** The real-life package at this point looks more attractive than the one for fantasy, especially when you factor in the age/risk. However, if he can continue to show the ability to take a walk and limit his strikeouts, Rondon could become an undervalued player in points leagues—even if he steals only 15-20 bases with a few homers sprinkled in.

**The Year Ahead:** Rondon is ready for the full-season challenge, as his advanced approach to the game and polish should allow him to have success. He lacks explosive tools, but a solid-average skill set at a premium position has a lot of value, even if the bat ends up playing down in the lineup. Rondon is unlikely to develop into a top-tier prospect, but a good performance in the Midwest League could elevate his stock and cement his place on the prospect landscape.

## 8.  Ricardo Sanchez   LHP

**Born:** 4/11/97  **Age:** 17  **Bats:** L  **Throws:** L  **Height:** 5' 10"  **Weight:** 170

| MLB ETA | CT | FB | CH | CB | SL | OFP | Realistic |
|---|---|---|---|---|---|---|---|
| 2018 | – | 60 | 60 | 60 | – | 60 NO.2-3 STARTER | 50 NO.4-5 STARTER |

| YEAR | TEAM | LVL | AGE | W | L | SV | G | GS | IP | H | HR | BB | SO | BB9 | SO9 | GB% | BABIP | WHIP | ERA | FIP | FRA | WARP |
|---|---|---|---|---|---|---|---|---|---|---|---|---|---|---|---|---|---|---|---|---|---|---|
| | | | | | | | | | No Professional Experience | | | | | | | | | | | | | |

**Drafted/Acquired:** International free agent, 2013, Venezuela

**What Happened in 2013:** The Angels signed the Venezuelan southpaw for $580,000, using more than a quarter of their international bonus pool.

**Strengths:** Easy, fluid delivery; fastball velo jumped during instructs; pitch worked comfortably in the low-90s; good movement; good feel for sharp curveball in the upper-70s; shows highly projectable changeup; good overall feel for command; high-end poise and makeup.

**Weaknesses:** Can rush the delivery; leave the ball arm side and up; changeup can get too firm; overthrows it; limited height; offerings can lack plane.

**Risk Factor/Injury History:** Extreme; no professional experience

**Bret Sayre's Fantasy Take:** The Angels' system is so bereft of players with potential fantasy impact that I'd likely take a gamble on Sanchez over nearly half of the players in front of him on this list. The chance that he's the pitching prospect everyone's talking about in 2016 is small, but at least there's a chance.

**The Year Ahead:** Sanchez is an exciting prospect, not only because of the promise found in the arsenal but the complete lack of professional experience. Sanchez gets to throw his first professional pitch in 2014, most likely at the complex level, but his showing at instructs was enough to force a Pavlovian prospect response. With a smooth and easy delivery, a present fastball that sits 91, a promising curveball that has touched 80, and the beginnings of a changeup that could develop into his money pitch, Sanchez is well on his way to becoming a very high-end prospect.

## 9.   Hunter Green   LHP

**Born:** 7/12/95   **Age:** 18   **Bats:** L   **Throws:** L   **Height:** 6' 4"   **Weight:** 175

| MLB ETA | CT | FB | CH | CB | SL | OFP | Realistic |
|---|---|---|---|---|---|---|---|
| 2018 | — | 60 | 60 | 50 | — | 60<br>NO.3 STARTER | 50<br>NO.5 STARTER |

| YEAR | TEAM | LVL | AGE | W | L | SV | G | GS | IP | H | HR | BB | SO | BB9 | SO9 | GB% | BABIP | WHIP | ERA | FIP | FRA | WARP |
|---|---|---|---|---|---|---|---|---|---|---|---|---|---|---|---|---|---|---|---|---|---|---|
| 2013 | ANG | Rk | 17 | 0 | 1 | 0 | 8 | 7 | 16.7 | 16 | 0 | 16 | 11 | 8.6 | 5.9 | 42% | .302 | 1.92 | 4.32 | 5.74 | 7.51 | -0.1 |
| 2014 | ANA | MLB | 18 | 1 | 3 | 0 | 8 | 8 | 30.3 | 39 | 4 | 21 | 11 | 6.2 | 3.3 | 43% | .312 | 2.00 | 7.10 | 6.77 | 7.72 | -0.7 |
| 2015 | ANA | MLB | 19 | 3 | 6 | 0 | 20 | 20 | 119.7 | 145 | 18 | 69 | 59 | 5.2 | 4.4 | 43% | .304 | 1.79 | 6.33 | 6.01 | 6.88 | -2.3 |

Breakout: 0%   Improve: 0%   Collapse: 0%   Attrition: 0%   MLB: 0%   *Comparables: Martin Perez, David Holmberg, Jordan Lyles*

**Drafted/Acquired:** 2nd round, 2013 draft, Warren East HS (Bowling Green, KY)

**Previous Ranking:** NR

**What Happened in 2013:** The Angels' second-round pick struggled in his brief professional debut, but the project-able lefty didn't even turn 18 until July.

**Strengths:** He's a 6'4'' lefty; projectable body and arsenal; good athlete; fast arm; from 3/4 slot, works fastball in 85-92 range; good life to the arm side; fastball projects solid-average to plus; upper-70s changeup is another plus potential offering; good sink and fade; big confidence in the pitch.

**Weaknesses:** Command is well below average at present; struggles to stay in his delivery/finish; fastball velo ebbs and flows; curveball is below average; limited depth.

**Risk Factor/Injury History:** High risk; limited professional record; underdeveloped at present

**Bret Sayre's Fantasy Take:** Solely for fantasy purposes, Green fits the bill of a chance to take. He may have plenty of risk, but you're making a play for the upside—and whether his downside is a back-end starter or a guy who never makes it out of Double-A isn't of much consequence for fantasy owners. He's a good use of a later draft pick if you want to take someone with a shot to be a tradable commodity after the 2014 season.

**The Year Ahead:** The Angels have a lot to work with in Green, a highly projectable left-handed pitcher with good athleticism and feel for craft. He's clearly raw, with poor command and delivery issues at present, but it's not a stretch to see a player that develops a consistent low-90s fastball to pair with a plus changeup and a passable breaking ball. The projection is substantial, but the journey is long and the risk is high.

## 10.   Zach Borenstein   OF

**Born:** 7/23/90   **Age:** 23   **Bats:** L   **Throws:** R   **Height:** 6' 0"   **Weight:** 205

| MLB ETA | Hit | Power | Run | Glove | Arm | OFP | Realistic |
|---|---|---|---|---|---|---|---|
| 2017 | — | 60 | 50 | — | — | 50<br>2ND DIV PLAYER | 45<br>PLATOON BAT |

| YEAR | TEAM | LVL | AGE | PA | R | 2B | 3B | HR | RBI | BB | SO | SB | CS | AVG/OBP/SLG | TAv | BABIP | BRR | FRAA | WARP |
|---|---|---|---|---|---|---|---|---|---|---|---|---|---|---|---|---|---|---|---|
| 2013 | SBR | A+ | 22 | 465 | 76 | 22 | 7 | 28 | 95 | 43 | 88 | 5 | 5 | .337/.403/.631 | 0.368 | 0.366 | -4.5 | LF(79): -3.0, RF(1): -0.0 | -5.7 |
| 2014 | ANA | MLB | 23 | 250 | 28 | 10 | 1 | 9 | 32 | 16 | 61 | 3 | 1 | .244/.297/.420 | 0.261 | 0.29 | -0.1 | LF -2, RF -0 | 0.3 |
| 2015 | ANA | MLB | 24 | 250 | 30 | 12 | 1 | 7 | 30 | 17 | 56 | 2 | 1 | .260/.315/.423 | 0.268 | 0.31 | -0.3 | LF -2, RF 0 | 1.8 |

Breakout: 1%   Improve: 14%   Collapse: 2%   Attrition: 8%   MLB: 27%   *Comparables: Corey Dickerson, Marc Krauss, Khris Davis*

**Drafted/Acquired:** 23rd round, 2011 draft, Eastern Illinois University (Charleston, IL)

**Previous Ranking:** NR

**What Happened in 2013:** Borenstein destroyed the California League to the point that even skeptics started wondering if the powerful bat had legit major-league potential.

**Strengths:** Good athlete; very strong; jacked upper body; shows some bat speed at the plate; crushes mistakes; plus raw power; controls the bat pretty well given the nature of the swing; average run; highly competitive type; plays above tools.

**Weaknesses:** Lacks much defensive versatility; arm is below average; left-field profile; bat speed is more strength derived; crushes mistakes but can get beat by stuff (velo inside/out; spin); hit tool likely to play below average at highest level; could limit power in game action.

**Risk Factor/Injury History:** Moderate risk; physically mature; limited upside.

**Bret Sayre's Fantasy Take:** You almost can't say Borenstein without boring, although he was anything but in the California League last year. Unfortunately for the 23-year-old, he doesn't project to be more than an extra out-fielder on a good team, so reading too much into the tea leaves his 2013 statistics were printed on will lead to bad decisions for your fantasy roster.

**The Year Ahead:** Borenstein will face the great prospect test in 2014: Double-A. He's more athletic than you might think, and his competitiveness really stands out and allows him to make plays despite limitations in the field. At the plate, his major-league-quality strength allows him to muscle balls out and crush mistakes in friendly conditions, but scouts aren't sold he can keep up with better stuff, as the bat speed is only average and he isn't a natural hitter. With a left-field-only profile in the outfield and a power-only bat at the plate, it's a tough profile to sell, but a strong Double-A campaign will silence some of the doubters.

## Prospects on the Rise

**1. LF Natanael Delgado:** Making a return trip to the On the Rise category, Delgado has a case for inclusion in the top 10 on the strength of his offensive projection alone. With bat speed and good pop from the left side, Delgado has impact potential with the bat, but his aggressive approach and lack of feel for the game have some questioning whether or not he will ever develop enough skills to make it work.

**2. RHP Keynan Middleton:** A highly projectable and athletic pitcher, Middleton can already work the fastball in the low-90s that touches higher, with multiple breaking ball looks. The command isn't there yet, and the changeup is still a baby, but Middleton is new to the mound and has already taken big developmental steps forward in a short amount of time. He could be ready for another jump in 2014.

**3. LHP Nate Smith:** Smith is a relatively unknown name, an eighth-round selection in the 2013 draft out of Furman. While Smith is unlikely to emerge as a name prospect, his combination of present stuff and polish will allow him to move very quickly. Smith is a strike-thrower with an upper-80s/low-90s fastball, good changeup, and plus pitchability.

## Factors on the Farm

### Prospects likely to contribute at the major-league level in 2014

**1. LHP Nick Maronde:** Maronde received a five-inning taste of the major-league level in 2013, showing a low-90s fastball and a good slider. Command isn't his friend, but with more refinement Maronde has the stuff to stick around in a major-league bullpen, most likely in middle relief but a chance for high leverage if he can stay healthy and stay consistent in his delivery.

**2. RHP Mike Morin:** With good command and a very good changeup, Morin crushed two stops in 2013, and looks to be a on the verge of a major-league contribution in 2014. The fastball isn't special—working in the low-90s—but he can spot it and set up his secondary arsenal, which includes a slower slider and the aforementioned changeup, a weapon he deploys to both lefties and righties.

**3. RHP Cam Bedrosian:** When healthy, Bedrosian can look the part of a nasty late-innings reliever, working his four-seamer in the mid-90s, with a low-80s slider and a hard cutter. But the command comes and goes, and when he works up in the zone, he flattens out and becomes hittable. If he can stay on the field, he can move fast through the upper minors, with a chance to reach the majors this season.

## 1. Julio Urias   LHP

**Born:** 8/12/96   **Age:** 17   **Bats:** L   **Throws:** L   **Height:** 5'11"   **Weight:** 160

| MLB ETA | CT | FB | CH | CB | SL | OFP | Realistic |
|---------|----|----|----|----|----|-----|-----------|
| 2015 | --- | 70 | 65 | 60 | --- | 65<br>NO.2 STARTER | 60<br>NO.3 STARTER |

| YEAR | TEAM | LVL | AGE | W | L | SV | G | GS | IP | H | HR | BB | SO | BB9 | SO9 | GB% | BABIP | WHIP | ERA | FIP | FRA | WARP |
|------|------|-----|-----|---|---|----|---|----|----|---|----|----|----|-----|-----|-----|-------|------|-----|-----|-----|------|
| 2013 | GRL | A | 16 | 2 | 0 | 0 | 18 | 18 | 54.3 | 44 | 5 | 16 | 67 | 2.7 | 11.1 | 54% | .320 | 1.10 | 2.48 | 3.01 | 3.59 | 1.4 |

**Drafted/Acquired:** International free agent, 2012, Mexico

**Previous Ranking:** On The Rise

**What Happened in 2013:** As a 16-year-old, Urias fluttered the hearts of many a prospectphile, jumping straight to the Midwest League and showing three above-average pitches, including a fastball that touched plus velocity in each start.

**Strengths:** Advanced pitchability; taller than listed height (more like 6'1''); easy and repeatable delivery; fastball works 91-93; touches 95 frequently; multiple fastball looks and actions; turns over highly projectable changeup with good arm-speed deception and fading action; projects as easy plus offering (and possibly higher); spins average curveball that already flashes plus potential, with a tight rotation and depth; above-average command projection; makeup for accelerated developmental schedule.

**Weaknesses:** Body could prove to be high maintenance; will need to maintain weight and athleticism as he matures; several sources question arsenal projection (more polish and present than projection); changeup can get too firm and lose action; limited exposure or experience with longer looks (starts).

**Risk Factor/Injury History:** High risk; mature stuff but 17 years old.

**Bret Sayre's Fantasy Take:** The fantasy profile here is just something we are really not used to seeing from an ETA standpoint, even if the stuff is more comfortable for evaluation. This could be an arm who impacts all four categories strongly—especially with that changeup as a big strikeout weapon against right-handed hitters. But the innings limits he's likely to be facing at the beginning of his career (if he does reach the majors in the next two seasons) will hurt his value slightly. Invest heavily, but wisely.

**The Year Ahead:** Urias is a very advanced prospect who could see the Double-A level at some point in the 2014 season, and perhaps reach the majors before his 19th birthday in 2015. The Mexican southpaw pitches well off his fastball, showing multiple looks, including a four-seamer he can push into the mid-90s when he needs it, and backing up the fastball with two secondary offerings that can already play as average and flash plus potential. I haven't seen a pitcher this advanced at this age since I started scouting, and if Urias can add strength and maintain his body without losing his delivery and command profile, his stuff will allow him to find results regardless of the level, major leagues included.

> **#35**
> BP Top 101 Prospects

## 2. Corey Seager   SS

**Born:** 4/27/94   **Age:** 20   **Bats:** L   **Throws:** R   **Height:** 6'4"   **Weight:** 215

| MLB ETA | Hit | Power | Run | Glove | Arm | OFP | Realistic |
|---------|-----|-------|-----|-------|-----|-----|-----------|
| 2016 | 60 | 60 | 50 | 55 | 65 | 60<br>1ST DIV PLAYER | 50<br>ML REGULAR |

| YEAR | TEAM | LVL | AGE | PA | R | 2B | 3B | HR | RBI | BB | SO | SB | CS | AVG/OBP/SLG | TAv | BABIP | BRR | FRAA | WARP |
|------|------|-----|-----|----|---|----|----|----|-----|----|----|----|----|-------------|-----|-------|-----|------|------|
| 2013 | GRL | A | 19 | 312 | 45 | 18 | 3 | 12 | 57 | 34 | 58 | 9 | 4 | .309/.389/.529 | .330 | .353 | -0.5 | SS(74): -5.5 | 3.2 |
| 2013 | RCU | A+ | 19 | 114 | 10 | 2 | 1 | 4 | 15 | 12 | 31 | 1 | 0 | .160/.246/.320 | .221 | .179 | 0.2 | SS(25): -4.1, 3B(1): -0.0 | -0.6 |
| 2014 | LAN | MLB | 20 | 250 | 25 | 9 | 1 | 8 | 28 | 17 | 66 | 2 | 1 | .221/.274/.363 | .235 | .270 | -0.2 | SS -8, 3B -0 | -0.4 |
| 2015 | LAN | MLB | 21 | 250 | 30 | 12 | 1 | 9 | 31 | 19 | 60 | 0 | 0 | .246/.305/.418 | .261 | .293 | -0.5 | SS -7, 3B 0 | 1.2 |

**Breakout:** 0%   **Improve:** 0%   **Collapse:** 0%   **Attrition:** 0%   **MLB:** 0%   **Comparables:** Nick Franklin, Xander Bogaerts, Matt Dominguez

**Drafted/Acquired:** 1st round, 2012 draft, Northwest Cabarrus HS (Concord, NC)

**Previous Ranking:** #3 (Org)

**What Happened in 2013:** As a 19-year-old, Seager crushed in his full-season debut in Low-A before struggling against better pitching in the California League and the Arizona Fall League.

**Strengths:** Excellent size/present strength; sweet swing from the left side; balanced with plus bat speed; projects for both power and average; tracks the ball well; puts himself in good hitting conditions; arm is plus; hands work well in the field; quality actions; runs well for his size; baseball skills and instincts.

**Weaknesses:** Can lengthen swing for power and open holes (inside); can get fastball happy and roll over off-speed early in counts; size limits projection at shortstop; lower-half movement can get stiff; good but not great range;

> **#44**
> BP Top 101 Prospects

straight-line speed will end up below average.

**Risk Factor/Injury History:** Moderate risk; yet to play at Double-A level; struggled against more advanced pitching.

**Bret Sayre's Fantasy Take:** Seager would be an even more interesting fantasy prospect if he had a better chance of sticking at shortstop. But even at third base, a .285 hitter with 20 homers is plenty valuable. On top of that, he's shown a good approach at the plate and the ability to take a walk, which could give him a slight boost in OBP leagues. The speed isn't a zero, but don't expect more than 5-10 steals annually.

**The Year Ahead:** Seager is a safe bet to end up at third base, which puts more pressure on his bat to carry the burden of value. With a smooth, fluid swing that produces bat speed and loft, the bat has a chance to hit for average and power, which could make him a first-division talent at the hot corner. The then-19-year-old did struggle against more advanced pitching, pulling off balls and losing his approach at times, but the offensive projections remain above average, and he should return to High-A and show more with the stick than he did in his 100 at-bat sample.

## 3. Joc Pederson CF

**Born:** 4/21/92  **Age:** 22  **Bats:** L  **Throws:** L  **Height:** 6' 1"  **Weight:** 185

| MLB ETA | Hit | Power | Run | Glove | Arm | OFP | Realistic |
|---------|-----|-------|-----|-------|-----|-----|-----------|
| 2014 | 55 | 60 | 55 | 55 | 55 | 60<br>1ST DIV PLAYER | 50<br>2ND DIV/PLATOON |

| YEAR | TEAM | LVL | AGE | PA | R | 2B | 3B | HR | RBI | BB | SO | SB | CS | AVG/OBP/SLG | TAv | BABIP | BRR | FRAA | WARP |
|------|------|-----|-----|----|----|----|----|----|-----|----|----|----|----|-------------|-----|-------|-----|------|------|
| 2013 | CHT | AA | 21 | 519 | 81 | 24 | 3 | 22 | 58 | 70 | 114 | 31 | 8 | .278/.381/.497 | .313 | .327 | 3.9 | CF(106): -0.3, LF(6): 0.5 | 5.3 |
| 2014 | LAN | MLB | 22 | 250 | 35 | 10 | 0 | 8 | 26 | 21 | 59 | 9 | 3 | .245/.314/.401 | .263 | .290 | 0.5 | CF -1, LF 1 | 0.7 |
| 2015 | LAN | MLB | 23 | 548 | 71 | 25 | 2 | 20 | 71 | 50 | 145 | 18 | 6 | .262/.331/.439 | .278 | .329 | 0.8 | CF -5 | 1.5 |

Breakout: 2%    Improve: 17%    Collapse: 1%    Attrition: 9%    MLB: 62%        *Comparables: Colby Rasmus, Brett Jackson, Wil Myers*

**Drafted/Acquired:** 11th round, 2010 draft, Palo Alto HS (Palo Alto, CA)

**Previous Ranking:** #5 (Org)

**What Happened in 2013:** In his steady climb up the minor-league ranks, Pederson more than held his own as a 21-year-old in Double-A, showing all five tools and becoming a highly coveted target around the league.

**Strengths:** Plus all-around athlete; natural hittability; good balance; great hands; creates plus bat speed; hit tool could play above average; tracks the ball well and forces a pitcher to beat him; raw power could grade as plus-plus; game power has a chance to play above average; strong arm in the field; above-average run/range; glove could play above average in center.

**#50**
BP Top 101 Prospects

**Weaknesses:** Overall profile is more solid-average than special; lacks high-end tools; sum-of-his-parts player; good bat but exposed by arm-side pitching; big swing-and-miss; power likely to play under projection; defense in center is good but shows some tweener qualities, and some see a better fit for left field.

**Risk Factor/Injury History:** Moderate risk; 123 games of Double-A experience.

**Bret Sayre's Fantasy Take:** With a classic five-category outfield profile, Peterson is someone to get excited about in both the short term and long term, despite not projecting to a superstar. There's real 20-20 potential here, and with an average that should hover around .270 and more upside in the power.

**The Year Ahead:** Pederson is a balls-out type of player with solid-average to above-average tools that he can bring into game action. While he might not be a premium up-the-middle talent, the former 11th rounder can make plays on all sides of the ball, showing a multidimensional offensive attack (hit, power, run), and strong fundamentals in the field. Sources are mixed about his long-term projection—be it as a first-division type or more of a league-average type in a corner—but several outside-the-organization sources suggested he was a player they highly recommended for acquisition should the opportunity present itself, as Pederson will be a no-doubt big-league contributor for a very long time.

## 4. Zach Lee RHP

**Born:** 9/13/91  **Age:** 22  **Bats:** R  **Throws:** R  **Height:** 6' 3"  **Weight:** 190

| MLB ETA | CT | FB | CH | CB | SL | OFP | Realistic |
|---------|----|----|----|----|----|-----|-----------|
| 2014 | —— | 55 | 55 | —— | 50 | 55<br>NO.3 STARTER | 50<br>NO.4 STARTER |

| YEAR | TEAM | LVL | AGE | W | L | SV | G | GS | IP | H | HR | BB | SO | BB9 | SO9 | GB% | BABIP | WHIP | ERA | FIP | FRA | WARP |
|------|------|-----|-----|---|---|----|----|----|-----|-----|----|----|-----|-----|-----|-----|-------|------|-----|-----|-----|------|
| 2013 | CHT | AA | 21 | 10 | 10 | 0 | 28 | 25 | 142.7 | 132 | 13 | 35 | 131 | 2.2 | 8.3 | 49% | .298 | 1.17 | 3.22 | 3.08 | 4.02 | 1.2 |
| 2014 | LAN | MLB | 22 | 6 | 9 | 0 | 23 | 23 | 114.7 | 120 | 16 | 35 | 79 | 2.7 | 6.2 | 46% | .311 | 1.35 | 4.69 | 4.71 | 5.10 | -0.4 |
| 2015 | LAN | MLB | 23 | 12 | 10 | 0 | 33 | 33 | 212.0 | 195 | 26 | 46 | 175 | 2.0 | 7.4 | 46% | .297 | 1.14 | 3.57 | 3.69 | 3.88 | 1.9 |

Breakout: 0%    Improve: 0%    Collapse: 0%    Attrition: 0%    MLB: 0%        *Comparables: Will Smith, Joe Wieland, Hector Rondon*

**Drafted/Acquired:** 1st round, 2010 draft, McKinney HS (McKinney, TX)

**Previous Ranking:** #2 (Org), #87 (Top 101)

**What Happened in 2013:** In a return to the Southern League, Lee built on his already strong professional resume, missing close to a bat an inning while limiting damage and holding Double-A hitters to a .247 average.

**Strengths:** Strong, athletic frame; repeatable delivery; arm works well/good release; fastball is solid-average offering; pitches well off it; velocity in the 90-93 range; can spike higher; can manipulate movement and shows good feel for location; slider can miss bats in the low- to mid-80s; can be thrown for strikes with some intensity to the break; changeup is solid-average and thrown well in sequence; good arm-speed deception and some sinking action; can drop a curveball for strikes; good overall command profile.

**Weaknesses:** Lacks plus stuff; fastball can play pedestrian; can move it around but struggles to live loose in the zone; slider isn't wipeout offering that forces bats out of the zone; changeup is more weak contact than whiff; curveball can get soft and easy to track; more of a steal-a-strike pitch at higher levels.

**Risk Factor/Injury History:** Low risk; 38 starts at Double-A level

**Bret Sayre's Fantasy Take:** The fantasy profile for Lee is more solid starter than impact one, as his stuff does not lend itself to missing a ton of bats at the major-league level. With that said, a slightly above-average pitcher in Dodger Stadium can be a number three fantasy starter even without an offering that looks like a separator.

**The Year Ahead:** Lee is going to be a good major-league starter, but his current stuff and limited arsenal projection point more to a solid number four type than the frontline arm many envisioned coming out of high school. The 22-year-old Texan is more command/control than power, but he can still dial up the fastball to the mid-90s on occasion, and the slider has been known to show some bat-missing intensity. But for the most part, Lee works his solid-average fastball in the 90-92 range, hitting his spots and setting up his deep secondary arsenal, which is geared more toward weak, off-balanced contact than swings and misses, at least as it is projected against more advanced hitters. Lee should move up to Triple-A in 2014, and could get a look at the major-league level in some capacity in 2014, either as a potential long man out of the bullpen (to break in), a back-end starter in case of injury or opportunity, or with another organization in the event of a trade.

#84<br>BP Top 101 Prospects

---

## 5.   Chris Anderson   RHP

**Born:** 7/29/92   **Age:** 21   **Bats:** R   **Throws:** R   **Height:** 6'4"   **Weight:** 215

| MLB ETA | CT | FB | CH | CB | SL | OFP | Realistic |
|---|---|---|---|---|---|---|---|
| Late 2015 | — | 60 | 50 | — | 60 | 55<br>NO.3 STARTER | 50<br>NO.4 STARTER |

| YEAR | TEAM | LVL | AGE | W | L | SV | G | GS | IP | H | HR | BB | SO | BB9 | SO9 | GB% | BABIP | WHIP | ERA | FIP | FRA | WARP |
|---|---|---|---|---|---|---|---|---|---|---|---|---|---|---|---|---|---|---|---|---|---|---|
| 2013 | GRL | A | 20 | 3 | 0 | 0 | 12 | 12 | 46.0 | 32 | 0 | 24 | 50 | 4.7 | 9.8 | 41% | .288 | 1.22 | 1.96 | 2.79 | 3.15 | 1.2 |
| 2014 | LAN | MLB | 21 | 2 | 3 | 0 | 9 | 9 | 35.7 | 35 | 4 | 18 | 29 | 4.5 | 7.3 | 42% | .316 | 1.48 | 4.65 | 4.71 | 5.06 | -0.1 |
| 2015 | LAN | MLB | 22 | 6 | 8 | 0 | 27 | 27 | 161.3 | 148 | 16 | 78 | 138 | 4.4 | 7.7 | 42% | .309 | 1.40 | 4.16 | 4.15 | 4.52 | 0.3 |

Breakout: 0%   Improve: 0%   Collapse: 0%   Attrition: 0%   MLB: 0%      *Comparables: Carter Capps, Yovani Gallardo, Randall Delgado*

**Drafted/Acquired:** 1st round, 2013 draft, Jacksonville University (Jacksonville, FL)

**Previous Ranking:** NR

**What Happened in 2013:** Selected 18th overall in the 2013 draft, Anderson moved straight to the full-season level and made 12 starts, missing 50 bats in only 46 innings of work.

**Strengths:** Excellent size/strength; good arm strength and speed; fastball is plus offering; working low-90s with good angle; can amp up velocity and work up in the zone; slider is above average and should get to consistent plus; mid-80s velocity and sharp two-plane break; hard pitch for right-handers to handle; changeup has some projection; works fringe-average at present; some late action; strike-throwing ability; aggressive approach.

**Weaknesses:** Fringe command at present; tendency to overthrow and lose his ability to locate; sources not as high on his curveball; can get loose and slurvy; changeup can get too firm; more deliberate than other offerings.

**Risk Factor/Injury History:** Moderate risk; limited professional experience.

**Bret Sayre's Fantasy Take:** Oft-overlooked in dynasty drafts due to the publicity of the arms ahead of him, Anderson carries the second most upside of any starter on this list. Of course, that's not the world's greatest compliment, as even if the change becomes an average pitch, his fantasy outlook is more number four starter in shallower leagues with a 3.50 ERA and 170 strikeouts over a full season.

**The Year Ahead:** Anderson has the size, strength, and delivery to log a lot of innings in a rotation, a potential mid-rotation workhorse. The 21-year-old has a solid four-pitch mix, with the fastball being his breadwinner and his slider as his complementary bat-misser. When/if the command improves, he can set the table with his fastball and use his secondary depth to make outs, which should allow the big right-hander to find sustainable success in a rotation. Because of the mature stuff, Anderson could move through the minors quickly, with a likely start in High-A and a chance to finish the season in the Southern League, positioning himself for a major-league call-up at some point in 2015.

## 6.  Chris Reed   LHP

**Born:** 5/20/90   **Age:** 24   **Bats:** L   **Throws:** L   **Height:** 6' 4"   **Weight:** 195

| MLB ETA | CT | FB | CH | CB | SL | OFP | Realistic |
|---|---|---|---|---|---|---|---|
| 2014 | – | 65 | 50 | – | 50 | 50<br>NO.4 STARTER | 50<br>LATE-INN RP (SETUP) |

| YEAR | TEAM | LVL | AGE | W | L | SV | G | GS | IP | H | HR | BB | SO | BB9 | SO9 | GB% | BABIP | WHIP | ERA | FIP | FRA | WARP |
|---|---|---|---|---|---|---|---|---|---|---|---|---|---|---|---|---|---|---|---|---|---|---|
| 2013 | CHT | AA | 23 | 4 | 11 | 0 | 29 | 25 | 137.7 | 128 | 9 | 63 | 106 | 4.1 | 6.9 | 62% | .295 | 1.39 | 3.86 | 3.73 | 5.60 | 0.0 |
| 2014 | LAN | MLB | 24 | 6 | 8 | 0 | 24 | 24 | 106.7 | 106 | 12 | 47 | 75 | 4.0 | 6.3 | 55% | .310 | 1.43 | 4.60 | 4.77 | 5.00 | -0.1 |
| 2015 | LAN | MLB | 25 | 9 | 11 | 0 | 31 | 31 | 195.3 | 193 | 22 | 75 | 140 | 3.5 | 6.5 | 55% | .310 | 1.37 | 4.42 | 4.33 | 4.80 | -0.4 |

Breakout: 0%     Improve: 0%     Collapse: 0%     Attrition: 0%     MLB: 0%          *Comparables: Cesar Carrillo, D.J. Mitchell, Mitch Talbot*

**Drafted/Acquired:** 1st round, 2011 draft, Stanford University

**Previous Ranking:** #4 (Org)

**What Happened in 2013:** After 11 Southern League starts in 2012, Reed logged a full season of work at that level in 2013, making 25 starts and accruing over 137 innings.

**Strengths:** Tall; remaining projection in body; very good arm strength; fastball is plus, with velocity in the low-90s (can bump mid-90s) and bowling ball weight; slider can flash plus; can show sharp tilt in the 82-85 range; changeup is average offering in the mid-80s with heavy action.

**Weaknesses:** Body teases more projection but has yet to fill out to projection; fastball can play down in games; heavy weight but average velocity and below-average command; slider struggles to achieve consistent sharp tilt; break can get soft; lacks true secondary weapon; overall command is below average.

**Risk Factor/Injury History:** Low risk; 36 starts at Double-A level; fastball to play in bullpen now.

**Bret Sayre's Fantasy Take:** Reed doesn't make for a great fantasy option in shallower leagues, as his lack of high-quality off-speed stuff will leave him lacking in the strikeout department. Plus, his control issues will leave him exposed to high WHIPs and diminished win potential. And all that is if he even ends up in the rotation.

**The Year Ahead:** Reed draws mixed reviews from scouts, with several doubting his ability to offer much impact in a major-league rotation because of his average secondary arsenal and poor command. It's easy to see a potential power arm out of the bullpen, with a heavy low-90s heater that could play up in bursts and a slider that tends to lose its intensity throughout games but could miss more bats in limited looks. The 24-year-old lefty is going to be a major leaguer in some capacity, but without improved command and a step forward with the secondary stuff, his likely contributions will come out of the bullpen, where he should be able to find some success and eventually develop into a quality late-innings option.

## 7.  Ross Stripling   RHP

**Born:** 11/23/89   **Age:** 24   **Bats:** R   **Throws:** R   **Height:** 6' 3"   **Weight:** 190

| MLB ETA | CT | FB | CH | CB | SL | OFP | Realistic |
|---|---|---|---|---|---|---|---|
| 2014 | --- | 60 | 50 | 50 | 50 | 50<br>NO.4 STARTER | 50<br>NO.4 STARTER |

| YEAR | TEAM | LVL | AGE | W | L | SV | G | GS | IP | H | HR | BB | SO | BB9 | SO9 | GB% | BABIP | WHIP | ERA | FIP | FRA | WARP |
|---|---|---|---|---|---|---|---|---|---|---|---|---|---|---|---|---|---|---|---|---|---|---|
| 2013 | RCU | A+ | 23 | 2 | 0 | 0 | 6 | 6 | 33.7 | 24 | 1 | 11 | 34 | 2.9 | 9.1 | 57% | .261 | 1.04 | 2.94 | 3.12 | 3.13 | 1.0 |
| 2013 | CHT | AA | 23 | 6 | 4 | 0 | 21 | 16 | 94.0 | 91 | 4 | 19 | 83 | 1.8 | 7.9 | 54% | .310 | 1.17 | 2.78 | 2.31 | 3.87 | 1.4 |
| 2014 | LAN | MLB | 24 | 5 | 6 | 0 | 21 | 21 | 93.0 | 93 | 10 | 28 | 68 | 2.7 | 6.6 | 53% | .311 | 1.30 | 3.99 | 4.16 | 4.33 | 0.6 |
| 2015 | LAN | MLB | 25 | 9 | 9 | 0 | 32 | 32 | 203.0 | 185 | 21 | 57 | 172 | 2.5 | 7.6 | 53% | .302 | 1.19 | 3.44 | 3.60 | 3.74 | 2.2 |

Breakout: 19%     Improve: 30%     Collapse: 12%     Attrition: 28%     MLB: 48%          *Comparables: David Phelps, Tommy Milone, Adam Warren*

**Drafted/Acquired:** 5th round, 2012 draft, Texas A&M University (College Station, TX)

**Previous Ranking:** NR

**What Happened in 2013:** In his full-season debut, the former A&M starter pitched his way to the Double-A level, mostly on the back of a plus fastball that he can locate.

**Strengths:** Good size; arm slot allows a steep plane on the fastball; pitch works low-90s with good tailing action; bumps a little higher; spots the ball; works east/west; shows multiple breaking-ball looks; curveball works well with sharp vertical spike; slider shows hard velocity and some tilt; changeup has tumbling action and plays as average offering; good control and improving command.

**Weaknesses:** Short-stride delivery; can get too arm heavy and lose velocity in starts; lacks plus secondary offerings; arm slot can work against breaking ball deception; slider is more weak contact than wipeout.

**Risk Factor/Injury History:** Low risk; mature stuff; 16 Double-A starts

**Bret Sayre's Fantasy Take:** Stripling isn't a particularly interesting name for fantasy, as he profiles as more of a back-end guy here. The strikeout potential is middling for a starter at the major-league level, as he doesn't have a true putaway pitch—though he could put up helpful ratios in a perfect world.

**The Year Ahead:** Stripling is a mature arm with a plus fastball and a deep secondary arsenal of playable pitches that he can throw for strikes. While he lacks the upside and stuff of his former A&M rotation-mate Michael Wacha, Stripling should be on a similar fast track to a major-league rotation, holding a fringe mid-rotation ceiling and a similar floor. Without knockout secondary stuff, Stripling needs his fastball command to be sharp to find sustainable success and to help get bats moving on the off-speed arsenal. The profile will be more weak contact than swing-and-miss, but with good size, an arm that works well, and a good overall feel for craft, the 24-year-old should pitch his way to the majors at some point in 2014, and could settle into the back end of the rotation by 2015.

## 8. Tom Windle    LHP

**Born:** 3/10/92    **Age:** 22    **Bats:** L    **Throws:** L    **Height:** 6' 4"    **Weight:** 215

| MLB ETA | CT | FB | CH | CB | SL | OFP | Realistic |
|---|---|---|---|---|---|---|---|
| Late 2015 | -- | 60 | 55 | -- | 60 | 55<br>NO.3 STARTER | 50<br>LATE INN RP (SETUP) |

| YEAR | TEAM | LVL | AGE | W | L | SV | G | GS | IP | H | HR | BB | SO | BB9 | SO9 | GB% | BABIP | WHIP | ERA | FIP | FRA | WARP |
|---|---|---|---|---|---|---|---|---|---|---|---|---|---|---|---|---|---|---|---|---|---|---|
| 2013 | GRL | A | 21 | 5 | 1 | 0 | 13 | 12 | 53.7 | 50 | 2 | 20 | 51 | 3.4 | 8.6 | 44% | .308 | 1.30 | 2.68 | 3.15 | 3.71 | 1.2 |
| 2014 | LAN | MLB | 22 | 2 | 3 | 0 | 9 | 9 | 38.7 | 41 | 5 | 18 | 26 | 4.2 | 6.0 | 43% | .317 | 1.52 | 5.03 | 5.11 | 5.47 | -0.3 |
| 2015 | LAN | MLB | 23 | 7 | 10 | 0 | 29 | 29 | 180.7 | 184 | 21 | 85 | 135 | 4.2 | 6.7 | 43% | .315 | 1.48 | 4.70 | 4.54 | 5.11 | -1.0 |

Breakout: 0%    Improve: 0%    Collapse: 0%    Attrition: 0%    MLB: 0%    *Comparables: Brian Flynn, Justin Wilson, Brett Marshall*

**Drafted/Acquired:** 2nd round, 2013 draft, University of Minnesota (Minneapolis, MN)

**Previous Ranking:** NR

**What Happened in 2013:** Popped in the second round of the 2013 draft, the former college reliever-turned-starter made his professional debut pitching in the Low-A rotation, making 12 starts and missing 51 bats in 53 innings.

**Strengths:** Excellent size; athletic; repeatable delivery with some deception; fastball can work 91-93; bump to 94+; some late action and thrown with good angle; good short, tight slider in the 82-84 range; feel for quality changeup; low-80s with some fade; shows good control; attacks the zone.

**Weaknesses:** Arm action can get stiff; fastball command is fringe-average at present; tendency to miss arm side and up; changeup receives average projections; good deception but can get too firm; overall command needs grade refinement.

**Risk Factor/Injury History:** Moderate risk; limited professional record; Low-A resume; shoulder injury (amateur).

**Bret Sayre's Fantasy Take:** A nice sleeper at the end of deep dynasty drafts this year, Windle has a strong arsenal that could lead to helpful ratios and a strikeout rate that would make him worth rostering in all leagues. However, the upside lies somewhere around Jonathon Niese—so don't go too crazy.

**The Year Ahead:** You can make a convincing case that Windle is underrated as a prospect, with excellent size, good athleticism and repeatability, and two above-average offerings from the left side, with enough feel for a changeup to project an average or better offering. Some sources have concerns about the stiff arm action and possible injury red flags as a result, coupled with more control than command at present, but even the rotation pessimists believe Windle could transition into a quality late-innings reliever. For now, Windle will get every opportunity to prove his mettle and merit in a rotation, and if he can iron out some of the rough edges in his delivery and improve his command, he could take a step forward in status and make his ultimate projection look more realistic.

## 9. Onelki Garcia    LHP

**Born:** 8/2/89    **Age:** 24    **Bats:** L    **Throws:** L    **Height:** 6' 3"    **Weight:** 220

| MLB ETA | CT | FB | CH | CB | SL | OFP | Realistic |
|---|---|---|---|---|---|---|---|
| Debuted in 2013 | -- | 65 | -- | 65 | -- | 55<br>LATE INN RP (CLOSER) | 50<br>LATE INN RP (SETUP) |

| YEAR | TEAM | LVL | AGE | W | L | SV | G | GS | IP | H | HR | BB | SO | BB9 | SO9 | GB% | BABIP | WHIP | ERA | FIP | FRA | WARP |
|---|---|---|---|---|---|---|---|---|---|---|---|---|---|---|---|---|---|---|---|---|---|---|
| 2013 | ABQ | AAA | 23 | 0 | 1 | 0 | 10 | 0 | 9.7 | 6 | 0 | 3 | 14 | 2.8 | 13.0 | 75% | .300 | 0.93 | 3.72 | 1.91 | 3.47 | 0.3 |
| 2013 | LAN | MLB | 23 | 0 | 0 | 0 | 3 | 0 | 1.3 | 1 | 1 | 4 | 1 | 27.0 | 6.8 | 75% | .000 | 3.75 | 13.50 | 20.27 | 25.75 | -0.3 |
| 2013 | CHT | AA | 23 | 2 | 3 | 1 | 25 | 6 | 52.3 | 41 | 3 | 32 | 53 | 5.5 | 9.1 | 61% | .277 | 1.39 | 2.75 | 3.58 | 5.81 | 0.4 |
| 2014 | LAN | MLB | 24 | 2 | 2 | 1 | 27 | 4 | 46.7 | 41 | 5 | 22 | 45 | 4.2 | 8.7 | 52% | .308 | 1.34 | 3.91 | 4.20 | 4.25 | 0.2 |
| 2015 | LAN | MLB | 25 | 3 | 1 | 0 | 51 | 0 | 54.0 | 47 | 6 | 27 | 53 | 4.5 | 8.8 | 52% | .305 | 1.35 | 3.99 | 4.14 | 4.33 | 0.4 |

Breakout: 17%    Improve: 29%    Collapse: 8%    Attrition: 24%    MLB: 39%    *Comparables: Phillippe Aumont, Jon Meloan, Juan Morillo*

**Drafted/Acquired:** 3rd round, 2012 draft, (Cuba)

**Previous Ranking:** #7 (org)

**What Happened in 2013:** Working mostly in relief, Garcia pitched his way to the major-league level after showing above-average bat-missing ability in the upper minors.

**Strengths:** Strong frame; intimidating presence; big arm strength from the left side; fastball works low- to mid-90s; can sit 93+; big life; curveball is big hammer; low-80s on the gun with serious bite; could end up playing well above average with better command; late-innings approach.

**Weaknesses:** Below-average command; limited pitchability; high effort; mostly a two-pitch reliever without rotational upside.

**Risk Factor/Injury History:** Low risk; achieved major-league level; minor injury concerns (bone spurs)

**Bret Sayre's Fantasy Take:** Even a slam-dunk closer prospect (which Garcia is not) isn't a great bet in the fantasy realm, and that makes Garcia someone worth keeping tabs on but not picking up at the moment. If your league counts holds, he'll be more valuable in the short term, but even then he's behind Paco Rodriguez as a lefty in the 'pen.

**The Year Ahead:** Garcia has a nasty two-pitch mix from the left side, and if he can stay healthy and refine his command, he has legit late-innings potential, perhaps even as a closer if the command improves beyond projection. He doesn't show a lot of pitchability, so his grip-it-and-rip-it approach proved to be a much better fit in short bursts than it projected in a rotation. He should continue to miss a lot of bats with his lively plus fastball and hard hammer curve, and could end up in a setup capacity very early in his major-league career.

---

## 10. Victor Arano RHP

**Born:** 2/7/95 **Age:** 19 **Bats:** R **Throws:** R **Height:** 6' 2" **Weight:** 200

| MLB ETA | CT | FB | CH | CB | SL | OFP | Realistic |
|---|---|---|---|---|---|---|---|
| 2017 | – | 65 | 55 | 60 | – | 60 NO.3 STARTER | 50 NO.4 STARTER |

| YEAR | TEAM | LVL | AGE | W | L | SV | G | GS | IP | H | HR | BB | SO | BB9 | SO9 | GB% | BABIP | WHIP | ERA | FIP | FRA | WARP |
|---|---|---|---|---|---|---|---|---|---|---|---|---|---|---|---|---|---|---|---|---|---|---|
| 2013 | DOD | Rk | 18 | 3 | 2 | 0 | 13 | 8 | 49.3 | 52 | 4 | 13 | 49 | 2.4 | 8.9 | 51% | .316 | 1.32 | 4.20 | 3.86 | 5.29 | 0.8 |
| 2014 | LAN | MLB | 19 | 1 | 2 | 0 | 9 | 5 | 34.3 | 40 | 5 | 20 | 17 | 5.2 | 4.5 | 45% | .319 | 1.77 | 6.27 | 6.09 | 6.81 | -0.7 |
| 2015 | LAN | MLB | 20 | 3 | 6 | 0 | 26 | 14 | 120.7 | 139 | 18 | 64 | 75 | 4.8 | 5.6 | 45% | .324 | 1.68 | 6.05 | 5.48 | 6.58 | -2.3 |

Breakout: 0%  Improve: 0%  Collapse: 0%  Attrition: 0%  MLB: 0%  *Comparables: David Holmberg, Kelvin Herrera, Will Smith*

**Drafted/Acquired:** International free agent, 2013, Mexico

**Previous Ranking:** NR

**What Happened in 2013:** In his professional debut, the Mexican right-hander showed off a mature fastball and promising secondary arsenal, missing a bat an inning.

**Strengths:** Mature body; clean delivery with good arm action; very loose and easy; fastball solid-average at present in the 89-92 range; can touch mid-90s; projects to be easy plus offering; can spin a quality breaking ball; curve can show tight rotation and some depth; good projection; some feel for a good changeup; shows some fade and sink; feel for control and pitchability.

**Weaknesses:** Body could be high maintenance; already showing some excess; inconsistent fastball velocity; would show 92-94 then fall to 88-90; breaking ball has tendency to get too loose and slurvy; changeup is inconsistent and can get deliberate in the release; can get very slow to the plate with runners on; struggles from stretch; more control than command.

**Risk Factor/Injury History:** High risk; complex-level resume

**Bret Sayre's Fantasy Take:** There is never a shortage of short-season or complex arms to take a chance on, and it's very likely that more interesting ones are out there in your league. Arano could turn into something, but his stuff isn't extreme enough to own outside of very deep leagues at the moment.

**The Year Ahead:** Arano has a very easy arm with good present strength, and can pound the zone with a low-90s fastball that can bump a little higher. He shows both a quality curveball and a changeup, although both offerings are inconsistent at present. The 19-year-old has a high mid-rotation projection, but needs to clean up his delivery and find more comfort working out of the stretch and with runners on base. While he lacks the same present polish or projection of Julio Urias, Arano isn't an arm to sleep on, as the fastball is really good and he could be ready to take a big step forward in 2014 if the secondary stuff finds more consistency.

### Prospects on the Rise

**1. LHP Victor Gonzalez:** An 18-year-old Mexican lefty with a good present fastball and changeup, Gonzalez should move up prospect lists in 2014. The body could escape him, and the breaking ball doesn't offer much projection at this point, but the low-90s fastball and quality changeup should allow him to miss bats and barrels, regardless if he starts at the short-season level or makes the jump to full-season ball.

**2. OF Jacob Scavuzzo:** After struggling in his complex-league debut, Scavuzzo erupted in the Pioneer League, hitting for average and power. The projectable outfielder has some limitations at the plate, and some sources aren't convinced he will hit against better pitching. But as he adds strength to the frame and refines his approach—putting himself in favorable hitting conditions and not

---

## FROM THE FIELD

### Joc Pederson

**Player:** Joc Pederson

**Team:** Los Angeles Dodgers

**Filed by:** Steffan Segui

**Date(s) Seen:** Every game during 2013 season

**Physical:** Slight, unassuming build. Thick legs.

**Hit:** 50 grade. Starts upright with substantial lunge but hands work so well that they stay back and explode through zone. Uncanny bat speed. Bails vs. left-handed pitching. Overall approach improving. Gives too much effort at times.

**Power:** 60 grade. Top-5 raw power in the minors. Uppercut swing and lightning hands produce loft. Drives ball out to any part of the field. More contact vs. left-handed pitching will allow him to hit 30+ home runs.

**Glove:** 60 grade. Natural center fielder. Excellent ball skills (former wide receiver). Puts head down and gets to almost every ball. Can play all three outfield spots well.

**Arm:** 50 grade. Plays down due to poor footwork and rushing throws.

**Speed:** 60 grade. 4.1-4.2 to first. Great instincts and jumps. Smart on basepaths. Routes in outfield can be cleaned up some.

**Makeup:** 60 grade. Very dedicated and hard worker with plus-plus instincts but very immature at times, which he often shows in game. Son of major leaguer.

**OFP:** 60; all-star outfielder

**Realistic Role:** 55; solid-average first-division starter

**Risk:** Low. MLB-ready now, should thrive at Triple-A Albuquerque.

trying to pull everything—the former 21st-round pick has a chance to be a very good prospect.

**3. 3B Adam Law:** I'm not usually in the habit of hyping 24-year-old prospects without full-season experience, but sources are high on Law, suggesting the combination of hittability, well-above-average speed, and feel for the game (bloodlines; son of Vance) could push the infielder up the list next season. He has a knack for hard contact, and the type of speed that would play very well in the outfield should his actions at third prove to be less than ideal.

## Factors on the Farm

### Prospects likely to contribute at the major-league level in 2014

**1. RHP Yimi Garcia:** The slender righty reliever has a knack for missing bats, using a lively low-90s fastball and a low-80s slider that can flash plus (but lacks consistency). After a strong run in Double-A and the AFL, the 23-year-old Dominican will be ready to make a major-league contribution at some point in 2014, most likely in middle relief.

**2. RHP Pedro Baez:** At one time, Baez's path to the majors was to be cut with his bat, but the conversion from the hot corner to high-leverage relief is what will take the 25-year-old to the highest level. With the potential to show a mid-90s heater and bat-missing curve, Baez has late-innings potential, and with more refined command and more experience in game situations, the transition from former positional prospect to present major-league pitcher will be complete.

**3. SS Miguel Rojas:** A super slick defender, Rojas will have an opportunity to carve out a home at the major-league level in 2014, either as a utility option or a starting second baseman, but the profile will have to pack more offensive punch than he provided in 2013. With Cuban import Alex Guerrero* in the best position to grab the most time at the keystone, Rojas will need to take a big step forward at the plate to justify any opportunity he might receive. (*Alexander Guerrero was not considered a prospect because he is likely to jump straight to the big leagues without any time in the minor league developmental system.)

**FROM THE FIELD**

## Zach Lee

**Player:** Zach Lee

**Team:** Los Angeles Dodgers

**Filed by:** Steffan Segui

**Date(s) Seen:** Every start during 2013 season

**Physical:** Well-built throughout. Powerful legs with broad shoulders and a big backside. Looks like a football player.

**Mechanics/Delivery:** Very controlled, continuous fluid delivery. Works at a good pace. Moderate-high leg lift with a bit of hip load at balance that allows his hand to get to the bottom of the circle and get around on time to his overhand delivery point. Also allows him to use legs for power. Good tilt at release, allowing arm to come through high slot naturally.

**Fastball:** 55 grade. 89-91 two-seam to right-handed hitters, harder four-seamers to left-handed hitters. Works down in zone. Two-seam has excellent sink down in zone. Elevates four-seam late.

**Slider:** 55 grade. Bigger break for slider wide berth with sharp two-plane break. Tough for hitters to square. Throws harder, more like cutter also.

**Curveball:** 45 grade. Inconsistent break and too loopy. Needs to be sharper. Occasionally shows better but doesn't use enough.

**Changeup:** 60 grade. Disguises well, mirrors fastballs. Pulls string effectively with some sink. Main out pitch.

**Makeup:** 70 grade. Former quarterback, high IQ. Understands himself, pitches within his means.

**OFP:** 60; no. 2 starter.

**Realistic Role:** 55; no. 3/4 starter.

**Risk:** Low; 208+ Double-A innings. Three full minor-league seasons. MLB ready.

## 1. Andrew Heaney LHP

**Born:** 6/5/91 **Age:** 23 **Bats:** L **Throws:** L **Height:** 6'2" **Weight:** 190

| MLB ETA | CT | FB | CH | CB | SL | OFP | Realistic |
|---|---|---|---|---|---|---|---|
| 2014 | – | 65 | 55 | –– | 65 | 65 NO.2 STARTER | 60 NO.3 STARTER |

| YEAR | TEAM | LVL | AGE | W | L | SV | G | GS | IP | H | HR | BB | SO | BB9 | SO9 | GB% | BABIP | WHIP | ERA | FIP | FRA | WARP |
|---|---|---|---|---|---|---|---|---|---|---|---|---|---|---|---|---|---|---|---|---|---|---|
| 2013 | JUP | A+ | 22 | 5 | 2 | 0 | 13 | 12 | 61.7 | 45 | 2 | 17 | 66 | 2.5 | 9.6 | 49% | .257 | 1.01 | 0.88 | 2.64 | 3.00 | 1.4 |
| 2013 | JAX | AA | 22 | 4 | 1 | 0 | 6 | 6 | 33.7 | 31 | 2 | 9 | 23 | 2.4 | 6.1 | 41% | .279 | 1.19 | 2.94 | 3.12 | 3.13 | 0.6 |
| 2014 | MIA | MLB | 23 | 4 | 5 | 0 | 14 | 14 | 71.7 | 69 | 6 | 27 | 55 | 3.4 | 6.9 | 45% | .309 | 1.35 | 4.12 | 4.06 | 4.48 | 0.2 |
| 2015 | MIA | MLB | 24 | 10 | 9 | 0 | 31 | 31 | 194.3 | 185 | 17 | 57 | 157 | 2.6 | 7.3 | 45% | .309 | 1.24 | 3.69 | 3.54 | 4.01 | 1.1 |

Breakout: 0%  Improve: 0%  Collapse: 0%  Attrition: 0%  MLB: 0%  *Comparables: Adam Warren, Erik Johnson, Alex Cobb*

**Drafted/Acquired:** 1st round, 2012 draft, Oklahoma State University (Stillwater, OK)

**Previous Ranking:** #5 (Org)

**What Happened in 2013:** Heaney really stepped forward in 2013, jumping from a "wait and see" college arm to a bona fide high-end prospect, pitching his way to the Double-A level in his first full season.

**Strengths:** Athletic and fluid delivery; good balance and tempo; arm works well; fastball is creeper pitch in the low-mid-90s; good deception in the delivery allows it to jump on hitters; velo ticks up deep into games; can touch 96+ when he needs it; slider is plus offering; multiple looks; can throw in the zone or chase; good vertical depth; turns over an average changeup; could play above average; repeats with good command profile.

**Weaknesses:** Needs to add strength to frame; fastball can play down early in games; will work 89-93 with some arm-side; slider can get too slurvy and loose; changeup has some vertical dive but lacks high projection; good control; command still needs refinement; can hang around the plate too much.

**Risk Factor/Injury History:** Low risk; limited Double-A experience; arsenal and pitchability for major-league level

**Bret Sayre's Fantasy Take:** Heaney is going to be the next prospect to take advantage of the Marlins' team philosophy on promoting players quickly and is likely to have some real fantasy value in 2014. He should be a very even fantasy performer, contributing nearly equally in all four categories. With the ballpark behind him and weak division in front of him, he can put up a 3.25 ERA, 1.20 WHIP and 170 strikeouts at peak.

**The Year Ahead:** Heaney is the top lefty starter prospect in the minors, with three average or better offerings and an athletic and fluid delivery that allows for strike-throwing ability. The fastball can play up or down, and the slider is both a chase pitch and a get-over offering when he needs to drop a strike. The changeup isn't a big weapon yet, but offers enough to keep righty bats honest with the fastball, and as the fastball control continues to refine into command, Heaney will be able to keep hitters from both sides of the plate off-balance. It's a very nice profile, and several sources think Heaney has the stuff and polish to start in the majors in 2014. Even if he doesn't break camp with the team, it won't be long until the 23-year-old joins Jose Fernandez in the Marlins rotation.

> **#30**
> BP Top
> 101
> Prospects

---

## 2. Colin Moran 3B

**Born:** 10/1/92 **Age:** 21 **Bats:** L **Throws:** R **Height:** 6'4" **Weight:** 190

| MLB ETA | Hit | Power | Run | Glove | Arm | OFP | Realistic |
|---|---|---|---|---|---|---|---|
| 2015 | 70 | 55 | – | – | 60 | 60 1ST DIV PLAYER | 50 ML REGULAR |

| YEAR | TEAM | LVL | AGE | PA | R | 2B | 3B | HR | RBI | BB | SO | SB | CS | AVG/OBP/SLG | TAv | BABIP | BRR | FRAA | WARP |
|---|---|---|---|---|---|---|---|---|---|---|---|---|---|---|---|---|---|---|---|
| 2013 | GRB | A | 20 | 175 | 19 | 8 | 1 | 4 | 23 | 15 | 25 | 1 | 0 | .299/.354/.442 | .300 | .323 | -1.0 | 3B(33): -0.5 | 1.0 |
| 2014 | MIA | MLB | 21 | 250 | 20 | 9 | 1 | 3 | 22 | 16 | 54 | 1 | 0 | .223/.273/.307 | .223 | .280 | -0.3 | 3B -2 | -0.5 |
| 2015 | MIA | MLB | 22 | 250 | 23 | 10 | 1 | 2 | 19 | 17 | 51 | 1 | 0 | .222/.275/.299 | .216 | .273 | -0.5 | 3B -1 | -1.5 |

Breakout: 0%  Improve: 0%  Collapse: 0%  Attrition: 0%  MLB: 0%  *Comparables: Taylor Green, Tony Cruz, Mat Gamel*

**Drafted/Acquired:** 1st round, 2013 draft, University of North Carolina (Chapel Hill, NC)

**Previous Ranking:** NR

**What Happened in 2013:** A legit 1:1 candidate in the 2013 draft, Moran fell to the Marlins with the sixth overall pick, and he started hitting immediately at the full-season level.

**Strengths:** Natural hitter; excellent bat-to-ball; excellent hand-eye; makes hard contact to all fields; swing has some leverage and power potential; hit tool could be a 7; power could play above average; arm is strong enough for third.

**Weaknesses:** Questions about game power; more of a line-drive stroke; can get tied up by arm-side stuff; not a great defender at third; well-below-average run limits range or defensive versatility in the outfield; some make-up concerns re: work ethic/dedication to baseball.

> **#74**
> BP Top
> 101
> Prospects

**Risk Factor/Injury History:** Moderate risk; hit tool is legit; questions about power and defensive profile

**Bret Sayre's Fantasy Take:** There's certainly upside here with Moran, especially if he can develop into a 20-homer hitter, but if the power doesn't develop, the skill set isn't that sexy for fantasy. A near .300 average at a below-average position is great and he should move fast, but fantasy owners may also have Stockholm Syndrome from waiting on the last UNC product with a very strong hit tool to develop into something.

**The Year Ahead:** Moran is going to hit the baseball, and that alone gives him the floor of a major-league regular. While the relatively safe floor is a selling point, the ultimate upside is the sex appeal, with a 7 potential bat and 5+ power potential, a third baseman with the ability to hit .300 and rip 15+ bombs a season. Moran isn't a great athlete, and some of his run times to first base are closer to 20-grade than anything else. But he has enough chops at third to stick around, and if the power can creep into the game without a big sacrifice from the hit tool, the offensive production will more than make up for a fringe-average profile at third. His bat is ready for a fast-track through the minors, and he should position himself for a role on the 25-man by 2015.

---

## 3. Jake Marisnick    CF

**Born:** 3/30/91   **Age:** 23   **Bats:** R   **Throws:** R   **Height:** 6'3"   **Weight:** 225

| MLB ETA | | Hit | Power | Run | Glove | Arm | | OFP | Realistic |
|---|---|---|---|---|---|---|---|---|---|
| Debuted in 2013 | | 50 | 60 | 60 | 60 | 60 | | 60<br>1ST DIV PLAYER | 50<br>ML REGULAR |

| YEAR | TEAM | LVL | AGE | PA | R | 2B | 3B | HR | RBI | BB | SO | SB | CS | AVG/OBP/SLG | TAv | BABIP | BRR | FRAA | WARP |
|---|---|---|---|---|---|---|---|---|---|---|---|---|---|---|---|---|---|---|---|
| 2013 | JUP | A+ | 22 | 15 | 2 | 1 | 0 | 0 | 0 | 0 | 1 | 0 | 0 | .200/.200/.267 | .221 | .214 | 0.0 | CF(3): -0.1 | 0.0 |
| 2013 | JAX | AA | 22 | 298 | 43 | 13 | 3 | 12 | 46 | 17 | 68 | 11 | 6 | .294/.358/.502 | .311 | .351 | 1.9 | CF(54): 3.4, LF(11): 0.3 | 3.3 |
| 2013 | MIA | MLB | 22 | 118 | 6 | 2 | 1 | 1 | 5 | 6 | 27 | 3 | 1 | .183/.231/.248 | .193 | .232 | 0.4 | CF(32): 0.8 | -0.1 |
| 2014 | MIA | MLB | 23 | 250 | 29 | 10 | 2 | 5 | 21 | 12 | 59 | 8 | 3 | .234/.284/.356 | .243 | .290 | 0.7 | CF 2, LF 0 | 0.6 |
| 2015 | MIA | MLB | 24 | 250 | 26 | 9 | 3 | 5 | 24 | 14 | 59 | 10 | 3 | .230/.287/.355 | .238 | .283 | 1.0 | CF 2 | 0.6 |

Breakout: 1%   Improve: 18%   Collapse: 6%   Attrition: 15%   MLB: 41%            *Comparables: Aaron Cunningham, Trayvon Robinson, Felix Pie*

**Drafted/Acquired:** 3rd round, 2009 draft, Riverside Poly HS (Riverside, CA)

**Previous Ranking:** #3 (Org), #71 (Top 101)

**What Happened in 2013:** Marisnick was promoted to the majors in late July, and despite 40 games and over 100 at-bats at that level, remains rookie (and therefore prospect) eligible.

**Strengths:** Can show all five tools; very athletic; excellent size/strength; run is plus; arm is plus; glove can play to plus; shows above-average power potential.

**Weaknesses:** Hit tool is shaky; struggles against quality secondary stuff; struggles to adjust against bad guesses; athleticism for center but doesn't always make it look easy.

**Risk Factor/Injury History:** Low risk; achieved major-league level

**Bret Sayre's Fantasy Take:** The fantasy upside has remained the same for Marisnick, even if he's firmly planted in post-hype prospect territory. A potential 20-homer and 20-steal outfielder, he will be in a fight for playing time to start 2014, but a job should be his by the All-Star break. If he does in fact end up back in Triple-A, it may be a good time to buy low from his likely frustrated owner.

**The Year Ahead:** Marisnick really struggled in his major-league debut, especially against quality off-speed stuff, but many sources felt he was rushed to the level and wasn't ready for the speed of the major-league game. The problem with Marisnick's five-tool profile is the hit tool, as it's currently below average and lacks the same game impact as some of his other now tools. Several sources love the player but have doubts about the hittability, as the swing is good but the bat speed isn't special and the feel for hitting can be lacking at times, especially against quality stuff. As a versatile defender with wheels and power potential, Marisnick can find value on a field even if the hit tool drags down the overall profile, but he could be a first-division player if the bat can play to solid-average. Some seasoning in the upper minors could benefit the 23-year-old, but you can't simulate the quality of talent (and speed of the game) in the minors, so learning to fail and recover at the highest level will be a necessary part of the developmental process.

---

## 4. Trevor Williams    RHP

**Born:** 4/25/92   **Age:** 22   **Bats:** R   **Throws:** R   **Height:** 6'3"   **Weight:** 228

| MLB ETA | | CT | FB | CH | CB | SL | | OFP | Realistic |
|---|---|---|---|---|---|---|---|---|---|
| 2015 | | — | 60 | 50 | 50 | 55 | | 60<br>NO.3 STARTER | 50<br>NO.4 STARTER |

| YEAR | TEAM | LVL | AGE | W | L | SV | G | GS | IP | H | HR | BB | SO | BB9 | SO9 | GB% | BABIP | WHIP | ERA | FIP | FRA | WARP |
|---|---|---|---|---|---|---|---|---|---|---|---|---|---|---|---|---|---|---|---|---|---|---|
| 2013 | GRB | A | 21 | 0 | 0 | 0 | 1 | 1 | 3.0 | 2 | 0 | 0 | 3 | 0.0 | 9.0 | 62% | .250 | 0.67 | 0.00 | 1.48 | 1.62 | 0.1 |
| 2013 | BAT | A- | 21 | 0 | 2 | 0 | 10 | 10 | 29.0 | 26 | 0 | 8 | 20 | 2.5 | 6.2 | 61% | .274 | 1.17 | 2.48 | 2.65 | 4.68 | 0.2 |
| 2013 | MRL | Rk | 21 | 0 | 0 | 0 | 1 | 1 | 2.0 | 3 | 0 | 0 | 1 | 0.0 | 4.5 | 44% | .333 | 1.50 | 4.50 | 2.46 | 3.70 | 0.1 |
| 2014 | MIA | MLB | 22 | 1 | 4 | 0 | 9 | 9 | 34.0 | 39 | 4 | 18 | 16 | 4.8 | 4.2 | 48% | .317 | 1.67 | 5.77 | 5.60 | 6.28 | -0.5 |
| 2015 | MIA | MLB | 23 | 5 | 8 | 0 | 29 | 29 | 183.0 | 197 | 18 | 74 | 112 | 3.6 | 5.5 | 48% | .318 | 1.48 | 4.91 | 4.43 | 5.33 | -1.7 |

Breakout: 0%   Improve: 0%   Collapse: 0%   Attrition: 0%   MLB: 0%            *Comparables: Esmil Rogers, Josh Wall, Pedro Beato*

**Drafted/Acquired:** 2nd round, 2013 draft, Arizona State University (Tempe, AZ)

**Previous Ranking:** NR

**What Happened in 2013:** The 44th overall pick in the 2013 draft, Williams is a polished college arm who felt the wear of a long season after signing, as the stuff was just a tick down from his established collegiate standard.

**Strengths:** Big, strong frame; arm works well; throws downhill; shows multiple fastball looks; heavy two-seamer in the 90-93 range; shows a lively 93- to 95-mph fastball with more arm-side tail; multiple breaking-ball looks; mid-70s downer curveball; harder breaker in the low-80s; two-plane action with more slider-like tilt; turns over an average low-80s changeup; plays well off fastball; has strike-throwing ability; aggressive approach; not afraid to challenge hitters.

**Weaknesses:** Thick build that could be high maintenance; some effort in the delivery; command is loose; secondary stuff lacks wipeout projection; curveball is more show/sight line; changeup isn't a big weapon; more present than projection.

**Risk Factor/Injury History:** Moderate risk; limited professional record; mature arsenal

**Bret Sayre's Fantasy Take:** Williams is a big boy with the potential to log a lot of innings, though he'll need all of those innings to rack up average strikeout number for a fantasy starter. He's worth gambling on (especially in deeper leagues) with a third- or fourth-round dynasty draft pick this year.

**The Year Ahead:** Williams is ready to move quickly in the Marlins system, most likely starting in High-A with a good chance to reach Double-A during the summer. With a fresh arm, Williams is going to pound the zone with his fastball looks, showing feel for changing speeds, and using his hard breaking ball to miss bats. The secondary arsenal isn't overwhelming, but he can mix his pitches and pitch well off the fastball, so he should find sustainable success in a rotation as long as he can set the table with the heater. The ceiling is a mid-rotation arm, but the present polish gives him a high floor and the opportunity for an accelerated developmental path to the majors. He should move up this list with a strong 2014, and could compete for a rotation spot at some point in 2015.

## 5.  Nick Wittgren  RHP

**Born:** 5/29/91  **Age:** 23  **Bats:** R  **Throws:** R  **Height:** 6'3"  **Weight:** 210

| MLB ETA | CT | FB | CH | CB | SL | OFP | Realistic |
|---------|-----|-----|-----|-----|-----|-----|-----|
| 2014 | — | 60 | 50 | 60 | — | 55<br>LATE INN RP (CLOSER) | 50<br>LATE INN RP (SETUP) |

| YEAR | TEAM | LVL | AGE | W | L | SV | G | GS | IP | H | HR | BB | SO | BB9 | SO9 | GB% | BABIP | WHIP | ERA | FIP | FRA | WARP |
|------|------|-----|-----|---|---|----|----|----|----|---|----|----|----|-----|-----|-----|-------|------|-----|-----|-----|------|
| 2013 | JUP | A+ | 22 | 2 | 1 | 25 | 48 | 0 | 54.3 | 42 | 1 | 10 | 59 | 1.7 | 9.8 | 50% | .289 | 0.96 | 0.83 | 1.97 | 2.49 | 1.3 |
| 2013 | JAX | AA | 22 | 0 | 0 | 1 | 4 | 0 | 4.0 | 0 | 0 | 0 | 4 | 0.0 | 9.0 | 56% | .000 | 0.00 | 0.00 | 0.91 | 2.35 | 0.1 |
| 2014 | MIA | MLB | 23 | 2 | 1 | 2 | 38 | 0 | 45.0 | 40 | 4 | 17 | 43 | 3.4 | 8.6 | 45% | .313 | 1.26 | 3.54 | 3.68 | 3.85 | 0.3 |
| 2015 | MIA | MLB | 24 | 3 | 1 | 3 | 58 | 0 | 68.7 | 57 | 4 | 20 | 69 | 2.6 | 9.0 | 45% | .311 | 1.12 | 2.85 | 2.80 | 3.09 | 1.5 |

Breakout: 0%    Improve: 0%    Collapse: 0%    Attrition: 0%    MLB: 0%    *Comparables: Cory Burns, Robbie Weinhardt, C.C. Lee*

**Drafted/Acquired:** 9th round, 2012 draft, Purdue University (West Lafayette, IN)

**Previous Ranking:** NR

**What Happened in 2013:** In his first full season, Wittgren blew up the Florida State League and then turned heads in the Arizona Fall League, where the then-22-year-old only allowed eight baserunners in 13 appearances.

**Strengths:** Excellent pitchability; repeatable mechanics; good balance and timing; fastball works 90-93; can spot it up; works east/west; good deception in the release; can get swings-and-misses with solid-average velocity; backs up fastball with quality hard curveball; upper-70s with tight rotation; mixes in low-80s changeup; good action and plays well off the fastball; sharp overall command; late-innings approach.

**Weaknesses:** Lacks a standard late-innings fastball; pitch can work pedestrian in the 90-91 range; has to spot it up for success; delivery has effort (he makes it work); smaller margin of error than closers.

**Risk Factor/Injury History:** Low risk; mature arsenal; limited exposure to upper minors.

**Bret Sayre's Fantasy Take:** I don't want to sound like a broken record here, but the pure relief profile is not something that dynasty league owners should be spending much time worrying about. The risk is twofold, as you're dealing with both performance and role anxiety. But if your league is deep enough, Wittgren is one of the better ones to speculate on.

**The Year Ahead:** I don't often rank relievers high on prospect lists, and I rarely go high on late-innings relievers that lack big heat and rely on location more than dominating stuff. But Wittgren can really pitch, and despite a fastball that plays in the low-90s and not the upper-90s, the ability to locate the offering forces bats to move, which then allows his solid-average (to plus) secondary stuff to really play up and miss bats. If he can maintain his delivery and continue to show sharp command, the ceiling is a closer at the major-league level, with a more likely outcome as a legit setup option at the back of a bullpen. Wittgren should return to Double-A to start the year, but should be pitching in games that count at some point over the summer.

# 6. Jose Urena RHP

**Born:** 9/12/91 **Age:** 22 **Bats:** R **Throws:** R **Height:** 6'3" **Weight:** 175

| MLB ETA | CT | FB | CH | CB | SL | OFP | Realistic |
|---|---|---|---|---|---|---|---|
| 2015 | — | 70 | 65 | — | 50 | 60 NO.3 STARTER | 50 LATE-INN RP (SETUP) |

| YEAR | TEAM | LVL | AGE | W | L | SV | G | GS | IP | H | HR | BB | SO | BB9 | SO9 | GB% | BABIP | WHIP | ERA | FIP | FRA | WARP |
|---|---|---|---|---|---|---|---|---|---|---|---|---|---|---|---|---|---|---|---|---|---|---|
| 2013 | JUP | A+ | 21 | 10 | 7 | 0 | 27 | 26 | 149.7 | 148 | 8 | 29 | 107 | 1.7 | 6.4 | 50% | .299 | 1.18 | 3.73 | 3.21 | 4.45 | 0.3 |
| 2014 | MIA | MLB | 22 | 5 | 8 | 0 | 24 | 18 | 125.7 | 137 | 14 | 46 | 69 | 3.3 | 4.9 | 46% | .311 | 1.46 | 4.85 | 4.81 | 5.27 | -1.0 |
| 2015 | MIA | MLB | 23 | 5 | 5 | 0 | 20 | 15 | 114.7 | 119 | 12 | 37 | 70 | 2.9 | 5.5 | 46% | .308 | 1.37 | 4.37 | 4.20 | 4.75 | -0.2 |

Breakout: 0%   Improve: 0%   Collapse: 0%   Attrition: 0%   MLB: 0%   *Comparables: Zeke Spruill, Robbie Ross, Jeanmar Gomez*

**Drafted/Acquired:** International free agent, 2008, Dominican Republic

**Previous Ranking:** On The Rise

**What Happened in 2013:** In his continued journey up the professional ranks, the projectable Dominican arm logged another heavy workload, making 26 starts and logging close to 150 innings.

**Strengths:** Easy cheese arm; from 3/4 slot, creates good angle with near-elite arm speed; fastball works comfortably in the 92-95 range; can bump elite velocity in bursts; turns over quality changeup; plays up because of arm speed and power of fastball; slider can flash average potential; can drop it for strikes; body to hold more strength/weight; good control.

**Weaknesses:** Needs to add strength; can struggle with arm-heavy/whippy delivery throughout a game; tendency to lose crispness of stuff (fastball velo); lacks above-average breaking ball; more of a get-over pitch; overall command is fringe; power arm that can struggle to put away hitters; limited pitchability.

**Risk Factor/Injury History:** Moderate risk; arm for late-innings work; yet to pitch at Double-A level.

**Bret Sayre's Fantasy Take:** There's certainly fantasy potential with Urena, but the most likely outcome is still him serving up cheese in the Marlins' 'pen. That would give him a shot at fantasy value, but again, it would be out of his (above-average) control. If he does make it to the rotation, he'll have a tough time getting punchouts at a rate his fastball deserves without a big jump in the breaking ball.

**The Year Ahead:** Urena has a special arm, but you won't find many sources that see a long-term starter in the profile; rather, most see a future late-innings reliever, one complete with a near-elite fastball in bursts and two usable off-speed pitches, including a plus changeup. I get that profile and can respect the likely role, but I'm still onboard the starter bus at present. The 22-year-old arm continues to take steps forward on the mound, and even without great feel, has more room to add pitchability to his game and improve his secondary utility. The fastball is a major-league pitch, so he's going to find success in some role at the end of the day. Double-A will be a big test, either pushing Urena toward his future in the bullpen or changing the minds of those who doubt his bona fides to start.

# 7. Justin Nicolino LHP

**Born:** 11/22/91 **Age:** 22 **Bats:** L **Throws:** L **Height:** 6'3" **Weight:** 190

| MLB ETA | CT | FB | CH | CB | SL | OFP | Realistic |
|---|---|---|---|---|---|---|---|
| 2015 | — | 50 | 65 | 50 | — | 55 NO.3 STARTER | 50 NO.5 SP/MIDDLE RP |

| YEAR | TEAM | LVL | AGE | W | L | SV | G | GS | IP | H | HR | BB | SO | BB9 | SO9 | GB% | BABIP | WHIP | ERA | FIP | FRA | WARP |
|---|---|---|---|---|---|---|---|---|---|---|---|---|---|---|---|---|---|---|---|---|---|---|
| 2013 | JUP | A+ | 21 | 5 | 2 | 0 | 18 | 18 | 96.7 | 89 | 4 | 18 | 64 | 1.7 | 6.0 | 50% | .286 | 1.11 | 2.23 | 3.08 | 4.38 | 0.5 |
| 2013 | JAX | AA | 21 | 3 | 2 | 0 | 9 | 9 | 45.3 | 63 | 2 | 12 | 31 | 2.4 | 6.2 | 42% | .386 | 1.65 | 4.96 | 3.04 | 4.02 | 0.6 |
| 2014 | MIA | MLB | 22 | 6 | 9 | 0 | 24 | 24 | 119.0 | 124 | 11 | 39 | 80 | 2.9 | 6.1 | 48% | .319 | 1.37 | 4.26 | 4.17 | 4.63 | 0.1 |
| 2015 | MIA | MLB | 23 | 7 | 7 | 0 | 22 | 22 | 131.7 | 120 | 11 | 54 | 100 | 3.7 | 6.8 | 48% | .299 | 1.33 | 3.91 | 3.98 | 4.25 | 0.5 |

Breakout: 0%   Improve: 0%   Collapse: 0%   Attrition: 0%   MLB: 0%   *Comparables: Brett Oberholtzer, Joe Wieland, Aaron Poreda*

**Drafted/Acquired:** 2nd round, 2010 draft, University HS (Orlando, FL)

**Previous Ranking:** #4 (Org), #73 (Top 101)

**What Happened in 2013:** Nicolino pitched his way to the Double-A level but saw his prospect stock fall because he found more barrels than he missed.

**Strengths:** Good size; clean delivery; repeatable mechanics; fastball can set the table when he hits his spots; works upper-80s/low-90s; some arm-side life; changeup is best offering; fastball disguise with some late sink; shows average curveball; good pitchability; command profile projects to be plus.

**Weaknesses:** Lacks big arm strength; fastball is average offering; working in fringe-to-solid average velocity; changeup is really nice pitch but lacks huge action; curveball is average; command has to be special to achieve ceiling.

**Risk Factor/Injury History:** Moderate risk; 9 Double-A starts

**Bret Sayre's Fantasy Take:** Like Robbie Erlin, Nicolino is in the perfect spot to maximize his fantasy value—which makes him a better bet in our game than real life. A strong command profile will help him keep low WHIPs, and a big ballpark will help keep his ERA around league average. He's better than he showed at Double-A, but this is not a frontline fantasy arm by any means.

**The Year Ahead:** Nicolino is a classic overrated prospect in the minors, a command/control profile with very good changeup who can dominate the lower levels but lacks the punch to miss more advanced bats. Pitchers who can spot up their arsenals will find success in the minors, but as you move up the chain, the command needs to be very good to find success with only an average fastball/breaking ball, and as good as Nicolino's command looks, it's far from elite. The margin of error is small, and without an uptick in velocity or breaking ball intensity, it's hard to see Nicolino finding sustainable success against better competition. It's a back-end starter/middle reliever for me.

## 8. Anthony DeSclafani RHP

**Born:** 4/18/90   **Age:** 24   **Bats:** R   **Throws:** R   **Height:** 6' 2"   **Weight:** 195

| MLB ETA | CT | FB | CH | CB | SL | OFP | Realistic |
|---|---|---|---|---|---|---|---|
| 2014 | – | 60 | 50 | – | 60 | 50<br>NO.4 STARTER | 50<br>LATE-INN RP (7TH) |

| YEAR | TEAM | LVL | AGE | W | L | SV | G | GS | IP | H | HR | BB | SO | BB9 | SO9 | GB% | BABIP | WHIP | ERA | FIP | FRA | WARP |
|---|---|---|---|---|---|---|---|---|---|---|---|---|---|---|---|---|---|---|---|---|---|---|
| 2013 | JUP | A+ | 23 | 4 | 2 | 0 | 12 | 12 | 54.0 | 48 | 3 | 9 | 53 | 1.5 | 8.8 | 54% | .304 | 1.06 | 1.67 | 2.56 | 3.94 | 0.6 |
| 2013 | JAX | AA | 23 | 5 | 4 | 0 | 13 | 13 | 75.0 | 74 | 7 | 14 | 62 | 1.7 | 7.4 | 49% | .309 | 1.17 | 3.36 | 3.19 | 4.69 | 0.4 |
| 2014 | MIA | MLB | 24 | 5 | 8 | 0 | 21 | 21 | 105.7 | 113 | 11 | 34 | 72 | 2.9 | 6.1 | 50% | .325 | 1.39 | 4.46 | 4.30 | 4.85 | -0.2 |
| 2015 | MIA | MLB | 25 | 10 | 11 | 0 | 31 | 31 | 198.0 | 214 | 20 | 51 | 150 | 2.3 | 6.8 | 50% | .336 | 1.34 | 4.26 | 3.69 | 4.63 | -0.3 |

Breakout: 0%   Improve: 0%   Collapse: 0%   Attrition: 0%   MLB: 0%      *Comparables: Tommy Milone, Nick Tepesch, Juan Nicasio*

**Drafted/Acquired:** 6th round, 2011 draft, University of Florida (Gainesville, FL)

**Previous Ranking:** NR

**What Happened in 2013:** The then-23-year-old pitched his way to the Double-A level, finishing strong with an impressive run through the Southern League.

**Strengths:** Athletic and aggressive on the mound; arm works well; fastball comfortable in the 90-94 range; can gain velo throughout games; good angle and late zip; slider is solid-average to plus offering; short and sharp; can turn over a decent changeup; average but playable and used in sequence; good command profile.

**Weaknesses:** Arsenal is more solid-average than special; fastball can play below plus; aggressive approach can put balls in danger zones; struggles when he elevates; breaking ball lacks big, wipeout break; more about missing barrels than bats; changeup isn't a weapon.

**Risk Factor/Injury History:** Moderate risk; achieved Double-A level; fastball/slider for bullpen.

**Bret Sayre's Fantasy Take:** If you're in a points league, or one that counts K/BB ratio in your format, DeSclafani gets a tick up for you. Congratulations! For everyone else, he is just a middling potential starting option who is best left for deep leagues. The strikeouts have been pretty good at the minor-league level, but don't expect him to miss a ton of bats in The Show.

**The Year Ahead:** DeSclafani is going to be a major-league arm, but the ultimate role still seems to be up in the air. He has the body/delivery and arsenal to start, but he lacks power stuff, although the fastball does show the ability to get into the mid-90s in bursts. The command is solid, but he likes to challenge hitters and can run into trouble when he elevates, and his secondary arsenal will struggle to play multiple times through a major-league lineup. His likely role will come out of the bullpen, where his stuff can play up a bit and the short-burst style will be better suited for his overall approach. He could continue in the Double-A rotation to start 2014 but could break into the majors in a relief role at some point during the season.

## 9. Brian Flynn LHP

**Born:** 4/19/90   **Age:** 24   **Bats:** L   **Throws:** L   **Height:** 6' 7"   **Weight:** 240

| MLB ETA | CT | FB | CH | CB | SL | OFP | Realistic |
|---|---|---|---|---|---|---|---|
| Debuted in 2013 | – | 55 | 50 | – | 50 | 50<br>NO.4 STARTER | 50<br>NO.5 SP/LONG RP |

| YEAR | TEAM | LVL | AGE | W | L | SV | G | GS | IP | H | HR | BB | SO | BB9 | SO9 | GB% | BABIP | WHIP | ERA | FIP | FRA | WARP |
|---|---|---|---|---|---|---|---|---|---|---|---|---|---|---|---|---|---|---|---|---|---|---|
| 2013 | MIA | MLB | 23 | 0 | 2 | 0 | 4 | 4 | 18.0 | 27 | 4 | 13 | 15 | 6.5 | 7.5 | 40% | .411 | 2.22 | 8.50 | 6.41 | 7.12 | -0.3 |
| 2013 | NWO | AAA | 23 | 6 | 11 | 0 | 23 | 23 | 138.0 | 127 | 7 | 40 | 122 | 2.6 | 8.0 | 55% | .302 | 1.21 | 2.80 | 3.42 | 3.79 | 2.1 |
| 2013 | JAX | AA | 23 | 1 | 1 | 0 | 4 | 4 | 23.0 | 18 | 2 | 3 | 25 | 1.2 | 9.8 | 47% | .298 | 0.91 | 1.57 | 2.39 | 2.41 | 0.7 |
| 2014 | MIA | MLB | 24 | 7 | 10 | 0 | 26 | 26 | 143.7 | 147 | 13 | 51 | 103 | 3.2 | 6.5 | 46% | .319 | 1.38 | 4.24 | 4.14 | 4.60 | 0.0 |
| 2015 | MIA | MLB | 25 | 11 | 10 | 0 | 32 | 32 | 207.0 | 199 | 14 | 58 | 165 | 2.5 | 7.2 | 47% | .320 | 1.24 | 3.52 | 3.24 | 3.83 | 1.7 |

Breakout: 17%   Improve: 36%   Collapse: 10%   Attrition: 26%   MLB: 56%      *Comparables: Garrett Richards, Zach McAllister, Felix Doubront*

**Drafted/Acquired:** 7th round, 2011 draft, Wichita State University (Wichita, KS)

**Previous Ranking:** NR

**What Happened in 2013:** The large lefty hit three spots on the year, including a late-season major-league call up, but his command never made the trip to Miami.

**Strengths:** Abnormally large human; creates tough angles from 3/4 slot; whippy arm; fastball plays solid-average; will work low-90s; can touch higher; good low-80s slider; sharp tilt; lower-70s curveball that he can drop for strikes; changeup can show average; plays well off the fastball; good strike-thrower with pitchability.

**Weaknesses:** Big stuff but lacks big stuff; fastball can play down in the upper-80s/90 range; long action and arm swing can affect command; slider can get slurvy and loose; curveball shows early hump and can lack deception; steal-a-strike pitch; changeup lacks much projection.

**Risk Factor/Injury History:** Low risk; achieved major-league level

**Bret Sayre's Fantasy Take:** On the bright side, being in Miami is probably the best thing for Flynn's fantasy value. On the other side, he's somewhat likely to never carry any value in non-deep leagues. He's not nearly as horrific as his major-league numbers from 2013 would suggest, but even if he had a rotation spot, the ratios would be middling, the strikeouts would be poor and the wins would be nonexistent.

**The Year Ahead:** Flynn can execute a four-pitch mix from the left side, and with his size and strike-throwing, profiles as a back-end starter at the major-league level. It's more control than command, and without improved stuff, the ceiling isn't much higher than the floor, which is an unexceptional long reliever. Assuming the control he showed in the upper minors returns, he should be able to spot his fastball, keep hitters off-balance with his secondary stuff, and chew some innings in a back-of-the- rotation role.

## 10.  Jesus Solorzano   OF

**Born:** 8/8/90    **Age:** 23    **Bats:** R    **Throws:** R    **Height:** 6'0"    **Weight:** 190

| MLB ETA | Hit | Power | Run | Glove | Arm | OFP | Realistic |
|---|---|---|---|---|---|---|---|
| 2016 | ---- | 65 | 60 | -- | 60 | 60<br>1ST DIV PLAYER | 45<br><AVG ML/BENCH OF |

| YEAR | TEAM | LVL | AGE | PA | R | 2B | 3B | HR | RBI | BB | SO | SB | CS | AVG/OBP/SLG | TAv | BABIP | BRR | FRAA | WARP |
|---|---|---|---|---|---|---|---|---|---|---|---|---|---|---|---|---|---|---|---|
| 2013 | GRB | A | 22 | 523 | 72 | 29 | 3 | 15 | 66 | 24 | 111 | 33 | 4 | .285/.325/.450 | .284 | .339 | 3.7 | RF(78): 4.8, CF(45): 2.0 | 3.6 |
| 2014 | MIA | MLB | 23 | 250 | 24 | 10 | 1 | 4 | 23 | 8 | 66 | 8 | 2 | .222/.252/.326 | .217 | .280 | 0.7 | RF 1, CF 0 | -0.2 |
| 2015 | MIA | MLB | 24 | 250 | 23 | 11 | 2 | 4 | 23 | 8 | 66 | 6 | 2 | .221/.250/.335 | .212 | .284 | 0.5 | RF 1, CF 0 | -1.3 |

Breakout: 0%    Improve: 0%    Collapse: 0%    Attrition: 0%    MLB: 0%          *Comparables: Scott Cousins, Matt Joyce, Lorenzo Cain*

**Drafted/Acquired:** International free agent, 2009, Venezuela

**Previous Ranking:** On the Rise

**What Happened in 2013:** After four short-season campaigns, the toolsy Venezuelan finally arrived at the full-season level, showing off the power and speed, hitting 47 extra-base hits and swiping 33 bags.

**Strengths:** Loud tools; runs well; runs smart; big raw pop; generates plus bat speed and can lift the ball; more gap-to-gap right now; five o'clock power impressive; range for center; arm for right; very good basestealer/-runner.

**Weaknesses:** Hit tool and approach could limit power/profile; trigger can be slow; attacks fastballs but can struggle against sequence; limited bat control; aggressive approach; poor reads/routes in center; better fit for a corner despite speed.

**Risk Factor/Injury History:** High risk; questionable hit tool; yet to play in upper minors.

**Bret Sayre's Fantasy Take:** The stat line in High-A was whiplash inducing from a potential fantasy standpoint, but this is not the type of performance that should be expected at the major-league level. The steals are more real than the power, but it could all come together in a very nice fantasy package if he can get on base.

**The Year Ahead:** Signed in 2009 but didn't reach the full-season level until 2013, the Marlins have been slow with Solorzano, whose overall approach is immature and could end up limiting his rise in the minors. The toolsy outfielder will move to the Florida State League in 2014, where the 23-year-old will face better arms with better secondary stuff, which given his fastball-hungry and aggressive approach, could expose him. But the pop and the speed are legit, and if he can take a step forward with the approach, he might just surprise some people and emerge as a prospect worth paying closer attention to. As of now, sources seem to like the tools but fear the ability to adjust and the approach, so 2014 will be a big test.

## Prospects on the Rise

**1. LHP Jarlin Garcia:** One of the better young arms I saw in short-season ball in 2013, Garcia has a chance to really step forward in full-season ball. The 21-year-old lefty has a good feel for pitching, with a clean and athletic delivery, and a crisp fastball, and as he adds strength and refines his secondary arsenal, he should blossom into a top-10 prospect in this system. I like this arm.

**2. 3B J.T. Riddle:** A 13th-round pick in 2013, Riddle didn't look the part in his professional debut, but reports from instructional league were glowing, as the 22-year-old can spray the ball all over the field and can play on the left side of the infield. Because of his maturity, the Marlins could get aggressive with his development and push him to the Florida State League to start the season, where Riddle might just surprise people with his solid-average skills.

**3. SS Javier Lopez:** A six-figure talent from the Dominican Republic, Lopez has impact projections, but a long way to go before he starts to actualize on the field. Having watched Lopez several times in 2013, I can see the tools; flashy glove and arm at short, and legit bat speed at the plate. The defensive skills need a lot of refinement, and the bat wasn't ready for the college-heavy New York-Penn League, but as he matures, this is a player to keep tabs on. I wouldn't be surprised if Lopez is an "On the Rise" type for a few years before he really emerges as a top talent. But I like it.

## Factors on the Farm
### Prospects likely to contribute at the major-league level in 2014

**1. RHP Arquimedes Caminero:** Let's not overthink things here. First of all, any 6'4", 255 lb. pitcher named Arquimedes belongs on a list, regardless of the list. Secondly—and most important—Caminero can really bring the heat, working with a mid- to upper-90s fastball that can touch 100, backing up the smoke with a trapdoor splitter and a slider that can miss bats. Command is loose, but if he can throw strikes with his near-elite fastball, he's going to find sustainable success at the back of a major-league bullpen.

**2. LHP Adam Conley:** Conley has a good case for inclusion on the top-10 list, as he's a lefty with a starter's arsenal and some strike-throwing ability. But the realities of his delivery and arsenal limit his upside in a rotation; more of a back-end type with a good low-90s fastball and a good change. But out of the bullpen, the stuff could tick up a bit and make him a legit bullpen weapon, especially against left-handed bats, who struggle to pick up the ball from his delivery.

**3. RHP Colby Suggs:** A short and thick fastball reliever, Suggs won't be long for the minors if he can improve his fastball command and breaking-ball utility. Selected in the second round of the 2013 draft, Suggs is a power 'pen arm in the making, with a max-effort plus-plus fastball that is both his bread and his butter, but he can also flash a plus hard curve in the low-80s and a mid-80s slider when the mood strikes. He's a legit closer prospect, but will need to add more quality to the secondary package to reach that ceiling.

## FROM THE FIELD

### Andrew Heaney

**Player:** Andrew Heaney

**Team:** Miami Marlins

**Filed by:** Steffan Segui

**Date(s) Seen:** August 1, October 22, and October 29, 2013

**Physical:** Average height and very slender. Could add some weight to help with durability going forward.

**Mechanics/Delivery:** Easy simple fluid mechanics with good rhythm and tempo. Active hands separate late and he hides the ball well behind slightly closed-off front side. That, along with whippy 3/4 arm slot, creates excellent deception. Can get somewhat rotational but always finishes strong down mound.

**Fastball:** 55 grade. 89-93 not explosive but carries late in games. Good sink/run down and away from right-handed hitters and bore it in on the hands.

**Slider:** 60 grade. Has good hard down break with some horizontal movement. Can get slurvy. Uses as two different pitches for strikes and chase.

**Changeup:** 55 grade. Typical lefty change with some dive. Little firm at times. Keeps down well.

**Makeup:** 60 grade. Very even-headed pitcher. Stays very calm and doesn't show his emotions.

**OFP:** 60; no. 2 starter

**Realistic Role:** 55; no. 3 starter

**Risk:** Low; advanced left-handed college arm who has pitched very well at every level thus far.

## 1. Tyrone Taylor CF

**Born:** 1/22/94 **Age:** 20 **Bats:** R **Throws:** R **Height:** 6' 0" **Weight:** 185

| MLB ETA | Hit | Power | Run | Glove | Arm | OFP | Realistic |
|---------|-----|-------|-----|-------|-----|-----|-----------|
| 2017 | 55 | 55 | 70 | 60 | 55 | 60<br>1ST DIV PLAYER | 45<br><AVG ML/BENCH |

| YEAR | TEAM | LVL | AGE | PA | R | 2B | 3B | HR | RBI | BB | SO | SB | CS | AVG/OBP/SLG | TAv | BABIP | BRR | FRAA | WARP |
|------|------|-----|-----|-----|----|----|----|----|-----|----|----|----|----|-------------|-----|-------|-----|------|------|
| 2013 | WIS | A | 19 | 549 | 69 | 33 | 2 | 8 | 57 | 35 | 63 | 19 | 8 | .274/.338/.400 | .266 | .299 | 2.4 | CF(108): 12.2, LF(4): 0.0 | 3.5 |
| 2014 | MIL | MLB | 20 | 250 | 23 | 10 | 1 | 4 | 23 | 10 | 49 | 5 | 2 | .229/.269/.331 | .215 | .270 | -0.1 | CF 4, LF 0 | 0.0 |
| 2015 | MIL | MLB | 21 | 250 | 25 | 9 | 1 | 4 | 23 | 11 | 42 | 3 | 1 | .237/.280/.335 | .224 | .266 | -0.2 | CF 4, LF 0 | -0.3 |

Breakout: 0%    Improve: 0%    Collapse: 0%    Attrition: 0%    MLB: 0%          *Comparables: Cedric Hunter, Che-Hsuan Lin, Abraham Almonte*

**Drafted/Acquired:** 2nd round, 2012 draft, Torrance HS (Torrance, CA)

**Previous Ranking:** #9 (Org)

**What Happened in 2013:** In his full-season debut, the former second-round pick showed prowess in the field and at the plate, pushing himself to the top of the Brewers prospect pyramid.

**Strengths:** High-end athlete; well-above-average run; tools to stick in center; good arm; bat projects to solid-average; good hand-eye; some pop in the stick; could find average or better power.

**Weaknesses:** Still transitioning from athlete to baseball player; reads/routes need refinement in center; struggles against arm-side stuff; struggles against spin; streaky hitter that will need to make quicker adjustments as he climbs.

**Risk Factor/Injury History:** High risk; limited experience at full-season level; questions about offensive profile.

**Bret Sayre's Fantasy Take:** Taylor is the guy to own in this system if forced to carry someone on a dynasty farm team. He could be a legitimate 20/20 candidate playing in Miller Park (where his power will be accentuated), and the combination of the scouting takes on his swing and his contact rate in the Midwest League leave open the possibility of some average as well.

**The Year Ahead:** Taylor has the highest ceiling on the Brewers farm, a five-tool player that projects to stick up the middle. But the 20-year-old is more raw tools than baseball skills at this point, and several sources are hesitant to profess much faith in the offensive profile, despite his solid season in the Midwest League. If he can take steps forward with his pitch-recognition and reaction skills, and learn to tap into his strength at the plate, he's going to offer more than just contact and speed. In the field, he has a chance to be very legit at a premium position, and that alone will end up eventually carrying him to the major leagues. If the bat steps up, Taylor will climb prospect lists as he climbs toward the highest level.

## 2. Jimmy Nelson RHP

**Born:** 6/5/89 **Age:** 25 **Bats:** R **Throws:** R **Height:** 6' 5" **Weight:** 245

| MLB ETA | CT | FB | CH | CB | SL | OFP | Realistic |
|---------|----|----|----|----|----|-----|-----------|
| Debuted in 2013 | ---- | 60 | 50 | ---- | 60 | 50<br>NO.4 STARTER | 50<br>NO.4 STARTER |

| YEAR | TEAM | LVL | AGE | W | L | SV | G | GS | IP | H | HR | BB | SO | BB9 | SO9 | GB% | BABIP | WHIP | ERA | FIP | FRA | WARP |
|------|------|-----|-----|---|---|----|----|----|------|-----|----|----|-----|-----|-----|-----|-------|------|------|------|------|------|
| 2013 | MIL | MLB | 24 | 0 | 0 | 0 | 4 | 1 | 10.0 | 2 | 0 | 5 | 8 | 4.5 | 7.2 | 42% | .083 | 0.70 | 0.90 | 2.92 | 3.47 | 0.1 |
| 2013 | NAS | AAA | 24 | 5 | 6 | 0 | 15 | 15 | 83.3 | 74 | 2 | 50 | 91 | 5.4 | 9.8 | 63% | .327 | 1.49 | 3.67 | 3.64 | 3.94 | 1.3 |
| 2013 | HUN | AA | 24 | 5 | 4 | 0 | 12 | 12 | 69.0 | 63 | 5 | 15 | 72 | 2.0 | 9.4 | 53% | .320 | 1.13 | 2.74 | 2.81 | 3.96 | 0.7 |
| 2014 | MIL | MLB | 25 | 7 | 9 | 0 | 23 | 23 | 126.7 | 125 | 14 | 63 | 100 | 4.5 | 7.1 | 54% | .313 | 1.48 | 4.76 | 4.81 | 5.17 | -0.2 |
| 2015 | MIL | MLB | 26 | 6 | 5 | 0 | 64 | 13 | 129.7 | 128 | 16 | 54 | 110 | 3.7 | 7.6 | 54% | .315 | 1.40 | 4.56 | 4.36 | 4.96 | 0.1 |

Breakout: 22%    Improve: 30%    Collapse: 9%    Attrition: 31%    MLB: 46%          *Comparables: Chris Carpenter, Justin Wilson, Mark Rogers*

**Drafted/Acquired:** 2nd round, 2010 draft, University of Alabama (Tuscaloosa, AL)

**Previous Ranking:** Factor on the Farm

**What Happened in 2013:** Nelson pitched his way to the major-league level, but his below-average command continued to cloud his potential.

**Strengths:** Big, sturdy frame; pitches with good angle and plane; fastball is plus offering; consistently in the low-90s with weight; slider is out pitch; 82-84 with tilt; shows changeup; attacks hitters.

**Weaknesses:** Below-average command; struggles with release points; won't finish and will miss arm side and up; changeup is fringe; gets firm and deliberate; what you see is what you get; several sources see a reliever.

**Risk Factor/Injury History:** Low risk; upper minors experience; achieved major-league level.

**Bret Sayre's Fantasy Take:** This is exactly what to expect from the Brewers' list. Nelson is not close to a top-100 fantasy prospect and is really ownable only in deeper formats. Could be a big ground-ball guy who logs a lot of innings, but the ERA and strikeout numbers are likely to leave him near replacement level in shallow leagues.

**The Year Ahead:** Nelson is a workhorse starter, with a big, physical body and two above-average offerings. The command is below average and could limit his effectiveness in a rotation, and the changeup is a fringe-pitch at present that is often too firm and lacking deception from the arm. If the command can refine, Nelson should enjoy a long career as a back-end starter, and even if the command remains below average, he can carve out a role in a major-league bullpen.

---

## 3.  Mitch Haniger   CF

**Born:** 12/23/90  **Age:** 23  **Bats:** R  **Throws:** R  **Height:** 6' 2"  **Weight:** 180

| MLB ETA | Hit | Power | Run | Glove | Arm | OFP | Realistic |
|---|---|---|---|---|---|---|---|
| 2015 | 50 | 60 | — | — | 60 | 55 >AVG PLAYER | 50 ML REGULAR |

| YEAR | TEAM | LVL | AGE | PA | R | 2B | 3B | HR | RBI | BB | SO | SB | CS | AVG/OBP/SLG | TAv | BABIP | BRR | FRAA | WARP |
|---|---|---|---|---|---|---|---|---|---|---|---|---|---|---|---|---|---|---|---|
| 2013 | WIS | A | 22 | 178 | 24 | 12 | 2 | 5 | 25 | 25 | 24 | 7 | 0 | .297/.399/.510 | .327 | .314 | 1.8 | RF(23): 0.9, CF(12): -0.7 | 2.0 |
| 2013 | BRV | A+ | 22 | 365 | 52 | 24 | 3 | 6 | 43 | 32 | 68 | 2 | 2 | .250/.323/.396 | .266 | .298 | 1.7 | RF(45): -3.1, CF(42): 6.1 | 1.7 |
| 2014 | MIL | MLB | 23 | 250 | 23 | 11 | 1 | 5 | 26 | 19 | 59 | 1 | 0 | .225/.288/.352 | .231 | .280 | -0.2 | RF -1, CF 1 | -0.1 |
| 2015 | MIL | MLB | 24 | 250 | 27 | 10 | 1 | 6 | 26 | 20 | 61 | 0 | 0 | .219/.286/.352 | .237 | .269 | -0.5 | RF -1, CF 1 | 0.0 |

Breakout: 0%    Improve: 0%    Collapse: 0%    Attrition: 0%    MLB: 0%    *Comparables: Andrew Lambo, Matt Joyce, Rene Tosoni*

**Drafted/Acquired:** 1st round, 2012 draft, California Polytechnic State University (San Luis Obispo, CA)

**Previous Ranking:** #8 (Org)

**What Happened in 2013:** A supplemental first-round pick in the 2012 draft, Haniger hit his way to the Florida State League in 2013, wrapping up his first full season with a successful 25-game run in the Arizona Fall League.

**Strengths:** Plus power potential; good hands; good present strength; feel for hitting; has a plan at the plate and forces pitchers to work; arm is above average; will play in a corner.

**Weaknesses:** Lacks high-end tools; hit tool only projects in the average range; can try to yank too many balls; struggles against balls on the outer half; game play might play under projection; fringe defensive profile; fringe run; bat has to play to projection (or above) for impact.

**Risk Factor/Injury History:** Moderate risk; yet to play at Double-A level.

**Bret Sayre's Fantasy Take:** A better fantasy prospect than real-life one, Haniger could hit his fair share of homers playing at Miller Park. However, the hit tool is going to have to play to at least a fringe-average level or else the power won't matter all that much. Upside is for .260 and 25 homers.

**The Year Ahead:** Haniger is a hitter, but just how much he will hit is a subject of debate. While he has good hands and can produce good bat speed, he has yet to find his over-the-fence stroke and might only profile for average game power. With defensive limitation, the bat will need to play for Haniger to profile as a major-league regular, and without loud physical tools, the margin of error is slim. But after a strong showing in the prospect-heavy Arizona Fall League, several sources were more confident that he can make the bat work against quality pitching, a vote of confidence as the 23 year-old will attempt to pass the Double-A test in 2014.

---

## 4.  Orlando Arcia   SS

**Born:** 8/4/94  **Age:** 19  **Bats:** R  **Throws:** R  **Height:** 6' 0"  **Weight:** 165

| MLB ETA | Hit | Power | Run | Glove | Arm | OFP | Realistic |
|---|---|---|---|---|---|---|---|
| 2016 | 55 | — | 50 | 60 | 60 | 60 1ST DIV PLAYER | 45 UT PLAYER |

| YEAR | TEAM | LVL | AGE | PA | R | 2B | 3B | HR | RBI | BB | SO | SB | CS | AVG/OBP/SLG | TAv | BABIP | BRR | FRAA | WARP |
|---|---|---|---|---|---|---|---|---|---|---|---|---|---|---|---|---|---|---|---|
| 2013 | WIS | A | 18 | 486 | 67 | 14 | 5 | 4 | 39 | 35 | 40 | 20 | 9 | .251/.314/.333 | .241 | .268 | 1.8 | SS(120): 7.3 | 2.4 |
| 2014 | MIL | MLB | 19 | 250 | 23 | 8 | 1 | 3 | 21 | 11 | 42 | 5 | 2 | .225/.263/.315 | .210 | .260 | 0.1 | SS 4 | 0.3 |
| 2015 | MIL | MLB | 20 | 250 | 24 | 7 | 1 | 3 | 22 | 12 | 34 | 3 | 2 | .235/.279/.321 | .224 | .257 | -0.1 | SS 2 | -0.1 |

Breakout: 0%    Improve: 0%    Collapse: 0%    Attrition: 0%    MLB: 0%    *Comparables: Ruben Tejada, Wilfredo Tovar, Carlos Triunfel*

**Drafted/Acquired:** International free agent, 2010, Venezuela

**Previous Ranking:** On The Rise

**What Happened in 2013:** The slick defender struggled in his full-season debut, which is to be expected given the fact that the 19-year-old lost a season to injury in 2012 and was last seen playing in the Dominican Summer League in 2011.

**Strengths:** Lean and athletic body; skinny but room to add more strength; impressive baseball instincts; fluid actions in the field; great hands; quick reads and reactions; natural shortstop; strong arm; good plan of attack at the plate; contact swing with some natural jump off the bat; hit tool projects to solid-average or better; average run.

**Weaknesses:** Needs to add strength; struggles against quality spin; fastball-first approach; well-below-average power; speed is average at best; glove-first profile.

**Risk Factor/Injury History:** High risk; yet to play in high minors; questions about bat.

**Bret Sayre's Fantasy Take:** Sort of a reverse Haniger, Arcia's strengths are on the defensive side of the equation, making him a guy not worth paying much attention to in fantasy leagues. There is a chance that he could be a .280 hitter with 15-20 steals per year, but if that's your fantasy ceiling, it's not worth much of an investment.

**The Year Ahead:** Arcia is a highly instinctual player with excellent hands on both sides of the ball, fluid actions, and a strong arm. He's not a burner but he has range, and he's not a power hitter but he can make hard contact, showing a good feel for squaring up velocity. He struggles against secondary stuff and the bat is more about consistent contact than impact, so the profile is more about his glove than his stick. Arcia could develop into a down-the-lineup bat with an above-average defensive profile at shortstop, making him a very valuable first-division player if everything comes together. There is a high risk involved because of the bat, but the glove should at least carry him to a utility position down the line, so the major-league floor is relatively high.

## 5. Johnny Hellweg RHP

**Born:** 10/29/88 **Age:** 25 **Bats:** R **Throws:** R **Height:** 6'9" **Weight:** 205

| MLB ETA | CT | FB | CH | CB | SL | OFP | Realistic |
|---|---|---|---|---|---|---|---|
| Debuted in 2013 | – | 75 | 50 | 50 | – | 55 NO.4 STARTER | 50 LATE INN RP (SU) |

| YEAR | TEAM | LVL | AGE | W | L | SV | G | GS | IP | H | HR | BB | SO | BB9 | SO9 | GB% | BABIP | WHIP | ERA | FIP | FRA | WARP |
|---|---|---|---|---|---|---|---|---|---|---|---|---|---|---|---|---|---|---|---|---|---|---|
| 2013 | NAS | AAA | 24 | 12 | 5 | 0 | 23 | 23 | 125.7 | 103 | 6 | 81 | 89 | 5.8 | 6.4 | 59% | .270 | 1.46 | 3.15 | 5.04 | 5.41 | 0.5 |
| 2013 | WIS | A | 24 | 1 | 0 | 0 | 1 | 1 | 6.0 | 5 | 0 | 2 | 4 | 3.0 | 6.0 | 47% | .263 | 1.17 | 3.00 | 3.51 | 4.29 | 0.1 |
| 2013 | MIL | MLB | 24 | 1 | 4 | 0 | 8 | 7 | 30.7 | 40 | 3 | 26 | 9 | 7.6 | 2.6 | 58% | .319 | 2.15 | 6.75 | 7.03 | 7.45 | -0.9 |
| 2014 | MIL | MLB | 25 | 6 | 9 | 1 | 40 | 21 | 133.3 | 127 | 14 | 87 | 99 | 5.9 | 6.7 | 54% | .303 | 1.60 | 5.24 | 5.45 | 5.69 | -0.9 |
| 2015 | MIL | MLB | 26 | 4 | 3 | 0 | 58 | 5 | 83.7 | 79 | 9 | 52 | 63 | 5.6 | 6.8 | 52% | .301 | 1.56 | 5.17 | 5.05 | 5.61 | -0.6 |

Breakout: 22%    Improve: 28%    Collapse: 3%    Attrition: 25%    MLB: 37%    *Comparables: J.D. Durbin, Charlie Haeger, Elvin Ramirez*

**Drafted/Acquired:** 16th round, 2008 draft, Florida College (Jacksonville, FL)

**Previous Ranking:** #3 (Org)

**What Happened in 2013:** Hellweg's control problems continued as he climbed all the way to the major leagues, struggling to miss bats and limit damage.

**Strengths:** Extreme height/length; excellent extension; fastball can show elite velocity; routinely works in the 93-97 range; shows big arm-side run; hard curveball in upper-70s/low-80s; two-plane break and occasional depth; average changeup; some fade and sink.

**Weaknesses:** Well-below-average command; struggles to control body/delivery; arm can show drag; excellent in bursts but struggles deeper into games; arsenal is fastball heavy; secondary arsenal is average at best; starter profile is shaky.

**Risk Factor/Injury History:** Low risk; achieved major-league level; some injury concerns.

**Bret Sayre's Fantasy Take:** Hellweg is best left to be someone else's problem in fantasy leagues. There was a time where he made for a nice upside play, but with less of a chance to stick in a rotation (and less upside there even if he makes it), the likelihood is that Hellweg has a Jon Rauch-type career as a huge man with little fantasy interest.

**The Year Ahead:** Hellweg has a lot of length to control in his delivery, and when he manages to repeat his mechanics, his fastball can be a monster offering, with the ability to work mid- to upper-90s with big arm-side life. The secondary arsenal often looks underdeveloped and struggles to find much utility; the curveball can get slurvy and loose, and the changeup can get too firm and flat. Command is his biggest hindrance, and without a step forward, high-leverage relief won't be an option, much less starting. But the length that is at times a detriment is also an asset, and if he can find a way to repeat with any consistency, he has a chance to be an impact arm in the back of a major-league bullpen.

## 6. Victor Roache OF

**Born:** 9/17/91 **Age:** 22 **Bats:** R **Throws:** R **Height:** 6'1" **Weight:** 225

| MLB ETA | Hit | Power | Run | Glove | Arm | OFP | Realistic |
|---|---|---|---|---|---|---|---|
| 2016 | – | 70 | – | 50 | 50 | 60 1ST DIV PLAYER | 45 <AVG ML PLAYER |

| YEAR | TEAM | LVL | AGE | PA | R | 2B | 3B | HR | RBI | BB | SO | SB | CS | AVG/OBP/SLG | TAv | BABIP | BRR | FRAA | WARP |
|---|---|---|---|---|---|---|---|---|---|---|---|---|---|---|---|---|---|---|---|
| 2013 | WIS | A | 21 | 519 | 62 | 14 | 4 | 22 | 74 | 46 | 137 | 6 | 2 | .248/.322/.440 | .274 | .302 | -1 | LF(86): 1.7 | 1.7 |
| 2014 | MIL | MLB | 22 | 250 | 24 | 7 | 1 | 9 | 30 | 15 | 81 | 0 | 0 | .207/.258/.361 | .223 | .270 | -0.3 | LF 1 | -0.4 |
| 2015 | MIL | MLB | 23 | 250 | 28 | 7 | 1 | 9 | 29 | 15 | 82 | 0 | 0 | .202/.255/.358 | .226 | .263 | -0.4 | LF 1 | -0.7 |

Breakout: 0%    Improve: 0%    Collapse: 0%    Attrition: 0%    MLB: 0%    *Comparables Jeremy Moore, Andrew Lambo, Joel Guzman*

**Drafted/Acquired:** 1st round, 2012 draft, Georgia Southern University (Statesboro, GA)

**Previous Ranking:** #5 (Org)

**What Happened in 2013:** In his professional debut, the former first-round pick managed 40 extra-base hits, including 22 bombs, but the swing-and-miss was a little more grotesque than anticipated, with 137 whiffs in 119 games.

**Strengths:** Monster raw power; leveraged swing capable of driving the ball out of the park; impressive strength; glove could play to average; raw arm strength is solid.

**Weaknesses:** Questionable hittability; struggles against arm-side stuff; pitch-recognition skills might be a problem; hit tool could pull game power down; limited defensive profile; most likely a left fielder because of range and arm utility.

**Risk Factor/Injury History:** High risk; limited professional experience; questions about hit tool.

**Bret Sayre's Fantasy Take:** It's easy to squint and imagine Roache as a solid fantasy contributor—that power could play to 30+ bombs in Milwaukee's homer haven. However, he has red flags that run from his injury history to his hit tool, which makes him an interesting flier and not much else. Better for shallow leagues.

**The Year Ahead:** Roache possesses the most sought-after attribute on the offensive side of the ball—big raw power—but his overall feel for hitting and defensive limitations make the profile tough to champion. If Roache can find a way to fully tap into his well-above-average raw power, his other shortcomings can be ignored, as we all can appreciate the beauty that is 35 bombs a season. But as a player that really struggles against arm-side stuff and seems to have a slower trigger because of pitch read/reaction skills, bringing that power into game action against better arms is as task with a low probability of success.

## 7. Devin Williams    RHP

**Born:** 9/21/94   **Age:** 19   **Bats:** R   **Throws:** R   **Height:** 6'3"   **Weight:** 165

| MLB ETA | CT | FB | CH | CB | SL | OFP | Realistic |
|---|---|---|---|---|---|---|---|
| 2017 | – | 70 | 60 | – | 50 | 60<br>NO.2 STARTER | 50<br>NO.4 STARTER |

| YEAR | TEAM | LVL | AGE | W | L | SV | G | GS | IP | H | HR | BB | SO | BB9 | SO9 | GB% | BABIP | WHIP | ERA | FIP | FRA | WARP |
|---|---|---|---|---|---|---|---|---|---|---|---|---|---|---|---|---|---|---|---|---|---|---|
| 2013 | BRR | Rk | 18 | 1 | 3 | 1 | 13 | 6 | 34.7 | 28 | 0 | 22 | 39 | 5.7 | 10.1 | 62% | .301 | 1.44 | 3.38 | 4.00 | 4.84 | 0.7 |
| 2014 | MIL | MLB | 19 | 1 | 2 | 0 | 11 | 4 | 33.0 | 37 | 5 | 22 | 20 | 6.0 | 5.5 | 48% | .321 | 1.79 | 6.35 | 6.30 | 6.90 | -0.5 |
| 2015 | MIL | MLB | 20 | 3 | 4 | 1 | 33 | 10 | 110.3 | 116 | 16 | 60 | 82 | 4.9 | 6.7 | 48% | .316 | 1.59 | 5.55 | 5.26 | 6.04 | -1.2 |

Breakout: 0%    Improve: 0%    Collapse: 0%    Attrition: 0%    MLB: 0%    *Comparables: Joe Wieland, Brad Hand, Stolmy Pimentel*

**Drafted/Acquired:** 1st round, 2013 draft, Hazelwood West HS (Hazelwood, MO)

**Previous Ranking:** NR

**What Happened in 2013:** The electric second-round arm turned a lot of heads in the Arizona League, missing more than a bat an inning despite wobbly control.

**Strengths:** Highly projectable body; athletic; big arm strength; fastball works 90-94; touches higher; good vertical life; projects to be a well-above-average offering; shows feel for 82- to 85-mph changeup; plays well off the fastball; shows confidence in the offering; slider can flash potential; low-80s with occasional sharp tilt.

**Weaknesses:** Inconsistent mechanics at present; needs to add strength; fastball command is below average; can overthrow changeup; breaking ball lacks an identity at present; slurvy slider without consistent velocity or tilt; long developmental road ahead.

**Risk Factor/Injury History:** High risk; limited professional experience; big gap between present/future

**Bret Sayre's Fantasy Take:** Williams was one of my favorite unheralded arms in the 2013 draft class, and is worth taking with a late second- or third-round dynasty league pick. It's going to be a slow burn with him, but there is more potential here than in any other arm in this system (admittedly, that's not saying much). He has the foundation to miss bats.

**The Year Ahead:** Williams has the highest ceiling of all the arms on the farm, but he's just starting his professional journey and he's not going to reach his ceiling overnight. With a projectable body and plenty of athleticism, Williams should be able to refine his command and pound the lower zone with his already plus fastball, which projects to develop into a 70-grade pitch. He shows some feel for the changeup, but the breaking ball will need to announce itself with more authority if the 19-year-old arm wants to climb on the national prospect radar in 2014. It shouldn't take long. This kid is going to be a stud.

## 8. Taylor Jungmann    RHP

**Born:** 12/18/89   **Age:** 24   **Bats:** R   **Throws:** R   **Height:** 6'6"   **Weight:** 210

| MLB ETA | CT | FB | CH | CB | SL | OFP | Realistic |
|---|---|---|---|---|---|---|---|
| 2014 | – | 55 | – | – | 55 | 50<br>NO.4 STARTER | 50<br>LONG RP/NO.5 |

| YEAR | TEAM | LVL | AGE | W | L | SV | G | GS | IP | H | HR | BB | SO | BB9 | SO9 | GB% | BABIP | WHIP | ERA | FIP | FRA | WARP |
|---|---|---|---|---|---|---|---|---|---|---|---|---|---|---|---|---|---|---|---|---|---|---|
| 2013 | HUN | AA | 23 | 10 | 10 | 0 | 26 | 26 | 139.3 | 117 | 11 | 73 | 82 | 4.7 | 5.3 | 58% | .253 | 1.36 | 4.33 | 4.55 | 6.48 | -1.8 |
| 2014 | MIL | MLB | 24 | 6 | 9 | 0 | 21 | 21 | 118.3 | 128 | 16 | 53 | 63 | 4.0 | 4.8 | 53% | .306 | 1.53 | 5.32 | 5.51 | 5.79 | -0.9 |
| 2015 | MIL | MLB | 25 | 9 | 11 | 0 | 30 | 30 | 191.3 | 193 | 26 | 70 | 109 | 3.3 | 5.1 | 53% | .291 | 1.38 | 4.71 | 4.91 | 5.12 | -0.2 |

Breakout: 0%    Improve: 0%    Collapse: 0%    Attrition: 0%    MLB: 0%    *Comparables: Charlie Leesman, Brandon Cumpton, Lucas Harrell*

**Drafted/Acquired:** 1st round, 2011 draft, University of Texas (Austin, TX)

**Previous Ranking:** #4 (Org)

**What Happened in 2013:** In his Double-A debut, the former 12th overall pick in the 2011 draft failed to gain any prospect traction, losing his feel for command and showing an average arsenal.

**Strengths:** Excellent size and present strength; creates good angle to the plate; multiple fastball looks; sinker in upper-80s/low-90s; can spike a little higher with four-seamer; good natural weight to the sinker; can cut the ball as well; slider is solid-average offering; upper-70s with some tilt; will show a playable changeup; durable.

**Weaknesses:** Lacks impact stuff; can lose his release points; tendency to miss arm side; doesn't pitch with a lot of athleticism; below-average command (present); changeup is average at best; routinely plays fringe or below; some sink, but mechanics can get deliberate and give away the pitch.

**Risk Factor/Injury History:** Low risk; mature arsenal; 26 starts at Double-A level.

**Bret Sayre's Fantasy Take:** That strikeout-to-walk rate of nearly 1:1 in Double-A speaks volumes about how interested I am in Jungmann from a fantasy perspective. He has name recognition at this point and little else. Pass.

**The Year Ahead:** Normally you wouldn't draft a nondescript workhorse starter with the 12th overall pick in a loaded draft, but that's the reality of the former Longhorns ace. He has the body to log a ton of innings, and the stuff is solid-average, so with sharp command he could find sustainable success at the highest level. But without bat-missing stuff, his pitch-to-weak-contact approach gets put to the test when he struggles with the free pass, a problem that he can successfully sidestep in the minors but one that will likely limit his major-league production if he doesn't take a step forward.

---

## 9.  David Goforth  RHP

**Born:** 10/11/88  **Age:** 25  **Bats:** R  **Throws:** R  **Height:** 6'0"  **Weight:** 190

| MLB ETA | CT | FB | CH | CB | SL | OFP | Realistic |
|---|---|---|---|---|---|---|---|
| 2014 | 55 | 70 | — | — | 55 | 50<br>LATE INN RP (SU) | 50<br>MIDDLE RP |

| YEAR | TEAM | LVL | AGE | W | L | SV | G | GS | IP | H | HR | BB | SO | BB9 | SO9 | GB% | BABIP | WHIP | ERA | FIP | FRA | WARP |
|---|---|---|---|---|---|---|---|---|---|---|---|---|---|---|---|---|---|---|---|---|---|---|
| 2013 | BRV | A+ | 24 | 7 | 5 | 0 | 14 | 14 | 78.3 | 67 | 4 | 28 | 58 | 3.2 | 6.7 | 51% | .270 | 1.21 | 3.10 | 3.69 | 4.71 | 0.2 |
| 2013 | HUN | AA | 24 | 4 | 3 | 5 | 20 | 4 | 46.7 | 32 | 1 | 18 | 36 | 3.5 | 6.9 | 54% | .233 | 1.07 | 3.28 | 2.87 | 3.56 | 0.5 |
| 2014 | MIL | MLB | 25 | 5 | 7 | 0 | 28 | 16 | 107.7 | 118 | 15 | 51 | 59 | 4.3 | 4.9 | 47% | .307 | 1.58 | 5.58 | 5.61 | 6.06 | -1.2 |
| 2015 | MIL | MLB | 26 | 4 | 6 | 0 | 24 | 14 | 101.3 | 108 | 14 | 44 | 67 | 3.9 | 6.0 | 47% | .311 | 1.50 | 5.23 | 4.97 | 5.68 | -0.7 |

Breakout: 0%   Improve: 0%   Collapse: 0%   Attrition: 0%   MLB: 0%      *Comparables: Steven Jackson, Joel Hanrahan, Cesar Carrillo*

**Drafted/Acquired:** 7th round, 2011 draft, University of Mississippi (Oxford, MS)

**Previous Ranking:** NR

**What Happened in 2013:** The diminutive righty eventually transitioned from starter to reliever, where he saw a spike in his stuff and put himself on the fast track to the major leagues with a strong showing in the Arizona Fall League.

**Strengths:** Near-elite arm strength; fastball can work in the mid- to upper-90s; power pitch; easy plus-plus offering; shows bat-breaking hard cutter in the upper-80s/low-90s; shows a low-80s slider that can miss bat; aggressive late-innings approach.

**Weaknesses:** Shorter than listed height; needs to work down to create plane; secondary arsenal comes and goes; hard slider/cutter can play too short/flat; shows below-average curveball and changeup; command is below average.

**Risk Factor/Injury History:** Low risk; limited Double-A experience.

**Bret Sayre's Fantasy Take:** There's really nothing to see here from a potential good middle reliever. Even if you're in an NL-only league that counts holds, you don't want to bother here.

**The Year Ahead:** What Goforth lacks in size he makes up for with fastball velocity, an attribute that will eventually carry him to the back of a major-league bullpen. He doesn't have wipeout secondary stuff, but if he can refine his command, he can pound with mid- to upper-90s fastball and make the slider/cutter combo more effective as a result. It shouldn't take the 25-year-old righty long to establish himself as a legit back-of-the-bullpen force at the major-league level.

---

## 10.  Yadiel Rivera  SS

**Born:** 5/2/92  **Age:** 22  **Bats:** R  **Throws:** R  **Height:** 6'2"  **Weight:** 175

| MLB ETA | Hit | Power | Run | Glove | Arm | OFP | Realistic |
|---|---|---|---|---|---|---|---|
| Late 2015 | — | 50 | — | 65 | 55 | 50<br>ML REGULAR | 45<br>UTILITY |

| YEAR | TEAM | LVL | AGE | PA | R | 2B | 3B | HR | RBI | BB | SO | SB | CS | AVG/OBP/SLG | TAv | BABIP | BRR | FRAA | WARP |
|---|---|---|---|---|---|---|---|---|---|---|---|---|---|---|---|---|---|---|---|
| 2013 | BRV | A+ | 21 | 524 | 51 | 16 | 2 | 5 | 37 | 32 | 80 | 13 | 8 | .241/.300/.314 | .242 | .279 | 1.4 | SS(129): 20.2 | 3.6 |
| 2014 | MIL | MLB | 22 | 250 | 23 | 8 | 1 | 4 | 20 | 8 | 67 | 2 | 1 | .207/.236/.303 | .196 | .260 | -0.2 | SS 2 | -0.4 |
| 2015 | MIL | MLB | 23 | 250 | 24 | 8 | 1 | 5 | 23 | 10 | 62 | 1 | 0 | .219/.255/.323 | .214 | .271 | -0.4 | SS 2 | -0.9 |

Breakout: 0%   Improve: 0%   Collapse: 0%   Attrition: 0%   MLB: 0%      *Comparables: German Duran, Argenis Diaz, Jordy Mercer*

**Drafted/Acquired:** 9th round, 2010 draft, Manuela Toro HS (Caguas, PR)

**Previous Ranking:** On The Rise

**What Happened in 2013:** In his first pass in the Florida State League, the Puerto Rican shortstop swung an empty stick, making weak contact and slugging an anemic .314.

**Strengths:** Excellent hands/actions on defense; fluid and effortless; arm is strong enough to make the throws; can stick at the position all the way up; bigger-than-expected raw power; has a plan at the plate.

**Weaknesses:** Hit tool is well below average; linear in-game stroke; fringe bat speed and weak contact; raw power doesn't translate into games; struggles against off-speed offerings and good velocity; lacks plus run; range built on instincts and positioning.

**Risk Factor/Injury History:** Moderate risk; glove can play; bat is a big question mark; yet to play at Double-A level

**Bret Sayre's Fantasy Take:** Rivera is like a poor man's Orlando Arcia from a fantasy standpoint, and Arcia wasn't all that interesting. He shouldn't be rostered outside of Yadiel-only leagues.

**The Year Ahead:** I'm still relatively high on Rivera despite the realities of his bat, as the fluid and natural actions in the field are above average at a premium defensive position. With a solid approach and good raw pop, you would think the bat had more projection and promise than it currently shows, which is possibly true. While the bat needs to step up for him to become a major-league regular, the baseball instincts and glovework will eventually carry him to the majors. But it's a utility-at-best profile if the stick doesn't start packing a bigger punch, and the pitching isn't going to get any easier at the Double-A level.

## Prospects on the Rise

**1. RHP Jorge Lopez:** I thought 2013 would be the breakout season for the Puerto Rican arm, but Lopez struggled with stuff and command in his full-season debut. The athletic and highly projectable righty has all the necessary components to right the command ship and let the plus stuff out in game action, an eventuality that will push him into the top-10 list and onto the national prospect landscape.

**2. 3B Tucker Neuhaus:** A second-round pick in the 2013 draft, Neuhaus has all the tools to blossom into a top-10 talent in this system, a distinction that his paper grades make a case for right now. With a very big arm in the field and a clean, powerful stroke at the plate, the 18-year-old brings a potent dual-threat profile to the field, a player with the potential to hit for average and power while showing a good glove at the hot corner (his eventual home). He's very young, so it's going to take time. But the projections make him a very interesting prospect to keep an eye on.

**3. SS Franly Mallen:** A recent signing in the J2 international market, Mallen was one of the top shortstop prospects available in the class. The 16-year-old Dominican will show good actions in the field with a strong, and enough bat speed and bat control at the plate to offer average or better offensive projections. Because of his age, the projection (both physically and emotionally) is very abstract, but in a system that is thin on Latin American talent, signing Mallen was a step in the right direction.

## Factors on the Farm

### Prospects likely to contribute at the major-league level in 2014

**1. 1B Hunter Morris:** With above-average pop from the left side, Morris was able to rip 53 extra-base hits in his Triple-A debut, but his struggles against arm-side stuff and high whiff rates could limit his major-league role to that of a platoon bat, assuming the opportunity opens up at the position at some point in 2014.

**2. 1B Jason Rogers:** With big boy raw power from the right side, Rogers has a chance to hit his way to the major-league level in 2014, but positional deficiency clouds the path, as does his struggles against arm-side pitching. If you put Hunter Morris and Jason Rogers together, you might just have a first-division first baseman: Hunter Rogers/Jason Morris.

**3. RHP Ariel Pena:** A large and in charge Dominican arm with a big fastball, Pena has the stuff to pitch at the major-league level in 2014, even though his below-average command points to a bullpen future.

## 1. Byron Buxton  CF

**Born:** 12/18/93  **Age:** 20  **Bats:** R  **Throws:** R  **Height:** 6' 2"  **Weight:** 190

| MLB ETA | Hit | Power | Run | Glove | Arm | OFP | Realistic |
|---------|-----|-------|-----|-------|-----|-----|-----------|
| Late 2014 | 60 | 70 | 80 | 70 | 60 | 80<br>ELITE POTENTIAL | 65<br>1ST DIV/ALL-STAR |

| YEAR | TEAM | LVL | AGE | PA | R | 2B | 3B | HR | RBI | BB | SO | SB | CS | AVG/OBP/SLG | TAv | BABIP | BRR | FRAA | WARP |
|------|------|-----|-----|-----|----|----|----|----|-----|----|----|----|----|-------------|------|-------|-----|------|------|
| 2013 | CDR | A | 19 | 321 | 68 | 15 | 10 | 8 | 55 | 44 | 56 | 32 | 11 | .341/.431/.559 | .349 | .402 | 4.6 | CF(66): 3.5 | 5.0 |
| 2013 | FTM | A+ | 19 | 253 | 41 | 4 | 8 | 4 | 22 | 32 | 49 | 23 | 8 | .326/.415/.472 | .320 | .404 | 5.0 | CF(55): 5.1 | 3.6 |
| 2014 | MIN | MLB | 20 | 250 | 33 | 8 | 3 | 5 | 21 | 22 | 63 | 13 | 5 | .250/.319/.374 | .257 | .320 | 1.2 | CF 4, LF 0 | 1.2 |
| 2015 | MIN | MLB | 21 | 607 | 75 | 22 | 8 | 15 | 69 | 66 | 147 | 28 | 10 | .261/.344/.416 | .284 | .330 | 2.3 | CF 8 | 3.7 |

**Breakout:** 10%   **Improve:** 16%   **Collapse:** 0%   **Attrition:** 6%   **MLB:** 20%   *Comparables: Mike Trout, Fernando Martinez, Justin Upton*

**Drafted/Acquired:** 1st round, 2012 draft, Appling County HS (Baxley, GA)

**Previous Ranking:** #1 (Org), #8 (Top 101)

**What Happened in 2013:** With only a short-season resume to work with, we decided to rank Buxton in the top 10 in baseball coming into the year, and he rewarded our faith by blossoming into the top overall prospect in baseball.

**Strengths:** Well-above-average athlete; elite run; glove could end up plus-plus or better; arm is plus; hit tool is advanced; lets balls travel deep into the zone; quick hands and explosive bat speed; power potential is plus (some sources suggest it could be plus-plus at maturity); advanced approach at the plate.

**Weaknesses:** Still transitioning from raw athlete to skill player; needs to refine base-running utility; scout sources are mixed on future game power output; has struggled against plus breaking stuff.

**Risk Factor/Injury History:** Moderate risk; yet to play at Double-A level.

**Bret Sayre's Fantasy Take:** Just give me a second to take a breath and collect my thoughts. The sky is the limit with Buxton, but you already knew that. He has a chance to be the best player in fantasy with his combination of tools—the same type of value that we've seen from Mike Trout the last two seasons. It's a clear five-category profile with impact potential in steals.

**The Year Ahead:** Buxton is a monster athlete, with elite speed, near-elite potential in center field, a potent hit tool, and raw power that some think could end up emerging as yet another plus-plus tool in the coming years. He will move to Double-A in 2014, and barring an unforeseen developmental setback, Buxton will likely taste major-league action as a 20-year-old. One scout suggested Buxton's career floor was Torii Hunter, which is both a ridiculous bar of success to reach and an absolutely justifiable suggestion based on the physical gifts. I don't even want to discuss what the ceiling might look like.

> #1
> BP Top 101 Prospects

## 2. Miguel Sano  3B

**Born:** 5/11/93  **Age:** 21  **Bats:** R  **Throws:** R  **Height:** 6' 4"  **Weight:** 235

| MLB ETA | Hit | Power | Run | Glove | Arm | OFP | Realistic |
|---------|-----|-------|-----|-------|-----|-----|-----------|
| Late 2014 | ---- | 80 | 50 | 55 | 70 | 70<br>ALL-STAR | 60<br>1ST DIV PLAYER |

| YEAR | TEAM | LVL | AGE | PA | R | 2B | 3B | HR | RBI | BB | SO | SB | CS | AVG/OBP/SLG | TAv | BABIP | BRR | FRAA | WARP |
|------|------|-----|-----|-----|----|----|----|----|-----|----|----|----|----|-------------|------|-------|-----|------|------|
| 2013 | NBR | AA | 20 | 276 | 35 | 15 | 3 | 19 | 55 | 36 | 81 | 2 | 1 | .236/.344/.571 | .312 | .265 | -0.9 | 3B(64): 2.8 | 2.4 |
| 2013 | FTM | A+ | 20 | 243 | 51 | 15 | 2 | 16 | 48 | 29 | 61 | 9 | 2 | .330/.424/.655 | .366 | .397 | 2.8 | 3B(56): -1.4 | 3.6 |
| 2014 | MIN | MLB | 21 | 250 | 32 | 10 | 2 | 13 | 38 | 24 | 79 | 1 | 1 | .228/.307/.460 | .272 | .280 | -0.2 | 3B -1, SS 0 | 0.9 |
| 2015 | MIN | MLB | 22 | 517 | 74 | 19 | 2 | 28 | 78 | 57 | 160 | 2 | 1 | .227/.318/.465 | .281 | .280 | -0.7 | 3B -1 | 1.3 |

**Breakout:** 5%   **Improve:** 24%   **Collapse:** 1%   **Attrition:** 7%   **MLB:** 32%   *Comparables: Giancarlo Stanton, Jay Bruce, Colby Rasmus*

**Drafted/Acquired:** International free agent, 2009, Dominican Republic

**Previous Ranking:** #2 (Org), #21 (Top 101)

**What Happened in 2013:** As a 20-year-old, Sano hit 70 extra-base hits over two stops, including 35 bombs—half of which have yet to land.

**Strengths:** Massive raw strength/power; 8 grade power potential; better athlete than people realize; can produce plus run times to first; arm is a 7; glove could end up being 5+; aptitude for the game.

**Weaknesses:** Leveraged swing with length; has swing-and-miss in the zone; can struggle against off-speed offerings; hit tool might play below average; hot-corner defense comes and goes; good coming in on balls but struggles going side-to-side.

**Risk Factor/Injury History:** Moderate risk; only 21 years old; struggled (somewhat) in Double-A debut.

> #14
> BP Top 101 Prospects

**Bret Sayre's Fantasy Take:** Sano's ability to contribute in home runs, RBI, and runs scored is rarely up for discussion among analysts, but the two categories that remain are where the debate lies. Sano could hit 40 homers annually and still not be a first-round talent (Adam Dunn never was), but if he can either hit at least .260 or steal double-digit bases, that's Giancarlo Stanton territory. With third-base eligibility, no less.

**The Year Ahead:** Sano is the best all-around power threat in the minors, with elite raw power and a hit tool that should allow most of it to show up in game action. His swing can get loose and he will chase outside the zone despite showing a willingness to take a walk when he's pitched around, so pitchers with a plan and command of off-speed offerings can trip him up. When he connects, the ball goes a long way, and if he can improve his bat control and ability to square up movement, he could develop into a middle-of-the-order monster and a future all-star at the major-league level.

---

## 3. Alex Meyer  RHP

**Born:** 1/3/90  **Age:** 24  **Bats:** R  **Throws:** R  **Height:** 6'9"  **Weight:** 220

| MLB ETA | CT | FB | CH | CB | SL | OFP | Realistic |
|---|---|---|---|---|---|---|---|
| 2014 | -- | 80 | 55 | -- | 65 | 60<br>NO.2-3 STARTER | 60<br>LATE INN RP (CL) |

| YEAR | TEAM | LVL | AGE | W | L | SV | G | GS | IP | H | HR | BB | SO | BB9 | SO9 | GB% | BABIP | WHIP | ERA | FIP | FRA | WARP |
|---|---|---|---|---|---|---|---|---|---|---|---|---|---|---|---|---|---|---|---|---|---|---|
| 2013 | TWI | Rk | 23 | 0 | 0 | 0 | 3 | 3 | 8.3 | 7 | 0 | 3 | 16 | 3.2 | 17.3 | 60% | .467 | 1.20 | 1.08 | 0.70 | 1.66 | 0.4 |
| 2013 | NBR | AA | 23 | 4 | 3 | 0 | 13 | 13 | 70.0 | 60 | 3 | 29 | 84 | 3.7 | 10.8 | 61% | .317 | 1.27 | 3.21 | 2.85 | 3.79 | 1.4 |
| 2014 | MIN | MLB | 24 | 4 | 5 | 0 | 14 | 14 | 72.7 | 72 | 7 | 32 | 66 | 4.0 | 8.2 | 51% | .306 | 1.43 | 4.27 | 4.26 | 4.64 | 0.5 |
| 2015 | MIN | MLB | 25 | 8 | 7 | 0 | 60 | 19 | 154.7 | 142 | 16 | 56 | 150 | 3.3 | 8.7 | 51% | .296 | 1.28 | 3.64 | 3.77 | 3.95 | 2.0 |

Breakout: 21%    Improve: 42%    Collapse: 10%    Attrition: 31%    MLB: 56%    *Comparables: Jake Arrieta, Jose Cisnero, James Paxton*

**Drafted/Acquired:** 1st round, 2011 draft, University of Kentucky (Lexington, KY)

**Previous Ranking:** #88 (Top 101)

**What Happened in 2013:** A shoulder injury limited Meyer's workload in 2013, but when healthy he was a force on the mound, looking dominant at times in Double-A and taking another step forward in the Arizona Fall League.

**Strengths:** Length you can't teach; good athlete for size; coordinated; big-time arm strength; fastball can work mid- to upper-90s; has touched triple digits; good vertical action; could grade to 8; slider is easy plus offering and possibly a 7; mid-80s with depth and sharp two-plane slice; has flashed plus changeup.

**Weaknesses:** Command is below average; athletic but lots of body to control; can lose delivery; struggle to repeat mechanics throughout a game; can slow body on secondary offerings; changeup can lose arm-speed deception.

**Risk Factor/Injury History:** Low risk; ready for major-league challenge; shoulder injuries are a concern.

**Bret Sayre's Fantasy Take:** The great thing about Meyer from a fantasy perspective is that even if it doesn't work for him in the rotation, his major-league fallback plan won't lower his draft slots much. In the rotation, he has the stuff to strike out close to a batter an inning, but with a slightly elevated WHIP (think around 1.25-1.30). In the bullpen, he could be a top-10 closer.

**The Year Ahead:** Industry sources continue to offer mixed prognostications about Meyer's long-term role, and I can honestly say that I don't have a strong feeling either way. The body is a paradox, with length you dream about but length you struggle to control over the course of a game. The arm strength is elite, and the fastball grade could reach that status with improved command. The slider is of the knockout variety, and even the changeup, which graded below average coming into the season, now has some sources putting a plus grade on its future. In a rotation, he has the stuff to stand out, but the command and mechanical inconsistency could lead to erratic production; a gem one start and an early exit the next. In the bullpen, he could develop into a top-shelf closer, even if the command is a little shaky. Meyer is a low-risk, role 6 arm regardless of whether he is pitching in a rotation or out of the bullpen. Impact talent.

> **#32**
> BP Top
> 101
> Prospects

---

## 4. Kohl Stewart  RHP

**Born:** 10/7/94  **Age:** 19  **Bats:** R  **Throws:** R  **Height:** 6'3"  **Weight:** 195

| MLB ETA | CT | FB | CH | CB | SL | OFP | Realistic |
|---|---|---|---|---|---|---|---|
| 2016 | -- | 70 | 55 | 55 | 70 | 70<br>NO.1-2 STARTER | 60<br>NO.3 STARTER |

| YEAR | TEAM | LVL | AGE | W | L | SV | G | GS | IP | H | HR | BB | SO | BB9 | SO9 | GB% | BABIP | WHIP | ERA | FIP | FRA | WARP |
|---|---|---|---|---|---|---|---|---|---|---|---|---|---|---|---|---|---|---|---|---|---|---|
| 2013 | ELZ | Rk | 18 | 0 | 0 | 0 | 1 | 1 | 4.0 | 1 | 0 | 1 | 8 | 2.2 | 18.0 | 20% | .200 | 0.50 | 0.00 | 0.93 | 2.25 | 0.1 |
| 2013 | TWI | Rk | 18 | 0 | 0 | 0 | 6 | 3 | 16.0 | 12 | 0 | 3 | 16 | 1.7 | 9.0 | 58% | .250 | 0.94 | 1.69 | 2.21 | 4.34 | 0.1 |
| 2014 | MIN | MLB | 19 | 1 | 2 | 0 | 9 | 5 | 30.7 | 39 | 4 | 20 | 15 | 5.9 | 4.4 | 45% | .316 | 1.91 | 6.72 | 6.35 | 7.30 | -0.6 |
| 2015 | MIN | MLB | 20 | 3 | 5 | 1 | 30 | 13 | 113.7 | 132 | 16 | 66 | 72 | 5.2 | 5.7 | 45% | .309 | 1.74 | 6.03 | 5.65 | 6.55 | -1.8 |

Breakout: 0%    Improve: 0%    Collapse: 0%    Attrition: 0%    MLB: 0%    *Comparables: Brad Hand, Stolmy Pimentel, Joe Wieland*

**Drafted/Acquired:** 1st round, 2013 draft, St. Pius X HS (Houston, TX)

**Previous Ranking:** NR

**What Happened in 2013:** After being drafted fourth overall, Stewart made the most of his brief 20-inning debut, striking out 24 while walking only four hitters.

**Strengths:** Athletic build; good delivery; arm is very fast; fastball is a future 7 pitch; works low-90s and can get to mid-90s; creates good angle; velocity will tick up; slider is second plus offering; mid-80s with big bite; curveball flashes plus, could play as average-or-better offering; good up/down pitch; changeup projects to be average or better; command profile could end up above average; big competitor.

**Weaknesses:** More polish than projection; body is mature for age; secondary command is below average; change-up can get too firm/overthrown.

**Risk Factor/Injury History:** High risk; health concerns on resume (type 1 diabetes); limited professional experience.

**Bret Sayre's Fantasy Take:** Stewart has the higher fantasy upside than Meyer, but clearly the risk is greater. With two potential plus-plus pitches, the strikeouts should come in spades if he hits anything resembling his ceiling. And with Target Field at his back, suppressing power from the left-hand side, it's not difficult to envision Stewart's path to being a top-10 fantasy starter.

**The Year Ahead:** Several sources thought Stewart was the best pitcher available in the 2013 draft, a future number one type that could move quickly through a developmental system. The profile is what you want to see in a frontline arm; plus-plus potential fastball, plus-plus potential slider, quality curveball for sight line/timing disruption, and a changeup that could be average or better. The command needs to improve, but with an athletic delivery and easy arm, the stuff could reach its potential. This is a very high-end talent that should move faster than most high-school arms, and by the end of next season, Stewart could find himself in the discussion for top pitcher in the minor-league class.

#54
BP Top
101
Prospects

## 5. Josmil Pinto  C

**Born:** 3/31/89  **Age:** 25  **Bats:** R  **Throws:** R  **Height:** 5'11"  **Weight:** 210

| | Hit | Power | Run | Glove | Arm | | OFP | Realistic |
|---|---|---|---|---|---|---|---|---|
| MLB ETA | 50 | 60 | – | 50 | 55 | | 55 | 50 |
| Debuted in 2013 | | | | | | | >AVG PLAYER | AVG ML REGULAR |

| YEAR | TEAM | LVL | AGE | PA | R | 2B | 3B | HR | RBI | BB | SO | SB | CS | AVG/OBP/SLG | TAv | BABIP | BRR | FRAA | WARP |
|---|---|---|---|---|---|---|---|---|---|---|---|---|---|---|---|---|---|---|---|
| 2013 | NBR | AA | 24 | 453 | 59 | 23 | 1 | 14 | 68 | 64 | 71 | 0 | 2 | .308/.411/.482 | .320 | .349 | -1.5 | C(60): 0.0 | 3.9 |
| 2013 | ROC | AAA | 24 | 75 | 6 | 9 | 0 | 1 | 6 | 2 | 12 | 0 | 0 | .314/.333/.486 | .248 | .356 | -1.3 | C(14): -0.3 | 0.1 |
| 2013 | MIN | MLB | 24 | 83 | 10 | 5 | 0 | 4 | 12 | 6 | 22 | 0 | 0 | .342/.398/.566 | .337 | .440 | -0.4 | C(20): -0.2 | 1.1 |
| 2014 | MIN | MLB | 25 | 250 | 26 | 12 | 1 | 7 | 30 | 19 | 52 | 0 | 0 | .262/.320/.414 | .265 | .310 | -0.5 | C -0 | 1.0 |
| 2015 | MIN | MLB | 26 | 530 | 61 | 26 | 1 | 13 | 58 | 42 | 110 | 0 | 0 | .248/.310/.389 | .256 | .293 | -1.3 | C -1 | 0.8 |

Breakout: 6%   Improve: 29%   Collapse: 7%   Attrition: 30%   MLB: 57%     *Comparables: Geovany Soto, Josh Donaldson, Ronny Paulino*

**Drafted/Acquired:** International free agent, 2006, Venezuela

**Previous Ranking:** NR

**What Happened in 2013:** After over 1,600 at-bats at the minor-league level, Pinto erupted in 2013, hitting for average and power over three stops, including a highly impressive 21-game run at the major-league level.

**Strengths:** Plus raw power; good overall feel for hitting; short to the ball; nothing fancy in the swing; stays balanced; good approach; works himself into favorable hitting conditions; arm is strong; good catch/throw skills; glove is at least average; good receiver with leadership skills.

**Weaknesses:** Well-below-average run; footwork behind the plate can be sluggish and slow; not an impact defender; potential to be good but not great hitter.

**Risk Factor/Injury History:** Low risk; major-league ready

**Bret Sayre's Fantasy Take:** The most exciting thing to happen in 2013 for Pinto's fantasy value wasn't his breakout performance at Double-A or taking it up a notch at the major-league level. It was the news of Joe Mauer being moved full-time to first base that gets Pinto shooting up draft boards. A catcher who could hit .270 with 20 homers in short order? Sign me up, please.

**The Year Ahead:** Pinto's 2013 breakthrough was legit, as I watched him in New Britain over the summer and came away impressed by his bat, his ability behind the plate, and his overall approach to the game. He's not a middle-of-the-order hitter and he's not a shutdown defender, but he is likely to be a consistent solid-average player at a premium position, one that could hit .275+ with 15 bombs while playing average (or better) defense. It's a very nice profile.

#56
BP Top
101
Prospects

## 6. Jose Berrios RHP

**Born:** 5/27/94 **Age:** 20 **Bats:** R **Throws:** R **Height:** 6'0" **Weight:** 187

| MLB ETA | CT | FB | CH | CB | SL | OFP | Realistic |
|---------|----|----|----|----|----|-----|-----------|
| 2016 | – | 60 | 60 | 60 | – | 60<br>NO.3 STARTER | 50<br>LATE INN RP (SU) |

| YEAR | TEAM | LVL | AGE | W | L | SV | G | GS | IP | H | HR | BB | SO | BB9 | SO9 | GB% | BABIP | WHIP | ERA | FIP | FRA | WARP |
|------|------|-----|-----|---|---|----|----|----|----|---|----|----|----|-----|-----|-----|-------|------|-----|-----|-----|------|
| 2013 | CDR | A | 19 | 7 | 7 | 0 | 19 | 19 | 103.7 | 105 | 6 | 40 | 100 | 3.5 | 8.7 | 45% | .330 | 1.40 | 3.99 | 3.58 | 4.69 | 1.5 |
| 2014 | MIN | MLB | 20 | 3 | 6 | 0 | 14 | 14 | 73.7 | 83 | 9 | 37 | 53 | 4.5 | 6.5 | 43% | .314 | 1.64 | 5.44 | 5.25 | 5.91 | -0.6 |
| 2015 | MIN | MLB | 21 | 8 | 10 | 0 | 27 | 27 | 162.0 | 172 | 20 | 78 | 125 | 4.3 | 6.9 | 43% | .303 | 1.54 | 5.05 | 4.83 | 5.49 | -0.7 |

Breakout: 0%   Improve: 0%   Collapse: 0%   Attrition: 0%   MLB: 0%   *Comparables: Jenrry Mejia, Jarrod Parker, Arodys Vizcaino*

**#75**
BP Top 101 Prospects

**Drafted/Acquired:** 1st round, 2012 draft, Papa Juan HS (Bayamon, PR)

**Previous Ranking:** #7 (Org)

**What Happened in 2013:** In his full-season debut, Berrios made 19 starts and logged over 100 innings, but started to fade down the stretch and the electric stuff was a little sapped.

**Strengths:** Extremely fast arm; athletic delivery; fastball routinely works 92-96; very lively when spotted lower in the zone; hard curveball offers plenty of snap and depth; swing-and-miss pitch; turns over a good changeup; good arm-speed deception; plus projection.

**Weaknesses:** Limited size (height); has to work down to create angle; struggles with hard contact when he elevates; struggled to maintain stuff in '13; shows control but command is presently below average; can slip to the side of the curve/get slurvy.

**Risk Factor/Injury History:** High risk; only 20 years old; limited professional experience.

**Bret Sayre's Fantasy Take:** There are ballparks where Berrios would not profile well. Fortunately for him, Target Field is not one of them. He's had a tough time keeping the ball on the ground in his short pro career thus far (less than 40 percent ground-ball rate), but the strikeout potential is real, even if he comes with a few too many long balls. He can be a very solid fantasy starter, just not someone to build a staff around.

**The Year Ahead:** I really like Berrios, and even though I listed his realistic role as a late-innings reliever, I think he has the stuff and the approach to make it work in a rotation. He needs to get stronger in order to maintain his stuff, and because of his size, he needs to refine his command and hit his spots lower in the zone. But with three quality pitches and feel for craft, he has a good chance of figuring it out and developing into a mid-rotation type.

## 7. Eddie Rosario 2B/CF

**Born:** 9/28/91 **Age:** 22 **Bats:** L **Throws:** R **Height:** 6'1" **Weight:** 180

| MLB ETA | Hit | Power | Run | Glove | Arm | OFP | Realistic |
|---------|-----|-------|-----|-------|-----|-----|-----------|
| Late 2014 | 60 | 50 | 60 | -- | -- | 55<br>>AVG PLAYER | 50<br>2ND DIV PLAYER |

| YEAR | TEAM | LVL | AGE | PA | R | 2B | 3B | HR | RBI | BB | SO | SB | CS | AVG/OBP/SLG | TAv | BABIP | BRR | FRAA | WARP |
|------|------|-----|-----|----|---|----|----|----|-----|----|----|----|----|-------------|-----|-------|-----|------|------|
| 2013 | FTM | A+ | 21 | 231 | 40 | 13 | 5 | 6 | 35 | 17 | 29 | 3 | 6 | .329/.377/.527 | .317 | .350 | -2.5 | 2B(50): 8.9 | 2.9 |
| 2013 | NBR | AA | 21 | 313 | 40 | 19 | 3 | 4 | 38 | 21 | 67 | 7 | 4 | .284/.330/.412 | .269 | .355 | -1.0 | 2B(65): -5.8 | 0.6 |
| 2014 | MIN | MLB | 22 | 250 | 25 | 12 | 2 | 5 | 27 | 11 | 56 | 4 | 3 | .251/.285/.385 | .241 | .300 | -0.3 | 2B -0, CF -0 | 0.3 |
| 2015 | MIN | MLB | 23 | 250 | 27 | 13 | 2 | 6 | 28 | 13 | 58 | 3 | 2 | .257/.297/.407 | .254 | .315 | -0.5 | 2B 0, CF 0 | 1.3 |

Breakout: 0%   Improve: 0%   Collapse: 0%   Attrition: 0%   MLB: 0%   *Comparables: Henry Rodriguez, Brandon Laird, Nick Franklin*

**#60**
BP Top 101 Prospects

**Drafted/Acquired:** 4th round, 2010 draft, Rafael Lopez Landron HS (Guayama, PR)

**Previous Ranking:** #6 (Org)

**What Happened in 2013:** Rosario crushed in the Florida State League, and after a promotion to Double-A, continued to show off his plus hit tool, racking up 82 hits in 70 games against older competition.

**Strengths:** Excellent bat-to-ball; fast hands and a pretty swing; pure hitter; runs well; very good athlete; has good pop in the stick; might end up with average game power.

**Weaknesses:** Can carry over bad batting-practice habits into game action; will drop shoulder and elevate plane for power; lacks the strength for this approach; glove at second is below average; arm can make throws but not a weapon; hit tool could end up being only carrying tool; could end up empty.

**Risk Factor/Injury History:** Moderate risk; room to grow; solid Double-A debut.

**Bret Sayre's Fantasy Take:** Here's where the real-life value and the fantasy diverge. Rosario is not a good defender at the keystone, but fantasy owners don't care as long as he has the eligibility. If he were to stick there, he'd have top-five second baseman potential, in the mold of a Jason Kipnis that just wasn't quite left in the oven long enough (think 20 steals instead of 30).

**The Year Ahead:** Rosario can hit a baseball, and that's going to take him to the major-league level. His swing is quick and fluid, but when he attempts to wear a power costume, it doesn't fit and the outcomes suffer. I didn't like his actions or approach at second, and I didn't see enough feel for big improvements on that side of the ball. I can see a move back to the outfield where the above-average speed and athleticism would play better, but if he stays at second, it's hard to envision an average defensive profile at the position. This is a bat-first player that could end up hitting .280+ at the highest level, with extra-base hit potential and good wheels.

## 8. Lewis Thorpe  LHP

**Born:** 11/23/95  **Age:** 18  **Bats:** R  **Throws:** L  **Height:** 6' 1"  **Weight:** 160

| MLB ETA | CT | FB | CH | CB | SL | OFP | Realistic |
|---|---|---|---|---|---|---|---|
| 2017 | – | 70 | 65 | 60 | – | 70 NO.2 STARTER | 50 NO.4 STARTER |

| YEAR | TEAM | LVL | AGE | W | L | SV | G | GS | IP | H | HR | BB | SO | BB9 | SO9 | GB% | BABIP | WHIP | ERA | FIP | FRA | WARP |
|---|---|---|---|---|---|---|---|---|---|---|---|---|---|---|---|---|---|---|---|---|---|---|
| 2013 | TWI | Rk | 17 | 4 | 1 | 0 | 12 | 8 | 44.0 | 32 | 2 | 6 | 64 | 1.2 | 13.1 | 45% | .319 | 0.86 | 2.05 | 1.69 | 3.08 | 1.3 |
| 2014 | MIN | MLB | 18 | 1 | 2 | 0 | 8 | 5 | 32.0 | 36 | 4 | 19 | 23 | 5.3 | 6.5 | 43% | .315 | 1.73 | 5.79 | 5.61 | 6.30 | -0.3 |
| 2015 | MIN | MLB | 19 | 5 | 6 | 1 | 32 | 19 | 147.7 | 149 | 18 | 68 | 111 | 4.1 | 6.8 | 43% | .291 | 1.47 | 4.54 | 4.75 | 4.94 | 0.2 |

Breakout: 0%   Improve: 0%   Collapse: 0%   Attrition: 0%   MLB: 0%   *Comparables: Jordan Lyles, Wilmer Font, Arodys Vizcaino*

**Drafted/Acquired:** International free agent, 2012, Australia

**Previous Ranking:** NR

**What Happened in 2013:** The then-17-year-old Aussie made his professional debut in the Gulf Coast League, and the scouting backed up the stats, as his advanced arsenal and execution made him one of the better prospects in the circuit.

**Strengths:** Projectable body; delivery is easy and repeatable; arm works very well; fastball works 89-93; touches 95; good arm-side life; shows plus potential curveball; tight rotation and vertical depth; good command of the pitch; can turn over a promising changeup; overall command profile is excellent; advanced pitchability.

**Weaknesses:** Still physically immature; velocity spike yet to be tested in workload; secondary stuff is still on the come (obviously); limited professional sample.

**Risk Factor/Injury History:** Extreme risk; will pitch '14 season at age 18; complex-league resume.

**Bret Sayre's Fantasy Take:** In a system with no shortage of dreams, Thorpe is the freshest one from a fantasy standpoint. Likely unowned in your league, unless you play extremely deep, it's tough to match his star upside—even among 2013 draftees. It makes sense to jump on him in offseason drafts, especially in shallower leagues, with his potential to break out in 2014.

**The Year Ahead:** Thanks to his international performances, Thorpe has been on the prospect radar for a while, but it wasn't until his GCL dominance that he became a name you can't forget. There is a lot of room to grow here, both physically and from an arsenal standpoint, so there will be ebbs and flows in the developmental process. If he can maintain control over his body as he fills out, while intensifying the stuff without losing his advanced feel, Thorpe could end up one of the better arms in the minors. At the end of the day (which is a long way off), the Australian southpaw could be a low- to mid-90s velo type, with multiple secondary looks that play above average or better, all delivered in a smooth, repeatable manner that allows everything to play up thanks to strong command. That's an abnormal profile. That could be a number two starter on a championship-caliber team. Look for another run in short-season ball in 2014 followed by a full-season breakout scheduled for 2015.

**#101**
BP Top 101 Prospects

## 9. Felix Jorge  RHP

**Born:** 1/2/94  **Age:** 20  **Bats:** R  **Throws:** R  **Height:** 6' 2"  **Weight:** 170

| MLB ETA | CT | FB | CH | CB | SL | OFP | Realistic |
|---|---|---|---|---|---|---|---|
| 2017 | – | 70 | 50 | – | 60 | 60 NO.3 STARTER | 50 LATE INN RP (SU) |

| YEAR | TEAM | LVL | AGE | W | L | SV | G | GS | IP | H | HR | BB | SO | BB9 | SO9 | GB% | BABIP | WHIP | ERA | FIP | FRA | WARP |
|---|---|---|---|---|---|---|---|---|---|---|---|---|---|---|---|---|---|---|---|---|---|---|
| 2013 | ELZ | Rk | 19 | 2 | 2 | 0 | 12 | 12 | 61.0 | 56 | 2 | 18 | 72 | 2.7 | 10.6 | 54% | .335 | 1.21 | 2.95 | 2.48 | 3.52 | 1.4 |
| 2014 | MIN | MLB | 20 | 1 | 4 | 0 | 11 | 8 | 41.7 | 51 | 5 | 27 | 25 | 5.8 | 5.4 | 45% | .317 | 1.86 | 6.48 | 5.91 | 7.04 | -0.7 |
| 2015 | MIN | MLB | 21 | 6 | 10 | 0 | 26 | 26 | 154.7 | 173 | 21 | 78 | 103 | 4.5 | 6.0 | 46% | .302 | 1.63 | 5.64 | 5.28 | 6.13 | -1.6 |

Breakout: 0%   Improve: 0%   Collapse: 0%   Attrition: 0%   MLB: 0%   *Comparables: Carlos Carrasco, J.C. Ramirez, Jon Niese*

**Drafted/Acquired:** International free agent, 2010, Dominican Republic

**Previous Ranking:** NR

**What Happened in 2013:** The highly projectable Dominican arm made 12 starts in the Appalachian League, missing 72 bats in only 61 innings, appearing to take steps forward with each subsequent start.

**Strengths:** Loose arm; electric; very good arm action; projectable body; athletic; fastball works 90-95; projects to be plus-plus offering at maturity; slider already flashes its potential; hard offering with tilt; turns over changeup and shows feel for the pitch; looks the part on the mound; plus makeup reports.

**Weaknesses:** Command is loose; fastball velocity fluctuates; arm will slow on secondaries; can lose pace/tempo in delivery; learning to attack with fastball, but can be passive at times and rely too much on secondary stuff

**Risk Factor/Injury History:** High risk; 20 years old; yet to pitch at full-season level.

**Bret Sayre's Fantasy Take:** Another potential 2014 breakout pick, Jorge doesn't have the ceiling that Thorpe does, but it's impressive nonetheless. His 4.0 strikeout-to-walk rate in Elizabethton hints at the ability to lay down strong ratios, but his changeup holds the key to his fantasy future.

**The Year Ahead:** This is a live arm that comes with some feel, a dangerous profile if everything clicks. With excellent reports on the makeup and aptitude, Jorge has a chance to not only stick around in a rotation but excel in that role. The fastball needs to find consistency, but it's highly projectable and could develop into a lively 93-95 offering (even higher in bursts), backed up by a hard breaking ball and a changeup that he already feels comfortable throwing in sequence. He will move up to the full-season level in 2014, and a strong showing will push him up the prospect ranks and possibly land him in the top 101 by the end of the season.

## 10. Jorge Polanco 2B

**Born:** 7/5/93  **Age:** 20  **Bats:** B  **Throws:** R  **Height:** 5'11"  **Weight:** 165

| Hit | Power | Run | Glove | Arm | OFP | Realistic |
|-----|-------|-----|-------|-----|-----|-----------|
| MLB ETA: 2016 | | | | | 55 >AVG PLAYER | 50 2ND DIV/GOOD UT |
| 60 | – | 60 | 55 | – | | |

| YEAR | TEAM | LVL | AGE | PA | R | 2B | 3B | HR | RBI | BB | SO | SB | CS | AVG/OBP/SLG | TAv | BABIP | BRR | FRAA | WARP |
|------|------|-----|-----|-----|-----|-----|-----|-----|-----|-----|-----|-----|-----|-------------|-----|-------|-----|------|------|
| 2013 | CDR | A | 19 | 523 | 76 | 32 | 10 | 5 | 78 | 42 | 59 | 4 | 4 | .308/.362/.452 | .297 | .336 | -0.4 | 2B(57): -0.2, SS(49): -4.5 | 2.9 |
| 2014 | MIN | MLB | 20 | 250 | 19 | 11 | 2 | 2 | 21 | 12 | 48 | 1 | 0 | .238/.275/.322 | .222 | .290 | -0.3 | 2B 0, SS -2 | -0.3 |
| 2015 | MIN | MLB | 21 | 250 | 24 | 12 | 2 | 2 | 21 | 13 | 42 | 0 | 0 | .251/.293/.345 | .240 | .294 | -0.4 | 2B 0, SS -2 | 0.3 |

Breakout: 0%  Improve: 0%  Collapse: 0%  Attrition: 0%  MLB: 0%  *Comparables: Jose Ramirez, Adrian Cardenas, Jonathan Schoop*

**Drafted/Acquired:** International free agent, 2009, Dominican Republic

**Previous Ranking:** #10 (Org)

**What Happened in 2013:** In his full-season debut, the switch-hitting Dominican continued his recent trend of hitting over .300, racking up 143 hits in 115 Midwest League games.

**Strengths:** Really quick hands; can put bat to the ball from both sides of the plate; line-drive stroke; pop for the gaps; runs well; good actions with the leather; can make plays; good overall approach.

**Weaknesses:** Lacks impact arm for the left side of the infield; better fit for second base; power is more doubles than over the fence; hit-tool second-base profile, so he has to really hit; good run but not a burner; body needs to add strength.

**Risk Factor/Injury History:** High risk; long developmental road ahead

**Bret Sayre's Fantasy Take:** For someone as fast as Polanco is, he's really not much of a basestealer. In fact, he's just 19-for-37 in his minor-league career. Without improvement in that area, he'll still clear the bar for ownership at second base because he can hit for average, but he won't be a player to get particularly excited about.

**The Year Ahead:** Polanco can really swing the bat, and that has the potential to carry him to a major-league future. He offers some versatility with the defensive profile, so there is a good utility floor, but he has the chops to develop into a regular at second base if he develops to potential. He's moving to the Florida State League in 2014, and given his balance at the plate, he's probably going to continuing making hard contact with the baseball. The test will arrive in Double-A, which could happen over the summer if the bat really takes off to start the season.

## Prospects on the Rise

**1. LHP Stephen Gonsalves:** The projectable lefty could have (and perhaps should have) been a first-round pick in 2013, but fell to the Twins in the fourth round after some off-the-field issues raised questions about his makeup and down spring. With impressive size, raw stuff to build on, and feel, it won't take long for the rest of baseball to mourn the decision to pass on Gonsalves, especially if that decision was based on a minor marijuana indiscretion. The arsenal isn't there yet, but the velocity will continue to creep up as the delivery refines, and with a very promising changeup already in the arsenal, a major breakout could be coming in 2014.

**2. RHP Luke Bard:** Assorted injuries have stalled the former first-rounder's progress since he was drafted in 2012, but if we get a chance to see a healthy arm in 2014, the results could push Bard up prospect lists and return him to the major-league fast track. It's a power reliever profile, but a good one, with an electric fastball/slider combination thrown with purpose.

**3. RHP Ryan Eades:** It's not the sexiest profile, and perhaps a throwback pitcher to the days when the Twins were known for their predilection of solid-average/pitch-to-contact types, but Eades might have more to offer than just a back-end projection. With a low-90s fastball and good feel for the secondary arsenal, the former

---

### FROM THE FIELD

#### Eddie Rosario

**Player:** Eddie Rosario

**Team:** Minnesota Twins

**Filed by:** Tucker Blair

**Date(s) Seen:** August 23-25, 2013

**Physical:** Scrappy build, room left for growth into slender frame.

**Hit:** 60 grade; excellent hand control, ability to cover the entire plate and push ball to all fields; occasionally wraps hands and drops shoulder; bat and hands quick through the zone.

**Power:** 50 grade; surprising pop from solid bat speed; alters swing in the name of power at times, sacrificing his true calling-card in contact.

**Glove:** 40 grade; footwork can be a mess at second base; not highly intuitive, but can make the routine plays.

**Arm:** 60 grade; plus arm, saves him from lack of instincts; would work in the outfield if Twins decided to move away from second base.

**Speed:** 60 grade; plus agility and ability for quick bursts; solid athlete with improving base-running skills.

**Makeup:** 40 grade; pouts at the plate, will take bad at-bats to the field; suspended first 50 games for 2014 season.

**OFP:** 60; first-division player

**Realistic Role:** 50; second-division player

**Risk:** Moderate; room for maturation left, demolished Double-A; improvements at second necessary.

LSU arm will look to take a step forward in 2014, perhaps emerging as yet another fast-moving pitcher in a very deep system.

## Factors on the Farm
### Prospects likely to contribute at the major-league level in 2014

**1. RHP Trevor May:** In all honesty, May should be a lot better prospect than he is; he has plus velocity and he shows the ability to execute a deep secondary arsenal. Perhaps it's a lack of feel or a delivery that works against his height advantage, but the full package rarely comes together on the mound. I think he finds his role in the back of a major-league rotation, but based on his size and stuff, the developmental outcome should have been better.

**2. RHP Michael Tonkin:** Abnormally large human with an angular 93-96 mph fastball and good, two-plane slider, Tonkin is ready for an extended look at the major-league level. He has good command for a max-effort power arm, and he should be able to find sustainable success at that level, most likely profiling as a quality 7th/8th inning type.

**3. IF Danny Santana:** I'm not sold that Santana's bat is going to play as regular, but with plus-plus speed, contact ability from both sides of the plate, and defensive versatility, I think he carves out a career as a utility player. Some believe in the bat more than I do and project a second-division future at shortstop, but I think major-league quality pitching is going to expose the bat for what it is. The aforementioned skills will still make him a valuable member of a 25-man roster at some point in 2014.

---

## FROM THE FIELD

### Miguel Sano

**Player:** Miguel Sano

**Team:** Minnesota Twins

**Filed by:** Chris Mellen

**Date(s) Seen:** March 19-21 and September 1-2, 2013

**Physical:** Strong body; muscular; athletic, with agility when he gets going; has considerably filled out and gotten firmer than early career.

**Hit:** 45 grade; leveraged swing; extends early; drives offerings out and over the plate with authority; gets tied up on inner third; can square velocity; doesn't presently adjust well to path of the ball.

**Power:** 70 grade; elite raw power; can drive balls with loft to all fields; does not have to crush offering to get it out; projecting power to play down a bit due to holes in swing, but capable of 35-plus home runs.

**Glove:** 50 grade; average reads at the crack of the bat; slow lateral movements; robotic at times; fronts balls well; will make routine plays; needs more confidence.

**Arm:** 70 grade; throws travel on a line across diamond; a tad slow with release; likes to show off; will play in outfield; average accuracy; strength enables to throw off-balances or on the move.

**Speed:** 50 grade; on the slower side out of the box; long swing takes momentum toward third; does accelerate once he gets moving; can take an extra base on ball hit into gap.

**Makeup:** 55 grade

**OFP:** 70; perennial all-star

**Realistic Role:** 55; solid-average regular

**Risk:** Moderate; must prove bat can adjust to higher caliber arms in upper minors; will have to always maintain swing to avoid extended valleys.

---

## FROM THE FIELD

### Josmil Pinto

**Player:** Josmil Pinto

**Team:** Minnesota Twins

**Filed by:** Chris Mellen

**Date(s) Seen:** April 19, May 5, and May 6, 2013

**Physical:** Strong body; catcher's build; developed lower body; wide; built to handle wear and tear behind the dish.

**Hit:** 50 grade; average to slightly above-average bat speed; covers plate with swing; short to the ball; not overly loose hands, but has enough life to turn around velocity; can be overaggressive.

**Power:** 50 grade; above-average raw power; lacks ideal leverage in swing; can generate some thump; will muscle up on mistakes.

**Glove:** 55 grade; firm receiver; controls the game; glove doesn't overly drift; can struggle with ball control, but gets big and will smother; feet don't quick fire when moving laterally; fringe-average range.

**Arm:** 55 grade; quick release; strong arm; comes out of crouch smoothly; at times feet will get tangled and throws will tail into runner.

**Speed:** 30 grade; station-to-station runner; consistent double-play candidate; ball needs to be into gap to score from second with less than two outs.

**Makeup:** 50 grade

**OFP:** 55; solid-average regular

**Realistic Role:** 50; average regular

**Risk:** Low; reached big leagues.

---

## FROM THE FIELD

### Alex Meyer

**Player:** Alex Meyer

**Team:** Minnesota Twins

**Filed by:** Chris Mellen

**Date(s) Seen:** May 5, 2013

**Mechanics/Delivery:** Between mid-and-3/4 arm slot; consistently lands square to plate with feet; natural motion takes body toward first base after finish; can drift too much toward first when overthrows.

**Fastball:** 65 grade; velocity: 93-97, top 98; command: below-average; movement: downward glove-side finish in lower tier of strike zone; ride when elevated; occasional bore on righties; plenty of life and hop.

**Slider:** 60 grade; velocity: 82-86; command: fringe-average; movement: late break, with heavy tilt off the table; will sweep at times; power pitch in upper velocity band.

**Changeup:** 40 grade; velocity: 83-86; command: below-average; movement: some arm-side fade; some drop; Lacks depth; too firm; looks like a fastball he is taking something off of.

**Other:** Composed on mound; competitor; imposing figure due to size; release appears to be right on top of hitter; held velocity throughout outing; predictable pitch sequences; solely relied on fastball and slider.

**Makeup:** 55 grade

**OFP:** 60; no. 3 starter/first-division closer

**Realistic Role:** 55; setup man

**Risk:** Moderate; reached upper levels; lack of diversity in arsenal can create strain against elite bats

## 1.  Noah Syndergaard   RHP

**Born:** 8/29/92   **Age:** 21   **Bats:** L   **Throws:** R   **Height:** 6' 6"   **Weight:** 240

| MLB ETA | CT | FB | CH | CB | SL | OFP | Realistic |
|---|---|---|---|---|---|---|---|
| 2014 | -- | 80 | 65 | 70 | -- | 70<br>NO.2 STARTER | 65<br>NO.2-3 STARTER |

| YEAR | TEAM | LVL | AGE | W | L | SV | G | GS | IP | H | HR | BB | SO | BB9 | SO9 | GB% | BABIP | WHIP | ERA | FIP | FRA | WARP |
|---|---|---|---|---|---|---|---|---|---|---|---|---|---|---|---|---|---|---|---|---|---|---|
| 2013 | BIN | AA | 20 | 6 | 1 | 0 | 11 | 11 | 54.0 | 46 | 8 | 12 | 69 | 2.0 | 11.5 | 43% | .304 | 1.07 | 3.00 | 3.36 | 3.97 | 1.3 |
| 2013 | SLU | A+ | 20 | 3 | 3 | 0 | 12 | 12 | 63.7 | 61 | 3 | 16 | 64 | 2.3 | 9.0 | 53% | .333 | 1.21 | 3.11 | 2.64 | 3.90 | 0.9 |
| 2014 | NYN | MLB | 21 | 5 | 7 | 0 | 23 | 19 | 99.0 | 88 | 11 | 36 | 98 | 3.3 | 8.9 | 49% | .310 | 1.26 | 3.72 | 3.89 | 4.05 | 0.8 |
| 2015 | NYN | MLB | 22 | 11 | 10 | 0 | 32 | 32 | 205.3 | 185 | 26 | 67 | 192 | 2.9 | 8.4 | 49% | .302 | 1.23 | 3.83 | 3.89 | 4.16 | 0.9 |

**Breakout:** 0%   **Improve:** 0%   **Collapse:** 0%   **Attrition:** 0%   **MLB:** 0%      *Comparables: Shelby Miller, Brett Anderson, Jake McGee*

> **#11**
> BP Top 101 Prospects

**Drafted/Acquired:** 1st round, 2010 draft, Legacy HS (Mansfield, TX)

**Previous Ranking:** #3 (Org), #28 (Top 101)

**What Happened in 2013:** Another developmental step forward for the big Texan, as Syndergaard pitched his way to the Double-A level flashing a power arsenal with sharp control.

**Strengths:** Impressive size and strength; very athletic; creates steep plane to the plate; elite arm strength; fastball can work 95-100; excellent manipulation of the pitch; can create big arm-side run; can cut the ball; true 80 grade offering; curveball is plus at present; projects to be plus-plus; upper-70s/low-80s with sharp vertical action; impressive depth; power pitch; changeup projects to plus (or better); shows feel for the offering; can show deception and plus arm-side life; control is very sharp for power arm; command projects to be plus; frontline profile.

**Weaknesses:** Tendency to elevate and work up in the zone; curveball can break early; easier to track the tumble; changeup is often overthrown and too firm; thrown into bat speed.

**Risk Factor/Injury History:** Low risk; 50+ innings at Double-A level; physically mature.

**Bret Sayre's Fantasy Take:** While it's easier to profile as a fantasy ace than a true ace in a scouting sense, it's still not something that gets thrown around too lightly. Syndergaard, with his strikeout-inducing stuff and WHIP-reducing control, has that upside—and he should be up as soon as he has cleared all necessary financial hurdles, given the current state of the team.

**The Year Ahead:** Syndergaard is one of the top arms in the minors, with impressive size and strength, an impact arsenal including an elite fastball and wipeout curveball, and the overall command to elevate an already intense arsenal. It's the prototypical profile of a power pitcher, and that's without giving the changeup its proper hype, as several sources think the changeup will blossom in the coming years, settling in as a plus offering and taking Syndergaard to his frontline projection. The big Texan could use more seasoning in the upper minors, but will likely make his major-league debut at some point in 2014, and should help the Mets compile the best young rotation trio in baseball in 2015, along with Harvey and Wheeler.

## 2.  Travis d'Arnaud   C

**Born:** 2/10/89   **Age:** 25   **Bats:** R   **Throws:** R   **Height:** 6' 2"   **Weight:** 195

| MLB ETA | Hit | Power | Run | Glove | Arm | OFP | Realistic |
|---|---|---|---|---|---|---|---|
| Debuted in 2013 | 55 | 55 | -- | 60 | 55 | 60<br>1ST DIV PLAYER | 50<br>ML REGULAR |

| YEAR | TEAM | LVL | AGE | PA | R | 2B | 3B | HR | RBI | BB | SO | SB | CS | AVG/OBP/SLG | TAv | BABIP | BRR | FRAA | WARP |
|---|---|---|---|---|---|---|---|---|---|---|---|---|---|---|---|---|---|---|---|
| 2013 | BIN | AA | 24 | 30 | 2 | 2 | 1 | 1 | 3 | 3 | 9 | 0 | 0 | .222/.300/.481 | .266 | .294 | -0.8 | C(7): 0.3 | 0.2 |
| 2013 | LVG | AAA | 24 | 78 | 19 | 8 | 0 | 2 | 12 | 21 | 12 | 0 | 0 | .304/.487/.554 | .355 | .349 | -1.2 | C(18): 0.6 | 1.1 |
| 2013 | MTS | Rk | 24 | 23 | 4 | 3 | 0 | 0 | 5 | 1 | 2 | 0 | 0 | .318/.348/.455 | .280 | .350 | -0.7 | C(5): 0.2 | 0.2 |
| 2013 | NYN | MLB | 24 | 112 | 4 | 3 | 0 | 1 | 5 | 12 | 21 | 0 | 0 | .202/.286/.263 | .205 | .244 | -0.5 | C(30): -0.3 | -0.2 |
| 2014 | NYN | MLB | 25 | 250 | 28 | 12 | 0 | 9 | 32 | 19 | 60 | 1 | 0 | .253/.314/.427 | .275 | .300 | -0.4 | C -0, 1B -0 | 1.5 |
| 2015 | NYN | MLB | 26 | 623 | 72 | 28 | 1 | 18 | 70 | 50 | 140 | 2 | 1 | .236/.299/.383 | .249 | .280 | -1.4 | C 0 | 1.1 |

**Breakout:** 7%   **Improve:** 34%   **Collapse:** 7%   **Attrition:** 25%   **MLB:** 69%      *Comparables: Ryan Lavarnway, Geovany Soto, Devin Mesoraco*

> **#48**
> BP Top 101 Prospects

**Drafted/Acquired:** 1st round, 2007 draft, Lakewood HS (Lakewood, CA)

**Previous Ranking:** #2 (Org), #15 (Top 101)

**What Happened in 2013:** An injury once again limited d'Arnaud's ability to stay on a field, but the long-time prospect finally made his major-league debut in 2013, although the bat showed up lighter than expected.

**Strengths:** Good frame; good strength; well-rounded skills on both sides of the ball; very good receiver with a plus glove; fundamentally sound; blocks well; calls well; frames well; strong arm; quick release; controls the running game well; shows both ability to put the ball in play and make hard contact; hit/power could play to solid-average (or better).

**Weaknesses:** Can't stay on the field; tools are more solid-average than plus; can sell out for power and lose bat control; tendency to wrap the bat; can get tied up by velocity.

**Risk Factor/Injury History:** Low risk; achieved major-league level; durability concerns.

**Bret Sayre's Fantasy Take:** The worst thing about having d'Arnaud as your dynasty league catcher is that you'll likely need to waste a roster spot on a backup, unless your league is particularly shallow. When healthy, he should be a capable starter on any team, with the potential for a .270 average and 20 homers. But it's going to take a long time to rid himself of that modifier.

**The Year Ahead:** I feel bad for d'Arnaud, a player who has been on the prospect landscape since 2007 yet has faced numerous (and often freak) injury hurdles on his journey to the majors. In his debut, he was pressing and selling out for more pop, which resulted in less pop and less contact. A run of good health could lead to a run of more comfort and confidence in the box, and the real d'Arnaud can emerge, a legit dual-threat catcher who has the overall skill set to develop into a first-division talent. It will all come down to healthy reps at the highest level, so staying on the field will be paramount.

---

## 3.   Wilmer Flores   3B

**Born:** 8/6/91   **Age:** 22   **Bats:** R   **Throws:** R   **Height:** 6' 3"   **Weight:** 190

| MLB ETA | Hit | Power | Run | Glove | Arm | OFP | Realistic |
|---|---|---|---|---|---|---|---|
| Debuted in 2013 | 50 | 60 | --- | 55 | 60 | 55 >AVG REGULAR | 50 ML REGULAR |

| YEAR | TEAM | LVL | AGE | PA | R | 2B | 3B | HR | RBI | BB | SO | SB | CS | AVG/OBP/SLG | TAv | BABIP | BRR | FRAA | WARP |
|---|---|---|---|---|---|---|---|---|---|---|---|---|---|---|---|---|---|---|---|
| 2013 | LVG | AAA | 21 | 463 | 69 | 36 | 4 | 15 | 86 | 25 | 63 | 1 | 3 | .321/.357/.531 | .300 | .342 | -1.2 | 2B(79): -4.8, 1B(11): 0.7 | 2.7 |
| 2013 | NYN | MLB | 21 | 101 | 8 | 5 | 0 | 1 | 13 | 5 | 23 | 0 | 0 | .211/.248/.295 | .200 | .264 | -0.3 | 3B(26): 1.8, 2B(2): -0.1 | -0.2 |
| 2014 | NYN | MLB | 22 | 250 | 22 | 12 | 1 | 6 | 28 | 10 | 47 | 0 | 0 | .244/.277/.377 | .245 | .280 | -0.5 | 3B -1, 2B -1 | 0.2 |
| 2015 | NYN | MLB | 23 | 374 | 42 | 20 | 1 | 10 | 43 | 17 | 66 | 0 | 0 | .257/.292/.406 | .253 | .285 | -1.0 | 3B -1, 2B -1 | 0.8 |

Breakout: 5%     Improve: 23%     Collapse: 10%     Attrition: 25%     MLB: 41%          *Comparables: Henry Rodriguez, Adrian Cardenas, Scooter Gennett*

**Drafted/Acquired:** International free agent, 2007, Venezuela

**Previous Ranking:** #5 (Org)

**What Happened in 2013:** It happened fast for Flores, who started the 2012 season in the Florida State League and finished the 2013 season at the major-league level, where the Triple-A bat failed to make the journey.

**Strengths:** Good feel for hitting; excellent hand-eye; added strength in 2013; power likely to play solid-average to plus; run producer; can catch up to velocity; hands to find contact when he's fooled; arm is left-side strong; soft hands; fluid actions; good footwork around the bag at second.

**Weaknesses:** Well-below-average run; range isn't sufficient for shortstop; aggressive approach at the plate; can get himself out early; hit tool might only play to average; game power could play down without approach refinement.

**Risk Factor/Injury History:** Low risk; achieved major-league level.

**Bret Sayre's Fantasy Take:** Flores is just in the wrong organization for his current fantasy value. The two half-decent offensive players the Mets finished the 2013 season with cover the only two places that Flores can potentially play (second and third base), so he's unlikely to be much help in 2014 barring injury. If given a full season, he could hit .275 with 25 homers and more RBI than you think given his propensity for contact.

**The Year Ahead:** Flores doesn't get enough credit, mostly due to his inability to project at shortstop and the organizational roadblock at third base; it gets forgotten that Flores has really nice hands and a very strong arm, and with his offensive upside, a third-base profile would make him a much more heralded prospect in the game. Despite the glove and overall coordination, Flores lacks average range, and that could limit his utility at second base, although he could certainly handle the fundamental aspects of the position. At the plate, Flores is going to hit for power; it's just a matter of time and a question of how much. He has a knack for putting the barrel on the ball, with excellent hand-eye coordination and improving strength in his body that allows him to get extension and drive the ball to right-center. This is a very legit player, and this will be true even if he struggles in a longer major-league look in 2014. I'm a fan.

**#71**
BP Top
101
Prospects

## 4. Rafael Montero   RHP

**Born:** 10/17/90   **Age:** 23   **Bats:** R   **Throws:** R   **Height:** 6'0"   **Weight:** 170

| MLB ETA | CT | FB | CH | CB | SL | OFP | Realistic |
|---|---|---|---|---|---|---|---|
| 2014 | – | 60 | 55 | – | 50 | 55 NO.3 STARTER | 50 NO.4 STARTER |

| YEAR | TEAM | LVL | AGE | W | L | SV | G | GS | IP | H | HR | BB | SO | BB9 | SO9 | GB% | BABIP | WHIP | ERA | FIP | FRA | WARP |
|---|---|---|---|---|---|---|---|---|---|---|---|---|---|---|---|---|---|---|---|---|---|---|
| 2013 | BIN | AA | 22 | 7 | 3 | 0 | 11 | 11 | 66.7 | 51 | 2 | 10 | 72 | 1.4 | 9.7 | 40% | .277 | 0.92 | 2.43 | 2.00 | 2.57 | 2.1 |
| 2013 | LVG | AAA | 22 | 5 | 4 | 0 | 16 | 16 | 88.7 | 85 | 4 | 25 | 78 | 2.5 | 7.9 | 40% | .316 | 1.24 | 3.05 | 3.24 | 3.59 | 2.5 |
| 2014 | NYN | MLB | 23 | 7 | 8 | 0 | 23 | 23 | 128.0 | 114 | 12 | 35 | 109 | 2.5 | 7.7 | 39% | .297 | 1.17 | 3.28 | 3.64 | 3.57 | 1.7 |
| 2015 | NYN | MLB | 24 | 7 | 4 | 0 | 81 | 10 | 134.7 | 119 | 13 | 32 | 123 | 2.1 | 8.2 | 39% | .301 | 1.13 | 3.14 | 3.25 | 3.41 | 2.3 |

Breakout: 13%   Improve: 24%   Collapse: 10%   Attrition: 22%   MLB: 40%   *Comparables: Jake Odorizzi, Chad Bettis, Kyle Gibson*

**Drafted/Acquired:** International free agent, 2011, Dominican Republic

**Previous Ranking:** #10 (Org)

**What Happened in 2013:** Montero continues to climb the professional ranks while being underappreciated (at least by this source), putting himself in a position to contribute to the major-league rotation in 2014.

**Strengths:** Fluid, easy arm; good arm strength; sneaky plus fastball in the low 90s; whippy 3/4 arm and good late explosion; good overall pitchability; can locate fastball; work east/west; changeup plays well from the arm; good disguise and solid-average action; slider can play average (or above); can log innings and hold stuff despite size.

**Weaknesses:** Lacks prototypical size; short/slender; lacks impact stuff; fastball can get to the mid-90s, but more comfortable in low-90s; tendency to get too fly-ball friendly; secondary arsenal lacks wipeout pitch; slider can play sharp but can also get slurvy and lose bite; more command/control profile than power.

**Risk Factor/Injury History:** Low risk; upper-minors experience; mature arsenal.

**Bret Sayre's Fantasy Take:** Montero has gotten the job done at the minor-league level, despite not having elite raw stuff, but he'll have more trouble putting up these types of numbers for your fantasy team. What he can provide is a decent number of strikeouts (think 160 or so over a full season) and a very strong WHIP, which could linger in the 1.10-1.15 range in his better seasons.

**The Year Ahead:** I often discount Montero because of his size and his good-but-not-great stuff, missing out on the fact that he can actually pitch, mixing his arsenal with a good feel for command execution and the ability to make outs. As long as Montero can stay healthy and continue to refine his command, he can find sustainable success in a rotation, but I see more of a back-end type than a pitcher likely to reach frontline status. Perhaps I'm still underselling the 23-year-old Dominican, for as much as I respect his ability to pitch, I'm still skeptical that his solid-average arsenal can push him that high in a major-league rotation without exceptional command. He should get a chance to make his case in 2014.

## 5. Amed Rosario   SS

**Born:** 11/20/95   **Age:** 18   **Bats:** R   **Throws:** R   **Height:** 6'2"   **Weight:** 170

| MLB ETA | Hit | Power | Run | Glove | Arm | OFP | Realistic |
|---|---|---|---|---|---|---|---|
| 2018 | 60 | 55 | 55 | 60 | 55 | 65 1ST DIV/ALL-STAR | 50 ML REGULAR |

| YEAR | TEAM | LVL | AGE | PA | R | 2B | 3B | HR | RBI | BB | SO | SB | CS | AVG/OBP/SLG | TAv | BABIP | BRR | FRAA | WARP |
|---|---|---|---|---|---|---|---|---|---|---|---|---|---|---|---|---|---|---|---|
| 2013 | KNG | Rk | 17 | 226 | 22 | 8 | 4 | 3 | 23 | 11 | 43 | 2 | 6 | .241/.279/.358 | .228 | .286 | -3.5 | SS(58): -3.7 | -0.4 |
| 2014 | NYN | MLB | 18 | 250 | 17 | 7 | 1 | 2 | 17 | 9 | 78 | 1 | 1 | .180/.212/.247 | .176 | .250 | -0.5 | SS -4 | -1.5 |
| 2015 | NYN | MLB | 19 | 250 | 19 | 6 | 1 | 2 | 18 | 8 | 77 | 0 | 0 | .186/.213/.254 | .175 | .256 | -0.4 | SS -3 | -4.0 |

Breakout: 0%   Improve: 0%   Collapse: 0%   Attrition: 0%   MLB: 0%   *Comparables: Hector Gomez, Juan Lagares, Juan Diaz*

**Drafted/Acquired:** International free agent, 2012, Dominican Republic

**Previous Ranking:** NR

**What Happened in 2013:** High-dollar international signee in 2012, Rosario made his professional debut in the rookie-level Appalachian League, holding his own as a 17-year-old.

**Strengths:** Physically projectable; good athlete; natural feel for the game; great actions; easy and fluid; glove projects to above-average; arm is solid-average to plus; can make left-side throws; quick first step and reactions; good range; solid-average run; projectable hit tool; impressive bat speed and hand-eye; stays inside the ball; drives through it; uses all fields; power potential down the line; high baseball IQ.

**Weaknesses:** More flash than fundamentals in the field; range could slow as he adds weight; not a speedster; swing mechanics are inconsistent; can load the hands too deep and arrive to the ball late; gets himself out; aggressive; raw power is present but game power might play below average.

**Risk Factor/Injury History:** High risk; rookie-level experience.

**Bret Sayre's Fantasy Take:** Rosario is forever away, and his impact will likely be much less important in fantasy than for the Mets, but he still is worth watching for our purposes as well. And while he's still just a flier at this point, if the .118 isolated power as a 17-year old in rookie ball is an indication of some future pop, he may graduate from that status in short order.

**The Year Ahead:** Rosario has the potential to blossom into a top-tier prospect in the game, with five-tool talent at a premium position and the type of natural bat-to-ball ability to produce at the plate. Add to the mix a noticeable feel for the game, work ethic, and intelligence, and you could have something very special. But Rosario has a long developmental road ahead, and needs refinement in all aspects of the game. The glove is slick, but the physical projection could end up limiting range, even though every source for this list had Rosario projected to stay at shortstop. The bat will play because of his quick hands and overall coordination, but if he is to really step forward with the stick, he will need to work himself into better hitting conditions and not give away at-bats with an overly aggressive approach and the need to swing just because he can. For some context on his potential, ask yourself how many stateside high school juniors could make the jump straight to the Appalachian League and hold their own at the plate while playing a premium position? The Mets have something here, but it's not going to be an overnight rise to glory for the 18-year-old Dominican.

## 6. Dominic Smith 1B

**Born:** 6/15/95  **Age:** 19  **Bats:** L  **Throws:** L  **Height:** 6' 0"  **Weight:** 185

| MLB ETA | Hit | Power | Run | Glove | Arm | OFP | Realistic |
|---|---|---|---|---|---|---|---|
| 2017 | 70 | 50 | – | 65 | 65 | 60 1ST DIV PLAYER | 50 2ND DIV PLAYER |

| YEAR | TEAM | LVL | AGE | PA | R | 2B | 3B | HR | RBI | BB | SO | SB | CS | AVG/OBP/SLG | TAv | BABIP | BRR | FRAA | WARP |
|---|---|---|---|---|---|---|---|---|---|---|---|---|---|---|---|---|---|---|---|
| 2013 | MTS | Rk | 18 | 198 | 23 | 9 | 1 | 3 | 22 | 24 | 37 | 2 | 4 | .287/.384/.407 | .289 | .346 | -0.2 | 1B(43): 1.4 | 1.2 |
| 2013 | KNG | Rk | 18 | 8 | 2 | 4 | 0 | 0 | 4 | 2 | 0 | 0 | 0 | .667/.750/1.333 | .580 | .667 | -0.3 | 1B(1): -0.0 | 0.3 |
| 2014 | NYN | MLB | 19 | 250 | 18 | 8 | 0 | 3 | 21 | 15 | 76 | 0 | 0 | .188/.239/.266 | .193 | .260 | -0.5 | 1B 1 | -1.4 |
| 2015 | NYN | MLB | 20 | 250 | 25 | 9 | 0 | 5 | 23 | 15 | 66 | 0 | 0 | .219/.266/.324 | .217 | .278 | -0.6 | 1B 1 | -1.5 |

Breakout: 0%   Improve: 0%   Collapse: 0%   Attrition: 0%   MLB: 0%   *Comparables: Cedric Hunter, Marcell Ozuna, Caleb Gindl*

**Drafted/Acquired:** 1st round, 2013 draft, Serra HS (Gardena, CA)

**Previous Ranking:** NR

**What Happened in 2013:** In a strong draft class, Smith was taken 11th overall and showed off his sweet left-handed swing, hitting over .300 in his first professional taste.

**Strengths:** Beautiful swing from the left side; shows natural feel for putting the barrel on the ball; can square velocity and keeps hands back on off-speed; hit tool could make him a .300 hitter; power could play to solid-average; good athlete with plus glove at first; strong arm; could hit 90+ off the mound as an amateur; natural leader on the field; high baseball IQ.

**Weaknesses:** Not physically imposing; limited defensively; run is below average; power potential is subject of debate; could play below average; swing more conducive for line-drive pop, not over-the-fence power.

**Risk Factor/Injury History:** High risk; limited professional experience; first-base-only profile.

**Bret Sayre's Fantasy Take:** There are a wide range of opinions on Smith's power potential, and that is a huge driver of his dynasty league value. I view him as the eighth-best option in dynasty drafts this year and a potential .300-hitting first baseman with 20-25 homers. Of course, like any first-base prospect, the fantasy upside is greater than the real-life upside.

**The Year Ahead:** Smith is going to hit; anybody who has ever seen him in person can tell you that after watching his swing against live pitching. The real question is whether or not he brings big power into the equation, which could take him from being a good major-league regular to a first-division/all-star type. As a first baseman, Smith is going to have to really hit to carve out his value, and as mentioned, he's going to make a lot of hard contact and should develop into a plus hitter at the highest level, and perhaps even a perennial .300 hitter if everything clicks. With his easy plus defensive profile at first and a monster hit tool, the Mets could be looking at a Keith Hernandez type, with more power potential than the former MVP but less mustache projection. Smith failed to crack the BP 101 heading into the season, but could hit his way there with a strong full-season debut in 2014.

## 7. Cesar Puello OF

**Born:** 4/1/91  **Age:** 23  **Bats:** R  **Throws:** R  **Height:** 6' 2"  **Weight:** 195

| MLB ETA | Hit | Power | Run | Glove | Arm | OFP | Realistic |
|---|---|---|---|---|---|---|---|
| 2015 | – | 60 | 60 | 55 | 60 | 60 1ST DIV PLAYER | 45 <AVG ML/BENCH OF |

| YEAR | TEAM | LVL | AGE | PA | R | 2B | 3B | HR | RBI | BB | SO | SB | CS | AVG/OBP/SLG | TAv | BABIP | BRR | FRAA | WARP |
|---|---|---|---|---|---|---|---|---|---|---|---|---|---|---|---|---|---|---|---|
| 2013 | BIN | AA | 22 | 377 | 63 | 21 | 2 | 16 | 73 | 28 | 82 | 24 | 7 | .326/.403/.547 | .350 | .391 | 3.7 | RF(85): 10.1, CF(4): -0.1 | 6.0 |
| 2014 | NYN | MLB | 23 | 250 | 28 | 10 | 1 | 6 | 26 | 8 | 69 | 10 | 3 | .234/.283/.371 | .247 | .300 | 1.0 | RF 2, CF 0 | 0.6 |
| 2015 | NYN | MLB | 24 | 250 | 26 | 11 | 1 | 5 | 25 | 8 | 66 | 9 | 3 | .234/.281/.358 | .238 | .301 | 1.0 | RF 3, CF 0 | 0.5 |

Breakout: 3%   Improve: 14%   Collapse: 4%   Attrition: 8%   MLB: 24%   *Comparables: Nate Schierholtz, Roger Kieschnick, J.D. Martinez*

**Drafted/Acquired:** International free agent, 2007, Dominican Republic

**Previous Ranking:** NR

**What Happened in 2013:** Puello was erupting as a prospect before a connection to the Biogenesis investigation brought a 50-game suspension, a connection that soured several sources on the then-22-year-old Dominican.

**Strengths:** Athletic with good present strength; loud raw tools; plus run; plus arm strength; versatile on defense, with some feel for center; good glove; showed ability to make improvements at the plate (improved hand position in the setup/swing allowed the bat to take off in 2013); power potential is plus; impressive bat speed and ability to lift the ball.

**Weaknesses:** Aggressive at the plate; looks fastball and struggles to recover from bad guesses; pitch-recognition concerns; balance needs work; lacks consistency; reads/routes need refinement up the middle; power likely to play down against better arms; more boom or bust than average player with Double-A experience; makeup concerns.

**Overall Future Potential:** 6; first-division player

**Realistic Role:** High 4; below-average major leaguer/bench outfielder

**Risk Factor/Injury History:** High risk; limited upper minors experience; makeup concerns; gap between present/future offensive grades.

**Bret Sayre's Fantasy Take:** Anytime you see plus grades on the run and power potential, you know you're looking at someone you should pay attention to for fantasy. Puello is no different, though he's going to have to show that his bat will allow those things to play without whatever he may have allegedly received from the Biogenesis clinic in order to make his 20/20 upside believable.

**The Year Ahead:** I have several outside-the-organization sources on Puello, and while each source can wax poetic about his tool-based potential, each source also found the projection to be very abstract and carrying more risk than most players with upper-minors experience. Puello has loud tools and was starting to bring them into game action before the suspension, which is another issue that raises red flags about his profile. Not that the results in 2013 weren't authentic; they likely were. But the stain of the association will follow Puello for the foreseeable future, casting doubt on his level of performance and his makeup for allowing the association in the first place. I have no idea what to expect from Puello in 2014, as the talented Dominican could continue where he left off in 2013 and mash his way to a big-league opportunity or he could suffer at the hand of his aggressive approach and general inconsistencies on all sides of the ball. The ceiling is high enough to justify this ranking—or even ranking him higher on a list—but the profile is still very cloudy and the risk is still high.

## 8. Kevin Plawecki  C

**Born:** 2/26/91   **Age:** 23   **Bats:** R   **Throws:** R   **Height:** 6' 2"   **Weight:** 205

| MLB ETA | Hit | Power | Run | Glove | Arm | OFP | Realistic |
|---|---|---|---|---|---|---|---|
| Late 2015 | 55 | 50 | -- | 50 | 50 | 55 >AVG REGULAR | 50 2ND DIV PLAYER |

| YEAR | TEAM | LVL | AGE | PA | R | 2B | 3B | HR | RBI | BB | SO | SB | CS | AVG/OBP/SLG | TAv | BABIP | BRR | FRAA | WARP |
|---|---|---|---|---|---|---|---|---|---|---|---|---|---|---|---|---|---|---|---|
| 2013 | SAV | A | 22 | 282 | 35 | 24 | 1 | 6 | 43 | 23 | 32 | 1 | 0 | .314/.390/.494 | .355 | .336 | -3.7 | C(46): 0.6 | 3.7 |
| 2013 | SLU | A+ | 22 | 239 | 25 | 14 | 0 | 2 | 37 | 19 | 21 | 0 | 0 | .294/.391/.392 | .295 | .319 | -1.9 | C(42): -1.0, 1B(17): 1.5 | 1.5 |
| 2014 | NYN | MLB | 23 | 250 | 23 | 11 | 0 | 5 | 25 | 16 | 46 | 0 | 0 | .237/.303/.349 | .248 | .270 | -0.5 | C -0, 1B 0 | 0.6 |
| 2015 | NYN | MLB | 24 | 250 | 29 | 10 | 1 | 6 | 26 | 16 | 42 | 0 | 0 | .244/.313/.374 | .254 | .272 | -0.5 | C 0, 1B 0 | 1.2 |

Breakout: 4%   Improve: 19%   Collapse: 1%   Attrition: 11%   MLB: 34%   *Comparables: Russell Martin, Jason Castro, Josh Thole*

**Drafted/Acquired:** 1st round, 2012 draft, Purdue University (West Lafayette, IN)

**Previous Ranking:** NR

**What Happened in 2013:** In his full-season debut, the former first-round pick hit his way to the Florida State League, showing a knack for contact while flashing playable skills behind the plate.

**Strengths:** Good build for backstop; good present strength; simple swing that is very contact heavy; doesn't swing just to swing; mature approach; hit tool projects to solid-average; power could play to average; good receiver; strong hands; fundamentals over flash; arm is average; can control the running game.

**Weaknesses:** Lacks plus tools; defensive profile is average; below-average run; lacks big boy pop; more contact heavy and gap power than over the fence; lacks projection.

**Risk Factor/Injury History:** Moderate risk; yet to play at Double-A level; dual-threat development.

**Bret Sayre's Fantasy Take:** Plawecki makes for a nice target in OBP leagues, as he could post .360-.370 marks at the major-league level—which is fantastic for a catcher. Unfortunately, he doesn't profile to do much else, as his power isn't much more than low double digits. However, the average/on-base profile is enough to keep him above the Blake Swihart line and makes him ownable in non-shallow formats.

**The Year Ahead:** Plawecki is a quality prospect, with playable tools at a premium position and the ability to swing a good bat. The problem is that it's more present than projection and the tools are more of the average variety than impact level. As a sum-of-his-parts player, Plawecki could end up an above-average talent, especially if the bat continues to play as he faces better pitching. But any setback to his defensive profile will retard his overall value, and right-handed first basemen that can hit left-handed pitching are vastly more abundant than well-rounded role 5 backstops. Double-A will be a big test for Plawecki.

## 9.  Brandon Nimmo   CF

**Born:** 3/27/93   **Age:** 21   **Bats:** L   **Throws:** R   **Height:** 6' 3"   **Weight:** 185

| MLB ETA | Hit | Power | Run | Glove | Arm | | OFP | Realistic |
|---|---|---|---|---|---|---|---|---|
| 2017 | 50 | 60 | 50 | 50 | 60 | | 60<br>1ST DIV PLAYER | 45<br><AVG ML/BENCH OF |

| YEAR | TEAM | LVL | AGE | PA | R | 2B | 3B | HR | RBI | BB | SO | SB | CS | AVG/OBP/SLG | TAv | BABIP | BRR | FRAA | WARP |
|---|---|---|---|---|---|---|---|---|---|---|---|---|---|---|---|---|---|---|---|
| 2013 | SAV | A | 20 | 480 | 62 | 16 | 6 | 2 | 40 | 71 | 131 | 10 | 7 | .273/.397/.359 | .301 | .402 | 2.0 | CF(106): -1.2 | 4.0 |
| 2014 | NYN | MLB | 21 | 250 | 25 | 8 | 1 | 3 | 17 | 27 | 82 | 1 | 1 | .197/.291/.278 | .222 | .300 | -0.4 | CF 0 | -0.3 |
| 2015 | NYN | MLB | 22 | 250 | 27 | 9 | 2 | 4 | 22 | 26 | 79 | 0 | 0 | .212/.303/.324 | .235 | .306 | -0.3 | CF 0 | 0.0 |

**Breakout:** 0%   **Improve:** 0%   **Collapse:** 0%   **Attrition:** 0%   **MLB:** 0%   *Comparables: Aaron Hicks, Michael Saunders, Brett Jackson*

**Drafted/Acquired:** 1st round, 2012 draft, East HS (Cheyenne, WY)

**Previous Ranking:** #9 (Org)

**What Happened in 2013:** In his full-season debut, the former first round pick (13th overall) was solid but not spectacular, making developmental progress on his long road to his projections.

**Strengths:** Good athlete; good baseball awareness; pretty swing from the left side; line-drive stroke with some power to come down the line; average run; average glove; arm is corner strong; can flash five-tool talent; more baseball skills than expected given his background.

**Weaknesses:** Lacks loud tools; can play soft in games; good athlete but lacks plus run; better profile in a corner; pretty swing but bat speed is average; tendency to wrap it; struggles against arm-side stuff and quality velocity can tie him up.

**Risk Factor/Injury History:** High risk; yet to play in upper minors; questions about his profile.

**Bret Sayre's Fantasy Take:** There is still the potential for Nimmo to be a 20+ homer/10+ steal player with an average that won't hurt you, but the combination of his rawness and his ETA keeps him from graduation out of the flier pool. He's a worthy risk if your league rosters 200 or more prospects, but if not, there's probably someone better out there.

**The Year Ahead:** Nimmo deserves some developmental space given his limited exposure to quality talent in high school, and he's made noticeable progress on all sides of the ball since signing with the Mets. He is athletic and physical, and when it works, it can look very good on the field. But the tools are more solid-average than high end, and the overall profile looks more like a tweener than a first-division player in either center field or a corner. Nimmo's bat speed has never impressed me, and the better velocity he faces, the more this particular attribute could be exposed. I still see a major-league future for the 21-year-old, but it might be more of a second-division/utility variety than the all-star caliber talent you expect from the 13th overall pick in a loaded draft.

## 10.  Marcos Molina   RHP

**Born:** 3/8/95   **Age:** 19   **Bats:** R   **Throws:** R   **Height:** 6' 3"   **Weight:** 188

| MLB ETA | CT | FB | CH | CB | SL | | OFP | Realistic |
|---|---|---|---|---|---|---|---|---|
| 2017 | — | 70 | 60 | 50 | — | | 60<br>NO.3 STARTER | 50<br>NO.4 STARTER |

| YEAR | TEAM | LVL | AGE | W | L | SV | G | GS | IP | H | HR | BB | SO | BB9 | SO9 | GB% | BABIP | WHIP | ERA | FIP | FRA | WARP |
|---|---|---|---|---|---|---|---|---|---|---|---|---|---|---|---|---|---|---|---|---|---|---|
| 2013 | MTS | Rk | 18 | 4 | 3 | 0 | 11 | 6 | 53.3 | 56 | 3 | 14 | 43 | 2.4 | 7.3 | 47% | .323 | 1.31 | 4.39 | 3.76 | 4.95 | 0.2 |
| 2014 | NYN | MLB | 19 | 1 | 1 | 0 | 10 | 3 | 44.3 | 52 | 6 | 26 | 21 | 5.3 | 4.3 | 46% | .316 | 1.76 | 6.32 | 6.06 | 6.87 | -1.0 |
| 2015 | NYN | MLB | 20 | 2 | 2 | 0 | 15 | 4 | 66.7 | 69 | 9 | 31 | 42 | 4.2 | 5.7 | 46% | .301 | 1.50 | 5.13 | 5.07 | 5.57 | -0.5 |

**Breakout:** 0%   **Improve:** 0%   **Collapse:** 0%   **Attrition:** 0%   **MLB:** 0%   *Comparables: Enny Romero, Zeke Spruill, Jake Odorizzi*

**Drafted/Acquired:** International free agent, 2012, Dominican Republic

**Previous Ranking:** NR

**What Happened in 2013:** In his stateside debut, the electric Dominican arm showed up better on the scouting report than he did on the stat sheet, missing bats but showing the inconsistency of a young, underdeveloped pitcher.

**Strengths:** Plus-plus athlete; physically projectable; fast-twitch; big arm strength; very quick arm; routinely worked 91-96 in the GCL; good feel for filling up the zone; turns over a promising changeup; excellent late action on the pitch; commands it; slurvy breaking ball shows some bat-missing potential; slower slider action; highly competitive on/off the mound.

**Weaknesses:** Still transitioning from thrower to pitcher; erratic stuff; flashes of brilliance followed by inconsistency; more control than command at present; turns over a quality changeup but can get deliberate in the delivery; breaking ball is inconsistent; more slurve than clear slider; lacks tight rotation and shows limited depth.

**Risk Factor/Injury History:** High risk; complex-league experience.

**Bret Sayre's Fantasy Take:** Here's a name to watch for the future. While Molina likely doesn't warrant a pickup in your league right now (unless you play in a league where 300+ minor leaguers are kept), he is someone to keep an eye out for as he moves up the ladder in the Mets system. With a strong fastball, and advanced development of a changeup for his age, Molina could blossom into a strong fantasy starter—it will just take a some time.

**The Year Ahead:** We might be a year premature by ranking a relative unknown like Molina this high in a very good system, but the scouting reports were excellent in his stateside debut, and a conversation with one front-office source (outside the organization) really sealed his placement on this list. When discussing Molina, it was mentioned that if the then-18-year-old were available for inclusion in the rule 4 draft, the highly athletic 6-foot-3, 190-pound righty would be considered a first-round talent. Add to that his strong complex debut and lofty projections, and the choice to include Molina became easier to justify. Molina isn't going to explode overnight, but as he improves his pitchability and finds more consistency on the mound, he has all the ingredients to develop into a high-end prospect, a super athletic righty with size, stuff, and a competitive edge to push him beyond his paper grades.

## Prospects on the Rise

**1. RHP Michael Fulmer:** A healthy Fulmer is a no-brainer top-10 prospect in this (or any other) system but an injury-plagued 2013 put his status in limbo. The reports are good coming into 2014, but knee injuries can linger, and when you add Fulmer's big boy size to the equation, the road to his former self could take some time. We can worry about the health, but we need not worry about the stuff, because even when he was dealing with the knee issue, the stuff was still sharp, with a plus fastball/slider combination delivered with the polish of a command/control arm. When Fulmer proves (on the field) that he is 100 percent, he's a legit mid-rotation starter in the making.

**2. RHP Casey Meisner:** A highly projectable Texan arm, Meisner's present stuff arrived on the professional scene better than advertised, sitting comfortably in the low-90s and showing good feel for his secondary arsenal, including a good changeup. The third-round pick is the rare lanky 6-foot-7 pitcher who can control his body and repeat his delivery, allowing the 18-year-old to throw strikes. As he adds strength to his frame, his fastball could blossom into a monster offering, but even without additional fuel to the heater, the combination of plane, location, and present velocity will allow him to find success as he climbs the professional ranks. If he does start to tick up, watch out. He will likely be a top 10 prospect in this system at this time next season.

**3. SS Luis Guillorme:** Arguably the slickest glove available in the 2013 draft, Guillorme is going to wow you with the leather and is worth the price of admission, but his bat could limit his upside. The 19-year-old can put the ball in play from the left side of the plate, which is a positive of his offensive skill set, but most sources don't think the bat will play to major-league standard. But the glove is slick, a potential 7-grade tool, and if he can just carve out a little offense, he could develop into a second-division type as a ceiling or a utility type as a floor. He's fun to watch.

## Factors on the Farm

### Prospects likely to contribute at the major-league level in 2014

**1. RHP Victor Black:** Acquired in the Marlon Byrd trade, Black is a hard-throwing reliever with heavy mid-90s smoke and a sharp slider, but struggles with command limited his effectiveness in his major-league debut. The big Texan can find late-innings success if he can find more consistency in his delivery, which will improve his strike-throwing ability and allow him to pound the lower zone with his plus-plus fastball and use his breaking ball to miss bats. It's a setup profile that could morph into a closer if the command really picks up.

**2. LHP Jack Leathersich:** A fifth-round selection in the 2011 draft, Leathersich's brief career has been built on grotesque strikeout totals, including missing a ridiculous 102 bats in only 58 innings in 2013. Aside from his plus name, the 23-year-old lefty brings a deceptive plus fastball to the table that he backs up with a playable hard curve. The short lefty's future will mostly likely be as a situational reliever at the highest level, mostly on the back of the sneaky low-90s fastball, but if he can refine his command and stay over the curve despite the slot and action, he can continue to miss bats and work himself into more high-leverage situations at the next level.

**3. RHP Jake deGrom:** It's not an overly sexy profile but it can be effective, as the former ninth-round pick in 2010 was able to build on a strong 2012 season and push himself up the ladder toward a major-league opportunity. With good size (long and lean) and athleticism, deGrom can throw strikes and log innings, using a 90- to 94-mph fastball with some sink to do most of his dirty work but flashing a quality slider and playable changeup as well. Sources aren't sold that he's a viable major-league starter, but he could find a home in the bullpen—where the 25-year-old arm could offer versatility, pushing the arsenal up a few ticks to work in bursts—or chew innings in a long relief/spot starter capacity.

## FROM THE FIELD

### Noah Syndergaard

**Player:** Noah Syndergaard

**Team:** New York Mets

**Filed by:** CJ Wittmann

**Date(s) Seen:** August 26, 2013

**Physical:** Huge, physical frame; good muscle tone on frame; long legs with sturdy, thick lower half.

**Mechanics/Delivery:** Good balance; high 3/4 arm slot creating extreme downhill plane; stays on top consistently; shorter arm action but was not a problem; average profile command.

**Fastball:** 80 grade; 96-100 mph; had ability to throw some with heavy arm-side life at 96-98 mph and also some with natural cut at 99-100 mph; extreme downhill plane.

**Curveball:** 70 grade; 76-80 mph; sharp, two-plane break with good depth; ability to throw for a strike in all counts.

**Changeup:** 55 grade; 86-88 mph; power fade; hard, sinking action; development in the future is key, below average at present.

**Makeup:** 60 grade; hard work ethic from scouts, very good competitive demeanor.

**OFP:** 70; no. 2 starter on championship-level team

**Realistic Role:** 60; no. 3 starter

**Risk:** Moderate; only 11 starts at Double-A.

## 1. Gary Sanchez   C

**Born:** 12/2/92   **Age:** 21   **Bats:** R   **Throws:** R   **Height:** 6' 2"   **Weight:** 220

| MLB ETA | Hit | Power | Run | Glove | Arm | OFP | Realistic |
|---|---|---|---|---|---|---|---|
| Late 2014 | ----- | 65 | ----- | ----- | 70 | 60<br>1ST DIV PLAYER | 50<br>ML REGULAR (1B/DH) |

| YEAR | TEAM | LVL | AGE | PA | R | 2B | 3B | HR | RBI | BB | SO | SB | CS | AVG/OBP/SLG | TAv | BABIP | BRR | FRAA | WARP |
|---|---|---|---|---|---|---|---|---|---|---|---|---|---|---|---|---|---|---|---|
| 2013 | TRN | AA | 20 | 110 | 12 | 6 | 0 | 2 | 10 | 13 | 16 | 0 | 0 | .250/.364/.380 | .285 | .280 | -0.5 | C(20): 0.2 | 0.8 |
| 2013 | TAM | A+ | 20 | 399 | 38 | 21 | 0 | 13 | 61 | 28 | 71 | 3 | 1 | .254/.313/.420 | .259 | .280 | -0.3 | C(76): -1.8, 1B(1): -0.0 | 1.8 |
| 2014 | NYA | MLB | 21 | 250 | 26 | 10 | 0 | 9 | 31 | 14 | 67 | 1 | 0 | .227/.276/.390 | .241 | .280 | -0.4 | C -0 | 0.5 |
| 2015 | NYA | MLB | 22 | 250 | 31 | 11 | 0 | 9 | 31 | 17 | 60 | 1 | 0 | .241/.299/.411 | .261 | .284 | -0.6 | C -1 | 1.6 |

**Breakout:** 0%   **Improve:** 0%   **Collapse:** 0%   **Attrition:** 0%   **MLB:** 0%     *Comparables: Chris Marrero, Anthony Rizzo, Brandon Laird*

**Drafted/Acquired:** International free agent, 2009, Dominican Republic

**Previous Ranking:** #1 (Org), #47 (Top 101)

**What Happened in 2013:** Sanchez finally reached the Double-A level, but the reviews were mixed on the high-ceiling talent, both at the plate and behind it.

**Strengths:** Big raw power; gets excellent extension and shows impressive opposite-field pop; controlled aggression at the plate; can identify balls/strikes; arm is very strong; easy plus-plus arm strength; above-average catch/throw skills.

**Weaknesses:** Makeup concerns; hitter-first approach to the game; swing has some miss (in the zone); struggles against arm-side stuff; hit tool might bring game power down; well-below-average run; receiving skills are still underdeveloped.

**Risk Factor/Injury History:** Moderate risk; limited Double-A exposure; dual-threat development.

**Bret Sayre's Fantasy Take:** A bigger deal than any other positional difference, the drop from catcher to first base eligibility is like falling out a three-story window. If Sanchez plays behind the plate (regardless of how well), he has top-five upside at the position with his potential 25-homer power. If he has to move off the position, he's just another corner infielder. Perhaps interestingly, his strikeout rate has dropped by around five percentage points at each level since Low-A. Then again, perhaps not.

**The Year Ahead:** Sanchez was once considered a premier prospect—a dual-threat player with plus potential behind the plate and middle-of-the-order power in the stick. While he's still a top-101 prospect in the game, his stock has slipped, and several scout sources continue to question his baseball makeup, and the likelihood that he reaches his tool-based ceiling. If the receiving can continue to take steps forward, he has the arm to offer impact on defense. However, Sanchez's future is tied to his bat, and if the power can play against high-end pitching, his prospect stock will once again soar.

> **#85**
> BP Top 101 Prospects

## 2. Jose Ramirez   RHP

**Born:** 1/21/90   **Age:** 24   **Bats:** R   **Throws:** R   **Height:** 6' 3"   **Weight:** 190

| MLB ETA | CT | FB | CH | CB | SL | OFP | Realistic |
|---|---|---|---|---|---|---|---|
| 2014 | ----- | 70 | 70 | ----- | 60 | 65<br>NO.2-3 STARTER | 55<br>LATE INN RP (SU) |

| YEAR | TEAM | LVL | AGE | W | L | SV | G | GS | IP | H | HR | BB | SO | BB9 | SO9 | GB% | BABIP | WHIP | ERA | FIP | FRA | WARP |
|---|---|---|---|---|---|---|---|---|---|---|---|---|---|---|---|---|---|---|---|---|---|---|
| 2013 | TRN | AA | 23 | 1 | 3 | 1 | 9 | 8 | 42.3 | 28 | 7 | 15 | 50 | 3.2 | 10.6 | 44% | .233 | 1.02 | 2.76 | 4.39 | 5.40 | 0.1 |
| 2013 | SWB | AAA | 23 | 1 | 1 | 0 | 8 | 8 | 31.3 | 29 | 3 | 21 | 28 | 6.0 | 8.0 | 46% | .321 | 1.60 | 4.88 | 5.06 | 6.34 | -0.3 |
| 2014 | NYA | MLB | 24 | 2 | 3 | 0 | 46 | 0 | 48.3 | 52 | 7 | 24 | 35 | 4.4 | 6.6 | 44% | .297 | 1.57 | 5.47 | 5.26 | 5.95 | -0.6 |
| 2015 | NYA | MLB | 24 | 2 | 1 | 0 | 38 | 0 | 40.0 | 42 | 5 | 21 | 34 | 4.8 | 6.6 | 44% | .310 | 1.59 | 5.27 | 4.80 | 5.72 | -0.4 |

**Breakout:** 0%   **Improve:** 0%   **Collapse:** 0%   **Attrition:** 0%   **MLB:** 0%     *Comparables: Steve Johnson, Corey Kluber, Henry Sosa*

**Drafted/Acquired:** International free agent, 2007, Dominican Republic

**Previous Ranking:** #3 (Org)

**What Happened in 2013:** Ramirez failed to log 100 innings for the second straight season, once again plagued by injuries that continue to keep the 24-year-old arm from blossoming into a frontline prospect.

**Strengths:** Excellent size/strength; athletic; arm speed is special; fastball is easy plus pitch; routinely works in the mid-90s; touches higher; late life; changeup is money pitch; excellent arm speed and late action; plus-plus potential with better command; slider flashes high quality; sharp with big tilt.

**Weaknesses:** Delivery is inconsistent; doesn't repeat/below-average command; slider can get too slurvy/loses arm speed and is deliberate; injuries limit potential.

**Risk Factor/Injury History:** Moderate risk; long history of injury

**Bret Sayre's Fantasy Take:** While he gets fewer press clippings than Rafael De Paula, Ramirez' stuff firmly places him as the top fantasy option among pitchers in this system. Fortunately for him, it's been historically easier for pitching prospects to find a place in the Bronx than it has for position players. In the rotation, he could be a reliable source of wins and strikeouts, but with some giveback in WHIP, a la Lance Lynn.

**The Year Ahead:** I'm a very big fan of Jose Ramirez, although he's probably a long shot to stick around in a rotation. That said, the arm is special, and the fastball/changeup combo will make him an impact pitcher at the highest level. If he can stay healthy (big if) and take steps forward with his delivery and overall command, Ramirez could develop into a high-leverage reliever, perhaps even a closer if it really comes together. The arm is that good.

## 3. J.R. Murphy    C

**Born:** 5/13/91    **Age:** 23    **Bats:** R    **Throws:** R    **Height:** 5'11"    **Weight:** 195

| MLB ETA | Hit | Power | Run | Glove | Arm | | OFP | Realistic |
|---|---|---|---|---|---|---|---|---|
| Debuted in 2013 | 50 | --- | --- | 50 | 50 | | 50<br>ML REGULAR | 45<br>BACKUP C/<AVG ML |

| YEAR | TEAM | LVL | AGE | PA | R | 2B | 3B | HR | RBI | BB | SO | SB | CS | AVG/OBP/SLG | TAv | BABIP | BRR | FRAA | WARP |
|---|---|---|---|---|---|---|---|---|---|---|---|---|---|---|---|---|---|---|---|
| 2013 | TRN | AA | 22 | 211 | 34 | 10 | 0 | 6 | 25 | 24 | 32 | 1 | 0 | .268/.352/.421 | .307 | .293 | 1.4 | C(49): 0.1 | 2.6 |
| 2013 | SWB | AAA | 22 | 257 | 26 | 19 | 0 | 6 | 21 | 23 | 41 | 0 | 1 | .270/.342/.430 | .264 | .304 | 0.6 | C(56): -0.8 | 1.5 |
| 2013 | NYA | MLB | 22 | 27 | 3 | 1 | 0 | 0 | 1 | 1 | 9 | 0 | 0 | .154/.185/.192 | .146 | .235 | 0.0 | C(15): 0.1 | -0.1 |
| 2014 | NYA | MLB | 23 | 250 | 23 | 12 | 0 | 6 | 28 | 16 | 49 | 0 | 0 | .235/.287/.370 | .240 | .270 | -0.5 | C 0, 3B 0 | 0.6 |
| 2015 | NYA | MLB | 24 | 250 | 28 | 12 | 0 | 7 | 27 | 21 | 51 | 0 | 0 | .227/.295/.370 | .244 | .261 | -0.7 | C 0, 3B 0 | 0.7 |

Breakout: 2%    Improve: 11%    Collapse: 1%    Attrition: 10%    MLB: 24%    *Comparables: Austin Romine, Jonathan Lucroy, Bryan Anderson*

**Drafted/Acquired:** 2nd round, 2009 draft, The Pendleton School (Bradenton, FL)

**Previous Ranking:** NR

**What Happened in 2013:** You can call it a breakout year for the then-22-year-old backstop, as he played 108 games in the upper minors, and even had a 16-game cup of coffee at the major-league level.

**Strengths:** Good swing; shows bat speed and strength; can lift the ball; has a chance to develop into solid-average hitter; good approach; has a plan at the plate; receiving skills project to solid-average; arm is solid-average; quick release; good catch/throw skills; good makeup.

**Weaknesses:** Lacks impact tools; power will likely play below average; hit tool lacks plus projection; struggles against velocity and arm-side stuff; well-below-average run; defensive profile is average (to solid-average) but not game changing; footwork/glovework still need refinement.

**Risk Factor/Injury History:** Low risk; achieved major-league level

**Bret Sayre's Fantasy Take:** Outside of deeper leagues, there's not a ton of upside with Murphy. However, in two-catcher formats, he can help in a Carlos Ruiz sort of way (without the power spike). The potential for strong plate discipline skills gives him a slight uptick in points league value, but with Brian McCann in town, he's going to need a change of scenery to find consistent playing time.

**The Year Ahead:** Murphy is going to be a major-league quality defender behind the plate, with a playable arm and improving catch/throw and receiving skills. The bat is likely to be down-the-lineup at best, but he brings a plan to the plate and isn't a giveaway out. His likely role will be as a backup, but he has the potential to develop into an average major-league regular at a premium defensive position, and despite a lack of loud tools, the sum of his parts could make him a very valuable player.

## 4. Slade Heathcott    CF

**Born:** 9/28/90    **Age:** 23    **Bats:** L    **Throws:** L    **Height:** 6'0"    **Weight:** 195

| MLB ETA | Hit | Power | Run | Glove | Arm | | OFP | Realistic |
|---|---|---|---|---|---|---|---|---|
| Late 2014 | 50 | --- | 70 | 60 | 60 | | 60<br>1ST DIV PLAYER | 45<br>BENCH OF/<AVG ML |

| YEAR | TEAM | LVL | AGE | PA | R | 2B | 3B | HR | RBI | BB | SO | SB | CS | AVG/OBP/SLG | TAv | BABIP | BRR | FRAA | WARP |
|---|---|---|---|---|---|---|---|---|---|---|---|---|---|---|---|---|---|---|---|
| 2013 | TRN | AA | 22 | 444 | 59 | 22 | 7 | 8 | 49 | 36 | 107 | 15 | 8 | .261/.327/.411 | .274 | .336 | 1.7 | CF(90): -5.8 | 1.6 |
| 2014 | NYA | MLB | 23 | 250 | 30 | 10 | 2 | 5 | 22 | 14 | 71 | 7 | 3 | .233/.282/.360 | .233 | .310 | 0.3 | CF -1, LF 0 | -0.1 |
| 2015 | NYA | MLB | 24 | 250 | 26 | 11 | 2 | 5 | 25 | 16 | 72 | 7 | 3 | .232/.288/.362 | .237 | .309 | 0.3 | CF -2, LF 0 | -0.1 |

Breakout: 1%    Improve: 8%    Collapse: 3%    Attrition: 9%    MLB: 24%    *Comparables: Trayvon Robinson, Austin Jackson, Xavier Paul*

**Drafted/Acquired:** 1st round, 2009 draft, Texas HS (Texarkana, TX)

**Previous Ranking:** #4 (Org)

**What Happened in 2013:** Even though he missed time with injury (a tradition for Heathcott), he still managed to play a career-high 103 games.

**Strengths:** Plus-plus athleticism; high-end physical tools; run is plus-plus; arm is plus; glove is above average; gap pop; some bat-to-ball ability; could develop into average hitter.

**Weaknesses:** Balls-to-the-wall approach on all sides of the ball; reckless; overly aggressive at the plate; struggles against spin; loses balance; noisy in preswing; limited bat control in the zone; game power to play below average.

**Risk Factor/Injury History:** Moderate risk; injury history; big gap between projection and present.

**Bret Sayre's Fantasy Take:** Heathcott's value will be predicated on his speed, and the lack of stolen-base attempts at the minor-league level isn't making his case particularly well. At his best, he could be a light version of Brett Gardner, with a .260-.270 average, a handful of homers and 25-30 steals. Of course, that power could tick up at Yankee Stadium, but the odds of him calling that stadium home are low compared to other similar prospects.

**The Year Ahead:** You can make the case that Heathcott has the highest tool-based ceiling in the entire organization, with impressive physical gifts and the ability to play an up-the-middle position. His game lacks nuance, with an all-or-nothing approach and a highly contagious but often reckless style of play that limits his ability to stay healthy. If he can put the bat to the ball with enough consistency, he can bring his legs into the equation and possibly hit for a respectable average. Along with his defensive ability, this would allow him to develop into a major-league regular, and perhaps more if the bat really steps up. The likely outcome is a versatile bench outfielder with speed and a soft bat, a valuable player but a fraction of what the physical tools suggested was possible.

## 5. Tyler Austin    RF

**Born:** 9/6/91   **Age:** 22   **Bats:** R   **Throws:** R   **Height:** 6' 1"   **Weight:** 220

| MLB ETA | Hit | Power | Run | Glove | Arm | OFP | Realistic |
|---|---|---|---|---|---|---|---|
| Late 2014 | 55 | 50 | – | 50 | 50 | 50<br>ML REGULAR | 45<br>BENCH OF/PLATOON |

| YEAR | TEAM | LVL | AGE | PA | R | 2B | 3B | HR | RBI | BB | SO | SB | CS | AVG/OBP/SLG | TAv | BABIP | BRR | FRAA | WARP |
|---|---|---|---|---|---|---|---|---|---|---|---|---|---|---|---|---|---|---|---|
| 2013 | TRN | AA | 21 | 366 | 43 | 17 | 1 | 6 | 40 | 41 | 79 | 4 | 0 | .257/.344/.373 | .260 | .321 | -0.4 | RF(69): -4.6 | 0.6 |
| 2013 | YAT | Rk | 21 | 7 | 1 | 0 | 0 | 0 | 0 | 1 | 0 | 0 | 0 | .667/.714/.667 | .491 | .667 | -0.1 | RF(2): 0.0 | 0.2 |
| 2014 | NYA | MLB | 22 | 250 | 27 | 11 | 1 | 7 | 28 | 19 | 65 | 4 | 0 | .242/.303/.385 | .251 | .300 | 0.4 | RF -2, 1B -0 | 0.0 |
| 2015 | NYA | MLB | 23 | 250 | 29 | 13 | 1 | 7 | 29 | 21 | 64 | 3 | 0 | .242/.310/.401 | .261 | .305 | 0.1 | RF -3, 1B 0 | 1.2 |

Breakout: 0%    Improve: 0%    Collapse: 0%    Attrition: 0%    MLB: 0%    *Comparables: Caleb Gindl, Domonic Brown, Carlos Gonzalez*

**Drafted/Acquired:** 13th round, 2010 draft, Heritage HS (Conyers, GA)

**Previous Ranking:** #5 (Org)

**What Happened in 2013:** Injuries prevented Austin from building on his breakout 2012 season, but when healthy, the bat speed and solid-average power potential could make him a major-league regular.

**Strengths:** Strong frame; short, compact stroke; produces very good bat speed; can drive the ball; solid-average power potential; advanced approach; average arm (can play in outfield); average glove; high baseball IQ; plus-plus makeup.

**Weaknesses:** Game power slow to come; lacks loud tools; defensive profile is average at best in a corner; below-average run; relies on instincts more than athleticism in the field; struggles against arm-side stuff.

**Risk Factor/Injury History:** Moderate risk; injury history

**Bret Sayre's Fantasy Take:** After a disappointing season, Austin's dynasty league value has taken a big tumble, but maybe the tumble shouldn't be quite so big. The potential is still there for a .275 hitter with 20-home-run power and enough smarts on the bases to steal double digits. After all, in 244 career minor-league games, he's 45-for-47 on the basepaths.

**The Year Ahead:** Austin has natural bat-to-ball ability, with a short stroke that produces bat speed and allows him to make hard contact. That contact has yet to manifest itself as over-the-fence power, at least against upper-minors pitching, but it has a chance to play to average, and the hit tool and approach could push it beyond that in a perfect-world scenario. It's not a sexy profile, but Austin has a strong feel for the game and plus makeup, so he has a chance to develop into a major-league regular.

## 6. Mason Williams    CF

**Born:** 8/21/91   **Age:** 22   **Bats:** L   **Throws:** R   **Height:** 6' 1"   **Weight:** 180

| MLB ETA | Hit | Power | Run | Glove | Arm | OFP | Realistic |
|---|---|---|---|---|---|---|---|
| 2015 | 50 | – | 65 | 60 | 50 | 60<br>1ST DIV PLAYER | 45<br>BENCH OF/<AVG ML |

| YEAR | TEAM | LVL | AGE | PA | R | 2B | 3B | HR | RBI | BB | SO | SB | CS | AVG/OBP/SLG | TAv | BABIP | BRR | FRAA | WARP |
|---|---|---|---|---|---|---|---|---|---|---|---|---|---|---|---|---|---|---|---|
| 2013 | TAM | A+ | 21 | 461 | 56 | 21 | 3 | 3 | 24 | 39 | 61 | 15 | 9 | .261/.327/.350 | .245 | .299 | 3.3 | CF(98): 6.6 | 1.7 |
| 2013 | TRN | AA | 21 | 76 | 7 | 3 | 1 | 1 | 4 | 1 | 18 | 0 | 0 | .153/.164/.264 | .146 | .189 | -0.5 | CF(15): 0.3 | -0.7 |
| 2014 | NYA | MLB | 22 | 250 | 29 | 10 | 1 | 5 | 21 | 11 | 51 | 7 | 4 | .231/.267/.346 | .218 | .270 | 0.0 | CF 2 | -0.1 |
| 2015 | NYA | MLB | 23 | 250 | 25 | 10 | 1 | 4 | 24 | 14 | 48 | 6 | 4 | .240/.283/.352 | .229 | .275 | -0.2 | CF 2 | -0.2 |

Breakout: 0%    Improve: 0%    Collapse: 0%    Attrition: 0%    MLB: 0%    *Comparables: A.J. Pollock, Rafael Ortega, Gerardo Parra*

**Drafted/Acquired:** 4th round, 2010 draft, West Orange HS (Winter Garden, FL)

**Previous Ranking:** #2 (Org), #51 (Top 101)

**What Happened in 2013:** After a very strong 2012 season—one that saw Williams shoot up prospect rankings—his stock came crashing down to earth after a lackluster 100-game run in the Florida State League.

**Strengths:** Impact athlete; well-above-average run; excellent range in center; glove projects to plus; arm is solid; shows contact ability at the plate; impressive hand-eye coordination.

**Weaknesses:** Contact is often weak; lacks punch; bails out on pitches; power will play well below average; speed is easy plus, but isn't a great baserunner; questions about work ethic/makeup.

**Risk Factor/Injury History:** Moderate risk; limited experience at Double-A; makeup concerns.

**Bret Sayre's Fantasy Take:** Valuing Williams for fantasy leagues is extremely difficult, as there's such a gap between what his raw tools say he should be and what he is. At best, he's a potential top-30 outfielder, capable of stealing 30+ bases and contributing a little everywhere else (like a Starling Marte type). But as Jason writes above, Williams' tool package does not nearly tell the whole story.

**The Year Ahead:** Williams has all the raw physical tools to be a major-league regular, and perhaps an impact first-division type if it all comes together. The bat isn't as good as some have suggested in the past, as the contact can be soft and lifeless. But the hand-eye and speed could allow him to hit for average, a top-of-the-lineup table-setter as the dream. The defensive profile in center will give him value even if the bat falls short of the mark, but the concerns about his work ethic and overall baseball makeup don't offer a lot of confidence that he will reach his potential, much less overachieve his projections.

---

## 7.  Gregory Bird    1B

**Born:** 11/9/92   **Age:** 21   **Bats:** L   **Throws:** R   **Height:** 6' 3"   **Weight:** 215

| MLB ETA | Hit | Power | Run | Glove | Arm | | OFP | Realistic |
|---|---|---|---|---|---|---|---|---|
| **2016** | **55** | **60** | --- | --- | --- | | **50**<br>ML REGULAR | **45**<br>PLATOON/<AVG ML |

| YEAR | TEAM | LVL | AGE | PA | R | 2B | 3B | HR | RBI | BB | SO | SB | CS | AVG/OBP/SLG | TAv | BABIP | BRR | FRAA | WARP |
|---|---|---|---|---|---|---|---|---|---|---|---|---|---|---|---|---|---|---|---|
| 2013 | CSC | A | 20 | 573 | 84 | 36 | 3 | 20 | 84 | 107 | 132 | 1 | 1 | .288/.428/.511 | .347 | .364 | -0.5 | 1B(90): -7.9 | 5.4 |
| 2014 | NYA | MLB | 21 | 250 | 28 | 10 | 0 | 8 | 30 | 33 | 70 | 0 | 0 | .228/.332/.386 | .262 | .290 | -0.5 | 1B -3, C -0 | 0.0 |
| 2015 | NYA | MLB | 22 | 250 | 33 | 10 | 1 | 8 | 30 | 35 | 65 | 0 | 0 | .236/.345/.406 | .275 | .297 | -0.6 | 1B -3, C 0 | 1.9 |

Breakout: 0%    Improve: 0%    Collapse: 0%    Attrition: 0%    MLB: 0%         *Comparables: Jaff Decker, Anthony Rizzo, Lars Anderson*

**Drafted/Acquired:** 5th round, 2011 draft, Grandview HS (Aurora, CO)

**Previous Ranking:** NR

**What Happened in 2013:** In his full-season debut, the former 5th round pick emerged as a legit prospect, clubbing 59 extra-base hits in 130 Sally League games.

**Strengths:** Physical player; generates very good bat speed; swing has power characteristics; plus in-game power potential; hit tool to let it play; excellent eye at the plate; takes counts deep; advanced overall approach; excellent makeup reports.

**Weaknesses:** Strong but not overly athletic; below-average run; limited on defense; swing can get can long/leveraged; hit-first profile.

**Risk Factor/Injury History:** Moderate risk; yet to play in upper-minors; bat-only profile.

**Bret Sayre's Fantasy Take:** He'll need the power to come through at the highest level to be a fantasy first baseman worth investing in. Of course, if he were to hold down the position with the Yankees, that short porch would help make him more fantasy viable, but it's too early to worry about that. At this point, you're hoping he becomes a .285 hitter with 15-20 homers—but even that wasn't enough to make Brandon Belt a top-15 option at the position in 2013.

**The Year Ahead:** Several industry sources were very high on Bird, including one front office (NL) source who said he would take the 21-year-old bat over every position player in the Yankees system other than Sanchez. The makeup gets positive reviews, which is encouraging, but the swing is what really matters, and Bird can hit, with bat speed and strength and the potential to bring legit power into game action. It's a tough profile but if the offense has a chance to play, I wouldn't be shocked if Bird climbs the list in 2014 and continues to bring it at the plate.

## 8. Eric Jagielo 3B

**Born:** 5/17/92  **Age:** 22  **Bats:** L  **Throws:** R  **Height:** 6' 2"  **Weight:** 195

| | Hit | Power | Run | Glove | Arm | OFP | Realistic |
|---|---|---|---|---|---|---|---|
| **MLB ETA** 2016 | 55 | 60 | --- | --- | 60 | 55 >AVG ML PLAYER | 45 <AVG ML PLAYER |

| YEAR | TEAM | LVL | AGE | PA | R | 2B | 3B | HR | RBI | BB | SO | SB | CS | AVG/OBP/SLG | TAv | BABIP | BRR | FRAA | WARP |
|---|---|---|---|---|---|---|---|---|---|---|---|---|---|---|---|---|---|---|---|
| 2013 | YAN | Rk | 21 | 3 | 1 | 0 | 0 | 0 | 0 | 0 | 0 | 0 | 0 | .000/.333/.000 | .197 | .000 | 0.0 | 3B(1): -0.0 | 0.0 |
| 2013 | YAT | Rk | 21 | 8 | 2 | 2 | 0 | 0 | 1 | 1 | 2 | 0 | 0 | .286/.375/.571 | .324 | .400 | 0.1 | 3B(3): -0.0 | 0.1 |
| 2013 | STA | A- | 21 | 218 | 19 | 14 | 1 | 6 | 27 | 26 | 54 | 0 | 0 | .266/.376/.451 | .315 | .344 | -1.9 | 3B(42): -1.3 | 1.6 |
| 2014 | NYA | MLB | 22 | 250 | 21 | 8 | 0 | 5 | 24 | 18 | 74 | 0 | 0 | .198/.263/.305 | .209 | .260 | -0.4 | 3B -2 | -0.9 |
| 2015 | NYA | MLB | 23 | 250 | 29 | 9 | 0 | 8 | 28 | 19 | 70 | 0 | 0 | .212/.282/.360 | .237 | .265 | -0.6 | 3B -2 | -0.2 |

**Breakout:** 0%   **Improve:** 0%   **Collapse:** 0%   **Attrition:** 0%   **MLB:** 0%        *Comparables: Mike Olt, Jedd Gyorko, Jesus Guzman*

**Drafted/Acquired:** 1st round, 2013 draft, University of Notre Dame (South Bend, IN)

**Previous Ranking:** NR

**What Happened in 2013:** The 26th overall pick in the draft, Jagielo was solid but not spectacular in his short-season debut, flashing the power potential but showing swing-and-miss against average pitching.

**Strengths:** Big, strong frame; potential for hit/power profile; good swing; good approach; power could reach plus; swing has lift; arm is strong enough for third or corner OF spot; okay actions in the field; works hard/good makeup.

**Weaknesses:** Hit tool might play fringe-average; swing-and-miss in the zone; below average at third; below-average rung; limited range.

**Risk Factor/Injury History:** Moderate risk; short-season resume.

**Bret Sayre's Fantasy Take:** A better fantasy prospect than real-life prospect, Jagielo has a chance to develop into the Yankees' best homegrown hitter since Robinson Cano. However, that's more of a reflection on the organization than Jagielo. A third baseman who could hit .275 with 25 homers is nothing to shake your head at, and he should be off the board within the first 20 names in 2013 dynasty drafts.

**The Year Ahead:** Jagielo was drafted for his polish and offensive potential, which means he should be facing an accelerated developmental plan and high expectations for immediate production. It was a small sample, but I wasn't blown away with Jagielo's bat in the New York-Penn League; the bat speed wasn't special and he was often behind average stuff located over the plate. But it was the end of a long season, and several sources think the 22-year-old product of Notre Dame is going to hit, for both average and power, and if he shines in his full-season debut, he could be sitting atop this list next season.

## 9. Ian Clarkin LHP

**Born:** 2/14/95  **Age:** 19  **Bats:** L  **Throws:** L  **Height:** 6' 2"  **Weight:** 186

| | CT | FB | CH | CB | SL | OFP | Realistic |
|---|---|---|---|---|---|---|---|
| **MLB ETA** 2017 | --- | 60 | 50 | 60 | --- | 60 NO.2-3 STARTER | 50 NO.4 STARTER |

| YEAR | TEAM | LVL | AGE | W | L | SV | G | GS | IP | H | HR | BB | SO | BB9 | SO9 | GB% | BABIP | WHIP | ERA | FIP | FRA | WARP |
|---|---|---|---|---|---|---|---|---|---|---|---|---|---|---|---|---|---|---|---|---|---|---|
| 2013 | YAN | Rk | 18 | 0 | 2 | 0 | 3 | 3 | 5.0 | 5 | 2 | 4 | 4 | 7.2 | 7.2 | 44% | .214 | 1.80 | 10.80 | 10.06 | 14.18 | -0.3 |

**Breakout:** 0%   **Improve:** 0%   **Collapse:** 0%   **Attrition:** 0%   **MLB:** 0%        *Comparables: Brandon Maurer, Jeurys Familia, David Holmberg*

**Drafted/Acquired:** 1st round, 2013 draft, Madison HS (San Diego, CA)

**Previous Ranking:** NR

**What Happened in 2013:** Selected 33rd overall in the 2013 draft, Clarkin has a higher ceiling than most of his organizational contemporaries (he actually projects to stick around in a rotation), with a projectable three-pitch mix from the left side.

**Strengths:** Athletic; physically projectable; creates good downhill plane from high 3/4 slot; fastball works upper-80s/low-90s; projects to be plus pitch; curveball has money potential; big tumbler with wipeout potential with better command; shows some feel for changeup; highly competitive background.

**Weaknesses:** Complicated delivery, with high hands and high leg; struggles with timing/finishing; command is below average (present); fastball is pedestrian (velo) and can lack movement; changeup is below average (present).

**Risk Factor/Injury History:** High risk; 5 professional innings; long developmental road.

**Bret Sayre's Fantasy Take:** He may not have the upside of some of his draft classmates, but Clarkin is plenty interesting for fantasy nonetheless. It's very early to know what he might be, but Clarkin isn't likely to be a pitcher that overwhelms with strikeouts—more of an above-average across-the-board contributor with a tough AL East task possibly ahead of him.

**The Year Ahead:** Clarkin will get to settle into a short-season assignment in 2014, where he can work to refine his delivery/command and develop his fastball. The secondary stuff will get there eventually, as the curveball already shows legit plus potential, but the first developmental steps will likely be taken through a heavy dose of four-seam fastballs. Clarkin is a long-term project, but an athletic lefty with a promising and projectable three-pitch mix is worth the developmental patience.

## 10.  Aaron Judge  OF

**Born:** 4/26/92   **Age:** 22   **Bats:** R   **Throws:** R   **Height:** 6'7"   **Weight:** 230

| MLB ETA | Hit | Power | Run | Glove | Arm | OFP | Realistic |
|---|---|---|---|---|---|---|---|
| Late 2016 | – | 80 | – | – | 60 | 60<br>1ST DIV PLAYER | 40<br>UPPER MINORS |

| YEAR | TEAM | LVL | AGE | PA | R | 2B | 3B | HR | RBI | BB | SO | SB | CS | AVG/OBP/SLG | TAv | BABIP | BRR | FRAA | WARP |
|---|---|---|---|---|---|---|---|---|---|---|---|---|---|---|---|---|---|---|---|
| | | | | | | | | | No Professional Experience | | | | | | | | | | |

**Drafted/Acquired:** 1st round, 2013 draft, California State University Fresno (Fresno, CA)

**Previous Ranking:** NR

**What Happened in 2013:** Built like a power forward but drafted as a power hitter, Judge is an abnormally large human that has more raw power than anybody on the Yankees farm.

**Strengths:** Enormous size, raw strength; excellent athlete for his size; 80 raw; power could play as well above average; solid run; strong arm.

**Weaknesses:** Hit tool could limit power; likely to feature big swing-and-miss; big strike zone; swing not tailored for power yet; strength-driven bat speed; enormous size could raise injury concerns (long term).

**Risk Factor/Injury History:** High risk; no professional record; questions about hit tool.

**Bret Sayre's Fantasy Take:** A great flier in dynasty drafts, Judge will set out to prove that his power can translate to the stat page. If it can, we're looking at a potential 30-homer hitter at his peak. If not, you'll probably be dropping him from your roster in 2015.

**The Year Ahead:** Judge has the potential to be a middle-of-the-order power monster, but he also has the potential to flame out before he reaches the highest level. Some scouts believe the hit tool and swing-and-miss tendencies could spoil the party for Judge, but without a professional record, it's all just speculation and projection at this point.

## Prospects on the Rise

**1. RHP Luis Severino:** You can make a case for Severino in the top 10, based solely on his incredible arm strength and fastball potential. The profile might end up being more reliever than starter, but you should never discount a mid-90s fastball (touches higher) that comes out with such ease and effectiveness. He's a promising prospect.

**2. C Luis Torrens:** A seven-figure Dominican signing in 2012, Torrens has the physical tools and feel for the game to develop into a promising prospect, with a quality swing and power potential at the plate and a big arm behind it, despite being raw on all sides of the ball. He could be ready to take a big step forward in 2014.

**3. RHP Jose Campos:** I loved Campos when I saw him in the Mariners system, so it's been highly disappointing to see injuries slow down his progress after coming over in the Montero/Pineda exchange in 2012. It's foolish to blindly assume health, but if Campos can stay on the mound and get back on his developmental trajectory, he's a top-10 player in this system and a legit major-league prospect. I still really like the stuff.

## Factors on the Farm

### Prospects likely to contribute at the major-league level in 2014

**1. LHP Manny Banuelos:** "Hey you, I know you, I know you." Before the elbow injury shut him down for the entire 2013 season, Banuelos was on the cusp of the majors and considered one of the top prospects in the Yankees system. Reports have the stuff back to normal—including the plus fastball and change—but the lengthy layoff could cover him in rust, especially when it comes to command. But it shouldn't take long for the 22-year-old lefty to find his form, and in the event of injury or ineffectiveness, he could then find himself pitching at the major-league level.

**2. RHP Rafael De Paula:** De Paula's stateside debut was both fantastic and frustrating, as his plus-plus bat-missing fastball made hitters look foolish, but his lack of control often offered up a free pass instead. Despite his limited professional resume, I think De Paula could be fast-tracked in the bullpen, a role that he is likely to end up in down the line anyway. The fastball is explosive, with velocity and incredible wiggle, and with a little refinement in his delivery, he should be able to throw enough strikes to ride that pitch all the way to the majors. It's a long shot in 2014, but I have a feeling he could be in for an accelerated ride this season.

**3. RHP Bryan Mitchell:** A live-armed righty with two major-league quality pitches, Mitchell could contribute to the 2014 major-league team as either a starter or a reliever. The latter is the likely outcome, as the 22-year-old brings a very big fastball (works with easy plus velocity and touches higher) and hard curveball (low-80s; big snap), but struggles to repeat his delivery and has below-average command at present. He will likely continue to start in Double-A, but the profile could have impact in bursts, especially if he can refine enough to throw more quality strikes and avoid barrels, and a step forward developmentally could put the former 16th-round pick on the biggest stage before the end of the season.

## 1. Addison Russell   SS

**Born:** 1/23/94   **Age:** 20   **Bats:** R   **Throws:** R   **Height:** 6'0"   **Weight:** 195

| MLB ETA | Hit | Power | Run | Glove | Arm | OFP | Realistic |
|---|---|---|---|---|---|---|---|
| Late 2014 | 60 | 60 | — | 60 | 60 | 70 ALL-STAR | 60 1ST DIV PLAYER |

| YEAR | TEAM | LVL | AGE | PA | R | 2B | 3B | HR | RBI | BB | SO | SB | CS | AVG/OBP/SLG | TAv | BABIP | BRR | FRAA | WARP |
|---|---|---|---|---|---|---|---|---|---|---|---|---|---|---|---|---|---|---|---|
| 2013 | SAC | AAA | 19 | 13 | 1 | 0 | 0 | 0 | 0 | 0 | 9 | 0 | 0 | .077/.077/.077 | .037 | .250 | 0.7 | SS(2): -0.2 | -0.2 |
| 2013 | STO | A+ | 19 | 504 | 85 | 29 | 10 | 17 | 60 | 61 | 116 | 21 | 3 | .275/.377/.508 | .321 | .338 | 1.0 | SS(105): -4.6 | 5.3 |
| 2014 | OAK | MLB | 20 | 250 | 29 | 10 | 2 | 5 | 21 | 20 | 67 | 6 | 1 | .226/.294/.348 | .246 | .300 | 0.8 | SS -3 | 0.5 |
| 2015 | OAK | MLB | 21 | 250 | 29 | 12 | 2 | 6 | 27 | 21 | 62 | 4 | 1 | .243/.314/.395 | .265 | .306 | 0.3 | SS -3 | 1.9 |

**Breakout:** 0%   **Improve:** 0%   **Collapse:** 0%   **Attrition:** 0%   **MLB:** 0%   *Comparables: Xander Bogaerts, Nick Franklin, Brett Lawrie*

**Drafted/Acquired:** 1st round, 2012 draft, Pace HS (Pace, FL)

**Previous Ranking:** #1 (Org), #22 (Top 101)

**What Happened in 2013:** As a 19-year-old, Russell jumped straight to the High-A level, and more than held his own against older competition, slugging 56 extra-base hits and stealing 21 bags.

**Strengths:** Legit offensive upside; hands are very good; gets extension and can drive the ball; plus raw power; shows bat speed; feeds on velocity; good baseball instincts; excellent actions in the field; can make the plays; arm is plus.

**Weaknesses:** Can get too fast on defense; will rush setup/footwork; good instincts but range could be issue in the future; bat can get loose; swing-and-miss; will expand and chase for spin.

**Risk Factor/Injury History:** Moderate risk; advanced player; ready for Double-A

**Bret Sayre's Fantasy Take:** A top-10 overall fantasy prospect, Russell has a shot at becoming one of the most sought-after commodities in fantasy baseball: a middle infielder who can contribute in all five categories. Playing in Oakland might put a slight damper on his raw stats, but this is still a player who could hit .280+ with 20-20 potential. He's a keeper.

**The Year Ahead:** Russell is on the fast track to the majors, and with a strong start in Double-A could find himself in Oakland before the end of the season. His overall profile is special, but you can raise some red flags if you use a sharp enough lens; the actions are sweet at short but the range isn't ideal and he can play a bit hard, and at the plate his swing can be too power driven with early extension on an exaggerated plane. Even if he moves to third down the line, which I don't think is a given, the bat will not only play but allow him to reach a first-division status. If he sticks at short—which I believe he can—he's a perennial all-star caliber player. Either way, the future is bright.

**#7**
BP Top 101 Prospects

## 2. Bobby Wahl   RHP

**Born:** 3/21/92   **Age:** 22   **Bats:** R   **Throws:** R   **Height:** 6'2"   **Weight:** 210

| MLB ETA | CT | FB | CH | CB | SL | OFP | Realistic |
|---|---|---|---|---|---|---|---|
| Late 2015 | — | 70 | 55 | — | 60 | 60 NO.2-3 STARTER | 50 LATE INN RP (SU) |

| YEAR | TEAM | LVL | AGE | W | L | SV | G | GS | IP | H | HR | BB | SO | BB9 | SO9 | GB% | BABIP | WHIP | ERA | FIP | FRA | WARP |
|---|---|---|---|---|---|---|---|---|---|---|---|---|---|---|---|---|---|---|---|---|---|---|
| 2013 | VER | A- | 21 | 0 | 0 | 2 | 9 | 4 | 20.7 | 20 | 3 | 6 | 27 | 2.6 | 11.8 | 32% | .321 | 1.26 | 3.92 | 3.24 | 4.17 | 0.2 |
| 2013 | ATH | Rk | 21 | 0 | 0 | 0 | 1 | 1 | 1.0 | 0 | 0 | 2 | 1 | 18.0 | 9.0 | 0% | .000 | 2.00 | 9.00 | 8.00 | 15.01 | -0.1 |
| 2014 | OAK | MLB | 22 | 1 | 2 | 0 | 11 | 4 | 32.0 | 37 | 4 | 19 | 20 | 5.3 | 5.6 | 41% | .306 | 1.72 | 5.71 | 5.70 | 6.21 | -0.4 |
| 2015 | OAK | MLB | 23 | 2 | 2 | 1 | 30 | 8 | 96.7 | 98 | 11 | 43 | 67 | 4.0 | 6.2 | 42% | .289 | 1.47 | 4.61 | 4.74 | 5.01 | -0.1 |

**Breakout:** 0%   **Improve:** 0%   **Collapse:** 0%   **Attrition:** 0%   **MLB:** 0%   *Comparables: Vic Black, Trevor Rosenthal, Michael Blazek*

**Drafted/Acquired:** 5th round, 2013 draft, University of Mississippi (Oxford, MS)

**Previous Ranking:** NR

**What Happened in 2013:** The A's got a steal when Wahl slipped to the fifth round of the 2013 draft, as the athletic righty has not only the stuff to move fast but also the arsenal to have impact potential at the major-league level.

**Strengths:** Good size/strength combo; pitches with athleticism; good angle on fastball from 3/4 slot; routinely works 92-95+; good vertical action; slider shows plus; 82-84 with two-plane break and depth; turns over usable changeup; low-80s with some sink; strong competitive background.

**Weaknesses:** Command comes and goes; can throw too many strikes; changeup is clear third offering; needs refinement/more consistency; delivery can show some effort; competitiveness and approach can rub some the wrong way.

**Risk Factor/Injury History:** Moderate risk; mature arsenal; ready for accelerated developmental pace.

**Bret Sayre's Fantasy Take:** This is where paying attention to pro scouting reports can come in very handy during your dynasty league drafts. While everyone else is scrambling for names once the top 20-30 players are off the board, Wahl is a great pick to have in your back pocket. There aren't more than a handful of pitchers from the 2013 draft with more fantasy upside than him, and he'll be available late.

**The Year Ahead:** Wahl was troubled by blisters and inconsistency during the spring, and that coupled with questions about his signability pushed him down the draft. The A's are going to look very smart for taking advantage of this outcome, as Wahl's stuff gives him a high ceiling and his polish allows for a high floor. Not that he is without any risk, but with a lively fastball that he can work in the mid-90s and a sharp two-plane slider, he's going to find his way to the major leagues in some capacity. If the command sharpens up and the changeup can step forward, he has a chance to pitch higher up in a major-league rotation. I expect him to move fast in 2014, possibly reaching Double-A in his first full season.

## 3. Daniel Robertson    SS

**Born:** 3/22/94    **Age:** 20    **Bats:** R    **Throws:** R    **Height:** 6'0"    **Weight:** 190

| MLB ETA | Hit | Power | Run | Glove | Arm | OFP | Realistic |
|---|---|---|---|---|---|---|---|
| 2016 | 60 | – | 50 | 50 | 50 | 55 >AVG PLAYER | 50 2ND DIV PLAYER |

| YEAR | TEAM | LVL | AGE | PA | R | 2B | 3B | HR | RBI | BB | SO | SB | CS | AVG/OBP/SLG | TAv | BABIP | BRR | FRAA | WARP |
|---|---|---|---|---|---|---|---|---|---|---|---|---|---|---|---|---|---|---|---|
| 2013 | BLT | A | 19 | 451 | 59 | 21 | 1 | 9 | 46 | 41 | 79 | 1 | 7 | .277/.353/.401 | .272 | .324 | -0.6 | SS(99): -8.9 | 1.6 |
| 2014 | OAK | MLB | 20 | 250 | 23 | 9 | 0 | 4 | 20 | 15 | 63 | 0 | 0 | .212/.264/.306 | .218 | .270 | -0.5 | SS -3, 3B 0 | -0.4 |
| 2015 | OAK | MLB | 21 | 250 | 27 | 10 | 1 | 5 | 25 | 15 | 56 | 0 | 0 | .235/.286/.356 | .238 | .281 | -0.6 | SS -3, 3B 0 | 0.1 |

Breakout: 0%    Improve: 0%    Collapse: 0%    Attrition: 0%    MLB: 0%          *Comparables: Yamaico Navarro, Lonnie Chisenhall, Tim Beckham*

**Drafted/Acquired:** 1st round, 2012 draft, Upland HS (Upland, CA)

**Previous Ranking:** #9 (Org)

**What Happened in 2013:** Robertson made his full-season debut, showing a steady and consistent approach day in and day out in the Midwest League, a tough feat for a 19-year-old at that level.

**Strengths:** Baseball skills; fundamentally sound player; quick hands at the plate; short, efficient stroke; uses the entire field; works counts; good pitch-recognition/reaction skills; can drive the ball into the gaps; makes the plays he's supposed to make in the field; makeup is lauded.

**Weaknesses:** Lacks impact tools; more polish than projection; arm isn't a weapon; range is underwhelming; move off shortstop is likely; power might not play to average.

**Risk Factor/Injury History:** Moderate risk; shows baseball skills and polish for age/level.

**Bret Sayre's Fantasy Take:** Without much upside to speak of, Robertson is not someone to target highly in fantasy leagues. With him unlikely to stay up the middle, his profile isn't sexy at a corner. And in an attempt to show off his wheels for future fantasy owners, he went 1-for-8 on the basepaths in 2013. Wait, what?

**The Year Ahead:** Players like Robertson are often undervalued, as the profile isn't sexy or suggestive and he's unlikely to find himself on a high prospect tier. But the baseball skills are present, the kind of skills that will propel him up the professional ladder and eventually land him in the major leagues. He can hit the baseball, he can field the baseball, he can throw the baseball, but he's not a loud player that will change the fortunes of a game or a team. But I bet he develops into a consistent major leaguer, most likely as a second-division third baseman that can hit for average with doubles power while giving you maximum effort on all sides of the ball. Call him a gamer, and whatever adjective fits the profile, but eventually you'll be calling him a major leaguer.

## 4. Billy McKinney    CF

**Born:** 8/23/94    **Age:** 19    **Bats:** L    **Throws:** L    **Height:** 6'1"    **Weight:** 195

| MLB ETA | Hit | Power | Run | Glove | Arm | OFP | Realistic |
|---|---|---|---|---|---|---|---|
| 2017 | 65 | 50 | – | – | – | 60 1ST DIV PLAYER | 50 2ND DIV PLAYER |

| YEAR | TEAM | LVL | AGE | PA | R | 2B | 3B | HR | RBI | BB | SO | SB | CS | AVG/OBP/SLG | TAv | BABIP | BRR | FRAA | WARP |
|---|---|---|---|---|---|---|---|---|---|---|---|---|---|---|---|---|---|---|---|
| 2013 | VER | A- | 18 | 37 | 5 | 2 | 1 | 1 | 6 | 3 | 4 | 1 | 1 | .353/.405/.559 | .371 | .379 | -0.5 | CF(9): 0.6 | 0.6 |
| 2013 | ATH | Rk | 18 | 206 | 31 | 7 | 2 | 2 | 20 | 17 | 29 | 7 | 0 | .320/.383/.414 | .296 | .364 | 3.3 | CF(29): -2.3 | 1.3 |
| 2014 | OAK | MLB | 19 | 250 | 21 | 8 | 1 | 2 | 17 | 11 | 65 | 1 | 0 | .200/.240/.272 | .197 | .260 | -0.2 | CF -1 | -1.1 |
| 2015 | OAK | MLB | 20 | 250 | 24 | 10 | 1 | 3 | 21 | 15 | 57 | 1 | 0 | .221/.270/.320 | .219 | .275 | -0.3 | CF -1 | -1.2 |

Breakout: 0%    Improve: 0%    Collapse: 0%    Attrition: 0%    MLB: 0%          *Comparables: Aaron Hicks, Che-Hsuan Lin, Joe Benson*

**Drafted/Acquired:** 1st round, 2013 draft, Plano West Senior HS (Plano, TX)

**Previous Ranking:** NR

**What Happened in 2013:** Selected 24th overall in the 2013 draft, McKinney wasted little time showing off his hyper hit tool, hitting a combined .326 over two short-season stops.

**Strengths:** Excellent bat-to-ball skills; fluid swing; short to the ball and strong through it; plus bat speed; some pop; could end up solid-average; brings it on the field; good approach.

**Weaknesses:** Bat-first profile; power future is mixed; several sources see empty batting average type; glove is average at best; arm is fringy; speed is below average; left-field profile at best.

**Risk Factor/Injury History:** High risk; short-season resume; hit tool only carrying weapon.

**Bret Sayre's Fantasy Take:** A more interesting fantasy prospect than real-life prospect, McKinney's value is tied to whether or not he can develop average power. With it, he could be a .300-15-15 guy. Without it, he's more of a Jon Jay type. Regardless, he gets a tick up in points leagues.

**The Year Ahead:** McKinney is ready for the full-season challenge, and it wouldn't shock me to see the bat continue to turn heads. The profile is a problem, so the bat will need to reach (or exceed) the projection to have value at the big-league level. He has a sweet left-handed swing and a feel for hard contact, so he should be able to hit for a high average with some secondary power and on-base skills. He could end up being a liability in the outfield, as the arm isn't strong and the speed is already below average and likely to trend down as he matures.

## 5. Raul Alcantara    RHP

**Born:** 12/4/92    **Age:** 21    **Bats:** R    **Throws:** R    **Height:** 6'3"    **Weight:** 180

| MLB ETA | CT | FB | CH | CB | SL | OFP | Realistic |
|---|---|---|---|---|---|---|---|
| 2015 | – | 65 | 60 | – | 50 | 60 NO.3 STARTER | 50 LATE INN RP (SU) |

| YEAR | TEAM | LVL | AGE | W | L | SV | G | GS | IP | H | HR | BB | SO | BB9 | SO9 | GB% | BABIP | WHIP | ERA | FIP | FRA | WARP |
|---|---|---|---|---|---|---|---|---|---|---|---|---|---|---|---|---|---|---|---|---|---|---|
| 2013 | BLT | A | 20 | 7 | 1 | 0 | 13 | 13 | 77.3 | 84 | 3 | 7 | 58 | 0.8 | 6.8 | 47% | .324 | 1.18 | 2.44 | 2.77 | 3.79 | 1.7 |
| 2013 | STO | A+ | 20 | 5 | 5 | 0 | 14 | 14 | 79.0 | 73 | 8 | 17 | 66 | 1.9 | 7.5 | 41% | .280 | 1.14 | 3.76 | 4.21 | 4.57 | 1.1 |
| 2014 | OAK | MLB | 21 | 5 | 7 | 0 | 24 | 17 | 116.7 | 139 | 15 | 47 | 50 | 3.6 | 3.9 | 45% | .301 | 1.60 | 5.49 | 5.60 | 5.96 | -1.4 |
| 2015 | OAK | MLB | 22 | 5 | 6 | 0 | 24 | 17 | 123.0 | 132 | 14 | 41 | 70 | 3.0 | 5.1 | 45% | .292 | 1.41 | 4.57 | 4.62 | 4.96 | -0.2 |

Breakout: 0%    Improve: 0%    Collapse: 0%    Attrition: 0%    MLB: 0%        *Comparables: Henderson Alvarez, Erasmo Ramirez, Alex Burnett*

**Drafted/Acquired:** International free agent, 2009, Dominican Republic

**Previous Ranking:** On The Rise

**What Happened in 2013:** Alcantara really broke out as a prospect, starting back in the Midwest League and pitching his way to High-A, where the then-20-year-old looked sharp in 14 California League starts.

**Strengths:** Prototypical pitcher frame; loose, easy arm; fastball is a plus offering; works low-90s and touches higher; good late finish; creates good angle from higher slot; slider can flash plus; thrown off fastball with good velocity and occasional sharp tilt; changeup took big step forward in 2013; good deception and fade.

**Weaknesses:** Improving control but command is still loose; can catch too much of the plate; tendency to work up in the zone; slider can lose bite; flashes but not a consistent knockout pitch yet; regressed a bit in 2013; can overthrow the changeup; lose movement.

**Risk Factor/Injury History:** Moderate risk; will pitch as a 21-year-old in '14; ready for Double-A level; arsenal for respectable major-league floor.

**Bret Sayre's Fantasy Take:** While there are certainly risks here, Alcantara's weaknesses align somewhat nicely with his potential future home. As a fly-ball pitcher who may not rack up a ton of strikeouts, the Coliseum would reduce some of the downside in his performance. Think A.J. Griffin type numbers if his secondaries both grade out as average.

**The Year Ahead:** Alcantara remains under the radar as a national prospect, but a strong showing in Double-A could change all of that. I'm quick to project Dominican arms to the bullpen, usually because of a lack of feel or an unrefined secondary arsenal. But Alcantara looks the part of a starter, and even though the realistic role suggests a late-innings outcome, I wouldn't discount his chance to stick in a rotation; he has the body to log innings, the arsenal for sequencing multiple times through an order, and the ability to throw strikes. In a perfect world, he's a quality number three starter, and the floor is quite high given his age, as he looks like a likely major-league arm regardless of the specific role.

## 6. Michael Ynoa    RHP

**Born:** 9/24/91    **Age:** 22    **Bats:** R    **Throws:** R    **Height:** 6'7"    **Weight:** 210

| MLB ETA | CT | FB | CH | CB | SL | OFP | Realistic |
|---|---|---|---|---|---|---|---|
| Late 2014 | – | 65 | 55 | 65 | – | 60 NO.2-3 STARTER | 50 LATE INN RP (SU) |

| YEAR | TEAM | LVL | AGE | W | L | SV | G | GS | IP | H | HR | BB | SO | BB9 | SO9 | GB% | BABIP | WHIP | ERA | FIP | FRA | WARP |
|---|---|---|---|---|---|---|---|---|---|---|---|---|---|---|---|---|---|---|---|---|---|---|
| 2013 | BLT | A | 21 | 2 | 1 | 0 | 15 | 15 | 54.7 | 45 | 3 | 18 | 48 | 3.0 | 7.9 | 51% | .275 | 1.15 | 2.14 | 3.67 | 4.50 | 1.1 |
| 2013 | STO | A+ | 21 | 1 | 2 | 1 | 7 | 6 | 21.0 | 23 | 2 | 17 | 20 | 7.3 | 8.6 | 37% | .333 | 1.90 | 7.71 | 5.82 | 6.80 | -0.1 |
| 2014 | OAK | MLB | 22 | 3 | 5 | 0 | 18 | 13 | 55.3 | 62 | 7 | 33 | 33 | 5.4 | 5.4 | 42% | .300 | 1.72 | 5.72 | 5.86 | 6.22 | -0.7 |
| 2015 | OAK | MLB | 23 | 5 | 7 | 0 | 35 | 23 | 157.7 | 162 | 19 | 78 | 127 | 4.5 | 7.2 | 42% | .300 | 1.52 | 4.82 | 4.73 | 5.24 | -0.8 |

Breakout: 0%    Improve: 0%    Collapse: 0%    Attrition: 0%    MLB: 0%        *Comparables: Ryan Pressly, Anthony Ortega, Rafael Dolis*

**Drafted/Acquired:** International free agent, 2008, Dominican Republic

**Previous Ranking:** On The Rise

**What Happened in 2013:** Ynoa logged a career high in innings in 2012, and more than doubled that total in 2013, but the 22-year-old has yet to log more than 100 innings in any season since signing in 2008.

**Strengths:** Remains a highly projectable, high-ceiling arm; arm strength is there; fastball sits easy plus and can touch higher; when he's over it, breaking ball has plus snap and bat-missing ability; changeup is more flash and future than present.

**Weaknesses:** Injury issues have limited developmental progress; makeup concerns; command is below average; loses his delivery; throws rather than pitches; secondary arsenal lacks consistency.

**Risk Factor/Injury History:** High risk; Tommy John surgery on resume; injury concerns

**Bret Sayre's Fantasy Take:** Ynoa is a poster child for why it's a mistake to reach for J2 signings in dynasty drafts. He still has a potential fantasy future, but it's both dimmer and more drawn out than originally anticipated. He's a worthy deep league flier regardless of role, but this is not an impact fantasy arm.

**The Year Ahead:** Ynoa remains an intriguing yet highly frustrating prospect, the kind that gets put on the 40-man despite a limited professional record yet struggles to put together the type of consistency you want to see in someone with such a roster distinction. The progress has been slow, but if Ynoa can build on 2013, the way he built on 2012, he can climb this list and pitch his way to the majors, mostly on the back of his low- to mid-90s fastball and erratic yet promising curveball. You can make a case that outside of Russell, Ynoa still has one of the highest ceilings in the system, but hope can only be sold for so long before the sell-by date makes the product unsafe for consumption. I still don't know how this ends up.

## 7.  Nolan Sanburn  RHP

**Born:** 7/21/91  **Age:** 22  **Bats:** R  **Throws:** R  **Height:** 6'0"  **Weight:** 175

| MLB ETA | CT | FB | CH | CB | SL | OFP | Realistic |
|---|---|---|---|---|---|---|---|
| 2016 | – | 60 | – | 60 | 55 | 55<br>NO.3-4 STARTER | 50<br>LATE INN RP (SU) |

| YEAR | TEAM | LVL | AGE | W | L | SV | G | GS | IP | H | HR | BB | SO | BB9 | SO9 | GB% | BABIP | WHIP | ERA | FIP | FRA | WARP |
|---|---|---|---|---|---|---|---|---|---|---|---|---|---|---|---|---|---|---|---|---|---|---|
| 2013 | BLT | A | 21 | 1 | 3 | 0 | 14 | 1 | 26.0 | 17 | 1 | 9 | 20 | 3.1 | 6.9 | 47% | .225 | 1.00 | 1.38 | 3.34 | 4.47 | 0.3 |
| 2013 | ATH | Rk | 21 | 0 | 0 | 0 | 2 | 1 | 4.0 | 3 | 0 | 1 | 6 | 2.2 | 13.5 | 67% | .333 | 1.00 | 2.25 | 2.50 | 2.31 | 0.1 |
| 2014 | OAK | MLB | 22 | 1 | 2 | 0 | 13 | 4 | 32.3 | 37 | 4 | 17 | 18 | 4.7 | 5.0 | 46% | .302 | 1.68 | 5.57 | 5.62 | 6.06 | -0.4 |
| 2015 | OAK | MLB | 23 | 3 | 3 | 1 | 39 | 8 | 105.0 | 111 | 12 | 49 | 73 | 4.2 | 6.3 | 46% | .297 | 1.52 | 4.82 | 4.80 | 5.24 | -0.4 |

Breakout: 0%    Improve: 0%    Collapse: 0%    Attrition: 0%    MLB: 0%    *Comparables: Trevor Rosenthal, Michael Blazek, Ryan Brasier*

**Drafted/Acquired:** 2nd round, 2012 draft, Kokomo HS (Kokomo, IN)

**Previous Ranking:** #6 (Org)

**What Happened in 2013:** A shoulder injury stalled the start to his season, and the diminutive righty worked out of the bullpen upon his return, trying to build up the arm strength that made him a second-round pick in 2012.

**Strengths:** High-end arm strength; can work the fastball 90-94; has touched the upper-90s before in bursts (when healthy); could offer plus-plus velocity out of the bullpen; can work to both sides of the plate; hard 12-6 curve-ball; good sight-line pitch; flashes plus and will eventually get there; slider could be second plus breaking ball; thrown in the 83-84 range with tilt; effective against right-handers; shows changeup; late-innings mentality.

**Weaknesses:** Injuries slowed development in rotation; limited height; lacks projection; delivery has effort; fastball can lack plane; struggles to hold his stuff; relief arsenal at present.

**Risk Factor/Injury History:** High risk; shoulder injury on resume; limited professional record.

**Bret Sayre's Fantasy Take:** Not a high-upside play for fantasy, as the odds of him both reaching the majors with success and making his way into a position for saves is a daunting task. He's likely not a big-strikeout reliever without a plus secondary pitch, which limits his value across the board.

**The Year Ahead:** Staying healthy and on the mound is key, as Sanburn's setback with the shoulder shifted his already debatable long-term projection toward a relief future. With a stressful delivery and a potential power arsenal, it's easy to see the short-in-stature Sanburn as a late-innings reliever. But let's see what happens if he can get back into a rotation, log innings, build up his arsenal, and refine his command. The ceiling is higher if he can start, but the arsenal offers impact potential even if he finds a home in the bullpen.

## 8.  Renato Nunez  3B

**Born:** 4/4/94  **Age:** 20  **Bats:** R  **Throws:** R  **Height:** 6'1"  **Weight:** 185

| MLB ETA | Hit | Power | Run | Glove | Arm | OFP | Realistic |
|---|---|---|---|---|---|---|---|
| 2017 | – | 60 | – | –– | 55 | 50<br>ML REGULAR | 45<br>PLTN 1B/<AVG ML |

| YEAR | TEAM | LVL | AGE | PA | R | 2B | 3B | HR | RBI | BB | SO | SB | CS | AVG/OBP/SLG | TAv | BABIP | BRR | FRAA | WARP |
|---|---|---|---|---|---|---|---|---|---|---|---|---|---|---|---|---|---|---|---|
| 2013 | BLT | A | 19 | 546 | 69 | 27 | 0 | 19 | 85 | 28 | 136 | 2 | 2 | .258/.301/.423 | .248 | .315 | -1.6 | 3B(114): 3.9 | 1.2 |
| 2014 | OAK | MLB | 20 | 250 | 20 | 9 | 0 | 6 | 26 | 7 | 76 | 0 | 0 | .203/.228/.323 | .205 | .260 | -0.5 | 3B 1 | -0.7 |
| 2015 | OAK | MLB | 21 | 250 | 26 | 11 | 0 | 8 | 28 | 9 | 72 | 0 | 0 | .219/.249/.368 | .224 | .275 | -0.7 | 3B 1 | -0.7 |

Breakout: 0%    Improve: 0%    Collapse: 0%    Attrition: 0%    MLB: 0%    *Comparables: Neftali Soto, Matt Davidson, Nick Castellanos*

**Drafted/Acquired:** International free agent, 2010, Venezuela

**Previous Ranking:** #7 (Org)

**What Happened in 2013:** After a standout season in complex ball, Nunez attempted to take a big step forward in a full-season league, but the reports were very mixed as to whether that step forward was as big as the numbers might suggest.

**Strengths:** Plus power potential; shows bat speed; good on fastballs; can extend and drive the ball; arm is average but strong enough for throws from third.

**Weaknesses:** Lots of swing-and-miss in his game; aggressive approach; secondary utility can eat him up; hit tool might limit power potential; footwork at third is rough; below-average range; arm isn't a weapon; likely a first baseman.

**Risk Factor/Injury History:** High risk; 20 years old in 2014; long developmental road ahead.

**Bret Sayre's Fantasy Take:** A potential 20+ homer bat from the third-base position is tempting from a fantasy perspective, but Nunez is not someone who profiles as much more than waiver wire fodder in shallower leagues. If it goes smoothly, he could have some 2013 Matt Dominguez seasons at the plate, but even that isn't exciting.

**The Year Ahead:** It almost seems foolish to knock a 19-year-old who ripped 48 extra-base hits in a full-season league, but we have to look at the realities of the profile and attempt to predict the future. Nunez isn't a graceful fielder, and the athleticism just isn't there to foresee big improvements through repetition. He's likely a first baseman, which puts a lot of pressure on the bat, and the power looks like the only carrying tool in his collection. If he can refine his approach and improve the hit tool enough for the power to play, he's a valuable player, even if he lacks a first-division label. But if the power doesn't play to potential, it's hard to see Nunez bringing much value to the table in the majors.

---

## 9.   Chris Kohler   LHP

**Born:** 5/4/95   **Age:** 19   **Bats:** L   **Throws:** L   **Height:** 6'3"   **Weight:** 195

| MLB ETA | CT | FB | CH | CB | SL | OFP | Realistic |
|---|---|---|---|---|---|---|---|
| 2018 | – | 50 | 55 | 55 | – | 50<br>NO.4 STARTER | 40<br>AAA/MR |

| YEAR | TEAM | LVL | AGE | W | L | SV | G | GS | IP | H | HR | BB | SO | BB9 | SO9 | GB% | BABIP | WHIP | ERA | FIP | FRA | WARP |
|---|---|---|---|---|---|---|---|---|---|---|---|---|---|---|---|---|---|---|---|---|---|---|
| 2013 | ATH | Rk | 18 | 1 | 2 | 1 | 13 | 4 | 22.7 | 19 | 0 | 9 | 32 | 3.6 | 12.7 | 60% | .345 | 1.24 | 2.78 | 2.50 | 3.72 | 0.7 |
| 2014 | OAK | MLB | 19 | 1 | 1 | 0 | 14 | 2 | 31.3 | 36 | 4 | 21 | 19 | 6.0 | 5.5 | 47% | .307 | 1.83 | 6.11 | 6.02 | 6.64 | -0.5 |
| 2015 | OAK | MLB | 20 | 1 | 1 | 1 | 22 | 2 | 48.7 | 52 | 6 | 29 | 29 | 5.4 | 5.4 | 47% | .288 | 1.65 | 5.52 | 5.54 | 6.00 | -0.6 |

Breakout: 0%   Improve: 0%   Collapse: 0%   Attrition: 0%   MLB: 0%   *Comparables: Michael Blazek, Luis Avilan, Matt Moore*

**Drafted/Acquired:** 3rd round, 2013 draft, Los Osos High School (Rancho Cucamonga, CA)

**Previous Ranking:** NR

**What Happened in 2013:** A fresh 18 years old when he was drafted, Kohler ended up missing 32 bats in less than 23 innings of work at the Arizona Complex.

**Strengths:** Ideal size; smooth delivery; very easy release; athletic; fastball shows good angle from higher slot; works fringe-average at present; shows average (or better) projection; changeup has good tumble and plays well in the delivery; shows feel for long curveball; good pitchability.

**Weaknesses:** Lacks plus stuff (at present); lacks big projection; arm action can get long; can struggle to finish his delivery from the high 3/4 slot; fastball lacks punch; changeup and curveball lack big deception; easy to pick up early; more slow tumble than sharp bite on both.

**Risk Factor/Injury History:** High risk; complex resume; lacks plus stuff.

**Bret Sayre's Fantasy Take:** There is fantasy upside in Kohler's arm, it's just tucked away behind a few layers of projection and development. As of right now, he's not worth rostering in fantasy leagues, but if he can tick his velocity up, he could grow into a strikeout source of slightly higher probability and make his way onto your radar.

**The Year Ahead:** Kohler is a long-term project, but he's a very young lefty with an ideal body, good athleticism, and good feel for pitching, so the A's have something to work with. The stuff at present is pedestrian at best, as the fastball is mostly in the upper-80s and straight, and the secondary stuff is below average. As he adds strength to his frame and adjusts to the professional grind, Kohler could start to tick up on the gun, which could elevate his status as he moves on to the New York-Penn League in 2014.

## 10. Matt Olson 1B

**Born:** 3/29/94 **Age:** 20 **Bats:** L **Throws:** R **Height:** 6' 4" **Weight:** 235

| MLB ETA | Hit | Power | Run | Glove | Arm | | OFP | Realistic |
|---------|-----|-------|-----|-------|-----|---|-----|-----------|
| 2016 | 50 | 60 | — | 50 | 60 | | 50<br>ML REGULAR | 45<br>PLATOON BAT |

| YEAR | TEAM | LVL | AGE | PA | R | 2B | 3B | HR | RBI | BB | SO | SB | CS | AVG/OBP/SLG | TAv | BABIP | BRR | FRAA | WARP |
|------|------|-----|-----|----|----|----|----|----|-----|----|----|----|----|-------------|-----|-------|-----|------|------|
| 2013 | BLT | A | 19 | 558 | 69 | 32 | 0 | 23 | 93 | 72 | 148 | 4 | 3 | .225/.326/.435 | .266 | .272 | 0.1 | 1B(127): 6.5 | 1.9 |
| 2014 | OAK | MLB | 20 | 250 | 24 | 9 | 0 | 8 | 28 | 21 | 81 | 0 | 0 | .191/.258/.340 | .224 | .250 | -0.5 | 1B 2 | -0.4 |
| 2015 | OAK | MLB | 21 | 250 | 30 | 11 | 0 | 9 | 30 | 25 | 74 | 0 | 0 | .210/.292/.380 | .246 | .266 | -0.7 | 1B 2 | 0.6 |

Breakout: 0%     Improve: 0%     Collapse: 0%     Attrition: 0%     MLB: 0%          *Comparables: Chris Marrero, Logan Morrison, Anthony Rizzo*

**Drafted/Acquired:** 1st round, 2012 draft, Parkview High School (Lilburn, GA)

**Previous Ranking:** #8 (Org)

**What Happened in 2013:** In his full-season debut, the former first-round pick struggled with consistency at the plate, but he did manage to hit 55 extra-base hits, including 23 bombs.

**Strengths:** Big size/strength; good athlete; moves well around the base at first; strong arm for the position; heady player; big boy raw power; natural power characteristics in the swing; will work counts; understands the strike zone.

**Weaknesses:** Really struggles against arm-side stuff; can beat him inside with velocity; swing can get long and leveraged; hit tool could drag game power down; limited to first defensively.

**Risk Factor/Injury History:** High risk; yet to play at Double-A level; questions about hit tool.

**Bret Sayre's Fantasy Take:** There's a pretty clear bar prospects must clear in fantasy if they are starting out at first base. If you really squint, maybe Olson peeks his head above that bar, but it's not by much. If you're in a deep OBP league, he could be worth a gamble as a potential 20-homer, .340-OBP hitter. In other formats, I'd look elsewhere.

**The Year Ahead:** Olson is an interesting prospect because of the impressive strength, big raw pop, and approach at the plate, but it's a profile that only works if the power really comes to play, as he's a first baseman without a highly projectable hit tool. Despite the struggles in Low-A, Olson was able to bring the power and the patience into action, and if he can continue that trend as the pitching improves, he will have a shot at being a major-league regular down the line.

## Prospects on the Rise

**1. LHP Dillon Overton:** While it might not come in 2014 thanks to Tommy John surgery, a healthy Overton will shoot up prospect rankings thanks to his mature approach and solid-average three-pitch mix from the left side. Don't forget about him.

**2. RHP Dylan Covey:** When the discovery of diabetes altered his professional course and pushed him to college instead of signing with the Brewers, many people forgot about the 6'2'' right-hander. But after finding his footing with his new disease, and returning to form, both physically and emotionally, Covey was selected by the A's in the fourth round of the 2013 draft. With a heavy low-90s fastball and two secondary offerings that could play to average or better, Covey has a big-league future. It's not a crazy ceiling, but he's a good bet to move up prospect lists in 2014.

**3. OF B.J. Boyd:** Boyd's body resembles that of Marlon Byrd, and I'm not sure that's a good thing for a 20-year-old to boast about. But Boyd is an interesting player because—like Byrd—he's a good athlete despite owning a supersized culo, and his quick little stroke can pop a baseball. The overall profile is probably a bat-first left-field type, but don't sleep on the bat. Boyd can hit a little bit, and I bet a strong full-season debut will push him up prospect lists.

## Factors on the Farm

### Prospects likely to contribute at the major-league level in 2014

**1. 1B Max Muncy:** This isn't a sexy choice, but Muncy could hit his way to the majors at some point in 2014, most likely as a bench bat. He lacks the profile of a major-league regular, but with some pop and a good approach, he could find a way to contribute.

**2. RHP Arnold Leon:** Although he worked as a starter in 2013, Leon has a chance to contribute to the major-league bullpen in 2014, most likely in middle/long relief. He lacks impact stuff, but can fill up the zone with a low- to mid-90s fastball that should play up a bit in bursts.

**3. IF/OF Shane Peterson:** Like Muncy, Peterson has decent pop and a solid approach, most likely filling a role as a fifth-outfielder type that can also play some first. He's not an impact talent, but he can rip a mistake and force a pitcher to work, giving him some value in a very limited role.

## FROM THE FIELD

### Addison Russell

**Player:** Addison Russell

**Team:** Oakland A's

**Filed by:** Steffan Segui

**Date(s) Seen:** October 1 - November 1, 2013 (during AFL)

**Physical:** Average athletic build that should fill out some without getting too bulky and limiting athletic ability.

**Hit:** 60 grade. Open but crouched stance. Hands stay in well without pulling off. Fast hands with plus bat speed. Good inside hitter but can go with balls away, too. Works into a lot of deep counts. Great bad-ball hitter that will chase spin in the dirt and have his share of swing-and-misses. Swing-and-miss should decrease as he learns to shrink his zone. Hit profile is good enough to play anywhere.

**Power:** 55 grade. Fast bat with lift. Pull-side power but extends barrel well through zone, allowing power to play. May lose a tick of pop going forward when he starts getting more soft away.

**Glove:** 60 grade. Great instincts allows to good range to play up. Still some inexperience with footwork and hands working, which hurts him fielding balls cleanly, but just needs time and he will be fine.

**Arm:** 60 grade. Can make any throw at shortstop. Doesn't always get in best positions to throw, more of an experience issue, should be fine. More than enough strength to stay at shortstop.

**Speed:** 60 grade. 4.2 to first consistently. Is fast but instincts and smarts allow it to play up. Doesn't get caught often.

**Makeup:** 70 grade. Very mature for age. Played in High-A and AFL in his first full season of pro ball.

**OFP:** 65; all-star-level talent

**Realistic Role:** 60; consistent above-average level player

**Risk:** Medium. Still young; only one full season of pro ball.

---

**Player:** Addison Russell

**Team:** Oakland Athletics

**Filed by:** Ronit Shah

**Date(s) Seen:** June 13-16 and August 13-14, 2013

**Physical:** Wide, broad-shouldered frame; strong legs.

**Hit:** 60 grade; simple swing with some length; lowers hands slightly; blazing quick hands that work in unison and create plus bat speed; explodes to the ball and uses all fields; a tad overaggressive and will expand zone, specifically up.

**Power:** 60 grade; plus bat speed combined with balance at the plate creates present above-average in-game power; doesn't have tremendous loft in swing; ability to drive the ball to all fields during batting practice and games; improved ability to use lower half strength into driving the ball between dates seen.

**Glove:** 50 grade; solid-average range; good actions and clean footwork, but not the quickest; it doesn't always look fluid and natural, but the plays get made; hands work well.

**Arm:** 60 grade; Plus arm strength that could play at third base if he's ever transitioned to the hot corner; can rush throwing motion on double-play balls.

**Speed:** 50 grade; not a burner, but possesses a second gear when he wants to be aggressive on the bases; will settle in as an average runner once player matures.

**Makeup:** 60 grade; turned a poor start in High-A into a great season that ended with a short promotion to Triple-A; made significant and loud improvements in all phases of the game between dates seen; works hard at his craft.

**OFP:** 70; all-star player

**Realistic Role:** 60, first division player

**Risk:** Moderate; player lacks experience in upper minors, but is advanced for his age.

## 1.  Maikel Franco  1B/3B

**Born:** 8/26/92  **Age:** 21  **Bats:** R  **Throws:** R  **Height:** 6' 1"  **Weight:** 180

| MLB ETA | Hit | Power | Run | Glove | Arm | OFP | Realistic |
|---|---|---|---|---|---|---|---|
| 2014 | 55 | 70 | — | 50 | 65 | 60<br>1ST DIV PLAYER | 50<br>ML REGULAR |

| YEAR | TEAM | LVL | AGE | PA | R | 2B | 3B | HR | RBI | BB | SO | SB | CS | AVG/OBP/SLG | TAv | BABIP | BRR | FRAA | WARP |
|---|---|---|---|---|---|---|---|---|---|---|---|---|---|---|---|---|---|---|---|
| 2013 | REA | AA | 20 | 292 | 47 | 13 | 2 | 15 | 51 | 10 | 31 | 1 | 2 | .339/.363/.563 | .336 | .338 | 0.9 | 3B(59): 3.4, 1B(8): -0.3 | 3.7 |
| 2013 | CLR | A+ | 20 | 289 | 42 | 23 | 1 | 16 | 52 | 20 | 39 | 0 | 0 | .299/.349/.576 | .315 | .297 | -0.5 | 3B(64): -6.1 | 2.2 |
| 2014 | PHI | MLB | 21 | 250 | 26 | 12 | 1 | 9 | 33 | 8 | 49 | 0 | 0 | .255/.282/.427 | .254 | .280 | -0.4 | 3B -3, 1B -0 | 0.1 |
| 2015 | PHI | MLB | 22 | 250 | 30 | 13 | 1 | 9 | 33 | 11 | 46 | 0 | 0 | .263/.298/.444 | .270 | .288 | -0.6 | 3B -3, 1B 0 | 1.9 |

**Breakout:** 5%   **Improve:** 14%   **Collapse:** 1%   **Attrition:** 15%   **MLB:** 25%        *Comparables: Lonnie Chisenhall, Josh Vitters, Wilmer Flores*

**#52**

BP Top
101
Prospects

**Drafted/Acquired:** International Free Agent, 2010, Dominican Republic

**Previous Ranking:** #2 (Org)

**What Happened in 2013:** Franco crushed in the Florida State League, and then took another step forward after his promotion to Double-A, hitting a combined 31 bombs.

**Strengths:** Electric bat speed; well-above-average hand-eye coordination; hit tool could play average or better; feel for hard contact; crushes fastballs; power potential is plus-plus; plane for over-the-fence power; backspins the ball; arm is easy plus; hands work well in the field.

**Weaknesses:** Deep hand load in setup (drawing back a bow); brings hands back/up and then back down into launch; excellent hand-eye allows him to recover from bad guesses; very aggressive approach; struggles against off-speed stuff; hit tool likely to pull power down; high-maintenance body; good hands in the field but sloppy footwork and fringe range.

**Risk Factor/Injury History:** Moderate risk; achieved Double-A level; questions about defensive profile and hit tool.

**Bret Sayre's Fantasy Take:** Here is a case where the eligibility could make a real difference. If Franco is a first baseman, his fantasy value takes a hit. But even if he plays third base only against lefties, that will still be enough for him to maintain those 20 games. At the plate, he could be a .275 hitter with 25 homers in that park, which is notoriously friendly to right-handed hitters (just ask Jayson Werth).

**The Year Ahead:** Franco was a monster in 2013, hitting for average and power, but sources question the utility of the hit tool against better arms, particularly arms that can beat him with sequence. His preternatural feel for contact helps him recover from a late trigger or a poor pitch read, so he should be able to keep the ball in play. But his impressive plus-plus power is likely to play down as a result of his swing and approach, which will limit his overall value, especially if he can't make the profile work at third base. I can see a .260+ hitter with 20+ bombs, most likely coming at first base, and I would probably be higher on the overall profile if the work ethic received praise from outside-the-organization sources rather than questions and red flags.

## 2.  Jesse Biddle  LHP

**Born:** 10/22/91  **Age:** 22  **Bats:** L  **Throws:** L  **Height:** 6' 4"  **Weight:** 225

| MLB ETA | CT | FB | CH | CB | SL | OFP | Realistic |
|---|---|---|---|---|---|---|---|
| 2014 | — | 55 | 55 | 50 | 50 | 55<br>NO.3 STARTER | 50<br>NO.4 STARTER |

| YEAR | TEAM | LVL | AGE | W | L | SV | G | GS | IP | H | HR | BB | SO | BB9 | SO9 | GB% | BABIP | WHIP | ERA | FIP | FRA | WARP |
|---|---|---|---|---|---|---|---|---|---|---|---|---|---|---|---|---|---|---|---|---|---|---|
| 2013 | REA | AA | 21 | 5 | 14 | 0 | 27 | 27 | 138.3 | 104 | 10 | 82 | 154 | 5.3 | 10.0 | 44% | .278 | 1.34 | 3.64 | 3.88 | 4.28 | 2.7 |
| 2014 | PHI | MLB | 22 | 6 | 9 | 0 | 23 | 23 | 118.3 | 111 | 14 | 64 | 105 | 4.9 | 8.0 | 41% | .310 | 1.48 | 4.65 | 4.77 | 5.05 | 0.0 |
| 2015 | PHI | MLB | 23 | 2 | 1 | 0 | 48 | 0 | 51.0 | 45 | 6 | 25 | 49 | 4.4 | 8.6 | 41% | .308 | 1.38 | 4.14 | 4.18 | 4.50 | 0.3 |

**Breakout:** 0%   **Improve:** 0%   **Collapse:** 0%   **Attrition:** 0%   **MLB:** 0%        *Comparables: Zack Wheeler, Dan Cortes, Carlos Carrasco*

**#94**

BP Top
101
Prospects

**Drafted/Acquired:** 1st round, 2010 draft, Germantown Friends HS (Philadelphia, PA)

**Previous Ranking:** #1 (Org), #67 (Top 101)

**What Happened in 2013:** In his first pass in Double-A, the former first-round pick made 27 starts, logged 138 innings and missed an impressive 154 bats, but he also allowed 82 free passes.

**Strengths:** Good size/present strength; athletic; fastball works solid-average; comfortable at 89-92; touches a bit higher; creates good plane to the plate; curveball is average offering; plays up against minor-league bats; can show a tight rotation and deception off the fastball; turns over a promising changeup; average at present but has some projection; shows slider that he can throw in the zone.

**Weaknesses:** Release-point inconsistency; poor fastball command at present; tendency to fly open in delivery and miss arm-side and up; curveball can get loopy and long; upper-60s/low-70s; changeup can get deliberate in the delivery; needs general mound refinement (holding runner, PFP, etc.).

**Risk Factor/Injury History:** Low risk; 27 starts at Double-A level; needs command refinement.

**Bret Sayre's Fantasy Take:** Shallow leaguers should take note that Biddle, despite his projection, isn't the kind of player who you should be stocking your farm team with. He'll have to max out his projection in order to be much above streamer level in 10- to 12-team leagues, but in deep formats, his stability and ability to eat innings will come in handy.

**The Year Ahead:** Biddle has one of those lefty curveballs that can freeze hitters or make their swings look like foolish attempts to make contact with air. But the pitch is better in the present (in the minors) than it projects to be in the future (in the majors), and without a true plus offering, Biddle doesn't have a large margin for error. It all starts with poor fastball command; without the ability to spot up the pitch, better sticks won't be triggering early to strike it, which will make a slow, long curveball easier to stay back on and track. Minor-league hitters struggle to accomplish this. If Biddle can correct his command woes, he has a good chance of developing into a solid back-end starter at the major-league level, and perhaps more if the changeup can blossom into a near-plus offering. But the robust minor-league curve isn't going to play without better fastball utility, and until Biddle takes steps forward on that front, his overall profile comes with more than questions than answers.

---

## 3. J.P. Crawford   SS

**Born:** 1/11/95   **Age:** 19   **Bats:** L   **Throws:** R   **Height:** 6' 2"   **Weight:** 180

| MLB ETA | Hit | Power | Run | Glove | Arm | OFP | Realistic |
|---------|-----|-------|-----|-------|-----|-----|-----------|
| 2017 | 55 | – | 60 | 60 | 55 | 60<br>1ST DIV PLAYER | 50<br>ML REGULAR |

| YEAR | TEAM | LVL | AGE | PA | R | 2B | 3B | HR | RBI | BB | SO | SB | CS | AVG/OBP/SLG | TAv | BABIP | BRR | FRAA | WARP |
|------|------|-----|-----|-----|-----|-----|-----|-----|-----|-----|-----|-----|-----|-------------|-----|-------|-----|------|------|
| 2013 | LWD | A | 18 | 60 | 10 | 1 | 0 | 0 | 2 | 7 | 10 | 2 | 1 | .208/.300/.226 | .220 | .256 | -0.3 | SS(14): 0.1 | 0.1 |
| 2013 | PHL | Rk | 18 | 168 | 24 | 8 | 3 | 1 | 19 | 25 | 25 | 12 | 5 | .345/.443/.465 | .327 | .414 | 0.6 | SS(31): 1.2 | 2.0 |
| 2014 | PHI | MLB | 19 | 250 | 26 | 9 | 1 | 3 | 17 | 18 | 66 | 6 | 2 | .209/.269/.292 | .208 | .270 | 0.1 | SS 0 | -0.3 |
| 2015 | PHI | MLB | 20 | 250 | 25 | 7 | 2 | 3 | 21 | 19 | 57 | 3 | 1 | .228/.291/.316 | .229 | .283 | 0.0 | SS 0 | -0.1 |

Breakout: 0%   Improve: 0%   Collapse: 0%   Attrition: 0%   MLB: 0%          *Comparables: Jonathan Schoop, Elvis Andrus, Ruben Tejada*

**Drafted/Acquired:** 1st round, 2013, Lakewood HS (Lakewood, CA)

**Previous Ranking:** NR

**What Happened in 2013:** Selected 16th overall in the 2013 draft, Crawford hit the ground hitting in his complex league debut, putting up a .345 average in a 39-game sample.

**Strengths:** Fast-twitch athlete; coordinated and graceful; plus run; plus range; natural feel for the glove; clean, fluid actions; excellent backhand pickup; left-side arm; shows some bat speed at the plate; quick hands with some bat control.

**Weaknesses:** Needs to add strength to lean/lanky frame; general refinement through repetition in the field; bat lacks power; contact-heavy swing; balance isn't great in setup/swing; can shift weight early to front foot and lose punch/control with the bat.

**Risk Factor/Injury History:** High risk; limited professional experience; questions about the bat/body.

**Bret Sayre's Fantasy Take:** Crawford may not have the fantasy upside of some of his first-round brethren, but he's a strong bet to stay at shortstop due to his defensive prowess, and his speed should be able to provide returns, even if the bat or fringy power don't work out so well. He is a strong second-round pick in dynasty drafts this year.

**The Year Ahead:** Crawford is ready for a full season in Low-A, where he will likely continue to flash the goods at shortstop and show enough promise at the plate to keep his stock high. There are some concerns about his physical projection and how it keeps the bat in his hands, but he shows the necessary work ethic and should be able to add strength without sacrificing his athleticism or game speed. I don't see an impact bat, as the power will likely play below average and the hit tool will be more about consistent contact than middle-of-the-order destruction. But the defensive profile at a premium position is legit, and the total package could be a first-division player at the major-league level. He just missed the cut for the BP 101 this season, and should find his way securely on the list as he climbs the corporate ladder.

---

## 4. Kelly Dugan   RF

**Born:** 9/18/90   **Age:** 23   **Bats:** L   **Throws:** R   **Height:** 6' 3"   **Weight:** 195

| MLB ETA | Hit | Power | Run | Glove | Arm | OFP | Realistic |
|---------|-----|-------|-----|-------|-----|-----|-----------|
| Late 2014 | 50 | 55 | – | 55 | 60 | 50<br>ML REGULAR | 45<br><AVG REG/BENCH |

| YEAR | TEAM | LVL | AGE | PA | R | 2B | 3B | HR | RBI | BB | SO | SB | CS | AVG/OBP/SLG | TAv | BABIP | BRR | FRAA | WARP |
|------|------|-----|-----|-----|-----|-----|-----|-----|-----|-----|-----|-----|-----|-------------|-----|-------|-----|------|------|
| 2013 | REA | AA | 22 | 226 | 25 | 12 | 1 | 10 | 23 | 5 | 54 | 0 | 1 | .264/.299/.472 | .273 | .309 | -0.8 | RF(28): 0.7, LF(24): 3.7 | 1.2 |
| 2013 | CLR | A+ | 22 | 248 | 37 | 12 | 3 | 10 | 36 | 24 | 60 | 1 | 3 | .318/.401/.539 | .334 | .401 | -0.8 | RF(50): 5.6 | 3.1 |
| 2014 | PHI | MLB | 23 | 250 | 25 | 11 | 1 | 8 | 30 | 12 | 74 | 0 | 0 | .237/.286/.391 | .242 | .310 | -0.4 | RF 2, LF 1 | 0.2 |
| 2015 | PHI | MLB | 24 | 250 | 28 | 12 | 1 | 7 | 28 | 13 | 72 | 0 | 0 | .244/.294/.395 | .249 | .319 | -0.5 | RF 2, LF 1 | 0.9 |

Breakout: 2%   Improve: 9%   Collapse: 1%   Attrition: 3%   MLB: 14%          *Comparables: Roger Kieschnick, Matt Joyce, J.D. Martinez*

**Drafted/Acquired:** 2nd round, 2009 draft, Notre Dame HS (Sherman Oaks, CA)

**Previous Ranking:** NR

**What Happened in 2013:** After a strong full-season debut in 2012, Dugan continued to progress in 2013, hitting his way to Double-A and racking up 48 extra-base hits on the season.

**Strengths:** Good athlete; good feel for baseball skills; strong upper body; generates good bat speed at the plate; hit tool could play to average; power could play above average; strong arm for a corner; good glove; good reads/routes.

**Weaknesses:** Top-heavy physique; can jump fastballs and struggle with off-speed pitches; can lose legs in his swing; hit tool lacks impact projection; power unlikely to play above plus; approach puts him in bad hitting situations; speed is below average.

**Risk Factor/Injury History:** Moderate risk; limited experience in upper minors.

**Bret Sayre's Fantasy Take:** There's just not a whole lot for fantasy owners to get too excited about here with Dugan. There could be 20-homer power at the major-league level, but it is likely to come with an average (or on-base percentage, if you're into that sort of thing) that will eat into the value you get from the middling power.

**The Year Ahead:** Dugan lacks big upside but the bat has a chance to make him a major-league regular, assuming his approach refines and he can make enough contact to let the power play in game action. The 23-year-old has bat speed and good upper-body strength, and when he can put some loft in his bat, he can drive the baseball out of the park. In his first pass in Double-A, arms could beat him with stuff and spin, so he will need to work himself into better counts and take advantage of mistakes if he wants to put himself into the major-league discussion for 2015.

---

## 5.  Carlos Tocci  CF

**Born:** 8/23/95   **Age:** 18   **Bats:** R   **Throws:** R   **Height:** 6' 2"   **Weight:** 160

| MLB ETA | Hit | Power | Run | Glove | Arm | OFP | Realistic |
|---|---|---|---|---|---|---|---|
| 2017 | 55 | --- | 70 | 60 | 65 | 60<br>1ST DIV PLAYER | 45<br><AVG REG/BENCH |

| YEAR | TEAM | LVL | AGE | PA | R | 2B | 3B | HR | RBI | BB | SO | SB | CS | AVG/OBP/SLG | TAv | BABIP | BRR | FRAA | WARP |
|---|---|---|---|---|---|---|---|---|---|---|---|---|---|---|---|---|---|---|---|
| 2013 | LWD | A | 17 | 459 | 40 | 17 | 0 | 0 | 26 | 22 | 77 | 6 | 7 | .209/.261/.249 | .206 | .253 | -0.3 | CF(116): 16.4 | 0.5 |
| 2014 | PHI | MLB | 18 | 250 | 19 | 9 | 0 | 2 | 18 | 8 | 57 | 3 | 2 | .204/.235/.272 | .184 | .250 | -0.4 | CF 7, LF 0 | -0.5 |
| 2015 | PHI | MLB | 19 | 250 | 22 | 10 | 0 | 3 | 20 | 9 | 51 | 1 | 1 | .207/.246/.292 | .204 | .249 | -0.6 | CF 6, LF 0 | -1.3 |

Breakout: 0%    Improve: 0%    Collapse: 0%    Attrition: 0%    MLB: 0%          *Comparables: Michael Brantley, Che-Hsuan Lin, Andrew McCutchen*

**Drafted/Acquired:** International free agent, 2011, Venezuela

**Previous Ranking:** #9 (Org)

**What Happened in 2013:** Tocci jumped to the full-season level as a 17-year-old, and despite an OPS that would suggest he was overwhelmed at the plate, the young Venezuelan didn't fold under the weight of the competition.

**Strengths:** Well-above-average athlete; lanky/projectable body; easy plus run; could end up plus-pus with more strength; arm is a weapon in center; easy plus and possible plus-plus; confidence in the arm; glove to play above average in center; good approach and contact ability at the plate.

**Weaknesses:** Body is very immature at present; lack of strength limits utility of all tools; hit tool is all projection at this point; poor power at present; below-average base-running utility at present; overall game needs refinement.

**Risk Factor/Injury History:** High risk; 18 years old; questions about physical projection/strength.

**Bret Sayre's Fantasy Take:** Outside of Franco, Tocci is the player with the highest fantasy upside on this list. Don't let the stats fool you; he was not good last season, but he played nearly the entire year at 17 years old. With the chance for 30+ steals down the road, he's a pure lottery ticket, but a lottery ticket is still better in fantasy than most of the other players on this list.

**The Year Ahead:** Tocci was one of my favorite prospects to watch in 2013, as the raw tools were louder than I expected, given the player's age and level. The body is very immature, and some sources question whether or not he has the frame to add enough mass to keep the bat in his hands against better arms. He's only 18, so if he can add strength over time, he has the type of athleticism and feel for the game to really shine as a prospect, the type of player who profiles in center with plus speed and a good swing/approach at the plate. I really like this prospect, and he could take a huge step forward if the body starts to show signs of maturity.

# 6.   Deivi Grullon   C

**Born:** 2/17/96   **Age:** 18   **Bats:** R   **Throws:** R   **Height:** 6' 1"   **Weight:** 180

| MLB ETA | Hit | Power | Run | Glove | Arm | | OFP | Realistic |
|---|---|---|---|---|---|---|---|---|
| 2018 | 55 | – | – | 65 | 80 | | 60<br>1ST DIV PLAYER | 45<br>BACKUP C |

| YEAR | TEAM | LVL | AGE | PA | R | 2B | 3B | HR | RBI | BB | SO | SB | CS | AVG/OBP/SLG | TAv | BABIP | BRR | FRAA | WARP |
|---|---|---|---|---|---|---|---|---|---|---|---|---|---|---|---|---|---|---|---|
| 2013 | PHL | Rk | 17 | 132 | 13 | 8 | 0 | 1 | 14 | 10 | 18 | 0 | 0 | .273/.333/.364 | .264 | .314 | -1.2 | C(38): -1.3 | 0.3 |
| 2014 | PHI | MLB | 18 | 250 | 17 | 8 | 0 | 3 | 21 | 11 | 74 | 1 | 0 | .193/.231/.273 | .185 | .260 | -0.4 | C -1 | -0.9 |
| 2015 | PHI | MLB | 19 | 250 | 24 | 9 | 1 | 5 | 23 | 11 | 69 | 1 | 0 | .223/.259/.327 | .217 | .290 | -0.5 | C -1 | -1.2 |

Breakout: 0%   Improve: 0%   Collapse: 0%   Attrition: 0%   MLB: 0%   *Comparables: Christian Bethancourt, Cedric Hunter, Caleb Gindl*

**Drafted/Acquired:** International free agent, 2012, Dominican Republic

**Previous Ranking:** NR

**What Happened in 2013:** In his professional debut, the six-figure international signee showed off one of the strongest arms in the minors, a true 8 weapon behind the plate, which pushes him up prospect lists despite an offensive profile that lacks big projection.

**Strengths:** Good size; strength projection; good athlete at the position; arm strength is elite; quick release and accurate; shows good footwork behind the plate and projectable glove; could end up a well-above-average backstop; hit tool projects to average; shows some bat speed and ability to drive the ball.

**Weaknesses:** Needs refinement behind the plate; can get overly confident with the arm; lacks impact offensive tools; struggles with arm-side stuff; struggles against soft/spin; power likely to play well below average; below-average run.

**Risk Factor/Injury History:** Extreme risk; 18 years old; limited professional experience; tough developmental profile

**Bret Sayre's Fantasy Take:** As exciting as it is to see an 8 on any prospect's tool, this one means nothing to fantasy players (unless a speedy player on your team is trying to steal against him). He's not a fantasy option at this point.

**The Year Ahead:** I'm a recidivist when it comes to falling in love with above-average defenders behind the plate, even more so when they come equipped with elite arms. Grullon has a very long way to go in all facets of his game, but the defensive projections could make him a well-above-average force, and even if the bat plays soft, a usable hit tool could keep him in a lineup for a very long time. It's still early in the developmental process and the bat could pull down his value for several years before he brings it together, but never turn away from a capable catcher with sniper arm strength.

# 7.   Severino Gonzalez   RHP

**Born:** 9/28/92   **Age:** 21   **Bats:** R   **Throws:** R   **Height:** 6' 1"   **Weight:** 153

| MLB ETA | CT | FB | CH | CB | SL | | OFP | Realistic |
|---|---|---|---|---|---|---|---|---|
| 2015 | 55 | 50 | 50 | 50 | – | | 50<br>NO.4 STARTER | 50<br>NO.5/LONG RELIEF |

| YEAR | TEAM | LVL | AGE | W | L | SV | G | GS | IP | H | HR | BB | SO | BB9 | SO9 | GB% | BABIP | WHIP | ERA | FIP | FRA | WARP |
|---|---|---|---|---|---|---|---|---|---|---|---|---|---|---|---|---|---|---|---|---|---|---|
| 2013 | LWD | A | 20 | 3 | 0 | 0 | 4 | 4 | 21.3 | 10 | 1 | 3 | 31 | 1.3 | 13.1 | 47% | .214 | 0.61 | 1.69 | 1.75 | 2.91 | 0.5 |
| 2013 | REA | AA | 20 | 1 | 0 | 0 | 1 | 1 | 6.7 | 8 | 0 | 0 | 6 | 0.0 | 8.1 | 35% | .400 | 1.20 | 2.70 | 1.52 | 2.60 | 0.2 |
| 2013 | CLR | A+ | 20 | 3 | 5 | 0 | 20 | 9 | 75.7 | 66 | 4 | 19 | 82 | 2.3 | 9.8 | 32% | .318 | 1.12 | 2.02 | 2.59 | 2.97 | 1.9 |
| 2014 | PHI | MLB | 21 | 2 | 2 | 1 | 20 | 5 | 83.7 | 79 | 10 | 30 | 76 | 3.2 | 8.2 | 44% | .314 | 1.31 | 4.16 | 4.22 | 4.52 | 0.3 |
| 2015 | PHI | MLB | 22 | 4 | 3 | 1 | 25 | 9 | 126.7 | 106 | 14 | 37 | 122 | 2.6 | 8.7 | 43% | .290 | 1.13 | 3.35 | 3.57 | 3.64 | 2.0 |

Breakout: 0%   Improve: 0%   Collapse: 0%   Attrition: 0%   MLB: 0%   *Comparables: Luis Marte, Phillippe Aumont, Eduardo Sanchez*

**Drafted/Acquired:** International free agent, 2011, Panama

**Previous Ranking:** NR

**What Happened in 2013:** In his stateside debut, the Panamanian arm pitched at three levels, finishing in Double-A and jumping from unknown status to top-10 prospect in only 100 innings of work.

**Strengths:** Plus pitchability; easy delivery; fluid arm; stays in a good line to the plate; fastball works in the upper-80s/low-90s; has some sneak to it; spots it up with sharp command; multiple breaking-ball looks; cut-slider has more bite to it; could play above average; good for forcing weak contact; curve can miss minor-league bats; changeup plays well off the fastball because of the consistent mechanics/release point; overall command is above average.

**Weaknesses:** Slight build; lacks big strength; fastball has pedestrian velocity; can sit in the upper-80s deeper into games; command has to be sharp for the pitch to play; curveball can get too long and soft; plays up because he can spot the fastball; lacks a true plus pitch; command/control profile.

**Risk Factor/Injury History:** Moderate risk; limited exposure to upper minors; lacks a power arsenal.

**Bret Sayre's Fantasy Take:** The stats have been solid, but Severino isn't a guy to concern yourself with much for fantasy. He's a very fly-ball-heavy pitcher headed to a park that does not treat fly-ball pitchers with kindness. Severino makes for a better stash in very deep leagues.

**The Year Ahead:** Gonzalez carved up the lower levels of the minors with a deep arsenal and the ability to spot his fastball, which allowed the secondary stuff to play up. The curve lacks plus projection but is effective in the minors because of the fastball, while the cutter should be a playable pitch for the slender righty as he matures. Because of the slight frame and average stuff, Gonzalez will need to be very sharp to find sustainable success at the next level, but his pitchability and clean mechanics will give him a chance. He should return to Double-A in 2014, and if he can continue to play wizard with his location, the 21-year-old has a chance to pitch in the big leagues at some point in 2015. Not bad for a prospect signed at age 18 for $14,000.

## 8. Cesar Hernandez    IF/OF

**Born:** 5/23/90   **Age:** 24   **Bats:** B   **Throws:** R   **Height:** 5' 10"   **Weight:** 175

| MLB ETA | Hit | Power | Run | Glove | Arm | | OFP | Realistic |
|---------|-----|-------|-----|-------|-----|---|-----|-----------|
| Debuted in 2013 | 50 | – | 60 | 55 | 50 | | 50<br>2ND DIV PLAYER | 50<br>SUPER UTILITY |

| YEAR | TEAM | LVL | AGE | PA | R | 2B | 3B | HR | RBI | BB | SO | SB | CS | AVG/OBP/SLG | TAv | BABIP | BRR | FRAA | WARP |
|------|------|-----|-----|----|----|----|----|----|-----|----|----|----|----|-------------|-----|-------|-----|------|------|
| 2013 | REA | AA | 23 | 13 | 2 | 1 | 0 | 0 | 3 | 1 | 1 | 1 | 0 | .500/.500/.600 | .440 | .500 | -0.8 | CF(3): 0.4 | 0.2 |
| 2013 | LEH | AAA | 23 | 440 | 59 | 12 | 9 | 2 | 34 | 41 | 81 | 32 | 8 | .309/.375/.402 | .281 | .384 | 3.8 | 2B(79): -2.5, CF(19): -0.0 | 2.4 |
| 2013 | PHI | MLB | 23 | 131 | 17 | 5 | 0 | 0 | 10 | 9 | 26 | 0 | 3 | .289/.344/.331 | .237 | .368 | -1.2 | CF(22): -1.0, 2B(10): -0.0 | -0.2 |
| 2014 | PHI | MLB | 24 | 250 | 28 | 9 | 3 | 2 | 19 | 12 | 50 | 9 | 4 | .264/.301/.357 | .241 | .320 | 0.5 | 2B -1, CF -0 | 0.3 |
| 2015 | PHI | MLB | 25 | 250 | 24 | 9 | 3 | 2 | 21 | 14 | 49 | 9 | 4 | .254/.297/.341 | .239 | .307 | 0.6 | 2B -1, CF 0 | 0.4 |

Breakout: 2%   Improve: 16%   Collapse: 6%   Attrition: 18%   MLB: 41%   *Comparables: Emilio Bonifacio, Hernan Iribarren, Jonathan Herrera*

**Drafted/Acquired:** International free agent, 2006, Venezuela

**Previous Ranking:** NR

**What Happened in 2013:** In a return to the International League, Hernandez took a step forward at the plate, and eventually found himself at the major-league level, where his defensive versatility made him a valuable player.

**Strengths:** Good athlete with legit baseball skills; plus run; above-average glove; arm plays as average; can make plays at second; can handle center field; good feel for the stick; contact oriented with some ability to make hard contact; good fundamental player.

**Weaknesses:** Lacks first-division tools; not physically imposing; lacks big strength; arm is only average and limits left-side utility; power is well below average; bat is of the down-the-lineup variety; bat speed is only average; utility profile.

**Risk Factor/Injury History:** Low risk; achieved major-league level

**Bret Sayre's Fantasy Take:** There's really not much to see here. Hernandez could weasel his way into a full slate of at-bats somewhere down the road, but even if he does, you're looking at an average that won't kill you and maybe 20 steals or so. That's not worth taking up a roster spot for.

**The Year Ahead:** Hernandez is a good baseball player, one with above-average speed, defensive versatility, and the ability to make contact at the plate, but despite the on-the-field skills, the 24-year-old lacks the impact-level tools to make him a sustainable force as a major-league regular. The likely outcome is a superutility type, a right-side infielder that can also handle center field duties, offering speed on base and a fundamental approach at the plate. These types of players don't make great prospects but can provide great value to a 25-man roster, especially when they are under team control for six years.

## 9. Yoel Mecias    LHP

**Born:** 10/11/93   **Age:** 20   **Bats:** L   **Throws:** L   **Height:** 6' 2"   **Weight:** 160

| MLB ETA | CT | FB | CH | CB | SL | | OFP | Realistic |
|---------|----|----|----|----|----|---|-----|-----------|
| 2017 | – | 60 | 65 | – | 50 | | 60<br>NO.3 STARTER | 50<br>NO.4 STARTER |

| YEAR | TEAM | LVL | AGE | W | L | SV | G | GS | IP | H | HR | BB | SO | BB9 | SO9 | GB% | BABIP | WHIP | ERA | FIP | FRA | WARP |
|------|------|-----|-----|---|---|----|---|----|------|-----|----|----|-----|-----|-----|-----|-------|------|------|------|------|------|
| 2013 | LWD | A | 19 | 4 | 3 | 1 | 13 | 11 | 57.0 | 53 | 3 | 25 | 70 | 3.9 | 11.1 | 52% | .338 | 1.37 | 3.79 | 3.08 | 2.97 | 1.2 |
| 2014 | PHI | MLB | 20 | 2 | 3 | 0 | 13 | 7 | 46.3 | 49 | 6 | 24 | 36 | 4.7 | 7.0 | 47% | .320 | 1.57 | 5.42 | 5.12 | 5.89 | -0.4 |
| 2015 | PHI | MLB | 21 | 5 | 6 | 1 | 34 | 17 | 143.3 | 138 | 19 | 63 | 115 | 4.0 | 7.2 | 47% | .301 | 1.41 | 4.65 | 4.61 | 5.05 | -0.1 |

Breakout: 0%   Improve: 0%   Collapse: 0%   Attrition: 0%   MLB: 0%   *Comparables: Chris Tillman, Wilmer Font, Jarrod Parker*

**Drafted/Acquired:** International free agent, 2010, Venezuela

**Previous Ranking:** NR

**What Happened in 2013:** Before coming down with a case of Tommy John surgery, Mecias was really starting to shine in his full-season debut, missing 70 bats in only 57 innings.

**Strengths:** Easy/fluid mechanics; arm is very quick; fastball works 88-92; projects to sit in plus range at maturity; can touch 94/95 in bursts; changeup is above average at present; could end up playing well above average; good fastball disguise in the arm and excellent late action; slider should also play to average or above; good overall feel for pitching.

**Weaknesses:** Thin, lanky frame; needs to add strength; preinjury questions about ability to hold velocity/workload; slider can get long and slurvy; effective against lefties but easier to read and track by righties; more control than command.

**Risk Factor/Injury History:** High risk; recovering from Tommy John surgery; limited professional experience.

**Bret Sayre's Fantasy Take:** The risk factor is extremely high here, but at least this is an arm with a little fantasy upside to it. A lefty with velocity and a real bat-missing changeup is always a factor at the major-league level, but the combination of distance and risk from the surgery just makes him an interesting deep-league flier.

**The Year Ahead:** It's a tough sell to rank a player in the top 10 with a recent Tommy John on the resume, but Mecias is pushing ahead on his rehab schedule, and could/should return to game action this summer, most likely toeing the rubber as a 20-year-old in the Florida State League, assuming the rehab continues on schedule. Despite limited experience on the mound, Mecias shows a lot of feel and a very fluid and easy arm, which allows the present fastball to jump and offer projection, and the changeup to play the role of the arsenal darling, missing bats and barrels of both righties and lefties. This is a very good prospect, and when he returns to action and refines the rough edges, he has a chance to move up in this system and become a national name. It could happen at the end of 2014, but the following year is when I expect Mecias to become a household name.

## 10.  Cord Sandberg  OF

**Born:** 1/2/95   **Age:** 19   **Bats:** L   **Throws:** L   **Height:** 6' 3"   **Weight:** 215

| | Hit | Power | Run | Glove | Arm | | OFP | Realistic |
|---|---|---|---|---|---|---|---|---|
| MLB ETA | | | | | | | 60 | 50 |
| 2017 | – | 60 | 55 | 50 | 60 | | 1ST DIV PLAYER | <AVG REG/BENCH |

| YEAR | TEAM | LVL | AGE | PA | R | 2B | 3B | HR | RBI | BB | SO | SB | CS | AVG/OBP/SLG | TAv | BABIP | BRR | FRAA | WARP |
|---|---|---|---|---|---|---|---|---|---|---|---|---|---|---|---|---|---|---|---|
| 2013 | PHL | Rk | 18 | 196 | 23 | 3 | 1 | 2 | 14 | 24 | 36 | 4 | 3 | .207/.313/.272 | .230 | .252 | -0.8 | LF(24): 5.9, CF(20): 2.5 | 0.7 |
| 2014 | PHI | MLB | 19 | 250 | 22 | 8 | 0 | 3 | 18 | 15 | 77 | 1 | 0 | .186/.237/.267 | .187 | .260 | -0.4 | LF 5, CF 1 | -0.6 |
| 2015 | PHI | MLB | 20 | 250 | 24 | 7 | 1 | 5 | 23 | 13 | 76 | 0 | 0 | .199/.245/.305 | .205 | .263 | -0.5 | LF 5, CF 1 | -1.3 |

Breakout: 0%   Improve: 0%   Collapse: 0%   Attrition: 0%   MLB: 0%   *Comparables: Marcell Ozuna, Caleb Gindl, Che-Hsuan Lin*

**Drafted/Acquired:** 3rd round, 2013 draft, Manatee HS (Bradenton, FL)

**Previous Ranking:** NR

**What Happened in 2013:** Another toolsy, multisport athlete stolen away from football by the Phillies, signed in the third round for a high-six-figure bonus.

**Strengths:** Can show five tool potential; good athlete; good present strength; highly competitive; power projects to plus; shows bat speed and the ability to make hard contact; arm is strong; runs well for his size; impact potential if tools come together.

**Weaknesses:** Raw at the plate; iffy balance; tendency to lunge at the ball; hit tool and power projections have a long way to go; not a true center fielder; okay glove but reads/routes need a lot of work; good present run but will likely slow as he physically matures.

**Risk Factor/Injury History:** High risk; complex league resume

**Bret Sayre's Fantasy Take:** If Sandberg can hit, he becomes a guy to watch for fantasy purposes, but as you can gather by this list, it's not a particularly great system for farm-team adds. He likely shouldn't be drafted in dynasty leagues this year, unless it's more than three or four rounds.

**The Year Ahead:** Sandberg has the tools to project to the first-division level, but the overall feel for the game and playable skills are still underdeveloped and immature, so the developmental journey could be long. I love it when toolsy multisport types pick baseball over football or basketball, but as is often the case, the overall feel for the game can be a little underwhelming and can limit the utility of the physical gifts. Sandberg is a long-term project and it could take several years to see the first-division future start to blossom on a field. But the reason for his inclusion on this list is that his physical tools create the possibility for impact down the line, and if he can refine and bring those tools into game action, that's when you really have something of value.

## Prospects on the Rise

**1. C Gabriel Lino:** I've long been a fan of the raw Venezuelan backstop, dating back to his days in the Orioles organization. The arm is really strong behind the plate, and you can see just enough with the bat to keep you hanging around. He took some developmental steps in the right direction in 2013, and could be ready for an even bigger step in 2014. It's more of a backup profile long term, but the size, strength, arm, and raw power create the possibility of a higher ceiling, and that keeps him on my prospect landscape.

**2. OF Dylan Cozens:** Cozens is a massive human, standing a legit 6'6" and weighing 240 pounds, with plenty of raw power in his game. As you would expect, the swing can get long and leveraged, and sources question how much of the power is just pure strength and not projectable bat speed that will play as he moves up to the full-season level in 2014. This is a boom/bust type that could develop into a prototypical corner power bat in the middle of a lineup or one that could flame out before he reaches the Double-A level.

**3. 3B Zach Green:** Athletic and strong, Green was popped in the third round in 2012 and started to show some of the big power potential in his run through the NY-Penn League in 2013, ripping 34 extra-base hits in 74 games. At the plate, the trigger can look delayed and the path into the hitting zone isn't short and sweet, so his game features a lot of swing-and-miss at present. I don't see a big hit tool or consistent contact in his future, but he can find success and climb prospect lists if he can refine his swing and approach enough to get his plus power to play as he climbs.

## Factors on the Farm
### Prospects likely to contribute at the major-league level in 2014

**1. C/1B Tommy Joseph:** 2013 was a lost season for Joseph, who suffered a concussion in early May and struggled with the side effects until he was shut down for the year. With plus power potential in the stick and a strong arm, Joseph could offer value if he can return to his pre-concussion form, something that is often easier said than done. Concussions are no joke and it can take a long time to recover, but if Joseph returns healthy in 2014, he could play his way to the major-league level, where he could find time behind the plate and at first base.

**2. RHP Ken Giles:** A seventh-round pick in the 2011 draft, Giles looked the part of a future power reliever in 2013, missing bats in the Florida State League and then flashing elite fastball velocity in the AFL. His command is fringe at best, and his secondary arsenal comes and goes. But if he can gain some command of his mid- to upper-90s smoke and back it up with his mid- to upper-80s power slider, the 23-year-old righty is going to be a late-innings force at the major-league level at some point in 2014.

**3. RHP Ethan Martin:** Another late-innings arm that can often masquerade as a starter, Martin was once the 15th overall pick in the 2008 draft and considered a top tier prospect. But the 24-year-old has struggled with command his entire career, which puts his likely home in a major-league bullpen, despite a deep arsenal of power stuff that projects him much higher in a major-league rotation. With a little more consistency, Martin could develop into a legit setup option, pushing his already plus fastball into the mid-90s and backing it up with a hard mid-80s slider with wipeout potential.

## 1. Jameson Taillon RHP

**Born:** 11/18/91 **Age:** 22 **Bats:** R **Throws:** R **Height:** 6'6" **Weight:** 235

| MLB ETA | CT | FB | CH | CB | SL | OFP | Realistic |
|---|---|---|---|---|---|---|---|
| 2014 | — | 70 | 55 | 65 | — | 70 NO.2 STARTER | 60 NO.3 STARTER |

| YEAR | TEAM | LVL | AGE | W | L | SV | G | GS | IP | H | HR | BB | SO | BB9 | SO9 | GB% | BABIP | WHIP | ERA | FIP | FRA | WARP |
|---|---|---|---|---|---|---|---|---|---|---|---|---|---|---|---|---|---|---|---|---|---|---|
| 2013 | IND | AAA | 21 | 1 | 3 | 0 | 6 | 6 | 37.0 | 31 | 1 | 16 | 37 | 3.9 | 9.0 | 36% | .288 | 1.27 | 3.89 | 3.18 | 3.58 | 0.6 |
| 2013 | ALT | AA | 21 | 4 | 7 | 0 | 20 | 19 | 110.3 | 112 | 8 | 36 | 106 | 2.9 | 8.6 | 52% | .322 | 1.34 | 3.67 | 3.46 | 3.95 | 1.2 |
| 2014 | PIT | MLB | 22 | 7 | 9 | 0 | 25 | 25 | 129.3 | 126 | 14 | 44 | 101 | 3.1 | 7.0 | 44% | .309 | 1.31 | 4.17 | 4.27 | 4.54 | 0.3 |
| 2015 | PIT | MLB | 23 | 11 | 10 | 0 | 32 | 32 | 206.7 | 190 | 21 | 56 | 170 | 2.4 | 7.4 | 45% | .301 | 1.19 | 3.57 | 3.66 | 3.88 | 1.6 |

**Breakout:** 0%  **Improve:** 0%  **Collapse:** 0%  **Attrition:** 0%  **MLB:** 0%  *Comparables: Patrick Corbin, Brandon Maurer, Jarrod Parker*

**Drafted/Acquired:** 1st round, 2010 draft, The Woodlands HS (The Woodlands, TX)

**Previous Ranking:** #2 (Org), #11 (Top 101)

**What Happened in 2013:** Despite making 25 starts and logging close to 150 innings in the upper minors—missing close to a bat an inning as a 21-year-old—Taillon's national prospect status took a bit of a step back and he lost some of his shine. Go figure.

**Strengths:** Big, physical frame; built for workload; big arm strength; fastball is easy plus offering; shows plus-plus velocity; comfortable in the 94-97 range; heavy life to the arm side; bat breaker; curveball is plus; flashes well-above-average potential; low-80s with sharp two-plane break; aggressive approach; frontline mentality.

**Weaknesses:** Questions about lengthy arm action; fastball command is below average; curveball plays down from paper grade because of command; changeup is below average at present; lacks impact projection; too firm and limited fading action at higher velocity.

**Risk Factor/Injury History:** Low risk; 28 starts in upper minors

**Bret Sayre's Fantasy Take:** The prospect fatigue in fantasy circles has certainly been in full swing, as Taillon has seen his perceived value drop over the past two seasons. Of course, we know better and the developmental process often leads to nice buy-low opportunities on players like this. Taillon should be a strong four-category contributor who will pitch in a great park for his raw stats. Just because he's not an "ace" doesn't mean he can't be a top-20 fantasy starter.

**The Year Ahead:** Taillon was once considered a future frontline arm, a true number one in the making. Based on the scouting reports, the reality is a little less spectacular, but everything still points to a high-quality major-league starter, one capable of logging 200 innings a year and making outs. With excellent size and strength, in combination with two well-above-average offerings, Taillon should be considered one of the best arms in the minors. But his command profile is below average at present and limits the utility of the plus-plus pitches, and his changeup flashes only average potential, so the overall forecast has more clouds than once observed. However, Taillon's command still has time to refine, and if he does step forward on that front, the Pirates might just have one of the most potent one-two rotation punches in baseball.

**#19**
BP Top 101 Prospects

## 2. Gregory Polanco CF

**Born:** 9/14/91 **Age:** 22 **Bats:** L **Throws:** L **Height:** 6'4" **Weight:** 220

| MLB ETA | Hit | Power | Run | Glove | Arm | OFP | Realistic |
|---|---|---|---|---|---|---|---|
| 2014 | 60 | 65 | 65 | 55 | 60 | 65 1ST-DIV/ALL-STAR | 60 1ST-DIV PLAYER |

| YEAR | TEAM | LVL | AGE | PA | R | 2B | 3B | HR | RBI | BB | SO | SB | CS | AVG/OBP/SLG | TAv | BABIP | BRR | FRAA | WARP |
|---|---|---|---|---|---|---|---|---|---|---|---|---|---|---|---|---|---|---|---|
| 2013 | BRD | A+ | 21 | 241 | 29 | 17 | 0 | 6 | 30 | 16 | 37 | 24 | 4 | .312/.364/.472 | .311 | .350 | 1.3 | CF(56): -0.0 | 2.3 |
| 2013 | ALT | AA | 21 | 286 | 36 | 13 | 2 | 6 | 41 | 36 | 36 | 13 | 7 | .263/.354/.407 | .286 | .282 | 1.7 | CF(58): 6.3, RF(6): -0.3 | 2.6 |
| 2013 | IND | AAA | 21 | 9 | 1 | 0 | 0 | 0 | 0 | 0 | 0 | 1 | 0 | .222/.222/.222 | .232 | .222 | 0.2 | CF(2): -0.0 | 0.0 |
| 2014 | PIT | MLB | 22 | 250 | 29 | 10 | 1 | 5 | 25 | 17 | 49 | 12 | 4 | .245/.298/.367 | .252 | .280 | 1.0 | CF 2, RF 0 | 0.8 |
| 2015 | PIT | MLB | 23 | 250 | 28 | 11 | 1 | 5 | 26 | 19 | 47 | 11 | 3 | .255/.312/.385 | .258 | .296 | 0.9 | CF 2, RF 0 | 1.8 |

**Breakout:** 8%  **Improve:** 22%  **Collapse:** 5%  **Attrition:** 22%  **MLB:** 44%  *Comparables: Andrew McCutchen, Jake Marisnick, Ryan Kalish*

**Drafted/Acquired:** International free agent, 2009, Dominican Republic

**Previous Ranking:** #3 (Org), #44 (Top 101)

**What Happened in 2013:** As a 21-year-old, the five-tool talent played his way to the upper minors before exploding in the Dominican Winter League, establishing himself as one of the most exciting position players in the minors.

**Strengths:** Well-above-average athlete; long legs; more room to add strength; easy plus run; big, graceful strides; excellent range in the field; arm is plus; glove could play above average; good bat-to-ball skills; makes a lot of

**#24**
BP Top 101 Prospects

contact; hit tool likely to play plus; power potential is easy plus; makes quick adjustments; plus makeup.

**Weaknesses:** Still raw in the field; several sources prefer him in a corner spot; needs to improve his tracking skills/ routes to the ball; swing can get long; could struggle with inside coverage against plus velo; game power is still more about projection than game utility.

**Risk Factor/Injury History:** Moderate risk; 70 games in the upper minors; needs more tool refinement.

**Bret Sayre's Fantasy Take:** Usually three sixes are the sign of the devil, but when they come in the form of potential hit, power, and run tools, they are anything but. Polanco will impact fantasy rosters most with his speed first (think 25-30 steals), but he has the potential to hit 25 homers at the major-league level in due time. However, he's unlikely to have the power and speed overlap all that much at once—meaning his upside is just substantial and not mind-bending.

**The Year Ahead:** Polanco is the total tool package, loud across the board with the potential to develop into an all-star-caliber player at the major-league level. He's still raw in some aspects of the game, including his reads/ routes in center and his ability to turn his impressive raw power into over-the-fence results. But developmentally speaking, and taking into account his plus physical gifts, his work ethic, and his ability to make adjustments on the field, you really can't ask for a better model than Polanco. There are still some questions about the stick, and a dose of Triple-A pitching might present a good challenge for the 22-year-old, but the future is incredibly bright and he should reach the major-league level at some point in 2014.

## 3. Tyler Glasnow  RHP

**Born:** 8/23/93  **Age:** 20  **Bats:** L  **Throws:** R  **Height:** 6' 7"  **Weight:** 195

| MLB ETA | | CT | FB | CH | CB | SL | | OFP | Realistic |
|---|---|---|---|---|---|---|---|---|---|
| Late 2015 | | – | 65 | 50 | 60 | – | | 60 NO.2-3 STARTER | 50 NO.3-4 STARTER |

| YEAR | TEAM | LVL | AGE | W | L | SV | G | GS | IP | H | HR | BB | SO | BB9 | SO9 | GB% | BABIP | WHIP | ERA | FIP | FRA | WARP |
|---|---|---|---|---|---|---|---|---|---|---|---|---|---|---|---|---|---|---|---|---|---|---|
| 2013 | WVA | A | 19 | 9 | 3 | 0 | 24 | 24 | 111.3 | 54 | 9 | 61 | 164 | 4.9 | 13.3 | 50% | .215 | 1.03 | 2.18 | 3.47 | 3.99 | 1.6 |
| 2014 | PIT | MLB | 20 | 4 | 6 | 0 | 19 | 19 | 83.3 | 69 | 9 | 47 | 90 | 5.1 | 9.7 | 46% | .306 | 1.38 | 4.06 | 4.34 | 4.41 | 0.4 |
| 2015 | PIT | MLB | 21 | 8 | 8 | 0 | 30 | 30 | 186.0 | 140 | 19 | 101 | 217 | 4.9 | 10.5 | 46% | .294 | 1.30 | 3.64 | 3.84 | 3.96 | 1.3 |

Breakout: 0%    Improve: 0%    Collapse: 0%    Attrition: 0%    MLB: 0%        *Comparables: Clayton Kershaw, Danny Duffy, Shelby Miller*

**Drafted/Acquired:** 5th round, 2011 draft, Hart HS (Santa Clarita, CA)

**Previous Ranking:** #8 (Org)

**What Happened in 2013:** Glasnow erupted as a prospect, missing a ton of bats in his full-season debut, showing a well-above-average fastball and a highly projectable profile.

**Strengths:** Impressive size; fast arm from 3/4 slot; long arms and steep downward plane; fastball works in the 93-96 range with ease; touches higher; attacks with fastball; upper-70s curveball flashes plus; sharp vertical break; changeup projects to average.

**Weaknesses:** Delivery can get funky; struggles to control body and loses release; fastball can sit in the mid-90s but control gets too loose at upper registers; fastball command is below average at present; tendency to over-throw the curveball; changeup is below average at present; limited action; pitchability needs improvement.

**Risk Factor/Injury History:** Moderate risk; Low-A resume; pitchability needs work

**Bret Sayre's Fantasy Take:** We know it's easier to rack up strikeouts in Low-A than in the upper minors or at the major-league level, but it's not supposed to be this easy. Glasnow's curveball could eventually help push him up to the 200+ strikeout range at the major-league level, but he'll need to limit the walks in order to be as strong of a ratio play (impact ERA will be more attainable than WHIP for him).

**The Year Ahead:** Glasnow blew up as a prospect in 2013, and despite a warranted rise in the national ranks, some of the hype surrounding the 20-year-old arm is quite overblown. You have to love the size and projection it offers, and the fastball is already a big-league-quality weapon, but the command isn't sharp and he can struggle with his length in the delivery. The fastball/curve combo is simply too good for lower-level hitters to deal with, so he will be able to hide the warts as he climbs the chain, but he could struggle once he reaches Double-A and sees more advanced sticks. I don't see a frontline projection in Glasnow—despite the frontline size and fastball— but I do see a future mid-rotation starter, one capable of workload and whiffs but one unlikely to blossom into a top-of-the-rotation arm because of the questions surrounding his pitchability.

**#42**
BP Top 101 Prospects

## 4.  Reese McGuire  C

**Born:** 3/2/95  **Age:** 19  **Bats:** L  **Throws:** R  **Height:** 6'0"  **Weight:** 181

| MLB ETA | Hit | Power | Run | Glove | Arm | OFP | Realistic |
|---|---|---|---|---|---|---|---|
| 2017 | 55 | 50 | 55 | 65 | 75 | 65<br>1ST-DIV/ALL-STAR | 60<br>1ST-DIV PLAYER |

| YEAR | TEAM | LVL | AGE | PA | R | 2B | 3B | HR | RBI | BB | SO | SB | CS | AVG/OBP/SLG | TAv | BABIP | BRR | FRAA | WARP |
|---|---|---|---|---|---|---|---|---|---|---|---|---|---|---|---|---|---|---|---|
| 2013 | JAM | A- | 18 | 17 | 3 | 0 | 0 | 0 | 0 | 1 | 1 | 1 | 0 | .250/.294/.250 | .237 | .267 | 0.5 | C(3): -0.0 | 0.1 |
| 2013 | PIR | Rk | 18 | 198 | 30 | 11 | 0 | 0 | 21 | 15 | 18 | 5 | 1 | .330/.388/.392 | .290 | .362 | 0.4 | C(25): 1.1 | 1.7 |
| 2014 | PIT | MLB | 19 | 250 | 16 | 8 | 0 | 1 | 19 | 10 | 63 | 1 | 0 | .202/.237/.259 | .191 | .260 | -0.4 | C 1 | -0.9 |
| 2015 | PIT | MLB | 20 | 250 | 23 | 8 | 0 | 3 | 21 | 10 | 56 | 1 | 0 | .235/.266/.313 | .216 | .289 | -0.5 | C 1 | -1.3 |

**Breakout:** 0%  **Improve:** 0%  **Collapse:** 0%  **Attrition:** 0%  **MLB:** 0%  *Comparables: Christian Bethancourt, Cedric Hunter, Caleb Gindl*

**Drafted/Acquired:** 1st round, 2013 draft, Kentwood HS (Covington, WA)

**Previous Ranking:** NR

**What Happened in 2013:** A rare five-tool talent behind the plate, McGuire has yet to receive the national love, but his time is coming as a top-tier prospect.

**Strengths:** Good athlete; good present strength/coordination; arm is a big weapon; receiving projects to plus or better; intelligence for calling games; shows a good swing at the plate; generates good bat speed and can drive the ball; above-average potential hit; average potential power; solid run; huge makeup.

**Weaknesses:** Still refining as a receiver; working on footwork/positioning; can get too aggressive with the arm; sources are mixed on the stick; pessimists see a fringe hit tool; likely to struggle against better velocity/secondaries; game power could play below average.

**Risk Factor/Injury History:** High risk; dual-threat development; limited professional experience.

**Bret Sayre's Fantasy Take:** McGuire is not Austin Hedges, as far as the gap between real-life and fantasy value goes, but he's certainly more valuable from a real-life standpoint. Right now, he offers enough fantasy upside to roster. He doesn't project to be a huge help in any individual categories, but could forge a fantasy future as an early-career Russell Martin type—a catcher who can hit a little, has some pop, and runs a bit.

**The Year Ahead:** I love plus defensive catchers with near-elite arms, especially when the profile is completed with makeup that scouts line up to champion. McGuire is incredibly underrated as a prospect, a legit five-tool backstop who is a better athlete than people realize and who could develop into a Gold Glove-caliber defender. If the bat is average, he could be a major-league regular for a very long time. He's an all-star if the bat offers anything close to its projection. I wouldn't be shocked if McGuire climbs the prospect lists in 2014 after a strong full-season campaign. I'm very high on this prospect.

> **#59**
> BP Top
> 101
> Prospects

## 5.  Josh Bell  RF

**Born:** 8/14/92  **Age:** 21  **Bats:** B  **Throws:** R  **Height:** 6'3"  **Weight:** 213

| MLB ETA | Hit | Power | Run | Glove | Arm | OFP | Realistic |
|---|---|---|---|---|---|---|---|
| Late 2015 | 60 | 60 | 50 | 50 | 55 | 60<br>1ST-DIV PLAYER | 50<br>ML REGULAR |

| YEAR | TEAM | LVL | AGE | PA | R | 2B | 3B | HR | RBI | BB | SO | SB | CS | AVG/OBP/SLG | TAv | BABIP | BRR | FRAA | WARP |
|---|---|---|---|---|---|---|---|---|---|---|---|---|---|---|---|---|---|---|---|
| 2013 | WVA | A | 20 | 519 | 75 | 37 | 2 | 13 | 76 | 52 | 90 | 1 | 2 | .279/.353/.453 | .318 | .319 | -1.1 | RF(83): 2.9 | 4.1 |
| 2014 | PIT | MLB | 21 | 250 | 22 | 11 | 0 | 5 | 26 | 14 | 58 | 0 | 0 | .232/.275/.350 | .237 | .280 | -0.5 | RF 0 | -0.2 |
| 2015 | PIT | MLB | 22 | 250 | 26 | 11 | 1 | 5 | 25 | 16 | 57 | 0 | 0 | .232/.283/.354 | .237 | .281 | -0.6 | RF 0 | -0.2 |

**Breakout:** 0%  **Improve:** 0%  **Collapse:** 0%  **Attrition:** 0%  **MLB:** 0%  *Comparables: Billy Butler, Moises Sierra, Oswaldo Arcia*

**Drafted/Acquired:** 2nd round, 2011 draft, Dallas Jesuit College Prep (Dallas, TX)

**Previous Ranking:** #6 (Org)

**What Happened in 2013:** An injury marred his full-season debut in 2012, but a return to health saw Bell take a step forward in his return in 2013, ripping 52 extra-base hits as a 20-year-old.

**Strengths:** Good athlete with size; good present strength; natural feel for hitting; right-handed stroke is easy and clean; quick to the ball and consistent hard contact; hit tool projects to plus; power is still developing, but projects to be plus; left-handed swing shows bat speed and lift; arm is above average; average run; can show all five tools.

**Weaknesses:** Power mechanics from the left side; tendency to drop his back shoulder and load up for the long ball; susceptible to quality secondary stuff; corner profile in the outfield; arm is strong but doesn't always show above-average utility; lacks big recovery speed on bad read/routes.

**Risk Factor/Injury History:** Moderate risk; Low-A experience; knee injury on resume (2012); early makeup concerns.

**Bret Sayre's Fantasy Take:** The bottom really fell out of Bell's value this season—to the point where I was called an idiot on Twitter for saying I would take him over Devon Travis in fantasy leagues. This is still a guy who could hit .280 and 25+ bombs with a lot of RBIs. If his current owner doesn't still believe, by all means step in and relieve him/her of Bell.

**The Year Ahead:** In 2013, Bell flashed the talent to justify his $5 million price tag, and should continue to build on the success in 2014. It's not an elite profile, but both the hit tool and the power could play to plus, and he has

> **#77**
> BP Top
> 101
> Prospects

more than enough athleticism to handle a corner-outfield spot. It will be interesting to see how he responds as a switch-hitter to better pitching, as he has a tendency to sell out from the left side and could open himself up to exploitation if he continues to cheat on the fastball and load up the power. I think Bell could be ready to take another step forward, with the potential to blossom into a top-50 player in the minors.

## 6. Nick Kingham RHP

**Born:** 11/8/91  **Age:** 22  **Bats:** R  **Throws:** R  **Height:** 6'5"  **Weight:** 220

| MLB ETA | CT | FB | CH | CB | SL | OFP | Realistic |
|---|---|---|---|---|---|---|---|
| Late 2014 | – | 60 | 50 | 60 | – | 60<br>NO.2-3 STARTER | 50<br>NO.4 STARTER |

| YEAR | TEAM | LVL | AGE | W | L | SV | G | GS | IP | H | HR | BB | SO | BB9 | SO9 | GB% | BABIP | WHIP | ERA | FIP | FRA | WARP |
|---|---|---|---|---|---|---|---|---|---|---|---|---|---|---|---|---|---|---|---|---|---|---|
| 2013 | BRD | A+ | 21 | 6 | 3 | 0 | 13 | 13 | 70.0 | 55 | 6 | 14 | 75 | 1.8 | 9.6 | 46% | .274 | 0.99 | 3.09 | 3.20 | 4.27 | 0.7 |
| 2013 | ALT | AA | 21 | 3 | 3 | 0 | 14 | 12 | 73.3 | 70 | 1 | 30 | 69 | 3.7 | 8.5 | 45% | .328 | 1.36 | 2.70 | 2.97 | 3.18 | 1.5 |
| 2014 | PIT | MLB | 22 | 6 | 9 | 0 | 24 | 24 | 117.7 | 116 | 13 | 43 | 91 | 3.3 | 7.0 | 44% | .309 | 1.35 | 4.35 | 4.40 | 4.73 | 0.0 |
| 2015 | PIT | MLB | 23 | 9 | 9 | 0 | 31 | 31 | 199.0 | 183 | 20 | 64 | 172 | 2.9 | 7.8 | 45% | .305 | 1.24 | 3.74 | 3.74 | 4.06 | 1.1 |

Breakout: 0%  Improve: 0%  Collapse: 0%  Attrition: 0%  MLB: 0%  *Comparables: Jarrod Parker, Alex Wood, Wade Davis*

**Drafted/Acquired:** 4th round, 2010 draft, Sierra Vista HS (Las Vegas, NV)

**Previous Ranking:** #9 (Org)

**What Happened in 2013:** The former fourth-round pick's 2012 season was solid, but his 2013 campaign was explosive, as he pitched his way to the Double-A level, missing a bat an inning and holding hitters to a .233 average.

**Strengths:** Excellent size and present strength; clean delivery and arm action; throws downhill and repeats; fastball is plus offering; routinely works 92-94; can spike in the 97 range; some late life to the arm side; curveball is a hard breaker that can show heavy depth; almost splitter-like at times because of the vertical action; feel for an average changeup that has more to offer; has pitchability and command projection.

**Weaknesses:** More control than command at present; can spot the fastball but struggles with secondary command; tendency to overthrow the curveball and lose the depth; changeup plays well because of deception but can lack big action.

**Risk Factor/Injury History:** Moderate risk; Double-A experience.

**Bret Sayre's Fantasy Take:** Kingham gets overlooked in the Pirates' system because Taillon and Glasnow are both top-tier pitching prospects, but that's not his fault. Kingham doesn't have that same upside, but he could be a very worthy shallow-league starter in relatively short order, with 170-175 strikeouts and an ERA which could hover below 3.50.

**The Year Ahead:** While the profile lacks the same sex appeal as that of Glasnow, several sources actually prefer Kingham as a prospect because of his overall feel for the mound and execution of his entire arsenal. The fastball is a true plus offering, with plus velocity and good life. He uses his size well on the mound and repeats his mechanics despite the length. The curveball will need to be tighter, but it can show plus because of its velocity and heavy vertical depth. A step forward in command could elevate the 22-year-old onto another prospect tier and set him up for a rotation spot in 2015. The ceiling isn't as high as those of Taillon and Glasnow, but I wouldn't be shocked if Kingham develops into a quality mid-rotation starter at the major-league level, one who lacks a frontline punch but makes up for it with consistency and dependability.

**#80**
BP Top 101 Prospects

## 7. Austin Meadows OF

**Born:** 5/3/95  **Age:** 19  **Bats:** L  **Throws:** L  **Height:** 6'3"  **Weight:** 200

| MLB ETA | Hit | Power | Run | Glove | Arm | OFP | Realistic |
|---|---|---|---|---|---|---|---|
| 2017 | 55 | 55 | 65 | 55 | – | 60<br>1ST-DIV PLAYER | 50<br>ML REGULAR |

| YEAR | TEAM | LVL | AGE | PA | R | 2B | 3B | HR | RBI | BB | SO | SB | CS | AVG/OBP/SLG | TAv | BABIP | BRR | FRAA | WARP |
|---|---|---|---|---|---|---|---|---|---|---|---|---|---|---|---|---|---|---|---|
| 2013 | JAM | A- | 18 | 22 | 8 | 0 | 0 | 2 | 2 | 5 | 4 | 0 | 0 | .529/.636/.882 | .506 | .636 | 0.5 | CF(5): 0.5 | 0.8 |
| 2013 | PIR | Rk | 18 | 189 | 29 | 11 | 5 | 5 | 20 | 24 | 42 | 3 | 2 | .294/.399/.519 | .316 | .372 | -2.4 | CF(36): 0.4 | 1.5 |
| 2014 | PIT | MLB | 19 | 250 | 21 | 7 | 1 | 5 | 24 | 16 | 77 | 0 | 0 | .197/.253/.303 | .212 | .270 | -0.4 | CF 1 | -0.5 |
| 2015 | PIT | MLB | 20 | 250 | 27 | 9 | 1 | 6 | 26 | 19 | 73 | 0 | 0 | .217/.283/.351 | .233 | .284 | -0.4 | CF 1 | -0.1 |

Breakout: 0%  Improve: 0%  Collapse: 0%  Attrition: 0%  MLB: 0%  *Comparables: Jaff Decker, Aaron Hicks, Fernando Martinez*

**Drafted/Acquired:** 1st round, 2013 draft, Grayson HS (Loganville, GA)

**Previous Ranking:** NR

**What Happened in 2013:** A highly touted amateur player, Meadows was popped with the ninth overall pick in the draft and started ripping the ball at the complex-level right out of the gate.

**Strengths:** Looks the part; size/athleticism/strength; easy plus run; swing is aesthetically pleasing; can drive the ball and will use all fields; hit tool could play to above average; raw power to play above average; comes from highly competitive amateur background.

**Weaknesses:** Speed could dip as body continues to mature/bulk up; arm is below average; bat speed isn't special; tendency to swing through average velocity; power will likely come from strength and leverage in the swing.

**#89**
BP Top 101 Prospects

**Risk Factor/Injury History:** High risk; short-season resume; questions about profile.

**Bret Sayre's Fantasy Take:** Meadows is essentially a compressed version of Polanco, but with that compression comes less fantasy ceiling. As of right now, he's a prospect who hasn't played full-season ball and doesn't project to have impact potential in homers, steals, or average—his value is likely to come in aggregation. He's a pick in the back of the first round for me in dynasty league drafts this year.

**The Year Ahead:** As a player who spent his amateur years on the showcase circuit, Meadows is very familiar to most evaluators. Dating back to those showcase days, it was clear that Meadows looked the part of a future first-division major leaguer, a player who had the body of a young Josh Hamilton, complete with wheels and a pretty swing from the left-side. Despite the physical qualities, Meadows can struggle with the stick, showing a tendency to swing and miss on fringy stuff in the zone. His short-season performance was much better than expected and could represent a true developmental step forward for the then-18-year-old, which if replicated could erase some of the early doubts about his bat. The arm issue and body projection (bulk) could force a move to left field, which will put more pressure on the bat to live up the lofty hype. I'm not sold that the bat can carry that burden, but will gladly change my mind after putting eyes back on Meadows in 2014 and beyond.

## 8. Alen Hanson  SS

**Born:** 10/22/92  **Age:** 21  **Bats:** B  **Throws:** R  **Height:** 5'11"  **Weight:** 170

| MLB ETA | Hit | Power | Run | Glove | Arm | OFP | Realistic |
|---|---|---|---|---|---|---|---|
| 2015 | 55 | 50 | 60 | 55 | – | 55 >AVG REGULAR | 45 UT/<AVG REG |

| YEAR | TEAM | LVL | AGE | PA | R | 2B | 3B | HR | RBI | BB | SO | SB | CS | AVG/OBP/SLG | TAv | BABIP | BRR | FRAA | WARP |
|---|---|---|---|---|---|---|---|---|---|---|---|---|---|---|---|---|---|---|---|
| 2013 | ALT | AA | 20 | 150 | 13 | 4 | 5 | 1 | 10 | 8 | 26 | 6 | 2 | .255/.299/.380 | .273 | .306 | -0.9 | SS(34): -1.6 | 0.6 |
| 2013 | BRD | A+ | 20 | 409 | 51 | 23 | 8 | 7 | 48 | 33 | 70 | 24 | 14 | .281/.339/.444 | .283 | .325 | 2.0 | SS(92): 2.4 | 3.4 |
| 2014 | PIT | MLB | 21 | 250 | 30 | 10 | 3 | 4 | 20 | 14 | 59 | 10 | 5 | .236/.281/.356 | .237 | .290 | 0.6 | SS -4, 2B -0 | 0.1 |
| 2015 | PIT | MLB | 22 | 250 | 28 | 11 | 3 | 5 | 26 | 18 | 53 | 10 | 5 | .259/.315/.398 | .259 | .308 | 0.4 | SS -4, 2B 0 | 1.5 |

Breakout: 0%   Improve: 0%   Collapse: 0%   Attrition: 0%   MLB: 0%   *Comparables: Nick Franklin, Joel Guzman, Yamaico Navarro*

**Drafted/Acquired:** International free agent, 2009, Dominican Republic

**Previous Ranking:** #5 (Org), #66 (Top 101)

**What Happened in 2013:** After ripping it in High-A, Hanson struggled in his first taste of the Eastern League, and carried over some of the offensive struggles in his fall and winter ball campaigns.

**Strengths:** Plus athlete; great hands on both sides of the ball; good feel for contact; controls the bat well and has bat speed; hit tool could play above average; good pop for his size; can make loud contact and drive the ball out of the park; plus run; glove could play solid-average or above at second.

**Weaknesses:** Not likely a shortstop at highest level; arm plays fringe or below; great hands but can struggle with routine plays; more flash than fundamentals; bat can get aggressive; tendency to roll over off-speed; can get caught cheating on heat; get to front foot too early and make weak contact; power might play below average.

**Risk Factor/Injury History:** Moderate risk; limited Double-A experience; questions about profile.

**Bret Sayre's Fantasy Take:** Hanson still ranks fourth on this list for fantasy purposes, as his defensive profile pulls him down this list. If Hanson is a second baseman, we don't really care, as it's not that much worse of a position than shortstop. He still can be a 15-homer/20-steal middle infielder with a pretty good average.

**The Year Ahead:** If you think Hanson is a shortstop all the way up the chain, he belongs much higher on this list. The kid can hit, and will most likely develop into a solid-average offensive force, with good contact ability, some pop, and the legs to add pressure to the equation. A solid-average offensive profile for a shortstop points to a first-division player and possible all-star, but the value doesn't play the same at second, where the bat needs to carry more of the weight. I don't see big power coming from the stick, and I don't see a .300 hitter, so the profile plays a little soft for me. A promising return to Double-A could push his stock up a bit in the short term, but the long-term projection looks more like a major-league regular than a first-division type. That's still a huge developmental win for the Pirates.

## 9. Luis Heredia  RHP

**Born:** 8/10/94  **Age:** 19  **Bats:** R  **Throws:** R  **Height:** 6'6"  **Weight:** 205

| MLB ETA | CT | FB | CH | CB | SL | OFP | Realistic |
|---|---|---|---|---|---|---|---|
| 2016 | – | 60 | 65 | – | 50 | 60 NO.3 STARTER | 50 NO.5 STARTER |

| YEAR | TEAM | LVL | AGE | W | L | SV | G | GS | IP | H | HR | BB | SO | BB9 | SO9 | GB% | BABIP | WHIP | ERA | FIP | FRA | WARP |
|---|---|---|---|---|---|---|---|---|---|---|---|---|---|---|---|---|---|---|---|---|---|---|
| 2013 | WVA | A | 18 | 7 | 3 | 0 | 14 | 13 | 65.0 | 52 | 5 | 37 | 55 | 5.1 | 7.6 | 39% | .272 | 1.37 | 3.05 | 4.77 | 4.70 | 0.1 |
| 2014 | PIT | MLB | 19 | 2 | 5 | 0 | 13 | 13 | 54.0 | 59 | 7 | 31 | 28 | 5.2 | 4.7 | 42% | .308 | 1.66 | 5.67 | 5.88 | 6.16 | -0.8 |
| 2015 | PIT | MLB | 20 | 7 | 10 | 0 | 29 | 29 | 176.3 | 175 | 21 | 89 | 118 | 4.5 | 6.0 | 42% | .300 | 1.50 | 4.97 | 4.90 | 5.40 | -1.7 |

Breakout: 0%   Improve: 0%   Collapse: 0%   Attrition: 0%   MLB: 0%   *Comparables: Julio Teheran, Jonathan Pettibone, Jenrry Mejia*

**Drafted/Acquired:** International free agent, 2010, Mexico

**Previous Ranking:** #4 (Org), #53 (Top 101)

**What Happened in 2013:** In his full-season debut, the full-bodied Heredia struggled with his control and secondary execution, watching his stock tumble as the system improved as a whole.

**Strengths:** Large frame; good strength; has pitchability; fastball was down in 2013, but can still work low-90s with occasional velocity spike; turns over a quality changeup; good arm speed and fading action; slider would flash average or better; could show sharp tilt; will show curveball; deep arsenal mix.

**Weaknesses:** High-maintenance body; lost fluidity in the delivery and mechanical consistency; fastball was very pedestrian at times; would dip into upper-80s; lacks a knockout breaking ball; can miss some bats; more about missing barrels; command and control were both below average; question the makeup/work ethic.

**Risk Factor/Injury History:** High risk; Low-A resume; only 19 years old

**Bret Sayre's Fantasy Take:** What Heredia likely won't give you in strikeouts, he will give you in innings. More of a target in points leagues, he doesn't miss as many bats as you'd like (although Pirate pitching prospect strikeout numbers can be deceiving), and the breaking ball may not develop enough to get him more than 150-160 in a season. The ratios should be strong, though.

**The Year Ahead:** Heredia is still very young and very promising, but showing up to camp out of shape raises a red flag, regardless of his age. The large and in charge righty has always been more about pitchability and making outs than filling up the stat sheet with whiffs, and there is some merit to the approach. But when the stuff ticks down and the command falls below average, the inability to hit spots and miss barrels limits the effectiveness of the arsenal. With his fastball/changeup, Heredia can force weak contact and escape at-bats, and the slider showed some bat-missing ability in 2014, so he has something to build on going forward. If he can control his body and his delivery, Heredia could once again climb the prospect ranks and regain his mid-rotation projection.

## 10. Harold Ramirez  LF

**Born:** 9/6/94  **Age:** 19  **Bats:** R  **Throws:** R  **Height:** 5'11"  **Weight:** 175

| MLB ETA | Hit | Power | Run | Glove | Arm | OFP | Realistic |
|---|---|---|---|---|---|---|---|
| 2017 | 55 | 50 | 65 | 50 | 50 | 60<br>1ST DIV PLAYER | 45<br>BENCH/<AVG REG |

| YEAR | TEAM | LVL | AGE | PA | R | 2B | 3B | HR | RBI | BB | SO | SB | CS | AVG/OBP/SLG | TAv | BABIP | BRR | FRAA | WARP |
|---|---|---|---|---|---|---|---|---|---|---|---|---|---|---|---|---|---|---|---|
| 2013 | JAM | A- | 18 | 310 | 42 | 11 | 4 | 5 | 40 | 23 | 52 | 23 | 11 | .285/.354/.409 | .293 | .332 | 1.6 | CF(31): -3.6, RF(22): 0.9 | 2.2 |
| 2014 | PIT | MLB | 19 | 250 | 23 | 8 | 1 | 3 | 19 | 10 | 64 | 9 | 5 | .206/.245/.284 | .203 | .270 | 0.1 | LF 2, CF -2 | -0.7 |
| 2015 | PIT | MLB | 20 | 250 | 24 | 9 | 1 | 3 | 21 | 14 | 59 | 8 | 4 | .213/.266/.306 | .215 | .268 | 0.0 | LF 2, CF -2 | -1.2 |

Breakout: 0%    Improve: 0%    Collapse: 0%    Attrition: 0%    MLB: 0%    *Comparables: Aaron Hicks, Che-Hsuan Lin, Engel Beltre*

**Drafted/Acquired:** International free agent, 2011, Colombia

**Previous Ranking:** NR

**What Happened in 2013:** In his New York-Penn League debut, the seven-figure talent was electric at the plate, showing an advanced feel for contact and the ability to drive the ball.

**Strengths:** Plus athlete; good present strength; strong lower half; excellent hands at the plate; feel for the barrel; puts himself in good hitting conditions and drives the ball; power could play above average down the line; easy plus run; shows good range in the outfield; arm can show average; glove could play to average with refinement.

**Weaknesses:** Struggles against off-speed; looks to attack fastballs early and often; struggled against pitchers with a plan; body could pull speed down as he matures; lower half already showing some thickness; reads/routes in center need a lot of work; arm strength is average but utility doesn't always play to grade; could end up a left-field profile.

**Risk Factor/Injury History:** High risk; short-season resume; sizeable gap between present/future.

**Bret Sayre's Fantasy Take:** If you're looking for a Pirates prospect who could take that Polanco/Hanson step forward in 2014, Ramirez is a good guy to gamble on. He doesn't project to have that kind of power, but the hit and speed tools are certainly interesting from a fantasy perspective.

**The Year Ahead:** Ramirez received a lot of love early this summer, as his New York-Penn League debut was highly successful; he hit for average with good pop and speed. But he struggled mightily in his final month, and some of the on-the-field reports weren't as glowing. Because of his combination of speed, hit tool, and power potential, Ramirez gets lumped in with the top-tier prospects, and perhaps he has the overall feel and makeup to turn the physical gifts into that reality. But sources are mixed on his defensive prow-

## FROM THE FIELD

### Nick Kingham

**Player:** Nick Kingham

**Team:** Pittsburgh Pirates

**Filed by:** Chris King

**Date(s) Seen:** June 4, 2013

**Physical:** Big and strong; powerful legs; moves well for his size.

**Mechanics/Delivery:** High 3/4 slot; low effort and repeats delivery; medium-high leg kick; drives off his legs; finishes square to the plate.

**Fastball:** 70 grade; 93-96 mph topped out at 97; above-average command; late movement; some arm-side run; heavy pitch down in the zone.

**Curveball:** 55 grade; 76-80 mph; fringe-average command; average spin with decent bite; did a good job staying on top of the pitch; seemed shy to throw it.

**Changeup:** 60 grade; 84-86 mph; average command; deceiving drop; decent depth; good arm speed; willing to throw in any count; showed a good feel.

**Other:** Ideal size and frame; worked off of his fastball all game; maintained velocity deep into the start; will attack inside with fastball; mixed in off-speed well to keep hitters off balance; had a plan and executed it; secondary offerings need to improve; would like to see him throw the curveball more; not many swing-and-misses.

**Makeup:** 60 grade; showed good mound presence; kept his composure when in tight spots.

**OFP:** High 5; solid no. 3 starter

**Realistic Role:** Low 5; no. 4/5 starter.

**Risk:** High

ess in center, with some suggesting left field is a more likely outcome, despite the plus speed and playable arm. Developmentally speaking, if he does have to shift to left, the bat will have to reach its projections (or beyond) for Ramirez to achieve a first-division status. Long way to go, but lots of tools to work with.

## Prospects on the Rise

**1. OF Michael De La Cruz:** A six-figure talent from the Dominican Republic, De La Cruz is a middle-of-the-diamond player who has good feel for hitting. It's raw, but he has baseball instincts and a lot of physical gifts to mold into form, and he will jump onto the national scene next year in his stateside debut. I think the Pirates have one of the top international departments under director Rene Gayo, and a track record for hitting on up-the-middle position players. Keep the name on your follow list for 2014.

**2. LHP Blake Taylor:** A second-round pick in the 2013 draft, Taylor has excellent size and present strength, and a fast arm that offers projection. As an amateur, the southpaw would work mostly in the upper-80s, touching the low-90s, with the ability to spin a quality curve, but he struggled with his delivery (high leg/struggled to get over and finish) and command in his small complex-league sample. As he starts to put the pieces together, he should climb the prospect ranks and jump into the top 10 within the next few seasons.

**3. LHP Cody Dickson:** A Sam Houston State lefty drafted in the fourth round in 2013, Dickson has a lively solid-average fastball that has some remaining projection, a quality changeup that plays well off the fastball with good arm-side action and a good tumbling curveball. Command needs work, but this is a lefty with a good combination of now stuff, feel for craft, and remaining projection. I feel confident saying he will be among the top 10 prospects in this system next season.

## Factors on the Farm

### Prospects likely to contribute at the major-league level in 2014

**1. C Tony Sanchez:** The former first-round pick finally made it the majors, although the bat stayed in the minors. Sanchez is most likely a backup catcher at the highest level, but one who can offer defensive value in addition to some pop at the plate, but the outcome is obviously a disappointment from the fourth overall pick in 2009.

### FROM THE FIELD

## Reese McGuire

**Player:** Reese McGuire
**Team:** Pittsburgh Pirates
**Filed by:** Chris King
**Date(s) Seen:** August 15 and August 26-28, 2013
**Physical:** Strong foundation and core; very athletic behind the plate and on base; solid footwork; durable build.
**Hit:** 60 grade; Wide stance; simple bat-to-ball approach; above-average bat speed; level swing.
**Power:** 50 grade; gap-to-gap; still developing strength; swing more geared to hard-contact line drives.
**Glove:** 65 grade; brick wall behind the plate; controls blocked pitches very well; solid footwork allows for quick pop times and quick transfers.
**Arm:** 65 grade; easy plus arm now; plus-plus potential; very accurate; quick release.
**Speed:** 50 grade; faster than expected; top end is a tick above-average; consistent average times to first base.
**Makeup:** 70 grade; natural leader; cerebral player with a high baseball IQ; handles the pitchers very well for his age.
**OFP:** High 60; first-division; all-star potential
**Realistic Role:** 60; first-division regular
**Risk:** Medium

### FROM THE FIELD

## Gregory Polanco

**Player:** Gregory Polanco
**Team:** Pittsburgh Pirates
**Filed by:** Chris King
**Date(s) Seen:** May 19, May 23, June 3, and June 4, 2013
**Physical:** Long and lanky; room to add weight; projectable; strong lower half.
**Hit:** 60 grade; above-average approach; covers the entire plate well; great bat speed; strong wrists allow him to control the bat; vulnerable to off-speed down; will chase and lunge at times.
**Power:** 60 grade; natural leverage creates good backspin; most power is pull side; has enough to go deep opposite field; uses his lower half well; more will come as he adds some weight.
**Glove:** 65 grade; steady improvements; good pre-pitch positioning; routes getting better, but still work to be done; still improving his reads off the bat; plus range in center field; excellent at cutting balls off in the gaps; has enough to stay in center field.
**Arm:** 60 grade; above average; accurate from all fields and on the run; stays accurate after quick transfers; consistently hits the cutoff man.
**Speed:** 60 grade; plus speed in the field and on base; gets to top speed quickly; athletic and agile, especially in the outfield.
**Makeup:** 70 grade; maintains positive body language even during a tough day; great teammate; doesn't dwell on bad at-bats.
**OFP:** High 6; first division; all-star potential
**Realistic Role:** 6; first-division regular
**Risk:** High; still have concerns how he will handle top-tier breaking balls and off-speed pitches as he advances.

---

**Player:** Gregory Polanco
**Team:** Pittsburgh Pirates
**Filed by:** CJ Wittmann
**Date(s) Seen:** June 22, 2013
**Physical:** Long, physical frame; room to add more muscle as he matures; very long legs; above-average athleticism.
**Hit:** 60 grade; good bat speed with natural bat-to-ball skills; line-drive-oriented swing where barrel stays in hitting zone a long time; lots of loud contact; swing can get long at times; struggled with quality spin.
**Power:** 60 grade; more raw strength than power at present; shows present gap-to-gap pop; ability to loft balls with slight bat angle through hitting zone.
**Glove:** 60 grade; swift movements in center field; tracks ball and runs/reads routes well but still a bit raw; excellent range; talked to multiple scouts who felt he could stay in center field, also some who preferred a corner outfield spot.
**Arm:** 60 grade; strong, accurate throws; gets behind ball well and uses whole body.
**Speed:** 60 grade; long strides with very good agility; consistently around 4.0 range (to 1B) from left side; think as he fills out, speed will only play to 60.
**Makeup:** 60 grade; very involved with teammates on occasion and strong work ethic
**OFP:** 65; all-star
**Realistic Role:** 60; first-division player
**Risk:** Moderate; limited experience in upper minors and could use work in field.

**2. OF Andrew Lambo:** A fourth-round pick in the 2007 draft, Lambo has seen his ups and downs as a prospect, including being traded for the great Octavio Dotel. But he finally got to taste the highest level in 2013 after close to 2,500 minor-league at-bats, and even though the sample was small and the contact inconsistent, the power from the left side makes him an interesting major-league option in 2014.

**3. RHP Stolmy Pimentel:** Signed by the Red Sox back in 2006, Pimentel has made 147 career minor-league starts but finally reached the major-league level pitching out of the bullpen, a role that could keep him at the level in 2014. He's always had the fastball, working in the plus velocity range as a starter and sitting mid-90s in bursts, and his cutter-like slider in the upper-80s with sharp glove-side slice can miss bats and barrels. But the once above-average changeup comes and goes, as does the command, so a max-effort arsenal out of the bullpen looks like the best chance for a sustainable future.

---

## FROM THE FIELD

### Austin Meadows

**Player:** Austin Meadows

**Team:** Pittsburgh Pirates

**Filed by:** Ethan Purser

**Date(s) Seen:** March 12, 2013

**Physical:** Impressive specimen (6'3", 200+ lbs.); major-league body with truckloads of projectability and athleticism; body should continue adding bulk as he matures physically.

**Hit:** 60 grade; tall, balanced setup; swing has some natural length due to long arms; will extend early on occasion and loop under the ball; stroke seems conducive to all-fields contact despite an overall lack of fluidity; above-average bat speed; keen pitch-recognition skills.

**Power:** 60 grade; impressive raw power to his pull side in BP; developing strength in the body; stroke is currently on the linear side and is more conducive to line drives to the gaps; a few alterations to the aforementioned swing mechanics paired with inevitable physical maturation should allow power to develop.

**Glove:** 50 grade; mature reads and routes in center; shows good instincts; has the speed to handle center currently; body maturation may force a move to left field.

**Arm:** 45 grade; center-field/left-field arm strength; fringe-average; wrist curl at bottom of arm swing; throws lack carry and velocity.

**Speed:** 55 grade; speed is currently plus (or a tick above); long strider; added mass via physical development should force speed component of game to diminish slightly at physical peak.

**Makeup:** Performance/effort didn't stand out in an environment with loads of heat; lets the game come to him; patient and tactful player; some will describe player as low-energy, but more views are required to make this determination.

**OFP:** 60; first-division player

**Realistic Role:** 50; major-league regular

**Risk:** High. Hit tool has underwhelmed against inferior stuff. Performance didn't match hype in this particular viewing. Projection to first-division regular requires large jumps for several tools, including hit. Lack of arm strength places emphasis on center-field development.

---

## FROM THE FIELD

### Jameson Taillon

**Player:** Jameson Taillon

**Team:** Pittsburgh Pirates

**Filed by:** Jeff Moore

**Date(s) Seen:** May 19, 2013

**Physical:** Ideal frame for a starting pitcher. Tall (6'6") and already physically developed with room to add more strength.

**Mechanics/Delivery:** Solid base, stays tall and uses his size well; has a long arm action that causes inconsistencies in his command.

**Fastball:** 70 grade; premium velocity (93-97 mph) with 40 current command; throws strikes but not always good strikes; gets away with mistakes within strike zone because of velocity and movement (hard two-seam action).

**Curveball:** 65 grade; a second true plus pitch; strong downward movement with ability to miss bats; average command of pitch.

**Changeup:** 50 grade; potentially average pitch, but below average at the moment; will never be a swing-and-miss pitch but needs it to keep hitters honest.

**Makeup:** 70; no makeup concerns; pitched for Team Canada in WBC against major-league competition and held his own.

**OFP:** 7; no. 2 starter

**Realistic Role:** 6; no. 3 starter

**Risk:** Low, will start season in Triple-A and should be in majors by summer.

---

**Player:** Jameson Taillon

**Team:** Pittsburgh Pirates

**Filed by:** CJ Wittmann

**Date(s) Seen:** Multiple times

**Physical:** Massive, physical frame; muscular build, looks very much the part of a workhorse.

**Mechanics/Delivery:** Traditional 3/4 arm slot; lengthy arm action causing arm to get offline at times and maximum effort to repeat mechanics; keeps balance and momentum throughout delivery but sometimes arm comes through late.

**Fastball:** 70 grade; 94-98 mph; heavy, late arm-side life; threw a few with natural cut; shatters bats on occasion; present below-average command profile.

**Curveball:** 70 grade; 80-83 mph; late downward break with great depth; two plane break type pitch; hammer.

**Changeup:** 50 grade; 85-88 mph; flashed fade at lower velo; higher velo causes pitch to be too firm and straight.

**Makeup:** 50 grade; visibly frustrated on mound at times; very good work ethic.

**OFP:** 65; no. 2 starter.

**Realistic Role:** 60; no. 3 starter.

**Risk:** Low; experience in all levels besides MLB.

# SAN DIEGO PADRES

## 1. Austin Hedges C

**Born:** 8/18/92 **Age:** 21 **Bats:** R **Throws:** R **Height:** 6' 1" **Weight:** 190

| MLB ETA | Hit | Power | Run | Glove | Arm | OFP | Realistic |
|---------|-----|-------|-----|-------|-----|-----|-----------|
| 2015 | 55 | — | — | 75 | 65 | 70 ALL-STAR | 60 1ST DIV PLAYER |

| YEAR | TEAM | LVL | AGE | PA | R | 2B | 3B | HR | RBI | BB | SO | SB | CS | AVG/OBP/SLG | TAv | BABIP | BRR | FRAA | WARP |
|------|------|-----|-----|----|----|----|----|----|-----|----|----|----|----|-------------|-----|-------|-----|------|------|
| 2013 | SAN | AA | 20 | 75 | 4 | 3 | 0 | 0 | 8 | 6 | 9 | 3 | 1 | .224/.297/.269 | .225 | .259 | 0.4 | C(18): 0.0 | 0.1 |
| 2013 | LEL | A+ | 20 | 266 | 34 | 22 | 1 | 4 | 30 | 22 | 45 | 5 | 4 | .270/.343/.425 | .279 | .314 | 0.7 | C(61): 0.9 | 2.2 |
| 2014 | SDN | MLB | 21 | 250 | 23 | 11 | 0 | 4 | 23 | 13 | 56 | 4 | 2 | .222/.270/.328 | .226 | .270 | -0.3 | C 0 | 0.3 |
| 2015 | SDN | MLB | 22 | 250 | 27 | 13 | 0 | 6 | 26 | 13 | 52 | 3 | 2 | .240/.287/.374 | .244 | .282 | -0.6 | C 0 | 0.7 |

**Breakout:** 0%   **Improve:** 0%   **Collapse:** 0%   **Attrition:** 0%   **MLB:** 0%   *Comparables: J.R. Murphy, Travis d'Arnaud, Hector Sanchez*

**Drafted/Acquired:** 2nd round, 2011 draft, Junipero Serra Catholic HS (San Juan Capistrano, CA)

**Previous Ranking:** #1 (Org), #19 (Top 101)

**What Happened in 2013:** After a successful full-season debut in 2013, Hedges took another step forward in 2013, playing his way to the Texas League to finish the regular season, and then showed off his impressive defensive chops in the prospect-heavy landscape of the Arizona Fall League.

**Strengths:** Near-elite defensive profile behind the plate; plus arm; quick release and accurate; excellent footwork; excellent receiver; strong hands and quick feet; high baseball IQ; excels at game management and battery relationship; good swing at the plate; tracks well; shows good bat speed and strength; has some pop; crazy makeup.

**Weaknesses:** Can get overly aggressive with the arm (back picks, etc); bat unlikely to achieve big impact; struggles against arm-side stuff; good not great bat speed; can drive the ball but power unlikely to play above average; below-average run.

**Risk Factor/Injury History:** Moderate risk; limited exposure to upper minors; questions about offensive utility.

**Bret Sayre's Fantasy Take:** The fact that I'd probably take Hedges seventh or eighth for fantasy purposes says everything you need to know about his defensive potential. Unfortunately, unless you're in a sim league, he's just not going to be much more than a borderline use of a farm spot—even if he maxes out and hits around .275 with 15 homers, that's barely above replacement level in one-catcher leagues. If you can shop him on his name value, do it.

**The Year Ahead:** Hedges is the best all-around defensive catcher I've had the privilege of scouting at the minor-league level, with a strong, accurate arm, quick and coordinated actions, and the in-game management qualities of a seasoned major-league veteran. The glove is going to carry him a long way, but the bat could make him a perennial all-star if he proves to be more than just a tough down-the-lineup out. He has some offensive qualities, with a sound swing and good strength, and it's not a stretch to envision a .275 hitter with 15-homer pop, a formidable profile given his near-elite defensive projections. We were high on Hedges last season (number one in the organization and top 20 overall in the game), and will continue to sing his praises heading into 2014, as he once again takes the top place in the system and will once again find himself ranked among the top 20 prospects in the game.

> **#18**
> BP Top 101 Prospects

## 2. Matt Wisler RHP

**Born:** 9/12/92 **Age:** 21 **Bats:** R **Throws:** R **Height:** 6' 3" **Weight:** 195

| MLB ETA | CT | FB | CH | CB | SL | OFP | Realistic |
|---------|-----|-----|-----|-----|-----|-----|-----------|
| 2014 | — | 60 | 55 | — | 60 | 60 NO.3 STARTER | 50 NO.4 STARTER |

| YEAR | TEAM | LVL | AGE | W | L | SV | G | GS | IP | H | HR | BB | SO | BB9 | SO9 | GB% | BABIP | WHIP | ERA | FIP | FRA | WARP |
|------|------|-----|-----|---|---|----|----|----|------|-----|----|----|-----|-----|-----|------|-------|------|------|------|------|------|
| 2013 | LEL | A+ | 20 | 2 | 1 | 0 | 6 | 6 | 31.0 | 22 | 1 | 6 | 28 | 1.7 | 8.1 | 43% | .253 | 0.90 | 2.03 | 3.06 | 3.46 | 0.7 |
| 2013 | SAN | AA | 20 | 8 | 5 | 0 | 20 | 20 | 105.0 | 85 | 7 | 27 | 103 | 2.3 | 8.8 | 39% | .281 | 1.07 | 3.00 | 2.79 | 3.42 | 1.8 |
| 2014 | SDN | MLB | 21 | 6 | 8 | 0 | 22 | 22 | 112.3 | 103 | 11 | 40 | 95 | 3.2 | 7.6 | 41% | .304 | 1.27 | 3.77 | 3.97 | 4.10 | 0.9 |
| 2015 | SDN | MLB | 22 | 10 | 9 | 0 | 32 | 32 | 207.7 | 185 | 22 | 65 | 174 | 2.8 | 7.5 | 41% | .294 | 1.20 | 3.56 | 3.76 | 3.87 | 1.8 |

**Breakout:** 0%   **Improve:** 0%   **Collapse:** 0%   **Attrition:** 0%   **MLB:** 0%   *Comparables: Carlos Martinez, Jarrod Parker, Shelby Miller*

**Drafted/Acquired:** 7th round, 2011 draft, Bryan HS (Bryan, OH)

**Previous Ranking:** #8 (Org)

**What Happened in 2013:** Early buzz in spring training turned into an industry choir over the course of the season, as Wisler proved to be more than just camp hype, pitching his way to Double-A and missing a bat an inning as a 20-year-old.

**Strengths:** Good size; athletic; big arm strength; fastball works comfortably in the 92-94 range; can touch 98 in

> **#47**
> BP Top 101 Prospects

shorter bursts; good arm-side life; slider is bat-misser; low- to mid-80s with sharp two-plane movement and excellent depth; punisher pitch against right-handed bats; changeup shows average potential; mid-80s with sink; good deception; flashes playable curveball; good feel for control.

**Weaknesses:** Delivery has some noise; tendency to cross-fire and lose release points; struggles to locate against left-handers; slider not as effective against left-handed hitters; overall command is fringe-average at present; changeup can get too firm; curveball can lose tight rotation and feature more tumble than snap.

**Risk Factor/Injury History:** Low risk; 20 Double-A starts; mature stuff.

**Bret Sayre's Fantasy Take:** Wisler offers that combination of upside, floor, attractive home park, and proximity that is so attractive to fantasy owners—especially ones in deeper leagues. The Padres rotation may be full to start the year, but with the way they go through UCLs, an opportunity is likely to present itself before midseason. He can do a pretty good Mat Latos-in-Petco impression, with a full tick down in strikeouts.

**The Year Ahead:** Wisler looked the part of a major-league arm during his stint in Double-A, so it's easy to forget the former seventh-round pick was only 20 years old and still in the developmental process. The delivery doesn't always look the part despite the utility he is able to achieve, and the command doesn't always allow the plus raw stuff to play to its potential. But with more refinement, Wisler can not only stick in a rotation long term, but thrive in the middle of it, with two easy plus weapons in the fastball and slider, and two playable change-of-pace pitches in the changeup and curve.

---

## 3.  Max Fried   LHP

**Born:** 1/18/94   **Age:** 20   **Bats:** L   **Throws:** L   **Height:** 6' 4"   **Weight:** 185

| MLB ETA | CT | FB | CH | CB | SL | OFP | Realistic |
|---------|----|----|----|----|----|----|-----------|
| 2016 | – | 60 | 65 | 65 | – | 65<br>NO.2 STARTER | 50<br>NO.4 STARTER |

| YEAR | TEAM | LVL | AGE | W | L | SV | G | GS | IP | H | HR | BB | SO | BB9 | SO9 | GB% | BABIP | WHIP | ERA | FIP | FRA | WARP |
|------|------|-----|-----|---|---|----|----|----|----|----|----|----|----|-----|-----|-----|-------|------|-----|-----|-----|------|
| 2013 | FTW | A | 19 | 6 | 7 | 0 | 23 | 23 | 118.7 | 107 | 7 | 56 | 100 | 4.2 | 7.6 | 59% | .304 | 1.37 | 3.49 | 4.04 | 5.46 | 0.6 |
| 2014 | SDN | MLB | 20 | 4 | 6 | 0 | 20 | 15 | 84.7 | 86 | 10 | 47 | 59 | 5.0 | 6.3 | 52% | .311 | 1.57 | 5.21 | 5.23 | 5.67 | -0.9 |
| 2015 | SDN | MLB | 21 | 7 | 9 | 0 | 35 | 24 | 165.3 | 167 | 21 | 81 | 122 | 4.4 | 6.6 | 52% | .313 | 1.50 | 5.07 | 4.85 | 5.51 | -1.6 |

Breakout: 0%   Improve: 0%   Collapse: 0%   Attrition: 0%   MLB: 0%      *Comparables: Brad Hand, Tyler Chatwood, Jarrod Parker*

**Drafted/Acquired:** 1st round, 2012 draft, Harvard-Westlake HS (Los Angeles, CA)

**Previous Ranking:** #3 (Org), #61 (Top 101)

**What Happened in 2013:** In his full-season debut, the much-hyped lefty flashed the stuff to justify the lofty praise, but battled command inconsistency throughout the year and struggled against right-handed bats.

**#55**
BP Top 101 Prospects

**Strengths:** Excellent size/physical projection; delivery is easy and smooth; excellent arm action; fastball has some jump in the low-90s; projects to settle in the plus velocity range; good late action to the arm side; snaps very good curveball (present); tight rotation and heavy break; bat-misser (at present); changeup might end up as best pitch; good arm deception and late action; will be difference-maker offering.

**Weaknesses:** Fastball command is below average; tendency to cast his pitches and lose deception and intensity; fastball is pedestrian at times; curveball might end up being a better minor-league pitch than major-league pitch; break can be long and easy to track; changeup can hang up in the zone.

**Risk Factor/Injury History:** High risk; yet to achieve Double-A level; sizeable gap between present/future.

**Bret Sayre's Fantasy Take:** Wisler vs. Fried is still a very tough decision, as no one in the Padres system can touch Fried's ceiling. I said before the season that I thought Fried would be top left-handed fantasy pitching prospect in the minors at the end of the 2013 season—and he is, although that's more because it's a weak group overall than his performance. A 3.25 ERA and nearly a strikeout per inning are possible if he can take that next step forward.

**The Year Ahead:** Fried's size, present stuff, and arsenal projection set a high bar of expectations, so when the results are only solid, the evaluation can read as a bit of a disappointment. Fried has a long way to go, but could/should end up with three above-average offerings from the left side, with enough athleticism and simplicity in the delivery to project for at least an average command profile. I think the changeup will eventually pass the curveball as his go-to secondary offering, but both have a chance to play as plus pitches at the end of the day. If the fastball velocity ticks up and holds steady, and the command refines, Fried is going to live up to the hype and then some. He will pitch the 2014 season as a 20-year-old, so the prospect explosion might be a year away.

## 4. Hunter Renfroe   OF

**Born:** 1/28/92   **Age:** 22   **Bats:** R   **Throws:** R   **Height:** 6'1"   **Weight:** 200

| MLB ETA | Hit | Power | Run | Glove | Arm | OFP | Realistic |
|---|---|---|---|---|---|---|---|
| Late 2015 | – | 70 | 55 | 55 | 60 | 60<br>1ST DIV PLAYER | 50<br>ML REGULAR |

| YEAR | TEAM | LVL | AGE | PA | R | 2B | 3B | HR | RBI | BB | SO | SB | CS | AVG/OBP/SLG | TAv | BABIP | BRR | FRAA | WARP |
|---|---|---|---|---|---|---|---|---|---|---|---|---|---|---|---|---|---|---|---|
| 2013 | FTW | A | 21 | 72 | 6 | 5 | 0 | 2 | 7 | 4 | 23 | 0 | 0 | .212/.268/.379 | .230 | .293 | -1.0 | RF(16): -1.2 | -0.4 |
| 2013 | EUG | A- | 21 | 111 | 20 | 9 | 0 | 4 | 18 | 5 | 26 | 2 | 0 | .308/.333/.510 | .335 | .368 | 1.1 | RF(25): 1.2 | 1.4 |
| 2014 | SDN | MLB | 22 | 250 | 20 | 8 | 1 | 6 | 25 | 11 | 80 | 1 | 0 | .196/.234/.308 | .201 | .260 | -0.3 | RF -2 | -1.3 |
| 2015 | SDN | MLB | 23 | 250 | 24 | 10 | 1 | 6 | 25 | 11 | 77 | 1 | 0 | .205/.242/.329 | .209 | .271 | -0.4 | RF -2 | -2.2 |

Breakout: 0%   Improve: 0%   Collapse: 0%   Attrition: 0%   MLB: 0%   *Comparables: Zoilo Almonte, John Mayberry, Melky Mesa*

**Drafted/Acquired:** 1st round, 2013 draft, Mississippi State University (Mississippi State, MS)

**Previous Ranking:** NR

**What Happened in 2013:** Selected 13th overall in the 2013 draft, Renfroe was considered one of the better college bats in the class, a well-rounded player with middle-of-the-lineup impact power.

**Strengths:** Excellent strength; good athlete; good bat speed; power is carrying tool; could play to plus-plus; swing geared for over-the-fence power; leverage, loft, and backspin; good run; coordinated; glove could play above average in a corner; arm is strong; run producer profile with some hittability.

**Weaknesses:** Swing-and-miss in the profile; tracks well but likes to swing and can get overly aggressive; can struggle against arm-side spin; power over hit; offensive profile could become one-dimensional at highest level.

**Risk Factor/Injury History:** Moderate risk; limited professional experience; questions about hit tool.

**Bret Sayre's Fantasy Take:** Having clocked in at number 14 in my Top 50 2013 Signees for Dynasty Drafts, Renfroe has the power/speed combo that fantasy owners look for—even if it comes packaged inside a questionable hit tool. He should move relatively fast as a college hitter, and it's not unreasonable to think he can hit 25+ homers and steal close to 20 bases in his prime.

**The Year Ahead:** Renfroe has well-above-average right-handed power, and if the hit tool can play to average, he has a chance to develop into a middle-of-the-order power bat from a prototypical right-field profile. His game is always going to feature a lot of swing-and-miss; not because of poor pitch recognition but because of an aggressive approach and hearty swing appetite. But Renfroe has more hittability than hack, and with a more refined approach and controlled attack, he can bring more power into game action and develop to potential. This is really promising offensive talent, and he is a good candidate to blossom in 2014.

## 5. Rymer Liriano   RF

**Born:** 6/20/91   **Age:** 23   **Bats:** R   **Throws:** R   **Height:** 6'0"   **Weight:** 225

| MLB ETA | Hit | Power | Run | Glove | Arm | OFP | Realistic |
|---|---|---|---|---|---|---|---|
| 2015 | –– | 60 | 60 | 55 | 60 | 60<br>1ST DIV PLAYER | 50<br>2ND DIV PLAYER |

| YEAR | TEAM | LVL | AGE | PA | R | 2B | 3B | HR | RBI | BB | SO | SB | CS | AVG/OBP/SLG | TAv | BABIP | BRR | FRAA | WARP |
|---|---|---|---|---|---|---|---|---|---|---|---|---|---|---|---|---|---|---|---|
| 2014 | SDN | MLB | 23 | 250 | 28 | 10 | 1 | 4 | 22 | 15 | 65 | 14 | 4 | .227/.280/.335 | .232 | .300 | 1.3 | RF -2, CF 0 | -0.3 |
| 2015 | SDN | MLB | 24 | 250 | 27 | 11 | 2 | 5 | 26 | 16 | 66 | 16 | 5 | .238/.291/.367 | .242 | .308 | 1.7 | RF -2, CF 0 | 0.3 |

Breakout: 0%   Improve: 0%   Collapse: 0%   Attrition: 0%   MLB: 0%   *Comparables: Andrew Lambo, Scott Van Slyke, Lorenzo Cain*

**Drafted/Acquired:** International free agent, 2007, Dominican Republic

**Previous Ranking:** #2 (Org), #39 (Top 101)

**What Happened in 2013:** Much like organization mate Casey Kelly, Liriano missed the entire 2013 season with a Tommy John related illness, but with a full recovery, the scouting report from last season has not changed.

**Strengths:** Physical player; plus present strength; plus runner; plus raw power; easy plus arm in right field; hit tool projects as a 5; plus bat speed; all the tools to be a first-division talent.

**Weaknesses:** Despite the athleticism, doesn't make it look easy; more raw tools than baseball-ready skills; power has yet to blossom; swing path isn't always efficient; can open holes on inner third; early extension; bat might underperform.

**Risk Factor/Injury History:** High risk; limited experience at Double-A; Tommy John surgery on resume.

**Bret Sayre's Fantasy Take:** The lost year for Liriano didn't suppress his fantasy upside, even if it made him a riskier proposition. There is still legitimate 20-20 potential in his bat, and Chris Young type upside—remember when he was a fantasy target? However, expect a slow burn with Liriano, who has historically struggled each time he has moved up a rung in the minors.

**The Year Ahead:** Liriano has a chance to develop into a middle-of-the-order bat from a prototypical right-field profile, but he comes at a higher risk than most prospects that have already achieved the Double-A level. Injury recovery and rehab aside (good reports on that front), Liriano struggles with consistency when it comes to putting his tools to use on the field; he can show all five, but teases more than showing full utility in the form of game skills and overall feel for execution. If he can step forward on the utility front, he has more than enough raw power to have impact at the highest level. I'm still high on this prospect, not only for the tool-based ceiling but the work ethic and makeup he brings to the equation. He's dealt with on-the-field failure and physical setback, but he keeps coming back with the same intensity and determination. I like his chances despite the risk factor on the report.

## 6. Burch Smith   RHP

**Born:** 4/12/90   **Age:** 24   **Bats:** R   **Throws:** R   **Height:** 6' 4"   **Weight:** 215

| MLB ETA | CT | FB | CH | CB | SL | OFP | Realistic |
|---|---|---|---|---|---|---|---|
| Debuted in 2013 | – | 70 | 60 | 50 | – | 55<br>NO.3 STARTER | 50<br>LATE-INN RP (SETUP) |

| YEAR | TEAM | LVL | AGE | W | L | SV | G | GS | IP | H | HR | BB | SO | BB9 | SO9 | GB% | BABIP | WHIP | ERA | FIP | FRA | WARP |
|---|---|---|---|---|---|---|---|---|---|---|---|---|---|---|---|---|---|---|---|---|---|---|
| 2013 | SAN | AA | 23 | 1 | 2 | 0 | 6 | 6 | 31.3 | 17 | 1 | 6 | 37 | 1.7 | 10.6 | 53% | .222 | 0.73 | 1.15 | 1.88 | 3.08 | 0.7 |
| 2013 | SDN | MLB | 23 | 1 | 3 | 0 | 10 | 7 | 36.3 | 39 | 9 | 21 | 46 | 5.2 | 11.4 | 27% | .330 | 1.65 | 6.44 | 5.44 | 5.37 | -0.3 |
| 2013 | TUC | AAA | 23 | 5 | 1 | 0 | 12 | 12 | 61.0 | 56 | 4 | 17 | 65 | 2.5 | 9.6 | 38% | .325 | 1.20 | 3.39 | 3.18 | 3.36 | 1.8 |
| 2014 | SDN | MLB | 24 | 6 | 8 | 0 | 22 | 22 | 110.7 | 99 | 13 | 37 | 111 | 3.0 | 9.0 | 40% | .309 | 1.23 | 3.71 | 3.85 | 4.03 | 1.0 |
| 2015 | SDN | MLB | 25 | 7 | 4 | 0 | 74 | 9 | 124.3 | 109 | 14 | 40 | 126 | 2.9 | 9.1 | 40% | .307 | 1.19 | 3.52 | 3.54 | 3.83 | 1.5 |

**Breakout:** 33%   **Improve:** 58%   **Collapse:** 8%   **Attrition:** 25%   **MLB:** 74%   *Comparables: Tyler Thornburg, Jason Windsor, Dan Straily*

**Drafted/Acquired:** 14th round, 2011 draft, University of Oklahoma (Norman, OK)

**Previous Ranking:** NR

**What Happened in 2013:** Smith shoved in his Double-A debut, was solid in his 12 Triple-A starts, and struggled with command in his major-league trial, but emerged as a future piece of the Padres future.

**Strengths:** Excellent size; huge arm strength; repeats; deception in the delivery; fastball is easy plus offering; often works in plus-plus range; sits comfortably in the 92-95 range; bumps 98; holds velocity; changeup is plus offering; good fastball disguise with some sink; shows average potential curveball; plays as change-of-pace off fastball.

**Weaknesses:** Fastball command is fringe; big velocity but can lack movement; drop and drive delivery and slot limits advantage of height; curveball is fringe offering; lacks bite; can show soft rotation and easy to track two-plane movement; struggles to stay over it because of lower arm slot.

**Risk Factor/Injury History:** Low risk; achieved major-league level.

**Bret Sayre's Fantasy Take:** There is a philosophy that supports taking Padres pitchers because of Petco, but Smith doesn't carry either the upside or certainty of the arms before him on this list. His potential lack of a breaking ball could lead to a career in the bullpen, and even if it doesn't, it will certainly inhibit his effectiveness.

**The Year Ahead:** Smith has big arm strength and some strike-throwing ability, but he stumbles when the command isn't sharp and the secondary stuff lacks the punch to bail him out of at-bats. Smith can miss bats with the fastball, especially when he can change sight lines and live above barrels. But the pitch can also play too firm at times, and without a solid breaking ball to back it up, he is at the mercy of his ability to locate his offerings with more precision than most power arms. The fastball will make him a bullpen arm as a floor, but he can stick around in the middle of a rotation if the command refines and the curveball improves enough to play or a slider is added to the mix.

## 7. Casey Kelly   RHP

**Born:** 10/4/89   **Age:** 24   **Bats:** R   **Throws:** R   **Height:** 6' 3"   **Weight:** 210

| MLB ETA | CT | FB | CH | CB | SL | OFP | Realistic |
|---|---|---|---|---|---|---|---|
| Debuted in 2012 | – | 55 | 60 | 60 | – | 50<br>NO.3 STARTER | 50<br>NO.4 STARTER |

| YEAR | TEAM | LVL | AGE | W | L | SV | G | GS | IP | H | HR | BB | SO | BB9 | SO9 | GB% | BABIP | WHIP | ERA | FIP | FRA | WARP |
|---|---|---|---|---|---|---|---|---|---|---|---|---|---|---|---|---|---|---|---|---|---|---|
| 2014 | SDN | MLB | 24 | 2 | 3 | 0 | 7 | 7 | 36.3 | 38 | 4 | 12 | 26 | 3 | 6.4 | 50% | .318 | 1.38 | 4.58 | 4.34 | 4.98 | -0.1 |
| 2015 | SDN | MLB | 25 | 8 | 6 | 0 | 71 | 15 | 145.7 | 136 | 14 | 47 | 114 | 2.9 | 7.0 | 49% | .303 | 1.25 | 3.76 | 3.78 | 4.09 | 1.2 |

**Breakout:** 20%   **Improve:** 43%   **Collapse:** 13%   **Attrition:** 29%   **MLB:** 61%   *Comparables: Alex Cobb, Felix Doubront, Justin Germano*

**Drafted/Acquired:** 1st round, 2008 draft, Sarasota HS (Sarasota, FL)

**Previous Ranking:** #4 (Org), #77 (Top 101)

**What Happened in 2013:** Tommy John surgery sapped the season, but a healthy Kelly should be able to mirror the scouting report prior to the injury setback.

**Strengths:** Plus athleticism; very good pitchability; fastball normally works in the 90-92 range, but can touch 95; shows good vertical action; good setup pitch; curveball is out pitch; tight rotation and quality depth; changeup can play as a 5; delivery is clean; good command profile.

**Weaknesses:** Lacks knockout stuff; fastball usually works a little below plus velocity; needs to hit his spots; changeup can get too firm; doesn't always turn it over; will always walk tight line because of solid-average arsenal.

**Risk Factor/Injury History:** Moderate risk; achieved major-league level; Tommy John on resume (2013).

**Bret Sayre's Fantasy Take:** I've long been a Casey Kelly believer, and that's not about to stop now. Assuming health, the big park should keep his ERA in the 3.50 and slightly under range with reasonable strikeout numbers (think 150-160 over the course of a full season). It's the profile of a solid number four fantasy starter, but he'll be healthy in short order and back in the majors not long after that.

**The Year Ahead:** Kelly is likely to stick around in extended spring training this season, before proving full health and comfort on the mound and making his way back to the upper minors. Because of the nature of the surgery and subsequent layoff, you can assume a certain amount of rust will form on the profile, but with any luck, Kelly can find his form quickly and climb back to the major-league level at some point in 2014.

## 8. Jace Peterson  SS

**Born:** 5/9/90  **Age:** 24  **Bats:** L  **Throws:** R  **Height:** 6'0"  **Weight:** 205

| MLB ETA | Hit | Power | Run | Glove | Arm | OFP | Realistic |
|---------|-----|-------|-----|-------|-----|-----|-----------|
| 2015 | 55 | — | 50 | 50 | 50 | 50 ML REGULAR | 45 UTILITY PLAYER |

| YEAR | TEAM | LVL | AGE | PA | R | 2B | 3B | HR | RBI | BB | SO | SB | CS | AVG/OBP/SLG | TAv | BABIP | BRR | FRAA | WARP |
|------|------|-----|-----|-----|----|----|----|----|-----|----|----|----|----|-------------|-----|-------|-----|------|------|
| 2013 | LEL | A+ | 23 | 496 | 78 | 17 | 13 | 7 | 66 | 54 | 58 | 42 | 10 | .303/.382/.454 | .314 | .332 | 4.7 | SS(106): -4.4 | 4.8 |
| 2014 | SDN | MLB | 24 | 250 | 30 | 8 | 2 | 2 | 15 | 22 | 47 | 15 | 4 | .227/.297/.306 | .230 | .270 | 1.7 | SS -3 | 0.2 |
| 2015 | SDN | MLB | 25 | 250 | 25 | 8 | 2 | 3 | 20 | 24 | 48 | 13 | 3 | .216/.293/.311 | .227 | .258 | 1.6 | SS -3 | -0.4 |

Breakout: 1%    Improve: 4%    Collapse: 6%    Attrition: 15%    MLB: 18%    *Comparables: Alberto Gonzalez, Paul Janish, Brian Dozier*

**Drafted/Acquired:** 1st round, 2011 draft, McNeese State University (Lake Charles, LA)

**Previous Ranking:** NR

**What Happened in 2013:** A first-round pick in 2010, Peterson had his best season as a professional, taking a big step forward in the second half of his California League debut, hitting .318/.414/.494 in his final 48 games.

**Strengths:** Strong and physical; good overall athlete; feel for game and baseball skills took big step forward; clean stroke at the plate; shows good bat speed and bat control; tracks well with a good approach; very good baserunner; good first step quickness on base and in the field; solid-average glove; average but playable arm.

**Weaknesses:** Lacks impact tools; sum-of-his-parts player; bat is more contact driven; power will play well below average; defensive profile is average; lacks plus defensive weapons; slower in the developmental process.

**Risk Factor/Injury History:** Moderate risk; yet to play at Double-A level; good baseball skills.

**Bret Sayre's Fantasy Take:** There's a lot to like on paper here, with his very solid strikeout-to-walk ratios (174:166 for his minor-league career) and high stolen-base totals (at an 80 percent clip), but he isn't likely to be another Jean Segura. A .275 average with 25 steals and very little else would be a pretty good outcome here—and his plate discipline should give him a tick up in points leagues.

**The Year Ahead:** Peterson isn't a flashy player, with a skill set that is more average than awe inspiring. But he brings playable baseball skills to the table, pushing his tools beyond their paper grade in game action. Sources are still mixed when it comes to his ultimate role, as the defensive chops are good enough if the bat is good enough, but everything has to max out if he has a chance to be a major-league regular at the position. Double-A will be a big test for the bat and will end up telling us a lot about the player, as a strong season could push his name up this list and in the queue for major-league action.

## 9. Alex Dickerson  1B/RF

**Born:** 5/26/90  **Age:** 24  **Bats:** L  **Throws:** L  **Height:** 6'3"  **Weight:** 235

| MLB ETA | Hit | Power | Run | Glove | Arm | OFP | Realistic |
|---------|-----|-------|-----|-------|-----|-----|-----------|
| Late 2014 | 50 | 65 | — | — | 50 | 50 ML REGULAR | 45 <AVG/PLATOON |

| YEAR | TEAM | LVL | AGE | PA | R | 2B | 3B | HR | RBI | BB | SO | SB | CS | AVG/OBP/SLG | TAv | BABIP | BRR | FRAA | WARP |
|------|------|-----|-----|-----|----|----|----|----|-----|----|----|----|----|-------------|-----|-------|-----|------|------|
| 2013 | ALT | AA | 23 | 491 | 61 | 36 | 3 | 17 | 68 | 27 | 89 | 10 | 7 | .288/.337/.494 | .304 | .325 | -1.8 | RF(114): -6.3, LF(6): -0.2 | 2.2 |
| 2014 | SDN | MLB | 24 | 250 | 25 | 13 | 1 | 7 | 29 | 11 | 58 | 3 | 2 | .245/.284/.394 | .251 | .300 | -0.3 | RF -2, 1B 1 | 0.1 |
| 2015 | SDN | MLB | 25 | 298 | 35 | 15 | 1 | 9 | 35 | 17 | 68 | 3 | 1 | .255/.307/.413 | .263 | .303 | -0.6 | RF -4 | 0.0 |

Breakout: 3%    Improve: 13%    Collapse: 4%    Attrition: 14%    MLB: 26%    *Comparables: John Bowker, Roger Kieschnick, Scott Van Slyke*

**Drafted/Acquired:** 3rd round, 2011 draft, Indiana University-Bloomington (Bloomington, IN)

**Previous Ranking:** NR

**What Happened in 2013:** Acquired in the offseason for Jaff Decker, Dickerson is a big man with big power, and a chance to make it play if the hit tool and approach cooperate.

**Strengths:** Big boy size and strength; simple left-handed stroke; game power could play to plus or above; hit tool could play to average; shows some barrel awareness and control; arm is average.

**Weaknesses:** Power can tease; more 5 o'clock at present; will struggle against quality arm-side stuff; swing can get long; bat speed more strength derived; can beat him with velocity; better profile at first base; below-average run; limited range.

**Risk Factor/Injury History:** Moderate risk; Double-A experience; difficult profile (bat has to play to potential or above); some injury concerns (back).

**Bret Sayre's Fantasy Take:** Dickerson is the kind of player who fantasy owners often overlook, as he does not have the draft/prospect pedigree to fall back on. However, he continues to hit as he moves up and there's plenty of value in a .270 hitter with 15 homers (even at outfield) in deeper leagues. He could provide underrated value in 20-team leagues, while doing a half-decent Garrett Jones impression.

**The Year Ahead:** Very mixed reports on Dickerson, all centered on the power tool and whether or not it plays to potential at the highest level. If you believe in the power, you can see a second-division type at first base—or perhaps a corner—as the strength is there to punish mistakes even if the hit tool is unlikely to offer much impact against plus stuff. The more pessimistic view is a platoon bat with a one-dimensional weapon and limited defensive value. Personally, I think the bat will play better than the scouting report might suggest, and even with average utility from the hit tool, I think the power can play enough to eventually keep his name in a major-league lineup.

---

# 10.  Joe Ross  RHP

**Born:** 5/21/93  **Age:** 21  **Bats:** R  **Throws:** R  **Height:** 6'3"  **Weight:** 185

| MLB ETA | CT | FB | CH | CB | SL | OFP | Realistic |
|---|---|---|---|---|---|---|---|
| 2016 | — | 65 | 50 | — | 60 | 55 NO.3 STARTER | 50 NO.5 STARTER |

| YEAR | TEAM | LVL | AGE | W | L | SV | G | GS | IP | H | HR | BB | SO | BB9 | SO9 | GB% | BABIP | WHIP | ERA | FIP | FRA | WARP |
|---|---|---|---|---|---|---|---|---|---|---|---|---|---|---|---|---|---|---|---|---|---|---|
| 2013 | FTW | A | 20 | 5 | 8 | 0 | 23 | 23 | 122.3 | 124 | 7 | 40 | 79 | 2.9 | 5.8 | 52% | .298 | 1.34 | 3.75 | 3.89 | 5.19 | 0.8 |
| 2014 | SDN | MLB | 21 | 4 | 8 | 0 | 20 | 20 | 94.7 | 104 | 12 | 45 | 54 | 4.3 | 5.1 | 48% | .311 | 1.57 | 5.34 | 5.34 | 5.80 | -1.1 |
| 2015 | SDN | MLB | 22 | 8 | 10 | 0 | 29 | 29 | 182.3 | 185 | 20 | 76 | 124 | 3.8 | 6.1 | 48% | .307 | 1.43 | 4.56 | 4.44 | 4.96 | -0.8 |

**Breakout:** 0%    **Improve:** 0%    **Collapse:** 0%    **Attrition:** 0%    **MLB:** 0%    *Comparables: Brett Marshall, Alex Sanabia, Vin Mazzaro*

**Drafted/Acquired:** 1st round, 2011 draft, Bishop O'Dowd HS (Oakland, CA)

**Previous Ranking:** #7 (Org)

**What Happened in 2013:** Ross returned to the Midwest League with better results, but the lack of punchouts troubled scouts and clouded Ross's ultimate projection.

**Strengths:** Prototypical size/strength; projectable; smooth in the delivery; Beckett-like mechanics; fast arm; fastball works low-90s; touches higher; heavy life; slider is plus potential pitch; two-plane with potential for good depth; shows average changeup potential; starter's arsenal and strike-throwing ability.

**Weaknesses:** More weak contact than bat missing; fastball command is fringe; secondary arsenal lacks big knockout potential; how will he gets outs against better bats?; fastball can play soft.

**Risk Factor/Injury History:** High risk; Low-A resume; questions about profile/arsenal.

**Bret Sayre's Fantasy Take:** The biggest risk of the Padres' upper echelon of arms, Ross could potentially make for a pretty dynamite closer if he ends up taking the bullpen route. However, if he can make it through the gantlet and into the Padres' rotation, he's likely to be a guy who should put up better numbers than he does—but Petco can cover up a lot of sins (just ask his older brother). I still prefer Kelly's certainty to Ross's upside for fantasy.

**The Year Ahead:** Ross is a frustrating prospect when it comes to what he appears to be versus what he actually is. Ross looks the part; body beautiful pitcher with the physical attributes you want in a prototypical starter, and the lively fastball to set the table for the secondary stuff. But the fastball can play soft, geared more for missing the barrel than missing the bat, and the secondary stuff lacks the type of knockout utility to force the big swing-and-miss. It forces scouts to question how he will be able to get outs against better bats, which could limit his effectiveness as he climbs the professional ladder. The California League will be a test for the 21-year-old, and if the profile stays the same and he struggles to miss bats, the stock could fall in 2014.

## Prospects on the Rise

**1. SS Franchy Cordero:** Signed out of the Dominican Republic in 2011, Cordero put his name on the world with a strong stateside debut in the Arizona complex league, showing a good stick with up-the-middle chops at shortstop. The 19-year-old infielder was in the running for the top 10 this year, thanks to his easy and fluid stroke from the left side that is likely to produce above-average power in the future, and good overall feel for the game; if he can continue to make progress on the field in 2014, his status as a no-brainer top-10 talent in the system will be confirmed. I like this prospect a lot.

**2. 3B Dustin Pederson:** A second-round selection in the 2013 draft, Peterson has a highly projectable offensive profile, and a chance to eventually make it work at the hot corner. The tools are still very raw, and the statistical output will likely back this up in 2014, but the 19-year-old will flash enough upside with the stick to offset any defensive concerns and push his way up prospect lists as a result.

**3. RHP Zach Eflin:** Eflin is a prospect tease, with excellent size and present pitchability, including good feel for execution of a solid-average fastball and promising and projectable changeup. But the stuff isn't always sharp, and as a result, the 19-year-old arm is more about missing the good part of the barrel than missing the bat. With an improved breaking ball and a little more meat to the fastball, Eflin has the potential to develop into a quality number four starter. Look for him to take a step forward in 2014 and start showing more signs of his potential.

## Factors on the Farm
### Prospects likely to contribute at the major-league level in 2014

**1. RHP Leonel Campos:** The 26-year-old Venezuelan has some of the nastiest stuff you will see at the minor-league level; a lively plus-plus fastball and an assortment of secondary pitches (changeup, splitter, hard curveball) that all featured intense trapdoor-like movement that would be easier to explain if everybody in the world took psychotropic drugs. He's a high-end bat-misser with legit late-innings relief potential, but the command profile is below average and would need refinement to keep a major-league manager from chewing off his own fingers in high-leverage situations. Fun arm to watch, though.

**2. RHP Keyvius Sampson:** A fourth-round selection in the 2009 draft, Sampson has masqueraded as a starter since he signed out of high school, but could develop into a major-league weapon out of the bullpen, a role he excelled in during the Arizona Fall League. With an easy plus fastball that can sit in the 92-95 range and touch higher in bursts, a sharp mid-80s slider, and usable changeup, Sampson has the makings of a deep and intense late-innings arsenal. His command is below average and limits his potential in a rotation. But in short bursts, the lively arsenal can play loose, missing bats and limiting damage despite a propensity for the free pass.

**3. 2B Cory Spangenberg:** Selected 10th overall in the 2011 draft, Spangenberg is on the cusp of the major leagues, but his profile as a player is closer to below average than anything of impact. The speed is a weapon, but the bat plays light, with a slappy, soft approach that doesn't force fear on any pitcher. The bat could improve—at least enough to play in some capacity—but the impact talent you would expect to find with a top-10 pick has yet to materialize at the professional level, and given the offensive projection, Spangenberg seems unlikely to ever live up to his lofty draft status and initial hype.

## FROM THE FIELD

### Austin Hedges

**Player:** Austin Hedges

**Team:** San Diego Padres

**Filed by:** Ronit Shah

**Date(s) Seen:** July 22-24 and July 26-27, 2013

**Physical:** Durable catcher's body with some bulk and athleticism; strong lower body.

**Hit:** 40 grade; displays balance and patience as a hitter; good hip rotation and incorporation of the lower half; doesn't have standout bat speed, but can drive fastballs to pull side; struggles against soft and away offerings.

**Power:** 50 grade; swing is conducive to power, specifically to pull side; creates some backspin with loft; strong lower body and rotation through swing should create solid-average over-the-fence power.

**Glove:** 70 grade; strong, quiet hands allow for great receiving and framing skills; plus pop times that play up because of great arm strength and quick release.

**Arm:** 70 grade; excellent arm strength that plays up even more because of a super-quick release; shuts down the running game and routinely catches runners asleep at first with back picks.

**Speed:** 40 grade; below-average run, but doesn't clog the bases.

**Makeup:** 70 grade; leader on the field; runs the pitching staff; aware of game situations through the lenses of a catcher and pitcher.

**OFP:** 60; first-division player.

**Realistic Role:** 60; first-division player.

**Risk:** Low; player lacks experience in upper minors, but calling card remains the special defensive talent that will translate in the majors.

## 1. Kyle Crick  RHP

**Born:** 11/30/92  **Age:** 21  **Bats:** L  **Throws:** R  **Height:** 6' 4"  **Weight:** 220

| MLB ETA | CT | FB | CH | CB | SL | OFP | Realistic |
|---|---|---|---|---|---|---|---|
| 2015 | – | 75 | 65 | 60 | 65 | 70<br>NO.2 STARTER | 60<br>LATE-INN RP/CLOSER |

| YEAR | TEAM | LVL | AGE | W | L | SV | G | GS | IP | H | HR | BB | SO | BB9 | SO9 | GB% | BABIP | WHIP | ERA | FIP | FRA | WARP |
|---|---|---|---|---|---|---|---|---|---|---|---|---|---|---|---|---|---|---|---|---|---|---|
| 2013 | SJO | A+ | 20 | 3 | 1 | 0 | 14 | 14 | 68.7 | 48 | 1 | 39 | 95 | 5.1 | 12.5 | 45% | .324 | 1.27 | 1.57 | 2.94 | 2.96 | 2.2 |
| 2014 | SFN | MLB | 21 | 4 | 4 | 0 | 13 | 13 | 65.0 | 56 | 5 | 40 | 65 | 5.5 | 9.0 | 45% | .314 | 1.48 | 4.21 | 4.25 | 4.57 | 0.2 |
| 2015 | SFN | MLB | 22 | 9 | 9 | 0 | 31 | 31 | 195.7 | 161 | 16 | 104 | 180 | 4.8 | 8.3 | 45% | .293 | 1.35 | 3.73 | 3.97 | 4.05 | 1.4 |

Breakout: 0%    Improve: 0%    Collapse: 0%    Attrition: 0%    MLB: 0%    *Comparables: Joel Zumaya, Chris Tillman, Trevor Cahill*

**Drafted/Acquired:** 1st round, 2011 draft, Sherman HS (Sherman, TX)

**Previous Ranking:** #1 (Org), #65 (Top 101)

**What Happened in 2013:** An oblique injury three starts into his season slowed his initial California League destruction, but it didn't take long after his return for him to emerge as one of the best young arms in the minors, a trend he carried over to the Arizona Fall League.

**Strengths:** Excellent size and present strength; arm is incredibly fast; fastball is easy plus-plus offering; pitch works in the 93-97 range; touches higher; big late life; changeup started out as a weakness but emerged as his best secondary offering; excellent arm speed and late action to the arm side; difference-maker pitch with more consistency; shows both curveball and hard slider; curveball with two-plane movement and some depth; plus is possible; slider is hard with sharp cutter-like slice to the glove side; mid-80s to low-90s; aggressive approach.

**Weaknesses:** Delivery can be problematic; can struggle with balance and rhythm (arm can be late); overall command is below average; secondary inconsistency; fastball-heavy attack; can overthrow the slider and lose depth.

**Risk Factor/Injury History:** Moderate risk; yet to pitch at Double-A level

**Bret Sayre's Fantasy Take:** The positive takeaway for fantasy is that Crick will miss bats regardless of his role. As a starting pitcher, Crick could be a big contributor in ERA and strikeouts, but his WHIP is likely to hold him back (unless he takes a big step forward in control) and his high pitch counts may inhibit his potential for wins. If he's a reliever, he can be an 80- to 90-strikeout closer—which installs a relatively high realistic floor into his fantasy value.

**The Year Ahead:** Crick is a monster, regardless of his ultimate role. Given his age and developmental progress of the changeup, you can see a frontline starter in the making, with size, strength, a deep plus potential secondary arsenal, and a near-elite fastball. The inconsistencies in the delivery and command woes could limit his upside in a rotation, which several sources cite when a bullpen projection is suggested. If he can iron out the delivery in the next few seasons and throw more strikes, Crick has the type of lively stuff that can survive in the zone, and if one of the breaking balls steps forward into a true plus pitch, the big Texan shouldn't have any trouble missing bats and barrels alike. I think Crick can stick around in a rotation for the foreseeable future, and any command refinement could launch him into the top 10 prospects in the game.

> #38
>
> BP Top 101 Prospects

## 2. Adalberto Mejia  LHP

**Born:** 6/20/93  **Age:** 21  **Bats:** L  **Throws:** L  **Height:** 6' 3"  **Weight:** 195

| MLB ETA | CT | FB | CH | CB | SL | OFP | Realistic |
|---|---|---|---|---|---|---|---|
| 2015 | – | 60 | 60 | – | 60 | 60<br>NO.3 STARTER | 50<br>NO.4 STARTER |

| YEAR | TEAM | LVL | AGE | W | L | SV | G | GS | IP | H | HR | BB | SO | BB9 | SO9 | GB% | BABIP | WHIP | ERA | FIP | FRA | WARP |
|---|---|---|---|---|---|---|---|---|---|---|---|---|---|---|---|---|---|---|---|---|---|---|
| 2013 | SJO | A+ | 20 | 7 | 4 | 0 | 16 | 16 | 87.0 | 75 | 11 | 23 | 89 | 2.4 | 9.2 | 38% | .277 | 1.13 | 3.31 | 4.20 | 4.50 | 1.2 |
| 2013 | FRE | AAA | 20 | 0 | 0 | 0 | 1 | 1 | 5.0 | 5 | 2 | 2 | 2 | 3.6 | 3.6 | 17% | .188 | 1.40 | 3.60 | 9.17 | 8.49 | -0.1 |
| 2014 | SFN | MLB | 21 | 4 | 5 | 0 | 18 | 13 | 81.0 | 88 | 10 | 30 | 48 | 3.3 | 5.3 | 41% | .312 | 1.46 | 4.91 | 4.90 | 5.34 | -0.5 |
| 2015 | SFN | MLB | 22 | 8 | 9 | 1 | 37 | 24 | 170.3 | 174 | 23 | 53 | 126 | 2.8 | 6.7 | 40% | .308 | 1.33 | 4.47 | 4.31 | 4.86 | -0.3 |

Breakout: 0%    Improve: 0%    Collapse: 0%    Attrition: 0%    MLB: 0%    *Comparables: Joe Wieland, Will Smith, Stolmy Pimentel*

**Drafted/Acquired:** International free agent, 2011, Dominican Republic

**Previous Ranking:** On The Rise

**What Happened in 2013:** Mejia built on his strong full-season debut in 2012 with an even better season in the hitter-friendly environments of the California League, using a plus potential three-pitch mix from the left side to miss more than a bat an inning.

**Strengths:** Smooth, easy delivery; creates good angles; fastball works low-90s; touches a bit higher; excellent late hop; slider is sharp in the 82-85 range; very tough on left-handed bats; turns over a very good changeup; projects to be third plus offering; arm speed offers deception; good fade to the arm side and some sink; strong command projection; good overall pitchability.

**Weaknesses:** Good delivery but doesn't always stay over the ball and finish; tendency to elevate and work up in the zone; more control than command at present; secondary stuff lacks knockout projections; more pitchability than power.

**Risk Factor/Injury History:** Moderate risk; yet to pitch at Double-A level.

**Bret Sayre's Fantasy Take:** The stuff may not be off the charts with Mejia, but this is another arm to get excited about for fantasy. Of course, some of that has to do with the ballpark he has to look forward to pitching in. Having fly-ball tendencies didn't derail his numbers in the Cal League this season, and will come in handy at AT&T Park.

**The Year Ahead:** Mejia was an "On the Rise" candidate coming into the season, and he really took a step forward, with enhanced stuff that didn't sell out at the expense of control. Any lefty that can work a lively fastball in the plus velocity range and back it up with two secondary pitches with above-average potential has a chance to reach the major-league level, and when you add pitchability and a good command profile into the equation, you could develop an impact starter. Mejia lives in a world in between power and finesse, and if the stuff continues to hold steady as the command refines, the Giants will have a future middle-of-the-rotation arm in the near future.

---

## 3. Edwin Escobar LHP

**Born:** 4/22/92 **Age:** 22 **Bats:** L **Throws:** L **Height:** 6' 2" **Weight:** 200

| MLB ETA | CT | FB | CH | CB | SL | OFP | Realistic |
|---|---|---|---|---|---|---|---|
| 2015 | — | 55 | 55 | — | 50 | 55 NO.3 STARTER | 50 NO.4 STARTER |

| YEAR | TEAM | LVL | AGE | W | L | SV | G | GS | IP | H | HR | BB | SO | BB9 | SO9 | GB% | BABIP | WHIP | ERA | FIP | FRA | WARP |
|---|---|---|---|---|---|---|---|---|---|---|---|---|---|---|---|---|---|---|---|---|---|---|
| 2013 | SJO | A+ | 21 | 3 | 4 | 0 | 16 | 14 | 74.7 | 68 | 3 | 17 | 92 | 2.0 | 11.1 | 41% | .323 | 1.14 | 2.89 | 2.55 | 2.93 | 2.3 |
| 2013 | RIC | AA | 21 | 5 | 4 | 0 | 10 | 10 | 54.0 | 44 | 2 | 13 | 54 | 2.2 | 9.0 | 44% | .286 | 1.06 | 2.67 | 2.64 | 3.31 | 1.2 |
| 2014 | SFN | MLB | 22 | 6 | 8 | 0 | 22 | 22 | 110.0 | 113 | 11 | 45 | 82 | 3.7 | 6.7 | 43% | .318 | 1.43 | 4.62 | 4.38 | 5.03 | -0.3 |
| 2015 | SFN | MLB | 23 | 9 | 10 | 0 | 30 | 30 | 191.0 | 194 | 19 | 69 | 149 | 3.3 | 7.0 | 42% | .319 | 1.38 | 4.38 | 3.94 | 4.76 | -0.2 |

Breakout: 0%    Improve: 0%    Collapse: 0%    Attrition: 0%    MLB: 0%          *Comparables: Liam Hendriks, Alex Wood, Josh Lindblom*

**Drafted/Acquired:** International free agent, 2008, Venezuela

**Previous Ranking:** NR

**What Happened in 2013:** Escobar arrived on the national prospect scene in 2012 with a strong Sally League season, but after pitching his way to the Double-A level in 2013, the 22-year-old southpaw could be knocking on the door of the majors with another step forward this season.

**Strengths:** Good strength; delivery works well; plus pitchability; fastball can pack a punch in the low-90s; plus offering at times with some arm-side life; changeup is best secondary pitch; good fastball disguise and late action; shows a playable slider with some tilt; good strike-thrower.

**Weaknesses:** Thick build with some maintenance concerns; can lose angle and work arm side and up; fastball can dip into upper-80s; can play pedestrian at times; breaking ball lacks big upside; slider can get too slurvy and loose; relies more on location and sequence than pure stuff.

**Risk Factor/Injury History:** Moderate risk; 54 innings at Double-A level; lacks much projection; solid-average stuff.

**Bret Sayre's Fantasy Take:** It's going to become painfully clear as this list continues, most of these guys are decent options for fantasy, but no one outside of Kyle Crick has real high-end stuff. With his strong command profile, Escobar is likely to be of most help in the non-strikeout categories—though he won't be a dud in the missing-bats department. Think more along the lines of good Matt Harrison value (from someone who likes Harrison).

**The Year Ahead:** I've been watching Escobar since he first signed with the Rangers back in 2008, and his developmental journey from lottery ticket trade throw-in to number three prospect in the Giants' system is quite remarkable. Back in his complex-league days, Escobar had a very promising high three-quarters curveball, a true plus potential offering that he could snap and throw for strikes. At present, Escobar's lack of highly projectable breaking ball has several sources thinking his future is more likely as a back-end starter or reliever than an impact arm in the middle of a rotation. The development journey can be strange. The Venezuelan southpaw mixes his pitches well, relying heavily on his solid-average fastball and quality changeup to miss bats and keep hitters off-balance, mixing in a slider that has been especially effective against left-handed bats. He's a good arm and a future major leaguer—which is a huge win for the Giants regardless of the outcome—but a long shot to reach his ultimate upside without a step forward in playable intensity from the slider and more consistent velocity from the fastball.

## 4. Kendry Flores  RHP

**Born:** 11/24/91  **Age:** 22  **Bats:** R  **Throws:** R  **Height:** 6' 2"  **Weight:** 175

| MLB ETA | CT | FB | CH | CB | SL | OFP | Realistic |
|---|---|---|---|---|---|---|---|
| Late 2015 | – | 65 | 60 | 50 | – | 55 NO.3 STARTER | 50 NO.4 STARTER |

| YEAR | TEAM | LVL | AGE | W | L | SV | G | GS | IP | H | HR | BB | SO | BB9 | SO9 | GB% | BABIP | WHIP | ERA | FIP | FRA | WARP |
|---|---|---|---|---|---|---|---|---|---|---|---|---|---|---|---|---|---|---|---|---|---|---|
| 2013 | AUG | A | 21 | 10 | 6 | 0 | 22 | 22 | 141.7 | 113 | 11 | 17 | 137 | 1.1 | 8.7 | 39% | .267 | 0.92 | 2.73 | 3.00 | 3.74 | 1.7 |
| 2014 | SFN | MLB | 22 | 5 | 7 | 0 | 19 | 19 | 100.0 | 107 | 13 | 37 | 62 | 3.3 | 5.6 | 38% | .311 | 1.45 | 4.97 | 4.91 | 5.41 | -0.7 |
| 2015 | SFN | MLB | 23 | 8 | 9 | 0 | 26 | 26 | 153.0 | 159 | 19 | 46 | 97 | 2.7 | 5.7 | 38% | .306 | 1.34 | 4.49 | 4.37 | 4.88 | -0.3 |

Breakout: 0%    Improve: 0%    Collapse: 0%    Attrition: 0%    MLB: 0%          *Comparables: Adam Wilk, Daryl Thompson, Jeanmar Gomez*

**Drafted/Acquired:** International free agent, 2009, Dominican Republic

**Previous Ranking:** NR

**What Happened in 2013:** After four years of short-season ball, Flores made his way to the Sally League, where the Dominican arm walked only 17 batters in over 141 innings of work.

**Strengths:** Smooth, athletic delivery; sharp command profile; repeats well/consistent release points; fastball jumpy in the low-90s; can work comfortably in the 92-93 range, touching 95; changeup plays up because of consistent mechanics/release; some late sink; shows average curveball with some depth; advanced pitchability.

**Weaknesses:** Recent uptick in stuff; previous profile was pitchability over power; fastball can still dip to fringe-average; work in the 89-91 range; can get vanilla; breaking ball lacks wipeout grade; needs to add strength to frame; questions about ultimate projection.

**Risk Factor/Injury History:** High risk; yet to pitch above Low-A; velocity uptick is new development.

**Bret Sayre's Fantasy Take:** There's risk and reward here with Flores, even more than with other pitchers who have completed a full season at Low-A. The combination of the potential stuff and park could make him a future number three or four starter in fantasy leagues, but if there's real regression in that department, he becomes much closer to waiver wire fodder. I'd prefer taking a flier on a short-season arm with bigger upside to grabbing Flores.

**The Year Ahead:** Flores is perhaps the most polarizing of arms in the Giants system, with sharp command and strong overall pitchability but stuff that can play sharp in one start and play down in another. Added strength could help with the arsenal consistency, but the concerns about his ultimate projection will remain until he can show an above-average arsenal for an entire season. At his best, Flores could spot up a 92-94 fastball, use his plus potential changeup to miss bats and barrels, and mix in a solid curveball to help change sight lines and disrupt timing. The feel for craft is very strong, and if the uptick in stuff proves to be legit, Flores could move quickly in 2014. Despite his low-level resume, the Giants elected to add the 22-year-old arm to the 40-man roster, a move that seems to suggest the organization believes the gains of 2013 will continue going forward.

## 5. Clayton Blackburn  RHP

**Born:** 1/6/93  **Age:** 21  **Bats:** L  **Throws:** R  **Height:** 6' 3"  **Weight:** 220

| MLB ETA | CT | FB | CH | CB | SL | OFP | Realistic |
|---|---|---|---|---|---|---|---|
| 2015 | – | 55 | 50 | 60 | 50 | 50 NO.4 STARTER | 50 NO.4 STARTER |

| YEAR | TEAM | LVL | AGE | W | L | SV | G | GS | IP | H | HR | BB | SO | BB9 | SO9 | GB% | BABIP | WHIP | ERA | FIP | FRA | WARP |
|---|---|---|---|---|---|---|---|---|---|---|---|---|---|---|---|---|---|---|---|---|---|---|
| 2013 | SJO | A+ | 20 | 7 | 5 | 0 | 23 | 23 | 133.0 | 111 | 12 | 35 | 138 | 2.4 | 9.3 | 49% | .280 | 1.10 | 3.65 | 3.86 | 4.25 | 2.0 |
| 2014 | SFN | MLB | 21 | 7 | 7 | 0 | 20 | 20 | 115.7 | 113 | 12 | 40 | 89 | 3.1 | 6.9 | 52% | .309 | 1.32 | 4.13 | 4.20 | 4.49 | 0.3 |
| 2015 | SFN | MLB | 22 | 11 | 10 | 0 | 31 | 31 | 193.3 | 180 | 18 | 59 | 148 | 2.7 | 6.9 | 51% | .301 | 1.24 | 3.71 | 3.75 | 4.03 | 1.4 |

Breakout: 0%    Improve: 0%    Collapse: 0%    Attrition: 0%    MLB: 0%          *Comparables: David Holmberg, Brett Anderson, Michael Bowden*

**Drafted/Acquired:** 16th round, 2011 draft, Edmond Santa Fe HS (Edmond, OK)

**Previous Ranking:** #2 (Org), #95 (Top 101)

**What Happened in 2013:** Big boy righty that logged 131 innings in his 2012 full-season debut, moved up to the California League and logged 133 more, missing more than a bat an inning in the process.

**Strengths:** Big, strong, physical body/frame; sound delivery; fastball is solid-average pitch; can work 90-93 with some weight; strike-zone pounder; curveball flashes plus potential; tight rotation and vertical depth; shows average changeup with sink; slider is fourth average (or better) offering; can show sharp tilt and good deception from fastball; good command profile.

**Weaknesses:** More command/control than a power arm; fastball can play as fringe-average offering at 88-90; secondary stuff lacks wipeout projections; more solid-average than special across the board; limited projection.

**Risk Factor/Injury History:** Moderate risk; yet to pitch in Double-A; lacks impact stuff or impact projection.

**Bret Sayre's Fantasy Take:** Blackburn is a safe pick to accrue fantasy value, but he lacks that above-replacement punch in shallower leagues. In deep leagues, he's an underrated prospect who has the potential to contribute strong ratios and win potential—however, the strikeouts are likely to underwhelm.

**The Year Ahead:** Blackburn is a workhorse prototype, a big, strong pitcher capable of taking the ball every fifth day and logging innings. He's more finesse than frontline, and he lacks much arsenal projection, so what you see now is likely what you will see when he arrives at the major-league level. But there is a lot of value to be found in a cost-controlled innings eater with only moderate risk attached. While he might lack the sexy ceiling of some of his organizational contemporaries, Blackburn is a good bet to eventually find a home at the back of a major-league rotation, where he could give you 200 innings of solid but not spectacular performance.

## 6.  Andrew Susac   C

**Born:** 3/22/90   **Age:** 24   **Bats:** R   **Throws:** R   **Height:** 6'2"   **Weight:** 210

| MLB ETA | | Hit | Power | Run | Glove | Arm | | OFP | Realistic |
|---|---|---|---|---|---|---|---|---|---|
| 2015 | | ---- | 60 | ---- | 50 | 55 | | 55 >AVG REGULAR | 45 <AVG REG/2ND C |

| YEAR | TEAM | LVL | AGE | PA | R | 2B | 3B | HR | RBI | BB | SO | SB | CS | AVG/OBP/SLG | TAv | BABIP | BRR | FRAA | WARP |
|---|---|---|---|---|---|---|---|---|---|---|---|---|---|---|---|---|---|---|---|
| 2013 | RIC | AA | 23 | 310 | 32 | 17 | 0 | 12 | 46 | 42 | 68 | 1 | 0 | .256/.362/.458 | .310 | .299 | -0.6 | C(71): -0.5, 1B(9): -0.7 | 3.0 |
| 2014 | SFN | MLB | 24 | 250 | 25 | 10 | 1 | 6 | 27 | 26 | 65 | 0 | 0 | .221/.306/.355 | .247 | .280 | -0.4 | C -0, 1B -0 | 0.7 |
| 2015 | SFN | MLB | 25 | 250 | 28 | 11 | 1 | 6 | 26 | 25 | 71 | 0 | 0 | .213/.298/.350 | .239 | .279 | -0.6 | C 0, 1B 0 | 0.3 |

Breakout: 2%   Improve: 7%   Collapse: 7%   Attrition: 11%   MLB: 25%        *Comparables: Josh Donaldson, Michael McKenry, Jeff Clement*

**Drafted/Acquired:** 2nd round, 2011 draft, Oregon State University (Corvallis, OR)

**Previous Ranking:** #6 (Org)

**What Happened in 2013:** The former Oregon State product started to show more thunder in his stick at the Double-A level, and was even more impressive in a small 17-game sample in the Arizona Fall League

**Strengths:** Good present strength; body for backstop; raw power is plus; game power could play above average; clean, no-frills stroke; shows some bat control; good approach; will force pitchers to work; glove could play to average; arm is solid-average to plus; good catch-and-throw skills.

**Weaknesses:** Shows swing-and-miss in the zone; struggles against velocity; hit tool likely to play below-average to fringe; could limit power utility; receiving skills need work; feet can get heavy; slow to the arm side on balls in the dirt; overall defensive profile lacks plus projection; well-below-average runner.

**Risk Factor/Injury History:** Moderate risk; 84 games at Double-A level; questions about hit tool/receiving skills.

**Bret Sayre's Fantasy Take:** Susac has a likely future behind the plate and potential 15-homer pop (even in that stadium) in his corner, but the batting average is likely to be an issue. That said, if you are in an OBP league (or a points league), Susac is a stronger option, as he has an advanced approach with strong walk rates to back it up.

**The Year Ahead:** Susac might appear as a power-first/only prospect, but he has enough chops behind the plate for a dual-threat profile, even if that profile is more solid-average than first-division or higher. The hit tool is a question mark, especially against quality stuff. But the strength in the swing is legit, and he's going to run into some power at the highest level. The arm [read: ability to throw out baserunners] is his best defensive attribute, while the receiving and blocking components still come off as unrefined; the hands can be stiff and the footwork can be casual and sloppy. Despite the shortcomings, the overall profile could be an above-average regular, a down-the-lineup catcher with playable power that can control the running game and manage a battery. The numbers might not be sexy, but a 55 (20/80) backstop is an extremely valuable commodity to have under team control.

## 7.  Keury Mella   LHP

**Born:** 8/2/93   **Age:** 20   **Bats:** R   **Throws:** R   **Height:** 6'2"   **Weight:** 200

| MLB ETA | | CT | FB | CH | CB | SL | | OFP | Realistic |
|---|---|---|---|---|---|---|---|---|---|
| 2017 | | ---- | 75 | 50 | 60 | ---- | | 65 NO.2 STARTER | 50 LATE-INN RP (SETUP) |

| YEAR | TEAM | LVL | AGE | W | L | SV | G | GS | IP | H | HR | BB | SO | BB9 | SO9 | GB% | BABIP | WHIP | ERA | FIP | FRA | WARP |
|---|---|---|---|---|---|---|---|---|---|---|---|---|---|---|---|---|---|---|---|---|---|---|
| 2013 | GIA | Rk | 19 | 3 | 2 | 0 | 10 | 9 | 36.0 | 34 | 0 | 11 | 41 | 2.8 | 10.2 | 67% | .358 | 1.25 | 2.25 | 2.73 | 4.10 | 0.7 |
| 2014 | SFN | MLB | 20 | 1 | 1 | 0 | 7 | 3 | 33.7 | 37 | 4 | 21 | 22 | 5.6 | 5.9 | 51% | .323 | 1.72 | 5.79 | 5.52 | 6.29 | -0.5 |
| 2015 | SFN | MLB | 21 | 1 | 1 | 0 | 14 | 4 | 71.7 | 75 | 7 | 34 | 51 | 4.3 | 6.4 | 51% | .321 | 1.52 | 4.90 | 4.48 | 5.33 | -0.4 |

Breakout: 0%   Improve: 0%   Collapse: 0%   Attrition: 0%   MLB: 0%        *Comparables: Luis Avilan, Yordano Ventura, Kevin Siegrist*

**Drafted/Acquired:** International free agent, 2011, Dominican Republic

**Previous Ranking:** NR

**What Happened in 2013:** In his stateside debut, Mella was electric on the mound, missing bats with his well-above-average fastball and showing more feel than expected.

**Strengths:** Big arm strength; good feel for a repeatable delivery; fastball is power offering; two-seamer works low-90s with weight; four-seamer can work in the mid-90s with room for more in the future; shows hard curveball with bite; projectable offering; some feel for changeup.

**Weaknesses:** Fastball-heavy arsenal at present; some pitchability and feel but still more thrower than pitcher; inconsistent release on breaking ball; wide gap between present and future; changeup is underdeveloped at present; can get too firm; deliberate in release; command is below-average at present.

**Risk Factor/Injury History:** High risk; complex-level resume; big gap between present and future.

**Bret Sayre's Fantasy Take:** Go ahead, live a little. The range of outcomes is so big here that it's not even worth speculating on what he could be for fantasy. But if the stuff is legit, he'll be something—and that's worth a flier.

**The Year Ahead:** Next to Crick, Mella might have the highest tool-based ceiling on the farm, with the type of fastball to project near the top of a major-league rotation. The secondary stuff is a long way away, but he already shows the ability to spin a hard breaking ball, and even though it's raw, the changeup has potential because of the delivery and utility of the fastball. At present, Mella pounds the zone with a lively two-seam fastball in the low-90s, and backs it up with a bat-missing four-seamer that can work up to 96 with late life. He can ride the fastball a long way on his developmental journey, but any step forward with the secondary stuff could launch him into the national spotlight as a top-tier prospect in the Giants system. It might not happen in 2014, but it's going to happen eventually.

## 8. Joan Gregorio RHP

**Born:** 1/12/92 **Age:** 22 **Bats:** R **Throws:** R **Height:** 6' 7" **Weight:** 180

| MLB ETA | | CT | FB | CH | CB | SL | | OFP | Realistic |
|---|---|---|---|---|---|---|---|---|---|
| 2016 | | — | 65 | — | — | 60 | | 60<br>NO.3 STARTER | 50<br>LATE-INN RP (SETUP) |

| YEAR | TEAM | LVL | AGE | W | L | SV | G | GS | IP | H | HR | BB | SO | BB9 | SO9 | GB% | BABIP | WHIP | ERA | FIP | FRA | WARP |
|---|---|---|---|---|---|---|---|---|---|---|---|---|---|---|---|---|---|---|---|---|---|---|
| 2013 | AUG | A | 21 | 6 | 3 | 0 | 14 | 13 | 69.7 | 65 | 3 | 17 | 84 | 2.2 | 10.9 | 35% | .341 | 1.18 | 4.00 | 2.45 | 2.94 | 1.8 |
| 2014 | SFN | MLB | 22 | 2 | 3 | 0 | 12 | 9 | 60.3 | 64 | 7 | 29 | 43 | 4.3 | 6.4 | 39% | .321 | 1.53 | 5.07 | 4.92 | 5.51 | -0.5 |
| 2015 | SFN | MLB | 23 | 5 | 6 | 0 | 26 | 18 | 148.0 | 147 | 17 | 59 | 111 | 3.6 | 6.8 | 38% | .308 | 1.40 | 4.55 | 4.29 | 4.95 | -0.3 |

Breakout: 0%    Improve: 0%    Collapse: 0%    Attrition: 0%    MLB: 0%        *Comparables: Adam Wilk, Daryl Thompson, Dan Straily*

**Drafted/Acquired:** International free agent, 2010, Dominican Republic

**Previous Ranking:** NR

**What Happened in 2013:** The projectable Dominican arm failed to eclipse the 100-inning mark in his full-season debut, making 13 starts but losing time to an oblique injury and a blister issue.

**Strengths:** Projectable size; length and leverage in delivery; fastball works in the low-90s; touches a little higher; could get a bump with added strength; flashes above-average slider; fastball plane with late tilt; good strike-thrower at present; his first name is Joan.

**Weaknesses:** Body can get out of sorts in the delivery; struggles to stay over his offerings; slider will flatten out and lose bite; fastball command is fringe; struggles to turn over the changeup; pitch can get too firm and flat.

**Risk Factor/Injury History:** High risk; Low-A resume; underdeveloped changeup.

**Bret Sayre's Fantasy Take:** The bottom of this list isn't filled with guys who are must-owns by any means in shallow and medium-sized dynasty leagues, but in a deep league, Gregorio is worth a pickup with that strikeout-to-walk rate. He has a nice strikeout/WHIP profile if he continues to progress.

**The Year Ahead:** Gregorio has size you can't teach, which is both appealing because of the length and leverage he can create, and detrimental because of the athleticism and body control necessary to be consistent in his mechanics. With room to add more strength, the 22-year-old righty could see a jump in his fastball, a pitch that can already show plus velocity in the 92+ range with good movement. The slider has potential, but is more flash than anything else right now, and the undeveloped changeup has many scouts putting a future bullpen label on Gregorio. He can quiet some of the bullpen chatter by staying healthy and logging a full season of starts in High-A, which should help with the development of his secondary offerings and fastball command. The ultimate ceiling is high, and with size and a projectable fastball/slider combo, the floor could be a late-innings reliever. He just needs to avoid the disabled list and log professional innings.

## 9. Martin Agosta RHP

**Born:** 4/7/91 **Age:** 23 **Bats:** R **Throws:** R **Height:** 6' 1" **Weight:** 180

| MLB ETA | | CT | FB | CH | CB | SL | | OFP | Realistic |
|---|---|---|---|---|---|---|---|---|---|
| 2015 | | 55 | 55 | 60 | — | 50 | | 50<br>NO.4 STARTER | 50<br>LATE-INN RP (SETUP) |

| YEAR | TEAM | LVL | AGE | W | L | SV | G | GS | IP | H | HR | BB | SO | BB9 | SO9 | GB% | BABIP | WHIP | ERA | FIP | FRA | WARP |
|---|---|---|---|---|---|---|---|---|---|---|---|---|---|---|---|---|---|---|---|---|---|---|
| 2013 | AUG | A | 22 | 9 | 3 | 0 | 18 | 18 | 91.7 | 57 | 4 | 43 | 109 | 4.2 | 10.7 | 37% | .254 | 1.09 | 2.06 | 3.31 | 4.17 | 0.6 |
| 2014 | SFN | MLB | 23 | 3 | 4 | 0 | 15 | 11 | 64.3 | 59 | 7 | 36 | 58 | 5.0 | 8.1 | 40% | .313 | 1.48 | 4.57 | 4.67 | 4.97 | -0.1 |
| 2015 | SFN | MLB | 24 | 8 | 9 | 0 | 35 | 26 | 179.7 | 160 | 16 | 93 | 169 | 4.7 | 8.5 | 40% | .311 | 1.41 | 4.20 | 3.96 | 4.56 | 0.3 |

Breakout: 0%    Improve: 0%    Collapse: 0%    Attrition: 0%    MLB: 0%        *Comparables: Jose Cisnero, Jake Arrieta, Bud Norris*

**Drafted/Acquired:** 2nd round, 2012 draft, St. Mary's College of California (Moraga,CA)

**Previous Ranking:** #9 (Org)

**What Happened in 2013:** A second-round pick in 2012, Agosta made his full-season debut in 2013, taking the mound for 19 starts and allowing only 57 hits in over 91 innings of work.

**Strengths:** Clean, athletic delivery; arm works very well; solid-average to plus fastball; velocity consistent in the low-90s; can bump higher; good movement; changeup is most consistent secondary pitch; plays well off fastball with good vertical action; playable slider; sharp mid-80s cutter in his bag; throws all offerings for strikes; pitchability.

**Weaknesses:** Lacks wipeout stuff in rotation; more control than command; fastball can play down over the course of a game; above-average cutter put on the developmental backburner; standard slider is more show than stud.

**Risk Factor/Injury History:** Moderate risk; mature stuff/feel; yet to pitch above Low-A level.

**Bret Sayre's Fantasy Take:** Agosta's story is not too dissimilar to Clayton Blackburn's, where the value comes in deeper leagues because he lacks the upside to own at this point in shallower formats. He's also not close enough to the majors to be as safe of an own as he will be next year.

**The Year Ahead:** Agosta can get lost in the Giants' voluptuous mid-rotation prospect mix, but I like his upside more than those of Stratton or Blach, mostly because of the deep arsenal that has enough meat to miss bats and enough velocity and movement variance to keep hitters off-balance and guessing. The command needs a grade jump, but the 23-year-old has a feel for the mound and should be able to refine enough for the command to play as average. The late-innings potential is there as a floor, but I'm still on the Agosta-as-a-starter bandwagon, and I wouldn't be shocked if he finds his way to Double-A in 2014 and proves up to the rotation task.

## 10. Ty Blach    LHP

**Born:** 10/20/90    **Age:** 23    **Bats:** R    **Throws:** L    **Height:** 6'1"    **Weight:** 200

| MLB ETA | | CT | | FB | | CH | | CB | | SL | | OFP | | Realistic |
|---|---|---|---|---|---|---|---|---|---|---|---|---|---|---|
| 2015 | | – | | 55 | | 60 | | 50 | | 50 | | 50 NO.4 STARTER | | 50 NO.4 STARTER |

| YEAR | TEAM | LVL | AGE | W | L | SV | G | GS | IP | H | HR | BB | SO | BB9 | SO9 | GB% | BABIP | WHIP | ERA | FIP | FRA | WARP |
|---|---|---|---|---|---|---|---|---|---|---|---|---|---|---|---|---|---|---|---|---|---|---|
| 2013 | SJO | A+ | 22 | 12 | 4 | 0 | 22 | 20 | 130.3 | 124 | 8 | 18 | 117 | 1.2 | 8.1 | 48% | .304 | 1.09 | 2.90 | 3.23 | 3.70 | 2.5 |
| 2014 | SFN | MLB | 23 | 5 | 6 | 0 | 16 | 16 | 91.3 | 95 | 9 | 28 | 59 | 2.8 | 5.8 | 46% | .312 | 1.34 | 4.25 | 4.24 | 4.61 | 0.1 |
| 2015 | SFN | MLB | 24 | 11 | 11 | 0 | 30 | 30 | 190.7 | 197 | 22 | 49 | 133 | 2.3 | 6.3 | 46% | .313 | 1.29 | 4.18 | 3.97 | 4.55 | 0.2 |

**Breakout:** 8%    **Improve:** 12%    **Collapse:** 5%    **Attrition:** 12%    **MLB:** 21%    *Comparables: Dallas Keuchel, Zach McAllister, Adam Wilk*

**Drafted/Acquired:** 5th round, 2012 draft, Creighton University (Omaha, NE)

**Previous Ranking:** On The Rise

**What Happened in 2013:** An "On the Rise" player on last season's list, Blach lived up to the hype in his professional debut, starting in the California League and displaying a very good feel for control in addition to some bat-missing prowess.

**Strengths:** Plus pitchability; good present strength and repeatability in the delivery; loud hip rotation/jerk in the delivery can distract the eye before release; multiple fastball looks; two-seamer with some sink in the upper-80s/low-90s; four-seamer with more giddy-up in the 91-94 range; changeup plays as plus offering; excellent deception in the arm and some arm-side action; shows multiple breaking balls; both slider and curveball should play as average offerings; sharp control; plus command projection.

**Weaknesses:** Can open up in the delivery and miss arm side and up; fastball is not a power pitch; relies more on location and movement than velocity; lacks plus breaking ball; command/control profile; questions about ability to miss bats at higher levels.

**Risk Factor/Injury History:** Moderate risk; yet to pitch at Double-A level; lacks plus stuff/small margin of error.

**Bret Sayre's Fantasy Take:** Another lower-upside Giants prospect and someone to ignore in anything but deep leagues with deep farm teams. Could be a Robbie Erlin type with the ability to put the ball where he wants to and the underwhelming stuff overall if it all works.

**The Year Ahead:** Blach is a command/control lefty with a deep mix of pitches that he sequences well. The stuff doesn't pack a big punch, but his pitchability allows it to play up, as he shows multiple fastball and breaking-ball looks, and a very good fading changeup that should be good enough to keep right-handed sticks off his fastball. He makes the delivery work, and the loud hip snap works to his advantage in the form of eye-line deception and not against his ability to repeat and locate the ball. Blach should continue to produce results at Double-A, and will eventually settle in as a solid back-of-the-rotation type at the major-league level. The command will have to be sharp for sustainable production, but the overall profile looks like a safe bet for league-average success in a rotation.

## Prospects on the Rise

**1. SS Christian Arroyo:** Excellent reports on the promise of the hit tool, but concerns about the defensive profile and projected value raised doubts about Arroyo and prevented him from cracking the top 10 this season. But with a strong full-season campaign, the former first-round pick should push into the top 10, especially if he can quiet some of the concerns about his ability to stick at shortstop.

**2. 3B Ryder Jones:** A second-round pick in the 2013 draft, Jones has the natural ability to rip a baseball, projecting to hit for both average and power. He has a long way to go in the field, but the arm could be a weapon at third, and he has plenty of time to iron out the actions. But his name will be made with the stick, and if the 19-year-old can bring his advanced hittability to a full-season league, he will move up the prospect ranks and into the top 10 next season along with draftmate Christian Arroyo.

**3. RHP Chase Johnson:** A college reliever turned starter at the professional level, Johnson has the size and stuff to project to the major-league level in either role. In bursts, Johnson can work into the mid-90s, showing a sharp slider and the feel to turn over a projectable changeup. Out of the rotation, the command inconsistencies could limit his overall utility, but the fastball will still play as a plus offering in the low-90s, with a secondary arsenal that could play to solid-average or higher if everything comes together. Reports were mixed in his short-season debut, with several sources keeping the reliever label on the 22-year-old righty despite initial success out of the rotation.

## Factors on the Farm
### Prospects likely to contribute at the major-league level in 2014

**1. RHP Heath Hembree:** I'm not big on ranking relievers high on prospect lists, especially when in competition against arms that feature legit rotation futures. But Hembree could have easily cracked this list based on his impact potential in a late-innings capacity and low risk factor involved. With a plus fastball that can show plus-plus velocity (but often at the expense of control), and a very sharp mid-80s slider, the 25-year-old righty will have a good chance to miss a lot of bats in a major-league bullpen going forward.

**2. RHP Derek Law:** Despite only 25 innings above the Low-A level, Law is a legit bullpen option for 2014, with an easy plus fastball in the 93-95 range, a very good curveball with bite, and an average but effective slider. The delivery makes command problematic, with a pronounced back turn and plenty of effort, but his stuff is good enough to live loose, and he should continue to miss plenty of bats as he makes an accelerated climb toward the major-league level.

**3. OF Gary Brown:** From first-division center fielder of the future in 2011 to below-average bench outfielder in 2013, Brown has experienced quite the drop in status since exploding on the scene in his full-season debut. The inability to make adjustments against quality arms has been his biggest weakness, and it's highly unlikely that his bat improves to the point where it plays as a major-league regular. But the defensive profile and speed should be enough to carry him to the highest level, which would be seen as a developmental success story for most players; however, when you have the physical tools of Brown—a former first-round pick—the bar for success is set much higher than it is for most players.

## FROM THE FIELD

### Kyle Crick

**Player:** Kyle Crick

**Team:** San Francisco Giants

**Filed by:** Chris Rodriguez

**Date(s) Seen:** July 17, 2013

**Physical:** Big size; prototypical workhorse body; built to log innings; body reminiscent of Matt Cain.

**Mechanics/Delivery:** Fast arm; good control of his big body; can overthrow the fastball; inconsistent release point inning to inning.

**Fastball:** 70 grade; near elite; sat 93-95 in this game; touched 96 and has gone even higher; heavy pitch; not a lot of good swings against it.

**Slider:** 65 grade; more of a short slider; hard, darting action; inconsistent; flashed plus-plus when thrown properly; also flattens out and loses movement; thrown in the high-80s; best secondary offering.

**Curveball:** 60 grade; big break; tight rotation and depth; can get a little loopy; used as chase pitch to right-handed hitters; thrown in the low-80s.

**Changeup:** 60 grade; good pitch with arm speed and arm-side sink; inconsistent velocity; touched 89 with it; struggled with it throughout the game; flashed some beautiful offerings mixed with some that were on a tee.

**Other:** Command needs to take a step up; lost his feel for release point of all his pitches and fought himself in his fifth and final inning, walking three in a row. I think he can start though because of his big body and four plus to plus-plus offerings. If the command jumps, the sky is the limit.

**Makeup:** 60 grade; loves to compete; likes to establish his big fastball early and often.

**OFP:** 70; no. 2 starter

**Realistic Role:** 60; no. 3 starter

**Risk:** Moderate; still working on command and control; ready for Double-A.

---

**Player:** Kyle Crick

**Team:** San Francisco Giants

**Filed by:** Steffan Segui

**Date(s) Seen:** October 10, 22, and 29, 2013

**Physical:** Big thick body. Durable filled-out frame.

**Mechanics/Delivery:** Almost mirror image of Matt Cain. Works very fast. Stays linear throughout but doesn't finish well. Instead of getting over his front side he goes around it, arm slot drops, front side pulls out, and his pitches miss.

**Command/Control:** 45 grade. Mechanical problems are fixable but tends to overuse stuff and tries to power by hitters.

**Fastball:** 70 grade. Hard and heavy. Up to 99, works in the mid-90s. Throws downhill with good angle. Tends to overthrow and pull off, losing control and effectiveness.

**Slider:** 60 grade. Short, late, hard and sharp with good two-plane break. Spots well arm-side down. Better control than fastball.

**Changeup:** 55 grade. Has some feel and great movement. Runs when up, sinks when down.

**Makeup:** 60 grade. Never any issues, works hard and has presence on the mound.

**OFP:** 65; no. 2 starter

**Realistic Role:** 60; no. 3 starter or closer

**Risk:** Moderate. Slight injury concerns, command issues.

## 1. Taijuan Walker  RHP

**Born:** 8/13/92  **Age:** 21  **Bats:** R  **Throws:** R  **Height:** 6' 4"  **Weight:** 210

| MLB ETA | CT | FB | CH | CB | SL | OFP | Realistic |
|---|---|---|---|---|---|---|---|
| Debuted in 2013 | 70 | 70 | 50 | 50 | — | 70<br>NO.2 STARTER | 70<br>NO.2 STARTER |

| YEAR | TEAM | LVL | AGE | W | L | SV | G | GS | IP | H | HR | BB | SO | BB9 | SO9 | GB% | BABIP | WHIP | ERA | FIP | FRA | WARP |
|---|---|---|---|---|---|---|---|---|---|---|---|---|---|---|---|---|---|---|---|---|---|---|
| 2013 | TAC | AAA | 20 | 5 | 3 | 0 | 11 | 11 | 57.3 | 54 | 5 | 27 | 64 | 4.2 | 10.0 | 49% | .331 | 1.41 | 3.61 | 3.99 | 3.87 | 1.2 |
| 2013 | WTN | AA | 20 | 4 | 7 | 0 | 14 | 14 | 84.0 | 58 | 6 | 30 | 96 | 3.2 | 10.3 | 47% | .259 | 1.05 | 2.46 | 2.84 | 3.66 | 1.2 |
| 2013 | SEA | MLB | 20 | 1 | 0 | 0 | 3 | 3 | 15.0 | 11 | 0 | 4 | 12 | 2.4 | 7.2 | 39% | .250 | 1.00 | 3.60 | 2.28 | 2.72 | 0.4 |
| 2014 | SEA | MLB | 21 | 8 | 8 | 0 | 24 | 24 | 126.3 | 119 | 14 | 51 | 118 | 3.6 | 8.4 | 45% | .296 | 1.35 | 4.03 | 4.31 | 4.38 | 0.7 |
| 2015 | SEA | MLB | 22 | 8 | 8 | 0 | 27 | 27 | 164.0 | 152 | 20 | 56 | 147 | 3.1 | 8.1 | 44% | .285 | 1.27 | 3.86 | 4.12 | 4.20 | 1.2 |

Breakout: 9%    Improve: 24%    Collapse: 3%    Attrition: 17%    MLB: 33%    *Comparables: Carlos Martinez, Julio Teheran, Shelby Miller*

**Drafted/Acquired:** 1st round, 2010 draft, Yucaipa HS (Yucaipa, CA)

**Previous Ranking:** #1 (Org), #9 (Top 101)

**What Happened in 2013:** Walker started at the Double-A level and finished his season with three starts at the major-league level, displaying not only high-level stuff but also the necessary makeup to stand on a major-league mound as a 21-year-old.

**Strengths:** Electric fastball from easy release; works in the 94-96 range; can get more when he needs more; good movement to the arm side; cutter is a monster pitch; 89-93 with late horizontal movement to the glove side; curveball has big depth in the 73-76 range; average but effective offering; excellent pickoff move; big competitor.

**Weaknesses:** Command is below average; lacks plus projection; can work up in the zone too often; curveball has nice shape but can get soft; tendency to start it too high in the zone; will struggle to be effective unless it plays with sharper fastball command; changeup can get too firm; lacks quality fade.

**Risk Factor/Injury History:** Low risk; ready for majors

**Bret Sayre's Fantasy Take:** One of the top fantasy pitching prospects in the game, Walker has the type of arm that can help contribute strongly across all categories. I'm not sold that he'll be someone who sits near the top of the league leaderboard in strikeouts, but there will be enough to go around (think around 190-200 at his peak).

**The Year Ahead:** Walker needs to refine his command and his secondary arsenal, but the fastball is a high-end major-league pitch, and the cutter can bail him out of situations. Oddly enough, the curve that received all the minor-league hype received the least amount of industry love, at least as far as major-league projection is concerned. Don't rule out his changeup becoming a much better pitch than people are projecting; it doesn't look good now, but he has feel for pitching and the power of the fastball will assist in the deceptive elements of the offering. I wouldn't be shocked if it develops into a plus pitch down the line. Give it time.

**#8**

BP Top
101
Prospects

## 2. D.J. Peterson  1B

**Born:** 12/31/91  **Age:** 22  **Bats:** R  **Throws:** R  **Height:** 6' 1"  **Weight:** 190

| MLB ETA | Hit | Power | Run | Glove | Arm | OFP | Realistic |
|---|---|---|---|---|---|---|---|
| 2015 | 60 | 60 | — | — | — | 60<br>1ST DIV 3B | 50<br>2ND DIV 1B |

| YEAR | TEAM | LVL | AGE | PA | R | 2B | 3B | HR | RBI | BB | SO | SB | CS | AVG/OBP/SLG | TAv | BABIP | BRR | FRAA | WARP |
|---|---|---|---|---|---|---|---|---|---|---|---|---|---|---|---|---|---|---|---|
| 2013 | EVE | A- | 21 | 123 | 20 | 6 | 0 | 6 | 27 | 13 | 18 | 0 | 1 | .312/.382/.532 | .331 | .326 | -0.6 | 3B(24): -2.9, 1B(1): -0.0 | 0.9 |
| 2013 | CLN | A | 21 | 107 | 16 | 5 | 1 | 7 | 20 | 7 | 24 | 1 | 0 | .293/.346/.576 | .321 | .324 | -0.1 | 3B(21): -0.6 | 0.9 |
| 2014 | SEA | MLB | 22 | 250 | 25 | 9 | 1 | 9 | 31 | 13 | 67 | 0 | 0 | .224/.265/.384 | .240 | .270 | -0.4 | 3B -4, 1B -0 | -0.4 |
| 2015 | SEA | MLB | 23 | 250 | 29 | 9 | 1 | 10 | 31 | 12 | 68 | 0 | 0 | .231/.271/.400 | .241 | .278 | -0.6 | 3B -4, 1B 0 | -0.1 |

Breakout: 0%    Improve: 0%    Collapse: 0%    Attrition: 0%    MLB: 0%    *Comparables: Alex Liddi, Brandon Laird, Matt Davidson*

**Drafted/Acquired:** 1st round, 2013 draft, University of New Mexico (Albuquerque, NM)

**Previous Ranking:** NR

**What Happened in 2013:** It's a small sample, but Peterson did exactly what a polished college bat should do in the lower minors, which is slug .553 over two spots, including 13 home runs in 55 games.

**Strengths:** Natural hitter; easy to the ball; good extension; uses the entire field; shows plus power potential; doesn't sell out for the tool; strength to lift the ball; arm is strong enough for third.

**Weaknesses:** Glove is below average at third; below-average range; likely home is across the diamond at first; has work ethic to improve at position, but the bat is the carrying tool; has to hit.

**Risk Factor/Injury History:** Moderate; difficult profile but good polish at present with plus projections on hit/power.

**#65**

BP Top
101
Prospects

**Bret Sayre's Fantasy Take:** The key with Peterson is how long he can maintain that third-base eligibility, even if his future eventually lies across the diamond. If his bat comes close to maxing out, that's the difference between a stud at the hot corner and a back-end starter at first base. However, it's a tough task to put up big power numbers as a right-handed bat at Safeco.

**The Year Ahead:** Peterson could be ready to move fast, possibly reaching Double-A by summer. The bat is his ticket to a first-division future, and the reports since he signed have been very positive; his bat-to-ball is very easy, and the power is already showing up in game action. He's going to hit. The big question is: Will he become a 6/6 hit/power type or will he fall short of those projections? Falling short with the stick could come with an even bigger sting if he does in fact shift over to first at some point in the development process, a move that my sources seem to think is a likely outcome.

## 3. James Paxton  LHP

**Born:** 11/6/88  **Age:** 25  **Bats:** L  **Throws:** L  **Height:** 6' 4"  **Weight:** 220

| MLB ETA | CT | FB | CH | CB | SL | OFP | Realistic |
|---|---|---|---|---|---|---|---|
| Debuted in 2013 | 50 | 70 | – | 50 | – | 55 NO.3-4 STARTER | 50 LATE INN RP |

| YEAR | TEAM | LVL | AGE | W | L | SV | G | GS | IP | H | HR | BB | SO | BB9 | SO9 | GB% | BABIP | WHIP | ERA | FIP | FRA | WARP |
|---|---|---|---|---|---|---|---|---|---|---|---|---|---|---|---|---|---|---|---|---|---|---|
| 2013 | TAC | AAA | 24 | 8 | 11 | 0 | 28 | 26 | 145.7 | 158 | 10 | 58 | 131 | 3.6 | 8.1 | 51% | .338 | 1.48 | 4.45 | 3.92 | 4.07 | 2.3 |
| 2013 | SEA | MLB | 24 | 3 | 0 | 0 | 4 | 4 | 24.0 | 15 | 2 | 7 | 21 | 2.6 | 7.9 | 59% | .203 | 0.92 | 1.50 | 3.28 | 4.40 | 0.2 |
| 2014 | SEA | MLB | 25 | 8 | 8 | 0 | 25 | 25 | 136.7 | 132 | 13 | 57 | 126 | 3.8 | 8.3 | 49% | .305 | 1.38 | 3.94 | 4.08 | 4.29 | 0.9 |
| 2015 | SEA | MLB | 26 | 9 | 9 | 0 | 30 | 30 | 191.7 | 186 | 18 | 72 | 178 | 3.4 | 8.4 | 48% | .305 | 1.34 | 3.82 | 3.71 | 4.15 | 1.4 |

**Breakout:** 32%  **Improve:** 51%  **Collapse:** 11%  **Attrition:** 30%  **MLB:** 73%        *Comparables: Lance Lynn, Eric Surkamp, Jason Windsor*

**Drafted/Acquired:** 4th round, 2010 draft, University of Kentucky (Lexington, KY)

**Previous Ranking:** #5 (Org), #92 (Top 101)

**What Happened in 2013:** Paxton logged 145 2/3 innings at the Triple-A level, but finally got a taste of the majors: four starts with surprisingly intense stuff and subsequent results.

**Strengths:** Plus-plus velocity from the left side; can work 94-95; touch higher; shows average curveball that has the shape and depth to play as plus when he commands it; has a usable cutter that could play to average; body to log innings.

**Weaknesses:** Long arms can get out of whack in the delivery; comes high front side and leaves it long in the back (mullet mechanics); command profile is below average; inconsistent secondary stuff; changeup is below average at present; lacks much projection.

**Risk Factor/Injury History:** Low risk; ready for major-league role

**Bret Sayre's Fantasy Take:** If Paxton does stick in the rotation, he'll do the most damage in strikeouts and ERA, as high walk rates and pitch counts could limit his impact in wins and WHIP. As a reliever, he'd have the whole "lefties can't be closers" thing going against him, but his stuff is good enough to break though that glass ceiling.

**The Year Ahead:** Paxton's call-up performance shocked me, as the velocity was better and more consistent than I recall seeing, and the overall command was better as well. I'm not sold that the Paxton of 2014 will look like the Paxton of late 2013, but I'll gladly admit I'm wrong. The delivery concerns me, and I think the length and the deep-arm pickup in the back will limit command and secondary utility, and major-league hitters will eventually adjust to his velocity. If he can maintain his delivery, getting over the front side, I think he has the stuff to stick in a rotation. If not, he's a nice weapon to have in the bullpen; a long-armed lefty who can pump fastballs in the mid-90s.

**#68** BP Top 101 Prospects

## 4. Victor Sanchez  RHP

**Born:** 1/30/95  **Age:** 19  **Bats:** R  **Throws:** R  **Height:** 6' 0"  **Weight:** 255

| MLB ETA | CT | FB | CH | CB | SL | OFP | Realistic |
|---|---|---|---|---|---|---|---|
| 2016 | – | 60 | 60 | 60 | – | 60 NO.3 STARTER | 50 NO.4-5 STARTER |

| YEAR | TEAM | LVL | AGE | W | L | SV | G | GS | IP | H | HR | BB | SO | BB9 | SO9 | GB% | BABIP | WHIP | ERA | FIP | FRA | WARP |
|---|---|---|---|---|---|---|---|---|---|---|---|---|---|---|---|---|---|---|---|---|---|---|
| 2013 | CLN | A | 18 | 6 | 6 | 0 | 20 | 20 | 113.3 | 106 | 4 | 18 | 79 | 1.4 | 6.3 | 46% | .282 | 1.09 | 2.78 | 3.01 | 4.02 | 1.8 |
| 2014 | SEA | MLB | 19 | 4 | 6 | 0 | 15 | 15 | 85.0 | 99 | 11 | 36 | 41 | 3.8 | 4.3 | 43% | .299 | 1.59 | 5.36 | 5.54 | 5.83 | -0.9 |
| 2015 | SEA | MLB | 20 | 9 | 11 | 0 | 29 | 29 | 179.3 | 202 | 22 | 59 | 105 | 3.0 | 5.3 | 43% | .300 | 1.46 | 4.94 | 4.71 | 5.37 | -1.1 |

**Breakout:** 0%  **Improve:** 0%  **Collapse:** 0%  **Attrition:** 0%  **MLB:** 0%        *Comparables: Julio Teheran, Taijuan Walker, Jonathan Pettibone*

**Drafted/Acquired:** International free agent, 2011, Venezuela

**Previous Ranking:** #8 (Org)

**What Happened in 2013:** Sanchez made 20 starts in the Midwest League at the age of 18, walking only 18 batters in 113 innings of work.

**Strengths:** Plus-plus pitchability; easy delivery; simple/no frills; despite short/squatty stature, can create angle by pounding the lower zone with lively fastball; can work low-90s; has touched higher; curveball and changeup will both flash plus potential; can locate secondary stuff for strikes; excellent command profile; advanced for age.

**Weaknesses:** Colon-ian body as a teenager; the delivery works and he can repeat, so it's not a major issue; lacks any physical projection; fastball velocity would ebb and flow; would dip into 80s; curveball and changeup can play but might not be impact pitches; curve can get too short and flat; changeup can get too firm in the mid-80s.

**Risk Factor/Injury History:** High risk; teenager with a bad body

**Bret Sayre's Fantasy Take:** If it weren't for his potential future home being a great place to pitch, Sanchez would be a better real-life pitcher than fantasy one. As a potential innings eater (pun intended), his rate stats won't likely cause you to swoon, but they'll add up.

**The Year Ahead:** Sanchez gets a bad rap because of the body, and I'm not suggesting it's something to overlook. But Sanchez makes things look easy, from the delivery and release to strike throwing and sequencing. He knows how to pitch, and his polish and poise on the mound should allow him to find success all the way up to the majors. The secondary stuff can play a little bland, and the fastball isn't so overpowering that he can live on its back forever, but he has a chance to develop into a mid-rotation horse if he can stay healthy and the secondary stuff can tick up.

## 5. Edwin Diaz   RHP

**Born:** 3/22/94   **Age:** 20   **Bats:** R   **Throws:** R   **Height:** 6'2"   **Weight:** 165

| MLB ETA | CT | FB | CH | CB | SL | OFP | Realistic |
|---|---|---|---|---|---|---|---|
| 2017 | — | 70 | 50 | 60 | — | 60 NO.2-3 STARTER | 50 NO.4-5 STARTER |

| YEAR | TEAM | LVL | AGE | W | L | SV | G | GS | IP | H | HR | BB | SO | BB9 | SO9 | GB% | BABIP | WHIP | ERA | FIP | FRA | WARP |
|---|---|---|---|---|---|---|---|---|---|---|---|---|---|---|---|---|---|---|---|---|---|---|
| 2013 | PUL | Rk | 19 | 5 | 2 | 0 | 13 | 13 | 69.0 | 45 | 5 | 18 | 79 | 2.3 | 10.3 | 49% | .260 | 0.91 | 1.43 | 3.04 | 4.37 | 0.8 |
| 2014 | SEA | MLB | 20 | 2 | 3 | 0 | 10 | 6 | 41.7 | 47 | 6 | 28 | 28 | 6.0 | 6.0 | 45% | .309 | 1.80 | 6.05 | 6.16 | 6.58 | -0.7 |
| 2015 | SEA | MLB | 21 | 6 | 8 | 1 | 32 | 18 | 137.7 | 145 | 18 | 81 | 104 | 5.3 | 6.8 | 45% | .298 | 1.65 | 5.56 | 5.31 | 6.04 | -1.7 |

Breakout: 0%     Improve: 0%     Collapse: 0%     Attrition: 0%     MLB: 0%          *Comparables: Carlos Carrasco, Jon Niese, Enny Romero*

**Drafted/Acquired:** 3rd round, 2012 draft, Caguas Military Academy (Caguas, PR)

**Previous Ranking:** On The Rise

**What Happened in 2013:** After starting in extended spring training, Diaz made 13 appearances in the rookie-level Appalachian League, finishing the year with a miniscule era and a prospect trajectory powered by jet fuel.

**Strengths:** Loose, easy arm action; fastball works 92-95; touches higher; big wiggle on the pitch; projects to be a plus-plus offering; can spin a tight curveball in the mid-70s; has depth and can use it as a weapon; skinny frame with some projection; good feel for control; good command projection.

**Weaknesses:** Changeup is below average; needs to improve the feel for the pitch; body needs to add strength; can revert to throwing instead of pitching; likes to live up in the zone.

**Risk Factor/Injury History:** High; has yet to reach full-season ball

**Bret Sayre's Fantasy Take:** It's easy to dream on Diaz being a high-end fantasy starter, and he hasn't given us any reason not to. The fastball/curveball combination could lead to large strikeout totals, and Diaz is a strong candidate to break out at Low-A next season.

**The Year Ahead:** Diaz could explode as a prospect in 2014, as he looks to make the jump to full-season ball. The delivery is smooth and easy, and the arm is very fluid and whippy. The fastball works low- to mid-90s, and he can sit in the higher range without much issue. The secondary stuff needs work, especially the feel for the changeup, but he has plenty of time to refine. This could be the top prospect in the system a year from now.

## 6. Luiz Gohara   LHP

**Born:** 7/31/96   **Age:** 17   **Bats:** L   **Throws:** L   **Height:** 6'3"   **Weight:** 210

| MLB ETA | CT | FB | CH | CB | SL | OFP | Realistic |
|---|---|---|---|---|---|---|---|
| 2018 | — | 60 | 60 | 60 | — | 70 NO.2 STARTER | 50 NO.4-5 STARTER |

| YEAR | TEAM | LVL | AGE | W | L | SV | G | GS | IP | H | HR | BB | SO | BB9 | SO9 | GB% | BABIP | WHIP | ERA | FIP | FRA | WARP |
|---|---|---|---|---|---|---|---|---|---|---|---|---|---|---|---|---|---|---|---|---|---|---|
| 2013 | PUL | Rk | 16 | 1 | 2 | 0 | 6 | 6 | 21.7 | 22 | 1 | 9 | 27 | 3.7 | 11.2 | 68% | .356 | 1.43 | 4.15 | 3.06 | 4.53 | 0.3 |

**Drafted/Acquired:** International free agent, 2012, Brazil

**Previous Ranking:** #7 (Org)

**What Happened in 2013:** The then-16-year-old Brazilian made six starts at rookie-level Pulaski, missing 27 bats in 22 innings against much, much older competition.

**Strengths:** Impressive arm strength; fastball can sit in the low-90s and has touched near-elite velocity in bursts; delivery isn't too complicated; manages size well; shows advanced pitchability; shows multiple breaking ball looks; changeup shows fading action and could end up over plus.

**Weaknesses:** He's a big boy; body could trend negative; fastball velocity was inconsistent; command is below average at present; secondary stuff flashes but lacks consistency; struggles to stay over the ball/finish his delivery.

**Risk Factor/Injury History:** Extreme risk; short-season resume; was born in 1996.

**Bret Sayre's Fantasy Take:** The upside is enormous with Gohara, but ETA matters when filling out a minor-league roster. Stashing a pitcher with his potential can pay off in spades, as he has the raw tools to develop into a front-line fantasy starter, but it's a long time to wait on an arm.

**The Year Ahead:** The Mariners don't have to rush the young Brazilian lefty, so another round of extended spring training and short-season ball could be the ticket, but don't rule out a jump to the full-season level in 2014. The pitchability is there, but the raw stuff is a bit too unruly at times and hard to gain command of. He's a long way off, but the ceiling is enormous. This is a big-bodied lefty with the potential for a plus-plus fastball and a plus secondary arsenal. That's a beast.

---

## 7.  Chris Taylor   SS

**Born:** 8/29/90   **Age:** 23   **Bats:** R   **Throws:** R   **Height:** 6'0"   **Weight:** 170

| MLB ETA | Hit | Power | Run | Glove | Arm | OFP | Realistic |
|---|---|---|---|---|---|---|---|
| 2014 | 50 | – | 60 | 55 | 50 | 50 ML REGULAR | 50 2ND DIV PLAYER |

| YEAR | TEAM | LVL | AGE | PA | R | 2B | 3B | HR | RBI | BB | SO | SB | CS | AVG/OBP/SLG | TAv | BABIP | BRR | FRAA | WARP |
|---|---|---|---|---|---|---|---|---|---|---|---|---|---|---|---|---|---|---|---|
| 2013 | WTN | AA | 22 | 300 | 46 | 12 | 4 | 1 | 16 | 40 | 55 | 18 | 3 | .293/.391/.383 | .296 | .368 | 5.3 | SS(39): 1.6, 2B(25): -0.4 | 3.3 |
| 2013 | HDS | A+ | 22 | 319 | 62 | 16 | 7 | 7 | 44 | 44 | 62 | 20 | 2 | .335/.426/.524 | .320 | .407 | 5.2 | SS(61): 3.6, 2B(2): 0.2 | 4.1 |
| 2014 | SEA | MLB | 23 | 250 | 29 | 10 | 1 | 2 | 17 | 23 | 57 | 10 | 2 | .247/.322/.327 | .250 | .320 | 1.0 | SS 1, 2B 0 | 1.0 |
| 2015 | SEA | MLB | 24 | 250 | 25 | 11 | 2 | 1 | 20 | 22 | 55 | 7 | 1 | .246/.317/.330 | .244 | .315 | 0.7 | SS 1, 2B 0 | 1.1 |

Breakout: 4%   Improve: 25%   Collapse: 2%   Attrition: 19%   MLB: 35%   *Comparables: Chase d'Arnaud, Brad Miller, Brent Lillibridge*

**Drafted/Acquired:** 5th round, 2012 draft, University of Virginia (Charlottesville, VA)

**Previous Ranking:** NR

**What Happened in 2013:** A polished college player, Taylor swung a good bat over two minor-league stops, and continued the trend in the Arizona Fall League, winning over doubters at every stop.

**Strengths:** Baseball skills/field IQ; plus run; above-average leather at short; makes the plays he is supposed to make; has good bat-to-ball skills; could end up a 5+ hitter.

**Weaknesses:** The bat isn't a special weapon; can sting the ball, but won't be a power threat; down-the-lineup glove-first type; solid but not spectacular.

**Risk Factor/Injury History:** Low risk

**Bret Sayre's Fantasy Take:** A 25- or 30-steal threat who can actually hit a little is a tempting package, especially when he comes with shortstop eligibility. Unfortunately, he's blocked by Brad Miller, so the opportunity he needs could be tough to come by in Seattle.

**The Year Ahead:** Taylor is the type of prospect I've traditionally overlooked; he plays the game with skill, but the overall profile isn't sexy and I like sexy. Do not overlook Chris Taylor! He might not end up being anything more than a second-division player, but he can bring a lot to a team with his glove at shortstop and his speed, and the bat might lack punch but he's going to battle at the plate. This is the type of player who sticks around the game for a decade or more, and will most likely have a better career than a healthy chunk of the sexy prospects who get more attention, including the ones ahead of him on this list.

---

## 8.  Tyler Pike   LHP

**Born:** 1/26/94   **Age:** 20   **Bats:** L   **Throws:** L   **Height:** 6'0"   **Weight:** 180

| MLB ETA | CT | FB | CH | CB | SL | OFP | Realistic |
|---|---|---|---|---|---|---|---|
| 2016 | – | 55 | 55 | 50 | – | 55 NO.3-4 STARTER | 50 NO.5 STARTER |

| YEAR | TEAM | LVL | AGE | W | L | SV | G | GS | IP | H | HR | BB | SO | BB9 | SO9 | GB% | BABIP | WHIP | ERA | FIP | FRA | WARP |
|---|---|---|---|---|---|---|---|---|---|---|---|---|---|---|---|---|---|---|---|---|---|---|
| 2013 | CLN | A | 19 | 7 | 4 | 0 | 22 | 22 | 110.3 | 73 | 5 | 57 | 90 | 4.6 | 7.3 | 41% | .233 | 1.18 | 2.37 | 3.87 | 4.73 | 0.9 |
| 2014 | SEA | MLB | 20 | 3 | 4 | 0 | 15 | 10 | 75.0 | 79 | 9 | 47 | 50 | 5.6 | 6.0 | 42% | .295 | 1.68 | 5.39 | 5.68 | 5.86 | -0.8 |
| 2015 | SEA | MLB | 21 | 5 | 6 | 0 | 26 | 16 | 139.3 | 129 | 16 | 78 | 108 | 5.0 | 7.0 | 42% | .274 | 1.49 | 4.51 | 4.91 | 4.91 | -0.1 |

Breakout: 0%   Improve: 0%   Collapse: 0%   Attrition: 0%   MLB: 0%   Comparables:  *Mauricio Robles, Wilmer Font, Phillippe Aumont*

**Drafted/Acquired:** 3rd round, 2012 draft, Winter Haven HS (Winter Haven, FL)

**Previous Ranking:** #9 (Org)

**What Happened in 2013:** Pike made the jump from the AZL in 2013 to full-season ball in 2014, making 22 starts, showing the ability to miss bats and force weak contact against older competition.

**Strengths:** Smooth delivery; pitches with athleticism; fastball can work low-90s, touched higher; good arm-side life on the offering; curveball and changeup can flash; both pitches project to at least solid-average; good feel for sequence.

**Weaknesses:** Fastball velocity would dip into upper-80s; stuff can get soft; curveball break can lack intensity; command is below average; doesn't always attack hitters.

**Risk Factor/Injury History:** High risk; good three-pitch mix but long way to go.

**Bret Sayre's Fantasy Take:** Not someone to target on skills alone from a fantasy perspective, but if he were afforded the opportunity to pitch in Safeco, his raw stats might make him appear more skilled than he actually is. More of a deeper-league flier.

**The Year Ahead:** Pike can flash above-average stuff, but I've never seen him look dominant in my limited sample with the player. The fastball velocity is inconsistent, but when the arm is feeling it, he can work low-90s and touch higher from the left side, showing two average secondary offerings that he can sequence. He's a nice prospect who has a chance to step forward with command refinement and secondary development, but the ceiling doesn't belong in the same building as some of the other young arms in the system.

## 9. Tyler Marlette  C

**Born:** 1/23/93  **Age:** 21  **Bats:** R  **Throws:** R  **Height:** 5' 11"  **Weight:** 195

| MLB ETA | | Hit | Power | Run | Glove | Arm | | OFP | Realistic |
|---------|---|-----|-------|-----|-------|-----|---|-----|-----------|
| 2016 | | 50 | 55 | --- | --- | 60 | | 60<br>1ST DIV PLAYER | 45<br>BACKUP C |

| YEAR | TEAM | LVL | AGE | PA | R | 2B | 3B | HR | RBI | BB | SO | SB | CS | AVG/OBP/SLG | TAv | BABIP | BRR | FRAA | WARP |
|------|------|-----|-----|-----|----|----|----|----|-----|----|----|----|----|-------------|-----|-------|-----|------|------|
| 2013 | CLN | A | 20 | 297 | 36 | 17 | 2 | 6 | 37 | 24 | 53 | 10 | 4 | .304/.367/.448 | .291 | .360 | 0.4 | C(73): 0.9 | 2.8 |
| 2014 | SEA | MLB | 21 | 250 | 21 | 10 | 0 | 4 | 23 | 11 | 68 | 2 | 1 | .218/.254/.312 | .214 | .280 | -0.3 | C 0 | 0.0 |
| 2015 | SEA | MLB | 22 | 250 | 25 | 11 | 0 | 5 | 24 | 12 | 65 | 1 | 0 | .226/.266/.335 | .222 | .289 | -0.6 | C 0 | -0.8 |

Breakout: 0%    Improve: 0%    Collapse: 0%    Attrition: 0%    MLB: 0%          *Comparables: Welington Castillo, Neil Walker, Devin Mesoraco*

**Drafted/Acquired:** 5th round, 2011 draft, Hagerty HS (Oviedo, FL)

**Previous Ranking:** NR

**What Happened in 2013:** With only a short-season resume since signing in 2011, Marlette finally advanced to the full-season level, and the offensive potential that made him a fifth-round pick was on display in the Midwest League.

**Strengths:** Comes from a highly competitive amateur background; shows bat speed; power potential; excellent raw strength and lift in the bat; arm is strong behind the plate; lauded work ethic and makeup; receiving skills improved.

**Weaknesses:** Offense is ahead of the glove; plate discipline and approach need work; needs to slow down on defense; rushes throws; footwork needs refinement; hit tool could limit game power.

**Risk Factor/Injury History:** High risk; dual-threat developmental plan

**Bret Sayre's Fantasy Take:** In leagues where fewer than 15 catchers are rostered, Marlette probably does not have the type of upside you'd want to see out of a prospect at the position. If he's a .260 hitter with 15-18 bombs, that's nice in deeper leagues, but it's essentially what Wilson Ramos did in 2013—and he didn't crack the top 15.

**The Year Ahead:** Scouts seem to like Marlette, dating back to his amateur days when his power was turning heads on the showcase circuit. As a receiver, he is still raw, and the bat is still the driving force in his status. But his makeup and competitive background offer hope when it comes to his defensive development behind the plate, and even though his road to the majors won't be expedited because of the dual-threat process, the long-term outcome could be a very good player, one who can show not only some bat-to-ball ability and pop, but also catch-and-throw skills behind the plate. That's a valuable player.

## 10. Gabriel Guerrero  CF

**Born:** 12/11/93  **Age:** 20  **Bats:** R  **Throws:** R  **Height:** 6' 3"  **Weight:** 190

| MLB ETA | | Hit | Power | Run | Glove | Arm | | OFP | Realistic |
|---------|---|-----|-------|-----|-------|-----|---|-----|-----------|
| 2016 | | --- | 70 | --- | --- | 60 | | 60<br>1ST DIV PLAYER | 40<br>FRINGE ML/AAA |

| YEAR | TEAM | LVL | AGE | PA | R | 2B | 3B | HR | RBI | BB | SO | SB | CS | AVG/OBP/SLG | TAv | BABIP | BRR | FRAA | WARP |
|------|------|-----|-----|-----|----|----|----|----|-----|----|----|----|----|-------------|-----|-------|-----|------|------|
| 2013 | CLN | A | 19 | 499 | 60 | 23 | 3 | 4 | 50 | 21 | 113 | 12 | 3 | .271/.303/.358 | .251 | .344 | 1.8 | RF(121): 10.0 | 1.3 |
| 2014 | SEA | MLB | 20 | 250 | 18 | 9 | 1 | 3 | 22 | 5 | 71 | 1 | 1 | .215/.230/.299 | .201 | .290 | -0.4 | RF 2, LF -0 | -0.8 |
| 2015 | SEA | MLB | 21 | 250 | 24 | 10 | 1 | 5 | 24 | 8 | 67 | 0 | 0 | .235/.259/.347 | .223 | .301 | -0.5 | RF 2 | -0.8 |

Breakout: 0%    Improve: 0%    Collapse: 0%    Attrition: 0%    MLB: 0%          *Comparables: Moises Sierra, Avisail Garcia, Domonic Brown*

**Drafted/Acquired:** International free agent, 2011, Dominican Republic

**Previous Ranking:** On The Rise

**What Happened in 2013:** After a slow start in an unforgiving environment for a hitter, Guerrero stepped forward in the second half of the season, hitting .306/.340/.396 in the warmer months of the summer.

**Strengths:** High-end bat speed; very loose; hand-eye coordination is ridiculous; raw power is a 7; game power could play as a 6; good athlete who can handle either left or right field; arm has plus arm strength; Hall of Fame bloodlines.

**Weaknesses:** Pitch-recognition skills are a concern; will expand and chase out of the zone; struggles with soft/spin; reactionary hitter who looks to rip regardless of sequence or setting; hit tool could pull the power down; not an up-the-middle defender.

**Risk Factor/Injury History:** High risk; very raw

**Bret Sayre's Fantasy Take:** With 30-homer potential, Guerrero is a pure upside play toward the end of your minor-league roster. But too many Guerrero types on your roster and you risk having a very dry pipeline.

**The Year Ahead:** I've been very high on Guerrero in the past, and I remain enamored by his offensive skill set. The bat speed is very good, and the easy, loose swing is reminiscent of his famous uncle and physical doppelganger. But the pitch-recognition issues are the red flag here, the kind of issue that can spoil the offensive potential. This year will be a very good test for the young hitter, as he will see better off-speed offerings as he climbs the ladder, and if he can refine his approach and work himself into more favorable fastball counts, the bat might let the power play. If that happens, Guerrero has impact potential.

## Prospects on the Rise

**1. OF Tyler O'Neill:** A third-round draft selection in 2013, O'Neill has drawn the obvious comparisons to fellow Canadian Brett Lawrie. Like Lawrie, O'Neill is a hyper-intense bulldog of a player, with an impressive hit tool and approach to the game. He could take a big step forward in 2014 and emerge as a top-10 prospect in the system.

**2. OF Wilton Martinez:** With a projectable body and highly project-able offensive tools, Martinez looks the part of a prototypical corner bat. He's still raw—and the numbers might not back up the hype for a while—but the bat speed and raw pop are there to develop into a legit middle-of-the-order prospect.

**3. SS Ketel Marte:** A 20-year-old Dominican with legit defensive skills at shortstop, Marte is a precocious talent who could end up developing into a dual-threat player at the highest level. Power will never be a part of his game, but with plus speed and very good bat-to-ball skills, he has a chance to hit for average from a premium spot on the diamond.

## Factors on the Farm

### Prospects likely to contribute at the major-league level in 2014

**1. RHP Carson Smith:** It's easy to make a case for Smith's inclusion in the top 10, as his fastball/slider combination gives him a high floor as a quality major-league reliever. The fastball is pretty nasty, thrown with plus velocity and lots of movement, and if the slider can tighten up, he has late-innings potential.

**2. RHP Dominic Leone:** An undersized righty with big stuff and a future in a big-league bullpen, Leone is a good bet to contribute to the major-league team in 2014. Working with a heavy mid-90s fastball, hard cutter, and slider combo, Leone has the ability to miss barrels and force a lot of weak contact.

**3. 1B Ji-Man Choi:** The 22-year-old South Korean isn't a big-name prospect—nor should he be considered a big-name prospect—but he does have some pop in his stick, and he could find his way into major-league action in 2014. The power could play to a 5, meaning he could probably hit 15-20 bombs over a full season, but it comes from a first-base profile, so don't expect anything more than a second-division player at best.

---

## FROM THE FIELD

### Taijuan Walker

**Player:** Taijuan Walker

**Team:** Seattle Mariners

**Filed by:** Steffan Segui

**Date(s) Seen:** April 25 and June 8, 2013

**Physical:** Big, imposing pitcher on mound. About filled out. Lean but strong and solid.

**Mechanics/Delivery:** Very controlled and quiet in his delivery. Hands and lead leg work in rhythm with a tick of pause at balance. Bit of a jab with a very fast arm to a high 3/4 arm slot with good angle. High finish causes some command inconsistency.

**Fastball:** 70 grade. Plus-plus pitch. Special life, especially arm side. Command is just okay. Maintains velocity, hit 99 on 108th pitch in April game.

**Cutter:** 70 grade. Sharp and late. Uses a lot early. Throws in low-90s. Good command.

**Curveball:** 60 grade. Potential to be a plus pitch. Can be a little firmer. Has bouts of control loss of it.

**Changeup:** 50 grade. A bit too hard. Straight. Decent effect.

**Makeup:** 70 grade. Reached the majors the month he turned 21.

**OFP:** 70; no. 1 starter.

**Realistic Role:** 65; no. 2 starter.

**Risk:** Very low; 53 starts at Double-A or higher. Will start 2014 in MLB rotation.

# ST. LOUIS CARDINALS

## 1. Oscar Taveras    CF

**Born:** 6/19/92   **Age:** 22   **Bats:** L   **Throws:** L   **Height:** 6' 2"   **Weight:** 200

| MLB ETA | Hit | Power | Run | Glove | Arm | OFP | Realistic |
|---|---|---|---|---|---|---|---|
| 2014 | 80 | 70 | 50 | 50 | 50 | 70 PERENNIAL ALL-STAR | 65 1ST DIV/ALL-STAR |

| YEAR | TEAM | LVL | AGE | PA | R | 2B | 3B | HR | RBI | BB | SO | SB | CS | AVG/OBP/SLG | TAv | BABIP | BRR | FRAA | WARP |
|---|---|---|---|---|---|---|---|---|---|---|---|---|---|---|---|---|---|---|---|
| 2013 | MEM | AAA | 21 | 186 | 25 | 12 | 0 | 5 | 32 | 9 | 22 | 5 | 1 | .306/.341/.462 | .288 | .324 | -1.0 | CF(34): -1.4, RF(6): -0.5 | 0.8 |
| 2013 | CRD | Rk | 21 | 2 | 0 | 1 | 0 | 0 | 0 | 1 | 0 | 0 | 0 | 1.00/1.00/2.00 | .712 | 1.000 | -0.1 | CF(1): -0.0 | 0.1 |
| 2014 | SLN | MLB | 22 | 250 | 28 | 14 | 2 | 7 | 32 | 13 | 37 | 2 | 1 | .288/.328/.456 | .283 | .310 | -0.1 | CF -1, RF -0 | 1.1 |
| 2015 | SLN | MLB | 23 | 616 | 76 | 38 | 5 | 19 | 79 | 34 | 93 | 5 | 2 | .287/.330/.468 | .287 | .313 | -0.4 | RF -9 | 1.6 |

**Breakout:** 5%   **Improve:** 31%   **Collapse:** 5%   **Attrition:** 24%   **MLB:** 66%   *Comparables: Colby Rasmus, Wil Myers, Adam Jones*

**Drafted/Acquired:** International free agent, 2008, Dominican Republic

**Previous Ranking:** #1 (Org), #2 (Top 101)

**What Happened in 2013:** A high-ankle injury spoiled what was to be his major-league breakout, limiting Taveras to only 46 games in Triple-A.

**Strengths:** Elite hit tool potential; natural feel for barreling the baseball; elite hands; elite bat speed; controlled chaos in the swing; batting title future; power will flow from the hit tool; raw power is near elite; game power likely to play above plus; arm is strong; good athlete with instincts for the game; average run; average (or better) glove; special offensive profile.

**Weaknesses:** Greedy at the plate; thinks he can hit every pitch thrown (usually can); can lose counts because of aggressive approach; reads/routes need work in center; good athlete but lacks plus run; baserunning needs refinement.

**Risk Factor/Injury History:** Low risk; ready for majors; ankle injury on resume (2013).

**Bret Sayre's Fantasy Take:** There's a group of four elite fantasy prospects right now, and Taveras is squarely in the middle of it. There's no one who can touch his batting average projection, which could be league-leading, but he's certainly no slouch in power either (think 25-30 homers, realistically)—and he can even sprinkle in a couple of steals. This is a potential future first-rounder here, and a player to build around for the future.

**The Year Ahead:** Taveras lost some of his high-gloss prospect shine in 2013, but only because he was limited by a nagging ankle injury that prevented him from climbing to the major-league level, becoming a media darling in the postseason, and admitting to a national audience that his long-term goal is to become my best friend. The bat is very special, with electric hands, ferocious bat speed, and contact so easy and natural that it's conceivable that Taveras shares a genetic relationship with the bat in his hand. He's ready to hit at the major-league level, and the medicals suggest the ankle will be ready to go for 2014, so whenever he gets to promotion, be prepared to watch a future batting champion and perennial all-star.

> #3
> BP Top 101 Prospects

## 2. Kolten Wong    2B

**Born:** 10/10/90   **Age:** 23   **Bats:** L   **Throws:** R   **Height:** 5' 9"   **Weight:** 185

| MLB ETA | Hit | Power | Run | Glove | Arm | OFP | Realistic |
|---|---|---|---|---|---|---|---|
| Debuted in 2013 | 65 | 50 | 50 | 60 | – | 60 1ST DIV PLAYER | 50 ML REGULAR |

| YEAR | TEAM | LVL | AGE | PA | R | 2B | 3B | HR | RBI | BB | SO | SB | CS | AVG/OBP/SLG | TAv | BABIP | BRR | FRAA | WARP |
|---|---|---|---|---|---|---|---|---|---|---|---|---|---|---|---|---|---|---|---|
| 2013 | MEM | AAA | 22 | 463 | 68 | 21 | 8 | 10 | 45 | 41 | 60 | 20 | 1 | .303/.369/.466 | .307 | .332 | 0.7 | 2B(102): 12.9 | 4.9 |
| 2013 | SLN | MLB | 22 | 62 | 6 | 1 | 0 | 0 | 0 | 3 | 12 | 3 | 0 | .153/.194/.169 | .143 | .191 | 0.6 | 2B(18): 1.3 | -0.4 |
| 2014 | SLN | MLB | 23 | 250 | 29 | 11 | 2 | 4 | 21 | 15 | 39 | 7 | 2 | .264/.311/.376 | .254 | .300 | 0.7 | 2B 4 | 1.2 |
| 2015 | SLN | MLB | 24 | 481 | 50 | 21 | 5 | 7 | 46 | 29 | 71 | 13 | 4 | .257/.308/.374 | .251 | .289 | 1.2 | 2B 8 | 2.4 |

**Breakout:** 3%   **Improve:** 33%   **Collapse:** 2%   **Attrition:** 15%   **MLB:** 46%   *Comparables: Steve Lombardozzi, Adrian Cardenas, Luis Valbuena*

**Drafted/Acquired:** 1st round, 2011 draft, University of Hawaii (Honolulu, HI)

**Previous Ranking:** #6 (Org), #90 (Top 101)

**What Happened in 2013:** Wong crushed in Triple-A, but struggled with the stick at the major-league level, retarding his prospect value in some circles.

**Strengths:** Tremendous feel for baseball; natural hitter; quick stroke; more pop than size suggests; hit tool projects to be plus (or better); several sources see a future .300 hitter; doubles power, but can put balls in the seats; above-average glove at second; overall defensive profile could play above average despite fringe arm; runs well; instincts and makeup.

> #33
> BP Top 101 Prospects

**Weaknesses:** Setup (leg lift) can affect balance/landing; can struggle with off-speed; lacks plus game power; likely to play below average; arm is fringe; accurate but lacks much arm strength; aside from hit tool, needs instincts and aptitude to play up to potential.

**Risk Factor/Injury History:** Low risk; achieved major-league level.

**Bret Sayre's Fantasy Take:** Power production will be the big driver of Wong's future value. He's ready to start for the Cardinals now, and he should be a good all-around player, especially in deep leagues. In shallow leagues, without 12- to 15-homer pop, he just becomes a guy who can hit around .280 with 20 steals—and while that's above replacement level, it's essentially a poor man's Jose Altuve.

**The Year Ahead:** It's generic to suggest, but the best way to describe Wong is to say he's a gamer, a player who shows obvious feel and instincts for the game, which allows his average physical tools to play up. The hit tool could actually play above plus, as he shows excellent bat-to-ball ability, but the rest of his game lacks much impact and could keep him from becoming more than just a major-league regular. With a longer look and time to adjust, Wong is going to hit at the highest level, and given his style and approach to the game, it won't take him long to establish himself as a fan favorite.

---

# 3.  Stephen Piscotty   RF

**Born:** 1/14/91   **Age:** 23   **Bats:** R   **Throws:** R   **Height:** 6' 3"   **Weight:** 210

| MLB ETA | Hit | Power | Run | Glove | Arm | OFP | Realistic |
|---|---|---|---|---|---|---|---|
| 2014 | 70 | 50 | 50 | 55 | 70 | 70<br>1ST DIV/ALL-STAR | 55<br>>AVG REGULAR |

| YEAR | TEAM | LVL | AGE | PA | R | 2B | 3B | HR | RBI | BB | SO | SB | CS | AVG/OBP/SLG | TAv | BABIP | BRR | FRAA | WARP |
|---|---|---|---|---|---|---|---|---|---|---|---|---|---|---|---|---|---|---|---|
| 2013 | SFD | AA | 22 | 207 | 17 | 9 | 0 | 6 | 24 | 19 | 19 | 7 | 3 | .299/.364/.446 | .292 | .304 | -4.3 | RF(48): 0.6 | 0.6 |
| 2013 | PMB | A+ | 22 | 264 | 30 | 14 | 2 | 9 | 35 | 18 | 27 | 4 | 5 | .292/.348/.477 | .296 | .300 | 1.1 | RF(59): -1.7 | 1.4 |
| 2014 | SLN | MLB | 23 | 250 | 26 | 11 | 1 | 6 | 28 | 14 | 38 | 3 | 1 | .261/.308/.394 | .259 | .280 | -0.4 | RF -0, 3B -0 | 0.4 |
| 2015 | SLN | MLB | 24 | 250 | 28 | 12 | 1 | 6 | 28 | 13 | 37 | 2 | 1 | .262/.308/.398 | .259 | .285 | -0.5 | RF -1, 3B 0 | 1.3 |

Breakout: 2%   Improve: 21%   Collapse: 2%   Attrition: 11%   MLB: 37%          *Comparables: Caleb Gindl, Moises Sierra, Adam Eaton*

**#66**
**BP Top 101 Prospects**

**Drafted/Acquired:** 1st round, 2012 draft, Stanford University (Palo Alto, CA)

**Previous Ranking:** NR

**What Happened in 2013:** TINSTAASS: There is no such thing as a Stanford swing

**Strengths:** Natural hitter; has a knack for making hard contact to all fields; can shorten up or add length/leverage to stroke; good balance; minimal movement in setup; good approach; hit tool could play to plus-plus; game power should play average or better; arm is easy plus-plus; weapon in right; athletic and runs well; good glove/range for position.

**Weaknesses:** Bat speed isn't special; can get tied up by inside velocity; doesn't project to hit for plus power; more doubles/gaps than over the fence; still refining as an outfielder; glove likely to play average.

**Risk Factor/Injury History:** Low risk; 49 games at Double-A level.

**Bret Sayre's Fantasy Take:** Piscotty is a potential .300 hitter at the major-league level and can augment that with 15-20 homers. That may not be a fantasy star, but it's certainly someone who will be plenty helpful in leagues of any size—especially in a points format. Like any other Cardinals position prospect, he may not get regular at-bats as quickly as his talent may dictate.

**The Year Ahead:** Piscotty can absolutely rake, plain and simple. He might not end up hitting for plus over-the-fence power, but you can see a projection where he hits .300 with 30+ doubles and 15 homers. Piscotty should develop into a solid-average right fielder, with a laser arm and more than enough athleticism for the position. It won't take long for Piscotty to force the issue at the major-league level; a logjam of first-division outfield talent waiting for the opportunity to make an already strong team even stronger. The first three prospects on this list could eventually end up hitting .300 at the major-league level. That's pretty crazy. LogJammin'.

---

# 4.  Alexander Reyes   RHP

**Born:** 8/29/94   **Age:** 19   **Bats:** R   **Throws:** R   **Height:** 6' 3"   **Weight:** 185

| MLB ETA | CT | FB | CH | CB | SL | OFP | Realistic |
|---|---|---|---|---|---|---|---|
| 2017 | – | 70 | 55 | 70 | – | 70<br>NO.2 STARTER | 55<br>NO.4 STARTER |

| YEAR | TEAM | LVL | AGE | W | L | SV | G | GS | IP | H | HR | BB | SO | BB9 | SO9 | GB% | BABIP | WHIP | ERA | FIP | FRA | WARP |
|---|---|---|---|---|---|---|---|---|---|---|---|---|---|---|---|---|---|---|---|---|---|---|
| 2013 | JCY | Rk | 18 | 6 | 4 | 0 | 12 | 12 | 58.3 | 54 | 1 | 28 | 68 | 4.3 | 10.5 | 45% | .349 | 1.41 | 3.39 | 2.97 | 4.25 | 1.1 |
| 2014 | SLN | MLB | 19 | 2 | 4 | 0 | 8 | 8 | 39.7 | 45 | 5 | 25 | 23 | 5.7 | 5.2 | 43% | .324 | 1.75 | 6.06 | 5.86 | 6.59 | -0.7 |
| 2015 | SLN | MLB | 20 | 8 | 10 | 0 | 29 | 29 | 181.7 | 181 | 19 | 95 | 128 | 4.7 | 6.3 | 43% | .308 | 1.52 | 4.89 | 4.69 | 5.32 | -1.1 |

Breakout: 0%   Improve: 0%   Collapse: 0%   Attrition: 0%   MLB: 0%          *Comparables: Jenrry Mejia, Jonathan Pettibone, Julio Teheran*

**Drafted/Acquired:** International free agent, 2012, Dominican Republic

**Previous Ranking:** NR

**What Happened in 2013:** In his professional debut, Reyes flashed his frontline upside in the Appalachian League, missing 68 bats in only 12 starts.

**Strengths:** Prototypical size; room for physical projection; electric arm speed; easy action and smooth release; fastball already works plus; projects to be plus-plus; 92-98 mph with late action; curveball could be second well-above-average offering; hard breaker with tight rotation and heavy vertical bite; feel for changeup; could end up playing above average; delivery conducive to command projection.

**Weaknesses:** Needs general refinement; still transitioning from thrower to pitcher; needs to sharpen up command; work on sequencing; PFP refinement; holding runners; changeup is third offering; can overthrow the pitch; more deliberate in release.

**Risk Factor/Injury History:** High risk; short-season resume.

**Bret Sayre's Fantasy Take:** One of two international arms to make the Fantasy 101, Reyes has enough upside to overcome his ETA right now. With his raw stuff and the Cardinals' ability to transform tools into performance, he could be a big riser on this list next season and has the potential to be a top fantasy pitching prospect in baseball not long after that.

**The Year Ahead:** It's a high-risk profile, but Reyes has the highest ceiling of any arm on the Cardinals farm, a frontline type who should eventually move into the upper tier of all prospects in the minors. He is still raw and needs refinement across the board, but has feel despite being a power arm, and could end up being a faster mover than his risk might suggest. With good present size and remaining physical projection, a clean delivery, a plus-plus potential arsenal, and pitchability, it would be difficult to build a more prototypical frontline pitching prospect, and with a strong debut at the full-season level in 2014, Reyes could rank among the top arms in the minors. This is legit.

---

## 5. Marco Gonzales LHP

**Born:** 2/16/92 **Age:** 22 **Bats:** L **Throws:** L **Height:** 6'0" **Weight:** 185

| MLB ETA | CT | FB | CH | CB | SL | | OFP | Realistic |
|---|---|---|---|---|---|---|---|---|
| Late 2015 | – | 55 | 75 | 50 | – | | 60 NO.3 STARTER | 50 NO.4 STARTER |

| YEAR | TEAM | LVL | AGE | W | L | SV | G | GS | IP | H | HR | BB | SO | BB9 | SO9 | GB% | BABIP | WHIP | ERA | FIP | FRA | WARP |
|---|---|---|---|---|---|---|---|---|---|---|---|---|---|---|---|---|---|---|---|---|---|---|
| 2013 | PMB | A+ | 21 | 0 | 0 | 0 | 4 | 4 | 16.7 | 10 | 1 | 5 | 13 | 2.7 | 7.0 | 33% | .214 | 0.90 | 1.62 | 3.36 | 4.48 | 0.1 |
| 2013 | CRD | Rk | 21 | 0 | 0 | 0 | 4 | 2 | 6.7 | 8 | 0 | 3 | 10 | 4.1 | 13.5 | 63% | .421 | 1.65 | 5.40 | 1.81 | 4.30 | 0.2 |
| 2014 | SLN | MLB | 22 | 2 | 3 | 0 | 10 | 7 | 35.3 | 37 | 4 | 16 | 24 | 4.1 | 6.1 | 44% | .317 | 1.50 | 4.95 | 4.85 | 5.38 | -0.1 |
| 2015 | SLN | MLB | 23 | 5 | 7 | 1 | 37 | 23 | 163.0 | 168 | 17 | 76 | 128 | 4.2 | 7.1 | 44% | .326 | 1.50 | 4.69 | 4.32 | 5.10 | -0.5 |

**Breakout:** 0% **Improve:** 0% **Collapse:** 0% **Attrition:** 0% **MLB:** 0% *Comparables: Matt Magill, Cesar Carrillo, Zach Phillips*

**Drafted/Acquired:** 1st round, 2013, Gonzaga University (Spokane, Washington)

**Previous Ranking:** NR

**What Happened in 2013:** Popped with the 19th overall pick in the 2013 draft, Gonzales has a changeup that one source referred to as the best secondary pitch in the minors.

**Strengths:** Fluid, athletic delivery; repeats mechanics and consistent with release point; fastball plays to solid-average; upper-80s/low-90s; grade elevated by command and late arm-side life; changeup is a religious experience pitch; easy plus-plus; some sources go to 8 with future grade; exceptional deception from the fastball/arm in combination with action; plays with two breaking balls; curveball should get to average; command should play to plus; great makeup.

**Weaknesses:** Athletic but not physically imposing; fastball velocity is pedestrian; has to hit his spots to find success; breaking balls lack plus potential; curveball is loose, not of the hammer variety; command needs refinement to hit projection.

**Risk Factor/Injury History:** Moderate risk; limited professional experience; ready to move fast.

**Bret Sayre's Fantasy Take:** Lefties with great changeups can miss bats just as well as right-handers with great breaking balls, so while Gonzales doesn't have a special fastball, he can provide a lot of fantasy value if the change is what it can be. In a beneficial home park and division, Gonzales could post an ERA south of 3.50 along with a strong WHIP.

**The Year Ahead:** Gonzales can ride his smutty changeup all the way to the majors, despite setting it up with an average fastball and a fringe (present) breaking-ball assortment. His command will have to be sharp to reach his ceiling, but getting bats moving with a decent fastball will allow the mighty changeup to disrupt the timing and balance of hitters and miss bats and barrels alike. The 22-year-old should reach Double-A very early in his professional career, and could challenge for a major-league job at some point in 2015. Given the explicit rating on his changeup, he probably won't face much of a challenge until he reaches that level.

## 6. Carson Kelly   C

**Born:** 7/14/94   **Age:** 19   **Bats:** R   **Throws:** R   **Height:** 6' 2"   **Weight:** 200

| MLB ETA | Hit | Power | Run | Glove | Arm | | OFP | Realistic |
|---|---|---|---|---|---|---|---|---|
| 2017 | 55 | 60 | – | 55 | 65 | | 60<br>1ST DIV PLAYER | 50<br>ML REGULAR |

| YEAR | TEAM | LVL | AGE | PA | R | 2B | 3B | HR | RBI | BB | SO | SB | CS | AVG/OBP/SLG | TAv | BABIP | BRR | FRAA | WARP |
|---|---|---|---|---|---|---|---|---|---|---|---|---|---|---|---|---|---|---|---|
| 2013 | PEO | A | 18 | 168 | 18 | 6 | 0 | 2 | 13 | 13 | 25 | 0 | 0 | .219/.288/.301 | .242 | .248 | 0.2 | 3B(31): -4.9 | -0.3 |
| 2013 | SCO | A- | 18 | 299 | 35 | 16 | 1 | 4 | 32 | 20 | 31 | 1 | 0 | .277/.340/.387 | .260 | .301 | -0.9 | 3B(64): -7.2 | -0.1 |
| 2014 | SLN | MLB | 19 | 250 | 19 | 9 | 0 | 4 | 23 | 10 | 55 | 0 | 0 | .211/.246/.301 | .204 | .250 | -0.5 | 3B -9 | -1.8 |
| 2015 | SLN | MLB | 20 | 250 | 27 | 11 | 0 | 7 | 28 | 9 | 41 | 0 | 0 | .242/.274/.380 | .240 | .261 | -0.6 | 3B -9 | -0.8 |

Breakout: 0%    Improve: 0%    Collapse: 0%    Attrition: 0%    MLB: 0%          *Comparables: Josh Vitters, Nolan Arenado, Matt Davidson*

**Drafted/Acquired:** 2nd round, 2012 draft, Westview HS (Portland, OR)

**Previous Ranking:** #10 (Org)

**What Happened in 2013:** A second-round pick in the 2012 draft, Kelly shows a lot of promise with the stick, but the overall value just received a shot in the arm with a positional move behind the plate.

**Strengths:** Good athlete, with size and strength; strong arm; good feel for hitting; has quality at-bats; hit tool projects to solid-average; bat speed and strength to project for solid-average to plus game power; high baseball IQ; top-shelf makeup.

**Weaknesses:** New to position; needs to learn/refine footwork; strong arm but limited experience throwing from behind the plate; game calling is at beginning stages; hit tool isn't impact; good swing but unlikely to develop into plus bat; swing can show some violence and could struggle against better arms/better secondary stuff.

**Risk Factor/Injury History:** High risk; new developmental trajectory; dual threat.

**Bret Sayre's Fantasy Take:** This is an interesting one. Kelly was a fringe fantasy prospect as a third baseman, but as a catcher, the bat becomes very interesting. He's a long way from realizing any of this, but he certainly falls above the Blake Swihart line as far as future potential goes. Could be a .270 hitter with 20-25 homers.

**The Year Ahead:** While Kelly might not have profiled as a solid third baseman, his skill set is a much better fit behind the plate, where his strong arm can be a weapon, his athleticism can be an asset instead of an obstacle, and his overall baseball aptitude can take a solid-average profile to a higher level. It's going to take time and patience, but the defensive opportunities and the offensive projections could make Kelly a first-division talent at a premium position. The bat has a good chance to take a step forward in 2014, and I expect more over-the-fence power to show up in another pass in Peoria. As he rounds into shape behind the plate, Kelly's prospect stock should soar.

## 7. Rob Kaminsky   LHP

**Born:** 9/2/94   **Age:** 19   **Bats:** R   **Throws:** L   **Height:** 5' 11"   **Weight:** 191

| MLB ETA | CT | FB | CH | CB | SL | | OFP | Realistic |
|---|---|---|---|---|---|---|---|---|
| 2017 | – | 60 | 55 | 70 | – | | 60<br>NO.3 STARTER | 50<br>NO.5 STARTER |

| YEAR | TEAM | LVL | AGE | W | L | SV | G | GS | IP | H | HR | BB | SO | BB9 | SO9 | GB% | BABIP | WHIP | ERA | FIP | FRA | WARP |
|---|---|---|---|---|---|---|---|---|---|---|---|---|---|---|---|---|---|---|---|---|---|---|
| 2013 | CRD | Rk | 18 | 0 | 3 | 0 | 8 | 5 | 22.0 | 23 | 1 | 9 | 28 | 3.7 | 11.5 | 53% | .373 | 1.45 | 3.68 | 2.87 | 3.31 | 0.3 |
| 2014 | SLN | MLB | 19 | 1 | 2 | 0 | 10 | 5 | 33.3 | 38 | 4 | 20 | 19 | 5.4 | 5.1 | 46% | .324 | 1.75 | 6.11 | 5.73 | 6.64 | -0.5 |
| 2015 | SLN | MLB | 20 | 4 | 5 | 1 | 34 | 15 | 133.7 | 137 | 17 | 68 | 98 | 4.6 | 6.6 | 46% | .314 | 1.54 | 5.12 | 4.89 | 5.57 | -1.0 |

Breakout: 0%    Improve: 0%    Collapse: 0%    Attrition: 0%    MLB: 0%          *Comparables: Brad Hand, Stolmy Pimentel, Jonathan Pettibone*

**Drafted/Acquired:** 1st round, 2013 draft, St. Joseph Regional HS (Montvale, NJ)

**Previous Ranking:** NR

**What Happened in 2013:** Diminutive southpaw with one of the best (if not the best) curveballs in the entire draft class, Kaminsky wasted little time showing off his bat-missing prowess in his eight Gulf Coast League appearances.

**Strengths:** Short but pitches tall with high slot; creates some plane; fastball is average at present, but can push the velocity into plus range; some action to the arm side; projects as plus offering; curveball is future plus-plus offering; big tumble with tight rotation and depth; hard for bats to adjust to; changeup plays well off fastball; fringe at present but projectable; solid-average command projection; competitive.

**Weaknesses:** Fastball command is fringe at present; can struggle to finish his delivery and work down (which is necessary for him to create plane); curveball is a developed pitch and is often used as the primary to a fault; fastball velocity can play down; upper-80s and flat when he elevates; changeup is fringe at present; can sail the pitch and lose action.

**Risk Factor/Injury History:** High risk; limited professional experience; 19 years old.

**Bret Sayre's Fantasy Take:** There may be more fantasy upside to Kaminsky than Gonzales, but there's also more risk and a longer timeline. Which you prefer may just come down to philosophy. The diminutive lefty will be pitching in a great park for his fly-ball-inducing skills, and he could rack up close to 200 strikeouts a year if the curveball develops into the monster pitch it could.

**The Year Ahead:** Kaminsky has all the necessary components to start, despite limited size or physical projection. He has some pitchability, and the fastball has more projection than fellow southpaw Gonzales. As he adds strength to his frame and settles into more consistent velocity, the fastball should develop into an excellent compliment to his already monster curveball, a pairing that should allow him to miss a lot of bats at the minor-league level. The changeup and command need work, but he's a 19-year-old arm with limited professional experience, so refinement will come in the developmental process.

## 8. Randal Grichuk    RF

**Born:** 8/13/91    **Age:** 22    **Bats:** R    **Throws:** R    **Height:** 6' 1"    **Weight:** 195

| MLB ETA | Hit | Power | Run | Glove | Arm | | OFP | Realistic |
|---|---|---|---|---|---|---|---|---|
| Late 2014 | ---- | 60 | ---- | 50 | 50 | | 50<br>2ND DIV PLAYER | 45<br>PLTN BAT/4TH OF |

| YEAR | TEAM | LVL | AGE | PA | R | 2B | 3B | HR | RBI | BB | SO | SB | CS | AVG/OBP/SLG | TAv | BABIP | BRR | FRAA | WARP |
|---|---|---|---|---|---|---|---|---|---|---|---|---|---|---|---|---|---|---|---|
| 2013 | ARK | AA | 21 | 542 | 85 | 27 | 8 | 22 | 64 | 28 | 92 | 9 | 5 | .256/.306/.474 | .285 | .272 | 3.0 | RF(95): 13.0, CF(23): -0.8 | 4.3 |
| 2014 | SLN | MLB | 22 | 250 | 25 | 11 | 2 | 7 | 29 | 6 | 52 | 3 | 1 | .242/.269/.397 | .243 | .280 | 0.1 | RF 2, CF 0 | 0.3 |
| 2015 | SLN | MLB | 23 | 250 | 29 | 11 | 3 | 8 | 31 | 10 | 51 | 2 | 1 | .247/.287/.428 | .260 | .279 | 0.0 | RF 2, CF 0 | 1.7 |

Breakout: 0%    Improve: 0%    Collapse: 0%    Attrition: 0%    MLB: 0%        *Comparables: Carlos Gonzalez, Josh Reddick, Aaron Cunningham*

**Drafted/Acquired:** 1st round, 2009 draft, Lamar Consolidated HS (Rosenberg, TX)

**Previous Ranking:** #4 (Org; Angels)

**What Happened in 2013:** Grichuk enjoyed good health for the second straight season, allowing him to take a step forward in his development and move beyond the injury issues that slowed his progress after being drafted.

**Strengths:** Good athlete; can handle the demands of right; arm is solid-average; has good raw strength and power; can drive the ball out of the ballpark; good natural lift to the swing; has some bat speed; good hitter against left-handers; leaves it all on the field.

**Weaknesses:** Doesn't make consistent contact; struggles against arm-side pitching; will get aggressive at the plate; susceptible to good off-speed stuff; lacks up-the-middle defensive profile; has power but hit tool could limit utility.

**Risk Factor/Injury History:** Low risk; injury free for two full seasons; 500 at-bats at Double-A level.

**Bret Sayre's Fantasy Take:** Outside of NL-only leagues, Grichuk has minimal value, as the combination of non-sexy eligibility and a fantasy ceiling that is barely above replacement leaves a lot to be desired.

**The Year Ahead:** Grichuk could develop into an average player at the highest level, which sounds like a pejorative outcome, but that is far from the truth. If you assume the hit tool manages to play to fringe-average, but he makes enough contact to let his raw power play, Grichuk could be a .250 type with 15-20 bombs, all from a decent defensive profile in right field. That's a second-division player, and that's probably the ceiling here, but that's still a valuable commodity to have under cost control for six seasons.

## 9. Tim Cooney    LHP

**Born:** 12/19/90    **Age:** 23    **Bats:** L    **Throws:** L    **Height:** 6' 3"    **Weight:** 195

| MLB ETA | CT | FB | CH | CB | SL | | OFP | Realistic |
|---|---|---|---|---|---|---|---|---|
| 2014 | 50 | 50 | 55 | 50 | --- | | 50<br>NO.4 STARTER | 50<br>NO.5 STARTER |

| YEAR | TEAM | LVL | AGE | W | L | SV | G | GS | IP | H | HR | BB | SO | BB9 | SO9 | GB% | BABIP | WHIP | ERA | FIP | FRA | WARP |
|---|---|---|---|---|---|---|---|---|---|---|---|---|---|---|---|---|---|---|---|---|---|---|
| 2013 | SFD | AA | 22 | 7 | 10 | 0 | 20 | 20 | 118.3 | 132 | 8 | 18 | 125 | 1.4 | 9.5 | 49% | .366 | 1.27 | 3.80 | 2.43 | 3.29 | 3.1 |
| 2013 | PMB | A+ | 22 | 3 | 3 | 0 | 6 | 6 | 36.0 | 38 | 1 | 4 | 23 | 1.0 | 5.8 | 43% | .316 | 1.17 | 2.75 | 2.74 | 4.16 | 0.2 |
| 2014 | SLN | MLB | 23 | 7 | 8 | 0 | 22 | 22 | 117.3 | 126 | 12 | 30 | 88 | 2.3 | 6.8 | 47% | .330 | 1.33 | 4.29 | 3.97 | 4.66 | 0.3 |
| 2015 | SLN | MLB | 24 | 9 | 9 | 0 | 28 | 28 | 170.7 | 181 | 17 | 35 | 125 | 1.8 | 6.6 | 47% | .326 | 1.27 | 4.12 | 3.61 | 4.48 | 0.6 |

Breakout: 8%    Improve: 15%    Collapse: 7%    Attrition: 17%    MLB: 28%        *Comparables: Burch Smith, Brett Oberholtzer, Adam Warren*

**Drafted/Acquired:** 3rd round, 2012, Wake Forest University (Winston-Salem, NC)

**Previous Ranking:** NR

**What Happened in 2013:** In his first-full season, Cooney pitched his way to the Texas League, where the former third-round pick made 20 starts and missed more than a bat an inning.

**Strengths:** Polished; sound delivery and good command profile; creates good angle; fastball velocity is average, but he spots the pitch well; good arm-side life; changeup is solid-average; plays well off the fastball; good deception and action; can throw curveball for strikes; cutter can force weak contact; plus pitchability.

**Weaknesses:** Lacks impact stuff; relies on sharp command and sequence to keep hitters off-balance and force bad swings; fastball plays in the zone too often in the 89-91 range; works in Double-A but likely to get hit in the majors; finds too many bats; lacks a wipeout breaking ball; unlikely to miss bats at the highest level.

**Risk Factor/Injury History:** Low risk; Double-A experience; could reach majors in 2014.

**Bret Sayre's Fantasy Take:** While the strikeout-to-walk rate is awfully pretty, Cooney isn't someone to target heavily in fantasy leagues. He could throw a lot of innings (if he can squeeze into that crowded rotation) with a strong WHIP (potentially under 1.20), but he may give back some of those gains in ERA and strikeouts.

**The Year Ahead:** Cooney is a polished arm with pitchability and a deep arsenal he can locate, which allows him to find success at the minor-league level. Despite the size, the angles, and the ability to change speeds, Cooney will need to have sharp command to have sustainable success against major-league bats, a starter's profile but more of a back-end variety than a pitcher capable of missing enough bats to be considered a mid-rotation type. He will reach the majors in 2014, but I wouldn't expect more than a number four starter at best, and most likely a capable and durable number five type.

## 10.  Vaughn Bryan    CF

**Born:** 6/5/93    **Age:** 21   **Bats:** B   **Throws:** R    **Height:** 6' 0"    **Weight:** 185

| MLB ETA | Hit | Power | Run | Glove | Arm | OFP | Realistic |
|---|---|---|---|---|---|---|---|
| 2017 | 50 | 60 | 75 | 60 | – | 65<br>1ST DIV/ALL-STAR | 45<br>BENCH OF/<AVG REG |

| YEAR | TEAM | LVL | AGE | PA | R | 2B | 3B | HR | RBI | BB | SO | SB | CS | AVG/OBP/SLG | TAv | BABIP | BRR | FRAA | WARP |
|---|---|---|---|---|---|---|---|---|---|---|---|---|---|---|---|---|---|---|---|
| 2013 | SCO | A- | 20 | 8 | 1 | 1 | 0 | 0 | 0 | 0 | 2 | 0 | 0 | .125/.125/.250 | .144 | .167 | -0.1 | CF(1): 0.0, LF(1): 0.3 | 0.0 |
| 2013 | JCY | Rk | 20 | 261 | 45 | 8 | 5 | 3 | 24 | 22 | 54 | 13 | 3 | .280/.341/.394 | .269 | .348 | 3.9 | CF(57): 1.9 | 1.8 |
| 2014 | SLN | MLB | 21 | 250 | 22 | 8 | 1 | 2 | 15 | 10 | 73 | 4 | 1 | .190/.226/.253 | .180 | .260 | 0.2 | CF 1, LF 0 | -1.1 |
| 2015 | SLN | MLB | 22 | 250 | 22 | 8 | 1 | 3 | 19 | 13 | 74 | 1 | 0 | .198/.242/.280 | .193 | .270 | -0.2 | CF 1, LF 0 | -2.6 |

Breakout: 0%    Improve: 0%    Collapse: 0%    Attrition: 0%    MLB: 0%    *Comparables: Kevin Kiermaier, Trayvon Robinson, Kirk Nieuwenhuis*

**Drafted/Acquired:** 35th round, 2013 draft, Broward Community College (Fort Lauderdale, FL)

**Previous Ranking:** NR

**What Happened in 2013:** The raw 35th-round talent showed a lot more on the field than some expected, and his physical electricity made him a much-talked-about sleeper to watch as he matures into a baseball player.

**Strengths:** Elite athleticism; good present strength; plus-plus run; covers a lot of ground in center; glove projects to plus; bat shows promise; good hip rotation and fluidity in the swing; has bat speed and power potential; work ethic is plus.

**Weaknesses:** Very raw; reads/routes need refinement in center; arm is below average; better stick from the right side; needs to improve left-handed swing; game power is more gaps than over the fence (at present); impact talent but a long way to go.

**Risk Factor/Injury History:** High risk; limited professional experience; big questions about raw tools playing against better competition.

**Bret Sayre's Fantasy Take:** This is a fun one. Someone who is undoubtedly unowned in your dynasty league, Bryan has tools to make fantasy owners drool. However, he's forever away (both developmentally and chronologically) from turning this into production. But a potential 20+ homer, 40+ steal player? That makes his extreme risk worth it now in deeper leagues.

**The Year Ahead:** Bryan is a classic boom or bust prospect, a high-impact athlete who might not be able to turn that premium athleticism into usable baseball skills. He can run for days, so his range in center will be a weapon if he can refine his reads off the bat and his path to the ball. His arm has strength but plays below average at present, but has a chance to improve a bit through instruction. The swing is actually quite pretty, with good hips and hands, capable of generating plus bat speed from both sides of the plate. He needs a lot of work, and this ranking might be a year premature, but the physical characteristics are hard to ignore; if he can take a step forward in 2014, he has the potential to develop into a significant prospect.

## Prospects on the Rise

**1. SS Chris Rivera:** One of the top national amateur talents in his early teen years, Rivera's stock fell because of poor performances at the plate, and he lasted until the seventh round in the 2013 draft as a result. With excellent defensive chops at shortstop and a laser arm, the future is wide open for the 18-year-old, even if the bat fails to stand next to the defensive gifts. His feel for the game and athletic gifts could make him a first-division talent, and if the bat doesn't pass the test, his arm could make him a candidate for the mound. Regardless of where he ends up on a diamond, this is a player worth keeping an eye on.

**2. OF Charlie Tilson:** The plus athlete took a big step forward in 2013, hitting his way to the Florida State League after missing the entire 2012 season with an injury and subsequent surgery to his shoulder. A fully healthy Tilson is an impact talent on all sides of the ball, and if he continues the healthy trend in 2014, his inclusion in the Cardinals top 10 will be a given.

**3. RHP Sam Tuivailala:** An infielder-turned-reliever, Tuivailala made his full-season debut in 2013, and despite some minor injury setbacks, he flashed his late-innings upside in a 35-inning sample. Working mainly off a fastball that routinely sits in the 97- to 100-mph range, the 21-year-old has the type of fastball to move through the minors very quickly. The command needs work, and his hard breaking ball comes and goes, but the fastball is special, so if Tuivailala can stay healthy, he should blossom into yet another successful conversion arm for the Cardinals.

## Factors on the Farm
### Prospects likely to contribute at the major-league level in 2014

**1. OF James Ramsey:** A first-round pick in the 2012 draft, Ramsey has moved quickly and will be knocking on the major-league door at some point in 2014. With a skill set that is more solid-average than special, it will be a difficult challenge for the 24-year-old to surpass fellow outfielders Oscar Taveras and Stephen Piscotty on the depth chart. But his well-rounded game and versatility in the field could make him a viable contributor this season, especially in the event of injury or inconsistency to those ahead of him in the line.

**2. LHP Lee Stoppelman:** Drafted in the 24th round in 2012, Stoppelman had a whirlwind run through the minors in his full-season debut, pitching across three levels and finishing the year in the Arizona Fall League. The arsenal isn't going to scare children or break radar guns, but the average arsenal (fastball/changeup/curveball) is brutal on lefties, and despite a limited ceiling, the 23-year-old is likely to carve out a long major-league career as a situational reliever.

**3. RHP Seth Blair:** It's been a rocky developmental path for the former supplemental first-round pick, with a poor debut season and a scrubbed 2012 season thanks to a tumor found on his pitching hand. But he found his stride in 2013, logging 22 starts at the Double-A level, battling with command issues but getting back on the developmental track. His most likely role will come out of the bullpen, where his low-90s fastball and hard breaking ball could play up and his command woes could play down.

# TAMPA BAY RAYS

## 1. Enny Romero  LHP

**Born:** 1/24/91  **Age:** 23  **Bats:** L  **Throws:** L  **Height:** 6'3"  **Weight:** 165

| MLB ETA | CT | FB | CH | CB | SL | OFP | Realistic |
|---|---|---|---|---|---|---|---|
| Debuted in 2013 | — | 70 | — | 70 | — | 60 NO.3 STARTER | 50 LATE-INN RP |

| YEAR | TEAM | LVL | AGE | W | L | SV | G | GS | IP | H | HR | BB | SO | BB9 | SO9 | GB% | BABIP | WHIP | ERA | FIP | FRA | WARP |
|---|---|---|---|---|---|---|---|---|---|---|---|---|---|---|---|---|---|---|---|---|---|---|
| 2013 | TBA | MLB | 22 | 0 | 0 | 0 | 1 | 1 | 4.7 | 1 | 0 | 4 | 0 | 7.7 | 0.0 | 64% | .071 | 1.07 | 0.00 | 5.65 | 5.26 | 0.0 |
| 2013 | DUR | AAA | 22 | 0 | 0 | 0 | 1 | 1 | 8.0 | 4 | 0 | 2 | 2 | 2.2 | 2.2 | 50% | .167 | 0.75 | 0.00 | 3.45 | 3.96 | 0.1 |
| 2013 | MNT | AA | 22 | 11 | 7 | 0 | 27 | 27 | 140.3 | 110 | 9 | 73 | 110 | 4.7 | 7.1 | 44% | .252 | 1.30 | 2.76 | 3.78 | 4.49 | 0.8 |
| 2014 | TBA | MLB | 23 | 6 | 9 | 0 | 24 | 24 | 117.7 | 116 | 14 | 75 | 86 | 5.7 | 6.6 | 47% | .284 | 1.62 | 5.03 | 5.51 | 5.47 | -0.7 |
| 2015 | TBA | MLB | 24 | 8 | 8 | 0 | 25 | 25 | 149.3 | 124 | 14 | 83 | 120 | 5.0 | 7.2 | 46% | .258 | 1.39 | 3.89 | 4.52 | 4.23 | 1.0 |

**Breakout:** 18%   **Improve:** 27%   **Collapse:** 6%   **Attrition:** 18%   **MLB:** 33%        *Comparables: Chris Archer, Justin Wilson, Jarred Cosart*

**Drafted/Acquired:** International free agent, 2008, Dominican Republic

**Previous Ranking:** NR

**What Happened in 2013:** After a somewhat disappointing 2012 campaign, Romero failed to crack the top 10 in a strong Rays system, but after a solid season in Double-A, nice flash appearances in the Futures Game and in the majors, and a downturn in status for the farm, Romero jumps the queue to claim the top prospect distinction.

**Strengths:** Excellent size; remaining projection; loose arm; big arm strength; fastball works in the low- to mid-90s; can sit in plus-plus velocity and touch higher; good movement; hard curveball has wipeout potential; slider velocity and two-plane break; changeup will flash above-average potential in the mid-80s with late action.

**Weaknesses:** Well-below-average command; release point/slot inconsistency; can get around on the curve and lose snap/rotation; more slurvy action and less bite; changeup is often overthrown and true; more deliberate with secondary stuff.

**Risk Factor/Injury History:** Low risk; 27 starts at Double-A level.

**Bret Sayre's Fantasy Take:** As a likely reliever, Romero is one of the least valuable of all the organizational top guns in this series in the fantasy world. Even if he does stick in the rotation, the lack of control will go a long way toward suppressing his potential in WHIP and wins. And if he ends up in the Tampa Bay 'pen soon, both the logjam of relievers ahead of him and the disincentive for small-market teams to give pre-arbitration players save opportunities will likely leave you looking elsewhere for saves.

**The Year Ahead:** My opinions on Romero have often been schizophrenic, as I dance between the reality of his skill set and the fantasy about what he has the potential to become. In bursts, Romero is a legit late-innings weapon, a lengthy lefty with a mid-90s heater (he can go get more) and a bat-missing breaking ball. The command is very limiting, but several industry sources suggested Romero could still find success in a rotation as an effectively wild type, and I'm starting to come around to the idea that he could find his way as a starter. Romero has made 77 minor-league starts the last three seasons, so he has the durability to take the ball every fifth day and log innings. His biggest roadblock is his command, and any step forward on that front could propel him into a major-league rotation, where the stuff will most definitely play.

> **#90**
> BP Top 101 Prospects

## 2. Jake Odorizzi  RHP

**Born:** 3/27/90  **Age:** 24  **Bats:** R  **Throws:** R  **Height:** 6'2"  **Weight:** 185

| MLB ETA | CT | FB | CH | CB | SL | OFP | Realistic |
|---|---|---|---|---|---|---|---|
| Debuted in 2012 | — | 55 | 55 | — | 50 | 50 NO.4 STARTER | 50 NO.4 STARTER |

| YEAR | TEAM | LVL | AGE | W | L | SV | G | GS | IP | H | HR | BB | SO | BB9 | SO9 | GB% | BABIP | WHIP | ERA | FIP | FRA | WARP |
|---|---|---|---|---|---|---|---|---|---|---|---|---|---|---|---|---|---|---|---|---|---|---|
| 2013 | DUR | AAA | 23 | 9 | 6 | 0 | 22 | 22 | 124.3 | 101 | 12 | 40 | 124 | 2.9 | 9.0 | 37% | .282 | 1.13 | 3.33 | 3.45 | 4.54 | 1.6 |
| 2013 | TBA | MLB | 23 | 0 | 1 | 1 | 7 | 4 | 29.7 | 28 | 3 | 8 | 22 | 2.4 | 6.7 | 34% | .287 | 1.21 | 3.94 | 3.92 | 3.61 | 0.4 |
| 2014 | TBA | MLB | 24 | 8 | 8 | 0 | 23 | 23 | 127.0 | 119 | 16 | 46 | 108 | 3.3 | 7.7 | 37% | .282 | 1.30 | 3.86 | 4.51 | 4.20 | 1.0 |
| 2015 | TBA | MLB | 25 | 11 | 9 | 0 | 31 | 31 | 199.7 | 171 | 25 | 63 | 175 | 2.8 | 7.9 | 37% | .264 | 1.17 | 3.29 | 4.06 | 3.58 | 2.9 |

**Breakout:** 29%   **Improve:** 50%   **Collapse:** 12%   **Attrition:** 28%   **MLB:** 68%        *Comparables: Jeremy Hellickson, Dan Straily, Eric Surkamp*

**Drafted/Acquired:** 1st round, 2008 draft, Highland HS (Highland, IL)

**Previous Ranking:** #5 (Org), #83 (Top 101)

**The Tools:** 5+ FB; 5 SL; 5+ potential CH

**What Happened in 2013:** Another strong minor-league season for Odorizzi and a good showing in his four major-league starts should put him in contention for a full-time gig in the 2014 rotation.

> **#92**
> BP Top 101 Prospects

**Strengths:** Consistent; clean, athletic delivery; repeats; throws strikes; fastball works in the low-90s; some late arm-side movement; slider is solid-average; works in the 82-84 range with some tilt; changeup is average/ flashes above-average potential; good deception and action; shows low-70s curveball; can locate his offerings; competitive approach.

**Weaknesses:** Lacks true plus offering; has to mix pitches and hit his spots; can run into hard contact; slider can get slurvy and loose; curveball is sequence dependent and easy to track; high floor/low ceiling.

**Risk Factor/Injury History:** Low risk; achieved major-league level.

**Bret Sayre's Fantasy Take:** Odorizzi is what he is, and at this point, he's essentially a replacement-level starter in shallower leagues. As the depth of your league increases, the more it makes sense to roster him, but without a strong strikeout profile or much of an ability to keep the ball on the ground, Odorizzi is on the outside looking in at the Top 100 Fantasy Prospects list this year.

**The Year Ahead:** After 114 career starts across all levels, Odorizzi has shown a consistency rarely found in the often-erratic developmental journey of a high-school arm. He's a solid but not sexy starter, with a four-pitch mix of average (or slightly better) pitches that he can locate and sequence. The ceiling and the floor exist in close proximity, and there is very little risk in the profile. Barring injury, Odorizzi is going to be a major-league-average starter, and that's a very valuable commodity to have while he's under team control.

---

## 3.  Alex Colome   RHP

**Born:** 12/31/88  **Age:** 25  **Bats:** R  **Throws:** R  **Height:** 6' 2"  **Weight:** 185

| MLB ETA | CT | FB | CH | CB | SL | | OFP | | Realistic |
|---|---|---|---|---|---|---|---|---|---|
| Debuted in 2013 | 60 | 70 | 60 | 60 | — | | **60**<br>NO.3 STARTER | | **50**<br>LATE INN RP (SETUP) |

| YEAR | TEAM | LVL | AGE | W | L | SV | G | GS | IP | H | HR | BB | SO | BB9 | SO9 | GB% | BABIP | WHIP | ERA | FIP | FRA | WARP |
|---|---|---|---|---|---|---|---|---|---|---|---|---|---|---|---|---|---|---|---|---|---|---|
| 2013 | TBA | MLB | 24 | 1 | 1 | 0 | 3 | 3 | 16.0 | 14 | 2 | 9 | 12 | 5.1 | 6.8 | 45% | .255 | 1.44 | 2.25 | 5.08 | 5.64 | -0.1 |
| 2013 | DUR | AAA | 24 | 4 | 6 | 0 | 14 | 14 | 70.3 | 63 | 5 | 29 | 72 | 3.7 | 9.2 | 42% | .301 | 1.31 | 3.07 | 3.49 | 4.01 | 1.2 |
| 2014 | TBA | MLB | 25 | 4 | 5 | 0 | 14 | 14 | 73.3 | 71 | 9 | 36 | 58 | 4.4 | 7.1 | 44% | .285 | 1.47 | 4.56 | 5.03 | 4.95 | 0.0 |
| 2015 | TBA | MLB | 26 | 5 | 4 | 0 | 61 | 8 | 103.3 | 97 | 14 | 46 | 86 | 4.0 | 7.5 | 44% | .277 | 1.38 | 4.36 | 4.74 | 4.74 | 0.2 |

Breakout: 16%   Improve: 27%   Collapse: 17%   Attrition: 35%   MLB: 52%       *Comparables: Brad Mills, Kyle Weiland, Scott Barnes*

**Drafted/Acquired:** International free agent, 2007, Dominican Republic

**Previous Ranking:** #10 (Org)

**What Happened in 2013:** Colome once again failed to eclipse the 100 innings mark on the year, as injuries continue to keep the live-armed righty from exploding as a frontline prospect.

**Strengths:** Electric arm; easy and explosive out of the hand; multiple fastball looks; can work mid-90s; sit higher in bursts; plus-plus offering with "rising" action; can show power sinker as well with good weight; cutter is above-average offering; looks like a short slider, thrown with velocity and late horizontal slice to the glove side; tight curveball will show plus; changeup plays well off fastball; impact arsenal.

**Weaknesses:** Inconsistent delivery/release points; command is below average; likes to work up with the fastball; inconsistent breaking balls; changeup can be overthrown; can get deliberate and lose deception in the delivery; struggles to stay healthy; limited pitchability.

**Risk Factor/Injury History:** Low risk; 20 starts in Triple-A/majors.

**Bret Sayre's Fantasy Take:** A lazier man would copy and paste much of Enny Romero's write-up and put it here as well, but I am not said lazier man. In another organization, I would like Colome's chances of pitching in the back of a rotation in 2014, but the Rays continue to be stacked with starting pitching; unless a David Price trade returns no major-league-ready pitching, Colome will take his plus stuff and shaky command to the bullpen, where he is also unlikely to get saves.

**The Year Ahead:** Colome has really, really nasty stuff, especially when he feels confident in the secondary arsenal and can locate the fastball early in counts. On paper, the stuff would make him a mid-rotation starter, and perhaps even more if the command were sharp. But the command isn't sharp, and the 25-year-old Dominican has struggled to stay healthy, so his likely home will come in the bullpen, where his deep mix of plus stuff could make him a late-innings weapon, perhaps even a closer if the command refines.

## 4. Nate Karns RHP

**Born:** 11/25/87　**Age:** 26　**Bats:** R　**Throws:** R　**Height:** 6'3"　**Weight:** 230

| MLB ETA | CT | FB | CH | CB | SL | OFP | Realistic |
|---|---|---|---|---|---|---|---|
| Debuted in 2013 | – | 60 | – | 60 | – | 50 LATE INN RP (CL) | 50 LATE INN RP (SU) |

| YEAR | TEAM | LVL | AGE | W | L | SV | G | GS | IP | H | HR | BB | SO | BB9 | SO9 | GB% | BABIP | WHIP | ERA | FIP | FRA | WARP |
|---|---|---|---|---|---|---|---|---|---|---|---|---|---|---|---|---|---|---|---|---|---|---|
| 2013 | WAS | MLB | 25 | 0 | 1 | 0 | 3 | 3 | 12.0 | 17 | 5 | 6 | 11 | 4.5 | 8.2 | 37% | .316 | 1.92 | 7.50 | 8.35 | 7.62 | -0.4 |
| 2013 | HAR | AA | 25 | 10 | 6 | 0 | 23 | 23 | 132.7 | 109 | 14 | 48 | 155 | 3.3 | 10.5 | 47% | .289 | 1.18 | 3.26 | 3.60 | 3.87 | 1.7 |
| 2014 | TBA | MLB | 26 | 7 | 7 | 0 | 22 | 22 | 113.7 | 103 | 14 | 52 | 113 | 4.1 | 8.9 | 46% | .291 | 1.36 | 4.04 | 4.51 | 4.39 | 0.7 |
| 2015 | TBA | MLB | 27 | 9 | 10 | 0 | 30 | 30 | 192.3 | 178 | 24 | 78 | 185 | 3.7 | 8.7 | 46% | .293 | 1.33 | 3.99 | 4.20 | 4.34 | 0.9 |

Breakout: 25%　Improve: 34%　Collapse: 16%　Attrition: 41%　MLB: 57%　　*Comparables: Joel Carreno, Collin McHugh, Corey Kluber*

**Drafted/Acquired:** 12th round, 2009 draft, Texas Tech University (Lubbock, TX)

**Previous Ranking:** #5 (Org)

**What Happened in 2013:** Karns had a very strong 2013 season, getting a forced major-league cup of coffee early, but showing two plus pitches in his 23 Double-A starts.

**Strengths:** Big, strong frame; physical pitcher; big arm strength; fastball is plus offering; works 92-95; can touch higher; curveball is big hammer; slider velocity with bottom-heavy action; plus offering that will miss bats at any level; shows some feel for throwing strikes; attacks hitters.

**Weaknesses:** Overall command is below average; delivery has some effort; struggles to remain consistent with his mechanics/release points; can overthrow the curve and lose his depth; changeup is below average; unlikely to find sustainable success as a starter.

**Risk Factor/Injury History:** Low risk; 26 years old; achieved major-league level; detailed injury history on resume (torn labrum).

**Bret Sayre's Fantasy Take:** The strikeout numbers he posted at Double-A look impressive, but without a better changeup, he's either going to be a disappointing starting pitcher who has trouble with lefties or a very good reliever who has trouble with lefties. The curveball is good enough to be a solid contributor in strikeouts regardless of role, but expecting him to be a starter (especially in Tampa Bay) is setting yourself up for disappointment.

**The Year Ahead:** Karns is a starter in name only, at least as far as sources are concerned, as the 26-year-old lacks the command and third pitch to find sustainable success in a major-league rotation. But he can be very nasty in short bursts, pushing the fastball to the mid-90s and backing it up with a hard mid-80s curveball that can miss bats and hurt feelings, so he should carve out a career as a late-innings reliever. If the command can sharpen, he has a chance to close, but could settle in as a setup reliever very soon.

## 5. Hak-Ju Lee SS

**Born:** 11/4/90　**Age:** 23　**Bats:** L　**Throws:** R　**Height:** 6'2"　**Weight:** 170

| MLB ETA | Hit | Power | Run | Glove | Arm | OFP | Realistic |
|---|---|---|---|---|---|---|---|
| 2014 | 50 | – | 60 | 65 | 65 | 55 >AVG REGULAR | 50 2ND DIV STARTER |

| YEAR | TEAM | LVL | AGE | PA | R | 2B | 3B | HR | RBI | BB | SO | SB | CS | AVG/OBP/SLG | TAv | BABIP | BRR | FRAA | WARP |
|---|---|---|---|---|---|---|---|---|---|---|---|---|---|---|---|---|---|---|---|
| 2013 | DUR | AAA | 22 | 57 | 13 | 3 | 1 | 1 | 7 | 11 | 9 | 6 | 2 | .422/.536/.600 | .387 | .514 | 2.7 | SS(15): -0.7 | 1.2 |
| 2014 | TBA | MLB | 23 | 250 | 30 | 7 | 3 | 3 | 18 | 18 | 56 | 12 | 4 | .239/.296/.338 | .240 | .300 | 1.4 | SS 0 | 0.8 |
| 2015 | TBA | MLB | 24 | 343 | 34 | 11 | 4 | 4 | 30 | 22 | 75 | 21 | 7 | .242/.295/.342 | .239 | .300 | 2.4 | SS 0 | 0.9 |

Breakout: 9%　Improve: 29%　Collapse: 7%　Attrition: 25%　MLB: 45%　　*Comparables: Josh Rutledge, Anderson Hernandez, Tim Beckham*

**Drafted/Acquired:** International free agent, 2008, South Korea

**Previous Ranking:** #4 (Org)

**What Happened in 2013:** 15 games into the 2013 season, Lee tore ligaments in his left knee and missed the remainder of the season.

**Strengths:** Assuming full recovery (same report preinjury), fast-twitch athlete; frame is lengthy and can hold additional strength/mass; high-end defensive profile at shortstop; actions are extremely fluid; soft hands; arm is very strong; first-step quickness and plus range; well-above-average speed; continues to improve as baserunner; hit tool has potential; will work himself into favorable counts; the bat has a chance to play.

**Weaknesses:** Bat can play empty; show some contact ability, but pitchers not afraid to challenge the zone; well-below-average power; questions about ability to square up velocity, especially stuff on the inner third; range questions because of knee injury.

**Risk Factor/Injury History:** Moderate risk; torn ligaments in knee; defensive chops for major-league level.

**Bret Sayre's Fantasy Take:** While his defense anchors his future real-life value, Lee's future fantasy value is tied directly to his speed. Without much pop or hope for a .300 average, he's going to need to steal 25-30 bases to be worth starting, even at a shallow position like shortstop. Prior to 2013, he had stolen 105 bases in his last three seasons—but major knee injuries don't tend to increase base-running skill.

**The Year Ahead:** Because his calling card was his defensive prowess, which included well-above-average range, the ability to return to form will be paramount to his status as a prospect and as a player. If you assume he makes a full recovery, which isn't farfetched, the speedy shortstop has impact potential at the highest level; Lee has plus-plus speed, excellent hand-eye coordination at the plate that should allow for consistent contact, and the defensive chops to play above-average defense at a premium up-the-middle position. It's a very nice profile, and a healthy Lee could find a way to contribute to the major-league team at some point in 2014.

## 6.  Nick Ciuffo   C

**Born:** 3/7/95    **Age:** 19    **Bats:** L    **Throws:** R    **Height:** 6' 1"    **Weight:** 205

| MLB ETA | Hit | Power | Run | Glove | Arm | OFP | Realistic |
|---|---|---|---|---|---|---|---|
| 2018 | 55 | 50 | – | 55 | 60 | 60 1ST DIV PLAYER | 50 2ND DIV PLAYER |

| YEAR | TEAM | LVL | AGE | PA | R | 2B | 3B | HR | RBI | BB | SO | SB | CS | AVG/OBP/SLG | TAv | BABIP | BRR | FRAA | WARP |
|---|---|---|---|---|---|---|---|---|---|---|---|---|---|---|---|---|---|---|---|
| 2013 | RAY | Rk | 18 | 169 | 11 | 6 | 1 | 0 | 25 | 9 | 40 | 0 | 0 | .258/.296/.308 | .224 | .342 | 0.0 | C(25): 0.0 | 0.0 |
| 2014 | TBA | MLB | 19 | 250 | 15 | 8 | 1 | 2 | 18 | 10 | 80 | 0 | 0 | .178/.212/.237 | .171 | .250 | -0.3 | C 0 | -1.4 |
| 2015 | TBA | MLB | 20 | 250 | 22 | 8 | 1 | 3 | 20 | 12 | 77 | 0 | 0 | .202/.240/.282 | .193 | .281 | -0.5 | C 0 | -2.7 |

Breakout: 0%    Improve: 0%    Collapse: 0%    Attrition: 0%    MLB: 0%    *Comparables: Christian Bethancourt, Matt Davidson, Cedric Hunter*

**Drafted/Acquired:** 1st round, 2013 draft, Lexington HS (Lexington, SC)

**Previous Ranking:** NR

**What Happened in 2013:** Selected 21st overall in the 2013 draft, Ciuffo projects to have one of the most sought-after profiles in the game: a dual-threat catcher.

**Strengths:** Strong, athletic build; short, quick actions behind the plate; projects to be above-average defensive catcher; arm is strong and accurate; aggressive and confident with actions; lefty swing is simple and easy; good plane to the ball; power potential; highly competitive with baseball IQ.

**Weaknesses:** Needs general refinement as a receiver; can get overly aggressive, especially with back picks; aggressive swinger at the plate; struggled against spin debut.

**Risk Factor/Injury History:** High risk; dual-threat development; limited professional experience.

**Bret Sayre's Fantasy Take:** As I continue to say, holding a catcher on your dynasty farm team is not the best use of a roster spot unless he has star-level upside offensively. Ciuffo, despite the strength of his all-around game, is not at that point and is forever away from contributing.

**The Year Ahead:** I'm actually pretty excited about Ciuffo, as every amateur source I contacted adored the young catcher, and Gulf Coast League eyes echoed the glowing reports. Dual-threat development is inherently high risk, and while that is true of Ciuffo, the makeup and natural aptitude for the game give him a big advantage and better odds than most high-ceiling dual-threat high-school draftees. It might take a few years to see the type of production the hype suggests, but the present skill set and promise of ceiling will keep him securely in the top 10 for years to come. In the direct parlance of amateur scouts, Ciuffo is "a dude."

## 7.  Taylor Guerrieri   RHP

**Born:** 12/1/92    **Age:** 21    **Bats:** R    **Throws:** R    **Height:** 6' 3"    **Weight:** 195

| MLB ETA | CT | FB | CH | CB | SL | OFP | Realistic |
|---|---|---|---|---|---|---|---|
| 2017 | – | 70 | – | 70 | – | 65 NO.2 STARTER | 50 NO.4 STARTER |

| YEAR | TEAM | LVL | AGE | W | L | SV | G | GS | IP | H | HR | BB | SO | BB9 | SO9 | GB% | BABIP | WHIP | ERA | FIP | FRA | WARP |
|---|---|---|---|---|---|---|---|---|---|---|---|---|---|---|---|---|---|---|---|---|---|---|
| 2013 | BGR | A | 20 | 6 | 2 | 0 | 14 | 14 | 67.0 | 54 | 5 | 12 | 51 | 1.6 | 6.9 | 67% | .266 | 0.99 | 2.01 | 3.77 | 5.03 | 0.6 |
| 2014 | TBA | MLB | 21 | 3 | 4 | 0 | 10 | 10 | 48.3 | 53 | 7 | 20 | 29 | 3.7 | 5.4 | 55% | .297 | 1.52 | 5.15 | 5.55 | 5.59 | -0.3 |
| 2015 | TBA | MLB | 22 | 8 | 10 | 0 | 30 | 30 | 188.3 | 187 | 23 | 70 | 141 | 3.3 | 6.7 | 55% | .289 | 1.36 | 4.34 | 4.54 | 4.72 | 0.1 |

Breakout: 0%    Improve: 0%    Collapse: 0%    Attrition: 0%    MLB: 0%    *Comparables: Vance Worley, Ian Krol, Patrick Corbin*

**Drafted/Acquired:** 1st round, 2011 draft, Spring Valley HS (Columbia, SC)

**Previous Ranking:** #3 (Org), #48 (Top 101)

**What Happened in 2013:** Fourteen starts into his full-season debut, injury forced Guerrieri to undergo Tommy John surgery, effectively halting his encouraging developmental progress.

**Strengths:** Ideal size/strength; delivery and arm work very well; fastball would routinely work in the low-90s and bump the mid-90s; excellent movement to the offering; can sink the ball, run the ball, and cut it; curveball is easy plus offering; big depth and tight rotation; bat-missing pitch; good pitchability and command profile.

**Weaknesses:** Tendency to overthrow the changeup; secondary delivery can look more deliberate; more control than command (at present); makeup concerns.

**Risk Factor/Injury History:** High risk; Tommy John surgery on resume

**Bret Sayre's Fantasy Take:** If I could take one player from this system for my dynasty league, it would be Guerrieri. No one can match his upside, and while the Tommy John surgery should push back his ETA, it doesn't detract much from the upside he has. With potentially top-notch ground-ball and walk rates, he projects as a very strong ratio play who can give enough strikeouts to be a top-20 starter. Don't let the risk scare you off.

**The Year Ahead:** Guerrieri is a power pitcher, one that can ride his lively fastball and wipeout curve all the way to a major-league rotation. The injury effectively presses pause on his development, and the late-season drug suspension adds to the already existing concerns about his overall approach. But a setback of this nature could be a blessing in disguise for the young arm, as Guerrieri will be forced to focus all of his attention on baseball to make a complete recovery, and the flash-boiled maturity could elevate his already impressive profile to the next level. He's going to be on the shelf for most of 2014, so it will be a lost year on the field. But the rehab process and road to recovery will be the most important test of Guerrieri's young career.

## 8. Kevin Kiermaier CF

**Born:** 4/22/90   **Age:** 24   **Bats:** L   **Throws:** R   **Height:** 6' 1"   **Weight:** 200

| MLB ETA | Hit | Power | Run | Glove | Arm | OFP | Realistic |
|---|---|---|---|---|---|---|---|
| Debuted in 2013 | — | — | 70 | 65 | 60 | 50 ML REGULAR | 45 BACKUP/<AVG REG |

| YEAR | TEAM | LVL | AGE | PA | R | 2B | 3B | HR | RBI | BB | SO | SB | CS | AVG/OBP/SLG | TAv | BABIP | BRR | FRAA | WARP |
|---|---|---|---|---|---|---|---|---|---|---|---|---|---|---|---|---|---|---|---|
| 2013 | MNT | AA | 23 | 417 | 65 | 14 | 9 | 5 | 28 | 31 | 61 | 14 | 11 | .307/.370/.434 | .302 | .354 | 2.5 | CF(89): 10.5 | 5.1 |
| 2013 | DUR | AAA | 23 | 154 | 24 | 7 | 6 | 1 | 13 | 14 | 26 | 7 | 1 | .263/.338/.423 | .258 | .315 | 3.6 | CF(38): 7.6 | 1.7 |
| 2013 | TBA | MLB | 23 | 0 | 0 | 0 | 0 | 0 | 0 | 0 | 0 | 0 | 0 | — | — | — | 0.0 | CF(1): -0.0 | 0.0 |
| 2014 | TBA | MLB | 24 | 250 | 27 | 8 | 4 | 2 | 18 | 16 | 55 | 7 | 3 | .237/.293/.333 | .234 | .290 | 0.6 | CF 7, RF 0 | 0.9 |
| 2015 | TBA | MLB | 25 | 250 | 26 | 8 | 4 | 3 | 23 | 19 | 53 | 7 | 3 | .247/.311/.366 | .244 | .299 | 0.7 | CF 7, RF 0 | 1.5 |

Breakout: 0%    Improve: 0%    Collapse: 0%    Attrition: 0%    MLB: 0%          *Comparables: Brandon Guyer, Brett Gardner, Clete Thomas*

**Drafted/Acquired:** 31st round, 2010 draft, Parkland College (Champaign, IL)

**Previous Ranking:** NR

**What Happened in 2013:** Kiermaier continued to flash his impressive outfield profile, establishing himself as one of the top defensive center fielders in the minors.

**Strengths:** Physical athlete; good present strength; plus-plus run; excellent range; reads/routes are very good; glove is easy plus; arm is plus; weapon defender in center; good approach at the plate; can swing the bat a little.

**Weaknesses:** Defense-first profile; struggles to drive the ball against arm-side pitching; hit tool likely to play below average; power to play well below average; baserunning needs work.

**Risk Factor/Injury History:** Low risk; 140 games of upper-minors experience.

**Bret Sayre's Fantasy Take:** The defense is spectacular, but unless you're playing in a sim league, Kiermaier is best left on the waiver wire. If he were to get time in center for Tampa, his speed would play up on the basepaths due to Joe Maddon's aggressiveness, but it wouldn't make up for his lack of offensive value.

**The Year Ahead:** Kiermaier is a fantastic defensive outfielder, with well-above-average speed, instincts for the position, and a strong arm. The bat isn't nearly as sexy, although he puts himself in good hitting conditions and isn't a pushover out. If the bat plays above expectations, he could be a second-division type, but he's a valuable major leaguer even if the bat is too light to start.

## 9. Ryan Brett 2B

**Born:** 10/9/91   **Age:** 22   **Bats:** R   **Throws:** R   **Height:** 5' 9"   **Weight:** 180

| MLB ETA | Hit | Power | Run | Glove | Arm | OFP | Realistic |
|---|---|---|---|---|---|---|---|
| 2015 | 60 | — | 60 | 55 | 50 | 55 >AVG REGULAR | 45 UTILITY |

| YEAR | TEAM | LVL | AGE | PA | R | 2B | 3B | HR | RBI | BB | SO | SB | CS | AVG/OBP/SLG | TAv | BABIP | BRR | FRAA | WARP |
|---|---|---|---|---|---|---|---|---|---|---|---|---|---|---|---|---|---|---|---|
| 2013 | MNT | AA | 21 | 114 | 19 | 6 | 1 | 3 | 16 | 8 | 14 | 4 | 0 | .238/.289/.400 | .257 | .247 | 1.8 | 2B(25): 1.1 | 0.5 |
| 2013 | PCH | A+ | 21 | 225 | 38 | 11 | 4 | 4 | 22 | 15 | 27 | 22 | 7 | .340/.396/.490 | .307 | .377 | 1.0 | 2B(47): -2.0 | 1.5 |
| 2013 | RAY | Rk | 21 | 4 | 0 | 0 | 0 | 0 | 0 | 0 | 2 | 0 | 0 | .000/.000/.000 | .007 | .000 | 0.0 | 2B(1): 0.0 | -0.1 |
| 2014 | TBA | MLB | 22 | 250 | 30 | 9 | 1 | 4 | 18 | 13 | 53 | 13 | 3 | .235/.278/.334 | .231 | .280 | 1.6 | 2B -3 | 0.0 |
| 2015 | TBA | MLB | 23 | 250 | 25 | 9 | 2 | 4 | 23 | 14 | 52 | 12 | 3 | .236/.283/.347 | .233 | .284 | 1.7 | 2B -3 | 0.0 |

Breakout: 0%    Improve: 0%    Collapse: 0%    Attrition: 0%    MLB: 0%          *Comparables: Adrian Cardenas, Tony Abreu, Logan Watkins*

**Drafted/Acquired:** 3rd round, 2010 draft, Highline High School (Burien, WA)

**Previous Ranking:** NR

**What Happened in 2013:** Coming off his 50-game drug suspension, Brett continued to hit ropes all over the Florida State League, earned a promotion to the Double-A level, and finished the season playing in the prospect-heavy Arizona Fall League.

**Strengths:** Excellent barrel control; great hands; hits lasers all over the park; stays inside the ball and makes consistent hard contact; hit tool could play above plus; runs well; good range in the field and smart baserunner; glove is above average at second; arm plays well on the right side; high-energy player.

**Weaknesses:** Can play too fast; rushes actions/throws in the field; good approach but can get too aggressive on the fastball and get jumpy on secondary stuff; limited power potential.

**Risk Factor/Injury History:** Moderate risk; limited experience at Double-A level; hit tool has to carry.

**Bret Sayre's Fantasy Take:** A points league late-round darling, Brett has the eligibility, hit tool, and speed to be worthy of ownership in dynasty leagues. He may not project to hit double-digit homers, but with usable 25- to 30-steal potential along with an average that could brush up against .300 in his better seasons, Brett has a shot to be a starter, even in shallow formats.

**The Year Ahead:** If you love small, grinder, proletariat gamers, Brett fits the profile perfectly, including an amphetamine suspension as the cherry on top. Put him in whatever box you need to, but this isn't a fringy player, as Brett has a very good (and real) hit tool, with above-average speed and glove at second. He plays with his hair on fire sometimes, but these tools show up in game action, and despite his limited size and power, Brett could end up a major-league regular if the bat plays to its projection. If not, he would make a decent utility option because of his overall feel for the game and athleticism. Fun player to watch. He should get a longer look in Double-A in 2014, and could put himself in the major-league discussion for 2015.

# 10. Andrew Toles  CF

**Born:** 5/24/92  **Age:** 22  **Bats:** L  **Throws:** R  **Height:** 5' 10"  **Weight:** 185

| MLB ETA | Hit | Power | Run | Glove | Arm | OFP | Realistic |
|---|---|---|---|---|---|---|---|
| 2017 | 50 | ---- | 70 | 60 | ---- | 55<br>>AVG REGULAR | 45<br>BENCH/<AVG ML PLYR |

| YEAR | TEAM | LVL | AGE | PA | R | 2B | 3B | HR | RBI | BB | SO | SB | CS | AVG/OBP/SLG | TAv | BABIP | BRR | FRAA | WARP |
|---|---|---|---|---|---|---|---|---|---|---|---|---|---|---|---|---|---|---|---|
| 2013 | BGR | A | 21 | 552 | 79 | 35 | 16 | 2 | 57 | 22 | 105 | 62 | 17 | .326/.359/.466 | .295 | .402 | 7.1 | CF(110): 1.6, RF(6): 0.1 | 4.6 |
| 2014 | TBA | MLB | 22 | 250 | 29 | 10 | 2 | 2 | 15 | 5 | 67 | 14 | 5 | .230/.249/.316 | .211 | .310 | 1.7 | CF 1, RF 0 | -0.3 |
| 2015 | TBA | MLB | 23 | 250 | 22 | 11 | 3 | 2 | 21 | 9 | 66 | 13 | 4 | .233/.265/.334 | .221 | .307 | 1.5 | CF 0, RF 0 | -0.7 |

Breakout: 0%    Improve: 0%    Collapse: 0%    Attrition: 0%    MLB: 0%          *Comparables: Juan Lagares, A.J. Pollock, Trayvon Robinson*

**Drafted/Acquired:** 3rd round, 2012 draft, Chipola College (Marianna, FL)

**Previous Ranking:** NR

**What Happened in 2013:** The former third-round pick had a breakout campaign in his full-season debut, ripping 169 hits in 121 games, while stealing 62 bags.

**Strengths:** Impact athlete; plus-plus run; above-average defensive profile in center, with obvious plus range; ball comes off the bat with some pop; shows backspin; gap ability; leadoff offensive profile.

**Weaknesses:** Aggressive approach; balance issues in swing/setup; fooled by breaking balls; will pull off; swing-and-miss; arm is fringe; needs refinement on reads/routes.

**Risk Factor/Injury History:** High risk; Low-A resume; more tools than skills.

**Bret Sayre's Fantasy Take:** Steal 62 bases in full-season ball, and you have my attention. Toles' fantasy relevance will be all about speed, but it will hinge on his hit tool, as he's going to have to have to earn enough playing time to allow those steals to pile up. The upside makes him the second-best fantasy investment in this system (behind Guerrieri), but there is a lot of work left to be done here.

**The Year Ahead:** Toles can really run, both as a base-stealing threat and as somebody who can go get it in center. He hit for a very high average in Low-A, but the swing [itself] might prove to be problematic as he climbs the professional ladder, with bat speed but balance issues and an approach that puts him at the mercy of secondary offerings. High floor because of the speed and the defensive profile, but the offensive prowess is overstated by the stats and not nearly as projectable as his defensive tools.

## Prospects on the Rise

**1. LHP Blake Snell:** Lefties with impressive size and stuff are rare breeds, and Snell would be a no-doubt top-10 prospect if the command concerns didn't exist. But after 73 walks in 99 Midwest League innings, the status launch remains in a holding pattern until he can show some refinement on that front.

**2. RHP Jeff Ames:** A supplemental first-round pick in the 2011 draft, Ames has been on the slow and steady developmental climb, reaching and pitching well in his full-season debut. The big, strong righty already has an above-average fastball, and the secondaries (slider/change) project to be average-or-better major-league offerings, although he lacks a true knockout weapon in the arsenal. Ames will continue his climb next season in the Florida State League, and with steady improvements, he could emerge as a top-10 prospect in the system at this time next year.

**3. CF Thomas Milone:** The tools are very raw, but the profile could offer impact, with plus power potential in the bat and a chance to stick around in center field. With his high-school football career behind him, a focus on baseball could push the Connecticut native up prospect lists in 2014.

## Factors on the Farm

### Prospects likely to contribute at the major-league level in 2014

**1. 1B Cameron Seitzer:** While not a name prospect, Seitzer has a chance to eventually contribute to a major-league team, as the abnormally large human from the University of Oklahoma has a very advanced approach at the plate and defensive chops at first, a profile with minimal value to most but one that could find utility for the Rays. The power is unlikely to impress and he doesn't project as a major-league regular, but the on-base ability is legit, and the major-league bloodlines won't hurt his cause.

**2. RHP Matt Ramsey:** A 19th-round pick in the 2011 draft, Ramsey is a short right-hander with a thick build, with the stuff to pitch in the major-league bullpen, perhaps as early as the 2014 season. While the arsenal isn't going to strike major-league hitters with fear, the 24-year-old has shown the ability to miss bats with his 92- to 94-mph fastball and two-plane breaking ball, but he also finds hard contact, so his command will have to improve if he wants to find sustainable success. He should start the season in Double-A, and a step forward could push him to the majors before the season is over.

**3. LHP Mike Montgomery:** It seems like I've been writing about Mike Montgomery for my entire adult life, as the 24-year-old has been on the prospect landscape since he was popped by the Royals in the first round of the 2008 draft. With suspect command and inconsistent stuff, Montgomery's future looks brighter in the bullpen, where his stuff could play up and hopefully avoid more barrels than he found as a starter.

## 1. Rougned Odor    2B

**Born:** 2/3/94   **Age:** 20   **Bats:** L   **Throws:** R   **Height:** 5' 11"   **Weight:** 170

| MLB ETA | Hit | Power | Run | Glove | Arm | OFP | Realistic |
|---|---|---|---|---|---|---|---|
| **2014** | **70** | **50** | **50** | **60** | **50** | **65**<br>1ST DIV/POT ALL-STAR | **55**<br>>AVG ML PLAYER |

| YEAR | TEAM | LVL | AGE | PA | R | 2B | 3B | HR | RBI | BB | SO | SB | CS | AVG/OBP/SLG | TAv | BABIP | BRR | FRAA | WARP |
|---|---|---|---|---|---|---|---|---|---|---|---|---|---|---|---|---|---|---|---|
| 2013 | FRI | AA | 19 | 144 | 20 | 8 | 2 | 6 | 19 | 9 | 24 | 5 | 2 | .306/.354/.530 | .314 | .337 | -0.4 | 2B(30): 2.5 | 1.6 |
| 2013 | MYR | A+ | 19 | 425 | 65 | 33 | 4 | 5 | 59 | 26 | 67 | 27 | 8 | .305/.369/.454 | .293 | .355 | 1.4 | 2B(84): 4.3 | 3.6 |
| 2014 | TEX | MLB | 20 | 250 | 28 | 11 | 1 | 4 | 21 | 8 | 52 | 7 | 3 | .240/.274/.355 | .231 | .290 | 0.3 | 2B 2, SS -0 | 0.4 |
| 2015 | TEX | MLB | 21 | 443 | 50 | 21 | 2 | 11 | 50 | 16 | 83 | 11 | 4 | .259/.298/.403 | .260 | .296 | 0.2 | 2B 4 | 1.8 |

Breakout: 0%    Improve: 0%    Collapse: 0%    Attrition: 0%    MLB: 0%        *Comparables: Jonathan Schoop, Jose Ramirez, Brett Lawrie*

**Drafted/Acquired:** International free agent, 2011, Venezuela

**Previous Ranking:** On The Rise

**What Happened in 2013:** As a 19-year-old, Odor crushed in High-A and finished the season with an impressive 30-game run in Double-A, hitting a combined 58 extra-base hits over the two stops.

**Strengths:** Natural bat-to-ball ability; shows impressive bat speed and the ability to make quick adjustments at the plate; can barrel velocity and track/stay back on off-speed; baseball instincts are elite; has the raw pop to drive the ball into the gaps; will develop average home-run power over time; glove at second base should be plus; arm is average but strong on turns; at least average run, but plays up in game action; plays with extreme confidence and swagger; big-league competitor.

**Weaknesses:** Can get overly aggressive on all sides of the ball; tendency to bring bad batting practice habits into games; will drop shoulder and try to be a power hitter; has the actions and the arm to play shortstop, but doesn't always play in control and can get sloppy; emotions can take him out of game.

**Risk Factor/Injury History:** Low risk

**Bret Sayre's Fantasy Take:** The top fantasy prospect at the keystone, Odor is the kind of player who won't dominate any individual categories but can offer reliable all-around production. And with the dearth of high-impact second basemen both in the majors and minors, his fantasy value is even higher than it appears, particularly in deeper leagues. Heck, Daniel Murphy was top five at the position this year, and Odor can do that.

**The Year Ahead:** As of this writing, Odor doesn't have a clear path to the majors, as Jurickson Profar is ahead of him in the keystone queue. But as far as the skill set is concerned, Odor will be ready for a big-league taste in 2014, and his emergence allowed the Rangers to trade Ian Kinsler this past offseason. Regardless of what happens, Odor is going to hit the baseball, and he's going to bring a very particular brand of intensity to the field, which can often alternate between a positive and a negative attribute. He has a chance to develop into a .300 hitter with gap power, coming from an above-average defensive profile at an up-the-middle position. That's an all-star if everything clicks.

> **#39**
> BP Top 101 Prospects

## 2. Jorge Alfaro    C

**Born:** 6/11/93   **Age:** 21   **Bats:** R   **Throws:** R   **Height:** 6' 2"   **Weight:** 185

| MLB ETA | Hit | Power | Run | Glove | Arm | OFP | Realistic |
|---|---|---|---|---|---|---|---|
| **2015** | — | **65** | **60** | **50** | **80** | **70**<br>ALL-STAR | **50**<br>ML REGULAR |

| YEAR | TEAM | LVL | AGE | PA | R | 2B | 3B | HR | RBI | BB | SO | SB | CS | AVG/OBP/SLG | TAv | BABIP | BRR | FRAA | WARP |
|---|---|---|---|---|---|---|---|---|---|---|---|---|---|---|---|---|---|---|---|
| 2013 | HIC | A | 20 | 420 | 63 | 22 | 1 | 16 | 53 | 28 | 111 | 16 | 3 | .258/.338/.452 | .280 | .324 | -0.4 | C(82): 1.4, 1B(17): -1.2 | 2.8 |
| 2013 | MYR | A+ | 20 | 13 | 4 | 0 | 0 | 0 | 0 | 2 | 5 | 0 | 0 | .182/.308/.182 | .195 | .333 | 0.2 | 1B(1): -0.1 | -0.1 |
| 2013 | RNG | Rk | 20 | 26 | 5 | 2 | 0 | 2 | 8 | 2 | 6 | 2 | 0 | .429/.500/.810 | .494 | .500 | -1.3 | C(4): -0.0 | 0.4 |
| 2014 | TEX | MLB | 21 | 250 | 23 | 9 | 1 | 6 | 26 | 10 | 82 | 3 | 1 | .210/.258/.336 | .217 | .290 | 0.1 | C 0, 1B -0 | -0.2 |
| 2015 | TEX | MLB | 22 | 250 | 26 | 10 | 1 | 6 | 25 | 12 | 81 | 1 | 0 | .204/.260/.335 | .221 | .279 | -0.3 | C 0, 1B -1 | -1.0 |

Breakout: 0%    Improve: 0%    Collapse: 0%    Attrition: 0%    MLB: 0%        *Comparables: Wilson Ramos, Welington Castillo, Kyle Skipworth*

**Drafted/Acquired:** International free agent, 2010, Colombia

**Previous Ranking:** #4 (Org), #76 (Top 101)

**What Happened in 2013:** After an injury-plagued 2012 campaign, Alfaro played in a career-high 113 games, not counting his breakout performance in the Arizona Fall League.

**Strengths:** Plus athlete; plus strength; arm is 8; routine sub-1.9 pops; catch-and-throw weapon; raw power is 7; could play over plus; above-average run; sub-4.2 times to first; glove improving; could develop to solid-average; hit could play to average.

> **#41**
> BP Top 101 Prospects

**Weaknesses:** Torque-heavy swing limits bat control; highly susceptible to off-speed offerings; aggressive approach; hit tool is below average; could limit power utility; glove can get sloppy behind the plate; rushes foot-work; needs more receiving refinement.

**Risk Factor/Injury History:** High risk; dual-threat development/yet to play at Double-A level.

**Bret Sayre's Fantasy Take:** There's not a single catching prospect in baseball who can match Alfaro's fantasy up-side, and frankly it's not particularly close. Even though he's full of risk, the evil temptress that is a catcher who can hit 25 homers and steal double-digit bases can be irresistible. If it all clicks for him, he will be the top fantasy catcher in baseball.

**The Year Ahead:** After a strong Arizona Fall League showing, Alfaro will be ready to tackle the biggest professional challenge of his career, a likely start back in High-A before eventually arriving at the Double-A level. Pitchers with a plan can exploit the aggressive hitter, so a more refined approach at the plate could do wonders for the five-tool catcher. If everything comes together, Alfaro is a superstar, a middle-of-the-order bat with impact defense at a premium spot on the diamond. I've been hyping Alfaro since he was first stateside at age 16, and with each year, he takes another step toward that exceptional eventuality. He still comes with a high risk, but the ceiling makes him one of the most valuable prospects in the minors.

## 3. Alex Gonzalez   RHP

**Born:** 1/15/92    **Age:** 22    **Bats:** R    **Throws:** R    **Height:** 6' 2"    **Weight:** 195

| MLB ETA | CT | FB | CH | CB | SL | OFP | Realistic |
|---|---|---|---|---|---|---|---|
| Late 2014 | -- | 70 | 60 | -- | 60 | 60<br>NO.3 STARTER | 55<br>NO.4 STARTER |

| YEAR | TEAM | LVL | AGE | W | L | SV | G | GS | IP | H | HR | BB | SO | BB9 | SO9 | GB% | BABIP | WHIP | ERA | FIP | FRA | WARP |
|---|---|---|---|---|---|---|---|---|---|---|---|---|---|---|---|---|---|---|---|---|---|---|
| 2013 | SPO | A- | 21 | 0 | 4 | 0 | 9 | 9 | 23.7 | 30 | 1 | 7 | 20 | 2.7 | 7.6 | 69% | .382 | 1.56 | 4.56 | 3.19 | 3.77 | 0.6 |
| 2013 | MYR | A+ | 21 | 0 | 0 | 0 | 5 | 5 | 19.0 | 15 | 1 | 9 | 15 | 4.3 | 7.1 | 59% | .264 | 1.26 | 2.84 | 3.88 | 5.59 | 0.1 |
| 2014 | TEX | MLB | 22 | 2 | 3 | 0 | 9 | 9 | 32.0 | 39 | 4 | 17 | 18 | 4.8 | 5.1 | 50% | .311 | 1.74 | 6.00 | 5.64 | 6.52 | -0.3 |
| 2015 | TEX | MLB | 23 | 5 | 8 | 0 | 28 | 28 | 174.7 | 193 | 23 | 76 | 125 | 3.9 | 6.4 | 50% | .308 | 1.54 | 5.01 | 4.85 | 5.44 | -0.5 |

Breakout: 0%    Improve: 0%    Collapse: 0%    Attrition: 0%    MLB: 0%    *Comparables: Robbie Ross, Alex Cobb, Michael Belfiore*

**Drafted/Acquired:** 1st round, 2013 draft, Oral Roberts University (Tulsa, OK)

**Previous Ranking:** NR

**What Happened in 2013:** The 23rd overall pick in the 2013 draft, Gonzalez started nine games in the Northwest League before finishing the season with five starts in High-A.

**Strengths:** Plus-plus fastball; velo in low- to mid-90s; three-way life; natural cut; can run and sink it as well; true slider is second plus offering; 85-88 with tilt and bigger shape than cutter; plays well off the fastball; changeup flashes above-average potential.

**Weaknesses:** Delivery can get stiff; command needs refinement; not a consistent strike-thrower; changeup at 85-87 can get too firm and flat.

**Risk Factor/Injury History:** Low risk; two plus pitches; ready for Double-A level.

**Bret Sayre's Fantasy Take:** A great fit for his likely future home in Arlington, Gonzalez should be able to put up strong fantasy numbers there despite its offensive tendencies. In a small sample, he's been able to keep the ball on the ground at a 60 percent rate in the minors, and it is backed up by the reports. He could put up Matt Harrison ratios with Derek Holland strikeout totals.

**The Year Ahead:** Chi Chi Gonzalez might like a top-of-the-rotation ceiling, but he's a safe bet to develop into a mid-rotation starter. On the back of an extremely lively fastball—one that often features natural cut to the glove side—Gonzalez can challenge hitters in the zone, forcing weak contact on the ground. His slider is a second plus offering, one that shows a bigger shape than the harder cut fastball, thrown in the mid- to upper-80s with tilt. He can turn over the changeup, and several sources think it eventually becomes a solid-average to plus offering, giving Gonzalez more than enough to find success in a rotation. He shouldn't have a long stay in the minors.

**#70**

BP Top 101 Prospects

## 4. Luis Sardinas   SS

**Born:** 5/16/93    **Age:** 21    **Bats:** B    **Throws:** R    **Height:** 6' 1"    **Weight:** 150

| MLB ETA | Hit | Power | Run | Glove | Arm | OFP | Realistic |
|---|---|---|---|---|---|---|---|
| 2015 | 60 | -- | 70 | 60 | 60 | 60<br>1ST DIV | 50<br>ML REGULAR |

| YEAR | TEAM | LVL | AGE | PA | R | 2B | 3B | HR | RBI | BB | SO | SB | CS | AVG/OBP/SLG | TAv | BABIP | BRR | FRAA | WARP |
|---|---|---|---|---|---|---|---|---|---|---|---|---|---|---|---|---|---|---|---|
| 2013 | FRI | AA | 20 | 141 | 12 | 4 | 0 | 1 | 15 | 4 | 21 | 5 | 2 | .259/.286/.311 | .225 | .301 | -1.7 | SS(29): 0.9 | 0.0 |
| 2013 | MYR | A+ | 20 | 432 | 69 | 15 | 3 | 1 | 31 | 32 | 54 | 27 | 8 | .298/.358/.360 | .261 | .339 | 3.9 | SS(92): -3.6, 2B(1): -0.1 | 2.0 |
| 2014 | TEX | MLB | 21 | 250 | 26 | 8 | 1 | 1 | 16 | 10 | 47 | 9 | 3 | .244/.277/.303 | .216 | .290 | 0.6 | SS -0, 2B -0 | 0.0 |
| 2015 | TEX | MLB | 22 | 250 | 26 | 9 | 1 | 2 | 22 | 14 | 44 | 8 | 3 | .282/.325/.363 | .257 | .330 | 0.4 | SS 0, 2B 0 | 1.7 |

Breakout: 0%    Improve: 0%    Collapse: 0%    Attrition: 0%    MLB: 0%    *Comparables: Carlos Triunfel, Leury Garcia, Alcides Escobar*

**Drafted/Acquired:** International free agent, 2009, Venezuela

**Previous Ranking:** #5 (Org), #86 (Top 101)

**What Happened in 2013:** After several years of developmental setbacks and struggles, Sardinas was finally able to build on a strong season with another strong season, finishing the year in Double-A and flashing all the tools that made him one of the premier signings back in 2009.

**Strengths:** Slick defender at shortstop; arm is easy plus; actions are smooth and easy; impact potential; run is plus-plus; contact ability from both sides of the plate; excellent bat-to-ball ability; good plan of attack at the plate.

**Weaknesses:** Limited physical projection (strength); narrow hips/shoulders; injury history leads to durability concerns; well-below-average power; slick defender, but lack of focus can lead to casual errors; work ethic and intensity have been questioned.

**Risk Factor/Injury History:** Moderate risk; injuries to both shoulders on resume.

**Bret Sayre's Fantasy Take:** The speed is the distinguishing factor here, but despite a strong fantasy profile, his lack of any semblance of pop (four homers in 262 career minor-league games) will keep a bit of an anchor on his upside. He's also slightly team dependent, as his profile is way more valuable at the top of a lineup than the bottom.

**The Year Ahead:** Sardinas held his own in his 29-game Double-A sample, and a return trip to the level will answer more questions about the overall quality of his bat. Based on conversations with other teams, Sardinas is a highly coveted prospect, mostly on the back of his legit plus defensive profile at short. Add to the mix his plus-plus speed and his contact ability from both sides of the plate and you get a promising player, one who could become a 1980s throwback type, a la Tony Fernandez.

> #72
> BP Top
> 101
> Prospects

---

## 5. Michael Choice CF

**Born:** 11/10/89  **Age:** 24  **Bats:** R  **Throws:** R  **Height:** 6'0"  **Weight:** 215

| MLB ETA | Hit | Power | Run | Glove | Arm | OFP | Realistic |
|---|---|---|---|---|---|---|---|
| Debuted in 2013 | – | 65 | 50 | – | – | 55<br>>AVG REGULAR | 50<br>AVG ML PLAYER |

| YEAR | TEAM | LVL | AGE | PA | R | 2B | 3B | HR | RBI | BB | SO | SB | CS | AVG/OBP/SLG | TAv | BABIP | BRR | FRAA | WARP |
|---|---|---|---|---|---|---|---|---|---|---|---|---|---|---|---|---|---|---|---|
| 2013 | SAC | AAA | 23 | 600 | 90 | 29 | 1 | 14 | 89 | 69 | 115 | 1 | 2 | .302/.390/.445 | .303 | .358 | -4.9 | LF(55): -4.5, CF(52): -2.5 | 3.0 |
| 2013 | OAK | MLB | 23 | 19 | 2 | 1 | 0 | 0 | 0 | 1 | 6 | 0 | 0 | .278/.316/.333 | .294 | .417 | 0.0 | RF(4): 0.1, LF(2): -0.0 | 0.1 |
| 2014 | TEX | MLB | 24 | 250 | 27 | 10 | 0 | 7 | 30 | 20 | 61 | 1 | 0 | .253/.322/.401 | .264 | .310 | -0.4 | CF -2, LF -1 | 0.3 |
| 2015 | TEX | MLB | 25 | 449 | 57 | 18 | 0 | 14 | 54 | 41 | 113 | 1 | 1 | .261/.334/.414 | .275 | .327 | -1.1 | LF -9 | 0.2 |

Breakout: 1%    Improve: 16%    Collapse: 10%    Attrition: 13%    MLB: 34%    *Comparables: Eric Thames, Khris Davis, Todd Frazier*

**Drafted/Acquired:** 1st round, 2010 draft, University of Texas at Arlington (Arlington, TX)

**Previous Ranking:** #2 (Org; A's), #82 (Top 101)

**What Happened in 2013:** After a fractured hand ended his 2012 campaign, Choice rebounded in 2013, playing a full-season in the PCL, and even getting a nine-game cup of coffee at the major-league level.

**Strengths:** Big boy raw power; game power could play above plus; has a plan at the plate; shows recognition/reaction skills; will draw some walks; good athlete for his size/body type; average run; short-term option in center field.

**Weaknesses:** Body can get big; not a long-term [realistic] option in center field; arm is fringe at best; swing can get long; will always have miss; hit tool projects to average.

**Risk Factor/Injury History:** Low risk; fractured hand (2012) on resume; achieved major-league level.

**Bret Sayre's Fantasy Take:** With the potential for a harmful batting average, Choice is a better option in leagues that use on-base percentage (and even more so in leagues that use OPS). The power is great, but unless he can either hit in the .260 range or steal double-digit bases, there's a cap to his value. I mean, Chris Carter hit 29 bombs in 2013 and wasn't even a top-50 outfielder.

**The Year Ahead:** Choice is ready for an extended look at the highest level, but the weaknesses in his game could limit his overall value. At the end of the day, it's a left-field power-first profile, with a hit tool that might drag the power utility down a grade. He could hit 25 bombs with good on-base skills, which is a quality player even if the average is low and the defensive profile is fringy. The swing-and-miss might be more grotesque at the major-league level, as Choice has been a good mistake hitter in the minors and is less likely to see as many mistakes against upper-level pitching. I think he struggles before eventually settling in as an average player, one that can beat you with power if you enter his comfort zone, but not a consistent middle-of-the-order threat.

> #79
> BP Top
> 101
> Prospects

## 6. Nick Williams    LF

**Born:** 9/8/93   **Age:** 20   **Bats:** L   **Throws:** L   **Height:** 6' 3"   **Weight:** 195

| MLB ETA | Hit | Power | Run | Glove | Arm | OFP | Realistic |
|---------|-----|-------|-----|-------|-----|-----|-----------|
| 2016 | 70 | 60 | 70 | – | – | 65<br>1ST DIV/ALL-STAR | 50<br>ML REGULAR |

| YEAR | TEAM | LVL | AGE | PA | R | 2B | 3B | HR | RBI | BB | SO | SB | CS | AVG/OBP/SLG | TAv | BABIP | BRR | FRAA | WARP |
|------|------|-----|-----|-----|----|----|----|----|-----|----|-----|----|----|-------------|-----|-------|-----|------|------|
| 2013 | HIC | A | 19 | 404 | 70 | 19 | 12 | 17 | 60 | 15 | 110 | 8 | 5 | .293/.337/.543 | .303 | .371 | -0.4 | LF(73): -3.7, CF(8): -1.8 | 2.3 |
| 2014 | TEX | MLB | 20 | 250 | 28 | 8 | 2 | 7 | 25 | 7 | 78 | 3 | 1 | .222/.254/.367 | .222 | .290 | 0.4 | LF -2, CF -1 | -0.5 |
| 2015 | TEX | MLB | 21 | 250 | 28 | 9 | 3 | 8 | 30 | 10 | 78 | 1 | 1 | .233/.272/.397 | .242 | .308 | 0.0 | LF -2, CF -1 | 0.1 |

**Breakout:** 0%   **Improve:** 0%   **Collapse:** 0%   **Attrition:** 0%   **MLB:** 0%     *Comparables: Andrew Lambo, Marcell Ozuna, Travis Snider*

#88
BP Top 101 Prospects

**Drafted/Acquired:** 2nd round, 2012 draft, Ball HS (Galveston, TX)

**Previous Ranking:** On The Rise

**What Happened in 2013:** On a Low-A team absolutely stacked with seven-figure talent, Williams's offensive prowess and potential pushed him to the top of the class.

**Strengths:** Innate bat-to-ball ability; can put the barrel on velocity and can track spin; hit tool could end up a plus-plus tool; raw power is plus; good chance to play to that level in game action; 7 run; would play center field in most organizations.

**Weaknesses:** Outside of natural hitting ability, lacks baseball skills; approach is very aggressive (see ball, hit ball); plus-plus run but below-average baserunner; arm isn't a weapon; reads and routes in outfield can be head-scratchers.

**Risk Factor/Injury History:** High risk; lacks baseball skills outside of hitting.

**Bret Sayre's Fantasy Take:** Yawn, just another Rangers prospect with the potential to be a fantasy monster. If there are better tools-based bets for your fantasy farm system, there are probably not enough to count on both hands. Williams is a better prospect in this realm than in real life, as we don't care if he's a center fielder or (to an extent) can draw a walk.

**The Year Ahead:** Williams is a hitting freak, meaning he just stands in the box and squares up baseballs like he was born to do it. Unfortunately, his other baseball tools are far from developing into usable skills, as his overall feel for the game is lacking. But his hit tool is so good that it might not matter all that much if his other skills are unrefined; he could hit .300 with 20 bombs and look like a complete mess on the field, and most teams would take that profile with a smile. If Williams can add to his baseball acumen, this could be a star-level player. But even if he falls short of tool refinement, the natural feel for hitting should carry him all the way to the majors.

## 7. Joey Gallo    3B

**Born:** 11/19/93   **Age:** 20   **Bats:** L   **Throws:** R   **Height:** 6' 5"   **Weight:** 205

| MLB ETA | Hit | Power | Run | Glove | Arm | OFP | Realistic |
|---------|-----|-------|-----|-------|-----|-----|-----------|
| Late 2015 | – | 80 | – | 50 | 70 | 70<br>ALL-STAR | 45<br>QUAD A PLAYER |

| YEAR | TEAM | LVL | AGE | PA | R | 2B | 3B | HR | RBI | BB | SO | SB | CS | AVG/OBP/SLG | TAv | BABIP | BRR | FRAA | WARP |
|------|------|-----|-----|-----|----|----|----|----|-----|----|-----|----|----|-------------|-----|-------|-----|------|------|
| 2013 | RNG | Rk | 19 | 21 | 4 | 4 | 0 | 2 | 10 | 2 | 7 | 1 | 0 | .368/.429/.895 | .444 | .500 | 0.2 | 3B(4): 0.2 | 0.5 |
| 2013 | HIC | A | 19 | 446 | 82 | 19 | 5 | 38 | 78 | 48 | 165 | 14 | 1 | .245/.334/.610 | .316 | .305 | 3.1 | 3B(100): -3.6 | 3.7 |
| 2014 | TEX | MLB | 20 | 250 | 34 | 7 | 1 | 16 | 41 | 21 | 98 | 3 | 0 | .209/.278/.465 | .262 | .270 | 0.2 | 3B -2 | 0.5 |
| 2015 | TEX | MLB | 21 | 250 | 38 | 7 | 1 | 17 | 43 | 25 | 95 | 1 | 0 | .218/.299/.491 | .280 | .278 | -0.2 | 3B -2 | 2.7 |

**Breakout:** 7%   **Improve:** 18%   **Collapse:** 1%   **Attrition:** 8%   **MLB:** 22%     *Comparables: Giancarlo Stanton, Xander Bogaerts, Marcell Ozuna*

#95
BP Top 101 Prospects

**Drafted/Acquired:** 1st round, 2012 draft, Bishop Gorman HS (Las Vegas, NV)

**Previous Ranking:** #10 (Org)

**What Happened in 2013:** Gallo hit 40 delicious bombs in 2013, which paired nicely with a slightly chilled bottle of 172 whiffs.

**Strengths:** Grotesque raw power; elite; great extension; shows impressive bat speed/not just raw strength; arm is plus-plus weapon; glove has improved and could play to average; shows necessary work ethic to improve in the field.

**Weaknesses:** Huge swing-and-miss in his game; struggles against spin; extreme hip rotation allows for bat speed but limits his ability to maneuver the barrel after he launches; contact ability could limit his elite power potential; footwork at third still needs refinement; arm is extremely strong but not accurate.

**Risk Factor/Injury History:** High risk; the swing-and-miss is 80-grade.

**Bret Sayre's Fantasy Take:** The inherent problem with power-hitting prospects that have questionable hit tools is if the contact never shows up, their value becomes slim-to-none. Gallo could be a future fantasy first rounder if the hit tool allows the power to play at a 40+ pace, but the odds are more likely that he's a Russell Branyan type—which, while not a dead spot, would be a huge disappointment.

**The Year Ahead:** Gallo's future profile is often compared to Adam Dunn's, and on the surface, it makes some sense: both have huge left-handed power, huge swing-and-miss, and the ability to take a walk. Three-outcome types.

The problem is that people often confuse the realities of what Dunn has accomplished at the major-league level with what Gallo accomplished in Low-A. For reference, at the same point in his career, Dunn hit over .300 in his first stop in Low-A, striking out around 17 percent of the time. Gallo's strikeout rate was 37 percent in 2013. Pitching doesn't get any easier as you climb the ladder, so Gallo is facing long odds if he wants to develop into Adam Dunn. I can honestly say that I've never seen a minor leaguer with such raw power, but the swing-and-miss rate is just as extreme, and without contact improvement, I don't see the power living up to its massive potential.

## 8. Luke Jackson RHP

**Born:** 8/24/91 **Age:** 22 **Bats:** R **Throws:** R **Height:** 6' 2" **Weight:** 185

| MLB ETA | CT | FB | CH | CB | SL | OFP | Realistic |
|---|---|---|---|---|---|---|---|
| 2014 | – | 70 | 60 | 55 | – | 60 NO.3 STARTER | 50 LATE-INN RP |

| YEAR | TEAM | LVL | AGE | W | L | SV | G | GS | IP | H | HR | BB | SO | BB9 | SO9 | GB% | BABIP | WHIP | ERA | FIP | FRA | WARP |
|---|---|---|---|---|---|---|---|---|---|---|---|---|---|---|---|---|---|---|---|---|---|---|
| 2013 | VIS | A+ | 20 | 2 | 0 | 0 | 5 | 5 | 28.7 | 22 | 1 | 10 | 43 | 3.1 | 13.5 | 44% | .362 | 1.12 | 1.26 | 2.48 | 2.41 | 1.2 |
| 2013 | MOB | AA | 20 | 12 | 5 | 0 | 21 | 21 | 123.3 | 93 | 5 | 59 | 119 | 4.3 | 8.7 | 47% | .276 | 1.23 | 1.97 | 3.04 | 3.70 | 1.4 |
| 2014 | ARI | MLB | 21 | 2 | 3 | 0 | 8 | 8 | 40.0 | 35 | 4 | 21 | 37 | 4.8 | 8.3 | 47% | .306 | 1.42 | 4.36 | 4.22 | 4.73 | 0.1 |
| 2015 | ARI | MLB | 21 | 10 | 10 | 0 | 32 | 32 | 202.3 | 170 | 22 | 95 | 173 | 4.2 | 8.3 | 47% | .284 | 1.31 | 3.98 | 4.29 | 4.33 | 1.2 |

Breakout: 0%   Improve: 0%   Collapse: 0%   Attrition: 0%   MLB: 0%   *Comparables: Casey Crosby, Jarrod Parker, Wade Davis*

**Drafted/Acquired:** 1st round, 2010 draft, Calvary Christian HS (Fort Lauderdale, FL)

**Previous Ranking:** NR

**What Happened in 2013:** After a return trip to High-A to start the season, Jackson took a big step forward, finishing the season with a tremendous run in Double-A.

**Strengths:** Big arm strength; creates good angle to the plate; fastball routinely works in 91-97 range; often 93-96 with late life; changeup offers good deception from fastball; some sink; could develop into plus pitch; curveball can flash plus; can show sharp vertical break and depth; slider could develop into promising secondary pitch; thrown with velocity and some tilt; high baseball IQ.

**Weaknesses:** Delivery has effort; tendency to miss arm side and up; struggles to get over high front side in delivery; fastball command is below average; curveball/changeup command is below average; lacks above-average command projection.

**Risk Factor/Injury History:** Moderate risk; limited exposure to Double-A; stuff to pitch in big leagues.

**Bret Sayre's Fantasy Take:** Jackson has his share of upside, but there are causes for concern from a fantasy standpoint—and it all hinges on whether he can maintain an above-average breaking ball. Without it, he is unlikely to post particularly strong strikeouts rates and becomes closer to replacement level in shallower leagues.

**The Year Ahead:** Jackson has nasty stuff, especially the lively mid-90s fastball, but the secondary utility comes and goes, and the command is below average. Because of the effort in the delivery and his struggles repeating and working low in the zone, I think he is a better fit for the bullpen. But he has the arsenal and the arm strength to start, so if the command takes a step forward, Jackson has the potential to not only stick around in a rotation, but offer impact potential in that role.

## 9. Nomar Mazara RF

**Born:** 4/26/95 **Age:** 19 **Bats:** L **Throws:** L **Height:** 6' 4" **Weight:** 195

| MLB ETA | Hit | Power | Run | Glove | Arm | OFP | Realistic |
|---|---|---|---|---|---|---|---|
| Late 2016 | 60 | 70 | — | — | 60 | 60 1ST DIV PLAYER | 50 2ND DIV PLAYER |

| YEAR | TEAM | LVL | AGE | PA | R | 2B | 3B | HR | RBI | BB | SO | SB | CS | AVG/OBP/SLG | TAv | BABIP | BRR | FRAA | WARP |
|---|---|---|---|---|---|---|---|---|---|---|---|---|---|---|---|---|---|---|---|
| 2013 | HIC | A | 18 | 506 | 48 | 23 | 2 | 13 | 62 | 44 | 131 | 1 | 2 | .236/.310/.382 | .254 | .301 | -2.5 | RF(114): -4.7 | 0.4 |
| 2014 | TEX | MLB | 19 | 250 | 20 | 9 | 1 | 5 | 24 | 17 | 77 | 0 | 0 | .201/.256/.310 | .207 | .270 | -0.4 | RF -2 | -1.1 |
| 2015 | TEX | MLB | 20 | 250 | 27 | 9 | 1 | 7 | 26 | 19 | 74 | 0 | 0 | .218/.279/.356 | .233 | .287 | -0.5 | RF -2 | -0.6 |

Breakout: 0%   Improve: 0%   Collapse: 0%   Attrition: 0%   MLB: 0%   *Comparables: Marcell Ozuna, Jason Heyward, Chris Marrero*

**Drafted/Acquired:** International free agent, 2011, Dominican Republic

**Previous Ranking:** #8 (Org)

**What Happened in 2013:** Mazara made his full-season debut as an 18-year-old, holding his own in an advanced league, racking up 38 extra-base hits.

**Strengths:** Excellent bat speed; good overall feel for hitting; raw power is plus-plus; game power has legit chance to play; tracks the ball well and is strong against right-handing pitching; moves well for his size; strong arm; prototypical right-field profile.

**Weaknesses:** Swing can get hitchy; can limit bat control; struggles against arm-side stuff; lots of swing-and-miss in his game; hit tool receives mixed reviews; some question how much it affects power potential.

**Risk Factor/Injury History:** High risk; will play '14 season at age 19; still unrefined.

**Bret Sayre's Fantasy Take:** On the one hand, Mazara could end up with more home runs at the major-league level than his teammate Joey Gallo. On the other, he has less fantasy upside than Gallo due to his eligibility and because no one has Gallo's raw. Rangers Ballpark would be a great place for him to showcase his skills.

**The Year Ahead:** Mazara is ready for the High-A level, but the bat might not be ready to take a huge step forward; developmentally speaking, Mazara could repeat Hickory for several years before he would fall behind the curve. The bat has always impressed me, and the raw power is a legit 7 on the 2/8 scale. It's a middle-of-the-order corner profile if everything clicks, and I think Mazara has a good chance to put the swing together and allow the impressive power to play. He might not look the part (at the plate) for a few years, but a little extra patience is necessary when the ceiling is a first-division talent.

## 10.  Lewis Brinson   CF

**Born:** 5/8/94   **Age:** 20   **Bats:** R   **Throws:** R   **Height:** 6' 3"   **Weight:** 170

| MLB ETA | Hit | Power | Run | Glove | Arm | | OFP | Realistic |
|---|---|---|---|---|---|---|---|---|
| 2017 | — | 60 | 65 | 60 | 60 | | 70 ALL-STAR | 45 4TH-5TH OF |

| YEAR | TEAM | LVL | AGE | PA | R | 2B | 3B | HR | RBI | BB | SO | SB | CS | AVG/OBP/SLG | TAv | BABIP | BRR | FRAA | WARP |
|---|---|---|---|---|---|---|---|---|---|---|---|---|---|---|---|---|---|---|---|
| 2013 | HIC | A | 19 | 503 | 64 | 18 | 2 | 21 | 52 | 48 | 191 | 24 | 7 | .237/.322/.427 | .268 | .362 | -0.1 | CF(119): 4.0 | 2.5 |
| 2014 | TEX | MLB | 20 | 250 | 30 | 7 | 0 | 8 | 23 | 16 | 99 | 6 | 2 | .191/.248/.327 | .210 | .290 | 0.5 | CF 0 | -0.4 |
| 2015 | TEX | MLB | 21 | 250 | 28 | 8 | 0 | 8 | 28 | 19 | 98 | 4 | 1 | .197/.261/.346 | .224 | .296 | 0.1 | CF 0 | -0.6 |

Breakout: 0%    Improve: 0%    Collapse: 0%    Attrition: 0%    MLB: 0%    *Comparables: Marcell Ozuna, Greg Halman, Travis Snider*

**Drafted/Acquired:** 1st round, 2012 draft, Coral Springs HS (Coral Springs, FL)

**Previous Ranking:** #6 (Org), #99 (Top 101)

**What Happened in 2013:** My biggest regret in 2013 was not dressing up like Lewis Brinson's 38 percent strikeout rate and scaring members of the Rangers' front office on Halloween.

**Strengths:** Loud impact tools; plus athlete; plus raw power; plus arm; plus-plus potential glove; no-doubt center fielder at the highest level; plus run; feel for the game; hard worker/good makeup.

**Weaknesses:** Elite level swing-and-miss; noisy feet in the box; inconsistent setups; recognition/reaction skills are lacking; hit tool is poor; could limit any/all of the power utility.

**Risk Factor/Injury History:** Extreme risk; more than a two-grade jump from realistic role to OFP.

**Bret Sayre's Fantasy Take:** It's much tougher to see a road to Brinson being a fantasy stud, but it's still there if you squint. In shallower leagues, he's a player to target later on in drafts because his potential is something that is very tough to find on the waiver wire. But in points leagues, his strikeouts are a huge drawback.

**The Year Ahead:** I really love to watch Lewis Brinson, as he has everything you want to see in a young superstar talent: four tools with plus (or better) projections and very good makeup. But the swing-and-miss he showed in 2013 was historically bad, and the list of players with 38 percent strikeout rates in Low-A that turned into quality major leaguers won't cramp your hand to produce. Because of the skill set in center field, as well as the raw power and the plus run, Brinson is still a safe bet to reach the highest level, but without substantial improvement to the hit tool, Brinson won't sniff the ceiling his raw physical gifts suggest is possible. I think he needs to repeat Low-A and find some consistency and comfort in his swing. Yet another player you can afford to be extra patient with in the developmental process. The end result is more than worth it.

## Prospects on the Rise

**1. RHP Akeem Bostick:** A second-round pick in the 2013 draft, the highly projectable righty arrived on the scene with a raw label as a high-risk/high-reward gamble. The 6-foot-4 18-year-old has a live arm and can already pump his fastball in the low-90s, and according to several reports, his nascent curveball was more advanced than advertised, giving him the arsenal to take a big step forward in 2014 and emerge as a top-10 prospect in the system.

**2. RHP Cole Wiper:** After undergoing Tommy John surgery in 2012, the former Oregon starter fell to the Rangers in the 10th round, and signed for a cool $700,000. Fully healthy, Wiper can show a low-90s fastball, a promising slider, and good feel for a plus potential changeup. He still has to put it all together, which means refining his command and holding his velocity in longer outings, but the combination of size and stuff could push Wiper through the system quickly and up prospect lists if he finds immediate success at the full-season level.

### FROM THE FIELD

**Nick Williams**

**Player:** Nick Williams

**Team:** Texas Rangers

**Filed by:** Chris Mellen

**Date(s) Seen:** June 7-9, 2013

**Physical:** Wiry body; frame to fill into; lean muscle; athletic.

**Hit:** 60 grade; innate hitting ability; easy, fluid stroke; generates plus bat speed; explosive hands; swing covers entire plate and adjusts to path of the ball.

**Power:** 55 grade; produces power via bat speed and backspin; swing shows upward plane through hitting zone; in the early stages of creating lift with swing; generates postcontact extension.

**Glove:** 50 grade; very raw presently; average reads at the crack of the bat; average range; makes the routine plays hit out his way; left-field projection.

**Arm:** 45 grade; Long release; throws lose steam on way into infield; average accuracy; limited to left field.

**Speed:** 50 grade; 4.23-4.26 down the line digging for hit/avoiding double play; kicks it into higher gear running first to third; doesn't presently read pitchers well.

**Makeup:** 50 grade

**OFP:** 60; first-division regular

**Realistic Role:** 50; major-league regular

**Risk:** High; multiple facets of game are presently underdeveloped.

**3. 3B Drew Robinson:** I've long been a fan of Robinson, mostly because he shows impressive bat speed and the ability to make hard contact with the baseball. I think the 21-year-old is ready to take the big step forward and put all the offensive tools together. This could be yet another role 6 player in the Rangers system, a left-side infielder with legit pop in the bat.

## Factors on the Farm

### Prospects likely to contribute at the major-league level in 2014

**1. RHP Wilmer Font:** Font is an abnormally large human with an abnormally large fastball, and if he finds his command and a reliable second pitch, he has closer potential. Until then, he's an intimidating flamethrower who could carve out a late-innings role, most likely as a seventh/eighth-inning type.

**2. OF Jared Hoying:** It's not a sexy profile, as Hoying lacks impact-level tools, but this is the type of player that not only finds his way to the highest level but finds a way to complete. He's probably a fifth outfielder, a guy who holds his own in the outfield (better in a corner) and offers enough at the plate to keep a pitcher honest. That's not a bad outcome for a 10th-round pick.

**3. RHP Keone Kela:** A 12th-round pick in the 2012 draft, Kela only has 19 innings of full-season experience, but I wouldn't be shocked if he steamrolls his way to the majors in 2014. A physically strong and compact righty, Kela turned heads in the Arizona Fall League, pumping his fastball in the 98- to 100-mph range. Despite the limited professional experience in the upper minors, elite-level velocity has a tendency to move fast, and with an intense late-innings mentality already built into the profile, Kela could find himself reaching triple-digits in the majors before the year is out.

### FROM THE FIELD

**Jorge Alfaro**

**Player:** Jorge Alfaro

**Team:** Texas Rangers

**Filed by:** CJ Wittmann

**Date(s) Seen:** May 16-19, 2013

**Physical:** Muscular build; body type that could withstand longevity of season behind the plate; very good athlete.

**Hit:** 50 grade; aggressive approach; lot of hand movement in load; wrist cock before starting swing, limiting true bat control; good bat speed; makes loud contact; needs development in pitch recognition and has trouble with velo up in the zone; could play average.

**Power:** 60 grade; great raw strength; raw is plus; hit tool will limit power; present pop to all areas of field; natural leverage in swing.

**Glove:** 55 grade; improving receiving skills; strong wrist when receiving; needs to slow footwork down at times but improving; smooth transfers from glove to strong throwing arm; can get sloppy at times with balls in dirt or off target.

**Arm:** 80 grade; extreme arm strength; quick release with improving footwork; sub-1.9 pop consistently; 1.81 pop on steal in game.

**Speed:** 50 grade; very athletic; swift strides from athletic stance; uncommon for a catcher; 4.2.-4.3 range to first base from right side; speed will play average at full maturity.

**Makeup:** 50 grade; visibly frustrated in box at times.

**OFP:** 70; all-star

**Realistic Role:** 55; solid-average regular; legit dual threat

Risk: High; only three games at High-A level, injuries on resume.

### FROM THE FIELD

**Jorge Alfaro**

**Player:** Jorge Alfaro

**Team:** Texas Rangers

**Filed by:** Chris Mellen

**Date(s) Seen:** June 7-9, 2013

**Physical:** Sturdy frame; some more room to fill out; athletic; may lose some athleticism as fills out or due to defensive rigors of catching position.

**Hit:** 50 grade; shorter swing; quick, strong hands; plus-plus bat speed; yank in swing; follow-through causes hands to roll early.

**Power:** 60 grade; possesses plus-to-better raw power in batting practice; easily drives ball out; presently an upper-body hitter; high in-game power potential if learns to use lower body.

**Glove:** 50 grade; raw receiver behind the dish; stiff at times with glove; target will drift; quick feet, but rough footwork; body to smother balls in the dirt; in the early stages of learning how to focus defensively and slow the game down.

**Arm:** 70 grade; plus-plus raw strength; slow, long release; can struggle with grip; gets tangled coming out of crouch.

**Speed:** 50 grade; runs well for catcher; accelerates on the bases; gets out of the box well; will slow down as ages.

**Makeup:** 45 grade

**OFP:** 65; first-division regular/occasional all-star

**Realistic Role:** 50; major-league regular

**Risk:** High; hit tool and approach left questions; defense has ways to go behind plate.

---

**Jorge Alfaro**

**Player:** Jorge Alfaro

**Team:** Texas Rangers

**Filed by:** Steffan Segui

**Date(s) Seen:** Spring training, Instructional League, and Arizona Fall League

**Physical:** Thick athleticism. Very muscular and solid throughout.

**Hit:** 50 grade. Starts very compact and then stretches out as his hands go back with long load before stride. Hurts him on balls in. Still learning to hit break. Stays on balls middle or away well with good approach and hands that carry through contact. Overaggressive, needs to improve discipline.

**Power:** 60 grade. Line-drive hitter with carry due to good extension. More doubles as a result. Opposite-field pop will play well in Texas.

**Glove:** 60 grade. Still learning the mental aspects of catching. Receiving improving, excellent blocker. Energy and effort massively improved in 2013.

**Arm:** 80 grade. Elite arm. 1.9 or less pop times. Quick, explosive fluid actions.

**Speed:** 50 grade. Consistently runs well (4.4 to first) for a catcher but keeps getting bigger. Likely to lose a bit of that speed and flexibility as he gets older.

**Makeup:** 60 grade. Really matured a lot in the last year. High-energy player now who is becoming a field general.

**OFP:** 65; all-star caliber

**Realistic Role:** 55; solid-average first division regular.

**Risk:** Moderate; played very well in fall league but hasn't played above A-ball during season.

## FROM THE FIELD

### Joey Gallo

**Player:** Joey Gallo

**Team:** Texas Rangers

**Filed by:** Chris Mellen

**Date(s) Seen:** June 7-9, 2013

**Physical:** Huge frame; muscular; still room to add even more, especially in lower body; athlete; extremely strong body.

**Hit:** 40 grade; early extension in swing; fully leveraged, with back shoulder dropping often; has trouble adjusting due to max lift approach; can get bat on velocity; loose hands; ultra-aggressive approach—needs to learn how to control his strike zone.

**Power:** 65 grade; elite raw power; can drive ball out to all fields; impressive power to opposite field; generates huge lift and loft with swing; wheelhouse out and over the plate; holes in swing can cause power to play down; 30-plus home-run potential.

**Glove:** 50 grade; stiff and rigid present actions; feet tend to get tangled; will front the ball; engaged in the field; needs to get lighter on his feet and trust reactions; first base or left field likely destination.

**Arm:** 70 grade; plenty of arm strength for third; throws travel on a line across diamond; can drop arm slot and sling the ball; accuracy suffers.

**Speed:** 45 grade; digs out of box and on the bases; can take an extra base; aggressive runner.

**Makeup:** 60 grade; approaches and plays game in a noticeable manner.

**OFP:** 65; first-division player/occasional all-star

**Realistic Role:** 45; up-and-down guy

**Risk:** High; considerable improvement developing hit tool is necessary for rest of game to translate.

---

### Joey Gallo

**Player:** Joey Gallo

**Team:** Texas Rangers

**Filed by:** Ryan Parker

**Date(s) Seen:** March 2013

**Physical:** Huge athletic frame. Can play at current weight or bulk up to maximize power. Adam Dunn type.

**Hit:** 40 grade; Grade comes from high-level batspeed and elite strength. Does not show ability to adjust barrel.

**Power:** 80 grade; absolute monster in BP. Power to all fields. 40+ homer future

**Glove:** 40 grade; stiff actions in the field but a hard worker. Bad first step. Risky bet at third but could handle first or a corner outfield spot.

**Arm:** 70 grade; 94+ on the mound and shows it off in the field. Long arm action and can't throw from multiple angles.

**Speed:** 40 grade; slow out of first gear but picks up steam. Decent baserunner. Will steal 5-10 bases.

**Makeup:** 50 grade; hard worker. Much improved on defense. Lets early bad at-bats get in his head and alter approach.

**OFP:** 60; Mark Trumbo type

**Realistic Role:** 55; Russell Branyan type

**Risk:** Moderate to high. Struggles with big-league velocity and hard breaking stuff. Will get multiple shots to stick in big leagues due to elite power.

## FROM THE FIELD

### Joey Gallo

**Player:** Joey Gallo

**Team:** Texas Rangers

**Filed by:** CJ Wittmann

**Date(s) Seen:** May 16-19, 2013

**Physical:** Massive frame; good build; thick base; sneaky athletic for big frame.

**Hit:** 45 grade; good bat speed; will crush mistakes; uses hips to create extreme torque when deciding to swing (making it difficult to adjust); not great barrel control; swing is very long; massive swing-and-miss; has trouble against average secondaries; will expand the zone greatly; quality of hit tool will make extreme raw pop play down.

**Power:** 70 grade; massive raw power; great extension through swing; extreme leverage in swing.

**Glove:** 50 grade; good instincts when reacting; can make backhand play down line; improving footwork; will play to average at full maturity.

**Arm:** 70 grade; great arm strength; throws made on a line consistently; accuracy is an issue presently.

**Speed:** 40 grade; long strides; not a burner; instinctive baserunner

**Makeup:** 60 grade; great work ethic and did not show visible frustration after bad at-bats

**OFP:** 65; first-division regular/all-star

**Realistic Role:** 50; major-league regular

**Risk:** Extreme; one year at Low-A and he swings and misses a lot.

## FROM THE FIELD

### Alex "Chi Chi" Gonzalez

**Player:** Chi Chi Gonzalez

**Team:** Texas Rangers

**Filed by:** CJ Wittmann

**Date(s) Seen:** August 29, 2013

**Physical:** Nice build; comfortable thick lower half; added weight not needed.

**Mechanics/Delivery:** Long stride and good momentum to the plate; short arm action; 3/4 arm slot but arm can come through a bit late; lands on stiff front side at times; athletic enough to make up for it.

**Fastball:** 70 grade; 93-97 mph; three-way pitch; some with natural cut at 96; some with heavy sink at 96; also some with natural two-seam run; good downhill plane.

**Slider:** 60 grade; 85-88 mph; short, tight breaker; good shape and flashed tilt; works very well off of fastball.

**Changeup:** 55 grade; 82-88 mph; flashed sinking action; can get firm and flat often; good arm action; best when 82-84 mph.

**Cutter:** 60 grade; 89-91 mph; short, late horizontal movement; breaks bats often.

**Makeup:** 70 grade; plus makeup with little concerns from scouts.

**OFP:** 65; no. 2/3 starter

**Realistic Role:** 55; no. 4 starter on a contending team

**Risk:** Low; college arm ready for upper minors.

## 1. Marcus Stroman   RHP

**Born:** 5/1/91   **Age:** 23   **Bats:** R   **Throws:** R   **Height:** 5'9"   **Weight:** 185

| MLB ETA | CT | FB | CH | CB | SL | OFP | Realistic |
|---|---|---|---|---|---|---|---|
| 2014 | 70 | 70 | 60 | --- | 70 | 65 NO.2 STARTER | 60 LATE-INN RP/CLOSER |

| YEAR | TEAM | LVL | AGE | W | L | SV | G | GS | IP | H | HR | BB | SO | BB9 | SO9 | GB% | BABIP | WHIP | ERA | FIP | FRA | WARP |
|---|---|---|---|---|---|---|---|---|---|---|---|---|---|---|---|---|---|---|---|---|---|---|
| 2013 | NHP | AA | 22 | 9 | 5 | 0 | 20 | 20 | 111.7 | 99 | 13 | 27 | 129 | 2.2 | 10.4 | 45% | .301 | 1.13 | 3.30 | 3.33 | 4.11 | 2.1 |
| 2014 | TOR | MLB | 23 | 4 | 4 | 0 | 21 | 12 | 78.7 | 76 | 11 | 27 | 78 | 3.1 | 8.9 | 45% | .298 | 1.31 | 4.01 | 4.36 | 4.36 | 0.7 |
| 2015 | TOR | MLB | 24 | 7 | 5 | 0 | 72 | 12 | 135.0 | 123 | 17 | 43 | 131 | 2.9 | 8.7 | 45% | .286 | 1.23 | 3.58 | 3.90 | 3.89 | 1.9 |

**Breakout:** 28%   **Improve:** 36%   **Collapse:** 5%   **Attrition:** 31%   **MLB:** 47%   *Comparables: Jeremy Hellickson, Matt Harvey, Jake McGee*

**Drafted/Acquired:** 1st round, 2012 draft, Duke University (Durham, NC)

**Previous Ranking:** #8 (Org)

**What Happened in 2013:** Stroman made 20 starts at the Double-A level, showing bat-missing ability and sharp command, doing everything in his power to convince the doubters that he can be a starting pitcher.

**Strengths:** Strong and athletic; generates power in his delivery with lower half; impressive arm strength; fastball works low/mid-90s; can sit mid-90s in bursts; slider is true wipeout pitch; easy 7 grade; mid-80s with sharp tilt; changeup flashes plus; projects to play at that grade; excellent action and deception from fastball; shows plus-plus cutter in the 91-93 range; nasty and late glove-side slice; plus command profile; big-time competitor.

**Weaknesses:** Short; has to work down to create plane; fastball can arrive flat/lack movement; if he works up, becomes hittable; changeup can get too firm/overthrown.

**Risk Factor/Injury History:** Low risk; ready for major leagues

**Bret Sayre's Fantasy Take:** Stroman is that perfect combination of high fantasy potential in the rotation and a high fantasy floor in the bullpen. As a starter, he can rack up the strikeouts with multiple pitches and has the control/command to have a very strong WHIP—though his ERA may lag behind due to potential troubles with the long ball. As a reliever, he could be one of the top fantasy closers in baseball, but like any relief prospect, just because he's awesome doesn't mean he'll get saves when you want him to.

**The Year Ahead:** Stroman might be even shorter than his listed height (5'9"), and normally I would be the first person to put him into the reliever box—especially given the fact that he could be an elite closer in that role. But I think Stroman is a starter all the way, with more than enough strength and athleticism for the workload and a deep arsenal that he can command. He's atypical and unorthodox, but Stroman is going to be an impact starter at the major-league level. The stuff is well above average, the delivery and arm work very well and should be able to handle a starter's workload, and the aggressiveness and poise fit the mold of a frontline starter just as much as they do a late-innings arm. If you focus too much on the height you are going to miss the realities of the overall profile. This is a starting pitcher.

**#27**
BP Top 101 Prospects

## 2. Aaron Sanchez   RHP

**Born:** 7/1/92   **Age:** 21   **Bats:** R   **Throws:** R   **Height:** 6'4"   **Weight:** 190

| MLB ETA | CT | FB | CH | CB | SL | OFP | Realistic |
|---|---|---|---|---|---|---|---|
| 2015 | — | 70 | 60 | 65 | — | 70 NO.2 STARTER | 60 NO.3 STARTER |

| YEAR | TEAM | LVL | AGE | W | L | SV | G | GS | IP | H | HR | BB | SO | BB9 | SO9 | GB% | BABIP | WHIP | ERA | FIP | FRA | WARP |
|---|---|---|---|---|---|---|---|---|---|---|---|---|---|---|---|---|---|---|---|---|---|---|
| 2013 | DUN | A+ | 20 | 4 | 5 | 0 | 22 | 20 | 86.3 | 63 | 4 | 40 | 75 | 4.2 | 7.8 | 61% | .250 | 1.19 | 3.34 | 3.67 | 5.19 | 0.3 |
| 2014 | TOR | MLB | 21 | 3 | 5 | 0 | 18 | 15 | 68.3 | 69 | 9 | 43 | 55 | 5.7 | 7.2 | 53% | .296 | 1.65 | 5.31 | 5.62 | 5.77 | -0.2 |
| 2015 | TOR | MLB | 22 | 5 | 7 | 0 | 30 | 22 | 157.7 | 151 | 20 | 87 | 130 | 5.0 | 7.4 | 53% | .287 | 1.51 | 4.73 | 4.95 | 5.14 | 0.1 |

**Breakout:** 0%   **Improve:** 0%   **Collapse:** 0%   **Attrition:** 0%   **MLB:** 0%   *Comparables: Wilmer Font, Zack Wheeler, Casey Crosby*

**Drafted/Acquired:** 1st round, 2010 draft, Barstow HS (Barstow, CA)

**Previous Ranking:** #3 (Org), #32 (Top 101)

**What Happened in 2013:** Top-shelf stuff, but a frustrating year that included some minor injury setbacks and on-the-field performances that failed to match the hype.

**Strengths:** Elite arm action; ball explodes out of his hand; fastball routinely works in the mid-90s; heavy life; hard curveball in the low-80s shows plus potential; changeup flashes plus; late arm-side action; frontline stuff.

**Weaknesses:** Below-average command; can get stiff and upright in the delivery; can struggle to stay over the ball; loses movement and flattens out; curveball can lack snap/get slurvy; changeup too firm; some sources question the passivity in his approach; pitchability needs work.

**#31**
BP Top 101 Prospects

**Risk Factor/Injury History:** Moderate risk; yet to pitch at Double-A level; some minor injury concerns.

**Bret Sayre's Fantasy Take:** Sanchez has the higher fantasy upside as a starting pitcher, but he's unlikely to take enough of a step forward with his control to be a strong contributor in WHIP—making him likely a three-category guy at peak. His ability to keep the ball on the ground (58 percent ground-ball rate during the past two seasons) may help neutralize some of the Rogers Centre's home run-inducing tendencies.

**The Year Ahead:** Sanchez has some of the best arm action you will see, a lightning fast arm that allows the ball to just explode out of his hand. His mechanics can get out of whack, and he struggles to stay over the ball and finish his pitches. This causes his fastball to elevate and lose life, and his power curveball to get too slurvy and lose its bite. If you are optimistic about his command and refinement of the secondary stuff, Sanchez is a legit frontline number two starter, but there is still a sizeable gap between the present and future.

---

## 3.  Alberto Tirado  RHP

**Born:** 12/10/94  **Age:** 19  **Bats:** R  **Throws:** R  **Height:** 6' 1"  **Weight:** 177

| MLB ETA | CT | FB | CH | CB | SL | OFP | Realistic |
|---|---|---|---|---|---|---|---|
| 2017 | -- | 70 | 65 | --- | 60 | 65 NO.2 STARTER | 50 NO.3-4 STARTER |

| YEAR | TEAM | LVL | AGE | W | L | SV | G | GS | IP | H | HR | BB | SO | BB9 | SO9 | GB% | BABIP | WHIP | ERA | FIP | FRA | WARP |
|---|---|---|---|---|---|---|---|---|---|---|---|---|---|---|---|---|---|---|---|---|---|---|
| 2013 | BLU | Rk | 18 | 3 | 0 | 0 | 12 | 8 | 48.3 | 41 | 1 | 20 | 44 | 3.7 | 8.2 | 54% | .301 | 1.26 | 1.68 | 3.62 | 4.42 | 0.5 |
| 2014 | TOR | MLB | 19 | 1 | 3 | 0 | 9 | 8 | 35.7 | 44 | 6 | 25 | 16 | 6.3 | 4.0 | 49% | .308 | 1.96 | 7.07 | 7.08 | 7.68 | -0.7 |
| 2015 | TOR | MLB | 20 | 3 | 7 | 0 | 24 | 18 | 131.3 | 150 | 21 | 88 | 84 | 6.0 | 5.8 | 49% | .300 | 1.81 | 6.39 | 6.18 | 6.95 | -2.3 |

Breakout: 0%    Improve: 0%    Collapse: 0%    Attrition: 0%    MLB: 0%

*Comparables: David Holmberg, Jeurys Familia, Brandon Maurer*

**Drafted/Acquired:** International free agent, 2011, Dominican Republic

**Previous Ranking:** #10 (Org)

**What Happened in 2013:** After another start in extended spring training and another pass through the Appalachian League, Tirado proved to be ready for a bigger challenge in his 48 innings of short-season work.

**Strengths:** Loose, easy arm; good release; fastball is plus offering; works 91-95; good arm-side life; changeup is advanced for age; good fastball disguise and late action; slider also looks like future plus offering; 82-84 with sharp tilt; more to project in the body.

**Weaknesses:** Inconsistent mechanics; arm is whippy and release points vary; command is below average (present); slider is behind changeup; can saucer the pitch; body is underdeveloped/immature; needs to add strength.

**Risk Factor/Injury History:** High risk; short-season resume.

**Bret Sayre's Fantasy Take:** For fantasy purposes, there may not be a more interesting pitching prospect who hasn't yet reached full-season ball than Tirado. He could be a lot of things at this point, but if you judge it off his raw stuff, the fantasy potential is there across the board. If you can get in on the ground floor now, he's a candidate to see a huge spike in dynasty league value during the 2014 season.

**The Year Ahead:** Tirado is a beast in the making, with three pitches that could end as plus offerings. The delivery is inconsistent at present, and the body needs to add strength to hold stuff and log innings. Despite the iffy command at present, Tirado shows pitchability and aptitude, and with a slow-and-steady approach, has a good chance to develop into a top-tier prospect in the coming years. His stock is going to soar when he shoves in full-season ball, and when the command starts to refine, look out. This is an impact prospect that could develop into an impact major-league starter.

**#76**
BP Top
101
Prospects

---

## 4.  Daniel Norris  LHP

**Born:** 4/25/93  **Age:** 21  **Bats:** L  **Throws:** L  **Height:** 6' 2"  **Weight:** 180

| MLB ETA | CT | FB | CH | CB | SL | OFP | Realistic |
|---|---|---|---|---|---|---|---|
| Late 2015 | -- | 60 | 55 | -- | 60 | 60 NO.3 STARTER | 50 NO.4 STARTER |

| YEAR | TEAM | LVL | AGE | W | L | SV | G | GS | IP | H | HR | BB | SO | BB9 | SO9 | GB% | BABIP | WHIP | ERA | FIP | FRA | WARP |
|---|---|---|---|---|---|---|---|---|---|---|---|---|---|---|---|---|---|---|---|---|---|---|
| 2013 | DUN | A+ | 20 | 1 | 0 | 0 | 1 | 1 | 5.0 | 1 | 0 | 2 | 1 | 3.6 | 1.8 | 53% | .067 | 0.60 | 0.00 | 4.04 | 4.77 | 0.0 |
| 2013 | LNS | A | 20 | 1 | 7 | 0 | 23 | 22 | 85.7 | 84 | 6 | 44 | 99 | 4.6 | 10.4 | 51% | .342 | 1.49 | 4.20 | 3.62 | 4.08 | 2.0 |
| 2014 | TOR | MLB | 21 | 3 | 7 | 0 | 18 | 18 | 67.3 | 75 | 10 | 40 | 52 | 5.3 | 7.0 | 46% | .310 | 1.71 | 5.81 | 5.75 | 6.31 | -0.5 |
| 2015 | TOR | MLB | 22 | 6 | 9 | 0 | 27 | 27 | 158.7 | 158 | 20 | 89 | 140 | 5.0 | 7.9 | 46% | .299 | 1.56 | 5.04 | 4.87 | 5.48 | -0.4 |

Breakout: 0%    Improve: 0%    Collapse: 0%    Attrition: 0%    MLB: 0%

*Comparables: Jeurys Familia, Matt Magill, Jordan Norberto*

**Drafted/Acquired:** 2nd round, 2011 draft, Science Hill HS (Johnson City, TN)

**Previous Ranking:** #7 (Org)

**What Happened in 2013:** In his full-season debut, Norris showed the stuff that made him a second-round pick back in 2011; a four-pitch mix that can miss bats and force weak contact.

**Strengths:** Athletic; excellent arm strength; fastball works 92-95; can touch 97; some arm-side wiggle; slider is bat-missing pitch; 82-84 and sharp; turns over a promising changeup; good velocity separation and some late action; shows a mid-70s curve that he can locate.

**Weaknesses:** Command is below average; can lose his delivery; changeup still a work in progress; curveball is more show-me than showcase.

**Risk Factor/Injury History:** Moderate risk; only one start above the Low-A level; minor injury concerns.

**Bret Sayre's Fantasy Take:** After being dropped in many leagues following his brutal 2012 season, Norris showed again this year why he's worth investing in. He may lack the fantasy upside of a Stroman or Sanchez, but he's capable of racking up strikeouts at any level. So check and see if he's available in your league prior to the start of your draft—you may be surprised.

**The Year Ahead:** While it's foolish to suggest a 20-year-old pitcher is a safe bet to develop, Norris has the type of arsenal, body, and approach to minimize some of the risk normally associated with the developmental process. He's not a finished product—the command needs a full-grade jump and the secondary stuff needs more consistency—but the profile is advanced, and he could move fast in 2014 if it continues to click. I think he reaches Double-A at some point in 2014, and could set himself up for a late-season debut in 2015, assuming the command takes a step forward.

---

## 5.  Sean Nolin   LHP

**Born:** 12/26/89  **Age:** 24  **Bats:** L  **Throws:** L  **Height:** 6' 5"  **Weight:** 235

| MLB ETA | CT | FB | CH | CB | SL | OFP | Realistic |
|---|---|---|---|---|---|---|---|
| Debuted in 2013 | — | 50 | 60 | 50 | 50 | 55 NO.3-4 STARTER | 50 NO.4 STARTER |

| YEAR | TEAM | LVL | AGE | W | L | SV | G | GS | IP | H | HR | BB | SO | BB9 | SO9 | GB% | BABIP | WHIP | ERA | FIP | FRA | WARP |
|---|---|---|---|---|---|---|---|---|---|---|---|---|---|---|---|---|---|---|---|---|---|---|
| 2013 | BUF | AAA | 23 | 1 | 1 | 0 | 3 | 3 | 17.7 | 13 | 1 | 10 | 13 | 5.1 | 6.6 | 39% | .267 | 1.30 | 1.53 | 4.34 | 4.97 | 0.0 |
| 2013 | TOR | MLB | 23 | 0 | 1 | 0 | 1 | 1 | 1.3 | 7 | 1 | 1 | 0 | 6.8 | 0.0 | 30% | .667 | 6.00 | 40.50 | 15.08 | 12.58 | -0.1 |
| 2013 | NHP | AA | 23 | 8 | 3 | 0 | 17 | 17 | 92.7 | 89 | 6 | 25 | 103 | 2.4 | 10.0 | 36% | .333 | 1.23 | 3.01 | 2.82 | 2.84 | 3.0 |
| 2014 | TOR | MLB | 24 | 5 | 6 | 0 | 18 | 18 | 89.7 | 93 | 12 | 36 | 78 | 3.6 | 7.8 | 40% | .305 | 1.44 | 4.60 | 4.71 | 5.00 | 0.3 |
| 2015 | TOR | MLB | 25 | 9 | 10 | 0 | 30 | 30 | 184.3 | 187 | 24 | 63 | 178 | 3.1 | 8.7 | 40% | .314 | 1.36 | 4.20 | 4.09 | 4.57 | 1.3 |

Breakout: 22%    Improve: 40%    Collapse: 9%    Attrition: 30%    MLB: 55%          *Comparables: Christian Friedrich, Scott Barnes, Lance Lynn*

**Drafted/Acquired:** 6th round, 2010 draft, San Jacinto Junior College (Pasadena, TX)

**Previous Ranking:** #4 (Org), #97 (Top 101)

**What Happened in 2013:** Nolin was solid across two minor-league stops, showing good control and strikeout ability, and even made a not-so-memorable appearance at the major-league level.

**Strengths:** Good size/strength; clean delivery; creates steep plane to the plate; fastball is setup pitch; can work all quadrants; some arm-side life; changeup plays well off fastball; good deception and action in the low-80s; shows both average slider and curveball; mixes well; changes sight lines and planes; good command profile.

**Weaknesses:** Fastball is pedestrian and average at best, often working 89-90 range; command has to be sharp; has to keep hitters off-balance; breaking balls lack plus projections; small margin of error.

**Risk Factor/Injury History:** Low risk; achieved major-league level.

**Bret Sayre's Fantasy Take:** Even if Nolin hits his ceiling, he will not be in a perfect environment for his skill set at the major-league level in Toronto. For a left-hander who is very fly-ball heavy, Rogers Centre (and most other AL East parks) may diminish some of his fantasy numbers—leaving him looking better in the context of neutralized stats. He can be a bulk contributor in wins and strikeouts, while not destroying your ratios.

**The Year Ahead:** Nolin is a very low-risk major-league starter, with average stuff but good pitchability and command profile. He can move the ball around, changing sight lines and planes by backing up his fastball with a good changeup with arm-side fade, a loopier curveball in the low- to mid-70s, and a hard slider in the mid-80s. He missed bats in the minors but might be more of a weak-contact arm at the highest level, keeping hitters off-balance and behind in counts. I think he develops into a solid number four starter with a chance for a little more if the fastball plays up.

---

## 6.  A.J. Jimenez   C

**Born:** 5/1/90  **Age:** 24  **Bats:** R  **Throws:** R  **Height:** 6' 0"  **Weight:** 210

| MLB ETA | Hit | Power | Run | Glove | Arm | OFP | Realistic |
|---|---|---|---|---|---|---|---|
| 2014 | ..... | 50 | ..... | 60 | 60 | 50 ML REGULAR | 45 BACKUP C/<AVG ML |

| YEAR | TEAM | LVL | AGE | PA | R | 2B | 3B | HR | RBI | BB | SO | SB | CS | AVG/OBP/SLG | TAv | BABIP | BRR | FRAA | WARP |
|---|---|---|---|---|---|---|---|---|---|---|---|---|---|---|---|---|---|---|---|
| 2013 | NHP | AA | 23 | 223 | 28 | 15 | 0 | 3 | 29 | 16 | 37 | 1 | 2 | .276/.327/.394 | .271 | .319 | -0.7 | C(40): 1.9 | 1.3 |
| 2013 | DUN | A+ | 23 | 29 | 5 | 3 | 0 | 1 | 9 | 1 | 3 | 0 | 0 | .429/.448/.643 | .391 | .458 | -2.4 | C(7): -0.1 | 0.3 |
| 2013 | BUF | AAA | 23 | 31 | 0 | 1 | 0 | 0 | 0 | 1 | 2 | 0 | 1 | .233/.258/.267 | .189 | .250 | -0.5 | C(7): -0.0 | -0.1 |
| 2014 | TOR | MLB | 24 | 250 | 21 | 13 | 0 | 4 | 24 | 12 | 48 | 2 | 1 | .242/.280/.346 | .227 | .280 | -0.5 | C 1 | 0.3 |
| 2015 | TOR | MLB | 25 | 250 | 26 | 13 | 0 | 5 | 25 | 14 | 48 | 2 | 1 | .242/.288/.361 | .238 | .281 | -0.6 | C 0 | 0.3 |

Breakout: 0%    Improve: 0%    Collapse: 0%    Attrition: 0%    MLB: 0%          *Comparables: Manny Pina, Jordan Pacheco, Tony Cruz*

**Drafted/Acquired:** 9th round, 2008 draft, Academia Discipulos de Cristo (Bayamon, PR)

**Previous Ranking:** NR

**What Happened in 2013:** In his return to action after Tommy John surgery, Jimenez still managed to throw out close to 50 percent of would-be basestealers in Double-A.

**Strengths:** Excellent catch-and-throw skills; arm is plus; footwork is excellent; slow runner but quick feet; good receiver; intangibles for position; good swing at the plate; has some pop; average raw power.

**Weaknesses:** Assorted injuries throughout his career; defense-first catcher; hit tool likely to play below average; game power likely to play below average; well-below-average run.

**Risk Factor/Injury History:** Moderate risk; numerous injuries on resume; Tommy John surgery in 2012.

**Bret Sayre's Fantasy Take:** The least interesting player on this list for fantasy purposes, Jimenez shows up here mostly due to his defensive prowess. He's really only worth picking up on spec if you're in a simulation league.

**The Year Ahead:** Jimenez is a very good catcher, a weapon in the running game and with the pitchers. The bat can show some promise, and I actually like his swing; good path to the ball and shows bat speed. I don't see an impact bat, but with his defensive skill set, a down-the-lineup stick would still give him value as a starter. If he can actually stay on the field for a full season, Jimenez might take a step forward at the plate and emerge as a challenger to Dioner Navarro in 2015 or a good trade chip if he forces the issue sooner.

## 7. Franklin Barreto   SS

**Born:** 2/27/96   **Age:** 18   **Bats:** R   **Throws:** R   **Height:** 5'9"   **Weight:** 174

| MLB ETA | Hit | Power | Run | Glove | Arm | OFP | Realistic |
|---|---|---|---|---|---|---|---|
| 2018 | 50 | 50 | 60 | — | 60 | 65 | 45 |
|  |  |  |  |  |  | 1ST DIV/ALL-STAR | UT/<AVG REG |

| YEAR | TEAM | LVL | AGE | PA | R | 2B | 3B | HR | RBI | BB | SO | SB | CS | AVG/OBP/SLG | TAv | BABIP | BRR | FRAA | WARP |
|---|---|---|---|---|---|---|---|---|---|---|---|---|---|---|---|---|---|---|---|
| 2013 | BLJ | Rk | 17 | 194 | 30 | 16 | 6 | 4 | 19 | 13 | 42 | 10 | 4 | .299/.368/.529 | .308 | .375 | 1.4 | SS(42): 0.8 | 2.0 |
| 2013 | BLU | Rk | 17 | 58 | 4 | 5 | 1 | 0 | 7 | 2 | 14 | 0 | 2 | .204/.259/.333 | .208 | .275 | -1.3 | SS(15): -2.2 | -0.3 |
| 2014 | TOR | MLB | 18 | 250 | 25 | 9 | 1 | 4 | 18 | 9 | 79 | 5 | 3 | .189/.227/.286 | .186 | .260 | 0.0 | SS -2 | -1.0 |
| 2015 | TOR | MLB | 19 | 250 | 22 | 9 | 1 | 4 | 22 | 9 | 80 | 3 | 2 | .196/.230/.299 | .195 | .270 | -0.2 | SS -2 | -2.5 |

Breakout: 0%    Improve: 0%    Collapse: 0%    Attrition: 0%    MLB: 0%         *Comparables: Chris Owings, Jonathan Schoop, Juan Lagares*

**Drafted/Acquired:** International free agent, 2012, Venezuela

**Previous Ranking:** On The Rise

**What Happened in 2013:** In his professional debut, the seven-figure Latin American signing was dynamic in the Gulf Coast League and finished the season as a 17-year-old in the Appalachian League.

**Strengths:** Plus athlete; excellent hand-eye coordination; barrels the ball at the plate; hands are extremely impressive; good strength for present body; line-drive stroke; hit tool could end up being plus; power could play to average; arm is plus; run is plus; impact potential talent.

**Weaknesses:** Still raw in all aspects on the game; reactive see-ball/hit-ball approach; will chase and lose his setup; arm is strong but wild; actions aren't smooth at short; glove unlikely to stick at short.

**Risk Factor/Injury History:** High risk; short-season resume.

**Bret Sayre's Fantasy Take:** He's forever away, but Barreto has the raw ingredients to be a strong fantasy middle infielder (assuming he stays there). In what categories that future upside materializes is yet to be determined, but he makes for an interesting flier regardless.

**The Year Ahead:** Barreto showed off his tools—especially his ability to put his bat on the ball—in his debut, and emerged as a legit professional prospect and not just an expensive amateur signing. There's a huge gap between present and future, and you will be hard pressed to find a source that likes his glove enough to project him at the position to the highest level. But he has more than enough arm for third and more than enough athleticism for the outfield, so the Jays have options should a move be required in the coming years. A return trip to the Appalachian League will be in order for Barreto, and given his precocious talent, this is must-see scouting in 2014.

## 8. D.J. Davis   CF

**Born:** 7/25/94   **Age:** 19   **Bats:** L   **Throws:** R   **Height:** 6'1"   **Weight:** 180

| MLB ETA | Hit | Power | Run | Glove | Arm | OFP | Realistic |
|---|---|---|---|---|---|---|---|
| Late 2017 | 50 | 50 | 80 | 65 | 50 | 65 | 45 |
|  |  |  |  |  |  | 1ST DIV/ALL-STAR | BACKUP/<AVG REG |

| YEAR | TEAM | LVL | AGE | PA | R | 2B | 3B | HR | RBI | BB | SO | SB | CS | AVG/OBP/SLG | TAv | BABIP | BRR | FRAA | WARP |
|---|---|---|---|---|---|---|---|---|---|---|---|---|---|---|---|---|---|---|---|
| 2013 | BLU | Rk | 18 | 258 | 35 | 8 | 7 | 6 | 25 | 26 | 76 | 13 | 8 | .240/.323/.418 | .253 | .329 | -1.4 | CF(57): -8.4 | -0.5 |
| 2014 | TOR | MLB | 19 | 250 | 28 | 7 | 1 | 5 | 17 | 15 | 87 | 9 | 4 | .180/.237/.280 | .189 | .260 | 0.4 | CF -3, LF 0 | -1.3 |
| 2015 | TOR | MLB | 20 | 250 | 24 | 9 | 1 | 5 | 22 | 17 | 83 | 7 | 4 | .193/.259/.307 | .210 | .275 | 0.2 | CF -3, LF 0 | -1.9 |

Breakout: 0%    Improve: 0%    Collapse: 0%    Attrition: 0%    MLB: 0%         *Comparables: Aaron Hicks, Joe Benson, Che-Hsuan Lin*

**Drafted/Acquired:** 1st round, 2012 draft, Stone County HS (Wiggins, MS)

**Previous Ranking:** #5 (Org)

**What Happened in 2013:** In his return trip to Bluefield, Davis had an up-and-down short-season, flashing the impact tools while wearing the inconsistency of a teenager.

**Strengths:** High-end athlete; can run with anybody; range for days; arm is solid; glove projects to plus; shows bat speed at the plate; can drive the baseball; power could be even better than projection (average).

**Weaknesses:** Still very raw on all sides of the ball; reads/routes need work; big swing-and-miss at the plate; struggles with velocity; struggles against spin; more of an athlete than a skill player at this stage.

**Risk Factor/Injury History:** High risk; short-season resume.

**Bret Sayre's Fantasy Take:** It's no exaggeration to say that Davis has the highest fantasy ceiling of anyone in this system. He's also pretty unlikely to reach it. The speed is tantalizing and unlike many other 80-grade runners, Davis actually has the potential to contribute some in the power categories. This is exactly the type of player who sees a value bump in shallower leagues with farm systems due to his extreme risk/reward.

**The Year Ahead:** Davis has a monster ceiling, a prototypical leadoff type with impact speed, enough thunder in the bat to keep pitchers honest, and a plus profile at a premium up-the-middle position. He has a very long way to go on all sides on the ball, and the raw tools are most certainly raw at this point, especially when it comes to game application/utility. But this is the type of developmental project that can pay huge dividends in a few years, as Davis has all-star level talent and five-tool potential.

---

## 9.  Chase DeJong  LHP

**Born:** 12/29/93  **Age:** 20  **Bats:** L  **Throws:** R  **Height:** 6' 4"  **Weight:** 185

| MLB ETA | | CT | FB | CH | CB | SL | | OFP | Realistic |
|---|---|---|---|---|---|---|---|---|---|
| 2017 | | – | 60 | 55 | 60 | – | | 60 NO.3 STARTER | 50 NO.4 STARTER |

| YEAR | TEAM | LVL | AGE | W | L | SV | G | GS | IP | H | HR | BB | SO | BB9 | SO9 | GB% | BABIP | WHIP | ERA | FIP | FRA | WARP |
|---|---|---|---|---|---|---|---|---|---|---|---|---|---|---|---|---|---|---|---|---|---|---|
| 2013 | BLU | Rk | 19 | 2 | 3 | 0 | 13 | 10 | 56.0 | 58 | 2 | 10 | 66 | 1.6 | 10.6 | 42% | .359 | 1.21 | 3.05 | 2.13 | 3.23 | 1.4 |
| 2014 | TOR | MLB | 20 | 1 | 2 | 0 | 10 | 5 | 36.0 | 43 | 6 | 23 | 22 | 5.8 | 5.5 | 42% | .312 | 1.84 | 6.49 | 6.52 | 7.05 | -0.6 |
| 2015 | TOR | MLB | 21 | 4 | 5 | 1 | 29 | 13 | 118.0 | 130 | 18 | 65 | 82 | 5.0 | 6.3 | 42% | .299 | 1.65 | 5.76 | 5.61 | 6.27 | -1.4 |

Breakout: 0%    Improve: 0%    Collapse: 0%    Attrition: 0%    MLB: 0%          *Comparables: Jarred Cosart, Enny Romero, Rafael Dolis*

**Drafted/Acquired:** 2nd round, 2012 draft, Woodrow Wilson HS (Long Beach, CA)

**Previous Ranking:** On The Rise

**What Happened in 2013:** In his professional debut, the former second-round pick made 13 appearances (including 10 starts), missing 66 bats in only 56 innings while walking only 10.

**Strengths:** Very projectable (physically); good pitchability; good arm action; fastball projects to be plus offering; curveball projects to plus; good depth/heavy vertical action; some feel for a changeup; projects to at least average; good command profile.

**Weaknesses:** Fastball is pedestrian at present; works 88-91; can flatten out; curveball can break too early out of the hand; start too high; changeup is below average at present; tendency to overthrow pitch.

**Risk Factor/Injury History:** High risk; short-season resume.

**Bret Sayre's Fantasy Take:** There's a lot to like about DeJong, and there's no shame in ranking behind the arms ahead of him. Like most everyone else here, he's a long way off, but he is a starter kit for someone who can have an above-average impact in all four starting pitching categories.

**The Year Ahead:** Several sources waxed poetic about DeJong's arm action and arsenal projection, suggesting the fastball velocity is going to arrive and take the 20-year-old arm to the next prospect level. He has feel for craft, and the curveball already shows its plus potential. If he can take a step forward in full-season ball, DeJong has a chance to emerge as a top-101 prospect in the game. If the fastball starts to tick up, look out.

---

## 10.  Jairo Labourt  LHP

**Born:** 3/7/94  **Age:** 20  **Bats:** L  **Throws:** L  **Height:** 6' 4"  **Weight:** 204

| MLB ETA | | CT | FB | CH | CB | SL | | OFP | Realistic |
|---|---|---|---|---|---|---|---|---|---|
| Late 2017 | | – | 65 | 50 | – | 60 | | 60 NO.3 STARTER | 50 NO.4 STARTER |

| YEAR | TEAM | LVL | AGE | W | L | SV | G | GS | IP | H | HR | BB | SO | BB9 | SO9 | GB% | BABIP | WHIP | ERA | FIP | FRA | WARP |
|---|---|---|---|---|---|---|---|---|---|---|---|---|---|---|---|---|---|---|---|---|---|---|
| 2013 | BLU | Rk | 19 | 2 | 2 | 0 | 12 | 8 | 51.7 | 39 | 3 | 14 | 45 | 2.4 | 7.8 | 56% | .248 | 1.03 | 1.92 | 3.43 | 4.77 | 0.4 |
| 2014 | TOR | MLB | 20 | 1 | 4 | 0 | 10 | 8 | 35.7 | 45 | 6 | 25 | 17 | 6.3 | 4.3 | 45% | .309 | 1.96 | 7.16 | 7.03 | 7.78 | -0.8 |
| 2015 | TOR | MLB | 21 | 3 | 7 | 0 | 23 | 17 | 124.0 | 138 | 20 | 77 | 78 | 5.6 | 5.7 | 45% | .293 | 1.74 | 6.15 | 6.06 | 6.68 | -1.9 |

Breakout: 0%    Improve: 0%    Collapse: 0%    Attrition: 0%    MLB: 0%          *Comparables: Matt Magill, Brandon Maurer, Patrick Corbin*

**Drafted/Acquired:** International free agent, 2011, Dominican Republic

**Previous Ranking:** NR

**What Happened in 2013:** After 12 complex-level starts in 2012, the then-19-year-old climbed a level to the Appalachian League, where the big-bodied Dominican allowed 39 hits in over 51 innings of work.

**Strengths:** Big frame; long legs; arm works well; fastball can sit 89-93; touches a little higher; projects to throw harder; slider has wipeout potential; mid-80s velocity and sharp slice; good pitchability.

**Weaknesses:** Body could be high-maintenance; fastball velocity has yet to regulate in plus range; slider can flatten out; changeup is underdeveloped; more control than command.

**Risk Factor/Injury History:** High risk; short-season resume.

**Bret Sayre's Fantasy Take:** The short-season levels of the Blue Jays system are like clown cars that fantasy-relevant pitchers keep climbing out of. As a left-hander who will need to develop a pitch to keep righties in check to remain a starter, Labourt is a slightly higher risk to end up in the 'pen than some of the other names on this list.

**The Year Ahead:** My sources absolutely love this arm, saying he has the potential to have three plus pitches to go along with good feel for craft. With a big, strong body and a clean arm, you can see a workhorse type as a floor, and if you really want to dream, Labourt could find a home in the middle of a major-league rotation (or perhaps higher if you think the fastball really ticks up during the developmental process). The Jays are ridiculously stacked at the short-season levels, and Labourt has the stuff and pitchability to stand out in a crowded prospect field.

## Notable Omission

**RHP Roberto Osuna:** A healthy Osuna is a likely top-five player in this system, but thanks to Tommy John surgery, the 18-year-old pitcher is on the shelf for the 2014 season. While it's quite common for arms to make a full recovery after such a procedure, the ones that improve their chances are the ones with advanced makeup and work ethic, two things that some sources have questioned about Osuna in the past. I can't speak to the specifics of such opinion, but I do have my own concerns about his already high-maintenance body, and how a prolonged recovery process could affect his physical form. This could either be viewed as an opportunity for Osuna to take a step forward with his physical work ethic or a substantial roadblock, as his approach could hinder his ability to fully recover.

## Prospects on the Rise

**1. RHP Clinton Hollon:** An athletic righty with big arm strength and feel for a deep arsenal, Hollon received several votes of confidence from scouts that encouraged me to include him in the top 10. He needs to stay healthy and stay on the field, but the profile is yet another impact rotation arm with projections in the two/three starter range. The Jays are growing these guys on trees in the lower minors.

**2. 3B Mitch Nay:** A supplemental first-round pick in 2012, Nay has legit above-average projections on the hit/power tools, but several questions about his athleticism and ultimate defensive profile pushed him off the top 10. If you really like the bat, the defensive limitations won't bother you much, but if he has to eventually move to first base, the bat needs to be a heavy player for him to have value.

**3. RHP Miguel Castro:** Stop me when this gets old: yet another highly projectable arm at the short-season level, Castro looks the part in the uniform and shows off the live arm on the mound, already working in the low-90s and touching 95-96. No doubt scheduled for another short-season assignment in 2014, Castro is going to be a national prospect after more people get to see this kid on the hill. It wouldn't shock me if he's securely in the top 10 at this time next season.

## Factors on the Farm

### Prospects likely to contribute at the major-league level in 2014

**1. RHP John Stilson:** It's most likely a 7th/8th inning profile rather than a closer, but the former Texas A&M arm can bring the funk in short bursts, routinely working his heater in the 95+ range and mixing in a hard, biting slider and heavy changeup. He's going to be a very good bullpen arm.

**2. 3B Andy Burns:** Burns turned heads with a strong offensive campaign in the Arizona Fall League, showing good bat-to-ball skills and a mature approach. Unless you really believe in the bat, Burns is probably not going to be a major-league regular, but with some defensive versatility and enough stick to keep pitchers honest, he could find a role as a bench bat or a second-division type if everything comes together at the plate.

---

## FROM THE FIELD

### Marcus Stroman

**Player:** Marcus Stroman

**Team:** Toronto Blue Jays

**Filed by:** Jeff Moore

**Date(s) Seen:** Spring training 2013

**Physical:** Short (5'9"), but has exceptional athleticism.

**Mechanics/Delivery:** Smooth mechanics and top-of-the-charts arm speed allow him to get the most out of his limited frame. Despite size, generates velocity without max-effort delivery.

**Fastball:** Two fastballs (four-seam and cutter) which are both 70 grade, premium velocity (94- to 96-mph four-seam, 91- to 93-mph cutter). Fastball tends to flatten out because of his size and he struggles to create downward plane. Throws a ton of strikes.

**Slider:** 60 grade. Hard, sweeping pitch that will dominate right-handed hitters.

**Changeup:** 60 grade currently, potential 70 pitch. Plus movement, fading hard to the arm side. His exceptional arm speed creates extra deception.

**Makeup:** 60 grade. Generally considered to have strong makeup. Went to a good school and comes from a good family, but has a 50-game drug suspension on his record.

**OFP:** 65; no. 2 starter

**Realistic Role:** 60; late-innings reliever

**Risk:** Low, to become an effective big league pitcher, but moderate to become a starter if you worry about the size.

---

### Marcus Stroman

**Player:** Marcus Stroman

**Team:** Toronto Blue Jays

**Filed by:** Steffan Segui

**Date(s) Seen:** October 16, 18, 23, and 31, 2013

**Physical:** Small and athletic but not thin.

**Mechanics/Delivery:** Free easy, smooth delivery. Very up-tempo, rotational mechanics. Not sustainable as a starter. Can stay on plane due to lack of height. Front side is soft and throws him off, inconsistent break and control. Command is below average. Will improve in the 'pen.

**Fastball:** 60 grade. Good late life, tail when on but flat if he isn't on top of it. Explodes out of hand and gets on hitter quick.

**Slider:** 70 grade. Hard late break. Inconsistent life currently; can be a plus-plus pitch. Starts behind right-handed hitters and has a hard sharp two-plane buckling break.

**Curveball:** 55 grade. Secondary off speed. Shows solid break and shape. May dump if he moves to 'pen full time.

**Changeup:** 50 grade. Tick below average now. Tough to throw with his delivery. Has some sink to it.

**Makeup:** 60 grade. Excellent poise and aggressive. Went to Duke. Was the starting second baseman and a pitcher. Three times Academic Honor Roll. 50-game suspension in 2013.

**OFP:** 60; no. 2/3 starter

**Realistic Role:** 60; closer in bullpen

**Risk:** Low. He will get MLB outs in some role, just not sure which one.

**3. RHP Deck McGuire:** Taken 11th overall in the 2010 draft, McGuire has yet to reach the heights suggested and projected by his lofty draft placement. Stuck in a Double-A purgatory since the end of the 2011 season, the 24-year-old righty has made 57 starts and logged over 320 innings at that level without advancement. It's a solid-average at best arsenal, but McGuire did show some signs of life in 2013; if he's actually allowed to pitch outside the Eastern League in 2014, he might find his way to the majors, where his likely role is a back-end starter or middle reliever.

## 1. Lucas Giolito  RHP

**Born:** 7/14/94  **Age:** 19  **Bats:** R  **Throws:** R  **Height:** 6'6"  **Weight:** 225

| MLB ETA | | CT | FB | CH | CB | SL | | OFP | Realistic |
|---|---|---|---|---|---|---|---|---|---|
| 2016 | | — | 80 | 70 | 80 | — | | 80<br>ELITE SP | 70<br>NO.1-2 STARTER |

| YEAR | TEAM | LVL | AGE | W | L | SV | G | GS | IP | H | HR | BB | SO | BB9 | SO9 | GB% | BABIP | WHIP | ERA | FIP | FRA | WARP |
|---|---|---|---|---|---|---|---|---|---|---|---|---|---|---|---|---|---|---|---|---|---|---|
| 2013 | AUB | A- | 18 | 1 | 0 | 0 | 3 | 3 | 14.0 | 9 | 1 | 4 | 14 | 2.6 | 9.0 | 67% | .250 | 0.93 | 0.64 | 3.31 | 3.56 | 0.3 |
| 2013 | NAT | Rk | 18 | 1 | 1 | 0 | 8 | 8 | 22.7 | 19 | 0 | 10 | 25 | 4.0 | 9.9 | 53% | .322 | 1.28 | 2.78 | 2.58 | 3.89 | 0.4 |
| 2014 | WAS | MLB | 19 | 2 | 3 | 0 | 9 | 9 | 33.7 | 38 | 4 | 20 | 21 | 5.3 | 5.6 | 48% | .325 | 1.71 | 5.90 | 5.49 | 6.41 | -0.4 |
| 2015 | WAS | MLB | 20 | 6 | 9 | 0 | 29 | 29 | 182.0 | 186 | 20 | 89 | 132 | 4.4 | 6.5 | 48% | .315 | 1.51 | 4.94 | 4.59 | 5.37 | -0.9 |

**Breakout:** 0%  **Improve:** 0%  **Collapse:** 0%  **Attrition:** 0%  **MLB:** 0%  *Comparables: Jonathan Pettibone, Jenrry Mejia, Julio Teheran*

**Drafted/Acquired:** 1st round, 2012 draft, Harvard-Westlake HS (Los Angeles, CA)

**Previous Ranking:** #2 (Org), #70 (Top 101)

**What Happened in 2013:** After only appearing in one game before falling victim to Tommy John surgery in 2012, Giolito returned to the hill the following summer, making 11 starts and hitting 100 on the gun.

**Strengths:** Elite size/strength; creates steep plane to the plate; elite arm strength; easy explosion from the hand; fastball works comfortably in the 94-97 range; can touch 100; big late life; future elite pitch; curveball is true hammer; thrown with slider velocity with big 12-6 shape; second elite future offering; changeup shows late vertical life and will eventually become monster pitch because of the arm action and fastball fear; good pitchability for a power arm.

**Weaknesses:** Easy release but delivery can show some effort; he has a lot of body to control; can struggle with mechanical consistency; command is fringe at present; changeup underdeveloped at present; good action but struggles to command the pitch.

**Risk Factor/Injury History:** High risk; Tommy John surgery on resume; yet to pitch at full-season level.

**Bret Sayre's Fantasy Take:** If everything breaks right, Giolito could end up as the best pitcher in the major leagues one day. On the other hand, acting like that's a given could get you into serious trouble in dynasty leagues. The fact that he's a top-20 fantasy prospect while not having thrown a pitch in full-season ball shows you the upside—he could be elite in all four categories. Ignore the uncertainty or time frame at your own risk.

**The Year Ahead:** On paper, Giolito has the highest ceiling of any arm in the minors, and that list includes Taijuan Walker and Archie Bradley. It's an almost irresponsible combination of size and stuff, a 6'6" power righty who can sit in the mid- to upper-90s with a lively fastball and back it up with an unhittable hard curveball that can show intense vertical depth. He's not far removed from Tommy John surgery, and the command profile needs refinement, but the 19-year-old arm should dominate at the A-ball level in 2014; when the Nationals take the governor off the semi in 2015, Giolito should erupt into the premier arm in baseball, if he doesn't already have claim on that distinction after his full-season debut. This is what it looks like, folks. This is a future number one starter at the major-league level.

> **#13**
> BP Top 101 Prospects

## 2. A.J. Cole  RHP

**Born:** 1/5/92  **Age:** 22  **Bats:** R  **Throws:** R  **Height:** 6'5"  **Weight:** 200

| MLB ETA | | CT | FB | CH | CB | SL | | OFP | Realistic |
|---|---|---|---|---|---|---|---|---|---|
| Late 2014 | | — | 70 | 60 | — | 50 | | 60<br>NO.3 STARTER | 50<br>NO.4 STARTER |

| YEAR | TEAM | LVL | AGE | W | L | SV | G | GS | IP | H | HR | BB | SO | BB9 | SO9 | GB% | BABIP | WHIP | ERA | FIP | FRA | WARP |
|---|---|---|---|---|---|---|---|---|---|---|---|---|---|---|---|---|---|---|---|---|---|---|
| 2013 | POT | A+ | 21 | 6 | 3 | 0 | 18 | 18 | 97.3 | 96 | 12 | 23 | 102 | 2.1 | 9.4 | 38% | .317 | 1.22 | 4.25 | 3.69 | 4.44 | 1.8 |
| 2013 | HAR | AA | 21 | 4 | 2 | 0 | 7 | 7 | 45.3 | 31 | 3 | 10 | 49 | 2.0 | 9.7 | 39% | .248 | 0.90 | 2.18 | 2.68 | 2.84 | 1.1 |
| 2014 | WAS | MLB | 22 | 7 | 8 | 0 | 24 | 24 | 120.7 | 124 | 15 | 39 | 100 | 2.9 | 7.5 | 39% | .324 | 1.36 | 4.46 | 4.27 | 4.85 | 0.2 |
| 2015 | WAS | MLB | 23 | 12 | 10 | 0 | 32 | 32 | 210.3 | 186 | 21 | 54 | 195 | 2.3 | 8.3 | 39% | .302 | 1.14 | 3.27 | 3.33 | 3.55 | 3.4 |

**Breakout:** 0%  **Improve:** 0%  **Collapse:** 0%  **Attrition:** 0%  **MLB:** 0%  *Comparables: Jeremy Hellickson, Hector Rondon, Eric Hurley*

**Drafted/Acquired:** 4th round, 2010 draft, Oviedo HS (Oviedo, FL)

**Previous Ranking:** #4 (Org)

**What Happened in 2013:** Cole survived the season without getting traded, and he rewarded the developmental patience with developmental progress, pitching his way to the Double-A level.

**Strengths:** Prototypical size; excellent arm action; easy plus arm strength; fastball is plus-plus; can work comfortably in the mid-90s; spots it up; changeup is solid-average to plus; smooth from the arm with good action to the arm side; commands blended breaking ball; effective in sequence; improved in Double-A; plus command profile.

> **#53**
> BP Top 101 Prospects

**Weaknesses:** Secondary stuff lags behind the fastball; breaking ball is often indistinguishable; slurvy and loose; can show occasional curveball depth but more often than not lacks sharp bite; utility of changeup is inconsistent.

**Risk Factor/Injury History:** Moderate risk; limited Double-A experience; questions about breaking ball.

**Bret Sayre's Fantasy Take:** The statistics look awfully impressive, but when you have good command of a 70 fastball, that's often enough against the level of competition. Without a step forward in the slider, he's going to have a tough time replicating a strikeout rate of 26 percent at the major-league level, but it should still remain above average and be flanked by strong ratios.

**The Year Ahead:** You can make a convincing argument that Cole is undervalued and underappreciated in the prospect community. Most 6'4'' power arms with sharp feel for command of a mid-90s fastball and fading change that have found success at the Double-A level tend to get acknowledged for their impact potential. Cole appears on most prospect lists, but often lacks helium because of his fringe-average and nondescript breaking ball, and the bias that some have against oft-traded players. I'm guilty of the latter, as I have consciously limited my glowing affection for Cole simply because he was traded twice before he even reached the Double-A level. Instead of scouting the arm and projecting accordingly, I was caught looking for the blemishes that made him expendable. Based on the scouting, Cole could develop into a number three starter at the major-league level, and if the breaking ball can continue to take steps forward, that reality could come sooner than most expect.

## 3. Brian Goodwin  CF

**Born:** 11/2/90  **Age:** 23  **Bats:** L  **Throws:** R  **Height:** 6' 1"  **Weight:** 195

| MLB ETA | Hit | Power | Run | Glove | Arm | | OFP | Realistic |
|---|---|---|---|---|---|---|---|---|
| Late 2014 | 55 | 55 | 60 | 50 | 50 | | 60<br>1ST-DIV PLAYER | 50<br>ML REGULAR |

| YEAR | TEAM | LVL | AGE | PA | R | 2B | 3B | HR | RBI | BB | SO | SB | CS | AVG/OBP/SLG | TAv | BABIP | BRR | FRAA | WARP |
|---|---|---|---|---|---|---|---|---|---|---|---|---|---|---|---|---|---|---|---|
| 2013 | HAR | AA | 22 | 533 | 82 | 19 | 11 | 10 | 40 | 66 | 121 | 19 | 11 | .252/.355/.407 | .286 | .321 | 2.0 | CF(116): -0.7 | 3.4 |
| 2014 | WAS | MLB | 23 | 250 | 31 | 9 | 2 | 5 | 22 | 24 | 63 | 6 | 3 | .232/.309/.357 | .247 | .300 | 0.1 | CF -2 | 0.2 |
| 2015 | WAS | MLB | 24 | 252 | 28 | 9 | 2 | 5 | 24 | 24 | 67 | 5 | 2 | .229/.307/.349 | .243 | .299 | 0.0 | CF -2 | 0.1 |

Breakout: 0%    Improve: 12%    Collapse: 4%    Attrition: 10%    MLB: 34%    *Comparables: Trayvon Robinson, Aaron Hicks, Austin Jackson*

**#86**
BP Top
101
Prospects

**Drafted/Acquired:** 1st round, 2011 draft, Miami Dade South Community College (Miami, FL)

**Previous Ranking:** #3 (Org), #74 (Top 101)

**What Happened in 2013:** In a return trip to the Eastern League, the former first-round pick showed all five tools but struggled with inconsistency at the plate and in the field.

**Strengths:** Strong/athletic build; incredible hands at the plate; very fast bat; very good low-ball hitter; can drop the bat head and drive the ball; hit could play solid-average to plus; raw power is plus; game power could play average or better; plus run; solid-average arm; glove to play center.

**Weaknesses:** Mechanically inconsistent at the plate; can get noisy; shows all five tools but can see them play down in game action; struggles against quality off-speed stuff; can get too pull happy when he looks for power; reads/routes aren't always crisp in center; can play with more athleticism than baseball instincts.

**Risk Factor/Injury History:** Moderate risk; achieved Double-A level; needs consistency against better pitching.

**Bret Sayre's Fantasy Take:** The results haven't always been pretty in pro ball for Goodwin, but the tools are all still there for him to be a five-category contributor. There is still opportunity to take advantage of the less-than-exquisite stats and deal for him at a discount. He could be a 20/20 player with a .270 average—and he even gets a tick up in OBP leagues.

**The Year Ahead:** Goodwin is a very good athlete, with a strong upper body and the ability to impact the game in all areas. But he struggles with consistency, and his feel for tool execution can come and go, causing the impressive physical gifts to play down in game action. He's a low-ball hitter that can do serious damage once he gets extended, and if he can keep himself in hitter's counts and stay back on secondary stuff, he should be able to hit for both reasonable average and power. He can play center field, but has the tool versatility to play in either corner, so if the bat fails to develop to projection, he can still carve out a long career as a fourth outfielder. This year should see Goodwin move up to Triple-A, where a steady diet of secondary junk will aid in his offensive development, and if everything breaks correctly he could become a lineup staple in 2015.

## 4. Michael Taylor    CF

**Born:** 3/26/91   **Age:** 23   **Bats:** R   **Throws:** R   **Height:** 6'3"   **Weight:** 210

| MLB ETA | Hit | Power | Run | Glove | Arm | OFP | Realistic |
|---------|-----|-------|-----|-------|-----|-----|-----------|
| 2016 | — | 65 | 60 | 65 | 60 | 65<br>1ST-DIV/ALL-STAR | 45<br><AVG ML/BENCH |

| YEAR | TEAM | LVL | AGE | PA | R | 2B | 3B | HR | RBI | BB | SO | SB | CS | AVG/OBP/SLG | TAv | BABIP | BRR | FRAA | WARP |
|------|------|-----|-----|-----|----|----|----|----|-----|----|-----|----|----|-------------|------|-------|------|------|------|
| 2013 | POT | A+ | 22 | 581 | 79 | 41 | 6 | 10 | 87 | 55 | 131 | 51 | 7 | .263/.340/.426 | .265 | .331 | 7.5 | CF(117): 14.3, RF(4): 0.1 | 5.0 |
| 2014 | WAS | MLB | 23 | 250 | 25 | 11 | 1 | 3 | 21 | 14 | 72 | 11 | 3 | .213/.260/.314 | .211 | .290 | 1.1 | CF 3, RF -0 | -0.1 |
| 2015 | WAS | MLB | 24 | 250 | 23 | 13 | 1 | 3 | 21 | 14 | 71 | 10 | 3 | .222/.268/.324 | .221 | .301 | 0.9 | CF 3, RF 0 | -0.4 |

Breakout: 0%    Improve: 0%    Collapse: 0%    Attrition: 0%    MLB: 0%    *Comparables: Collin Cowgill, Drew Stubbs, Jai Miller*

**Drafted/Acquired:** 6th round, 2009 draft, Westminster Academy (Fort Lauderdale, FL)

**Previous Ranking:** On The Rise

**What Happened in 2013:** In a return trip to the Carolina League, the toolsy Taylor showed some developmental progress, putting more bat to the ball and putting his speed to use on base.

**Strengths:** Excellent size; improving strength; plus athlete; shows loud raw tools; very big raw power; leveraged swing capable of distance bombs; game power could play above average; plus run; plus range in center; potential for a well-above-average glove; strong arm; complete package in center; weapon on base.

**Weaknesses:** Lacks consistency at the plate; below-average balance; swing can get too long and leveraged; struggles with velocity inside; will expand his zone and chase off-speed; hit tool could spoil the party.

**Risk Factor/Injury History:** High risk; yet to play at Double-A level; hit tool likely to play below-average.

**Bret Sayre's Fantasy Take:** You could make the argument that Taylor has the second highest fantasy upside in this system, next to Giolito. The only problem is that if he's going to hit 25+ homers and steal 20 bases at the major-league level, he's going to have to take a big step forward in the hit tool. This could be a George Springer-light profile for fantasy, as there's a good chance he could be a .220 hitter in the end.

**The Year Ahead:** Taylor has the highest tool-based ceiling on the Nationals farm (position player), but the profile comes with a great deal of risk. A high-end athlete with improving strength, Taylor's pop took a step forward in 2013, with 57 extra-base hits in 133 games, including 10 bombs. With well-above-average potential in the field and well-above-average utility on base, Taylor could blossom into an all-star if everything clicks, but the hit tool could end up playing below average, dragging down the raw power and limiting his ability to stay in a lineup. As a floor, Taylor is going to have value at the major-league level because of his glove and run, but if he can continue to progress at the plate, shortening his stroke and finding more consistency in his mechanics, he could really step up in the prospect world and develop into a future first-division talent. Double-A will be the big test.

## 5. Jake Johansen    RHP

**Born:** 1/23/91   **Age:** 23   **Bats:** R   **Throws:** R   **Height:** 6'6"   **Weight:** 235

| MLB ETA | CT | FB | CH | CB | SL | OFP | Realistic |
|---------|----|----|----|----|----|-----|-----------|
| Late 2015 | — | 70 | — | — | 65 | 60<br>NO. 3 STARTER | 50<br>LATE-INN RP (SETUP) |

| YEAR | TEAM | LVL | AGE | W | L | SV | G | GS | IP | H | HR | BB | SO | BB9 | SO9 | GB% | BABIP | WHIP | ERA | FIP | FRA | WARP |
|------|------|-----|-----|----|----|----|----|----|------|-----|----|----|-----|-----|-----|------|-------|------|------|------|------|------|
| 2013 | HAG | A | 22 | 0 | 2 | 0 | 2 | 2 | 9.3 | 13 | 1 | 5 | 7 | 4.8 | 6.8 | 53% | .364 | 1.93 | 5.79 | 4.98 | 5.87 | -0.1 |
| 2013 | AUB | A- | 22 | 1 | 1 | 0 | 10 | 10 | 42.3 | 22 | 1 | 18 | 44 | 3.8 | 9.4 | 71% | .200 | 0.94 | 1.06 | 2.67 | 3.84 | 0.7 |
| 2014 | WAS | MLB | 23 | 2 | 3 | 0 | 8 | 8 | 34.7 | 39 | 4 | 19 | 21 | 4.9 | 5.4 | 52% | .323 | 1.66 | 5.67 | 5.33 | 6.16 | -0.4 |
| 2015 | WAS | MLB | 24 | 7 | 10 | 0 | 29 | 29 | 181.3 | 191 | 22 | 83 | 135 | 4.1 | 6.7 | 52% | .321 | 1.51 | 5.04 | 4.60 | 5.48 | -1.1 |

Breakout: 0%    Improve: 0%    Collapse: 0%    Attrition: 0%    MLB: 0%    *Comparables: Josh Collmenter, Rob Scahill, Joel Carreno*

**Drafted/Acquired:** 2nd round, 2013 draft, Dallas Baptist University (Dallas, TX)

**Previous Ranking:** NR

**What Happened in 2013:** Despite an uneven amateur career, Johansen was selected in the second round of the 2013 draft, and made 12 starts across two levels after signing.

**Strengths:** Huge size; excellent present strength; physical and intimidating on the mound; elite arm strength; fastball works in the mid- to upper-90s; leveraged offering with weight; plus-plus offering; hard slider is second plus offering; sharp with late glove-side slice.

**Weaknesses:** Despite size and stuff, can lack confidence on the mound; command is fringe at present; can work up in the zone and lose size advantage; changeup is below average at present; overthrows the pitch with more deliberate mechanics; shows fringe curveball; can get too loose and loopy.

**Risk Factor/Injury History:** Moderate risk; limited professional experience; 23 years old with two plus pitches

**Bret Sayre's Fantasy Take:** Johansen may have the upside of a starting pitcher, but there's a very high probability that he will end up as a reliever. Of course, a reliever with two pitches of this quality would be one that matters for fantasy, it's just that the bullpen is not where you should be spending your minor-league roster spots.

**The Year Ahead:** Johansen is a power arm with a power build, but at the end of the day it's probably more of a late-inning profile than a workhorse starter. The 23-year-old is behind the developmental curve, so you can expect to see an accelerated timetable going forward, and with only average pitchability and a fringe changeup, the big Texan might end up in the bullpen before he arrives at the major-league level. But even out of the 'pen, Johansen is going to be a weapon, with a plus-plus fastball and hard slider, both pitches capable of missing bats and barrels alike.

## 6. Jefry Rodriguez    RHP

**Born:** 7/26/93   **Age:** 20   **Bats:** R   **Throws:** R   **Height:** 6' 5"   **Weight:** 185

| | CT | FB | CH | CB | SL | | OFP | Realistic |
|---|---|---|---|---|---|---|---|---|
| MLB ETA | | | | | | | 60 | 50 |
| 2017 | – | 70 | 50 | 60 | – | | NO.2-3 STARTER | LATE-INN RP (SETUP) |

| YEAR | TEAM | LVL | AGE | W | L | SV | G | GS | IP | H | HR | BB | SO | BB9 | SO9 | GB% | BABIP | WHIP | ERA | FIP | FRA | WARP |
|---|---|---|---|---|---|---|---|---|---|---|---|---|---|---|---|---|---|---|---|---|---|---|
| 2013 | NAT | Rk | 19 | 3 | 0 | 0 | 12 | 12 | 47.7 | 40 | 1 | 20 | 43 | 3.8 | 8.1 | 51% | .295 | 1.26 | 2.45 | 3.56 | 4.60 | 0.6 |
| 2014 | WAS | MLB | 20 | 1 | 2 | 0 | 9 | 5 | 37.7 | 44 | 5 | 25 | 20 | 6.0 | 4.8 | 46% | .326 | 1.85 | 6.53 | 6.18 | 7.10 | -0.7 |
| 2015 | WAS | MLB | 21 | 2 | 4 | 0 | 19 | 9 | 100.7 | 113 | 14 | 58 | 62 | 5.2 | 5.5 | 46% | .321 | 1.69 | 6.09 | 5.53 | 6.62 | -1.7 |

Breakout: 0%   Improve: 0%   Collapse: 0%   Attrition: 0%   MLB: 0%   *Comparables: Allen Webster, Jake Odorizzi, Brett Oberholtzer*

**Drafted/Acquired:** International free agent, 2012, Dominican Republic

**Previous Ranking:** NR

**What Happened in 2013:** The former shortstop continued to take steps forward on the mound in his stateside debut, showing a plus-plus potential fastball and a graphic amount of physical projection.

**Strengths:** Highly projectable; long and lean; very athletic; leveraged fastball already works 92-95; touches 97; shows the ability to spin a projectable curveball; pitch has good 11/5 shape and can show depth; changeup is new but looks good out of the hand with some late action; good feel for pitching despite limited experience.

**Weaknesses:** Raw; needs to add strength and stamina; fastball-heavy approach at present; curveball is inconsistent; changeup is underdeveloped; command has a long way to go.

**Risk Factor/Injury History:** High risk; complex-league resume.

**Bret Sayre's Fantasy Take:** Another very exciting rookie ball arm, Rodriguez could be almost anything at the major-league level. But with his stuff, he should miss bats regardless of role. If you're looking for a breakthrough arm for 2014, and a guy who could move up the rankings in a big way, Rodriguez is a pretty good arm to take a chance on.

**The Year Ahead:** Rodriguez has impact upside regardless of future role, but the risk is very high because the converted shortstop is relatively new to pitching and the overall utility is still very raw. With a highly projectable body and a present fastball that already works comfortably in the 92-95 range, Rodriguez could really step forward as he adds strength and experience. The breaking ball shows promise, and despite the inexperience, the 20-year-old shows some feel for the mound and the work ethic to put in the necessary wrench work to improve. It's not going to be an overnight success story, but he's definitely a high-ceiling talent to follow closely in the coming years.

## 7. Matt Skole    1B

**Born:** 7/30/89   **Age:** 24   **Bats:** L   **Throws:** R   **Height:** 6' 4"   **Weight:** 220

| | Hit | Power | Run | Glove | Arm | | OFP | Realistic |
|---|---|---|---|---|---|---|---|---|
| MLB ETA | | | | | | | 50 | 45 |
| 2015 | 50 | 65 | – | – | 55 | | ML REGULAR | PLATOON/<AVG REG |

| YEAR | TEAM | LVL | AGE | PA | R | 2B | 3B | HR | RBI | BB | SO | SB | CS | AVG/OBP/SLG | TAv | BABIP | BRR | FRAA | WARP |
|---|---|---|---|---|---|---|---|---|---|---|---|---|---|---|---|---|---|---|---|
| 2013 | HAR | AA | 23 | 7 | 1 | 1 | 0 | 0 | 2 | 2 | 2 | 0 | 0 | .200/.429/.400 | .323 | .333 | 0.4 | 1B(2): -0.2 | 0.1 |
| 2014 | WAS | MLB | 24 | 250 | 28 | 9 | 0 | 9 | 31 | 31 | 73 | 0 | 0 | .225/.321/.389 | .258 | .290 | -0.4 | 3B -5, 1B -0 | 0.0 |
| 2015 | WAS | MLB | 25 | 250 | 31 | 9 | 0 | 8 | 27 | 37 | 72 | 0 | 0 | .197/.317/.351 | .251 | .254 | -0.6 | 3B -5, 1B 0 | 0.4 |

Breakout: 3%   Improve: 13%   Collapse: 4%   Attrition: 11%   MLB: 22%   *Comparables: Aaron Bates, Taylor Teagarden, Rene Tosoni*

**Drafted/Acquired:** 5th round, 2011 draft, Georgia Institute of Technology (Atlanta, GA)

**Previous Ranking:** #7 (Org)

**What Happened in 2013:** It was a lost year for the former fifth-round pick, as an early-season collision fractured his wrist and damaged his elbow to the point that Tommy John surgery was required.

**Strengths:** Big raw power; shows bat speed and the ability to lift the ball; makes pitchers work; can discern balls and strikes and will wait for his pitch; game power could play to plus; strong against right-handed pitching; run producer; arm is average.

**Weaknesses:** Limited defensive profile; below average at third; hit tool lacks big projection; likely to play average or below; struggles against quality arm-side stuff; can bust him inside with velocity; well-below-average run.

**Risk Factor/Injury History:** Moderate risk; limited experience in the upper minors; wrist/elbow (Tommy John) injury in 2013.

**Bret Sayre's Fantasy Take:** Skole is far more interesting from a fantasy perspective than in real life because if he can be a .270 hitter with 20-25 homers, he'll be owned in nearly all leagues, regardless of eligibility. Until then, he'll just have to settle for being Craig Goldstein's favorite player.

**The Year Ahead:** Skole projects to hit for power from the left side of the plate, and that alone makes him a top-10 prospect, despite his limitations on defense and a lost season in 2013 that put the 24-year-old behind the developmental curve. At the end of the day, Skole might not be more than a platoon bat at first with enough versatility to play a below-average third base in a pinch, but if he can return to form and continue to rip right-handed pitching, he's going to end up playing at the major-league level for a long time. I expect Skole to step forward at the Double-A level in 2014, likely showing power to go along with a strong approach, and positioning himself for a major-league opportunity in some form in 2015.

## 8. Pedro Severino    C

**Born:** 7/20/93    **Age:** 20    **Bats:** R    **Throws:** R    **Height:** 6' 1"    **Weight:** 180

| MLB ETA | Hit | Power | Run | Glove | Arm | | OFP | Realistic |
|---------|-----|-------|-----|-------|-----|---|-----|-----------|
| 2017 | 50 | – | – | 65 | 70 | | 60<br>1ST DIV PLAYER | 45<br>BACKUP C |

| YEAR | TEAM | LVL | AGE | PA | R | 2B | 3B | HR | RBI | BB | SO | SB | CS | AVG/OBP/SLG | TAv | BABIP | BRR | FRAA | WARP |
|------|------|-----|-----|-----|-----|----|----|----|-----|----|----|----|----|-------------|-----|-------|-----|------|------|
| 2013 | HAG | A | 19 | 302 | 28 | 19 | 2 | 1 | 45 | 13 | 54 | 1 | 0 | .241/.274/.333 | .244 | .291 | 0.9 | C(81): 0.5 | 1.2 |
| 2014 | WAS | MLB | 20 | 250 | 17 | 10 | 1 | 2 | 18 | 8 | 57 | 0 | 0 | .210/.235/.277 | .191 | .260 | -0.4 | C 0 | -0.6 |
| 2015 | WAS | MLB | 21 | 250 | 21 | 9 | 0 | 2 | 19 | 9 | 46 | 0 | 0 | .207/.235/.275 | .195 | .241 | -0.6 | C 0 | -2.5 |

Breakout: 0%    Improve: 0%    Collapse: 0%    Attrition: 0%    MLB: 0%    *Comparables: Miguel Gonzalez, C. Bethancourt, Salvador Perez*

**Drafted/Acquired:** International free agent, 2010, Dominican Republic

**Previous Ranking:** NR

**What Happened in 2013:** After two years at the complex level, Severino moved up to full-season ball and was named a mid-season Sally League all-star, mostly on the back of his plus defensive profile behind the plate.

**Strengths:** Athletic with improving strength; arm is a weapon; plus-plus raw strength with a quick release; projectable glove; receives well; learned English; short to the ball at the plate; bat speed improved in 2013; contact bat with easy plus potential behind the dish.

**Weaknesses:** Offensive profile is light; well-below-average power; lacks plate coverage; needs to use more of the field; struggles against velocity and quality spin; hit tool likely to play below average; glove-first profile.

**Risk Factor/Injury History:** High risk; yet to play in upper minors; questions about the bat.

**Bret Sayre's Fantasy Take:** This isn't the first one of these comments I've written, and it won't be the last, but Severino isn't worth rostering in fantasy at this point. He could get to where his bat has enough upside to be worth picking up, but right now he's ranked here for his defense.

**The Year Ahead:** Severino has the type of defensive profile to get excited about, with a well-above-average arm and all the necessary ingredients to develop into a plus receiver. The bat is light, but he showed improved bat speed in 2013, and as he continues to add strength to his frame and learn how to find his pitch, he could develop into a down-the-lineup contact bat. The 20-year-old Dominican can ride his defensive chops all the way up the chain, but his ultimate upside will depend on the development of his stick, which could be the difference between a first-division type if everything clicks and a backup catcher at the major-league level if the profile remains lopsided.

## 9. Drew Vettleson    RF

**Born:** 7/19/91    **Age:** 22    **Bats:** L    **Throws:** R    **Height:** 6' 1"    **Weight:** 185

| MLB ETA | Hit | Power | Run | Glove | Arm | | OFP | Realistic |
|---------|-----|-------|-----|-------|-----|---|-----|-----------|
| Late 2015 | 50 | 60 | – | 55 | 65 | | 55<br>>AVG ML | 50<br>2ND DIV PLAYER |

| YEAR | TEAM | LVL | AGE | PA | R | 2B | 3B | HR | RBI | BB | SO | SB | CS | AVG/OBP/SLG | TAv | BABIP | BRR | FRAA | WARP |
|------|------|-----|-----|-----|-----|----|----|----|-----|----|----|----|----|-------------|-----|-------|-----|------|------|
| 2013 | PCH | A+ | 21 | 516 | 50 | 29 | 6 | 4 | 62 | 40 | 78 | 5 | 7 | .274/.331/.388 | .257 | .318 | -5.4 | RF(118): -6.1, CF(1): -0.1 | -0.3 |
| 2014 | WAS | MLB | 22 | 250 | 23 | 9 | 1 | 4 | 23 | 14 | 62 | 4 | 2 | .231/.275/.331 | .224 | .290 | -0.3 | RF -1, CF -0 | -0.6 |
| 2015 | WAS | MLB | 23 | 250 | 24 | 9 | 1 | 3 | 22 | 15 | 61 | 2 | 1 | .233/.279/.323 | .224 | .297 | -0.4 | RF -2, CF 0 | -1.1 |

Breakout: 0%    Improve: 0%    Collapse: 0%    Attrition: 0%    MLB: 0%    *Comparables: Moises Sierra, Zoilo Almonte, Abraham Almonte*

**Drafted/Acquired:** 1st round, 2010, Central Kitsap HS (Silverdale, WA)

**Previous Ranking:** #7 (Org; Rays)

**What Happened in 2013:** Acquired in an offseason trade with the Rays, Vettleson lacks the flash of a top prospect but brings playable baseball skills to the table.

**Strengths:** Good athlete; good feel for the game; good path to the ball at the plate; gets good extension and can drive through it; raw power is plus; game power could play average or better; hit tool shows average or better; strong against right-handed pitching; good approach; very strong arm in the field; plays plus or better; glove is solid-average or better.

**Weaknesses:** Lacks high-end impact tools at the plate; hit tool is more average; struggles against arm-side pitching; game power is more gap-to-gap than over-the-fence; power could end up playing light for an outfield corner; tweener profile.

**Risk Factor/Injury History:** Moderate risk; yet to play at Double-A level.

**Bret Sayre's Fantasy Take:** If it seems like Vettleson's pro career has gone in slow motion, it's because it has. But if he can show some of that power in Double-A, he can move toward becoming a 20+ homer bat at the major-league level. And if he can keep improving his contact rate as he moves up, the batting average won't hurt you either.

**The Year Ahead:** Vettleson is a solid-average prospect with a solid-average profile if everything clicks; a strong right fielder with a bat that might play a little below standard for a corner spot. Vettleson shows a lot of present baseball skills, with some feel for contact and the strength and bat speed to drive the ball into the gaps. Double-A pitching will present a challenge for the 22-year-old, and his production at that level will elevate Vettleson up this list or push him off completely. Despite a clear major-league projection and good overall feel for the game, the margin of error is small because the bat isn't likely to put him in the middle of a major-league lineup, making Vettleson more of a tweener type: a player with a corner profile but an up-the-middle bat.

## 10. Drew Ward 3B

**Born:** 11/25/94 **Age:** 19 **Bats:** L **Throws:** R **Height:** 6' 4" **Weight:** 210

| MLB ETA | Hit | Power | Run | Glove | Arm | OFP | Realistic |
|---|---|---|---|---|---|---|---|
| 2017 | 50 | 70 | – | 50 | 60 | 60 1ST DIV PLAYER | 50 ML REGULAR |

| YEAR | TEAM | LVL | AGE | PA | R | 2B | 3B | HR | RBI | BB | SO | SB | CS | AVG/OBP/SLG | TAv | BABIP | BRR | FRAA | WARP |
|---|---|---|---|---|---|---|---|---|---|---|---|---|---|---|---|---|---|---|---|
| 2013 | NAT | Rk | 18 | 199 | 24 | 13 | 0 | 1 | 28 | 25 | 44 | 2 | 4 | .292/.402/.387 | .270 | .390 | -1.3 | 3B(35): -0.9 | 0.7 |
| 2014 | WAS | MLB | 19 | 250 | 17 | 8 | 0 | 2 | 19 | 15 | 77 | 0 | 0 | .190/.242/.250 | .185 | .270 | -0.5 | 3B -2 | -1.5 |
| 2015 | WAS | MLB | 20 | 250 | 26 | 10 | 0 | 5 | 23 | 16 | 67 | 0 | 0 | .223/.276/.328 | .224 | .288 | -0.7 | 3B -1 | -1.0 |

Breakout: 0%    Improve: 0%    Collapse: 0%    Attrition: 0%    MLB: 0%    *Comparables: Matt Davidson, Nolan Arenado, Alex Liddi*

**Drafted/Acquired:** 3rd round pick, 2013 draft, Leedey High School (Leedey, OK)

**Previous Ranking:** NR

**What Happened in 2013:** In his professional debut, the third-round pick showed a very advanced approach and feel for hitting in his limited complex-league sample.

**Strengths:** Excellent size/strength; athletic for his size; big boy raw power; capable of tape-measure bombs; power projects to play plus (or better); leveraged left-handed swing that shows bat speed; very mature approach at the plate; excellent pitch-recognition ability; makes pitchers work; strong arm in the field; hands work well; glove could play average or better at third; big makeup reports.

**Weaknesses:** Swing can get long; more line-drive stroke at present; hit tool lacks same projection as power; can get too passive at the plate; looks for perfect pitch; below-average run; fringe range at third; physical projection could limit his profile at third.

**Risk Factor/Injury History:** High risk; limited professional experience.

**Bret Sayre's Fantasy Take:** A very sneaky pick late in dynasty drafts this year, Ward has the potential to move his stock upward in short order. A third baseman who could hit .280 with 20+ homers is not something to shake your head at, but he's got a long road ahead of him to get there.

**The Year Ahead:** Ward is a big, strong kid with a smooth left-handed stroke, and the type of power potential and patience to get very excited about. He can play third at present (was a shortstop in high school), with a strong arm and a decent glove, but he could end up outgrowing the position and putting all the pressure of value on his stick. The ceiling is very high, regardless of where he ends up playing on the diamond, mostly on the back of his well-above-average raw power that has a good chance to arrive in game action because of his functional hit tool and ability to recognize pitches early and react accordingly. Ward could use another year of short-season ball in 2014, but scouts universally praise the 19-year-old for his makeup and work ethic, so I wouldn't be shocked to see a more advanced assignment if he shows up strong in camp.

## Prospects on the Rise

**1. OF Rafael Bautista:** In his stateside debut, the 20-year-old Dominican really stepped forward on both sides of the ball, showing a leadoff profile at the plate and up-the-middle chops in center. While Bautista isn't a big power threat, he is very strong and physical, and has a linear, line-drive stroke capable of sending balls to all fields. He's a 7 runner with plus range in center and a solid-average arm, so he can provide defensive value even if the bat plays a little light.

**2. SS Osvaldo Abreu:** Another product of the Nationals' Latin American program, Abreu made his Gulf Coast League debut in 2013, making good contact and flashing his defensive potential at shortstop. The 19-year-old has really fast hands and strong wrists, which gives him bat control at the plate and the necessary actions in the field. A plus athlete, Abreu projects to stick around at the position for the foreseeable future, and if the bat can continue to take steps forward in 2014, he should jump into the conversation for top 10 prospects in the system. Legit upside.

**3. LHP Felipe Rivero:** Not new to the prospect world. Rivero was acquired in an offseason trade with Rays, along with current top-10 prospect Drew Vettleson. Baseball Prospectus ranked Rivero number nine in the Rays system last season, but he fell off the list for 2014, mostly because of an inconsistent campaign in the Florida State League that saw his command abandon him. Taller than his listed height of 6', the slender southpaw will eventually pitch in the major leagues because of an easy-cheese mid-90s fastball that can just explode on hitters, but he could really jump up prospect lists next season if he can refine his delivery enough to throw more strikes and take steps forward with his curveball that can flash hammer potential when he stays over it.

## Factors on the Farm

### Prospects likely to contribute at the major-league level in 2014

**1. IF Zach Walters:** A ninth-round pick in the 2010 draft (D-Backs), Walters finally played his way to the major-league level in 2013 after close to 2,000 at-bats in the minors. It's more of a utility profile than a regular, but unlike most utility types, Walters brings some legit thunder in the stick, especially from the left side, where the 24-year-old blasted 25 bombs in Triple-A.

**2. RHP Aaron Barrett:** Also a ninth-round pick in the 2010 draft, Barrett was added to the 40-man roster this off-season, and projects to be a late-innings reliever at the highest level. With a heavy plus fastball and a very good hard slider, the 26-year-old right-hander will be able to miss bats and keep the ball on the ground, and if the command steps up, he could eventually settle in as a setup arm in the back of the bullpen.

**3. OF Eury Perez:** You can make a case that Perez belongs in the top 10 based on his defensive profile in center and his easy plus speed, which gives him impressive range in the field and a weapon in the box and on base. Several sources questioned the utility of Perez's hit tool, seeing more of a bench profile than a regular, and those doubts helped push him off the initial list, and could eventually prove prophetic and push him out of the Nationals' long-term plans in center. It's a crowded outfield at present, and with higher-ceiling forces like Brian Goodwin and Michael Taylor on the rise in the minors, Perez needs to make the most of his opportunities in 2014 and step forward with the bat in order to stay on the radar.

# 2014 Farm System Rankings

*Note: Players mentioned in the "Prospects To See There" sections aren't necessarily starting the season at the "Must-See Affiliate." However, they may appear there at some point in 2014*

## 1. Minnesota Twins

**Farm System Ranking in 2013:** 4

**State of the System:** No team in baseball can boast the same level of top-tier talent on both sides of the ball and impressive depth at every level.

**Top Prospect:** Byron Buxton (1)

**Breakout Candidates for 2014:** Lewis Thorpe and Jorge Polanco

**Prospects on the BP 101:** 8

**Must-See Affiliate:** Low-A Cedar Rapids

**Prospects to See There:** Kohl Stewart, Felix Jorge, Stephen Gonsalves, Ryan Eades, Lewis Thorpe

**Farm System Trajectory for 2015:** Down. It's hard to stay on top, especially with some of the top talent in the system likely to graduate to the highest level (Miguel Sano, Alex Meyer, Josmil Pinto)

## 2. Chicago Cubs

**Farm System Ranking in 2013:** 12

**State of the System:** Thanks to a strong draft, clever trades, an aggressive acquisition plan in the international market, and developmental progress from some of the big names in the system, the Cubs became one of the strongest systems in the game.

**Top Prospect:** Javier Baez (4)

**Breakout Candidates for 2014:** Jeimer Candelario and Paul Blackburn

**Prospects on the BP 101:** 7

**Must-See Affiliate:** Double-A Tennessee

**Prospects to See There:** Kris Bryant, Albert Almora, Jorge Soler, C.J. Edwards, Pierce Johnson, Dan Vogelbach

**Farm System Trajectory for 2015:** Up. While it's likely that several of the Cubs' top prospects will get a taste of the majors in 2014, the majority of the talent will remain eligible for next season's list; if you add to the mix a high draft pick this June and an extreme amount of young depth ready to make their stateside debuts, the system could take over the coveted rank of number one in baseball.

## 3. Pittsburgh Pirates

**Farm System Ranking in 2013:** 6

**State of the System:** The Pirates are loaded with impact talent on both sides of the ball, with major-league-quality depth at the complex level through Triple-A.

**Top Prospect:** Jameson Taillon (19)

**Breakout Candidates for 2014:** Josh Bell and Cody Dickson

**Prospects on the BP 101:** 7

**Must-See Affiliate:** Low-A West Virginia

**Prospects to See There:** Austin Meadows, Reese McGuire, Harold Ramirez, Cody Dickson

**Farm System Trajectory for 2015:** Steady. The farm could lose the top two horses in Taillon and Gregory Polanco, but the depth is strong and should keep the Pirates' farm in the top three for years to come.

## 4. Boston Red Sox

**Farm System Ranking in 2013:** 16

**State of the System:** The Red Sox have impact talent at premium up-the-middle positions and major-leaguer-caliber arms in the upper minors.

**Top Prospect:** Xander Bogaerts (2)

**Breakout Candidates for 2014:** Blake Swihart and Trey Ball

**Prospects on the BP 101:** 6

**Must-See Affiliate:** Triple-A Pawtucket

**Prospects to See There:** Garin Cecchini, Matt Barnes, Henry Owens, Christian Vazquez, Anthony Ranaudo

**Farm System Trajectory 2015:** Down. As good as the depth is in the Red Sox system, losing Bogaerts, Jackie Bradley Jr., and Allen Webster (they could also lose Barnes and Cecchini) will weaken the farm as a whole.

## 5. Houston Astros

**Farm System Ranking in 2013:** 9

**State of the System:** The system is top-heavy, with three prospects in the top 25 in the game followed by a deep roster of prospects with legit major-league futures.

**Top Prospect:** Carlos Correa (5)

**Breakout Candidates for 2014:** Rio Ruiz and Michael Feliz

**Prospects on the BP 101:** 5

**Must-See Affiliate:** High-A Lancaster

**Prospects to See There:** Carlos Correa, Mark Appel, Vince Velasquez, Lance McCullers, Rio Ruiz, Teoscar Hernandez, Andrew Thurman

**Farm System Trajectory for 2015:** Up. Losing does have its advantages, as the Astros will once again be picking 1:1 in the June draft and will be allotted more money to spend on amateur acquisition than any other team in baseball.

## 6. St. Louis Cardinals

**Farm System Ranking in 2013:** 1

**State of the System:** Even after losing Shelby Miller, Michael Wacha, Trevor Rosenthal, Matt Adams, and Carlos Martinez to the major-league level, the Cardinals remain a strong system, built on the star power of Oscar Taveras and the mixture of high-ceiling depth and high-floor role players throughout the system.

**Top Prospect:** Oscar Taveras (3)

**Breakout Candidates for 2014:** Alexander Reyes and Carson Kelly

**Prospects on the BP 101:** 4

**Must-See Affiliate:** Low-A Peoria

**Prospects to See There:** Alexander Reyes, Carson Kelly, Rob Kaminsky, C.J. McElroy, Vaughn Bryan

**Farm System Trajectory for 2015:** Down. Losing Taveras and Kolten Wong will sting the system, but several prospects could step forward in 2014 to keep the Cardinals in the discussion for the top 10, most notably right-hander Alex Reyes, who has a chance to follow in the footsteps of Cardinals' recent power arms Miller, Wacha, and Martinez.

## 7. Kansas City Royals

**Farm System Ranking in 2013:** 7

**State of the System:** The Royals system remains quite strong thanks to a talent infusion from the Rule 4 draft and developmental progress from some of the high-ceiling talent scattered across every level.

**Top Prospect:** Yordano Ventura (12)

**Breakout Candidates for 2014:** Christian Binford and Hunter Dozier

**Prospects on the BP 101:** 7

**Must-See Affiliate:** High-A Wilmington

**Prospects to See There:** Raul Mondesi, Miguel Almonte, Sean Manaea, Hunter Dozier, Bubba Starling, Christian Binford, Daniel Rockett, Aroni Nina

**Farm System Trajectory for 2015:** Up. The Royals will lose Ventura and possibly Jason Adam, but the lower levels are stacked with talent on the developmental upswing.

## 8. New York Mets

**Farm System Ranking in 2013:** 10

**State of the System:** The Mets boast a solid blend of pitching and positional talent, ranging from high-risk/high-reward types at the lower levels to safer high-floor prospects nearing the major-league level.

**Top Prospect:** Noah Syndergaard (11)

**Breakout Candidates for 2014:** Amed Rosario and Marcos Molina

**Prospects on the BP 101:** 3

**Must-See Affiliate:** Short-Season Brooklyn

**Prospects to See There:** Amed Rosario, Marcos Molina, Casey Meisner, Chris Flexen, Champ Stuart

**Farm System Trajectory for 2015:** Steady. The Mets will likely graduate four of the top five prospects in their system, but the helium from low-level talents like Rosario, Molina, and Meisner could keep the system holding strong in the top 10 in the game, despite the graduations.

## 9. Texas Rangers

**Farm System Ranking in 2013:** 2

**State of the System:** Losing Jurickson Profar and Martin Perez to the majors left a mark, and trading away Mike Olt and C.J. Edwards drew some blood, but the foundation of the system is still extremely strong because of the organization's ability to recognize and acquire high-ceiling talent in the amateur markets.

**Top Prospect:** Rougned Odor (39)

**Breakout Candidates for 2014:** Marcos Diplan and Joey Gallo

**Prospects on the BP 101:** 7

**Must-See Affiliate:** Double-A Frisco

**Prospects to See There:** Rougned Odor, Luis Sardinas, Drew Robinson, Jorge Alfaro, Luke Jackson, Chi Chi Gonzalez

**Farm System Trajectory for 2015:** Up. Alfaro is about to explode into a top-tier prospect in the game, and the stockpile of talent at the lower levels of the minors should start taking developmental steps forward. This should be a top-five system next season.

## 10. Colorado Rockies

**Farm System Ranking in 2013:** 22

**State of the System:** Eddie Butler exploded, Jonathan Gray fell in the draft, and the Grand Junction team seems to multiply talent like water being poured on a mogwai.

**Top Prospect:** Jonathan Gray (16)

**Breakout Candidates for 2014:** David Dahl and Raul Fernandez

**Prospects on the BP 101:** 4

**Must-See Affiliate:** Low-A Asheville

**Prospects to See There:** Raimel Tapia, David Dahl, Ryan McMahon, Terry McClure

**Farm System Trajectory for 2015:** Up. Butler and Chad Bettis will likely graduate, and Gray could force the issue by dominating in the minors. But the rest of the farm should continue to develop and evolve, and if the Low-A roster shines like the scouting reports suggest, the Rockies could be looking at a very, very strong system for the foreseeable future.

## 11. San Diego Padres

**Farm System Ranking in 2013:** 3

**State of the System:** Injuries to key prospects in 2013 hurt the stock, but high-ceiling arms, the top backstop in the minors, and a strong draft haul keep the farm on the edge of the top 10.

**Top Prospect:** Austin Hedges (18)

**Breakout Candidates for 2014:** Franchy Cordero and Zach Eflin

**Prospects on the BP 101:** 3

**Must-See Affiliate:** High-A Lake Elsinore

**Prospects to See There:** Max Fried, Zach Eflin, Joe Ross, Walker Weickel, Rodney Daal, Hunter Renfroe, Mallex Smith

**Farm System Trajectory for 2015:** Up. The meat of the Padres system won't graduate to the majors in 2014, and as Hedges, Renfroe, Fried, and Cordero continue to develop, the system as a whole is likely to take steps forward—if they can avoid the injury bug.

## 12. Baltimore Orioles

**Farm System Ranking in 2013:** 20

**State of the System:** Kevin Gausman and Dylan Bundy are still frontline monsters, but a strong draft in 2013 (Hunter Harvey, Josh Hart) and the continued development of Eduardo Rodriguez and Mike Wright have taken the system up a few notches.

**Top Prospect:** Kevin Gausman (10)

**Breakout Candidates for 2014:** Chance Sisco and Stephen Tarpley

**Prospects on the BP 101:** 5

**Must-See Affiliate:** Double-A Bowie

**Prospects to See There:** Eduardo Rodriguez, Tim Berry, Zachary Davies, Christian Walker

**Farm System Trajectory for 2015:** Down. The Orioles are likely to graduate five of their top six prospects to the majors, leaving the fate of the farm on the young talent at the lower levels of the minors.

## 13. Toronto Blue Jays

**Farm System Ranking in 2013:** 13

**State of the System:** Despite a recent penchant for using prospects as currency to acquire major-league talent, the Jays system remains thick with high-ceiling players on both sides of the ball.

**Top Prospect:** Marcus Stroman (27)

**Breakout Candidates for 2014:** Miguel Castro and Mitch Nay

**Prospects on the BP 101:** 3

**Must-See Affiliate:** Low-A Lansing

**Prospects to See There:** Alberto Tirado, D.J. Davis, Chase DeJong, Jairo Labourt, Mitch Nay, Matt Dean, Rowdy Telez

**Farm System Trajectory for 2015:** Up. The Jays have some of the best young prospect depth in baseball, and as the short-season talent starts to develop at the full-season level, the system as a whole should jump into the top 10, where they are likely to stay for a very long time.

## 14. Los Angeles Dodgers

**Farm System Ranking in 2013:** 21

**State of the System:** Most of the top talent is more solid-average than special, but the system has a lot of major-league-quality depth, and should start to push that talent to the major-league level in 2014.

**Top Prospect:** Julio Urias (35)

**Breakout Candidates for 2014:** Victor Arano and Jesmuel Valentin

**Prospects on the BP 101:** 3

**Must-See Affiliate:** Double-A Chattanooga

**Prospects to See There:** Julio Urias, Corey Seager, Chris Anderson, Ross Stripling, Tom Windle

**Farm System Trajectory for 2015:** Down. Urias and Seager should continue to move up the prospect hierarchy, but the Dodgers are likely to graduate several top-10 prospects to the majors in 2014.

## 15. Arizona Diamondbacks

**Farm System Ranking in 2013:** 17

**State of the System:** On the surface, prospect graduations and trades appear to have thinned the system, but the continued maturation of Archie Bradley and Chris Owings, the theft of Braden Shipley in the draft, and the frontline projections attached to Jose Martinez have the system ranked higher than last season.

**Top Prospect:** Archie Bradley (9)

**Breakout Candidates for 2014:** Jose Martinez and Justin Williams

**Prospects on the BP 101:** 3

**Must-See Affiliate:** Low-A South Bend

**Prospects to See There:** Jose Martinez, Stryker Trahan, Justin Williams, Jose Munoz, Brad Keller

**Farm System Trajectory for 2015:** Up. The D-Backs will likely graduate Bradley and Owings, but Shipley and Martinez are ready to step into the spotlight to take their place, and if the lower-level talent really blossoms, this farm could end up looking even better than it does now.

## 16. Cincinnati Reds

**Farm System Ranking in 2013:** 15

**State of the System:** The top tier of the farm is flashy with loud tools and high projections, and the middle contains a healthy amount of solid-average types with realistic major-league futures.

**Top Prospect:** Robert Stephenson (22)

**Breakout Candidates for 2014:** Ben Lively and Jose Ortiz

**Prospects on the BP 101:** 3

**Must-See Affiliate:** Double-A Pensacola

**Prospects to See There:** Robert Stephenson, Phillip Ervin, Yorman Rodriguez, Jesse Winker, Jon Moscot, Ben Lively, Michael Lorenzen, Seth Mejias-Brean

**Farm System Trajectory for 2015:** Up. Losing Billy Hamilton isn't going to break the farm, especially with impact names like Stephenson, Winker, and Ervin moving up the chain; if the aforementioned middle tier of talent can carve out their prospect identities, the system as a whole will improve as a result.

## 17. Seattle Mariners

**Farm System Ranking in 2013:** 5

**State of the System:** Major-league graduations to Nick Franklin, Mike Zunino, and Brad Miller—and a substantial injury to former number two pick Danny Hultzen—helped depress the farm despite the frontline upside of Taijuan Walker.

**Top Prospect:** Taijuan Walker (8)

**Breakout Candidates for 2014:** Edwin Diaz and Tyler O'Neill

**Prospects on the BP 101:** 3

**Must-See Affiliate:** High-A High Desert

**Prospects to See There:** D.J. Peterson, Victor Sanchez, Tyler Pike, Tyler Marlette, Gabby Guerrero, Ketel Marte

**Farm System Trajectory for 2015:** Steady. The Mariners are going to lose Walker and James Paxton to the majors, but the system should hold steady thanks to expected developmental progress from Peterson and A-ball arms like Edwin Diaz, Luiz Gohara, and Victor Diaz.

## 18. Washington Nationals

**Farm System Ranking in 2013:** 23

**State of the System:** They have Lucas Giolito.

**Top Prospect:** Lucas Giolito (13)

**Breakout Candidates for 2014:** Jefry Rodriguez and Drew Ward

**Prospects on the BP 101:** 3

**Must-See Affiliate:** Low-A Hagerstown

**Prospects to See There:** Lucas Giolito, Drew Ward

**Farm System Trajectory for 2015:** Up. Giolito could emerge as the top pitching prospect in the game, and with toolsy positional talent and projectable arms, the system as a whole could jump into the top half in the game.

## 19. Miami Marlins

**Farm System Ranking in 2013:** 11

**State of the System:** Losing Jose Fernandez, Christian Yelich, and Marcell Ozuna hurt the system, but a strong campaign from Heaney and a strong 2013 draft class keeps the farm in the top 20.

**Top Prospect:** Andrew Heaney (30)

**Breakout Candidates for 2014:** Jarlin Garcia and J.T. Riddle

**Prospects on the BP 101:** 2

**Must-See Affiliate:** Double-A Jacksonville

**Prospects to See There:** Colin Moran, Trevor Williams, Jose Urena, Justin Nicolino, Anthony DeSclafani, Colby Suggs

**Farm System Trajectory for 2015:** Up. Heaney and Jake Marisnick will likely lose eligibility, but with expected developmental progress from Moran and Williams, and a slew of early draft picks—including the number two overall selection, the farm system is likely to take a few steps forward.

## 20. Cleveland Indians

**Farm System Ranking in 2013:** 19

**State of the System:** The system is top-heavy with two studs in Francisco Lindor and Clint Frazier, and a lot of promising Latin American depth spread across the entire system, but the majority of that depth comes with considerable risk.

**Top Prospect:** Francisco Lindor (6)

**Breakout Candidates for 2014:** Francisco Mejia and Dace Kime

**Prospects on the BP 101:** 2

**Must-See Affiliate:** Double-A Akron

**Prospects to See There:** Tyler Naquin, Cody Anderson, Luigi Rodriguez, Tony Wolters, Joe Wendle

**Farm System Trajectory for 2015:** Up. Lindor is ready for the major-league test and will likely lose his prospect eligibility, but Frazier is ready to emerge as a top-tier prospect in the minors; if some of the depth can take a step forward and minimize some of the attached risk, the system as a whole should tick up a bit.

## 21. Chicago White Sox

**Farm System Ranking in 2013:** 28

**State of the System:** A strong draft class and a splash in the Latin American market have given the White Sox a much-needed talent infusion on the farm.

**Top Prospect:** Erik Johnson (67)

**Breakout Candidates for 2014:** Tim Anderson and Francellis Montas

**Prospects on the BP 101:** 2

**Must-See Affiliate:** High-A Winston-Salem

**Prospects to See There:** Tim Anderson, Courtney Hawkins, Francellis Montas, Jacob May, Chris Freudenberg, Keon Barnum

**Farm System Trajectory for 2015:** Up. The White Sox will lose Johnson, Matt Davidson, Marcus Semien, and Carlos Sanchez to the majors, but a strong wave of talent is forming at the lower levels, and new alpha prospect Tim Anderson is ready to emerge as a frontline talent.

## 22. San Francisco Giants

**Farm System Ranking in 2013:** 26

**State of the System:** Kyle Crick leads a pitching-heavy farm, with a seemingly endless supply of future number four starters up and down the system.

**Top Prospect:** Kyle Crick (38)

**Breakout Candidates for 2014:** Keury Mella and Ryder Jones

**Prospects on the BP 101:** 1

**Must-See Affiliate:** Double-A Richmond

**Prospects to See There:** Kyle Crick, Adalberto Mejia, Clayton Blackburn, Martin Agosta, Ty Blach, Derek Law

**Farm System Trajectory for 2015:** Up. As the wave of solid-average pitching talent continues to climb toward the majors, and the lower-level bats like Christian Arroyo and Jones take their cuts at the full-season level, the system as a whole should take several steps forward over the course of the next season.

## 23. New York Yankees

**Farm System Ranking in 2013:** 14

**State of the System:** The Yankees have talent in the minors—which helps separate them from the poorer systems in baseball—but down years from key prospects caused the system to yo-yo from middle of the pack to the bottom third.

**Top Prospect:** Gary Sanchez (85)

**Breakout Candidates for 2014:** Luis Severino and Luis Torrens

**Prospects on the BP 101:** 1

**Must-See Affiliate:** Short-Season Staten Island

**Prospects to See There:** Luis Severino, Luis Torrens, Ian Clarkin, Gosuke Katoh, Thairo Estrada

**Farm System Trajectory for 2015:** Up. In a talented yet schizophrenic system, all it takes is a return to form from some of the more heralded names on the farm and the Yankees will shoot back up the organizational rankings.

## 24. Atlanta Braves

**Farm System Ranking in 2013:** 18

**State of the System:** The Braves have a knack for acquiring and developing Latin American players, but the economical approach to the Rule 4 draft has left the system thin on high-ceiling stateside talent.

**Top Prospect:** Lucas Sims (40)

**Breakout Candidates for 2014:** Jose Peraza and Mauricio Cabrera

**Prospects on the BP 101:** 2

**Must-See Affiliate:** High-A Lynchburg

**Prospects to See There:** Lucas Sims, Mauricio Cabrera, Jose Peraza, Jason Hursh, Wes Parsons

**Farm System Trajectory for 2015:** Up. The bulk of the talent is still at the A-ball level, and with expected developmental progress, the system as a whole could jump up a few spots on the list.

## 25. Philadelphia Phillies

**Farm System Ranking in 2013:** 24

**State of the System:** Injuries to several top prospects have taken the system down a few pegs, but the organization's ability to find and acquire Latin American talent could pay off in a big way in the coming years.

**Top Prospect:** Maikel Franco (52)

**Breakout Candidates for 2014:** J.P. Crawford and Yoel Mecias

**Prospects on the BP 101:** 2

**Must-See Affiliate:** Low-A Lakewood

**Prospects to See There:** Dylan Cozens, Yoel Mecias (when he returns from Tommy John surgery); J.P. Crawford, Zach Green, Gabriel Lino, Cord Sandberg, Carlos Tocci

**Farm System Trajectory for 2015:** Up. The Phillies should lose Franco and Jesse Biddle to the majors, but good young talent at the lower levels should help push the system up, assuming they can stay on the field and avoid injury.

## 26. Tampa Bay Rays

**Farm System Ranking in 2013:** 8

**State of the System:** Major-league graduations and a slew of injuries to key prospects have the Rays toward the back of the pack of all farm systems in the game.

**Top Prospect:** Enny Romero (90)

**Breakout Candidates for 2014:** Nick Ciuffo and Blake Snell

**Prospects on the BP 101:** 2

**Must-See Affiliate:** Triple-A Durham

**Prospects to See There:** Enny Romero, Jake Odorizzi, Alex Colome, Hak-Ju Lee, Nate Karns, Kevin Kiermaier, Matt Ramsey

**Farm System Trajectory for 2015:** Down. Based on the fact that the must-see affiliate is Triple-A, the Rays are likely to lose a healthy chunk of talent to the majors in 2014, taking a slice out of an already shaky farm system.

## 27. Detroit Tigers

**Farm System Ranking in 2013:** 29

**State of the System:** Adding Robbie Ray helped, but this is a system built on Venezuelan dreams and a lot of really fringy stateside talent.

**Top Prospect:** Nick Castellanos (37)

**Breakout Candidates for 2014:** Javier Betancourt and Joe Jimenez

**Prospects on the BP 101:** 1

**Must-See Affiliate:** Double-A Erie

**Prospects to See There:** Corey Knebel, Drew VerHagen, Steven Moya, Devon Travis, Robbie Ray

**Farm System Trajectory for 2015:** Steady. Without a talent infusion, the system as a whole is unlikely to improve much, and with their only top-101 talent (Castellanos) graduating to the majors, holding steady in 2014 could be seen as a victory.

## 28. Oakland Athletics

**Farm System Ranking in 2013:** 25

**State of the System:** Addison Russell is going to be a very good player, but the rest of the system is either high risk/moderate reward or moderate risk/low reward.

**Top Prospect:** Addison Russell (7)

**Breakout Candidates for 2014:** Bobby Wahl and Billy McKinney

**Prospects on the BP 101:** 1

**Must-See Affiliate:** High-A Stockton

**Prospects to See There:** Bobby Wahl, Daniel Robertson, Raul Alcantara, Michael Ynoa, Nolan Sanburn, Renato Nunez, Dylan Covey

**Farm System Trajectory for 2015:** Up. It's not a deep system, but if you project strong years from prospects like Wahl, Robertson, Alcantara, and Billy McKinney—in addition to continued excellence from Russell—the farm should jump a few spots.

## 29. Milwaukee Brewers

**Farm System Ranking in 2013:** 27

**State of the System:** It's pretty rough, but at least the lower levels can offer some high-ceiling talent, even though it comes with considerable risk.

**Top Prospect:** Tyrone Taylor (NR)

**Breakout Candidates for 2014:** Devin Williams and Tucker Neuhaus

**Prospects on the BP 101:** 0

**Must-See Affiliate:** High-A Brevard County

**Prospects to See There:** Tyrone Taylor, Orlando Arcia, Victor Roache, Jorge Lopez

**Farm System Trajectory for 2015:** Up. I actually like some of the aforementioned lower-level talent, especially Williams, and if those higher risk types can start to actualize on the field, the farm will take a much-needed step forward.

## 30. Los Angeles Angels

**Farm System Ranking in 2013:** 30

**State of the System:** Losing early draft picks hasn't helped the Angels restock the farm, as the system is rich with fringe prospects and thin on high-ceiling upside.

**Top Prospect:** Taylor Lindsey (NR)

**Breakout Candidates for 2014:** Ricardo Sanchez and Natanael Delgado

**Prospects on the BP 101:** 0

**Must-See Affiliate:** Double-A Arkansas

**Prospects to See There:** Kaleb Cowart, R.J. Alvarez, Mark Sappington, Alex Yarbrough, Cam Bedrosian

**Farm System Trajectory for 2015:** Up. After two straight years on the bottom, the Angels will likely take a small step forward in 2014 thanks to emerging lower-level talent like Ricardo Sanchez, Keynan Middleton, Delgado, and Hunter Green, and a pick in the first round (15th) this June. ∎

# 2014 Top 100 Draft Rankings

*Compiled by Allan Simpson/Perfect Game USA*

Junior College Player
High School Player

| RANK | PLAYER | POS | YR | B-T | HT | WT | COLLEGE | HOMETOWN | ST | DOB | LAST DRAFTED | COMMITMENT |
|---|---|---|---|---|---|---|---|---|---|---|---|---|
| 1 | Carlos Rodon | LHP | JR | L-L | 6-3 | 235 | North Carolina State | Holly Springs | NC | 12/10/1992 | Brewers '11 (16) | |
| 2 | Jeff Hoffman | RHP | JR | R-R | 6-4 | 190 | East Carolina | Latham | NY | 1/8/1993 | Never drafted | |
| 3 | Tyler Kolek | RHP | R-R | R-R | 6-5 | 230 | Shepherd | Shepherd | TX | 12/15/1995 | | Texas Christian |
| 4 | Nick Burdi | RHP | JR | R-R | 6-3 | 220 | Louisville | Downers Grove | IL | 1/19/1993 | Twins '11 (24) | |
| 5 | Trea Turner | SS | JR | R-R | 6-1 | 170 | North Carolina State | Lake Worth | FL | 6/30/1993 | Pirates '11 (20) | |
| 6 | Tyler Beede | RHP | JR | R-R | 6-4 | 215 | Vanderbilt | Auburn | MA | 5/23/1993 | Blue Jays '11 (1) | |
| 7 | Michael Gettys | OF/RHP | SR | R-R | 6-2 | 220 | Gainesville | Gainesville | GA | 10/22/1995 | | Georgia |
| 8 | Alex Jackson | C/OF | SR | R-R | 6-2 | 215 | Rancho Bernardo | Escondido | CA | 12/25/1995 | | Oregon |
| 9 | Brandon Finnegan | LHP | JR | L-L | 5-11 | 185 | Texas Christian | Fort Worth | TX | 4/14/1993 | Rangers '11 (45) | |
| 10 | Michael Cederoth | RHP | JR | R-R | 6-6 | 210 | San Diego State | Spring Valley | CA | 11/25/1992 | Diamondbacks '11 (41) | |
| 11 | Nicholas Gordon | SS/RHP | SR | L-R | 6-2 | 170 | Olympia | Windermere | FL | 10/24/1995 | | Florida State |
| 12 | Max Pentecost | C | JR | R-R | 6-2 | 190 | Kennesaw State | Winder | GA | 3/10/1993 | Rangers '11 (7) | |
| 13 | Kodi Medeiros | LHP | SR | L-L | 6-0 | 180 | Waiakea | Hilo | HI | 5/25/1996 | | Pepperdine |
| 14 | Derek Fisher | OF | JR | L-R | 6-3 | 210 | Virginia | Rexmont | PA | 8/21/1993 | Rangers '11 (6) | |
| 15 | Michael Conforto | OF | JR | L-R | 6-2 | 215 | Oregon State | Redmond | WA | 3/1/1993 | Never drafted | |
| 16 | Aaron Nola | RHP | JR | R-R | 6-2 | 185 | Louisiana State | Baton Rouge | LA | 6/14/1993 | Blue Jays '11 (22) | |
| 17 | Luke Weaver | RHP | JR | R-R | 6-2 | 170 | Florida State | DeLand | FL | 8/21/1993 | Blue Jays '11 (19) | |
| 18 | Grant Holmes | RHP | SR | L-R | 6-2 | 210 | Conway | Conway | SC | 3/22/1996 | | Florida |
| 19 | Sean Reid-Foley | RHP | SR | R-R | 6-3 | 210 | Sandalwood | Jacksonville | FL | 8/3/1995 | | Florida State |
| 20 | Sean Newcomb | LHP | JR | R-L | 6-5 | 245 | Hartford | Middleboro | MA | 6/12/1993 | Never drafted | |
| 21 | Kyle Schwarber | C/OF | JR | L-R | 6-0 | 230 | Indiana | Middletown | OH | 3/5/1993 | Never drafted | |
| 22 | Luis Ortiz | RHP | SR | R-R | 6-3 | 220 | Sanger | Sanger | CA | 12/30/1995 | | Fresno State |
| 23 | Bradley Zimmer | OF | JR | L-R | 6-5 | 205 | San Francisco | San Diego | CA | 11/27/1992 | Cubs '11 (23) | |
| 24 | Jacob Gatewood | SS | SR | R-R | 6-5 | 190 | Clovis | Clovis | CA | 9/25/1995 | | Southern California |
| 25 | Touki Toussaint | RHP | SR | R-R | 6-2 | 195 | Coral Springs Christian | Coral Springs | FL | 6/20/1996 | | Vanderbilt |
| 26 | Braxton Davidson | 1B/OF | SR | L-L | 6-3 | 215 | T.C. Roberson | Arden | NC | 6/18/1996 | | North Carolina |
| 27 | Brady Aiken | LHP | SR | L-L | 6-3 | 210 | Cathedral Catholic | Jamul | CA | 8/16/1996 | | UCLA |
| 28 | Michael Chavis | 3B | SR | R-R | 6-0 | 185 | Sprayberry | Marietta | GA | 8/11/1995 | | Clemson |
| 29 | Matt Chapman | 3B/SS | JR | R-R | 6-2 | 215 | Cal State Fullerton | Trabuco Canyon | CA | 4/28/1993 | Never drafted | |
| 30 | Cobi Johnson | RHP | SR | R-R | 6-4 | 180 | J.W. Mitchell | New Port Richey | FL | 11/6/1995 | | Florida State |
| 31 | Kyle Freeland | LHP | JR | L-L | 6-4 | 190 | Evansville | Denver | CO | 5/14/1993 | Phillies '11 (35) | |
| 32 | Dylan Cease | RHP | SR | R-R | 6-2 | 180 | Milton | Milton | GA | 12/28/1995 | | Vanderbilt |
| 33 | Erick Fedde | RHP | JR | R-R | 6-4 | 170 | Nevada-Las Vegas | Las Vegas | NV | 2/25/1993 | Padres '11 (24) | |
| 34 | Scott Blewett | RHP | SR | R-R | 6-6 | 210 | Baker | Baldwinsville | NY | 4/10/1996 | | St. John's |
| 35 | Alex Verdugo | LHP/OF | SR | L-L | 6-1 | 190 | Sahuaro | Tucson | AZ | 5/15/1996 | | Arizona State |
| 36 | Chris Ellis | RHP | JR | L-R | 6-5 | 205 | Mississippi | Birmingham | AL | 9/22/1992 | Dodgers '11 (50) | |
| 37 | Jack Flaherty | 3B/RHP | SR | R-R | 6-4 | 210 | Harvard-Westlake | Burbank | CA | 10/15/1995 | | North Carolina |
| 38 | Daniel Mengden | C/RHP | JR | R-R | 6-1 | 215 | Texas A&M | Houston | TX | 2/19/1993 | Never drafted | |
| 39 | Greg Deichmann | SS | SR | L-R | 6-2 | 185 | Brother Martin | Metairie | LA | 5/31/1995 | | Louisiana State |
| 40 | Taylor Sparks | 3B | JR | R-R | 6-4 | 220 | UC Irvine | Bellflower | CA | 4/3/1993 | Indians '11 (24) | |
| 41 | Brian Anderson | 2B/OF | JR | R-R | 6-3 | 185 | Arkansas | Edmond | OK | 5/19/1993 | Twins '11 (20) | |
| 42 | Dylan Davis | OF/RHP | JR | R-R | 6-0 | 215 | Oregon State | Redmond | WA | 7/20/1993 | Never drafted | |
| 43 | Mac Marshall | LHP | SR | R-L | 6-2 | 180 | Parkview | Lilburn | GA | 1/27/1996 | | Louisiana State |
| 44 | Alex Blandino | 3B/SS | JR | L-R | 6-0 | 190 | Stanford | Mountain View | CA | 11/6/1992 | Athletics '11 (38) | |
| 45 | Matt Imhof | LHP | JR | L-L | 6-5 | 230 | Cal Poly | Fremont | CA | 10/26/1993 | Never drafted | |
| 46 | Marcus Wilson | OF | SR | R-R | 6-3 | 175 | J Serra | Los Angeles | CA | 8/15/1996 | | Arizona State |
| 47 | Cameron Varga | RHP/SS | SR | R-R | 6-3 | 205 | Cincinnati Christian Academy | West Chester | OH | 8/19/1994 | | North Carolina |

| RANK | PLAYER | POS | YR | B-T | HT | WT | COLLEGE | HOMETOWN | ST | DOB | LAST DRAFTED | COMMITMENT |
|------|--------|-----|-----|-----|-----|-----|---------|----------|-----|-----|--------------|------------|
| 48 | Chad Sobotka | RHP | JR | R-R | 6-6 | 195 | USC Upstate | Sarasota | FL | 7/10/1993 | Never drafted | |
| 49 | Parker French | RHP | JR | L-R | 6-2 | 210 | Texas | Dripping Springs | TX | 3/19/1993 | Never drafted | |
| 50 | Justus Sheffield | LHP | SR | L-L | 6-2 | 195 | Tullahoma | Tullahoma | TN | 5/13/1996 | | Vanderbilt |
| 51 | Karsten Whitson | RHP | JR | R-R | 6-4 | 220 | Florida | Chipley | FL | 8/25/1991 | Nationals '13 (37) | |
| 52 | Ti'quan Forbes | SS/RHP | SR | R-R | 6-4 | 170 | Columbia | Columbia | MS | 8/26/1996 | | Mississippi |
| 53 | Casey Gillaspie | 1B/OF | JR | B-L | 6-4 | 230 | Wichita State | Omaha | NE | 1/25/1993 | Never drafted | |
| 54 | Jace Fry | LHP | JR | L-L | 6-0 | 195 | Oregon State | Beaverton | OR | 7/9/1993 | Athletics '11 (9) | |
| 55 | Jordan Brink | RHP/OF | JR | L-R | 6-1 | 180 | Fresno State | Fresno | CA | 3/18/1993 | Never drafted | |
| 56 | Keith Weisenberg | RHP | SR | R-R | 6-4 | 185 | Osceola | Seminole | FL | 12/6/1995 | | Stanford |
| 57 | Aramis Garcia | C | JR | R-R | 6-2 | 200 | Florida International | Pembroke Pines | FL | 1/12/1993 | Cardinals '11 (20) | |
| 58 | Robbie Dickey | RHP | SO | R-R | 6-3 | 205 | Blinn (Texas) | Austin | TX | | Never drafted | Texas State |
| 59 | Derek Hill | OF | SR | R-R | 6-2 | 180 | Elk Grove | Sacramento | CA | 12/30/1995 | | Oregon |
| 60 | Zech Lemond | RHP | JR | R-R | 6-4 | 195 | Rice | Houston | TX | 10/9/1992 | Pirates '11 (50) | |
| 61 | Scott Heineman | 3B | JR | R-R | 6-0 | 205 | Oregon | Pacfic Palisades | CA | 12/4/1992 | Never drafted | |
| 62 | Foster Griffin | LHP | SR | R-L | 6-5 | 190 | The First Academy | Orlando | FL | 7/27/1995 | | Mississippi |
| 63 | Jake Cosart | RHP/OF | FR | R-R | 6-2 | 210 | Seminole State (Fla.) | League City | TX | 2/11/1994 | Never drafted | |
| 64 | Chris Oliver | RHP | JR | R-R | 6-4 | 180 | Arkansas | Farmington | AR | 7/8/1993 | Orioles '11 (27) | |
| 65 | James Norwood | RHP | JR | R-R | 6-2 | 200 | St. Louis | New York | NY | 12/24/1993 | Never drafted | |
| 66 | Dillon Peters | LHP | JR | L-L | 5-11 | 200 | Texas | Fishers | IN | 8/31/1992 | Indians '11 (20) | |
| 67 | Brandon Downes | OF | JR | R-R | 6-3 | 200 | Virginia | South Plainfield | NJ | 9/29/1992 | Red Sox '11 (43) | |
| 68 | Joey Pankake | 3B/SS | JR | R-R | 6-1 | 200 | South Carolina | Easley | SC | 11/23/1992 | Rangers '11 (42) | |
| 69 | Sam Coonrod | RHP/OF | JR | R-R | 6-2 | 205 | Southern Illinois | Carrolton | IL | 9/22/1992 | Never drafted | |
| 70 | Wyatt Strahan | RHP | JR | R-R | 6-3 | 190 | Southern California | Villa Park | CA | 4/18/1993 | Diamondbacks '11 (27) | |
| 71 | Grayson Greiner | C | JR | R-R | 6-5 | 220 | South Carolina | Lexington | SC | 1/20/1993 | Never drafted | |
| 72 | Forrest Wall | SS | SR | L-R | 6-0 | 180 | Orangewood Christian | Winter Park | FL | 11/20/1995 | | North Carolina |
| 73 | J.D. Davis | OF/RHP | JR | R-R | 6-3 | 215 | Cal State Fullerton | Elk Grove | CA | 4/27/1993 | Rays '11 (5) | |
| 74 | Jordan Foley | RHP | JR | R-R | 6-3 | 215 | Central Michigan | The Colony | TX | 7/12/1993 | Yankees '11 (26) | |
| 75 | Jakson Reetz | C/RHP | SR | R-R | 6-1 | 195 | Norris | Hickman | NE | 1/3/1996 | | Nebraska |
| 76 | A.J. Reed | LHP/1B | JR | L-L | 6-2 | 255 | Kentucky | Terre Haute | IN | 5/10/1993 | Mets '11 (25) | |
| 77 | Zack Shannon | RHP | SR | R-R | 6-3 | 220 | Moeller | Cincinnati | OH | 6/22/1996 | | Ohio State |
| 78 | Greg Allen | OF | JR | B-R | 6-0 | 170 | San Diego State | Chula Vista | CA | 3/15/1993 | Never drafted | |
| 79 | Keaton McKinney | RHP/1B | SR | R-R | 6-5 | 220 | Ankeny Centennial | Ankeny | IA | 1/3/1996 | | Arkansas |
| 80 | Ashton Perritt | OF/RHP | JR | R-R | 6-4 | 195 | Liberty | Whiteland | IN | | Never drafted | |
| 81 | A.J. Vanegas | RHP | SR | R-R | 6-3 | 215 | Stanford | Alameda | CA | 8/16/1992 | Athletics '13 (19) | |
| 82 | Spencer Turnbull | RHP | JR | R-R | 6-3 | 220 | Alabama | Madison | AL | 9/18/1992 | Never drafted | |
| 83 | Patrick Weigel | RHP | SO | R-R | 6-6 | 210 | Oxnard (Calif.) | Camarillo | CA | 7/8/1994 | Never drafted | Houston |
| 84 | Justin Smith | OF | SR | R-R | 6-2 | 200 | Bartram Trail | St. John's | FL | 2/29/1996 | | Miami |
| 85 | Michael Kopech | RHP | SR | R-R | 6-4 | 195 | Mt. Pleasant | Mt. Pleasant | TX | 4/30/1996 | | Arizona |
| 86 | Joey Gatto | RHP | SR | R-R | 6-5 | 215 | St. Augustine Prep | Hammonton | NJ | 6/14/1995 | | North Carolina |
| 87 | Brandon Woodruff | RHP | JR | L-R | 6-2 | 230 | Mississippi State | Wheeler | MS | 2/1/1993 | Rangers '11 (5) | |
| 88 | Nick Howard | 3B/RHP | JR | R-R | 6-3 | 215 | Virginia | Olney | MD | 4/6/1993 | Never drafted | |
| 89 | Jon Littell | OF/3B | SR | R-R | 6-4 | 190 | Stillwater | Stillwater | OK | 8/16/1995 | | Oklahoma State |
| 90 | Sean Bouchard | 3B | SR | R-R | 6-3 | 190 | Cathedral Catholic | San Diego | CA | 5/16/1996 | | UCLA |
| 91 | Milton Ramos | SS | SR | R-R | 6-0 | 150 | Florida Christian | Hialeah Gardens | FL | 10/26/1995 | | Florida Atlantic |
| 92 | Austin Byler | 1B/3B | JR | L-R | 6-3 | 215 | Nevada | Peoria | AZ | 10/15/1992 | Never drafted | |
| 93 | Josh Dezse | RHP/1B | JR | R-R | 6-5 | 225 | Ohio State | Powell | OH | 6/18/1992 | Yankees '10 (28) | |
| 94 | Pat Connaughton | RHP | JR | R-R | 6-5 | 215 | Notre Dame | Danvers | MA | 1/6/1993 | Padres '11 (38) | |
| 95 | Ben Smith | LHP | JR | L-L | 6-3 | 195 | Coastal Carolina | Wichita Falls | TX | | Never drafted | |
| 96 | Jake Reed | RHP | JR | R-R | 6-2 | 190 | Oregon | La Mesa | CA | 9/29/1992 | White Sox '11 (40) | |
| 97 | Stone Garrett | OF | SR | R-R | 6-2 | 200 | George Ranch | Sugar Land | TX | 11/22/1995 | | Rice |
| 98 | Shane Benes | SS | SR | R-R | 6-3 | 200 | Westminster Christian | St. Louis | MO | 2/16/1996 | | Missouri |
| 99 | Alex Destino | LHP | SR | L-L | 6-3 | 210 | North Buncombe | Weaverville | NC | 10/24/1995 | | South Carolina |
| 100 | David Peterson | LHP | SR | L-L | 6-6 | 220 | Regis Jesuit | Denver | CO | 9/3/1995 | | Oregon |

# Perfect Game Presents:
# Before They Were Pros

*by Patrick Ebert, Todd Gold, and David Rawnsley*

As part of Perfect Game's partnership with Baseball Prospectus, David Rawnsley, Todd Gold, and Patrick Ebert conducted a "Before They Were Pros" series, providing scouting reports on some of the top prospects in baseball from when they were in high school attending PG events.

## AL WEST

## Houston Astros

### Carlos Correa – SS

The first Perfect Game event that dynamic shortstop Carlos Correa attended was the 2010 16u BCS Finals held in late July in Fort Myers, Florida. Fort Myers served as Correa's home away from home the next few years, as he returned five more times, the last of which was his incredibly impressive performance at the 2012 World Showcase. In 2011, Correa was the first Puerto Rican named to the Perfect Game All-American Classic,

prior to becoming the highest-drafted Puerto Rican ever when the Astros took him no. 1 overall in 2012.

While Correa's tools were always evident, including his large, modern-day shortstop build, smooth, gliding infield actions, strong arm and budding power potential, he firmly put himself in the conversation for the no. 1 pick in the draft with that performance. He set an event record by throwing 97 mph across the infield, took one of the more impressive rounds of batting practice, and looked even better in game situations against elite pitching.

In his first at-bat of the event, Correa showed the ability to pull his hands in and drive a 93 mph fastball out of the hand of fellow Puerto Rican J.O. Berrios and drove the pitch hard over the left fielder's head for a double. In his second at-bat, against hard-throwing left-hander Anthony Siese, Correa drove an upper-80s fastball over the wall in left-center field for a booming home run. Not only were his bat speed, strength, and leverage already evident, but his pitch recognition and ability to make adjustments against high-level pitching were even more impressive.

Here is his PG report from that showing:

Outstanding athletic build, inevitable comparisons with Alex Rodriguez at same age. Unparalleled infield arm strength,

PG record 97 mph in drills, does it with game actions and footwork, smooth quick soft hands, could work through ball more aggressively but doesn't need to with arm strength. Big improvement with bat, showed plus leverage and bat speed, long loose extension, back spins the ball with plus carry, consistent hard contact, can make swing adjustments and pull hands in but wants to extend. Huge BP and game home runs to left-center field.

The biggest question at the time involved his eventual position. Although he always displayed deft infield actions at the shortstop position, his body size and type led to questions about whether or not he would have to move to third base, where he would have more than enough arm strength and power potential to fit the mold at the hot corner. However, that was and continues to be a long-range conversation and not something that will need to be addressed at any point in the near future.   —*Patrick Ebert*

## Mark Appel – RHP

Mark Appel's arm strength has always been evident, and he showed encouraging development in a seven-month span when his fastball velocity spiked from 87 mph at the National Underclass Showcase late in 2007 to 92 mph at the National Showcase in June 2008.

At the National, Appel showed the full three-pitch repertoire that continues to serve as the foundation of his current arsenal. In addition to his fastball, he threw an upper-70s slider and low-80s changeup. A good overall athlete, Appel also offered some promise as an outfielder, where he displayed his usual strong arm to go along with good foot speed and the ability to drive the ball when he squared it up.

Here is his scouting report from the National Showcase:

> Appel has a very good pitchers build and uses a 3/4 arm slot and touched 92 with his fastball. He can easily throw 90 and has good arm speed. His fastball also has good life. He compliments his fastball with a 78 mph slider that works, 82 mph change and also threw a 85 mph cutter. He projects well and showed athleticism by running a 6.94 sixty. He keeps improving each time we see him and will be interesting to follow over the next year. He is also an outstanding student.

After being selected by the Tigers in the 15th round of the 2009 draft, Appel opted to honor his commitment to Stanford, where his stuff continued to improve. His statistical performance didn't reflect his dominant stuff until his junior year in college, when he truly found comfort changing speeds between his fastball, which now sat in the 93-97 range peaking a few ticks higher, a biting mid-80s slider, and a polished fading changeup. His fastball can flatten out at times and can be hittable despite the gaudy velocity readings, but he routinely displayed the stuff, in addition to the prototypical size and stature, to develop in a future staff ace at the big-league level.   —*Patrick Ebert*

## Mike Foltynewicz – RHP

Before the start of his junior campaign at Minooka High School in the southwestern suburbs of Chicago, Foltynewicz put himself on the radar 15 months prior to the 2010 draft by showing a lot of potential at the 2009 PG Pitcher/Catcher Indoor Showcase. He topped out at 90 mph and showed bite on his curveball in that outing, earning himself an invitation to the PG National Showcase. The Illinois native showed consistent development through the spring of his high school season, seeing his fastball velocity climb occasionally into the mid-90s, and while he wasn't able to consistently show a reliable breaking ball, he did flash elite potential with it frequently enough for scouts to project it to become a plus offering over time.

The following February (2010) Foltynewicz returned to the PG Pitcher/Catcher Indoor Showcase, where his fastball velocity showed a significant uptick in velocity. Here's his report from that event:

> Pro profile build, good overall strength, some physical maturity. Outstanding power arm, comes through fast and clean, hip turn delivery, gets plenty of power from lower half, does tend to occ drift to the plate and leave FB up. FB to 94 mph, lots of 93/94s, gets late hard running action even at 94, flashed power CB with sharpness, big 11/5 shape, inconsistent release this date, change also had good deception and running action. Potential first round pick, keeps improving. Signed with Texas.

In hindsight his commitment to Texas wasn't a huge factor to his draft stock, as he went on to become a first-round pick. But as a relatively late bloomer, he didn't firmly establish himself as a first-round candidate until the spring of his senior season, and prior to that development there was some uncertainty about whether he'd pass on the Longhorns if he were to last until the second or third round.

Foltynewicz is the kind of story that scouts really enjoy watching unfold. He went from a potential D-I recruit to a solid draft prospect before working his way into first-round prospect status through a steady rate of development over time.
—*Todd Gold*

## Lance McCullers – RHP

McCullers' appearance on the mound on the final day of the 2011 National Showcase in Fort Myers, Florida, was enough reason for scouts to stick around for the entire four-day event. He flashed his usual incredible arm strength that day, with his first two pitches recording 97 mph and his third hitting 98. He also showed the ability to snap off a very nasty curveball that peaked at 86 mph while mixing in a handful of low-80s changeups.

Pitching in the mid-90s is something McCullers did with great regularity at numerous PG showcase and tournament events, and he also offered pro-level promise as an infielder, matching his fastball by throwing 98 mph across the infield—even if a few crop-hops were included—while showing good power potential from the left side of the batter's box.

Here's his report from the National Showcase:

> Solid athletic body, good present strength. Full delivery, long loose arm action, outstanding arm speed, high 3/4s release point, some effort on release, good downhill angle. Elite-level fastball velocity, 94-98 mph, lots of 96-97s, fastball mostly straight. Threw better curveball/changeup in warmups, humps up and tries to be too nasty in games. Curveball shows plus/plus power and spin at times, nice changeup with sink when in the zone. Potential for 3 plus/plus pitches. Very athletic, would be a definite top 3 round pick strictly as a shortstop/third baseman, left-handed hitter with present bat speed, good extension, power approach. Special arm.

Although McCullers' arm strength certainly was never in question, there was a lingering starter vs. closer debate since everything he threw he threw hard and his aggressive approach made some believe he may be better suited finishing games, where he wouldn't have to worry about pacing himself. That said, he also showed the ability to paint the corners with his fastball and effectively changed speeds between his three pitches.

McCullers sat at or near the top of the class of 2012 rankings for quite some time during his high school career, and started the 2011 Perfect Game All-American Classic for the East squad, where he peaked at 96 mph.   —*Patrick Ebert*

# Seattle Mariners

### Taijuan Walker – RHP

Taijuan Walker was best known athletically in high school initially as a top-level basketball player with Division I potential. His early high school baseball experience was playing shortstop beside future first-round pick and current Chicago White Sox third baseman Matt Davidson at Yucaipa High School in Southern California, where Davidson was a year ahead of Walker.

Walker's first exposure as a pitcher on the national scouting stage didn't occur until the summer before his senior year, when he appeared at the 2009 16u BCS Finals and the WWBA 17u National Championship. Here are the Perfect Game scouting notes from the 16u BCS Finals:

> Projectable 6-4, 190, very lean and rangy. Some actions at SS but bat is far away. Showed mid-high-80s on the mound, might be his better spot. D-I prospect, pro follow as pitcher.

But Walker's big event when he created a buzz and sense of urgency to catch up on rapidly improving right-hander was in Jupiter at the 2009 WWBA World Championship in late October. Performing as only a pitcher with the Southeast Texas Sun Devils, Walker sat steadily in the 91-93 mph range with a 77 mph curveball in front of a huge crowd of scouts. The PG scout notes from that day read as follows:

> Long arm action, arm speed, arm works, 11-5 CB, bite on CB, live arm, high leg kick, some down plane, extension, nice shape CB, FB explodes, balanced, maintained velo well, very projectable, quick arm, lower 1/2 opens a little early, good arm speed, going to throw hard, no drive w/ legs, 12-6 sharp CB, good feet on move to 1st, CB could be plus pitch.

Walker continued to improve his velocity during the spring of

his senior season, topping out regularly at 95-96 mph, although he never showed quite the consistency and quality with his curveball that scouts wanted to see. That and Walker's relative inexperience on the mound were the reasons he slid to the Mariners at the 43rd overall pick in the 2010 draft.
—*David Rawnsley*

### Edwin Diaz – RHP

Built long and loose with broad shoulders and a high waist, it was easy to dream on Puerto Rican right-hander Edwin Diaz. His first PG event was the 2010 16u BCS Finals in which he played for the same team as Carlos Correa. He was listed at 6-foot-2, 165 pounds and peaked at 87 mph with his fastball.

Diaz was part of the same Puerto Rican draft class as the aforementioned Correa as well as Jose Berrios and Jesmuel Valentin, all of whom were selected among the top 100 picks in the 2012 draft. All four also attended the 2011 National Showcase in Fort Myers, Florida, with Diaz making a favorable impression by taking significant step forward.

At the National, Diaz threw easily and steadily in the low 90s, peaking at 92 mph, while mixing in two solid off-speed pitches in his mid-70s curve and low-80s change. Similar to Correa, Diaz's stuff took another step up just seven months later at the 2013 World Showcase, peaking at 94 mph and seeing a similar uptick in velocity on his secondaries. Here's the PG report on Diaz from the World Showcase:

> Slender build, long arms and legs, loose whippy actions. Busy delivery with big leg raise, hands over head, extended mid 3/4's to 3/4's release point, works downhill at times. Very inconsistent front side/front leg position, will cruise for 4-5 pitches, then lose it completely for 2-3 pitches. Dominant fastball, sits at 93 mph, touched 94 mph, very good run down in the zone, could throw harder with strength. Flashes tight spin on curveball, proper shape and velocity, throws CB for strikes, CB has improved considerably. Rare changeup shows quality, nice run and arm speed. Can be first round talent with improved consistency, has the pitches, arm strength and projection.

As noted in that report, Diaz did have some mechanical issues that needed to be addressed, none of which were believed to be of concern, which was easy to overlook given his arm speed and how easily he threw, not to mention his seemingly endless growth potential. Reports continued to surface from the island later that spring that Diaz's velocity had continued to improve, with some indicating he had thrown as hard as 97 mph on more than one occasion.   —*Patrick Ebert*

### Tyler Marlette – C

The Baseball Prospectus report written by Jason Parks contains several phrases about Marlette that are very telling, insightful, and accurate, because they go beyond what you would normally expect to find in a minor-league prospect report on a 20-year-old Midwest League catcher.

Comes from a highly competitive amateur background... lauded work ethic and makeup...Scouts seem to like Marlette, dating back to his amateur days when his power was turning heads on the showcase circuit...his makeup and competitive background offer hope when it comes to his defensive development behind the plate.

Jason gets that the analysis of a top young prospect should go beyond just what he's done since signing a professional contract. The information is out there, especially with a high-profile player such as Marlette.

After reading Baseball Prospectus' report on Marlette, Jered Goodwin, who coached the Florida native both at Hagerty High School near Orlando during the spring and for FTB Mizuno during the summer and fall, responded to these by comments by saying quite simply, "Wow, that's awesome!" There is no one in baseball who knows Marlette better than Goodwin does.

Marlette appeared in more than 20 Perfect Game tournaments and showcases between the 2008 BCS 18u Finals and the 2011 World Showcase, highlighted by his MVP performance in the 2010 Perfect Game All-American Classic. During this time Marlette would regularly and very consistently post the best pop times. His best in drills was a 1.72-second throw, and drill throws in the 1.7s were commonplace. His throws in between innings were almost always in the 1.8 to 1.9 range and his game throws between 1.9 and 2.0. His reputation was such that he didn't have much opportunity to throw in games.

While there are many other things that go into evaluating catchers defensively, some of them much more important, it's worth recognizing that Marlette had—and still has—almost the perfect combination of physical traits to get the ball down to second base quickly. He's generously listed at 5-foot-11, giving him short levers and compact actions. He's a quick-twitch athlete who has run in the 6.8-second range in the 60. And he has plus raw arm strength, regularly registering in the mid-80s on his throws to second base. It's the same combination of physical tools that Pudge Rodriguez had in his prime.

But even more than his catch-and-throw ability, Marlette was known for his surprising power. As noted, he wasn't a physical presence on the field, but he was a middle-of-the-order power hitter with strength, raw bat speed, and a very aggressive approach at the plate. When Marlette launched a two-run no-doubt home run to left-center field at San Diego's spacious Petco Park in the 2010 All-American Classic, no one at Perfect Game was especially surprised.

But in the end, Marlette's lasting trademark was that he epitomized the intense, highly competitive redhead. It's a matter of lore in the scouting industry that many old-time scouts steer clear of redheads, and maybe that's why Marlette surprisingly lasted until the fifth round of the 2011 draft (it didn't seem to affect Clint Frazier last year, on the other hand). Marlette always played the game at the high school level like someone told him he couldn't do something and he was out to prove that he could. One presumes that he still does today professionally.

—David Rawnsley

# Los Angeles Angels

## Kaleb Cowart – 3B

If Perfect Game had a Hall of Fame for achievements related to PG events, Kaleb Cowart would find his way into it very quickly.

The Georgia native participated in his first event in 2006 just after leaving eighth grade and celebrating his 14th birthday. He was listed at 6-foot-1, 165 pounds at the 2006 National Underclass Showcase and is undoubtedly one of the youngest participants ever in that prestigious event. And not only did he play well, he stood out both as a shortstop and as a pitcher. Here's the report from that event.

He has a tall, lean young frame that could really fill out and get strong as he gets older. Cowart has very good two-way prospect tools and was named to the showcase Top Prospect Team. As a position player, Cowart had middle infield athleticism and very, very good arm strength for his age. He can make plays in both directions and has a live, flexible body. His hands work and he has a quick exchange and release. His 7.34 speed will improve with age and strength and he looks like the type of athlete who will be able to play all over the field. Cowart is a switch-hitter who is more advanced with better bat speed right now from the right side. He has good rhythm and a crisp, quick swing right handed. His left-handed swing is longer but shows promise, as the bat speed and balance are there. Despite his position/hitting tools, Cowart might be a better pitching prospect. He has an athletic, easy delivery with good arm speed and a mature ability to repeat his release point. His fastball was up to 86 mph and he pounded his riding fastball inside to right-handed hitters. Cowart threw both a curveball and slider and both were good pitches. His slider had very good spin and 2-plane tilt, while his curveball had 12/6 dower break. He also showed a changeup. Cowart has the pitches and mechanics in place as a pitcher, it's just a matter of getting stronger. Right now Cowart is one of the top 2010 players in the country and he should just keep getting better.

Cowart would go on to play in 26 Perfect Game tournament and showcase events, mostly for the East Cobb Astros, and eventually ended up as the no. 2 ranked prospect in the 2010 class rankings just prior to the draft.

There is one notable thing from that report on the 14-year old Cowart above that was an issue all the way through his high school development and even was a factor in the Angels decision to pick him with the 18th overall pick in the draft. It lies in the sentence "Despite his position/hitting tools, Cowart might be a better pitching prospect."

Cowart always was a primary infielder for East Cobb and pitched primarily as a closer, often seemingly reluctantly. But he had a special arm and couldn't hide it. He was topping out at 94 mph on the mound as early as his sophomore year and eventually threw even harder, topping out at 95 mph at the 2009 Perfect Game All-American Classic. Cowart took drills in the outfield at one showcase, even though he didn't play the position, and threw 100 mph. He played absurdly deep defensively at third base when there was no threat of a bunt because that long throw wasn't a challenge for him.

It was widely circulated before the 2010 draft that Cowart wouldn't consider signing with a team that wanted him as a primary pitcher and would instead honor his commitment to Florida State instead, as he also shined the classroom.

It's also notable that the report written after the 2009 National Showcase, where Cowart was listed as a primary infielder, discusses his pitching first and leaves his hitting ability for last.

> Loose athletic build, good strength potential. Top two way potential. Fast easy arm, loose athletic actions on the mound. Long powerful arm stroke, FB 90-92 this outing, often 94-95 in recent past. Hard spinning CB with very good depth, good 2 plane shape, developing changeup. Outstanding defensive infielder, quick feet, athletic movements/balance, cannon arm. Switch-hitter, very good bat speed RH'd, ball jumps hard, long and smooth LH'd, shows power both ways, 6.84 runner. Ethan Martin comp but better overall athlete. Early draft prospect. Very good student, verbal to Florida State.

It was always clear to the Perfect Game scouts that Cowart's biggest challenge moving on in his baseball career was going to be to develop as a hitter, but his athleticism and tools are just as obvious.  —David Rawnsley

# Texas Rangers

### Rougned Odor – 2B, Luis Sardinas – SS

Every year a handful of top international prospects make it to the States to play in select Perfect Game events and further showcase themselves to the scouting community. In 2009, young Venezuelan infielders Rougned Odor and Luis Sardinas were among them. Each played at the 2009 Perfect Game National Showcase and Odor stayed around to play in the WWBA 17u and 18u National Championships as well.

Sardinas had turned 17 years old in May and his age fit squarely into the 2010 draft class he was playing with at the Metrodome. Odor was eight months younger, though, and would have been a member of the 2011 class if he attended a high school in the United States.

Despite the age difference, Odor was clearly the more polished player at the time both offensively and defensively. His left-handed bat and his overall skills stood out more than his athleticism. Here is the report filed after the National Showcase:

> Left-handed hitter, straight stance, good balance, busy hands, simple swing approach, good bat speed, smooth extension out front, line drive plane, squares it up well, hard contact, gap power. Smooth and easy infield actions, quick first step, works through the ball well, charges aggressively, good arm strength with carry, footwork still developing. Nice looking young athlete with skills.

The PG scout notes from the 17u and 18u National Championships were just as enthusiastic:

> Can really play defense, strong arm, great actions at SS, aggressive hitter, quick hands, some pop, good balance and patience, big prospect if he gets stronger

Sardinas had a very slender and physically immature build at 6-foot, 150 pounds. He ran a 6.83 60-yard dash and had a slashing swing from the left side that got him out of the box quickly enough to run a 3.96-second home-to-first time. His right-handed swing had more strength to it at that time, although his highlight of the showcase might have been squarely lining a 95 mph fastball from Jameson Taillon up the middle for a hit.

Sardinas' easy middle infield actions also stood out. Here is his report from the National:

> Very lean, loose build. Very easy infield actions, glides effortlessly, very loose sure hands, quick release charging, arm strength presently short. Switch-hitter, busy load, run and slash swing, short to ball, good extension out front, handles the bat head, quick out of box, battled hard vs. Jameson Taillon.

In retrospect, and looking at just their showings in the United States, Odor looked like the better prospect at the time. He wasn't the defender at shortstop that Sardinas was, but he still was a middle infield athlete with skills. His bat, however, was better than Sardinas', and he had a quiet maturity to his game that was easy to notice. Sardinas had the build and athleticism to project and dream on but had further to go despite being the older player.

At the time the Rangers clearly thought Sardinas the better prospect and signed him for a $1.5 million bonus. Odor signed his first professional contract for a relatively modest $425,000. Both look like very sound investments today.  —David Rawnsley

### Nick Williams – OF

Following his sophomore season at Galveston Ball High School in the Houston area, Williams burst onto the national scene during the summer of 2010. It was one of the loudest debuts in WWBA history, and included a four-homer game, a key home run in the semifinals, and MVP honors at the 16u National Championship. His electric tools across the board caused Williams to soar as high as the no. 2 position in the PG Class of 2012 rankings entering the summer of 2011. He wasn't quite as productive during his senior season, in which he hit one home run and tallied nine extra-base hits.

While these developments scared away some organizations, there is an adage regarding player makeup that the most difficult thing to do in scouting is to walk away from talent. A lot of teams did just that with Williams. But other scouts saw his willingness to use the whole field as evidence of a high offensive IQ. Despite having obvious top-of-the-first-round physical tools, his stock was quite cloudy as the 2012 draft approached. In PG's Texas state draft preview, David Rawnsley highlighted Williams as the state's biggest wild card, writing:

> Williams' raw physical tools and overall athletic profile have

drawn comparisons to some of the most talented baseball players of this generation, including Ken Griffey Jr., but his play this spring has rarely reflected his tools. Given his immense talent he still could be taken in the first or second round by a team that has done its homework and isn't willing to let his talent slide past them, but his eventual draft position remains up in the air.

That high-risk, high-reward profile aligned perfectly with the goals of the Texas Rangers in that draft, and they snagged him in the second round along with slugging third baseman Joey Gallo. It was a noisy pick that served as an exclamation point for an ultra-aggressive draft approach by the Rangers in 2012. That draft strategy has a chance to pay major dividends, and Williams is arguably the strongest bet in the system for those rewards to manifest.    —Todd Gold

### Joey Gallo – 3B

Power has come easily for Gallo throughout his baseball career, setting numerous records at the high school level and frequently providing tape-measure shots at notable, national events. The biggest of such hits came at the 2011 Perfect Game All-American Classic, where Gallo stroked a 92 mph fastball out of the hand of current Atlanta Braves farmhand Lucas Sims to right-center field, a 442-foot shot that still stands as the 10th-longest home run ever hit at Petco Park, home of the San Diego Padres.

With a 6-foot-5, 220-pound build, he generated that power easily with an easy and free swing generating great bat speed and leverage to drive the ball with authority to all parks of the ballpark.

That easy power was also on display at the 2011 National Showcase in which every ball he hit during batting practice was hit high in the air to a different part of the park. The length in his swing due to his size has always been evident, as those that watched him play in high school knew that high strikeout totals would also come with his desire to hit the long ball, but he also displays a keen eye at the plate and is able to work pitchers deep into counts, which also will allow him to reach base at a high rate.

Due to that, player comparisons for Gallo at the time varied from Troy Glaus to Adam Dunn and Russell Branyan.

One aspect of Gallo's game at the time was just how good he was as a pitcher. In addition to his incredible power potential, he offered a first-round arm, with the ability to sit in the low-to-mid-90s fastball—which approached triple digits during his senior year at national powerhouse Bishop Gorman High School—while dropping in a hammer of a curveball.

Here's Gallo's report from the 2011 National Showcase, where he played on the same team as other notable prospects including Addison Russell, Lance McCullers, and current Florida State star quarterback Jameis Winston:

> Large well-proportioned athletic build, very good present strength. Smooth and polished defensive actions, soft hands, charges well, good balance, outstanding arm strength, accurate on line lasers. Left-handed hitter, extraordinary strength and leverage, light tower power in

batting practice, 100 mph + off the bat in games even when not squared, lets the ball travel deep, hands can be late at times and pull barrel through zone, can be beat by well placed velocity at present. Also pitches, easy leg raise delivery, extended 3/4's release point with good angle. Fastball 92-94 mph, good hard run/bore at times, throws strikes with his fastball, nice changeup with fading action, tends to get under curveball, shows polish on the mound considering inexperience. Huge tools, very high ceiling talent, scouts split on 3B vs. RHP future.

—Patrick Ebert

### Michael Choice – OF

When you think of Michael Choice, you think of the big, strong power-hitting outfielder who was the 10th pick in the 2010 draft after a dominant college career at Texas-Arlington. That present impression is nowhere close to what Choice, a native of the Dallas area, left after the 2006 Southeast Top Showcase in Atlanta prior to his senior year in high school.

First, Choice was listed at 6-foot-1, 180 pounds. However, there are many references in the notes from the event that say he was closer to 195 pounds, with a thick, muscular lower half. He is listed today on MLB.com at 6-foot, 215 pounds.

Most intriguingly, though, Choice came to the event as a primary second baseman, secondary pitcher. He played some shortstop in the games as well and threw 83-87 mph with a big sweeping curveball off the mound. Here are his fielding notes from the event:

> Listed as 2B, has 3B tools and look. More like 195, strong lower half/hips. Very good arm strength, quick actions. Actually a C type build and arm strength. Athletic actions, very good game arm strength.

The full report that was published afterward shows some other nuggets of Choice's potential for growth, although in retrospect his PG Grade of 8.5 should have been a 9. It mentions that Choice had an exaggerated no stride/no trigger, still bat approach, and if he could make adjustments he had a high ceiling as a hitter. It also mentioned his plus makeup and energy on the field, which is always a big plus in projecting talent.

> Mike Choice is a 2007 2B/P with a 6'1", 180 lb. frame from Arlington TX, who attends Mansfield Timberview HS. He has a strong, loose body, especially in his lower half, and looks bigger than his listed 180 pounds. Choice listed himself as a primary 2B but that's probably the last position we would considered him at. Choice is a 7.02 runner who showed very good arm strength in drills and during the games from shortstop. As an infielder Choice profiles at third base but if you'd had no background and just saw him and his tools on the field you'd think he should be catching. He has athletic actions at any position. Offensively, Choice hits out of an exaggerated pre-load, no-stride approach, which doesn't do him any favors. He manages to generate very good bat speed and stays on the plane of the ball for a long time, with nice extension out front. The ball jumps off his bat and he has quick, strong hands. Give Choice a trigger and some rhythm to the ball and he could really develop. To show he had the full package of tools, Choice also took the mound and threw

a very heavy 83-87 mph fastball with a big sweeping 72 mph curveball and a very nice changeup, all from a rather raw delivery. Overall, Choice has a strong set of tools and once he defines his position and batting style a bit better, has a very high ceiling. He played hard and really enjoyed himself on the field.

If Choice becomes a future standout big league outfielder, remember that he was a pretty decent high school second baseman. —*David Rawnsley*

# Oakland Athletics

## Addison Russell – SS

Russell established himself as a prominent prospect in the 2012 class at an early age. After a strong tournament debut following his freshman year of high school, Russell turned heads at the 2009 PG Southeast Underclass Showcase. His report from that event reads:

Broad-shouldered, high-waisted build, very athletic. Outstanding bat speed for age, quick hands, no problem with 90 mph velo, aggressive swing, good balance and rhythm, extends through contact, potential to be a top-level hitter. 6.75 runner, plays faster on field, excellent range at shortstop, quick release, arm strength good now with more to come. Plays the game hard. Chance to be a special player. Good student.

He built off of that showing and remained among the most well-known and scrutinized prospects in the 2012 class throughout his prep career. But by the end of his junior season, Russell began to develop the kind of physicality you'd expect from a football prospect. With that physical change, he lost a bit of his range and began to be viewed as a future third baseman by a lot of scouts. While he was a standout defender at third, his prospect profile value remained higher as a shortstop, where his power potential was considered a plus-plus attribute. In PG's draft focus feature on Russell, David Rawnsley wrote:

Russell has changed physically since (2009) but the tools and potential remain. His broad shoulders have filled out and he was a rock-solid 210 pounds last summer. That extra strength and mass has cost him a step of quickness and raised the inevitable questions about his future defensive position. Most scouts have consigned him to third base in the near future... If Russell can remain quick and lean enough to stay at shortstop, his offensive potential is a huge asset. A right-handed hitter, Russell has the strength and bat speed to overpower the ball when he gets his arms extended and is an intelligent and mature hitter who is advanced at looking for the pitch he wants during an at bat and jumping on it.

Heading into his senior year, Russell refocused his training and converted himself back into the physical mold of a prototypical shortstop. During the spring of his senior season he began to show the high-level ability at shortstop that had been instrumental in vaulting him to the top of the class a few years prior. As a result, as he climbed back toward the top of draft boards, eventually being selected 11th overall by the A's.
—*Todd Gold*

## Bobby Wahl – RHP

Wahl was already throwing in the low-90s by his junior year in high school, and peaked at 92 mph at the 2009 National Showcase. Given his athletic 6-foot-4, 195-pound frame and easy, repeatable delivery it was obvious at the time that it was only a matter of time before he was throwing in the mid-90s with greater regularity.

It was also obvious that the biggest thing holding Wahl back was improving the consistency of the break on his breaking pitches as well as the command of his changeup. He flashed the ability to do so, so similar to him throwing in the mid-90s it seemed as though it would be only a matter of time, with more experience, that he would do so.

Here's his report from the National Showcase:

Long and slender build, projects physically. Nice delivery, throws under control, fast loose arm, good direction, repeats well. Primary FB pitcher, topped at 92 mph, can see mid-90s in future, tries to spot FB. Limited present feel for off speed, CB/SL both tend to be flat, throws change too hard, no mechanical reason he can't develop secondary pitches.

The fastball velocity did indeed increase, often settling in at his showcase high of 92 mph, with Ole Miss while touching the 94-96 range with frequent regularity. He also improved the break on his breaking ball, developing a sharp low-to-mid-80s slider that he's able to drop in the zone for strikes as well as burying in the dirt to record strikeouts. His changeup has also developed to give him the requisite three pitches for a starter. Wahl's success in college was predicated on him establishing his fastball early in the count and pitching aggressively while not being afraid to elevate his fastball.

The biggest thing that kept Wahl from being a first-round pick this past June was a blister problem that effected his velocity, command, and ability to consistently snap off an effective breaking ball, although he battled through these issues to go 10-0 with a 2.03 ERA his junior year. —*Patrick Ebert*

## Daniel Robertson – 3B

The SoCal product always stood out for his polished hitting ability as an amateur. Robertson was selected to the 2011 PG All-American Classic at Petco Park and was consistently ranked among the top 50 high school prospects in the nation in PG's Class of 2012 rankings. A look through his scout notes from his PG career returns a consistent theme: hittability. His notes from the PG National Showcase read:

Strong, strides in, swings hard, good load, extends on ball, hits through, all fields, good barrel. Crushed 2 balls to CF in games, including 84 SL off LCF wall. Mashed the next game as well, can flat out hit.

Six weeks later his Area Code Games notes included:

Natural hitter, sees the ball, consistent hard contact, all fields, gets hits on weak swings, finds the barrel.

His right-handed swing was more sound than sexy, and while he never showed the kind of massive raw power to captivate the imaginations of scouts, he gave plenty of reason to believe he would continue to hit at the next level. He also consistently showed the requisite defensive ability and arm strength to be able to handle third base at the professional level well, and scouts acknowledged his ability to handle that spot throughout his career, barring injury.

While it's not the most exciting profile in baseball, a player who is expected to continue hitting at a high level as a professional while contributing quality defense at a skill position is certainly an attractive prospect. As a result, the A's supplemented their first round selection of Addison Russell by snagging Robertson with the 34th overall pick in the 2012 draft.    —*Todd Gold*

# AL CENTRAL

## Chicago White Sox

### Erik Johnson – RHP

Johnson was named to a pair of top prospect lists from PG showcase events he attended: the 2006 Nor Cal Underclass and the 2007 National. Although those two events were eight months apart, Johnson showed significant improvement between the two; his fastball velocity rose from 84-86, while peaking at 87 mph, to 90-92. He also firmed up his curveball, adding more power to the pitch and turning it from a low-70s offering to an upper-70s one.

Here's his report from the National Showcase:

> He has a power pitcher's body, with good body strength and long and loose limbs. Johnson has a low-effort delivery with good extension out front over his front leg. He'll occasionally fall of to first base. Johnson's fastball was very consistently in the 90-92 mph range with some late sink and run to it. He threw a slurve type curveball at 78 mph that had very good depth at times and was a solid secondary pitch for him. He also mixed in a couple of 81 mph changeups. Johnson's arm strength and easy fastball velocity make him a pitcher that scouts' can dream about. He is a good student who has a verbal commitment to Cal Berkeley.

As noted, Johnson's physical stature on the mound has always been evident, and despite his larger size he did a very nice job repeating his delivery with simple, on-line mechanics. He added 30-40 more pounds at the college level pitching for the Cal Bears, and he carried that added weight well while continuing to build on his profile as durable, middle-of-the-rotation innings eater. He initially began his college career as Cal's closer before moving to the team's Friday ace role. There he continued to work on developing his changeup, which was a clear third pitch behind his fastball and curveball.
—*Patrick Ebert*

### Courtney Hawkins – OF

The Houston native was considered one of the top prospects in the 2012 high school class from an early age. After pitching his high school team to a state championship as a sophomore, Hawkins slowly began to develop into an even better outfield prospect over the next couple of years, and he took a significant step forward athletically between his sophomore and junior years. He improved his 60-yard-dash time from 7.15 in 2010 to 6.62 as he grew into a body type that now resembles that of a middle linebacker.

The transition was complete by the summer of 2011, when he began showing tremendous raw power. He hit one of the longest home runs of the 2011 Area Code Games, and that power was on display again in batting practice at the PG All-American Classic. He continued to show off the plus raw power in tournament settings as one of the top prospects on the highly visible Houston Banditos. The notes from his breakout showing at the Area Code Games read:

> Calmer swing, occasionally swung and missed but much more consistent contact, showed as much power as any player here, big HR, multiple gap shots, 400+ BP bomb, drove RCF gap, tends to jump out at the ball occasionally, likes ball down in zone, made effective OF plays, strong throws, routes can be adventuresome. Stock WAY UP.

He built off that strong summer with a dominant showing in pool play at the WWBA World Championship in Jupiter, amateur scouting's biggest stage. That momentum carried through the spring at Carroll High School, as Hawkins led them to a return trip to the state championship en route to becoming the 13th overall pick. Late that spring he was featured in the PG top 50 prospects for the 2012 (as the 13th-ranked prospect), and David Rawnsley wrote:

> Hawkins has firmly established himself as one of the elite high school power bats in the country, if not the best, and his name consistently comes up in the first round in the 8-15 range. The 6-foot-3, 210-pound right-handed hitter has superior bat speed and strength, and the ability to drive balls out of the park to all fields. He is also a free swinger, however, who will expand the strike zone on breaking balls and probably post some high strikeout numbers early in his professional career. But he rarely swings and misses on pitches over the plate and can handle any degree of velocity.

—*Todd Gold*

### Tyler Danish – RHP

Tyler Danish was a sophomore at Durant High School when his baseball future changed. He was a primary third baseman, and a pretty good one, who also threw in relief at times with a fastball that sat in the mid-80s.

One day he and a few of his teammates were messing around in the bullpen when Danish dropped down from his normal high three-quarters arm slot to a crossfire low three-quarters slot. The results were immediate. Not only could Danish throw the ball harder, it had huge tailing and running life at the plate. And it seemed like it was easier to throw from the lower arm slot as well. The conversion to full-time pitcher wasn't immediate, but it began that day.

By the time Danish graduated from Durant and was drafted in the second round by the White Sox he had become one of the most impressive pitchers ever to pass through the Perfect Game system. One could also make a compelling argument that he was the best high school player in the country in 2013 in terms of his overall performance.

Strangely, Danish didn't participate in a single Perfect Game Showcase. He did, however, play in nine WWBA tournaments with Chet Lemon's Juice and was a dominant factor in most of those events. He won the Most Valuable Pitcher award at two of Perfect Game's most prestigious and competitive events, the 2011 WWBA Underclass World Championship and the 2012 WWBA World Championship.

At the 2011 Underclass, Danish threw in four different games, going 3-0 with a save while throwing 14 innings, allowing three hits, and striking out 15 hitters while only walking one. It's likely the only time that a pitcher has won three games at a four-day Perfect Game tournament. In Jupiter in 2012, Danish almost duplicated that achievement, again throwing in four games, going 2-0 in 13 1/3 innings, striking out 20 hitters, and allowing only six hits, including a dominant performance over Connor Jones and the EvoShield Canes in the semifinals that propelled the Juice to the championship game.

That type of performance points to another part of Danish's overall package, one that doesn't often come into play for a high school pitcher but that is inescapable in this case. He has a rubber arm and can throw every day and maintain his raw stuff. Whether that is because of his delivery and arm slot or just because of his athletic makeup is impossible to tell, but it is yet another established part of his resume.

As a senior Durant, Danish threw in 17 games, going 15-1 with a 0.00 ERA in 94 innings. That is not a misprint. Playing at the 5A level in one of the most competitive baseball areas in the country, Durant didn't allow an earned run all season (he allowed five unearned runs). He allowed 32 hits, 16 walks, and struck out 156 batters, and also hit .411-9-27.

Danish created a huge dilemma for the scouting community last spring because he broke all the normal criteria they look for in a top high school pitching prospect. He's listed at 6-foot-1, 190 pounds. He throws from a highly unusual arm angle and delivery. It's very easy to immediately classify him as a reliever due to his entire package, including his competitiveness (Florida head coach Kevin O'Sullivan, where Danish was committed, was very open about his plans for Danish to immediately become his closer). And it's impossible to project him.

Even Danish's raw stuff numbers weren't nasty by top round numbers. He's topped out at 94-95 mph on his fastball but regularly pitches in the 90-92 mph range. But he gets such consistent huge life on the pitch that the velocity plays up, especially to right-handed hitters. Danish's slider comes in at 76-79 mph, more of the speed of a curveball for a low-90s thrower, so it isn't a power pitch by that definition. But again the pitch plays up given how sharp and big the break is, combined with how well Danish commands it.

For some scouts it all added up: Danish is a plus athlete with two nasty pitches and the chance for a third in the changeup. He displays plus command, huge competitiveness, absurd performance numbers, and proven durability.  —*David Rawnsley*

# Minnesota Twins

### Byron Buxton – OF

Had Buxton been born a couple of decades earlier, he could have represented the kind of hidden gem that gets all but one scout in the area fired. Hailing from the small town of Baxley in rural southern Georgia, Buxton was a two-sport star at 2A Appling County High School. His time on the gridiron limited his baseball exposure to the summer months, and when he did compete in national level summer baseball tournaments, he didn't begin drawing large crowds until the summer after his junior year.

Despite the lack of early buzz, the scouts that saw Buxton play as an underclassmen had very positive things to say about his raw tools. The internal PG notes on Buxton from the 2009 16u WWBA National Championship read:

> Athletic build, 7 runner, pull power, good bat speed, sees ball well, quick hands, good hitter, smoked a ball back through the box at 92 mph off the bat.

He continued to impress in his one tournament in 2010, as the notes from the 18u WWBA National Championship, playing up as a 16-year-old. That summer Buxton committed to the University of Georgia, and the word began to spread. By the time he returned to the Atlanta area the following summer for the 2011 18u and 17u National Championships the scouting community eagerly awaited their opportunity to finally see the electric tools they'd been hearing about.

Buxton did not disappoint. After a breakout showing at the WWBA tournaments, Buxton cemented his status as one of the top prospects in the 2012 draft with a standout showing at the East Coast Pro Showcase, after which David Rawnsley wrote:

> Pull approach hitting, bit long and will hit around the ball, ball comes off barrel hard, showed pull power off low 90s stuff, does not like off-speed, aggressive approach. Impact speed, 3.89 H to 1B, 3.18 on SB, intimidates the defense. Plays hard and likes to play. Top of the 1st round talent, best prospect here.

Buxton, however, was still earlier in the development curve as a hitter than most of the other elite 2012 draft prospects. Because of that, he wasn't able to separate himself from the pack as the top prospect in the draft, despite having the highest ceiling. Power-armed right-hander Lucas Giolito had been the top-ranked prospect in the class prior to straining his UCL, ultimately requiring Tommy John surgery. Puerto Rican shortstop Carlos Correa showed a similarly high ceiling and paired it with more advanced skill development at a younger age. Giolito's injury pushed him down to the middle of the first round, leaving the Astros to choose between Buxton and Correa with the first overall pick. Houston saved millions of dollars by cutting a deal with Correa, allowing the Twins to snatch up Buxton with the second overall pick.   —*Todd Gold*

### Alex Meyer – RHP

With a towering, 6-foot-7, 200-pound build, Meyer offered an imposing presence on the mound on the final day of the 2007 National Showcase. He used that size and long levers well to throw on a downward plane with great extension, making his 92-94 mph fastball, which peaked at 95, look that much harder out of the hand. His low-80s slider gave him a second, legitimate strikeout pitch, as he was virtually unhittable when both pitches were working for him. That performance led to him being selected to participate in the PG All-American Classic later that summer.

Here is his report from the National:

> Meyer has a very long, tall, and loose build that hasn't come close to reaching physical maturity yet. Meyer throws from a low-effort tall delivery that he repeats well and maintains good balance from. He arm stroke is clean and extremely fast; he has as much pure arm speed as any pitcher in the 2008 class and has excellent extension out front. Meyer's fastball topped out at 95 mph and was rarely under 92 mph from a good downward plane. His breaking ball was an 80-81 mph slurve type slider that had some downward break to it. Meyer's delivery lacks deception and his slider isn't a swing/miss pitch at this point, so hitters got reasonably good cuts at him despite his raw ability, but he has a first-round-type arm and could be throwing very hard by next year's draft. Scouts will certainly dream on him.

Because of the dominance of his fastball/slider one-two punch, Meyer didn't need to develop his changeup as much at the high school level. He continued to work on this pitch at the college level playing for Kentucky after an inconsistent spring during his senior year in high school caused him to fall to the 20th round of the 2008 draft, although the Red Sox reportedly still offered him $2 million to sign.

The biggest question surrounding Meyer in both high school and college is whether or not he could develop the tempo and command to remain in a starting role. It was something he clearly worked on while pitching for the Wildcats, but it wasn't something that came to him overnight, as he continues to work on some of the finer nuances to taking the ball every five days. Even then, a worst-case scenario of him being moved to the back end of the bullpen isn't a bad consolation prize, where he wouldn't have to worry about pacing himself, given his large stature and overpowering arsenal. *—Patrick Ebert*

### Jose Berrios – RHP

One of a handful of promising Puerto Rican players that attended the 2011 National Showcase in Fort Myers, Florida, Jose Orlando (J.O.) Berrios made the most of his time on the big stage the National offered, working steadily in the low-90s with a peak velocity of 93 mph, while mixing in a sharp curveball and a promising changeup.

Here's his report from that event:

> Medium athletic build. Standard leg tuck delivery, high 3/4s release point, gets downhill, arm is smooth and quick, ball comes out of his hand easy with low effort. Steady low 90s fastball, topped at 93 mph, mostly straight from regular release point. Will drop down low 3/4s with same velocity for running action or cut fastball at 87 occasionally. Flashes plus spin on mid-70s curveball, good bite with hard downer action, tends to cut curveball out front at times. Rare changeup. Throws strikes, especially with his curveball, and will come inside aggressively to right-handed hitters. Quality arm with a feel for pitching.

As noted in the report, his feel for pitching was also evident, and while he wasn't built as lean, loose, and projectable as his island-mate Edwin Diaz, he too offered plenty of projection thanks to a loose, live arm with minimal effort and late, boring movement on his fastball.

Berrios showed roughly the same stuff at the 2012 World Showcase seven months later, giving the 2012 draft class a pair of promising pitchers from the island. The Twins selected Berrios in the supplemental first round of that year's draft, 32nd overall, making him the highest-drafted Puerto Rican pitcher ever the same year Carlos Correa went no. 1 overall. Not surprisingly Berrios has hit the ground running in the lower levels of their minor-league system.   *—Patrick Ebert*

## Kansas City Royals

### Sean Manaea – LHP

A classic case of projection, Sean Manaea didn't stand out nearly as much in high school as a 6-foot-4, 200-pound left-handed pitcher that peaked at 86 mph at the four Perfect Game tournament and showcase events he attended. One of those events was the 2009 National Underclass Main Event Showcase held annually right after the Christmas holiday in Fort Myers, Florida. There he threw in the low-80s, peaking at 85, but his tall, projectable frame made it easy to see much more could be on the way, earning him a PG grade of 8.5 and a spot on the event's top prospect team. Here is his report from that event:

> Tall athletic build, good projection. Short compact arm action, some wrap, works well out front, low 3/4s release, FB to 85 mph, some arm-side run, nice feel for changeup, CB sweeps away from LHHs, delivery and arm both projectable, should keep improving.

Manaea continued to enjoy slow and steady development over his first couple of years at Indiana State, and by the summer of 2011, after his freshman season, he was now pitching in the upper-80s to low-90s consistently, peaking at 93 mph. That development led to him being named the no. 1 prospect in the Prospect League, once again noting that the young lefty still had plenty more room to improve.

Fast-forward one more year to the summer of 2012 where Sean Manaea, now 6-foot-5 and 235 pounds, firmly put his name in the conversation for the no. 1 overall pick for the 2013 draft thanks to a dominant summer performance in the Cape Cod League. He posted video game-like numbers on his way to being named the league's no. 1 overall prospect as well as Perfect Game's Summer Collegiate Player of the Year, thanks to a fastball that now peaked at 97 mph while sitting 93-95 to go along with a wicked slider and solid changeup.

Unfortunately a lingering hip injury followed by shoulder stiffness clouded Manaea's draft status during his junior season. He still threw in the 92-94 range when healthy during the spring for the Sycamores, but the health concerns caused him to slip to the 34th overall pick, where the Kansas City Royals scooped him up. They were able to sign Manaea to first-round money to get him in the fold, as they signed their first selection, Hunter Dozier, the eighth overall pick, to a signing bonus nearly $1 million less than the slotted value.    —*Patrick Ebert*

### Bubba Starling – OF

The 2011 draft, where Starling (his given name is Derek) went fifth overall to the Royals and received a $7.5 million signing bonus (spread over three years due to the dual-sport language available under the CBA at that point) isn't that far in the past, so followers can still recall his incredible high school athletic achievements.

Playing at Gardner-Edgerton High School southwest of Kansas City, Starling was All-State in three sports—baseball, football, and basketball. He was probably best known for his football exploits as a 6-foot-4, 180-pound running quarterback. As a senior, Starling ran for 2,417 yards and 31 touchdowns, including 395 yards and five touchdowns in the state championship game. He only threw 81 passes that year, completing less than 50 percent. He was recruited by all the big-name schools, eventually signing a dual-sport scholarship with Nebraska, and was considered the top prize in the Huskers' 2011 recruiting class.

In basketball, all Starling did was average 28.3 points a game as a senior. He has been quoted in feature stories as saying the single most fun thing to do in sports is to dunk on someone.

In Kansas, high school baseball takes a back seat to other sports, but Starling was still a nationally known, if somewhat mysterious, prospect from early in his high school career. Although he was rostered for a couple of WWBA tournaments, conflicts with football kept him from attending a single Perfect Game event. He was only scouted on a national basis twice before his senior high school season, once playing for the 2010 USA National 18u team and again at the 2010 Area Code Games.

The USA 18u team went 19-2 and included top prospects such as Francisco Lindor, Blake Swihart, Albert Almora, Lance McCullers, and Henry Owens. Starling played in 19 games, hitting .339-3-12, and interestingly finished with 16 walks (second on the team) against only 12 strikeouts. His .474 on-base percentage was second on the team to Swihart's .491. He also pitched three times, holding foes scoreless in 4 1/3 innings while striking out seven.

Starling was the focus of everyone's attention at the Area Code Games and performed very well. He ran a 6.56 60 (he had a 4.36 electronically timed 40 to his credit from football camps), played center field, hit with power, and was up to 92 mph on the mound. There was plenty of scout talk that Starling could be a better pitching prospect, with work, than a hitting prospect.

Here are the Perfect Game notes from the event:

> Superior athlete. Sound balanced hitting approach, calm in the box, good leverage, plus bat speed, big-time power projection, squares up well, quality at-bats, some back-side

collapse, loose and extended out front, short to the ball for his size, plus OF arm strength, good OF instincts. Raw mechanics (on the mound), drop and drive, compact quick arm, loses leverage, throws strikes, pretty hard spin on SL, good bite. MUCH better hitting prospect, very raw on the mound.

It was almost preordained that the hometown Royals (Kauffman Stadium is 36 miles from Gardner-Edgerton High School) were going to select Starling if he was available. A story went around the scouting community that spring that the Royals area scout was told that he or one of his associates should be there every time Starling played as a senior, regardless of the sport. That might have been an exaggeration, but no one was surprised when the Royals did pick, and eventually sign, Starling.

The Bubba Starling football legend still lives on, too, courtesy of the rabid Nebraska football fans. When Starling was struggling in the middle of the 2013 summer and momentum was building for the start of football practice, an article appeared in the Omaha paper speculating that Starling might be interested in returning to football if his baseball career continued on its present path.    —*David Rawnsley*

## Cleveland Indians

### Francisco Lindor – SS

Lindor was born in Puerto Rico and lived there until 2006, when he and his family moved to the Orlando area. He played in the same youth leagues in Toa Alta, Puerto Rico, as Cubs 2011 first-round pick Javier Baez, who also later moved to Florida. Having started his schooling in Puerto Rico, Lindor was actually a year younger than most of his peers in the 2011 draft class, and if he'd been in Florida his entire life he likely would have been in the 2012 class.

Carrying on the Lindor/Baez connection, the early-season matchup in 2011 between Lindor's Montverde Academy and Baez's Arlington Country Day High School team was one of the most scouted games of the 2011 spring, with well over 100 scouts purportedly in attendance.

Lindor made his first impression on Perfect Game a very strong one. Playing for the Apopka Black Sox as a sophomore at the 2008 WWBA Underclass World Championship, and still more than a month shy of his 15th birthday, Lindor blasted a home run early in pool play and word quickly circulated about this 150-pound switch-hitting 14-year-old with surprising power and flashy defensive skills. Lindor followed up that early game with two more extra-base hits and some multihit games and vaulted right into the top 20 in the early Class of 2011 rankings.

A number of very consistent tool-oriented themes developed with Lindor over the next three years leading up to his being selected by the Indians with the eighth overall pick in the 2011 draft.

Lindor made his debut on the national stage showing power from both sides of the plate and continued to do so throughout his pre-professional career, even winning the home-run contest while hitting right-handed at the 2010 Perfect Game All-American Classic. Although he only has eight home runs in over 1,000 professional at-bats, the potential is there for more power production.

In professional scouting terms, Lindor only had "average" running speed and arm strength in high school. The best 60-yard dash he ran was 6.78 seconds, and he was consistently in the 4.3 area from home to first base. He lacked plus arm strength from the hole at shortstop, but his arm strength played up because he was so adept at charging the ball and working around and through difficult plays, and his release was lightning quick. There isn't much precedent for a teenage shortstop being a top-10 draft pick without true plus run and throw tools but Lindor was an exception.

The reason that Lindor was a top-10 draft pick is a reoccurring theme in the Perfect Game notes and in scout discussions in the spring prior to the draft. He played the game so easily—you could see the game happening in slow motion in his eyes, whether it was hitting or on the bases or playing defense. Lindor was always quick but was always on balance and was never athletically rushed. Much is made about young, very talented players learning to slow the game down before they are able to be truly successful, and Lindor was always able to do that from a very young age.

That is undoubtedly one of the reasons he was immediately successful upon reaching the Double-A level as a 19-year-old in 2013. Take a quick look at some of his peripheral numbers from 2013: 25-for-32 in stolen base attempts despite average speed, and a 49-to-46 walk-to-strikeout ratio as a teenager. Those are signs of someone who understands the game and slows it down.   —*David Rawnsley*

# Detroit Tigers

### Nick Castellanos – 3B/OF

Castellanos got an early start to his Perfect Game career, attending the 2006 WWBA Underclass World Championship early in his freshman year with the Deep South Florida team, and made his first showcase appearance at the 2007 Southeast Underclass Showcase in Atlanta at the start of his sophomore season. He went on to participate in 12 WWBA tournaments, mostly with the All American Prospects, and stood out at the 2009 Perfect Game National Showcase.

He received a PG Grade of 9 at that Southeast Underclass, a grade that in retrospect might have been a bit higher if he hadn't run 7.35 in the 60-yard dash and only thrown 81 mph during infield drills. While Castellanos' run and throw tools were never stellar, he did get his 60 time down to 6.70 on the turf at the Metrodome in 2009 at the National Showcase. His fastest infield throw was 87 mph.

What stood out about Castellanos even back then was his ability with the bat and how well he projected both physically and with his hitting skills. Here are the notes from that initial showcase, when Castellanos was 15 years old and listed at 6-foot-3, 180 pounds:

> Tall, good looking projectable athlete, has some bat speed, swing is long and loopy, showed oppo pop, looks to lift, has hitting tools to develop. Game swings were shorter, crisper but as a long levered athlete, will always have to work to stay short. Long arm, strong arm, corner guy, very good

fundamentals, soft hands, player, smooth actions at 3B. Hit everything hard.

Perhaps because of his running speed and arm strength, Castellanos was always a better player to watch and evaluate in game situations, where his hitting ability and high baseball IQ had a better stage to stand up and perform. The left side of the All American Prospects infield for two years consisted of Castellanos at third base and PG All-American Yordy Cabrera, later a second-round pick of the Oakland A's, at shortstop. That talented combo led All American Prospects to the championship at the 2008 WWBA Underclass World Championship, where they shared Most Valuable Player honors.

Castellanos was one of the final players considered but not selected for the 2009 Perfect Game All-American Game that featured players such as Bryce Harper, Jameson Taillon, and Kris Bryant, while Angels top prospect Kaleb Cowart was the starting third baseman for the East team. Cabrera won the Rawlings Home Run Challenge that year.

Castellanos was obviously very well known to scouts at that point, but his draft stock really blossomed during his senior season at Archbishop McCarthy High School. He played so well defensively at shortstop during the spring that there was talk about his potential ability to play that position as a professional, just as there was similar conversation about another fast-rising infield prospect in Miami at the same time named Manny Machado. And, of course, Castellanos did what he'd always done offensively: crush the ball consistently (.542 with 42 RBI) and run the bases with plus instincts (22 steals).

While Castellanos was considered a solid first-round talent on the field, there was a significant concern about his signability going into the draft. Castellanos was a solid student in the classroom and was an articulate young man with a scholarship to the hometown Miami Hurricanes, while his father Jorge is a physician. The Tigers ventured where many decided to shy away, picking Castellanos with the 44th overall pick and signing him to a $3.45 million signing bonus.   —*David Rawnsley*

### Jake Thompson – RHP

Thompson was certainly no stranger to the showcase circuit, attending his first showcase as a freshman in high school. At a young age Thompson was a two-way prospect, showing a steady development of raw power at the plate in addition to his ability on the mound. Over time his arm strength began to create separation in that two-way profile, as his development as a pitcher outpaced that as a hitter.

One side affect of his two-way profile was that he often pitched while dealing with considerably more fatigue than the "pitcher-only" prospects in his class. His fastball velocity climbed steadily and was toward the top of his class, but never reached eye-popping levels. He didn't surpass the 91 mph mark until the 2011 WWBA World Championship, where he sat 90-93 in the early innings. But what Thompson always showed was a bulldog mentality on the mound, pitching aggressively and backing his fastball with a tight slider that he commanded well at an early age.

And while his raw stuff was certainly prospect caliber, it is only part of what stood out about Thompson. He was a big-game pitcher throughout his prep career, stepping up in several big spots. He punched out 11 in a win against powerhouse East Cobb in the 17u WWBA National Championship before a packed house of scouts. He struck out seven while pitching Rockwall-Heath High School to the Texas 5A state championship game. In his outing in Jupiter he allowed two runs over three innings, but they were of the unearned variety, and he impressed with his ability to maintain his composure.

Entering the draft, David Rawnsley wrote the following about Thompson as part of the Texas State Preview:

> He solidified his new-found standing as a top prospect this spring by continuing to throw his fastball steadily in the low-90s with good sinking action. Thompson comes from a mid- to low-three-quarters release point with very good extension out front, and though his delivery is somewhat unconventional for a pitcher with his size and build, it works very well for him and shows his athletic looseness. Thompson's strikeout pitch is a big-breaking, low-80s slider that he commands very well and is especially tough on right-handed hitters.

His combination of polish and stuff led to his projection as a Group 1 (rounds 1-3) prospect entering the draft, and the Tigers made him their first pick of the 2012 draft in the second round.  —Todd Gold

### James McCann – C

McCann has fit the profile of a take-charge, defensive-oriented catcher whose bat shows promise, but likely will rise based on the strength of his skills behind the plate for quite some time. As a young high school player from California, McCann attended the 2007 Sunshine West Showcase the summer prior to his senior year. There he showed his lateral quickness, release, and arm strength, and at the time swung the bat from both sides of the plate. Here is his report from that event:

> McCann has a nice long and lanky frame that is projectable. Defensively he has an accurate arm from behind the plate with a good release. He has solid arm strength (75 mph), and he produced good pop times, including a 2.05 game pop. He keeps the ball in front of him well, and he has soft hands. McCann also has the ability to play 3B as well. At the plate he is a legitimate switch-hitter who has a solid approach from both sides. He has bat speed through the zone, and he has a nice line-drive swing plane. He stays inside the ball with the ability to hit to all fields. McCann has a nice approach, and he centers the ball consistently. Even though he is not listed as a pitcher, he threw at the event touching 84 mph. He throws from a 3/4 arm slot with a loose arm. He stays balanced and has good arm speed. McCann struck out five in two innings of work. He is an excellent student as well.

Although the White Sox drafted McCann in the 31st round in 2008 coming out of high school, McCann took his talents to Arkansas to continue to improve his hitting skills while honing his defensive talents. He handled a very talented and young Razorbacks pitching staff that reached the College World Series the following year, serving as his team's leader that finished 40-22 while hitting .306-6-38. Leading up to the draft that year, here is what was written about McCann as part of the Arkansas state preview:

> With his superior defensive skills, refined mechanics and take-charge approach, the 6-foot-3, 210-pound McCann could catch in the big leagues right now. He is regarded in a class of his own defensively among college catchers. Not only is he strong, durable and athletic behind the plate, but has very mature instincts for catching...Where McCann's athleticism is readily evident defensively, he struggles to show the same kind of consistent athleticism in his approach at the plate. He hit just .105 last summer as the regular catcher for Cotuit, the Cape Cod League champion, as pitchers routinely exposed his long swing and stride. He has quickened the hip rotation in his swing this spring, though, enabling him to turn on balls more consistently and he has shown marked improvement with the bat, also hitting a number of timely home runs.

Identified as one of the best overall defensive players available for the 2011 draft, McCann's profile led to him being selected by the Tigers in the second round, the team's first selection that year.  —Patrick Ebert

## AL EAST

## Toronto Blue Jays

### Marcus Stroman – RHP

The discussion about whether Stroman's long-term future as a big leaguer is as a starter or reliever has been a constant ever since the Blue Jays drafted him in the first round out of Duke in 2012. There just aren't many 5-foot-9 right-handers who have long-term success as starters at the highest level in baseball, so Stroman will have to prove himself every step of the way.

The fact that Stroman has been dominant in his few short stints as a closer, including in the Cape Cod League in 2010 and for the Collegiate National Team in 2011 has helped feed the starter/reliever discussion as well.

But well before the Long Island native turned professional, the topic was very different. Stroman was considered a primary middle infielder in high school, although everyone realized he had a special arm. When the Washington Nationals took a flier on him with their 18th-round pick as a high school senior in 2009, he was drafted as a shortstop.

Stroman was a do-everything type of athlete in high school. He lettered for four years as a point guard in basketball and was All-County as a senior, which resonates in that sport playing so close to New York City and attests to his overall athleticism. During the spring he excelled both at shortstop and on the mound, but gained more recognition for his pitching, as he was named the Paul Gibson Pitcher of the Year on Long Island after his senior year when he went 9-1, 0.25 with 126 strikeouts. And of course, Stroman was getting the types of grades in the classroom that enabled him to go to Duke.

But during the summers Stroman was primarily a shortstop and didn't even take the mound at a number of events, including the 2007 Northeast Top Prospect Showcase, the 2008 PG Aflac Showcase, and the 2008 Area Code Games. He did throw an inning at the 2008 PG National Showcase, topping out at 91 mph with an 81-mph breaking ball that was sharp and deep. That breaking ball, of course, has become his signature pitch and is now an 85-87-mph slider. Stroman also pitched at a couple of WWBA events for the South Florida Bandits.

The notes on Stroman as a shortstop prospect are consistent across the board:

> Good feet, bounce in step, easy arm, little erratic, hands work quickly, good body control; Small kid, open stance, easy loose swing, + extension out front, good bat speed, some gap pop, squares well, nice looking swing, + BP, open, fast bat, decent pop, quiet pro swing, good baseball player, steps in bucket some, short glide, good rhythm, short to ball, slight loft, solid LDs, hands work easy, simple, gap pop; ++ Balance/flow at plate, good bat speed, quick twitch, will reach outside, looks like RH'd Ray Durham w/o the speed, very slick in IF, hands were inconsistent in games, looked tentative on D at times.

Stroman was a still a primary shortstop at Duke as a freshman, or at least he was for the first half of the season, when he hit .265-2-20 in 166 at-bats. Stroman also worked as a long reliever out of the bullpen, a somewhat unusual combination, but was moved into the starting rotation in late April and threw well in that role, including a complete game against Wake Forest with 10 strikeouts. Stroman then went to the Cape Cod League as a reliever, notching 11 saves without allowing a run in 27 innings.

He continued in much the same pattern as a sophomore, starting 33 games at shortstop, eight games as a pitcher and appearing nine times as a reliever. It wasn't until his junior season that Stroman became a full-time starting pitcher and saw his stuff and prospect status explode, going 6-5, 2.39 with 136 strikeouts in 98 innings. —David Rawnsley

### Aaron Sanchez – RHP

Sanchez grew up in a baseball family in Barstow, California, as his father, Mike Shipley, was drafted twice by the California Angels as a right-handed pitcher out of Barstow Community College in 1976, first in the 10th round of the regular phase and again in the fourth round of the now-defunct secondary phase.

While Barstow is in the baseball hotbed of Southern California, it's well off the beaten path, and Sanchez was little known nationally before he participated in his first Perfect Game event, the 2009 National Showcase. Part of the reason that Sanchez was a late rising prospect was that he was a primary middle infielder his first two years in high school and didn't start pitching full time until his junior year.

Once Sanchez took the mound in Minneapolis it was obvious that he was an All-American and a potential first-round draft choice. He had a slender and very projectable 6-foot-3, 170-pound build and a lightning quick right arm. Sanchez's fastball sat in the 91-94 mph range and he had present quality to both his 75-mph curveball and his 80-mph changeup. Here are the notes from PG database on his performance:

> Slender long legs, arm is smooth/fast, stays over rubber well, arm accelerates, looks athletic, projects, CB flashes

quality spin, gets on side for sweeping break mostly, blows FB by hitters upstairs, should throw Chg more, big velocity arm ... Long legs, put together well, easy velo and can repeat, inconsistent with CB but is there, ok feel ... Very lanky, small-framed, shallow-chested righty w/chance to be 1st-round pick as pitcher. Loose arm and excellent athleticism in delivery, excellent balance, clean finish. Some loop in arm-action. Threw easy 91-94 MPH w/two-seam running action that projects to ave MLB movement. mid-70s CB was at times very sharp, downward bite, chance to become plus MLB pitch but needs much better command. Lots of projection, but needs to go slow at first because he's not very physical. One of the best arms this week.

Sanchez later went on to pitch at the Area Code Games as well as the PG All-American Classic in August, and he threw for the San Gabriel Valley (SGV) Arsenal at the 2009 WWBA World Championship in late October. It's interesting to note in the context of Sanchez's occasional command problems as a professional (134 walks in 256 innings) and his cautious workload by the Blue Jays that there were consistent scouting notes from those events in high school referring to him struggling with his command at times and that he appeared to tire quickly.

The impression that Sanchez left at the PG All-American Classic was a bit different than most players. A large and very boisterous crowd of Sanchez's family and friends made the 180-mile trip from Barstow to San Diego and stood out among the 8,000-plus fans at the game, literally taking over a whole section in the stands.

Sanchez went on to go 7-0, 0.73 with 104 strikeouts in 57 innings his senior year while also hitting .403-5-20 at the plate. The Blue Jays selected him with the 34th overall pick, just before they grabbed another tall, slender right-hander, Noah Syndergaard, with the 38th pick. The Mariners then choose Taijuan Walker with the 43rd overall selection, completing a great run of young, projectable high school right-handers that all look like future big-league stars. —David Rawnsley

### Daniel Norris – LHP

Norris offered one of the fastest arms and most explosive fastballs of any left-handed pitcher that has attended a Perfect Game event. His status as one of the top prospects available for the 2011 draft was established for several years, as he sat at no. 1 in the Perfect Game rankings for his class for the two years leading up to his senior year. Prior to the draft, Dylan Bundy leapfrogged Norris after his own impressive high school career (detailed below), but Norris still entered the 2011 draft as one of the most exciting and still-projectable pitchers of those eligible.

The 6-foot-2, 180-pounder peaked at 96 mph while in high school, doing so at the 2010 18u WWBA National Championship pitching for the East Cobb Yankees. It was the third year in a row he pitched at the 18u for the EC Yankees, touching 94 the summer before and 87 in 2008, doing so a couple of months after his 15th birthday.

Norris made that velocity look easy, with a smooth, repeatable, and athletic delivery, leading many to believe his radar gun readings could continue to climb at the next level, whether that be in college—he committed to play for Clemson—or as a pro.

His performance at the 2010 PG National, where he peaked at 94 mph and mixed in a sharp mid-70s curveball and promising low-to-mid-80s changeup, cemented his selection to participate in the PG All-American Classic later that summer. It was noted at the time, and the following spring leading up to the draft, that Norris' secondary offerings still needed to be tightened up and thrown with greater consistency, but all of the pieces were there for him to succeed at a high level. Here's his report from the National:

> Long-armed athletic build. Hands over head delivery, good pace, hard front side on landing, quick and athletic off the mound, 3/4's release point. Easy velocity, sat 92-94 mph, lots of 94s, fastball runs, good angle to the plate, threw strikes to spots with fastball. CB lacks ideal velocity but has big hard break, consistent spin and location, some changeups have big fade, good feel for off speed, throws strikes with all pitches, minimum effort to everything. Outstanding prospect.

Norris' prospective status led to equally lofty expectations leading up to draft day in June 2011. Word spread that his price tag to sign was $3.9 million, and he was identified as a player that could potentially fall in the draft due to those aspirations. Norris did indeed fall further than where his talents warranted, but the Blue Jays stopped that slide in the second round, taking him with the 74th overall pick. That year the Blue Jays owned seven picks in the top two rounds, and took a very aggressive approach with those selections.

Their first-round pick was Tyler Beede, who had lofty bonus aspirations of his own, as well as another Vanderbilt commit, Kevin Comer, who they took in the sandwich round. When Beede opted not to sign, it opened an opportunity for the Blue Jays to get Norris (and Comer) in the fold, which they did so for a $2 million bonus. That number fell short of Norris' original hope, but was a significant amount of money given to a second-round selection, even before the new draft pools were introduced.

*—Patrick Ebert*

### Chase DeJong – RHP

Typically, miles per hour translate to dollar signs in the draft. The hardest-throwing pitchers tend to come off the board earliest and thus command the highest bonuses. But there are exceptions, and Chase DeJong is a good example. The Southern California native wasn't exactly a soft-tosser, frequently working in the 88-90 mph range as a member of the San Gabriel Valley (SGV) Arsenal at numerous national level tournaments. DeJong was one of the better pitching prospects in the 2012 high school class, but not simply on the merit of his raw stuff. It was his command, pitchability, and quality of off-speed pitches that allowed DeJong to dominate his competition on a consistent basis as an amateur.

DeJong sparked a lot of debate amongst scouts prior to his senior spring, as on the one hand he was a right-hander who lacked an explosive high-velocity fastball, yet at the same time commanded three quality pitches and already had polish beyond his years. When his senior season at Wilson High School

in Long Beach got underway he saw an uptick in velocity, with reports of him settling in around 90 and climbing up to 93 at times. That changed the equation entirely, as even though 93 isn't the kind of velocity that pitchers can get away with mistakes at, it was firm enough that organizations had to begin taking him seriously as an early-round draft prospect. In PG's draft preview article highlighting California's top prospects for 2012, David Rawnsley wrote the following of DeJong:

> DeJong throws from a simple turn-and-throw delivery with a long, deep arm action and comes straight over-the-top which provides some deception. His 88-91-mph fastball comes in at a hard downhill angle and gets both sinking and cutting life at the plate. DeJong's best pitch is a nasty 82 mph changeup that is one of the best in the 2012 draft class, and is his separator when throwing to elite hitters. His 75 mph curve comes from a similar release point as his fastball and changeup, and gets big downer shape and bite to change the hitter's eye level.

The arsenal suggested a ceiling of a middle of the rotation starting pitcher, though his body had plenty of room to fill and his clean arm action suggested that he may have another uptick in velocity in his future. This allowed him to firmly establish himself as a top-two-round prospect in the eyes of some organizations. Even if he isn't able to develop his raw stuff another grade, DeJong has the ability to be an asset to the Blue Jays given his command and pitchability.   *—Todd Gold*

## Baltimore Orioles

### Kevin Gausman – RHP

With a perfectly projectable 6-foot-4, 180-pound build coming out of high school, with broad shoulders, long, wiry-strong limbs and a high waist, while throwing on a pronounced downhill plane, Gausman was arguably the most projectable pitcher eligible for the 2010 draft. He peaked at 94 mph at all three of the Perfect Game events he attended in high school—the National Showcase, the PG All-American Classic, and the WWBA World Championship—all of which he attended in the summer and fall of 2009 prior to his final spring tune-up as a senior leading up to the draft.

In addition to his fastball, he also flashed promising secondary offerings, although none showed the consistent break, or command, needed for him to be ranked higher on draft boards. He was ranked 17th in the 2010 class by Perfect Game prior to his being drafted, a testament to just how easy it was to dream on his future.

Here's his report from the 2009 PG National:

> Athletic lean pitcher's build, excellent physical projection. Very polished delivery, very good balance, arm works extremely well, hides ball in delivery, repeats. Velo comes easy, first warm up at 91, sits between 91-94 mph, good heaviness down in zone, can spot FB glove side with maturity. CB has hard spin/sharp bite at 72 mph, could add more velo, will shorten up CB break for soft SL, has feel for change. Very high ceiling talent. Early draft prospect.

Gausman made no secret of his willingness to honor his commitment to play for Louisiana State, although the Dodgers did draft him in the sixth round in 2010. At the time that seemed to be more as a backup plan if they were unable to sign their first-round pick, fellow right-hander and LSU commit Zach Lee, although Lee also had a promising football career to contend with, which was reflected by the $5.25 million bonus it took to sign him away from both LSU and football.

The summer after his senior year Gausman headed to the California Collegiate League where he reportedly flirted with triple digits prior to ever stepping on LSU's campus as a student. When he did, the initial results were promising, posting a 5-6, 3.51 record in an aggressive appointment as a weekend starter in the SEC as a freshman. For as obvious as his talent continued to be, it was also clear that his secondary pitches still needed refinement as his fastball velocity continued to climb.

Gausman pitched both on the Cape and for Team USA during the summer of 2011, where his game continued to evolve, and while he entered the following spring as a likely first-round pick as a draft-eligible sophomore, his draft status really exploded when he suddenly mastered a wipeout breaking pitch, a newly developed slider that he had tinkered with before but had yet to fully grasp. That pitch complemented his fastball, now thrown consistently at 93-95 while peaking 97/98 early in games, a softer yet big-breaking low- to mid-70s curveball, and a nice fading low-80s change. All of which led to an impressive 12-2, 2.77 season serving as the Tigers' Friday ace.

That complete package and overall development allowed him to be considered a realistic candidate to go no. 1 overall in 2012, and ended up being the Baltimore Orioles selection with the fourth overall pick. —*Patrick Ebert*

## Dylan Bundy – RHP

The Bundy name was fresh in the minds of scouts before Dylan took the mound at the 2008 17u WWBA National Championship following his freshman year of high school. His older brother Bobby had been considered a potential early-round pick heading into his senior year, but a knee injury and signing bonus demands caused him to slip to the eighth round of the 2008 draft.

Dylan quickly began to establish his own reputation, topping out at 88 mph at the WWBA National Championship before running his fastball up to 92 at the Area Code Games late that summer. His work ethic and training regimen would later become the stuff of legend, and the YouTube video of his boxing workout with his older brother would pile up views as the younger brother began to make a name for himself on the travel ball circuit.

Dylan followed up his brother's Gatorade Oklahoma Player of the Year award winning season by winning the award for himself as a sophomore in 2008. He continued to establish himself as a top prospect in the 2011 class as he followed up that sophomore season with a standout performance at the 2009 Junior National Showcase and then running his fastball up to 96 mph at the 2009 17u WWBA National Championship. Here's his scouting report from the Junior National Showcase:

> Bundy has a strong athletic build, three-quarters arm slot, fast arm, ball explodes out of hand, fastball has good life, clean effortless delivery, excellent change, good feel for change, hard slider, excellent off-speed, very good pitch-ability, commands all of his pitches, Highest level pitching prospect, shows pop with the bat, good power potential, has bat speed, strength in swing, quick hands, can hit, also high-level hitting prospect.

Bundy would transfer to local powerhouse Owasso High School for his junior and senior seasons, and would help the Rams reach the state championship in each of his two seasons there. It also gave him a slightly larger stage upon which to showcase his elite ability. He would go on to have the kind of dominant career at Owasso that would be expected of a pitcher with his combination of raw stuff, command, and pitchability. He would run his streak of Gatorade State Player of the Year awards to three straight, being named the Gatorade National Athlete of the Year (all sports) as a senior in 2011. That year he struck out 158, compared to just four walks, over 78 innings. Bundy threw a complete game and won each of the 11 starts he made that spring. Not only did he issue very few walks, he rarely even found himself in a three-ball count.

Bundy's draft stock was very strong despite belonging to the riskiest group of prospects—high school pitchers. His 6-foot-1 frame was the biggest flaw that scouts could find in a nearly flawless prospect. His fastball would sit comfortably in the mid-90s, touching the upper-90s while showing plus command from a mechanically sound, low-effort delivery. He backed his present big-league fastball with an even better cutter that sat in the 88-92-mph range with depth and advanced feel. His curveball lagged a bit behind but featured hard bite and looked to be another future plus pitch, and he had already begun working on developing his changeup. Here's part of Bundy's pre-draft writeup from David Rawnsley:

> That combination of command and raw stuff is key to why Bundy's relatively short and mature build doesn't seem to be even a passing concern to scouts, who often prefer their top high school pitching prospects to be more physically projectable. The bottom line is that Bundy simply doesn't need to get any better in the ways that classic projectability would impact a normal pitcher's future.

There was little question during the spring of 2011 that Bundy was the top prospect from the high school ranks, regardless of position. Rather, the questions about his draft stock centered around how he compared to the cadre of college power arms projected for the top of the first round. Given the dominance of UCLA's Gerrit Cole, there wasn't much buzz about Bundy potentially becoming the first high school righty to be selected first overall despite his rare and obvious talent. But it was clear that he would come off the board very early and scouts would often debate how well Bundy would have fared if he were sent directly to the major leagues that season. To this day, one of the most popular responses amateur scouts give to the question "who is the best prospect you've ever scouted?" is Dylan Bundy. —*Todd Gold*

# New York Yankees

## J.R. Murphy – C

John Ryan Murphy was one of the most dominant hitters in the 2009 class. However, until he made a full-time position switch from the outfield to behind the plate during his senior year in high school, he wasn't considered a serious draft prospect. Six-foot, 180-pound right-handed hitters (Murphy is now listed at 5-foot-11, 195 pounds) with big-league average running speed at best are not a popular draft demographic.

Murphy played during the summers for the Florida Bombers team that featured many future big leaguers—including Eric Hosmer, J.P. Arencibia, and Yonder Alonso—and the Bombers won an incredible six WWBA 18u National Championships in an eight-year period. He hit .439-10-66 for the Bombers the summer before his senior season at IMG Academy, then hit .627-11-66 during the spring for IMG.

While Murphy didn't stand out physically for his size, he was very strong and athletic. But almost every scouting comment in the Perfect Game database mentions the same thing—how quick his hands were at the plate. Here are the notes from multiple scouts from the 2008 WWBA 18u National Championship:

> Good power the other way, takes his hacks, quick hands, loads well, Top Prospect, possible draft, lower half can be more explosive, 4.25 H-1B, lets ball travel, very good approach, short but built well, looks like a big leaguer in the box approach-wise.

Murphy attended only one Perfect Game showcase, the 2006 National Underclass after his freshman year, where he received a PG Grade of 8.5. Interestingly, he's listed as a primary outfielder at the event but he did catch, throwing 78 mph with a best pop time of 1.97 during drills, both outstanding for his age. However, the scout notes do reflect that his receiving skills were very raw, and again, it was Murphy's bat that stood out:

> Athletic build, wide rock back load, open stance, mid-field contact, strong hands, good bat speed, consistent hard contact, showed LCF pop, good BP, gap 2B RF, uses all fields, med build, open stance, quick compact stroke ... + balance, leverage, strength in swing, nice swing mechs, nice hands to ball (8+), ball jumps off bat, nice hitter.

The 2009 high school catching class was one of the best in recent memory, and Perfect Game made the unprecedented decision to put six catchers on the 2008 PG All-American rosters: Luke Bailey, Austin Maddux, Max Stassi, Andrew Susac, Jonathan Walsh, and Mike Zunino. Murphy, of course, wasn't a primary catcher at that point and was not considered. But it became obvious as the draft drew closer that Murphy had impressed enough scouts with his work defensively behind the plate that he would be among the first high school catchers selected.

The Yankees made him their second-round pick and the fourth high school catcher chosen overall. Not a scenario that many could have imagined a year before.   —David Rawnsley

## Tyler Austin – OF

Tyler Austin played in twelve Perfect Game events as a high school player from Conyers, Georgia, including the 2009 National Showcase and the 2009 PG All-American Classic. But despite being one of the most prolific home-run hitters in Georgia high school history, Austin wasn't a particularly well-known player in the scouting community until the National. He played at WWBA and BCS tournaments for a small local team named the Rockdale Rhinos and hadn't been to any previous showcases prior to that June.

With that background he was on no one's short list to make the All-American roster prior to the event. But he blew away the Perfect Game scouting staff in Minneapolis with his tools and was immediately considered the second best catcher in the 2009 class behind Bryce Harper. And as Harper really wasn't in the 2009 class, just leaving high school early after getting his GED, it was easy to tout Austin as the top receiver in his peer group of seniors.

Austin had been only catching a year at that point and his defense was still unpolished, as shown in the notes below. But his athletic tools stood out, including running a 6.8 60-yard dash, throwing 84 mph from behind the plate and popping 1.78 in drills. He also topped out at 89 mph on the mound.

> High set, falls off, good arm, not directional, can improve mech's, quick but very raw. No block fundamentals, throws body forward at balls in dirt. Plus arm-strength that will make him a plus thrower when he gets the footwork figured out. Struggles w/ crouch, has good athleticism and can shift his feet, but hasn't found a comfortable sitting position. Hands are okay. Athletic enough to play OF/1B/3B.

The Yankees obviously had different ideas about Austin defensively, as he has never caught a game in professional baseball and actually was considered at first base before moving briefly to third and eventually to his present position, right field. The final line of the defensive notes from the National Showcase certainly seems prophetic.

It was offensively, though, that Austin really stood out. He had outstanding raw bat speed and big power potential, and attacked the ball as if he was looking to hurt it. Here are his hitting notes from the National Showcase:

> + build, strong, good swing, shows power, short to ball, pulls, good simple swing, ball jumps hard ... amazing power ... RHH w/outstanding hitting tools. 6-2, 215, and strong. Generates above-average MLB bat-speed right now w/ strong hitting actions and solid-ave raw power that projects to plus-plus ... Compact stroke with small load. Tools to become middle-order big league hitter, but is carved up by good curveballs right now. Just needs to refine approach. Potential 1st-round pick. Average runner.

Austin's life changed shortly after the National Showcase, however, when he was diagnosed with testicular cancer. He underwent surgery in early August to remove the tumor but was able to resume baseball activities almost immediately.

Perfect Game President Jerry Ford summarized Austin's PG All-American experience as part of his notes published on the PG website shortly after the game, including being the recipient of the first-ever Nick Adenhart Award in 2009:

Tyler Austin is an outstanding big strong athlete from Conyers Georgia. He is a very good student and always conducts himself in a first class manner. About a month before this year's Aflac Classic, Tyler got some bad news. He was diagnosed with testicular cancer. Shortly before report day to San Diego, Tyler had a tumor removed. He still awaits treatment and hopes for the best, remission. Most would have stayed home worrying about their condition. Most in his position would have a hard time going to an event that is geared toward cancer charity, let alone visit sick young kids at the Children's Hospital. But most people are not Tyler Austin. Tyler not only wanted to attend, he actually wanted to try and play. The stitches from surgery presented a problem and the pain was obvious. The doctor had said if he can stand the pain, he could try to play. We really didn't expect Tyler to play, especially when his primary position is catcher. We hoped we could get a plate appearance for him. However, Tyler had other thoughts. He did visit the kids at the hospital. He never missed a day of the activities or practices and he did want to play, even catch, in the game. Tyler Austin did play in the game and he did win the inaugural Nick Adenhart Award. After all, he did exemplify the overall spirit and character of a true Aflac All American.

*—David Rawnsley*

### Greg Bird – 1B

Scouts first noticed Bird at Grandview High School in Colorado when he was a young catcher handling his year older teammate, right-handed pitcher Kevin Gausman.

Of course, Bird wasn't hard to notice on his own. First, he was a 6-foot-3, 205-pound left-handed-hitting catcher, and those stand out on any field. But more obviously, Bird was in the middle of putting together three of the best high school seasons one can imagine.

As a sophomore, Bird hit .500-14-32. He followed that up with a .660-13-42 junior season and hit .553-12-38 when he was named the Colorado state player of the year as a senior. During his junior and senior seasons Bird also combined to draw 56 walks while striking out only eight times. His extremely high walk totals in professional baseball (125 walks in 162 games) had some precedent in his high school days.

Bird attended the 2010 Perfect Game National Showcase and received a PG Grade of 9.5. His strength and raw power were obvious and he crushed a couple of balls that stayed in the Metrodome air for a long, long time. There were two questions that resonated with Perfect Game scouts, however, that kept Bird from getting a 10 grade.

The first was whether Bird would be able to hit high-level pitching. His swing was long and lacked the versatility and explosiveness to really project as a "hit" tool. The second was whether Bird would be able to stay behind the plate due to his size and relative athleticism. Here is his report from the event:

Comfortable catching set up, shifts well, soft hands, some arm strength, tends to stand up when throwing, 1.99 best

pop time. Left-handed hitter, open stance, long extended swing, gets to his front side well, lots of lift in swing, big power on his pitch, mistake hitter but can really put a charge into the ball.

Those were also questions that much of the scouting world shared going into the 2011 draft. When Bird, who was a very good student in high school and had a scholarship to Arkansas, was open about his need to get first-round money to forgo that scholarship, that seemed to seal his short-term baseball plans. When the Yankees picked Bird in the fifth round anyway there were plenty of raised eyebrows.

Bird then did something that strongly contributed to his eventually signing a $1.1 million contract at the signing deadline. He traveled out to California to play in the California Collegiate League and proceeded to hit .273-3-17 with 24 walks in 23 games while being first-team All CCL. The swing and approach that worked so well against Colorado high school pitching, but that many scouts doubted (including this one), worked pretty well against older college-level pitching as well.

His 2013 season (.288-20-84, 102 walks, .938 OPS) shows that it works pretty well against South Atlantic League pitching, too.   *—David Rawnsley*

## Tampa Bay Rays

### Jake Odorizzi – RHP

Checking in at 6-foot-2, 175 pounds at the 2007 PG Pitcher/Catcher Indoor Showcase, Jake Odorizzi may very well have made his the last case needed to prompt the Milwaukee Brewers to draft him in the first round just four months later. On that day he peaked at 93 mph, sitting at 90-91 mph while mixing in three other pitches that all flashed plus potential. Those pitches included a slider that was nasty at times in the mid-80s, a hard, sharp downer curveball that was thrown in the mid-to-upper-70s, and a fading, low-80s changeup.

The fastball velocity was particularly impressive, thrown indoors in the month of February prior to Odorizzi's high school season even starting. However, the velocity wasn't surprising, as the looseness in his arm action and ease to his overall delivery were quite apparent for some time. Odorizzi, a talented overall athlete, also made the middle infield look pretty easy with gliding, graceful actions. Odorizzi took part in the 2007 PG National, where he showcased his two-way abilities. Here is his report from that event:

He has a young, loose and very projectable build. Odorizzi is one of the top 2-way prospects in the 2008 class. He's a primary pitcher but some scouts have told us that they like him more as a shortstop. On the mound, Odorizzi has a low effort delivery with a long and loose arm action. He showed good command of a 88-92 mph fastball and a big breaking 75 mph slurve type breaking ball. Odorizzi really projects with his velocity and we've heard reports of him being up to 95 mph in the weeks after the PG National. As a shortstop, Odorizzi has smooth middle infield actions and shows his athletic ability. His arm strength obviously isn't an issue and he's a 6.78 runner. Odorizzi has a short, whippy swing the mirrors his arm action on the mound in its easiness and fluidness. He hits calm and balanced and knows how to hit. It will be interesting to watch him develop on both sides of the ball.

The University of Louisville, where Odorizzi had committed, had hoped that his two-way abilities might prove to be troublesome enough to allow their prized recruit, who also excelled in the classroom, to make it to campus. His showing at the Indoor Showcase the following February, and his subsequent performances that spring, cemented his case as a legitimate first-round arm.

For as projectable as Odorizzi was coming out of high school, he hit the ground running upon making his professional debut. As a result his prospective status has already allowed the now 23-year-old to be involved in two major trades that included one past (Zack Greinke, 2009 AL Cy Young) and one current (Wil Myers, 2013 AL Rookie of the Year) major postseason award winner.    —*Patrick Ebert*

### Andrew Toles – OF

Toles was one of the highest drafted players from the 2010 draft that didn't sign, as he opted to honor his commitment to Tennessee after failing to come to an agreement with the Marlins as their fourth-round pick. An extremely athletic player thanks to his bloodlines—his father Alvin was drafted in the first round of the 1985 NFL Draft and played four years with the New Orleans Saints—Toles' game has always been fueled by his speed. However, he was far from one-dimensional, and he routinely proved the part playing with and against the top players in the nation at notable showcase and tournament events.

At the 2009 National Showcase he ran a 6.44 second 60-yard dash, and also threw 91 mph from the outfield. Three months later he ran a 6.40 60-yard dash at the Southeast Top Prospect Showcase. A smaller 5-foot-9, 180-pound athlete, Toles even took the mound at previous PG Showcase events with a personal best fastball velocity of 89 mph. Here's his report from the PG National:

> Not tall, but athletic build, good strength, quick twitch actions. 6.44 runner, aggressive on the bases, good jumps, will steal bases. Short swing, stays inside the ball, very balanced, quick hands, flashes gap power, good approach for tool set. Very good defensive OF'er, good jumps/routes, very strong arm, accurate throws, easy actions to the ball, projects as high-level CF'er. Could create lots of draft interest, he can really play.

When the Volunteers hired Dave Serrano to become their new Head Coach in 2011, Toles' departure from the program was one of many changes the program endured as part of the house cleaning. He transferred to Chipola (Florida) College in Florida, where he emerged as one of the top junior college prospects eligible for the 2012 draft. He sustained that status throughout the spring as he continued to show off his dynamic toolset highlighted by his game-changing speed, but also proved there was some developing pop in his swing as well.

With a package similar to that of big-league burner Michael Bourn, here's part of his Draft Focus report leading up to the 2012 MLB Draft:

Toles is far from just a burner, however, as he began to drive balls more consistently this spring. He finished the 2012 season by leading Chipola with a .367 average and 29 stolen bases, and also tied for second on the team with five home runs as his power began to evolve ... Toles is an excellent defensive center fielder, capable of running down balls in all directions with his impressive speed and making highlight-reel catches. He also has a strong accurate arm. His speed is a significant asset on the bases, as well, and combined with his aggressiveness and instincts, projects to be an impact basestealer.

That package led to him being drafted by the Rays in the third round of the 2012 draft, and so far in 172 games as a pro, he has continued to prove that he "is far from just a burner" with just as many extra-base hits as stolen bases (76).    —*Patrick Ebert*

## Boston Red Sox

### Jackie Bradley – OF

Bradley was a fixture in center field and in the leadoff spot for the Richmond Braves at WWBA tournaments from 2006 to 2008, playing in each of three 18u and 17u National Championships and twice at the WWBA World Championship. Although the Braves were always very competitive and usually made the playoffs at those events, Bradley was never in position to take home an MVP trophy despite almost always posting offensive performances worthy of attention.

While Bradley's ability to drive the ball despite his slender, greyhound build and his plus speed and instincts on the bases were impact tools, it was his defense in center field that stood out the most when one looks back at the notes in the Perfect Game database. The same notes and impressions are repeated again and again over a two-and-a-half year period:

> Great range in CF. Defensively cover ground well in CF. Quick hands, strong arm, good range, good speed. Athletic 2008. solid arm ... Great jumps on balls to center field ... Good range OF, makes things happen, hose, glides to fly balls.

For some reason, despite having three legitimate plus tools in his speed, throwing arm, and defense at a premium position, and for being a left-handed hitter, Bradley was never considered a top draft prospect while in high school. Perfect Game had him ranked 222nd in the 2008 high school class prior to the draft and he went undrafted, although it should be noted that Bradley was a top-level student in high school with a South Carolina scholarship in hand.

Bradley never attended a national level showcase until he came out to Cedar Rapids, Iowa for the 2008 PG Pre-Draft Showcase. The highlight of that performance was when Bradley threw a PG record 101 mph from the outfield during drills. However, he only ran a 7.06 in the 60. He had consistently shown impact speed both defensively and on the bases throughout his high school career in games but it didn't translate to that distance. One would have guessed he would run in the 6.5 to 6.65 range based on his game speed.

Here is Bradley's full report from the event:

He has an athletic build and is an excellent baseball player. Bradley stole the show in the outfield workout tying the Perfect Game record with a throw of 101 from the outfield. He has an incredibly fast arm and no one will want to run on him at the next level. He has a good smooth stroke at the plate and sprays line drives all over the field. He looked very good in the games with multiple hits and really projects with added strength at the next level. He also pitched an inning and touched 90. Expect big things from Jackie in the future.

And here's a snippet of Bradley's Draft Focus profile prior to the 2011 draft:

Bradley was undrafted and largely overlooked by colleges out of a Virginia high school three years ago, but had become a no-brainer first-round talent by his junior year at South Carolina before a nagging wrist injury led to a subpar 2011 season. Bradley was the centerpiece of South Carolina's 2010 national-championship team. He earned Most Outstanding Player honors at the College World Series, and hit .368-13-60 on the season overall. He then excelled last summer with Team USA's college-national team (.318-1-12), all but solidifying himself as a top selection in the 2011 draft. He generates good bat speed from the left side, and projects to be an above-average hitter with average power. It's on defense that Bradley truly excels, and he has become an elite-level center field with a strong, accurate arm.

*—David Rawnsley*

## Henry Owens – LHP

It was impossible not to appreciate Owens' ability and skill pitching the first time I laid eyes on him as an underclassman at the Area Code Games in 2009. But while there was lots of buzz about him in the SoCal scouting community, it was obvious from my notes that I wasn't buying in yet:

Profile build, long and loose, projects physically. Directional delivery, big leg raise, arm works well, effort at release, double head jerk, poor balance at release, H 3/4's release, 87-89/T90 FB, weak CB spin, limited Chg use, primary FB pitcher, thrower now. Lots to like, plenty to dislike.

A couple of months later, Owens came back at the 2009 WWBA World Championship and pitched the ABD Bulldogs junior team to the championship while being named the Most Valuable Pitcher.

Fast forward eight months to the 2010 Perfect Game National Showcase. Owens pitched at 88-90 and touched 91 while throwing a curveball that topped out at 73 mph and a 76-mph changeup. His performance led to him being named to the PG All-American Classic team. Here are my notes from that event:

Looks taller than 6-5/185 list, long lean build, busy hand drop delivery, hands overhead first, extended 3/4's release, FB straight, shows ball, some cross body, pitches up with FB, hitters swing through 88 for some reason, occ cuts FB, + SL release point but throws soft CB, fair change, off speed better the harder it's thrown, limited feel, 4.65 from windup, WAY TOO SLOW to plate. Obvious physical projection.

Later in the summer at the 2010 Area Code Games it was more of the same. Owens threw exactly the same velocity ranges with the same dominance.

K'd 6 in 2 innings pitched, hitters don't see ball, pitched up with FB and little contact, threw 2 types of CB, one at 73, the other at 67, softer more a show me type, good feel for changeup, hits spots, + downhill.

It should be noted that at the same time, Owens was having his way with the Southern California high school hitters, going 29-3 over three years with a 1.14 ERA in one of the most competitive leagues in the country. So his dominance at WWBA events and in small sample size showcase environments was very consistent with his overall performance.

But these simply are not the notes one would realistically be expecting to take on a 6-foot-7 left-hander who was touching 91 mph and dominating hitters at every turn. As a scout I wasn't buying into Owens as a potential first rounder, or certainly someone who should be considered a potential first rounder. Everyone used the word "projectable" with Owens like it was his first name, but I saw a pitcher who threw the same velocity every outing. His curveball was not close to an average big-league pitch and rarely even flashed the potential to be. His delivery was complicated and cumbersome and slow. His best pitch was an 88-mph fastball up in the zone. He looked like a long haired 6-foot-7 Jim Deshaies to me and that's the epitome of damning with faint praise.

That winter I had long conversations with Red Sox Southern California area scout Tom Battista, a former Perfect Game staff member, and the late Mike Spiers, who coached Owens with the ABD Bulldogs program. Both said basically the same thing about Owens in answer to my concerns, which can be paraphrased as follows:

"You're missing all the best things about Owens and focusing on the lesser parts. He has the absolute perfect demeanor for a big-league starting pitcher. He's competitive and relaxed at the same time. He's highly intelligent about pitching but doesn't overthink it at all. He's deceptive as hell on the mound without it being an issue mechanically. He's going to get hitters out at every level and that's all that matters."

At that point I started thinking about Owens differently. Both experienced baseball men were very convincing and they both knew Owens much better than I did. Of course, Battista was Owens signing scout when the Red Sox went on to select him with the 36th overall pick in the 2011 draft. My thinking had shifted enough that I'm sure that, along with being happy for Tom, I thought the Red Sox had made a very astute pick.

Move forward one more step. When Jason Parks did an Eyewitness Account on Owens after seeing him pitch for the Carolina League Salem Red Sox on July 11, he saw basically the same thing I'd been seeing for years on Owens, and his report was hardly glowing.

I looked up the box score from that game to see how Owens actually performed. Six 2/3 innings, three hits, zero earned runs, four walks, and four strikeouts. The strikeouts clearly show he didn't have his best stuff that night, as he struck out 169 hitters in 135 innings in 2013. But he still threw 6 2/3 innings and didn't allow an earned run (two unearned) and his team ended up winning the game in extra innings.

I wasn't surprised at all by the performance. It's what Owens has always done.   *—David Rawnsley*

## Garin Cecchini – 3B

Garin Cecchini is a coach's son—twice over. Glenn Cecchini is one of the more decorated high school baseball coaches in the nation, having won seven state championships in his 27 years as the head coach at Barbe High School in Lake Charles, Louisiana. Raissa Cecchini, Garin's mother, served as an assistant on Glenn's coaching staff at Barbe for two decades. Garin is the eldest son of the Cecchini family, with a younger brother Gavin, who was a first-round pick of the Mets in 2012.

Given his upbringing, it should come as no surprise that Garin was one of the more polished high school players in the country during his high school career. While he showed quality athleticism and tools all around, his hit tool was the carrying tool that put him within striking distance of the first round of the 2010 draft heading into his senior season. He showed advanced instincts on the bases and in the field and performed at a high level across numerous national level tournaments.

Cecchini was a good enough athlete that scouts were reluctant to write off his ability to stay at shortstop at a young age, even though his defensive profile was always a tighter fit for third base. Once he tore his ACL in the spring of 2010, it essentially sealed the deal on the anticipated transition. With that positional adjustment, injury question mark, and commitment to LSU, Cecchini slipped beyond the second round and appeared to be headed to college before the Red Sox finally acquiesced to a well-over-slot bonus of $1.3 million.

It was a bit of a risky proposition, as Gavin's polished left-handed swing was a safe bet to produce enough contact to be a quality offensive shortstop, but his power projection was a topic of debate. While he was a strong fit for third base defensively, some questioned whether he'd hit for enough power to make an impact at a corner position. In PG's 2010 Draft Preview, David Rawnsley wrote the following of Garin:

> The 6-foot-2, 200-pound Cecchini is a very good all-around athlete, but his best tools are his smooth left-handed swing and promising power potential ... Understandably, Cecchini is one of the more advanced players in this year's prep class. He plays shortstop at the high school level, but projects to move to third base immediately at the next level, though could also end up at second base or in the outfield. He was a 6.8 to 7.0-second runner in the 60 before his knee surgery, so his move to third base was anticipated as speed wasn't a primary part of his game. His base-stealing exploits are a factor of his superior technique and instincts. Cecchini's arm strength is solid big-league average if not a tick above, and he's thrown in the upper-80s off the mound.

The ingredients for that power development were present; bat speed, contact skills, athleticism, and strength projection to his late maturing body. It was more a matter of his not showing that power on a consistent basis that led some to question how much development could realistically be expected and whether it was worth risking a seven-figure bonus on a healthy recovery from the then-recent ACL tear, power developing, and a successful transition to a relatively new position. The Red Sox were willing to take their chances on Cecchini, given that he possessed all of the physical tools to become a high-level third baseman at the professional level and had advanced instincts and feel for the game to go with the physical tools. —*Todd Gold*

## Blake Swihart – C

Blake Swihart first appeared on the Perfect Game radar at as early an age as any player ever. That single statement is because in late 2005 and in 2006 PG ran a series of events around the country called "Pre-High School" showcases. This short-running series wasn't big in overall numbers but attracted some very notable future prospects, including Swihart, Bryce Harper, Albert Almora, Travis Harrison, Stefan Sebol, Dominic Jose, Robert Ray, Vincent Velazquez, and Stephen Gonzalves.

At the time of the 2010 PG National, Swihart's next PG event, he had recently converted to catcher from shortstop and first base. Although a native of Texas, Swihart was from New Mexico and became the first PG All-American from that state, beating out current LSU shortstop Alex Bregman by one year. Swihart's father, Arlan, was a 6-foot-8 former college basketball player who worked at the Los Alamos Nuclear Laboratory, giving the youngster a pretty interesting overall genetic base.

But the most notable things that Swihart did at the National Showcase were on the field. He took an outstanding batting practice from the right side of the plate, hitting a couple of lasers into the left field seats that got out right away and showing a strong, although different, swing from the left side. He then stepped up in the games left-handed and got multiple hits, including one hard single up the middle against Lance McCullers' mid-90s fastball that was especially impressive. Swihart was a legitimate switch-hitter, with bat speed and bat control left-handed and big power potential right-handed.

Swihart ran a 6.95 in the 60, threw 85 mph from behind home plate, and had a best pop time of 1.86 in drills. It was obvious that he was inexperienced behind the plate, although not as inexperienced as has been reported since in the Boston media, with an especially long release, but it was equally obvious that Swihart's athleticism and quickness would make him a top-level defensive catcher in the future. He looked like the type of athlete who you could put at any position on the field and he would be a top prospect.

Most of the rest of Swihart's summer was spent being the dominant player on the 2010 USA National 18u team that went 19-2 and won the IBAF World Championship. Swihart nearly won the team's triple crown, hitting .448-5-17, losing out to Marcus Littlewood by one RBI. Among his teammates were McCullers, Albert Almora, Francisco Lindor, Bubba Starling, and current Red Sox hurler Henry Owens.

During his senior year, Swihart added one more small item to his scouting resume, throwing in relief for his high school team and reaching 96 mph from the mound.

The fact that Swihart was a 4.0-plus student with a father who was a nuclear physicist and who had a close connection to his future college, Texas, made his signability more uncertain than most. That led to him falling to the deep-pocketed Red Sox with the 26th overall pick, and he eventually signed just before the deadline for $2.5 million. —*David Rawnsley*

### Mookie Betts – 2B

Betts, whose given name is Markus, was a three-sport star at Overton High School in Tennessee and played very little baseball on the national stage prior to signing with the Red Sox as their fifth-round pick in 2011. In fact, the only Perfect Game event he appeared at was after he was drafted and graduated, when he played for Dulin's Dodgers at the 2011 WWBA 18u National Championship. He left quite an impression on the PG scouts in Marietta that week:

> Stays inside ball well, short compact swing, Balanced swing, Excellent bat speed, Loose strong wrists, Line drive swing plane, Good eye, Sound hitting approach, Lead-off type hitter, Confident approach ... Ball jumps off bat, Makes very hard contact. Easy, fluid defensive actions, Can throw from all arm angles, Makes all plays, Soft, sure hands, Good fielding actions, Has lateral agility, Reads hops well, Gets in good position to throw, Quick feet, Quick, smooth transfer Makes game look easy, Great athlete, Good instincts, Scrappy player, Good makeup, Gamer.

The only national level showcase that Betts participated was the 2010 East Coast Professional Showcase, held that year in Lakeland, Florida. He played both middle infield and center field, and switch-hit, and was one of the stars of the event, especially with his speed. The PG notes from the event were:

> Plays way faster than 60 speed (6.75), impact guy on the bases, always on base, steals, takes extra base. Free swinger, fast bat, slashes and runs, contact guy, 4.19. Played both OF and IF, looked most comfortable at 2B, good footwork, accurate throws, playable arm strength, quick release.

It is usually assumed that any mention of a three-sport star includes baseball, football, and basketball, but that wasn't the case with Betts.

Betts of course excelled at baseball, where he hit .549-6-37 with 24 steals as a senior. He was also his district's Most Valuable Player and third team All-State as a point guard in basketball, where he averaged 14 points, nine assists, and four rebounds as a senior.

The third sport was bowling. Betts was named the Tennessee Boys Bowler of the Year in 2010 and boasts a high game of 290 according to published reports.   *—David Rawnsley*

## NL WEST

## Colorado Rockies

### Eddie Butler – RHP

With a pair of WWBA National Championships under his belt—the 16u in 2007 and the 18u in 2008—Timothy Edward Butler's first and only Perfect Game showcase was the 2008 Mid-Atlantic Top Prospect Showcase. Built tall and lanky at 6-foot-2 and 160 pounds, the right-hander peaked at 90 mph at the event, comfortably sitting in the upper-80s while showing plenty of room for added velo as he continued to fill out his projectable frame. Here is his report from that event:

> Lean athletic build, body projects well on the mound, long loose arm action, 3/4 arm slot, good arm speed, very live arm, arm works well, shows a tight slider, pitches with his fastball well, solid command, big upside, barrels the ball up well at the plate, consistent solid contact, ball jumps some on contact, good leverage, big raw arm strength in the field, accurate outfield arm, sound outfield tools, soft hands, solid student, highest-level prospect.

Butler earned a PG grade of 9 at that event, and although he did show legitimate two-way talents, he took those talents to Radford after he was drafted in the 35th round of the 2009 draft by the Rangers.

At Radford, Butler continued to progress, initially beginning his college career as a reliever before being inserted into the Highlanders' starting rotation by the end of his freshman year. His velocity gradually climbed and soon he was pitching at 93-95 at his best, with the ability to peak at 97 when used in shorter spurts. He was part of a dominant Harwich pitching staff on the Cape during the summer of 2012 that included fellow future first-round picks Kevin Gausman, Pierce Johnson, and Chris Stratton.

That performance on the Cape allowed Butler to enter the spring of 2012 as a potential first-round pick, and he was eventually selected by the Rockies in the supplemental first round, although there continued to be a debate in the scouting community as to where his talents would be best served.

Here's part of Butler's Draft Focus report prior to the 2012 draft:

> (Butler) is not overly physical at 6-foot-2 and 165 pounds, but has a very live body and quick arm, and his aggressive demeanor is ideal with a game on the line. Butler is also essentially a two-pitch pitcher as he rarely uses his changeup. He has demonstrated a good feel for spinning a breaking ball and his slider has become a nice complement to his overpowering fastball. As he embarks on the next stage of his blossoming career, Butler will just need to continue to work on developing some of the finer points of pitching, such as moving the ball around the strike zone with purpose and utilizing his off-speed stuff more efficiently.

*—Patrick Ebert*

### David Dahl – OF

2011 PG All-American outfielder David Dahl began to impress the PG scouting staff at a very early age, impressing as a shortstop at the 2008 14u WWBA National Championship. He would also see time on the mound during his early years, running his fastball up to 91 mph the summer following his sophomore season at Oak Mountain (Alabama) High School. The fact that he showed talent all over the diamond as an underclassmen should come as no surprise, given how well-rounded his tools became by the time the 2012 draft rolled around.

Dahl's prospect resume was already long and well-rounded entering his draft year in 2012, though it was a bit unconventional for a prospect who had been on the radar from an early age. He saw a lot of time on the mound in the summer of 2010 and he missed a significant chunk of the summer of 2011 due to mononucleosis. While scouts had plenty of chances to see him do a variety of things on the field and get a feel for his tools, it wasn't until the 2011 WWBA World Championship in Jupiter, Florida, that he really got to show off the overall package in center field while playing at 100 percent health.

The 2012 draft class was very deep on high school outfielders, and Dahl was just one of several prospects that showed high-level upside entering the draft. Interestingly, there wasn't a single area in which Dahl was the cream of the crop, yet he belonged on the short list along with some highly impressive peers in every single category. Here's a snippet of Dahl's Draft Focus report from 2012:

> There are seven outfielders ranked by Perfect Game among the top 20 prospects in the 2012 high school class. This is one of the top groups of high school outfielders since the renowned 2005 class that saw Justin Upton, Andrew McCutchen, Cameron Maybin, Jay Bruce, and Colby Rasmus picked in the first round. Of those seven, David Dahl probably has the best combination of tools and present skills across the board, although he doesn't really rank first in any single category. Despite running a 6.49 at the Perfect Game National, Dahl's speed ranks behind Byron Buxton and Lewis Brinson...Dahl doesn't have a pure power stroke at the plate but has the bat speed and strength in his 6-2/190 frame to drive the ball out of the park...but Courtney Hawkins, Jesse Winker, and Nick Williams will all grade out with more power potential among the top outfield prospects. Dahl's defensive tools and skills in the outfield will rank him right near the top of any prospect list, right along with Buxton, and he projects to be able to play center field at the highest levels of the game. His 95 mph arm strength from the outfield is a big weapon.

The across-the-board tools were supplemented by an advanced feel for the game that would have put him in the pole position in that category in nearly every high school class, though he had stiff competition from Albert Almora in that category as well. Yet despite not possessing the best individual tool in any category, he was one of the most popular responses when scouts were asked "which high school player in this draft are you most confident will play in the big leagues?"

The only think that lacked from Dahl's profile entering the 2012 draft was present power, and even in that category he clearly possessed the necessary ingredients to develop average or better power without projecting aggressively. He also earned high praise for his makeup and work ethic from coaches and scouts who knew him well as an amateur, and thus it should come as little surprise that he became the 10th overall pick.

—Todd Gold

### Kyle Parker – OF

It's always been somewhat curious, if not ironic, that the Colorado Rockies have advanced Kyle Parker, their top pick (26th overall) in the 2010 draft, so conservatively. He spent an entire year at age 21 in Low-A, an entire year in High-A as a 22-year-old, and all of 2013 as a 23-year-old in Double-A. It's curious because as a first-round pick who has performed admirably and very consistently, one would think the Rockies would want to test one of their top prospects, especially at Parker's age.

But it's ironic because Parker's history before he became a professional was as a very fast learner and precocious performer in both baseball and football.

Parker was much better known as a football quarterback at Bartram Trail High School in Jacksonville, Florida. ESPN had him ranked as the no. 4 quarterback and no. 34 overall recruit in the nation, which isn't quite Jameis Winston territory but is still

very, very good. At that age in baseball he was a power-hitting catcher with plus arm strength and he also pitched.

It's not unusual for a football player to enroll in college a semester early if he has the academics, and Parker did that at Clemson. In addition to participating in spring football practice and going to class, he also played baseball for Clemson, in what should have been his senior high school season. Parker was a dominant player from the start of the season and was named All-ACC after hitting .303-14-50 with 32 walks.

On the football field it was more of the same story. Parker became the starting quarterback as a redshirt freshman in 2009 and threw for 2,526 yards and 20 touchdowns while leading Clemson to nine wins and a bowl victory.

In 2010, Parker became the first and so far only college player hit 20 home runs (.344-20-64) and throw for 20 touchdown passes in the same academic year. On April 11 of that year, he threw for 171 yards and a touchdown in the Clemson spring game, then came back and went 3-for-7 with two home runs in a Clemson baseball doubleheader.

So if there was ever a logical candidate for a player an organization could push up the ladder based on past performance and aptitude before he became a professional, it would probably be Kyle Parker. It just hasn't happened that way.

—David Rawnsley

### Trevor Story – SS

Story was a classic shortstop prospect from Irving, Texas, whose development followed an advisable script. He was a well-known high school player locally as an underclassman who began competing on a national level following his sophomore year. He was a secondary pitcher, and given that he boasted plenty of arm strength it should come as no surprise that he ran has fastball into the mid-90s by the end of his high school career.

He and Josh Bell were the two big-time 2011 prospects on the Dallas Patriots, a program that was still emerging on the national scene at the time and didn't have a bid to the WWBA World Championship in Jupiter. Story almost single-handedly changed that with his performance at the 2010 WWBA South Qualifier, going 5-for-6 with four doubles and a championship-game-winning three-run homer in the semifinal and championship games to send the Patriots to Jupiter.

It was in Jupiter where he and Bell put up big-time performances that cemented their statuses as top 50 draft prospects. Story's plus power, plus arm strength and athleticism combined for a clear cut top two round draft profile coming out of high school.   —Todd Gold

## San Diego Padres

### Austin Hedges – C

Southern California is known for producing slick-fielding shortstops who can impact the game with their defense and are highly sought-after draft prospects as a result. But it is rare to find a catcher who fits the same profile. The stereotypical glove-first catcher is seen as a blue-collar tough guy with a big barrel-chested build and plenty of accompanying physical strength.

Yet Hedges was a mold-shattering

prospect. A 6-foot, 170-pound, defense-first catcher is rarely the description of a high-round draft prospect, and had never been the profile of one of the best prospects in the talent-rich area of Southern California. But Hedges was unlike anyone that came before him, a finesse catcher with incredibly smooth and athletic actions behind the plate who caught the way fellow 2010 PG All-American and 2011 draftee Francisco Lindor played shortstop. Hedges had soft hands and a highly advanced understanding of framing and blocking, and even as a high school player was easily the most polished catcher in the draft. He was a Renoir of receiving, and his plus-plus arm strength was only part of the defensive equation.

Scouts were completely sold on his defense, but the question that he raised was about the value of an elite defensive catcher who wasn't projected to be more than an average offensive player at the major-league level. There weren't historical case studies from prior drafts to compare him to, and so while he was seen as a potential first rounder, nobody was exactly sure where he belonged in the pecking order of 2011 draft prospects.

There was also the issue of college, as Hedges was a 4.0 student in high school and was committed to UCLA, a national powerhouse program located near his home with an academic pedigree to rival their on-field prominence. Hedges was in a position of great leverage, which typically causes a player's draft position to dip in exchange for that additional signing bonus money. While he was actually selected in the second round, he received first-round money, which is a better indication of how a player is valued by an organization.    —*Todd Gold*

## Matt Wisler – RHP

Wisler wasn't a high-profile pitching prospect in high school, and it wouldn't be a stretch to guess that the strong majority of big-league scouting staffs were content to let him attend Ohio State for three or four years and see how his stuff developed and how he filled out his slender 6-foot-3, 175-pound frame. He finished his high school career in northern Ohio rated no. 192 in the Perfect Game class of 2011 rankings.

The Padres thought differently, though, and picked him in the seventh round and eventually offered him $500,000 to sign. For that modest cost they found themselves one of the top young pitching prospects in baseball.

Wisler appeared at five WWBA tournaments while in high school, including pitching for Bo Jackson Midwest at the 2009 WWBA World Championship and for the Marucci Elite at the same event in 2010. He topped out at 91 mph for Marucci in Jupiter, pitching in the upper-80s with a sharp 74-mph curveball.

His defining event though was at the 2010 East Coast Pro Showcase. He pitched in his usual 87-89 range, touching 91, with a 75-mph curveball and 82-mph changeup. Here are the scouting notes from that event:

> Easy well-paced rotational delivery, 3/4s release, some wrap in back, works very quickly, loose and projectable, dominant CB, commands CB + well, hard bite, overmatched hitters.

Wisler's curveball that day was as good as a 17-year-old can throw a curveball, combining all aspects. It had power velocity, it had power spin, it was sharp and deep, and he threw it where he wanted to consistently.

A very important but often overlooked aspect of projecting a young pitcher's future fastball velocity gains is considering what his present curveball is like. A loose and physically immature pitcher who is in the mid- to upper-80s but throws a mid-70s hammer with hard spin and bite is almost always going to add velocity as he physically matures. It's just going to happen if he stays healthy and gets stronger.

Unless you asked them directly, there's no way of telling whether the Padres scouts figured this axiom into their decision to spend $500,000 on Wisler out of high school when virtually everyone else was loudly saying "pass" by their inaction. But it would be a good bet that they did.    —*David Rawnsley*

## Max Fried – LHP

Elite-level pitching prospects are typically tall flamethrowers who don't quite posses command before they get into the professional ranks. Max Fried was not a typical elite pitching prospect. He was a slender built, loose athlete whose fastball velocity was of secondary importance to his prospect profile. It should not be inferred that he was a soft-tossing lefty, as he would reach the mid-90s and work comfortably in the 90-92 mph range during his senior year of high school.

But in terms of pure stuff, it was Fried's hammer curveball that highlighted his arsenal, showing big-time depth and sharp downer break with 12-to-6 shape. While his fastball featured requisite prospect grade velocity, it was more notable for its late movement. His changeup was also highly advanced for a high school pitcher—it wasn't necessarily the best changeup in the class or a present plus offering, but within the context of his ability to throw it for strikes from the same plane and arm speed as his fastball, it was well ahead of the development curve.

Fried was firmly established on the national radar as an underclassman, having been selected for the 2009 Area Code Games, and was committed to national powerhouse UCLA. But when his high school dropped its athletics programs for financial reasons he transferred to Harvard-Westlake, where he became teammates with the highest profile pitcher in the country and fellow 2011 PG All-American, Lucas Giolito.

Giolito was viewed at the time as a viable candidate to become the first high school right-hander to ever be selected first overall. The addition of Fried, who was already considered a safe bet to be taken in the first round by that time, put even greater attention on Harvard-Westlake that spring. Giolito's season lasted just two starts before he suffered a UCL injury, leaving Fried as the lone ace on a nationally ranked team. Fried was also a prospect-level hitter who likely could have been a two-way player at UCLA, and he did his part that spring, having a big year both on the mound and at the plate. It wasn't enough to deliver a championship, but it was more than enough for him to be selected in the first round.    —*Todd Gold*

## Joe Ross – RHP

Ross was a pretty quick study at the 2010 PG National Showcase at Tropicana Field, home of the Tampa Bay Rays. He came out firing low-90s heat, peaking at 94 mph and throwing a sharp low-80s slider. That performance made it a fairly easy decision for him to be added to the PG All-American Classic roster that same summer. There he pitched at another big-league stadium, Petco Park, which he may call home for years to come as he ascends to his eventual debut with the Padres.

The scouting profile below on Ross posted on the Perfect Game website prior to the 2011 draft pretty much sums up Ross prior to his being drafted and signing with the Padres with the 25th overall pick. Robert Stephenson, it should be noted from the comparison below, went three picks later to the Reds.

Ross signed for a $2.75 million bonus.

> Ross is the brother of Oakland A's right-hander Tyson Ross, a second-round pick of the A's in 2008 who also attended Bishop O'Dowd High before going on to nearby Cal-Berkeley. Aside from being right-handed and throwing a 90-plus fastball/slider combination, the two don't resemble each other as pitchers. Tyson was a big-framed 6-foot-5, 200-pounder at the same age and threw from an extremely compact arm action that concerned scouts; almost the exact opposite is true of brother Joe's smooth, easy arm stroke. Ross has actually been more closely linked to fellow Northern California right-hander Robert Stephenson over the past year, and both should go in approximately the same area of the draft, likely between picks 25 and 40—if signability doesn't complicate their draft status.
>
> While Ross and Stephenson are very similar physically with long-limbed and loose athletic builds, their pitching styles and present stuff are not alike, giving scouts a good opportunity to see the differences between the two and make decisions based on those evaluations. Ross has a very clean, polished delivery that he repeats effortlessly. He already has solid command of all his pitches, and there is nothing to indicate that he might have control issues in the future. His three-quarters release point creates a nice angle to the plate, and his arm is loose and easy out front. Ross' fastball is regularly in the 91-94 mph range and while it is fairly straight at present, he has the ability to spot the pitch well, especially on the inside half of the plate to right-handed hitters. His breaking ball is a low-80s slider that has good tilt and sharpness. He continues to develop his changeup. Ross has gone 3-4, 1.20 with two saves this spring and in 46 innings, he has walked just 12 and struck out 59.

*—David Rawnsley*

## San Francisco Giants

### Andrew Susac – C

The Giants have drafted heavily for pitching in the last couple of years, and as noted in the Baseball Prospectus Top 10 prospect list, catcher Andrew Susac is the only position player who made the cut for the top 10. It certainly makes sense if you are going to go all-in developing pitchers to acquire talented catchers to handle them, and Susac came to the Giants in the second round in 2011 with a first class resume.

He played with an immensely talented team at Jesuit High School on the east side of Sacramento that featured at least nine other players who received Division I scholarships, including his future Giant teammate, right-hander Martin Agosto. Susac led a 27-5 team in hitting at .443-8-34 as a senior in 2009.

Susac attended the 2008 Perfect Game National Showcase and was an easy selection to that year's PG All-American Classic. He especially stood out defensively, where he had a physical presence on the field with his strong and mature 6-foot-1, 190-pound build and his very advanced tools and skills. He popped 1.75 with 83-mph arm strength, and then threw 1.87 in game action to nail a runner. Susac also blocked and received the ball very well, showing soft hands and quick, fluid hips. Part of the Perfect Game notes from the event simply read "don't run on!"

Susac's swing and approach were a matter of much conversation and debate in the scouting community back then. There was no question about his bat speed, the way the ball came off his bat, or his power potential. Those were all in the plus category. But like many hitters from the West Coast, and particularly from California, Susac had a very pronounced glide into contact and could often get too far out on his front side and off balance at contact. It's one of those things where if the timing works, it's a strength for a hitter, and if the timing doesn't work, it's a negative. For Susac it worked far more than not but it was still a concern.

This was because he was already 19 years old and would be draft-eligible after two years in college, and Susac was very firm in his commitment to Oregon State. The Phillies took him in the 16th round anyway and reportedly offered him $850,000 to sign.

A couple of times over the next two years, passing on that money might have seemed easy to second guess. Susac struggled more than expected as a freshman for the Beavers, splitting playing time at catcher and hitting only .260-2-13 in 96 plate appearances. He came back strong as a sophomore, hitting .364-4-25 in his first 26 games before breaking his hamate bone, missing the next 16 games, and being hampered in his swing the rest of the season. Scouts had seen enough during the first two months of the season, though, to secure Susac a spot in the second round and an above-slot $1.1 million signing bonus.

*—David Rawnsley*

## Arizona Diamondbacks

### Archie Bradley – RHP

The prospect origin story of Archie Bradley would have featured a narrative of how he was easily the best high school pitching prospect in the nation in his draft year, were it not for one remarkable coincidence. The fact that Bradley was born in the same year and grew up in the same area as fellow elite pitching prospect Dylan Bundy makes the script more interesting.

Bradley made his debut on the national prospect scene when he made the 2008 Area Code Games as a sophomore. He showed impressive arm strength for his age and topped out at 88 mph, but it was when he returned to the Area Code Games in 2009 that he firmly established himself as an elite prospect in the class of 2011. It was there that he ran his fastball up to 95 mph, 22 months prior to becoming draft-eligible.

All of this led to him being named the starting pitcher for the West squad at the 2010 PG All-American Classic, where Bradley struck out four of the six batters he faced in his near-flawless two-inning stint.

Typically, a 6-foot-4 pitcher who touches 95 as an underclassman and can impart hard spin on the baseball goes on to be the top arm in the class, as was the case the following year with Lucas Giolito who featured a similar profile. But fellow Oklahoman and Bradley's summer teammate Dylan Bundy was showing the same kind of velocity and ability to spin the baseball at the same time.

While the comparisons to Bundy dominated the story about Bradley in the year-plus buildup to the 2011 draft, there was a variable with far more significance to Bradley's draft stock. Bradley was also a highly sought-after quarterback recruit who was a dual-sport commit to the University of Oklahoma who had planned to pitch for the Sooners in the spring and play quarterback for Bob Stoops' national powerhouse college football program in the fall. Another quirk about the 2011 class saw Bradley somehow not even be the slam dunk top dual-sport prospect, as Bubba Starling was also an elite two-sport recruit who was a likely top-10 draft pick if he were willing to choose baseball.

Bradley did in fact want to play professional baseball and assured organizations of it. He also had a dominant spring which saw him lead Broken Arrow High School to its first state championship in 20 years. In the state championship game Bradley faced Dylan Bundy, who had pitched earlier in the playoffs and was in the lineup as a third baseman, striking him out in all three at-bats. Bradley would strike out 14 in a complete-game shutout, topping out at 97 mph and getting swings and misses at will with his plus-plus low-80s curveball. A few weeks later he and Bundy were the first two high school pitchers selected in the 2011 draft.   —*Todd Gold*

### Chris Owings – SS

Owings grew up in a small South Carolina town (Gilbert, population 500) and was not a very high-profile player heading into the summer of his senior year. That changed when he hit the road with the Diamond Devils, standing out first at the heavily scouted 2008 17u WWBA National Championship. Here are some of his notes from that event:

> Smallish, ok frame, has some lean muscle, athletic. Good SS actions, quick hands. S1 open, smoked 2B down LF line, 4.36, goes after first pitch, good BS, rotational hitter, nice quick swing on pitch down and in, kept hands in well, compact and short to ball, + massive rotational power, quick to ball, explosive bat speed, + speed, HR 340ft., runs well, hustles.

Owings was listed at 5-foot-10, 165 pounds back then, and the thing that stood out at the 2008 Area Code Games was the rare bat speed and power potential he had for a young player that size. It was also obvious that this was an athlete who could stay at shortstop for a long time.

> Uses hands well hitting, good bat speed, quick hands, good balance, some pop for his size. Very smooth defender, + on routine plays, high-level SS, should be immediate ACC/SEC starter or draft.

That surprising power and the ability to drive the ball was even more obvious playing for the Diamond Devils at the 2008 WWBA World Championship in Jupiter that October. The notes certainly acknowledge the speed and defensive ability, but the multiple extra-base hits take precedence for the PG scouts.

> Bat speed, swings hard, athletic look, even stance, gets barrel to ball, 11.56 to 3B, 11.83 to 3B, short stroke, fast hands, broken/shattered bat 2B to fence. Strong, can really run, nice safety bunt (safe), hit to RF warning track, stand up triple, can play, + arm at SS, smooth around bag.

Owings had signed with South Carolina, but the Diamondbacks drafted him with the 41st overall pick and signed

him a week before the signing deadline for $950,000, $130,000 over the MLB recommended bonus for that slot.
   —*David Rawnsley*

### Stryker Trahan – C

Stryker Trahan left about as good a first impression on the Perfect Game scouts as is possible. His first event was the 2009 Sunshine South Showcase in Brenham, Texas, just after the Louisiana native finished his freshman year at Acadiana High School.

To say he stood out with his barrel-chested, 6-foot-1, 205-pound build would not be an understatement. He looked like a senior All-State linebacker as a freshman. Then he went out and ran a 6.67, popped a 1.85 with 78-mph arm strength behind the plate, and dropped bombs in batting practice.

From then on Trahan was a regular on the Perfect Game circuit, appearing in 18 events, many with the Southeast Texas Sun Devils, during his high school career, plus numerous other events such as the Area Code Games and East Coast Pro Showcase. Although he was an All-State football player on a state championship football team, Trahan's baseball time or ability never seemed impacted by football. He was always a baseball-first athlete.

Just as Trahan's physical strength and athleticism stood out in a positive way, there were persistent flaws in his skills that kept him from being considered a truly elite-level prospect for some time. Many were on defense. Although Trahan's foot quickness and raw arm strength were very good, if not exceptional at times, he had trouble with his glove, both in receiving the ball cleanly and consistently and in game exchanges when throwing. Offensively, he tended to be overly pull happy at the plate, which resulted in the occasional majestic home run but more frequently in rolled-over groundballs and empty swings on off-speed pitches.

Something clicked with Trahan in late July 2011. He was part of the grueling 10-day coast-to-coast gauntlet of the East Coast Pro and Area Code Games and had the best 10 days of his baseball life to that point. He essentially discovered that there was a big open, previously unexplored area in left-center field that he could hit the ball very, very hard to. And he did repeatedly, racking up five to six doubles and triples in those two events, most of them crushed with authority to that part of the field with a new swing approach. The national-level scouts were sold, and it was easy to see why with the rest of his tools. The concerns with his catching future remained, but the realistic option of a strong-armed right fielder with a big power bat came more into play as a backup. As a result, the Diamondbacks picked him with the 26th pick in the first round of the 2012 draft.   —*David Rawnsley*

## Los Angeles Dodgers

### Corey Seager – SS/3B

Corey Seager is the younger brother of Mariners third baseman Kyle, although it's difficult to compare the two, as Corey, at 6-foot-3 and 190 pounds, had a much more physical presence with the build of a modern-day shortstop even while in high school. Kyle, who enjoyed a successful three-year collegiate career at North Carolina, was taken by Seattle in the third round of the 2009 draft.

Both Corey and Kyle played at numerous PG tournament events for the dominant North Carolina-based Dirtbags program, as did a third Seager brother, Justin. Justin played for UNC Charlotte before he was drafted by the Mariners in 2013, while Corey was committed to play for South Carolina prior to being drafted by the Dodgers in the first round of the 2012 draft.

Corey's success at the 2011 PG National Showcase in Fort Myers, Florida, led to him being selected to play in the PG All-American Classic that same summer. Here's his report from the National:

> Excellent physical build, square shoulders with tons of projection. Left-handed hitter, big hand coil and wrap to start swing, generates very good bat speed, loose extended swing with lift, ball jumps hard, hand action creates length at beginning of swing. 6.85 runner, very good infield arm strength, plus carry on throws, accurate, third base future but all the tools to be a defensive standout. Outstanding student.

With that larger, square-shouldered build and plenty of room to add strength to his still-projectable frame, his size evoked the usual questions about whether he may outgrow the shortstop position and have to slide over to man the hot corner. But that same size gave him excellent leverage and overall power potential to fit at third base if a move was, and is still, needed down the road. —*Patrick Ebert*

### Joc Pederson – OF

I had the pleasure of playing against Joc Pederson's father, Stu, in 1977 and 1978 while he was starring at Palo Alto High School in the San Francisco Bay Area, the same school that Joc attended. I attended Menlo School about three miles north along El Camino Real. Comparing a father and son as players is an obvious thing to do in this case, as they are very similar players with the same build, the same left/left profile, and roughly the same tools.

It's worth noting that while Stu Pederson had only five plate appearances for the Dodgers in 1985, he was a much better player than that and could have played for many, many years in the big leagues under different circumstances. He spent all or parts of nine years at the Triple-A level, spending all of that time with either the Dodgers or the Blue Jays, two of the most talented teams of that generation.

I saw Joc play at the 2009 Area Code Games before his senior year. It's obvious from my notes that making a father/son comparison was appropriate at that time as well.

> Very advanced hitter, + hand/eye coordination, busy in box, hand drop load, squares up hard to all fields, will go hard oppo, hitters hands, aggressive hitter who won't draw many walks or K. Dad got to MLs on bat and kid is

better. BA OF arm but accurate, good range, uses speed well on bases. Ballplayer.

I was definitely wrong on the "won't draw many walks or K" comment, as Pederson had 70 walks and 114 strikeouts last year as a 21-year old in Double-A, but the comparison between him and his dad seems like a good one.

Joc was committed to Southern California, where his father had gone, and reportedly told scouts that it would take a $1 million signing bonus to get him to turn professional. The Dodgers took a chance on him in the 11th round nonetheless. Southern California head coach Chad Kreuter was fired a week before the signing deadline and Pederson decided to go a different direction as well, signing with the Dodgers for $600,000.   —*David Rawnsley*

### Zach Lee – RHP

Zach Lee had one of the more interesting and winding roads to professional baseball of any other top prospect in the last decade or so.

There was no question that he was a primary football quarterback for most of his athletic development. Lee threw for 2,565 yards and 31 touchdowns as a junior at McKinney (Texas) High School, and 2,935 yards and 33 touchdowns as a senior. He was rated a four-star prospect by Rivals.com and ranked as the ninth best quarterback prospect in the country, with a scholarship to Louisiana State to back it up.

His star receiver, who had an offer to Alabama himself, was also his teammate on the baseball field, Braves 2010 supplemental first-round pick Matt Lipka. Lipka caught 55 of Lee's passes as a senior, averaging almost 25 years per catch and scoring 22 touchdowns.

Lee was a well-known pitching prospect leading into his senior year but threw infrequently on a national stage due to his football commitments and inconsistent raw stuff. His notes in the Perfect Game database from the 2009 Area Code Games, held well after Lee had started preparing for the fall football season, reflected this.

> Looks smaller than listed, basic delivery, cross body release, works fast, pitches to outside corner with all pitches, good feel for off speed, mixes it up, H 3/4 with cross body looks awkward, hard to project stuff, SL will flash good hard spin and is best pitch, has an idea, good college pitcher but don't see out pitch for high level. FB: 87-89/90, SL: 78, Chg: 81.

As a high school senior, though, with football temporarily behind him, Lee's stuff spiked. His fastball began working in the 93-95 mph range, touching higher, and his slider picked up similar power. Lee always had command of his pitches, with the ability to mix it up and change speeds, and he was considered a consensus first-round talent by the time the draft approached.

Lee's situation with football complicated his signability understandably, especially as he was enrolling at summer school at LSU, and Tigers head coach Les Miles was already talking loudly and often about how Lee could potentially play as a freshman instead of redshirting. Most teams considered him unsignable.

Thus it was a shock to almost everyone in the scouting community when the Dodgers, at the worst depths of the Frank McCourt ownership crisis, picked Lee with the 28th overall pick in the first round.

The immediate thought was that Dodgers had done what the Reds did in 2001 when they selected high school left-hander Jeremy Sowers with the 20th overall pick even though Sowers was considered perhaps the least signable player in that draft. It was an ownership-mandated pick engineered to not sign the player and therefore save the signing bonus money.

The second shock came literally minutes before the signing deadline in mid-August when Lee signed a $5.25 million deal to end his potential football career and play professional baseball.
—*David Rawnsley*

# NL CENTRAL

## Chicago Cubs

### Javier Baez – SS

Baez, a native of Puerto Rico, was a bit late to arrive on the national prospect scene, but he was a well-known player within the Jacksonville area, where he attended high school at Arlington Country Day School. He made up for lost time, opening eyes in his first WWBA appearance after being scooped up by East Cobb's highly visible program for an early summer tournament. He was immediately invited to the PG National Showcase, where he earned himself an invitation to the PG All-American Classic. At that game he shared the left side of the infield with fellow Puerto Rican native and 2011 first-round pick Francisco Lindor, whom he also teamed with at the WWBA World Championship in Jupiter that October as members of the loaded Cardinals Scout Team.

Baez's offensive upside was highly regarded in the prospect community, and his power projection made him a household name amongst scouts within weeks of landing on the national radar. The question about his long-term future was his eventual defensive home. His quick actions, smooth hands, and plus arm strength assured that he could be at least an above-average infielder playing on the left side of the diamond. The question was whether or not he could stay at shortstop as he matured and his body began to add mass. He also made a few cameos behind the plate as a catcher, though his offensive upside prevented that idea from picking up much steam given the time and attention that would have been required for him to learn the finer points of the position.

While there was a considerable amount of swing-and-miss to his game due to his super aggressive hitting approach, he was widely considered a safe bet to come off the board in the first round because of his elite bat speed and power projection. Those who had faith in both his ability to make frequent contact against professional pitching and stick at shortstop saw him as one of the elite prospects in a top heavy 2011 draft class. The Cubs fell into the latter group and selected him with the ninth overall pick.    —*Todd Gold*

### Albert Almora – OF

There haven't been many players at Almora's prospect level who followed the mantra "play as often as possible against the best players as possible as soon as possible" any more actively in pursuing becoming a better player.

With all his high-level experience as a teenager it is no wonder that Almora's top attributes as a baseball player are often considered to be his skills and makeup rather than his physical

tools. They've been developed differently than most teenagers.

Consider this resume: Almora played for various USA National teams for four consecutive years. He hit .667-3-14 in eight games for the 2008 14u Team. He spent the next two years playing for the 16u team, hitting .356-1-15 in 2009 and .455-1-5 in 2010. In 2011 he graduated to the 18u National team and was the Most Valuable Player at the Pan American championship.

Almora played in four different WWBA World Championships beginning his freshman year, the first two with the All-American Prospects, followed by a year each with the Florida Legends and FTB Mizuno. There is no official record kept for players who have done this, but if there were, it would be a very short and exclusive list.

Almora also played in two WWBA World Junior Championships, the Perfect Game Junior National and National Showcases, the East Coast Professional Showcase, and the 2011 Perfect Game All-American Classic.

At no event did Almora ever have the best tools. His fastest recorded 60 in the PG database is a 6.78, and his best outfield velocity was 89 mph. At 6-foot-2 and a slender 180 pounds, he didn't stand out as the alpha prospect in any crowd of athletic teenagers either. But he was frequently the best baseball player.

Almora's defining moment as a prospect was at the 2011 East Coast Professional Showcase in Lakeland, Florida. That was an absurdly talented gathering of players, highlighted by Byron Buxton and Carlos Correa in full tool mode and Lance McCullers hitting 100 mph on the scoreboard radar gun. But Almora stole the show from the very beginning. As the first batter in the first game on the first day of the four-day event, Almora blasted a deep home run to left-center field. He did the same thing in his second at-bat. The final score of the game was 2-0.

Almora grabbed everyone's attention that day and carried it all the way through the next year, when the Cubs picked him with the sixth pick in the 2012 draft and signed him to a $3.9 million bonus. Even though he was advised by Scott Boras, Almora carried no signability issues into the draft as the scouting community knew he was a 100-percent-dedicated ballplayer who should and would be playing professionally.
—*David Rawnsley*

### C.J. Edwards – RHP

Edwards pre-professional background is the stuff that movies could be made from if he makes it big in the major leagues. He was a 48th-round draft choice in 2011 by the Texas Rangers out of Mid-Carolina High School about a half-hour north of Columbia, South Carolina. 2011 was, of course, the last year the draft went 50 rounds—it was reduced to 40 rounds in 2012. It's safe to say that Edwards will be the last top prospect ever picked in the 48th round.

That Edwards reportedly received a $50,000 bonus to buy him out of a scholarship to Charleston Southern is pretty impressive for that round. The Rangers knew they had something.

Prosperity, South Carolina, is a town with a listed population of 1,184. Only Edwards didn't really live in Prosperity, he lived about six miles outside of Prosperity down a couple of dirt roads. If you've driven around the rural Deep South much, it isn't hard to picture. Edwards had two nicknames growing up due to his baseball prowess and build, the "String Bean Slinger" and "Satch"—the latter after the great Satchel Paige.

Perhaps somewhat surprisingly given his background, Edwards did play at three WWBA tournaments in high school, two for the Carolina Cyclones and one for the Diamond Devils. He wasn't a hidden player by any means, just an obscure one. His first event was at the 2009 16u WWBA National Championship coming out of his sophomore year. He threw in the 82-86 mph range with a 72-mph curveball and 77-mph changeup. The scout notes on him from that event read:

> Low effort, raw, whippy AA, not real great mechanics, doesn't follow through, w/coaching could be a great pitcher, FB has cut and ASR, can mix them up, once he warmed up his CB was sick-nasty.

Edwards' final appearance was at the 2011 18u WWBA National Championship about a month after he was drafted. It's easy to imagine that the Rangers had multiple scouts in attendance to see Edwards pitch. He threw 87-90 mph on his fastball with a 73-mph curveball and 85-mph cutter/slider. His notes from that event read:

> Overtop arm angle, Good command, Throws strikes, Arm works well, Effortless arm action, Good follow through, Sharp downhill, Throws easy, Quick arm, Works fast, Attacks hitters, Stays tall on backside, Smooth delivery.

*—David Rawnsley*

### Dan Vogelbach – 1B

Vogelbach most certainly did not fit the mold of an elite draft prospect as a teenager. For starters, organizations are typically very hesitant to invest heavily in high school first basemen. In the five drafts prior to Vogelbach's 2011 draft class only two high school first basemen were selected in the top 50 picks.

Eric Hosmer, who is the kind of athlete who would've been a high-level third-base prospect if he were born a right-handed thrower, was selected third overall in 2008. Christian Yelich was selected by the Marlins in 2010 and was immediately shifted to center field.

But even within the high school first-base demographic, Vogelbach didn't fit the mold of a prototypical prospect due to his thick, stout build. Many scouts either wrote him off completely as a result, or were slow to come around on him. This was certainly not a secret to Vogelbach himself, who was fueled by the doubters and played with an obvious chip on his shoulder.

The son of a personal trainer, Vogelbach was and is a much better athlete than he is generally given credit for. He ran a 7.20 60-yard dash as an underclassman, which while below average is not at a level that precludes him from being able to run the bases competently as a professional. After being measured at 5-foot-10 and 250 pounds at the 2010 East Coast Pro Showcase, Vogelbach worked hard over the off-season heading into his senior year, shedding 20 pounds. Of course, that would've gone unnoticed were it not for the fact that over his high school career Vogelbach had clearly established himself as one of the best, if not the best, hitters in the country.

Vogelbach had one of the most prolific careers in the World Wood Bat Association's history, consistently putting up huge offensive numbers while hitting in the middle of the order for one of the top travel baseball programs on the national circuit, FTB (Florida Travel Ball). He showed the ability to drive the ball out of every part of the park with ease, using a well-controlled swing with plus bat speed and tremendous strength at contact, and an advanced approach with no glaring flaws.

In the year leading up to the 2011 draft there was a philosophical debate taking place amongst scouts, and Vogelbach was clearly the catalyst. It was generally phrased along the lines of, "if a player is projected to be a legitimate plus hitter at the major-league level, but doesn't project as an average defender at any position, is he worth a first-round pick?" There wasn't a consensus as to whether or not Vogelbach could develop into a serviceable defensive first basemen with time in a player development system, or if he would live up to his lofty offensive ceiling. But it was plainly clear that Vogelbach was at least one of the best hitters in the class, with many feeling he was the best, and that he was never going to win a Gold Glove.

There was a general feeling heading into the 2011 draft that Vogelbach was likely to be taken by an American League club. But it was the Cubs, spending aggressively on the best available player on the board, who took advantage of the industry's skepticism, landing a first-round-caliber bat with their second-round pick. *—Todd Gold*

## Milwaukee Brewers

### Tyrone Taylor – OF

Taylor was a two-sport star in high school and played in only one national-level event, the 2011 Area Code Games. With all his achievements in football and the energy it probably took, that's probably not surprising.

During his senior year at Torrance High School between Los Angeles and Long Beach, Taylor rushed for 1,521 yards and 20 touchdowns and also added 25 more receptions good for 10 more touchdowns. He excelled on defense as well, making 190 tackles and intercepting three passes. He also kicked off for Torrance and recorded 29 touchbacks and even picked up seven more points on PATs. In an evident attempt to make sure he never left the field, Taylor also returned punts and kickoffs.

Taylor produced at much the same level on the baseball field, hitting .488-4-29 as a senior and .473-6-25 as a junior.

Taylor's baseball skills were understandably raw, especially for a top prospect from Southern California, but his athleticism stood out. He had easy-plus speed, and was big and strong enough to be showing present power and plenty of offensive projection. His Perfect Game notes from the Area Code Games certainly reflect that:

> 4.10 runner, plays the game fast, raw hitting mechanics, pulls up and out, finds the barrel consistently, has hitting skills despite mechanics, surprising pop, ball jumps, could be a big surprise over the next year.

The Brewers selected Taylor with their second-round pick in the 2012 draft and eventually signed him for a $750,000 bonus, well over the recommended slot of $523,000. Taylor passed on a baseball scholarship to Cal State Fullerton to enter professional baseball. *—David Rawnsley*

### Jimmy Nelson – RHP

The big-bodied Jimmy Nelson already checked in at 6-foot-5, 220 pounds when he made his first Perfect Game showcase appearance at the 2006 Florida Showcase. At the event Nelson pumped his sinking fastball up to 86 mph while also throwing both a promising slider and a changeup.

A year later at the 2007 World Showcase—where he earned a PG grade of 9.5 and was named to the event's top prospect list—Nelson's fastball was now thrown consistently as his previous peak velocity, touching 89 while throwing a harder, firmer slider and his usual polished change. Here's his report from that event:

> (Nelson) has a big and tall country strong type of build that could get really strong in the future. Nelson throws from a complicated, multipiece delivery with a full arms over head takeaway and a high 3/4s release point. There are plenty of inconsistencies he'll have to iron out at the next level. His arm works very well through all of it. His best pitch was an 80 mph slider that had a sharp 2-plane break and was nasty at times and will be a major weapon for him in the future. Nelson had much better command of his slider than his other pitches and lots of confidence in the pitch. His fastball was 86-89 mph from a good downhill plane and it had excellent sink at times when he got it low in the strike zone. Nelson's changeup also showed quality and he should consider throwing it more often. Nelson is a very good prospect now and when he gets his delivery under control and his strength grows into his frame, he could be something special. That slider will be unhittable when he's throwing it 85 mph. Nelson is a very good student who will be attending Alabama.

Nelson did indeed attend Alabama after going undrafted out of high school. He continued to work on his delivery while in college, and his fastball continued to add velocity, thrown consistently in the upper-80s—where it showed more sinking life—and peaking in the low-90s. Nelson's slider also continued to be a plus offering for him, thrown with the same arm speed and action as his fastball, giving him the profile of a sinker-slider innings eater.  —*Patrick Ebert*

### Taylor Jungmann – RHP

Jungmann's reputation led to his being selected to participate in the 2007 PG All-American Classic despite not attending a Perfect Game event prior to that. Here is the report from his performance at the Classic:

> Jungmann started off a little shaky, as he appeared to be overthrowing while not incorporating his whole body into his delivery as he was out of rhythm and all over the place. The good thing is that he was missing low, and the better thing is that he started to settle down and pitched quite well despite giving up a walk and a base hit to (Tim) Beckham and (Ethan) Martin respectively. He showed once he settled down that he does have pretty good fastball command and a nasty slider, using one such pitch to set Destin Hood down swinging.

Although the Angels selected him in the 24th round out of high school in the 2008 draft, it wasn't nearly early enough to sway him from him strong commitment to his home-state Texas Longhorns. There Jungmann enjoyed immediate success, and was remarkably consistent during his three-year stay with the Longhorns, collectively going 32-6 with a 1.63 ERA and highlighted by his 13-0, 0.95 campaign as a junior, which cemented his status as a first-round pick in the 2011 draft.

At Texas his success was predicated largely on his command, effectively changing speeds between his low-90s fastball, which would peak in the mid-90s and usually settle into the upper-80s later in games, a slider, curveball, and changeup. He grew more confident throwing his curveball during his college career, effectively dropping it in for strikes to induce weak, early contact, but none of his secondary pitches projected as much more than average.

Based on this profile, since he wasn't overpowering, his ceiling was that of a no. 3 starter. Because he consistently displayed plus command of four offerings he could throw for strikes, he also had a high floor, and was believed a safer bet to contribute effective innings at the major-league level.  —*Patrick Ebert*

## Cincinnati Reds

### Robert Stephenson – RHP

Stephenson grew up in the San Francisco Bay Area, and like many young top players from that region, didn't travel much in high school until the beginning of his senior year. His first national level event was the Perfect Game National Showcase in June 2010. He quickly showed that he was a top pitching prospect, sitting steadily at 92-93 mph during his outing with a mid-70s curveball and a 77-mph changeup. Stephenson was an easy choice for the 2010 PG All-American Classic based on his stuff and very projectable build, but the package was still pretty raw.

The scouting notes from that event read as follows:

> Long slender build, not close to mature, big leg raise delivery, drift in delivery, some effort, quick arm, loose actions, CB has v. short flat break, FB runs arm side, Good change but rarely uses, some head jerk, misses arm side, command improved 2nd IP, spin/effort not ideal but a power arm.

Later in the summer it was obvious that Stephenson was doing exactly what one wants to see a young high-level pitching prospect do; improve in noticeable and multiple ways. At the Area Code Games and PG All-American Classic in August, Stephenson upped his velocity to the 93-95 mph range and developed more depth to his curveball and better relative velocity to his more frequently used changeup. His notes from the Area Code Games read:

> Big leg raise delivery, rocks back, sometimes gets off balance, + athletic build, projects, occ has trouble working down in zone, mixes pitches well for a young power pitcher, change was very nice at times.

Stephenson's senior year, when scouts frequently got to double up on days with him and fellow first round pick Joe Ross in nearby Oakland, was more of the same. He opened the season with a pair of no-hitters and ended up striking out 119 batters in 61 innings. Stephenson generally worked in the 92-94 mph range, topping out at 97 mph, and he frequently maintained that velocity through a full seven innings. The debate between Stephenson and Ross centered around Ross being smoother with less effort in his delivery versus Stephenson's lightning fast arm and tick better raw stuff.

Ross won on draft day by going two picks higher than Stephenson's 27th slot to the Reds, where he received a $2 million signing bonus. Thus far it looks like Stephenson has the edge as a professional, however.   —David Rawnsley

### Billy Hamilton – OF

When Billy Hamilton made his first appearance at a Perfect Game tournament event—the 2006 16u WWBA National Championship—he was a 5-foot-6, 115-pound shortstop/right-handed pitcher whose athleticism was obvious. Not surprisingly, his game was highlighted by his quickness and speed even if he didn't have the strength necessary to consistently drive the ball.

Two years later Hamilton had grown to 6-foot, 150 pounds, and while he still needed to continue to add strength to improve his impact at the plate, his game-changing speed allowed him to wreak havoc simply by putting the ball in play.

That isn't to say Hamilton was weak, as he had visible, wiry strength, and even took to the mound with the ability to reach 90 mph with a promising curveball.

Here is a collection of reports from the tournament events he attended:

> 60 runner, great range in CF, 4.46 RH turn. Good range at ss, in CF w/ above avg HS arm. When he physically matures he could blow up. Smooth CF. Good wheels. Fast out of the box, good swing, kid flies, can go the other way. 4.22 H-1B. Hustle double, baseball instincts, runs well. Tall thin RH, slow delivery, good arm action, over the top delivery, quick to plate, early control trouble, good CB with weak command.

Hamilton made one more appearance at a PG tournament in 2009 at the 18u National Championship prior to signing with the Reds as their second-round pick that year. At that event he showed the promise as to why he was selected as early as he was, although there was still the need for him to improve as a hitter. His athleticism with three plus tools—arm strength, defense, and foot speed—made it easy for the Reds to select him as early as they did, and those tools continue to be the foundation to his success.   —Patrick Ebert

### Jesse Winker – OF

Winker was as well traveled as a teenage baseball prospect could be, competing in 25 Perfect Game events during his high school career, many with the FTB Mizuno organization, along with a pair of East Coast Pro Showcases, an Area Code Games, and the 2011 USA National 18u team. On top of that, he played on a top flight Olympia High School team with first-round right-handed pitcher Walker Weickel—now a member of the Padres organization—and a young shortstop named Nick Gordon.

What playing in all those high-profile events enabled Winker to do for the scouts was to give them the opportunity to track the huge improvements he made as an athlete over that time. Winker already had a national reputation as a hitter during his sophomore year, but was somewhat of a slow-twitch athlete who had below-average speed (7.5 second in the 60-yard dash) and arm strength on the professional grading scale. At that point he looked like a future sweet-swinging college left fielder.

That changed significantly over the next two years, as Winker got stronger and quicker. He got his 60 times down around 7.0 and his arm went from being a non-factor to a plus weapon. The extra strength and quickness in his body found its way into the barrel of his bat in the form of big power.

There was an ironic side to Winker's improved arm strength. The left-hander rarely pitched for either Olympia High School or for FTB Mizuno, but was pressed into pitching for the 2011 USA National 18u team. He went 2-0, 0.00, with a save, including a complete-game seven-inning shutout featuring only 66 pitches and was named the top pitcher at the Pan Am Championship. Winker did pitch in relief during his senior high school season, usually topping out in the 93-94 mph range.

Winker's defining moment as a prospect came in the same place as it does for many top prospects, in Jupiter at the WWBA World Championship. FTB Mizuno coach Jered Goodwin put together an unparalleled outfield featuring a trio of PG All-Americans including Winker, Albert Almora, and David Dahl. Winker outshined both the future top-10 picks, leading all Jupiter players in RBI and hitting a pair of long home runs. In the playoff quarterfinals, with FTB Mizuno down 5-3 in the bottom of the fifth inning, two outs, and the bases loaded, Winker took a mighty cut and just got under a ball that was caught on the warning track in right field. A grand slam could have very well changed the entire course of the tournament.

—David Rawnsley

## Pittsburgh Pirates

### Jameson Taillon – RHP

Taillon very well may have been a legitimate choice for the no. 1 overall pick in the 2010 draft if it weren't for the simple fact that young phenom Bryce Harper was also available. Built tall and strong at 6-foot-7, 230 pounds, Taillon had the workhorse frame and the stuff to match to project as a staff ace.

What made Taillon even more impressive was his athleticism and body control, as young pitchers of his stature often have difficulty repeating their deliveries. He also threw from a pronounced downhill plane, which made his fastball—which could sit in the 93-96 range while flirting with triple digits at times—that much harder to catch up to. He also threw a low-80s hammer curve, giving him two distinct swing-and-miss pitches.

That profile allowed Taillon to start the 2009 PG All-American Classic for the West squad, coincidentally throwing to the aforementioned Harper behind the plate. In that game he struck out four of the six batters he faced, three of them swinging on fastballs.

Taillon pitched at numerous PG events, including the 2009 National Showcase, where his report read as follows:

Extra large athletic build, plus strong, very well coordinated actions. Well paced 3/4s cross body release, long extended arm action, repeats + well. Maintained 95 mph FB from stretch, outstanding angle to RHHs. Present plus true CB at times, hard and late with big break, commands CB plus well. Only 1 change this outing, has flashed plus change in past. No doubt #1 guy in class, special talent. Very good student, early draft prospect, verbal to Rice.

Taillon continued his dominance on the travel circuit, including his appearance at the Classic. He showed much of the same the following spring, leading to the Pirates taking him with the no. 2 overall pick in June, right behind Harper.  —*Patrick Ebert*

### Nick Kingham – RHP

Nick Kingham's career as a prospect got off to a bumpy start, but once he got moving forward it took off quickly. He didn't pitch in high school during his junior (2009) season due to transfer rules enforced in Las Vegas. His first Perfect Game showcase was the 2009 Sunshine West Showcase, which is held in early June just prior to the National Showcase.

One of the primary functions of the Sunshine Showcases (there will be five in 2014) is a final sweep of the country to find any overlooked players that belong at the National Showcase. Numerous top prospects, including Marlins catcher Jarrod Saltalamacchia and Cubs first baseman Anthony Rizzo were first seen at these events.

Kingham threw very well at Sunshine West, pitching in the 85-88 mph range, with a hard 75-mph curveball and an 80-mph changeup. Here are his notes from that event:

> Arm works, good pitcher's build, arm speed, projects, long levers, low effort, balanced, some extension, can stay back better, opens a bit early with front hip, sharp CB, 11/5 CB, pot 92-93 arm, some down plane, 84-86 from stretch, comes out clean, can get more from midsection, occ ASR FB, occ GSR FB, quick move.

Kingham did earn his invitation to the National Showcase and his first exposure before a national scouting audience. He threw even better at that event, throwing in the 88-90 range with two quality secondary pitches. My own notes on Kingham's performance didn't understate how much I liked him:

> Profile build, well-paced balanced delivery, loose athletic actions, downhill, stays behind the ball, projects ++ well, compact in back, Chg was very good, + arm speed, CB has hard spin/good shape, has an idea how to pitch. Really LIKE this kid's potential.

Kingham stayed in that 88-90 mph range for the rest of the summer and fall while maintaining his high-level secondary pitches and ability to mix. One just knew that it was only a matter of time before he started throwing harder and he did, bumping up his comfort range the next spring to 90-92 and touching 94 mph regularly.

Knowing he had a scholarship to Oregon in hand, the Pirates selected Kingham with their fourth-round pick, the 117th overall selection. They signed him for $480,000 about 10 days before the signing deadline.  —*David Rawnsley*

### Josh Bell – OF

Bell was a well-known prospect after hitting .412-11-36 as a junior at Jesuit Prep in Dallas and was on his way to experiencing the full force of the summer showcase circuit in the summer of 2010 until he fractured his right kneecap in a high school playoff game and missed the entire summer.

That put the scouting community well behind on Bell compared to his peers in the class of 2011. It was frequently written and commented on that Bell would be the most-watched player at the WWBA World Championship in late October, where he was playing for the Dallas Patriots. With a huge contingent of scouts following his every move, Bell proceeded to put on one of the best performances in Jupiter history. He blasted three home runs in pool play to lead the Patriots to the playoffs. In the quarterfinals, the Patriots were the victims of one of the most brilliant pitching performances ever at that level of baseball, facing off against Jose Fernandez at the peak of his abilities. While Fernandez threw mid-90s with a disappearing slider and pinpoint control for six innings, Bell had a pair of quality at-bats, including a hard base hit, and looked remarkably comfortable against the otherwise dominant Cuban.

Bell went on to hit an eye-opening .552-14-55 as a senior, with 19 stolen bases, 48 walks and only five strikeouts.

Bell's non-hitting tools were frequently described as fringy average leading up to the draft. He was a 6.9 to 7.0 runner with fair arm strength, tools that both played up because Bell showed very good instincts on the bases and in the outfield. But it was his ability to hit equally well and with power from both sides of the plate that made up almost his entire value as a prospect.

Bell's path leading up to the draft and to signing with the Pirates was not as pretty as his swing, however. As a very hot commodity with Scott Boras as his advisor and a strong commitment to Texas, it had all makings of a player with complicated signability issues. Late in the spring Bell sent a letter to all 30 major-league teams that he was firm in his commitment to Texas and would be going to school. Even though Bell was perceived as having potential top-10-overall-pick talent, he slid to the Pirates with the 61st overall pick. The Pirates then surprised virtually everyone by finding Bell's price, which turned out to be an even $5 million.  —*David Rawnsley*

## St. Louis Cardinals

### Kolten Wong – 2B

Wong's talents were evident at an early age, and it was never a surprise that he could hit, as his father, Kaha, spent two years in the minor leagues, posting a .280/.345/.351 slash line, and is now one of the more respected hitting instructors on the Big Island.

Kolten first attended a PG event as a high school sophomore, the Hawaii Showcase in 2006, and came to the mainland during the summer of 2007 to attend the National Showcase in Cincinnati, Ohio. A very good overall athlete with great versatility and a wide array of tools from a compact, 5-foot-9, 175-pound frame, Wong was a catcher early in high school before eventually making the permanent switch to second base. He also played in the outfield, as well as some time at shortstop while at the University of Hawaii.

With a compact left-handed swing, Wong proved to be one of the better hitters in the nation, routinely smoking line drives to all parts of the field while also displaying surprising pop for a player of his stature. He also exhibited good foot speed and quickness, giving him a well-rounded toolset. Here's his report from the National where he earned a PG grade of 9.0 (out of 10):

> (Wong) has a short, compact build with good present strength. Wong has swung between catcher and second base and played mostly catcher in Cincinnati. His tools and actions are better suited for second base, where he has good quickness and speed (6.88 in the 60), and we are told that is the position that he is going to play in college. Wong's left-handed bat will play well at either premium defensive position. He hits from a balanced coil at the plate with very quick hands and a pull type of approach. For much of the showcase Wong seemed to be content to make contact and didn't elevate his bat speed and ability to drive the ball like we've seen frequently in the past. When Wong stepped up against 6-8 Kyle Long and his 94-96 mph fastball, we saw the true Wong, though. He was unfazed by the velocity and showed the bat speed we knew he had, along with the aggressiveness. Wong's bat plays and he has an aggressive ballplayer's approach to the game.

The Twins took Wong in the 16th round of the 2008 draft, but he opted to take his talents to the University of Hawaii and ended up being a first-round pick three years later. He was a College All-American at Hawaii, and also was named the MVP on the Cape Cod League during the summer of 2010.

Here's a snippet of his Draft Focus report prior to the 2011 draft:

> Pound for pound, there may not be a better prospect in the 2011 draft class than the 5-foot-9, 190-pound Wong. He has well-rounded skills and may have solidified his status as a potential first-rounder last summer by passing up an offer to return to Team USA's college national team for a second season. He elected instead to play in the Cape Cod League, where he earned league MVP honors for a .341-3-11 season along with a league-best 22 stolen bases. Wong showcased polished offensive skills with a sound approach from the left side of the plate, and surprising pop for a player his size. He drove the ball hard consistently. He also became an accomplished basestealer ... Wong had been an extremely versatile player earlier in his career, and spent most of freshman season at Hawaii in center field, while earning national acclaim by hitting .341-11-52 with 11 stolen bases. After initially being tried as a catcher as a sophomore, he settled in at second base and hit a solid .357-7-40 with 19 stolen bases ... Though not blessed with blazing speed, Wong is aggressive on the bases and has excellent base-running instincts.

Kolten's success from high school to college and now as a pro led the Tampa Bay Rays to draft his younger brother, Kean, a similar prospect, in the fourth round of the 2013 draft.

—Patrick Ebert

## Carson Kelly – 3B

The state of Oregon has received plenty of baseball attention in the last decade due to the pair of NCAA championships won by Oregon State, plus the reemergence and immediate success of the baseball program at Oregon.

But the state rarely produces much in the way of high school baseball talent. Carson Kelly had the distinction of probably being the state's best high school hitting and pitching prospect in the last two decades while he was at Westview High School in Portland. The last high school player to be selected in the first round of the draft from Oregon was first baseman Matt Smith by the Royals in 1994. The only prep pitcher selected in the top three rounds during the same time was the late Steve Bechler, taken in the third round by the Orioles in 1998.

Kelly was picked in the second round with the 86th overall selection.

More so than any player in the 2012 draft, Kelly was a true two-way prospect who had scouts lined up on both sides of the fence as to his future role in professional ball. Here is what was written in late March 2012 in Kelly's Perfect Game Draft Focus report:

> Kelly is a primary third baseman. He's very athletic defensively at third base, the kind of defender who plays on his toes and is very quick laterally on groundballs and line drives. His arm strength is a clear plus tool both on the mound and throwing across the infield, and he has a flexible, quick release. Offensively, Kelly has a very nice load and hitting rhythm with a bit bigger leg raise trigger than some scouts prefer. He shows plus raw power from the right side and has nice lift in his swing when he's pulling the ball. Kelly will get long at times and expand the strike zone, especially on off-speed pitches, but he handles high velocity stuff well.
>
> Surprisingly perhaps, Kelly is more polished on the mound. He has a simple, repeatable delivery and sits in the 90-92 mph range with minimal effort on release. For a pitcher who throws in the low-90s so consistently, it's somewhat unusual that there have never been reports that he'll touch 94-95 at times as most young strong armed pitchers do occasionally. That's a sign for me that his present mechanics work well for him and he's throwing in his envelope right now with his fastball.
>
> Kelly has shown less consistency with his breaking ball. I've seen him with a mid-70s curveball, but the best breaking ball I've seen him throw was at the 2011 Area Code Games, when he was throwing an 80 mph pitch I called a slider but which had tight, hard bite, good depth and was buckling hitter's knees with consistency. Kelly has a changeup that still is in the developing stages, and he throws consistent strikes with all three pitches. If he can develop consistency with the 80 mph hard biting version of his breaking ball, I can see more and more scouts leaning toward his future as a pitcher.

—David Rawnsley

### Tim Cooney – RHP

Although Cooney displayed solid baseball skills while in high school, it was clear at the time that his body needed to mature physically before he could reach his potential. At the time, that potential was unclear with a slight 6-foot-1, 165-pound frame. He did attend the Northeast Showcase after his sophomore year in high school, topping out at 84 with a sharp 74 mph curveball, earning a PG grade of 8.0 and this report:

Pitches from a high 3/4 arm slot, solid mechanics, clean arm action, straight FB at 84 mph, tight CB at 74 mph, CB has depth, mixes in a 74 mph CH, hits from a slightly open stance, high hands, top hand release, level swing plane, makes consistent contact, excellent student.

His velocity held throughout his high school career, peaking at 85 mph during his senior year while pitching for All Star Baseball Academy at the 2008 WWBA World Championship in Jupiter, Florida, and he went undrafted the following June.

Cooney elevated his game to another level while in college at Wake Forest, adding two inches and 30 pounds to his previously slight frame. He made a strong initial impression during his freshman year at Wake Forest, pitching in 14 games, 13 of which were starts, and served as the Demon Deacons' Friday ace during his junior season. His fastball sat in the upper-80s to low-90s, peaking a few ticks higher, and he routinely displayed a well-rounded four-pitch mix and advanced sense for changing speeds.

Here's part of his Draft Focus pre-draft report from 2012:

Cooney emerged as a solid second- or third-rounder with a breakthrough sophomore season, and he essentially solidified his standing in the draft as a junior ... Typically, (his fastball) ranges from 88-91 mph, but Cooney tried to overthrow it, at times, to achieve a little more velocity, and while it often reached 92-93 mph, his command suffered in the process. He threw quality strikes with his fastball more consistently toward the end of the season as he made a more-conscious effort to stay within himself. He did not have the same kind of command issues with any of his three off-speed pitches, a change, cutter and breaking ball. His cutter, which normally sits in the mid-80s, is considered his best secondary offering. Cooney typical relies on an advanced sense of pitchability for his success, and precise command is critical in his approach. At his best, Cooney excels at mixing his four pitches efficiently to get hitters guessing and keeping them off balance, and he is able to create deception with his loose, easy, free arm action.

—Patrick Ebert

### Randal Grichuk – OF

While Houston area native Randal Grichuk will always be known as the high school outfielder the Angels took just before Mike Trout in the 2009 draft, the selection actually made sense in the context of the time that the decision was made. Trout was a late bloomer in high school, especially with the bat, and New Jersey had an especially cold and rainy spring that year, making it difficult for cross-checkers and scouting directors to get a thorough read on him. Trout wasn't an unknown by any means, but there wasn't much surety on him.

Grichuk, on the other hand, had been putting up eye-opening home-run numbers in the Houston area since he was in Little League. He was the dominant performer on the 2007 Team USA 16u National Team, which included players such as Nick Franklin, A.J. Cole, Matt Davidson, and Zach Lee, and he hit .563-3-6 in six games. He played in Jupiter twice with the Houston Heat and won the 2009 International High School Power Showcase, blasting 20 home runs overall. In his senior year in high school, Grichuk hit .613-21-46.

The ball made a different sound when it came off Grichuk's bat at that age; it just exploded. It wasn't a classic or even pretty swing by any means, as he hit down to the ball in an almost exaggerated way and didn't have the lift and extension out front that one normally sees in power hitters. He just overpowered the ball with strength and bat speed.

Grichuk was also a 6.85 runner and regularly ran in the 4.2- to 4.3-second range to first base from the right side of the batter's box. He was considered a plus makeup young man with a plus motor on the field.

Here are the notes on Grichuk from the 2008 Area Code Games:

Strong kid, quick hands, live body look, kind of stiff at ball, level to almost downward swing, hits bombs, 420' to LCF off 90 mph FB, can flat hit, very hard contact, ball explodes, will fish at outside CBs, one of the best hitters in the 2009 class. Arm is marginal, likely LF future.

—David Rawnsley

# NL EAST

# Miami Marlins

### Andrew Heaney – LHP

Heaney participated in four Perfect Game tournament events while in high school, three of those with the powerful Texas Sun Devils program. A 6-foot-1, 150-pound athlete, Heaney worked in the mid-to-upper-80s back then with good feel for both a sharp overhand curveball and a changeup. Although it wasn't expected that he would ever be a flamethrower, it was evident that he had plenty of room to fill out, and as a result it was expected that one day he would be throwing consistently in the low-90s, peaking several ticks higher.

Although he was drafted in the 24th round in the 2009 draft by the Rays out of high school, Heaney decided to honor his commitment to Oklahoma State, where the transformation of his size and stuff occurred. Adding 25 pounds to his frame, by the end of his sophomore season he routinely sat in the 90-94 range early in games with his usual sharp curveball. Prior to assuming the Cowboys' Friday ace role during his junior season, he did alternate between a starting and relief role, but showed to have the requisite three-pitch repertoire to remain in a starting spot long term. In addition, his command and advanced sense for changing speeds really stood out, even at a young age, and his stuff was sharp enough for him to avoid the "finesse lefty" label.

Here's part of his PG Draft Focus report leading up to the 2012 draft:

Heaney has always had quality stuff for a left-hander, but it wasn't until he settled in as a regular starter that he displayed much-improved command of his lively 90-94 mph fastball, sharp curve and changeup. With his advanced feel for pitching, scouts say that he could become one of the first players from the 2012 draft class to reach the big leagues ... He also is adept at mixing his pitches, and has an advanced feel for generating cutting action on his fastball, varying the speed on his breaking stuff and creating tumbling action on his change ... Heaney is viewed as a safe college lefty with solid stuff and competitiveness, and is the kind of pitcher that rarely slides very far in the draft.

*—Patrick Ebert*

### Jake Marisnick – OF

Marisnick was considered one of the best athletes in the 2009 class as a graceful 6-foot-4, 200-pound outfielder with plus speed and big power potential. He was already considered an above-average defensive player in the outfield, with center-field range and a right-field throwing arm. Perhaps not surprisingly in retrospect, scouts considered Marisnick's least advanced tool to be his bat/hit tool.

Also not surprisingly for his type of athleticism, Marisnick was a two-sport star his first three years in high school before giving up football as a senior to concentrate on baseball. He caught 56 passes as a junior for 866 yards and also excelled at safety, making 62 tackles and intercepting four passes. Marisnick signed to play baseball at Oregon but was also extended an invitation to walk on for the Oregon football team, and would undoubtedly have been able to play Division I football if he had continued on that path.

Marisnick was a steady performer on the baseball field at Riverside Poly High School, hitting in the low .400s each of his final three years, including .404-6-31 with 22 stolen bases as a senior. Perhaps as a precursor to his professional hitting numbers—he has 119 walks in 1,600-plus minor-league plate appearances—Marisnick didn't walk much in high school either despite his top-prospect status, drawing 35 walks versus 48 strikeouts in 376 high school plate appearances.

Interestingly, Marisnick participated in two WWBA events, the 2007 17u WWBA National Championship and the 2008 WWBA World Championship, with teams from the East Coast, playing for the Mid-Atlantic Rookies and the Orioles Scout Team, respectively.

Here are some of the notes in the PG database from the 2008 Area Code Games:

> + build, + projection, very easy athletic actions, + RF arm, hitter's hands, very good bat speed, good looking swing, hit bomb off CF wall, swing can get long. Wouldn't be surprised if he's a 1st rounder.

For those who follow agent/advisor dealings, Marisnick was probably the easiest sell ever. His mother, Jennifer, is the Senior Director of Marketing for Larry Reynolds at Reynolds Sports Management. Marisnick signed for a $1 million signing bonus after being selected in the third round (104th overall pick) of the 2009 draft by the Toronto Blue Jays. *—David Rawnsley*

### Anthony DeSclafani – RHP

In high school, Anthony DeSclafani was a long and lean 6-foot-3, 175-pound right-hander from New Jersey with a very long and loose arm action and easy release that was very easy to project. He pitched in numerous WWBA tournaments in 2007-2008 for the South Florida Bandits and the Tri-State Arsenal, and was a regular on the 2007 summer showcase circuit, including throwing at the 2007 Perfect Game National Showcase. His

report from that event read:

> He has a slender, young build and hasn't started to get strong yet. DeSclafani has a low effort delivery and very long and loose whippy arm action and an extended mid 3/4's release point. He threw a 4 seam fastball that topped out at 92 mph and a 2-seamer that had nice sink and run at 87 mph and was able to throw both pitches to spots low in the zone. With his loose and easy arm, DeSclafani projects more velocity in the future. His slider and changeup are still in the developing stages. Like many pitchers with similar arm actions/release points, getting a feel for a breaking ball is difficult and DeSclafani's slider is soft with an early break. With his easy delivery, long arm action and lack of off speed pitches, he lacks deception right now.

DeSclafani would flash a better breaking ball at times for scouts but didn't develop any consistency with it during high school and was a primary fastball pitcher. When his fastball stayed in the 88-92 mph range as a senior, the Red Sox made him a 22nd-round draft pick in 2008 before DeSclafani headed south to attend Florida.

The Gators used DeSclafani as a starter early in his career in Gainesville but realized eventually that with one plus pitch that he had outstanding command of, the now low- to mid-90s sinking fastball, DeSclafani had more value in the bullpen than in the starting rotation. He went 5-3, 4.33 with six saves as a junior in 2011, striking out 39 hitters in 43 innings and only issuing three walks, leading to his being selected by the Toronto Blue Jays in the sixth round of the draft that year. He was part of the huge salary-dump trade with the Marlins that sent Jose Reyes, Mark Buerhle, and Josh Johnson to Toronto in November 2012.

DeSclafani has been a starter since he signed professionally, and according to the Baseball Prospectus scouting reports, the Blue Jays and Marlins development staffs have been able to finally coax at least an MLB-average slider and an improved changeup out of the long-arming right-hander. *—David Rawnsley*

## Philadelphia Phillies

### Jesse Biddle – LHP

Much of the evaluation of Jesse Biddle from his high school days has remained true to form, almost as if the Phillies have let him develop in his own vacuum. That is not necessarily a bad thing.

Biddle, who grew up and went to high school at Germantown Friends Academy, a Quaker institution in suburban Philadelphia, had a very symmetrical development curve as a teenager. He first started throwing at WWBA events for the Philadelphia Senators team coming out of his freshman year in 2007 and generally topped out at 83-84 mph with a big mid-60s curveball at that age. His arm action was long and loose, with some cross-body action at release that was noted from his first scouting reports and has remained with him since. He gradually bumped that up to the 87-88 mph range coming off his sophomore season and was up to 89-92 during the summer before his senior year. What really garnered him attention, and his eventual first-round status (27th overall) for his hometown Phillies, was topping out at 94-95 mph during the spring of his senior year.

He has taken pretty much the same development path since signing as well, with the slight downtick in velocity as a professional due to the workload of pitching every fifth day.

A few things have always stood out about Biddle from the beginning of his time on the national stage, starting with the Perfect Game National Showcase in 2009:

- His curveball has always been big and deep, but a relatively slow pitch, topping out at 71-73 mph in high school. It's not a power pitch, but it is one that he commands effectively, and its size and plane make it hard to square up.

- It has always seemed to this scout that Biddle's arm action is highly conducive to a slider or a cutter, but that hasn't happened yet. My notes have frequently made mention of that potential and a comp with the recently retired Andy Pettitte. It wouldn't be surprising if Biddle eventually developed a Pettitte-type cutter.

- The other thing that Biddle has consistently done is induce swing-and-miss tendencies in hitters without an obvious swing-and-miss pitch. Hitters at elite events in high school swung through far too many 88-89-mph fastballs to not know as a scout that there was some serious deception happening, even though it wasn't readily obvious where it was coming from. The same thing has happened at the professional level as well.

- Biddle has always drawn very positive comments from scouts and coaches for his quiet confidence and positive mature makeup. That seems to still be the case today.

—David Rawnsley

## New York Mets

### Kevin Plawecki – C

Plawecki played in a pair of WWBA National Championships in consecutive years for the Indiana Dirtbags while in high school, starting with the 16u in 2007 and following with the 17u in 2008. Although his power potential was evident, hitting a towering home run to the pull-side at the 17u event, his catching skills were considered to be well ahead of his bat.

Here is a collection of scouting notes from those two events:

> Tall athletic frame ... quick footwork and release, 2.04, 2.07, 2.09 (Pop times), good catch and release, throws easy, good soft receiver ... easy swing, long bomb down LF line, hustles, hands inside ball, balanced, nice stick.

At Purdue he grew from 5-foot-11, 165 pounds to 6-foot-1, 215 pounds while in college, and not only did he consistently tap into his considerable power potential more often, but he also matured into a vocal team leader behind the plate.

Here's his PG scouting report prior to the 2012 MLB Draft:

> When Plawecki enrolled at Purdue, he was considered a defensive-minded catcher with the potential to develop into a middle-of-the-order run producer. His bat definitely has stepped forward as he now has a very sound approach to hitting, and the ability to consistently square up balls and drive them to the gaps. His power continues to emerge in concert with his improvement as a hitter ... He shows good lateral movement and improving blocking skills, and his quick release overcomes the lack of ideal arm strength for the position.

It should be noted that Plawecki was part of a very promising draft class during his junior year at Purdue that included third baseman Cameron Perkins (sixth round, Phillies) and right-hander Nick Wittgren (ninth round, Marlins), and is further proof of the increased talent coming out of the Indiana high school and college ranks in recent years.    —Patrick Ebert

### Brandon Nimmo – OF

As has been well documented, Brandon Nimmo has one of the most unusual backgrounds of any top prospect in baseball.

He grew up in Cheyenne, Wyoming, a state that doesn't have high school baseball. He played for American Legion Post 6, a regionally prominent program, hitting .448-16-84 with 34 stolen bases in 70 games during the spring and summer of 2010. And while Nimmo did have short appearances on the national stage, including the 2010 Tournament of Stars and a four-day team-funded spring-break trip to Arizona in 2011, scouts had to primarily travel to Wyoming and South Dakota to see and evaluate Nimmo. It was the first time that many of those road warriors had ever been to either of those states.

Despite those obstacles, Nimmo was selected with the 13th overall pick in the 2011 draft and signed for a $2.1 million bonus. He became the highest Wyoming high school age player ever drafted, easily surpassing right-hander Michael Beaver, who was the Phillies sixth-round pick back in 1966. (The University of Wyoming, which no longer has a baseball team, produced fourth-round outfielder Bill Ewing in 1976.)

Nimmo's sweet left-handed swing, combination of power and speed, and projected ability to stay in center field all contributed to his being evaluated as a first rounder by many teams in addition to the Mets. This occurred despite the nagging reality that he had never faced quality competition over an extended length of time, or had rarely been evaluated against that level. Nimmo also had an injury background, having torn his ACL before giving up football in 2009, which didn't keep him from winning the state 400 meter championship as a senior at 51.45 seconds.

Mets Vice President of Player Development and Scouting Paul DePodesta said in an MLB.com article after the 2011 draft, "This certainly isn't without risk. But as we went into this, to be quite frank with you, we weren't that interested in making what we thought was the safest pick. We were interested in making the pick that we thought had the chance to make the most impact."

Hindsight is always 20/20 of course, and Nimmo still has plenty of time to develop into an impact Major League outfielder. However, the Florida Marlins picked immediately after the Mets in 2011 and selected another high school player with a high perceived risk level due to his unusual background, Jose Fernandez.    —David Rawnsley

# Washington Nationals

### Lucas Giolito – RHP

Lucas Giolito's Hollywood background, prodigious talent, and frustrating and ill-timed elbow injury have combined to make him perhaps the highest profile high school pitching prospect of the last decade.

He is the son of long-time television actress Lindsey Frost and video game executive (EA, Trilogy Studios) Rick Giolito, and comes from an extended Hollywood family. Although he was very young for the 2012 class and could have easily been a 2013 based on his birthdate—he is two months older than Kohl Stewart and three weeks younger than Trey Ball, the first two high school pitchers selected in the 2013 draft—Giolito grew to his present 6-foot-6, 230 pounds early and never experienced any young oversized awkwardness athletically.

Giolito made his first appearance on the national stage at the 2010 Area Code Games shortly before the beginning of his junior year at Harvard-Westlake High School. As one of the few underclassmen in Long Beach, he wowed the scouts, topping out at 96 mph with a 78 mph curveball. The Perfect Game notes from that event reflected that:

> ++ build for age, could be a 2013 with his B/D, slow paced delivery, hand drop set, long loose arm, warms up at 91-93, + fast arm, limited feel for off speed, CB spin not tight, not wild but not throwing to spots, very young but very, very good.

Giolito didn't really gain much velocity over the next year, not that he really needed to. He couldn't attend the Perfect Game National Showcase due to a prior commitment, but threw at the PG Sunshine West Showcase the previous week and also pitched at the 17u WWBA National Championship for the San Gabriel Valley (SGV) Arsenal, the Area Code Games again and topped off his summer by hitting 97 mph at the Perfect Game All-American Classic, starting the game for the West squad.

The big difference in Giolito's stuff, though, was the development of his curveball. It went from a mid- to upper-70s pitch with limited feel to an 82-84 mph hammer with plus/plus potential. Part of my notes from the 2011 Area Code Games read:

> Throws + easy, for all his velo CB is potentially a better pitch, scouts rave on CB, Young approach but #1/#1 talent.

The intrigue continued to grow for Giolito's senior season. First, fellow PG All-American SoCal top prospect Max Fried decided to join Giolito at Harvard-Westlake after his previous high school discontinued their baseball program, giving the school perhaps the best pitching duo in the history of high school baseball. Fried would end up being the seventh overall selection by the Padres in the 2012 draft.

Secondly, the bump in velocity that most scouts had been expecting from Giolito happened, as he was clocked at 100 mph in preseason scrimmages by numerous scouts. With no obvious no. 1 pick already established for the 2012 draft, there was already talk that Giolito could become the first high school right-hander ever selected first overall. He certainly seemed worthy of it.

Of course, everything unraveled quickly from there, as Giolito sprained his ulnar collateral ligament in his right elbow in another scrimmage and missed the entire spring while rehabbing the injury. He was the big wild card in the 2012 draft that saw Carlos Correa and Byron Buxton go nos. 1 and 2 and was eventually selected by the Nationals with the 16th pick and signed for a $2.925 million bonus despite not having thrown competitively in five months.   —David Rawnsley

### A.J. Cole – RHP

Andrew "A.J." Cole has always come about his velocity pretty easily and was already throwing Major League velocities coming out of his freshman year at Oviedo High School in Florida. He came to the 2007 Perfect Game Junior National Showcase as a 6-foot-4, 180-pound 15-year-old and threw steadily in the 88-90 mph range with an upper-70s slider.

His notes from that event read as follows:

> Easy arm, little hitch on backside, 3/4 arm slot, solid mechanics, good sink, held velocity from stretch, worked runners, good pitchers body, makings of a thick trunk with maturity, located FB and SL to both sides of plate, good hard SL, showed some ASR, fielded position well, good composure and presence.

Cole would continue to gradually improve and fulfill his young projection through the remainder of his high school days. His velocity moved up to 90-93 in the summer of 2008 while pitching for the Orlando Scorpions and was steadily in the mid-90s, topping out at 98 mph at the 17u WWBA National Championship in July of 2009. He was named a Perfect Game All-American and pitched in the 2009 PG All-American Classic.

Two things at that point kept scouts from going completely all-in on Cole despite the easy plus/plus velocity and the profile pitcher's build and looseness. First, while his breaking ball would flash hard spin and bite, it wavered between slider and curveball shape in the upper 70s and was never a consistent potential plus offering. Secondly, Cole showed good control of his fastball in terms of throwing strikes but had below-average command, as he was often up in the strike zone and straight. Hitters got better swings at times off Cole than one would expect given his raw stuff.

Cole went into the 2010 draft ranked seventh in the 2010 high school class by Perfect Game and was expected to be a first-round draft pick. However, concerns about his signability and scholarship to Miami caused Cole to slide out of the first round, and he was eventually selected by the Nationals in the fourth round.

Given that the new draft slot guidelines had Cole's slot listed at $258,000, the Nationals at the time didn't have a reputation for overspending, and that they were believed to be mustering all their resources for their first pick, no. 1 overall selection Bryce Harper, it seemed like a strange place for the hard throwing high school right-hander to land.

But the Nationals carried the day, not only signing Cole for a fourth-round-record $2 million bonus, but of course getting Harper into the organization as well.   —David Rawnsley

## Brian Goodwin – OF

Goodwin's talents were well known in high school, as he was named to the 2008 PG All-American, where he garnered MVP honors by hitting the go-ahead two-run single in the top of the ninth inning at Dodgers Stadium. Overall in that game he was 2-for-4 with a double, and also scored an insurance run in the final frame.

Leading up to the 2009 draft he was ranked the 34th-best high school player in the nation, although Goodwin's commitment to North Carolina caused him to slide to the 17th round, where he was taken by the White Sox, a team that is known to covet premium athletes such as Goodwin.

Goodwin played at a handful of PG/WWBA tournament events with his home-state Dirtbags, including back-to-back World Championships in Jupiter, Florida, in 2007 and 2008. His five-tool talents were easy to see on the baseball field, with game-changing speed, an impact bat from the left-handed batter's box, and the ability to pitch in the mid-80s off the mound. Most of his power was to the alleys at the time, but due to an aggressive approach and good natural strength, more over-the-fence power was expected to emerge as he continued to fill out his 6-foot-1, 190-pound frame.

His polished profile in high school led to his enjoying immediate success during his freshman year for the Tar Heels, although he spent only one year there prior to transferring to Miami-Dade College for his sophomore year after he was suspended for violating team policy at UNC. While this made him eligible for the draft a year earlier than if he had remained at North Carolina, it also led to some off-the-field questions.

Goodwin's superior athleticism and maturing baseball skills make him an obvious first-round candidate, no matter what the draft year. He has all the raw tools to excel in the big leagues, and his combination of hitting skills, emerging power, superior speed and stellar defense makes him one of the best all-around outfield prospects in the 2011 draft. Goodwin is a 6.5-second runner with outstanding range in center field. He also has one of the top outfield arms in the class. Offensively, Goodwin has a quick, effortless left-handed swing and stays inside the ball with a level, line-drive type swing. His raw strength enables him to generate bat speed and drive balls into the gaps, although his present approach at the plate limits his loft power ... Goodwin is far from a finished product, however, and scouts say he'll need to continue to refine both his approach at the plate and defense in center field. More than anything, he needs to develop more consistent breaks on balls hit his way in order to settle in as an everyday center fielder.

The Nationals, another organization that has valued impact overall athletes in recent years, took Goodwin in the supplemental first round of the 2011 draft.   —*Patrick Ebert*

# Atlanta Braves

## Lucas Sims – RHP

Sims, a Georgia native, began his high school career as a primary shortstop who also pitched. He attended his first showcase, the 2011 PG Southeast Underclass Showcase, as his sophomore year at Brookwood High School began. During the infield workout

the 15-year-old Sims threw 92 mph across the infield from shortstop, with a lot of movement. The next day he took the mound and sat 88-90 with that same movement, and it became quite obvious where his future would be on the baseball diamond.

Wisely, Sims technically remained a primary infielder until the summer after his junior year of high school, limiting the mileage on his arm until his final draft evaluation year arrived. He was a relatively advanced prep arm despite dividing his efforts, showing good command of his fastball when working in the 90-92 range, and several ticks higher whenever he decided to reached back for more. He registered as high as 97 mph with his fastball at the East Coast Pro Showcase. He didn't just flash velocity in showcase settings, though; he touched 96 in multiple WWBA tournaments, where he continued to play for his hometown Team Gwinnett, rather than leaving them for an all-prospect conglomerate team.

Beyond the velocity, Sims' curveball showed good potential, with sharp break and a hard spin rate, one of the primary indicators scouts look for when projecting breaking balls. His changeup was ahead of the developmental curve as well, and he showed a consistent ability to compete in tough spots and make necessary in-game adjustments throughout his amateur career.

His success the summer prior to his senior year, which began with an appearance at the 2011 National Showcase in Fort Myers, Florida, reached its pinnacle at the PG All-American Classic, where he took the mound in the second inning for the East squad. At both events Sims' fastball peaked at 94 mph.

Sims came into his senior spring as a viable first-round candidate, but in a very deep 2012 high school class he was seen as a bubble candidate for the first round. As it turned out, his hometown Atlanta Braves, who built a dynasty around drafting and developing pitching, particularly from players plucked up from their own backyard, tabbed Sims with the 21st pick.
   —*Todd Gold*

## J.R. Graham – RHP

Perfect Game's Allan Simpson wrote the following draft profile for Graham prior to the 2011 draft. It summarizes Graham's amateur years well and sets the stage for his somewhat ironic professional career thus far.

Even with his slight frame, Graham has one of the most electric arms in this year's draft class. His fastball reached 97-98 mph this spring as a matter of routine, and often peaked out at 100. For a time, it looked like Graham's overpowering fastball alone would vault him into the first round, especially when he didn't walk a batter through his first 12 relief appearances, spanning 24 innings. At the time, he had no walks and 26 strikeouts.

But Graham's performance started to level off after he made a rare start in the final game of Santa Clara's West Coast Conference season-opening, three-game series against Loyola Marymount on April 10, when he was rocked for eight runs in five-plus innings, and walked his first batter of the season. With Santa Clara posting just a 17-32 record (4-15 in conference) this season, save opportunities were tough to come by for Graham, and he ended up making three more starts to get in some meaningful innings. Overall, he went 3-4, 3.54 with four walks and 41 strikeouts in 53 innings.

As the season wound down, most of the talk about Graham going in the first round had pretty much subsided, and the consensus among scouts is that he'll be a second-rounder, though could possibly slip into the sandwich round. Graham is highly athletic and very competitive, but his issue as a prospect has always revolved around his big arm—and small, wiry frame.

As a senior in high school, Graham weighed only 165 pounds, but had little trouble reaching 92 mph and showcasing his impressive arm strength from the hole at shortstop. He was a solid two-way prospect at the time, with speed (6.68 in the 60) and sound infield actions, and actually saw significant time at third base in his first two seasons at Santa Clara. But when he struggled to hit at the college level, and it was becoming increasingly clear that his future was on the mound, Graham settled in as a closer for the Broncos over the latter part of the 2010 season.

In 23 appearances, he saved four games while going 1-1, 5.27. During the summer in the Northwoods League, Graham focused on pitching and earned strong reviews for his quick arm and ability to pound the strike zone with easy 92-94 mph velocity. By this spring, Graham had jacked up his velocity another 4-5 mph. Though he also has a quality slider and changeup, giving him the three pitches he would need to work as a starter, Graham's startling performance this spring in an end-of-game role, where he has been able to air out his fastball almost exclusively, has left little doubt in the minds of scouts that his future role is at the back end of the bullpen.

Evidently, the one organization that had doubts about Graham's future role as a back-end bullpen guy was the Braves, who grabbed him when Graham unexpectedly slid to the fourth round and immediately transitioned him to a full-time starter role. —David Rawnsley

### Jason Hursh – RHP

 Jason Hursh came to the Perfect Game Sunshine South Showcase in early June 2009, after his junior year as a primary shortstop and secondary outfielder. He ran a 6.96 60-yard dash and showed plus arm from both shortstop (91 mph) and the outfield (93) but did not grade out nearly as well as a hitter, grading out at 7.5/7 on the Perfect Game scouting scale that goes up to 10. With that in mind, the PG scouts at the event asked Hursh if he would like to throw an inning on the mound on the event's second day. He readily agreed.

It was a very good decision, as Hursh threw in the 89-91-mph range and did it easily with simple mechanics. He was immediately invited to the PG National Showcase two weeks later and duplicated his performance while adding a mid-70s curveball that showed some promise once his young mechanics become consistent. He reaffirmed in batting prospect that he wasn't a next-level hitter and showed all the colleges in attendance that he was a top-level pitching prospect.

Armed with a 4.0-plus GPA in addition to a fastball that started peaking in the 93-94 mph range during his senior year (11-2, 2.47, 123 strikeouts in 70 innings), Hursh bypassed a sixth-round selection by the Pittsburgh Pirates in the 2010 draft to attend Oklahoma State.

After an uneventful freshman season, Hursh tore an elbow ligament pitching in the Cape Cod League in the summer of 2011 and had to sit out the entire 2012 spring season after undergoing Tommy John surgery. He recovered quickly and had already returned to the mound by that summer, showing a steady mid-90s fastball in the California Collegiate Summer League.

Early in the spring of 2013, Hursh was one of hottest commodities on the scouting circuit, regularly topping out at 97-98 mph and showing very good command of his heavy sinking fastball. His slider and changeup were workable but not advanced secondary pitches, however. As Hursh lost some velocity and the edge on his command under a heavy workload at Oklahoma State (16 starts, 106 innings), he lost some of his luster in scouts' eyes but was still selected by the Braves with the 31st overall pick, receiving a $1.7 million signing bonus.

Yes, Hursh would have probably figured out at some point that his career was on the mound if he had declined to throw an inning that morning in Brenham, Texas, in 2009. But it still was a very good spur-of-the-moment decision. —David Rawnsley ∎

# Making Sense of Pitching Prospects

*by Paul Sporer*

If you bought this guide, you're already aware of the dangers of "box-score scouting"—using minor-league numbers as a primary means of evaluation—and you've decided to equip yourself with the best, most comprehensive minor-league coverage available at a single outlet. If you also play fantasy baseball, it's hard not to get enticed by gaudy numbers as you mine the prospect rivers for fantasy gold. Navigating the terrain can be tough, but if you keep your eye on certain aspects, you can help increase the success rate of your picks.

## Size

Size matters. Statistically, the data has been inconclusive regarding success and failure according to height, and I'm not here to suggest that smaller pitchers can't succeed. However, there is a reason that it is discussed so much when they do make it: they beat the odds—the odds of an institutional bias, but stacked odds nonetheless.

Even when they succeed, durability can be an issue. Johnny Cueto is listed at 5'11". He has one 200-inning season among his six as a major leaguer and followed that 217-inning campaign with just 61 in 2013.

Going back further, Ben Sheets (6'1") was an early first-rounder who zipped through the minors with major prospect appeal, but only managed enough innings to qualify for the ERA title four times in 10 years. His career was essentially done at age 29. In his thirties, Sheets threw a total of 168 2/3 innings over four seasons, missing all of 2009 and 2011 before retiring after a brief stint with the Atlanta Braves in 2012.

Shaun Marcum was a third-rounder and didn't make much noise on the prospect circuit, but the 6'0" righty has more DL trips (six) than he does seasons of even 100 innings (five) let alone the ERA-qualifying 162- (two) or 200-inning (one) campaigns in his seven years and change as a major leaguer.

Wait, it gets worse. The five names in the chart below would be considered successes by any reasonable measure and yet they averaged 8.4 trips to the DL in their careers (which averaged 13.6 years):

| Pitcher | Height | DL trips | Seasons |
|---|---|---|---|
| Mike Hampton | 5'10" | 10 | 16 |
| Roy Oswalt | 6'0" | 9 | 13 |
| Ted Lilly | 6'0" | 10 | 15 |
| Johan Santana | 6'0" | 6 | 12 |
| Jake Peavy | 6'1" | 7 | 12 |

To pick one example from this list, Santana had elbow surgery in 2001 and held up until 2010, but only five of those seasons (2004-2008) were full starter workloads. He has dealt with injuries every year since, and missed all of 2011 and 2013. Now 35, he has worked just 482 2/3 innings in his thirties. With two Cy Young Awards to his credit, Santana's career has been a resounding success—especially as a Rule 5 pick back in 1999—but he has fallen off the Hall of Fame trajectory he appeared to be on in 2008.

Looking at the last 14 years, we see that there hasn't been a single year of more 6'0" and under pitchers making 30-plus starts than 6'4" or taller, and the gap is growing. The first five years saw a single-digit difference between the two groups, while the last nine have an average of 17.9, including four years with more than 20.

More starts means more innings, which is a good thing. You rarely hear a pitcher's innings total cited as a reason to draft him, but logging innings might be the single most underrated factor of fantasy pitchers today.

In an era when starter innings are being curtailed and we accept a 180-inning season as strong, we don't also add a bonus to those consistently north of 215 innings. Look at the pitchers who populate the top of the innings leaders on a yearly basis: Justin Verlander (6'5", 225 lbs.), James Shields (6'4", 215 lbs.), Clayton Kershaw (6'3", 220 lbs.), Matt Cain (6'3", 230 lbs.), and Adam Wainwright (6'7", 235 lbs.) to name a few. Those guys are kind of good.

Piling up innings adds to the strikeout volume, but it also gives more weight to the ratios and can improve the chances of racking up wins. Guys like Archie Bradley (6'4", 225 lbs.), Noah Syndergaard (6'6", 240 lbs.), Jameson Taillon (6'6", 235 lbs.), and Jonathan Gray (6'4", 255 lbs.) look like they will be the next generation of workhorses. Not only do they have frontline stuff, but they have the size to endure the grind of a 162-game season and take their 32-34 turns every year.

| Year | ≤ 6'0" | ≥ 6'4" |
|---|---|---|
| 2000 | 11 | 16 |
| 2001 | 10 | 19 |
| 2002 | 16 | 18 |
| 2003 | 18 | 21 |
| 2004 | 14 | 21 |
| 2005 | 14 | 30 |
| 2006 | 8 | 31 |
| 2007 | 14 | 31 |
| 2008 | 11 | 23 |
| 2009 | 6 | 30 |
| 2010 | 11 | 32 |
| 2011 | 11 | 31 |
| 2012 | 11 | 26 |
| 2013 | 9 | 22 |
| AVG | 11.7 | 25.1 |

## Health

Related to durability is health. Size doesn't prevent you from getting injured, just as being 6-foot or under doesn't prevent you from succeeding. But let's take size out of the equation with regard to health. The best predictor of injury is previous injury; as such, when it comes to a fantasy investment, I severely ding guys who get hurt in the minors. We are already dealing with a high fail rate proposition; why increase my chances of failing by adding a checkered injury history to the mix?

For example, Tommy John surgery is more successful than ever, but the notion that it's a rite of passage with a 100 percent return rate is taking it a little too far. Ask Cory Luebke and Daniel Hudson about that. Unfortunately, this lowers my interest in a 6'6", 225-pound Lucas Giolito, who has all the makings of an ace, but also Tommy John surgery on his right arm. Throw in how far away he is from fruition, and the battle between him and Taillon is a no-brainer in favor of the latter even though Giolito slots higher on the Top 100.

When dealing with the elite pitching prospects—the ones getting the most fantasy consideration—everyone carries knockout stuff and a high ceiling, so we have to look for tiebreakers. Size translates to durability, which yields production.

Many pitchers get through rough patches in health to have long, excellent careers, but most deal with more health problems down the line. In fantasy baseball, we only care about production as soon as possible, so even if the guy who recovers from Tommy John surgery in Low-A becomes an ace five years down the line, I would much rather have the Double-A pitcher with third-starter ceiling giving me value on my team for three or four of those five years.

## Advancement

This one is easy and straightforward, but I place a lot of emphasis on advancement in the minors when assessing pitchers as fantasy commodities. Everyone loves a stratospheric ceiling, but the further away a guy is from reaching it, the more unlikely he is to pan out. Baby arms ripping through the low minors just don't carry the appeal of guys making their way through the high minors, even if the latter have lower ceilings. Now, I'm not suggesting you favor the fifth-starter ceiling in Triple-A over the frontline potential torching A-ball, but I will personally take a Matt Barnes over a Tyler Glasnow in fantasy.

Barnes is a college product, so he already entered pro ball with a bit more polish after 252 innings at Connecticut. Now he has added 233 more in the pros, with 133 1/3 of those coming in the high minors.

Glasnow is a high-school product with 150 pro innings, peaking at A-ball. The excitement surrounding him is merited, but time is a precious commodity in fantasy baseball and for me, it can make up a 22-spot difference in ranking at the draft table. Those drafting straight off the 101 see Glasnow at 42 and Barnes at 64, but I see someone likely not contributing meaningful innings until 2016 against someone poised for a 2014 debut.

Let's be honest, you don't really know how long your fantasy league will be around. So while it's great to have a loaded farm system ready to dominate from 2016 through 2020, you could have two leaguemates get married, a third get pregnant and decide the game has to take a backseat, and a fourth get some awesome promotion that puts him in Tokyo for the next three years and unable to play fantasy baseball. All of sudden your league of best friends is essentially defunct because life happened.

Focusing on a pitcher's advancement is about him specifically and how much closer he is to reaching his ceiling and delivering value. But it's also about the simple fact that no league is guaranteed beyond the current season.

I also strongly favor guys who are ahead of the advancement curve through the minors. This is another spot where box-score scouting can really hurt you. If a 21-year-old is getting knocked around a bit at Triple-A, I'm unlikely to instantly hit the panic button, especially if there aren't corresponding reports suggesting that his stuff has waned or injuries are behind the struggle.

Consider the cases of Julio Teheran and Martin Perez. Both zipped through the minors but sputtered somewhat during their age-21 seasons at Triple-A. Their prospect status dipped and their fantasy status fell even further. Fast forward a year and a half later, and both have been signed to long-term deals by their teams after excellent 2013 seasons at the major-league level.

Players seem to be moving through the minors faster than ever, leading to a youth movement unlike any we have ever seen (well, short of something prompted by a World War), but

the community has to be careful not to overadjust on either end. When a 19-year-old is tearing through Double-A, it doesn't mean he'll be an instant success at the big-league level later that summer. But when he inevitably hits that first road bump, whether in Triple-A or during his first taste of the majors, you shouldn't start severely downgrading the ceiling he built up during that minor-league ascension.

There was a colossal overreaction to the road bumps suffered by Teheran and Perez, particularly in the fantasy community, where you seemingly have to be Jose Fernandez or Shelby Miller upon arrival or risk becoming an afterthought. Don't make that mistake.

## Tools

Raw tools still matter. I favor the following:

**Velocity:** It's sexy and it can carry a pitcher a long way. Velocity doesn't guarantee success, or even strikeouts, but it lengthens a pitcher's leash and boosts his overall ceiling.

**Changeup:** Few things excite me more than "6 CH" or "7 CH," especially from a young arm. It is often the sign of an advanced arm. Consider that most high-school products don't even need a changeup because their fastball and breaking pitch (and maybe even just the former) are enough to dominate the competition. So if they come into the pros with a changeup in tow, it shows an advanced feel for the craft that often bodes well for the future.

**Command:** It's hard to determine just how strong a pitcher's command is in the minors, as walks alone can indicate control, but not necessarily command. Meanwhile, a high walk rate doesn't mark an absence of command. Without actually seeing a pitcher yourself, you have to rely on reports like the ones featured in this guide, written by people who have observed and studied these young arms.

## Conclusion

Prospecting for pitching is tough, especially when you are trying to extract fantasy value. A 200-inning arm who puts up a 4.40 ERA has immense value at the back end of a rotation and is considered a successful prospect/draft pick for a ballclub but doesn't bring much value in any fantasy league. So we are tasked with finding the biggest hits in a field rife with volatility and failure. This is why I try so hard to eliminate the factors that create the most variability: injury and time.

Don't get too enamored with the high-ceiling pitchers who are far away. Luis Heredia had a ceiling as high as orgmates Gerrit Cole and Jameson Taillon two years ago, but now he's down to a no. 3 starter ceiling. That's a strong ceiling, but he's still only 19 years old and hasn't yet hit full-season ball.

Heredia is just one example, but he's hardly an exception. As enticing as those long-distance arms (such as Minnesota's Lewis Thorpe) can be, don't be afraid to bypass them in favor of someone like Rafael Montero, who projects as a no. 3 or no. 4 but who will be knocking on the door of the majors after a big season across Double- and Triple-A in 2013. Sometimes the safe pick is the smart pick.

Size, health, advancement, tools. These won't guarantee success, but they will help you mitigate risk, which is the name of the game with pitchers. Good luck and happy prospecting! ■

# Fighting Prospect Fatigue and Learning to Love Again: Identifying Post-Prospect Sleepers

*by Ben Carsley*

Fatigue is a common theme within baseball. Odds are, at least one pitcher on your favorite team will hit the DL with arm fatigue at some point in 2014. Hitters receive intermittent off-days as they push through the fatigue that comes with playing 162 games per season. Once, Roger Clemens was shelved with groin fatigue. And fans of the Padres may even have fatigue fatigue, thanks to their team's alternate uniforms.

There's another kind of fatigue creeping into the world of baseball, especially among fantasy owners, and that's the idea of "prospect fatigue." It's a term my colleague Craig Goldstein introduced me to a few years back, and it's one that's becoming increasingly prevalent as interest in minor leaguers and prospects continues to sweep through the baseball world. We've never come up with a strict definition for prospect fatigue, but essentially, it deals with an unwillingness to accept and adjust to the developmental hurdles that accompany players on their ascent through the minors, and an unfortunate willingness to abandon said players once they reach the majors and their flaws are revealed.

Recent success stories we've seen with some of the game's best players have only exacerbated this problem. Mike Trout went from being drafted 25th overall to posting an 8.3-WARP season in less than three years. Jose Fernandez finished as the seventh most valuable starting pitcher in fantasy leagues 671 days after he was drafted. And Michael Wacha started Game Two of the World Series a whopping 508 days after the Cardinals selected him 19th overall in the 2012 draft.

The impression these players have left upon many in the fantasy community is significant. They have skewed our expectations and wreaked havoc on our evaluations by being so good. High-school players who take four years to reach the majors are viewed as slow movers now. College athletes who need more than two seasons are looked down upon.

We want draft picks to impact our teams now, and the endless cycle of hype created online and fueled by Twitter only strengthens our desire for prospects to impact our fantasy teams immediately. Whether prospects struggle due to standard developmental hurdles, organizational roadblocks, or injuries, fantasy owners obsess over every hiccup on the road to glory, mediocrity, or disappointment each minor leaguer must travel.

The irony is that once a player loses his magical prospect status—by exceeding the 130-at-bat, 50-innings-pitched, or service time thresholds used to determine his eligibility—fantasy owners tend to lose interest if the payoff isn't immediate. A prospect who ranks in the midst of the ever-popular annual top-100 lists may be quickly forgotten in a year if he fails to perform well immediately upon his ascension to the majors. Young pitchers who suffer injuries (aka most pitchers) are cast aside in the minds of fantasy owners who don't do well with delayed gratification. Even post-prospects who go on to have decent MLB debuts can be left in the dust by the newer, shinier, unblemished prospects who follow them. These new prospects have yet to have their flaws exposed to us at the highest level, and so we may still dream of their limitless potential.

Ultimately, this creates a sort of post-prospect fatigue phenomenon that sees players caught between "sexy bundle of potential" and "established MLB presence" vastly underrated in the fantasy community, particularly in redraft leagues. Identifying who among these players you should target and who you should avoid can pay huge dividends, and can transform the back halves of your drafts from crapshoots to a key factor in your success. Each year's crop of post-prospects is different, and the availability of said players will fluctuate with the type of league you're playing in, but we can identify some central sources of post-prospect fatigue and how to combat them in your drafts and auctions.

## Standard developmental hurdles

The first and perhaps most common source of post-prospect fatigue occurs when a player does not immediately dominate in the majors, no matter how unreasonable the expectations of dominance may be. We're loathe to recognize that players still develop once their minor-league days are over, and we punish those who aren't approaching their ultimate upsides as soon as they arrive.

To combat the first source of post-prospect fatigue, it's important to pay attention to scouting reports for each individual player, and not simply glance at minor-league stat sheets or the often overly optimistic ETAs that adorn offseason prospect rankings. A 21-year-old prep draftee or J2 player putting up league-average numbers in Double-A, where the median age is around 24, isn't struggling, even if he's already been in the minors for three-plus years.

Scouting reports are also of paramount importance when a player reaches the majors at a young age, as the reasons for his struggles are more important than the struggles themselves. For example, a young batter who's yet to grow into his power but who can really hit has a better chance of reaching his ceiling some day than does a young player with plenty of pop but a questionable hit tool. Power is useless if you can't make contact.

Similarly, pitchers who need refinement in terms of command or control but have good stuff are better bets for fantasy dominance than are pitchers who know how to throw the ball over the plate, but who lack two or more above-average pitches. It doesn't pay to throw strikes if your strikes aren't missing any bats.

This sounds simple, but practicing such patience can become quite frustrating. When you've been on a player since he was drafted out of high school as an 18-year-old, it's natural to be disappointed when he's still not showing major-league power at age 22. When you follow a Dominican arm from his early days as a 17-year-old and then watch him struggle to throw strikes in his first MLB starts at age 23, it's easy to lose patience. But it's important to remember that when players reach the majors at a young age, it means they're ahead of the curve already, and their development is far from complete even if their prospect status is in the rear-view mirror.

For a recent example of a talented post-prospect who simply needed time to find his way in the majors, let's turn our attention to Chris Tillman. A 2006 second-round pick by the Mariners, Tillman was a high-profile prospect sent to Baltimore along with Adam Jones in 2008. He ranked no. 16 on the Baseball Prospectus Top 101 list before the 2009 season, in which he made his MLB debut. That year, Tillman lost his rookie eligibility after 65 innings of uninspiring baseball at the major-league level. After similarly disappointing MLB stints in 2010 and 2011, Tillman was labeled a bust by many until a more respectable 86-inning stretch in Baltimore in 2012 revived some interest in his career.

A dip in velocity did add a legitimate red flag to Tillman's resume, but the right-hander struggled in the majors early on in large part because his command slipped, leading to higher walk rates and hittable strikes. Tillman made his major-league debut as a 21-year-old but was viewed as a failure for not seeing MLB success until the ripe old age of 24. And yet despite Tillman's prospect pedigree and solid 2012 performance, he finished the 2013 preseason with an ADP of 327 in ESPN leagues, meaning he was likely undrafted in most 10- and 12-team leagues.

Tillman rewarded owners with long memories handsomely by posting 16 wins, 179 strikeouts, a 3.71 ERA, and a 1.22 WHIP in 2013. He finished as fantasy's 123rd-best player per the ESPN Player Rater and the 30th-best starter in standard formats, ahead of Justin Verlander, Gio Gonzalez, and Matt Moore.

## Organizational roadblocks

A second source of post-prospect fatigue can stem from a player facing organizational roadblocks due to a star player ahead of him, a contending team showing reluctance to trust a rookie with a key position, or a team keeping a player in the minors in the interest of cost and years of control. The downside with post-prospects who face this challenge is there's no telling when the proverbial dam may proverbially break, allowing the player to see consistent major-league time. Erratic playing time can lead to poor performance and small sample sizes, making it difficult to adequately judge a player, and can perpetuate a team's belief that said post-prospect isn't yet ready for The Show.

The good news is that every fantasy player can forecast such situations though a simple understanding of depth charts and organizational tendencies. The offseason is a hectic time, but by late-February/early-March, we generally have an idea of which post-prospects will be given full-time jobs, which will have to fight for their right to playing time, and which face an uphill battle in terms of seeing regular starts. And knowing that teams like the Marlins and Orioles promote prospects aggressively while the Rays and Cubs tend to be conservative can go a long way toward forecasting fantasy relevancy, too.

A good example of a recent post-prospect who faced undue difficulty in securing playing time is Brandon Belt. An unheralded fifth-round pick in 2009, Belt popped up on prospect lists after showing an advanced hit tool in the minors and ranked no. 22 on the 2011 Baseball Prospectus Top 101. Promoted to the Giants as a 23-year-old, Belt understandably struggled in 209 plate appearances, hitting just .225/.306/.412.

Despite the down performance, the #FreeBrandonBelt movement was already underway, and for good reason. The Baby Giraffe had dominated in Double-A in 2010 and Triple-A in 2011, and while his power was not yet fully present, nearly all reports safely projected him to become a plus hitter.

The Giants did give Belt a good amount of playing time in 2012, but he still lost nearly 200 plate appearances to Brett Pill and the sentient remains of Aubrey Huff. His playing time was especially sporadic in the first half, and the then-24-year-old struggled a bit as a result.

When San Francisco finally let Belt off the leash in the second half, he hit .293/.362/.423, giving him an overall line of .275/.360/.421 for the season. Still, questions about Belt's power—often the last offensive tool to develop—plagued the fantasy community. Even though the Giants seemingly committed to playing him every day in 2013, fantasy owners jumped ship, apparently tired of waiting for his modest upside to show up over a full season. Belt's ESPN ADP prior to the 2013 season sat at 350, behind Garrett Jones, Trevor Plouffe, and Justin Ruggiano.

Belt answered his critics by hitting .289/.360/.481 in 2013, finishing as fantasy's 113rd-best player overall according to ESPN's Player Rater. He placed ahead of first basemen like Mike Napoli, Anthony Rizzo, and Adam Dunn.

## Injuries

Finally, a third, perhaps more justifiable cause for post-prospect fatigue stems from a factor that is impossible to predict, may strike at any time, and can render even the most promising players useless: injuries. For hitters, even minor injuries can disrupt timing at the plate, leading to depressed minor-league stats or lost development time. For pitchers, well, the TINSTAAPP theory exists for a reason, and while the frequency of pitching injuries may be somewhat overstated, they still play a prominent role in deciding who wins and loses fantasy leagues every year. It's also important to pay attention to lingering injuries that may not land a prospect or post-prospect on the disabled list, but which could impact performance.

As with our first cause for post-prospect fatigue, it's hugely important to pay attention to scouting reports when evaluating whether an injured player represents a solid gamble. Here's your stock disclaimer that I'm not a doctor, but in general, steer clear of shoulder injuries to pitchers and wrist injuries to hitters. It's smarter to bet on recoveries by athletic prospects who've suffered non-chronic injuries, even if misfortune leads to many of those injuries piling up. Pitchers recovering from Tommy John surgery are worth gambling on as well, though the view that Tommy John recovery is "automatic" is a flawed one, as John Lamb, Cory Luebke, and Ryan Madson can attest. And soft-tissue injuries garner more skepticism than do simple broken bones when it comes to projecting long-term ramifications.

For a recent example of a high-profile prospect who the fantasy community gave up on too soon thanks to injuries, let's look to Domonic Brown, whose story should still be fresh in the minds of fantasy players everywhere. A 20th-round pick of the Phillies in 2006, he began his career as an unheralded 18-year-old in rookie ball and soared through the minors, never facing a true statistical bump in the road until his second stint in Triple-A at age 23.

The problem is that amidst Brown's strong minor-league performances sits a lengthy and diverse list of injuries that slowed his ascent to the majors:

- **2009:** Finger fracture
- **2010:** Thigh and hamate injuries; the latter tends to sap hitters of their power for quite some time
- **2012:** Thumb and knee injuries

Brown missed significant time in each of his minor-league seasons, even if some of his injuries did not result in trips to the disabled list, and the cumulative impact of that missed developmental time could easily have led to his early career struggles. For the sins of struggling in sporadic MLB starts from 2010 to 2012 and failing to find meaningful MLB success until age 25, Brown saw his ESPN ADP fall to 324 before the 2013 season.

Brown did miss more time in 2013 thanks to a concussion and a foot injury, but he still finished as the 76th-most valuable asset in fantasy baseball. He hit .272/.324/.494 with 27 homers, outperforming Jose Bautista, Mark Trumbo, Yoenis Cespedes, and even Bryce Harper.

## Other factors

There are many more common traps fantasy owners fall into when it comes to undervaluing post-prospects. One of the simplest comes from a lack of exposure. Non-star players on bad, boring teams lend themselves to anonymity, which leads to low ADP.

Name me every Yankees right fielder of the past decade. You probably can, right? Now name me every Twins second baseman who played during the same span. Womp womp.

Post-prospects also become overlooked if they turn into solid MLB players, but don't live up to their once-extraordinary hype. That's why you'll see Matt Wieters and Trevor Cahill underdrafted this year, as others reach for Travis d'Arnaud and Danny Salazar.

## The next wave

Still, lack of immediate impact, obvious playing time, and health are the three main causes of post-prospect hype that I can identify. Owners who combat the urge to overlook players for these reasons will be in good shape.

Keeping those factors in mind, the most obvious question becomes: Who belongs in the next wave of post-prospects the fantasy community is likely to undervalue in the next few years?

Many come to mind for 2014. Tyler Skaggs ranked no. 17 on the 2013 Baseball Prospectus Top 101 and appears poised to grab 20-plus starts in a favorable home ballpark this season. Anthony Rendon ranked no. 35 on the BP 101 last season and looks to build upon a solid 2013 campaign. Nolan Arenado, no. 57 last season, could quietly end up as a top-15 option at third base. And Martin Perez, who I feel as though I've been covering since 1994, could take a step forward after he was "dropped" in the BP rankings to no. 59 overall prior to 2013.

But perhaps no player better embodies the idea of post-prospect fatigue than Minnesota Twins corner outfielder Oswaldo Arcia, ranked no. 60 by Baseball Prospectus last year, no. 41 by *Baseball America*, and no. 59 by Keith Law. Yet now Arcia finds himself in the midst of a perfect storm that's led to him being quite underrated. Consider the following:

- He had a solid but underwhelming 2013 campaign, registering enough plate appearances to no longer count as a prospect despite still being in a developmental phase.
- He doesn't have absurd upside—there will be no 40-homer or 20/20 campaigns here. You can't "dream on him" the way you can other prospects.
- He plays for a bad team that no one paid mind to in 2013 and no one will pay much mind to in 2014. For many national baseball fans, he's anonymous.
- Despite his talent, he doesn't project like a Byron Buxton or a Miguel Sano. He's been lost among myriad high-upside prospects in his own system, even sharing some of the limited limelight last year with fellow outfield prospect Aaron Hicks.

Arcia's 2013 MLB debut was solid if unspectacular, as he hit .251/.304/.430 with 14 homers in 378 plate appearances. The advanced approach he demonstrated throughout the minors left him; the 22-year-old left-handed hitter struck out in 31 percent of his plate appearances while walking in just 6.1 percent of them. Arcia projects to be a player with a fair share of whiffs, to be sure, but such an extreme shift is the mark of a player adjusting to the rigors of the majors at a young age, not of someone whose scouting profile shifted overnight.

Despite his solid debut and once-lofty prospect status, no one seems to care much about Arcia anymore. He's being drafted 73rd among outfielders with an ADP of 265, according to Mock Draft Central, behind stalwarts (sarcasm font) like Marcell Ozuna, Ryan Ludwick, and teammate Josh Willingham. He's going nearly 50 picks after Nick Swisher, who may not outproduce him in 2014, and nearly 55 picks after Kole Calhoun and Khris Davis, neither of whom was viewed highly by the prospect community.

The argument here isn't that Arcia is a star in the making. It's that he's likely to recoup significant value for where he's being drafted, and a big part of the reason he's being overlooked is that he no longer appears on top-100 prospect lists we so look forward to each year. Arcia is more than capable of hitting .270 with 20-plus homers and useful runs and RBI totals this season, and he represents the modest but meaningful reward fantasy owners can expect to gain by being savvy when it comes to evaluating post-prospects.

## Conclusion

Prospects, as the Baseball Prospectus series alerts us to, will nearly always break your heart. It is not so much their nature as ours, as no matter how often we tell ourselves not to expect perfection, we demand it. Such high expectations naturally lead to disappointment, and such disappointment leads to these assets being wildly undervalued at the beginning of each season. Knowing who among these undervalued assets to target and who to avoid will help you target high-upside forgotten youngsters late in your drafts, rather than settling once again for a boring, low-upside veteran or reaching for a current prospect with no clear path to playing time.

To be sure, some of the post-prospects you target will still fail you. And targeting post-prospects can lead to buyer's remorse—as soon as you purchase a Jean Segura, baseball comes out with a Xander Bogaerts. But if you're going to follow prospects all throughout their minor-league careers, you might as well hold on a little longer and bank on their skill and the impatience of other owners to provide you with a fantasy market inefficiency to exploit.

Besides, if the post-prospects you target do let you down, there will always be a new, shiny prospect to dream on right around the corner. ■

# The Top 101 Dynasty League Prospects for 2014

*by Bret Sayre*

In an age where there's more statistical information available on players than ever before, you've come to the right place to differentiate yourself from your leaguemates. Even if you don't play in a keeper or dynasty league where you can own minor leaguers without wasting a roster spot, the importance of reading scouting reports and knowing who these players are becomes obvious when a few years later you are faced with the dilemma of choosing them for your roster.

If you are in a dynasty league, you can take advantage of the box-score scouts by knowing more tangible details about a player. How can his power tool progress as he develops? How much of his speed at the minor-league level is sustainable for major-league stolen-base success? Does he lack high-end bat speed and can he potentially be exposed as the pitching he's facing improves?

The more you know, the more you'll win. And the more you win, the happier you'll feel. So let's start your journey toward nirvana.

Within this list, you'll find some fantasy-specific information about each player—namely where their impact lies and how much you can expect to one day pay for their services if they reach the heights they are capable of. Also included this year are "Realistic Ceiling" and "Realistic Floor" designations, which are meant to give a more tangible idea of who these players can be from a statistical standpoint or compared to their peers. So when I say that Rougned Odor could be Martin Prado, I do not mean it in any scouting sense—strictly in the type of value they can have for a fantasy team.

I also won't go too in depth with the commentary here, as you've just combed through hundreds of pages of scouting reports and I'm not going to add anything earth shattering. Plus, more detailed fantasy takes are already sprinkled throughout the top 10 lists.

Finally, like any list, there are some disclaimers to go over before we get started. These rankings are for fantasy purposes only, and do not directly take into account things like an outfielder's ability to stick in center or a catcher's pop time.

Of course, these things often matter indirectly, as they affect a player's ability to either stay in the lineup or maintain eligibility. So, while Austin Hedges is a top-20 prospect on Jason's Top 101 list, this is largely due to his defensive value. Hedges doesn't make the Fantasy 101 list because underneath that glossy defense is a bat that doesn't profile so well in our world.

Additionally, home environments and league differences need to be factored in, just as when we are when talking about a major-league player. If Josh Johnson's fantasy potential skyrockets from moving both from the American League to the National League and from a hitters' park in Toronto to a pitchers'

paradise in San Diego, we can't pretend that these prospects operate in a vacuum, unaffected by such factors. Of course, there's no guarantee that they will reach the majors with their current organization, so while it is not a heavy consideration, it is reflected.

In the end, the intention of this list is to balance the upside, probability, and proximity of these players to an active fantasy lineup. These rankings should be viewed in the context of a medium-sized mixed dynasty league where you have a separate minor-league farm team. That means if you're in a deep league, you can bump up some of the names that have higher probability and lower ceiling, like Matt Davidson and Rafael Montero. The opposite also applies with shallower leagues, where the focus should be upside, upside, and more upside—in those leagues, players like Tim Anderson and Joey Gallo will have increased value due to the elevated replacement level and likely shallowness of the minor-league systems.

## The List

### 1. Xander Bogaerts, SS, Boston Red Sox
*Age: 21, Previous Rank: 5*

**Potential Earnings:** $35+

**Risk Factor:** Low

**Fantasy Overview:** Four-category contributor; impact potential in HR, RBI

**Realistic Ceiling:** Troy Tulowitzki with health

**Realistic Floor:** J.J. Hardy with better on-base skills

No other prospect on this list combines Bogaerts' level of combined floor and ceiling for fantasy—and he'll be receiving regular at-bats in April. Playing half his games in Fenway will only magnify the positives of his game by allowing him to take aim at the Monster.

### 2. Byron Buxton, OF, Minnesota Twins
*Age: 20, Previous Rank: 18*

**Potential Earnings:** $35+

**Risk Factor:** Medium

**Fantasy Overview:** Five-category contributor; impact potential in AVG, R, SB

**Realistic Ceiling:** Perennial top-five pick overall

**Realistic Floor:** Carlos Gomez with less power

The only thing more dynamic than Buxton's fantasy upside may be his smile. What's keeping him from the top spot on this list is the fact that he has no experience in Double-A yet—not that it should be an issue for him.

### 3. Oscar Taveras, OF, St. Louis Cardinals
*Age: 21, Previous Rank: 2*

**Potential Earnings:** $35+

**Risk Factor:** Low

**Fantasy Overview:** Four-category contributor; impact potential in AVG, HR, RBI, R

**Realistic Ceiling:** Vladimir Guerrero without the speed

**Realistic Floor:** Matt Holliday without Coors Field

Taveras was supposed to have gotten a half-season of playing time by now, but his ankle did not go along with the plan. The 2014 season will be take two, and while the Cardinals' major-league lineup looks full, like the Red Sea, it will part for him when he's ready.

### 4. Javier Baez, SS, Chicago Cubs
*Age: 21, Previous Rank: 16*

**Potential Earnings:** $35+

**Risk Factor:** Medium

**Fantasy Overview:** Five-category contributor; impact potential in HR, RBI

**Realistic Ceiling:** 1b to Byron Buxton's 1a in the first round

**Realistic Floor:** The better half of Danny Espinosa

Baez has upside and bat speed for days. He also has nowhere near the floor of the first three names on this list for fantasy purposes. The other complicating factor (though it shouldn't matter with how Baez is valued) is that his major-league defensive home is up for debate.

### 5. Carlos Correa, SS, Houston Astros
*Age: 19, Previous Rank: 17*

**Potential Earnings:** $35+

**Risk Factor:** Medium

**Fantasy Overview:** Five-category contributor; impact potential in HR, RBI

**Realistic Ceiling:** Top-3 fantasy shortstop

**Realistic Floor:** An average fantasy third baseman

The first overall pick from 2012 only got better as the 2013 season went on. It will be fun to see what kind of numbers he can put up in Lancaster, as the Astros haven't had an offensive prospect this advanced (or good) in recent memory.

### 6. Billy Hamilton, OF, Cincinnati Reds
*Age: 23, Previous Rank: 3*

**Potential Earnings:** $35+

**Risk Factor:** Medium

**Fantasy Overview:** Three-category contributor; impact potential in R, SB

**Realistic Ceiling:** First-round pick and category winner

**Realistic Floor:** Top-50 fantasy outfielder on speed alone

All systems are go for Hamilton to start Opening Day in center field for Cincinnati. He is the only player in professional baseball who has the potential to steal 100 bases in the major leagues, but he's going to have to get on base (either by hitting or walking) to come close.

### 7. Miguel Sano, 3B, Minnesota Twins
*Age: 19, Previous Rank: 11*

**Potential Earnings:** $30-35

**Risk Factor:** Medium

**Fantasy Overview:** Four-category contributor; impact potential in HR, RBI, R

**Realistic Ceiling:** Top-three fantasy third baseman

**Realistic Floor:** Mark Reynolds part deux

The power is real and is beloved in fantasy circles. The hit tool scares some, but more than it should. No one is expecting a near-.300 average out of Sano, but with the fantasy stars at the hot corner aging (or losing eligibility), 40 homers at that spot is elite—even if he hits .250.

### 8. George Springer, OF, Houston Astros
*Age: 24, Previous Rank: 35*

**Potential Earnings:** $30-35

**Risk Factor:** Medium

**Fantasy Overview:** Four-category contributor; impact potential in HR, RBI, R

**Realistic Ceiling:** A 25/25 outfielder you wished hit for a higher average

**Realistic Floor:** A 20/20 outfielder you really wished hit for a higher average

Last season went a long way toward showing that Springer is not going to follow Brett Jackson's career path. The contact rate improved without damaging the beloved secondary skills. He'll likely start the year back in Triple-A, but through no fault of his own.

### 9. Addison Russell, SS, Oakland Athletics
*Age: 20, Previous Rank: 20*

**Potential Earnings:** $30-35

**Risk Factor:** Medium

**Fantasy Overview:** Five-category contributor; impact potential in RBI, R

**Realistic Ceiling:** An era-adjusted Miguel Tejada

**Realistic Floor:** A healthier Stephen Drew

Russell doesn't share the same lofty fantasy ceiling as the three shortstops ranked ahead of him, but that's a reflection on the forest, not this individual tree. Importantly, he's also the likeliest of the bunch to stay at the position long term.

### 10. Kris Bryant, 3B, Chicago Cubs
*Age: 22, Previous Rank: NR*

**Potential Earnings:** $30-35

**Risk Factor:** Medium

**Fantasy Overview:** Four-category contributor; impact potential in HR, RBI

**Realistic Ceiling:** Josh Willingham with health and third-base eligibility

**Realistic Floor:** Just another 20-plus-homer outfielder

The top fantasy prospect from the 2013 draft, Bryant is already one of the most powerful prospects in the minor leagues. Don't stress about whether he'll end up at third or in the outfield, as the latter isn't nearly as deep as it seems.

### 11. Taijuan Walker, RHP, Seattle Mariners
*Age: 21, Previous Rank: 13*

**Potential Earnings:** $25-30

**Risk Factor:** Low

**Fantasy Overview:** Four-category contributor; impact potential in W, K, ERA, WHIP

**Realistic Ceiling:** Mat Latos if he never left Petco

**Realistic Floor:** Solid no. 4 fantasy starter

If they pitched in neutral parks/leagues, Walker and Bradley would be a coin flip, but with Safeco being a more pleasant place to pitch than Chase Field, the Seattle righty gets the nod. To be fair, it's like choosing between cake and pie.

## 12. Archie Bradley, RHP, Arizona Diamondbacks
*Age: 21, Previous Rank: 30*

**Potential Earnings:** $25-30

**Risk Factor:** Low

**Fantasy Overview:** Four-category contributor; impact potential in W, K, ERA, WHIP

**Realistic Ceiling:** Top-10 fantasy starter

Realistic Floor: A Jeff Samardzija-type frustration special

The hammer is potentially special and could go a long way toward buoying the rest of his fantasy game, even if he regressed in command at the major-league level. It's not unrealistic to think that he'll to lead the National League in strikeouts at some point before the end of the decade.

## 13. Noah Syndergaard, RHP, New York Mets
*Age: 21, Previous Rank: 38*

**Potential Earnings:** $25-30

**Risk Factor:** Low

**Fantasy Overview:** Four-category contributor; impact potential in W, K, ERA, WHIP

**Realistic Ceiling:** Jordan Zimmermann with a few more strike-outs

**Realistic Floor:** A good no. 4 fantasy starter

It's tough to follow in the footsteps of Matt Harvey and Zack Wheeler, but the big right-hander is up to the challenge. Plus, if you draft him you can name your team "Stand Gaard" and your team logo can be the picture of Syndergaard working out in his Thor costume.

## 14. Gregory Polanco, OF, Pittsburgh Pirates
*Age: 22, Previous Rank: 46*

**Potential Earnings:** $30-35

**Risk Factor:** Medium

**Fantasy Overview:** Five-category contributor

**Realistic Ceiling:** Alex Rios in his better years

**Realistic Floor:** Colby Rasmus with better hair

The problem with trying to translate Polanco into fantasy categories is that he projects to have real impact in all five, it just likely won't happen at the same time. He'll be more steal-heavy when he arrives, and once the power develops, he'll likely be slowing down.

## 15. Kevin Gausman, RHP, Baltimore Orioles
*Age: 22, Previous Rank: 29*

**Potential Earnings:** $25-30

**Risk Factor:** Low

**Fantasy Overview:** Four-category contributor; impact potential in W, K, WHIP

**Realistic Ceiling:** A top-20 fantasy starter with 200+ strikeouts

**Realistic Floor:** Lance Lynn in the American League

Gausman was far better than he's being given credit for in his brief 2013 major-league debut. He's unlikely to crack the Orioles rotation out of Spring Training, but it wouldn't be shocking if he were their best pitcher by year's end.

## 16. Yordano Ventura, RHP, Kansas City Royals
*Age: 22, Previous Rank: 75*

**Potential Earnings:** $20-25

**Risk Factor:** Low

**Fantasy Overview:** Four-category contributor; impact potential in K

**Realistic Ceiling:** A top-20 fantasy starter

**Realistic Floor:** Kelvin Herrera

A contender for Rookie of the Year honors in the American League this season, Ventura's heat added some spice to the end of the Royals' 2013 season. He may struggle to throw 200-plus innings, but the rate stats have the potential to be high end.

## 17. Lucas Giolito, RHP, Washington Nationals
*Age: 19, Previous Rank: 62*

**Potential Earnings:** $30-35

**Risk Factor:** High

**Fantasy Overview:** Four-category contributor; impact potential in W, K, ERA, WHIP

**Realistic Ceiling:** The best fantasy starter in baseball

**Realistic Floor:** You mean there's another option here?

There's been no shortage of Giolito love this offseason after he showed his preinjury raw stuff in the minors—it's top of the pops. But don't lose sight of how much risk is still here. If he had just pitched in Double-A, he'd be right up there with the big four.

## 18. Dylan Bundy, RHP, Baltimore Orioles
*Age: 21, Previous Rank: 7*

**Potential Earnings:** $25-30

**Risk Factor:** Medium

**Fantasy Overview:** Four-category contributor; impact potential in W, K, ERA, WHIP

**Realistic Ceiling:** Fantasy ace

**Realistic Floor:** The good Edwin Jackson

While Cory Luebke, Ryan Madson, and Daniel Hudson have reminded us that Tommy John surgery is no sure thing, Bundy will look to be back on the mound this summer and could make a fantasy impact even in a relief role this season, if the Orioles let him.

## 19. Clint Frazier, OF, Cleveland Indians
*Age: 19, Previous Rank: NR*

**Potential Earnings:** $35+

**Risk Factor:** Extreme

**Fantasy Overview:** Five-category contributor; impact potential in HR, RBI, R

**Realistic Ceiling:** Perennial first-round pick

**Realistic Floor:** Jeff Francoeur with red hair

If fantasy upside is what you seek, Frazier is where you need to go. Armed with bat speed that could seriously injure a water buffalo, he has the raw tools to be a fantasy superstar. He could be the one who forces teams to change their stance on drafting redheads.

## 20. Jonathan Gray, RHP, Colorado Rockies
*Age: 22, Previous Rank: NR*

**Potential Earnings:** $25-30

**Risk Factor:** Medium

**Fantasy Overview:** Four-category contributor; impact potential in W, K

**Realistic Ceiling:** A fantasy ace despite Coors

**Realistic Floor:** A shallow league streamer on the road

There are less than one handful of arms on this list with higher ultimate fantasy upside than Gray, and that's despite him pitching half his games at altitude. Don't be surprised if he moves very quickly and sees action in Denver before rosters expand in 2014.

## 21. Jameson Taillon, RHP, Pittsburgh Pirates
*Age: 22, Previous Rank: 15*

**Potential Earnings:** $20-25

**Risk Factor:** Low

**Fantasy Overview:** Four-category contributor; impact potential in W, ERA

**Realistic Ceiling:** A solid no. 2 fantasy starter

**Realistic Floor:** A great no. 4 fantasy starter

Taillon gets lost in the shuffle behind the present dream of Gerrit Cole and the future dream of Tyler Glasnow, but that's ridiculous. He'll set out to prove this to be comical in Pittsburgh as soon as May or June 2014.

## 22. Nick Castellanos, 3B, Detroit Tigers
*Age: 22, Previous Rank: 19*

**Potential Earnings:** $35+

**Risk Factor:** Low

**Fantasy Overview:** Four-category contributor; impact potential in AVG

**Realistic Ceiling:** The good version of Pablo Sandoval

**Realistic Floor:** A near-replacement-level outfielder in shallow leagues

The Prince Fielder-for-Ian Kinsler swap gave Castellanos the clear inside track to playing time in Detroit until he proves he doesn't deserve it. The batting-gloveless wonder will have an adjustment period in 2014, but can hit right through it.

## 23. Robert Stephenson, RHP, Cincinnati Reds
*Age: 21, Previous Rank: 77*

**Potential Earnings:** $25-30

**Risk Factor:** Medium

**Fantasy Overview:** Four-category contributor; impact potential in K

**Realistic Ceiling:** Homer Bailey

**Realistic Floor:** A more athletic Wily Peralta

Cheese is delicious, but cheese alone does not make a meal. The Reds flamethrower has work ahead of him to satisfy those counting on him upon his arrival in the Queen City—the triple-digit heat will get him in the door, but won't unlock the key to fantasy stardom.

## 24. Travis d'Arnaud, C, New York Mets
*Age: 25, Previous Rank: 12*

**Potential Earnings:** $20-25

**Risk Factor:** Low

**Fantasy Overview:** Four-category contributor

**Realistic Ceiling:** Brian McCann with a little less average

**Realistic Floor:** The Chris Snelling of catchers

The offensive environments d'Arnaud has frequented in his march up the minor league ranks may overstate his case at the plate slightly, but the power is real and will show up in games if

he stops showing up in the trainer's office.

## 25. Kyle Zimmer, RHP, Kansas City Royals
*Age: 22, Previous Rank: 47*

**Potential Earnings:** $25-30

**Risk Factor:** Medium

**Fantasy Overview:** Four-category contributor; impact potential in K, ERA, WHIP

**Realistic Ceiling:** 90 percent of a healthy Ben Sheets

**Realistic Floor:** A solid back-end fantasy starter

Common sense states that Zimmer will be helped pitching in Kauffman Stadium, but then again, he spent the first couple of months in 2013 getting knocked around in Wilmington—one of the ultimate minor-league pitchers' parks.

## 26. Mark Appel, RHP, Houston Astros
*Age: 22, Previous Rank: NR*

**Potential Earnings:** $20-25

**Risk Factor:** Low

**Fantasy Overview:** Four-category contributor; impact potential in W, WHIP

**Realistic Ceiling:** A consistent top-25 starter

**Realistic Floor:** A consistent top-40 starter

The fantasy ceiling usually associated with a 1-1 pick in the draft isn't quite there with Appel, as he's unlikely to find a home as a fantasy ace. However, in deeper leagues his value shoots up due to his floor—which is as high as that of any other arm on this list.

## 27. Jorge Alfaro, C, Texas Rangers
*Age: 20, Previous Rank: 99*

**Potential Earnings:** $30-35

**Risk Factor:** High

**Fantasy Overview:** Four-category contributor; impact potential in HR, RBI

**Realistic Ceiling:** The best fantasy catcher in two decades

**Realistic Floor:** A high-end AL-only backup catcher

It's tough to overstate the ceiling in play here, as Alfaro could be a 30-homer, middle-of-the-lineup hitter, also capable of stealing double-digit bags. Unfortunately, it's also tough to overstate the risk, as he just may never hit enough for it to matter.

## 28. Jonathan Singleton, 1B, Houston Astros
*Age: 22, Previous Rank: 22*

**Potential Earnings:** $20-25

**Risk Factor:** Low

**Fantasy Overview:** Three-category contributor; impact potential in HR, RBI

**Realistic Ceiling:** The guy people think Anthony Rizzo will be

**Realistic Floor:** The guy Anthony Rizzo is now

If you believe in either second chances of the legalization of marijuana, Singleton is your kind of guy. He was bad, out of shape, and suspended for portions of the 2013 season, but still carries plenty of upside as a power prospect—and showed it off in winter ball.

## 29. Carlos Martinez, RHP, St. Louis Cardinals
*Age: 22, Previous Rank: 33*

**Potential Earnings:** $20-25

**Risk Factor:** Low

**Fantasy Overview:** Four-category contributor; impact potential in K, ERA

**Realistic Ceiling:** A waaaaay shorter Shelby Miller

**Realistic Floor:** Himself from the 2013 post-season

There's a real risk with Martinez that, despite the opportunity he should get in the rotation, the combination of organizational depth and his sheer awesomeness coming out of the bullpen will keep him there for good. This would deprive fans everywhere.

### 30. Marcus Stroman, RHP, Toronto Blue Jays
*Age: 22, Previous Rank: NR*

**Potential Earnings:** $20-25

**Risk Factor:** Low

**Fantasy Overview:** Four-category contributor; impact potential in K, WHIP

**Realistic Ceiling:** A no. 3 fantasy starter

**Realistic Floor:** A top-10 fantasy closer

Martinez gets the nod over Stroman because he's done it on the big stage, but they both have excellent stuff. He'll get opportunities north of the border, but if he doesn't make the most of them, he could get put back into the reliever box quickly.

### 31. Chris Owings, SS, Arizona Diamondbacks
*Age: 22, Previous Rank: NR*

**Potential Earnings:** $20-25

**Risk Factor:** Low

**Fantasy Overview:** Five-category contributor

**Realistic Ceiling:** A poor man's Ian Desmond

**Realistic Floor:** A poor man's Danny Espinosa (it's not as bad as it sounds!)

Owings will have that pesky Didi Gregorius And Kevin Towers, by extension) in the way of his playing time for 2014, but the job should be his before long. He can do a little of everything, which goes a long way when a player is shortstop eligible.

### 32. Joc Pederson, OF, Los Angeles Dodgers
*Age: 21, Previous Rank: NR*

**Potential Earnings:** $25-30

**Risk Factor:** Medium

**Fantasy Overview:** Five-category contributor

**Realistic Ceiling:** A 20/20 outfielder

**Realistic Floor:** A 15/15 outfielder

Pederson has the unfortunate (if you can call it that) luck of being known as a gritty gaming gamer who knows how to play the game the right way and maximizes his tools. It's unfortunate because it overshadows his actual tools, which are very real (including his surprising power).

### 33. Francisco Lindor, SS, Cleveland Indians
*Age: 20, Previous Rank: 59*

**Potential Earnings:** $20-25

**Risk Factor:** Low

**Fantasy Overview:** Four-category contributor; Impact potential in AVG

**Realistic Ceiling:** Jean Segura with a 25-steal governor

**Realistic Floor:** Jean Segura with a 25-steal governor

Yes, that is done to make a point. Lindor may not have extreme ceiling in fantasy (unlike he does in real life with that defense),

but he's this high on the list because he is a very safe pick. He'll hit enough, have enough pop, and steal some bases.

### 34. Andrew Heaney, LHP, Miami Marlins
*Age: 22, Previous Rank: NR*

**Potential Earnings:** $20-25

**Risk Factor:** Low

**Fantasy Overview:** Four-category contributor; impact potential in W, ERA

**Realistic Ceiling:** Mike Minor in a better ballpark

**Realistic Floor:** Jonathan Niese

Being caught between an organization no one pays attention to and a younger/better pitcher in Jose Fernandez helps Heaney fly under the radar in South Florida. However, expect him to flash brightly in air traffic control booths as soon as June of this year.

### 35. Maikel Franco, 3B/1B, Philadelphia Phillies
*Age: 21, Previous Rank: NR*

**Potential Earnings:** $20-25

**Risk Factor:** Medium

**Fantasy Overview:** Four-category contributor; impact potential in RBI

**Realistic Ceiling:** A 25-homer third baseman

**Realistic Floor:** A very vanilla first baseman

The fact that the Phillies are starting to get him some action at first base in 2014 doesn't mean he's doomed to a fantasy life of poor eligibility. His high-contact approach for a potential power source, combined with a future in a park very friendly to right-handed hitters, is attractive.

### 36. Corey Seager, 3B/SS, Los Angeles Dodgers
*Age: 19, Previous Rank: 88*

**Potential Earnings:** $20-25

**Risk Factor:** Medium

**Fantasy Overview:** Four-category contributor

**Realistic Ceiling:** Josh Donaldson

**Realistic Floor:** A slightly worse version of his brother

There is potential in both the average and power departments with Seager, but how much depends on whose eyes he is being viewed through. Still more safety than ceiling at this point, he will fit in nicely at a weak position in Los Angeles.

### 37. David Dahl, OF, Colorado Rockies
*Age: 20, Previous Rank: 45*

**Potential Earnings:** $30-35

**Risk Factor:** Extreme

**Fantasy Overview:** Five-category contributor; impact potential in AVG, R, SB

**Realistic Ceiling:** Prime Shane Victorino in Coors

**Realistic Floor:** Current Shane Victorino at peak

It's not very common for a player to miss nearly a whole season and move up in these rankings, but with great reports about his makeup and work ethic, Dahl may be more likely to reach his lofty ceiling than originally anticipated.

### 38. Matthew Wisler, RHP, San Diego Padres
*Age: 21, Previous Rank: NR*

**Potential Earnings:** $15-20

**Risk Factor:** Low

**Fantasy Overview:** Four-category contributor

**Realistic Ceiling:** A very good no. 3 fantasy starter

**Realistic Floor:** A very good no. 5 fantasy starter

Wisler ranks high here because he's close and San Diego is a wonderful place to ~~live~~ pitch. He should be a very popular name in deep leagues as, while he won't have huge impact on any one category, he'll help in all four.

## 39. Dan Vogelbach, 1B, Chicago Cubs
*Age: 21, Previous Rank: 67*

**Potential Earnings:** $25-30

**Risk Factor:** High

**Fantasy Overview:** Four-category contributor; impact potential in AVG, HR, RBI, R

**Realistic Ceiling:** Prince Fielder with less power

**Realistic Floor:** Billy Butler with less average

Vogelbach is the first name on the Fantasy 101 that does not show up on Jason's Top 101, and for good reason—he can't play the field. For better or worse, we don't care about that. We care that it's always autumn in Vogelbach's world, since there will be a lot of raking in his future.

## 40. Max Fried, LHP, San Diego Padres
*Age: 20, Previous Rank: 42*

**Potential Earnings:** $25-30

**Risk Factor:** High

**Fantasy Overview:** Four-category contributor; impact potential in W, K, ERA, WHIP

**Realistic Ceiling:** A back-end fantasy ace

**Realistic Floor:** A back-end fantasy starter

Even with a year that looked deceptively pedestrian on a statistical level, Fried still maintains some of the highest upside in the minor leagues in that left arm of his. However, someone needs to hide him from the UCL Boogeyman in San Diego.

## 41. Eddie Butler, RHP, Colorado Rockies
*Age: 23, Previous Rank: NR*

**Potential Earnings:** $20-25

**Risk Factor:** Medium

**Fantasy Overview:** Four-category contributor; impact potential in K

**Realistic Ceiling:** A top-25 fantasy starter despite Coors

**Realistic Floor:** Just another guy keeping Rex Brothers from getting saves

In a context-neutral setting, Butler probably deserves to be 5-10 spots higher, but Coors is Coors, and it remains a force to be reckoned with. If he's a starter, he should be good. If he's a reliever, he should be great.

## 42. Alex Meyer, RHP, Minnesota Twins
*Age: 24, Previous Rank: 82*

**Potential Earnings:** $20-25

**Risk Factor:** Medium

**Fantasy Overview:** Three-category contributor; impact potential in K

**Realistic Ceiling:** A 200-strikeout starter

**Realistic Floor:** A gentler Kyle Farnsworth

There's a wide range of outcomes with Meyer because, despite the strides he's made in the last two years, it's anything but a

lock that he'll stick in the rotation long term. Don't lose patience with him though—sometimes it just takes super tall guys longer.

## 43. Arismendy Alcantara, 2B/SS, Chicago Cubs
*Age: 22, Previous Rank: NR*

**Potential Earnings:** $20-25

**Risk Factor:** Medium

**Fantasy Overview:** Four-category contributor; impact potential in SB

**Realistic Ceiling:** A more fun-to-pronounce Jason Kipnis

**Realistic Floor:** A replacement-level middle infielder in shallow leagues

There's plenty of excitement in the range of tools here—especially with Alcantara's speed—but the ability to hit for average and power is still up in the air. Without help in those categories, he becomes a decent steals guy, but not much else.

## 44. Rougned Odor, 2B, Texas Rangers
*Age: 20, Previous Rank: NR*

**Potential Earnings:** $15-20

**Risk Factor:** Low

**Fantasy Overview:** Five-category contributor

**Realistic Ceiling:** Martin Prado with double-digit steals

**Realistic Floor:** Omar Infante with a killer name

The Odor/Alcantara debate was one that raged from the zygote stage of this list. In the end, it just depends on league size. In a deeper league, Odor is the better play, but in a shallower format, Alcantara has the requisite upside.

## 45. Julio Urias, LHP, Los Angeles Dodgers
*Age: 17, Previous Rank: NR*

**Potential Earnings:** $25-30

**Risk Factor:** High

**Fantasy Overview:** Four-category contributor; impact potential in W, ERA, WHIP

**Realistic Ceiling:** Doogie Howser, M.D.

**Realistic Floor:** Drew Barrymore

When someone has success at such a young age, it's tough to gauge how high his star can rise. For all of his press And deservedly so), Urias benefited from not having to turn over a lineup often in 2013. He could take a step forward and be great, or begin his descent into darkness.

## 46. Jorge Soler, OF, Chicago Cubs
*Age: 22, Previous Rank: 28*

**Potential Earnings:** $25-30

**Risk Factor:** High

**Fantasy Overview:** Four-category contributor; impact potential in HR, RBI

**Realistic Ceiling:** Ninety percent of Jay Bruce

**Realistic Floor:** Ninety percent of Ryan Ludwick

The power potential is there, and it is tempting, but Soler is going to have to show that he can stay healthy and tap into that power the way someone with his thunder is intended to. He may not have the fantasy pull of Baez or Bryant, but that's not his fault.

## 47. Tyler Glasnow, RHP, Pittsburgh Pirates
*Age: 20, Previous Rank: NR*

**Potential Earnings:** $25-30

**Risk Factor:** High

**Fantasy Overview:** Four-category contributor; impact potential in W, K, ERA

**Realistic Ceiling:** High-strikeout no. 2 fantasy starter

**Realistic Floor:** Inconsistent starter who frustrates the heck out of you

On the one hand, Glasnow gets less attention in fantasy leagues because everyone is busy losing their minds over Giolito. On the other, his strikeout numbers were ridiculous (164 in 111 1/3 innings). Where there's smoke, there's fire.

## 48. Kohl Stewart, RHP, Minnesota Twins
*Age: 19, Previous Rank: NR*

**Potential Earnings:** $25-30

**Risk Factor:** High

**Fantasy Overview:** Four-category contributor; impact potential in W, K, ERA

**Realistic Ceiling:** A top-20 fantasy starter

**Realistic Floor:** Good streaming starter at Target Field

The best prep pitcher in the 2013 draft, Stewart was taken by the Twins despite his ability to miss bats. As long as they don't try to get him to stop doing that, he could be a fantasy force in another three or four years.

## 49. Kolten Wong, 2B, St. Louis Cardinals
*Age: 23, Previous Rank: 65*

**Potential Earnings:** $15-20

**Risk Factor:** Low

**Fantasy Overview:** Four-category contributor

**Realistic Ceiling:** The best of Daniel Murphy

**Realistic Floor:** The worst of Daniel Murphy

What's a fantasy prospects list without invoking Charles Dickens? Wong is going to play now in St. Louis, and he has enough all-around skill to warrant ownership in all leagues right away (though he's more of a middle-of-the-road middle infield option in shallow formats). But will the Cards let him run?

## 50. Gary Sanchez, C, New York Yankees
*Age: 21, Previous Rank: 44*

**Potential Earnings:** $20-25

**Risk Factor:** Medium

**Fantasy Overview:** Three-category contributor

**Realistic Ceiling:** Wilson Ramos with health

**Realistic Floor:** A low-end first baseman

How highly Sanchez is valued is directly proportional to how likely he is to stay behind the plate. This story is just one of the many reasons catching prospects in dynasty leagues are highly volatile propositions—many trapdoors to fall through.

## 51. Aaron Sanchez, RHP, Toronto Blue Jays
*Age: 21, Previous Rank: 41*

**Potential Earnings:** $25-30

**Risk Factor:** High

**Fantasy Overview:** Three-category contributor; impact potential in K, ERA

**Realistic Ceiling:** The good version of Francisco Liriano

**Realistic Floor:** The bad version of Francisco Liriano

If Sanchez could consistently figure out where the ball was going, he'd likely be a top-25 prospect—his raw stuff would certainly support it. Even if he "makes it" and misses bats at the major league level, he still might be a drag on your WHIP.

## 52. Garin Cecchini, 3B, Boston Red Sox
*Age: 22, Previous Rank: NR*

**Potential Earnings:** $20-25

**Risk Factor:** Medium

**Fantasy Overview:** Four-category contributor

**Realistic Ceiling:** A slightly better Martin Prado

**Realistic Floor:** A slightly worse Nick Markakis

Cecchini will be one of those guys who gets underrated in fantasy because he doesn't do the sexy things all that well. He has the curse of being a strongest play in batting average and runs scored.

## 53. Kyle Crick, RHP, San Francisco Giants
*Age: 21, Previous Rank: 83*

**Potential Earnings:** $35+

**Risk Factor:** Low

**Fantasy Overview:** Three-category contributor; Impact potential in K, ERA

**Realistic Ceiling:** A top-20 starter, despite his WHIP

**Realistic Floor:** The good version of Carlos Marmol

See Sanchez, Aaron. As you can tell by my dropping of the M word above, Crick is also in serious need of stuff harnessing. If he can put the whole package together, he's a pitcher you build a fantasy staff around.

## 54. Raimel Tapia, OF, Colorado Rockies
*Age: 20, Previous Rank: NR*

**Potential Earnings:** $30-35

**Risk Factor:** Extreme

**Fantasy Overview:** Five-category contributor; Impact potential in R, RBI

**Realistic Ceiling:** Carlos Gonzalez

**Realistic Floor:** A bottomless pit

The first real high-payout lottery ticket here, Tapia has all of the requisite tools to be a future fantasy stud, including the most optimal home park known to man.

## 55. Henry Owens, LHP, Boston Red Sox
*Age: 21, Previous Rank: NR*

**Potential Earnings:** $20-25

**Risk Factor:** Medium

**Fantasy Overview:** Four-category contributor; Impact potential in W

**Realistic Ceiling:** The non-elite version of Jon Lester

**Realistic Floor:** A good back-end fantasy starter

It seems strange that a Red Sox prospect may actually be underrated, but I guess the shadow of Xander Bogaerts extends to somewhere south of Hartford. Which is amusing because that's only slightly smaller of a shadow than Owens himself has.

## 56. Miguel Almonte, RHP, Kansas City Royals
*Age: 20, Previous Rank: NR*

**Potential Earnings:** $20-25

**Risk Factor:** Medium

**Fantasy Overview:** Four-category contributor; Impact potential in ERA, WHIP

**Realistic Ceiling:** A solid no. 3 fantasy starter

**Realistic Floor:** Dillon Gee

The changeup is awe-inspiring, and Kauffman Stadium will be a nice place to call home. But unless the breaking ball maxes out its projection, he's probably never going to be a huge strikeout guy.

### 57. Albert Almora, OF, Chicago Cubs
*Age: 19, Previous Rank: 81*

**Potential Earnings:** $20-25

**Risk Factor:** Medium

**Fantasy Overview:** Four-category contributor

**Realistic Ceiling:** Andre Ethier

**Realistic Floor:** Lorenzo Cain, complete with injuries

The big question with Almora is how much power he'll have, but don't assume that because he projects to be a very good defensive center fielder, he will be able to help you on the basepaths. He's not that type of runner.

### 58. Dominic Smith, 1B, New York Mets
*Age: 18, Previous Rank: NR*

**Potential Earnings:** $20-25

**Risk Factor:** Medium

**Fantasy Overview:** Four-category contributor; impact potential in AVG

**Realistic Ceiling:** Billy Butler with first-base eligibility

**Realistic Floor:** James Loney, after we all accepted who James Loney was

Smith is a much more interesting fantasy proposition than real-life one. Most evaluators agree that he will hit for average wherever he is, but whether he has 15 or 25 homers with it will go a long way toward determining his future value.

### 59. James Paxton, LHP, Seattle Mariners
*Age: 25, Previous Rank: 70*

**Potential Earnings:** $15-20

**Risk Factor:** Low

**Fantasy Overview:** Three-category contributor; impact potential in K

**Realistic Ceiling:** Matt Moore if he never breaks out

**Realistic Floor:** Rex Brothers

Paxton was more or less a forgotten man before putting an exclamation point on his season in September with the big club. He'll have an uphill battle to post a helpful WHIP, but has upside everywhere else.

### 60. Mookie Betts, 2B, Boston Red Sox
*Age: 21, Previous Rank: NR*

**Potential Earnings:** $20-25

**Risk Factor:** Medium

**Fantasy Overview:** Three-category contributor

**Realistic Ceiling:** A borderline top-five second baseman

**Realistic Floor:** A part-time player who is still pretty valuable in deeper leagues

Despite the impressive numbers in 2013, the jury is still out on just how valuable Betts will be in the batting average and power categories. Plus, he's blocked for the foreseeable future in Boston—which possibly pushes back his ETA.

### 61. Tim Anderson, SS, Chicago White Sox
*Age: 20, Previous Rank: NR*

**Potential Earnings:** $25-30

**Risk Factor:** High

**Fantasy Overview:** Five-category contribution; impact potential in SB

**Realistic Ceiling:** Ian Desmond with more speed

**Realistic Floor:** A fourth outfielder

The range of outcomes is very wide with Anderson, but the tool set is enticing and U.S. Cellular would be a great place to draw some extra power out of his bat. He becomes even more delectable in shallower leagues, where upside is king.

### 62. Lucas Sims, RHP, Atlanta Braves
*Age: 19, Previous Rank: NR*

**Potential Earnings:** $20-25

**Risk Factor:** Medium

**Fantasy Overview:** Four-category contributor; impact potential in K

**Realistic Ceiling:** A pre-Tommy John Brandon Beachy

**Realistic Floor:** A valuable middle reliever

There's plenty to like about Sims, from the athleticism to the development of the change. However, he's got a ways to go to prove that he can pitch a lot of innings in a rotation.

### 63. Alen Hanson, 2B, Pittsburgh Pirates
*Age: 21, Previous Rank: 39*

**Potential Earnings:** $20-25

**Risk Factor:** Medium

**Fantasy Overview:** Five-category contributor

**Realistic Ceiling:** A slightly better Howie Kendrick

**Realistic Floor:** A low-end middle-infield option

It was difficult not to mention Hanson and Gregory Polanco in the same sentence last year after they both broke out in Low-A, but if you took Hanson first between the two in your 2013 draft, you're probably regretting that right about now.

### 64. Sean Manaea, LHP, Kansas City Royals
*Age: 22, Previous Rank: NR*

**Potential Earnings:** $25-30

**Risk Factor:** High

**Fantasy Overview:** Four-category contributor; impact potential in W, K, ERA, WHIP

**Realistic Ceiling:** A top-20 starting pitcher

**Realistic Floor:** A Kyle Gibson-esque journey

The hip injury clouds his potential value, but all signs point to him being strong and healthy heading into 2014. If that is the case, the owners who took a shot on him in their dynasty drafts will be well rewarded.

### 65. Hunter Harvey, RHP, Baltimore Orioles
*Age: 19, Previous Rank: NR*

**Potential Earnings:** $25-30

**Risk Factor:** High

**Fantasy Overview:** Four-category contributor; Impact potential in W, K, WHIP

**Realistic Ceiling:** A top-20 fantasy starter

**Realistic Floor:** Chris Tillman before he turned his career around
One of the big risers after the 2013 draft was in the books, Harvey has gained enough steam that he should be taken in the first round of most dynasty drafts.

## 66. Jake Marisnick, OF, Miami Marlins
*Age: 23, Previous Rank: 61*

**Potential Earnings:** $20-25

**Risk Factor:** Medium

**Fantasy Overview:** Four-category contributor
Realistic Ceiling: Alex Gordon with fewer runs scored
Realistic Floor: A poor man's Will Venable
While he may not be as revered as he was a year or two ago, forget about Marisnick at your own risk. He still carries enough talent to turn himself into an everyday outfielder in all leagues.

## 67. D.J. Peterson, 3B, Seattle Mariners
*Age: 22, Previous Rank: NR*

**Potential Earnings:** $20-25

**Risk Factor:** Medium

**Fantasy Overview:** Four-category contributor

**Realistic Ceiling:** Ryan Zimmerman in Safeco

**Realistic Floor:** A fringy fantasy first baseman
It may not be as tough to be a right-handed hitting prospect in Seattle as it used to be, but it's still not the friendliest assignment. Peterson could have a long career of strong park-adjusted stats ahead of him (which doesn't help for fantasy).

## 68. Braden Shipley, RHP, Arizona Diamondbacks
*Age: 22, Previous Rank: NR*

**Potential Earnings:** $25-30

**Risk Factor:** High

**Fantasy Overview:** Four-category contributor; impact potential in W, K

**Realistic Ceiling:** Solid no. 2 fantasy starter

**Realistic Floor:** An inconsistent swingman with flashes
Even if he doesn't live up to his lofty potential, the odds are still pretty good that Shipley will end his career with the highest WARP of any pitcher named Braden—this distinction now belongs to Braden Looper at 5.3 WARP.

## 69. Brian Goodwin, OF, Washington Nationals
*Age: 23, Previous Rank: 34*

**Potential Earnings:** $20-25

**Risk Factor:** Medium

**Fantasy Overview:** Five-category contributor

**Realistic Ceiling:** Shin-Soo Choo with less average/OBP

**Realistic Floor:** 80 percent of Denard Span
Hidden within the not overly impressive statistics is a near 20/20 player waiting to come out. Of course, if that were more certain to come out of Goodwin, he wouldn't have taken a 35-spot tumble from last year's list.

## 70. Michael Choice, OF, Texas Rangers
*Age: 24, Previous Rank: 89*

**Potential Earnings:** $15-20

**Risk Factor:** Low

**Fantasy Overview:** Three-category contributor

**Realistic Ceiling:** A good-enough no. 3 outfielder

**Realistic Floor:** A not-good-enough no. 4 outfielder
Choice was likely bumped from a starting spot to begin the 2014 season once Shin-Soo Choo and his glorious hair came to town. However, he can overtake Mitch Moreland for the DH spot during the season if he shows some of that power.

## 71. Mike Foltynewicz, RHP, Houston Astros
*Age: 22, Previous Rank: NR*

**Potential Earnings:** $20-25

**Risk Factor:** Medium

**Fantasy Overview:** Four-category contributor; impact potential in ERA

**Realistic Ceiling:** A good no. 4 fantasy starter

**Realistic Floor:** A very valuable middle reliever
The fastball is great, but if the breaking ball doesn't come around a little more, this is looking more and more like an eventual bullpen future. He could be great in that role, but that's not what you want in fantasy.

## 72. Mason Williams, OF, New York Yankees
*Age: 22, Previous Rank: 53*

**Potential Earnings:** $25-30

**Risk Factor:** High

**Fantasy Overview:** Five-category contributor; impact potential in SB

**Realistic Ceiling:** Brett Gardner with 15-homer power

**Realistic Floor:** A victim of his own makeup
The problem with Williams has never been his tools, it's been his ability to develop them as he moves up the developmental ladder. If Williams had Joc Pederson's #want, he'd be a top-25 prospect on this list.

## 73. Delino DeShields Jr., OF, Houston Astros
*Age: 21, Previous Rank: 27*

**Potential Earnings:** $25-30

**Risk Factor:** High

**Fantasy Overview:** Three-category contributor; Impact potential in R, SB

**Realistic Ceiling:** A 60+ steal monster

**Realistic Floor:** A player who gets way too many second chances in dynasty leagues
It's either coincidence or fate that Williams and DeShields are back-to-back here. The bigger issues with the embattled Astro are that he is moving down the defensive spectrum and that he plays like he reads too many of his own press clippings.

## 74. Hunter Renfroe, OF, San Diego Padres
*Age: 22, Previous Rank: NR*

**Potential Earnings:** $25-30

**Risk Factor:** High

**Fantasy Overview:** Four-category contributor; impact potential in HR, RBI

**Realistic Ceiling:** A healthy Carlos Quentin with speed

**Realistic Floor:** The bad version of Colby Rasmus
It's not as tough to be a power hitter in Petco as it used to be, but it's still not an ideal venue for the skill set. Fortunately, Renfroe can also contribute on the basepaths, leaving him with a second way to add value.

### 75. Matt Davidson, 3B, Chicago White Sox
*Age: 23, Previous Rank: 66*

**Potential Earnings:** $15-20

**Risk Factor:** Low

**Fantasy Overview:** Three-category contributor

**Realistic Ceiling:** A back-end top-10 third baseman

**Realistic Floor:** Joe Crede without the outlier 2006 season

It's tough to pull off an upgrade in home park when you're already staring Chase Field in the face, but Davidson did it. And if U.S. Cellular can't draw out his power, no park can.

### 76. Jackie Bradley Jr., OF, Boston Red Sox
*Age: 23, Previous Rank: 80*

**Potential Earnings:** $10-15

**Risk Factor:** Low

**Fantasy Overview:** Two-category contributor; impact potential in R

**Realistic Ceiling:** Daniel Nava with a few more steals

**Realistic Floor:** Daniel Nava with a few more steals

Bradley is as safe of a prospect as there is on this list, but that doesn't make him all that interesting long-term. He'll get on base and score a lot of runs if he is at the top of the Boston lineup, but don't expect much firepower in the glory stats.

### 77. Eduardo Rodriguez, LHP, Baltimore Orioles
*Age: 20, Previous Rank: NR*

**Potential Earnings:** $10-15

**Risk Factor:** Low

**Fantasy Overview:** Three-category contributor

**Realistic Ceiling:** A solid no. 5 fantasy starter

**Realistic Floor:** A solid no. 6 fantasy starter

Rodriguez is kind of like the pitching equivalent of Jackie Bradley—he doesn't offer much upside anywhere, but he should be good enough to stick on your roster for a long time.

### 78. C.J. Edwards, RHP, Chicago Cubs
*Age: 22, Previous Rank: NR*

**Potential Earnings:** $20-25

**Risk Factor:** High

**Fantasy Overview:** Four-category contributor; impact potential in ERA

**Realistic Ceiling:** A top-25 starting pitcher

**Realistic Floor:** A high-strikeout reliever

Edwards is going to look slighted here, especially when compared with some of his other small-statured brethren, but I have a lot less confidence in his ability to stick in the rotation than guys like Ventura, Martinez, and Stroman.

### 79. Eddie Rosario, 2B/OF, Minnesota Twins
*Age: 22, Previous Rank: 54*

**Potential Earnings:** $15-20

**Risk Factor:** Medium

**Fantasy Overview:** Four-category contributor

**Realistic Ceiling:** The current version of Brandon Phillips

**Realistic Floor:** Dexter Fowler without Coors

The suspension hurts in the short term, as he could have gotten to the major-league level in 2014 with another strong showing in the upper minors, but Rosario can hit. Someone has to stop him

from (or teach him the art of) running, though, as he's 21-for-42 over the last two years.

### 80. Rymer Liriano, OF, San Diego Padres
*Age: 22, Previous Rank: 56*

**Potential Earnings:** $20-25

**Risk Factor:** High

**Fantasy Overview:** Four-category contributor

**Realistic Ceiling:** The player we thought Cameron Maybin would be

**Realistic Floor:** The player Cameron Maybin is

The lost season hurt Liriano more than it would have hurt a more polished prospect, as he really needed the reps. However, the power/speed combo is still there in spades, and his injury should not have any lingering affect on either tool.

### 81. J.P. Crawford, SS, Philadelphia Phillies
*Age: 19, Previous Rank: NR*

**Potential Earnings:** $20-25

**Risk Factor:** High

**Fantasy Overview:** Five-category contributor

**Realistic Ceiling:** Not Jimmy Rollins

**Realistic Floor:** Yunel Escobar with more speed and fewer bad life decisions

Crawford may show up as high risk here, but he's on the shallower end of that pool because of his advanced approach and likeliness to stick at shortstop. He may end up even better in OBP leagues.

### 82. Josh Bell, OF, Pittsburgh Pirates
*Age: 21, Previous Rank: 98*

**Potential Earnings:** $20-25

**Risk Factor:** High

**Fantasy Overview:** Four-category contributor

**Realistic Ceiling:** Domonic Brown, if you're a believer

**Realistic Floor:** Matt Joyce

Coming off a lost season, Bell looks to reclaim the trajectory that was taking him toward the middle of the Pirates' lineup. The $5 million man makes for a nice trade target before the real games start.

### 83. Joey Gallo, 3B, Texas Rangers
*Age: 20, Previous Rank: NR*

**Potential Earnings:** $25-30

**Risk Factor:** Extreme

**Fantasy Overview:** Three-category contributor; impact potential in HR, RBI, R

**Realistic Ceiling:** Adam Dunn at third base with less OBP

**Realistic Floor:** Not a major leaguer

There's so much swing-and-miss in Gallo's game right now that it could provide enough wind power for the eastern half of the United States while he toils and hammers in Hickory and Myrtle Beach. Texas, you're up next.

### 84. Austin Meadows, OF, Pittsburgh Pirates
*Age: 18, Previous Rank: NR*

**Potential Earnings:** $20-25

**Risk Factor:** High

**Fantasy Overview:** Four-category contributor

**Realistic Ceiling:** Alex Gordon

**Realistic Floor:** The disappointing version of Austin Jackson
Everyone was happy and children were smiling until someone decided to drop a casual Mike Trout reference in regards to Meadows. Then a storm circled the village as the elders shouted, "There are no casual Mike Trout references!"

### 85. Alex "Chi Chi" Gonzalez, RHP, Texas Rangers
*Age: 22, Previous Rank: NR*

**Potential Earnings:** $15-20

**Risk Factor:** Medium

**Fantasy Overview:** Four-category contributor; impact potential in W

**Realistic Ceiling:** Our dream version of Ricky Nolasco

**Realistic Floor:** Kyle Lohse
The advanced right-hander should be on the fast track to making an impact in Texas, where his ability to keep the ball on the ground will help limit the damage of his surroundings.

### 86. Stephen Piscotty, OF, St. Louis Cardinals
*Age: 23, Previous Rank: NR*

**Potential Earnings:** $15-20

**Risk Factor:** Medium

**Fantasy Overview:** Four-category contributor; impact potential in AVG

**Realistic Ceiling:** A slightly lesser Allen Craig

**Realistic Floor:** Michael Brantley without the speed
Piscotty is exactly what you expect out of a Cardinals prospect these days. Somewhere deep in St. Louis there is a tree that grows .300 hitters, but it's too close to the shade for defensive value to sprout.

### 87. Jonathan Schoop, 2B/3B, Baltimore Orioles
*Age: 22, Previous Rank: 73*

**Potential Earnings:** $10-15

**Risk Factor:** Low

**Fantasy Overview:** Three-category contributor

**Realistic Ceiling:** The best of Neil Walker

**Realistic Floor:** A waiver-wire-dwelling third baseman
The Orioles have a Schoop-sized hole in their lineup at second base, which is awfully convenient for the honkbal enthusiast. Average pop should be there at the major-league level, but how much average and speed flank it will determine his value.

### 88. Raul A. Mondesi, SS, Kansas City Royals
*Age: 18, Previous Rank: 76*

**Potential Earnings:** $20-25

**Risk Factor:** High

**Fantasy Overview:** Five-category contributor

**Realistic Ceiling:** A top-five fantasy shortstop

**Realistic Floor:** A good defender
We're still a while away from finding out what the #SORBOR (Son of Raul, Brother of Raul) is from a fantasy perspective, but there are multiple roads to very good value embedded in his skill set.

### 89. A.J. Cole, RHP, Washington Nationals
*Age: 22, Previous Rank: NR*

**Potential Earnings:** $20-25

**Risk Factor:** High

**Fantasy Overview:** Four-category contributor; impact potential in K

**Realistic Ceiling:** A top-25 starting pitcher

**Realistic Floor:** The not-so-good Jeremy Hellickson
Cole took a nice step forward in 2013, as he finally made it through High-A without self-immolating, and even saw success in Double-A. But if the breaking ball doesn't improve, he's just another guy.

### 90. Rafael Montero, RHP, New York Mets
*Age: 23, Previous Rank: NR*

**Potential Earnings:** $10-15

**Risk Factor:** Low

**Fantasy Overview:** Two-category contributor

**Realistic Ceiling:** Ricky Nolasco

**Realistic Floor:** A decent add for holds
The Mets continue to pump out pitcher after pitcher, and while Montero doesn't have the upside of the more well-known names in their system, he'll likely be the first man up this season in case of injury.

### 91. Tyler Austin, OF, New York Yankees
*Age: 22, Previous Rank: 58*

**Potential Earnings:** $15-20

**Risk Factor:** Medium

**Fantasy Overview:** Four-category contributor

**Realistic Ceiling:** A good no. 4 fantasy outfielder

**Realistic Floor:** A replacement-level outfielder in mixed leagues
The sheen certainly wore off Austin's prospect star this year, but he was banged up all season. Although the Yankees may be allergic to promoting from within, Austin will do his best to force their hand.

### 92. Lance McCullers, RHP, Houston Astros
*Age: 20, Previous Rank: 100*

**Potential Earnings:** $20-25

**Risk Factor:** High

**Fantasy Overview:** Four-category contributor; impact potential in K

**Realistic Ceiling:** A top-30 fantasy starter

**Realistic Floor:** A high-strikeout reliever
Every year McCullers goes without imploding, he gets closer and closer to being a starter long term, but at some point he's going to have to show an average changeup or he'll just be another big-armed reliever.

### 93. Justin Nicolino, LHP, Miami Marlins
*Age: 22, Previous Rank: 85*

**Potential Earnings:** $15-20

**Risk Factor:** Medium

**Fantasy Overview:** Three-category contributor; impact potential in WHIP

**Realistic Ceiling:** Cliff Lee (kidding!)

**Realistic Floor:** An up-and-down fifth starter
The margin for error with Nicolino is smaller than for almost anyone else on this list because he gets by on command and guile. Even with that said, his innate ability to locate can get him there.

## 94. Nick Williams, OF, Texas Rangers
*Age: 20, Previous Rank: NR*

**Potential Earnings:** $25-30

**Risk Factor:** Extreme

**Fantasy Overview:** Five-category contributor

**Realistic Ceiling:** Not quite Adam Jones, but not far off

**Realistic Floor:** Tyler Colvin

Usually when a hitter strikes out 110 times against only 15 walks, it's a sign that things are going terribly wrong—and while Williams did that, he also flashed tools that could make those numbers not matter much in fantasy.

## 95. Jorge Bonifacio, OF, Kansas City Royals
*Age: 20, Previous Rank: 92*

**Potential Earnings:** $20-25

**Risk Factor:** High

**Fantasy Overview:** Four-category contributor

**Realistic Ceiling:** A top-25 fantasy outfielder

**Realistic Floor:** Delmon Young, the baseball player

The power hasn't shown up in games yet, but this is still a player who could hit 25 homers at the major-league level. Injuries haven't helped with that either, as his hamate bone injury in 2013 (combined with Wilmington's power-suppressing ways) led to a depressed stat line.

## 96. Lewis Thorpe, LHP, Minnesota Twins
*Age: 18, Previous Rank: NR*

**Potential Earnings:** $25-30

**Risk Factor:** Extreme

**Fantasy Overview:** Four-category contributor; impact potential in W, K, ERA, WHIP

**Realistic Ceiling:** The best Aussie pitcher ever

**Realistic Floor:** Josh Edgin

There are few propositions in baseball riskier than a short-season teenage arm, but Thorpe's combination of advanced pitchability and very strong raw stuff gives him as much upside as anyone in the group.

## 97. Adalberto Mejia, LHP, San Francisco Giants
*Age: 20, Previous Rank: NR*

**Potential Earnings:** $15-20

**Risk Factor:** Medium

**Fantasy Overview:** Three-category contributor; Impact potential in ERA

**Realistic Ceiling:** A top-40 fantasy starter

**Realistic Floor:** A decent streamer at AT&T Park

It's unwise to overlook a left-handed starter who will be pitching half of his games in San Francisco, where right-handed hitters to go cry. There's not top-shelf stuff here, but it's enough.

## 98. Colin Moran, 3B, Miami Marlins
*Age: 21, Previous Rank: NR*

**Potential Earnings:** $15-20

**Risk Factor:** Medium

**Fantasy Overview:** Four-category contributor

**Realistic Ceiling:** Dave Magadan with a little more pop

**Realistic Floor:** The guy we're afraid Dustin Ackley is

History has given us reasons to be leery of projecting big batting averages out of excellent contact hitters from the college ranks, but Moran has enough pop to make it matter in the pros.

## 99. Blake Swihart, C, Boston Red Sox
*Age: 21, Previous Rank: 96*

**Potential Earnings:** $15-20

**Risk Factor:** Medium

**Fantasy Overview:** Four-category contributor

**Realistic Ceiling:** Jonathan Lucroy

**Realistic Floor:** Welington Castillo without another step forward

The "Blake Swihart Line" is named that for a reason. Swihart doesn't have the highest upside in the world, but it's enough to warrant owning—and his defense/makeup will go a long way toward his reaching a relatively high floor.

## 100. Alexander Reyes, RHP, St. Louis Cardinals
*Age: 19, Previous Rank: NR*

**Potential Earnings:** $25-30

**Risk Factor:** Extreme

**Fantasy Overview:** Four-category contributor; impact potential in W, K, ERA

**Realistic Ceiling:** The next Shelby Miller

**Realistic Floor:** A pre-international draft fun fact

Let's be honest, what Reyes will be is still a mystery. But if he lives up to the quality of his raw stuff, he will return value—and that's really all you can ask for.

## 101. Bubba Starling, OF, Kansas City Royals
*Age: 21, Previous Rank: 51*

**Potential Earnings:** $25-30

**Risk Factor:** Extreme

**Fantasy Overview:** Four-category contributor; impact potential in HR, RBI, R, SB

**Realistic Ceiling:** A 25/25 outfielder, or better

**Realistic Floor:** Manager of a Kansas City McDonald's

No, I am not trolling you. Starling still possesses intense fantasy upside, and is not worth giving up on for that next new shiny thing at this point (unless said shiny thing ranks higher on this list).

# Just Missed (in alphabetical order)

## Matt Barnes, RHP, Boston Red Sox
*Age: 23, Previous Rank: 40*

**Potential Earnings:** $20-25

**Risk Factor:** High

**Fantasy Overview:** Four-category contributor; impact potential in W

**Realistic Ceiling:** A decent no. 3 fantasy starter

**Realistic Floor:** A name you don't bring up in Boston

## Jose Berrios, RHP, Minnesota Twins
*Age: 19, Previous Rank: NR*

**Potential Earnings:** $15-20

**Risk Factor:** Medium

**Fantasy Overview:** Four-category contributor

**Realistic Ceiling:** What the Twins hope Phil Hughes is

**Realistic Floor:** A fringy closer option

### Kaleb Cowart, 3B, Los Angeles Angels
*Age: 21, Previous Rank: 52*
**Potential Earnings:** $20-25
**Risk Factor:** High
**Fantasy Overview:** Four-category contributor
**Realistic Ceiling:** A 25-homer third baseman
**Realistic Floor:** Matt Dominguez lite

### C.J. Cron, 1B, Los Angeles Angels
*Age: 24, Previous Rank: NR*
**Potential Earnings:** $15-20
**Risk Factor:** Medium
**Fantasy Overview:** Four-category contributor
**Realistic Ceiling:** Mark Trumbo with less power
**Realistic Floor:** A Quadruple-A slugger

### Hunter Dozier, 3B, Kansas City Royals
*Age: 22, Previous Rank: NR*
**Potential Earnings:** $15-20
**Risk Factor:** Medium
**Fantasy Overview:** Four-category contributor
**Realistic Ceiling:** A poor man's Ryan Zimmerman
**Realistic Floor:** A poor man's Chris Johnson

### Edwin Escobar, LHP, San Francisco Giants
*Age: 21, Previous Rank: NR*
**Potential Earnings:** $10-15
**Risk Factor:** Low
**Fantasy Overview:** Four-category contributor
**Realistic Ceiling:** Matt Harrison in AT&T park
**Realistic Floor:** Matt Harrison in Coors Field

### Wilmer Flores, 3B/2B, New York Mets
*Age: 22, Previous Rank: NR*
**Potential Earnings:** $15-20
**Risk Factor:** Medium
**Fantasy Overview:** Four-category contributor; impact potential in AVG, HR, RBI
**Realistic Ceiling:** Brandon Phillips without the steals
**Realistic Floor:** A man without a defensive home

### Rosell Herrera, SS/3B, Colorado Rockies
*Age: 21, Previous Rank: NR*
**Potential Earnings:** $20-25
**Risk Factor:** High
**Fantasy Overview:** Five-category contributor
**Realistic Ceiling:** The guy we thought Trevor Story could be
**Realistic Floor:** Another Josh Rutledge

### Pierce Johnson, RHP, Chicago Cubs
*Age: 22, Previous Rank: NR*
**Potential Earnings:** $15-20
**Risk Factor:** Medium
**Fantasy Overview:** Four-category contributor
**Realistic Ceiling:** A strong no. 4 fantasy starter
**Realistic Floor:** A strong no. 6 fantasy starter

### Casey Kelly, RHP, San Diego Padres
*Age: 24, Previous Rank: 36*
**Potential Earnings:** $10-15

**Risk Factor:** Low
**Fantasy Overview:** Four-category contributor
**Realistic Ceiling:** A good no. 4 fantasy starter
**Realistic Floor:** A streaming option when at home

### Zach Lee, RHP, Los Angeles Dodgers
*Age: 22, Previous Rank: NR*
**Potential Earnings:** $15-20
**Risk Factor:** Medium
**Fantasy Overview:** Four-category contributor
**Realistic Ceiling:** A good no. 4 fantasy starter
**Realistic Floor:** A fringe shallow-league starter

### Jose Martinez, RHP, Arizona Diamondbacks
*Age: 19, Previous Rank: NR*
**Potential Earnings:** $20-25
**Risk Factor:** Extreme
**Fantasy Overview:** Four-category contributor; impact potential in K
**Realistic Ceiling:** A no. 2 fantasy starter
**Realistic Floor:** An erratic reliever with poor ratios

### Kyle Parker, 1B/OF, Colorado Rockies
*Age: 24, Previous Rank: NR*
**Potential Earnings:** $15-20
**Risk Factor:** Medium
**Fantasy Overview:** Four-category contributor; impact potential in RBI
**Realistic Ceiling:** A 25-plus-home-run-hitting outfielder
**Realistic Floor:** Lucas Duda, complete with defensive hilarity

### Joe Ross, RHP, San Diego Padres
*Age: 20, Previous Rank: NR*
**Potential Earnings:** $20-25
**Risk Factor:** High
**Fantasy Overview:** Four-category contributor; impact potential in ERA
**Realistic Ceiling:** A strong no. 3 fantasy starter
**Realistic Floor:** A strong holds guy

### Vincent Velasquez, RHP, Houston Astros
*Age: 21, Previous Rank: NR*
**Potential Earnings:** $15-20
**Risk Factor:** High
**Fantasy Overview:** Four-category contributor
**Realistic Ceiling:** A top-25 fantasy starter
**Realistic Floor:** The pitcher who's never the best option on the waiver wire

### Allen Webster, RHP, Boston Red Sox
*Age: 24, Previous Rank: 78*
**Potential Earnings:** $15-20
**Risk Factor:** Medium
**Fantasy Overview:** Three-category contributor
**Realistic Ceiling:** A high-WHIP no. 4 starter
**Realistic Floor:** A strong strikeout reliever ■

# The Ones Who Could Jump

*by Craig Goldstein*

We here at Baseball Prospectus like to give the people what they want, and it's been made abundantly clear that the people want rankings. We've done our best to shovel as many lists into the gaping maw that hungers for such things, but like the waves lapping against a shore, the demand is unceasing.

Our lists are created, debated, torn down, and built up, and ultimately a finished product arrives to you, the reader. The first thing done upon devouring each list is to ask, "what about ____?" or, alternatively, "who just missed?" To that end, we create "just missed" articles to satiate. From there the questions evolve, turning into "who could be on this list next year?" Thus the list below has been generated, ridiculed, adjusted, and refined just for you.

To be clear, this is not a ranking. It is an alphabetical list of 24 players who I believe could go from unranked on Bret Sayre's fantasy 101 to on it, and I tried as hard as possible to exclude names from his "just missed" section (including some favorites such as Joe Ross, Vincent Velasquez, and Rosell Herrera). The difficulty here is twofold: 1) these are players/sleepers that I have a personal preference for, and 2) I am trying to project them to make someone else's rankings. This means that my devotion to catchers may not be rewarded, as Bret doesn't share the same love for the position. Nevertheless, it is my list, and as such I'm going to place players who I think are deserving of your fantasy attention. I hope it serves you well.

## Chris Anderson, SP, Los Angeles Dodgers

The 18th overall pick in the 2013 draft, Anderson doesn't boast top-of-the-rotation upside like some of the other names on this list, but he does stand a good chance of contributing to the middle of a major-league rotation. He doesn't display the best command, but he's got a four-pitch mix, with a fastball and slider that grade out as plus. He was dominant in Low-A in a small sample and has the chance to move quickly, as the Dodgers won't let him languish in the High-A California League for long. He could enter the 2015 offseason with Double-A experience, a mid-rotation upside, and the ability to miss bats. It's not the sexiest profile, but those types of pitchers populate top 101s with frequency.

## Lewis Brinson, CF, Texas Rangers

Scootch closer children, I'm not going to tell you again about the scootching. Now that you're close, here's a secret: for as much criticism and questioning that Joey Gallo gels for striking out 37 percent of the time in Low-A, Brinson struck out more. He whiffed in 38 percent of his at-bats which is… bad. So much swing-and-miss could be a fatal flaw. There's a good chance Brinson repeats Low-A, and if he can cut down on the prodigious number of strikeouts, it will be hard to ignore his other tools. He's a plus runner (possibly better), with plus power, and if he can hit enough to access that power, he's going to be a fantasy factor. Even if it's a .230 batting average, his stolen bases (he does walk—9.5%) and home runs will make him worth owning in some form. As much risk as there is thanks to questions about the hit tool, that's someone to gamble on at the back end of a 101.

## Mauricio Cabrera, SP, Atlanta Braves

An upper-90s fastball will put anyone on the map, but back it up with a potential plus change and average breaking ball, and you're cooking with gas. Cabrera completed a full season at Low-A Danville, tossing 131 1/3 innings, striking out 107, and walking batters every other inning or so. His control needs refinement, but the relatively average strikeout rate belies the quality of his stuff. He also tired midseason, but returned looking sharp after a two-week break. A good changeup is a likeable quality in a prospect, though that pitch tends not to miss as many bats at the upper levels, so a polished curveball is a necessity. Realistically he is a mid-rotation starter, but if he can hone his breaking ball, he could miss more bats, raising his ceiling in the process. Even without that development, he'll be worthy of a top-101 ranking on the verge of Double-A.

## Franchy Cordero, SS, San Diego Padres

A strong stateside debut including hitting for power, hitting for average, getting on base, and swiping a few all while playing an up-the-middle position will make one take notice, and notice Cordero we did. That he's eons from the majors, having yet to play full-season ball, hurts his case as a future top 101, but shortstops are always desirable. Although complex league statistics aren't worth the grain of salt you'd have to take them with, the scouting reports on Cordero are positive as well, as he has both bat speed and strength. The risk you take here is a longer-than-expected development path and/or a possible position switch in the end, but Cordero is a player on the rise. If he holds his own in short-season or Low-A, he'll have lots of callers come 2015.

## Michael De La Cruz, OF, Pittsburgh Pirates

This is aggressive. De La Cruz hasn't even debuted stateside yet, but then… if he performs when he does, people are going to get excited. We love to dream big, and De La Cruz gives us the necessary accoutrements to do so. He received a big bonus from the Pirates thanks to his impressive feel for hitting and physical prowess. Pittsburgh has a positive track record with international talent, and De La Cruz could be the next name on the list. This is more of a name to keep an eye on than a legitimate option for a 101 next year, but if he performs like he can, it's not out of the question.

### Edwin Diaz, SP, Seattle Mariners

Where there is risk there is reward; as with many other prospects on this list, Diaz has yet to reach full-season ball. Polished prospects catch our eyes most often, as they're able to exploit those who aren't allowing their statistics to cast a bigger shadow than their tools. Others take incremental steps forward—not thriving, but not merely treading water either—slowly fulfilling their promise and giving us reason to believe they'll take yet another step next year. Diaz is more the latter than the former, as his big fastball (with movement) should enable him to overpower lower-minors hitters, while the real steps will come in moving his changeup closer to an average pitch and sharpening his curveball into a bat-missing offering. He could falter, finding hitters who will punish his mistakes more severely and won't flail at offerings off the plate—but the fundamental building blocks are good enough to make me believe he won't.

### Philip Ervin, OF, Cincinnati Reds

The question Ervin has to answer is whether he can handle center field all the way up the chain. If he can, he could be a dynamic option, especially in leagues that use LF/CF/RF designations. He was extremely impressive in his professional debut, backing up his statistical breakout by showing all five tools. Ervin could be a better fantasy player than real-life player if he ends up in a corner, as he'll lose the defensive value but still retain his 20/15 potential. He currently shows a short stroke, enabling him to put bat to ball very well, but as he gets older he may trade some of that for power, resulting in more of a 25-home-run-type bat with a bit lower average. There's a wide range of outcomes currently, though all them appear to be rosy.

### Marco Gonzales, SP, St. Louis Cardinals

Advanced command and the ability to sequence can allow lesser pitchers to eat up the lower minors, but this doesn't mean that such qualities and performances qualify one as a lesser pitcher. Gonzales fell to the 19th overall pick, where St. Louis nabbed him (sound familiar? *cough* Wacha *cough*), and was pushed to High-A by year's end. He experienced success in his 16 2/3 innings cameo there, and should continue to do so if he's not bumped to Double-A to start 2014. His fastball is pedestrian, but he locates it well, and upper-80s/low-90s is acceptable from the left side, especially with late life. The fastball will likely play up at times, as hitters will start to anticipate the mother****er of a changeup he throws, as his arm speed and release point mimic that of the fastball. Hitters are also treated to a gospel choir and a generous helping of fade each time he throws the pitch. He offers two breaking balls at present, with some aptitude for the curveball, though it doesn't project as more than solid-average. Of course, Wacha also was a fastball/changeup pitcher, and look how he turned out. Gonzales doesn't have front-of-the-rotation upside, but by this time next year he should be within shouting distance of the major leagues with enough strikeout ability to offset his "safe" profile.

### J.R. Graham, SP, Atlanta Braves

Perhaps one of the more known quantities on the list, Graham has already reached the Double-A level. He gets love from scouts for his ability to pound the lower portion of the zone with a hard sinker (93-96 mph), as well as a slider that has the ability to miss bats. A third pitch will be vital to Graham's chances at remaining a starter, as his build (he's listed at 5'10") is already working against him. Graham made progress on that front, showing a power changeup that graded as average but featured good fade in toward right-handed batters. A strained shoulder shelved Graham for much of 2013, but it didn't require surgery; he's 100% healthy and his stuff has returned to previous levels. He's likely to appear in the Atlanta bullpen in 2014, and if he is still prospect eligible come next offseason, he'll be in the top 101.

### Gabriel Guerrero, OF, Seattle Mariners

A high beta entrant, Guerrero (the nephew of Vladimir) didn't show much in the early months of the season before heating up with the weather. Impressive bat speed and hand-eye coordination are the foundation of his extreme raw power. He can get fooled by off-speed pitches, and whether he's able to develop his ability to recognize pitches will determine whether he lands on top prospect lists, and more importantly becomes a major leaguer. If he can't do that, the power won't function enough, though at 20 years old, he'll continue to be young for his level.

### Ronald Guzman, 1B, Texas Rangers

For a 6'5" player, Guzman controls the length of his swing well. He barrels the ball nicely and could end up with a plus hit tool. His size portends power, but that doesn't mean it will come. Learning to cover the inside of the plate will be paramount, as he will find pitchers who can exploit that hole more and more as he moves up the chain. He should play 2014 at High-A as a 19-year-old, allowing him to be merely okay and retain his prospect status. Guzman is the rare legitimate first-base prospect, and a steady year at High-A should push his stock even higher.

### Rob Kaminsky, SP, St. Louis Cardinals

At less than six feet tall, Kaminsky literally faces an uphill climb to remain a starter. In his favor, he's got the chance for three better-than-average pitches, including a curveball that projects as plus-plus. Kaminsky will likely work in the lower minors for the upcoming season, where his developed curveball could overwhelm inexperienced hitters. He can rely on the pitch too much, though, pitching off of it instead of his fastball. This approach may work early on, but eventually he'll need to learn to establish the fastball, a pitch he's had trouble commanding at times. He could be a 200-plus-strikeout pitcher down the line, but there could be some growing pains along the way, a la Sonny Gray.

### Manuel Margot, CF, Boston Red Sox

Distance from the majors is working against him, but Margot should debut in full-season ball this year and on the fantasy 101 next year. His carrying tool (in the fantasy world) is his speed, though he's got a chance for a plus hit tool and average power as well. Even if the power doesn't come, Margot's defense should get him to the majors and his speed should make him viable in fantasy, with everything else acting as gravy to those delicious potatoes.

### Nomar Mazara, OF, Texas Rangers

Another of Texas' bonus babies, Mazara features a feel for hitting and impressive bat speed that allows his power to play up into the plus-plus range. He can struggle against left-handed pitching, though that's not uncommon for left-handed hitters who rarely see quality same-side pitching early on. Well ahead on the age curve, Mazara should play at High-A as a 19-year-old; additional exposure against quality pitching could dampen the production while strengthening the player in the process. With the ceiling of a middle-of-the-order hitter, Mazara should be a coveted asset, but it won't happen quickly, as there's no reason to rush a prospect of his class. The Rangers will promote him when he's ready, but if you can get in on the ground floor, he'll be a worthy investment.

## Reese McGuire, C, Pittsburgh Pirates

While McGuire will always suffer from the gap between his real-life and fantasy value thanks to his considerable defensive talents, that doesn't mean he's not worth owning in the fantasy realm. Despite his backstop duties, McGuire runs well—with an above-average grade hung on the tool—and has the potential to develop into an above-average hitter with average power. Good bat speed allows him to generate power despite a short swing. This might be a year early on him thanks to certain people's irrational distaste for the position. Top 101 or no, McGuire has easy top-10 fantasy catcher upside down the line and solid offensive tools at a position with a stunning lack of average bats.

## Ryan McMahon, 3B, Colorado Rockies

Already being labeled as a steal, McMahon was taken by the Rockies in the second round of the 2013 draft. He's got first-round tools with possible plus grades on his hit and power tools. The best part is, as a former multisport athlete in high school, he might well outperform those projections now that he's focusing on baseball full time. Throw in the ultimate destination of Coors Field and hitter-friendly environments all the way up the chain, and McMahon's prospect stock should be like any good mix CD (er, playlist?): all rise.

## Francisco Mejia, C, Cleveland Indians

This pick is cheating on a fastball with no idea if one is coming. There's massive risk with Mejia, but there's everything to gain as well. We're talking about an 18-year-old backstop with a raw approach at the plate, who is equally unrefined defensively. Catchers are fraught with downside. If they move off the plate due to lack of defensive ability or a desire to hasten their ascent to the big leagues, their fantasy value is greatly diminished. If they don't move, they may not bloom offensively until later thanks to the defensive burden they carry. Knowing these things, this could be a foolish selection. And yet… Mejia might have the most upside of any catcher in the minors not named Jorge Alfaro. He's got the type of bat speed that will cause an irregular heartbeat, plus projections on his hit and power tools, and an arm that might be his best weapon. He should stay behind the plate long term, but "should" doesn't carry a lot of weight with 18-year-old catchers. There's a good chance he's not even in full-season ball in time for next year's version of the fantasy 101, but the chances are equally good he's placed prominently within those ranks.

## Harold Ramirez, OF, Pittsburgh Pirates

Unlike his orgmate De La Cruz, Ramirez has been stateside for two years, producing a .285/.354/.409 slash line in 71 games in the short-season New York-Penn League last season. Ramirez garnered attention for his five-tool package, showing a plus run to go with solid-average potential on his hit and power tools. He might end up a left fielder, putting more pressure on the offensive portion of his game, but he's got enough talent in the bat to be worthwhile either way. An impressive full-season debut will vault Ramirez up rankings, where he can then be turned for profit before his defensive limitations set in.

## Rio Ruiz, 3B, Houston Astros

Dropped to the fourth round due to blood clots, Ruiz was signed for over slot money, which put him on the fantasy prospect hound's radar. Ruiz improved each month of the season, with April serving as a particularly heavy anchor on his season's numbers. He has the potential for a plus hit and power tool, and has a good chance of being assigned to the launching pad that is the California League. While there's the risk that Ruiz moves off of third base in the long run, the short term should be kind to his prospect stock, thanks to his advanced approach and beneficial offensive environment. He should  move from the prospect background to foreground with a strong season at High-A.

## Domingo Santana, OF, Houston Astros

It's easy to lose Santana in the shuffle of Houston's bevy of prospects, but he doesn't deserve to be overlooked. He's already recorded a full season at Double-A, and while his .252 average won't excite anyone, his .498 slugging percentage should (Santana deposited 25 balls over the fence in 112 games). His hit tool might ultimately land at below-average, impeding the function of his impressive raw power, but 20-25 home runs doesn't seem out of reach. Houston has no reason to rush the 21-year-old, making him likely to be eligible for the 2015 version of Bret's top 101. When he's ready, he should function as a solid partner for George Springer in Houston's future outfield.

## Jacob Scavuzzo, OF, Los Angeles Dodgers

This is a long shot, I admit, but part of the purpose of this list is to shine a light on some of the dimly lit corners of the prospect universe, not merely to be "right." Still, it's not impossible that Scavuzzo ends up on a list. He broke out in 2013, overwhelming the Pioneer League with a .307/.350/.578 slash line, showing the ability to hit for average and power. Again, rookie-league stats can be deceiving, and there are questions about Scavuzzo's ability to execute against more advanced pitching, but this is an under-the-radar player who has a lot of projection to him. If he can add good weight to his 6'4", 195-pound frame and continue to develop, he could be the guy who comes from nowhere.

## Alberto Tirado, SP, Toronto Blue Jays

It might be an overstatement to say that Tirado eviscerated the opposition in his return to rookie ball, but his 44 strikeouts in 48 1/3 innings coupled with a 1.68 ERA would at least make a decent case. He walked too many, as young pitchers will do, but the scouting report tells the true story. There's potential for a plus-plus fastball, with two plus secondaries in his changeup and slider. The presence of an advanced changeup is pleasant, but even more so is the advanced slider. It will play off the fastball well and gives Tirado multiple options to miss bats with, which will enable him to sequence better once he reaches higher levels. He lacks command at present, but that's not unexpected in a prospect this young. Tirado should attack Low-A in 2014 at age 19, where he'll be forced to smooth out the rough edges of his game. Doing so should land him comfortably in the mix for next year's list.

## Andrew Toles, CF, Tampa Bay Rays

Toles faces an uphill climb to fantasy relevance because he doesn't offer the most sought-after tool: power. He can run like crazy, though, with a grade 7 run and the potential for a solid hit tool. He performed well at Low-A but will face a steeper test in the pitcher-friendly Florida State League in 2014. That could depress his potential breakout, but either way he'll remain a top-of-the-order-type hitter with impressive stolen-base ability and nonzero power. He doesn't project for even average power, though that doesn't mean he'll be a negative in the category. While he only hit two home runs in 2013, he did have 35 doubles and 16 triples.

### Devin Williams, SP, Milwaukee Brewers

Another arm that holds immense potential but could take its sweet time getting to the majors, Williams is all fastball at present, with an easy motion generating an already plus pitch with nice movement. He needs to be more consistent getting the pitch down in the zone and work on his promising changeup. He'll flash a slider, but there's no authority to the pitch. Williams impressed at the complex level, blowing his fastball by hitters, but walking far too many as well. Adding a second competent pitch and finding more of the zone will be huge steps for Williams, and while his ascent to the majors might be steady, he could find the spotlight quickly. ■

# The Top 50 2013 Signees for Dynasty Drafts

### by Bret Sayre

*This list was originally published at BaseballProspectus.com on January 9, 2014.*

Once the holidays have moved on and the calendar has flipped, dynasty leaguers all start to crawl out of the woodwork to submit their rosters for the current season and draft the new group of eligibles to dream on. As Wooderson would say, "That's what I love about these current-year draftees, man. I get older, they stay the same age." The promise of the 2013 signees collectively pool together to give dynasty-league rebuilders new hope of contention and dynasty-league contenders new trade chips with which to get the pieces to put them over the top.

And while the 2013 crop isn't the strongest we've seen in recent memory, there are still high-upside options from which to choose. The slight quirk of this year is that the options with the most fantasy upside are, for the most part, not the high-school players. In fact, only one of the top six players on this list fit into that category—which is a change of pace from last season, when Carlos Correa, Byron Buxton, and Addison Russell all fell into that space (and are all now top-10 prospects in the game). There is no prep arm with more impact potential than Jonathan Gray and no prep bat with more power potential than Kris Bryant. On the international front, just like last year, the crop is headlined by a Cuban hitter and a Japanese pitcher who have impact upside—though for fantasy purposes, they may be less exciting than Yu Darvish and Yoenis Cespedes. Then again, that's not much of a knock on Masahiro Tanaka or Jose Abreu, as you'd be hard pressed to find a one-two punch to match them in most seasons.

This is also the time of year that I get a lot of questions about trades involving draft picks. Like every other year, there is a drop-off after the first tier of players available, but 2014 drafts will see more dramatic tiering in the first round than we're used to. So when someone asks me on Twitter, "Should I trade player X and a first-round pick for player Y," the answer is inevitably another question: What pick is that? There is a very sizable difference between the fifth pick and eighth pick in drafts this year, so even small differences matter. And to expound on that a little further, if you don't have a pick in the top six this year (or top five if Tanaka is not available in your draft), it might be a good time to explore trade options. The biggest weakness of this class of fantasy prospects is in the midsection, and you can take advantage of that by dealing picks for players or pulling a Bill Belichick and securing more picks for 2015—which will have a much deeper draft pool.

These rankings assume a standard 5x5 rotisserie 16-team league where you can keep players forever without restriction. In a deeper league, guys like Mark Appel and Colin Moran will get a slight bump up, just like upside-driven names like Tim Anderson or Aaron Judge will get that same treatment in shallow leagues. "Get on with the list already," you're probably thinking and potentially saying out loud to no one in particular (although most of you probably went straight to the names first and are backfilling with the content). Don't worry, I forgive you. But yes, the list (in tiers):

1. Kris Bryant, 3B, Chicago Cubs
2. Jose Abreu, 1B, Chicago White Sox
3. Masahiro Tanaka, RHP, New York Yankees
4. Clint Frazier, OF, Cleveland Indians
5. Jonathan Gray, RHP, Colorado Rockies
6. Mark Appel, RHP, Houston Astros

Let's start at the top. Despite Tanaka and Abreu heading straight to the majors and both having chances at stardom, I'm still taking Bryant with the first pick in drafts this year. As a rather polished college hitter, he's not going to be too far behind the pair as far as ETA goes, and the power is just too tantalizing to pass up. That said, it's certainly defensible to take any of the top three with your first selection, depending on how much you believe in the international products. Abreu could be pre-injury Kendrys Morales, but he also has lingering questions about ability to catch up to velocity and his hit tool. Tanaka could be a healthier and slightly better version of Hisashi Iwakuma and slot in as a very good no. 2 fantasy pitcher for your squad, but he's got a ton of miles already on his arm (without the support of a Darvish-like frame).

My love of Clint Frazier is well documented, and frankly, I very nearly put him ahead of Tanaka. It's just the ETA that pushes him back. Then comes the big decision: Gray or Appel? It's close and I've flip-flopped them a couple of times during the process of researching and making this list. In the end, Gray has the upside to overcome the Coors Field factor and I prefer his strikeout potential to Appel's safety.

This is the part of the list where the fantasy values drop pretty dramatically.

7. Kohl Stewart, RHP, Minnesota Twins
8. Dominic Smith, 1B, New York Mets
9. Tim Anderson, SS, Chicago White Sox
10. Sean Manaea, LHP, Kansas City Royals
11. Hunter Harvey, RHP, Baltimore Orioles
12. D.J. Peterson, 3B, Seattle Mariners

The second group of six here certainly has potential, but it's a real step down either in upside or safety. Stewart will get billing as the top name in this group, but he's much closer to Smith's value than Appel's. Smith and Peterson both could be very solid fantasy bats, but since neither has huge power or stolen-base ability, their upsides are somewhat limited. The remaining three players have the upside you want, but all carry real risk. Anderson could be an Ian Desmond-type or he could flame out as a utility guy. Manaea has an injury history, and though the reports are good now, he could see a setback. Harvey has a lot of upside, but his division and ballpark won't help and he's still a long way away.

13. Braden Shipley, RHP, Arizona Diamondbacks
14. Hunter Renfroe, OF, San Diego Padres
15. J.P. Crawford, SS, Philadelphia Phillies
16. Austin Meadows, OF, Pittsburgh Pirates
17. Alex Gonzalez, RHP, Texas Rangers
18. Colin Moran, 3B, Miami Marlins
19. Alexander Guerrero, 2B, Los Angeles Dodgers
20. Hunter Dozier, 3B, Kansas City Royals

The upside in this third grouping is underwhelming. Shipley and Renfroe lead the charge, as they both can reach that next level of prospect status by honing their skills—Renfroe in particular, as a potential power/speed combo (albeit one likely with a low batting average). I'm not the world's biggest Meadows believer, at least not at a star level, but he's going to be a fantasy contributor. Moran should be able to hit and starred at North Carolina, but his position and power potential are up in the air—that doesn't sound at all like Dustin Ackley, right? And Guerrero is a gamble, just without the type of offensive payoff we generally see from Cuban defectors.

21. Reese McGuire, C, Pittsburgh Pirates
22. Trey Ball, LHP, Boston Red Sox
23. Rob Kaminsky, LHP, St Louis Cardinals
24. Devin Williams, RHP, Milwaukee Brewers
25. Ryan McMahon, 3B, Colorado Rockies
26. Eric Jagielo, 3B, New York Yankees
27. Bobby Wahl, RHP, Oakland Athletics
28. Billy McKinney, OF, Oakland Athletics
29. Ian Clarkin, LHP, New York Yankees

There's some talent still in the pool at this point, but once you get outside the top 20, it starts to drop off rapidly. If you're looking for the most potential bang for your buck in this group, I'd look at numbers 24 and 25. Williams is athletic, but raw, and could take a nice step forward and solidify himself as the Brewers' top prospect. McMahon is a guy who could hit for power and average—calling Coors Field home is just the icing on the cake.

30. Josh Hart, OF, Baltimore Orioles
31. Aaron Judge, OF, New York Yankees
32. Rafael Devers, 3B, Boston Red Sox
33. Chance Sisco, C, Baltimore Orioles
34. Eloy Jimenez, OF, Chicago Cubs
35. Marco Gonzales, RHP, St Louis Cardinals
36. Jonathan Denney, C, Boston Red Sox
37. Dustin Peterson, SS, San Diego Padres
38. Chris Anderson, RHP, Los Angeles Dodgers
39. Nick Ciuffo, C, Tampa Bay Rays
40. Austin Wilson, OF, Seattle Mariners
41. Gleyber Torres, SS, Chicago Cubs
42. Hunter Green, LHP, Los Angeles Angels
43. Travis Demerritte, 3B, Texas Rangers
44. Clinton Hollon, RHP, Toronto Blue Jays
45. Jordan Paroubeck, OF, San Diego Padres
46. Ryne Stanek, RHP, Tampa Bay Rays
47. Cord Sandberg, OF, Philadelphia Phillies
48. Corey Knebel, RHP, Detroit Tigers
49. Jason Hursh, RHP, Atlanta Braves
50. Tyler Danish, RHP, Chicago White Sox

The rest of this list is filled with lottery tickets (Judge, Devers, Jimenez, Hollon) and likely lower-level contributors (Gonzales, Anderson, Knebel, Danish). If you're counting on these guys for anything other than minor-league depth, it's very likely to end in disappointment. ∎

# Top 50 Prospects for 2014 Fantasy Value Only

*by Mike Gianella*

When I started playing in competitive fantasy baseball leagues in the mid-1990s, there was plenty of viable prospect information available for fantasy players to review. Unfortunately, despite the tremendous amount of data, little was geared toward fantasy.

We have come a long way since those somewhat darker days. Toolsy players like Glenn Williams and Derrick Gibson are avoided in all but the deepest of dynasty leagues, and most prospect rankings provide a good deal of insight into what a player's fantasy impact will be throughout his career.

If there is a gap in today's fantasy landscape, it comes when fantasy owners try to balance present-day considerations with a player's long-term outlook. In keeper (non-dynasty) leagues, owners tend to overvalue rookies, but this tendency exists in redraft leagues as well.

To remedy this, Baseball Prospectus has put together a list of the top 50 prospects for one-year, non-keeper leagues. While it's obviously an inexact science, the list below attempts to value players based on what they might do this year only if they are called up.

## 1. Billy Hamilton, OF, Cincinnati Reds

Hamilton isn't the best real-life prospect on this list by any stretch of the imagination, but it isn't an exaggeration to say that his speed is generational. Even if the Reds are conservative with Hamilton on the basepaths, an 80 stolen-base season is a realistic possibility if he can reach base even 30 percent of the time. While some fantasy analysts believe that he might not be valuable if he doesn't get on base enough, zero home runs, 29 RBI, a .232 batting average, 94 runs, and 107 steals from Hamilton would have been worth $43 last year. Those numbers are what Vince Coleman put up in 1986. All Hamilton needs to do is own one category in fantasy to be a monster, and he is capable of doing exactly that.

## 2. Masahiro Tanaka, SP, New York Yankees

Tanaka's ridiculous ERAs in Japan's Pacific League make everyone stand up and take notice, but the more modest strikeout rates are best to use as a fantasy baseline. Tanaka is likely to be very good, but despite the gaudy Japanese numbers, the consensus seems to lead more to a pitcher with a non-ace ceiling. Pitching in Yankee Stadium won't help his cause either. All of these caveats aside, the floor with Tanaka is relatively low, making him a safe bet compared to nearly every other rookie on this list.

## 3. Jose Abreu, 1B, Chicago White Sox

Yoenis Cespedes and Yasiel Puig have made forecasting the success or failure of Cuban players in the majors somewhat less risky than it used to be, but it remains difficult to translate statistics from Cuba into major-league numbers. Abreu's monstrous numbers in Cuba could make him a big-time power hitter at the position, but he could also be a relative bust. He should stick with the White Sox and produce, though it remains an open question if Abreu will be a stud or just a middle-of-the-pack first baseman.

## 4. Xander Bogaerts, SS, Boston Red Sox

There is little doubting Boegarts' long-term potential; only the question of what he will do in 2014 keeps him from topping this list. He has the opportunity to shine at the big-league level but is no lock to do so this year. Although his 16/72/8/79/.293 line across three levels last season is nice fantasy production, it doesn't speak to an immediate superstar level of performance. Improvement should be anticipated, but the question of whether it comes right away or takes a while keeps Bogaerts from a top ranking...at least this year.

## 5. Nick Castellanos, 3B, Detroit Tigers

In the short term, Castellanos could be a reliable performer, but the ceiling shouldn't be expected for some time. A .276 Triple-A batting average suggests that there could be some batting average questions in 2014, and the power profile doesn't scream 30 home runs and 100 RBI. If you buy or draft Castellanos this year, you are paying for reliability and the security of a starting job in Detroit, not a sudden breakthrough.

## 6. Taijuan Walker, SP, Seattle Mariners

Walker looked terrific in his late-season promotion and is a virtual lock for the Mariners rotation in 2014. He is still a work in progress, but with a fastball that can touch the upper-90s and a sick cutter, it might be enough to propel him into the top 30 starting pitchers as soon as this year. Walker is that rare fantasy pitcher who could provide instant dividends as a rookie. The caveat is the other side of this very coin: Walker is a rookie, and while the ceiling is exciting, attention must be paid to how the hitters adjust to his stuff upon repeated viewings.

## 7. George Springer, OF, Houston Astros

Springer is the first player on the top 50 who isn't assured of an Opening Day job. Despite this, Springer's dynamic power/speed combination makes him an instant fantasy commodity when he gets promoted, and that promotion should come at some point in 2014 barring a setback. Even 300-350 plate appearances of Springer at a 25-homer, 25-steal pace would offer plenty of fantasy viability. It is difficult to recommend players in redraft leagues who won't play a full season, but Springer will be impossible to pass up in all but the shallowest of leagues.

## 8. Kolten Wong, 2B, St. Louis Cardinals

Wong is the antithesis of Springer: a somewhat boring fantasy player who should produce decent stats all season long. Wong's ranking is helped by the strength of his organization: the Cardinals have an amazing track record of promoting players at exactly the right time and giving them every opportunity to succeed. A repeat of his 10-homer, 20-steal line from Triple-A last year is very realistic, although Mike Matheny's aversion to the running game might hamper Wong and keep the value down.

## 9. Jackie Bradley Jr., OF, Boston Red Sox

Like Wong, Bradley has job security on his side, which enhances his ranking more than a spectacular minor-league resume. Bradley could put up solid numbers this year but could also struggle with both his power and speed. Although the ceiling for 2014 appears to be Michael Brantley, there is also plenty of floor. It's a small sample (107 plate appearances), but his 617 OPS in Boston in 2013 was underwhelming, and to some degree illustrates the short-term risk.

## 10. Oscar Taveras, OF, St. Louis Cardinals

Taveras could spend most of 2014 in the minors and not even get a cup of coffee until September. But remember that it was injury and not performance that kept him down last year, and the talented package that was there in 2013 remains. Taveras appears to be blocked by an outfield/first-base logjam in St. Louis, but he will find a way to the majors if the early performance at Triple-A dictates it. Even in non-keeper leagues, it is mandatory that he stays on your radar.

## 11. Travis D'Arnaud, C, New York Mets

D'Arnaud has a clear path to the starting job in New York. Catchers are a difficult proposition in fantasy, though, as it often takes a while for the offense to come around due to the rigors of the position. D'Arnaud's overall package makes him a good bet for major-league success, but whether these real-life dividends come with fantasy success remains to be seen. Regardless, the playing time and power make D'Arnaud a solid bet even if he isn't a first-tier catcher this year.

## 12. Kevin Gausman, SP, Baltimore Orioles

Gausman struggled in his first time through the majors, but this shouldn't dampen his overall outlook one bit. The question is whether success comes quickly or if there will be more bumps and bruises along the way. The stuff is legit and will eventually play at any level. The ranking and the bid are an attempt to balance whether or not that eventual success comes in 2014 or later.

## 13. Matt Davidson, 3B, Chicago White Sox

Davidson might be in open competition for the White Sox starting third-base job, but with only Jeff Keppinger and Conor Gillaspie ahead of him, he should get a significant portion of at-bats at the position whether he starts with the White Sox on Opening Day or not. Davidson looks more like a reliable mainstay than a potential superstar, but a .250 batting average with 15-20 home runs from the hot corner isn't anything to lightly dismiss, even if this winds up being his ceiling.

## 14. Carlos Martinez, RP, St. Louis Cardinals*

*Martinez isn't a rookie due to service time; he spent more than the minimum 45 days on the active 25-man roster last year.*

It is rare to recommend a pitcher whose path to either starting or closing is blocked, but Martinez is so good that even in a non-keeper league he's worth owning in deeper formats. The relief strikeouts will be there, and despite last year's underwhelming numbers, Martinez should dominate on the ERA/WHIP front as well. Even if Martinez doesn't wind up in the Cardinals rotation by midseason, this is a case where paying for the skills and worrying about the role later is a good plan.

## 15. Jameson Taillon, SP, Pittsburgh Pirates

Taillon is unlikely to grace the Pirates' Opening Day roster, but like last year's Pirate sensation Gerrit Cole it's only a matter of time before he does. Taillon doesn't quite have Cole's ceiling but could turn into a legit no. 2 starter for Pittsburgh. One hundred innings of Taillon in 2014 could provide a significant boost for his fantasy owners.

## 16. Chris Owings, SS, Arizona Diamondbacks

Owings and Didi Gregorius will compete for Arizona's shortstop job, but Owings has the much higher fantasy ceiling. Although the PCL may have inflated Owings' raw numbers, a 10-homer, 20-steal season at the major-league level wouldn't come as a big surprise in 2014. Owings has a lower floor than fellow middle infielder Wong but arguably a higher ceiling if he gets the opportunity to play.

## 17. Alexander Guerrero, 2B, Los Angeles Dodgers

The ceiling isn't as high for Guerrero as it is for fellow Cuban import Jose Abreu, but the floor is lower than it is for many prospects on this list. Although Guerrero is unlikely to bust out and hit 25-30 home runs, a 15-homer/10-steal season is well within the realm of possibility. Guerrero could wind up being a boring option, but if he is healthy and the scouting reports are accurate, he will produce.

## 18. Mike Olt, 3B, Chicago Cubs

Depending on what happens in spring training, the bid—and the ranking—could easily be higher. Olt's power potential is still strong, and if his eye issues are behind him (and were the culprit for his lost 2013), then he could still be the big-time power hitter that he was projected to be with the Rangers. At 25 years old, the clock is ticking, but his age isn't a concern in redraft leagues.

## 19. James Paxton, SP, Seattle Mariners

Paxton's 24 strong MLB innings are too small of a sample size to be predictive; then again, his struggles at hitter-friendly Tacoma might not be too instructive either. The safest bet is probably the one in the middle: as a reliable, back-of-the-rotation guy who won't be great but will provide quality innings. The concerns about Paxton sticking in the rotation are for down the road; for 2014, he will be starting and will provide deeper mixed and only value at a minimum.

## 20. Jonathan Singleton, 1B. Houston Astros

The path to the majors isn't as clear or obvious for Singleton as it is for fellow Astro Springer, but if Singleton can get back on track this year, he has a shot to be in Houston by midsummer. That doesn't make this automatic. Singleton's struggles in Triple-A mean that he might need to spend an entire year at the level. However, this is a case where one bad year might be a blip on the radar, and the skills will outweigh (so to speak) the stats going forward.

## 21. Michael Choice, OF, Texas Rangers

Although Choice will start the year in a platoon with Mitch Moreland at DH, he could see a larger role if the bat plays in Texas. Choice didn't hit for big-time power in the high minors, but Arlington might help. It is more likely that Choice is solid all around, and his value will hinge on how many at-bats he can take away from Moreland and others on the Rangers roster.

## 22. Erik Johnson, SP, Chicago White Sox

Johnson dominated at every stop in the minors but—despite the solid ERA—struggled a bit in the majors. A high WHIP, so-so whiff rate, and mediocre K/BB isn't reason to stay away entirely but could signify a short term where he doesn't dominate immediately. Penciled into the White Sox rotation, Johnson's pitch-to-contact, nondominant approach makes him look more like a mid-tier guy, though savvy pitchers like this have proven us all wrong before.

## 23. Jake Odorizzi, SP, Tampa Bay Rays

An elbow injury to Jeremy Hellickson opens the door for Odorizzi to crack the Rays' Opening Day rotation. Odorizzi doesn't have any A+ pitches, but he compensates by throwing four pitches for strikes. The Rays have had success in the past working with pitchers like this in improving their sequencing, so Odorizzi could exceed his projection. More likely, he is what he is, a solid fantasy starter who should command a single-digit bid this year. Don't pay for potential growth in a non-keeper league.

## 24. Yordano Ventura, SP, Kansas City Royals

On potential alone, Ventura belongs much higher on this list, but multiple free-agent signings by the Royals push him back to Triple-A to start 2014. Although Bruce Chen shouldn't be a significant obstacle, the signing likely buys Kansas City and Ventura time to work on his secondary offerings to go with that ridiculous, Bugs Bunny fastball. Ventura should be up at some point this year, but it wouldn't shock anyone if that point was in August rather than May.

## 25. Archie Bradley, SP, Arizona Diamondbacks

With all due respect to the pitchers ranked above him, if there is a guy on this list who will surprise all of us and take the Jose Fernandez path to rapid superstardom, it's Bradley. The recent signing of Bronson Arroyo buys the Diamondbacks more time, but when Bradley is ready, Arizona won't use a stacked rotation as an excuse to keep him down on the farm. Consistency with his secondary offerings is all that stands between Bradley and the majors, and even if he makes it without that consistency he could still be very, very good.

## 26. Gregory Polanco, OF, Pittsburgh Pirates

Some of Polanco's short-term appeal comes because Jose Tabata and Travis Snider aren't exactly significant obstacles. Polanco still needs a little work in the minors, but a midseason promotion isn't out of the question. Although the power might be slow to come, Polanco could be a poor man's Starling Marte for half a season in 2014 if everything breaks right.

## 27. Andrew Lambo, 1B/OF, Pittsburgh Pirates

Lambo gets overlooked on fantasy prospect lists because he is considered old for a prospect. While this might be true, Lambo showed true growth in the power department in the minors last year and isn't facing stiff competition at first base from Gaby Sanchez. He should start the year on the Opening Day roster and could be a cheap source of low average, moderate power on the Pirates. Even in only leagues, the price will be right on this gamble.

## 28. Jake Marisnick, OF, Miami Marlins

Marisnick struggled in his first taste of big-league exposure in 2013, so it's likely he starts 2014 in the minors. There is a good chance he makes it back up again this year and becomes a fixture in the Marlins outfield. His minor-league numbers have never been exciting, but Marisnick is young enough that he could still see some growth there. He is ranked here due to potential opportunity, not for any anticipation of a statistical breakthrough.

## 29. Henry Urrutia, OF/DH, Baltimore Orioles

Urrutia doesn't project as a big impact bat, but with Nolan Reimold in front of him on the depth chart, there's a good chance he sees significant time at DH this season. Urrutia, who projects as a fourth or fifth outfielder in deeper mixed leagues assuming he gets outfield eligibility, will probably be unspectacular but has a chance to be solid.

## 30. Miguel Gonzalez, SP, Philadelphia Phillies

Gonzalez falls into the "your guess is as good as anyone else's" mold of most Cuban imports. Scouts were talking about him as a potential ace or no. 2 starter right before he signed, but once the Phillies made it official, that rapidly slipped to anything between a no. 3 and a bullpen arm. Gonzalez should provide serviceable innings at the back end of Philadelphia's rotation, but it's hard to predict much more from him.

## 31. Josmil Pinto, C, Minnesota Twins

Pinto's youth and bat make him an exciting long-term play, but the offseason signing of Kurt Suzuki pushes his timetable back to at least this summer. Given his age and the fact that it's not ideal breaking a minor-league catcher in midseason, the Twins could give Pinto a full year at Triple-A. Still, Pinto is likely to be up in 2014, although Suzuki's acquisition makes him less of an obvious prospect add in non-keeper leagues than he was a few short months ago.

## 32. Jonathan Schoop, 2B, Baltimore Orioles

The Orioles have pushed Schoop aggressively throughout the minors, but the addition of Jemile Weeks may be a subtle admission that the aggressive timetable needs to be scaled back. Schoop's ceiling has been compared to Daniel Murphy and Neil Walker's, but without more consistency, he might not even realize that. Although Schoop could change hearts and minds in Baltimore with a hot minor-league start, he probably won't be up until the All-Star break at the earliest.

## 33. Marcus Stroman, SP, Toronto Blue Jays

Stroman's future might be in the bullpen, but if he makes it to the majors in 2014, it will be as a starting pitcher. Although he only has 131 professional innings under his belt, he came out of college as a polished product, so this shouldn't be an impediment to his eventual promotion. Stroman is unlikely to begin 2014 in the majors, but a fast start will move him up fast. J.A. Happ and Kyle Drabek won't be roadblocks when he is ready.

### 34. Noah Syndergaard, SP, New York Mets

Syndergaard only has 54 innings in the high minors, but his delivery and mechanics make some believe that he could start in the majors in 2014 without missing a beat. Although this is unlikely, the Mets haven't ruled out a big-league call-up this year. Syndergaard probably doesn't see the majors until August or September, but he ranks this high because there is a good chance at success whenever he gets the call.

### 35. Wilmer Flores, 3B, New York Mets

Flores has leveled off as a prospect since the days when he was compared to Miguel Cabrera, but there is still the potential for a 20- to 25-home-run hitter with a good batting average. Although he's ready now, there doesn't seem to be a position for him to play unless the Mets give up on both Ike Davis and Lucas Duda. Flores could make an impact in 2014, but he'll need either an injury or work at another position to make it happen.

### 36. Mark Appel, SP, Houston Astros

Forget that Appel only has 38 professional innings under his belt. He is an extremely polished pitcher and is very likely to see time in Houston this summer. The scouting knock is that he is unlikely to be a no. 1 starter. This is a concern in a dynasty league, but in a one-and-done, Appel's polish gives him a leg up on a number of other pitchers. He could return $10-15 in value right away.

### 37. Byron Buxton, OF, Minnesota Twins

We all know that Buxton could eventually be one of the great ones. He sits here because even though he hasn't played an inning above High-A ball, a strong season could land him in the majors by August. This doesn't necessarily portend success; Mike Trout arrived in the bigs in August 2011 as a 19-year-old, and while he showed some power and speed, the overall numbers weren't terrific. Buxton is here because of what might be, even though it probably won't happen for him in 2014.

### 38. Miguel Sano, 3B, Minnesota Twins

As with many of the players toward the bottom of this list, Sano is unlikely to make a significant impact in 2014. He is included here because if he does get promoted, he could be a strong power producer: think 10-15 home runs. For that to happen, though, Sano must take a leap forward. His strikeout rate jumped in Double-A, and he will need to improve his approach against more advanced pitchers to arrive this year.

### 39. Trevor Bauer, SP, Cleveland Indians

You could make an argument for leaving Bauer off of this list entirely and you wouldn't necessarily be wrong, but he is close to the majors, will probably be the first or second arm called up if the Indians need a starter, and has the talent to be a useful pitcher even if he doesn't project to be an ace. You're better off stashing Bauer in a redraft league than some of the more highly regarded arms higher on this list if you're just looking for big-league innings in 2014.

### 40. Javier Baez, SS, Chicago Cubs

Baez is the infield version of Buxton: a highly touted top prospect who could accelerate the timetable if he dominates in the early going. If he makes it to Chicago by June or July, expect good power right away but with a low batting average. If your league plays with major-league position eligibility, keep in mind that Baez won't be shortstop eligible unless Starlin Castro is traded. Baez will likely be up at some point in 2014, but as with any hitter with only half a season at Double-A or higher, that projection won't hold up if he struggles.

### 41. Jesse Biddle, SP, Philadelphia Phillies

Biddle seemed to be on the fast track to Philadelphia entering 2013, but his command was a major mess and has probably pushed him back to 2015, with September 2014 looking like a best-case scenario. He is listed here due to the Phillies' lack of major- and minor-league depth. Biddle's arrival could be accelerated if he improves and/or if the team has a pressing need for his services. He would be a risky ERA/WHIP fantasy play, but the high strikeout totals would play in any format.

### 42. Maikel Franco, 3B, Philadelphia Phillies

Franco is yet another exciting third-base power prospect whose near-term future depends on how he adjusts to more advanced pitching. He maintained his power after a midseason promotion to Double-A but his batting average was a BABIP-fueled mirage. Cody Asche isn't any kind of roadblock, and a strong first half in the minors from Franco will lead to a promotion. He isn't as highly touted as Baez and Sano for good reasons, but in 2014 Franco could have just as much or more impact if everything breaks right.

### 43. Tommy La Stella, 2B, Atlanta Braves

La Stella is unexciting from a fantasy standpoint, as you're probably looking at a 10-homer/10- steal ceiling with decent batting averages. He is listed here because if Dan Uggla continues to struggle to make contact, La Stella could find his way to Atlanta this year. There is virtually no upside, but he could be a stable option at the keystone if he breaks through.

### 44. Rafael Montero, SP, New York Mets

Although Montero has an outside shot to crack the Mets rotation in spring training, it is much more likely he will return to Triple-A. His ceiling isn't nearly as high as Syndergaard's, but Montero has a better chance of logging major-league innings this year. If his control holds, he could be a solid WHIP guy with decent strikeout totals at Citi Field. Although his ceiling isn't near that of many pitchers on this list, he could have have an impact on fantasy teams in 2014, which is why he makes the cut.

### 45. Jimmy Nelson, SP, Milwaukee Brewers

Nelson's ceiling isn't anything to write home about, but he could be a solid back-of-the-rotation starter for years. He gets knocked down this list because the Brewers' acquisition of free agent Matt Garza makes his arrival more likely to happen later rather than sooner. Nelson isn't a standard mixed-league play; his impact will probably come in deeper mixed and only formats.

### 46. Arismendy Alcantara, SS, Chicago Cubs

It's hard to see where Alcantara fits in with the Cubs in 2014, but if he gets off to a fast start he could beat Baez to Wrigley Field and wrest the second base job from Darwin Barney some time this summer. Long term, the ceiling for Alcantara is high, but in 2014 a 10-homer/25-steal full-season pace is a realistic ceiling. Although Alcantara likely won't be up until September or 2015, he is worth including here because of the potential if he accelerates the timetable.

### 47. Allen Webster, SP, Boston Red Sox

Webster would be higher on this list if he toiled for a different organization that had a more pressing need for a midseason rotation replacement. But the Red Sox rotation is deep, and while anything could happen, it's more likely that Webster reprises his role as spot starter fill-in as opposed to midseason replacement who sticks. He could produce solid stats—particularly in the strikeout department—if he does stick, but that doesn't look likely. He could also land in the bullpen instead.

### 48. Alex Meyer, SP/RP, Minnesota Twins

Meyer's timetable was slowed by a shoulder injury that limited him to 8 1/3 innings at Double-A in 2013. His ceiling is that of a no. 2 starter, and a strong performance out of the gate could land him in Minnesota this summer, though a late-season promotion or a 2015 ETA is more likely. Meyer is another pitcher who ranks higher from a pure prospect perspective but is dinged on a 2014-only list. Some analysts believe that his strong AFL showing puts him on track for an early promotion, but don't be surprised if the Twins exercise caution.

### 49. Joc Pederson, OF, Los Angeles Dodgers

Pederson might have the ability and polish to make an impact now, but he is in a tough situation with the Dodgers, who have four quality outfielders in front of him. Carl Crawford and Matt Kemp aren't paragons of health, so if Pederson is to get a shot this year, that is likely where the path lies. Pederson's 20/20 potential makes him worth mentioning, and if the aforementioned injuries happen, he rises up this list with a silver bullet.

### 50. Marcus Semien, 2B, Chicago White Sox

Semien's ceiling isn't exciting, and he is blocked in Chicago at second, short, and third. But Gordon Beckham and Matt Davidson aren't insurmountable obstacles, and Semien could eventually replace one of them. Despite the minor-league 15-home-run power, Semien probably won't reach that in the majors. However, the 10/15 potential makes him worthwhile in deeper leagues as a middle-infield option if he can stick. If playing-time questions get resolved, Semien will make a fantasy impact in 2014. ∎

# The Top 40 Fantasy Prospects Outside of Major League Baseball

*by Bret Sayre*

In the wake of Masahiro Tanaka's signing with the New York Yankees for $155 million over seven years in January, now seems like a perfect opportunity to talk about who that next group of prospects/players to come into Major League Baseball will be. And I'm not just talking about Japanese imports, I'm talking about a group far more expansive and important to the shape of fantasy leagues to come.

Over the last half-decade, there's been a small, but noticeable movement to allow players outside of professional baseball (as we know it) to be owned in deep fantasy leagues. Permitting these players to be rostered prior to signing with an MLB team brings new challenges and opportunities to get a head start on your leaguemates. Whether you're reading the information produced at Baseball Prospectus by our prospect team (especially Nick Faleris, who leads our internal draft coverage) or everything that the Perfect Game guys put out, there's more available on amateur players now than ever before.

However, what's lacking are fantasy takes on this information. And with the help of some of the names mentioned earlier (along with others who are closely involved in this arena), I have put together a list of players you should get an early jump on in your leagues. The process of combining draft-eligible players for upcoming classes and international players, many of whom have unknown ETAs, was a challenge, but then again this isn't meant as a strict list of any sort. It's really more of an organized "get-to-know-you" for the next wave of players who you're going to wish you'd gotten to know earlier in two years.

Just remember that there will be so much movement, even with the 2014 draftees alone, over the next few months that having the background knowledge is only the first step. These names could be important. Know them, track them, love them, and reap the benefits.

## The List

### 1. Carlos Rodon, LHP (2014 draft, college)

The near-consensus no. 1 pick in the 2014 draft as of this writing, Rodon is the top pitching prospect available in the MLB draft since Stephen Strasburg. Armed with plus-plus velocity and a plus-plus slider from the left side, he'll move fast and arrive with much fanfare. You could argue that Rodon would be the top pitching prospect in the minors right now if eligible, though I'd put him slightly behind Taijuan Walker and Archie Bradley.

### 2. Jeff Hoffman, RHP (2014 draft, college)

If Rodon wasn't out capturing the hearts and minds of baseball evaluators everywhere, Hoffman would be getting more press. Armed with a mid-90s fastball and a potentially plus-plus curveball, he could be a big strikeout pitcher who can handle a lot of innings with a solid 6'4" frame. The command needs to take a step forward, but Hoffman opened eyes on the Cape last summer, and he'll look to keep them focused squarely on him this spring.

### 3. Alex Jackson, C/OF (2014 draft, high school)

Jackson is all about risk and reward. He has a bat that could play anywhere on the diamond with very big raw power, and a legitimate chance to stay at catcher. In fact, there may not be anyone in pro ball with more fantasy upside behind the plate than the Baseball Prospectus Prospect of the Year. And if he has to move off the position (or the team that drafts him does it voluntarily, a la Wil Myers), he can carry plenty of fantasy value from the outfield as well.

### 4. Kenta Maeda, RHP (Japan)

This is not another Yu Darvish, or even another Tanaka. However, Maeda brings great command/control and a vast arsenal of off-speed pitches that can miss bats. What he doesn't bring is heat—his fastball seesaws between the high-80s and low-90s. However, the 25-year-old's track record is impressive and includes a 2010 Sawamura Award (the Japanese Cy Young). He is much more about safety than upside, and is expected to be posted after the 2014 season.

### 5. Trea Turner, SS (2014 draft, college)

Speed is the name of Turner's game, as he could be a 40- to 50-steal type at the major-league level. Whether he turns into a top-flight fantasy option very much depends on how his hit tool develops. If he can keep his average respectable and knock a few over the fence, he can become a top-five fantasy shortstop.

### 6. Derek Fisher, OF (2014 draft, college)

A five-category threat who should move quickly upon entering the pros, Fisher doesn't have one standout tool that makes him drool-worthy. He's also likely to see his real-life draft value stagnate a bit because he'll probably be a left fielder. However, the overall value and decreased risk should make him a high pick in 2015 dynasty drafts.

### 7. Touki Toussaint, RHP (2014 draft, high school)

Toussaint is the top prep arm on this list. He has the chance for three plus pitches, including a potentially devastating curve that gets potential plus-plus grades from the scouts and induces faints from the weak of heart. He also gets bonus points for being one of the youngest players in the 2014 draft class and having an awesome name.

## 8. Ian Happ, 2B/OF (2015 draft, college)

The 2015 draft looks like a potentially strong one for college bats, and Happ leads the charge. A strong bet to hit for both average and power, his upside is higher from a fantasy perspective than that of any hitter from the 2014 draft class. Plus, he's athletic and quick enough to avoid being a zero in the steals category. If he can stay at the keystone, his fantasy value would benefit.

## 9. Aledmys Diaz, SS (Cuba)

The recently defected (but still awaiting OFAC clearance) Cuban shortstop ranks prominently on this list because he has a chance to post strong batting averages and have power (several scouts have put potential 6's on both). There are questions as to whether he'd stay at shortstop at the major-league level, but if the bat is as good as some believe, he'll have carry value anywhere.

## 10. Skye Bolt, OF (2015 draft, college)

Bolt, whose name rivals Toussaint's in awesomeness, is somewhat of an anomaly for highly touted college players—he's longer on tools than on present-level skills. A switch-hitter who has plenty of raw power from both sides, he also has the potential to contribute on the basepaths. There are questions about how his hit tool will play once he gets into pro ball, but the surrounding tools are there to make him a potentially high-end fantasy option.

## 11. Braxton Davidson, 1B/OF (2014 draft, high school)

Davidson is one of the most polished prep bats available in the 2014 draft. A finalist in the Perfect Game National Showcase Home Run Derby in June, he has the potential for plus power and a hit tool that shows flashes of the same possibility. However, it would take either a lot of work or a team that overlooks defense a bit for him to garner outfield eligibility as a pro.

## 12. Alex Bregman, 2B/SS (2015 draft, college)

Named the 2012-13 Freshman of the Year by Baseball America, Bregman may be the best pure hitter in college after slashing .369/.417/.546 with six homers and 16 steals. And his potential for fantasy would go up if he ever returned to his high-school position of catcher. Elite-level performance also runs in Bregman's blood: his uncle, Larry Schechter, is a six-time Tout Wars winner and author of Winning Fantasy Baseball.

## 13. Tyler Kolek, RHP (2014 draft, high school)

There is no prep pitcher in the 2014 draft class who brings more heat than the big Texan. Routinely clocked in the upper-90s, he has the size and potential with both the fastball and secondary offerings to flash frontline status. However, it's a riskier profile, as he needs a good amount of work on both the breaking pitch and changeup side.

## 14. Jose Fernandez, 2B (Cuba)

There may not be a better pure hitter in Cuba than Fernandez. However, unlike a few of the other Cuban names on this list, he has not defected, and any ETA you could assign to the 25-year old would be a guess. Statistically, he could be a Matt Carpenter type with high average, good on-base skills, and the potential for mid-teens pop. If I knew he was defecting tomorrow, he'd be no. 2 on this list.

## 15. Michael Gettys, OF (2014 draft, high school)

Maybe the toolsiest position player currently projected as a first-round pick in June, Gettys has a power/speed combination (both could eventually grade out as plus simultaneously). However, he's raw and there are plenty of questions about the hit tool. We know the range of outcomes here.

## 16. Grant Holmes, RHP (2014 draft, high school)

Holmes draws mixed opinions on his delivery, which can get a little long, but the stuff coming out of his right arm makes him one of the top prep pitchers available in this deep pool of young pitchers. He can sit in the mid-90s with his fastball and flash a plus curveball, but has rarely needed the change in high school. Good frame, good potential.

## 17. Jacob Gatewood, SS (2014 draft, high school)

One of the ultimate risk/reward picks on this list, Gatewood has immense power, but may not make enough contact for it to matter or stay at shortstop. If he is what his tools can be, he's an all-star-level shortstop with big-time power who will be in high demand in fantasy leagues. If the hit tool fails, he may never make it out of Double-A.

## 18. Nick Burdi, RHP, Louisville (2014 draft, college)

There may not be a better one-two punch than Burdi's fastball (which can touch triple digits) and his slider that gets some love as a future 70 pitch. He is a reliever, but don't be surprised if he's popped by a contending team and sees major-league action shortly after the All-Star break.

## 19. Rusney Castillo, OF (Cuba)

He's not a big guy at 5'9", but Castillo was a big-time performer in Serie Nacional up until a poor final season. In 2011-12, he hit .332 with 16 homers and 22 steals, but he's not expected to provide as much pop in the majors (though he is a deft basestealer). The 26-year old defected in December and is expected to sign with a major-league team during the first half of 2014.

## 20. Kyle Schwarber, 1B/C (2014 draft, college)

The catcher designation is still on there more for effect than anything else, as the chances of Schwarber catching in the majors are slim. However, he does carry 30-homer potential and what could be a solid-average hit tool—that'll play in fantasy, even if he is a first baseman.

## 21. Brady Aiken, LHP (2014 draft, high school)

Possibly the best left-handed prep pitcher available in the 2014 draft, Aiken boasts strong potential across the board from a strong 6'3" frame. He is an advanced high-school arm with early fastball command and a curveball that flashes plus (along with a change that's not far behind). He's also going to be one of the youngest players available this summer, as he won't turn 18 until mid-August.

## 22. Nathan Kirby, LHP (2015 draft, college)

The 6'2" left-hander was a potential first-round pick out of high school in 2012, but had no intention of passing on a college career at the University of Virginia. With the potential for two plus secondary pitches (including a curveball that could be plus-plus down the road) and low-to-mid-90s velocity from the left side, he could in high demand next summer.

### 23. Aaron Nola, RHP (2014 draft, college)

The LSU junior and Friday night starter does not have the highest upside on this list, but what he lacks there, he makes up for in extreme strikeout-to-walk ratios. However, this is an example where a pitcher's control is much more advanced than his command—and despite the gaudy numbers, he doesn't put the ball where he wants to. Yet.

### 24. Dazmon Cameron, OF (2015 draft, high school)

One of the players with a shot at going first overall in the 2015 draft, Cameron has all of the tools you're looking for in a potential fantasy stud. That he has power and speed potential shouldn't be surprising, as his father, Mike Cameron, did both of those things well at the major-league level for a long time. He also may be further from the majors than anyone on this list.

### 25. Sean Reid-Foley, RHP (2014 draft, high school)

Another candidate to be the top prep arm selected in this summer's draft, Reid-Foley has the potential to tick up in velocity this spring and add to an already impressive arsenal that includes four pitches that flash at least average potential, including an out pitch in his slider. It also doesn't hurt that he's been at his best when the showcase lights have shone brightest.

### 26. Yasmani Tomas, OF (Cuba)

If you're looking for the next Cuban power export, Tomas is probably your guy. The 22-year old stepped into the spotlight after the departures of Yoenis Cespedes and Leonys Martin. With strong bat speed, the potential to hit 25 homers, and steal a few bases, Tomas is a lottery ticket like all other Cuban players yet to defect, but a good one to purchase.

### 27. Tyler Beede, RHP (2014 draft, college)

Beede has been one of the better known names available in the 2014 draft ever since he spurned the Toronto Blue Jays in the first round of 2011 to attend Vanderbilt. The stuff has been there for him to get plenty of strikeouts most of the time, including a plus-plus fastball and bat-missing secondaries, but inconsistency in both command and stuff has caused his stock to drop a bit.

### 28. Nick Gordon, SS (2014 draft, high school)

If you're talking about deeper league formats, Gordon probably ranks higher than this, as his floor is higher than that of most prep players from the 2014 draft class. However, he doesn't have immense pop or the speed of his brother (Dee), so the fantasy upside is somewhat limited. On the plus side, he's a good bet to stay at the position.

### 29. Kodi Medeiros, LHP (2014 draft, high school)

Evaluators rarely are lukewarm on Medeiros—either they love him or likely won't touch him. The stuff can be intense, but he has trouble maintaining it over more than a couple of innings. If he can build into a starter's workload, he could be a steal. If he's a reliever, he's probably ranked too high here.

### 30. Ti'Quan Forbes, SS/3B (2014 draft, high school)

Stop me if you've heard this before. Forbes is a raw talent with the potential to be a five-category fantasy player with a lot of speed on the basepaths. He might the best athlete on this list and has a chance to stay at shortstop, and his 6'4" frame looks like roses and unicorns. He's also extremely young for his draft class and will have a long developmental path.

### 31. Eric Fedde, RHP (2014 draft, college)

The UNLV junior has the rare trifecta of college success, Cape success, and projectability. His changeup needs development, but he could be a solid no. 4 fantasy starter even if he doesn't have a jump up in stuff. The fact that scouts see potential to develop into more of a frontline starter is icing on the cake. He could be a fast riser this spring.

### 32. Michael Cederoth, RHP (2014 draft, college)

Another very hard-throwing college pitcher, Cederoth has touched triple digits at San Diego State. The jury is out on whether he can start, but even if he's relegated to the bullpen, he has the big-time stuff needed to be a big-time closer. He can hold velocity deep into games, so that's a check in the right column

### 33. Yusei Kikuchi, LHP (Japan)

Kikuchi was the original Shohei Otani (who we'll get to later). He very publicly considered bypassing the NPB and coming straight to the United States out of high school in 2009, but eventually decided against it. Now he is a 22-year-old burgeoning Japanese star coming off a 1.92 ERA and 92 strikeouts in 108 innings. Look for rumors of him being posted around 2017.

### 34. Brendan Rodgers, SS (2015 draft, high school)

The second of two 2015 prep players on this list, Rodgers has an ETA as far away as anyone included here (it could be 2019). But he is a middle infielder with the potential for plus grades in his hit and power tools, which will make him a very in-demand commodity come next summer.

### 35. Shohei Otani, RHP (Japan)

Best known as that Japanese kid who almost bypassed the NPB to come straight to the United States, Otani also has possibly the best raw stuff of any pitcher in Japan. Unfortunately for fantasy owners, he's still just 19 years old and won't be posted for another five or so seasons (at the earliest). There's only one Yu Darvish, but Otani can be damn good in his own right.

### 36. Michael Conforto, OF (2014 draft, college)

One of the better power bats in the college crop for the 2014 draft, Conforto could be a 25-homer outfielder at the major-league level. Unfortunately, the hit tool lags behind, leaving him with a diminished fantasy ceiling. He should be a relatively fast mover whose value could fluctuate based on landing spot.

### 37. Brandon Finnegan, LHP (2014 draft, college)

You get a little more leeway when you're a short left-handed pitcher than if you throw right handed, but there's nothing small about Finnegan's stuff. With a mid-90s fastball and two strong secondary pitches in his slider and change, he could develop into a high-strikeout fantasy option in a couple of years.

### 38. Norge Ruiz, RHP (Cuba)

Possibly the best pitching prospect in Cuba, Ruiz turns 20 in March, but is not the imposing figure that Aroldis Chapman was. Standing 5'9" and 170 pounds, Ruiz has advanced command of his secondary arsenal and low-90s velocity to back it up. His ETA is as unknown as unknown can be, but if he defects, he'll draw a lot of attention.

### 39. Ryan Boldt, OF (2016 draft, college)

One of my favorite sleepers in the 2013 draft, Boldt ended up in college due to the combination of a high signing bonus and a knee injury that wrecked his senior season. When on the field, he flashes five-tool potential and could be a very fast mover upon being drafted in two years.

### 40. Luke Weaver, RHP (2014 draft, college)

Weaver must build off his strong fastball to project as much more than an innings eater at the major-league level, and while the secondary stuff can flash, it doesn't hold at this point. He's a guy who could raise his stock significantly this spring if he can show more with a breaking ball.

## Honorable Mentions

Here are a few more names to stash in your back pocket:

- Max Pentecost, C (2014 draft, college)
- Luis Ortiz, RHP (2014 draft, high school)
- Shintaro Fujinami, RHP (Japan)
- John Aiello, SS/3B (2015 draft, high school)
- Alfredo Despaigne, OF (Cuba)

Also, Suk-Min Yoon was going to be number 23 on this list, but he signed with the Baltimore Orioles just before we went to press. You'll still want to know about him, so here's the scoop:

The Korean right-hander is more of a solid back-end pitcher than a front-of-the-rotation option. However, since he is already in a major-league organization, he gets a bump here. None of his pitches likely grade as plus, but he knows where the ball is going and he has no fewer than four pitches that he can command with movement.

### Conclusion

There might not be another Darvish or Cespedes in this group, but some of these guys will make an impact. As I said earlier: Know them, track them, love them, and reap the benefits. If you don't do it, your competition will. ■

# Statistical Appendix

**W**hy don't you get your nose out of those numbers and watch a game? It's a false dilemma, of course. Chances are, Baseball Prospectus readers watch more games than the typical fan. They also probably pay better attention when they do. The numbers do not replace observation, they supplement it. Having the numbers allows you to learn things not readily seen by mere watching, and to keep up on many more players than any one person could on their own.

So this book doesn't ask you to choose between the two. Instead, we combine numerical analysis with the observations of a lot of very bright people. They won't always agree. Just as the eyes don't always see what the numbers do, the reverse can be true. In order to get the most out of this book, however, it helps to understand the numbers we're presenting and why.

## Offense

The core of our offense measurements is True Average, which attempts to quantify everything a player does at the plate—hitting for power, taking walks, striking out and even "productive" outs—and scale it to batting average. A player with a TAv of .260 is average, .300 exceptional, .200 rather awful.

True Average also accounts for the context a player performs in. That means we adjust it based on the mix of parks a player plays in. Also, rather than use a blanket park adjustment for every player on a team, a player who plays a disproportionate amount of his games at home will see that reflected in his numbers. We also adjust based upon league quality: The average player in the AL is better than the average player in the NL, and True Average accounts for this.

Because hitting runs isn't the entirety of scoring runs, we also look at a player's Baserunning Runs. BRR accounts for the value of a player's ability to steal bases, of course, but also accounts for his ability to go first to third on a single, or advance on a fly ball.

## Defense

Defense is a much thornier issue. The general move in the sabermetric community has been toward stats based on zone data, where human stringers record the type of batted ball (grounder, liner, fly ball) and its presumed landing location. That data is used to compile expected outs for comparing a fielder's actual performance.

The trouble with zone data is twofold. First, unlike the sorts of data that we use in the calculation of the statistics you see in this book, zone data wasn't made publicly available; the data was recorded by commercial data providers who kept the raw data private, only disclosing it to a select few who paid for it. Second, as we've seen the field of zone-based defensive analysis open up—more data and more metrics based upon that data coming to light—we see that the conclusions of zone-based defensive metrics don't hold up to outside scrutiny. Different data providers can come to very different conclusions about the same events. And even two metrics based upon the same data set can come to radically different conclusions based upon their starting assumptions—assumptions that haven't been tested, using methods that can't be duplicated or verified by outside analysts.

The quality of the fielder can bias the data: Zone-based fielding metrics will tend to attribute more expected outs to good fielders than bad fielders, irrespective of the distribution of batted balls. Scorers who work in parks with high press boxes will tend to score more line drives than scorers who work in parks with low press boxes.

Our FRAA incorporates play-by-play data, allowing us to study the issue of defense at a granular level, without resorting to the sorts of subjective data used in some other fielding metrics. We count how many plays a player made, as well as expected plays for the average player at that position based upon a pitcher's estimated ground-ball tendencies and the handedness of the batter. There are also adjustments for park and the base-out situations.

## Pitching

Of course, how we measure fielding influences how we measure pitching. Most sabermetric analysis of pitching has been inspired by Voros McCracken, who stated, "There is little if any difference among major-league pitchers in their ability to prevent hits on balls hit in the field of play." When first published, this statement was extremely controversial, but later research has by-and-large validated it. McCracken (and others) went forth from that finding to come up with a variety of defense-independent pitching measures.

The trouble is that many efforts to separate pitching from fielding have ended up separating pitching from pitching—looking at only a handful of variables (typically walks, strikeouts, and home runs—the "three true outcomes") in isolation from the situation in which they occurred. What we've done instead is take a pitcher's actual results—not just what happened, but when it happened—and adjust it for the quality of a pitcher's defensive support, as measured by FRAA.

Applying FRAA to pitchers in this sense is easier than applying it to fielders. We don't have to worry about figuring out which fielder is responsible for making an out, only identifying the likelihood of an out being made.

So there is far less uncertainty here than there is in fielding analysis.

Note that Fair RA means exactly that, not his earned runs allowed per game. Looking only at earned runs tends over time to overrate three kinds of pitchers:

1. Pitchers who play in parks where scorers hand out more errors. Looking at error rates between parks tells us scorers differ significantly in how likely they are to score any given play as an error (as opposed to an infield hit);

2. Ground-ball pitchers, because a substantial proportion of errors occur on groundballs; and

3. Pitchers who aren't very good. Good pitchers tend to allow fewer unearned runs than bad pitchers, because good pitchers have more ways to get out of jams than bad pitchers. They're more likely to get a strikeout to end the inning, and less likely to give up a home run.

For a metric that provides a more forward-looking perspective, we have Fielding Independent Pitching, a metric developed independently by Tom Tango and Clay Dreslough that says what a pitcher's expected ERA would be given his walks, strikeouts, and home runs allowed. FIP is attempting to answer a different question than Fair RA; instead of saying how well a pitcher performed, it tells us how much of a pitcher's performance we think is due to things the pitcher has direct control over. Over time, we see pitchers who consistently over- or underperform their FIPs through some skill that isn't picked up by the rather limited components. FIP may be useful in identifying pitchers who were "lucky" or "unlucky," but some caution must be exercised.

## Projection

Of course, many of you aren't turning to this book just for a look at what a player has done, but a look at what a player is going to do—the PECOTA projections.

PECOTA, initially developed by Nate Silver (who has moved on to greater fame as a political analyst), consists of three parts:

1. Major league equivalencies, to allow us to use minor-league stats to project how a player will perform in the majors;

2. Baseline forecasts, which use weighted averages and regression to the mean to produce an estimate of a player's true talent level; and

3. A career path adjustment, which incorporates information on how comparable players' stats changed over time.

Now that we've gone over the stats, let's go over what's inside the book.

## Position Players

As an example, take a look at the position player statistical block for the leader of our Top 101 Prospects list, Byron Buxton.

| YEAR | TEAM | LVL | AGE | PA | R | 2B | 3B | HR | RBI | BB | SO | SB | CS | AVG/OBP/SLG | TAv | BABIP | BRR | FRAA | WARP |
|------|------|-----|-----|-----|----|----|----|----|-----|----|-----|----|----|-------------|-----|-------|-----|----------|------|
| 2013 | CDR | A | 19 | 321 | 68 | 15 | 10 | 8 | 55 | 44 | 56 | 32 | 11 | .341/.431/.559 | .349 | .402 | 4.6 | CF(66): 3.5 | 5.0 |
| 2013 | FTM | A+ | 19 | 253 | 41 | 4 | 8 | 4 | 22 | 32 | 49 | 23 | 8 | .326/.415/.472 | .320 | .404 | 5.0 | CF(55): 5.1 | 3.6 |
| 2014 | MIN | MLB | 20 | 250 | 33 | 8 | 3 | 5 | 21 | 22 | 63 | 13 | 5 | .250/.319/.374 | .257 | .320 | 1.2 | CF 4, LF 0 | 1.2 |
| 2015 | MIN | MLB | 21 | 607 | 75 | 22 | 8 | 15 | 69 | 66 | 147 | 28 | 10 | .261/.344/.416 | .284 | .330 | 2.3 | CF 8 | 3.7 |

The player-specific sections begin with biographical information before moving onto the column headers and actual data. The column headers begin with more standard information like year, team, level (majors or minors, and which level of the minors), and the raw, untranslated tallies found on the back of a baseball card: PA (plate appearances), R (runs), 2B (doubles), 3B (triples), HR (home runs), RBI, (runs batted in), BB (walks), SO (strikeouts), SB (stolen bases), and CS (caught stealing).

Following those are the untranslated triple-slash rate statistics: batting average (AVG), on base percentage (OBP), and slugging percentage (SLG). Their "slash" nickname is derived from the occasional presentation of slash-delimitation, such as noting that Robinson Cano hit .314/.383/.516. The slash line is followed by True Average (TAv), which rolls all those things and more into one easy-to-digest number.

BABIP stands for Batting Average on Balls in Play and is meant to show how well a hitter did when he put the ball in play. An especially low or high BABIP may mean a hitter was especially lucky or unlucky. However, line-drive hitters will tend to have especially high BABIPs from season to season; so will speedy hitters who are able to beat out more grounders for base hits.

Next is Baserunning Runs (BRR) which, as mentioned earlier, covers all sorts of base-running accomplishments, not just stolen bases. Then comes Fielding Runs Above Average; for historical stats, we have the number of games played at each position in parentheses.

The last column is Wins Above Replacement Player. WARP combines a player's batting runs above average (derived from a player's True Average), BRR, FRAA, an adjustment based upon position played, and a credit for plate appearances based upon the difference between the "replacement level" (derived from looking at the quality of players added to a team's roster after the start of the season) and the league average.

## Pitchers

Now let's look at how pitchers are presented, looking at the top pitching prospect on our list, Mark Appel:

| YEAR | TEAM | LVL | AGE | W | L | SV | G | GS | IP | H | HR | BB | SO | BB9 | SO9 | GB% | BABIP | WHIP | ERA | FIP | FRA | WARP |
|------|------|-----|-----|---|---|----|----|----|------|-----|----|----|-----|-----|------|-----|-------|------|------|------|------|------|
| 2013 | TCV | A- | 21 | 0 | 0 | 0 | 2 | 2 | 5.0 | 6 | 0 | 0 | 6 | 0.0 | 10.8 | 71% | .429 | 1.20 | 3.60 | 0.70 | 2.67 | 0.2 |
| 2013 | QUD | A | 21 | 0 | 0 | 0 | 8 | 8 | 33.0 | 30 | 2 | 9 | 27 | 2.5 | 7.4 | 54% | .277 | 1.18 | 3.82 | 3.40 | 4.58 | 0.4 |
| 2014 | HOU | MLB | 22 | 1 | 3 | 0 | 8 | 8 | 32.0 | 38 | 5 | 16 | 18 | 4.5 | 5.1 | 47% | .308 | 1.70 | 5.89 | 5.96 | 6.40 | -0.4 |
| 2015 | HOU | MLB | 23 | 8 | 11 | 0 | 28 | 28 | 172.0 | 190 | 24 | 79 | 115 | 4.1 | 6.0 | 47% | .302 | 1.57 | 5.21 | 5.12 | 5.67 | -1.1 |

The first line and the YEAR, TM, LVL, and AGE columns are the same as in the hitters' example above. The next set of columns—W (wins), L (losses), SV (saves), G (games pitched), GS (games started), IP (innings pitched), H (hits), HR, BB, SO, BB9, SO9—are the actual, unadjusted cumulative stats compiled by the pitcher during each season.

Next is GB%, which is the percentage of all batted balls that were hit on the ground including both outs and hits. The average GB% for a major league pitcher in 2007 was about 45%; a pitcher with a GB% anywhere north of 50% can be considered a good ground-ball pitcher. As mentioned above, this is based upon the observation of human stringers and can be skewed based upon a number of factors. We've included the number as a guide, but please approach it skeptically.

BABIP is the same statistic as for batters, but often tells you more in the case of pitchers, since most pitchers have very little control over their batting average on balls in play. A high BABIP is most likely due to a poor defense or bad luck rather than a pitcher's own abilities, and may be a good indicator of a potential rebound. A typical league-average BABIP is around .295–.300.

WHIP and ERA are common to most fans, with the former measuring the number of walks and hits allowed on a per-inning basis while the latter prorates earned runs allowed on a per-nine-innings basis. Neither is translated or adjusted in any way.

Fair RA (FRA) has been gone into in some depth above and is the basis of WARP for pitchers. Incorporating play-by-play data allows us to set different replacement levels for starting pitchers and relievers. Relief pitchers have several advantages over starters: they can give their best effort on every pitch, and hitters have fewer chances to pick up on what they're doing. That means that it's significantly easier to find decent replacements for relief pitchers than it is for starting pitchers, and that's reflected in the replacement level for each.

We also credit starters for pitching deeper into games and "saving the 'pen"—a starting pitcher who can go deep into a game (while pitching effectively) allows a manager to keep his worst relievers in the 'pen and bring his best relievers out to preserve a lead.

All of this means that WARP values for relief pitchers (especially closers) will seem lower than what we've seen in the past—and may conflict with how we feel about relief aces coming in and "saving" the game. Saves give extra credit to the closer for what his teammates did to put him in a save spot to begin with; WARP is incapable of feeling excitement over a successful save and judges them dispassionately.

## PECOTA

Both pitchers and hitters have PECOTA projections for next season, as well as a set of biographical details that describe the performance of that player's comparable players according to PECOTA.

The 2014 line is the PECOTA projection for the player in the upcoming season. Note that the player is projected into the league and park context as indicated by his team abbreviation. All PECOTAs represent a player's projected major-league performance. The numbers beneath the player's name—Breakout, Improve, Collapse, and Attrition—are also a part of PECOTA. These estimate the likelihood of changes in performance relative to a player's previously established level of production, based upon the performance of the comparable players:

- **Breakout Rate** is the percent chance that a player's production will improve by at least 20 percent relative to the weighted average of his performance over his most recent seasons.

- **Improve Rate** is the percent chance that a player's production will improve at all relative to his baseline performance. A player who is expected to perform just the same as he has in the recent past will have an Improve Rate of 50 percent.

- **Collapse Rate** is the percent chance that a position player's equivalent runs produced per PA will decline by at least 25 percent relative to his baseline performance over his past three seasons.

- **Attrition Rate** operates on playing time rather than performance. Specifically, it measures the likelihood that a player's playing time will decrease by at least 50 percent relative to his established level.

Breakout Rate and Collapse Rate can sometimes be counterintuitive for players who have already experienced a radical change in their performance levels. It's also worth noting that the projected decline in a given player's rate performances might not be indicative of an expected decline in underlying ability or skill, but rather something of an anticipated correction following a breakout season. MLB% is the percentage of similar players who played at the major-league level in the relevant season. Note that players who have an MLB% of 0 also have Breakout, Improve, Collapse, and Attrition Rates of 0.

The final pieces of information, listed just to the right of the player's Attrition Rate, are his three highest scoring comparable players as determined by PECOTA. Occasionally, a player's top comparables will not be representative of the larger sample that PECOTA uses. All comparables represent a snapshot of how the listed player was performing at the same age as the current player, so if a 23-year-old hitter is compared to Sammy Sosa, he's actually being compared to a 23-year-old Sammy Sosa, not the decrepit Orioles version of Sosa, nor to Sosa's career as a whole.

# Minor League Team Codes

| CODE | TEAM | LEAGUE | AFFILIATION | Name |
|------|------|--------|-------------|------|
| ABE | Aberdeen | NYP | Orioles | IronBirds |
| ABQ | Albuquerque | PCL | Dodgers | Isotopes |
| AKR | Akron | EAS | Indians | Aeros |
| ALT | Altoona | EAS | Pirates | Curve |
| ANA | Los Angeles | AL | - | Angels |
| ANG | AZL Angels | AZL | Angels | - |
| ARI | Arizona | NL | - | D-backs |
| ARK | Arkansas | TEX | Angels | Travelers |
| ART | Artemisa | CNS | - | |
| ASH | Asheville | SAL | Rockies | Tourists |
| AST | GCL Astros | GCL | Astros | GCL Astros |
| ATH | AZL Athletics | AZL | Athletics | - |
| ATL | Atlanta | NL | - | Braves |
| AUB | Auburn | NYP | Nationals | Doubledays |
| AUG | Augusta | SAL | Giants | GreenJackets |
| BAK | Bakersfield | CAL | Reds | Blaze |
| BAL | Baltimore | AL | - | Orioles |
| BAT | Batavia | NYP | Marlins | Muckdogs |
| BGR | Bowling Green | MID | Rays | Hot Rods |
| BIL | Billings | PIO | Reds | Mustangs |
| BIN | Binghamton | EAS | Mets | Mets |
| BIR | Birmingham | SOU | White Sox | Barons |
| BLJ | GCL Blue Jays | GCL | Blue Jays | GCL Blue Jays |
| BLT | Beloit | MID | Athletics | Snappers |
| BLU | Bluefield | APP | Blue Jays | Blue Jays |
| BNC | Burlington | APP | Royals | Royals |
| BOI | Boise | NOR | Cubs | Hawks |
| BOS | Boston | AL | - | Red Sox |
| BOW | Bowie | EAS | Orioles | Baysox |
| BRA | GCL Braves | GCL | Braves | GCL Braves |
| BRD | Bradenton | FSL | Pirates | Marauders |
| BRI | Bristol | APP | White Sox | White Sox |
| BRO | Brooklyn | NYP | Mets | Cyclones |
| BRR | AZL Brewers | AZL | Brewers | - |
| BRV | Brevard County | FSL | Brewers | Manatees |
| BUF | Buffalo | INT | Blue Jays | Bisons |
| BUR | Burlington | MID | Angels | Bees |
| CAR | Carolina | CAR | Indians | Mudcats |
| CCH | Corpus Christi | TEX | Astros | Hooks |
| CDR | Cedar Rapids | MID | Twins | Kernels |
| CFG | Cienfuegos | CNS | - | |
| CHA | Chicago | AL | - | White Sox |
| CHB | Chiba Lotte | NPB | - | Marines |
| CHN | Chicago | NL | - | Cubs |
| CHR | Charlotte | INT | White Sox | Knights |
| CHT | Chattanooga | SOU | Dodgers | Lookouts |
| CHU | Chunichi | NPB | - | Dragons |
| CIN | AZL Reds | AZL | Reds | - |
| CIN | Cincinnati | NL | - | Reds |
| CLE | Cleveland | AL | - | Indians |
| CLE | AZL Indians | AZL | Indians | - |

| CODE | TEAM | LEAGUE | AFFILIATION | Name |
|------|------|--------|-------------|------|
| CLN | Clinton | MID | Mariners | LumberKings |
| CLR | Clearwater | FSL | Phillies | Threshers |
| COH | Columbus | INT | Indians | Clippers |
| COL | Colorado | NL | - | Rockies |
| CRD | GCL Cardinals | GCL | Cardinals | GCL Cardinals |
| CSC | Charleston | SAL | Yankees | RiverDogs |
| CSP | Colorado Springs | PCL | Rockies | Sky Sox |
| CUB | AZL Cubs | AZL | Cubs | - |
| DAC | DSL D-backs/Reds | DSL | - | - |
| DAN | DSL Angels | DSL | Angels | - |
| DAS | DSL Astros | DSL | Astros | - |
| DAT | DSL Athletics | DSL | Athletics | - |
| DAY | Daytona | FSL | Cubs | Cubs |
| DBL | DSL Blue Jays | DSL | Blue Jays | - |
| DBR | DSL Braves | DSL | Braves | - |
| DBW | DSL Brewers | DSL | Brewers | - |
| DCA | DSL Cardinals | DSL | Cardinals | - |
| DCH | DSL Cubs2 | DSL | Cubs | - |
| DCU | DSL Cubs1 | DSL | Cubs | - |
| DDI | DSL D-backs | DSL | D-backs | - |
| DDO | DSL Dodgers | DSL | Dodgers | - |
| DDR | DSL Rays | DSL | Rays | - |
| DEL | Delmarva | SAL | Orioles | Shorebirds |
| DET | Detroit | AL | - | Tigers |
| DGI | DSL Giants | DSL | Giants | - |
| DIA | AZL D-backs | AZL | D-backs | - |
| DIN | DSL Indians | DSL | Indians | - |
| DME | DSL Mets 1 | DSL | Mets | - |
| DML | DSL Marlins | DSL | Marlins | - |
| DMR | DSL Mariners | DSL | Mariners | - |
| DNV | Danville | APP | Braves | Braves |
| DOD | AZL Dodgers | AZL | Dodgers | - |
| DOR | DSL Orioles | DSL | Orioles | - |
| DPA | DSL Padres | DSL | Padres | - |
| DPH | DSL Phillies | DSL | Phillies | - |
| DPI | DSL Pirates1 | DSL | Pirates | - |
| DPT | DSL Pirates2 | DSL | Pirates | - |
| DRD | DSL Reds | DSL | Reds | - |
| DRG | DSL Rangers | DSL | Rangers | - |
| DRO | DSL Rockies | DSL | Rockies | - |
| DRS | DSL Red Sox | DSL | Red Sox | - |
| DRY | DSL Royals | DSL | Royals | - |
| DTI | DSL Tigers | DSL | Tigers | - |
| DTW | DSL Twins | DSL | Twins | - |
| DUN | Dunedin | FSL | Blue Jays | Blue Jays |
| DUR | Durham | INT | Rays | Bulls |
| DWA | DSL Nationals | DSL | Nationals | - |
| DWS | DSL White Sox | DSL | White Sox | - |
| DYA | DSL Yankees1 | DSL | Yankees | - |
| DYN | DSL Yankees2 | DSL | Yankees | - |
| DYT | Dayton | MID | Reds | Dragons |

| CODE | TEAM | LEAGUE | AFFILIATION | Name |
|------|------|--------|-------------|------|
| ELZ | Elizabethton | APP | Twins | Twins |
| ERI | Erie | EAS | Tigers | SeaWolves |
| EUG | Eugene | NOR | Padres | Emeralds |
| EVE | Everett | NOR | Mariners | AquaSox |
| FKU | Fukuoka | NPB | - | Hawks |
| FRD | Frederick | CAR | Orioles | Keys |
| FRE | Fresno | PCL | Giants | Grizzlies |
| FRI | Frisco | TEX | Rangers | RoughRiders |
| FTM | Fort Myers | FSL | Twins | Miracle |
| FTW | Fort Wayne | MID | Padres | TinCaps |
| GIA | AZL Giants | AZL | Giants | - |
| GJR | Grand Junction | PIO | Rockies | Rockies |
| GRB | Greensboro | SAL | Marlins | Grasshoppers |
| GRF | Great Falls | PIO | White Sox | Voyagers |
| GRL | Great Lakes | MID | Dodgers | Loons |
| GRN | Greenville | SAL | Red Sox | Drive |
| GRV | Greeneville | APP | Astros | Astros |
| GWN | Gwinnett | INT | Braves | Braves |
| HAB | La | Habana | CNS | - |
| HAG | Hagerstown | SAL | Nationals | Suns |
| HAR | Harrisburg | EAS | Nationals | Senators |
| HDS | High Desert | CAL | Mariners | Mavericks |
| HEL | Helena | PIO | Brewers | Brewers |
| HIC | Hickory | SAL | Rangers | Crawdads |
| HNS | Hanshin | NPB | - | Tigers |
| HOU | Houston | AL | - | Astros |
| HRO | Hiroshima Toyo | NPB | - | Carp |
| HUD | Hudson Valley | NYP | Rays | Renegades |
| HUN | Huntsville | SOU | Brewers | Stars |
| IDA | Idaho Falls | PIO | Royals | Chukars |
| IND | Indianapolis | INT | Pirates | Indians |
| IOW | Iowa | PCL | Cubs | Cubs |
| JAM | Jamestown | NYP | Pirates | Jammers |
| JAX | Jacksonville | SOU | Marlins | Suns |
| JCY | Johnson City | APP | Cardinals | Cardinals |
| JUP | Jupiter | FSL | Marlins | Hammerheads |
| KAN | Kannapolis | SAL | White Sox | Intimidators |
| KCA | Kansas City | AL | - | Royals |
| KNC | Kane County | MID | Cubs | Cougars |
| KNG | Kingsport | APP | Mets | Mets |
| LAK | Lakeland | FSL | Tigers | Flying Tigers |
| LAN | Los Angeles | NL | - | Dodgers |
| LEH | Lehigh Valley | INT | Phillies | IronPigs |
| LEL | Lake Elsinore | CAL | Padres | Storm |
| LEX | Lexington | SAL | Royals | Legends |
| LKC | Lake County | MID | Indians | Captains |
| LNC | Lancaster | CAL | Astros | JetHawks |
| LNS | Lansing | MID | Blue Jays | Lugnuts |
| LOU | Louisville | INT | Reds | Bats |
| LOW | Lowell | NYP | Red Sox | Spinners |
| LTU | Las Tunas | CNS | - | |
| LVG | Las Vegas | PCL | Mets | 51s |
| LWD | Lakewood | SAL | Phillies | BlueClaws |
| LYN | Lynchburg | CAR | Braves | Hillcats |
| MEM | Memphis | PCL | Cardinals | Redbirds |
| MET | DSL Mets2 | DSL | Mets | - |
| MHV | Mahoning Valley | NYP | Indians | Scrappers |
| MIA | Miami | NL | - | Marlins |
| MID | Midland | TEX | Athletics | RockHounds |
| MIL | Milwaukee | NL | - | Brewers |
| MIN | Minnesota | AL | - | Twins |
| MIS | Mississippi | SOU | Braves | Braves |
| MNT | Montgomery | SOU | Rays | Biscuits |
| MOB | Mobile | SOU | D-backs | BayBears |
| MOD | Modesto | CAL | Rockies | Nuts |
| MRL | GCL Marlins | GCL | Marlins | GCL Marlins |
| MRN | AZL Mariners | AZL | Mariners | - |
| MSO | Missoula | PIO | D-backs | Osprey |
| MTS | GCL Mets | GCL | Mets | GCL Mets |
| MYR | Myrtle Beach | CAR | Rangers | Pelicans |
| NAS | Nashville | PCL | Brewers | Sounds |
| NAT | GCL Nationals | GCL | Nationals | GCL Nationals |
| NBR | New Britain | EAS | Twins | Rock Cats |
| NHP | New Hampshire | EAS | Blue Jays | Fisher Cats |
| NIP | Nippon Ham | NPB | - | Fighters |
| NOR | Norfolk | INT | Orioles | Tides |
| NWA | NW Arkansas | TEX | Royals | Naturals |
| NWO | New Oleans | PCL | Marlins | Zephyrs |
| NYA | New York | AL | - | Yankees |
| NYN | New York | NL | - | Mets |
| OAK | Oakland | AL | - | Athletics |
| OGD | Ogden | PIO | Dodgers | Raptors |
| OKL | Oklahoma City | PCL | Astros | RedHawks |
| OMA | Omaha | PCL | Royals | Storm Chasers |
| ONE | Connecticut | NYP | Tigers | Tigers |
| ORI | GCL Orioles | GCL | Orioles | GCL Orioles |
| ORM | Orem | PIO | Angels | Owlz |
| ORX | Orix | NPB | - | Buffaloes |
| PAW | Pawtucket | INT | Red Sox | Red Sox |
| PCH | Charlotte | FSL | Rays | Stone Crabs |
| PDR | AZL Padres | AZL | Padres | - |
| PEN | Pensacola | SOU | Reds | Blue Wahoos |
| PEO | Peoria | MID | Cardinals | Chiefs |
| PHI | Philadelphia | NL | - | Phillies |
| PHL | GCL Phillies | GCL | Phillies | GCL Phillies |
| PIR | GCL Pirates | GCL | Pirates | GCL Pirates |
| PIT | Pittsburgh | NL | - | Pirates |
| PMB | Palm Beach | FSL | Cardinals | Cardinals |
| PME | Portland | EAS | Red Sox | Sea Dogs |
| POT | Potomac | CAR | Nationals | Nationals |
| PRI | Princeton | APP | Rays | Rays |
| PUL | Pulaski | APP | Mariners | Mariners |
| QUD | Quad Cities | MID | Astros | River Bandits |
| RAK | Rakuten | NPB | - | Golden Eagles |
| RAY | GCL Rays | GCL | Rays | GCL Rays |
| RCU | Rancho Cucamonga | CAL | Dodgers | Quakes |
| REA | Reading | EAS | Phillies | Fightin Phils |
| RIC | Richmond | EAS | Giants | Flying Squirrels |
| RNG | AZL Rangers | AZL | Rangers | - |
| RNO | Reno | PCL | D-backs | Aces |

| CODE | TEAM | LEAGUE | AFFILIATION | Name |
|------|------|--------|-------------|------|
| ROC | Rochester | INT | Twins | Red Wings |
| ROM | Rome | SAL | Braves | Braves |
| ROU | Round Rock | PCL | Rangers | Express |
| ROY | AZL Royals | AZL | Royals | - |
| RSX | GCL Red Sox | GCL | Red Sox | GCL Red Sox |
| SAC | Sacramento | PCL | Athletics | River Cats |
| SAN | San Antonio | TEX | Padres | Missions |
| SAV | Savannah | SAL | Mets | Sand Gnats |
| SBN | South Bend | MID | D-backs | Silver Hawks |
| SBR | Inland Empire | CAL | Angels | 66ers |
| SCO | State College | NYP | Cardinals | Spikes |
| SDN | San Diego | NL | - | Padres |
| SEA | Seattle | AL | - | Mariners |
| SEI | Seibu | NPB | - | Lions |
| SFD | Springfield | TEX | Cardinals | Cardinals |
| SFN | San Francisco | NL | - | Giants |
| SJO | San Jose | CAL | Giants | Giants |
| SLC | Salt Lake | PCL | Angels | Bees |
| SLM | Salem | CAR | Red Sox | Red Sox |
| SLN | St. Louis | NL | - | Cardinals |
| SLO | Salem-Keizer | NOR | Giants | Volcanoes |
| SLU | St. Lucie | FSL | Mets | Mets |
| SPO | Spokane | NOR | Rangers | Indians |
| STA | Staten Island | NYP | Yankees | Yankees |
| STO | Stockton | CAL | Athletics | Ports |
| SWB | Scranton/WB | INT | Yankees | RailRiders |
| SYR | Syracuse | INT | Nationals | Chiefs |
| TAC | Tacoma | PCL | Mariners | Rainiers |
| TAM | Tampa | FSL | Yankees | Yankees |
| TBA | Tampa Bay | AL | - | Rays |
| TCV | Tri-City | NYP | Astros | ValleyCats |

| CODE | TEAM | LEAGUE | AFFILIATION | Name |
|------|------|--------|-------------|------|
| TEN | Tennessee | SOU | Cubs | Smokies |
| TEX | Texas | AL | - | Rangers |
| TGR | GCL Tigers | GCL | Tigers | GCL Tigers |
| TOL | Toledo | INT | Tigers | Mud Hens |
| TOR | Toronto | AL | - | Blue Jays |
| TRI | Tri-City | NOR | Rockies | Dust Devlis |
| TRN | Trenton | EAS | Yankees | Thunder |
| TUC | Tucson | PCL | Padres | Padres |
| TUL | Tulsa | TEX | Rockies | Drillers |
| TWI | GCL Twins | GCL | Twins | GCL Twins |
| VAN | Vancouver | NOR | Blue Jays | Canadians |
| VER | Vermont | NYP | Athletics | Lake Monsters |
| VIS | Visalia | CAL | D-backs | Rawhide |
| VPH | VSL PHI | VSL | Phillies | - |
| VSE | VSL SEA | VSL | Mariners | - |
| VTB | VSL TB | VSL | Rays | - |
| VTI | VSL DET | VSL | Tigers | - |
| WAS | Washington | NL | - | Nationals |
| WIL | Wilmington | CAR | Royals | Blue Rocks |
| WIS | Wisconsin | MID | Brewers | Timber Rattlers |
| WMI | West Michigan | MID | Tigers | Whitecaps |
| WNS | Winston-Salem | CAR | White Sox | Dash |
| WPT | Williamsport | NYP | Phillies | Crosscutters |
| WTN | Jackson | SOU | Mariners | Generals |
| WVA | West Virginia | SAL | Pirates | Power |
| YAK | Hillsboro | NOR | D-backs | Hops |
| YAN | GCL Yankees1 | GCL | Yankees | GCL Yankees |
| YAT | GCL Yankees2 | GCL | Yankees | GCL Yankees2 |
| YKL | Yakult | NPB | - | Swallows |
| YKO | Yokohama DeNa | NPB | - | BayStars |
| YOM | Yomiuri | NPB | - | Giants |

# Contributors

**Jason Parks** joined Baseball Prospectus in 2010, first as the co-host for the Up-and-In Podcast and then as a bi-weekly columnist, writing under the handle "Prospects Will Break Your Heart." Since the fall of 2012, the Texan (by birth) has been the director of prospects and player development coverage for the site, managing an ever-growing team of evaluators and spending a healthy chunk of his life on the road, watching players on the amateur side (both stateside and international) and at every level in the minors. In addition to his scouting duties, Jason currently co-hosts baseball's most casual podcast, "Fringe-Average" with XM's Mike Ferrin. When he's not at the fields, you can find Jason secluded in his Brooklyn apartment with his wife Jackie and their cat P.M. Nut, watching Paul Verhoeven films and assorted PBS programming.

**Nick J. Faleris** is a practicing attorney and member of the Sports Industry Team with Foley & Lardner LLP. He has been involved in player evaluation at the amateur and professional ranks for eight years, including three seasons as an associate scout for a Major League organization. Nick has worked with Baseball Prospectus since 2012, authoring various articles relating to scouting and player evaluation, in addition to contributing to the Baseball Prospectus Annual Publication and the Futures Guide.

Chris Mellen joined Baseball Prospectus in 2012, specializing in scouting and player development. He spends the season in the field watching pro games across all levels to contribute first-hand reports and scouting updates throughout the year. Prior to joining BP, Chris was Director of Scouting and part owner of SoxProspects.com, where he authored the site's scouting reports on Red Sox prospects and collaborated on player rankings. In addition to spending the offseason assisting with BP's Top 10s and preseason rankings, he roots on his Boston Bruins as a loyal season ticket holder.

**Mark Anderson** pitched at the collegiate level for Division III Clarkson University in northern New York from 1998 to 2003. After college he began scouting and writing for TigsTown.com as Director of Scouting and Managing Editor, focusing on scouting and evaluation of Detroit Tigers prospects. His work for TigsTown.com continues today. Mark's scouting experience led him to work as a Senior Minor League Analyst for Scout.com from 2009 to 2011, developing prospect rankings and reports for the annual Scout.com Prospect Guide. From November 2011 through June 2013, Mark conducted scouting and analysis for his own site, BaseballProspectNation.com. Added to the Baseball Prospectus Prospect Team in September 2012, Mark has continued to refine his scouting skills as one of BP's national scouts with coverage focusing in the northeast.

**Geoff Young** founded Ducksnorts, writing a regular column and three books about the Padres under that title from 1997 to 2011. He has written for Baseball Prospectus, The Hardball Times, and ESPN.com, and his words have appeared in many books. Geoff currently writes for PadresPublic.com and plays ukulele in San Diego, where he lives with his patient wife, Sandra.

---

**Additional contributors:** Jeff Moore, Steffan Segui, CJ Wittmann, Chris Rodriguez, Jordan Gorosh, Ethan Purser, Ryan Parker, Ronit Shah, Chris King, Bret Sayre, Paul Sporer, Ben Carsley, Craig Goldstein, Mike Gianella, Patrick Ebert, Todd Gold, David Rawnsley.

# Index of Names

# Baseball Prospectus Premium